TEMPLES & TOWNS

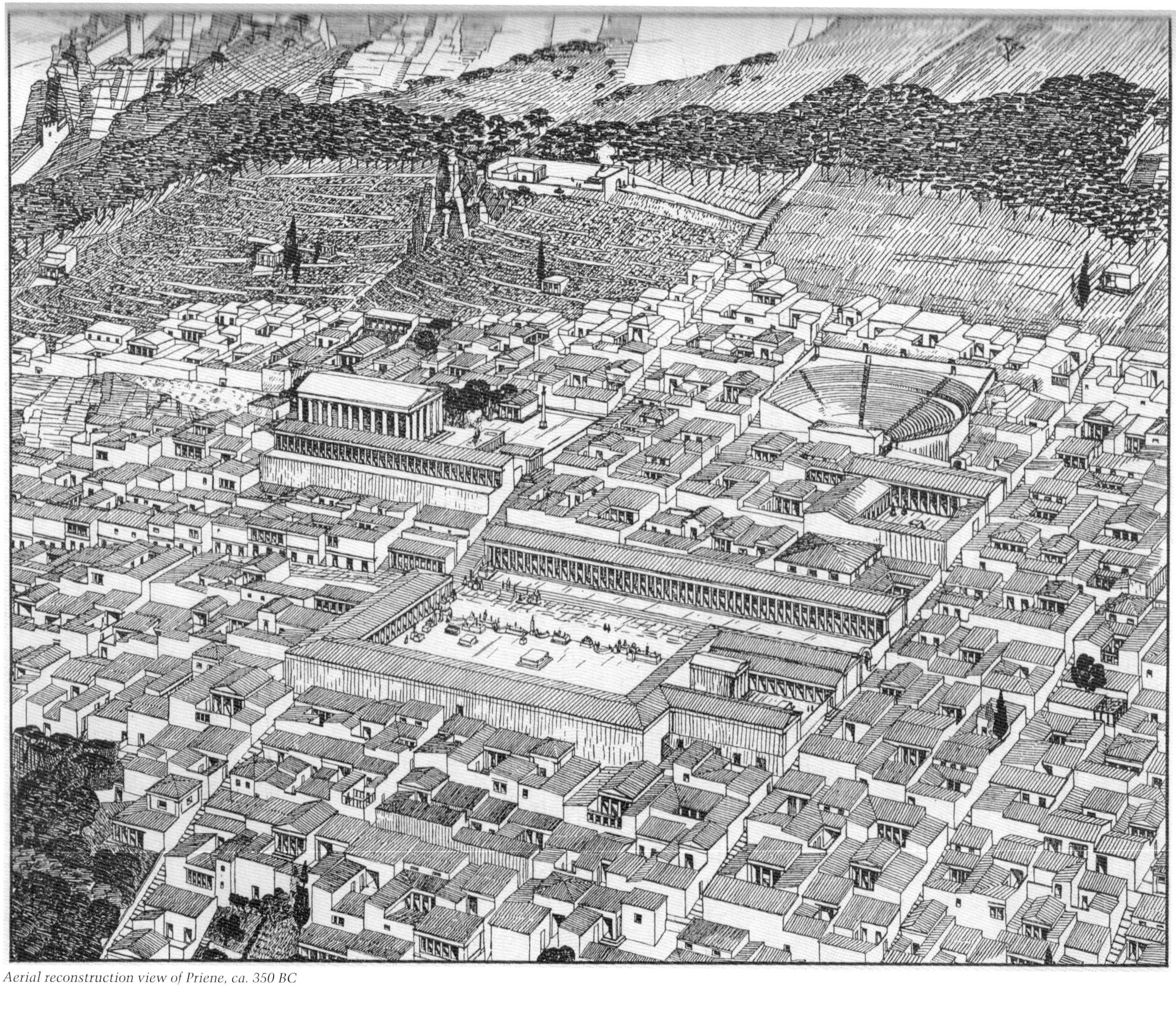

Aerial reconstruction view of Priene, ca. 350 BC

TEMPLES & TOWNS

The Form, Elements, and Principles of Planned Towns

Michael Dennis

Foreword by Steven K. Peterson

ORO
EDITIONS

ORO Editions
Publishers of Architecture, Art, and Design
Gordon Goff: Publisher

www.oroeditions.com
info@oroeditions.com

Published by ORO Editions

Author: Michael Dennis
Foreword: Steven K. Peterson
Book Design: Michael Dennis
Project Manager: Jake Anderson

10 9 8 7 6 5 4 3 2 1 First Edition

ISBN: 978-1-957183-02-2

Color Separations and Printing: ORO Group Inc.
Printed in China.

AR+D Publishing makes a continuous effort to minimize the overall carbon footprint of its publications. As part of this goal, AR+D, in association with Global ReLeaf, arranges to plant trees to replace those used in the manufacturing of the paper produced for its books. Global ReLeaf is an international campaign run by American Forests, one of the world's oldest nonprofit conservation organizations. Global ReLeaf is American Forests' education and action program that helps individuals, organizations, agencies, and corporations improve the local and global environment by planting and caring for trees.

Acknowledgments

This book grows out of studies made during the fall of 2009 by students and faculty of the SMarchS Architecture and Urbanism program in the Department of Architecture at the Massachusetts Institute of Technology. As such, it follows in a long tradition of informal publications of ongoing research at academic institutions. Most remain as useful "unpublished manuscripts." Often, however, these studies result in public lectures; occasionally in published articles; and sometimes they are preludes to finished books.

The following people contributed to the initial research: Allison Albericci, Matthew Bindner, Kathleen Dahlberg, Laura Delaney, Chris De Vries, Yashar Ghasemkhani, Theodossius Issaias, Priyanka Kapoor, Amrita Mahindroo, Mahsan Mohsenin, Nathan Prevendar, Eva Strobel, Sagarika Suri, Tony Vanky, Matti Wirth, and Kui Xue.

Copy editing at various stages was done by Judy Feldman, Evan Anderson, and Christie Monroe Dennis. Christie, however, contributed ideas and improvements well beyond what I could ever have imagined. For all the above contributions, I am profoundly grateful.

Michael Dennis
Boston, MA
2022

For Christie

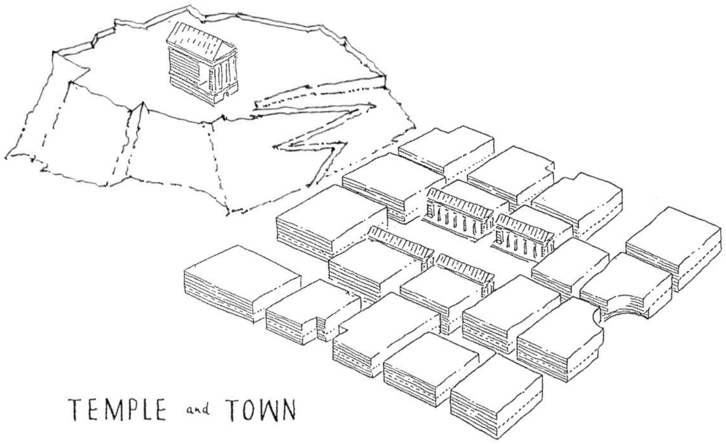

TEMPLE and TOWN

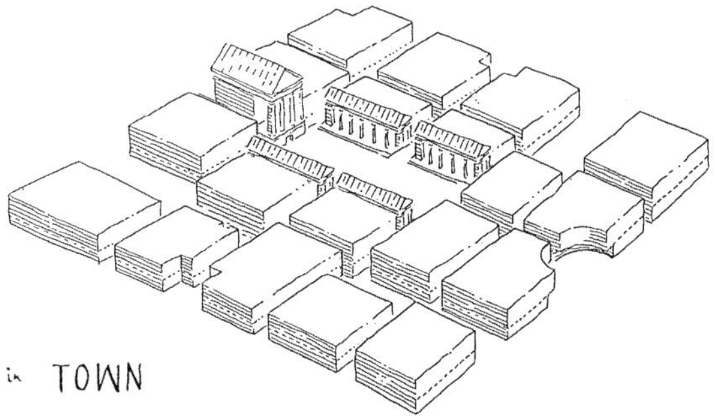

TEMPLE in TOWN

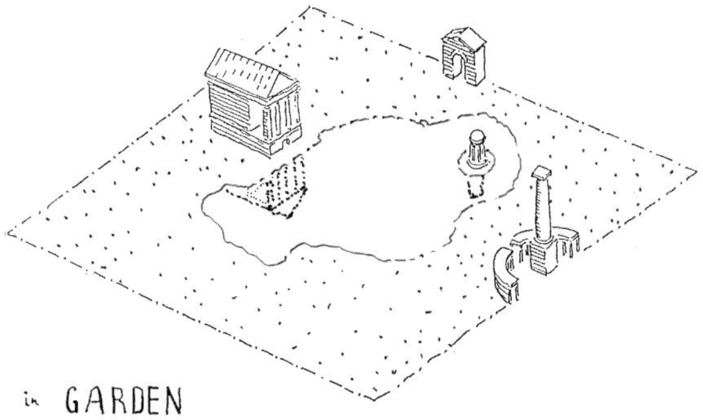

TEMPLE in GARDEN

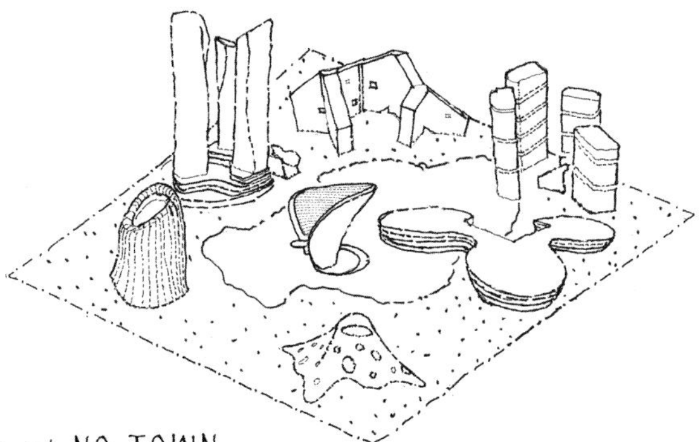

TEMPLES and NO TOWN

Temples and Towns

In Classical Greece the most sacred temples were often located on the acropolis, separate from the town. In Hellenistic Greek towns and Roman towns, however, the temples were usually within the town. This condition of reciprocity between architectural monuments and urban fabric remained until approximately the mid-eighteenth century, when important Western institutions began to be expressed as articulate architectural monuments—free-standing icons—often in gardens.

This Neoclassical change in sensibility re-emerged after the frenzy of nineteenth-century city building as the spatial and philosophical underpinning of modern architecture and town planning. Essentially, the city disappeared; architecture became more and more assertive and violent; and the private realm of architecture finally achieved hegemony over the public realm of the city.

During this process, society lost its sense of community and urbanity; staggering amounts of finite resources were consumed; and our planet became so polluted that the damage may be irreversible.

"Temples" without "Towns" is untenable. Both temples and towns are needed. Hence, the title and content of this book.

Illustrations with gratitude and apologies to Leon

Contents

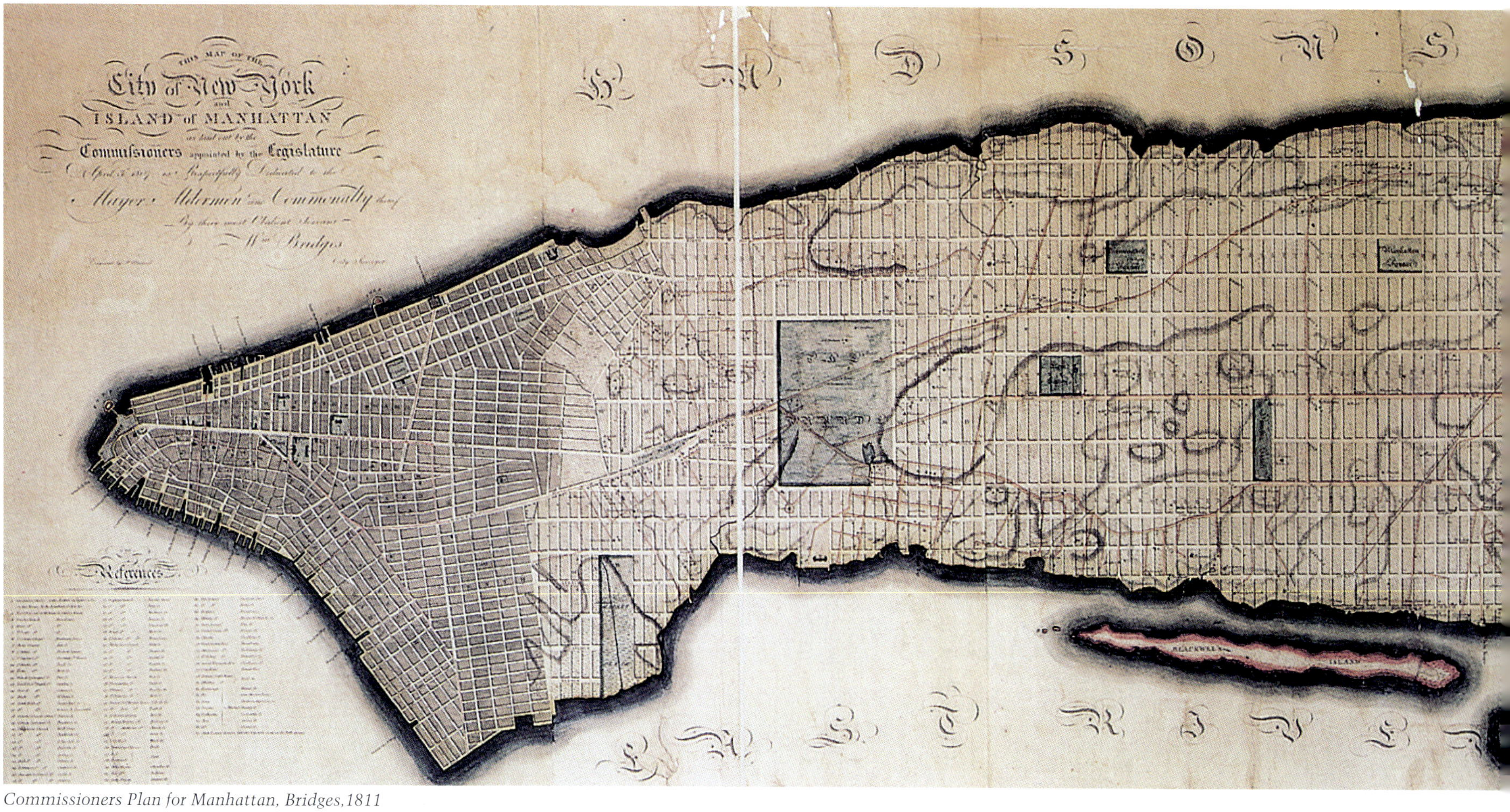

Commissioners Plan for Manhattan, Bridges, 1811

Foreword

Steven K. Peterson

The importance of this book by Michael Dennis, following his *Court and Garden*, published in 1986, is its assertion of the imperative presence of the urban plan. This book contains such a dense compilation of city plans and aerial views, that it can almost be "read" without the words as a visual narrative of the formal urban layouts covering 3,000 years of Western building. The book makes apparent that plans endure as a language in themselves, commenting on each other as protagonists of thought and engines of criticism. The city plan is the essential notational grammar of urban form.

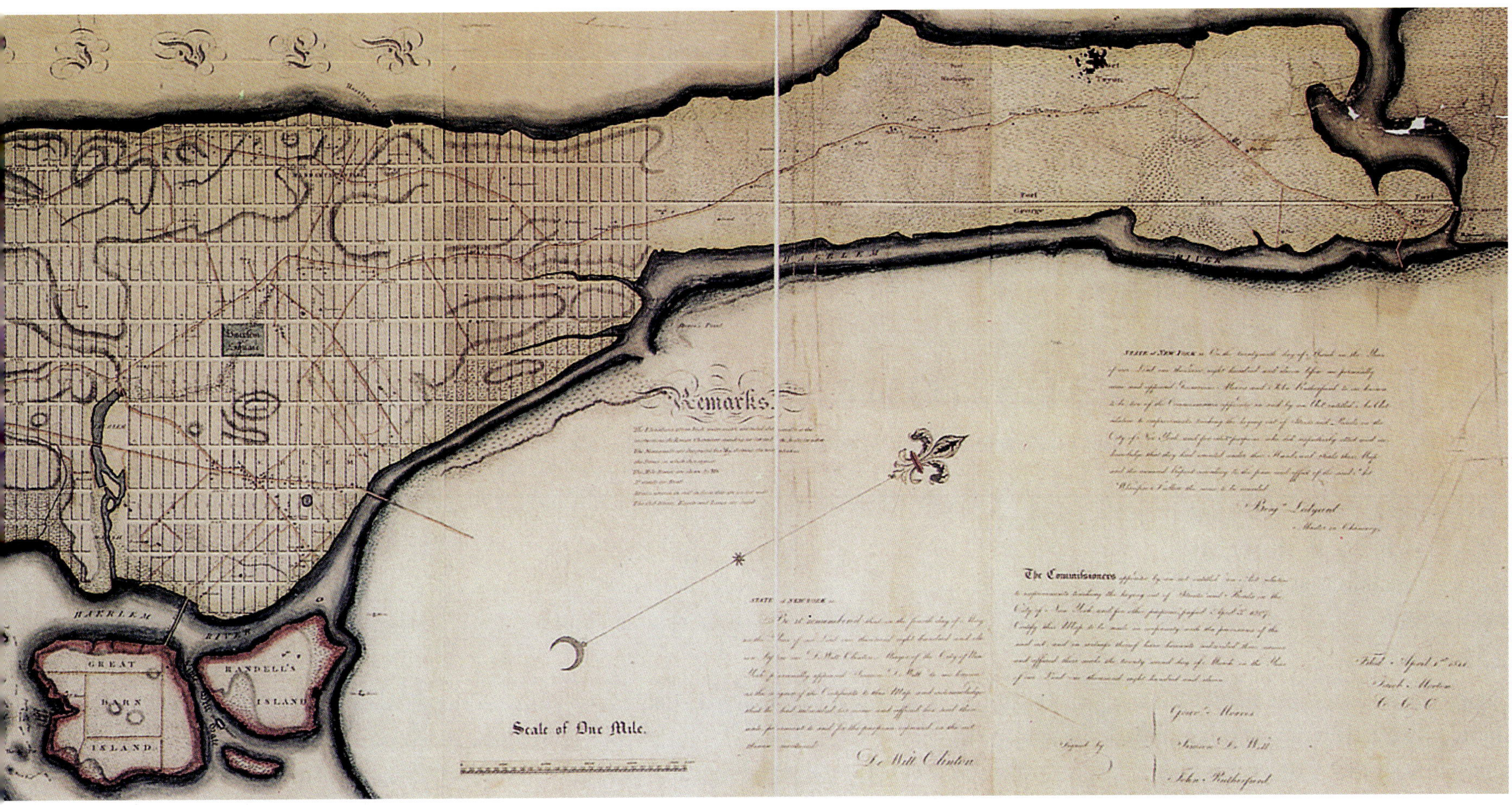

New York street view at Park and 65th Street

City and Town

To begin this discussion of cities, let me tell you a story about New York.

Our five-year-old granddaughter, Esmee Elisa Sherrill, lives in the small town of Hollidaysburg, Pennsylvania. It is, just as it sounds, a charming, tiny place with handsome brick Craftsman-style houses on tree-lined streets. Esmee comes with her parents to visit us in Manhattan about twice a year. This time, and at her age, she had become especially fascinated by all things in the city, and was excited to see and ask questions. She wanted my wife Barbara to take her out for a walk to look at our Manhattan neighborhood—the buildings, the streets, and Central Park. The view of Park and 65th Street is what it looks like in our neighborhood.

She heard the trains under the street. She saw the steam rising from the red and white cones over manholes. She asked about everything, and Barbara, holding her hand as they walked, explained: about the trains under the grass center strip of Park Avenue that could take you to Buffalo and Chicago; about the dragons below the street that heat the buildings and spew their steam; about the baby alligator pets brought back from Florida that are flushed down toilets to grow up in the sewers. Esmee smiles. She has a kind of W. C. Fields skepticism that comes from an experienced life of cartoon television.

Back at the house after their walk, Barbara told me Esmee's last question: "Why do people in the city live in apartments instead of houses?"

Barbara and I looked at each other, jaws dropped, eyebrows arched. Of course, this was not a question at all, but a child's accurate, innocent (and because of its directness), very potent observation: "People in cities live in apartments instead of houses." That is the whole deal. It is radical. This is an aspect that is common to all urban places as different as New York, Paris, or Rome. There are no separate houses, and very few object buildings. All the buildings touch. They go together wall to wall. This discussion about "urban" is not just about the definition of words. It is a recognizable physical condition sensed intuitively, even by a five year old, but it flies under the radar of professionals with vast amounts of analysis and discussion.

Aerial view of Chicago

Not all cities are urban. To statisticians the word "urban" literally means "not rural," and their word "city" just means a gathering of 100,000 people or more. Not very helpful at all as to shape and form.

This is obvious enough since most of what is being rapidly built and called cities today are actually not urban at all, and this is a real problem.

As of 2010, more than 50 percent of all people in the world lived in an urban area. Of all these urban dwellers 60 percent live in cities defined as 100,000 people or more. By 2050, 70 percent of all people will be living in urban areas.

What does this mean for us? What form will these places have?

What Is Urban?

What is urban? How can we make it? It is not a matter of density, or size, or a particular architectural style. Large cities, medium towns, and even small villages can be urban.

We already know that, both Los Angeles, California, and Savannah, Georgia, are not really urban. Everybody in those places lives in houses. To Esmee, they would look like big versions of Hollidaysburg. "Urban" means no houses. Both the historical center of New Orleans and the city of Manhattan are urban. Rome is urban, while large parts of London are not.

Urban is a special condition of cities and towns independent of their size or density, and results when buildings touch and are not free standing. Attached buildings combine into common urban walls, which are necessary to both define exterior space and subdivide it. This continuous wall is the essential urban element; it makes precise edges to streets, defines squares and parks like exterior rooms, and closes blocks, dividing outside from inside, front from back, public from private. A one-street English village can be urban, while a big city of millions like Detroit might not be. I realized the importance of this a few years back when Mike Dennis called me to talk. It was part of our ongoing conversation about cities and urban design that began at Cornell University in Ithaca, New York, in 1969.

Mike is always calling to test his observations, and being a Texan, he charms you by disguising assertions as questions: "Steven, I want to ask you a question about something. Do you think there are any real cities in America?" What? Well, I knew the answer. No, there are very few real "cities" in America. We both knew this was true. But it was a shock to say it out loud. I was raised in Chicago, which is a vast sprawl of free-standing houses and small walk-up apartments. Except for New York and some downtown cores, most US cities are really just vast grids of mostly wooden houses. Of course, this, like all useful characterizations, is also somewhat of an exaggeration.

The Urban Block

The first urban condition is the closed block. Only without houses (also, without free-standing buildings) does a city or town become truly urban. This is because, instead of houses, everything gets pushed together and becomes a closed block, a compound form, another entity. The closed block with its compressed, multiple architectures is a somewhat illusive and singular aggregate form. The enclosed block is the miraculous key from which every urbanity flows.[1]

The block provides:

Density, and sharing of services and costs. Every apartment building is a community secured by a doorman, with garbage removal, mail delivery, and all commonly managed. It is urbane and civilized.

The block provides:

Diversity. Many different people with different incomes can live in the same place—in apartment buildings—without knowing each other.

The block provides:

Privacy. In Hollidaysburg, Esmee's side window looks into the neighbors's dining room. In the city, you can't even see the building next door because you are attached to it.

The block provides:

Mixed use. In Hollidaysburg you can't buy a lightbulb or get groceries down the street in shops under your neighbor's house.

The block provides:

Conjunctions of potentially conflicting uses. In the view along Park Avenue, the three-story private club at the far end doesn't disturb the next two four-story residential town houses, and they are unperturbed by the twelve-floor hotel at the corner, with its busy French restaurant's entrance around the corner.

Notice, too, the detailed architectural relationship of cornices, openings, and materials among the very different styles and sizes of the buildings. It is conversation in architectural language.

Plan of Kirchsteigfeld, Potsdam, Krier Kohl Architects

Urban Space

The second urban condition and the primary medium of city design is space.[2]

The next time Esmee came to New York, I took her to the Museum of Natural History. We went to the planetarium first for the new show about outer space. The lights dimmed, the stars appeared, and the vast empty universe surrounded us. Esmee cried in terror. We left in a total state. She was not amused. Back at the apartment, her mother Lee tried to understand: "But Esmee, you like the stars in the night sky. What was wrong?" Puzzled, she thought, and responded: "I don't know Mom, I think I am just space shy."[3]

"Space shy," the terror of vast emptiness. This is part of why we make cities, to corral space and make it our own size, to divide it into discernible packages. We invent enclosure to protect us, boundaries to define our place, and to guide the order of our movement. Cities are the created world that substitutes for emptiness and the undefined. We make the design of bounded urban places because we are all fundamentally "space shy." We need the discipline of contained public space, the security of defined streets, and enclosed squares and parks. Only the walls of urban form mediate between the calm of private apartments in the midst of public chaos. This is not historical, modern, or traditional; it is universal to any urban city: space formed by the walls of attached buildings enclosing blocks for private use.

Rob Krier and his partner Christian Kohl have built new towns, such as Kirchsteigfeld, outside of Potsdam, using these urban conditions.[4] It is the essence of urban form in woven patterns, and varieties of places; an amazingly inventive and richly varied plan of particular spaces and blocks. Although the buildings, unlike New York's, are three and four stories, Kirchsteigfeld nonetheless epitomizes what is urban. Its block scale is flexible and adaptable.

There is a real joy in just squinting at the white spaces and the variety of urban elements: grids, boulevards, squares, lozenge-shaped piazzas, round points, rotated urban fabric of blocks and streets. Why couldn't this be built outside Washington, DC, or in downtown Newark, New Jersey?

The closed figural spaces shown here have to be consciously made and carved from the plasticity of solid blocks. You can't have one without the other. Incidentally, depending on the height and depth of buildings, this plan could probably be one for an urban city of 100,000 people.

The new cities we build tomorrow can be just as urban as our existing historical ones because the urban structure of cities is independent of the architecture it contains. The city does not have to be reinvented with each era or change of style, because it is already the container for change and the structure for a conjunction of differences. If so, why isn't real urbanism happening in the vacuous new cities being rapidly built around the world?

Antiurban Hyper-Architecture

It is easy to blame the famous designers of hyper-architecture for the lack of urbanism because they reject city contexts and just emphasize superficial shapes. But they are caught in their own spiraling bind as architectural entertainers. To be continually noticed in the competitive context of explosive world growth, more extreme notorious gestures will be required each time successively.

The world of hyper-architecture does not cause a rejection of urban form. It is just the inevitable fallout from a culture driven by the desire for fast cities (like fast food) that are banal, expedient, and technically proficient. They fill up quickly, but cannot satisfy or sustain a public life of genuine urbanity. They derive from the politics of power and image, from economic speculation, and from an excessive imbalance of wealth.

The Urban Plan

The failure of contemporary "fast cities" to be designed as urban places that are culturally sustainable over time is due to a societal void, the lack of political will, and the complacency of technocratic consultants. It is not caused by the arrogance and indifference of individual architects.

A city is the broader plan, an independent urban formal structure that has values and assets that even the most entertaining acts of architecture can never provide alone.

Look at New York City. Since the 1970s, the number and types of buildings have radically expanded and changed, but the urban structure, the basic armature of spaces, blocks, and streets, are still the same. It did not need reinvention or rethinking to accommodate the changes in architecture and scale because, in a very real sense, the urban form of New York City did not change at all.

Conclusion

This book illustrates the vast story of settlement plans, blocks, and spaces. It is a potent reference source of urban knowledge that might easily be subtitled "Templates for Towns." So, as you look through this marvelous and useful collection of town and city plans, be careful and participate. Watch out for city designs that are just large patterns made of individual houses and free-standing buildings. Instead, be aware of subtle differences: look for blocks; pry out public space; and keep asking: is it urban?

1. Street view, Kirchsteigfeld

2. The French Building, 1927, Sloan and Robertson

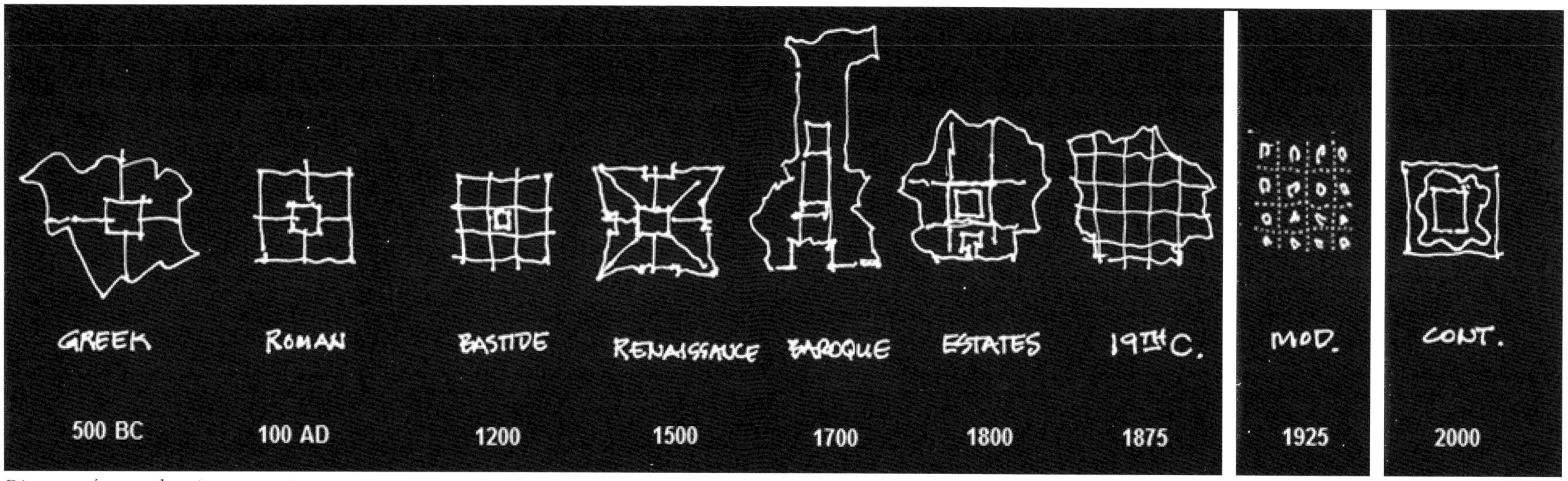

Diagram of town planning types

Preface

This book may be seen as a companion to my first book, *Court & Garden: From the French Hôtel to the City of Modern Architecture* (1986). Both books chronicle the disintegration of the city and long for its reconstruction, but *Court & Garden* traces the formal and social transformation of an architectural type from embedded urban buildings to free-standing private icons, while *Temples & Towns* focuses on the larger issue of town planning—a discipline that too many conceive as large-scale architecture.

This book has three aims: to trace the historic evolution of urban form, principles, and design; to serve as a compendium, or reference, of city design; and to polemicize the necessity for the recovery of the city and a contemporary urban architecture. As such, it may be read graphically, textually, or both. I like to think that it falls into the long tradition of illustrated treatises in which theory is embedded in the projects, with only occasional assistance or clarification from the text. Architecture and urban design are physical arts, not verbal arts, and they are best understood from graphic representations.

Illustrations graphically represent the urban language and the architectural language just as words represent spoken languages. At one time architecture and urbanism were analogous to slightly different dialects of Latin, but today they have come to be separate, but related languages, like Spanish and Italian. Despite their common base, however, today many people who understand one do not understand the other. Nevertheless, both can be understood without being verbally described. Mathematicians do not need verbal descriptions of their equations; they understand them directly. Architects should be able to read the drawings and pictures without reading someone else's description of them.

From eighteenth-century French treatises on domestic architecture to Rob Krier's 1982 monograph, architects have understood their profession through graphic representation, bolstered by a few facts. For those who understand architecture and urban design without assistance, this study can be "read" without literally reading the text. The text does add something, however. For example, it is good to know that, contrary to common assumptions, Cerdà did not win a competition for the Barcelona expansion plan. (He did not even enter the competition.) It is also useful to understand the difference and development sequence of the Roman cross-axial plan versus the Roman castrum plan. But these are clarifications that augment understanding, rather than being necessary.

Finally, a word about terminology: *town* and *city* are used interchangeably, but *town planning* is preferred over *city planning* because, though old-fashioned, it implies design more than the contemporary use of *planning*. The terms *city* and *urban* are more problematic. At one time *urban* was synonymous with *city*. Cities were urban. In our time, however, not all cities are urban. In fact, many are not—especially new ones. More like warehouses for people, cities in rapidly developing parts of the world are built quickly and expediently to house urban immigrants, but with little regard for the quality of urban life. To be genuinely urban two things are required: sufficient continuity of buildings to define the public space of the city—the civic structure—and mixed-use neighborhoods that provide a variety of social and functional amenities. In his Foreword, Steven Peterson discusses the formal requisites for urbanity, and why small towns like San Jose del Cabo in Mexico are urban, but most American cities are not.

1. Aerial view of Chicago

2. San Jose del Cabo, street view

Introduction

This study grew out of curiosity about two contrasting but interrelated issues: the pervasive estrangement of contemporary architecture and the city; and—in complete contrast—the apparently sudden sophistication of late-nineteenth-century city expansion plans, such as those by Poggi for Florence, and Cerdà for Barcelona.

For about 2,500 years town planners designed and drew cities, or parts of cities, and architects designed and drew buildings that occupied them; but in the late nineteenth century, and early in the twentieth century, town planners began to draw buildings rather than cities—which has created enormous confusion about the relationship between architecture and the city.

We therefore set out to trace the long evolution of urban design, or town planning, through planned cities and towns—not urban interventions such as Vienna's Ringstrasse, and not organic, or cumulative, cities such as Athens and Rome.

We begin with the planned cities of Greece and the Roman Empire from about 500 BC, through the late-medieval Bastides, the ideal Renaissance cities, and Baroque new towns, to the urban planning strategies of the nineteenth and twentieth centuries. Town planning will again be crucial in a world of diminishing resources.

View of Rome from the dome of St. Peter's

On City Form, Theory, and History

Confrontation with the complexity of the city is daunting—unlike science and mathematics where, according to Richard Feynman, problems are nearer the surface and significant work can be achieved at a relatively young age. With architecture and the city, problems and solutions are more elusive. Architecture and the city are slow maturation fields where history and culture are essential. The issues are less clear, and significant work tends to come later in life.

It is difficult to find clarity or consensus, for example, regarding the questions: *What is a city? What is urban? What is urbanism? What is urban design? What is planning?* There is little consensus today regarding answers to these questions, partially because the terms themselves have become confused, co-opted, and disconnected from meaning. Experience and conviction are required.

The terms *design, theory,* and *history* further confound the discussion, even if we speak of *urban design, urban design theory,* and *urban design history.* The articulation of these three terms is a distinctly modern (post-Kantian) phenomenon. The ancient Greeks, for example, steeped as they were in the concreteness of Homeric precedent, would not have understood such a distinction.[1] In our own time, Leon Krier has observed that you only need a theory if you don't know how to do something. But today there is little consensus about architecture and urbanism, and theory is a necessity.

At its purest, design is the manipulation of form and space. It is also about something, however, and throughout most of history, design was accomplished within a set of conventions. These conventions formed the theory base that guided design decisions. (Not everything had to be reinvented every Monday morning.) Indeed, it could be argued that theory grew out of design practice, and that design practice grew out of societal circumstance. Because design was embedded in the circumstance of culture and politics, it was part of the continuity of history. Within this framework better designers made better designs: e.g., Michelangelo versus Bandini. On occasion, great inventions transcended the conventional, or revolutionary ruptures precipitated an abrupt change in either form or society, but the norm was a condition of evolution or continuity.

Much has been written about the fact that this all changed in the twentieth century; theory now often precedes—and sometimes replaces—practice; major architectural designers are often trivial or disastrous urbanists; and the design professions have a generally uncertain relationship with the society of which they are a part.

According to William Westfall, a city has three constituent elements:[2]

the political character of its citizens;
their institutional arrangements; and
the embodiment of their politics and institutions in architectural and urban form.

As architects and citizens we should be mindful of the first two of these. As architects and urban designers, however, our focus should be on urban form as the physical embodiment of the idea of the city. The city may also represent the political aspirations of its citizens, but most cities have reflected different political aspirations throughout their history.

The most fundamental characteristics of urbanity are *spatial definition, density,* and *mixed uses.* Other physical characteristics are also important: continuity, scale, pedestrian orientation, varied neighborhoods, uniqueness of place, possibilities of both community and anonymity, incremental growth, and possibility of movement—ideally through public transit.

Worldwide, cities exhibit more similarities than differences. Many physical attributes, such as typology, are persistent and cross-cultural. Indeed, it can be argued that the biggest changes in the long evolution of traditional urban form have been prompted by changes in technology—especially the technology of movement: e.g., the invention of the sprung carriage in the eighteenth century; the advent of the railroad and the elevator in the nineteenth century; and the advent of the motor car, and perhaps the airplane, in the twentieth century. In the nineteenth century the traditional city "loosened" to accommodate this new condition of movement, and expanded to accommodate the urban population explosion precipitated by the industrial revolution. But until the twentieth century all these changes utilized traditional urban typologies. Cerdà's Barcelona is a particularly beautiful example.

Cities are composed of *buildings, blocks, streets, squares, parks, neighborhoods,* and a legible *civic structure,* and this—the form of the city—was the beginning point of this study. In other words, the concreteness of town plans was used to reveal the principles, or urban design theory, behind them, and this in turn led to authors, philosophy, culture, and history. The intent was to bring the professional artifacts themselves to the foreground for comparative purposes. This revealed a surprisingly consistent (and surprisingly continuous) tradition of urban design, or town planning theory—at least until the twentieth century. What follows are the components of the study that have been outlined above.

On Urban Design

Urban design is the design of the physical framework of cities within which architects design buildings. More precisely, it is the design of the public realm of the city, including specific landscape and public space design. Architectural design is the design of the private realms of the city, but also its civic buildings. Urban and architectural design occasionally overlap, and the "fit," or relationship, between the two is a contentious issue today.

Cities have always been composed of monuments and fabric, but until the middle of the eighteenth century the city's monuments, or civic buildings, were embedded within the city fabric. There was hegemony of the public realm. But in the eighteenth century formal sensibilities changed as societal institutions expanded, and public buildings became articulated from the urban fabric. Gradually this formal propensity toward free-standing objects extended to private buildings as well, and the private realm achieved hegemony over the public realm in the early twentieth century.[3]

The dilemma of urban design today: even the most inconsequential private buildings are often considered "art," and few buildings contribute to the urban fabric and space—the matrix of the city.

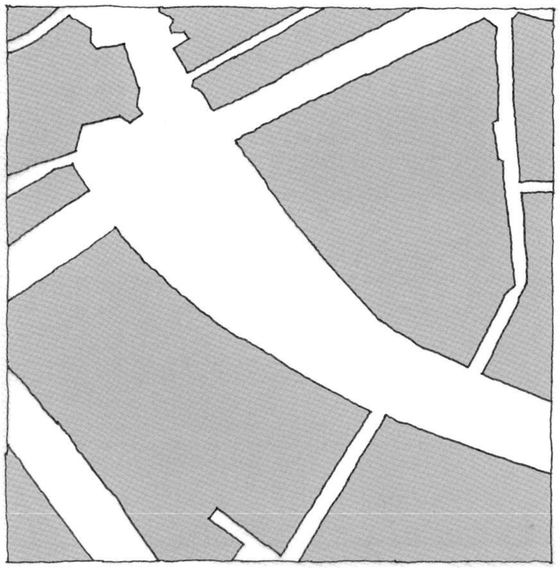

1. Town plan: Streets, Blocks, and Spaces

2. Land use pattern: Parcels

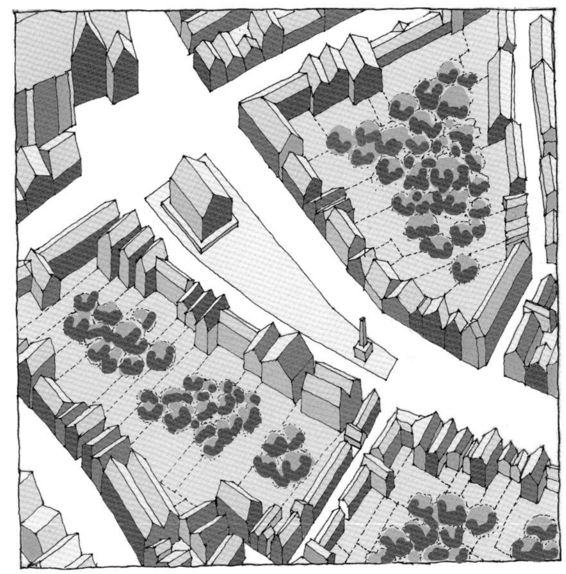

3. Building fabric: Architectural design

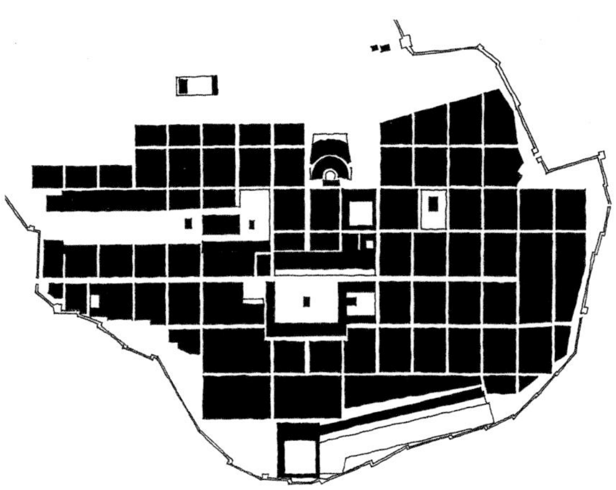

4. Town plan of Priene, ca. 350 BC

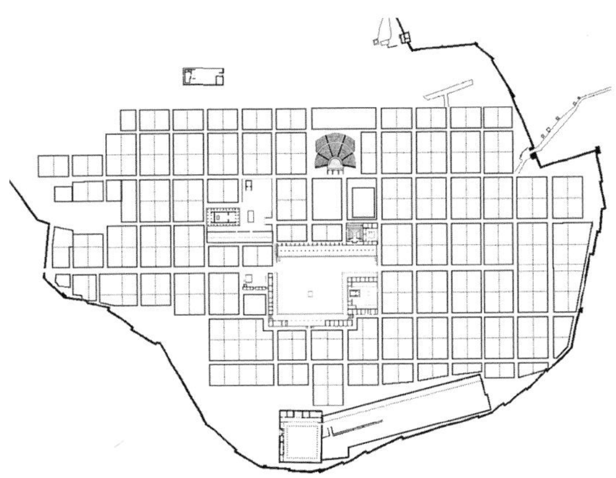

5. Land use pattern of Priene

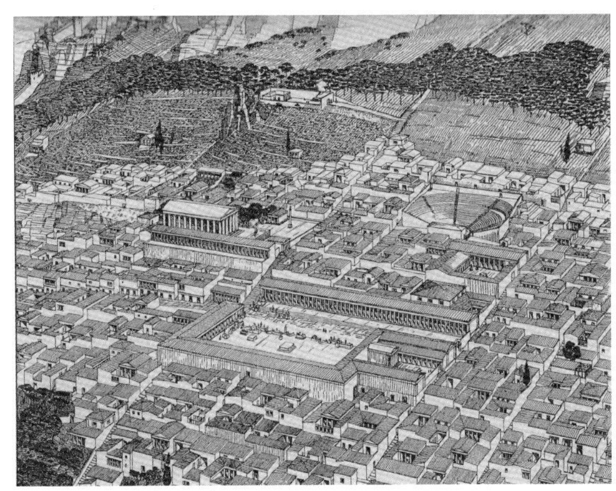

6. Building fabric of Priene

Urban Fabric

Spiro Kostof points out that in the morphogenetic approach to urban geography by M. R. G. Conzen, "urban fabric" comprises three interlocking elements: (1) the town plan of streets, blocks, and spaces; (2) the land use pattern of parcels; and, (3) the three-dimensional building fabric.[4]

Generally speaking, this is also a rough description of the differences between what town planners, or urban designers, have traditionally done (1 & 2), and what architects have done (3). Town planners had to be conversant with the building typologies for which they were planning, but they usually were not involved with the specific design of buildings that filled the urban fabric.

The size, scale, and block structure of the private parcels is a primary determinant in the character of the city, and the argument has been made that as the size of the parcels goes up, the quality of the environment goes down.

Planned and Unplanned Cities

Both regular, planned cities, and irregular, unplanned cities grow incrementally—usually over a long period of time—to become cumulative cities. We often associate cumulative cities with organic or picturesque patterns, such as Rome, or irregular medieval cities, such as Brussels. But in fact, Manhattan is a cumulative city despite its grid and relatively short life, as is Turin, with its much longer life.

Types of Urban Design

There are three types of urban designs: *planned cities and expansions*; *urban interventions*; and *architectural interventions*.

Planned Cities and Expansions

Planned cities and their major expansions are the subject of this study. Urban and architectural interventions happen within a plan, and may support or contradict it. They are also, by definition, a blend of architecture and urban design. But the design of an urban plan must stand alone. It is also not large-scale architectural design. Pure—perhaps ideal—values are visible and essential in designed plans, as the nuance and variation of years of incremental development cannot be envisioned and designed. This is why there have never been designed irregular town plans, nor unplanned grid towns. This is also why the new world was colonized almost entirely with planned grid towns. The very tip of Manhattan is a bit irregular, but the only city in America with an irregular plan is Boston. Because of their interest, however, a section on irregular plans is included at the end of this study.

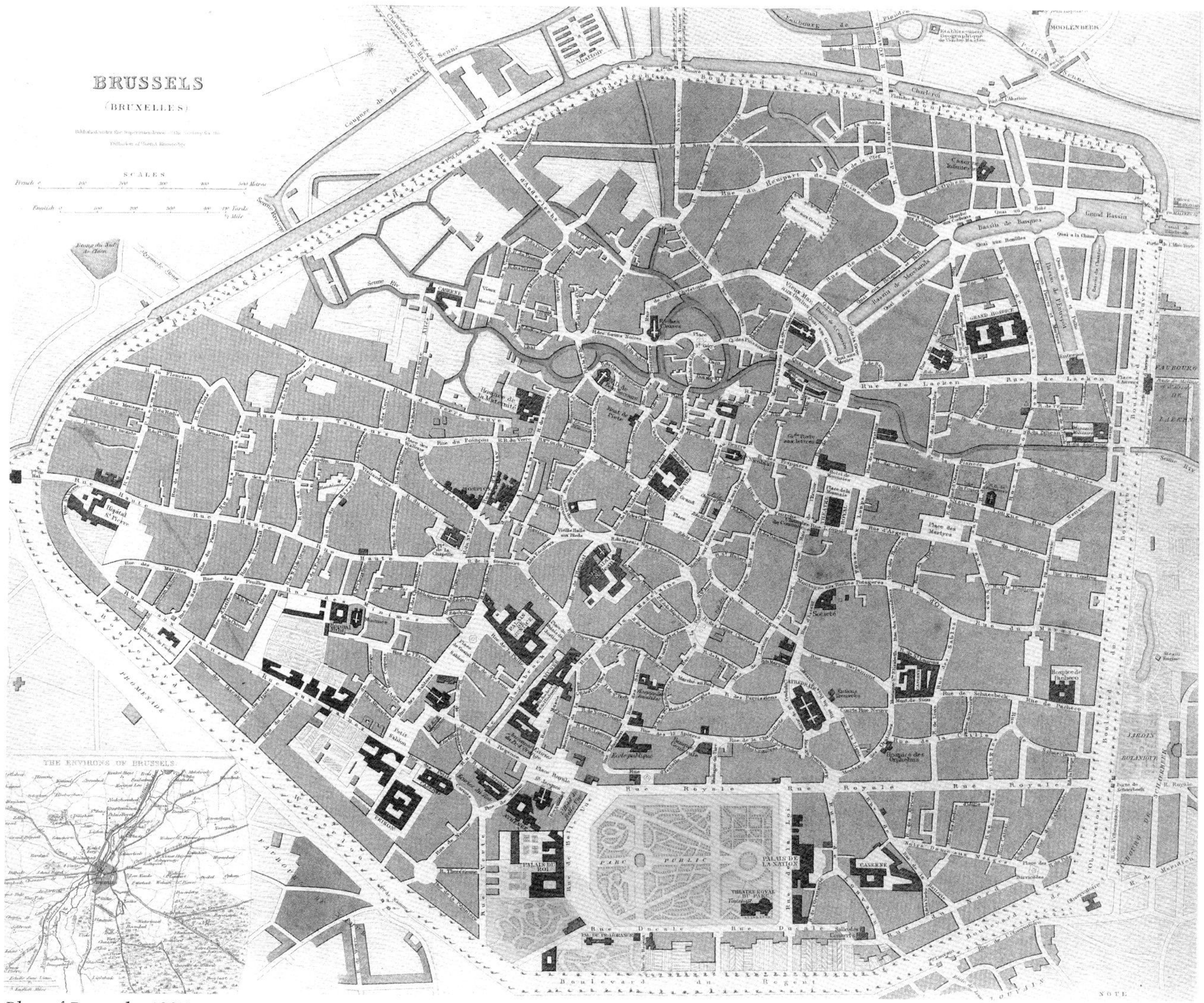

Plan of Brussels, 1837

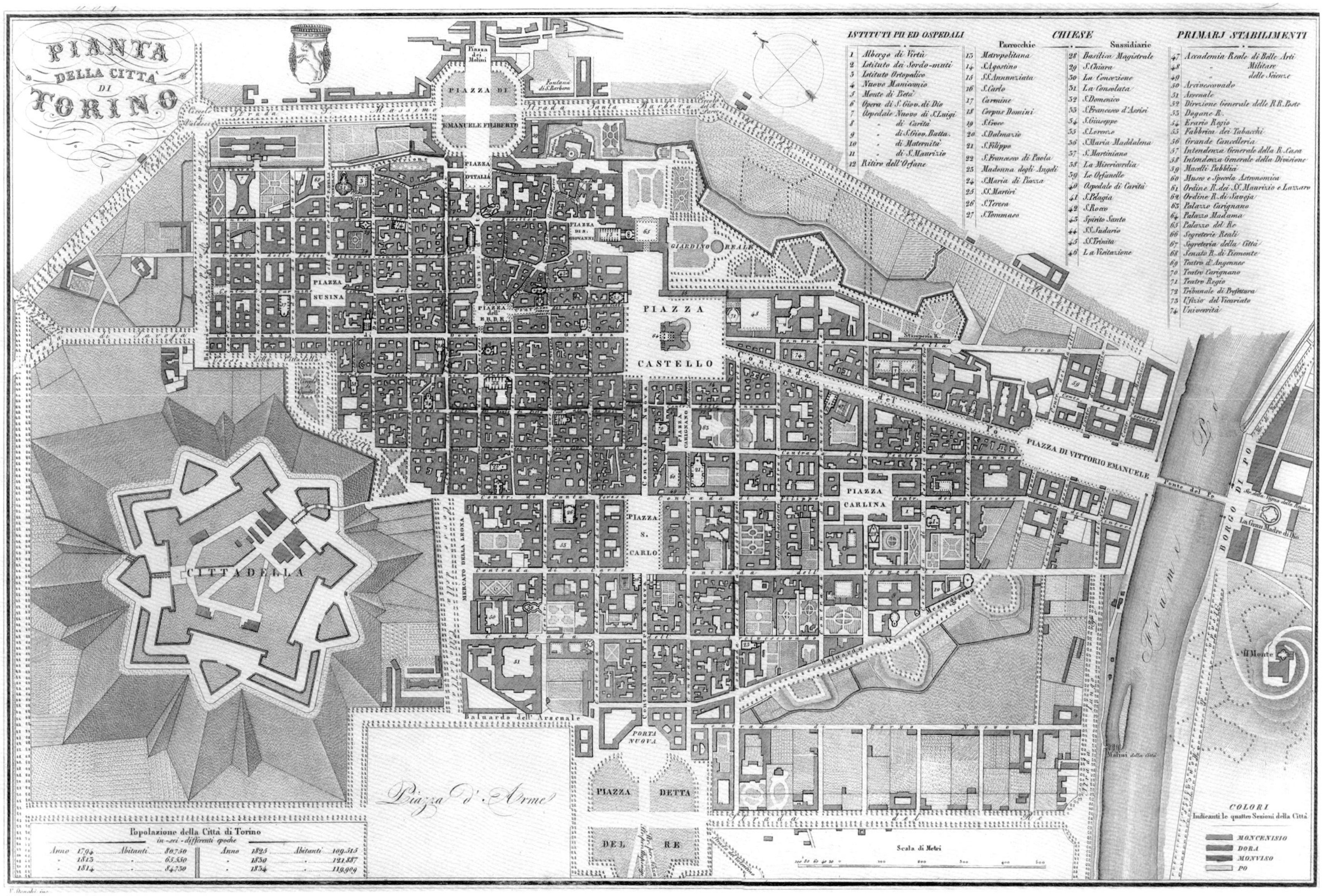

Plan of Turin, 1844

Urban Interventions

For present purposes, urban interventions are sizable urban design projects that alter existing urban fabric. An intervention may be destructive—as by fire, war, or "urban renewal"—or constructive—in order to connect, alter, or revise parts of the city.

The Ringstrasse in Vienna, for example, filled a previously open space, to bind the existing inner and outer parts of the city together. In fact, many European cities found urban design opportunities after the fortification walls were torn down during the Napoleonic era. Another superb example is the Baroque sequence of spaces designed by Héré in Nancy, to bind two distinct parts of the town together.

Other notable urban interventions include: the Roman designs for Sixtus V; Paris streets by Percier and Fontaine; London projects by John Nash and George Dance; and Vasari's Corridor in Florence.

1. Plan of Vienna, showing the Ringstrasse, begun 1857

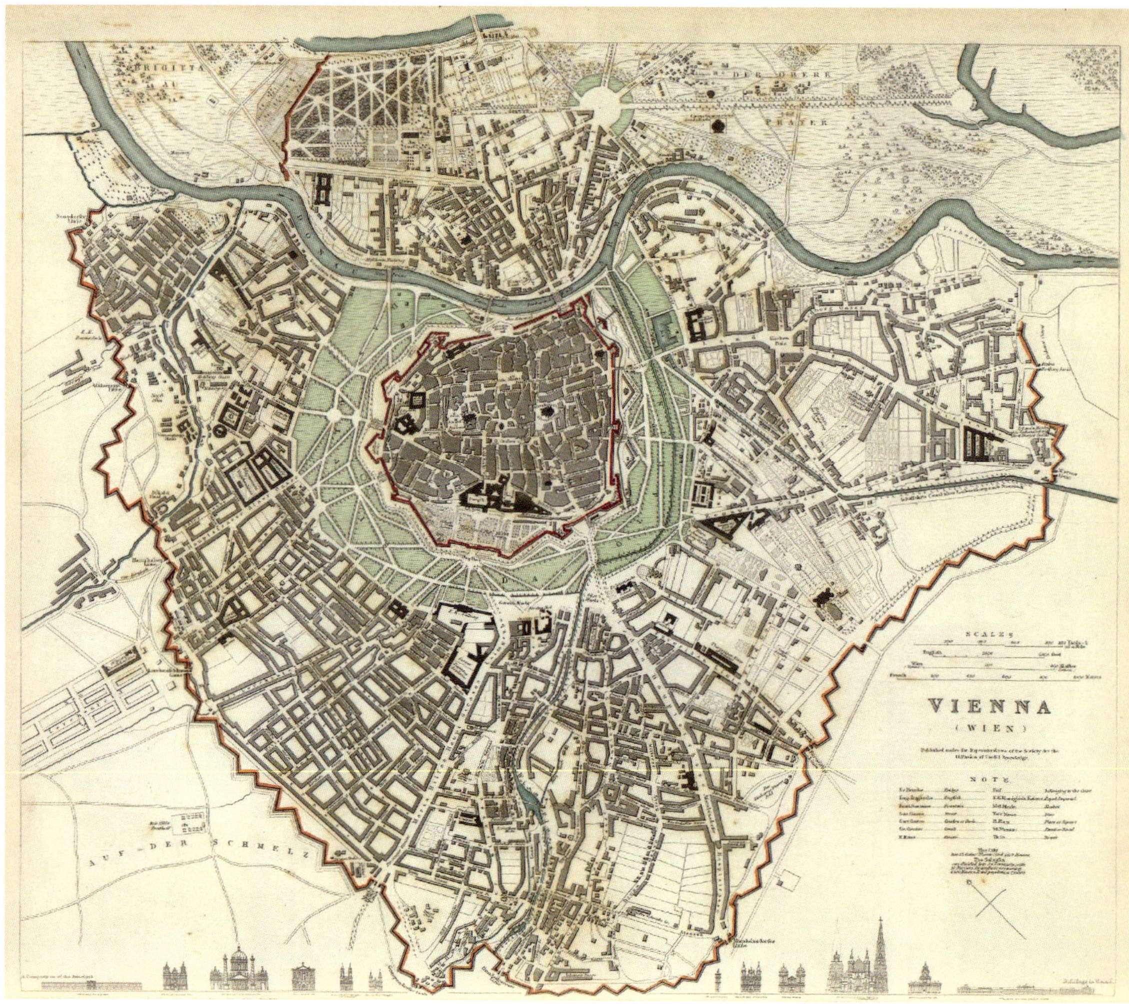

2. Plan of Vienna before the Ringstrasse, 1840

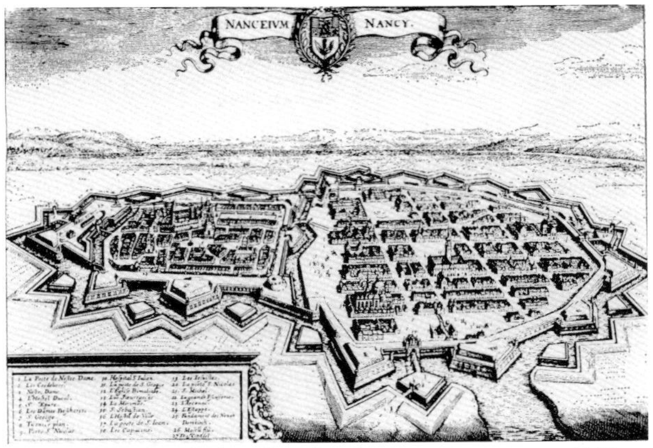

1. Nancy, the fortified medieval and Renaissance towns, 1645

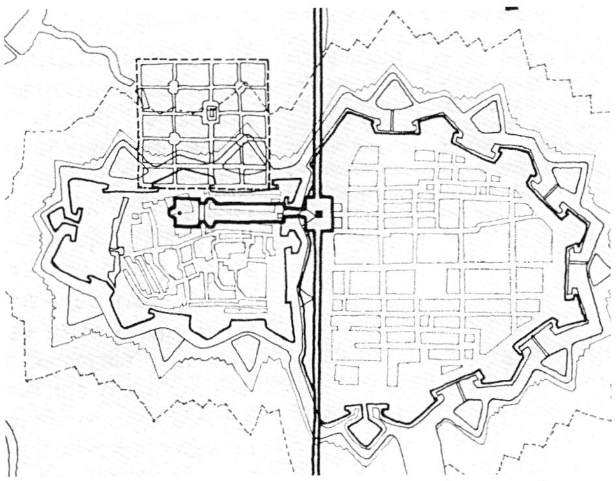

2. Plan of Nancy, showing Héré's intervention, begun 1753

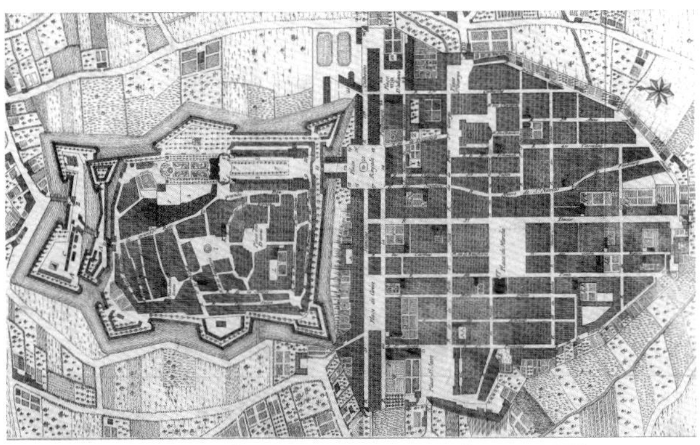

3. Plan of Nancy, with Héré's intervention, begun 1753

4. Aerial view of Héré's spatial sequence

Composite Architectural Interventions

Cities often have mega-buildings that are accumulations of interconnected buildings. The best ones, like the Hofburg in Vienna, respond, reflect, and enhance the urban context. Others, like the Massachusetts State House in Boston, are more modest in scale. Still others, such as Rockefeller Center, are primarily public spaces and extensions of the urban fabric. Other notable composite buildings include: the Vatican; the Quirinale; and the Palais Royale.

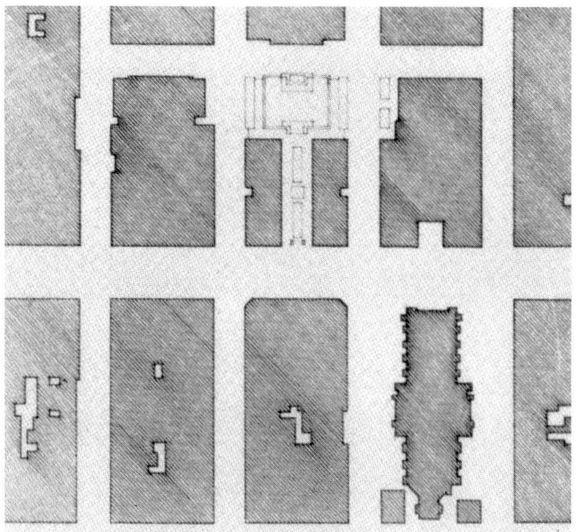

1. Rockefeller Center, plan

2. Rockefeller Center, aerial view

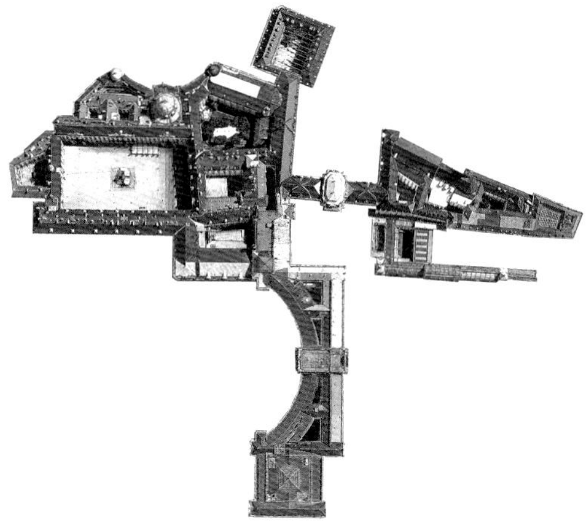

3. Hofburg, aerial plan

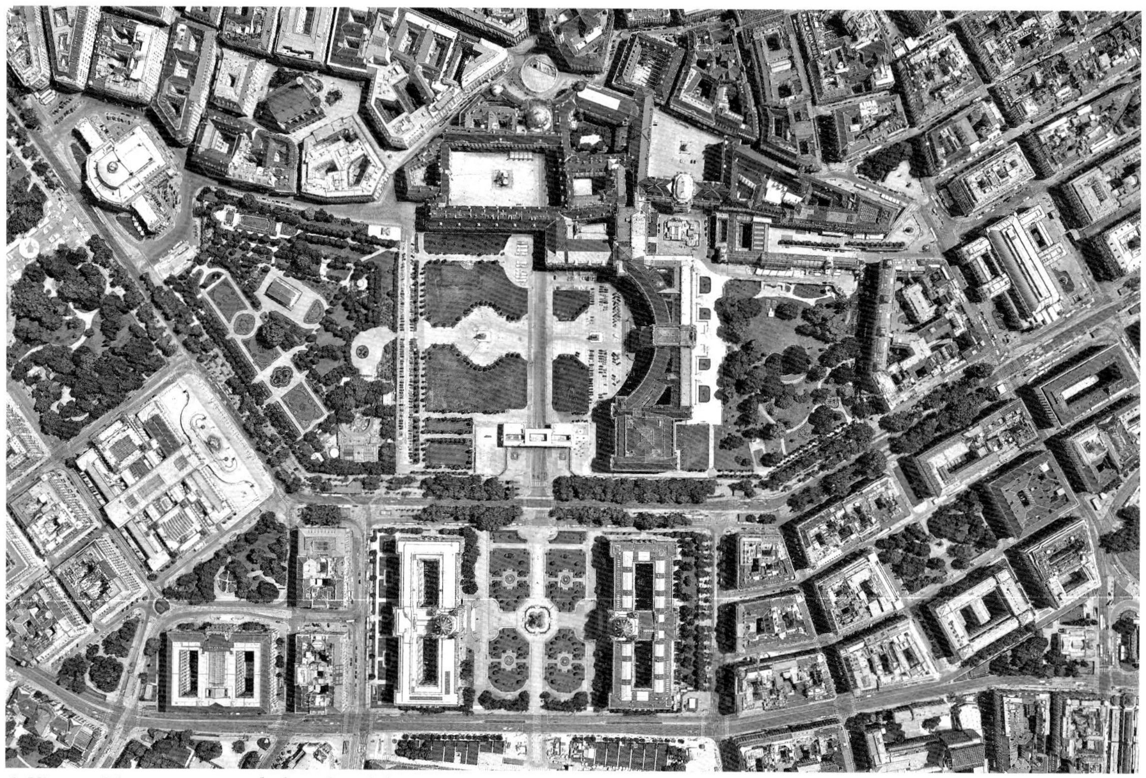

4. Vienna, Ringstrasse, aerial plan, detail, begun 1857

1. The Uffizi, view

2. The Uffizi, aerial plan

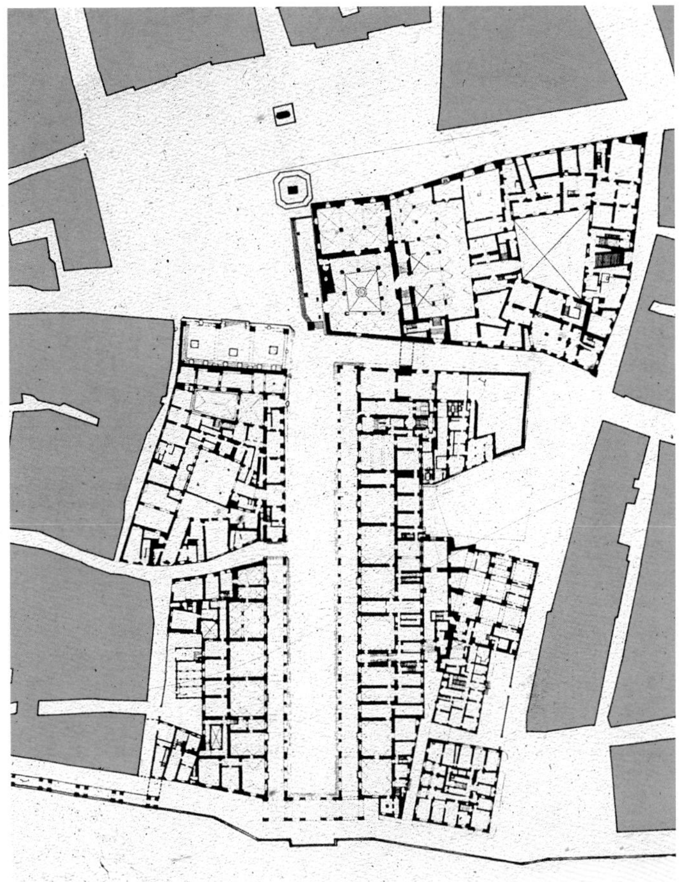

3. The Uffizi, plan

Architectural Interventions

Buildings that define public space and function as urban fabric—such as the Uffizi—buildings that function as monuments, and ambiguous buildings can all serve as positive urban interventions.[5]

Other notable architectural interventions include: the Zwinger in Dresden, and the Palazzo Montecitorio in Rome.

4. The Zwinger, aerial view

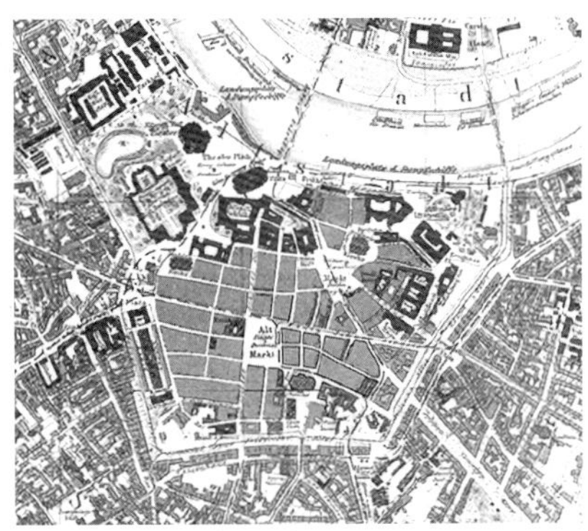

5. Prewar Dresden, plan

1. Athens Acropolis

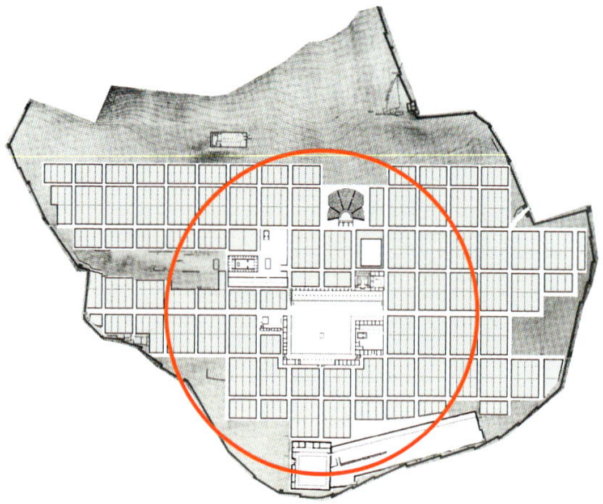

2. Plan of Priene with five min. walk shed

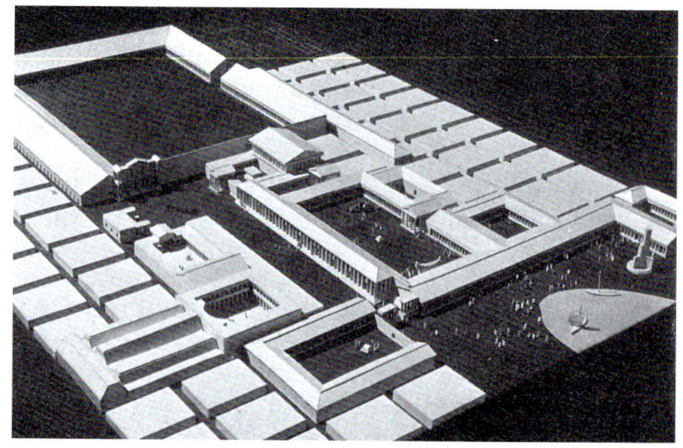

5. Model of the core of Miletus, second c.

Greek Temples and Towns

Traditional treatises on ancient Greece tend to emphasize temples rather than towns. Thus, our mental image is typically that of an Acropolis of picturesquely arranged temples separated vertically from the town—as at Sunium, Aegina, or the Acropolis in Athens. These complexes were usually unrelated directly to the town itself, but were always related to the larger landscape.[6] The sacred precincts at Delphi and Pergamon are extreme examples of a collection of temples.

With the advent of planned Hellenistic colonial cities, however, the temples were usually brought "down" and integrated into the fabric of the town.[7] They were more articulate and emphatic than the civic buildings, such as the stoa, gymnasium, bouleterion, and ekklesiasterion, but they were organized into the grid of the town, thus fundamentally changing their relationship to both the town and the landscape. The civic buildings were integrated into the fabric of the town as at Priene and Miletus, and the housing blocks were generally small and uniform. The original parcels were usually rectangles of about 2,500 square feet—oddly enough, the same area as the typical 25' x 100' New York City block.[8]

Thus, a dialogue was established: between the sacred and profane; between temple and town; or, formally, between monument and urban fabric.

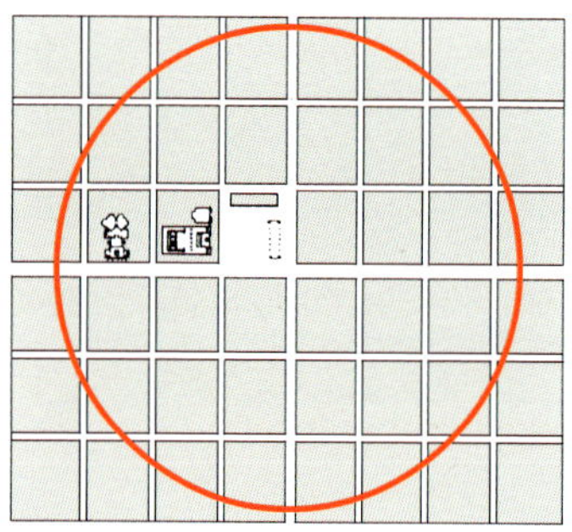

3. Plan of Roman Florence with five min. walk shed

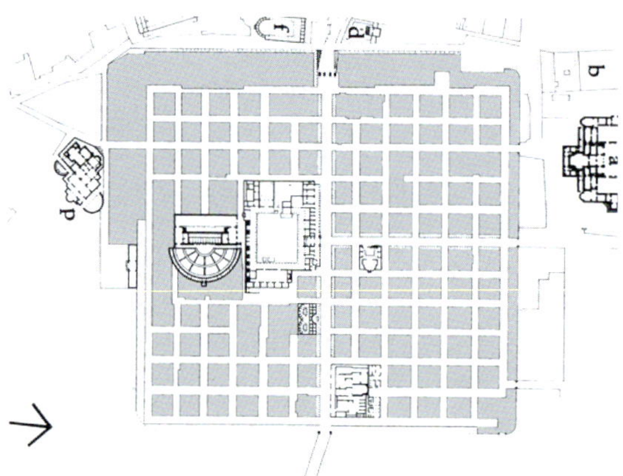

4. Plan of Roman Timgad, 100 AD

Roman Towns

Beyond Rome, the Roman colonies and *castra* followed Greek and Etruscan precedent—as grid towns that included the temple within the fabric of the town. The forum was located at the center of the town, like the agora at Priene, but unlike Greek towns, the original Roman towns had clear geometric perimeters. Roman blocks were often more squarish in proportion than Greek blocks, but the parceling system is unclear due to medieval rebuilding.

It can be argued that the Greeks were not interested in space, but the opposite may be argued for the Romans.[9] This can be seen most clearly at Miletus. Begun in about 466 BC, the planned Greek town was extended and completed by the Romans. The southern portion of fabric is Roman, but it is in the central civic sequence of spaces that the Roman system of spatial enclosure is most evident.

Timgad was founded in north Africa for retired Roman soldiers in 100 AD, and was one of the last Roman towns. As the Roman Empire disintegrated, towns and town planning in the West ceased for several hundred years.

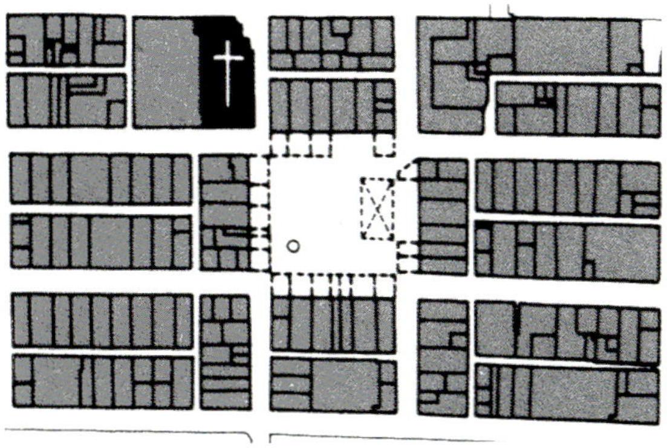

1. Plan detail of Monpazier

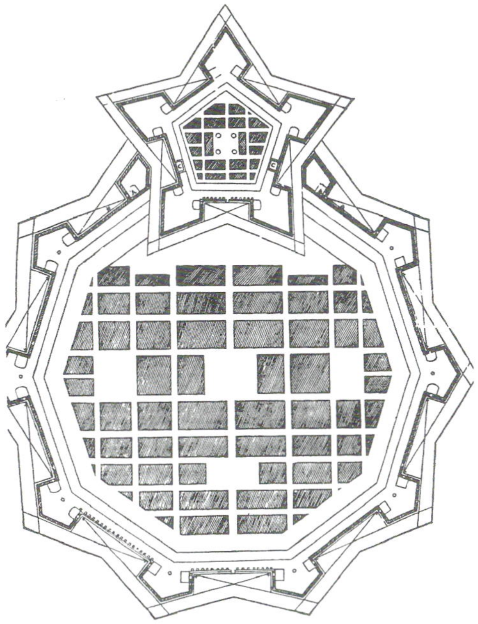

2. Plan of an ideal city by Pietro Cataneo

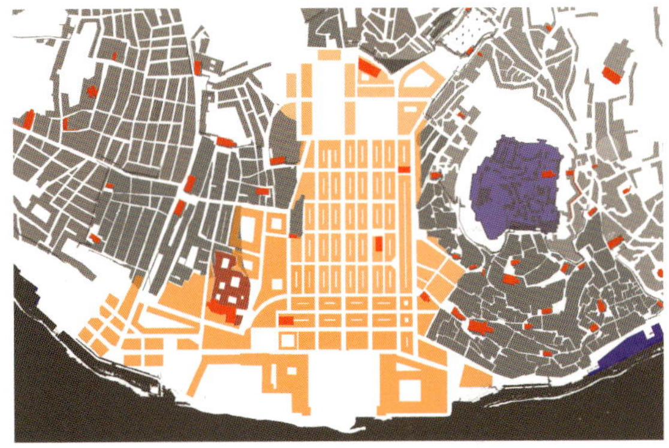

3. Plan of Lisbon, 1756

Bastide Towns

As trade grew, and western Europe began to emerge from the so-called dark age, medieval towns also began to grow—mostly incrementally, and sometimes over the remains of Roman towns.

But after a lapse of about eleven centuries, a series of regular grid towns began to be founded, primarily in southwestern France. Between 1200 and 1400, nearly 700 Bastides were built in this area.[10]

Following the Roman pattern, the town's market square was located in the center of the grid plan, usually with a colonnade around the square. The square was complete and open, the town church being located outside the square. The residential blocks were modest in size, with long narrow parcels, and alleys down the middle.

4. Aerial view of Monpazier

Ideal Renaissance Towns

Although the first planimetric maps of cities did not appear until the middle of the sixteenth century, the reconnection with antiquity through the discovery of Vitruvius's *Ten Books* in 1414 sponsored a seemingly endless series of ideal town plans beginning in the middle of the fifteenth century.[11]

These proposed city plans were centralized and fortified. They were of two types: radial and orthogonal. And though many plans were proposed from the middle of the fifteenth century, built examples—such as Sabbioneta and Palmanova—did not occur until almost 1600. The practice continued, however, until after the earthquake in Sicily in 1693, with the construction of Grammichele and Avola.

The "New World" was also touched by colonization and the grid tradition. The "Law of the Indies" evolved between 1512 and 1680, and was the basis for most towns in Latin America, including the southwestern United States.[12]

5. Aerial view of Palmanova

Baroque New Towns

Destruction by earthquakes also precipitated Baroque plans such as those for the reconstruction of Noto after the 1693 earthquake, and Lisbon after the earthquake of 1756.[13]

These plans might be seen as fragments of ideal Renaissance plans, except for their organization around a civic structure comprised of a theatrical, Baroque sequence of spaces and buildings. Major buildings are not articulated as "temples," but form an integral part of the spatial sequence. Blocks are modest in size with varied parcels.

6. Plan detail of Noto

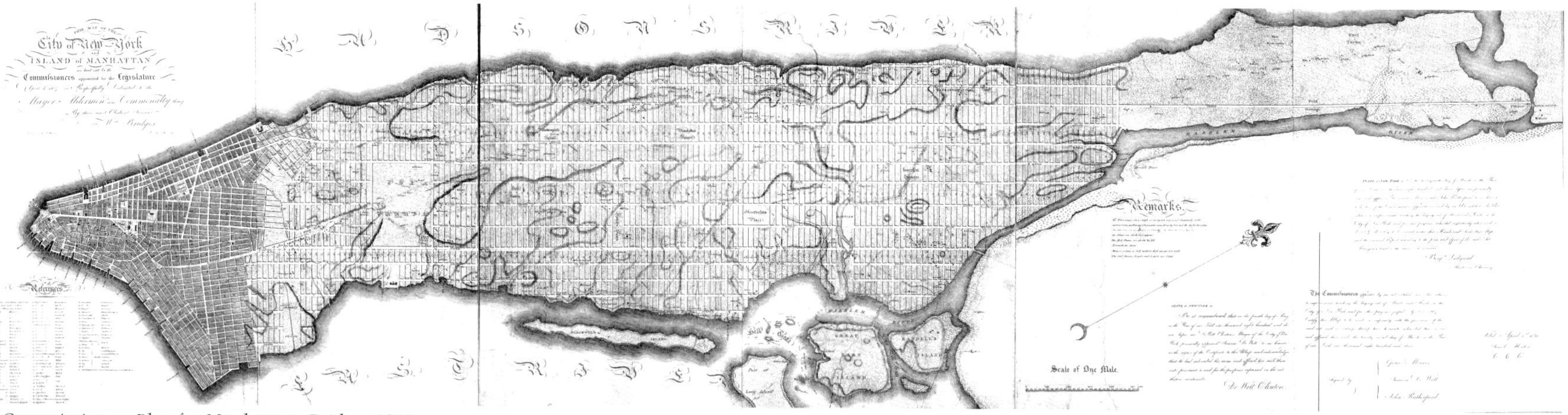

1. *Commissioners Plan for Manhattan, Bridges, 1811*

The Early Nineteenth Century

While Napoleon was conquering Europe and tearing down city fortification walls, a startling event was initiated in New York City: "The Commissioner's Plan" for the expansion of the city was approved in 1811. A regular grid composed of 200' x 800' blocks, divided into 25' x 100' parcels, was proposed to cover the entire undeveloped part of the island, flattening the topography as it moved north. Minor variations of the plan appeared until 1821, and by 1836, as the Coulton Plan illustrates, the armature of New York City was established.[14]

The first half of the nineteenth century in Europe—at least until 1835 or '40, if not 1850—was involved on the one hand with the late phase of Neoclassicism: detached, small-scale buildings, and the beginning of suburban residential quarters in Paris.

On the other hand, since the late eighteenth century there were the important urban interventions of George Dance, John Nash, and the Napoleonic forays into urban design by Percier and Fontaine. But for the most part, these were the beginnings of unified nineteenth-century street design, not the large-scale production of urban fabric. These projects did, however, establish a precedent, and an unbroken line of development for the Parisian boulevards of Haussmann and Napoleon III.

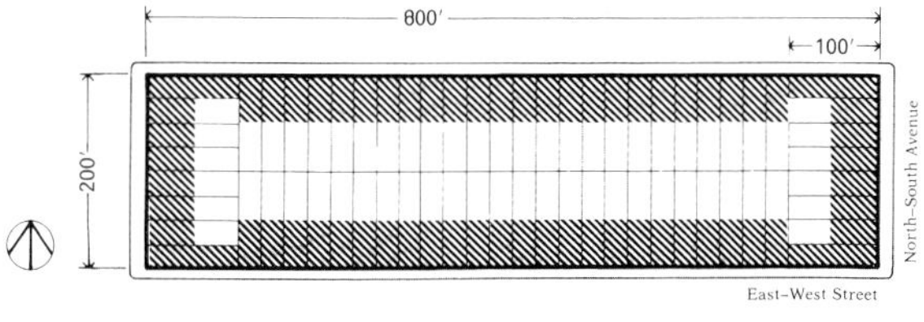

3. *Plan of New York City block*

The Great London Estates

Another notable early nineteenth-century planning model—one that could be a precedent for the many late nineteenth-century urban expansion plans—was the continued planning of the "great estates," such as Belgravia, in London. This tradition of new, planned towns-within-the-town began in the seventeenth century and continued unabated throughout the first half of the nineteenth century (while Napoleon III was in exile in London). None of these plans were on the scale of the late nineteenth-century expansion plans, but other than this, there appears to be no obvious, continuing tradition of town planning that could be drawn upon to respond to new demands that began around the mid-nineteenth century.[15]

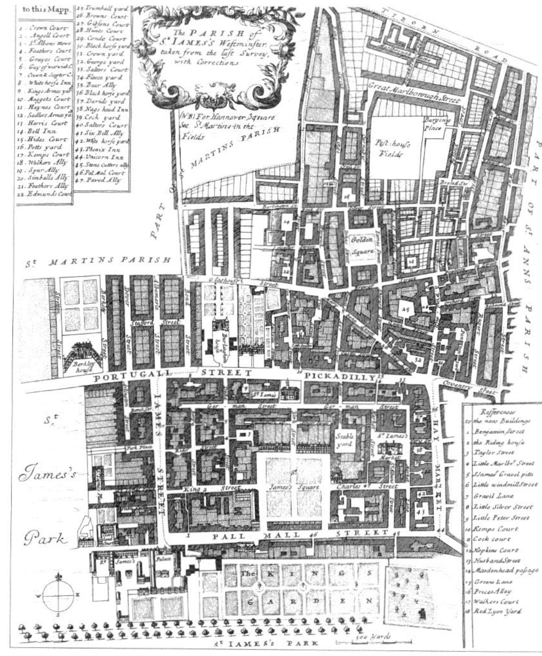

2. *Plan of St. James, 1660s*

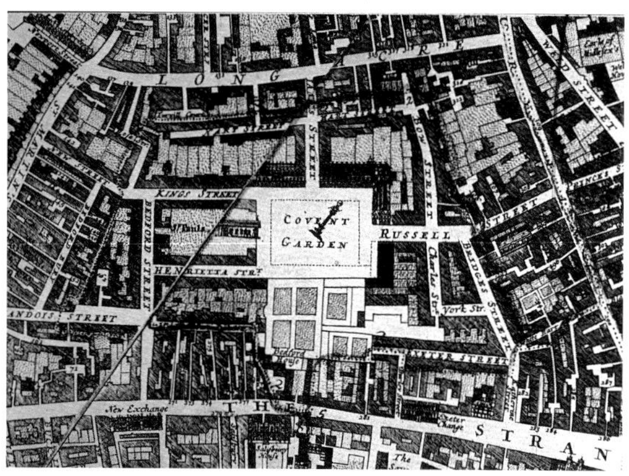

4. *Plan of Covent Garden, 1631–37*

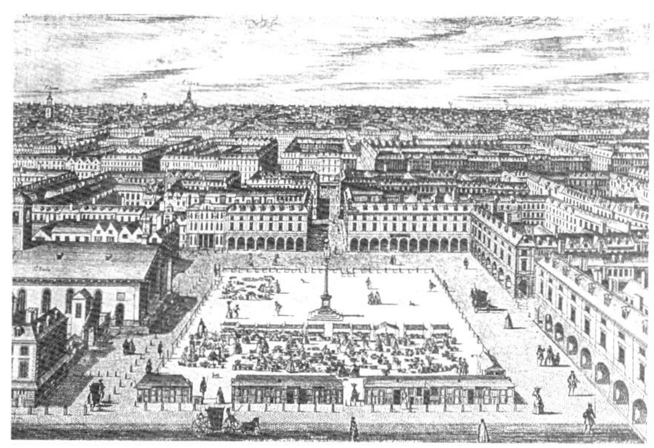

5. *View of Covent Garden, engraving*

1. View of Champs Élysée, Paris

The Late Nineteenth Century

Within a relatively brief period—approximately from 1860 to 1890—very sophisticated plans for the urban expansion of major American and European cities were designed, drawn up, and implemented by architects and engineers. These plans included comprehensive infrastructure (sewers, water, lighting), urban parks and landscape, new methods of finance, accommodation of increased urban movement via carriages, and the incorporation of a fashionable new building type, the *apartment building*.

One notable characteristic of these nineteenth-century urban expansion plans—one that they did share with the long tradition of planned towns—is that their urban authors did not draw buildings. During this time, the production of urban plans consisted of designing and drawing cities, and parts of cities, not buildings.

In other words, consistent with M. R. G. Conzen's theory of urban geography, urban planners designed the public realm of the city—the streets, blocks, and squares, and sometimes the parcel divisions—while architects designed the buildings within the urban framework. This period, on the eve of massive change, might therefore be seen as both the zenith and the twilight of what used to be called town planning.

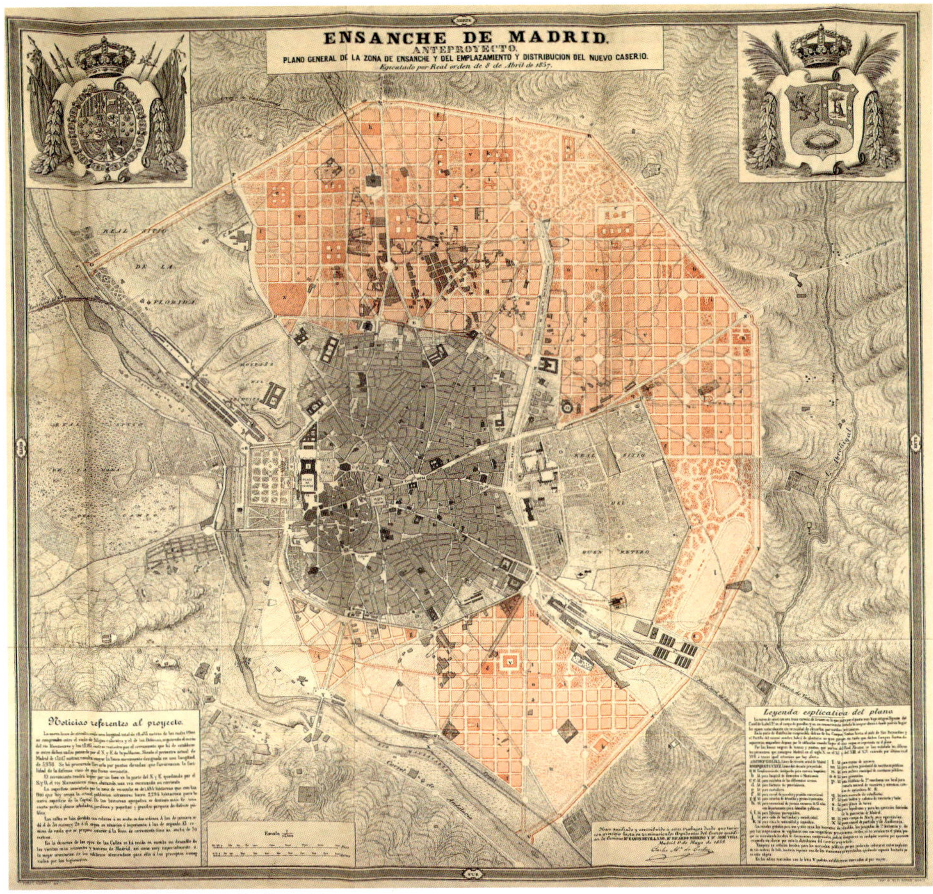

2. Expansion plan for Madrid, 1860

3. Aerial plan of Back Bay, Boston, begun 1859

Proto-Modernist Town Planning

With the rapid urban expansion in the second half of the nineteenth century, new urban issues emerged. Architects and town planners of the period between 1890 and 1910, however, did not question the validity of the traditional elements of the city: the streets, squares, and blocks. Rather, they tried to rationalize them and adapt them to "modern" demands. They also still utilized urban building types—buildings that defined the public space of the city.

This general consensus unites such otherwise disparate planners as Eugène Hénard, Camillo Sitte, Joseph Stübben, and Otto Wagner; and this consensus renders trivial the commonly framed oppositions, such as that between Sitte and Wagner. As either traditionalists or proto-modernists, these planners were united in their acceptance of the city. It remained for Le Corbusier and the other modernists to jettison the city.

The proto-modernists did, however, begin to draw buildings as well as plans; buildings tended to become as large as blocks; and planners did propose state management and distribution of land, as well as monofunctional zoning—all characteristics of later modernist planning.

1. Perspective of the core of the expansion plan for Vienna, Otto Wagner, 1910

2. City of the Future, Hénard

3. Intersection, Hénard

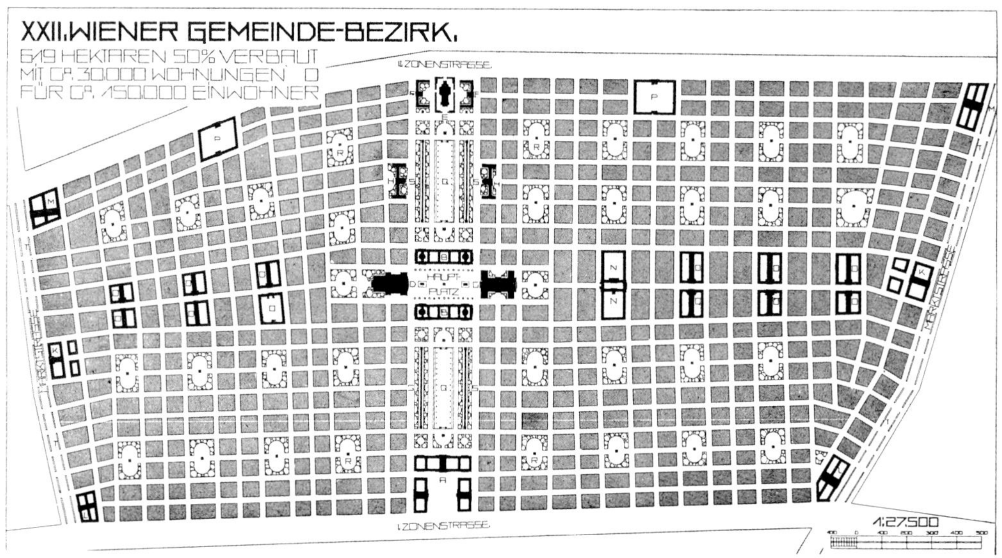

4. Expansion plan for Vienna, Otto Wagner, 1910

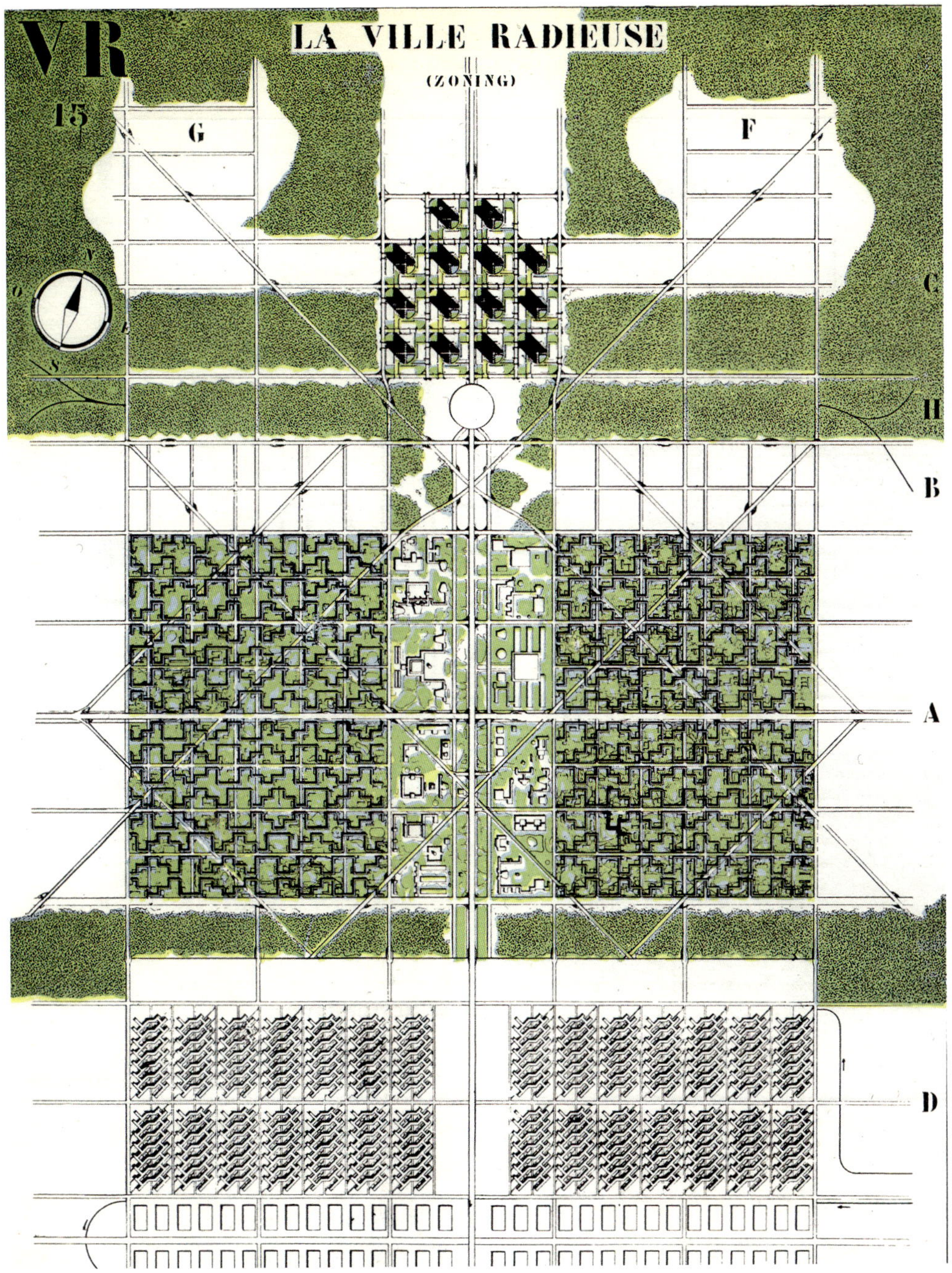

1. Le Corbusier, Ville Radieuse, Plan, 1933

Modernist Town Planning

The original thesis of this study was that sometime in the early 1920s, architects and town planners, such as Le Corbusier and his CIAM colleagues, began to draw buildings rather than cities, and that this has created confusion and promoted the degradation of the urban environment.

Until this time there had been a symbiotic relationship between architecture and urbanism: architectural styles could change as desired because there was hegemony of the urban realm; when architecture achieved hegemony over urbanism, however, the public realm disappeared as a legible, spatial entity.

New, fundamentally antiurban architectural typologies conspired with increased freedom of movement and monofunctional zoning to challenge the hegemony and validity of traditional urban form.

This period marks nothing less than a complete inversion of urban form and design principles. In simple terms it marks the death of the street, the end of legible urban space, the end of mixed-use zoning, and the hegemony of movement over place.[16]

2. Le Corbusier, Ville Radieuse, 1933

Postwar Planning

The Second World War was devastating for many European cities. Dresden was almost totally destroyed. Before the war Dresden had been one of Europe's most beautiful cities. Afterward, there were competing strategies for rebuilding the city, but the death of Joseph Stalin in 1953 freed the planners to establish a socialist utopia based on modernist typologies and principles.

In America, "urban renewal" accomplished at the hands of planners what the bombings had in Europe. White flight to the suburbs and the Highway Act conspired with the planners in the disintegration of American cities. The influx of European modernists, such as Gropius (and later Sert) at Harvard, and Mies at Chicago, helped ensure that reconstruction would be based on modernist—fundamentally anti-urban—principles.

Beginning in 1959, the successors to the Congrès International d'Architecture Moderne (CIAM), the members of Team X, tried to modify and transform the limitations of CIAM principles, and to extend their influence in America. Jose Sert introduced the urban design program at Harvard in 1956, and although his was a "softer" agenda, it was nevertheless an extension of CIAM principles.[17]

1. Aerial view of the historic core of Dresden, before the war

2. Aerial view of the Prager Strasse, 1960s

3. Contemporary aerial view of the inner city of Dresden looking west

4. Aerial view of the historic core of Boston, before the war

5. Aerial view of the historic core of Boston, 1960s

6. Aerial view of the historic core of Boston, 1970s

The Recovery of the City

As the limitations and reality of the modernist agenda became visible in the late 1960s and early 1970s, reaction against CIAM planning principles had already begun—as early as the 1960s. For many architects and urbanists the reconstruction, or rediscovery, of the city—its typologies and morphology—was a prerequisite for the recovery of quality urban life.

In Europe, the so-called rationalists—Aldo Rossi, Rob and Leon Krier, and others—began to revise architecture within the context of the city. As Andres Duany has pointed out, Leon Krier was the first in forty years to comprehensively draw the city, and his principles were, brashly, the complete opposite of those of CIAM.

In America, urbanists from Jane Jacobs to Denise Scott Brown advocated a gentler return to traditional urban ideas. The preservation movement and "advocacy planning" both emerged in resistance to the destruction of neighborhoods and cities.

Also, during the 1960s and early 1970s, Colin Rowe and colleagues at Cornell University began to explore ways to combine modernist and normative urban form strategies in order to produce a habitable contemporary urbanism. For about twenty years the urban design studio at Cornell was a continuous urban research lab.[18]

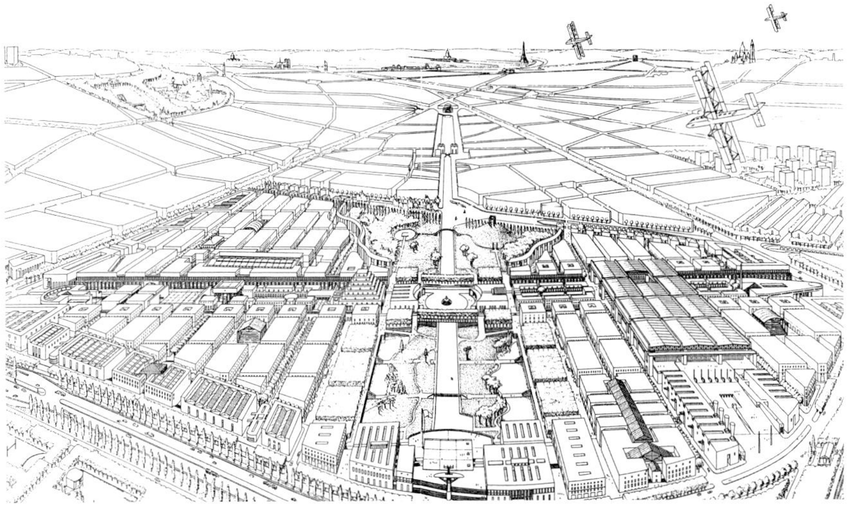

1. Leon Krier, La Villette, Perspective, 1976

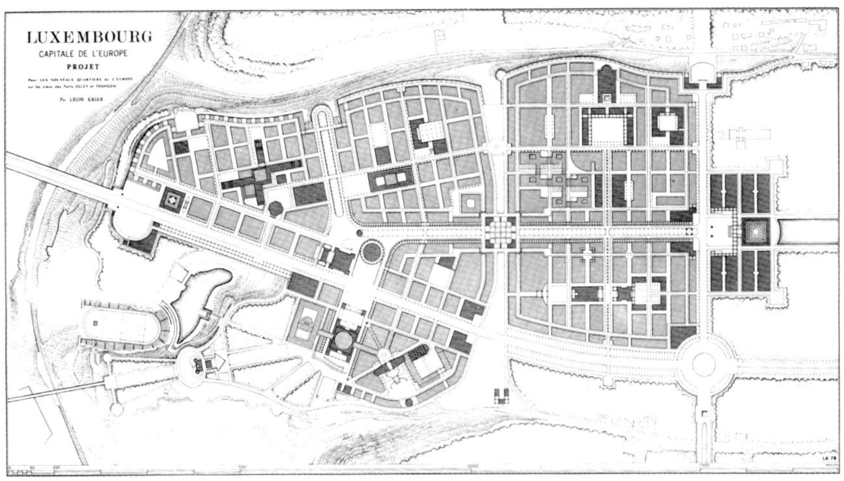

2. Leon Krier, proposed plan for Luxembourg, 1978

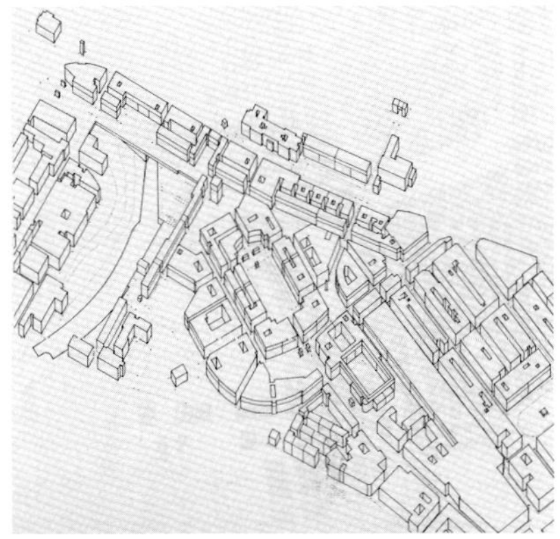

3. Steven Fong, Marylebone Project, 1979

4. Rowe Studio, Buffalo, model, 1966

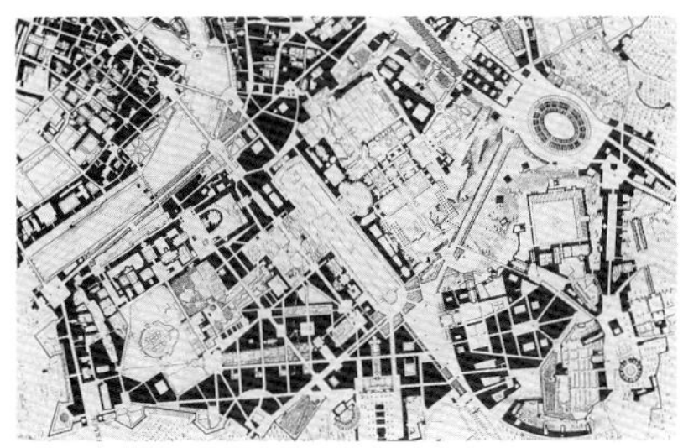

5. Rowe, et. al., Roma Interrotta, 1978

Contemporary Architecture

Despite efforts to redefine architecture and urbanism during the last quarter of the twentieth century, contemporary architecture has become ever more narcissistic and autonomous—the result of a three-hundred-year formal and social transformation, from near complete hegemony of the public realm in the seventeenth century to a no less tyrannical hegemony of the private realm in our time. The physical civic realm has all but disappeared.

Legible urban space is required for a physical public realm, but little architecture today contributes. This may be the most crucial professional issue of our time.

As the world continues to urbanize (over 50 percent of the world's population now lives in cities); as population increases (it is predicted to increase from six billion to nine billion by 2050); and as the world's resources diminish (especially petroleum); it will become imperative to reexamine architecture and its relationship to the city.

2. Aerial perspective of "Downtown" Dubai

1. Popstage, Breda, NL, E. van Egeraat

3. London City Hall, Foster + Partners

4. Performing Arts Center, F. Gehry

5. Global urbanism, W. Alsop

Three Contemporary New Towns

Despite the propensity of many contemporary architects to favor narcissistic anti-urban buildings, some of a series of new, planned towns have explored the relationship between architecture and urbanism.

Three such new towns are: Masdar City in Abu Dhabi, by Foster + Partners; Poundbury in Dorset, by Leon Krier; and Rak Gateway in Dubai, by the Office for Metropolitan Architecture.

All three are compact, with finite limits, and all three claim to be "sustainable," even though two are located in the desert. None of the three have traditional urban design plans showing blocks and parcels, and all illustrate building types and volumetric development, and sometimes the architectural character of the buildings.

One of these new towns has been built (Poundbury), and has been socially and financially successful—to the consternation of "avant-garde" architects.

1. Perspective interior view, Masdar

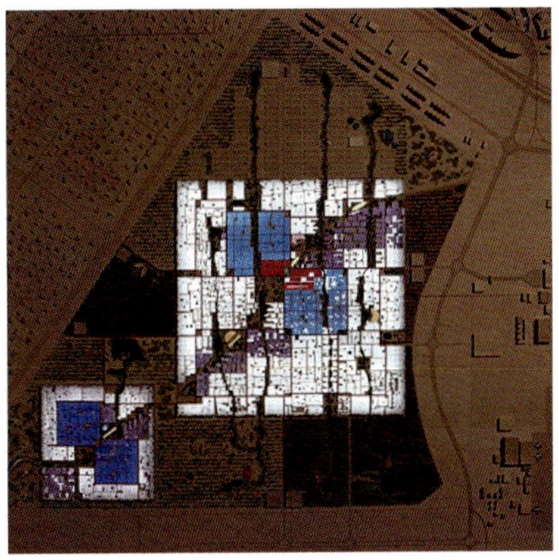
2. Plan of Masdar City, Abu Dhabi

3. Aerial perspective of Masdar City

4. Aerial perspective of Masdar City

5. View of Poundbury

6. Plan of Poundbury, UK

7. Aerial perspective of Poundbury

8. View of town square, Poundbury

9. Perspective view of RAK Gateway

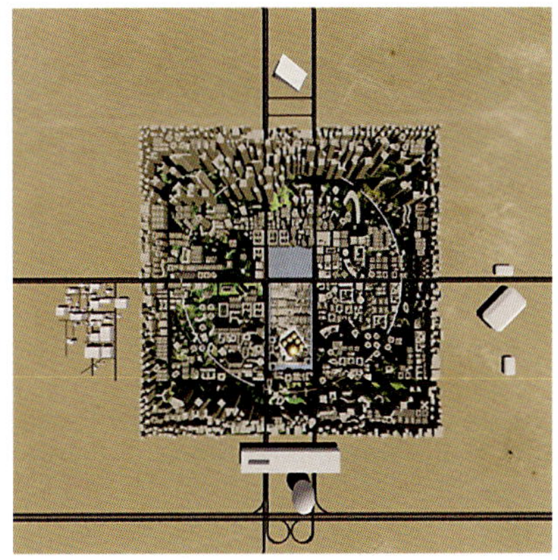
10. Plan of RAK Gateway, Dubai

11. Aerial perspective of RAK Gateway

12. Aerial perspective of RAK city center

1. *View of Earth from space*

Contemporary Environmental Issues

Data indicate that in the beginning of the twenty-first century, our planet has passed into an irreversible environmental crisis—one that, without intervention, could result in the extermination of human life within the not-too-distant future. This outcome may still be averted, but it will be difficult, and life will be radically different than that of the twentieth century.[19]

The size and lifestyle of our human population are the drivers of this crisis through production of food and materials, consumption of renewable and nonrenewable resources, and waste and pollution.

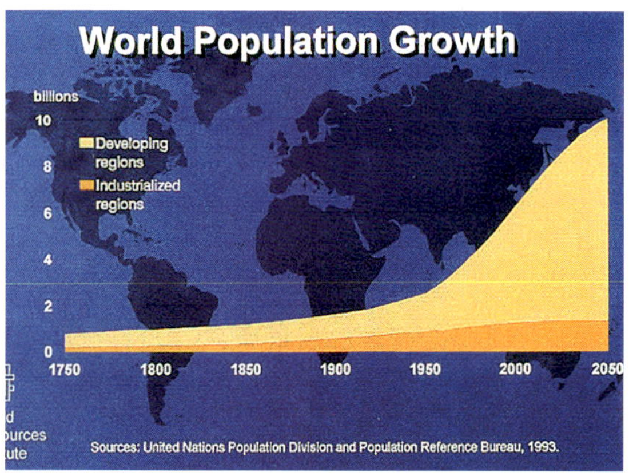

2. *World population growth, 1750–2050*

3. *Atlanta highway infrastructure*

Population and Lifestyle

The Earth can naturally support about 2.5 billion people. Population size beyond that has only been supported by technology in the production of food, with some segments of world population living in marginal conditions at best. Production of food has plateaued, however, and population continues to increase.

The production of material goods in the developed part of the world has also increased to an extravagant degree. The lifestyle to which we have become accustomed demands the production of ever more massive amounts of "stuff."

4. *Suburban family*

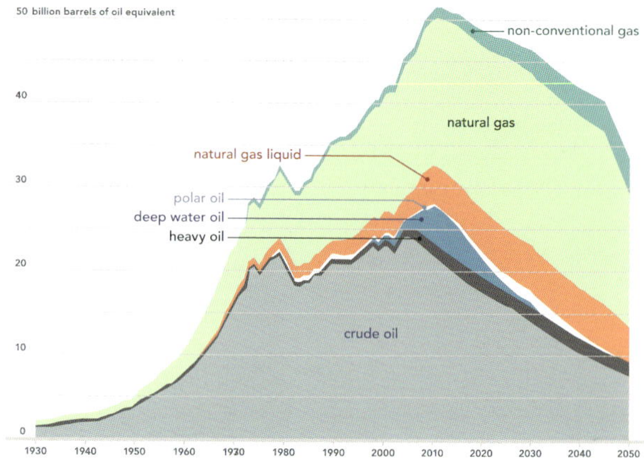

5. *Nonrenewable resource depletion*

Consumption

Humans are consuming the Earth's nonrenewable resources, such as petroleum, gas, coal, and metals, at a geometrically increasing rate. There are relatively fine-grained arguments about the remaining amounts of these resources, but nonrenewable means that when they are gone, they are gone. Tragically, an excessive proportion of nonrenewable resources are squandered on America's predominantly suburban lifestyle. We have 4.6 percent of the world's population, but we use almost one-third of the world's petroleum. World population is also consuming renewable resources at a greater rate than can be replenished. As population increases, consumption grows, and as diets in the developing world become more protein-centered, consumption expands further.

6. *West Virginia strip mine*

1. *Air pollution in Shanghai*

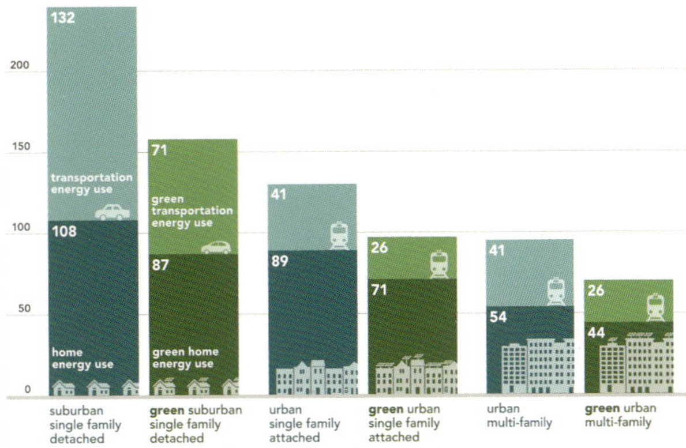

3. *Comparison of single-family energy use*

4. *Bordeaux urban life*

Pollution and Global Warming

The results of our complex, modern lifestyle of consumption are no longer unseen, but visible: from toxic pollution of the food chain and water system to melting ice and snow caps, rising sea level, acid seas, deforestation, desertification, fresh water loss, soil erosion and loss, and species extinction. Of all of the results of our lifestyle, however, global warming is by far the most devastating. We can live without oil, but we cannot live on an excessively warm planet.

The political excuse for non-action is always economic. But remediation is more expensive than prevention, and extinction is even cheaper. All we have to do is continue what we are doing, and natural forces will purge the Earth of the problem—us. Even if it takes a millennium or more for the Earth to come back to equilibrium this is an insignificant period in the timeline of the world.

2. *Modern life*

Urbanism and the Environment

What do environmental issues have to do with architecture and urbanism? Almost everything. The form of our cities and buildings is the solution, not the problem. Our whole culture is based on the idea of limitless resources and continuous growth, and we have become so accustomed to the idea that we have forgotten that we live on a finite planet. Urbanism is crucial to a solution of environmental problems as it is the most efficient form of inhabitation with the smallest ecological footprint on a per capita basis.[20] We need to use fewer resources and less infrastructure, and create less pollution. This means living smaller, closer, denser, simpler—more urban. We need to (again) conceive architecture and urbanism in these terms.

Most architectural and urban design proposals today derive from the facts—the *status quo*—of our contemporary society, not from scientific environmental projections. From urban farming to driverless cars to social media to big data, most proposals are technologically hopeful extensions of the status quo rather than radical rethinking of the basic conditions of the way we live.

Our industrial society has evolved incrementally over a century and a half to our current environmental crisis with most of that evolution happening within the last fifty or sixty years. To continue to rely on incremental change without a long-range strategy would be catastrophic.

Principles for a Sustainable Urbanism

The basic form guidelines for good, sustainable urbanism are simple. They are revolutionary only because they have been abandoned for so long that their value is no longer recognized. These are a good start:

Dense, contiguous urban buildings forming modestly sized blocks;

Streets as narrow as possible, designed primarily for people, not cars (or diesel buses);

A pattern of plazas or squares of moderate size;

Neighborhood and civic parks and gardens;

Mixed-use, walkable neighborhoods;

A legible civic structure of public spaces and buildings; and,

Efficient public transportation systems.

Technology has been the enabler to the problem of population growth and lifestyle. It is important, but should be used to enhance basic decisions, not supplant them—the final step, not the first.

I. THE PREINDUSTRIAL CITY: 800 BC–1850

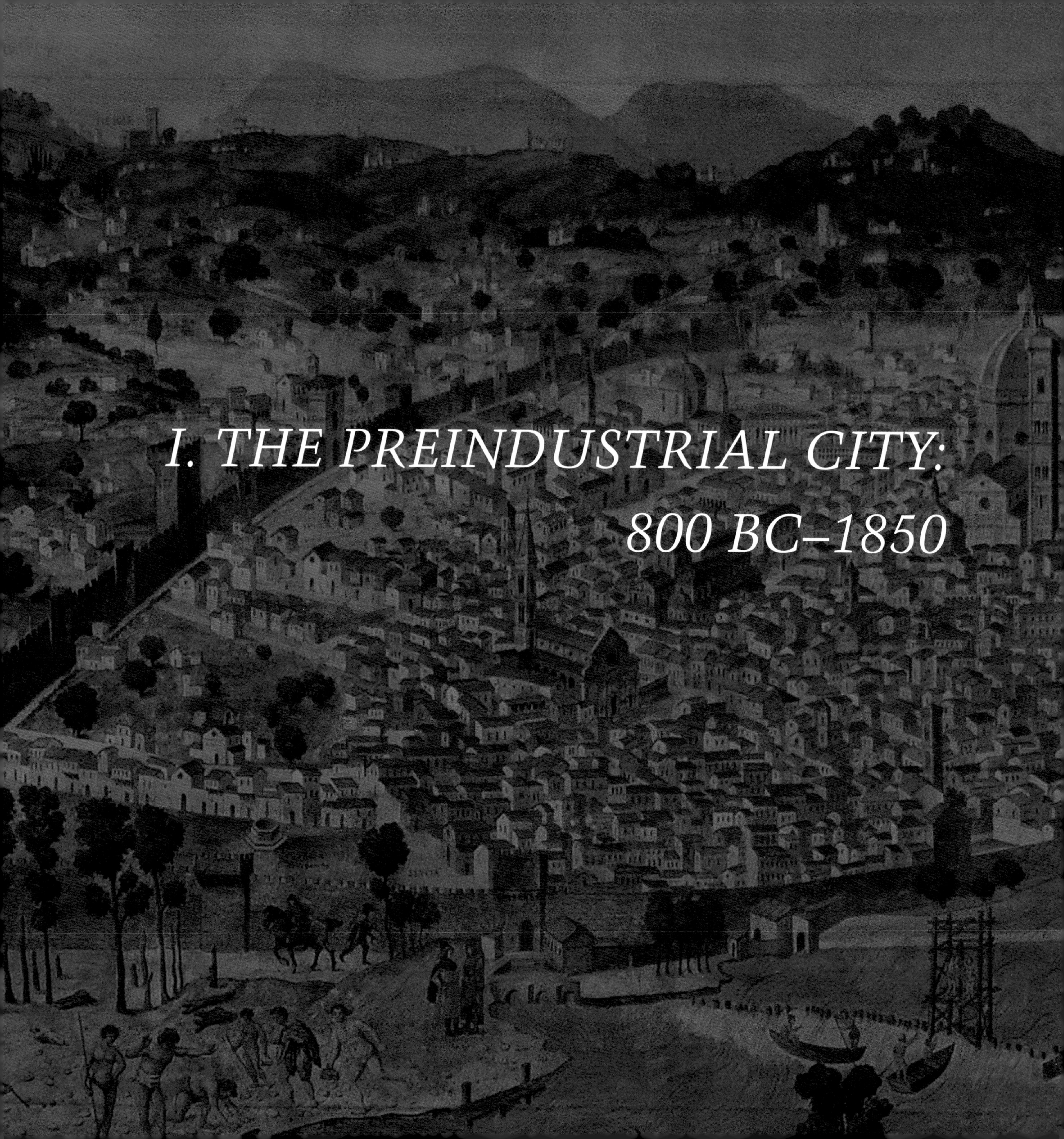

From the earliest planned Greek cities to the railroad age, Western cities had several characteristics in common: relatively small size, dense urban fabric, legible public spaces, multifunctional neighborhoods of walkable dimensions, limited vehicular circulation, and a limited range of known building types.

Maps of many of these cities were published by the Society for the Diffusion of Useful Knowledge in the middle of the nineteenth century. Beautifully drawn, these maps illustrate the cities at the last moment of preindustrial innocence, just as the railroads enter.

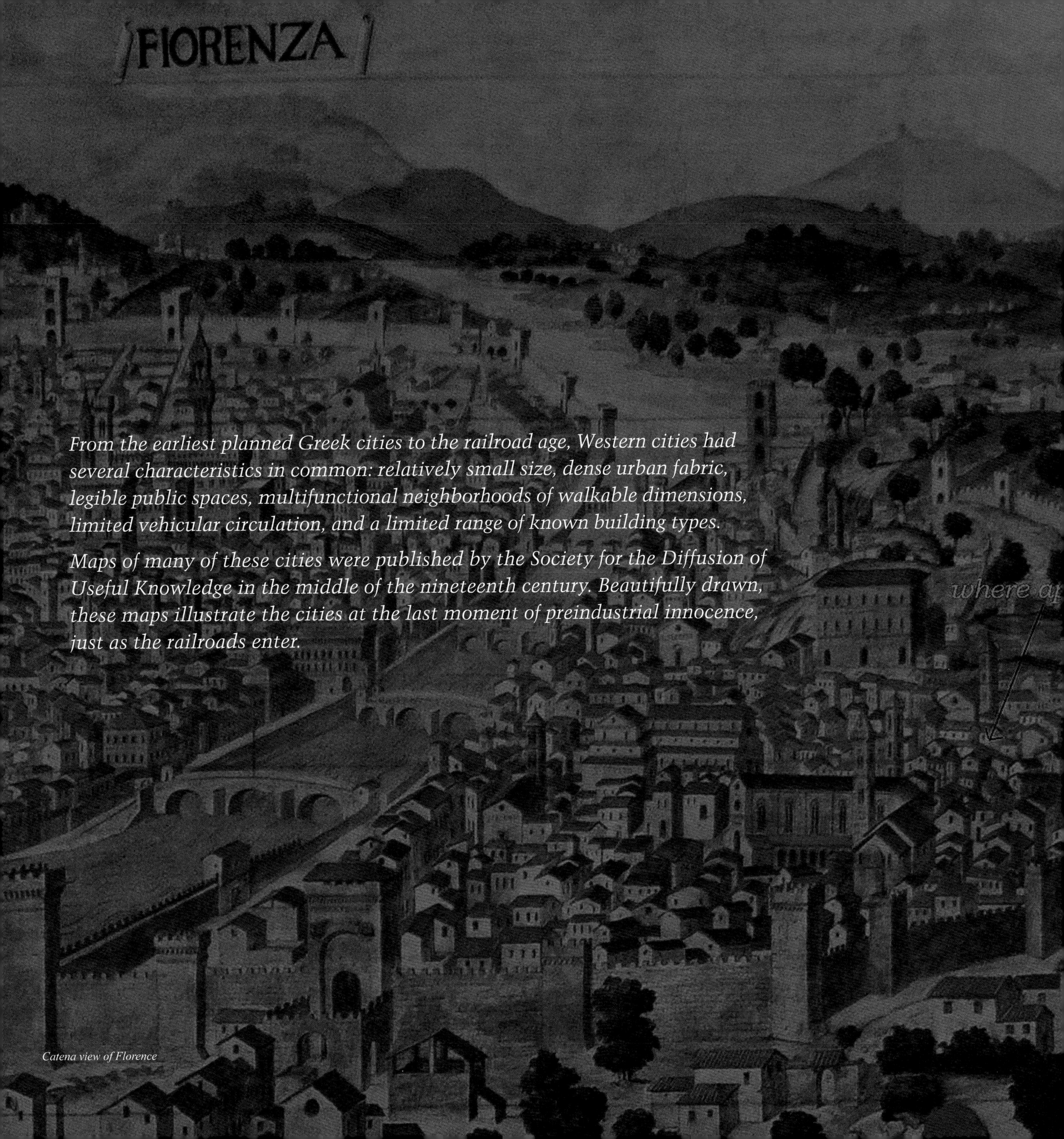

Catena view of Florence

Map of Greek and Phoenician colonies in the Mediterranean

Greek Cities: 800–200 BC

The sophisticated achievements of Greek architecture, as well as the apparent lack of interest in the form of Greek cities by Greek philosophers, have both tended to deflect attention from Greek town planning. But over the course of six centuries the Greeks formed a staggering number of new towns in Magna Grecia: Sicily, the Italic peninsula, and the east. As planning evolved from the diagrammatic orthogonal plans of the Classical period to the sophisticated Hellenistic compositions, a base was created not only for Roman towns, but for Western towns in general.

Antiquity

The roots of western town planning begin in what is often called antiquity—the ancient world of Etruscans, Greeks, and Romans. Too often, however, the periods of this fertile millennium are lumped together as "Classical Antiquity," thus blurring crucial architectural and town planning distinctions. It is therefore important to articulate Classical Greek, Hellenistic Greek, and Roman architecture and town planning.

Greek Town Planning

Ancient Greek sites cannot be understood from plans and pictures; they must be experienced. This is because the ancient Greeks may not have been interested in architectural and urban space *per se*, but they were masters at relating the individual to the space and iconography of the larger landscape through the design and siting of temple complexes,[1] and later—during the Hellenistic period—towns.

Between the eighth and second centuries BC the Greeks founded scores of new towns—in the east, in Sicily, and on the Italic peninsula. Formally, the towns fall into two distinct categories: those of the Archaic and Classical periods (ca. 800–336 BC), and those of the Hellenistic period (ca. 336–200 BC).

Greek town plans had no real religious content, but they were imagined as political constructs. To Plato and Aristotle they were sociopolitical entities rather more than formal ones. In the development of town planning, however, their formal structure is extremely important.

In town planning terms, the earliest Greek cities, such as Naxos, Poseidonia (Paestum), and Akragas (Agrigento), were primitive. They were diagrammatic, political arrangements consisting of large, even, gridded areas of urban fabric, with open areas reserved for the agora and temples.

The urban fabric consisted of long narrow blocks that were more or less equal and "democratically" divided into equal parcels for houses. The streets were unremarkable. There was no urban landscape, no neighborhood spaces. It was a practical arrangement. Indeed, these Archaic towns may be seen as the forerunners of twentieth-century monofunctional town planning—the Ville Contemporaine, minus the landscape.

Temples, on the other hand, received the highest architectural and site design attention—in the center of the town at Poseidonia, and on the edge of the town at Akragas. Despite the perfunctory nature of town plans, temple complexes, such as the temple of Aphaia at Aegina, had spectacular relationships to the landscape—relationships that cannot be imagined from plans.

By the Hellenistic period, the planning art that had been exercised in the design and siting of temples was applied to whole towns, their plans, and sites: e.g., Priene, Ephesus, Miletus, Pergamon, and Assos. By this time, the ideal of the Greek town was fully developed in its form and institutional components.[2]

Although Priene remained a basically pure, Hellenistic town, many other Greek towns were transformed by Roman urban and architectural renovations. Among them: Miletus, Ephesus, and Taormina. In essence, the Romans emphasized and exaggerated the existing Hellenistic civic structure of streets, squares, and public buildings by providing a more legible and elaborate spatial structure.

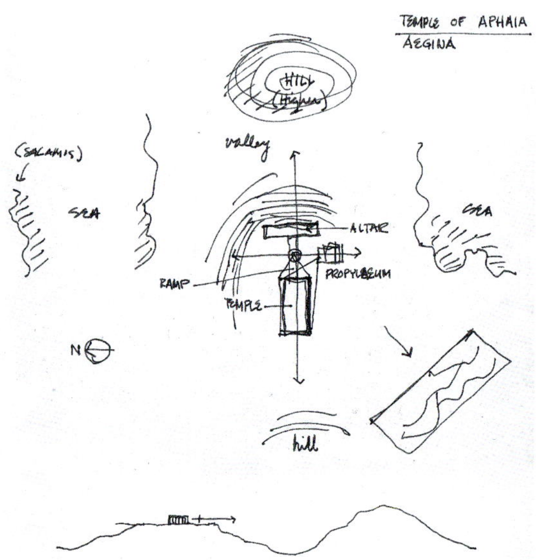

1. Temple of Aphaia, Aegina, sketch site plan and section. The temple and platform sit on the edge of a saddle of a hill, oriented east-west. The entry axis, perpendicular to that of the temple, is oriented to the coastline to the south and to the island of Salamis on the north. The higher hill to the east forms a backdrop for the altar.

2. Athens, view of theater, acropolis, and Mount Lycabettus

Classical Greek Cities

In contrast to the sophistication of the temples, classical Greek cities are surprisingly banal. Cities, such as Poseidonia (Paestum), were diagrammatic. Like modernist cities, they were based on mono-functional zoning. The plans consisted of large, gridded urban areas of housing surrounding open areas of relatively few civic building types. The private housing areas were formed of inwardly focused courtyard houses, originally on equally sized parcels on long, narrow blocks with narrow streets. The architectural language of civic buildings consisted of simple, flat stone walls and a trabeated system of free-standing stone columns and beams. This system was used most elaborately, for temples, which were always free-standing and often separated from the city—on an acropolis or in an open central area. Temples had pedimented "fronts" and lateral "sides," which made them even more articulate from the more prosaic urban buildings. Greek cities of the classical period did not develop formed, or conspicuous, urban space, but they did often emphasize their relationship with the larger landscape. The vitality and excellence of classical Greek architecture was expressed in civic buildings, not town planning.

Cities require walls to define urban space. Greek buildings were generally one story (sometimes two), and because of the climate and building openness, there were rarely windows to the public exterior. It is noteworthy that there are almost no examples of engaged columns and walls in classical Greek architecture. Rare exceptions are the temple of Zeus at Agrigento, the rear facade of the temple of Asclepius at Agrigento, and the west face of the Erechtheion in Athens. Engaged columns and elaborate walls were developed by the Romans, not the Greeks, thus providing architectural language for subsequent urban development.

Hellenistic Greek Cities

By the middle of the fourth century BC, the idea of the Greek city had matured. Hellenistic Greek cities, such as Priene, Assos, and Pergamon, were more conspicuously designed as sophisticated compositions, with designed public space, but they were still one story, and the architectural language still consisted of simple walls and free-standing columns. Temples and other public buildings were absorbed into the fabric of the cities, and the long, narrow blocks of earlier Greek cities became more nearly square, which increased the frequency of streets for a richer urban fabric. The private realm of the city consisted of introverted courtyard housing with little engagement of the streets. There were no secondary plazas and no landscape within the city.

1. Selinunte, conjectural restoration of main street

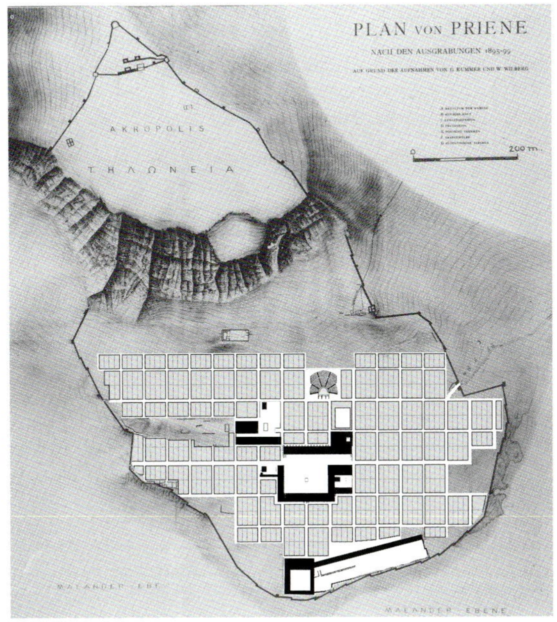

2. Plan of Priene

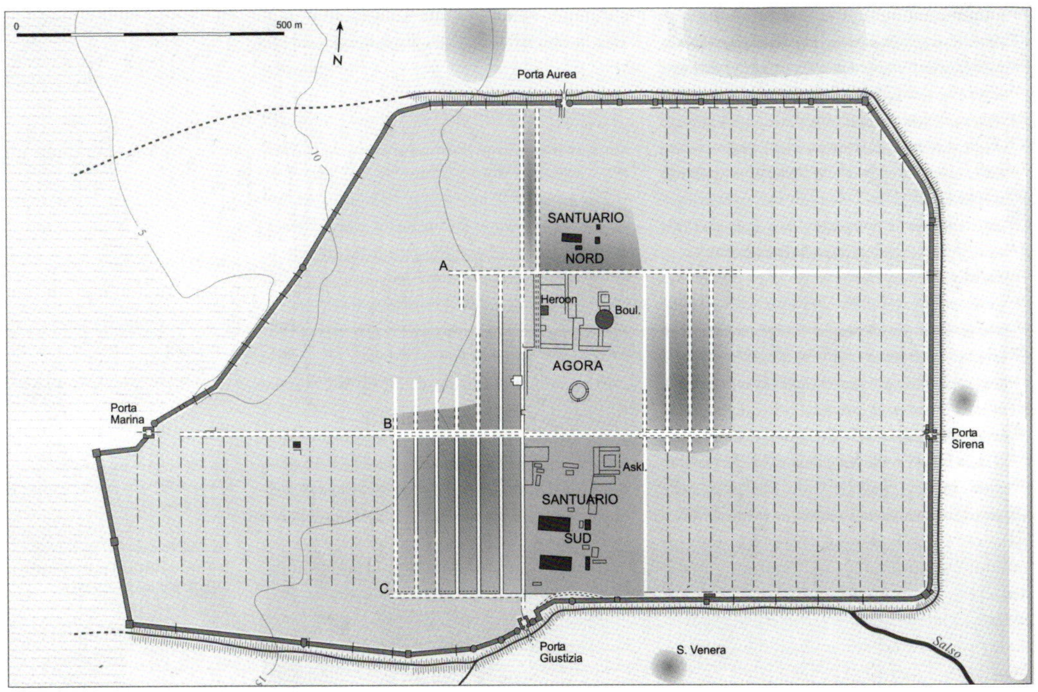

3. Poseidonia (Paestum), plan without Roman additions, ca. 600 BC

Selinunte

Selinunte was founded between 650 and 628 BC as the most western of Greece's Sicilian colonies. The city was destroyed by the Carthaginians in 409 BC and rebuilt on a grid plan. The new city became important again in Sicily until its final destruction by the Carthaginians in ca. 250 BC.

The beautiful, often published, reconstruction plan of the acropolis at Selinunte by Jean Hulot, below, gives little indication of the city's extent, or spectacular context on a high plateau overlooking the Mediterranean, and flanked by two ports. The plan also gives no indication of the additional temple site to the east. But Hulot also made the more comprehensive plan to the right, which illustrates the full extent of the city, the ports, and the eastern temple area.

This site must be seen to really be appreciated, as there are spectacular views up and down the coast and into the valley as well as the surrounding countryside.

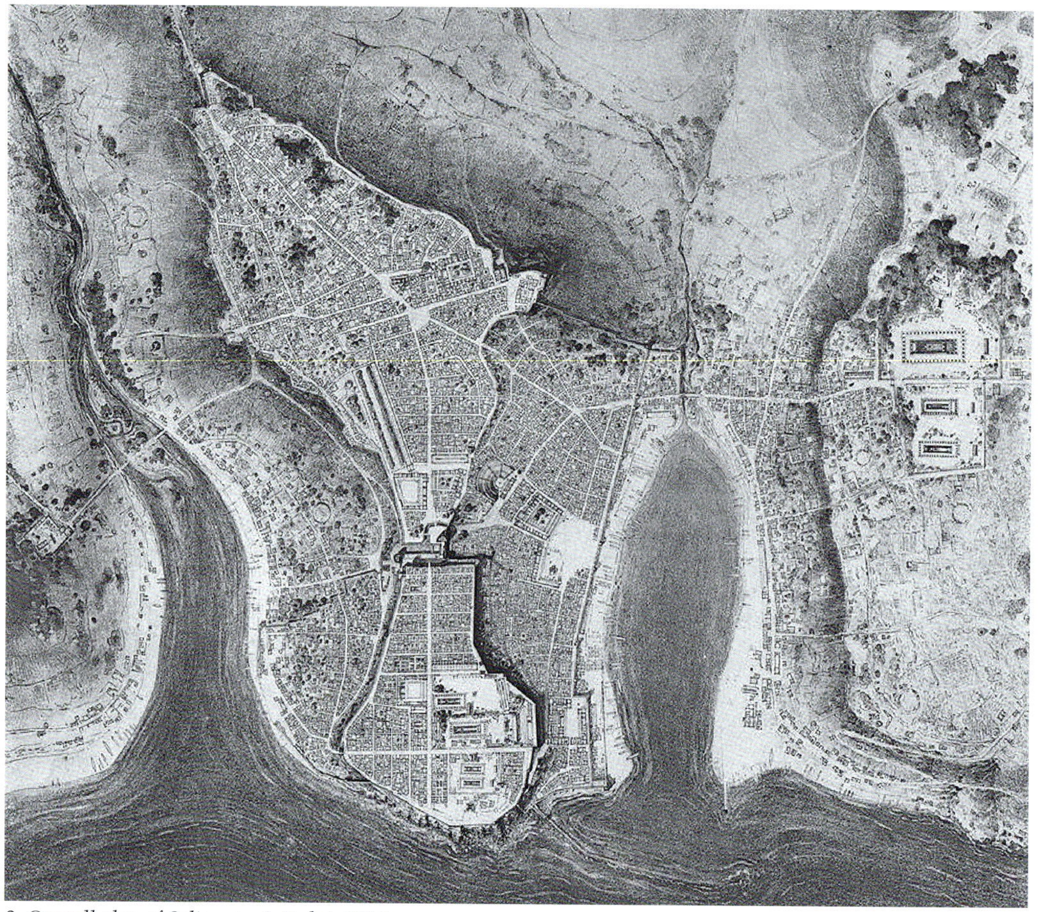

2. Overall plan of Selinunte, J. Hulot, 1904

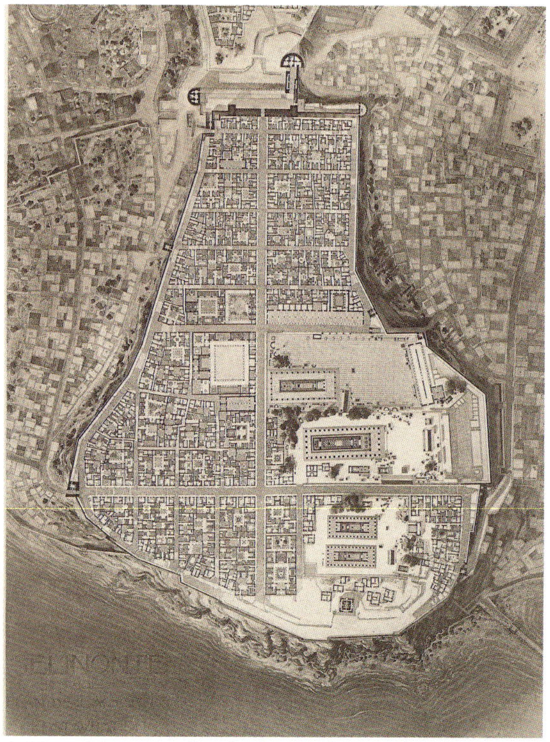

1. Plan of the acropolis of Selinunte by J. Hulot, 1904

3. View from the acropolis of Selinunte

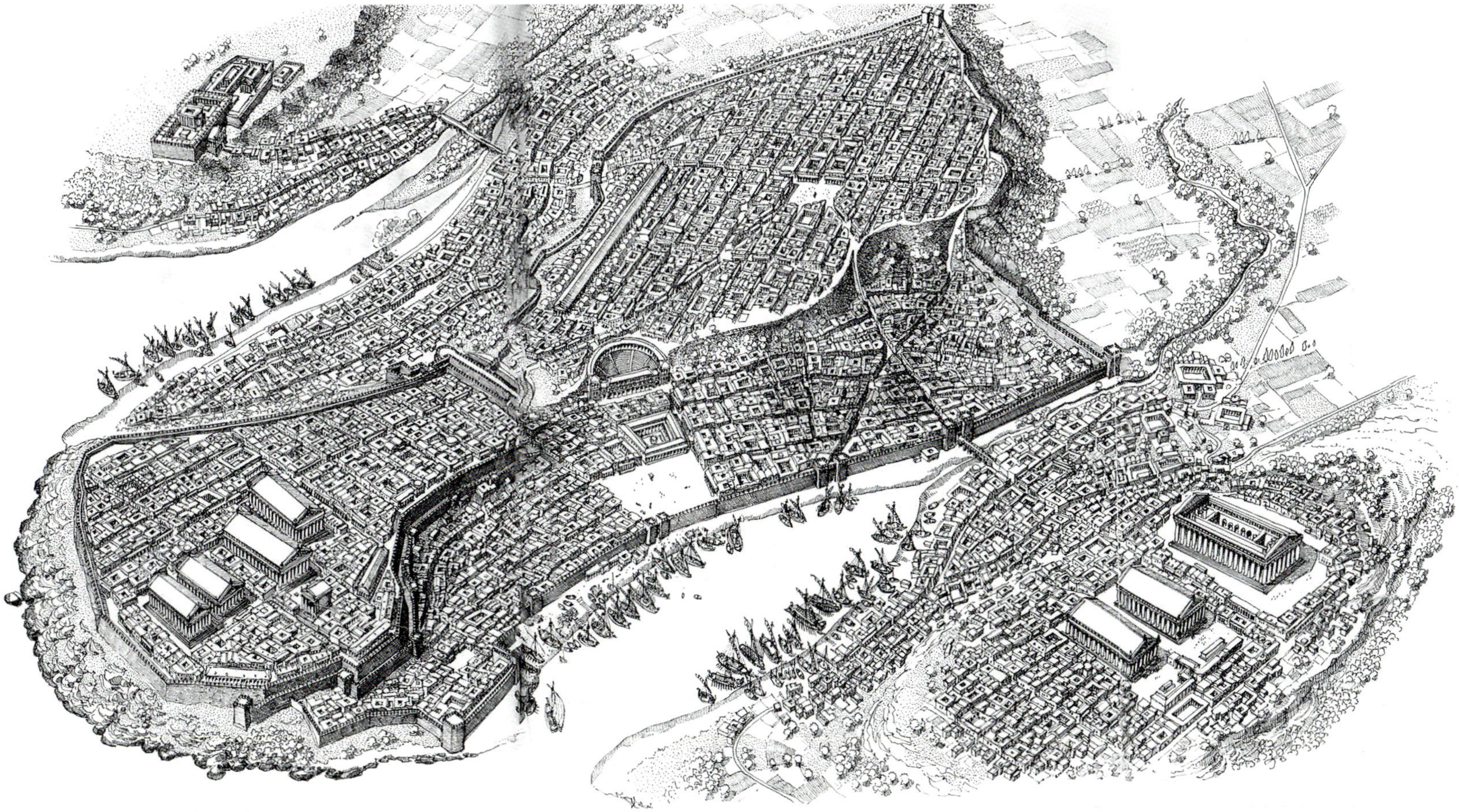

1. Aerial reconstruction, Hulot and Fougeres, 1910

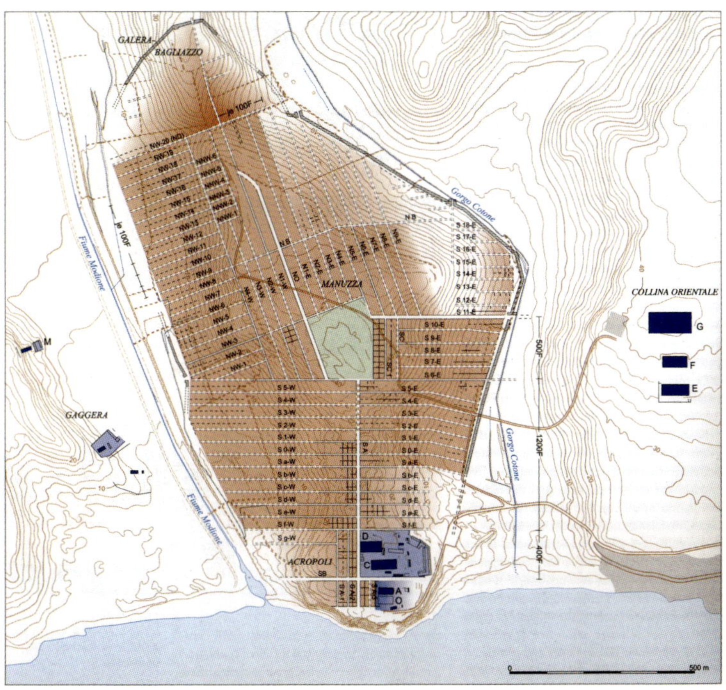

2. Plan of Selinunte, Dieter Mertens, 1:20,000

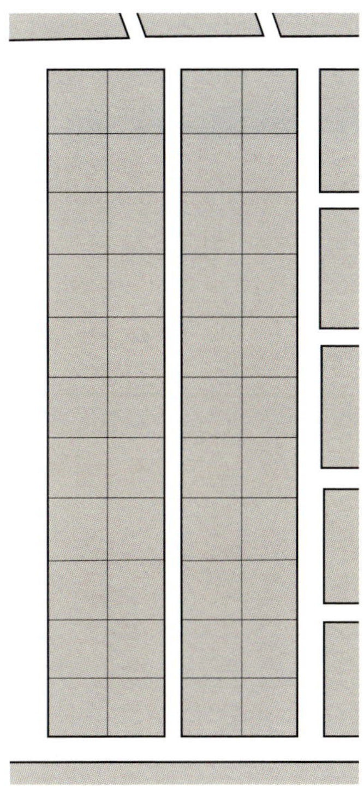

3. Plan of blocks and parcels, 1:2,000

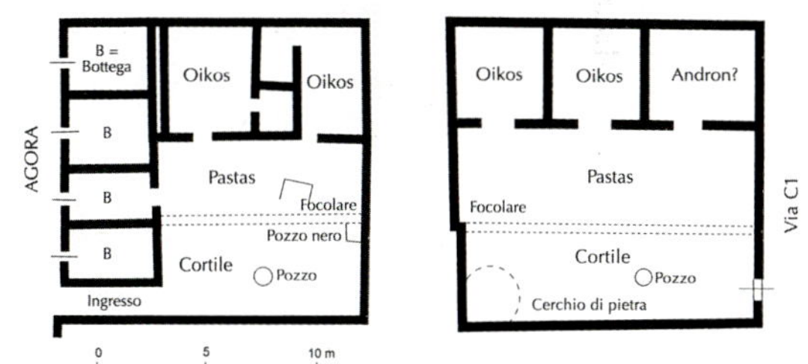

4. House plans, 1:500

Civic Structure and Urban Fabric

A more recent archaeological plan indicates that the city was composed of two regular grids of long, narrow blocks, each about 100' wide x 525' or more long. The blocks were mostly divided into courtyard house parcels of about 50' x 50'.[3] The urban fabric is relentless and diagrammatic. There are are no urban squares, and no urban landscape.

The civic structure consists of a main central street, ca. 29' wide, connecting the temple complex to the south with the trapezoidal agora to the north. Only residential blocks define the edges of the agora.

Poseidonia (Paestum)

Poseidonia was founded around 600 BC. Around 400 BC, the city was taken over by the indigenous Lucanians, who probably changed the name to Paestum.[4] The city became a Roman colony in 273 BC, and although major changes were made—most notably the addition of the Roman forum—the plan is Greek, with very long, narrow blocks, or *strigas*.

The Plan

The plan is diagrammatic: the residential areas are divided by a wide strip reserved for public buildings, with the *agora* in the center between sanctuaries to the north and south. Two main streets, *plateiai*, crossed at the center. The north–south street was 33' (10 m) wide. The main east–west street was 66' (20 m) wide. Two other streets divided the plan into three zones.[5]

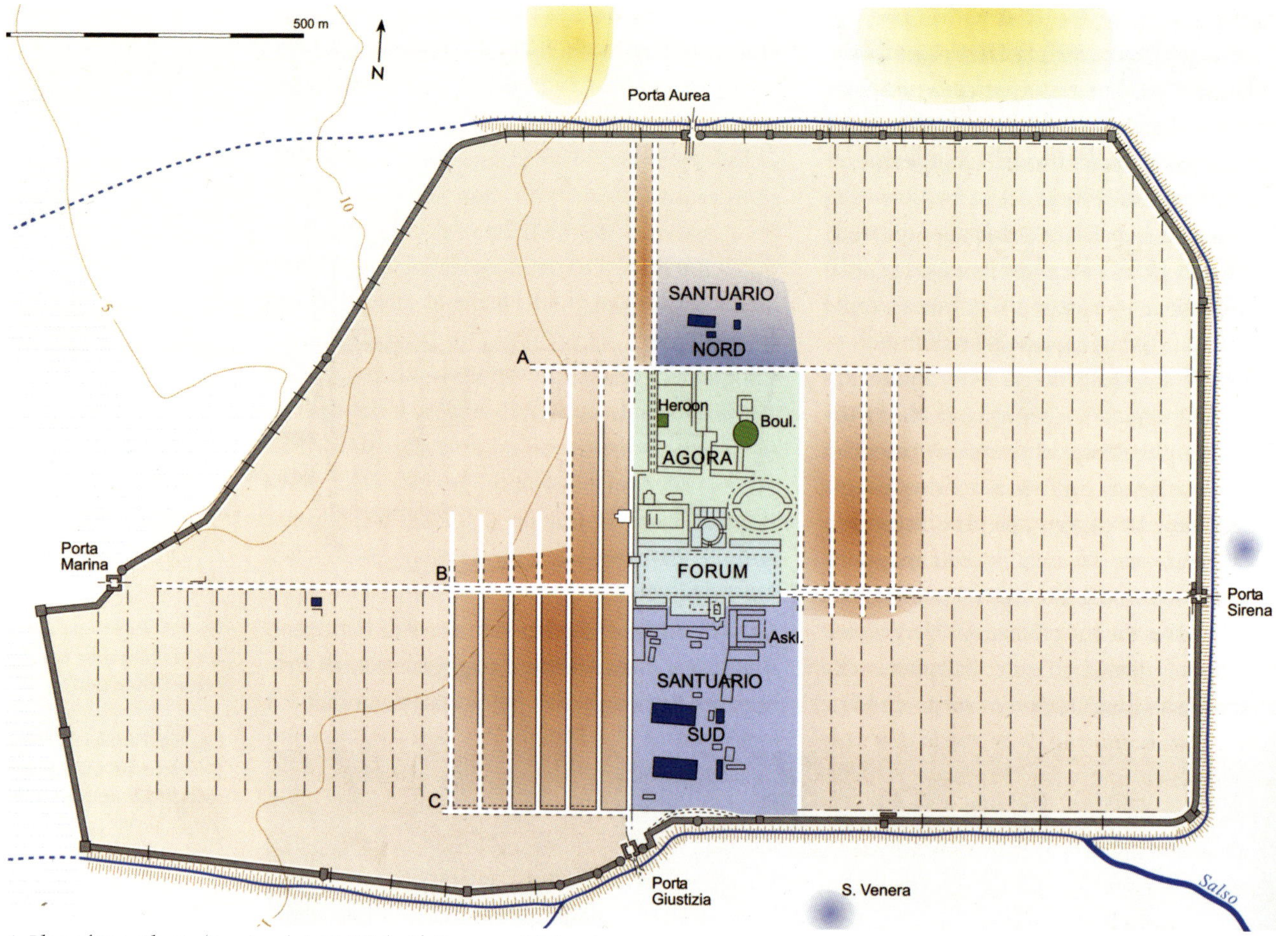

1. Plan of Poseidonia (Paestum), 1:10,000 (with Roman additions)

2. View of the temples by A. Joli, 1759

3. Temple of Neptune and the Basilica

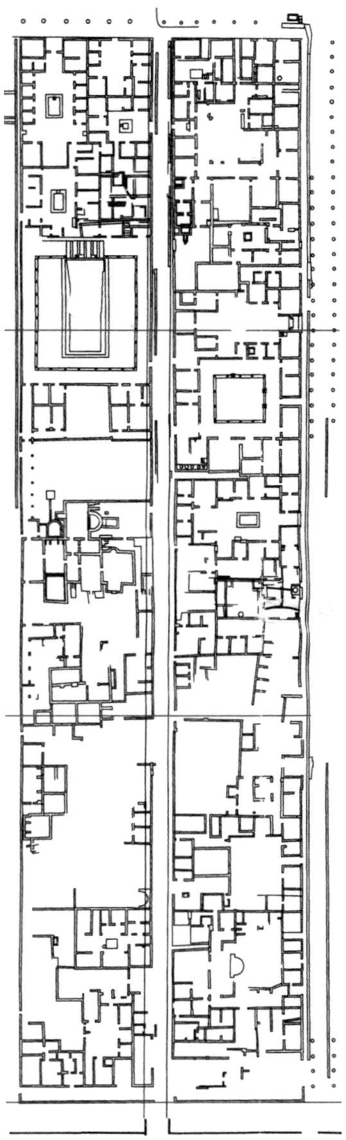

1. Plan of two residential blocks adjacent to the south sanctuary, 1:2,000

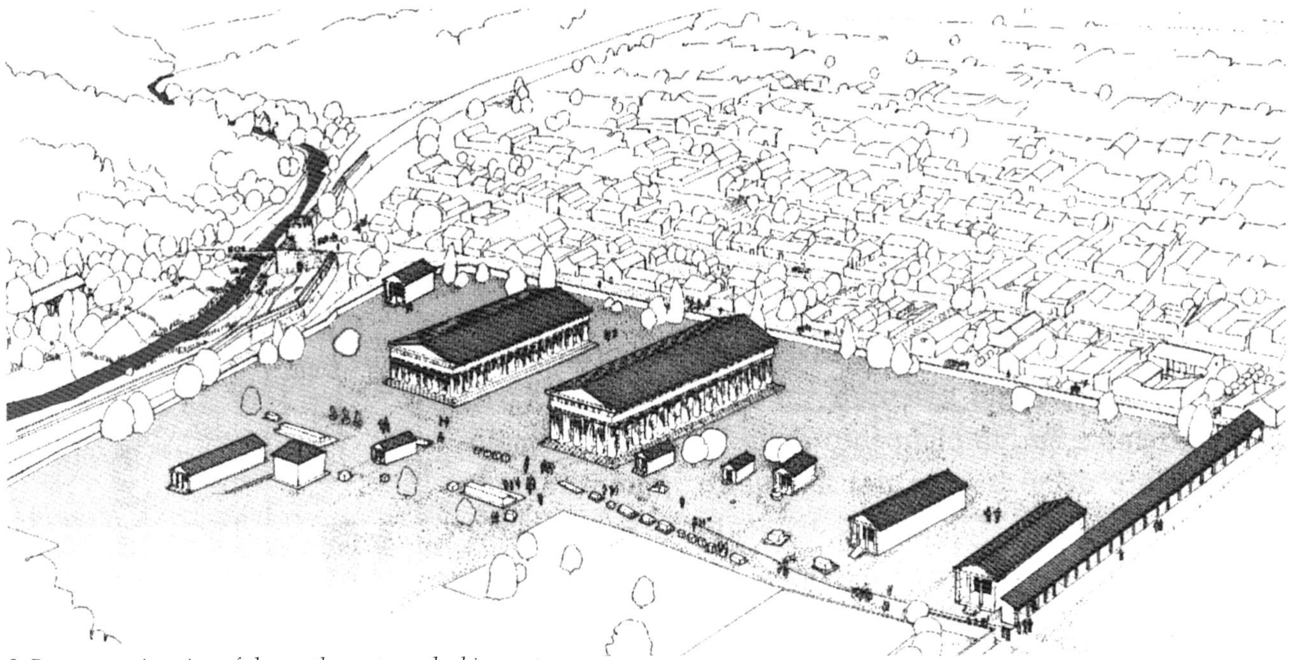

2. Reconstruction view of the south sanctuary looking east

Temples

Before Paestum became a Roman colony, the public areas of the city—the sanctuaries and the *agora*—were simply large open areas containing temples and other free-standing public buildings. The temples are at a slight angle to the grid of the city, further articulating them from the residential fabric.

Blocks and Parcels

The three east–west *plateiai* were intersected by residential streets, *stenapoi*, 16' (5 m) wide, forming blocks approximately 115' (35 m) x 900' (273 m). Few blocks have been excavated, and since those are near the forum, the houses are large Roman ones, such as the Casa con piscina. The original Greek parcels are not evident.

Roman Forum

The regular, enclosed space of the *forum romanum* was superimposed on the *agora* at the intersection of the two primary streets, encroaching slightly on the south sanctuary.

The enclosed space is approximately 165' x 550', and like that of Pompeii, it is surrounded by attached public buildings.

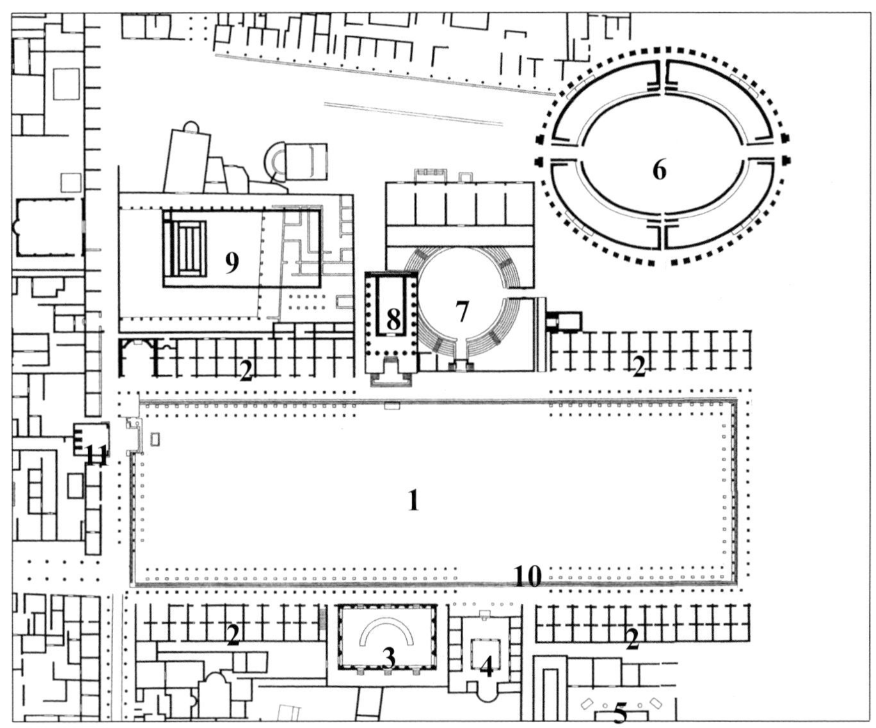

3. Plan of the Forum area, 1:2,000. (The east end of the Forum is approximate.)
1. Forum Romanum, 2. Tabernae, 3. Curia, 4. Macellum, 5. Aeskliepion, 6. Amphitheater, 7. Comitium, 8. Tempio della Pace, 9. Pool sanctuary, 10. Roman entrance to south sanctuary, 11. Lararium

1. *Map of the region of Priene*

Asia Minor

The Greek colonies in Asia Minor exhibit distinctly different characteristics from most of the western colonies. The blocks are shorter rectangles, rather than the very long blocks (*strigas*) of the west; the temples and public buildings are absorbed and integrated into the grid of the urban fabric; the civic spaces are more defined and spatially legible; and the cities are more holistic urban compositions. Many of these cities, as well as those in the west, were remade under the Romans, e.g., Miletus and Ephesus in the east, and Taormina in the west. Priene, however, remains the quintessential (almost) pure Hellenistic city; i.e., it was barely touched by the Romans.

Priene was located on the south-facing slope of Mount Mykale in a coastal region that included Miletus, Samos, and Ephesus. Fields could be reached without major exhaustion, and the city wall performed well, together with the sloping terraces.

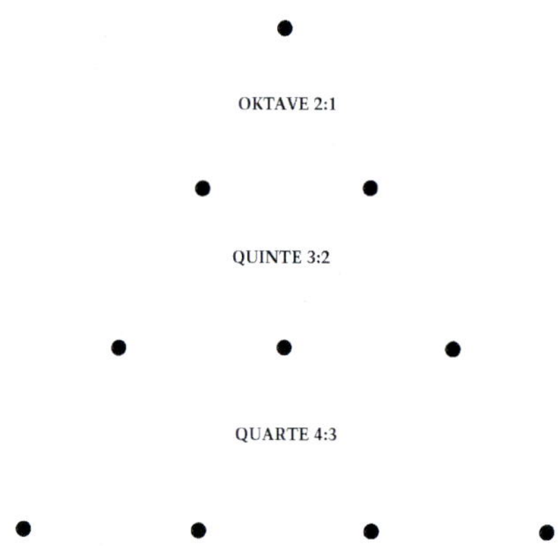

2. *Pythagorean numbers of the tetraktys*

Priene

Priene is an example of a comprehensive, unified design idea for a small city of about 5,000 inhabitants. Architecture and planning worked together, and even the details seem to be in harmony with the overall city form. Because it was not remade by the Romans, it has at once an intimate human scale and a spectacular relationship to the landscape and the sea.

The city was refounded in its current location in the fourth century BC (ca. 352 BC). As with many other Greek towns, Priene was refounded in a grid-plan layout—originally with equal house parcels configured for a typical courtyard house.

The architect Pythius is credited with both the design of the city and the design of the Temple of Athena Polius, one of the most admired designs in antiquity. Pythius is also considered to have belonged to the Pythagorean school. Indeed, the city is proportioned according to the system of the *tetraktys*, the symbol of the Pythagorean school. The basic residential block has a proportional ratio of 4:3, for example. This block determines the grid of the urban fabric, and all of the public buildings are related to the grid. Thus, both private and public buildings are integrated into a unified system.[6]

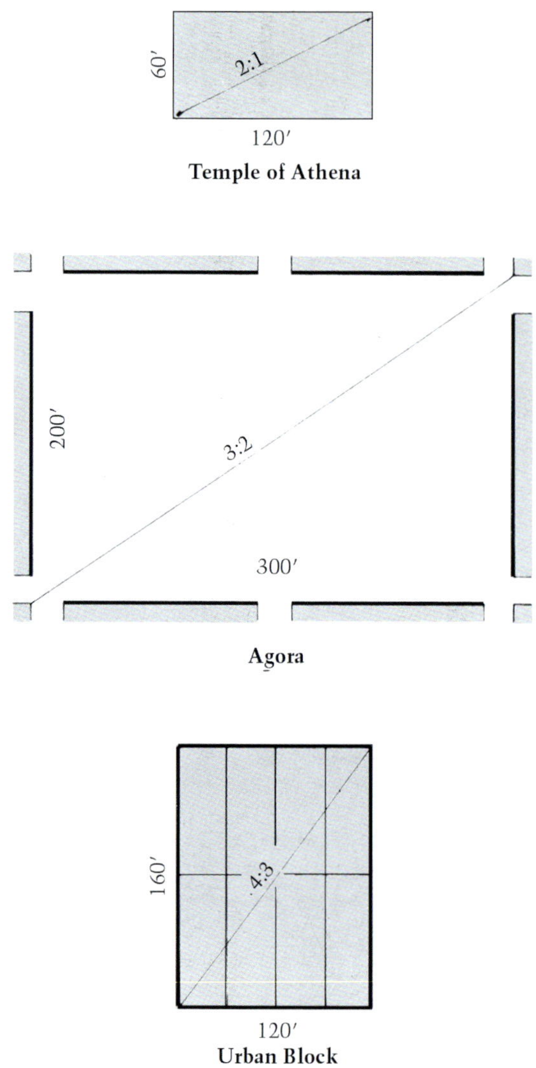

3. *Pythagorean proportions of Priene*

Reconstruction of Priene in the late Hellenistic period, (After Zippelius)

Urban Fabric

All of the original *insulae* of Priene were 120' x 160' (3:4), and contained eight equal-sized plots of 80' x 30'. There is a very clear, consistent street order. The width of each street was related to its function, and followed a hierarchical system: commercial streets were wider than streets of residential areas. The main east–west street was the widest at 24'. Three dominating streets in north–south orientation (20') crossed the main street and defined the rectangle of the Agora.[7]

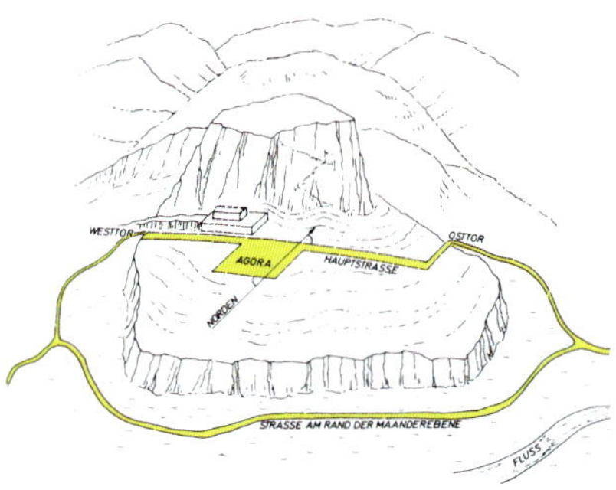

1. Access strategy

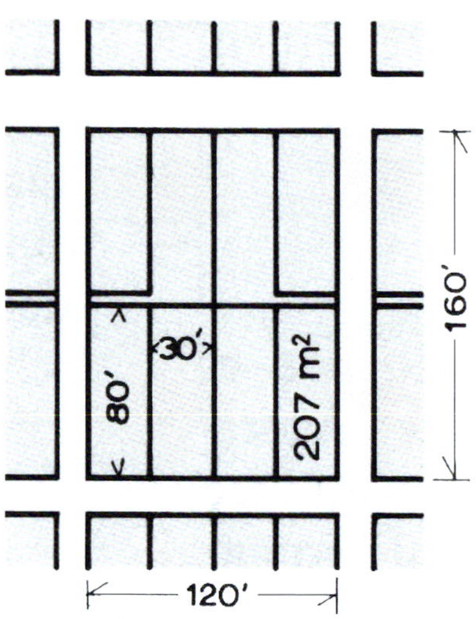

2. Original urban block

3. Plan of Priene, 1:5,000

1. Typical houses as they were designed originally, 1:500
1. Entrance, 2. Courtyard, 3. Prostas, 4. Oikos, 5. Andron, 6. Auxiliary space, 7. Storeroom, 8. Shop

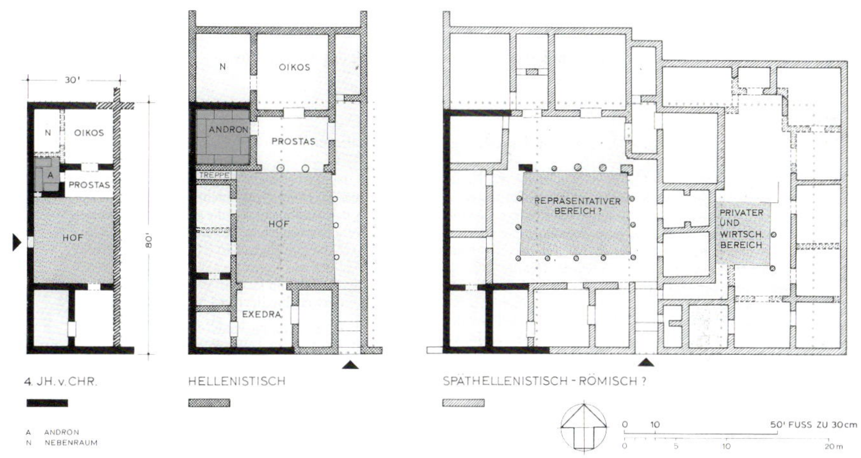

2. Development of the house type

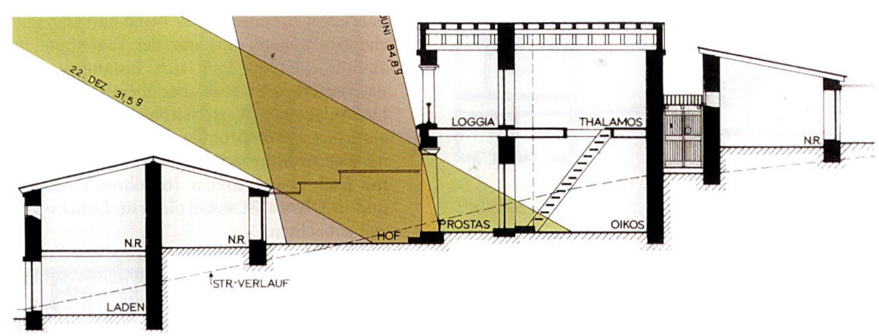

3. Typical house section

Typical Houses

When Priene was refounded, every citizen received an equal-sized plot and the obligation to build a "typical house," even if they owned a larger property before. The typical house was designed to meet the multiple needs of a family (around ten people). All houses faced south, and each plot was divided into three parts: the northern part served as the living quarters, the central part consisted of a rectangular courtyard, and the southern part had auxiliary rooms or shops, depending on the position of the house in relation to the main commercial street. The houses were accessed from the street through the courtyard.

Over time the houses underwent changes. During the middle Hellenistic period, an increase in population led to a different distribution of wealth in the city. Houses were divided to accommodate more people, or extended by those who could afford it. Poor citizens moved to residences closer to the city walls, whereas more affluent citizens occupied the center, which led to tension among the citizens.

The Agora

As stated above, the blocks of the city formed a grid in which public buildings and spaces had to fit. Thus, the civic structure (*agora*, temples, etc.) was integrated into the urban fabric.

As in most Greek city-states, the *agora* served mainly as the religious and political, rather than commercial, center of the city. The dimensions of the *agora* usually reflected its social and political significance. In its final phase, the *agora* of Priene is a typical example of an *agora* in small and middle-sized cities of the Hellenistic period. The basic open space defined by the stoas is about 213' x 250'.

It acquired its complete form with the construction of the Ekkleiasterion (the supreme political institution of the city, a place of assembly), and with the building of the Prytaneion (containing the "common hearth" of the city) to the north of the Sacred Stoa. The Stoa works as a filter from the open space of the *agora*, and dramatizes the entry to the adjacent rooms.

The Sacred Stoa enclosed the north side of the *agora*, and was raised 2.4 meters above ground level. The interior (6.47 m wide), gave shelter and connected the Ekklesiasterion and the Prytaneion with the *agora*. After the construction of the surrounding buildings, the central open space was clearly enclosed and was no longer crossed by secondary streets, thus emphasizing its identity.

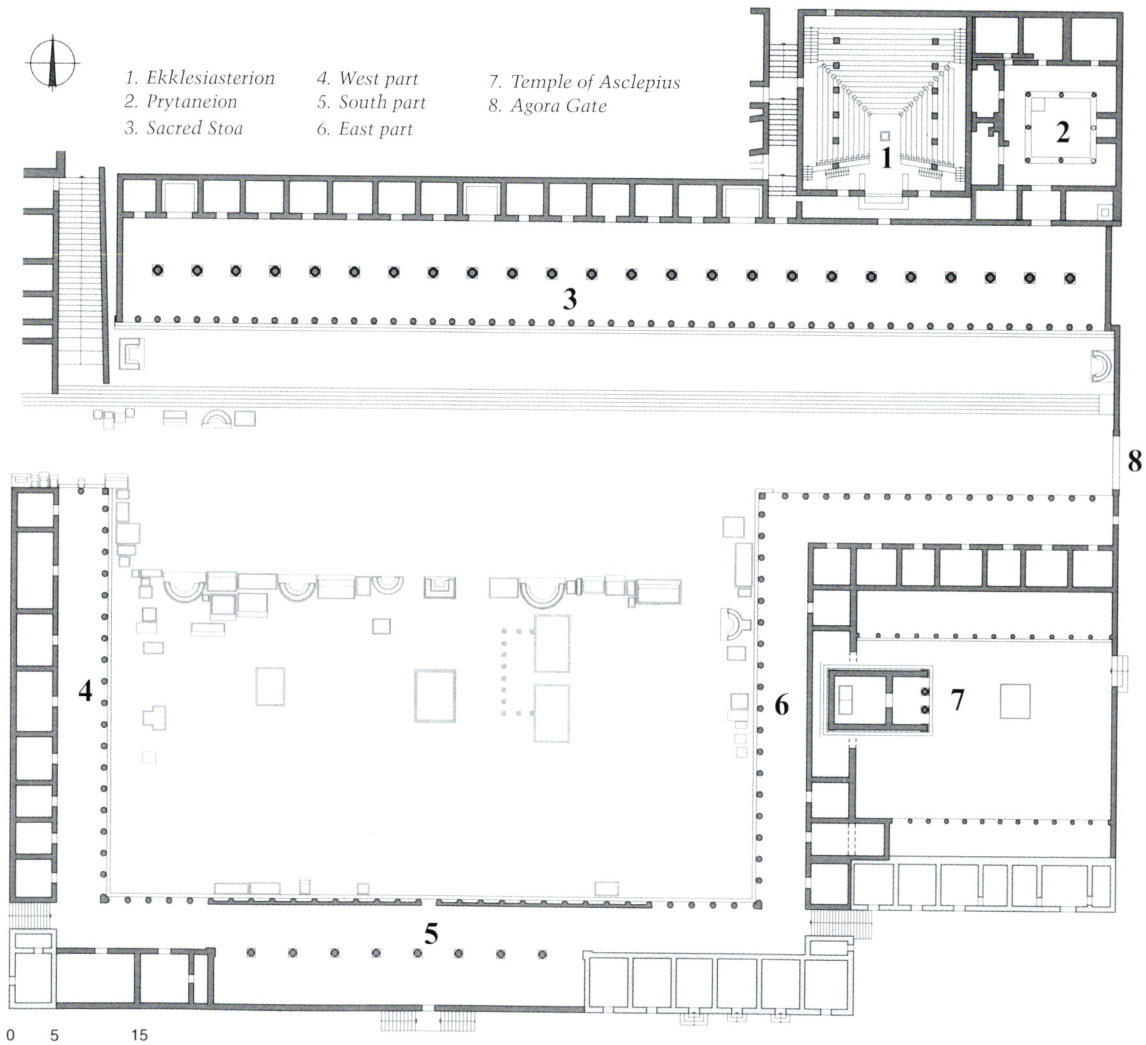

2. Plan of the Agora, 1:1,000

1. Excavated Ekklesiasterion

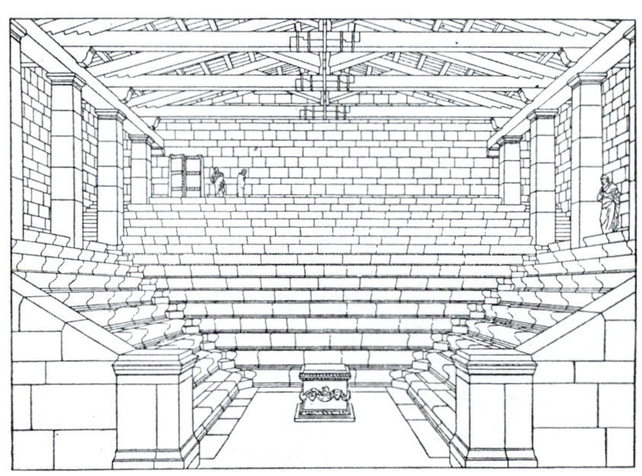

3. Perspective of the Ekklesiasterion

4. Temple of Asclepius, restoration

1. Bird's-eye model view of the town

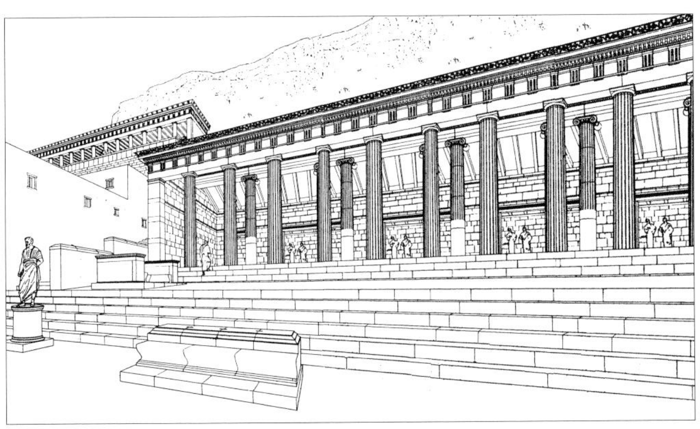

2. Restoration view of the west end of the Sacred Stoa

3. Sacred Stoa interior, restoration

1. Restoration perspective view of the theater in the late Hellenistic period

1. Propylon
2. Altar
3. Temple
4. Foundations of pedestals
5. Doric Stoa
6. Treasury
7. Later houses
8. Street leadings towards the Sanctuary of Athena Polias
9. Non-excavated area

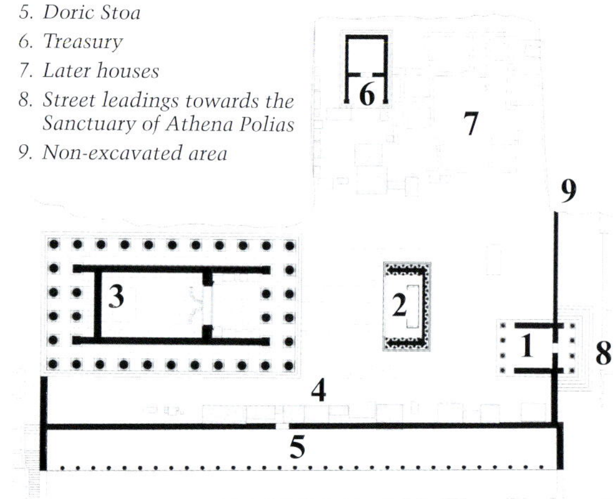

4. Plan of the sanctuary

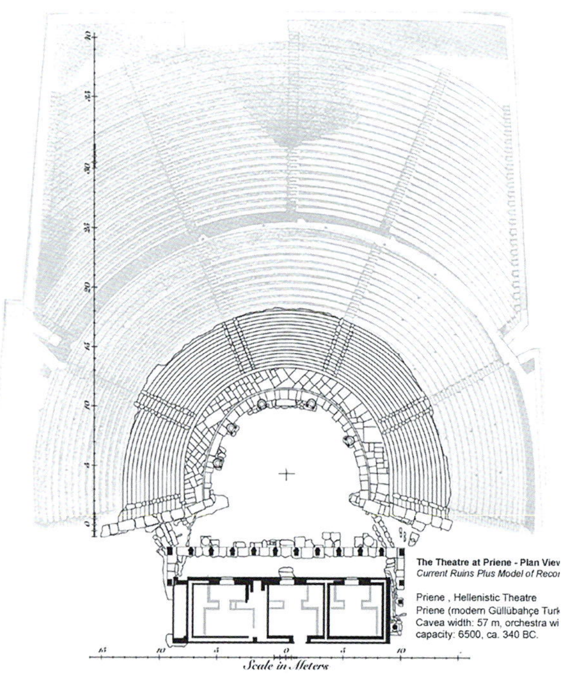

2. Plan of the theater in the Hellenistic period

Theater

The Theater is one of the oldest in Asia Minor, and displays the basic features of a third-century BC theater. It takes up two urban blocks and is integrated into the grid system. It is oriented to the south, thereby taking advantage of the sloping hillside to grade seats, to create an unobstructed view of the city and the plains. In the fourth and third centuries BC tragedies were performed, and later it served for flute as well as pantomime contests. Before the construction of the Ekklesiasterion, it served as a place for assembly of the citizens.

3. View over the theater

Sanctuary of Athena

The sanctuary's courtyard occupied two urban blocks, and was distinctly separated from the neighboring houses. Because of the sloping ground, a large terrace was created to accommodate the temple, altar, Doric stoa, and a treasury. It is known that Alexander the Great covered the expenses to build the temple, as a gift to the city. The architect Pythius designed the temple with all dimensions being multiples of the attic foot. The proportions are harmonious, a feature that characterized the academicism of the late Hellenistic era.[8]

5. Reconstruction of the sanctuary

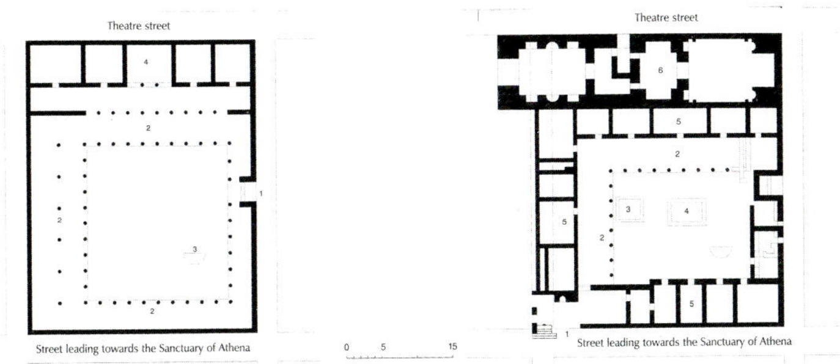

1. Upper gymnasium, conjectural plans of the Hellenistic and Roman periods

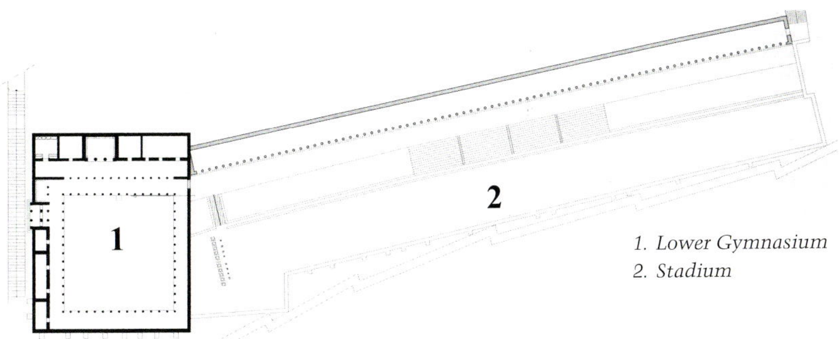

1. Lower Gymnasium
2. Stadium

2. Plan of the lower gymnasium and stadium

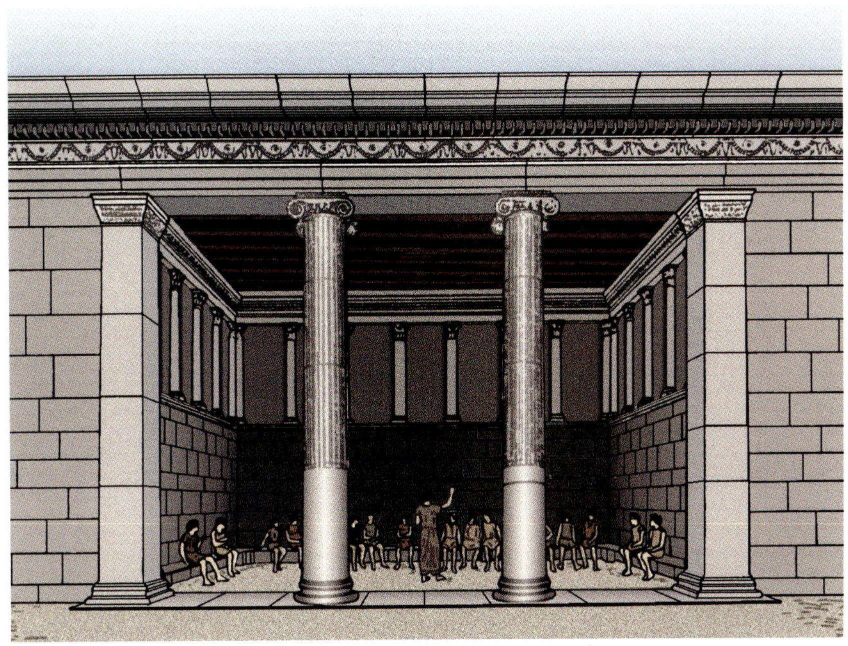

3. Central hall of the lower gymnasium

Lower and Upper Gymnasia

Gymnasia were public institutions for education, musical training, and athletic practice for the young. The upper gymnasium occupies one building plot in the north section of the city, between the Ekklesiasterion and the Theater. The initial plan (third c. BC) included a large, rectangular peristyle with rooms on the north side. Later, the north section was taken up by public baths, and the west and east colonnades were reconstructed by adding several rooms.

The lower gymnasium and the adjoining stadium were not included in the initial planning of Priene, and were only constructed in the late second century BC, which explains its position, not aligning with the city's grid. Like other buildings in Priene, the lower gymnasium is characterized by the mathematical relationship of its structural elements. In contrast to the upper gymnasium, whose initial structure was gradually altered as its functions changed with the passage of time, the lower gymnasium preserved its simple layout and initial character.

4. Perspective of lower gymnasium

1. Map of Greece and Asia Minor

Pergamon

Pergamon is a superb example of Greek talent for the scenographic arrangement of independent temples and public buildings, but applied to complex urban plans. After Alexander the Great, the nature of Greek towns changed radically, and this new Hellenistic art of town planning rapidly penetrated the east.

Under the Attalid dynasty, between 282 and 133 BC, Pergamon was a wealthy, important capital of a powerful kingdom[9]—especially under Eumenes II (197–159 BC), when it was an important Hellenistic center of art and culture.[10] The theater, for example, was built by Eumenes early in the second century BC.

The Plan

Strictly speaking, Pergamon is not a planned town, but an urban composition consistently developed over at least a century. It occupies a spectacular, steep, hillside site, and is spread over 700' vertically. The lower town was connected by a single road through a residential area to the upper town comprising the theater and other civic buildings. The plan complexity of the upper town is due to the sectional characteristics of the site, which cannot be understood from the plan alone.

2. Pergamon, reconstruction view of the city

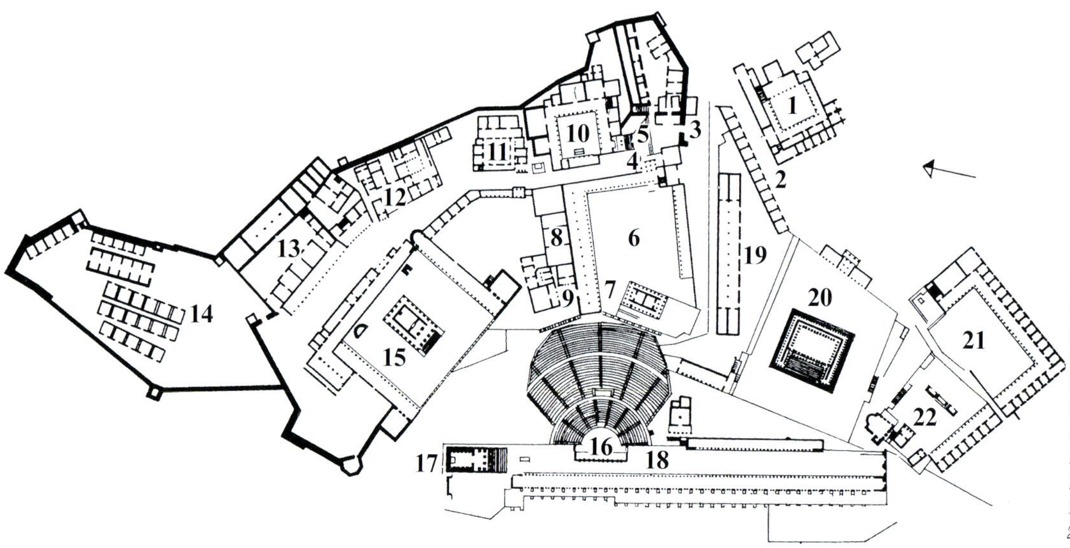

3. Pergamon, detail plan of upper town

1. *Heroum (building for the cult of hero worship)*
2. *Shops*
3. *Main entrance to Acropolis*
4. *Foundations of the Propylon (entrance porch)*
5. *Steps to the palace*
6. *Precinct of Athena*
7. *Temple of Athena*
8. *Library*
9. *A house*
10. *Palace of Eumenes II*
11. *Palace of Attalus I*
12. *Hellenistic houses*
13. *Barracks & command tower*
14. *Arsenal*
15. *Temple of Trajan*
16. *Theatre*
17. *Temple of Dionysos*
18. *Colonnaded terrace*
19. *Portico with two aisles*
20. *Altar of Zeus*
21. *Upper agora*
22. *Agora temple*

1. Pergamon, theater

2. Pergamon, reconstruction view of upper town

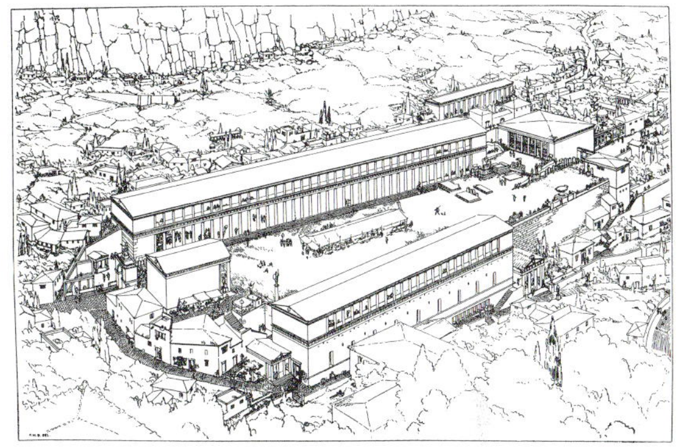

3. Assos, reconstruction view of agora

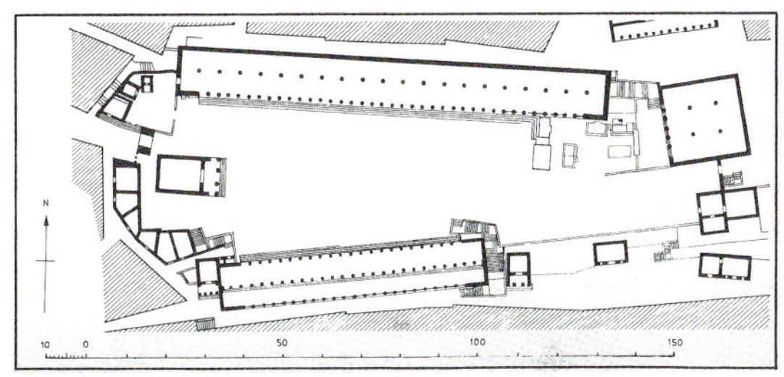

4. Assos, plan of agora

Assos

A near contemporary of Pergamon, Assos was partially rebuilt in the early second century BC. The stoas that define the space of the agora absorb the rather steep slope of the site and provide a splendid terrace overlooking the valley below. A temple occupies the west end of the agora, and the *bouleutrion* is at the east end. Aristotle established an Academy in Assos after leaving Athens.

1. Geographical map of Miletus

Miletus

The original Ionic city of Miletus had founded eighty colonies and was economically and culturally one of the leading city-states in the Greek world before it was destroyed by the Persians around 494 BC. Hippodamos may have been born there around 500 BC, and he may have been involved with the layout of the new city that was planned and built on the same site after the expulsion of the Persians from Greece in 479 BC.[11]

The Plan

The plan of Miletus is perhaps the most formally elaborate and interesting of all the planned Greek towns. This is partially because of the irregular perimeter, but also because of the variety of connected public spaces in the center. This is especially remarkable because unlike Priene, which was designed by one hand and built at once on a hillside site, Miletus was built over more than 600 years on a relatively flat site.

The beginning plan was typical of other fifth-century BC Greek plans in that gridded sections of urban fabric left large open areas for public spaces and buildings.

Urban Fabric

The areas of urban fabric were unique for the time, however, in that the blocks were not the typical long, narrow blocks, but rectangular, near-square blocks.

The northern *insulae* were 100' x 180' (5:9); in the south 120' x 150' (4:5)—all divided in six parcels. The blocks are different in proportion but equal in area, which results in equally sized plots for the whole city (2600 sf). The city's extent to the south is unclear, but historians assume a hypothetical number of 300 blocks, or 1,800 houses, which gives a population of 15,000 to 20,000 people.[12]

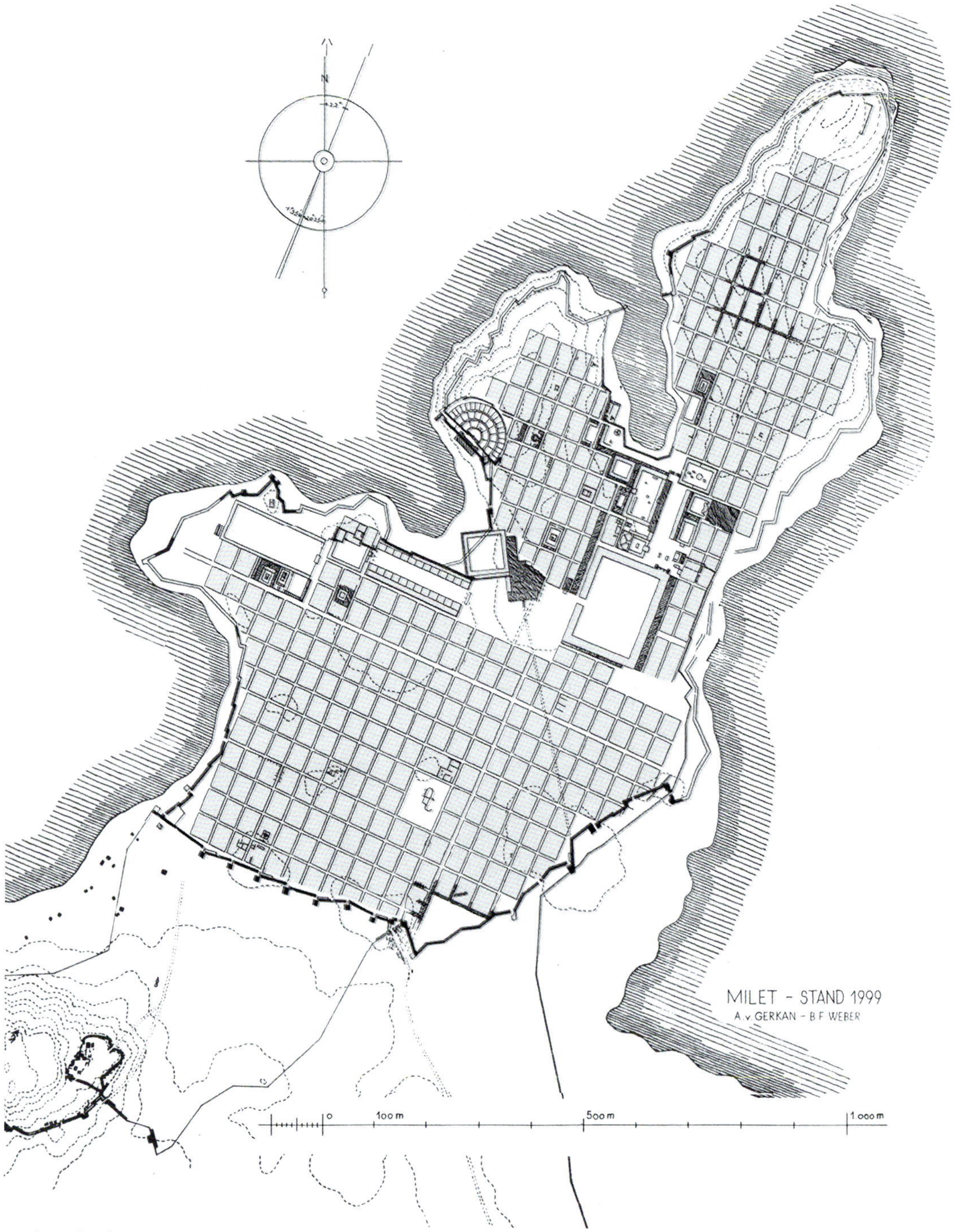

2. Plan of Miletus, 1:8,000, (After von Gerkan. For a more up-t-date archaeological plan of blocks (see Haus und Stadt.)

The Agoras

The three model photos show how a very distinct sequence of spaces evolved within the rhythm of the street grid.

Three different phases and approaches to design were implemented: the Greek work (ca. 300 BC), which left open the space of the Agora, but introduced the stoa connecting it to the harbor; the Hellenistic work (ca. 150 BC), which gave more formal character to the spaces, with architectural forms projecting into the spaces; and the Roman work (ca. 150 AD), colonnades that surrounded the spaces and divided the spaces into separate units. Each unit had its own architectural language, but the whole was unified.[13]

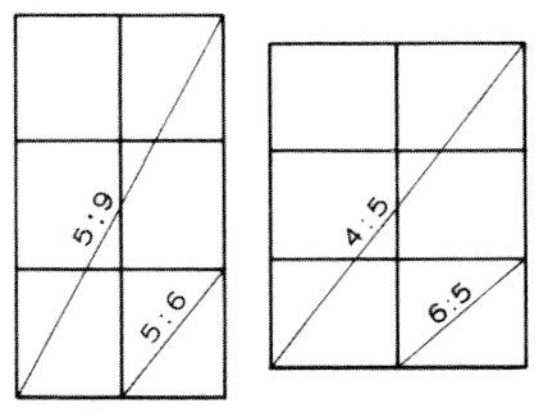

1. Block and parcel proportions

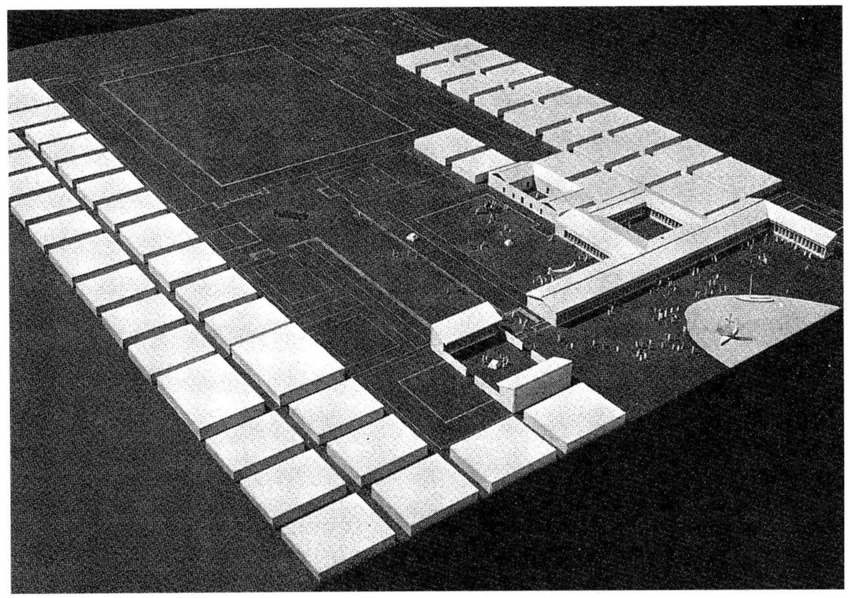

2. Greek development of the Agoras of Miletus, fourth century BC

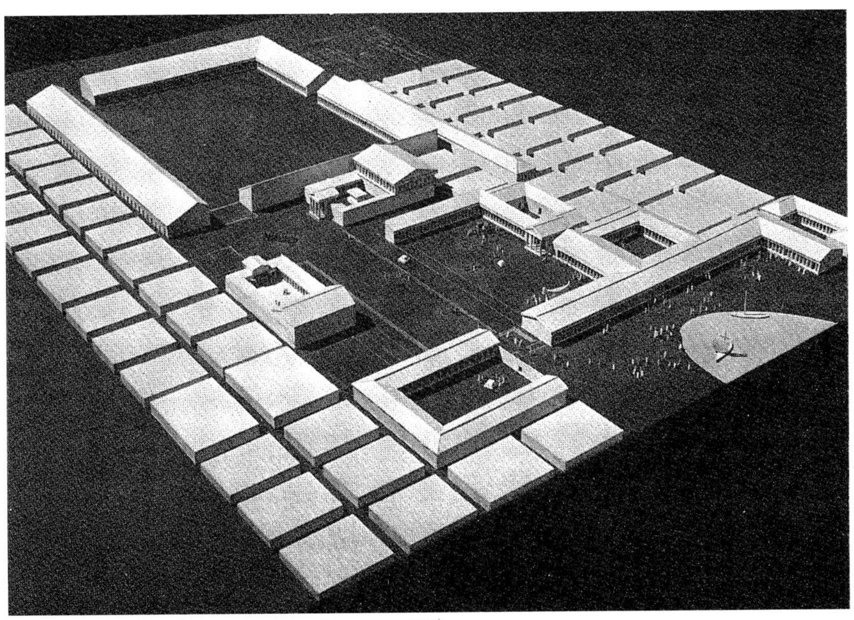

3. Hellenistic development, second century BC

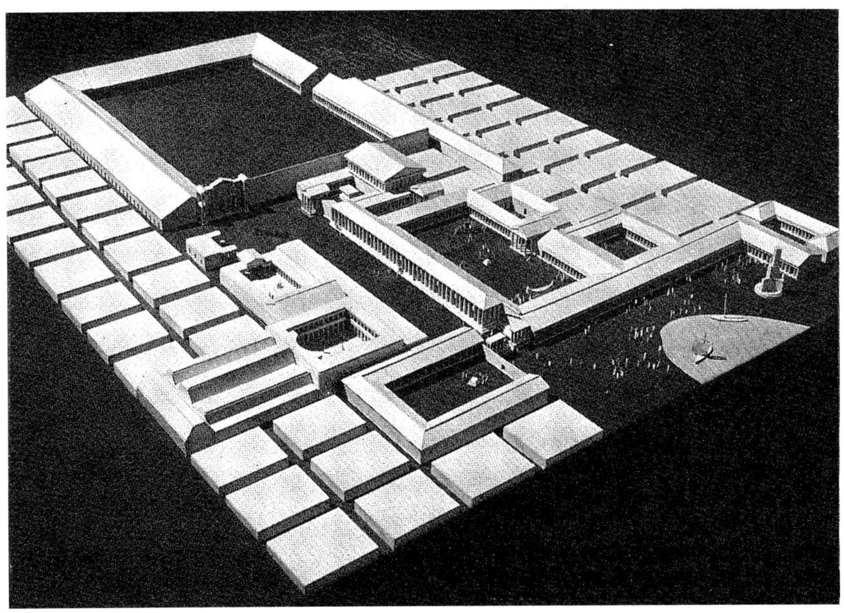

4. Roman development, second century AD

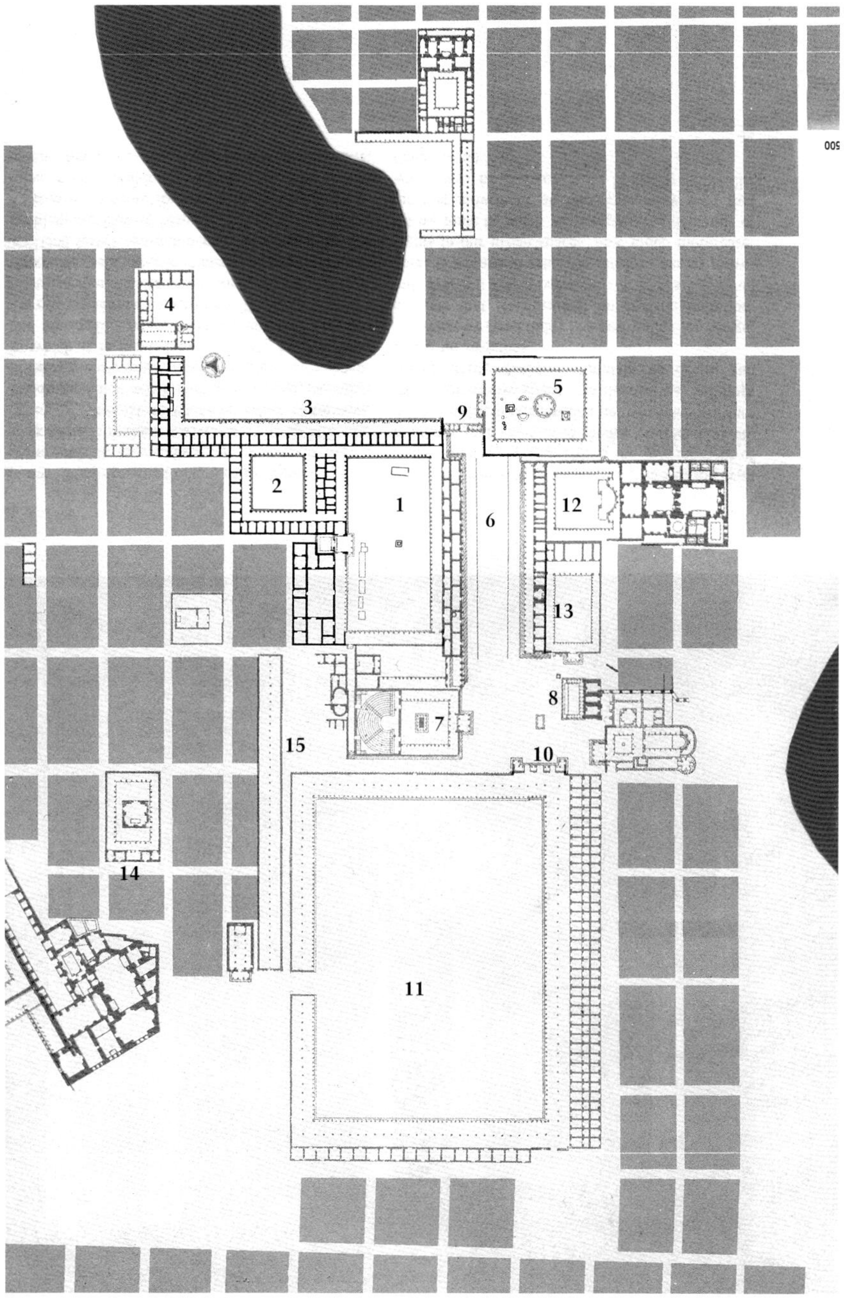

1. Agoras, Roman period

LEGEND

1. *Northern Agora*
2. *Small Market*
3. *Harbor Portico*
4. *Synagogue*
5. *Delphinion*
6. *Processional Road*
7. *Bouleterion*
8. *Nymphaeum*
9. *Harbor Gate*
10. *Northern Gate*
11. *Southern Agora*
12. *Baths of Capitus*
13. *Gymnasium*
14. *Roman Heroun*
15. *Storehouses*

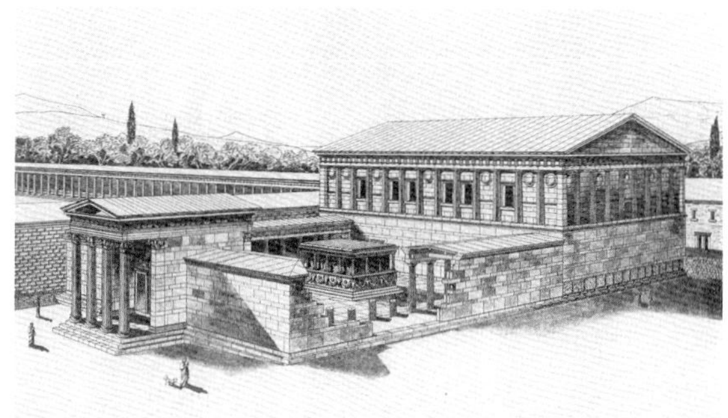

3. Bouleterion

North and South Agora

The Northern Market was the original Agora of the city, close to which is the old Delphinion (Temple of Apollo Delphinios), as well as other public buildings. Later, due to lack of space, the Bouleterion was erected on the place itself. The whole area of the Southern Market was formerly patterned with residential blocks, which had to be destroyed to accommodate more space for trade and markets. On the shore were places for markets, warehouses, halls, and commercial premises.

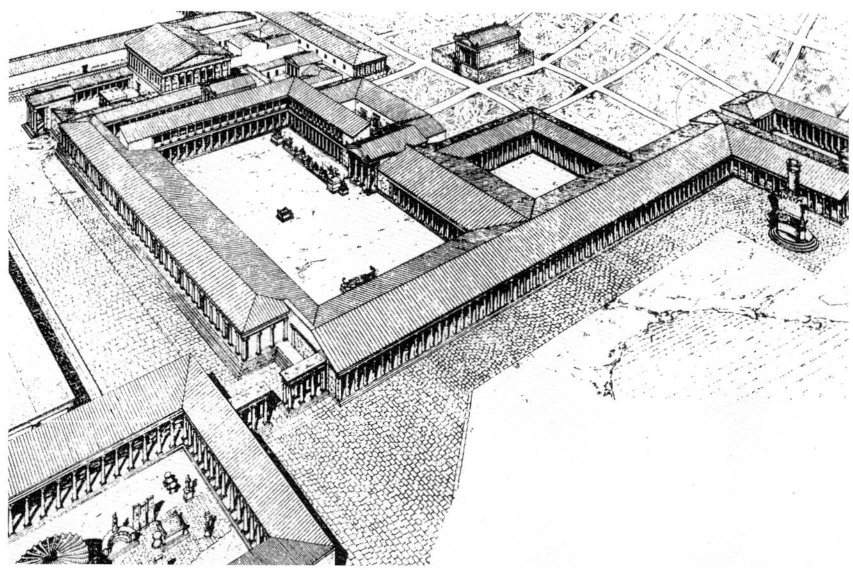

2. Bird's-eye view of reconstruction of the harbor and Agora

1. Roman Northern Gate

3. Bouleterion

The Harbor Gate and Northern Gate are elements that contribute architecturally to the sequence of public spaces. Probably they were intended to provide an impressive reception for visitors or merchants. The Processional Road connects the Harbor Gate with the southern Agora in a *promenade*. Overall, the market places in Miletus developed into a sequence of distinct spaces, each of them with a different geometry, and a defined, staggered, quality.

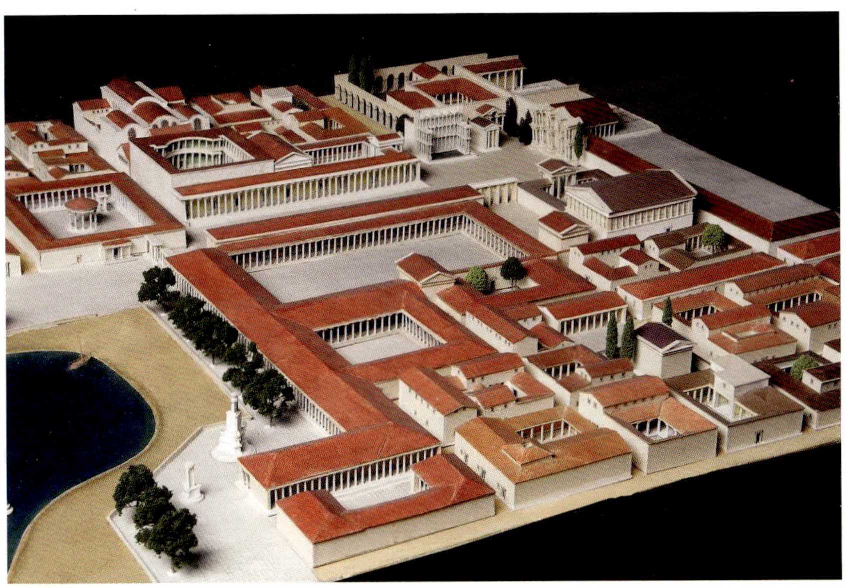

2. Model of the Agoras

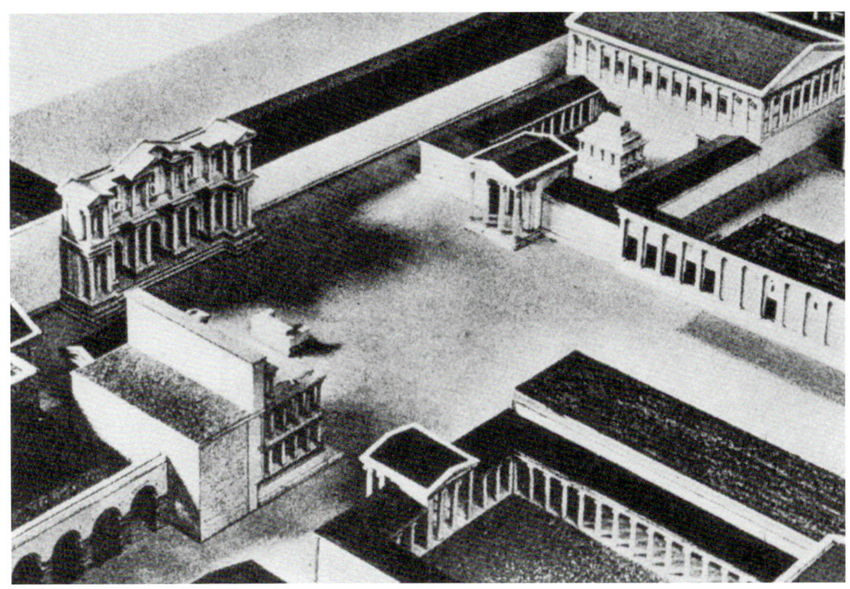

4. Model view of the Northern Gate and Bouleterion

Map of Roman cities

Roman Cities: 350 BC–100 AD

There are compelling reasons to consider the world of antiquity as a whole, but there are more compelling reasons for articulating the differences between Greek and Roman town planning. The primary reason is that the cultural and political roles of Greek and Roman colonies were completely different, as were their respective forms.

The Western Roman world lasted from the presumed founding of Rome in 753 BC to the unnoticed demise of the last emperor in 476 AD, but the planned towns were concentrated within the period of great Roman expansion, from about 350 BC to about 100 AD.

The Romans founded hundreds of towns throughout the empire. This study focuses primarily on those of the Italic peninsula.

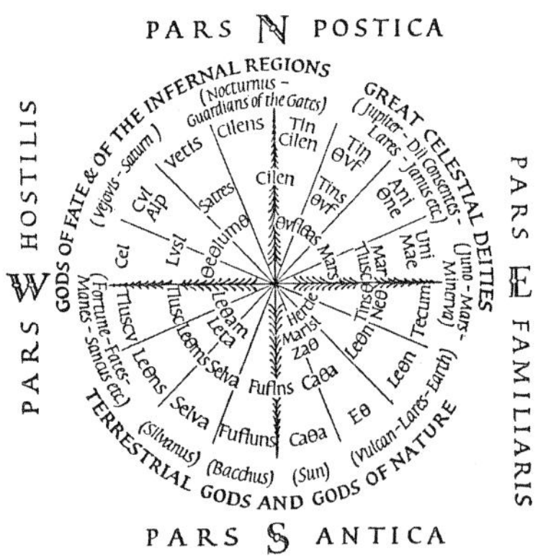

1. *Diagram of the Etruscan Templum*

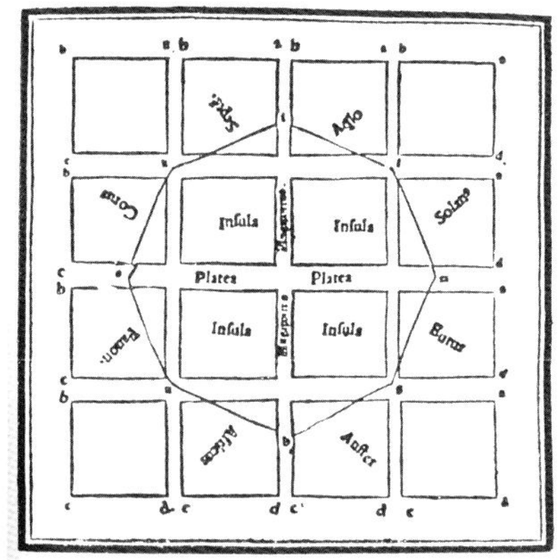

2. *Vitruvian diagram of a cross-axial town*

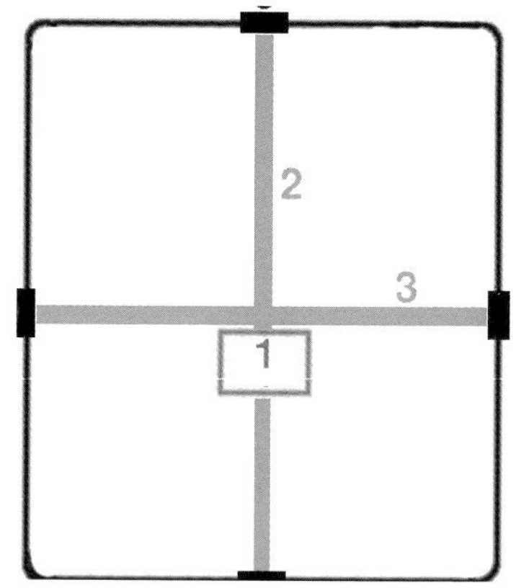

3. *Civic structure diagram of a Roman* castru

Roman Town Planning

In contrast to the relative independence of the founded Greek colony, or *polis*, Roman towns were primarily instruments of civil stabilization, defense, and centralized economic administration in the Roman world.

Another important difference is that Greek towns and sites usually focused out, in relationship to the surrounding landscape, while Roman towns tended to be inwardly focused urban compositions. The Romans exploited space—enclosed architectural and urban space—in a way that the Greeks did not. Vaulting, closed-corner public spaces, colonnaded compositions, closed rather than open theaters, and rudimentary perspective all contributed to this new sense of space.

As the Romans expanded outward from Rome into the Italic world they came into confrontation with the parallel civilizations of the Etruscans and Greeks. From the Greeks they inherited the orthogonal planning system, sometimes referred to as Hippodamean planning; from the Etruscans they inherited the idea of the cross-axis of *cardo* and *decumanus*—the terrestrial, astronomic manifestation of the celestial division of the circle of heaven into a *templum* of four quadrants, and then sixteen segments, representing the seats of the gods.[1]

This cross-axial "civic structure" of *cardo maximus* and *decumano maximus* forms the core of an expanded urban street system of *decumani* and *cardines*, sometimes oriented to the cardinal points. The *forum* was located at the center, and the perimeter of the town was enclosed by a wall. The overall form was usually square or rectangular, but not always. Thus, the ideal diagram of a Roman town—a square bisected by perpendicular streets with an open space at the center—is an unforgettable urban image, characteristic in formal town planning terms of both city and neighborhood: i.e., (1) clear center; (2) consistent fabric; and (3) clear edge.

This was also the basis of the grid system for organizing the agricultural territory beyond the city, the *centuriatio*. The *decumani* either ran east–west, or parallel to the lay of the land or natural features, while the *cardines* were perpendicular to the *decumani*.

There were two basic types of founded Roman towns: colonies, *colonie*, and military encampments, *castra*. The colonies were initially cross-axial towns and preceded the *castra*, but gradually the two types were often combined.[2]

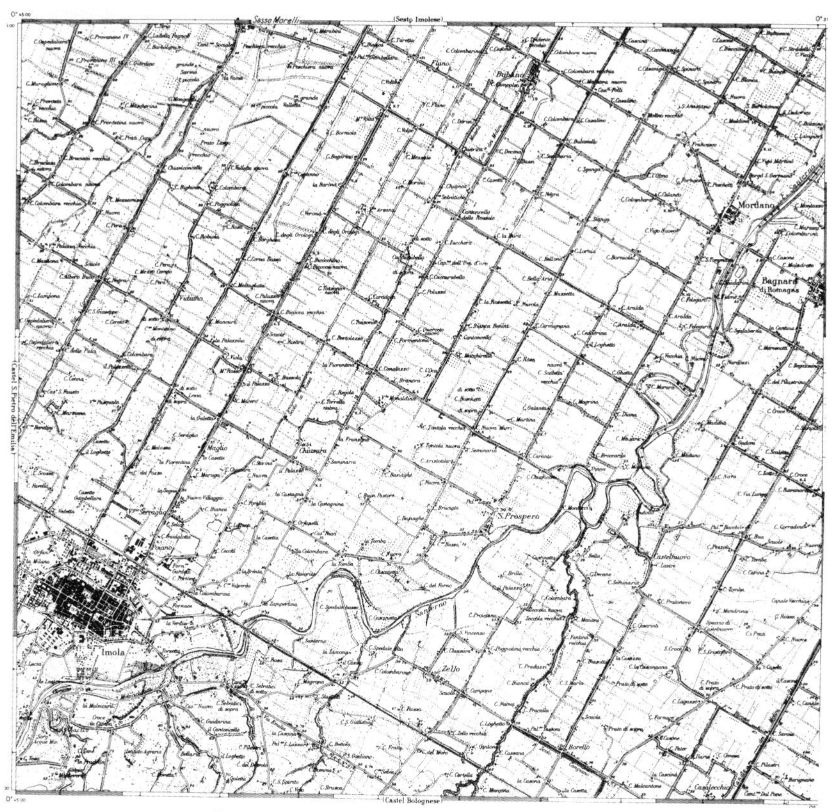

4. *Roman* centuriatio *above Imola*

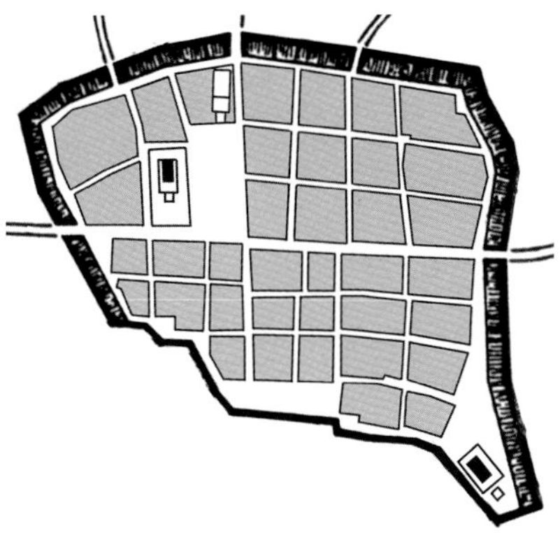

1. *Archaic Pompeii, plan, seventh century BC (after A. von Gerkan)*

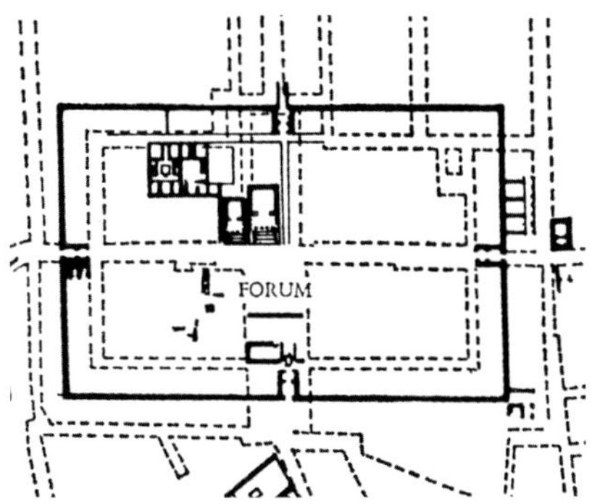

2. *Ostia, plan, ca. 310–300 BC*

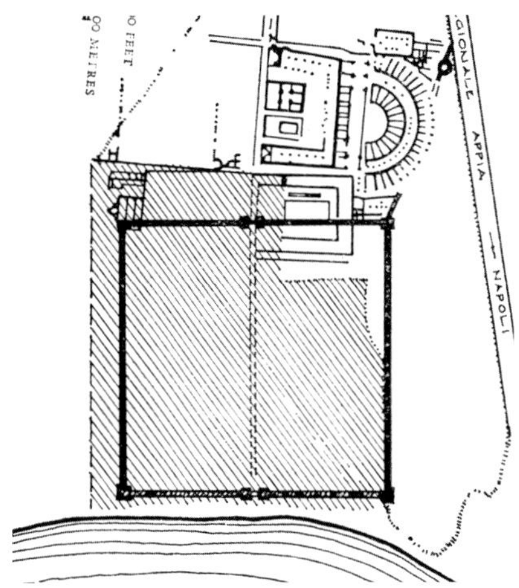

3. *Minturno, plan, ca. 295 BC*

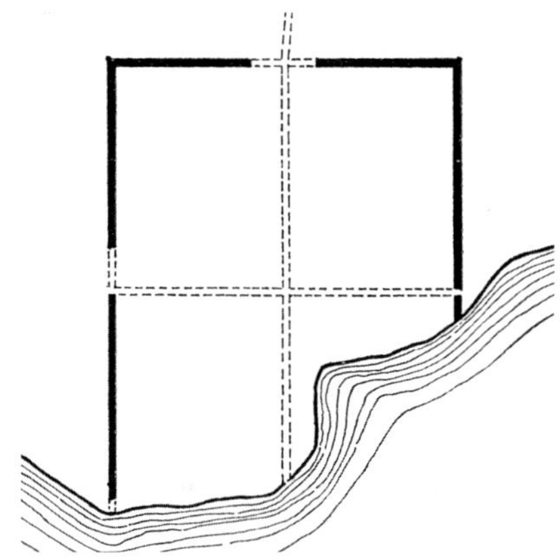

4. *Pyrgi, plan, before 264 BC*

Pre-Roman Towns

The cross-axial plan associated with the Etruscan idea of a terrestrial *templum* reflecting the celestial *templum* is at best faintly apparent in the early sixth-century BC Etruscan grid towns of Marzabotto and Capua.

A clearer predecessor of the Roman cross-axial plan is the archaic core of Pompeii, founded by the Oscans in the sixth century (?) BC. Archaic Pompeii had a clear cross-axis of primary streets intersecting at the *forum*. The surrounding wall was irregular in plan, like those of the Greeks, but the blocks were small and nearly square, rather than the long narrow blocks of the Greeks.

Roman Colonies

Between the sack of Rome by the Gauls in 386 BC and ca. 200 BC the Romans achieved hegemony in the Italic peninsula, first in the south (Latium and Campania) and then in the north (Etruria and beyond). As they expanded out from Rome they founded colonies and divided the surrounding agricultural territory. Each settler family was given a town parcel and an agricultural parcel, and the majority of the settlers lived on their farms.[3] Among the first towns were Cales (344 BC), Norba (342 BC), Terracina (329 BC), and Alba Fucens (303 BC).

Cross-axial Towns

The first cross-axial Roman town plan was Ostia, a military colony founded in the last decade of the fourth century BC to defend the mouth of the Tiber River. Although referred to as a *castrum*, or fort-town, it was in fact a cross-axial rectangular plan with an enclosing wall and four gates—like a regularized version of Archaic Pompeii.[4]

The second founded cross-axial Roman town plan was Minturno (ca. 295 BC), and the third was Pyrgi (before 264 BC).[5] After Minturno, the Romans founded fifteen other Latin colonies before founding Cosa in Etruria in 273 BC.

Cosa: An Early Roman Colony

In 273 BC the Romans founded the town of Cosa on a rocky outcrop in Etruria, overlooking the Tyrrhenian coast. The purpose of the colony was as a defensive frontier outpost at a strategic location.[6] Cosa was intended for about 2,500 families, or ca. 9,000 people, of which about half would live in the countryside.[7]

The plan comprised a grid of rectangular blocks, an irregular perimeter wall, and primary streets that intersected at the forum. But this was not yet the classic Roman cross-axial town plan with square or nearly square blocks and a rectangular perimeter. Rather, the plan and its elements still reflected strong Greek and Etruscan influences.

Typical streets are 20' wide with a 15' roadway. The block sizes vary, but the majority are long and narrow—about 108' wide by ca. 170', 270', and 360' long. Based on the excavated houses, the grid of parcels seems to be a module of about 27' x 54' (1,458 sf), or 27' x 108' (2,916 sf). Most of the modest courtyard houses run through the width of the block, with a garden occupying half the parcel. All of the town's public buildings fit within the urban fabric except the temples on the Arx.

The Arx is a citadel, the Roman equivalent of the Greek acropolis. At Cosa the Arx is located on a high southern precinct and is connected to the *forum* by the Sacred Way. The Arx contained two temples: the Mater Matuta and the Capitolium, both strongly Etruscan.

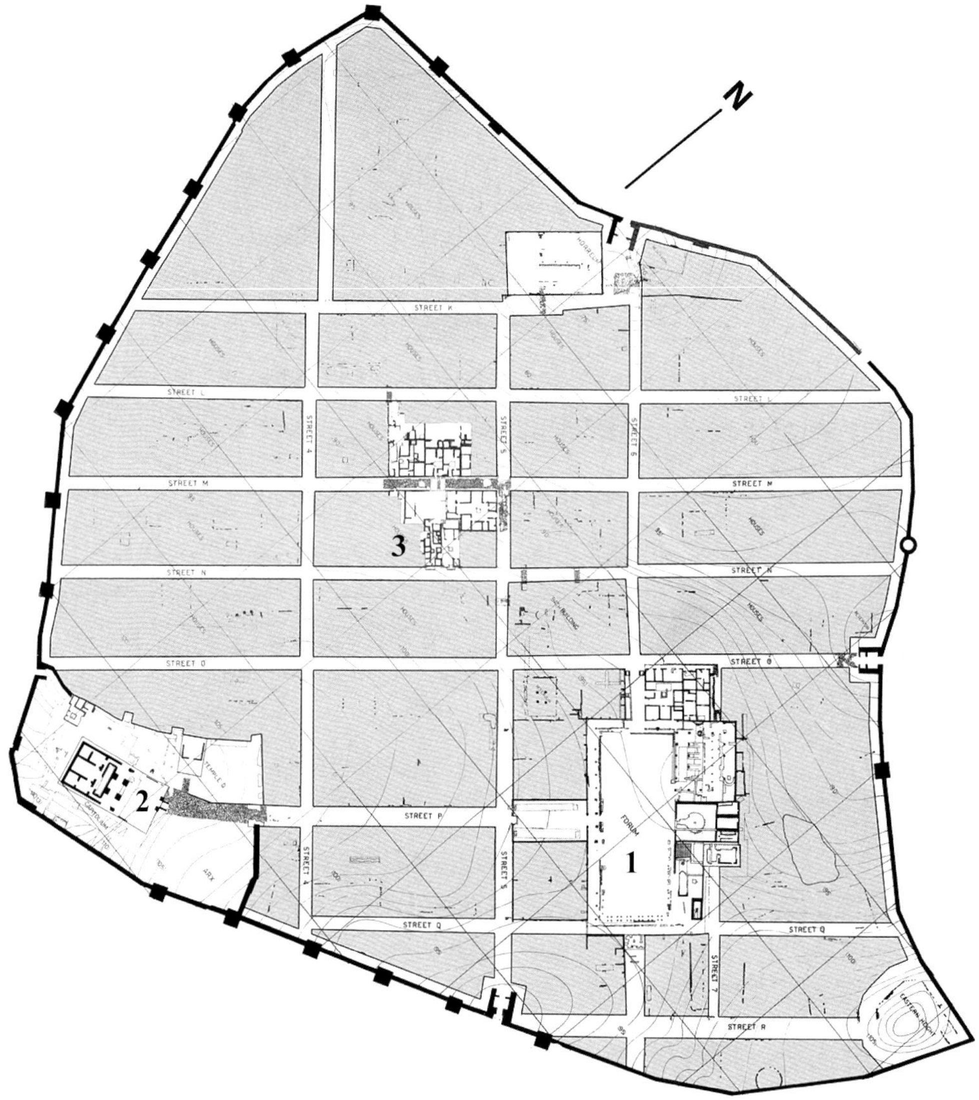

2. Plan of Cosa, 1:5,000:
1. Forum; 2. Arx; 3. Excavated houses

1. Cosa, Capitolium and Temple of Mater Matuta, restoration

3. Early house plans, 1:500

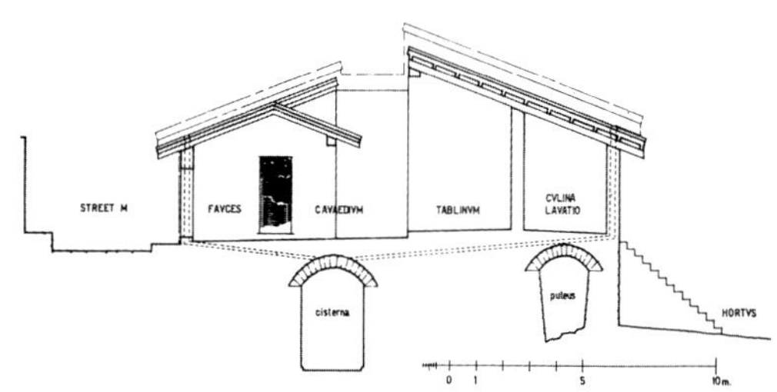

4. Section of an early house

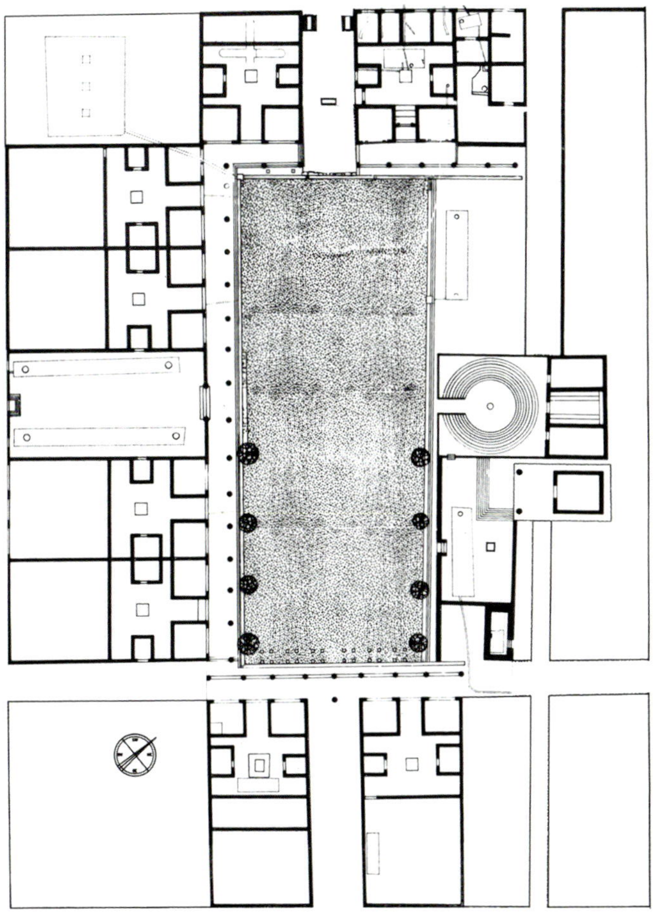

1. *Plan of the fifth phase of the forum restored, 1:1,250*

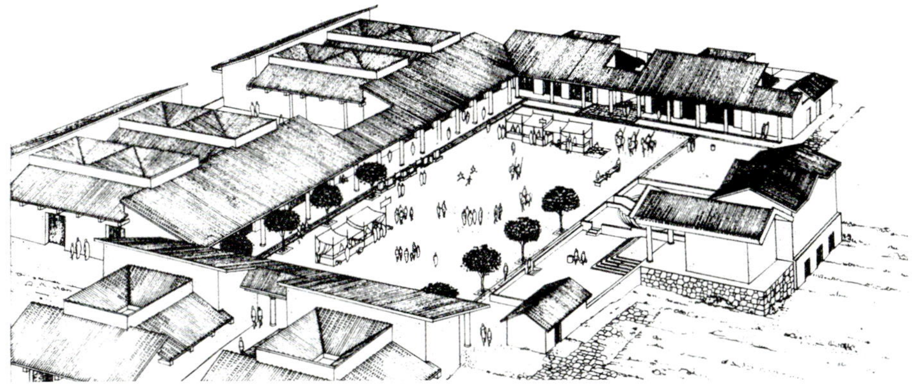

2. *Aerial perspective of the fifth phase of the forum, restoration*

3. *Aerial perspective of the sixth phase of the forum showing the addition of the Basilica, restoration*

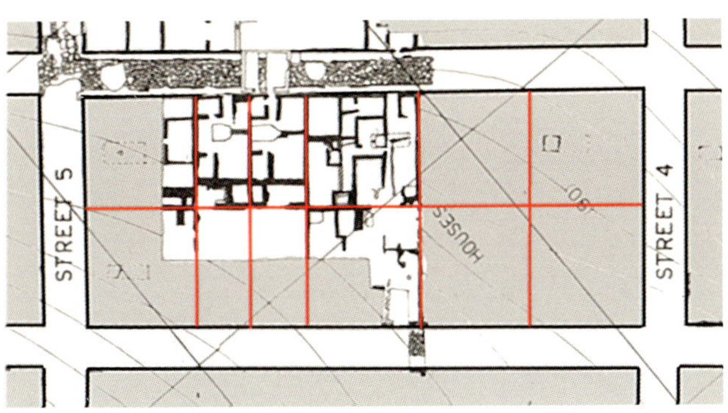

4. *Plan of excavated urban block, 1:1,250*

The Forum

Unlike other Roman *fora*, such as that at Pompeii, the *forum* at Cosa was not dominated by a temple. Rather, it was a unified space that was small in scale and size. One-story porticoes were built in about 170 BC to enclose three sides of the space, and later the basilica was added to the northeast corner, further increasing the spatial enclosure.

The defined open space of the *forum* is about 105' x 280'—almost the same dimensions as the medium-size urban blocks.

The *fora* of Cosa and Pompeii are currently regarded as the first regular Italian squares.[8]

Roman *Castra*

According to Frontius, the typical Roman military camp was an irregular grouping of tents before the Romans defeated Pyrrhus in 275 BC. But after they discovered the highly organized, orthogonal grid of Pyrrhus' military camp they developed their own version of the *castrum*, which was described by Polybius in 175 BC.[9]

Unlike the founded town with square or nearly square blocks and two primary streets intersecting at the center (as illustrated by Vitruvius), the civic structure of the castrum plan was "T"-shaped with rectangular blocks. The plan was often oriented according to the cardinal points, with the cap of the "T," the via Principalis, running east–west between gates, and the stem of the "T," the via Praetoria, running north–south from a gate to the *forum*, or *principalis*, in the center of the plan. There was often another primary street, the via Quintana, running parallel to the via Principalis. The commander's quarters, the paymaster, and the public facilities were located in the center. The soldiers' barracks formed long narrow blocks, and an open area encircled the camp just inside the walls. Despite the clarity of the prototype, endlessly varied *castra* were established as the empire expanded. Some ultimately disappeared, while others became the foundations of future cities.

The two types of founded towns, *colonia* and *castrum*, were also sometimes blended, as at Thamugadi (Timgad). Taken together, they provide the formal infrastructure of hundreds of European cities. In Italy alone, founded towns included Piacenza, Bologna, Imola, Pesaro, Parma, Lucca, Roman Pompeii, Verona, Como, Florence, Pavia, and Turin. The last founded town in Italy was Aosta.

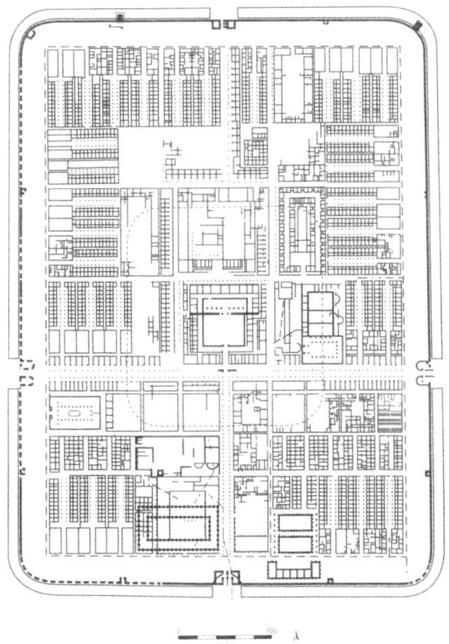

2. Plan of the castrum *of Nuess*

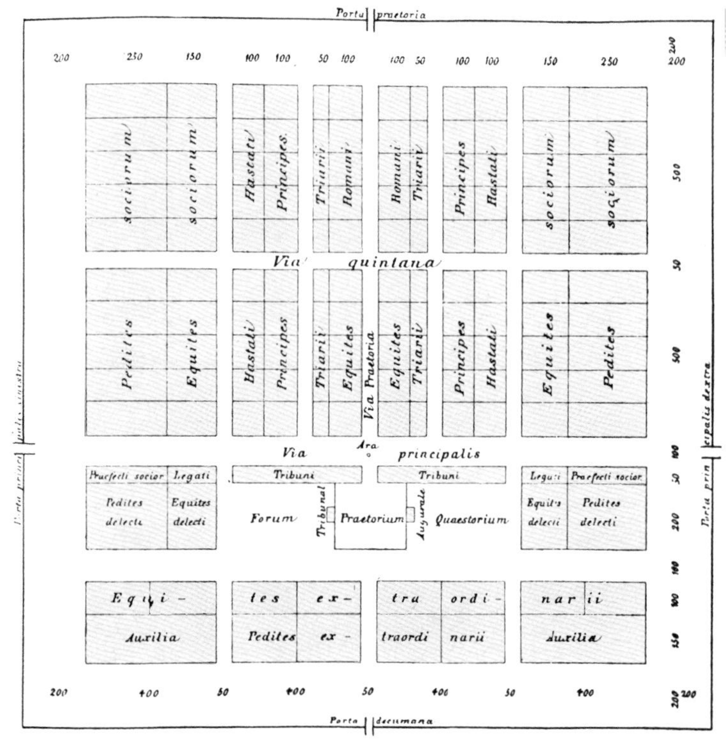

3. Typical castrum *plan as described by Polybius, 175 BC*

1. Timgad, view of the Decumanus Maximus

4. Reconstruction of the castrum *of Caerleon (Wales) in 79 AD by Alan Sorrell*

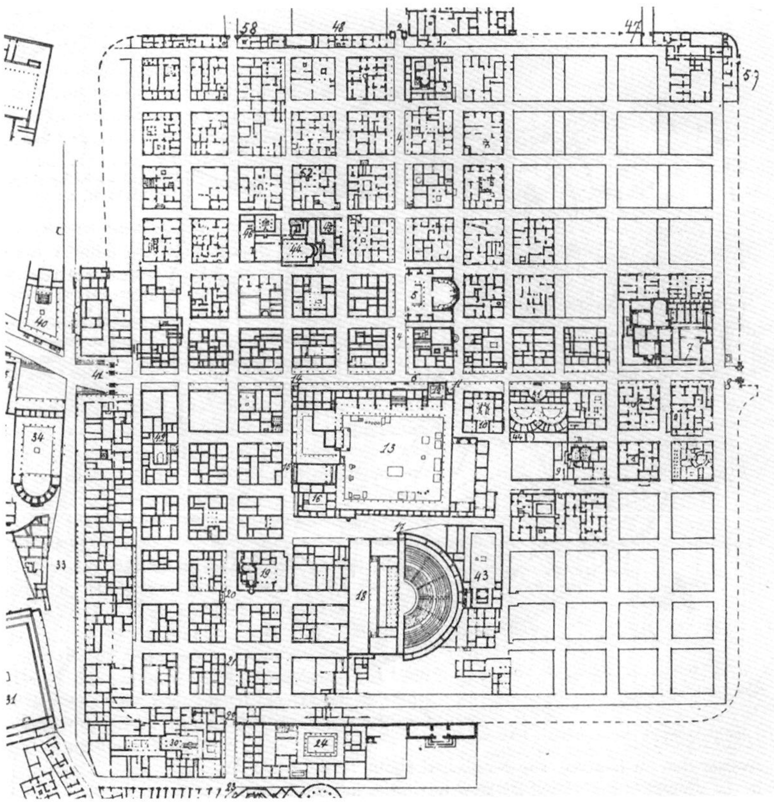

1. *Plan of Timgad*

2. *Timgad, aerial view of Forum and Theater*

TIMGAD

Located in the North African colonies, Timgad was built from 100 AD onward. It is almost a square of 1,150' consisting of 106 square blocks with the dimensions of 66' by 66'. Each block is divided among two or three families. The whole city is designed to accommodate 200 or 300 veteran families. At the intersection of main axes is the forum and all its associated public buildings, including the library and theater. There were also at least fourteen baths in the city. From the mid-second century, the extension of the city beyond its walls became inevitable. Large public buildings in autonomous arrangements were built outside the gates in clear contrast with the order of the grid. The major streets of Timgad were colonnaded, like many Roman towns in north Africa and the east.

3. *Timgad, aerial view*

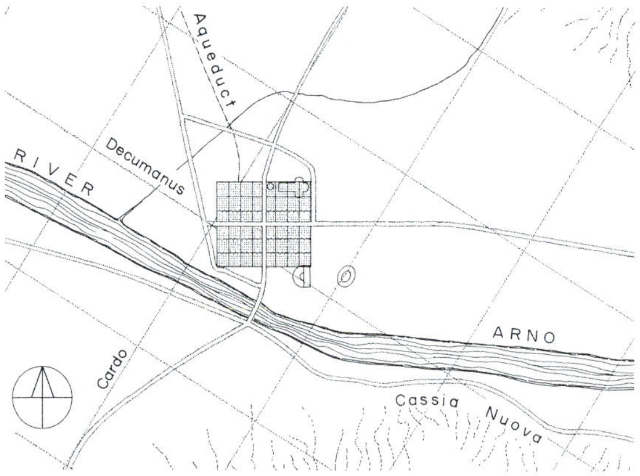

1. Florence, Roman grid and centuriation

Roman progress into the northern part of the Italic peninsula during the second and first centuries BC produced countless founded towns and garrisons that persist today as thriving cities—their formal infrastructure provided by the grid of the original Roman town plan. Among these towns were Piacenza, Bologna, Imola, Parma, Lucca, Verona, Como, Florence, Pavia, Turin, and Aosta. Of these, Florence is a classic example.

Florence

Traditionally, the founding of Florence has been attributed to Julius Caesar in 59 BC. The city is thought to have grown to a population of 10,000 by the second century AD.

The Plan

There is some archaeological evidence of the Roman plan, but it is scant, and the reconstructions vary considerably. Generally, the plan was a rectangle approximately 1,400' x 1,600', with a grid of six by eight blocks. The *cardo* and *decumanus* crossed at the *forum* in the center (today the Piazza della Repubblica); there were gates at the center of each side; and the grid was aligned with the cardinal points. The centuriation, however, aligned with the plain parallel to the Arno and the general direction of the valley.[10]

Because Florence disintegrated after the fall of the Roman Empire and was rebuilt irregularly, precise dimensions of streets and blocks cannot be determined, but basic street width was about 25', with the *cardo* and *decumanus* being around 35' and 40' respectively. The blocks were almost square—approximately 170' x 200'. The parcel sizes and configurations are also not known due to successive rebuilding.

The aerial plan clearly illustrates the medieval character of the urban fabric east of the "cardo," while the more regular blocks and wider streets west of the "cardo" are the result of Poggi's mid-nineteenth-century renewal plan.

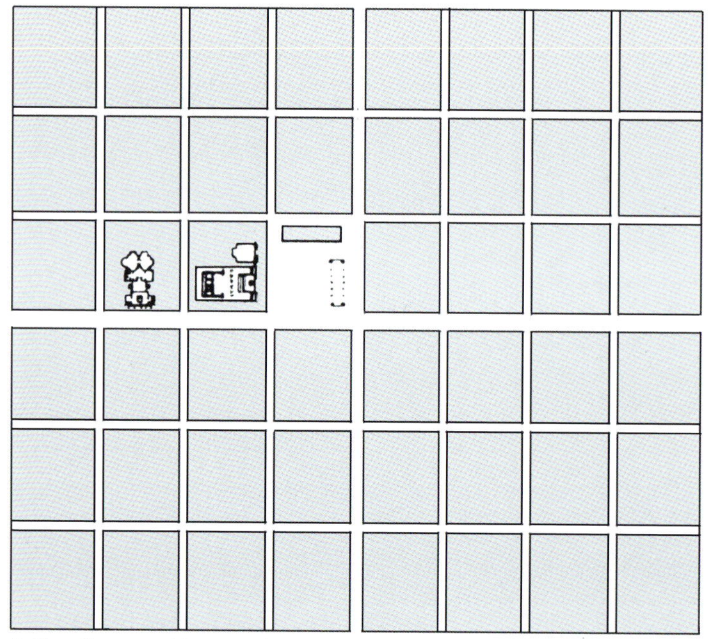

2. Plan diagram of Roman Florence, 1:5,000

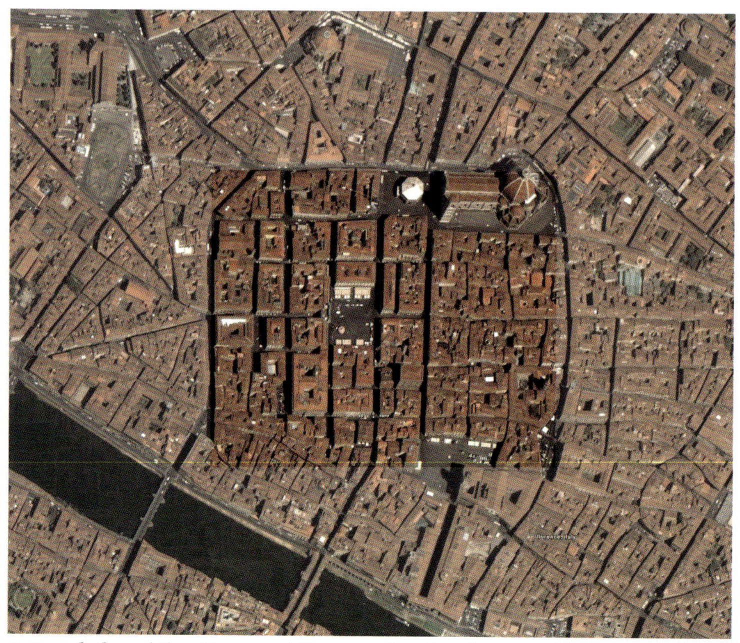

3. Aerial plan of the city core of Florence showing the area of the Roman plan

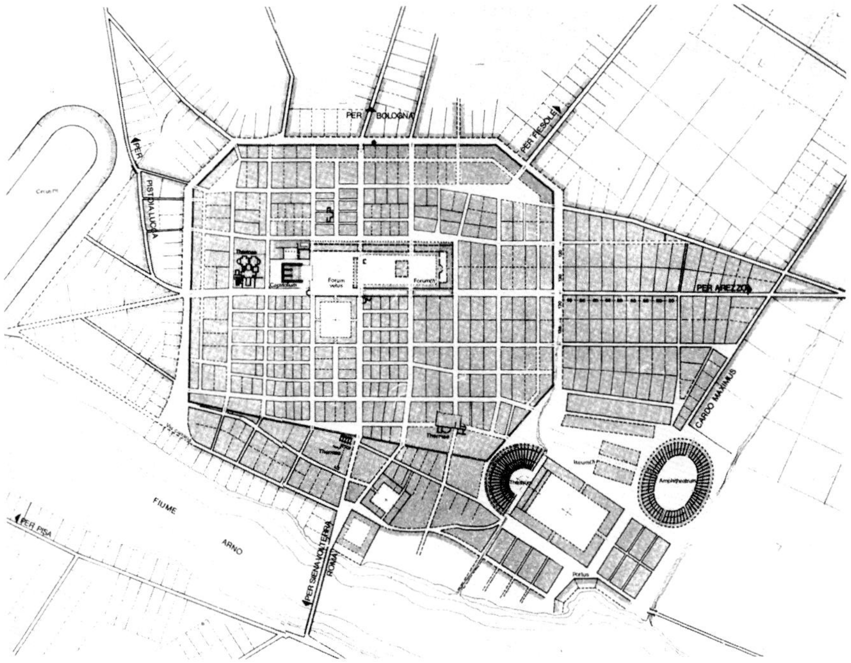

1. Plan of Roman Florence during the Empire

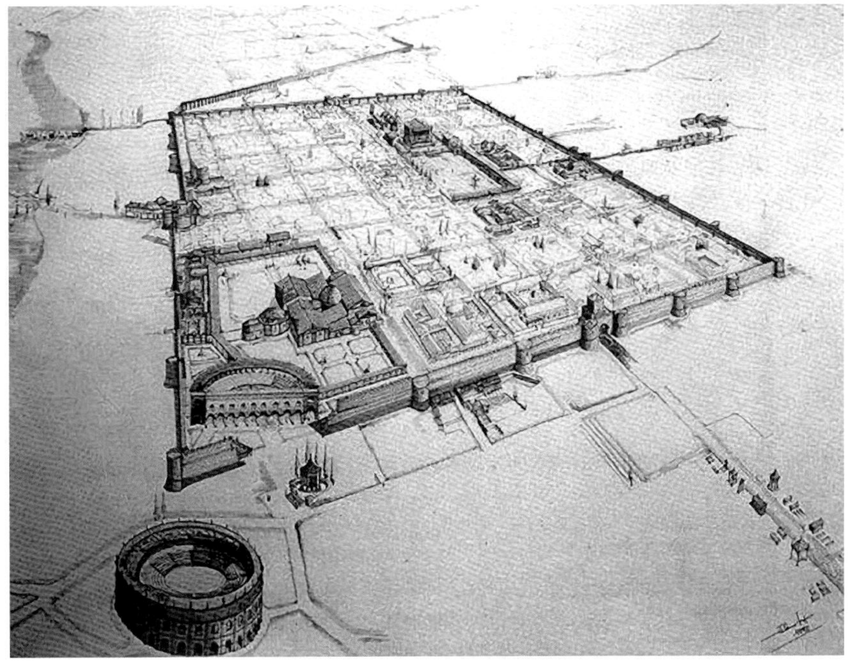

4. Aerial perspective of Imperial Roman Florence, restoration

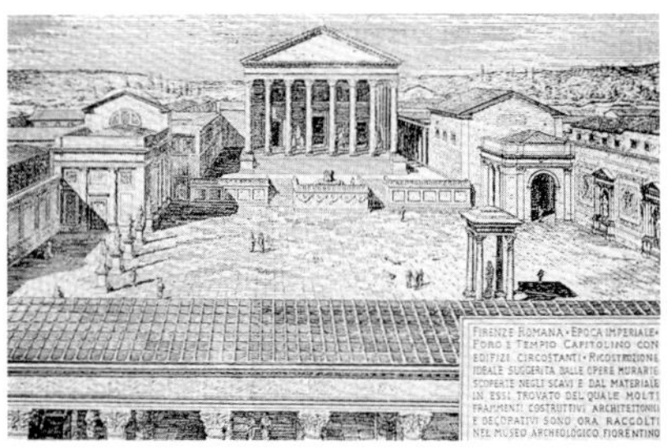

2. Imperial Forum, restoration

3. Mercato Vecchio (before Poggi)

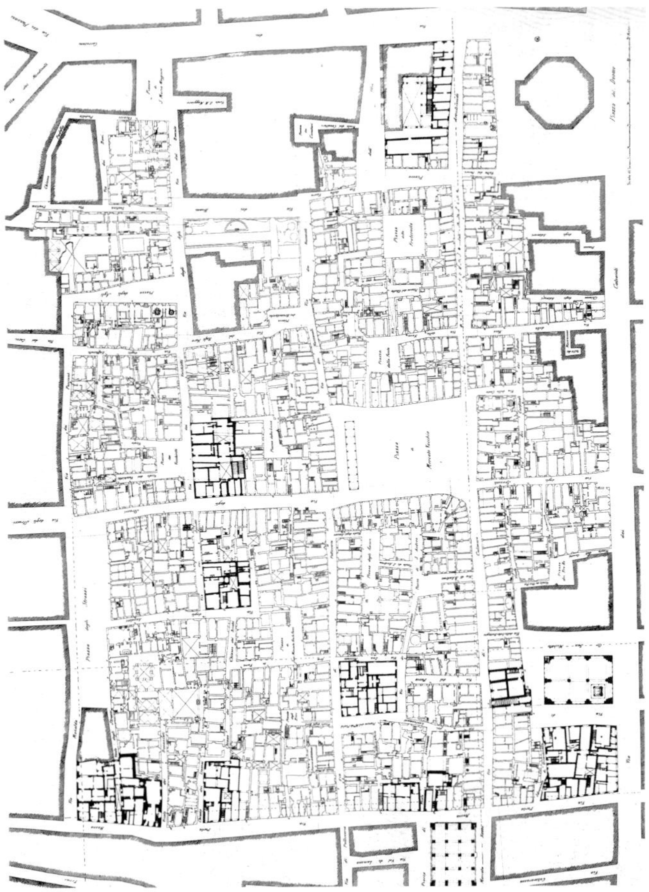

5. Plan of the Mercato Vecchio area

The Forum

During the empire, Florence grew beyond the original walls, the *forum* was expanded, and the theater (mid-first century AD) and amphitheater (124–130 AD) were added.

Before Poggi's urban renewal project the size of the *forum* had been reduced and was known as the Mercato Vecchio.

6. Mercato Vecchio (before Poggi)

Verona

Strategically located on a bend of the Adige river, and at the intersection of four main roads, Verona became a Roman colony in 89 BC (the same year that Pompeii was conquered), and a *municipium* in 49 BC.

Roman Verona was a large town, similar in size to Roman Turin—a rectangle of about 2,200' x 2,500' with two sides trimmed off irregularly by the river. Superimposing the Roman grid over a contemporary aerial plan reveals that the course of the river to the southeast was straightened and tightened, so that the original course of the river may now be seen in the urban fabric on the southeast side of the river. Both the theater and amphitheater were outside the walls.

Urban Fabric

Verona blocks are rather large—about 245' square—and because they have been built over there is no trace of the original parcels. They still form the pattern of the city, however.

The Forum

The forum is also rather large, about 245' x 560', or approximately two urban blocks. The famous Piazza delle Erbe occupies the same location, although in reduced and irregular form.

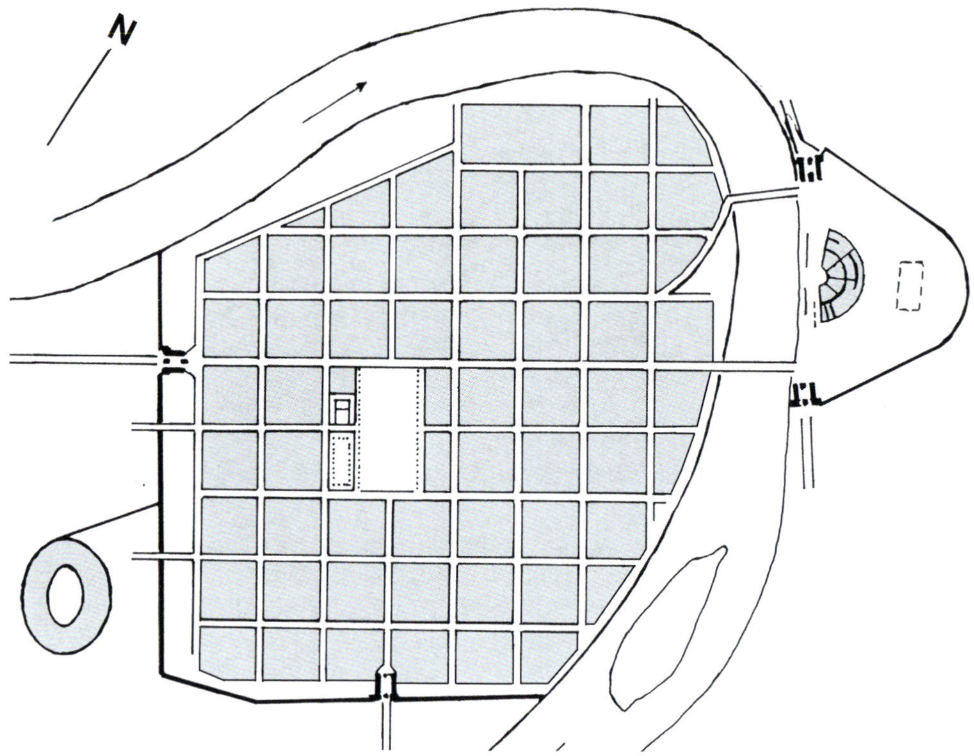

1. Plan of Roman Verona, 1:10,000

2. Verona, Roman gate, the Porta Borsari

3. Piazza delle Erbe

1. Aerial plan of Verona with the Roman plan superimposed, 1:10,000

2. Aerial view of the Roman amphitheater

3. Roman wall and gate

3. Roman Theater

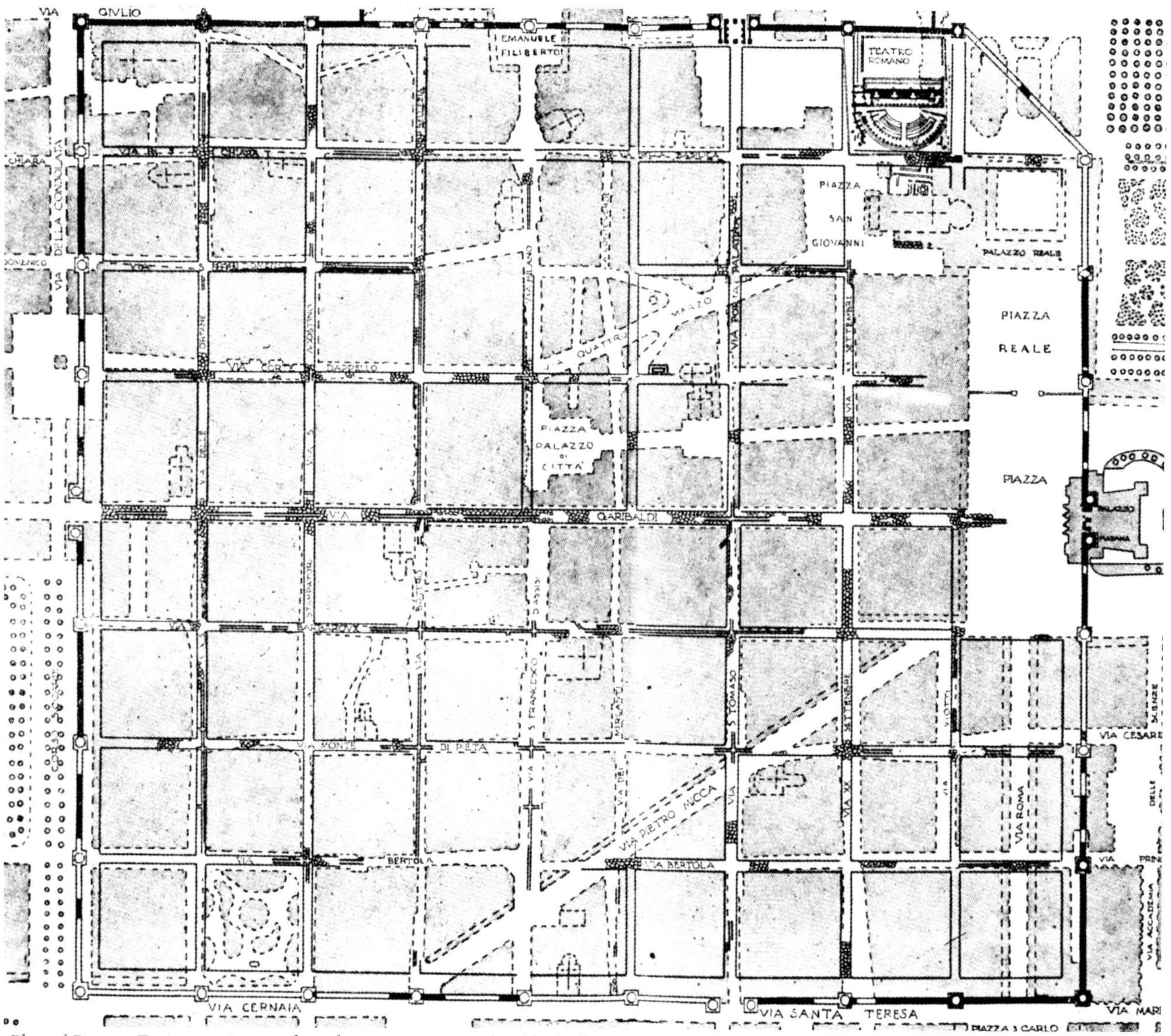

Plan of Roman Turin superimposed on the contemporary plan (dashed), 1:5,000

Turin

Turin was founded about 27 BC as a Roman military camp, *Castra Taurinorum,* and later as *Augusta Taurinorum*. The Roman town reached a population of about 5,000.

The Plan

The historic core of Turin has maintained a fairly consistent relationship between its block structure and that of the original Roman plan. The walled city was considerably larger than Florence. The plan was almost square: approximately 2,300' x 2,500' in contrast to Florence at 1,400' x 1,600', and the grid of blocks is eight by nine instead of six by eight. The *decumanus* bisected the plan, but the *cardo* was displaced toward the east, at the third point. There was one gate on each side, at the ends of the *cardo* and *decumanus* (the *via principalis*).

Urban Fabric

The typical street width is about 25', and the typical block is about 245' square. Because of overbuilding, the original parceling system is not known.

Remarkably, Roman Turin was expanded consistently as a grid pattern, and is today one of the most elaborate and sophisticated examples of urban fabric.

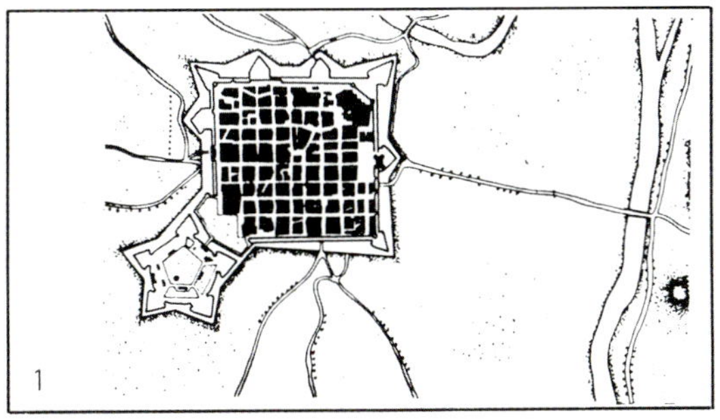

1. Plan in early 1600s, 1:50,000

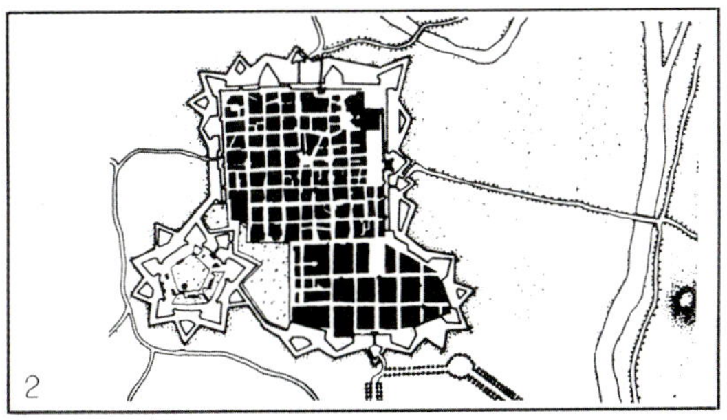

2. Plan of 1620 expansion, 1:50,000

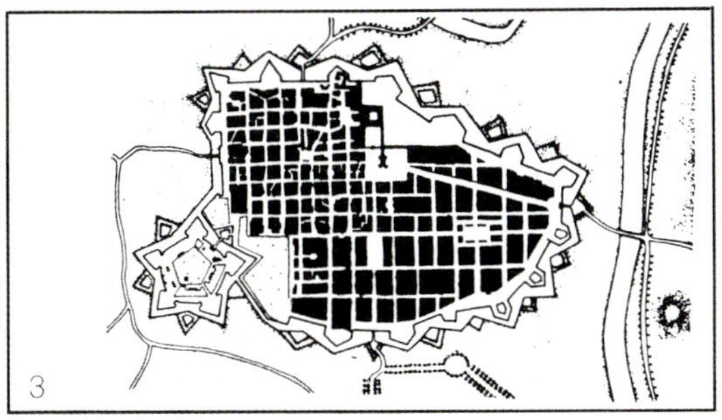

3. Plan of 1673 expansion, 1:50,000

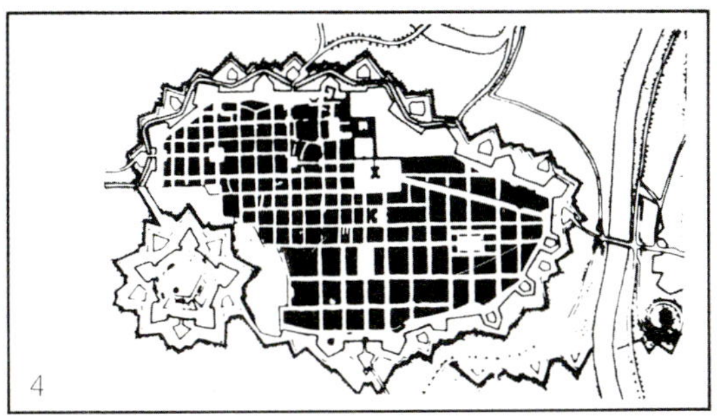

4. Plan of 1714 expansion, 1:50,000

5. Aerial plan of contemporary Turin illustrating area of the Roman city, 1:20,000

6. Roman gate, the Porta Palatina

7. Piazza San Carlo

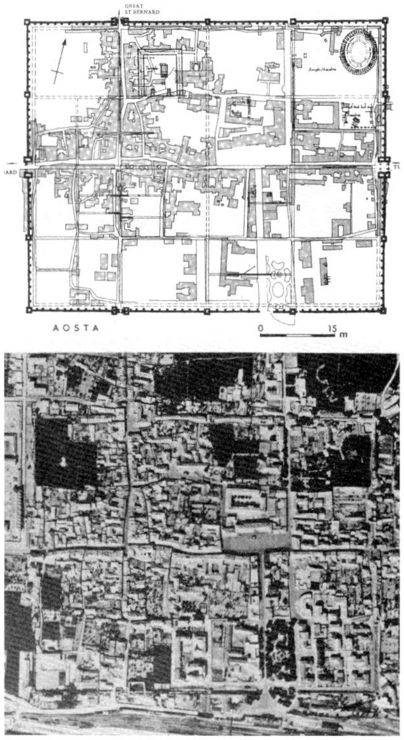

1. Roman plan of Aosta showing the medieval city (above), and contemporary aerial plan (below), 1:15,000

Aosta

The area of Aosta was captured by the Romans in 25 BC, and the Roman town was founded as a military camp for some 3,000 retired veterans. It was the last founded Roman town in Italy. The strategic location of the fort at the conjunction of two rivers gave it major importance.

The Plan

The form of the town was a rectangle about 1,900' x 2,400', divided into 64 rectangular blocks 210' x 280'. The typical streets were about 25' wide; the main streets were 32.5'.

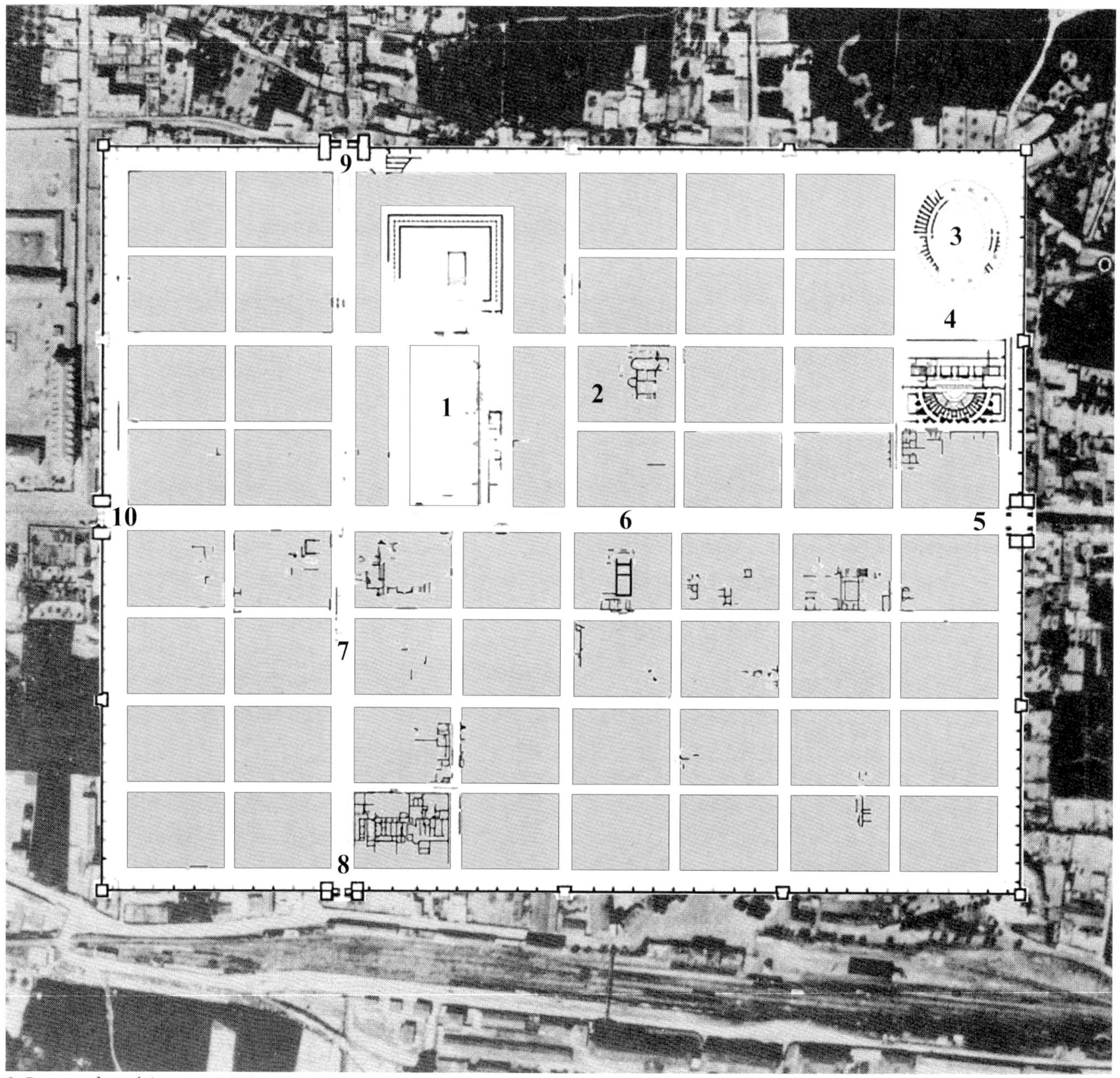

2. Roman plan of Aosta, 1:5,000
1. Forum, 2. Baths, 3. Amphitheater, 4. Theater. 5. Porta Praetoria, 6. Decumanus Maximus, 7. Cardo Maximus, 8. Porta Principalis Dextera, 9. Porta Principalis Sinistra, 10. Porta Decumana

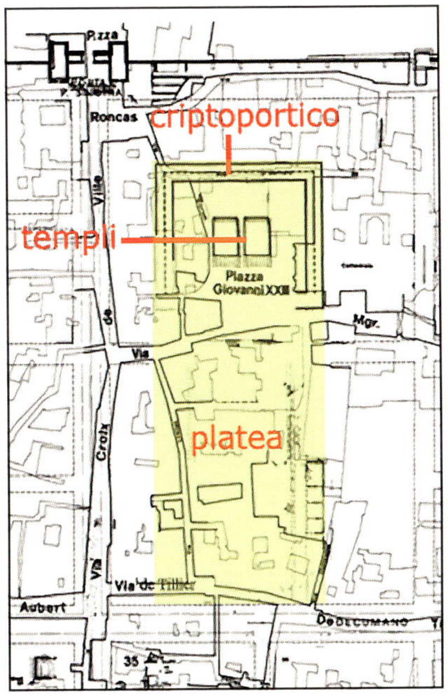

1. Roman Forum

The Forum

The ancient *forum* consisted of two parts. The forum proper (*platea*), 180' x 394', was defined by two-story colonnades on each of the long sides; and the temple complex, a space 187' x 236' enclosed by a *cryptoporticus*, and containing twin temples. The medieval town square was not built on the site of the ancient forum.

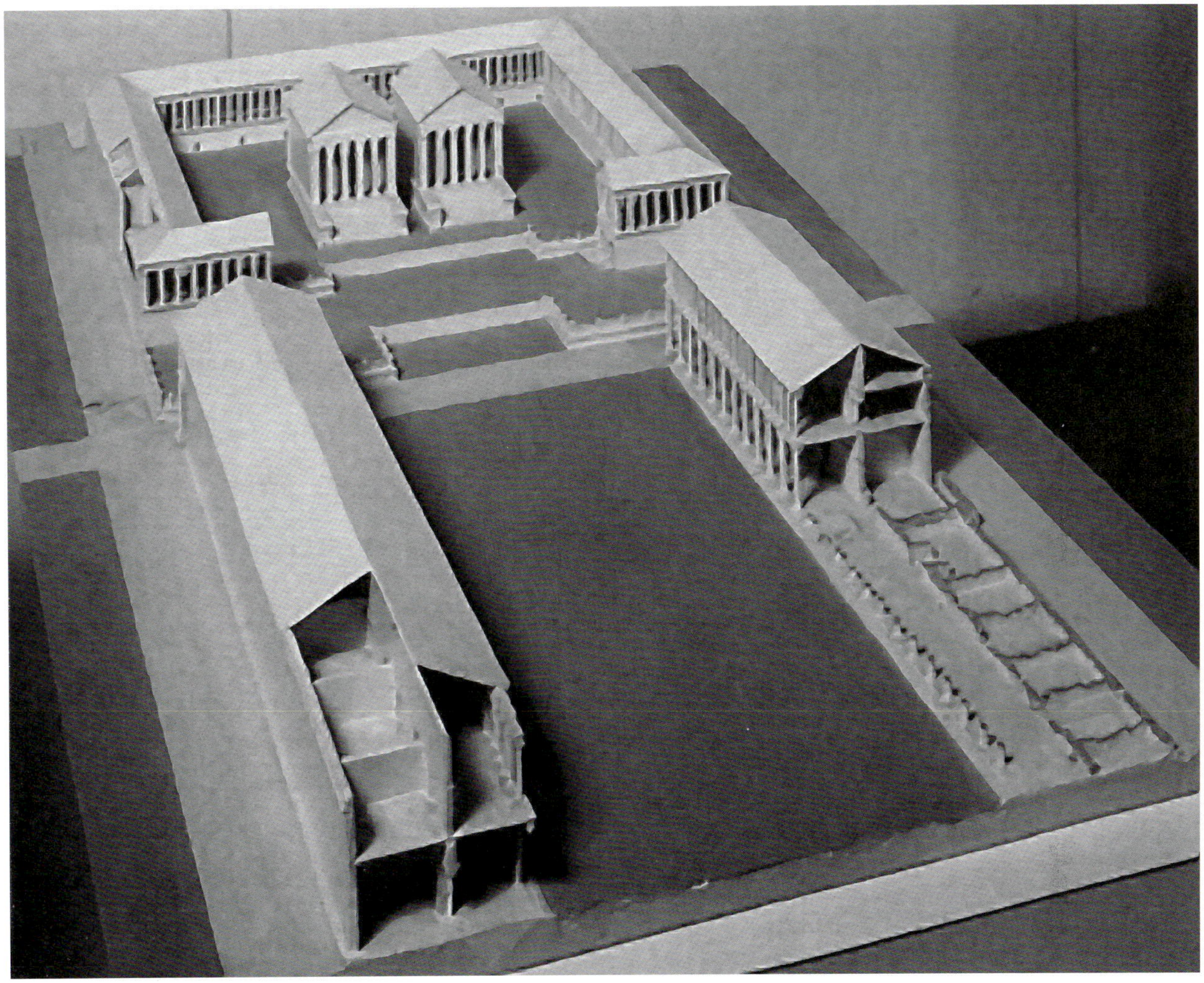

3. Model of the forum, restoration

2. Arch of Augustus

4. Contemporary piazza

5. Porta Praetoria

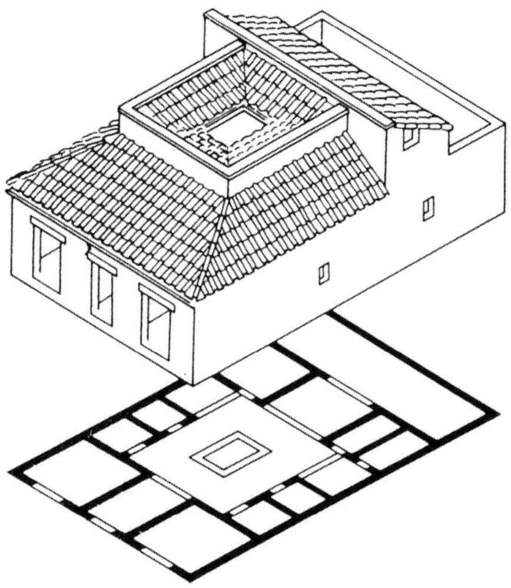

1. Ground floor plan of an atrium house

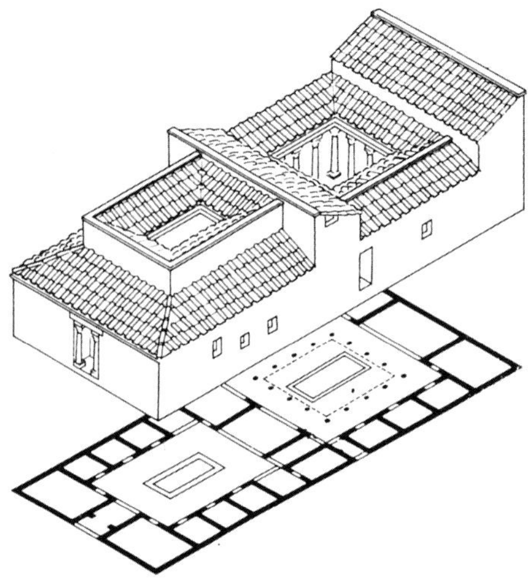

2. Ground floor plan of a peristyle house

Roman Dwellings

Three basic types of dwellings formed the urban fabric of Roman towns: *tabernae,* shops; *domus,* a courtyard house; and *insulae,* apartment buildings.

The *tabernae* were generally one-room shops that lined the major streets. There was often a second level. They also served as the living quarters of the workers and artisans.

The *domus* was a party-wall courtyard house of one, or sometimes two, stories. This is the classic Roman townhouse derived from the ancient Italic house. Early versions consisted of a variety of rooms arranged around an *atrium,* sometimes with a small garden, or *hortus,* at the rear. After contact with the Greeks during the Hellenistic period, the *hortus* was replaced by the peristyle.

The courtyard house was inwardly focused, with shops opening to the street—a type that allowed for infinite variation and adaptability. There were smaller, simpler versions for the less wealthy, and very large houses with multiple peristyles for the very rich. At Pompeii some houses occupied a whole block.

The street entrance to the *domus* had a recessed door (*inau*) between the *vestibulum* outside and the *fauces* inside, with space for a doorman.

The *atrium* had a roof opening, the *compluvium,* and a pool, the *impluvium,* for collecting rainwater to be stored in a cistern below. Around the *atrium* were a series of multi-use rooms, *cubicula,* two open, symmetrical rooms, *aulae,* and the *lararium,* the shrine for the divine protector of the family. Across from the entry was a public room for the head of the house, the *tablinum.* Adjacent to this was a dining room, the *triclinium,* and the passage to the peristyle.

The peristyle was a garden surrounded by a colonnade and important public rooms, including dining. The *exedra* corresponded to the *tablinum,* and the *oecus* corresponded to the *triclinium.* Sometimes larger sleeping rooms opened to the peristyle. There was also a secondary exit from the peristyle called the *posticulum.*

In theory the basic components of the typical *domus* were arranged symmetrically along a central axis on a regular rectangular site. In practice, however, there were few examples of this. At Pompeii, for example, most sites were irregular in plan, or had dimensional restrictions. Even the House of the Faun, which had a regular site, had an asymmetrical plan. The most stable component was the *atrium;* the peristyle could vary considerably; and the enclosed rooms were often freely arranged.

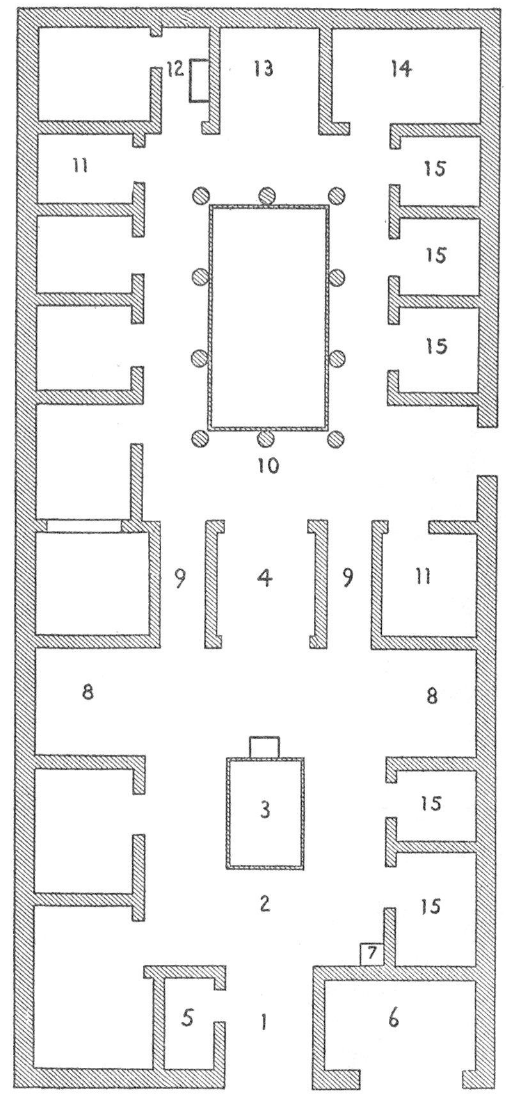

3. Plan of a typical domus*:*

1. vestibulum & fauces, 2. atrium, 3. impluvium, 4. tablinum, 5. doorman, 6. taberna, 7. lararium, 8. alae, 9. andron (corridor), 10. peristyle, 11. triclinium, 12. culina (kitchen), 13. exedra, 14. oecus (living room), 15. cubicola (bedrooms)

1. *Facade reconstruction of an insula, Ostia*

2. *Plans of a Roman apartment house in Ostia, Casa dei Dipinti, 127 AD*

As Roman cities became more populated, increased density created the need for a new form of urban dwelling: the *insula*, or apartment building. Typically, these were found in Rome, Ostia, and larger cities, but the remaining examples are almost entirely in Ostia.

In general, the *insulae* were courtyard buildings with a fountain connected to the public aqueduct system. Shops were on the ground floor and mezzanine, and apartments on the upper floors, with windows and balconies to the street. Many were poorly constructed, dangerous, up to eight stories high, and built for low-income inhabitants. There were also many higher-class apartment buildings, however, such as the Casa dei Dipinti in Ostia. It seems likely that the more populous Roman cities had variations of the apartment building, but none survive.

3. *Model reconstruction of an insula, Ostia, second century AD*

Pompeii

Modern knowledge of Roman cities would be far poorer if not for the preservation of Ostia, Herculaneum, and Pompeii. Indeed, the discovery of Herculaneum and Pompeii in the mid-eighteenth century revolutionized our view of the ancient world.

Pompeii is not fundamentally a Roman town, nor does it have a Roman plan. It is an Italic town transformed by the Romans—one of many spectacular Roman renovations of Greek and/or Italic cities, including Miletus, Ephesus, and Taormina.

The earliest findings in the historic core were Etruscan,[11] but the city is generally considered to have been founded by the Oscans. Located in Campania between the sophisticated cultures of the Etruscans and the Greeks, it was taken over by the Samnites in the fifth century BC and was expanded by the Samnites until it was conquered by Sulla in 89 BC. In 80 BC it became a Roman colony.[12]

The complete town plan has distinctive areas of contrasting urban fabric. The historic core is comprised of squareish, irregular blocks, and might be seen as a precedent for the cross-axial Roman plan. It is surrounded on the north and east by a zone of irregular blocks, and this layer is bounded on the north and east by regular areas of long narrow blocks in the Greek manner. The primary streets, whose configuration closely follows the pattern of roads outside the historic core, are thought to have divided the agricultural area before the expansion. In other words, the antique roads provided the framework, or infrastructure, for the new neighborhoods.

The sequence in which this expansion took place has been controversial among archaeologists. One theory has been that all the expansion happened in one or two phases.[13] A more recent theory is that an irregular defensive wall was erected around a large agricultural area in the first half of the sixth century BC, and that the expansion developed in a series of phases between the fourth and second centuries BC.[14] This theory is not supported by contemporary archeologists; but for contemporary architects and town planners, however, the issue of phasing is not central to the lessons of Pompeii. The primary lesson is that urbanism had hegemony over architecture and that architectural types had the flexibility to adapt to the urban patterns of both the core and the expansion.

1. Pompeii, conjectural restoration aerial view

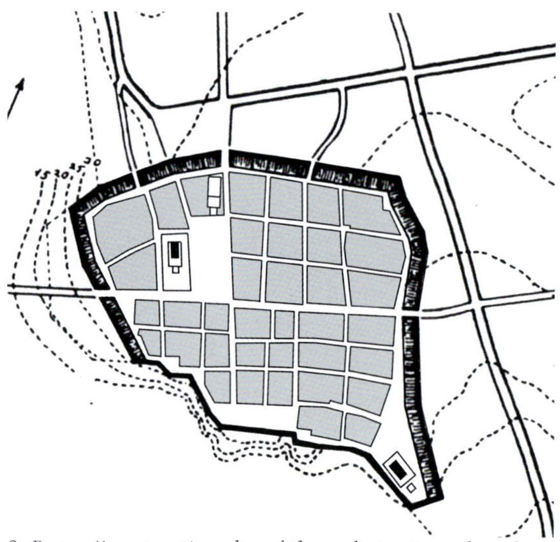

2. Pompeii, restoration plan of the archaic city and roads (after A. von Gerkan)

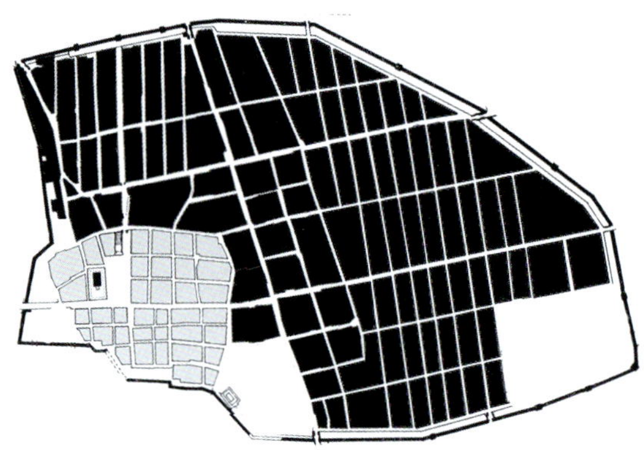

3. Archaic city with expansion to the north and east before Roman interventions

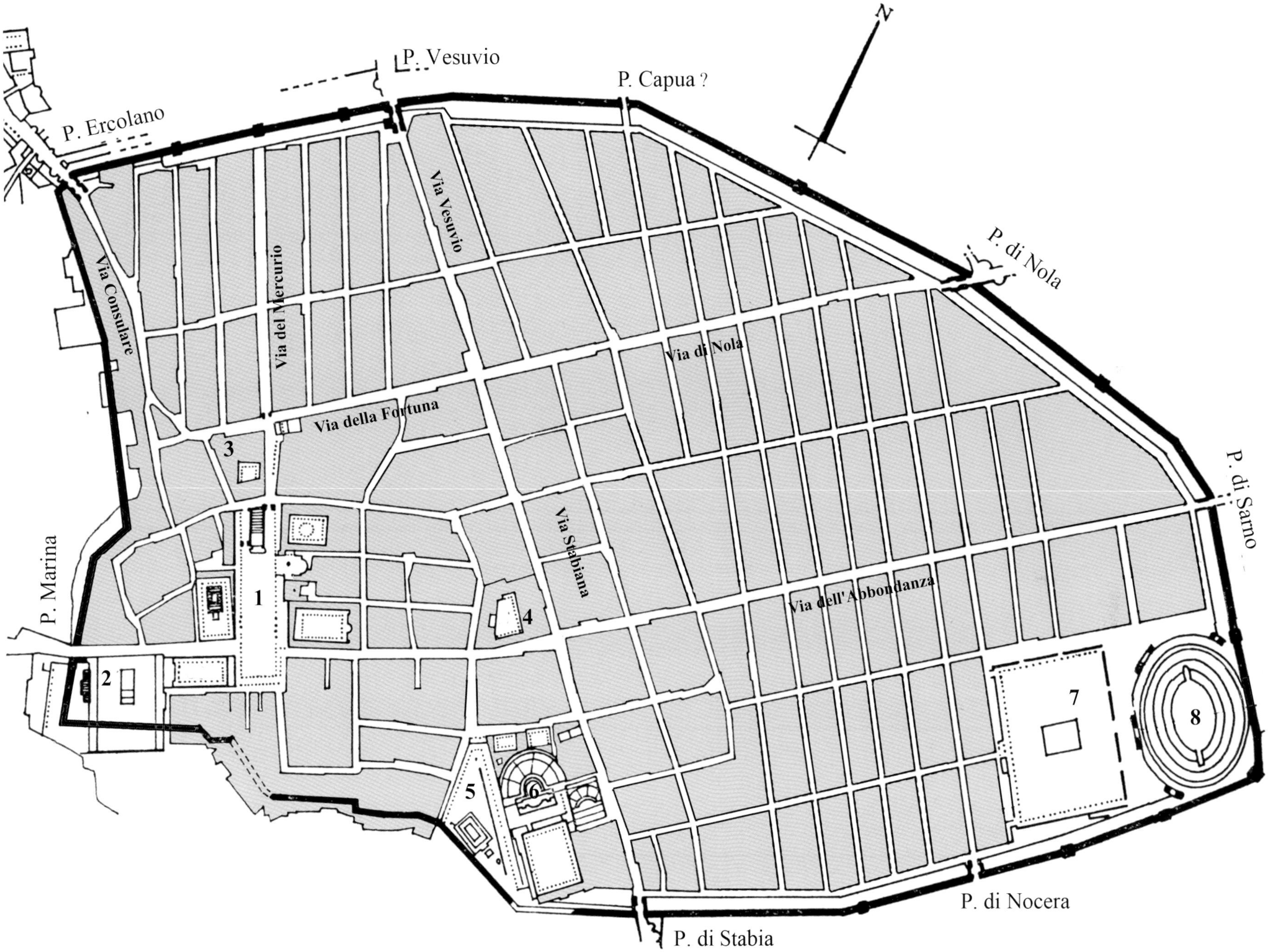

Plan of Roman Pompeii, showing the block pattern extended through the unexcavated areas, 1:5,000.
1. Forum, 2. Temple of Venus, 3. Forum Baths, 4. Stabian Baths, 5. Triangular Forum, 6. Theaters, 7. Palestra, 8. Amphitheater

1. Plan of the city core and forum by Gromort, 1:2,000.

1. Forum, 2. Temple of Jupiter (Capitolium), 3. Macellum, 4. Lararium, 5. Sanctuary of Augustus (Temple of Vespasian), 6. Eumachia, 7. Comitium, 8. Civic Buildings, 9. Basilica, 10. Sanctuary and Temple of Apollo, 11. Northwest Building, 12. Forum Baths

2. View of the Forum looking toward Vesuvius

The *Urban Core* and the *Forum*

There is little certainty about the historic urban core of Pompeii. The most common theory is that it was the original nucleus of the town. (See the plan diagram after A. von Gerkan above.) The blocks are relatively small and somewhat irregular, and the forum and its public buildings seem disproportionately large.

The exact historic development of the forum is not known—even the pre-Roman state—but there is now a provocative, if controversial, theory that its "final" form was the result of a Roman effort to create a unified urban ensemble.[15] The dimensions of the space are 107' x 484' to the back of the Temple of Jupiter, or the Capitolium. Like the forum at Cosa, it is almost identical to the proportions of one of the "Greek" blocks in Pompeii.

The forum at Pompeii is a compelling urban form in the evolution of urban design: a stable, legible public space surrounded by a constellation of idiosyncratic but distinctive public buildings embedded in the urban fabric of the city. Thus, the forum is to the city as the courtyard is to the *domus*.

The Gromort plan illustrated here is not the most up-to-date plan in some of its details, but it is still the most beautifully drawn.

1. Aerial view of the ruins

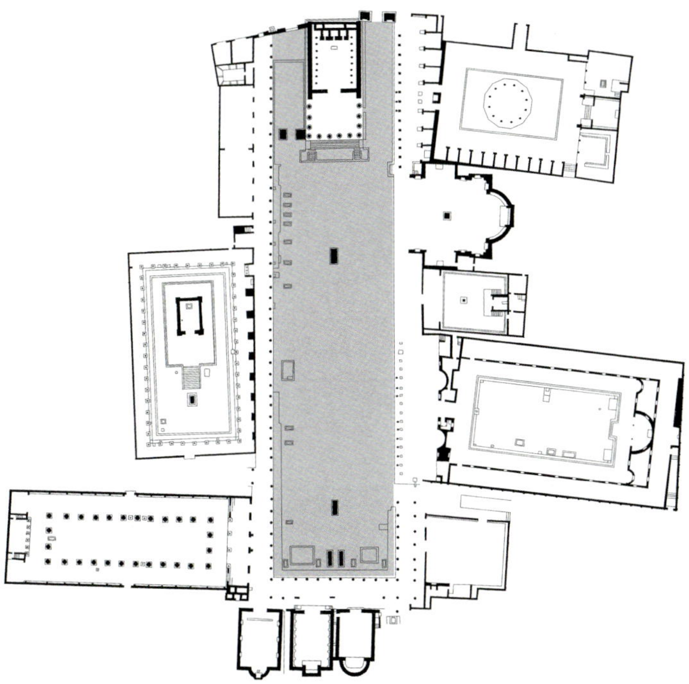

2. Plan of the Forum and public buildings, 1:2,000

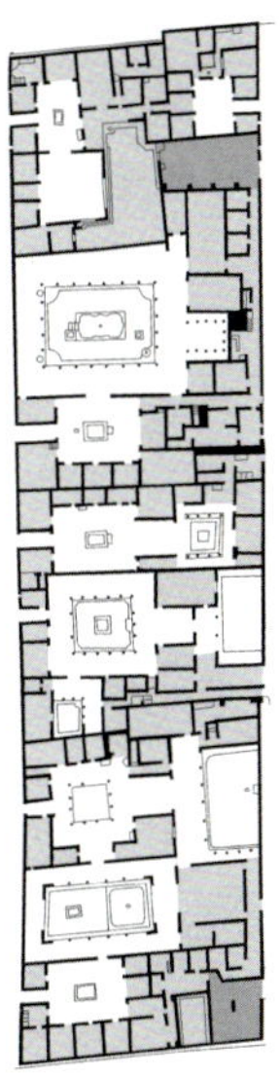

3. Block VI.9. 1:2,000

4. View of the Forum toward Vesuvius

5. Partial reconstruction view toward Vesuvius giving an idea of the proportions of the space

1. Via di Mercurio

Urban Fabric

Major portions of the urban fabric of Pompeii consist of long, narrow, Greek-type blocks almost entirely composed of a one to two-story party wall and courtyard houses. Unlike Greek blocks, however, which originally consisted of equally sized parcels, the Pompeii blocks have parcels of great variety and randomness.

The first area of expansion beyond the historic core, Region VI to the north, exhibits a remarkable range of houses, from small, to modest, to large, to very large. Among the smallest are *atrium* houses approximately 30' wide by 50' deep, or a parcel size of 1,500 square feet. There are modest peristyle houses about 33' x 105', or a parcel size of 3,465 square feet, and relatively generous peristyle houses of about 50' by 105' deep, or a parcel size of 5,250 square feet. Finally, there are large, lavish houses that occupy a full block, such as the House of Panza and the House of the Faun. These are almost 108' x 295' for a parcel size of almost 32,000 square feet. Many of the parcels and houses are irregular as a result of acquisition and remodeling, but the courtyard type is very flexible and adaptable.

In this section of Pompeii the typical streets are about 16' wide, and the Via di Mercurio is about 30' wide. Major streets are lined with shops.

The blocks in Region VI are generally 105-110' wide by 295–465' long. The block dimensions of the eastern expansion area are similar in size.

2. Porta di Mercurio

3. Restoration street view

4. Plan of the northern expansion, by Gromort, 1:2,000

LEGEND

1. House of Salusto, 2. House of Panza, 3. House of the Tragic Poet, 4. House of Apollo, 5. House of Meleagro, 6. House of the Labarinth, 7. House of the Vettii, 8. House of the Faun, 9. TempWle of Fortuna Augusta, 10. Porta di Mercurio, 12. Forum Baths

1. Blocks and parcels of the northern expansion, 1:2,000

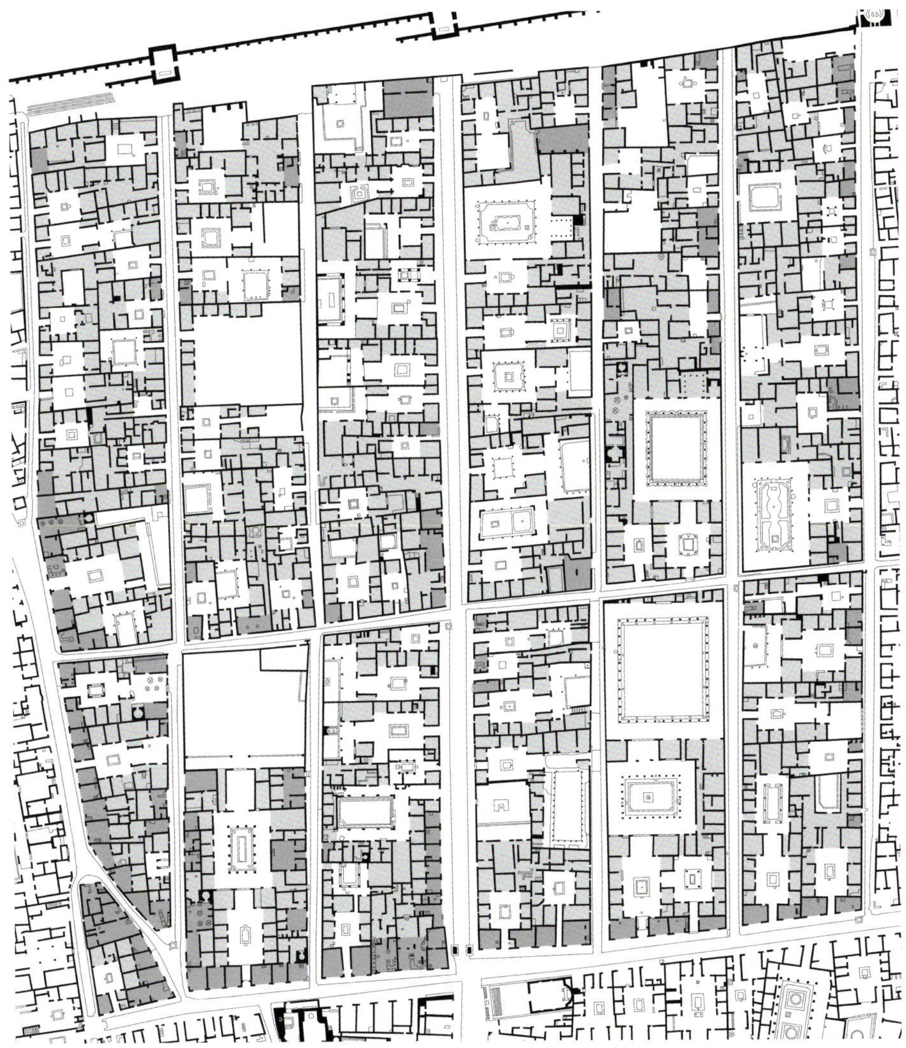

2. Northern expansion with interior sequences and shops, after Dobbins, 1:2,000

If the northern neighborhood of Pompeii is rendered in a manner similar to Giambattista Nolli's famous 1748 plan of Rome, the rich private "civic structure" of Pompeii is revealed. Like an elaborate urban garden, the fine-grained porosity of poché and platonic spaces weave an infinitely varied spatial fabric. The "irrationality" of the parcels—probably the result of convenient land swaps over the years—contributes to the gentle practicality of stable spatial centers and flexible perimeters. The idea of landscape as we know it today did not exist, but on a private level it was provided by the numerous gardens and private open spaces, the public faces of the shops shielding the private realm.

1. House of the Faun, conjectural restoration view of the atrium

2. House of the Faun, actual view

3. Atrium in Herculaneum

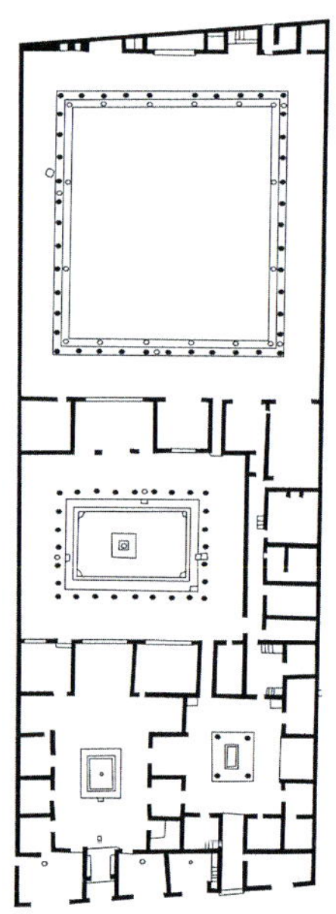

4. Plan of the House of the Faun

5. Mosaic of the battle between Alexander and Darius, from the exedra of the House of the Faun

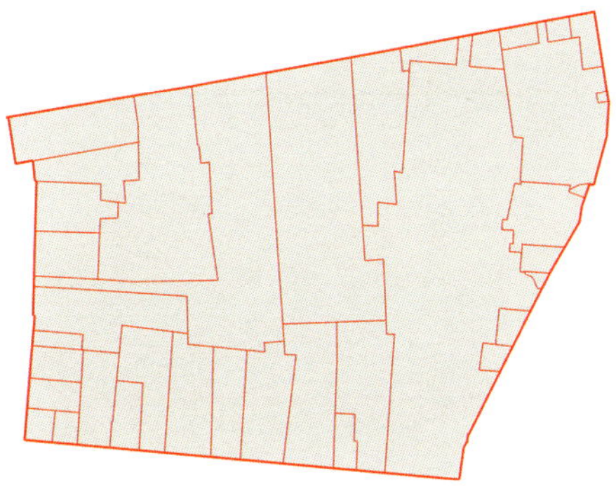

1. Block VII-4 and parcels, 1:2,000

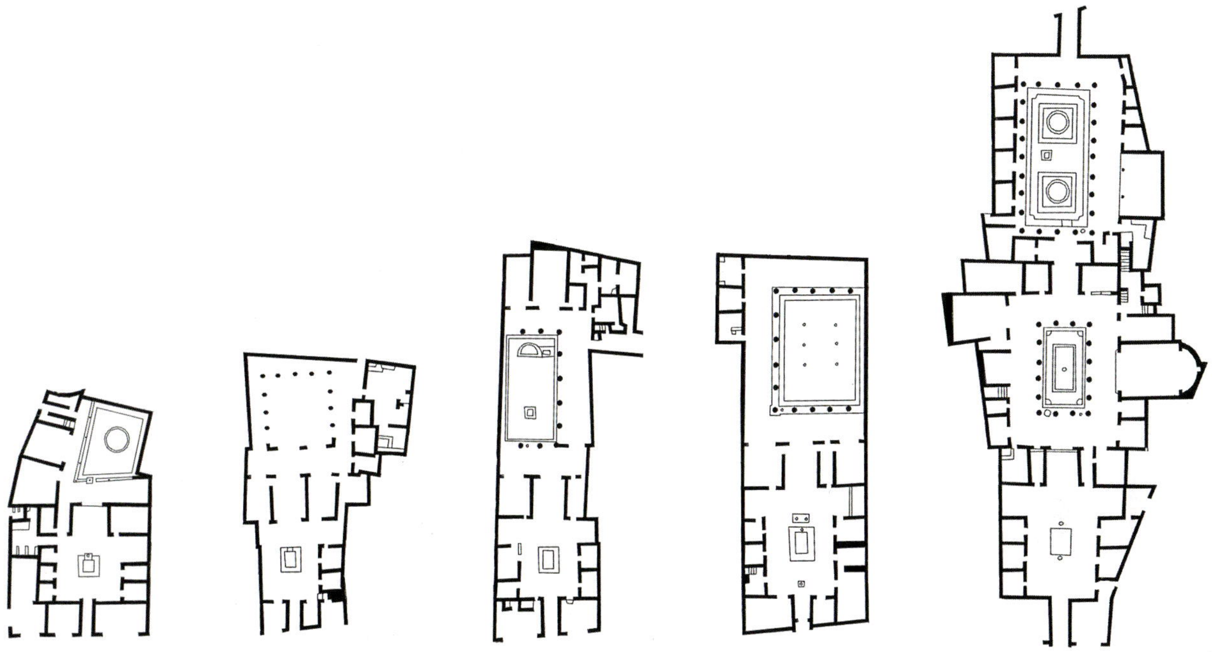

4. House of the Hunt | *Samnite House* | *House of the Black Wall* | *House of the Figured Capitals* | *House of Ariadne, 1:1,000*

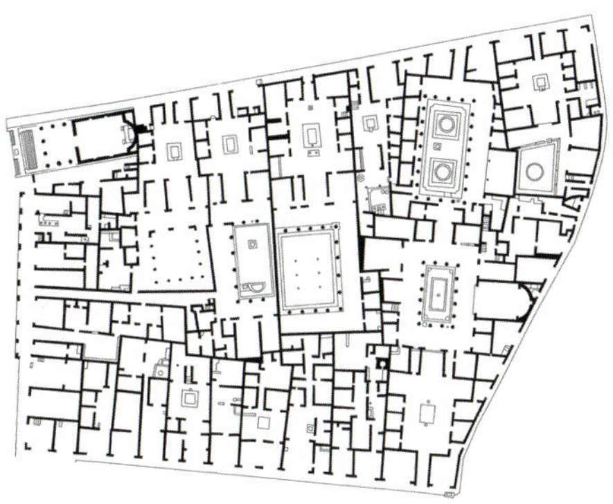

2. Block VII-4 and buildings, 1:2,000

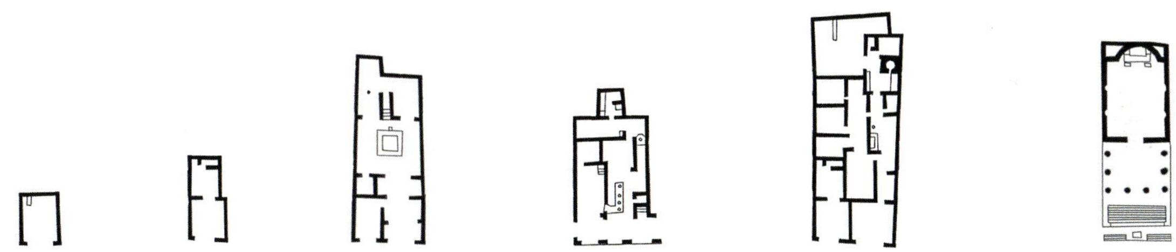

5. Shop | *Shop House* | *House and shop* | *Shop at colonnade* | *Shop and workshop* | *Temple of Fortuna Augusta*

3. Block VII-4 with shops and courts 1:2,000

Irregular Urban Fabric

Block VII-4 is one of the most architecturally challenging blocks in Pompeii. It occupies a strategic position at the intersection of the via del Foro and the via della Fortuna, between the city core and the northern expansion. The block is a large irregular trapezoid that is an average of 250' deep north–south, and 330' deep east–west. Because of its strategic location the perimeter of the block is almost continually lined by shops, and the northwest corner is anchored by the Temple of the Fortuna Augusta. The primary spatial organization of the block is provided by five large Samnite houses along the via della Fortuna.[16] The large peristyles of four of these houses occupy the center of the block. One house, the House of Ariadne, extends 275' through the entire block along an axis of atrium, peristyle, and great peristyle. The southern part of the block is largely occupied by small houses and workshops. In general the parcels and buildings are fairly regular and relate to their principal streets, with the odd resulting angles being taken up by secondary and tertiary rooms.

3. Pompeii, large theater

Temples and Public Buildings

The Romans conquered Pompeii in 89 BC, made it a colony in 80 BC, and inserted Roman citizens into the city and surrounding areas. They also began to build and renovate public buildings and spaces in order to transform Pompeii from a Samnite town into a Roman town.

The public buildings and spaces that were either built or renovated by the Romans included temples, baths, theaters, palaestra, an amphitheater, an aqueduct bringing fresh water, and most important, the forum.

With the exception of the amphitheater, however, none of these facilities were free-standing; they were integrated into the fabric of the city.

In the cases of some temple complexes, the Romans made formal adjustments at the expense of adjacent private fabric, but these were relatively minor.[17]

The temples themselves were almost always enclosed in a colonnaded courtyard, or sanctuary, such as the Temple of Apollo, the Temple of Isis, and the Capitolium in the Forum. One exception was the Temple of the Fortuna Augusta, which juts out of the block at an angle so that it may be seen from the Forum and the Via del Foro—an overt gesture of flattery from a provincial town to Emperor Augustus.[18]

1. Temple of Isis, engraving

2. Amphitheater

4. Pompeii, aerial view of the palaestra, small theater, and large theater

1. Taormina, Greco-Roman theater

Ephesus and Taormina

Ephesus, in Asia Minor, and Taormina, in Sicily—both Greek cities with spectacular sites—were taken over by the Romans, and in typical Roman fashion were refitted with grander buildings and monumental civic structures that enhanced their relationships to the landscape.

Taormina is a hilltop city with spectacular views to the sea, and a theater focused on Mount Etna. In Ephesus a colonnaded street led from the harbor to the theater, with a view of an island with a conical hill. The harbor is now silted-in, but the view remains.

Neither city can be fully appreciated from pictures.

The End of the Western Roman Empire

The transformation of the Western Roman Empire began long before Odoacer replaced Romulus Augustus in 476 AD, and as the physical environment gradually disintegrated, the Roman idea of cities as the primary instruments of civilization also disappeared for centuries. Indeed, almost 1,000 years would pass before cities revived and new towns would again be planned. Surprisingly, after 1,000 years, the planning tradition of gridded new towns would begin again—as if nothing had intervened.

2. Ephesus, view of theater from colonnaded street

3. Ephesus, view from the theater to the harbor and conical island

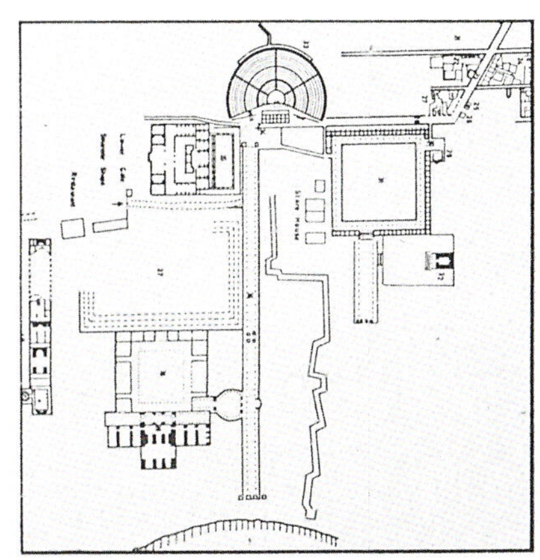

4. Ephesus, plan of Roman civic structure

Roman Fora

The core of every Roman town was the forum. It was the center of the city, and the center of public life—political, religious, commercial, and legal.

In form, Roman fora were usually unified, regular, rectangular spaces, whether they were imperial fora or those of planned towns—the Forum Romanum being the exception because it grew by accretion over many years. The fora of Cosa and Pompeii are regarded as the first regular Italic squares. The fora were also rather modest in size, even the imperial fora. Their widths ranged from ca. 115' to 260'; the lengths from 260' to 476'.

In planned towns the Fora were organic parts of the grid; i.e., they were either the size of a block, as in Cosa and Pompeii, or multiples of blocks, as in Imperial Florence, Verona, or Aosta. Thus, as the blocks got bigger (Verona and Aosta) the Fora consequently became larger.

In Imperial Rome the strategy for the fora was the opposite. Rather than fitting into an organizing grid, the fora were either loosely related set-pieces or larger composite constellations, around which the urban fabric grew. The spectacular plan of the monuments of Imperial Rome on the next page contrasts starkly with the planned towns at the same scale.

115' x 260'

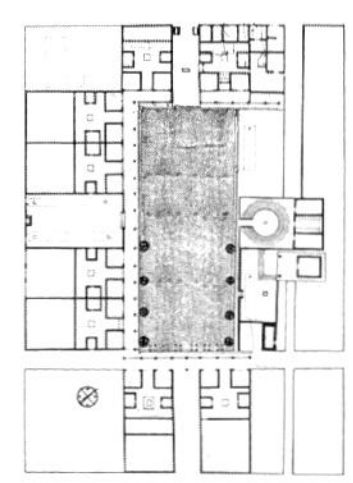

1. Cosa, Forum, 1:5,000

115' x 476'

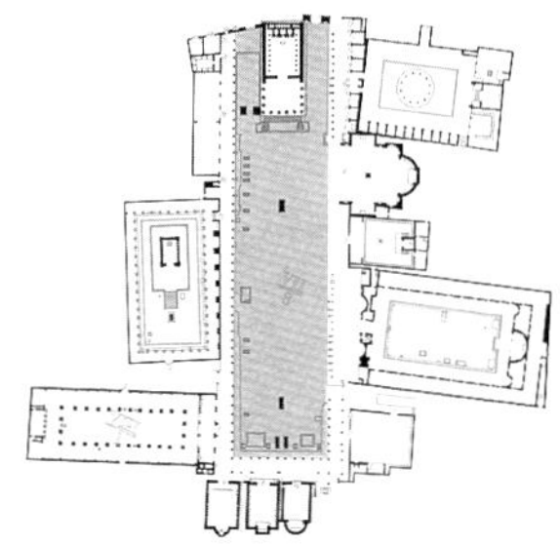

2. Pompeii, Forum, 1:5,000

172' x 148'

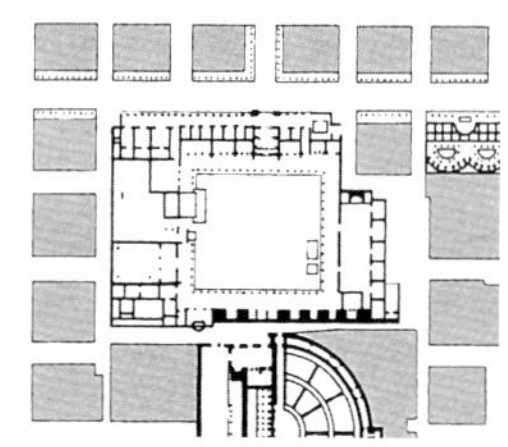

3. Timgad, Forum, 1:5,000

197' x 394'

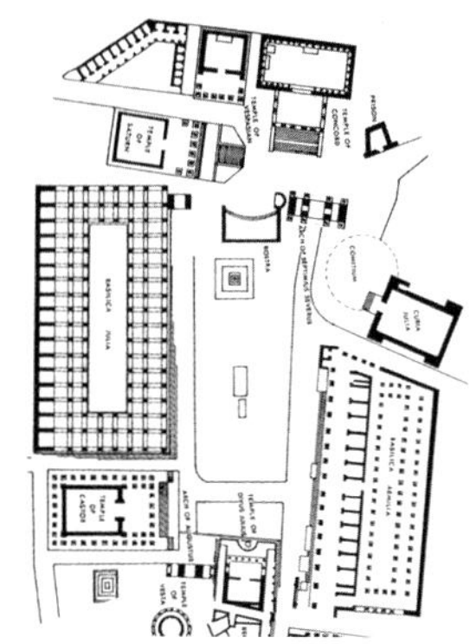

4. Rome, Forum Romanum, 1:5,000

197' x 213'　115' x 312'

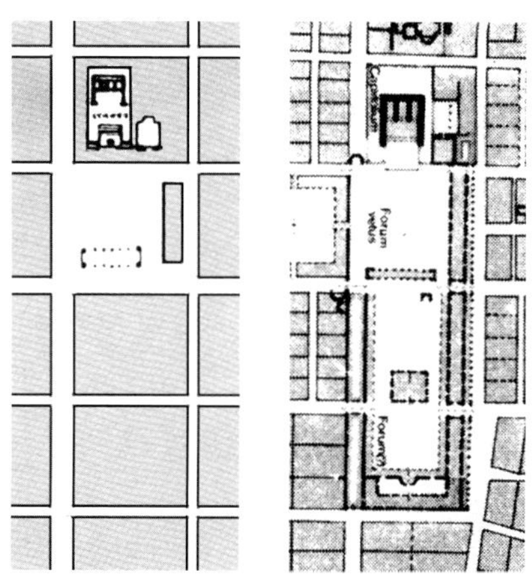

5. Florence, Republic & Imperial Fora

245' x 525'

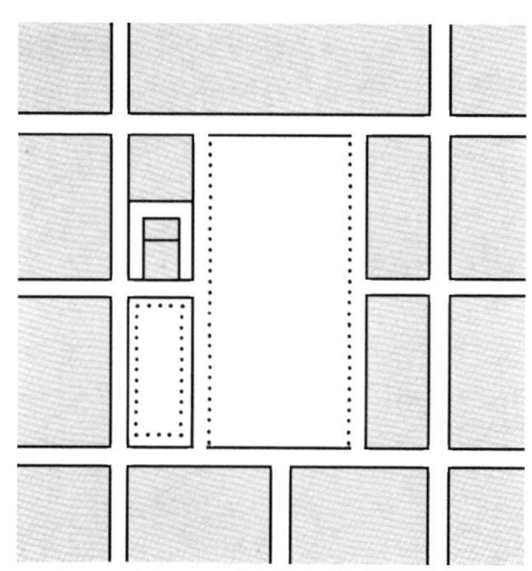

6. Verona, Forum, 1:5,000

187' x 394'

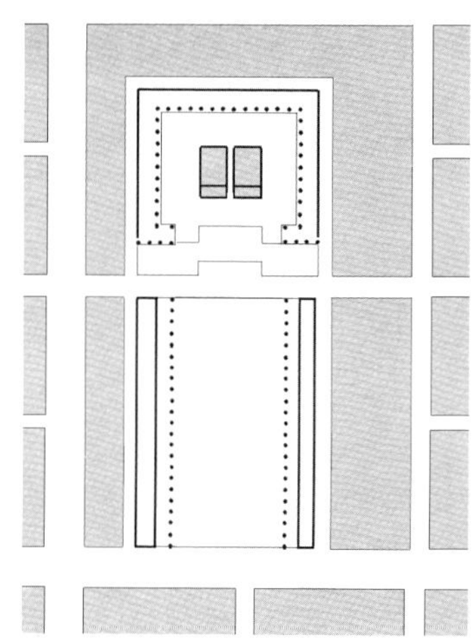

7. Aosta, Forum, 1:5,000

131' x 328'

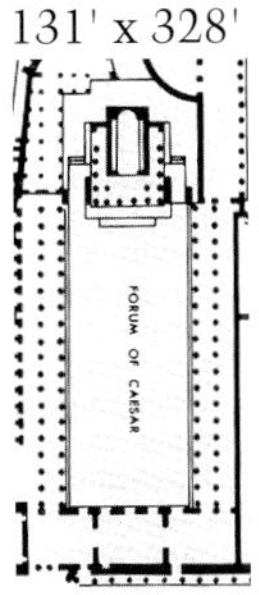

1. Rome, Forum of Caesar, 1:5,000

164' x 312'

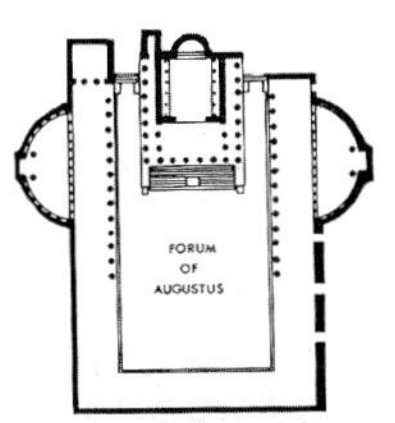

2. Rome, Forum of Augustus, 1:5,000

260' x 360'

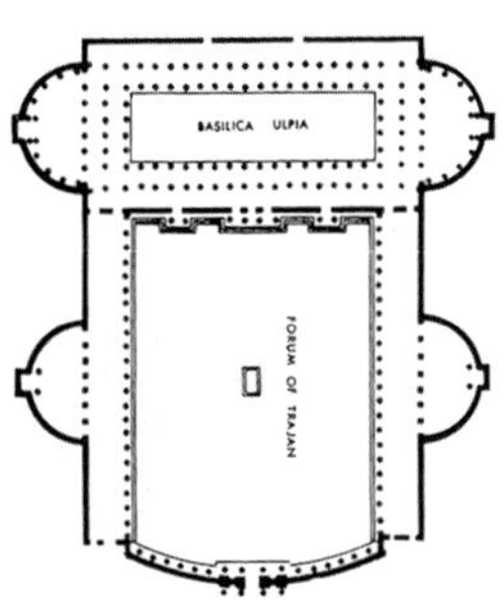

3. Rome, Forum of Trajan, 1:5,000

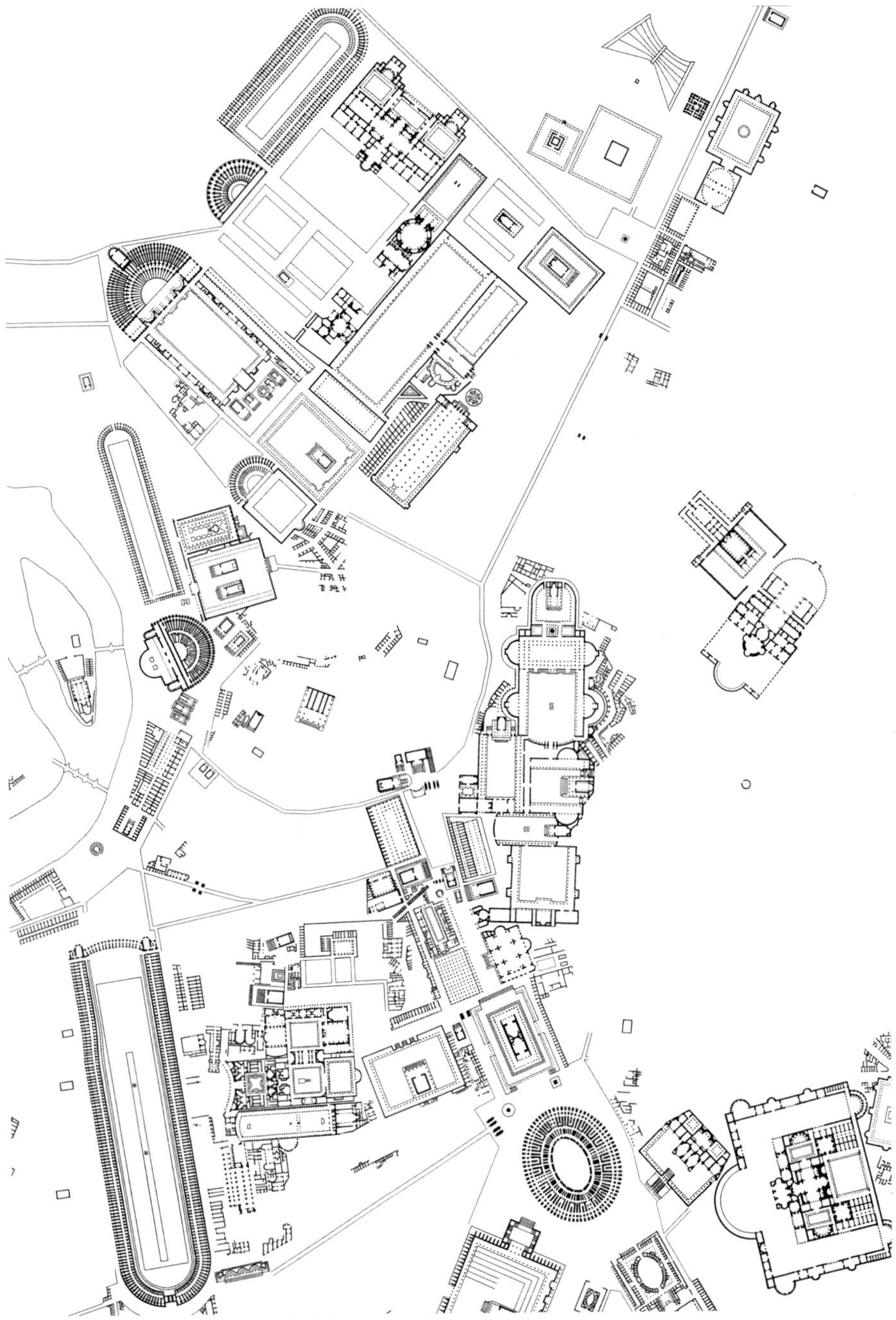

4. Rome, plan of Roman civic buildings, 1:12,500

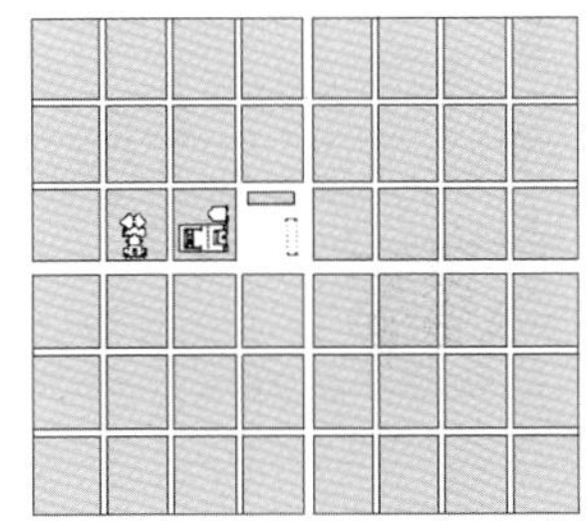

5. Plan of Roman Florence, 1:12,500

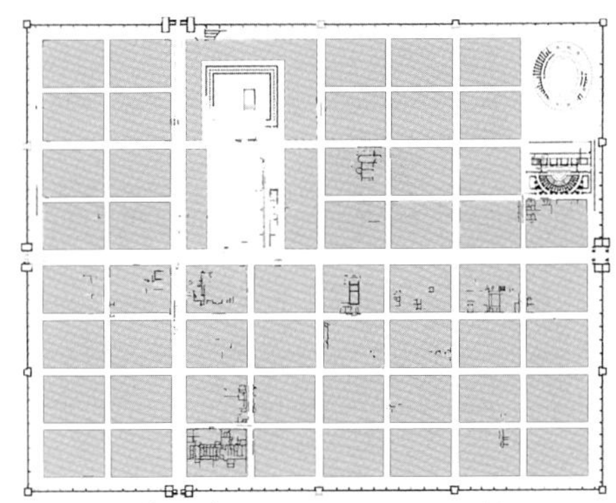

6. Plan of Roman Aosta, 1:12,500

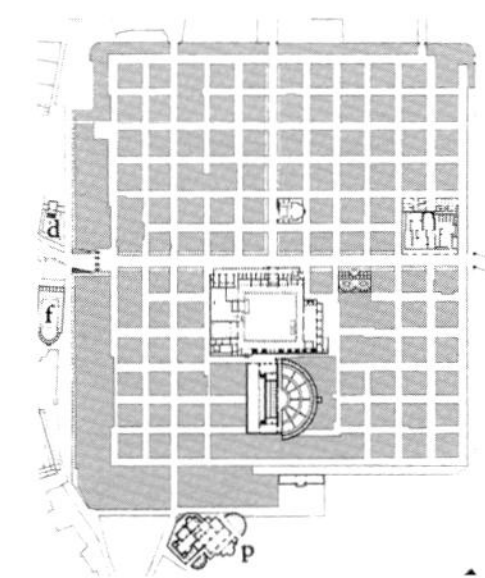

7. Plan of Roman Timgad, 1:12,500

Depiction of the Battle of Courtrai during the Hundred Year's War

Medieval Bastides: 1200–1400

Map of the Angevin Empire

As the Western Roman world disintegrated after 476 AD, cities shrank and ceased to be central to society. Trade and urban life began to revive around 1000, however, and cities again became instruments of commerce, culture, and defense. New towns began to be founded again.

In southwest France some 700 new towns—Bastides—were founded between 1200 and 1400. During this period France and England were not yet clear either politically or geographically, and disputes about this led directly to the infamous Hundred Years' War. It was within this context that the Bastide towns were established as fort towns for defensive, commercial, religious, and political reasons.

Cordes-sur-Ciel, Tarn, founded in 1222, is generally considered the first founded Bastide. This was approximately 1,100 years after the last Roman colony was founded, and much of the Roman world had vanished. Nevertheless, the Bastide towns were mostly founded and designed as grid towns—as if the intervening millennium had not happened. Why this urban form tradition was picked up again is not completely clear.

Context

The word *Bastide* denotes a new chartered town founded in the thirteenth or fourteenth centuries in southwest France. Cordes-sur-Ciel, Tarn, founded in 1222, is considered the earliest Bastide, and La Bastide d'Anjou, Tarn, built in 1373, as the most recent. Almost 700 such towns were founded in the region of Languedoc, Gascony, and Aquitaine in an effort to urbanize the area, to establish claim to the territory, and for commercial gain. They were an effective way to consolidate the population into profitable, tax-generating economic units.[1]

The Bastides were laid out on fairly regular grid plans with an arcaded market square at the center of the town. The regular geometry of the Bastides can be attributed to a combination of factors—juridical, geographical, political, and economic.[2]

The Bastides developed in an area subject to rival claims by both the French and the English crowns. The development of the towns occurred largely through the initiatives of Alphonse of Poitiers, the Count of Toulouse, and King Edward I of England, for whom the towns provided economic control over a subject population.

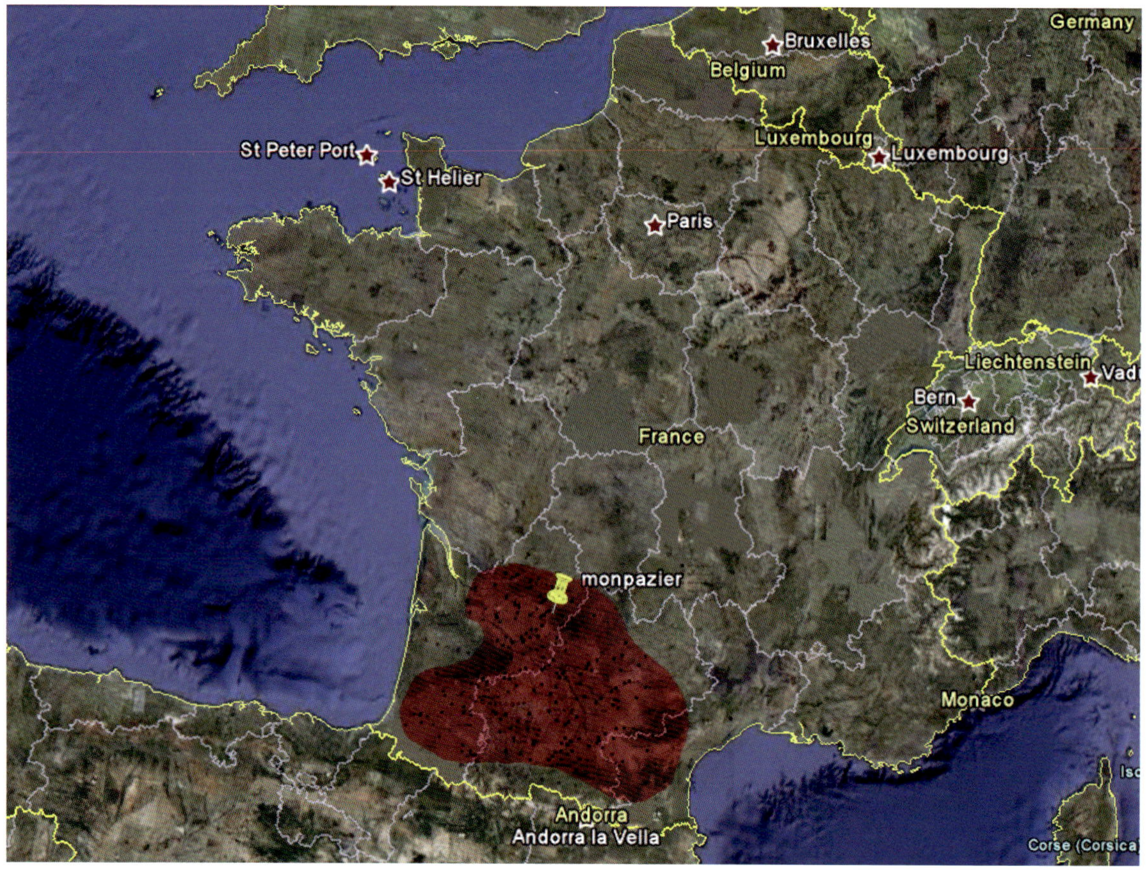

1. Location of Bastide towns in southwest France

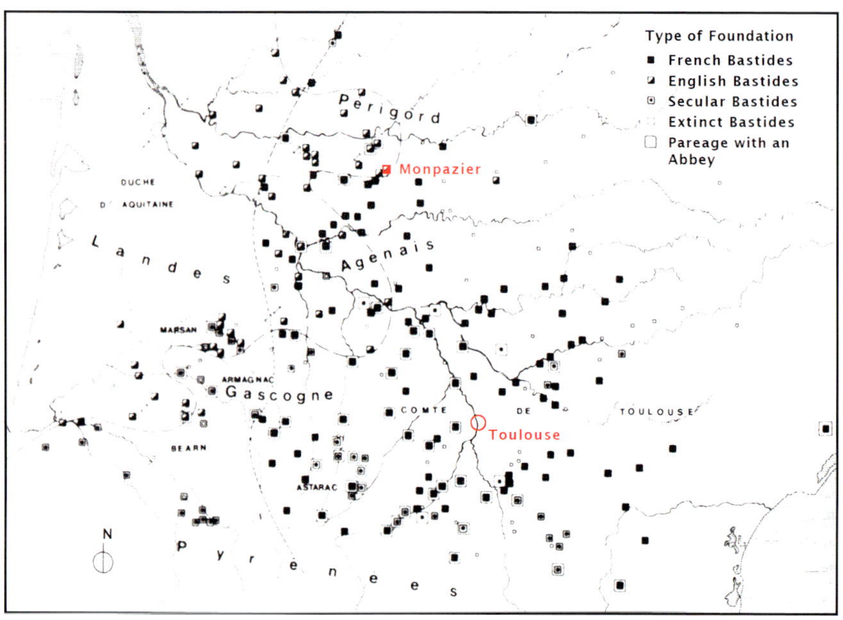

2. Foundation and extent of Bastides

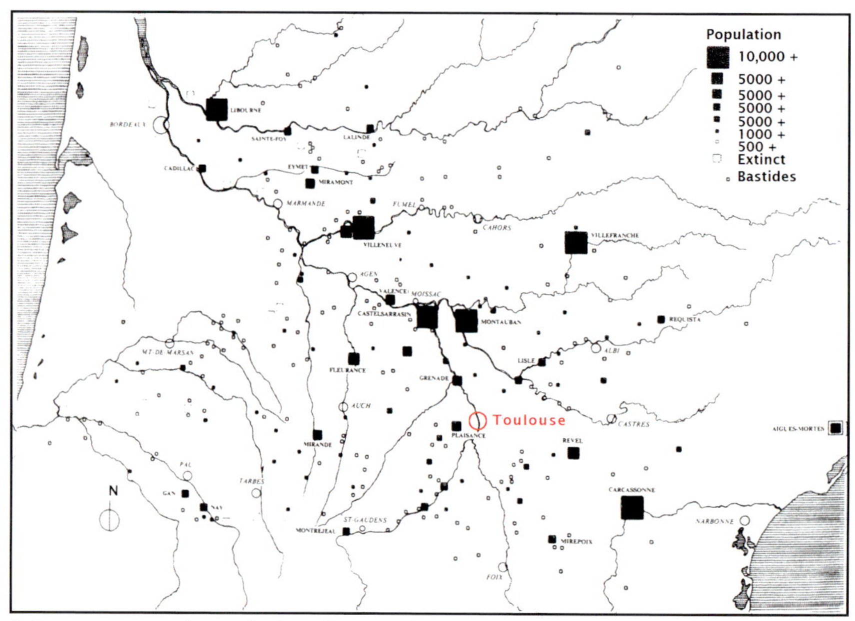

3. Representation of Bastides based on population

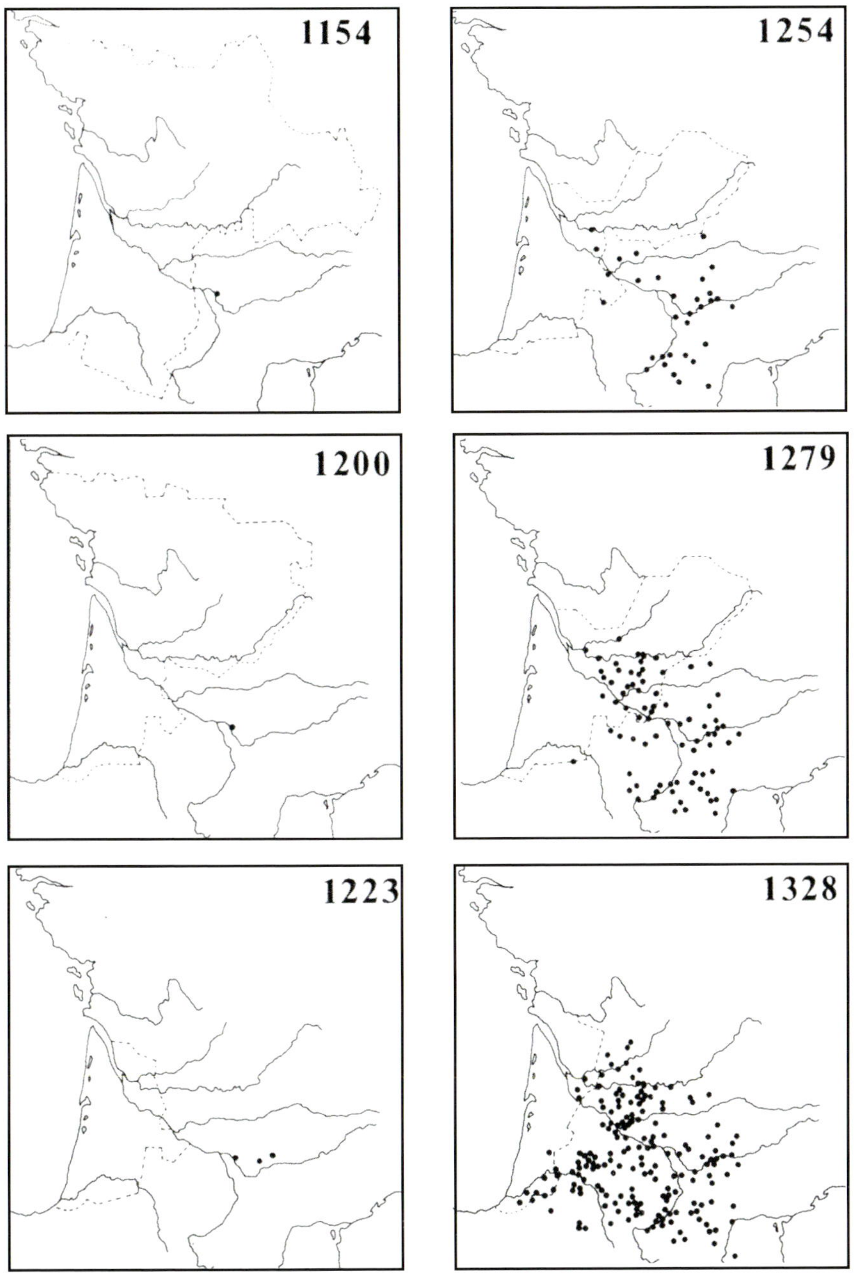

1. Town development between 1154 and 1328

2. Aerial plan of Villeneuve-sur-Lot, 1:5,000

LEGAL BASIS: THE *PARÉAGE*

The first stage in the foundation of a Bastide was a legal partnership between individual lords at the local level, or between the ecclesiastical heads of a monastery in the region and a *seigniorial* overlord, like the count of Toulouse, the king of England, or the king of France. This contract was called a *paréage* and enabled the consolidation of land and legal powers for the creation of a new town, the profits from which were shared by all the parties involved. The sovereign ruler was invested with the feudal rights and with ensuring security and legal rights in the Bastide, which he did through his representatives, while the local lords were responsible for supplying the land and for enforcing some level of local justice. The *paréage* included a mutual defense agreement where the king guaranteed protection to the Bastide and the local lords in exchange for military support. Clauses in the *paréage* required the construction of houses within a stipulated time—usually a year, ensuring the prompt construction and settlement of the towns.[3]

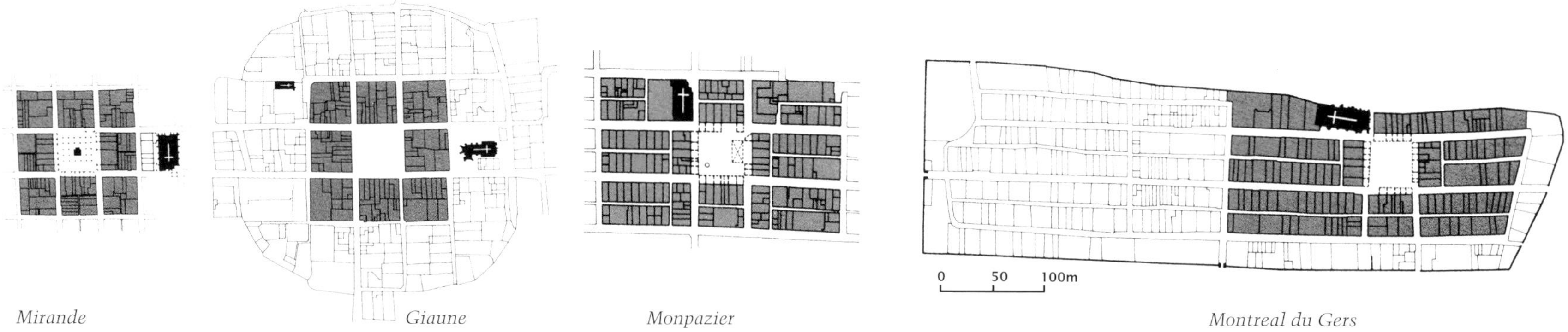

1. Plans of Bastide towns showing the organization of intersecting streets, blocks, and the market square

Legal Basis: Town Charter

The *paréage* was followed by a separate town charter that delineated the legal and economic rights, privileges, and customs for the inhabitants of the Bastide. The local lords ceded the property to the new settlers; hence by moving to a Bastide, the settlers became free of feudal obligations and no longer remained the serfs of a local lord. This was a huge incentive for the inhabitation of the towns and a mechanism for reducing feudalism.

Town and Country

Each settler was given a plot in town, an *ayral*, on which to build a house; a vegetable garden, a *cazal*; and farm land, *arpent* or *journaux*, outside the town.[4]

Physical Structure

The physical structure of the Bastide town enabled efficient remote control, both in the laying out of the town and in its subsequent functioning. The standardized and regularized grid structure was a function of the centralized planning control by the sovereign founders in London, Paris, and Toulouse. It further enabled the seneschals of the sovereign founder to exercise a certain degree of autonomy in taking extemporaneous decisions, thereby expediting the creation of the towns.

A Bastide is described by a grid network of streets, varying between six and ten meters in width, which run through the length and breadth of the town and divide it into residential blocks. The primary streets form the edges of the centrally located market square. The grid is the organizing principle of the town; however, it was not a rigid framework and was adapted according to local factors, like the topography of the land.[5]

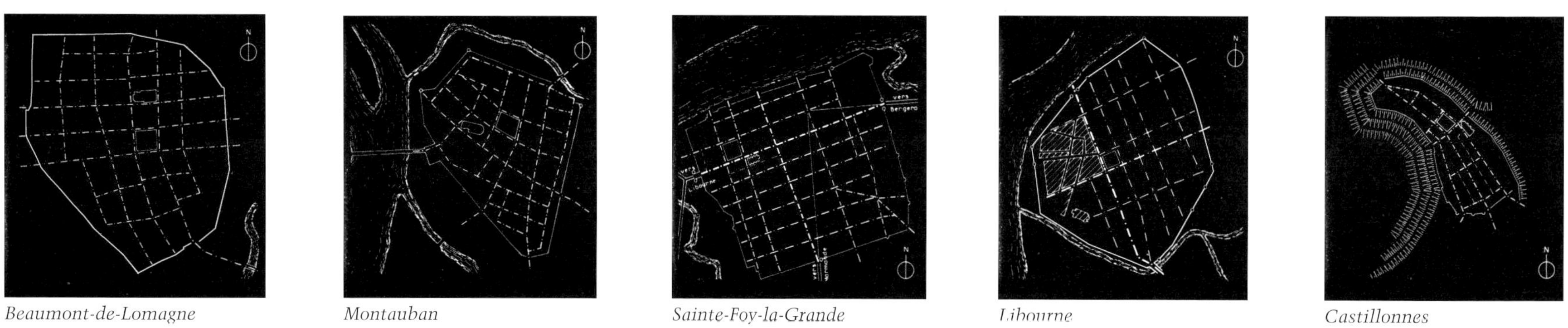

2. Schematics of Bastide Towns showing the grid as the determinant of organization

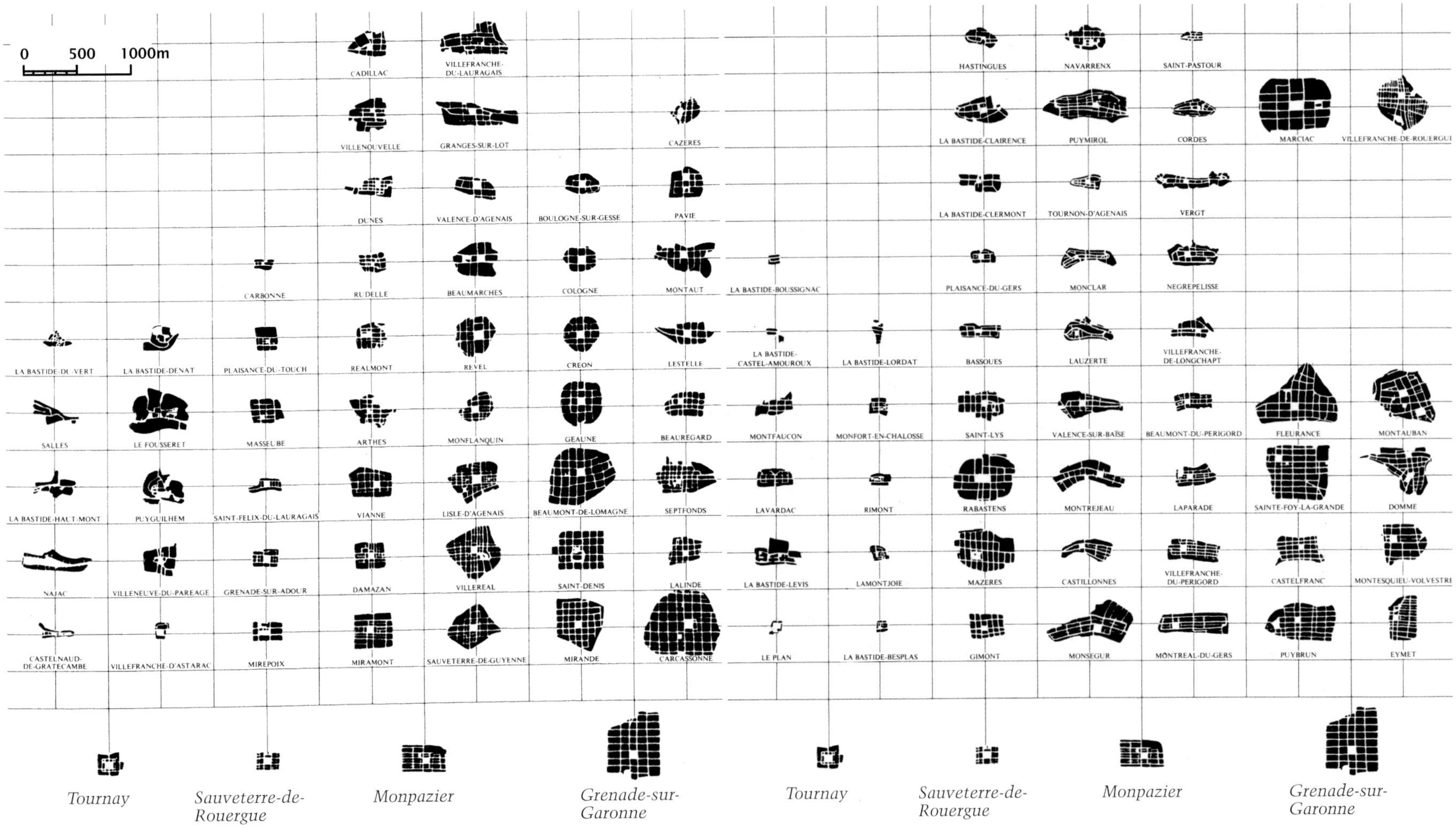

Typical models of Bastide towns and their variations, from the study by Divorne, et al.

1. Typical elevation of a dwelling unit

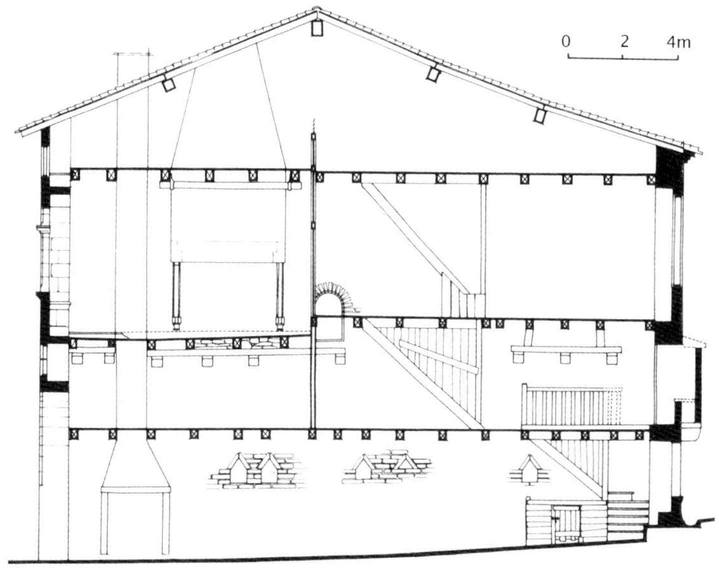

2. Typical section of a dwelling unit

The Dwelling Unit

Each settler was entitled to a lot on which the house was built, a garden in the town, and a plot of land for cultivation outside the town. The size of the lots was determined in the paréage and was probably analogous with the lowest taxable unit in the land. The size of the lot was more or less consistent and measured on average about 8 x 18 m.

The inhabitants were encouraged to cultivate the land around the Bastide, which generated trade in the form of merchants and markets. The lord taxed dwellings in the Bastides and all trade in the markets. These taxes were then shared between the different signatories of the paréage. Hence the inhabitants of the Bastide provided economic viability for the town by paying taxes, and in return they were granted freedom and security.[6]

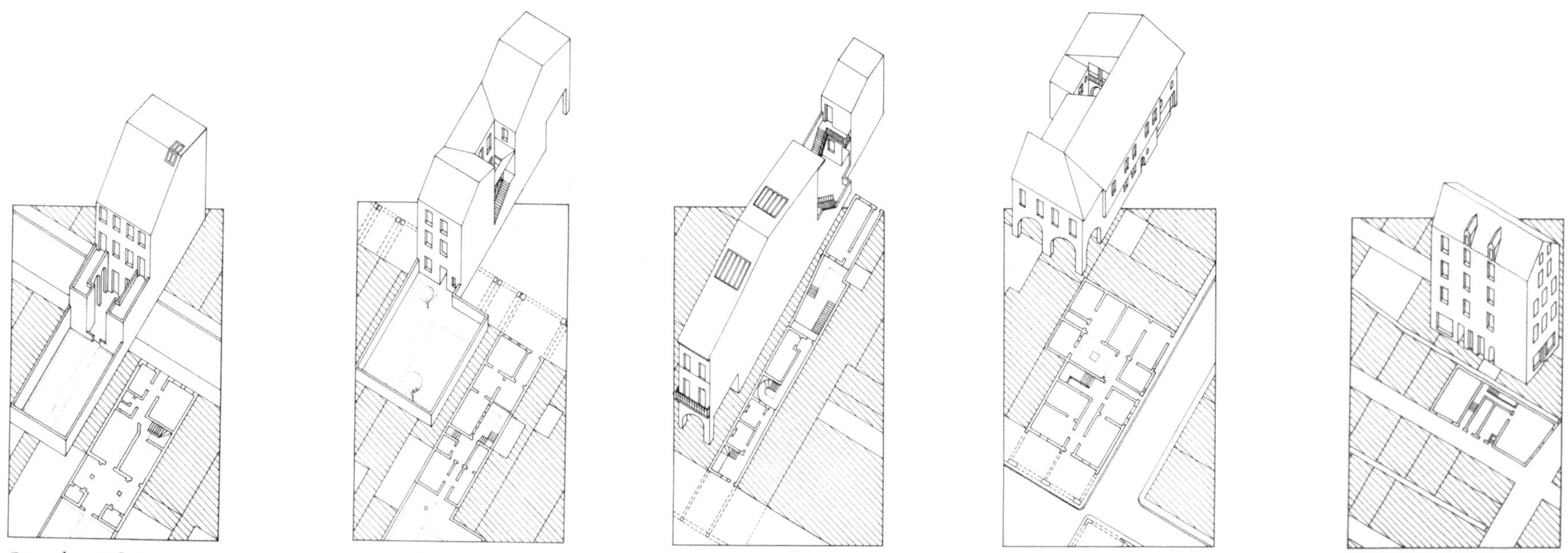

Grenade-sur-Garonne *Mirepoix* *Sainte-Foy-la-Grande* *Mirande* *Villefranche-de-Rouergue*

3. Typical dwelling unit plans and their axonometric projections

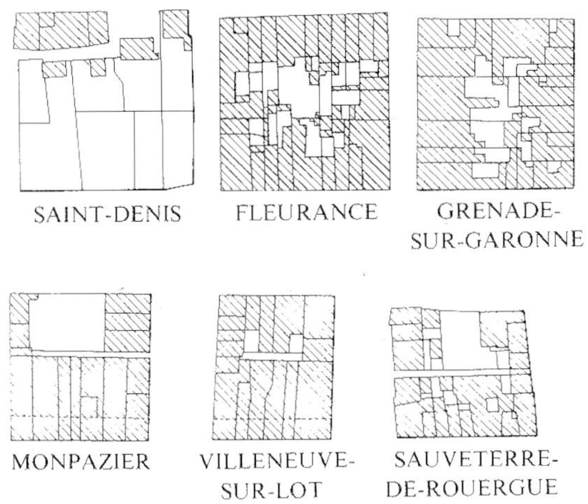

1. *Parcel divisions of square blocks*

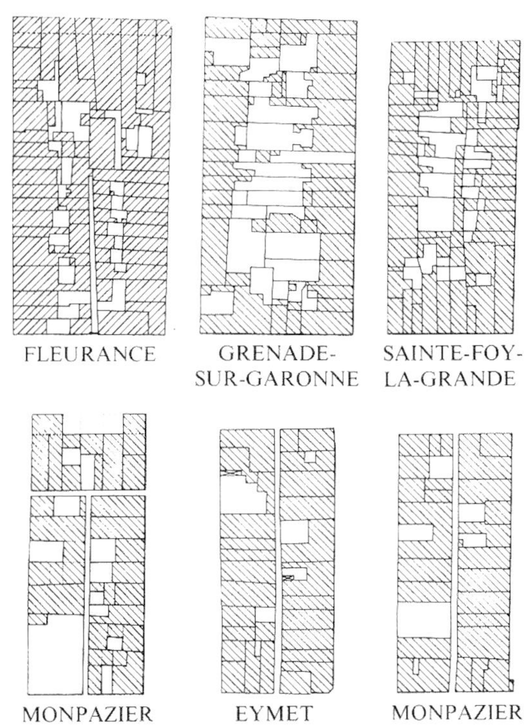

2. *Parcel divisions of rectangular blocks*

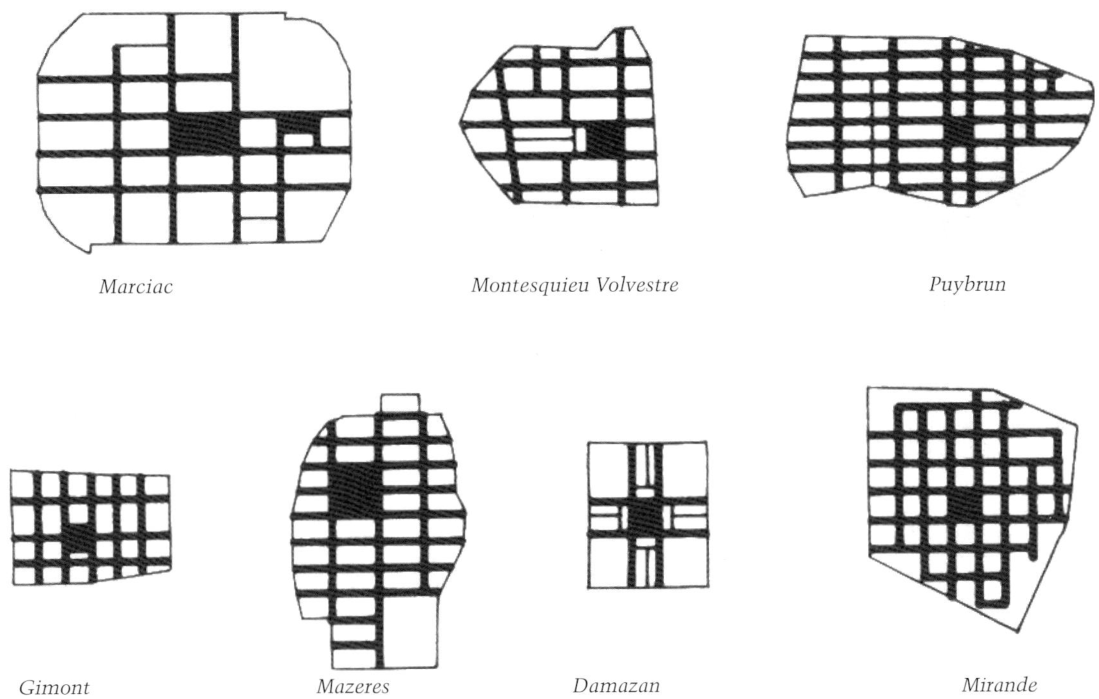

3. *Market squares and street patterns*

The Block

The market square provides the generative dimension for the blocks, which vary in size and generally have one of two proportions—1:1 and 1:2. In many cases an alleyway, called a *carreyou,* runs along the center of the block, dividing it into two separate sets of residential plots back to back. In addition, a gap was provided between individual dwellings, which served as an open sewer as well as a fire break.

The Market Square

The center of the town is the market square surrounded by arcades or *couverts,* under which pass the principal intersecting thoroughfares that frame the square. These arcades were probably required by municipal law, as the houses bordering the square were privately owned.

The market square formed the economic core; its location and description provided an efficient place for trade, which was easily controlled as there were only four entrances to the square. This was especially necessary during markets and fairs, when outsiders were taxed in order to participate and trade. Since many Bastides were built without walls and gates, the collection of a toll would occur at the market place.

1. Beaumont-de-Lomagne

2. Beaumont-de-Lomagne

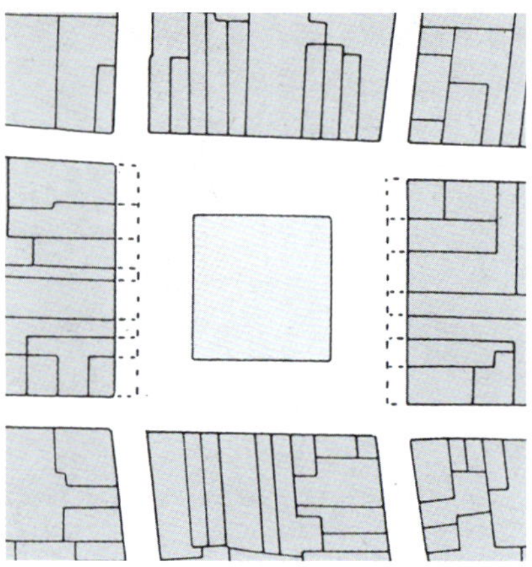

3. Beaumont-de-Lomagne, plan, 1:2,500

4. Beaumont-de-Lomagne

5. Beaumont-de-Lomagne, aerial view

6. Villefranche-du-Périgord

7. Monflanquin

8. Villeréal

9. Ste-Foy-la-Grande

1. Fleurance

2. Fleurance

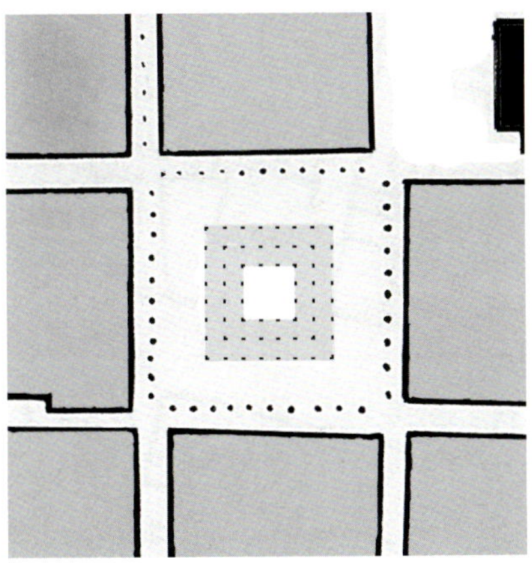

3. Fleurance, plan of market square, 1:2,500

Market Halls

Most of the Bastide town squares contained a market hall. Some are wood-framed pavilions, such as that of Beaumont-de-Lomagne, while others are stone-framed pavilions or arcaded masonry buildings. Many market halls also contained the mayor's office. The hall of Fleurance is one of the most substantial. The ground floor is open and fully arcaded with a two-story central court surrounded by the town offices on the second floor.

4. Fleurance

5. Fleurance, aerial view

6. Valence-d'Agen

7. Miramont-de-Guyenne

8. Monségur

9. Eymet

Monpazier

Monpazier is the most often cited example of a Bastide, probably because it is largely intact and well preserved. It was founded in 1284 by King Edward I of England in collaboration with the Duc de Biron, but during the reign of King Charles V of France (r. 1366–1380) the Bastide came under French control. The town is characterized by a regular geometry and was divided into nearly equal-sized parcels.[7]

The town measures about 400 m x 240 m and is perfectly quadrilateral. It is a typical Bastide, described by a central market square, which measures 50 x 50 m. Five streets run parallel to the longest sides from one end of the town to the other and are crossed by four transverse streets, thus dividing the town into rectangular compartments and providing a regular grid network for the organization of the parcels. The central square is surrounded by medieval and seventeenth-century houses. The fronts of the houses on the ground floor, facing the square, have continuous arcades, the facades of which touch at the corners providing spatial closure while allowing open passage into the square.

3. *Aerial plan of Monpazier*

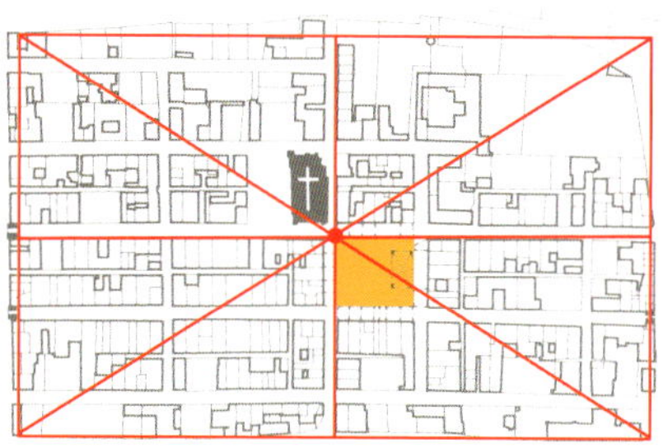

1. *Geometric determinants of the actual plan*

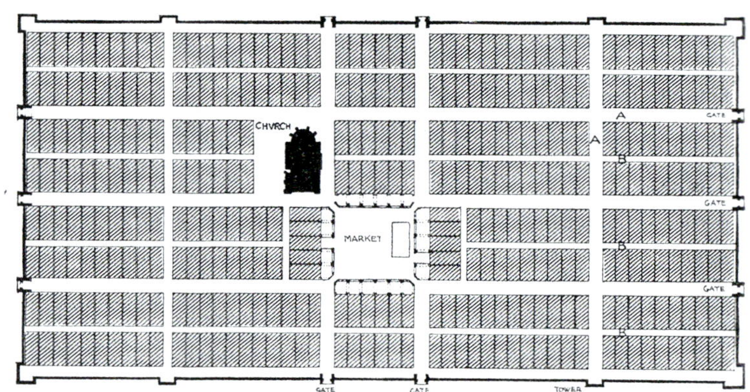

2. *The often published idealized plan of Monpazier*

4. *The actual plan of the town*

1. Aerial view of the market square

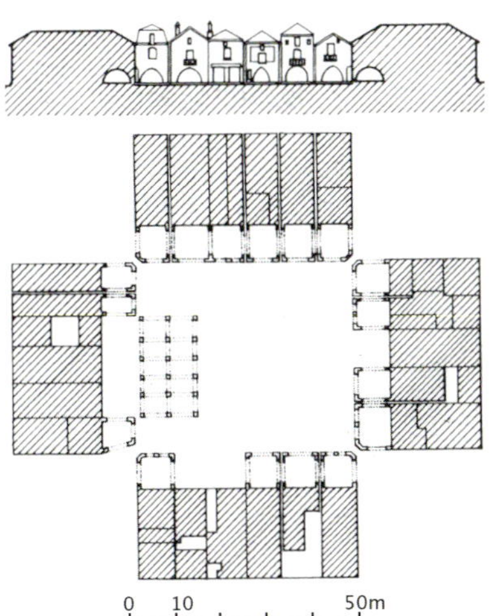

2. Plan and section of the square

3. Market square axon

4. View of a typical street

5. View of the market square

Parcels

Monpazier's house lots were originally set out in a consistent manner. They were more or less the same size, and were separated from one another by narrow side alleys to prevent the spread of fire. The more recently constructed houses did not maintain this gap, which would explain some discrepancies. The average width of a lot is about 7.8 meters throughout the town.

7. View of the arcade

6. Block type

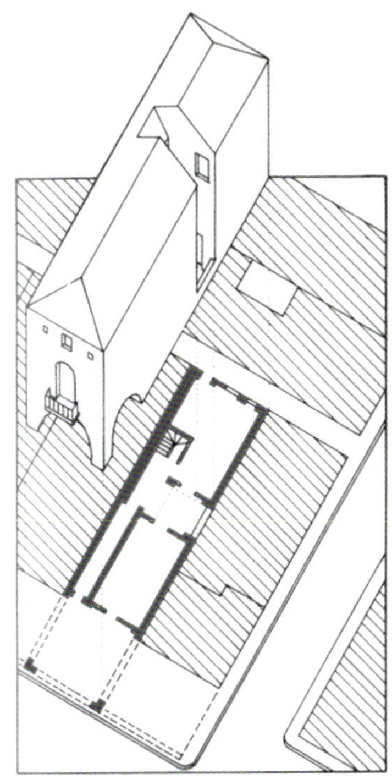

8. Dwelling type

1. *Aerial plan of Grenade-sur-Garonne, 1:7,500*

2. *Market aerial view*

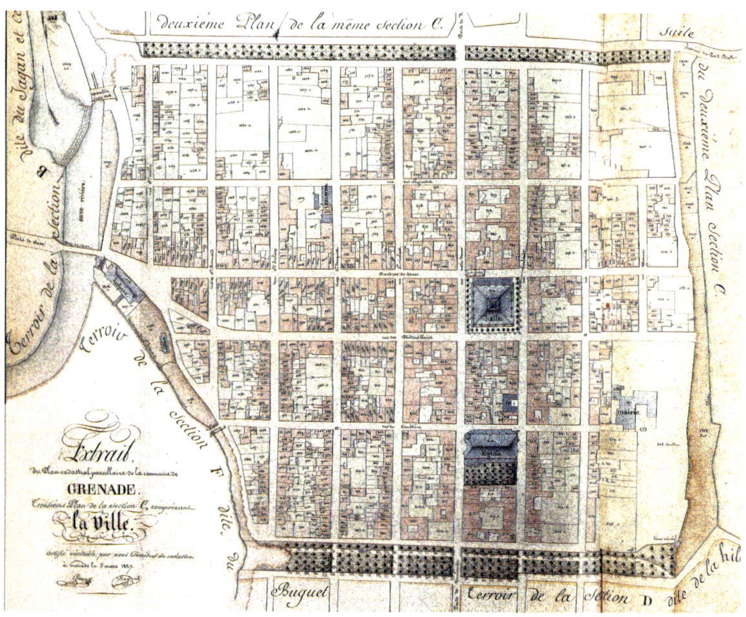

3. *Plan of Grenade-sur-Garonne, 1827, 1:7,500*

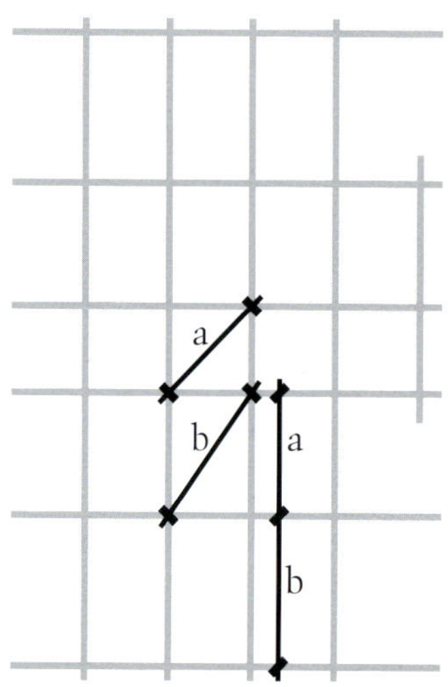

4. *Proportional system of planning grid*

Grenade-sur-Garonne

Founded in 1290 by Philippe le Bel in a *paréage* with the abbey of Grandselve, Grenade-sur-Garonne has a grid plan in which the proportions of the blocks are derived from the dimensions of the market square—similar to the plan of Ste.-Foy-la-Grande (1255).[8]

The space of the market square is approximately 230' x 230', and the market pavilion in its center is about 150' square. The diagonal of the market square (a) determines the length of the adjacent east and west blocks, and the diagonal of those blocks, and (b) determines the length of the next east and west blocks. Thus, the blocks sizes are approximately 180' x 180',180' x 280', and 180' x 380'. The parcel sizes vary considerably, but the original ones may have been about 30' wide.

The market hall is an open pavilion, built in the eighteenth century. A grid of 36 octagonal brick piers support a timber-framed roof, and the pavilion is ringed by curbside street trees that reinforce the continuity of the surrounding streets. The church is located a full block away from the market square.

1. Market pavilion interior

2. Market square

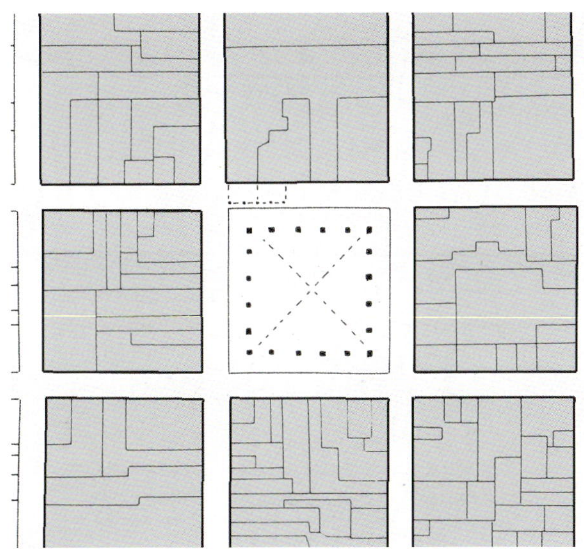

3. Market square plan (ca. 235′ x 235′), 1:2,500

1. Plan of Villefranche-de-Rouergue, 1:5,000

2. Aerial plan of the town

3. Aerial view of the cathedral and square

4. Aerial view of the town square

5. Town square arcade

6. View of the square from the bell tower porch

1. The town square

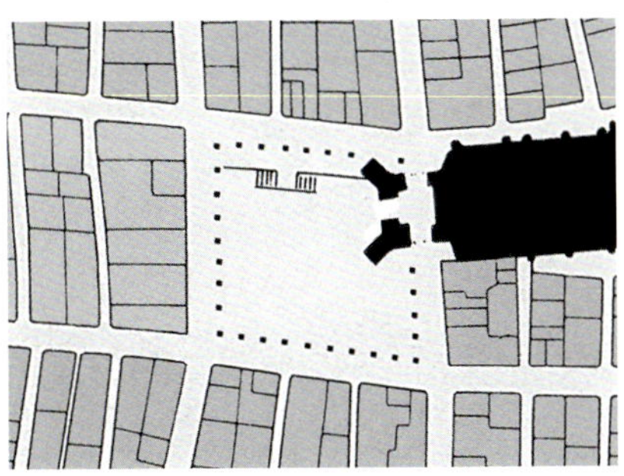

2. Town square plan, 1:2,500

Villefranche-de-Rouergue

Villefranche-de-Rouergue, located in the Aveyron Department, was founded in 1252 by Alphonse de Poitiers.[9]

The town has a slightly warped grid plan with an arcaded town square in the center, but it is unique for the long, narrow house types running generally north–south, and for the direct relationship of the church to the square. The town square is the most spectacular of all the Bastides—partially because the tall, stone houses clearly define the sloping square, but mainly because of the startling, colossal bell tower of the church of Notre-Dame that dominates the square. The bell tower's open porch straddles the north–south street and provides a covered entrance to the church. The square is about 140' x 140'.

Architectural perspective, attributed to Francisco di Giorgio Martini, ca. late 1400s

Renaissance Cities: 1400 –1700

It is difficult to overstate the importance of the invention of perspective in Florence in the early 1400s. This device permeated painting, sculpture, architecture, and town planning, and allowed for the conceptual and perceptual location of man at the center of his spatial and ideological universe.

It also introduced a dichotomy, between a natural condition of frontality in painting, sculpture, and architecture, and a condition of centrality in architecture and town design. Purely centralized buildings were few, but new towns—especially defensive towns—lent themselves easily to in-the-round, idealized design solutions.

Timeline of ideal Renaissance cities

Piero della Francesca, Ideal City (oil painting) ca. 1470. Galleria Nazionale in Urbino. Illustrates absolute geometric order and symmetry. Focus is on the civic center with a clear regularity and definition of street edges, as well as a uniformity of massing and classical architectural style. The perfection of architectural and urban form as the representation and manifestation of a harmonious political and social order—a vision of utopia.

Origins

The great social, cultural, and political transformations in fifteenth-and sixteenth-century Italy cannot be overstated. The impact of this metamorphosis and the resultant development of humanistic culture had far-reaching consequences on every aspect of society. Indeed, the Italian Renaissance may be seen as the beginning of modern society as we know it.

Frontality and Centrality

Two contrasting principles were fundamental to form and space in Renaissance art, architecture, and urbanism: *frontality* and *centrality*.

Frontality is the principle of a dominant point of view—of planar and spatial layers perpendicular to an observer's line of sight. This was an intrinsic characteristic of one-point perspective developed in Florence by Filippo Brunelleschi around 1420. It was implicitly spatial and led to the development of architectural and urban spatial progression and sequence. Essential to painting, frontality was also important to Renaissance architecture and to urban interventions, as well as sculpture.

Centrality, on the other hand, is the principle of multiple points of view—of space and figures in-the-round—of cosmic unity with man at the center of the universe. Centrality was explored primarily through the architecture of centrally planned churches and the urban planning of centralized, ideal cities. It should be noted that the centralized church had a limited program and a largely symbolic value. The centralized, ideal city, however, had a complex program in contrast to its symbolic value.

If frontality involved shallow, layered space and a balance of figure and field, centrality involved deep, oblique space and the predominance of figure over field.

Interestingly, these same themes were played out again in the twentieth century: frontality and shallow, layered space (growing out of cubism) in the architecture of Le Corbusier and others, and centrality and deep space in the architecture of Wright, the Dutch de Stile, the Russian Constructivists, and paradoxically, the town planning of Le Corbusier. Thus, if it can be argued that Le Corbusier was a great architect but a poor town planner, it might equally be argued that Renaissance architects produced magnificent buildings and urban interventions, but remarkably simplistic and boring town plans. In short, a city is not a building.

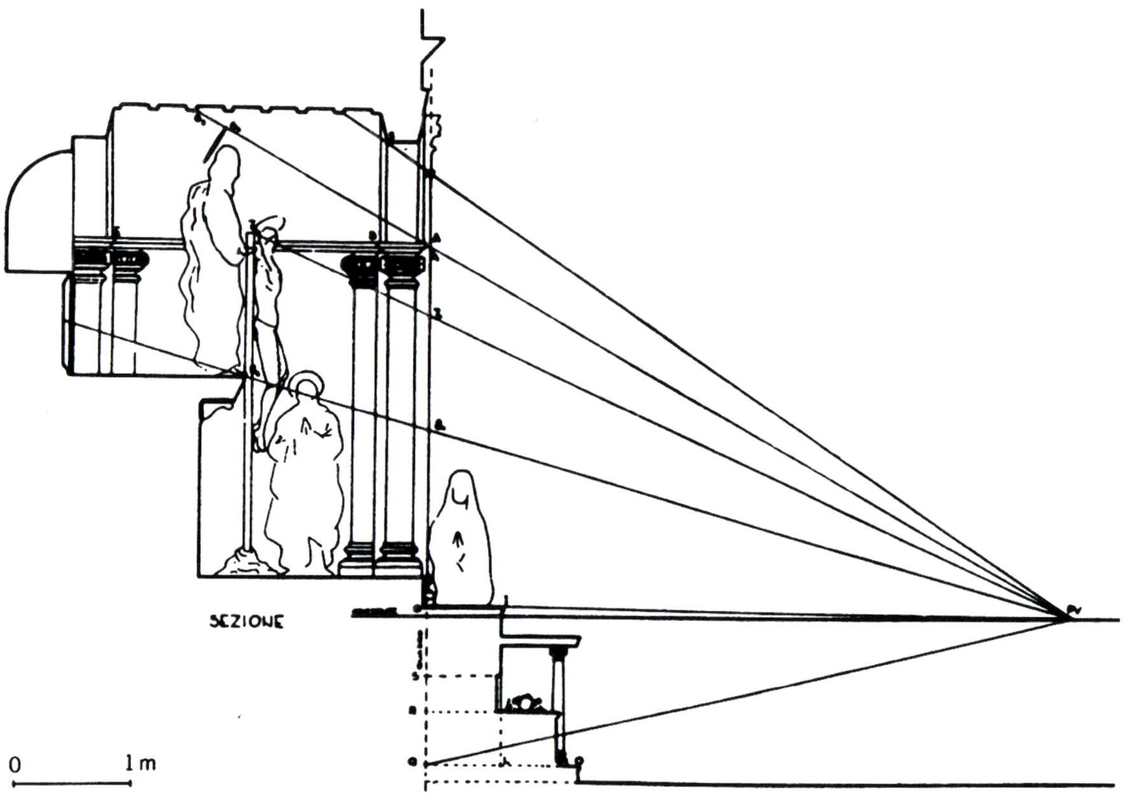

1. Section diagram of Masaccio's Trinity fresco

2. Masaccio, Trinity fresco, probably 1425

Perspective and Painting

The principles of central, or one-point, perspective were developed by Brunelleschi in Florence around 1420. For the first time it was possible to accurately delineate three-dimensional space in two dimensions, locate figures in proportional depth within it, and empathetically involve the viewer in the composition. This was revolutionary—the beginning of a humanistic spatial sensibility, or an anthropocentric relationship to space—in contrast to the awe-inspiring spatial distance of Gothic compositions.

Brunelleschi's artist friends, the painter Masaccio and the sculptor Donatello, were among the first to employ and exploit the discovery, but all the great fifteenth-century Florentine painters explored and developed the new art of perspective, as did Mantegna and the incomparable Piero della Francesca.

Some painters, such as Andrea del Castagno and Paolo Uccello, exploited the technical aspects of perspective, while others, such as Masaccio, Piero della Francesca, and Mantegna, went further, developing its phenomenal aspects.

1. *Piero della Francesca, The Flagellation of Christ, 1455–65*

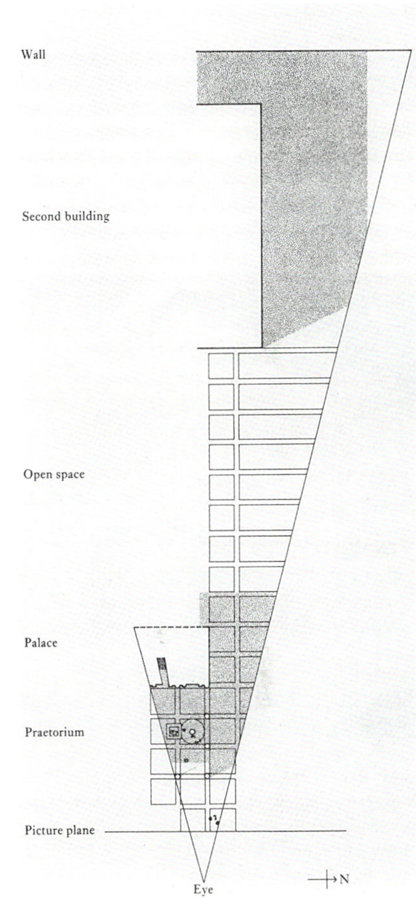

2. *Plan reconstruction of the Flagellation*

Both Masaccio's *Trinity* and Piero's *Flagellation* studiously obey the laws of perspective, but in both paintings the strongest perspectival cues—the diagonals—are minimal. In the *Trinity* the strongest depth cue is the vaulted ceiling. In the *Flagellation* it is the diagonal beam and the highly differentiated size of the figures. Both compositions depict relatively deep actual scenes, but in both the actual depth appears to be flattened into a series of shallow layers of space. This contradiction is heightened by color and light.

In the *Trinity* the section reveals that the figure of Christ is actually located several feet behind the arched opening, but in the painting his figure appears to be mystically suspended between the columns of the arch.[1] Further, two of the lower figures are located inside the arch, and two are located outside the arch; but they all appear to be nominally in the same plane, however, forming with Christ a large symmetrical, pyramidal composition.

In the *Flagellation* even greater actual depth is flattened into a series of orthogonal planes and spaces.[2] The most notable characteristic, however, is the asymmetry and multiple foci of the composition. The three figures in the foreground form a screen for the figures in the middle ground, but because the proportions of the painting are the square root of two, the figures of Christ and the red-robed figure are both contained within squares from each side of the painting. The colors tend to operate independently of perspective depth. Indeed, this might be considered the first cubist painting.

1. San Lorenzo, Brunelleschi, begun 1419

Perspective and Architecture

Brunelleschi's development of perspective was concurrent with his early architectural works, within which perspective was fundamental to a radically new architecture.

For example, in the church of San Lorenzo, for which he received the commission in 1418, the arches of the nave are in the ratio of eight to five with the arches of the side chapels, thus making a perspectival suggestion of depth without any vanishing diagonals (except the floor pattern). The round columns of the nave also collaborate with the pilasters of the side chapel wall in another suggestion of perspectival depth. Because the walls separating the side chapels are not seen, and because the back wall is flat, there appear to be three successive, parallel layers of space perpendicular to the axis of view. Thus, the observer is engaged in the space of the composition.

2. Pazzi Chapel, Brunelleschi, begun 1434

Perspective and Centrality

Similar perspectival devices were employed in the Pazzi Chapel (b. 1434), and the Old Sacristy of San Lorenzo (1419–1424), where a gridded perspectival structure of gray stone is combined with a centralized—in-the-round—idea, since Brunelleschi could not do a literally centralized form.

In the Pazzi Chapel, round arches delineate both literal and phenomenal spatial depth within the grid system of the rectangular space. A similar effect occurs in the Old Sacristy. In both cases, real centrality is suggested by a dome on pendentives, and is reinforced by the rondele in the pendentives and on the vertical walls. Indeed, even the perspectives of the rondele are designed to be seen by an observer at the center of the space. In the Pazzi Chapel, the illlusion of the end walls bowing in apse-like depth is "corrected" by the small bracket that snaps the reading back to a planar surface.

3. Old Sacristy, Brunelleschi, begun 1419

5. Old Sacristy, San Lorenzo, begun 1419

Centrality and Architecture

Brunelleschi's plan for Santa Maria degli Angeli, begun in 1434 and abandoned in 1437, was the first truly centralized church. The radial plan with eight side chapels and an octagonal

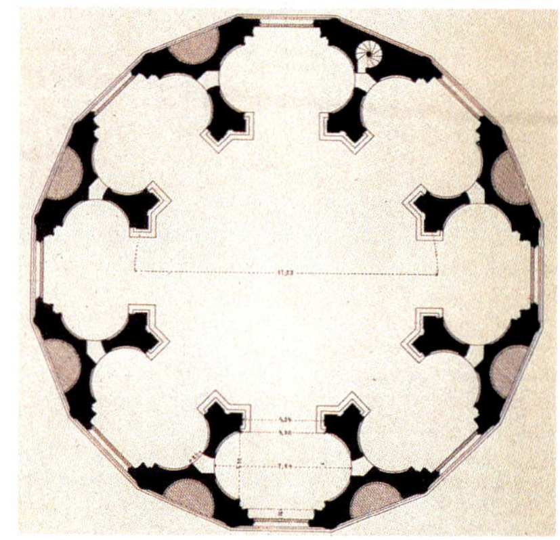

4. Plan, S.M. degli Angeli, Brunelleschi, b. 1434

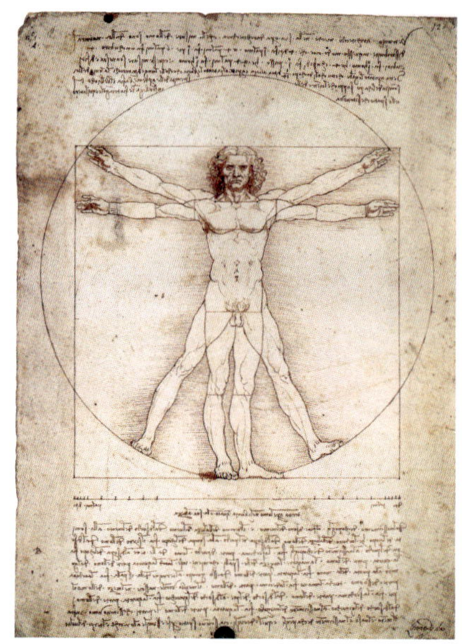

6. Universal Man, Leonardo da Vinci

central space was prophetic of later fifteenth-century and early sixteenth-century developments—as in the High Renaissance architecture of Leonardo's centralized church studies of the 1490s and Bramante's Tempietto of 1501.

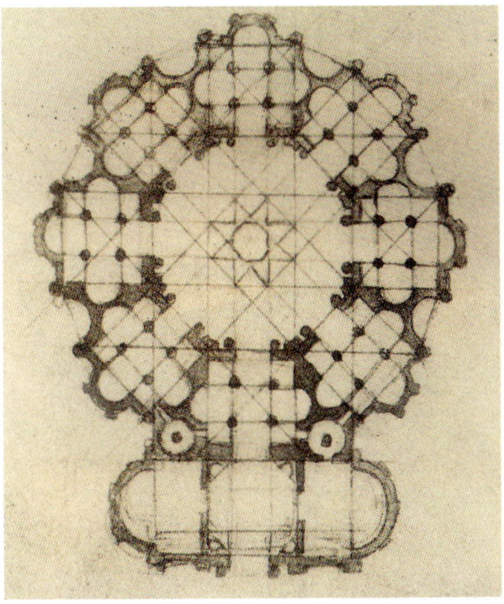

1. Plan for a centralized church, Leonardo

2. Drawing of a centralized church, Leonardo

3. S.M. della Consolazione, Todi

4. Tempietto, Bramante, 1501

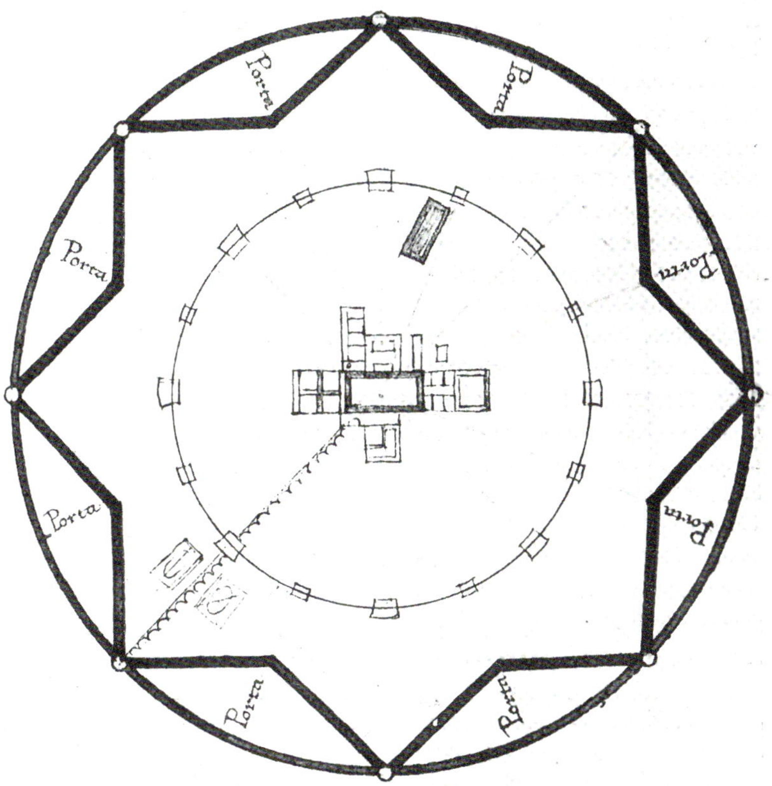

5. Filarete's plan for the ideal city of Sforzinda

Ideal Cities

The "rediscovery" in 1414 of Vitruvius's *Ten Books on Architecture* (written ca. 25 BC) by the Florentine humanist Poggio Bracciolini helped initiate a flood of interest in every aspect of classical culture, giving rise to a self-conscious culture that, as Argan explains, "was the first to take a conscientious view of the city as the heart of an organized society and as the visible expression of the functions of that society."[3]

In this atmosphere of cultural rebirth, treatises proliferated. As Argan states, "Treatises on architecture in the fifteenth and sixteenth centuries were full of ideal cities, that is, of cities planned ex novo, based on purely rational or geometric criteria."[4] Significant among these was Leon Battista Alberti's *De re aedificatoria*, written in Rome between 1443 and 1452, with the idealistic aim of realizing "the rebirth of the ancient city; [in which] the single building was always conceived as an element in a natural or urban context: that is, it is always part of a much larger composition, which is in turn subordinate to norms of symmetry, perspective, and proportion."[5]

Also influential was Filarete's *Trattato di architettura*, written between 1451 and 1464. Filarete's treatise reveals a more direct interest in city planning and includes a detailed description of an ideal city: Sforzinda.

The perimeter of the plan of Sforzinda is shaped like an octagonal star with an implied radial interior. The center of the city is distinguished by administrative areas including the prince's palace and cathedral—the seat of power and the symbol of order and civil society.

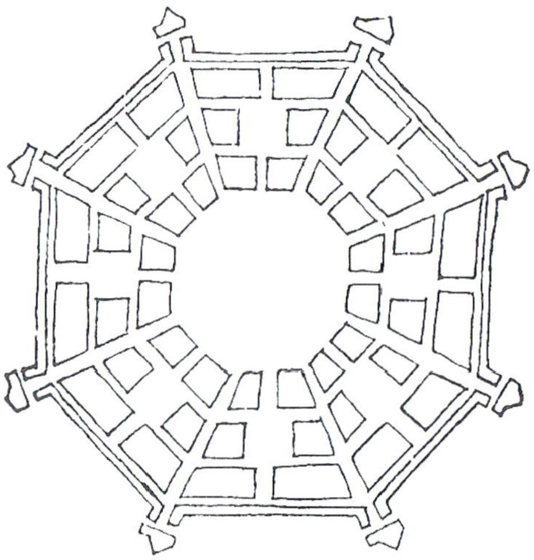

1. Plan of a City on a Plain, Francesco di Giorgio Martini, 1464

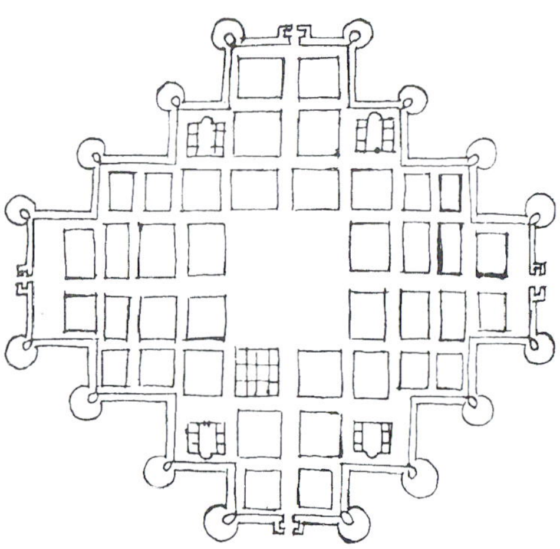

2. Plan of an Ideal City, Francesco di Giorgio Martini, 1464

3. Map of Palmanova, 1593, by Joris Hoefnagel, plan attributed to Vincenzo Scamozzi

Two Ideal Plan Types

Two main ideal plan types developed during the course of the sixteenth century: radial and orthogonal. In both cases the interest in idealized forms was combined with the latest thinking in military fortification. Both plan types are illustrated in Francesco di Giorgio Martini's treatise *Trattato di architettura, ingegneria e arte militare*, written circa 1451–64. He included various plans for ideal cities displaying a distinct relationship between the internal arrangement and the city walls. Both radial and orthogonal alignments were typically organized around a central plaza with a hierarchy of smaller open spaces, and displayed symmetry and rigorously structured order.

Palmanova

Palmanova is a radially organized fort town designed by Vincenzo Scamozzi. The city was constructed by the Venetians between approximately 1593 and 1603 as a defensive outpost against possible Austrian and Turkish invasions. The city plan represents the unity of military fortification engineering with Renaissance ideal geometry. The city is symmetrically planned as a static whole, with no future adaptation or expansion anticipated, and with social amenities playing no part in the design. Indeed, it might be seen as a Renaissance update of the Roman *castrum*.

The central plaza is a hexagonal space with a central tower, from which six streets radiate directly out to small plazas and the fortifications. (Three lead to city gates.) These allow continuous visual communication between the tower and the fortifications. Another twelve streets lead radially out to the fortifications from the first of four concentric streets, and six of these pass through neighborhood plazas. This represents an important new contribution to planned towns—for the first time the civic structure is expanded to include neighborhood spaces.

1. Aerial plan of Palmanova from Google Earth

2. Aerial view of Palmanova

3. Aerial view of Palmanova town square

4. View of the town square

5. City gate

1. Aerial plan of Grammichele

2. Aerial View of Grammichele

Grammichele, Sicily

In 1693 southeast Sicily was hit by a devastating earthquake that destroyed many towns. Three were rebuilt as planned new towns on new sites: Grammichele, Avola, and Noto. Grammichele and Avola were built according to centralized Renaissance ideal city principles on flat sites, but Noto was rebuilt on a sloping site according to Baroque principles. As such it will be discussed later.

Grammichele, like Palmanova, has a hexagonal plan with six streets radiating out from the hexagonal plaza in the center. Each is lined by nearly square blocks, and each passes through a plaza toward the outer edge of the original hexagon, thus establishing a hierarchical civic structure which helps with orientation. The six main streets are connected by a series of concentric streets lined by continuous blocks that get longer further from the center.

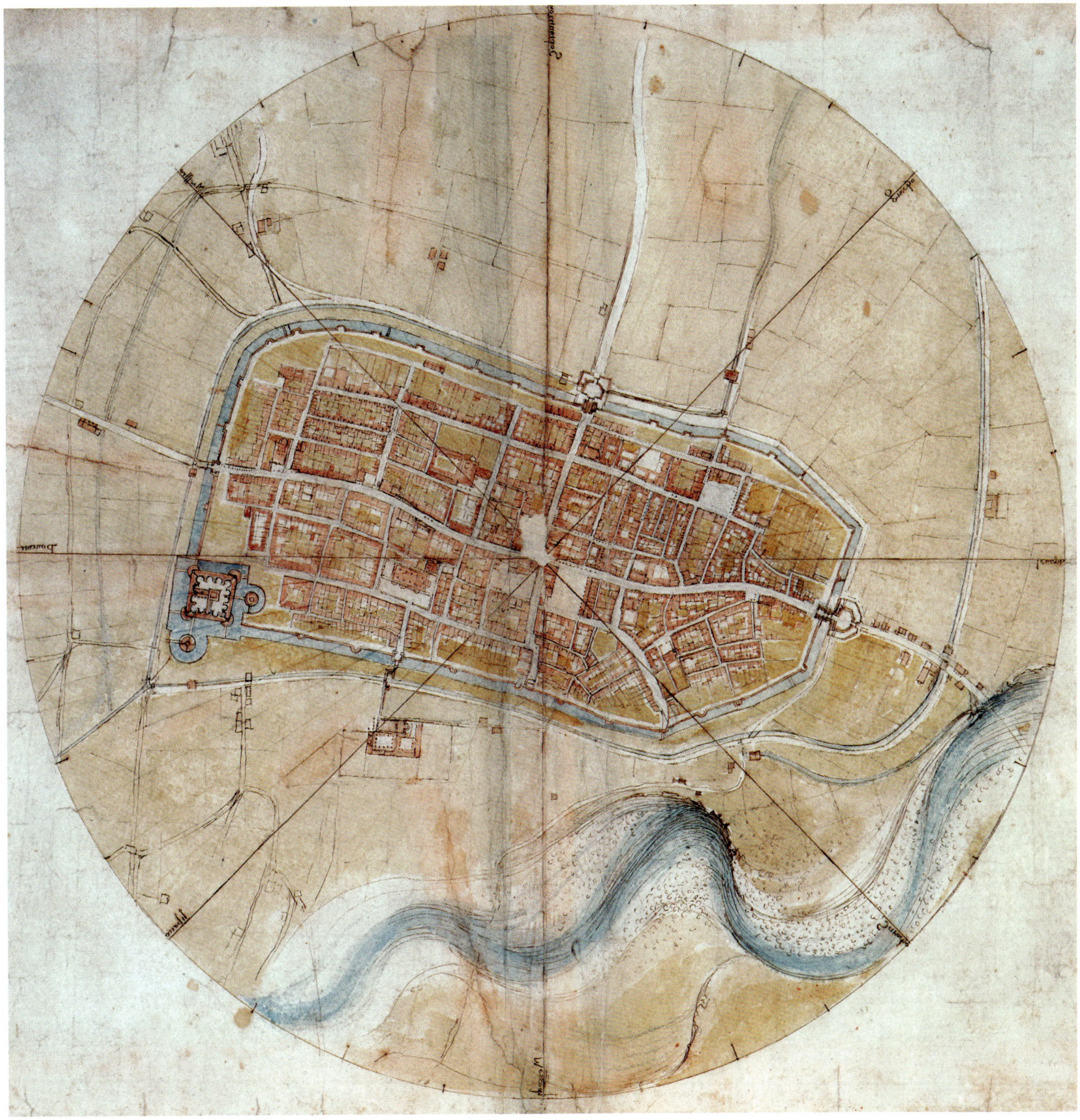

Plan of Imola, 1502, Leonardo da Vinci

Cartography

The means of representing the planimetric abstraction of cities did not exist until the sixteenth century. It was the development of new cartographic techniques by Leon Battista Alberti, Leonardo da Vinci, and others that allowed the potential of these ideal cities to be realized.

Pinto states that: "A more accurate means of representing cities was perfected at the very time that military technology and urban design were being revolutionized by the introduction of mobile artillery. The development of improved instruments and techniques of surveying and the graphic abstraction of cities which they permitted also coincided with renewed interest in the city as an ideal architectural form. Once the various organs of civic life began to be structured according to overriding principles of defence, communication, and visual coordination, a new means of representing cities which met specific functional requirements came to be formulated."[6]

Leonardo's remarkably accurate plan of Imola, of 1502, was prescient, as it would not be until mid-century that city maps would be produced by Braun and Hogenberg, and others.

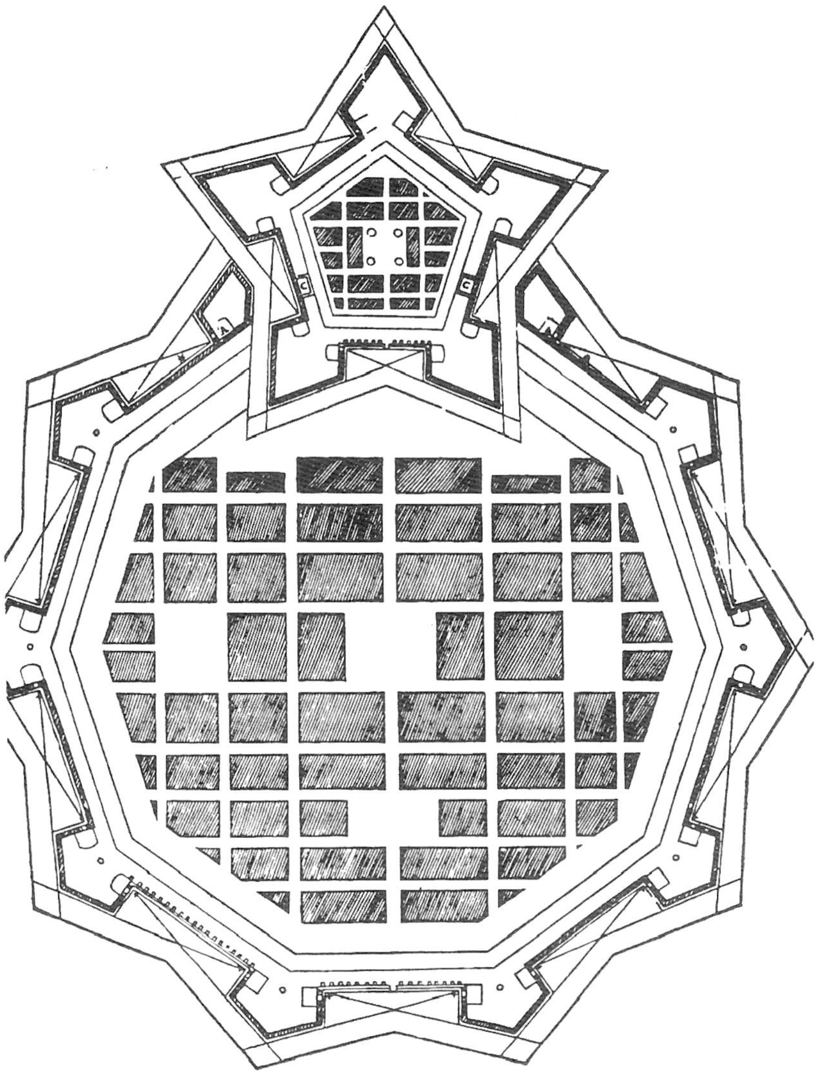

1. Land Fortress, published in Quattro Primi Libri di Architettura by Pietro Cataneo, 1554

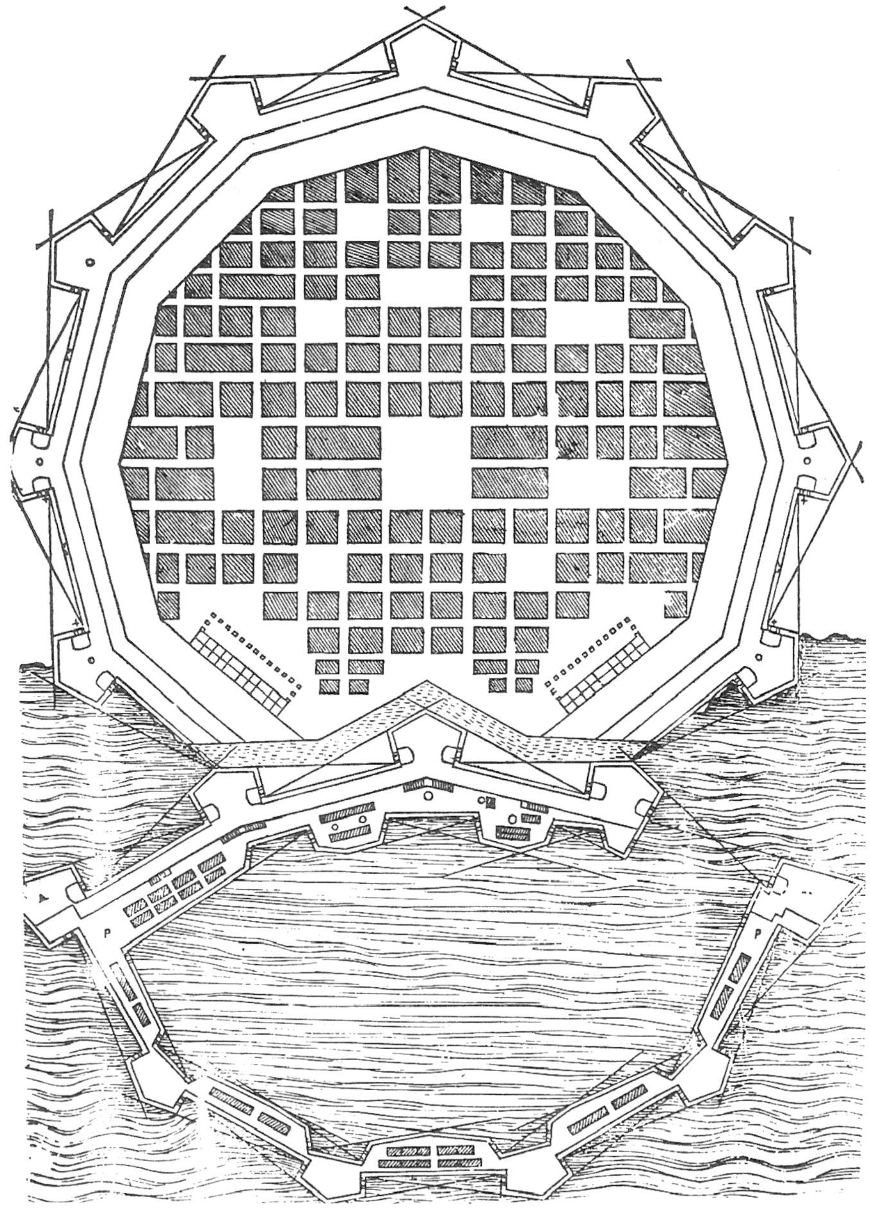

2. City on the Sea, Pietro Cataneo, 1554

Orthogonal Plans

Military fortifications have tended to homogenize both radial and orthogonal Renaissance plans into one centralized, ideal city type. Despite the fact that both plan types exhibit expanded patterns of civic space, each has radically different characteristics and implications.

If radial plans might be considered the urban equivalent of centralized churches, orthogonal plans have characteristics of frontal perspective and spatial extension—characteristics that heralded a whole new range of town planning possibilities in Europe, but especially in the new world.

A major source of town planning inspiration for almost two centuries was the *Quattro Primi Libri di Architettura* by the Sienese theoretician Pietro Cataneo. Volume 1 was published in 1554; volume 2 was published in 1567.

Cataneo illustrated both fortified towns and *castra*, and although all of his plans had a central square and a bounding fortification wall, the presence of secondary "neighborhood" squares and the orthogonal grid had both immediate and long-term influence, as well as a flexibility not achievable by the radial plans.

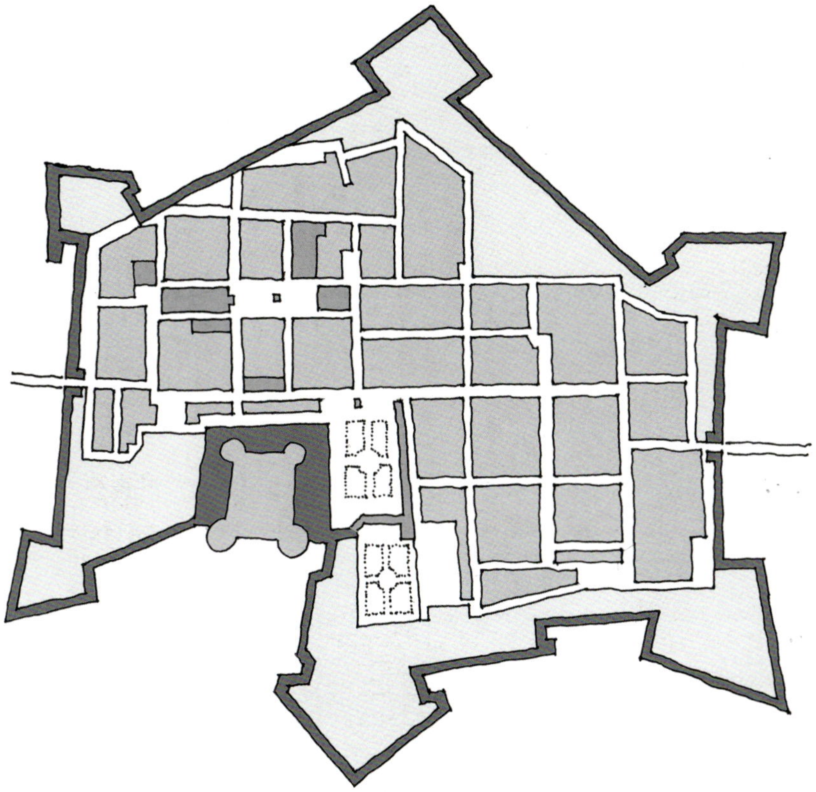

1. Plan of Sabbioneta, 1550s

2. Aerial plan of Sabbioneta from Google Earth

3. Aerial view of Sabbioneta

Sabbioneta

Sabbioneta, built for Vespasiano Gonzaza in the 1550s, was approximately contemporaneous with Cataneo and was the first fortified, ideal city in Italy with an orthogonal street plan. The grid is organized within a fortified polygonal perimeter. Its form recalls the Roman *cardo* and *decumanus* leading to the city gates and intersecting in the forum. The town center contains a church, schools, a library, a hospital, a mint, the Gallery of Antiquities, and the Olympic Theater completed by Vincenzo Scamozzi.

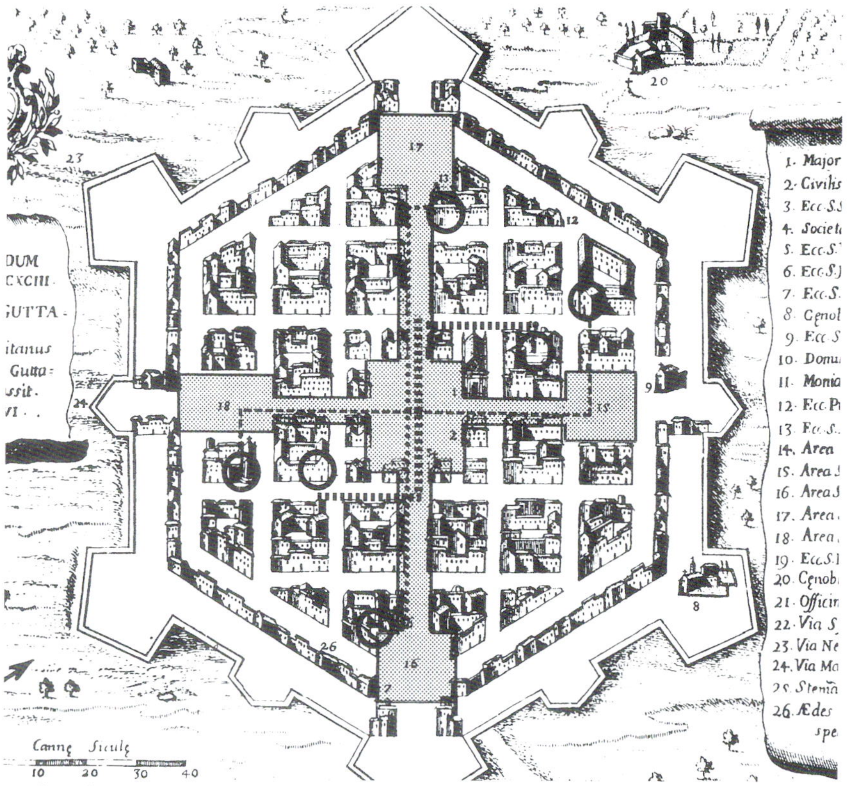

1. *Plan of Avola, attributed to Fra Angelo Italia, 1693*

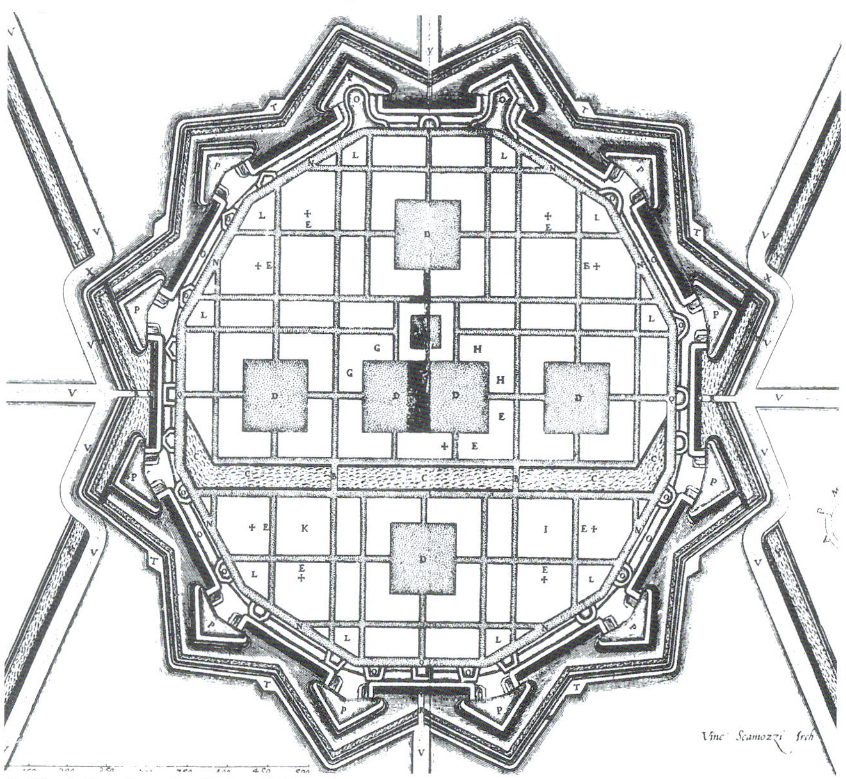

2. *Ideal City from Dell'idea dell architettura universale by Vincenzo Scamozzi, 1615*

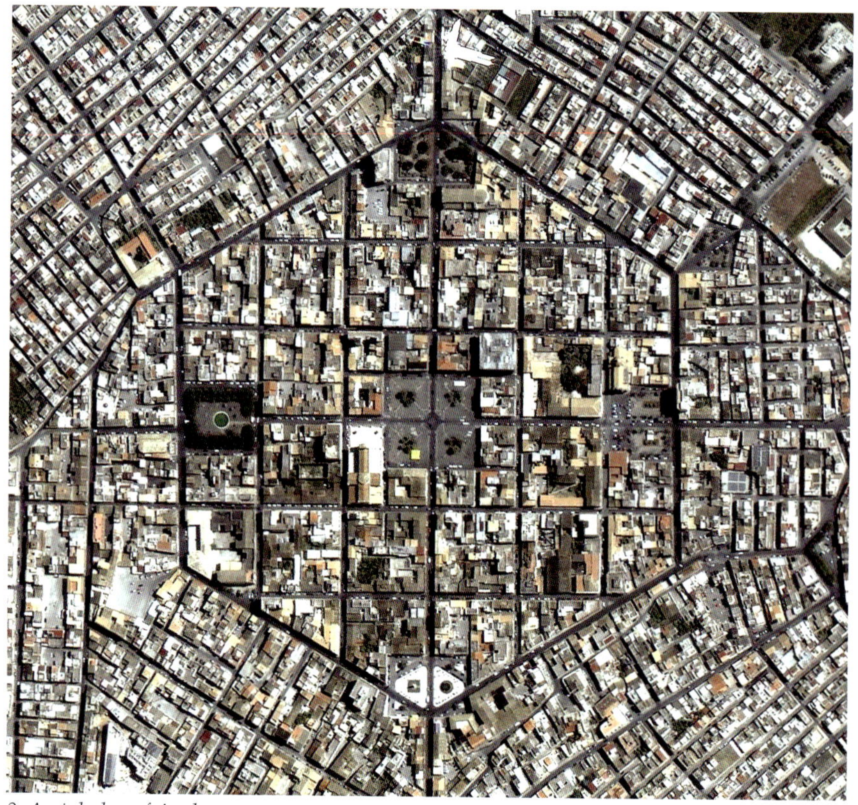

3. *Aerial plan of Avola*

Avola

The 1693 earthquake in the Valle di Noto destroyed many existing towns, following which approximately forty towns were constructed in just a few decades, though only a few were relocated and built from scratch. Avola and Grammichele are two such examples—executed as rigorously geometric plans over about a ten-year period.

These former hill towns were rebuilt on flatter, more easily accessible sites, with less risk for damage from earthquakes. In a further display of rational order, even the site of Avola was chosen by a qualified authority that assessed a wide range of alternatives and selected the best possible location.

Unlike Grammichele, Avola is an orthogonal plan within a hexagonal perimeter. Oddly, when the wall was removed, the town expanded as a series of radial grids, each oriented to the original edges of the hexagon. The plan is by Angelo Italia, based on a plan by Cataneo.

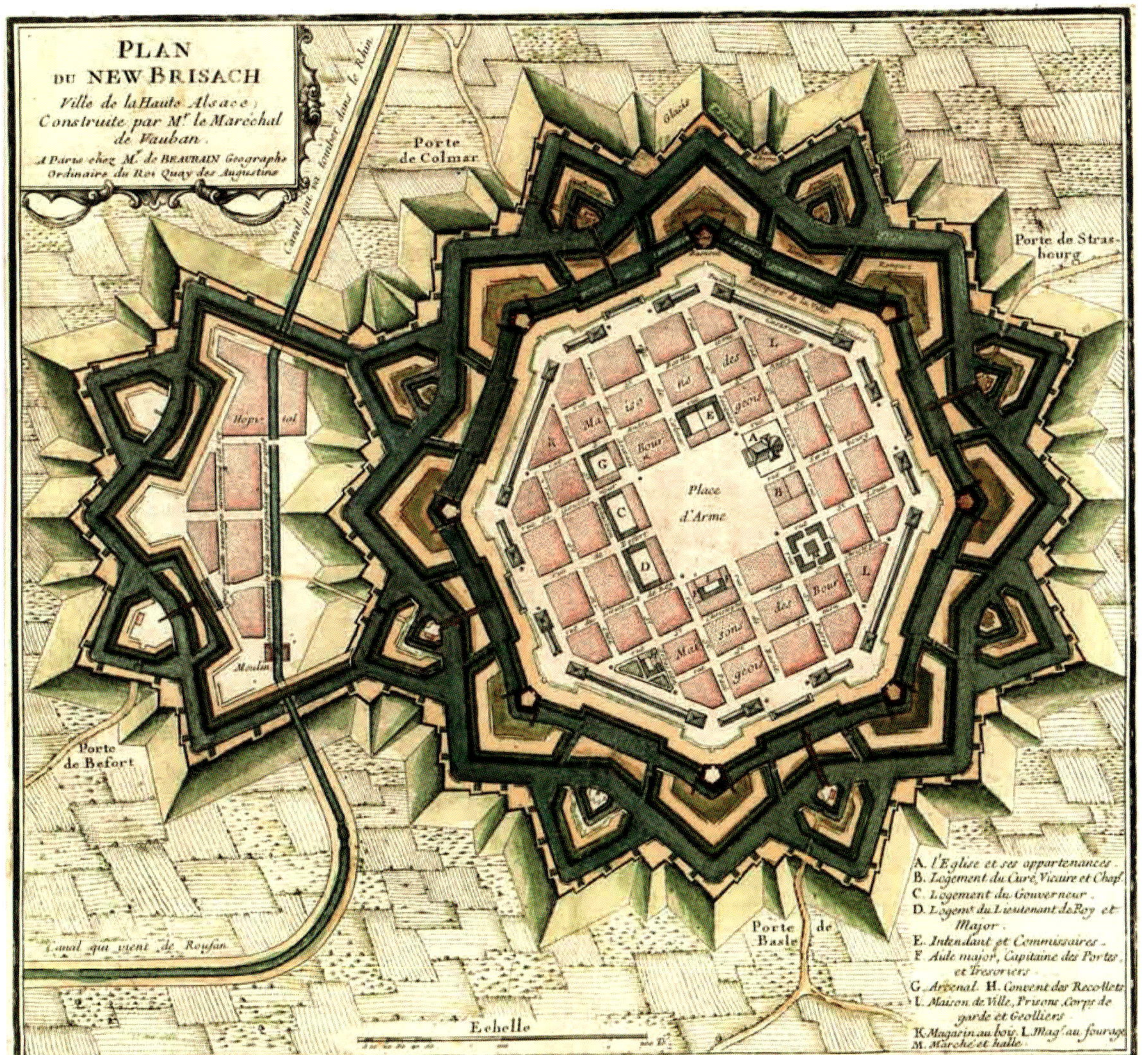

1. Antique plan of Neuf Brisach

2. Aerial view of Neuf Brisach

Neuf Brisach

The fortified town of Neuf Brisach was the last design by Vauban (1633–1707), the great French military engineer. It was intended to guard the northeast frontier in Alsace, and work on the town was begun in 1698.

The orthogonal plan is like a combination of a Roman cross-axial plan and a French Bastide. The central plaza is approximately 450' x 450', and the blocks are nearly square—approximately 165' x 185'.

3. View of Neuf Brisach Town Hall

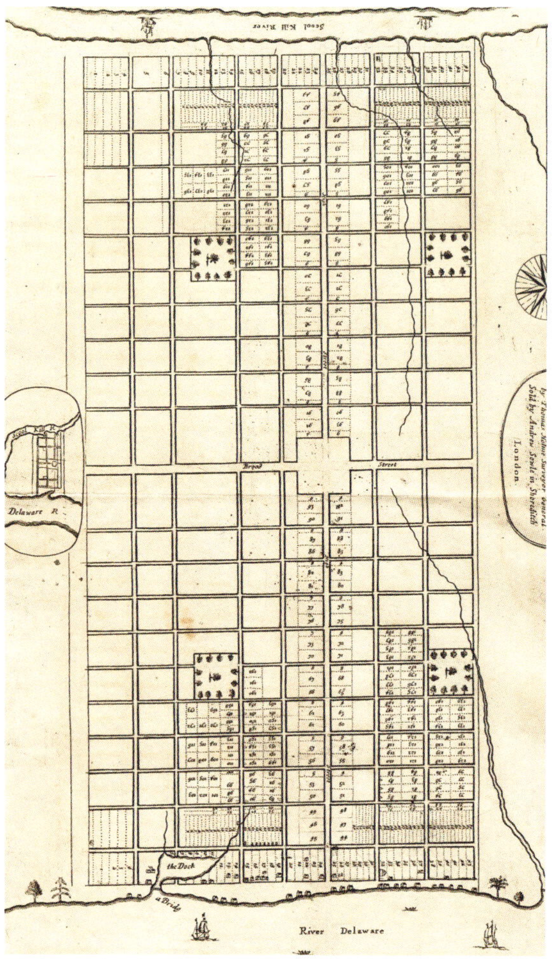

1. *Penn's plan for Philadelphia, 1682*

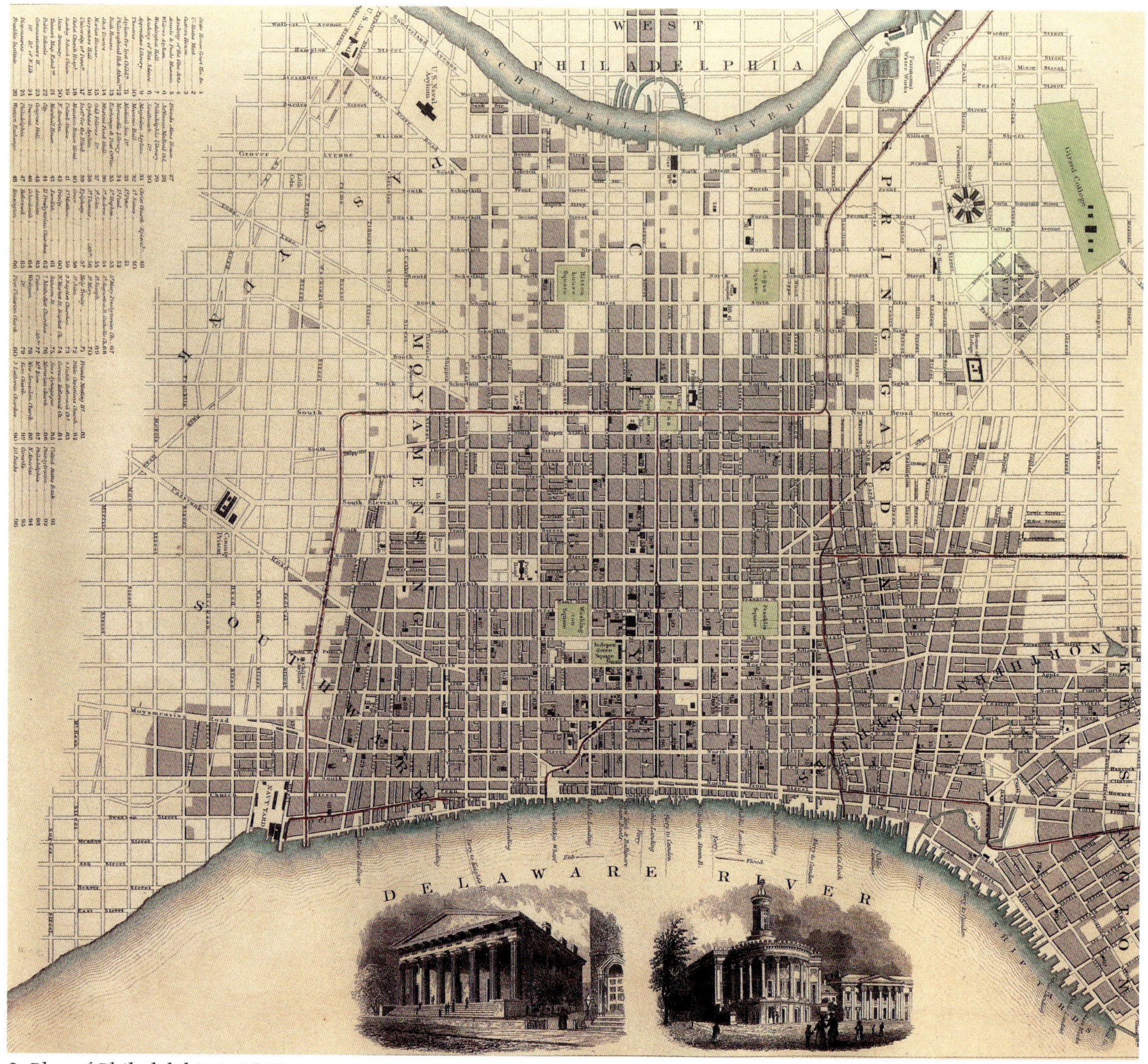

2. *Plan of Philadelphia in 1840*

Philadelphia

The relationship of the plans of Philadelphia and Savannah to those of Cataneo is obvious, and has often been noted.[7] Penn's plan of 1683 is a cross-axial plan with the town square at the intersection, and each resulting quadrant has its own "neighborhood" square. The original street grid was orthogonal but irregular, and the block sizes were relatively large. Penn intended the blocks to be filled with large plots and freestanding houses, but the city quickly became dense, and the blocks were divided.

Savannah

The sophisticated plan of Savannah, Georgia is the darling of American grid towns, and has been written about extensively.[8] The town was founded by James Oglethorpe in 1733, on a plan that called for six "Wards," consisting of a square with public buildings to the east and west, and blocks for private houses to the north and south. Over time this expanded to 24 wards. The size and character of the squares vary, but the average size is about 275' x 325'. Many are filled with what are now gigantic live oak trees.

The north–south streets between the wards are utilitarian and carry most of the north–south traffic; the east–west streets are tree-lined, and are fronted by houses and public buildings.

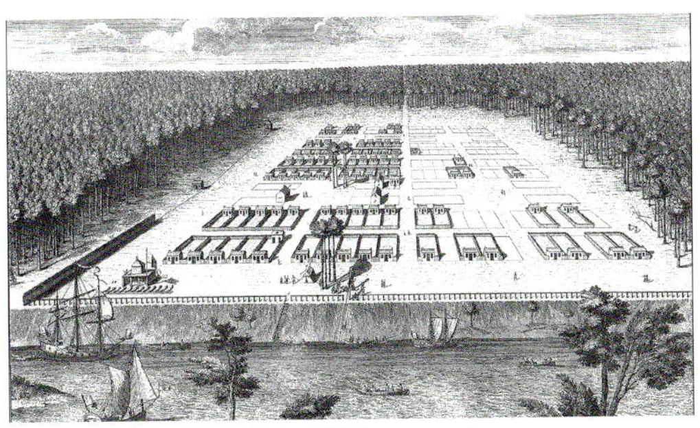

1. View of Savannah in 1734, engraving

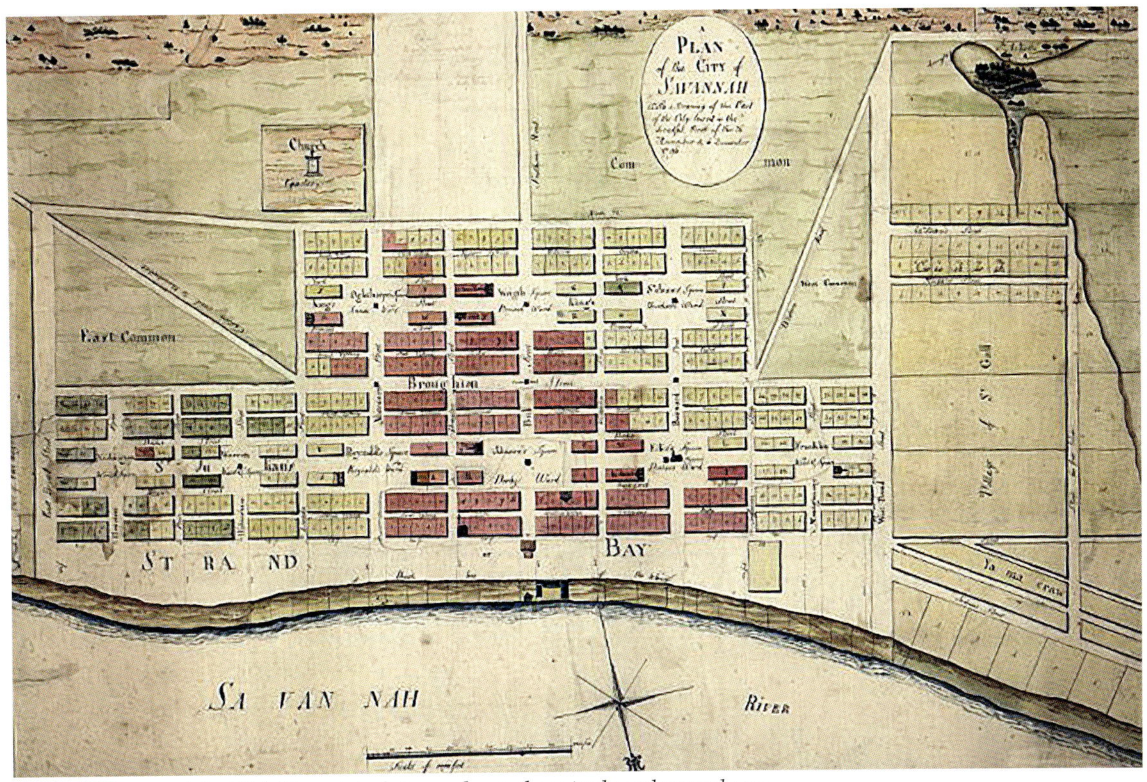

2. Plan of Savannah in 1796. The original six wards are those in the red central area

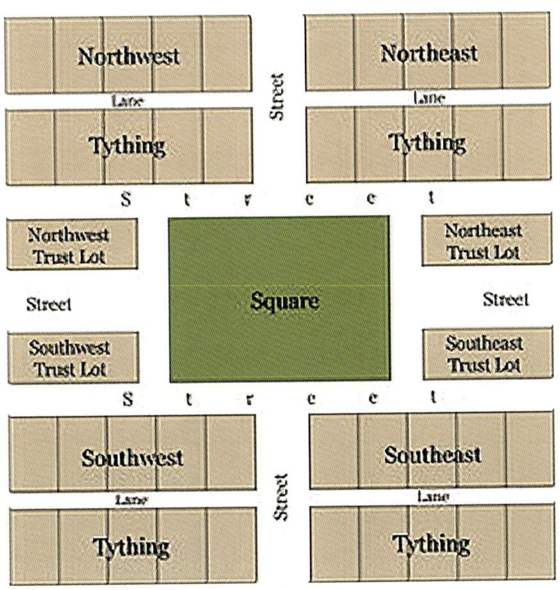

3. Plan diagram of a Savannah ward

4. View of a Savannah square

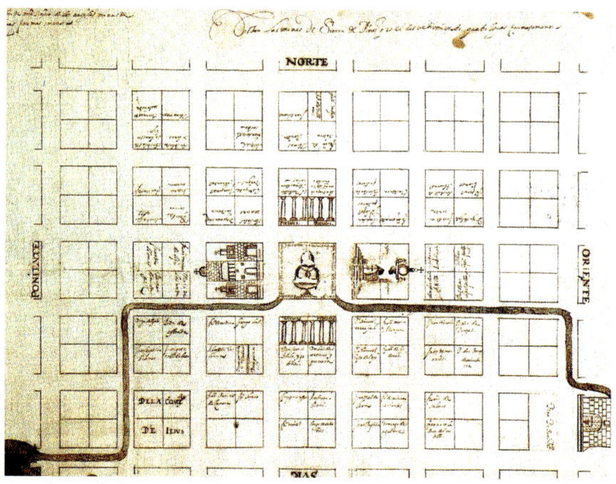

1. Plan of the City of Concepción, Mexico, by Juan Gutierrez, 1603

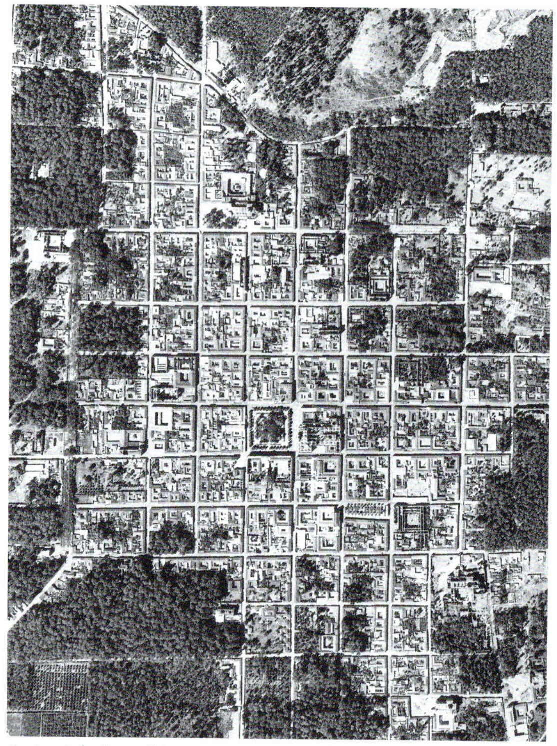

2. Aerial plan of Antigua, Guatemala, founded in 1519

3. Plan of second founding of Panama, 1673

The Laws of the Indies

The Laws of the Indies comprise an entire body of Spanish imperial law, issued by the crown, regulating every aspect of social, political, and economic life throughout their colonial holdings in the Americas and the Philippines. From the early years of the colonial period the Spanish realized the need for a mechanism that would allow them to maintain firm centralized control over the subjugated territories.

The Laws of the Indies served as the mechanism of control. Issued first as the Laws of Burgos (1512), they continued to evolve over a nearly 200-year period, with major issuances in 1542 (The New Laws of the Indies), in the *Ordenanzas de descubrimientos, nueva población y pacificación de las Indias* by Phillip II of 1573, and a further edition issued in 1680 as the *Recopilación de las Leyes de los Reynos de Indias* by Charles II. These proclamations of the Crown served many goals, including the organization of defensive outposts that also formed a social network for colonists, and the regularization of land distribution practices (including the surveying, subdivision, and legal processes).

The part of the Laws of the Indies regarding the physical environment—the principles of city development—is a very small part of the document.[9] It is an important part, however, because it was the part that had the most lasting impact.

Most of the town planning ordinances deal with site selection criteria. The more concrete planning criteria begin with: "The main plaza is to be the starting point for the town." They then prescribe that the main plaza should be square or rectangular, in which case it should have the proportion of 1:1.5, be at least 200' x 300', not more than 530' x 800', and that a good size is 400' x 600'. Four main streets are to begin in the middle of each side, and two at each corner. Finally, the plots fronting the plaza are to contain public buildings, not private houses. Smaller well-proportioned plazas may also be provided.

The physical form of the city is not prescribed in the laws, but orthogonal planning is implied by the proportional description of plazas and plots. The town plans are typified by an orthogonal gridiron structure, however (adapted locally as topography demanded). The plaza serves as the civic center of the colony; with the church and government facilities watching over the symbol of imperial governance and power.

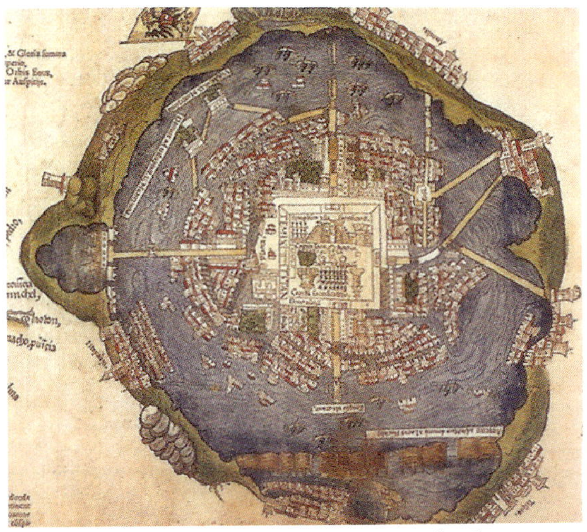

1. Plan of Tenochtitlan by Hernán Cortes in his letter to Philip II, 1524

2. Aerial plan of central Mexico City

This scheme is the basis of hundreds of towns in the Americas, and in the configuration of Mexico City, built by Hernán Cortes on the former site of Tenochitlan. In choosing this location, Cortes was cleverly able to co-opt the rigorously developed physical and social structure already ingrained by the conquered Aztecs, and put these to the purposes of the Spanish authority. Both Cortes's description to Phillip II of Tenochtitlan and the city subsequently built on its site were widely influential in the further colonization of Latin America and in later settlements across vast parts of North America.

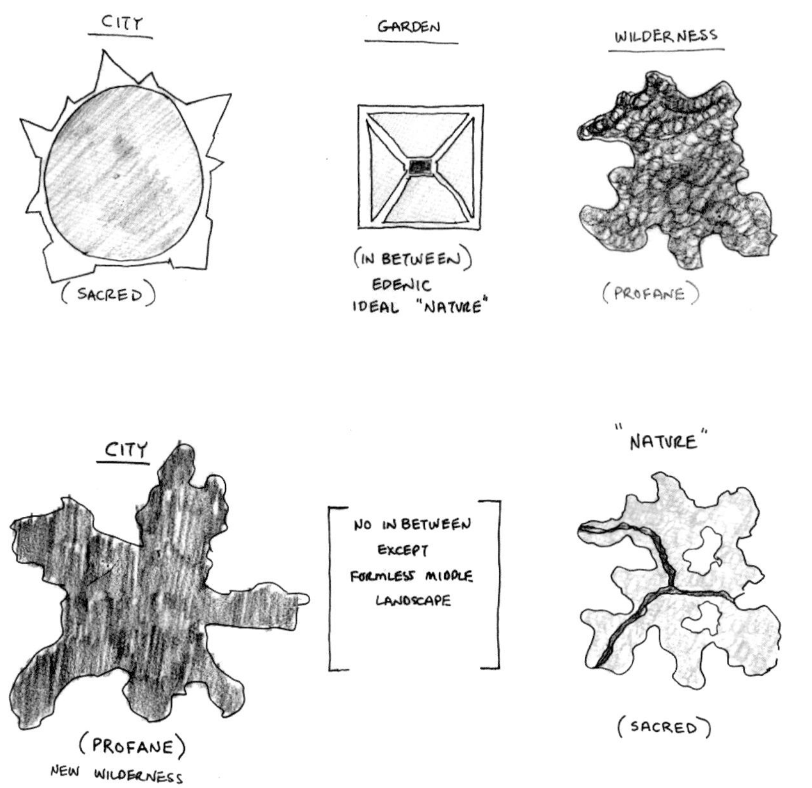

1. Diagrams of the evolution of the relationship of City:Garden:Country, Steven Peterson

2. Plan and section of Villa d'Este gardens at Tivoli

Landscape and the City

The interrelationship of landscape and the city has undergone a formal and philosophical transformation over the last 550 years: from landscape *and* the city during the Renaissance, to landscape *in* the city during the nineteenth century, to the city *in* the landscape in the twentieth century. This transformation from complete hegemony of the urban to equal hegemony of the natural represents nothing less than the demise of the city. Romanticism has been replaced by ecology, and architecture has been divorced from the city and reduced to the trivial.[10]

The Garden and the City

Steven Peterson has observed that, traditionally, the city was considered sacred and the country profane, and the garden was the mediator between the two. Gradually, however, the "natural landscape" became sacred and the city profane. Dense, compact cities were replaced by "towers-in-the-park" and suburbia, and the garden disappeared, as mediation was not required. Thus, the long-standing, fruitful relationship between landscape planning and the city was lost.[11]

Renaissance Gardens

Renaissance and Baroque gardens have a clear and unequivocal relationship to town planning. Gardens could at once be more immediate and more fanciful than cities. Often they were associated with country villas such as the Villa d'Este at Tivoli (begun in 1560), but others enjoyed a more direct relationship with a town or city, such as the Boboli Gardens in Florence (begun in 1549) and the Villa Lante at Bagnaia (begun in 1568).

2. Aerial view of the Boboli Garden, Pitti Palace, and Florence

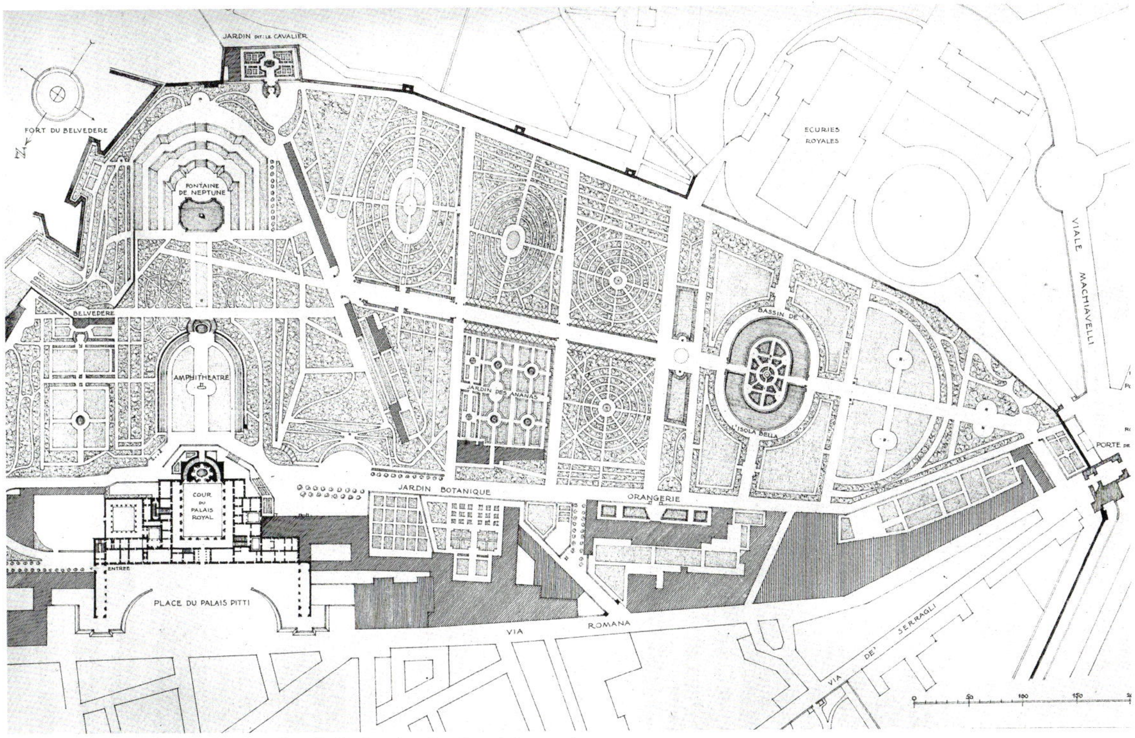

1. Plan of the Palazzo Pitti and Boboli Garden in the eighteenth century

3. Aerial view of the Boboli Garden, Pitti Palace, and Florence

The Villa d'Este at Tivoli

The plan of the Villa d'Este gardens by Pirro Ligorio could easily be imagined the plan of an ideal Renaissance town. The core of the plan is an orthogonal pattern of square and nearly-square blocks organized by a grid of streets. The town center would be asymmetrical, but otherwise only the section and absence of fortification walls would contradict the ideal city. Further, the presence of gods, goddesses, nymphs, demons, trees, and above all, the proliferation of water and fountains—in short, all the elements of a pleasure garden—would not be found in a city.

The Boboli Garden in Florence

Begun by Niccolò Tribolo for Eleonora de Toledo and Cosimo I in 1549, the original garden was continued after Tribolo's death in 1550 by Bartolomeo Ammannati, and then by Bernardo Buontalenti. The original sixteenth-century garden is shown in the lunette painting by Giusto Utens; the plan above illustrates eighteenth-century renovations and extensions up and down the hill. The plan, like that of the Villa d'Este, could be imagined to be an urban one, but slightly more Baroque with larger blocks and more flamboyant shapes.

4. Painting by Guisto Utens, 1599, of the Pitti Palace and the original extent of the Boboli Garden

Villa Lante at Bagnaia

The gardens of the Villa Lante (begun in 1568) are generally regarded as among the most beautiful in Italy. It is the villa's relationship with the town, however, that is most compelling—a clear expression of Peterson's idea of the garden as mediator between sacred and profane. The villa consists not only of the famous walled garden, but also the adjacent "wild" wooded area. The parterre of the garden relates directly to the town square, cementing the connection of *city:garden:nature*.

2. Aerial plan of Bagnaia and the Villa Lante

1. Aerial view of the villa and town

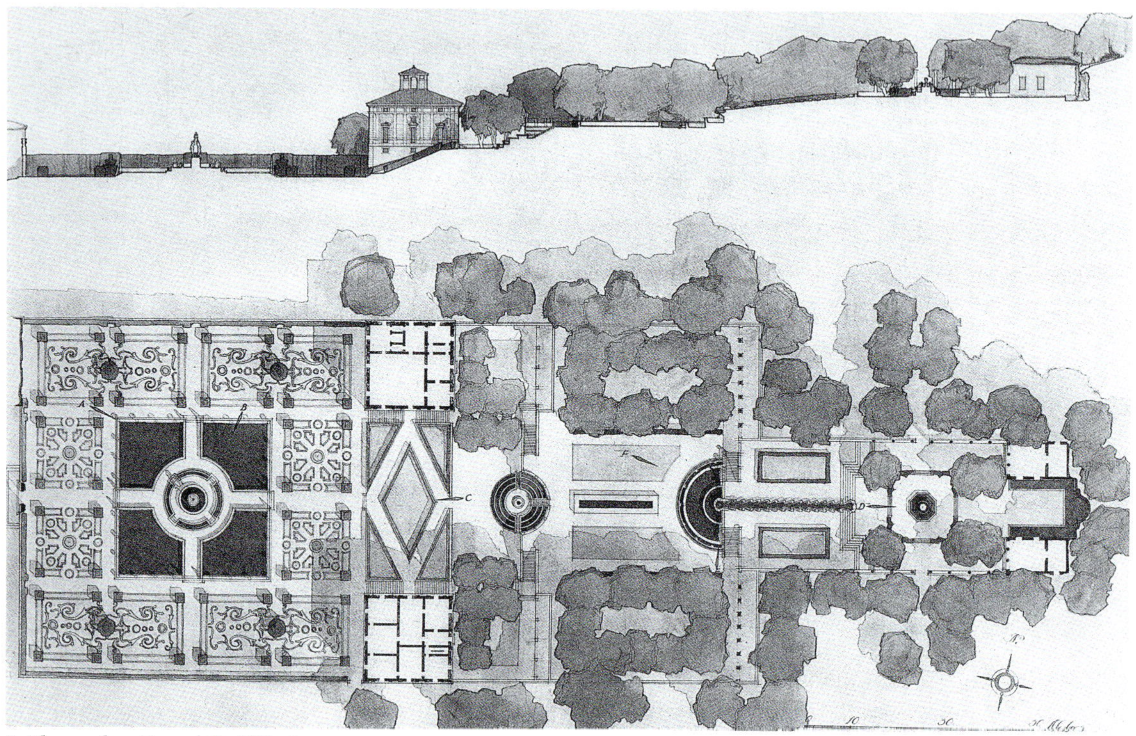

3. Plan and section of the Villa Lante

Richelieu

Richelieu, designed by Jacques Lemercier in 1628 for Cardinal Richelieu, owed an obvious debt to Cataneo. It did not literally have a square in the center, however, but two squares at each end of the main street. On the other hand, the main square, the Place Cardinal, was roughly in the center between the Cardinal's Chateau and the residential square, the Place Royale, at the north end of town. The town and garden form one unified composition. The Place Cardinal is about 290' square and is surrounded by the church, the town hall, and the market hall.

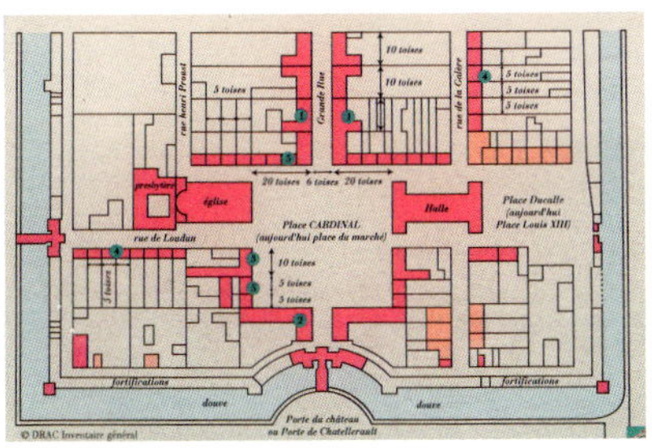

1. Plan of Place Cardinal

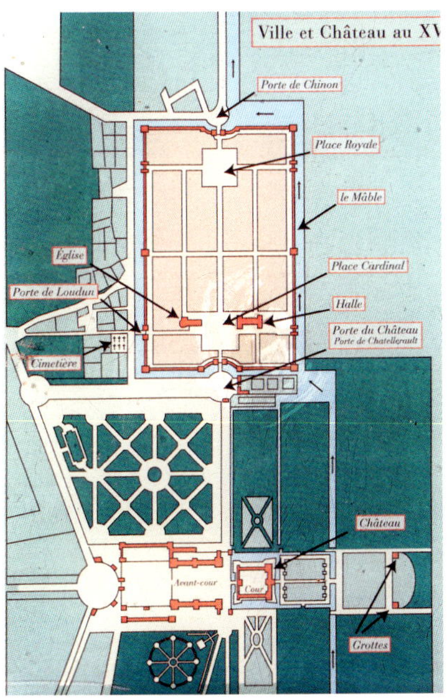

2. Plan of town and chateau

3. View of the Grande Rue toward the chateau

4. Allée leading to the chateau

5. Aerial plan of Richelieu and the grounds of the Chateau Richelieu

6. View of Place Cardinal

Painting of Versailles in 1668 by Pierre Patel

Baroque Cities: 1700–1800

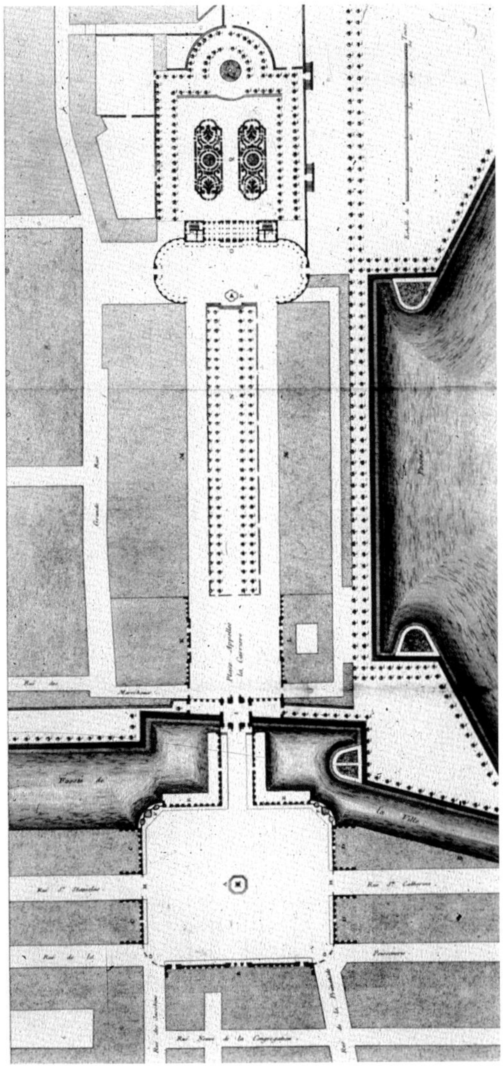

Plan of the spatial sequence in Nancy by Héré, 1752–59

The Baroque clearly favored the dynamics of spatial extension—of frontality—over the stasis of centrality. Urban spaces were linked along an axis, and both public and private buildings were used to shape and extend the civic structure of cities. This period was marked by a vast array of Baroque urban interventions, but circumstances also provided opportunities for large-scale town planning initiatives.

Smaller cities, such as the new towns that were developed after earthquakes, extended the practice of orthogonal Renaissance planning, but with more elaborate spatial sequences, and controlled, unified scenographic effects. Landscape, and objects such as statues, played a role in the composition, but the primary emphasis was on the spaces.

In larger existing cities, long, straight streets were used to connect important monuments and buildings. Pope Sixtus V (1585–90) and other popes provided the model with the renovation of Rome, beginning in the sixteenth century. L'Enfant's 1792 plan for the new capital city of Washington, DC, owed much to Sixtus V, and especially to classic French garden design.

Plan of fifteenth and sixteenth-century Rome with street projects by the popes

Sixtus V: Water and Streets

By the sixteenth century, Rome had shrunk to approximately a third of its imperial limits, leaving several important religious monuments exposed and isolated. Pope Sixtus V recognized the problem, and during his brief reign between 1585 and 1590 he had the ancient Alexandrina aqueduct repaired (and renamed Aqua Felice) to provide the city with water; he and his architect, Domenico Fontana, erected obelisks as focal points for major churches and outlined a series of streets to connect the various monuments. Very little was actually completed during his reign, but a plan for the civic infrastructure was in place to be fleshed out and completed by successive generations.

The resulting armature not only provided an improved circulation system and a stable, legible pilgrimage route, but together with the water supply, it also promoted the redevelopment of long-abandoned parts of the city. Moreover, it provided a precedent for the grand Baroque city and garden schemes of the seventeenth and eighteenth centuries.

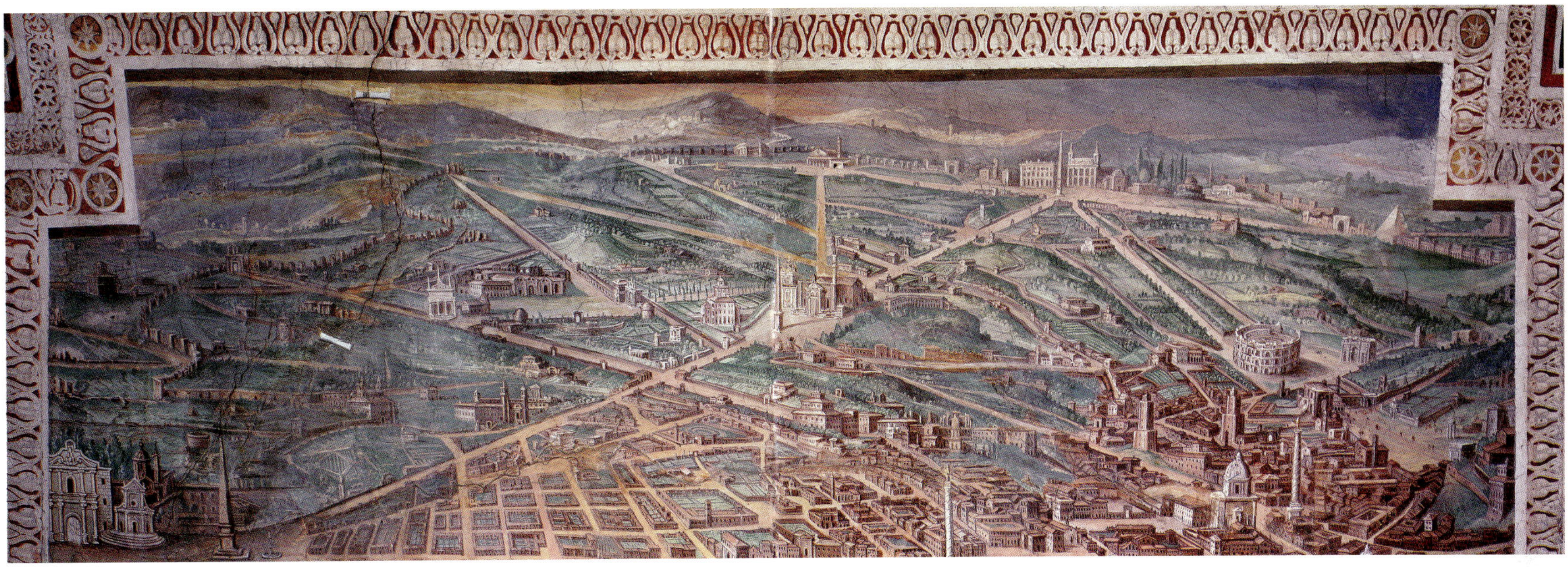

1. Fresco in the Vatican Library showing Sixtus V's plan for Rome

2. Engraving of the pilgrimage churches of Rome, A. Lafréry, 1575

3. Engraving, 1612, with architectural revisions and placement of obelisks

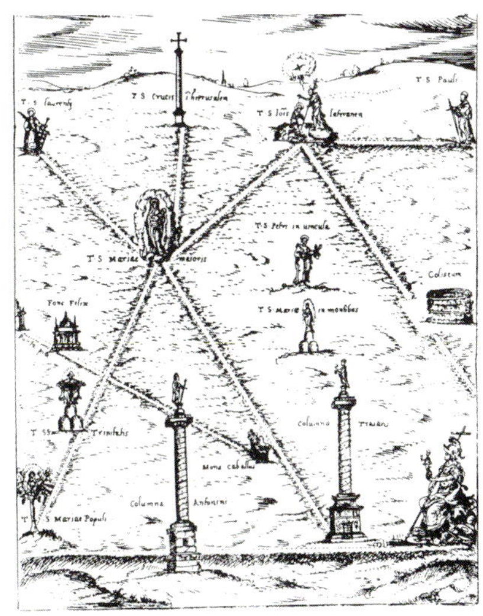

4. Connections between monuments, Bordino, 1588

Baroque Gardens and Cities

If walled Italian Renaissance gardens like the Villa Lante and the Boboli gardens could be seen as relating to urban models and as mediating between the city and country, French Baroque parks and gardens might be seen as more direct models for the city. Indeed, the Bois de Boulogne was bigger than the city of Paris, and twice as big as the city of London.

Liberated from the actual constraints of cities, French Baroque parks and gardens could be composed more freely. They were composed of long, straight streets and allées arranged orthogonally and diagonally through woods and parterres. Curves were rarely used except for intersections that were often *round points* and, unlike Sixtus V's plan for Rome, the "streets" did not terminate in objects, but in spaces.

Wren's 1666 plan for the reconstruction of London was based on similar principles, except that the diagonal streets were superimposed over a pronounced orthogonal urban block system.

Le Notre's design for the gardens of Versailles was a major influence on L'Enfant's plan for Washington, DC, a century later, and might also be seen as a dry run for mid-nineteenth-century Paris.

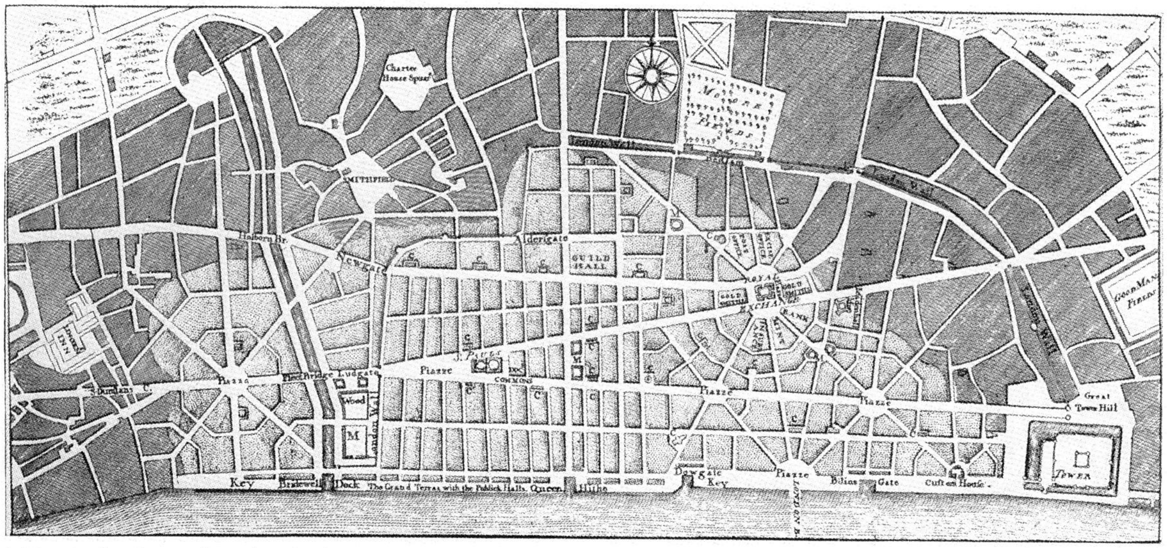

1. Wren's plan for London after the fire of 1666, 1:20,000

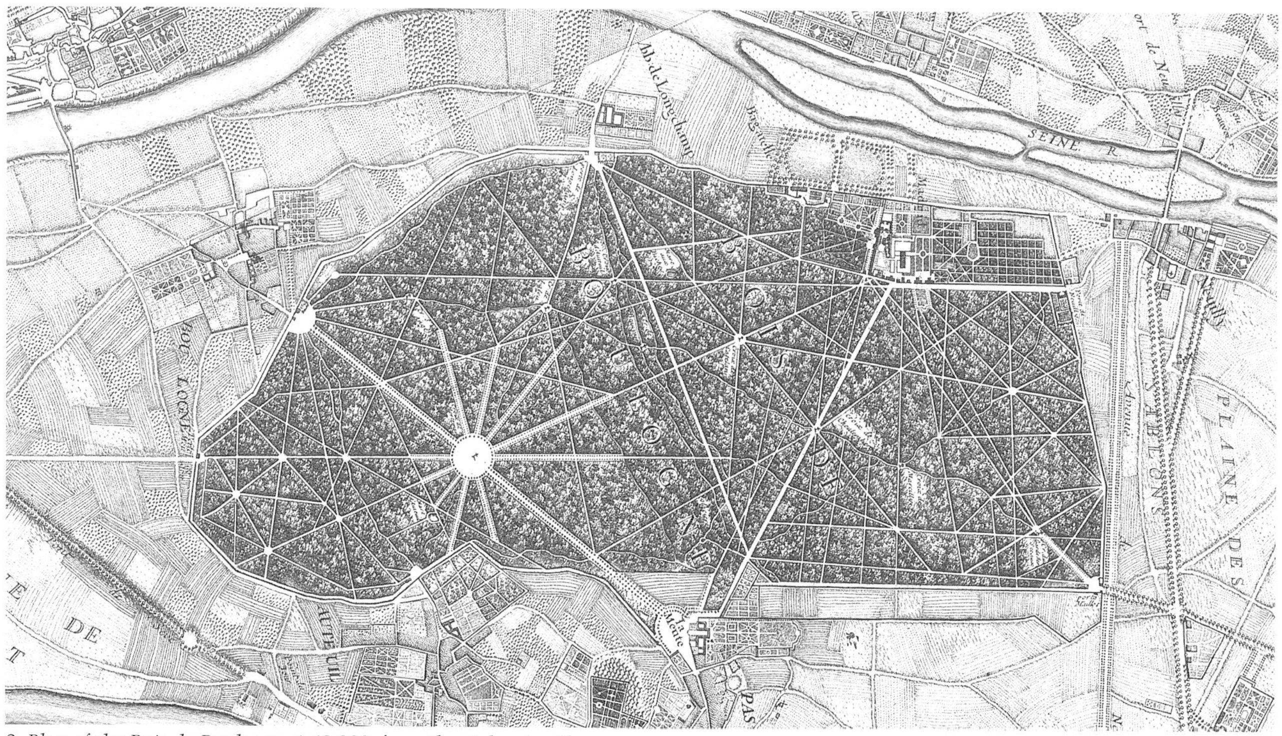

2. Plan of the Bois de Boulogne, 1:40,000, from the Delagrive Plan

Plan of Versailles by P. le Pautre, begun in the 1660s, 1:20,000

L'Enfant plan for Washington, DC, 1792, 1:40,000

Washington, DC

The plan of Versailles is an obvious ancestor of the plan for Washington, DC. The original author of the plan, Major Pierre Charles L'Enfant, grew up at Versailles where his father was a court painter for Louis XIV. The relationship between the plans can be overstated, however, for three major reasons.

The first and perhaps most obvious reason is that Washington is (finally) a city, not a park. The interstitial areas defined by the allées are not transparent woods or parterres, but dense urban fabric of blocks and streets.

The second is that Versailles is composed primarily of diagonals, whereas Washington is primarily an orthogonal grid plan. L'Enfant himself described the plan: "I made the distribution regular, with every street at right angles ... and afterwards, opened ... avenues to and from every principal place."[1]

The third is that at Versailles, the diagonals connect spaces, but in the original plan for Washington they connect monuments, and this is more neoclassical than Baroque. In other words, it is a late-eighteenth-century, neoclassical plan that articulates an enlightenment society's institutions as detached civic monuments.

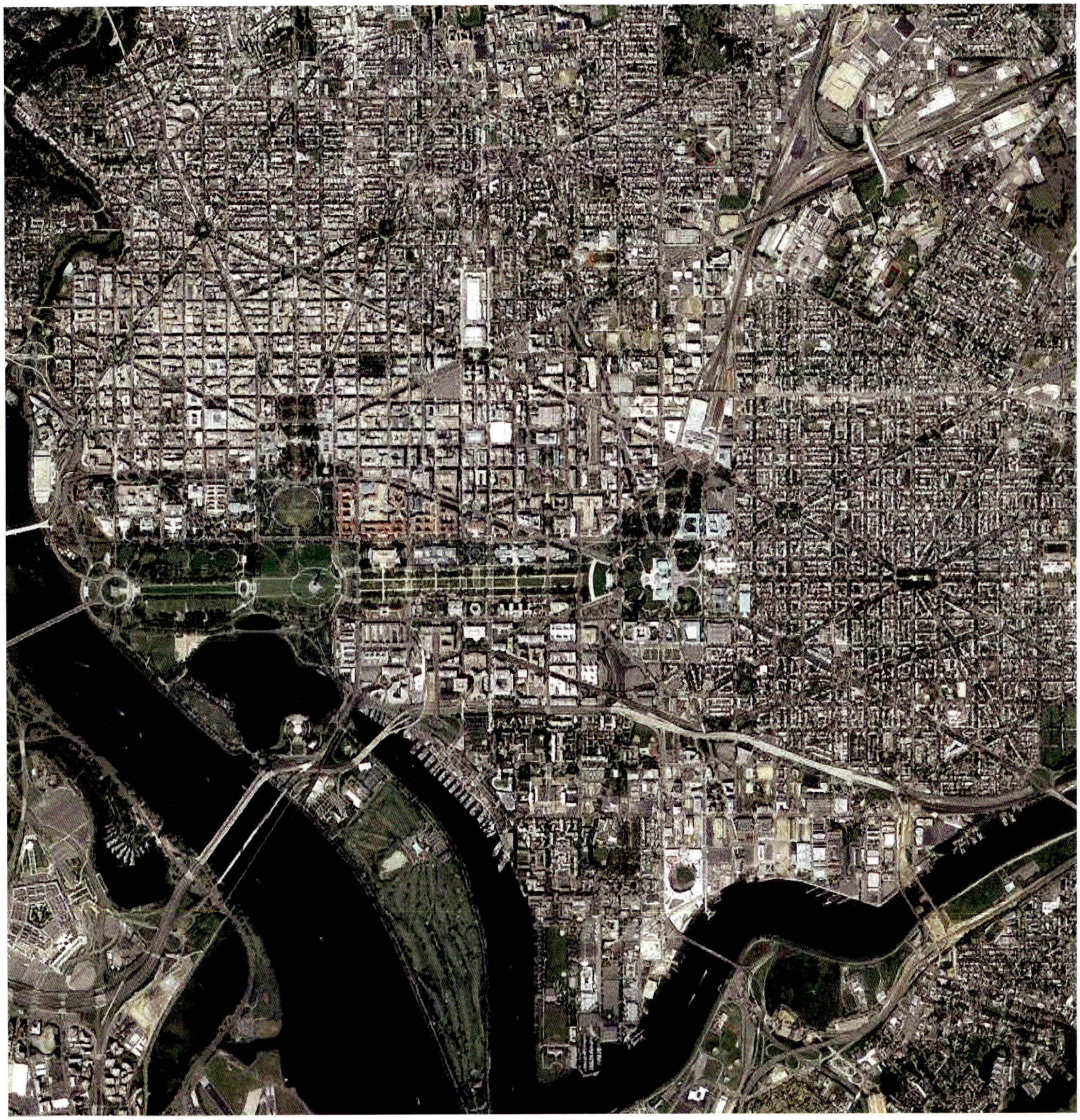

Aerial plan of Washington, DC, 1:40,000

Noto, Piazza del Municipio. View of the Duomo, San Nicolo, and SS. Salvatore

Noto

The Baroque is ubiquitous in Sicily. In many ways it is *the* language of Sicily, owing to Spanish domination and the relative absence of the Renaissance. But the new town of Noto is a special example of the integration of Baroque town planning and architecture, and is the product of a single event.

The earthquake of January 11, 1693, altered the face of Sicilian towns and communities throughout southeastern Sicily in a series of shock waves that caused the destruction of more than forty cities and the death of thousands of citizens.[2] It destroyed the medieval town of Noto Antica.

The earthquake also precipitated a debate regarding the practice of rebuilding cities. The question of whether to rebuild on the ruins of the destroyed city, build a new town adjacent to the ruins, or build a new city in a new location, one that would ideally be less susceptible to future environmental disasters, was a debate that would take many different paths throughout Sicily. The responses varied, but they all illustrated the practices of Renaissance and Baroque city-planning models as a departure from previous medieval urban development. In the case of Noto, the building of a completely new town on a different site put into practice contemporary Roman Baroque design principles, leading to a unique integration of urban and architectural design. In fact, if not for the architecture, Noto would have had an unremarkable plan.

1. Plan of Noto Antica, 1692

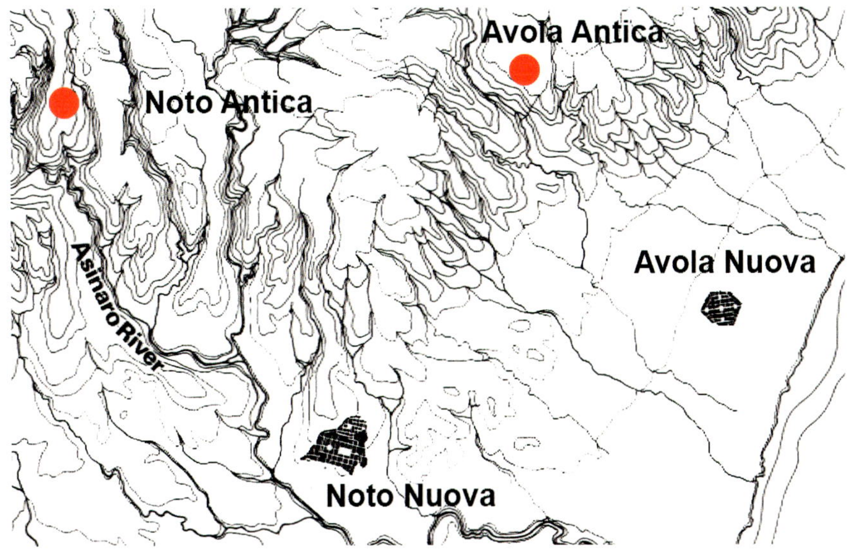

2. Locations of Noto and Avola

Noto Antica

Noto Antica is located roughly 13.5 kilometers inland from the sea. Originally a settlement founded in the late Bronze Age by the Sikels, the indigenous inhabitants, the town was ruled in succession by the Greeks, Romans, Byzantines, Arabs, Normans, Germans, French, and Spanish. The name came from the Arabs who called the city Noto, or "Eminent Place." The city was dependent on land, water rights, and agriculture rather than commerce, owing to its lack of proximity to a port or trade route.

The city layout was a function of the topography of the site. Noto Antica was a walled city organized around a central core containing two major piazzas—S. Venera and Piazza Maggiore—and was connected axially from this center to the north and south. The city blocks reflected a common practice in Medieval Europe, allowing organic geomorphic streets to extend and contain the city within the fortifications.[3] It is in this medieval freedom that the city embodied a harmony between the geography, fortification, and territory of the site.

The Earthquake

On the morning of January 11, 1693, the second of two earthquakes hit the southeast corner of Sicily. Word was immediately sent back to the Spanish Government. The Viceroy of Messina paints the picture of destruction:

"The coastal area is broken up in several places.... No one dares walk in the streets....The after-shocks still continue but they are very light. At the least trembling one anticipates a quake, so great is the state of fear we are all in."[4]

In the aftermath of the quake Noto Antica was left destroyed. The only remnants of the urban fabric were the remains of the south fortification wall, along with foundations littering the landscape. Through this drastic lens the city sought a new location for rebuilding.

The Political Landscape

Proceeding with unyielding haste the Viceregal Government of Spain took steps to rebuild Sicily. The Spanish government was greatly concerned with halting the diminishing economic and political problems in Sicily. Through the mismanagement of the agrarian sector numerous revolts and uprooting of peasants from the countryside amounted to diminishing population throughout Sicily.[5] This—along with the lack of return on investments in the New World—began to have drastic affects, and on Spain itself. Therefore, within months of the earthquake, a body of men was charged with orders to examine and move forward in the pursuit of rebuilding Sicily. A council was elected under the leadership of the Viceroy of Sicilia, who had a task force of aristocrats and clergy to assist in the study of a new city versus the resurrection of the old. By the powers of the Viceroy, the Duke of Uzeia, a new site was established seven kilometers from the site of Noto Antica.

Relocation

One can surmise that the site for Noto Nuova was chosen based on opposite characteristics from those of the medieval city. Yet, Noto Antica was a site rich in water, agriculture, and mills, and was easily accessible from the rest of Sicily. Ultimately, a site was selected based on the ability to initially provide adequate water to the city. The new site was flatter than the previous one—a common trait of the post-earthquake new towns in Sicily.

Noto Nuova

The form of Noto is the result of three interrelated factors: the grid(s), the topography, and the civic structure of Baroque architecture and spaces. The development process was confused, however, resulting in peculiarities and imperfections in the plan.

Thus, Noto would not be memorable for its plan alone, despite its spectacular south-facing site between two valleys. Rather, it is the power of Noto's civic structure of spaces and its Roman Baroque architecture that make it unique. The most important buildings and piazzas are arrayed horizontally along its main street, the Corso Vittorio Emanuele.

The Corso progresses from a belvedere on the west overlooking the valley, through the Piazza XVI Maggio with the church of San Domenico and the theater, through the Piazza del Municipio with the Duomo (San Nicoló) and City Hall, through the Piazza Immacolata with the church of San Francesco, then out through the Arch of Ferdinand II, and through the tree-lined allée of the Viale Marconi to the eastern belvedere overlooking the eastern valley.

1. Plan of Noto Nuova, 1:7,500

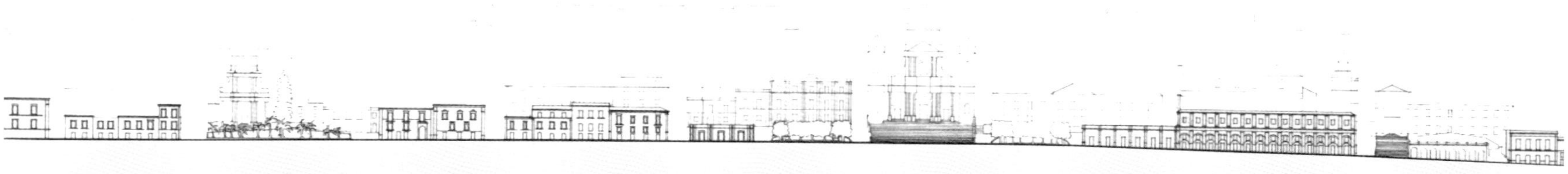

2. Section through the Corso

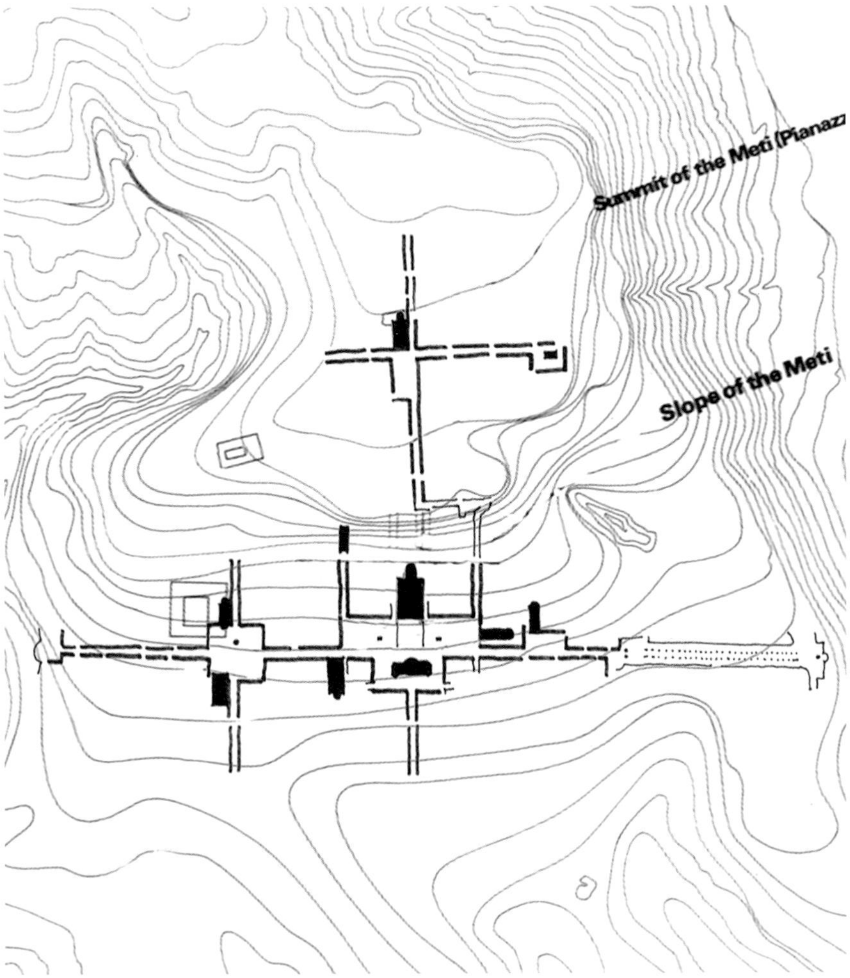

1. The topography and civic structure of Noto, 1:10,000. The Duomo and City Hall are in the center.

2. Aerial photo from the south

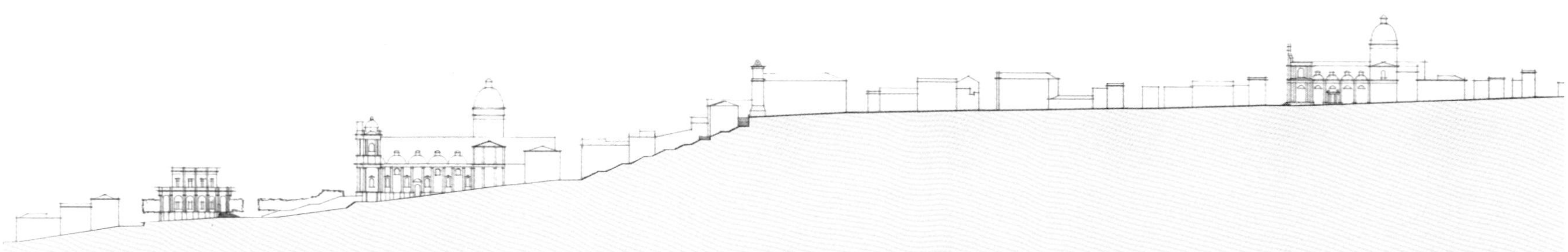

3. Section down the slope through the Via Vicere

Street Grids

Rebuilding on the new site was not embraced willingly by the citizens of Noto. There was a general fear that the community would dissolve. Citizens understood only their specific block and neighborhood in the city, so the consensus was that by moving to a new city whole neighborhoods would collapse. Thus, during the first five years, growth of the new town was slow. Rulers and citizens went back and forth regarding staying or leaving the old city, until finally the Spanish Crown had to step in and declare the new site as the location for Noto Nuova. Over the course of the next ten years Noto's plan was set, leading to the definition of the town as seen today.[6]

Noto is organized on two non-aligned grids separated by the steepest part of the site. Initially, the town was to be built on the upper plateau, but many settlers, including many of the nobility, preferred the lower slope. Confusion ensued. Ultimately, the two grids of Noto were constructed in conjunction with each other.

The church of SS. Crocefisso and its piazza form the center of the upper grid, while San Nicoló and the Piazza Municipio form the center of the lower grid.

No street extends through both grids owing to misalignment and the steepness of the intervening slope. Connections are therefore circuitous and somewhat difficult, thereby emphasizing the difference in character between the two parts of the city.

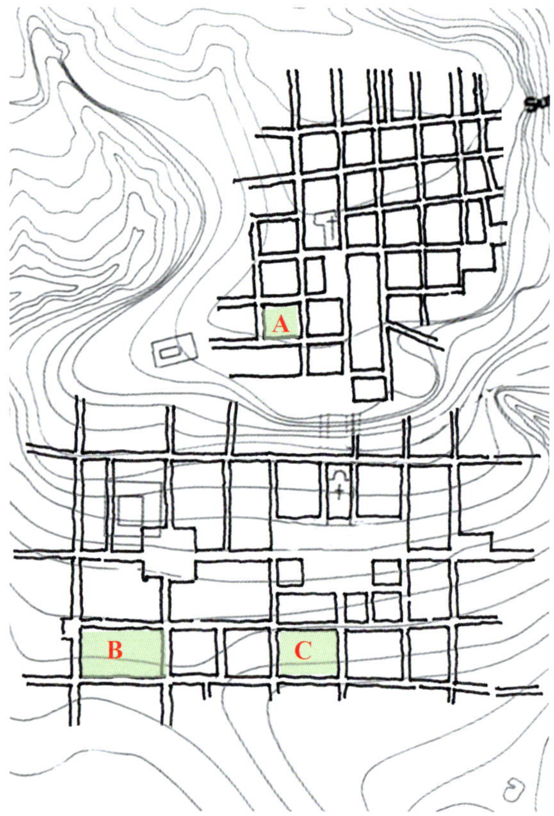

1. Upper and lower grids and contours, 1:10,000

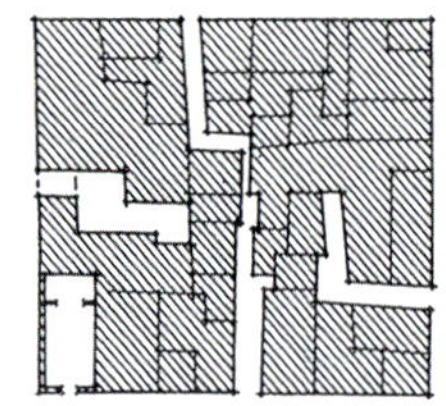

2. Typical upper block, 1:2,000

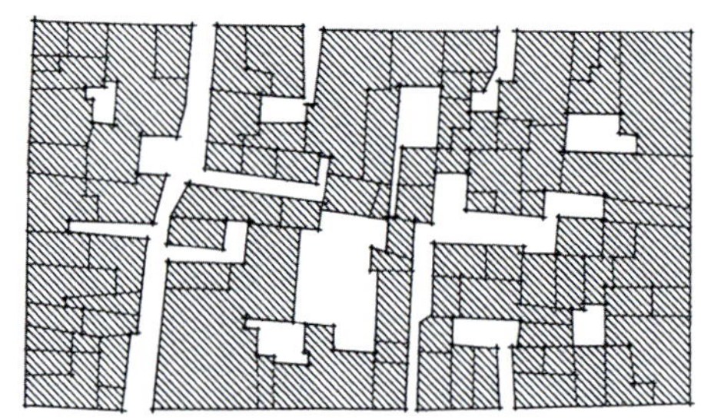

3. Plan of large block in lower town, 1:2,000

Urban Blocks:

Noto's urban blocks also differ between the upper and lower parts of the city.

The blocks in the upper grid are smaller and more nearly square. The dimensions vary, but the basic block module is approximately 170'. The only public space in the upper town—the Piazza Mazzini, in front of SS. Crocefisso—is a half a block in size. In other words, it is the result of the grid.

The blocks of the lower grid are larger and more varied in proportion, but generally with a narrow dimension of approximately 260–270' and a length of 275–400'. If the upper town is formed by the block grid, in the lower town the blocks are the result of the spatial pattern.

In both cases the parcels are surprisingly irregular, especially toward the edges. Typically, planned towns with regular blocks start out with regular parcels, which may become irregular over time. In Noto, however, it appears that the parcels were never regular. Indeed, it is as if a regular Baroque street pattern was draped over a medieval town plan.

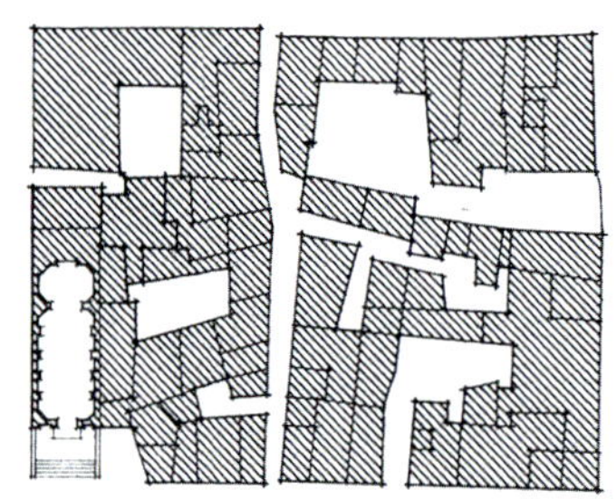

4. Plan of block in lower town, 1:2,000

1. Corso Vittorio Emanuele

2. Via Nicolaci

Streets

The typical streets of both grids have a width of 20–25', while the primary street, the Corso Vittorio Emanuele, is approximately 30' wide. Within this matrix there are many, many irregular streets 10–15' wide—especially internal to the blocks.

3. Stairs to upper Noto

4. Via Vincenzo Gioberti

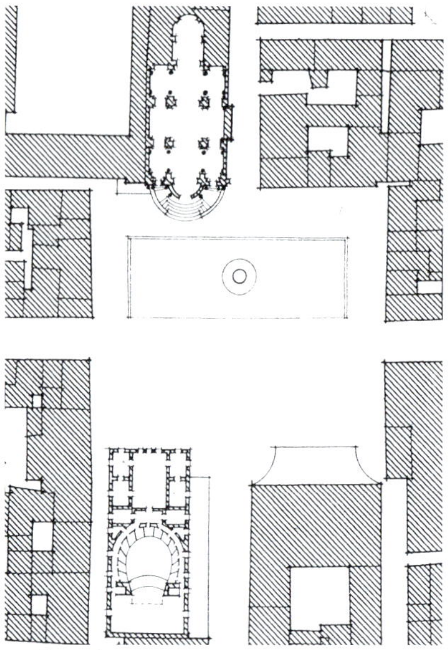

1. Plan of Piazza XVI Maggio, 1:2,000

2. San Nicolo

3. Municipio, City Hall

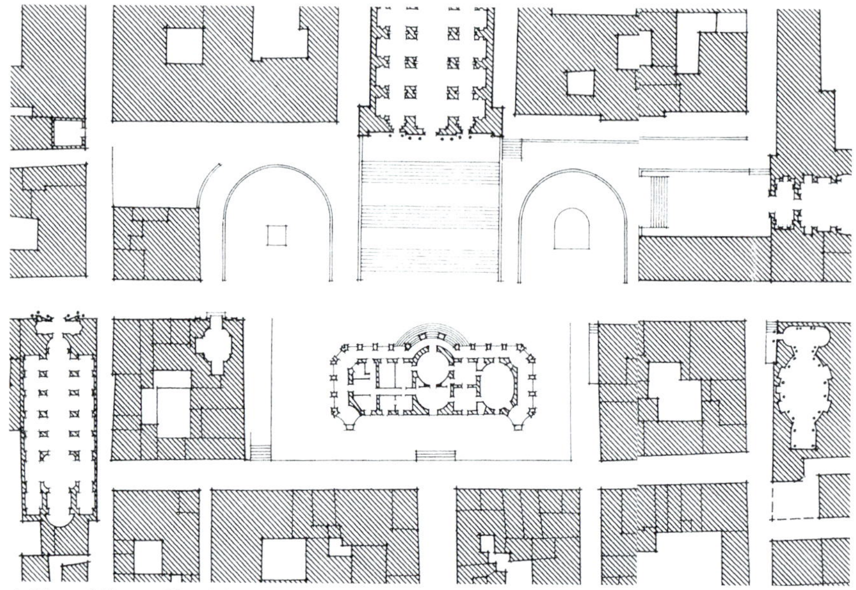

4. Plan of Piazza Municipio, 1:2,000

5. Convent of San Domenico

Squares

Noto's three main squares are linked into one unified, theatrical, Baroque composition along the town's main street, the Corso Vittorio Emmanuele.

6. View of Piazza Municipio looking west

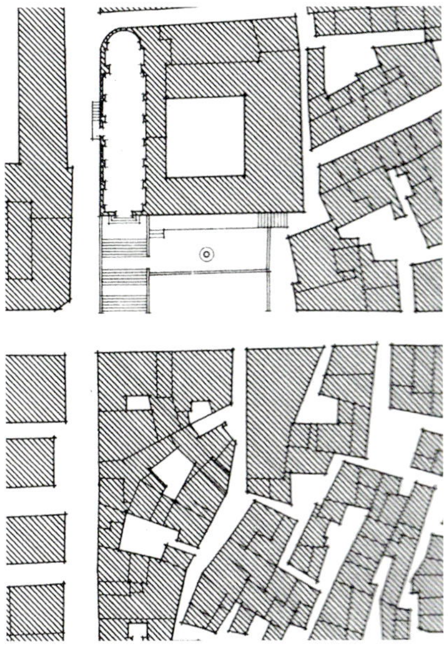

1. Plan of Piazza Immacolata, 1:2,000

2. Piazza Immacolata

3. San Francesco

4. Aerial view of the town

5. Corso Vittorio Emanuele

6. Porta Reale, entry gate to the Corso

7. Viale Marconi

8. View of landscape at end of the Corso

Aerial plan of Noto

1. Caltagirone

2. Ragusa Nuova and Ragusa Ibla

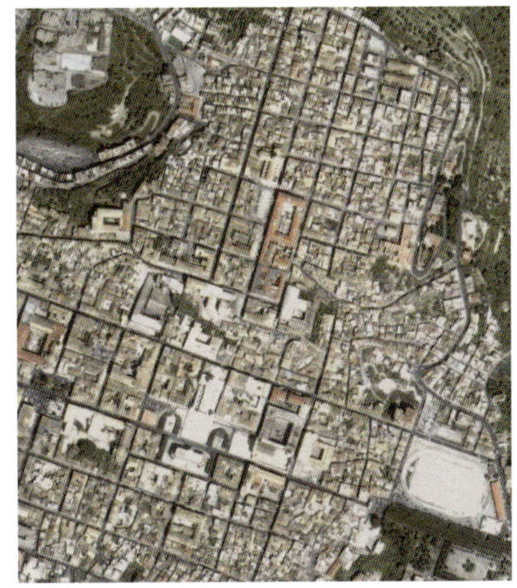

3. Noto

4. Avola

5. Grammichele

6. Ferla

7. Ispica

Earthquake Rebuilding in Sicily

In response to the earthquake of 1693 Sicilian towns had multiple, correlating, and differing urban responses, creating both new cities and interventions into the old fabric. Similarly, across the whole of Europe the same issues and responses were expressed in dealing with the dilemmas caused by natural disasters. Most famous of all these responses is the rebuilding of the core of Lisbon, which was completely destroyed by the 1755 earthquake.

The multiple schemes carried out in Sicily at the same time provide the greatest insight into what city planners, politicians, rulers, clergy, and surveyors were thinking in terms of solutions for "new cities." Within these solutions we see the creation of new Baroque and Renaissance cities on new sites. There was also a desire to merge medieval urban structures with then-current urban planning practices, as in the case of Ragusa.

On the far end of the spectrum is the case of Caltagirone, where the medieval fabric was retained but given a Baroque face lift. The buildings were updated and the major access into the city center was widened to create a straight access in juxtaposition to the organic narrow streets of the previous structure. Only a handful of Sicilian cities were rebuilt on new sites: Noto, Avola, Grammichele, Ferla, Sortino, Ispica, Buscemi, and Ragusa.[7]

Pombaline Lisbon

For over two centuries central Lisbon had been a source and a center of the Age of Discovery, when on November 1, 1755, the core of the city was destroyed by a catastrophic earthquake and its subsequent tidal waves and fire. The devastation was almost total in the Baixa area between the hills.

The Prime Minister, the Marquis de Pombal, immediately decreed that no construction would take place until a plan was made and approved. The same year, the Royal Engineer, Manuel da Maia, made a complete survey of the destroyed area and compiled a list of important urban issues. He also submitted five proposals for the reconstruction of the city. These proposals ranged from reconstructing the city largely as it had been, to a completely new plan, which was approved.[8]

The structure of the new town plan consisted of a large regular square on the waterfront measuring 550' x 640', the Praca do Comercio, connected to two squares up the slope, the Praca do Rossio and the Praca da Figueria, by a regular grid of rectangular blocks about 88' x 230'. Each block accommodated twelve four-story buildings with commercial on the ground floor, plus a habitable mansard roof. The architecture is modest, reflecting the difficulty of the economy as well as taste. The edges of the new pattern adapted as necessary to the irregularities of the adjacent existing urban fabric. The composition is like an adaptation of Héré's famous sequence in Nancy, published in 1752.

1. Plan of Lisbon before the earthquake

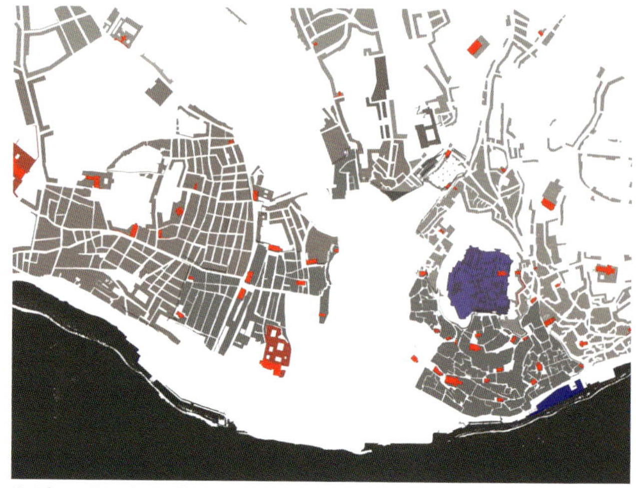

2. Plan of Lisbon showing destruction

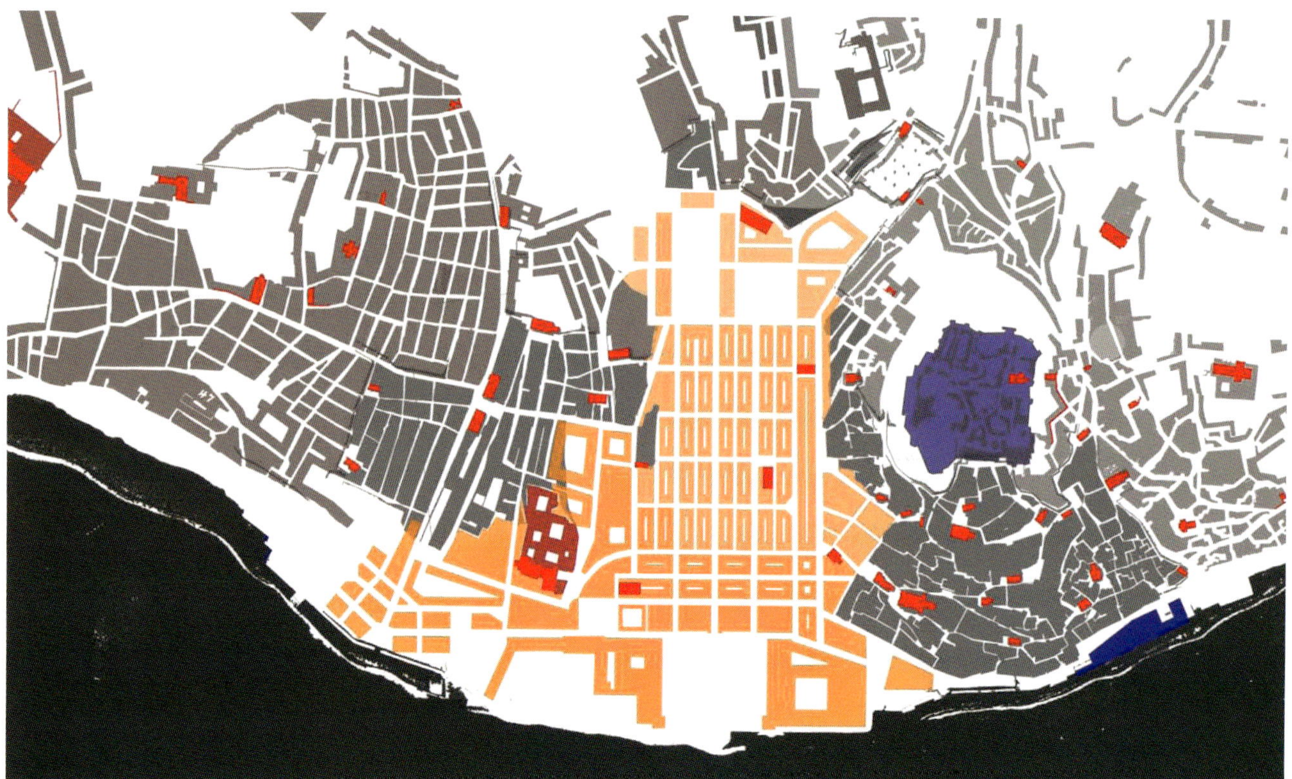

3. Plan of Lisbon with approved rebuilding plan

1. Urban plan of streets and blocks

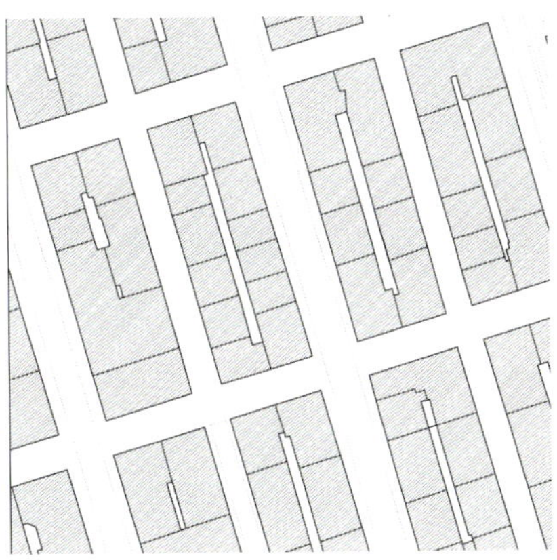

2. Urban plan of parcels

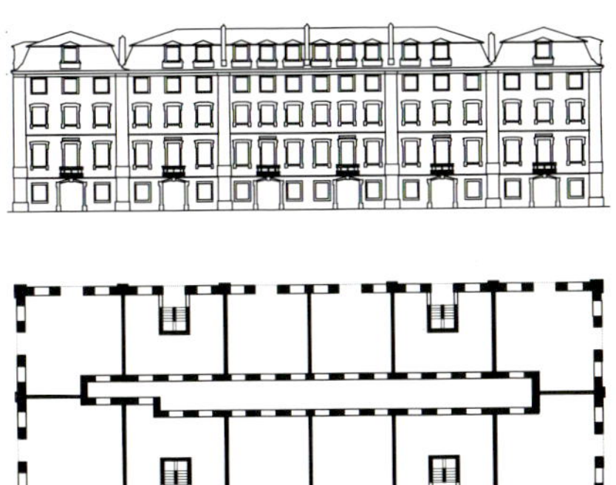

3. Typical block plan and elevation

4. Aerial view of rebuilt Lisbon

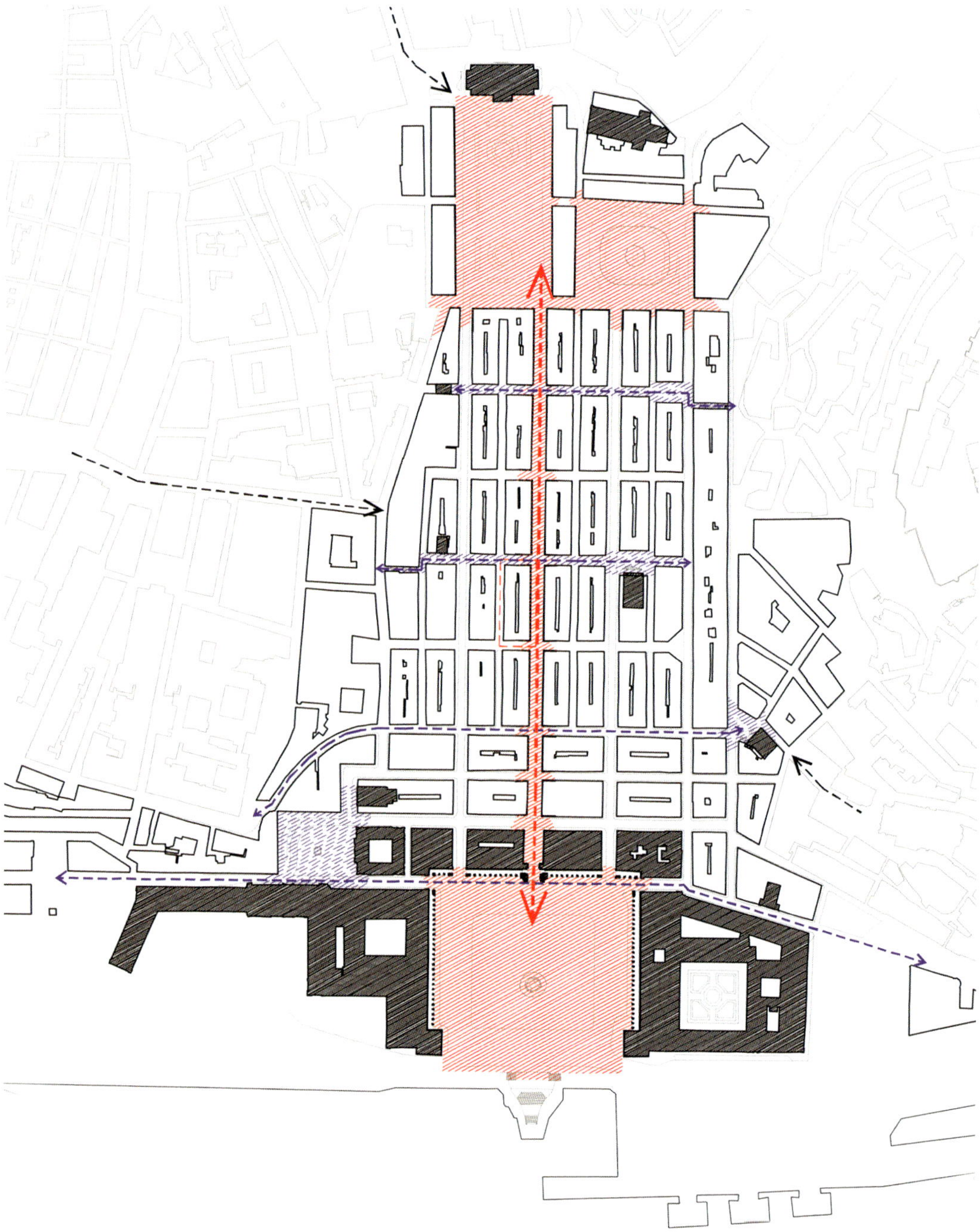

1. Civic structure diagram

2. Aerial view of the Praca do Rossio

3. Praca da Figueria

4. Praca do Comercio

Aerial plan of Lisbon

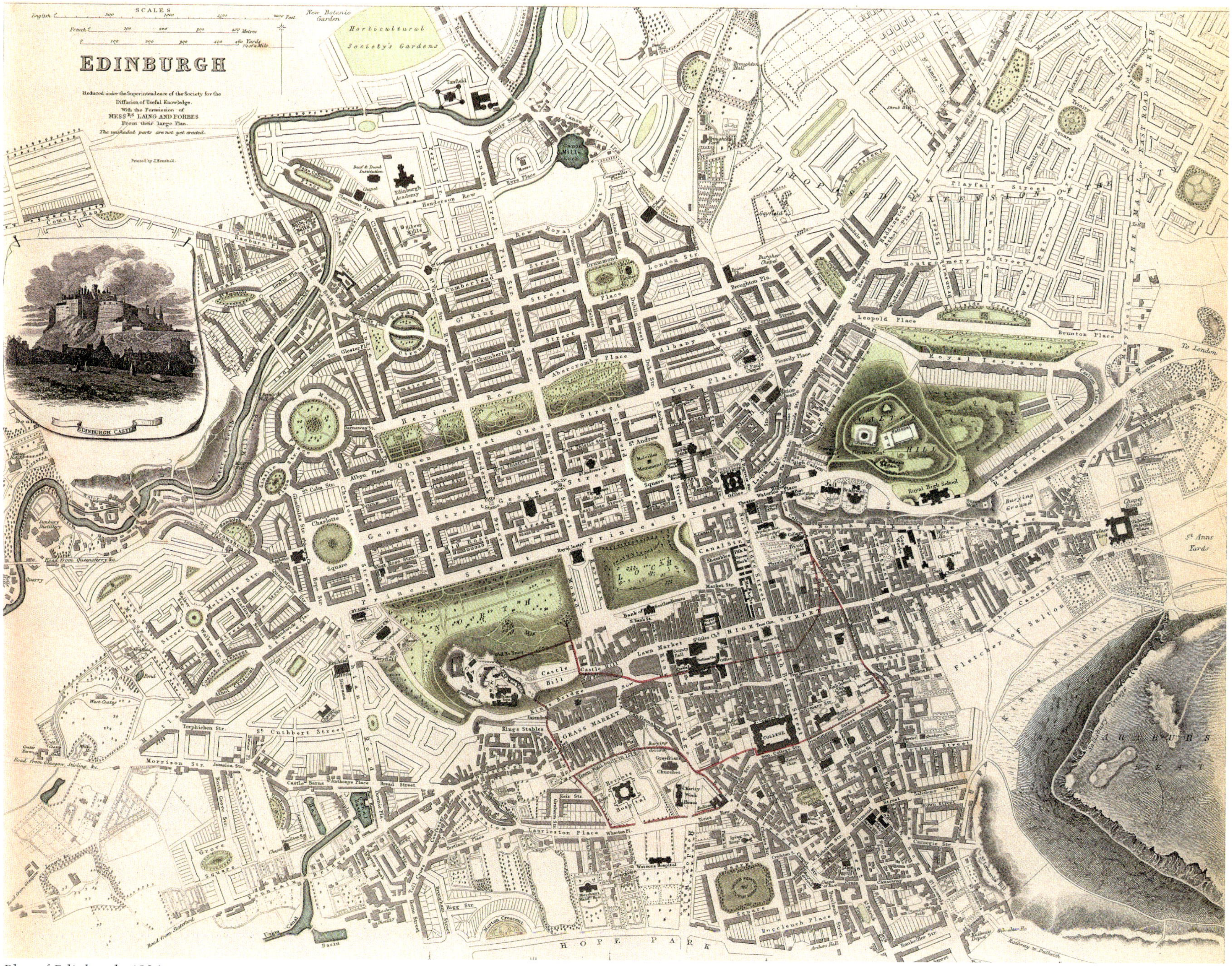

Plan of Edinburgh, 1834

Edinburgh

In 1767, James Craig won the competition for the plan of the expansion of the medieval town of Edinburgh, Scotland.[9]

Medieval Edinburgh was essentially a one-street town. Running along the crest of a hill, High Street connected the Palace, Holyrood House, on the east to Edinburgh Castle uphill on the west.

Compared to the sophistication of Bath, or London's squares and great estates, or Héré's refined sequence of squares at Nancy in 1752, Craig's plan would have been unremarkable were it not for two factors: topography and the form of the blocks.

1. High Street

2. Aerial view of Holyrood Palace

3. View of the old town

4. Plan of Edinburgh before the expansion

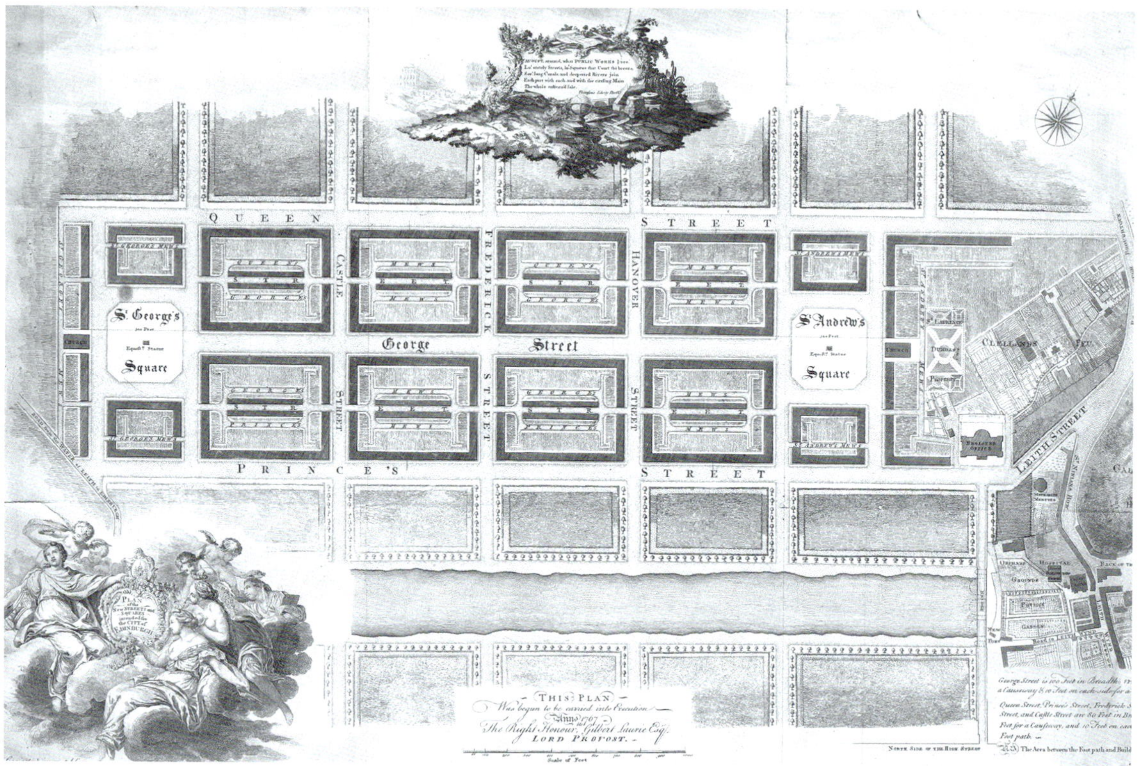

1. Proposed plan of Edinburgh New Town, James Craig, 1767, 1:10,000

Craig's New Town Plan

The new town was planned north of the old town, across the valley of the North Loch. The plan consisted of a central street, George Street, running through four large blocks, and connecting two large squares, St. Andrew's Square to the east and George's Square, later Charlotte Square, to the west. This pattern was bounded by Queen Street on the north and Princes Street on the south, overlooking the valley.

Blocks

The blocks are large, 450' x 570', but they are divided in the long direction by a narrow lane, and then by a unique double mews, thus providing for a great variety of development patterns. There were no parcel divisions; each client could buy whatever frontage he wished. In the main streets the height was limited to three stories and 48', and the intermediate streets or lanes were limited to two stories in height.

Streets

The main streets are 110' wide; the cross streets are 80' wide.

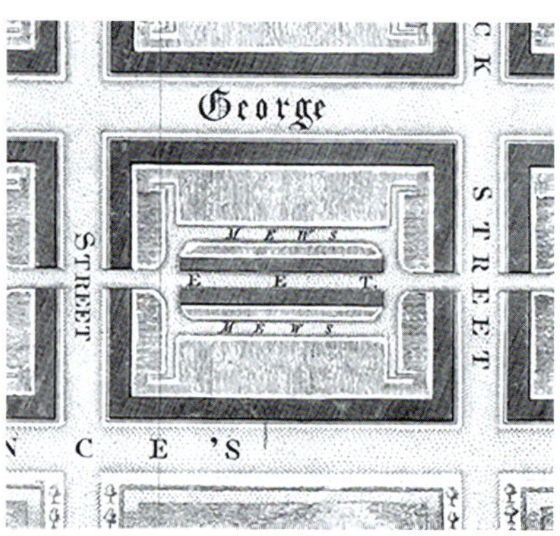

2. Plan of a typical block, 1:5,000

3. Aerial plan of a typical block, 1:5,000

4. Aerial view of a typical block

5. George Street, mid-nineteenth-century engraving

1. Aerial view of Edinburgh New Town with St. Andrew's Square in the foreground

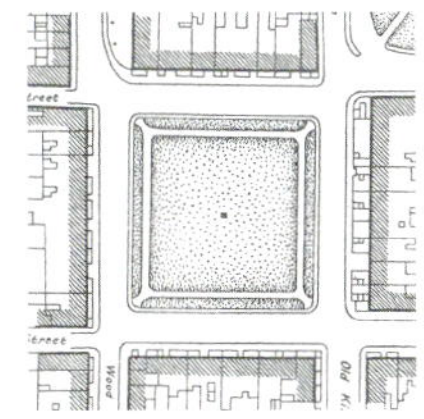

3. Queen's Square, Bath,1:5,000

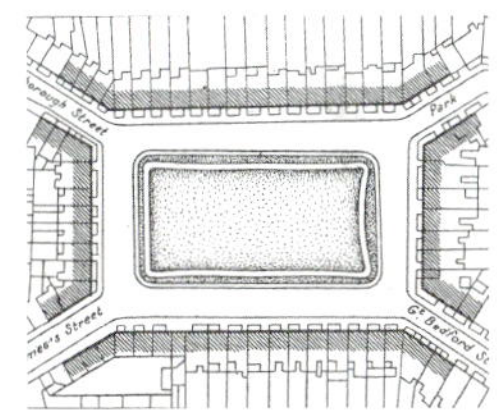

4. St. James Square, Bath,1:5,000

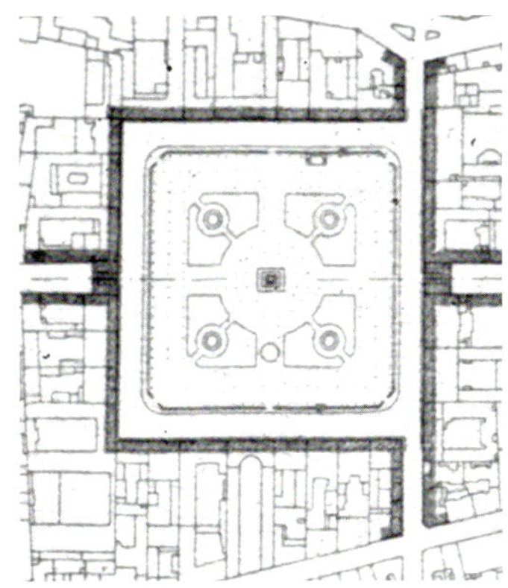

5. Place des Vosges, Paris, 1:5,000

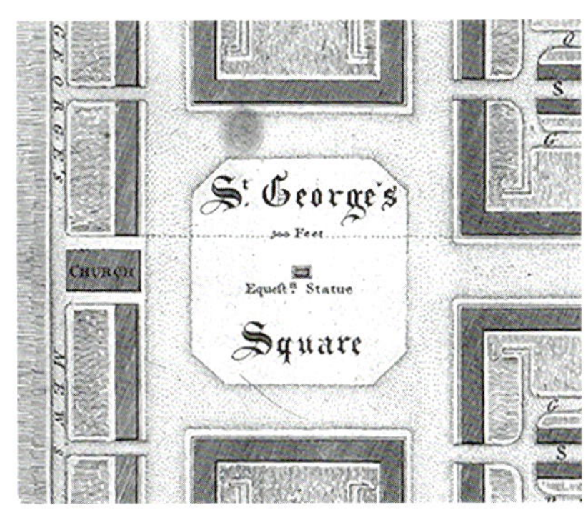

6. Charlotte Square, 1:5,000

Squares

The two squares of Craig's new town, Charlotte Square and St. Andrew's Square, are very large: each is 500' square. In comparison, Queen's Square in Bath is approximately 325' square. Even the Place des Vosges in Paris is smaller. Thus, from the beginning Craig's squares were more like urban parks than plazas.

Build-out of the new town began at the east end and proceeded west, Charlotte Square being the last increment. The houses around St. Andrew's Square and along George Street were simple, repetitive, and a bit bland—so much so that by the time Charlotte Square was about to be developed, Robert Adam was commissioned to design the facades around the square as unified palace fronts, similar to what he had done in Bath. Only the north side was built as he designed it, but the architectural and urban character of the two squares is still remarkably different.

The buildings defining Charlotte Square are more unified than those of St. Andrew's Square. The landscape is also different. The center of St. Andrew's Square is mostly lawn and open to the public, but the landscape center of Charlotte Square is dense and still private, open only to surrounding residents.

2. Robert Adam design for Charlotte Square (north)

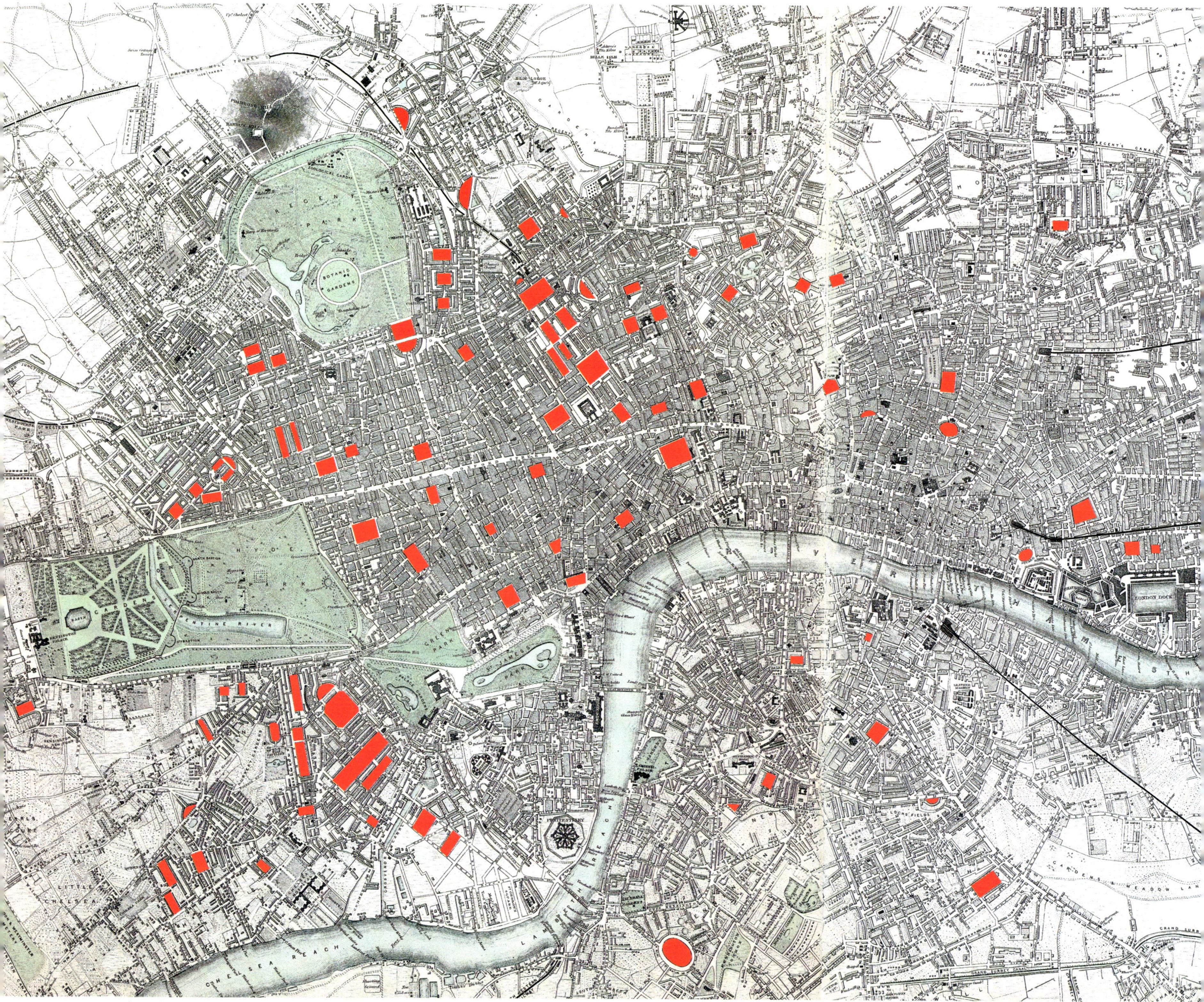

Map of London in 1840 showing the residential squares of the Great London Estates

Great London Estates: 1750–1850

For over two centuries a town planning tradition evolved in London through the development of the estates of the aristocracy as mini new towns. The plans for these estates consisted of a central urban square, a series of streets, and individual plots for private houses built by developers. Most often the row houses were uniform, even though they were sometimes built individually.

The prototype, Covent Garden, was laid out by Inigo Jones in 1631 for the Earl of Bedford, behind his house along the Strand, west of the City. Covent Garden was followed by Bloomsbury (1660–65), St. James (1660s), and Grosvenor (1723–30), among many others. This tradition continued unabated throughout the first half of the nineteenth century, with Belgrave (1825–35), Eaton, and Chester, all by Thomas Cubitt.

The planning of these estates provides an almost uninterrupted connection to mid-nineteenth-century European cities and the urban expansion plans of the second half of the nineteenth century.

Map of London, ca. 1550, Franz Hogenberg

Elizabethan London

Between 1550 and 1600 Italy had already experienced almost two centuries of the Renaissance, and was on the edge of the Baroque age. Italian Renaissance ideas had taken hold in France since the 1550s, but despite English advances in poetry, music, literature, and worldly exploration, Elizabethan London was a crowded warren of narrow, medieval streets and half-timber houses, with virtually no public open space.

Farmland surrounded the city, which consisted of the dense "City of London," connected to Westminster by princely houses along the Strand facing the Thames River. This rough civic and political diagram would form the backbone, or formal infrastructure, for the growth of London for the next 250 years, as the city expanded to the north and west.

Inigo Jones

The absorbtion of Italian Renaissance principles into France was slow and impure, but after Inigo Jones's trip to Italy in ca. 1601, Palladianism and the Italian Renaissance immediately began to transform English architecture and urbanism. Upon his return from Italy, Jones built the Queen's Banqueting House in 1619–22, and in 1631 designed Covent Garden, the beginning of the urban transformation of London.

1. Piazza Ducale, Vigevano, 1492–94

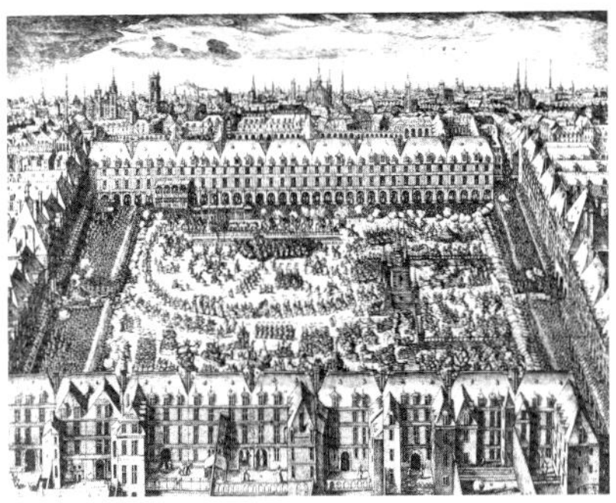

2. Place Royale, Paris, engraving, 1605–11

3. The Banqueting House, Inigo Jones, 1619–22

4. Elizabethan house, engraving, 1596

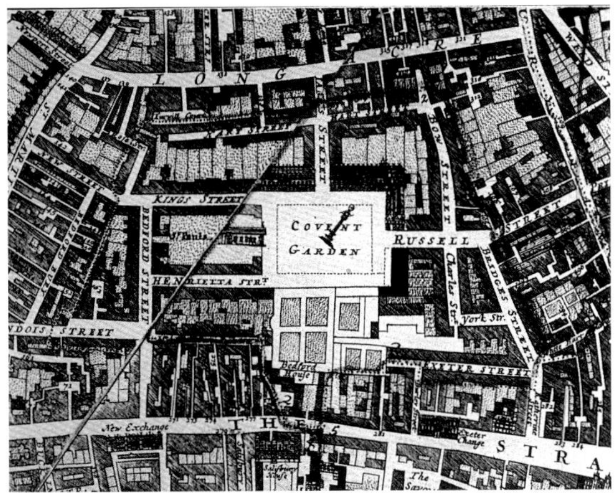

5. Plan of Covent Garden, Inigo Jones, 1631–37

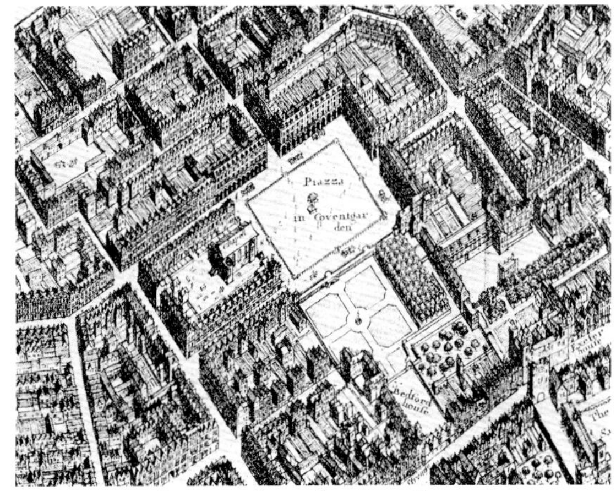

6. Covent Garden, aerial view by W. Hollar

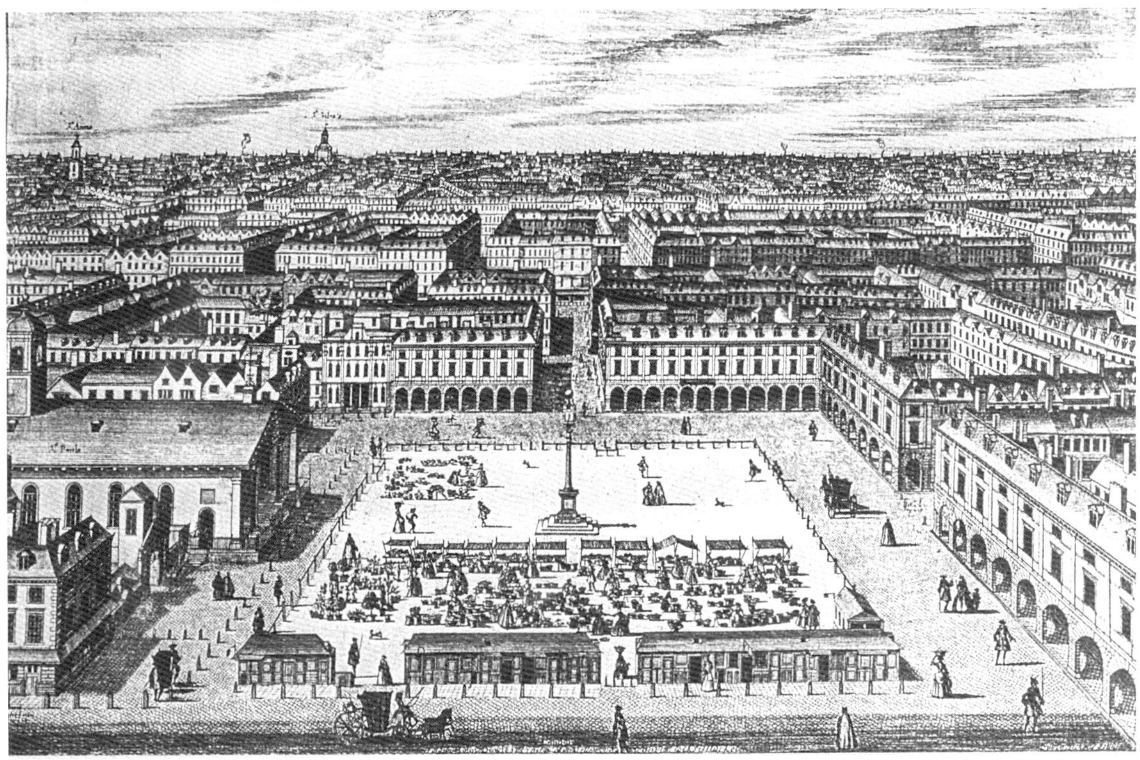

7. Covent Garden, engraving, 1631–37

Covent Garden

In addition to Palladianism, Inigo Jones also introduced Italian Renaissance urban space into England. Covent Garden was almost contemporary with the Place Royale in Paris. Modeled on Italian and French precedents, especially the church and piazza at Leghorn,[1] the square of Covent garden (316' x 420') was enclosed by uniform, arcaded residences on two sides, St. Paul's church on a third, and the garden of the earl's house on the fourth. The surrounding urban fabric consisted of row houses aligned on the gridded pattern of streets. As a venture for profit and public display—a city within the city—Covent Garden was the first London square, and the forerunner of scores of London estate developments. It was followed by Leicester Square in 1635, and Lincoln's Inn Fields in 1639–41.

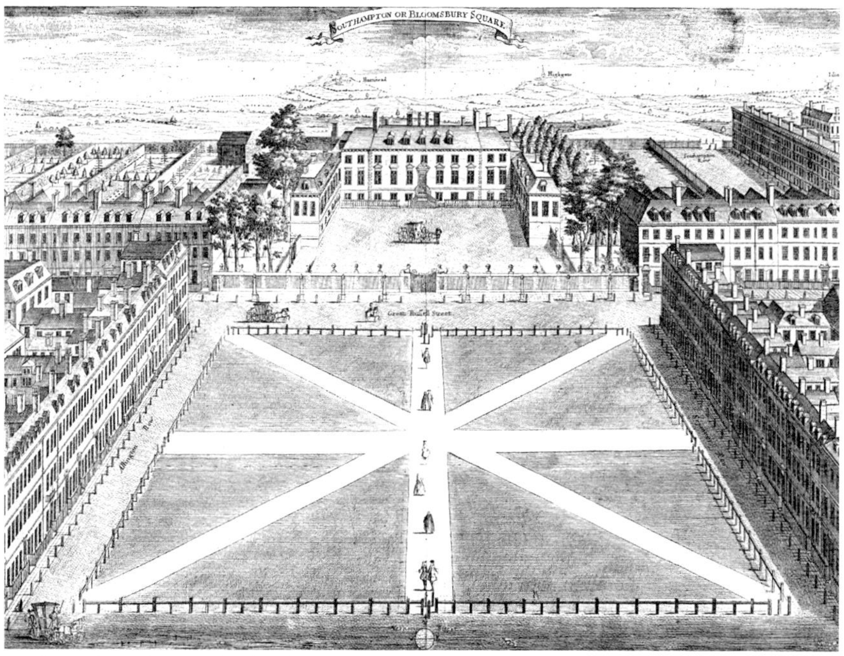

1. Bloomsbury Square, 1660–65, engraving

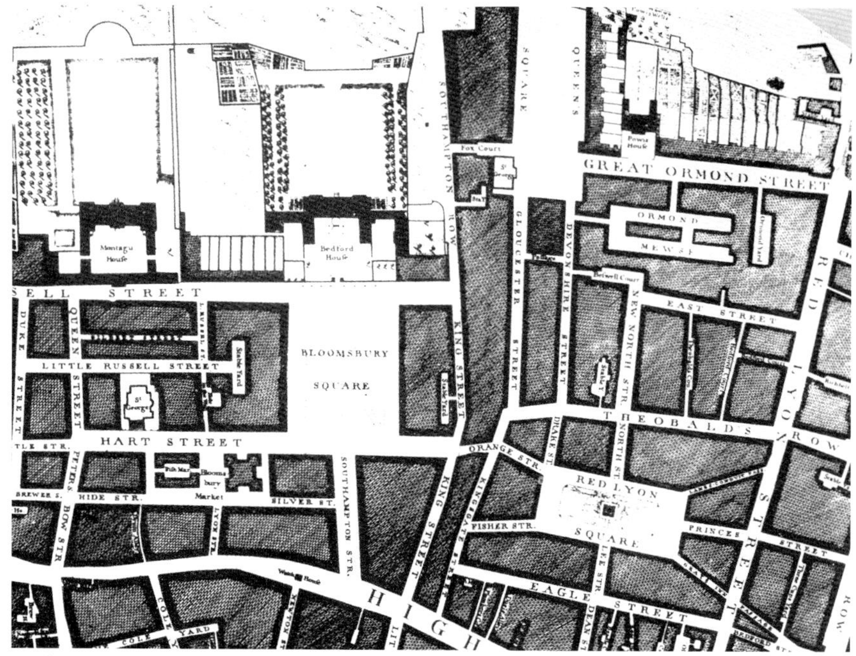

3. Bloomsbury Square, plan, 1660–65

2. Bloomsbury Square, 1660–65, engraving

The Commonwealth

During the revolution of 1642–49, and the period of the Commonwealth from 1649–60, London urban development ceased; but after the reinstatement of the aristocracy, the development of Bloomsbury in 1660–65 began a flood of estate development that continued largely unabated until the mid-nineteenth century.

Bloomsbury

The center of Bloomsbury, Bloomsbury Square, was developed by Thomas Wriothesley, fourth earl of Southampton, and became the model for all future estate development. The urban plan was based on plots twenty-four feet wide, which were leased to home builders on a long-term basis (ultimately 99 years), after which the buildings became the property of the land owner.[2]

This system was not only profitable in perpetuity, but it provided an elegant addition to London, and a neighborhood of friends and like-minded people for the earl. It also enabled development to proceed on a small-scale, incremental basis—often one house at a time.

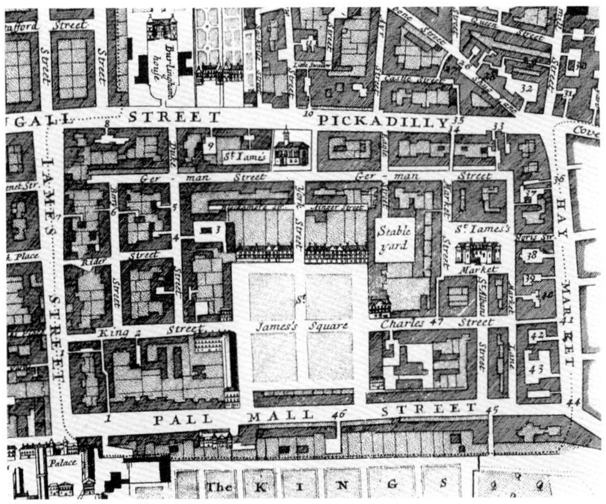

1. St. James Square, plan

2. St. James Square, 1670s, engraving

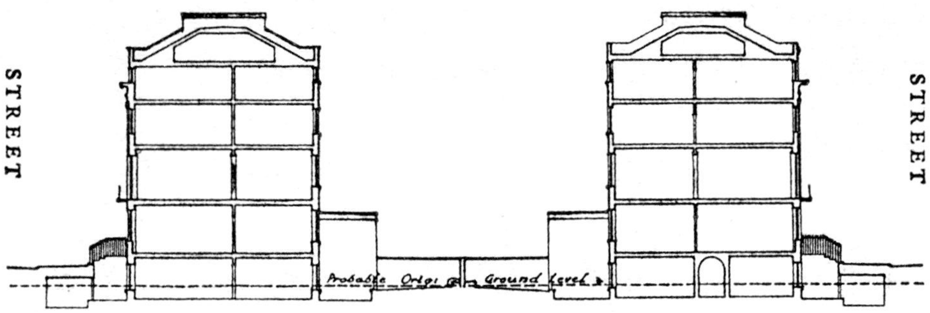

3. Typical block section in Bloomsbury

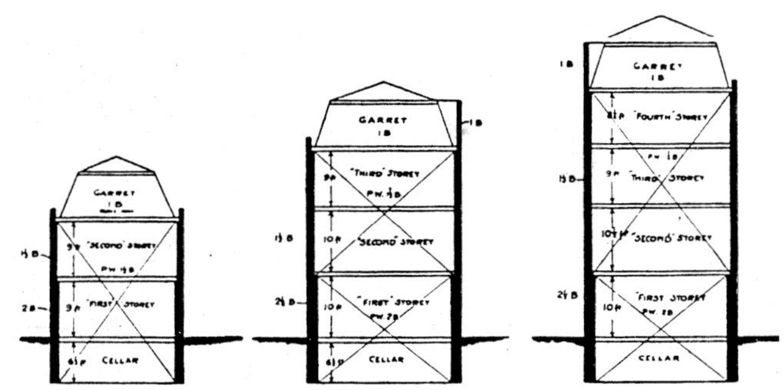

6. Building regulation of 1667 for houses in lanes, typical streets, and wide streets

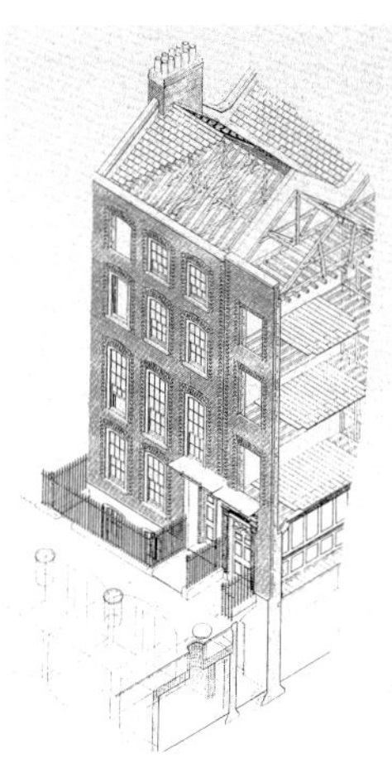

4. Typical Georgian row house

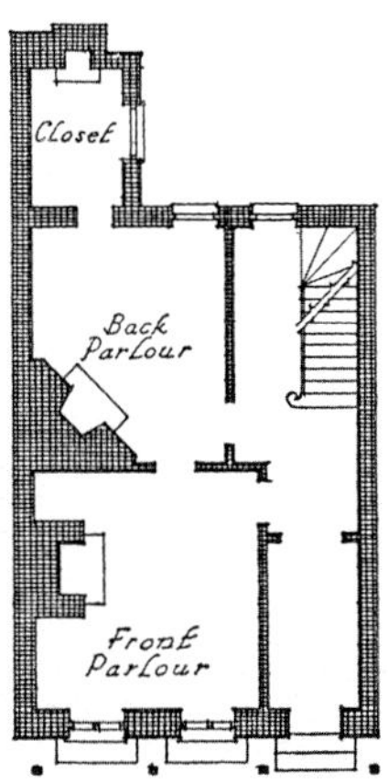

5. Typical plan of post-fire house

The London Row House

In contrast to Paris's aristocratic residential town house, the *hôtel particulier*, the London row house is inseparable from its urban context. Indeed, it is to urban ideas that the housing of Georgian London accedes.

The original ground plane was often manipulated—up on the street side, and down on the mews side—to give the main floor slightly more privacy from the street, and the basement a more direct relationship to the garden.

After the great fire of 1666 devastated most of the City of London, the building regulations of 1667 expanded the architecture-urban relationship by linking the height of building to the width of street.

St. James

The development of St. James was conceived by Henry Jermyn, first earl of St. Albans, before the great fire, but was built on a somewhat more modest basis during the westward rush after 1666.

Summerson points out that the estate as a planned town was based on three principles of development: (1) an aristocratic enclave, including the owner's house; (2) a complete town unit including a square, blocks, secondary streets, markets, churches, etc.; and (3) a speculative builder (or builders) as a middle man.[3]

The basic outlines of the system were in place—awaiting only master developers and architects.

Georgian London

George I ascended the throne in 1714 and George IV died in 1830. During this "Georgian" era there were three periods of prolific development of private estates: one after the Treaty of Utrecht in 1713, one after the Peace of Paris in 1763, and another from about 1800 until the Victorian era—almost mid-century.

Mayfair

Among the first developments after the 1713 Treaty were the large, West End estates of Hanover, Grosvenor, Cavendish-Harley, and Berkeley.

Hanover Square

Hanover Square and its surrounding neighborhood were developed by Richard Lumley, the first earl of Scarborough in 1717–19.[4] The square is 275' x 370' with closed corners. The horizontal streets and the central street are mostly orthogonal, but diagonal streets define the edges, thus producing modestly sized, irregular blocks.

Grosvenor Square

The Grosvenor estate consisted of large open fields at the beginning of the eighteenth century. The plan of the development, begun in about 1721, is the quintessential idea of estate-as-new-town: a large public space at the center, a grid of urban blocks, and an irregular perimeter connecting to the surrounding city. The square is about 500' x 700'. On the east side of the square the individual units were covered with a facade emphasizing the center and two end wings—perhaps the first of the neoclassical blocks as at Bath.

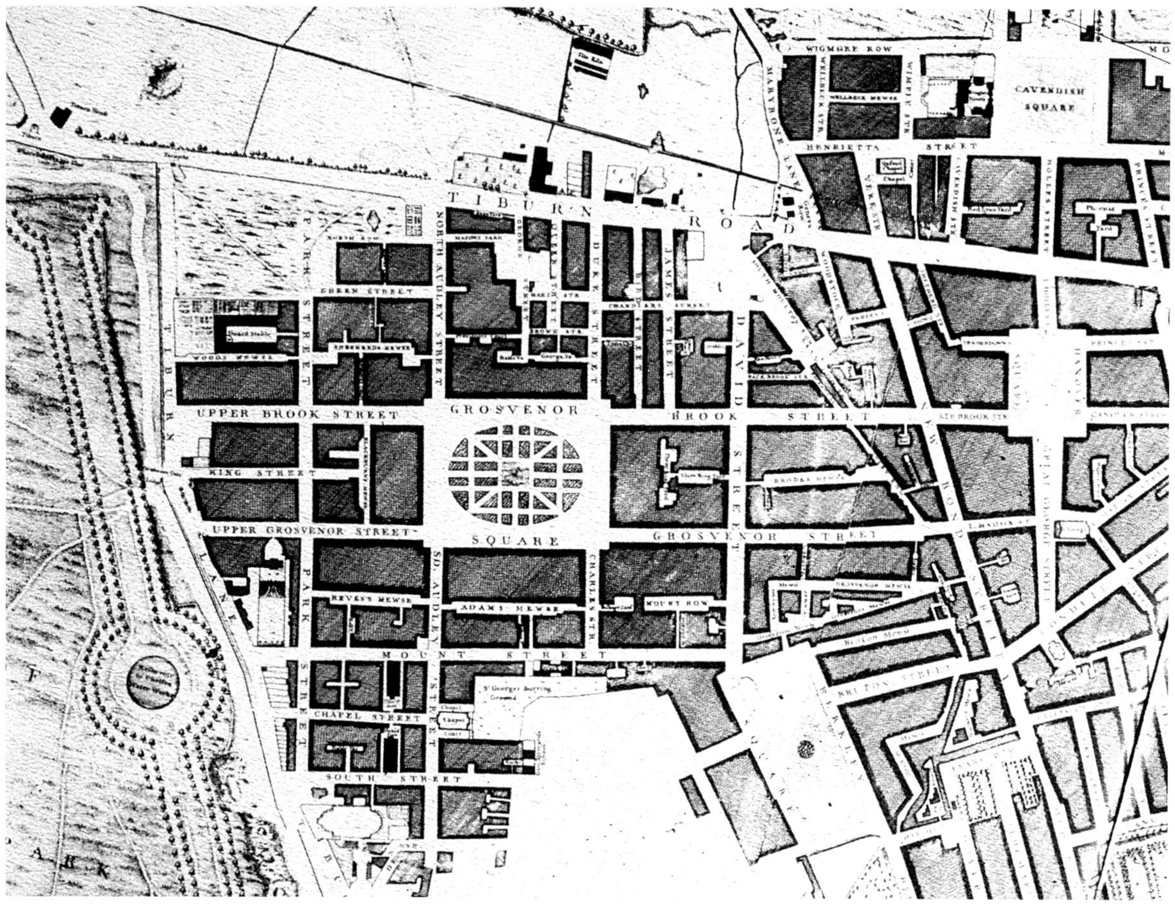

1. *Plan of Mayfair, detail from John Rocque's Plan of London, 1746*

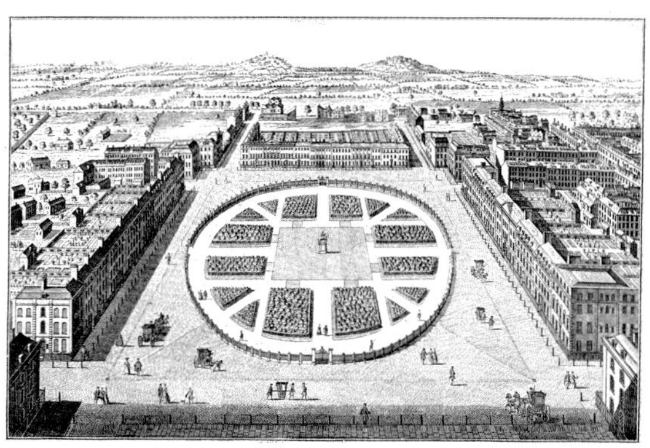

2. *Grosvenor Square, engraving*

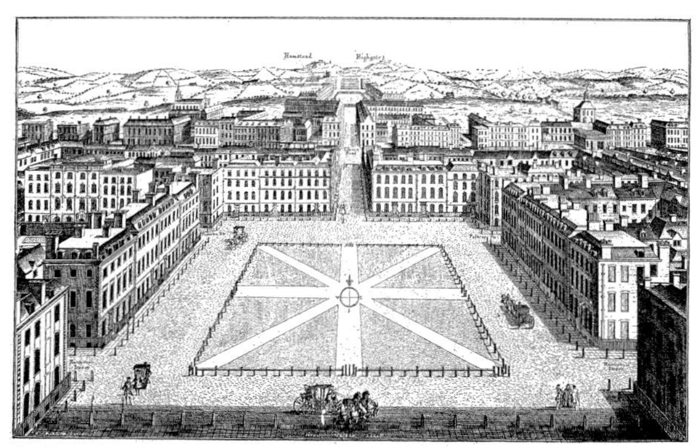

3. *Hanover Square, engraving*

Bedford Square

A unified residential square about 380' x 520', Bedford Square is the center of another Bedford estate development in Bloomsbury. Begun in 1775 amid one of Britain's international hostilities, the development was nevertheless built in one go and survives largely intact today.

The square is open at the corners, but is firmly defined by relentlessly repetitive, elegant facades, behind which the plans vary. It was the first fully unified square in London, and contributes to the extensive pattern of public squares in Bloomsbury.

1. Typical house, Bedford Square

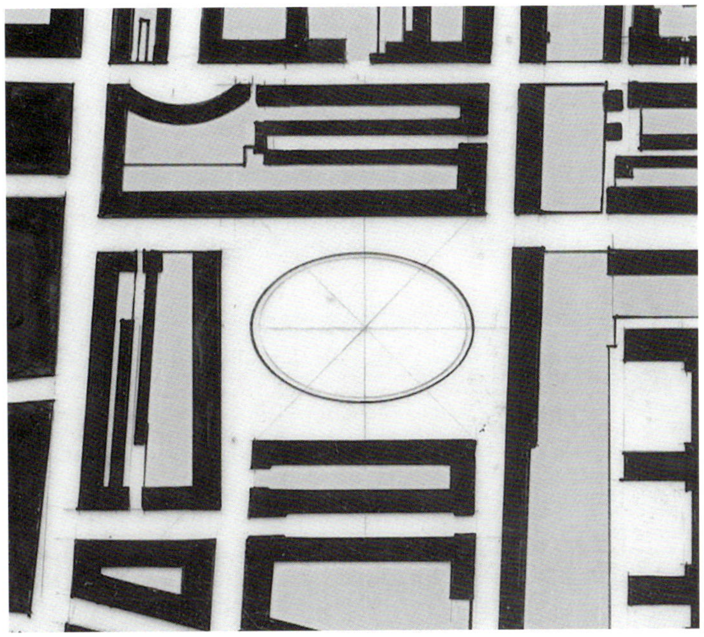

2. Bedford Square, plan

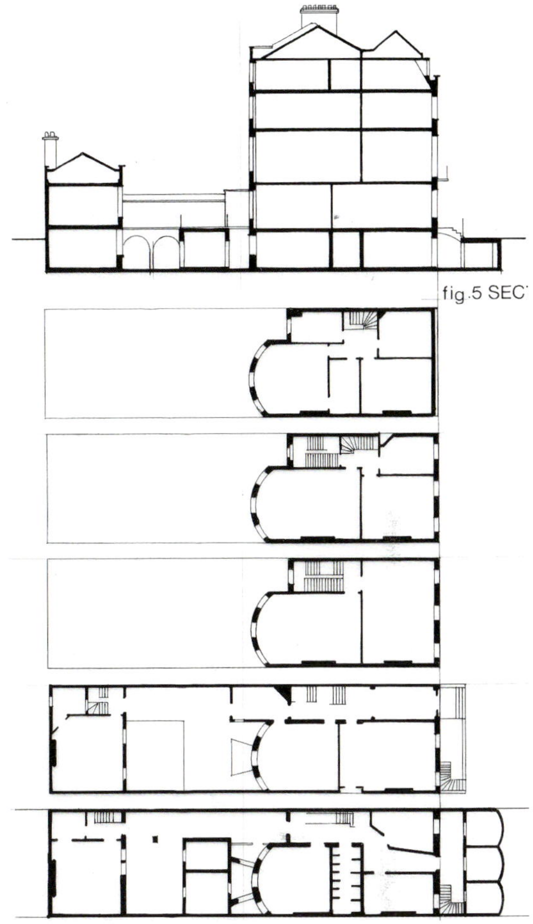

3. Typical house plans and section

4. Bedford Square terrace houses

5. Aerial view of Bedford Square

Knightsbridge and Belgravia

After the international disruption caused by the French Revolution, the period from ca. 1800 to 1835 and beyond was one of prolific urban development in London. The plan showing the residential squares in Knightsbridge and Belgravia gives an idea of the porosity of development. Squares, crescents, and long, park-like spaces provide an infinite variety of urban conditions, while the architecture is generally simple and repetitive—a continuation of the English tradition of subjugating architecture to the hegemony of the public realm, or the architectural idea to the civic idea. This must not have gone unnoticed by Napoleon III during his exile in London from 1846 to 1848. In both London and Paris, architecture—the apartment building and the row house—were subordinate parts to a more important whole, the city.

1. Aerial view of Eaton Square, 1825–35

3. Aerial plan of Knightsbridge and Belgravia illustrating residential squares

2. Aerial view of Trafalgar Square, 1820

4. Aerial view of Belgrave Square, 1825–35

5. Street off Belgrave Square

6. Pelham Crescent

Aerial plan of Belgravia, with Eaton and Chester Squares, Thomas Cubitt, 1825–40

II. THE INDUSTRIAL CITY: 1800–1975

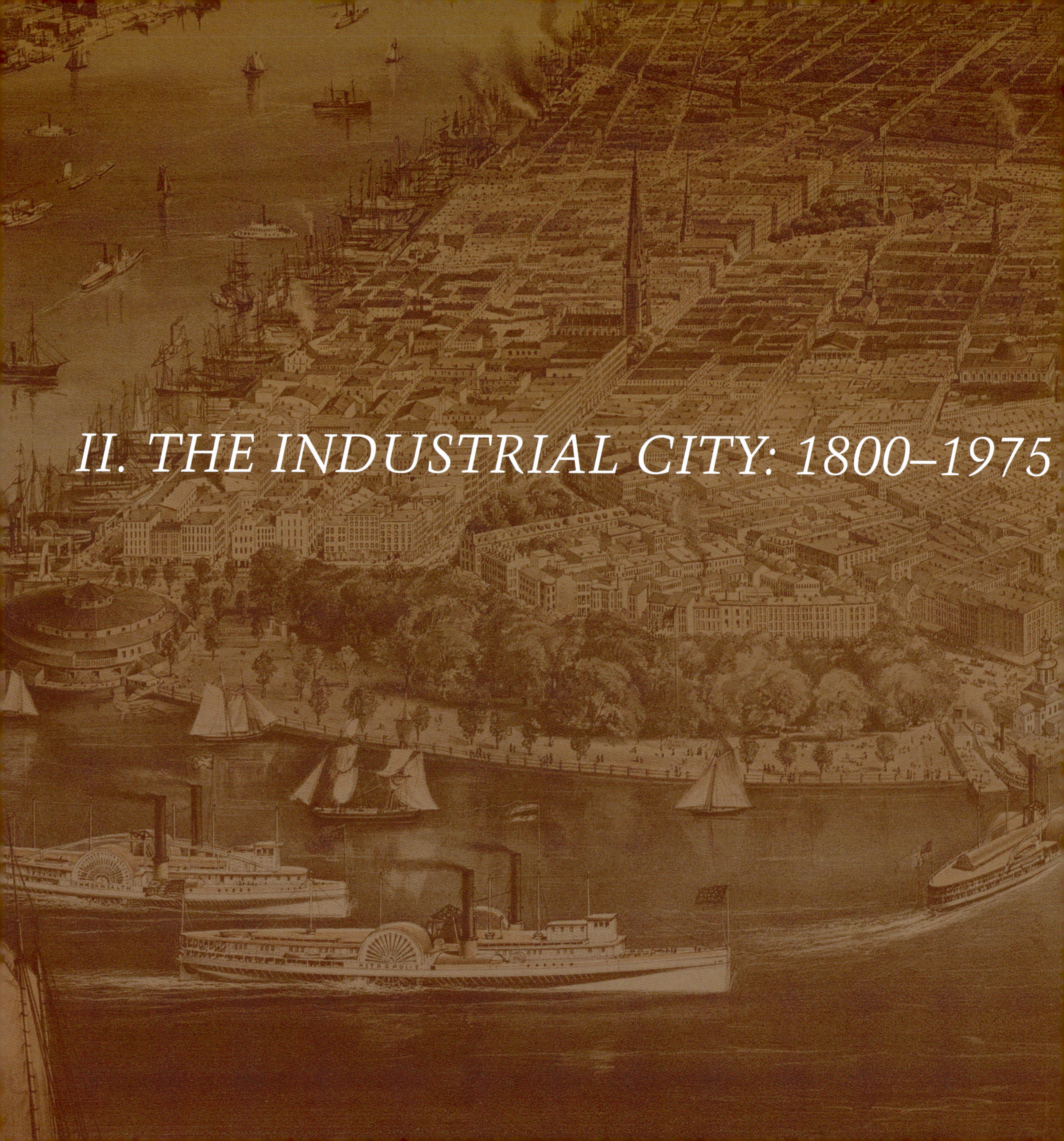

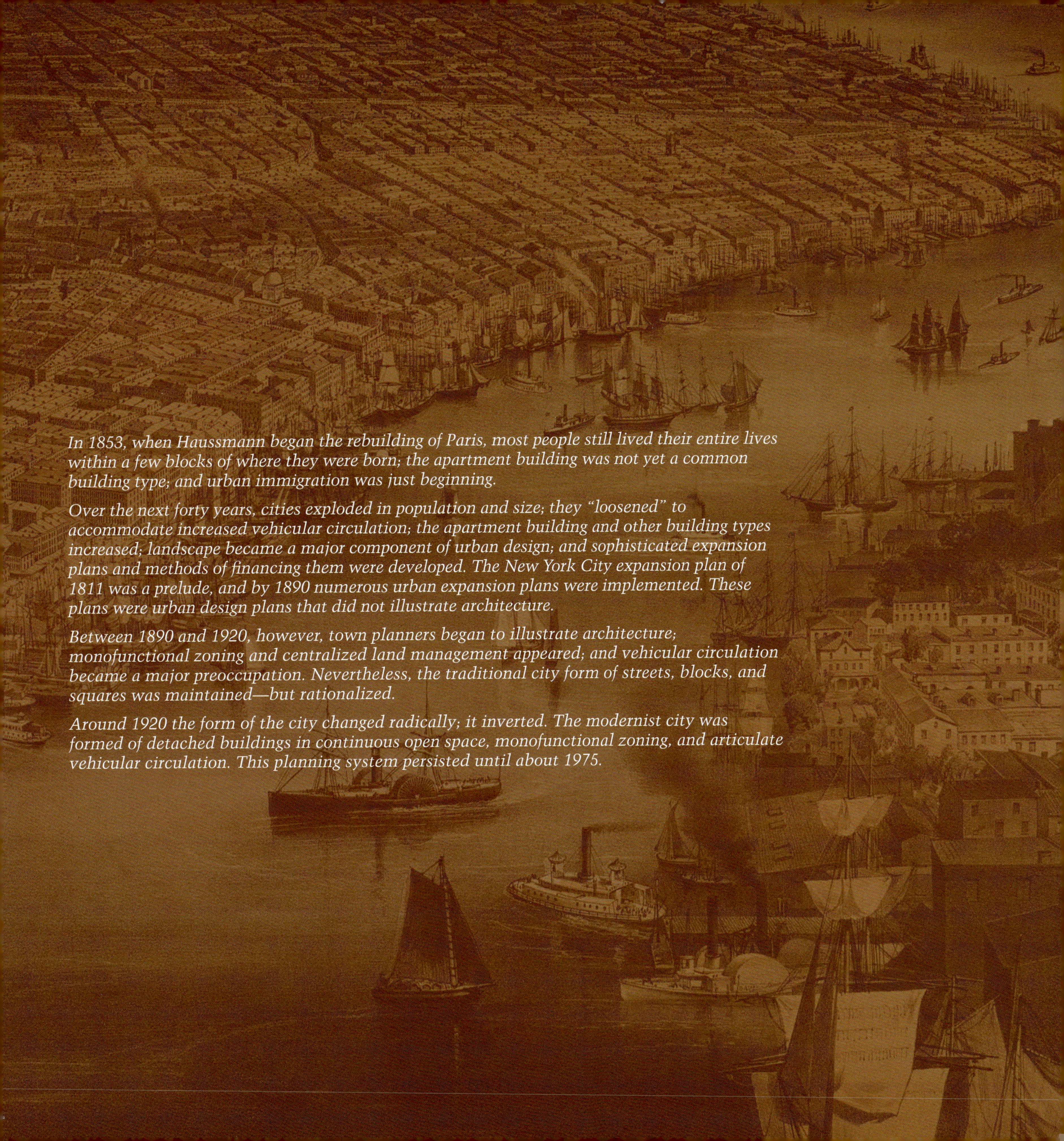

In 1853, when Haussmann began the rebuilding of Paris, most people still lived their entire lives within a few blocks of where they were born; the apartment building was not yet a common building type; and urban immigration was just beginning.

Over the next forty years, cities exploded in population and size; they "loosened" to accommodate increased vehicular circulation; the apartment building and other building types increased; landscape became a major component of urban design; and sophisticated expansion plans and methods of financing them were developed. The New York City expansion plan of 1811 was a prelude, and by 1890 numerous urban expansion plans were implemented. These plans were urban design plans that did not illustrate architecture.

Between 1890 and 1920, however, town planners began to illustrate architecture; monofunctional zoning and centralized land management appeared; and vehicular circulation became a major preoccupation. Nevertheless, the traditional city form of streets, blocks, and squares was maintained—but rationalized.

Around 1920 the form of the city changed radically; it inverted. The modernist city was formed of detached buildings in continuous open space, monofunctional zoning, and articulate vehicular circulation. This planning system persisted until about 1975.

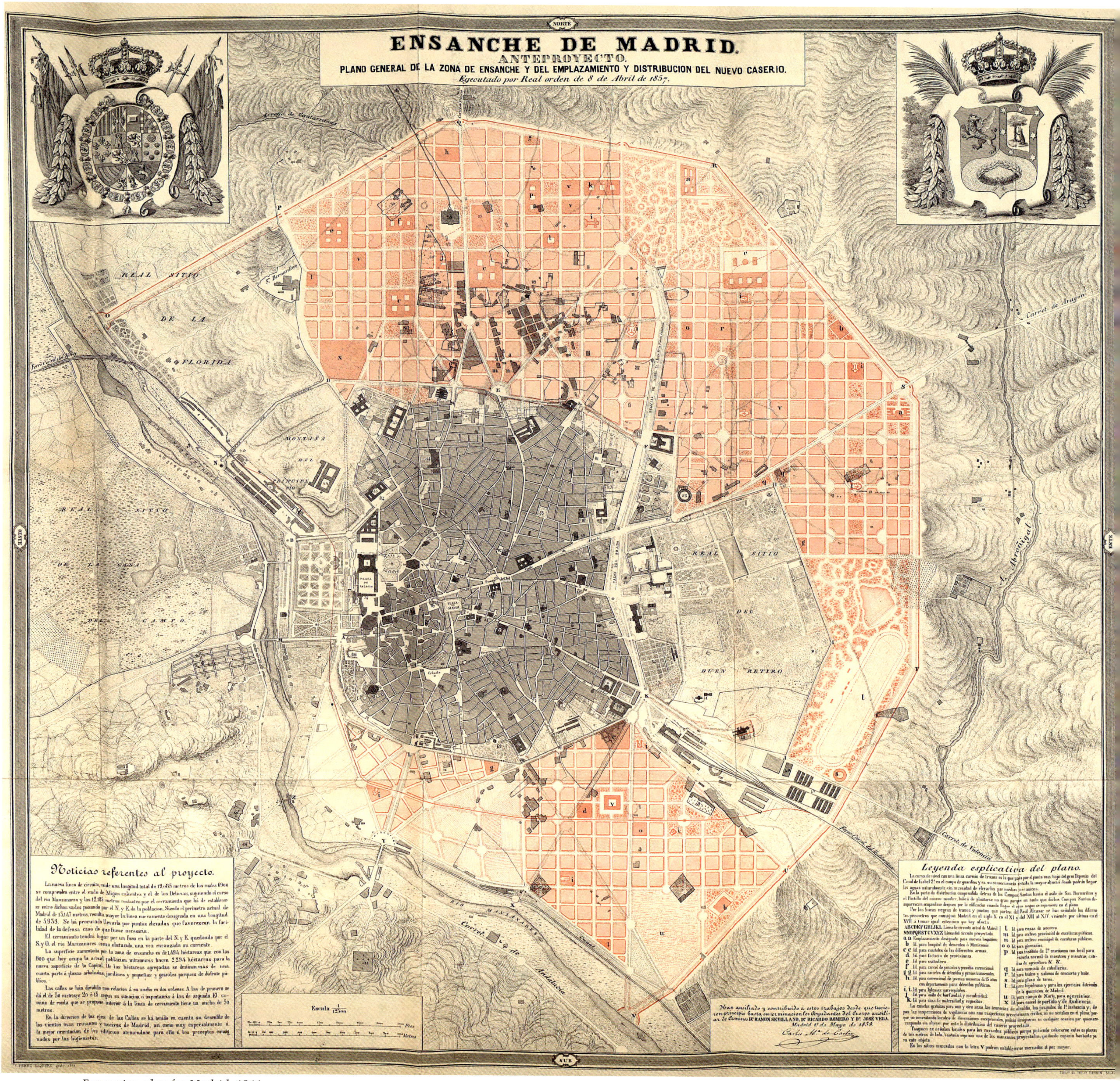

Expansion plan for Madrid, 1861

Nineteenth-Century Expansion: 1800–1890

The second half of the nineteenth century is almost unprecedented in the evolution of town planning. The explosion of urban population between 1850 and 1890 required rapid and extensive accommodation, and the urban plans developed in response to this growth were remarkable for their sophistication, their integration, and the relative speed with which they were produced. Although there were some planning precedents, such as the Great Estates in London, the expansion plans were wholly new plans to accommodate unprecedented problems of infrastructure and society. Indeed, these plans were the framework for a completely new kind of city, and the development of the designed street was fundamental.

In addition to the development of designed streets and the integration of infrastructure, one of the most important innovations was the introduction of landscape into the city. For the first time landscape entered the city as a major component of urban design. Tree-lined streets, planted squares, and urban parks extended and enriched the urban vocabulary both functionally and socially. Street trees helped articulate increased circulation of pedestrians and vehicles, and urban parks provided relief and recreation within expanded urban environments.

Some expansion plans, such as those for Barcelona and Madrid, were outside the historic cores; others, such as those for Florence and Paris, were largely internal expansions and renovations.

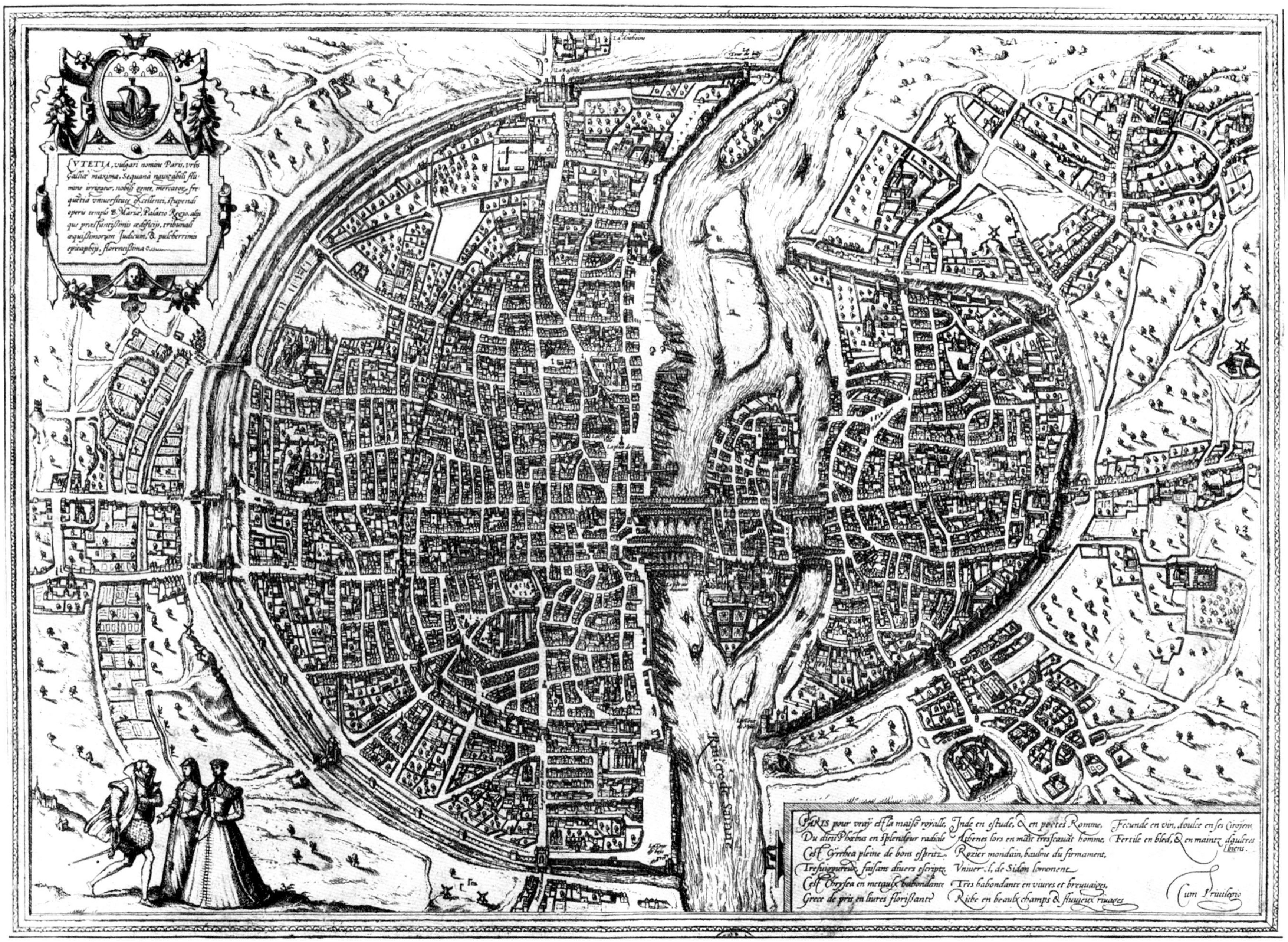

The Braun plan, called "Aux Trois Personnages," Paris ca. 1540

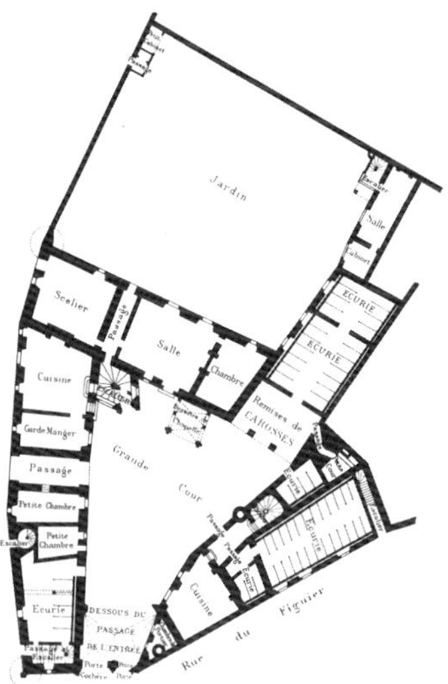

1. Hôtel de Sens, plan, 1475–1507

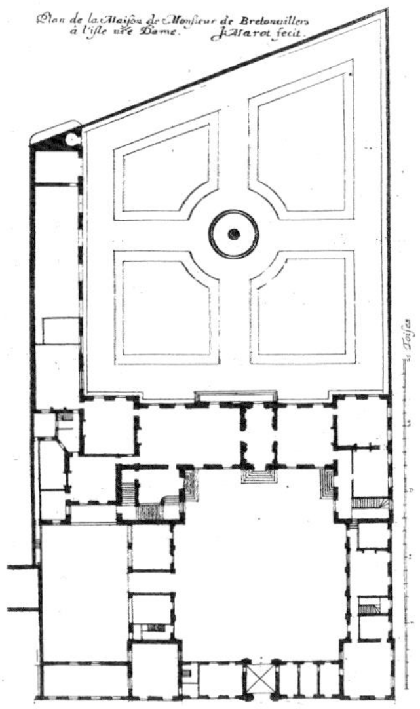

2. Hôtel de Bretonvilliers, Du Cerceau, b. 1635

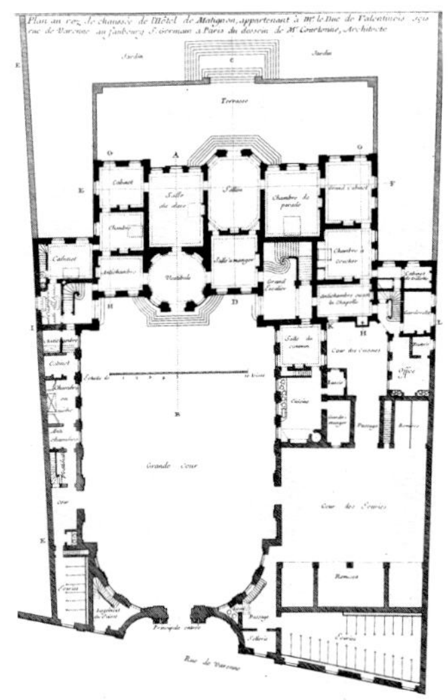

3. Hôtel de Matignon, Courtonne, 1722–24

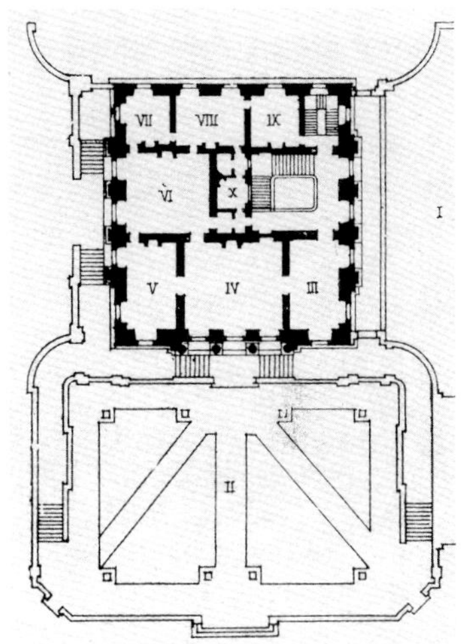

4. Petit Trianon, A.-J. Gabriel, b. 1762

Preindustrial Paris

The urban development of Paris may be seen as a continuous stream of change and evolution, or alternatively, as a series of important periods marked by significant shifts in thought and practice.

The transformations begun by Napoleon III and Georges Haussmann in the mid-nineteenth century are perhaps the most abrupt, but there were preceding milestones of consequence, if somewhat less noticeable.

The transformation of medieval Paris into the capital of a unified France was marked by two waves of Italian Renaissance ideas. The first followed the invasion of Italy in 1494 by Charles VIII. The second was due to the efforts of François I in the early 1500s. Serlio, Leonardo, Primaticcio, and others worked in France around mid-century when the prototypes for the hôtel, the Royal Square, and the architectural treatise were developed.

Renaissance Paris

Before the efforts of François I, France had been feudal with a nomadic court moving from chateau to chateau, and Paris had no conspicuous public spaces. The influx of Italian spatial ideas resulted in both urban townhouses and urban public spaces, and together, these began to establish Paris as the capitol and launched its development—especially under Henry IV at the beginning of the seventeenth century.

5. Place des Vosges, 1605–11

The French Hôtel

The evolution of the hôtel and the royal square illustrates a formal and social transformation that was the preface to bourgeois Paris of the nineteenth century.

The Baroque hôtel was an urban party-wall building organized around a courtyard that defined a garden and produced continuous urban fabric. The Rococo hôtel was a transitional type that articulated the main block between the court and garden, and produced less continuous urban fabric.

6. Place Vendôme, 1699–1722

The Neoclassical hôtel was the opposite of the Baroque hôtel, i.e., a freestanding individual building—ideally in a Romantic landscape. At the beginning of the nineteenth century, this was the preferred French residential model.[1]

There was also a similar transformation of public space from the spatial closure of the Place des Vosges and Place Vendôme to the openness of the Place de la Concorde. In 1752, Laugier railed against the "closure" of older squares.[2]

7. Place Louis XV, b. 1753, engraving by Le Rouge

Paris, "Plan des Artistes," 1793

1. Rue des Colonnes, 1793

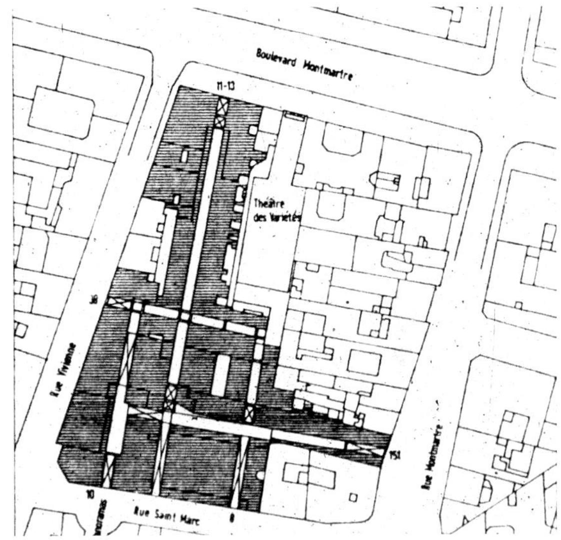

2. Passage des Panoramas and Passage Jouffroy

The Nineteenth-Century Street

If the seventeenth and eighteenth centuries were the centuries of the royal square, the nineteenth century was the century of the bourgeois street.

Five street types were developed: (1) the neoclassical street of detached urban villas, in the early part of the century; (2) the unified street, during the first decades after the French Revolution; (3) the arcade, or covered private street, during the first half of the century; (4) the boulevards, from 1853; and, (5) the mechanized street, during the last decades of the century.

The so-called Plan des Artistes of 1793 illustrates various projects for streets, some of which were actually carried out in the years following the revolution. The Rue des Colonnes was the first unified street in 1793 and the predecessor of the Rue de Rivoli. It still exists, although cut through.

3. Hôtel Dervieux, 1774

Between 1800 and 1830 several neoclassical streets of detached urban villas were built, but these were erased by subsequent urban development.

Countless covered arcades were also built during the first half of the nineteenth century, and they too served as models for the unified street.[3]

4. Galleries St. Hubert, Brussels, 1839

The Rue de Rivoli

Voltaire described the center of eighteenth-century Paris as "dark, hideous, closed in as in the age of the most frightful barbarism." Napoleon I also understood Paris's problems, remarking: "Paris is suffering from an aneurism of the heart." He was only able to accomplish the Arc de Triomphe, however, and his other major project, the Rue de Rivoli, by Percier and Fontaine, built 1806–35.

The contrast between the straight, unified, and repetitive form of the Rue de Rivoli, and the necessarily flexible idiosyncrasy of John Nash's Regent Street (designed in 1811, built 1814–25) could not be more exaggerated. Like the designs of Nash and George Dance, the urban plan, the bay elevation, and the section of the Rue de Rivoli were designed by Percier and Fontaine. The developer was responsible for the buildings behind.

1. Napoleon I with Percier and Fontaine

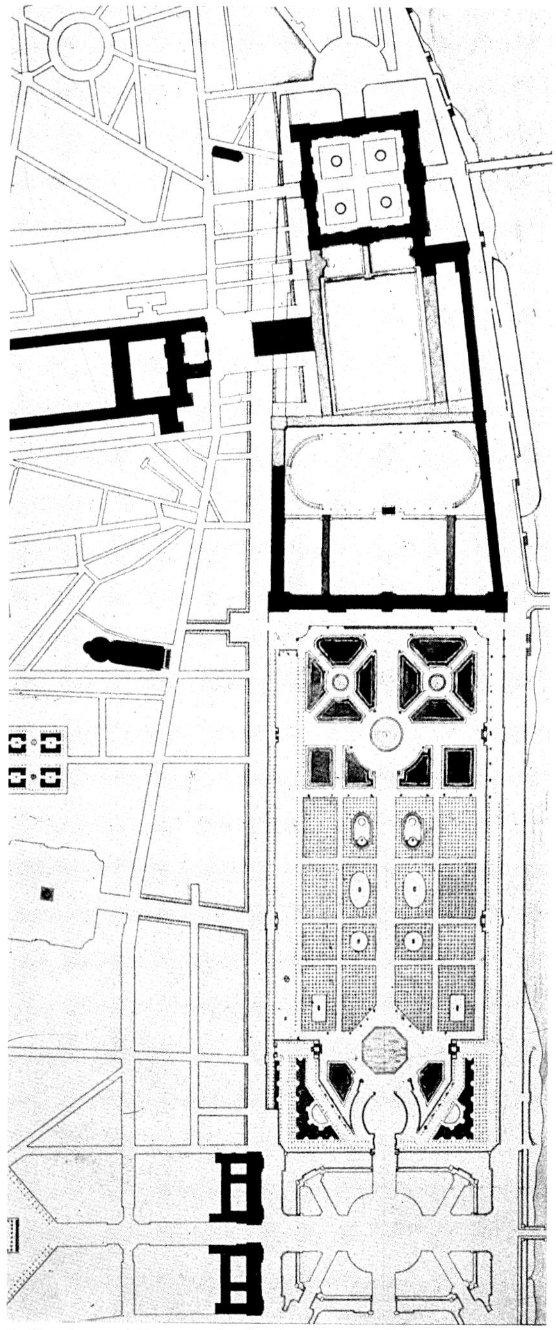

2. Percier and Fontaine's plan for the Rue de Rivoli, 1806–35

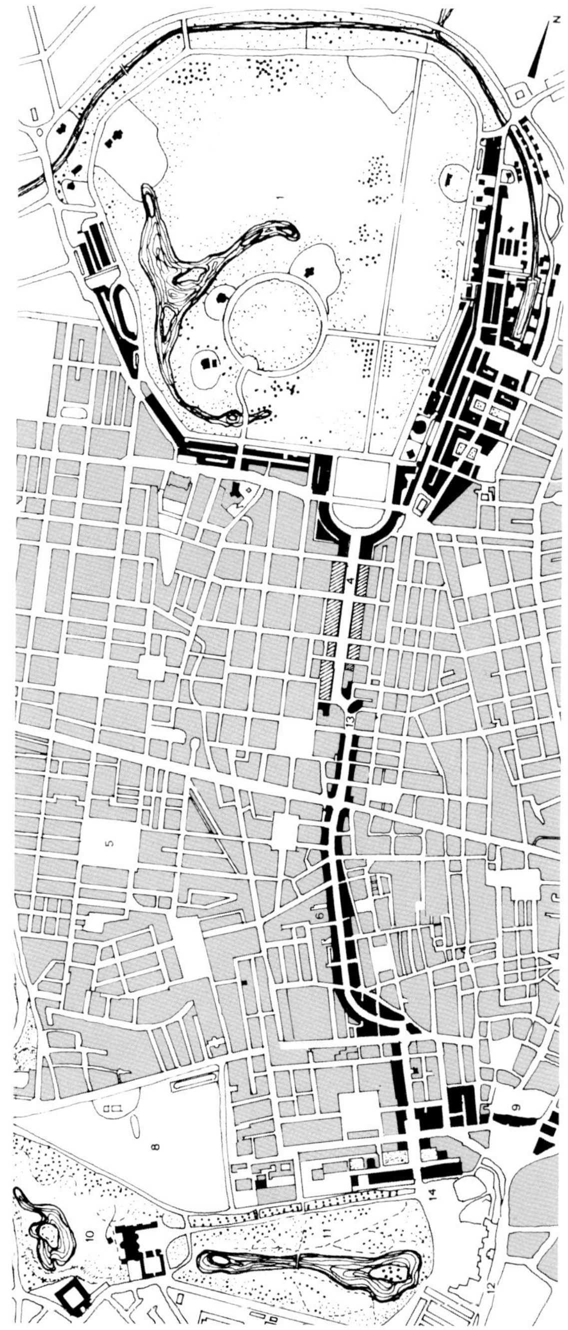

3. Regent Street, John Nash, designed 1811, built 1814–25

1. Panoramic view showing the Rue Vendôme and the Rue de Rivoli

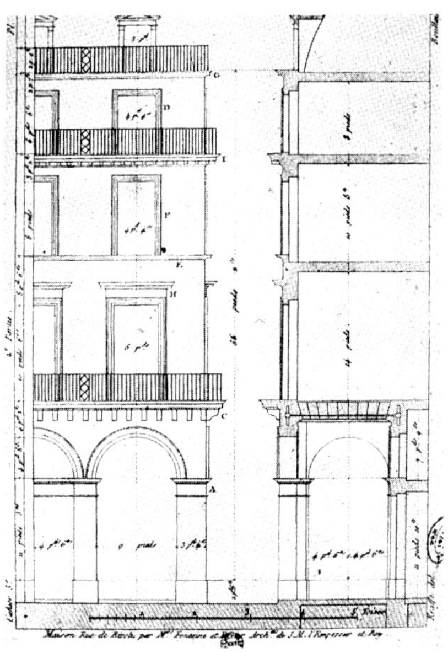

2. Bay elevation and section

3. Rue de Rivoli bays

4. View showing the corner of Rue de Rivoli and Rue Vendôme

1. Villa at Croissy

2. Hôtel design by Labrouste

Mid-Nineteenth-Century Paris

In 1850, Paris was on the cusp of revolutionary urban changes with far-reaching consequences. Three major new urban ideas would result from the collaboration of Napoleon III and Georges Haussmann in transforming Paris. First, a major city was (re) designed comprehensively, including streets, parks, sewers, and water supply. Second, landscape came into the city as an essential component of urban design. Third, a new system of finance was developed to accomplish the unprecedented transformation. All of this was in stark contrast to the state of the city in the first half of the century.[4]

3. A typical Parisian streeet in 1850

Paris before Haussmann

Prevailing theory and taste still preferred free-standing neoclassical houses as a model for urban living. This was promoted in Cesar Daly's *Revue générale de l'architecture*. Despite the example of the Rue de Rivoli and other street initiatives, little had been accomplished. At mid-century, most people lived their whole lives within a few blocks' radius of where they had been born. Haussmann himself lived on the right bank and went to the Sorbonne on the left bank. He later described his daily walk with disapproval—through squalor, stench, and tangled streets—in contrast to his education and preferences. In 1850, the need for a fundamental change was drastic. Paris's population was rapidly increasing in the face of industrialization. Houses were overcrowded, sanitation and street lighting were insufficient, and traffic flow was often stagnant. The public spaces lacked light and air and the density of the city had provided an attractive battleground for the 1848 Revolution. The new empire would be based on the poor and the *bourgeoisie*, whose culture needed a spatial matrix.

Napoleon III

Charles Louis Napoleon Bonaparte, nephew of Napoleon I, fancied himself as something of an architect and landscape architect. He had been in exile in one of the London estates between 1846 and 1848, and had started to work on a preliminary plan for a new network of thoroughfares for Paris. After returning to Paris in 1848, he was elected president of the Second Republic. In 1851 he precipitated a coup d'état, and in 1852 made himself emperor, as Napoleon III. In 1853 he appointed Georges Haussmann prefect of the Seine—effectively city planner, even mayor of Paris—and explained his plan and intentions for renovating the city.

Georges Haussmann

Haussmann was imposing and arrogant, but a consummate bureaucrat and technocrat. He was also honest and completely dedicated to the emperor and his charge. Haussmann quickly discovered that his predecessor, Berger, had routinely underestimated revenue and overestimated costs. Haussmann knew that the small revenues would not be enough to renovate Paris, but could attract loans, which could be paid off as work progressed. This, deficit financing, was the key to accomplishing the goals.

Planning Structure

Haussmann established three *bureaux* to direct the rebuilding of Paris. Eugéne Deschamps was chief planner, responsible for developing an accurate, detailed base plan, the Plan de Paris, on which the new streets were drawn. Eugéne Belgrand was the chief engineer, responsible for water and sewers. Adolphe Alphand was the chief landscape architect, responsible for the design of the boulevards and parks. Haussmann himself was in charge of finances. Together, between 1853 and 1872, they redesigned the water supply, sewers, boulevards, and parks of Paris. Alphand completed the work after 1872, and the debt was finally retired in 1929.[5]

1. Fighting in Rue St. Antoine during the Revolution of 1848

2. Perspective illustrating the sewer system of Paris before its transformation

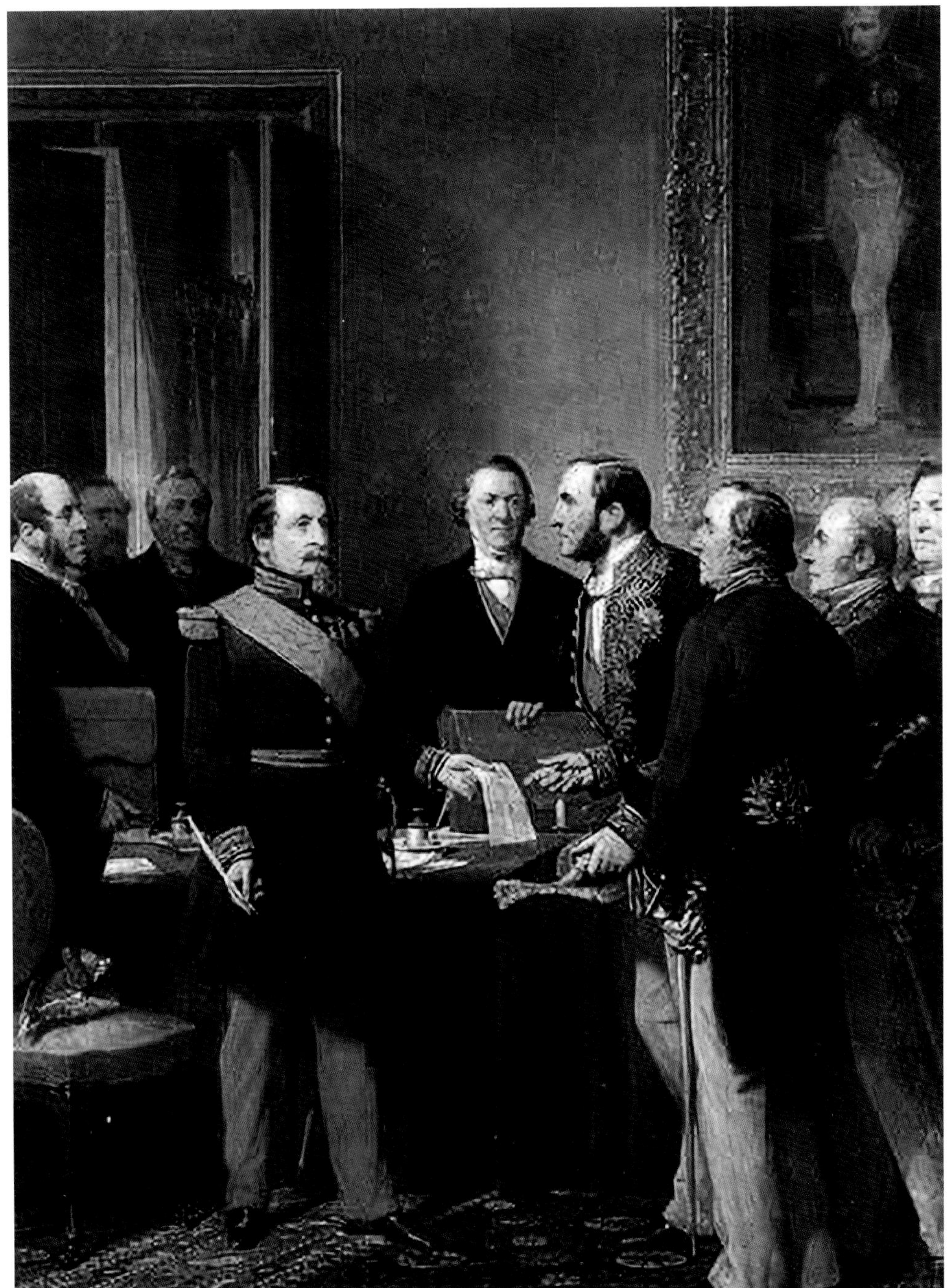

3. Napoleon III (l) and Haussmann (r) discussing plans for the transformation of Paris in 1859

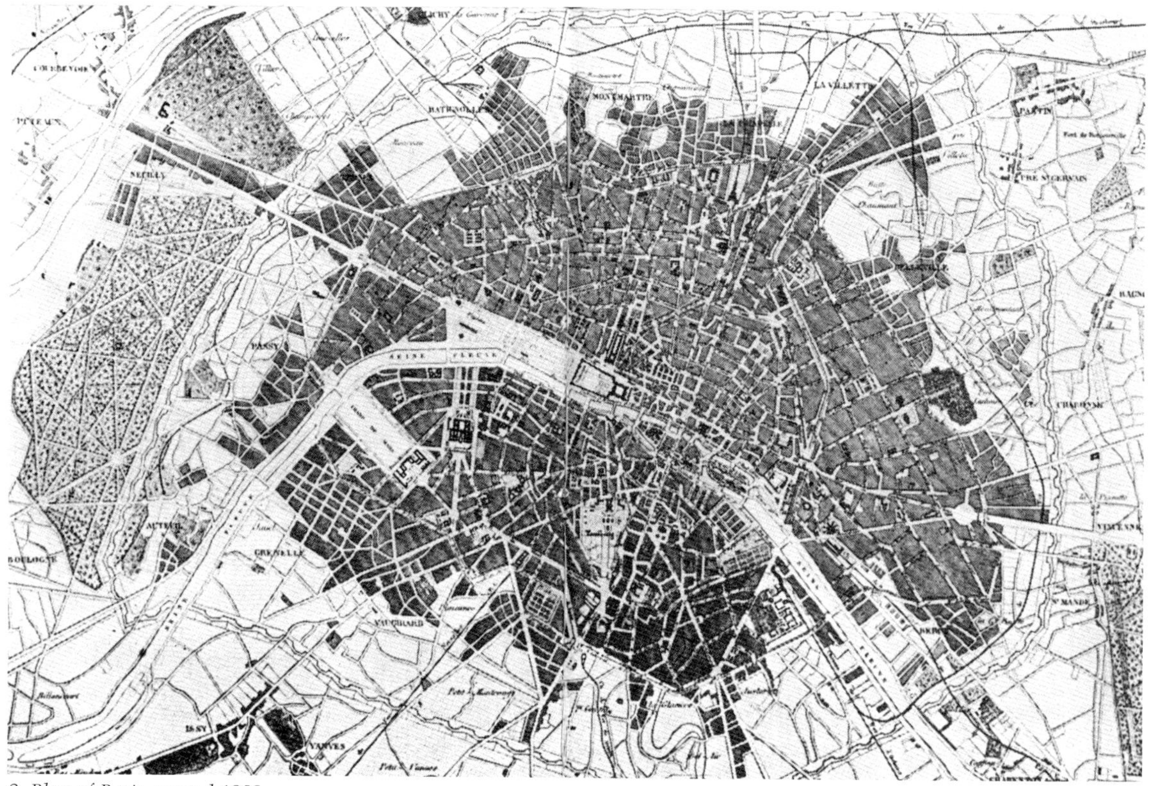

2. *Plan of Paris around 1850*

Transforming Paris

The transformations of Paris comprised an integrated system, including landscaped streets and boulevards, a comprehensive water and sewer network, train lines and stations, parks, and street lighting. For military, traffic, recreational, sanitary, and aesthetic purposes, Haussmann executed major thoroughfares, which were often cut directly through densely populated quarters of the city fabric.

The core of the street system was the cross-axis formed by the Boulevard Sebastopol forming a north–south line with the Boulevard St. Michel, and the extension of the Rue de Rivoli to the Rue Saint-Antoine, forming an east–west axis. A ring of boulevards was completed via the creation of the Boulevard Richard Lenoir and others. The network of boulevards was complemented by monuments, like the Opéra de Paris, which were often positioned at the end of vistas. The network was also complemented by a variety of parks, ranging from small squares to the conversion of urban forests, namely the Bois de Boulogne and the Bois de Vincennes.

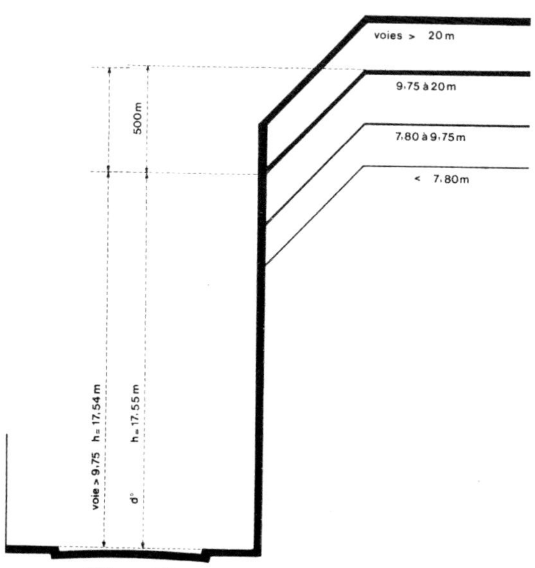

1. *Diagram showing revision of building height regulations in order to achieve more monumental facades*

3. *The Boulevard St. Germain showing apartment buildings, traffic separation, street trees, and sewer system. Houses of "old Paris" are on the left*

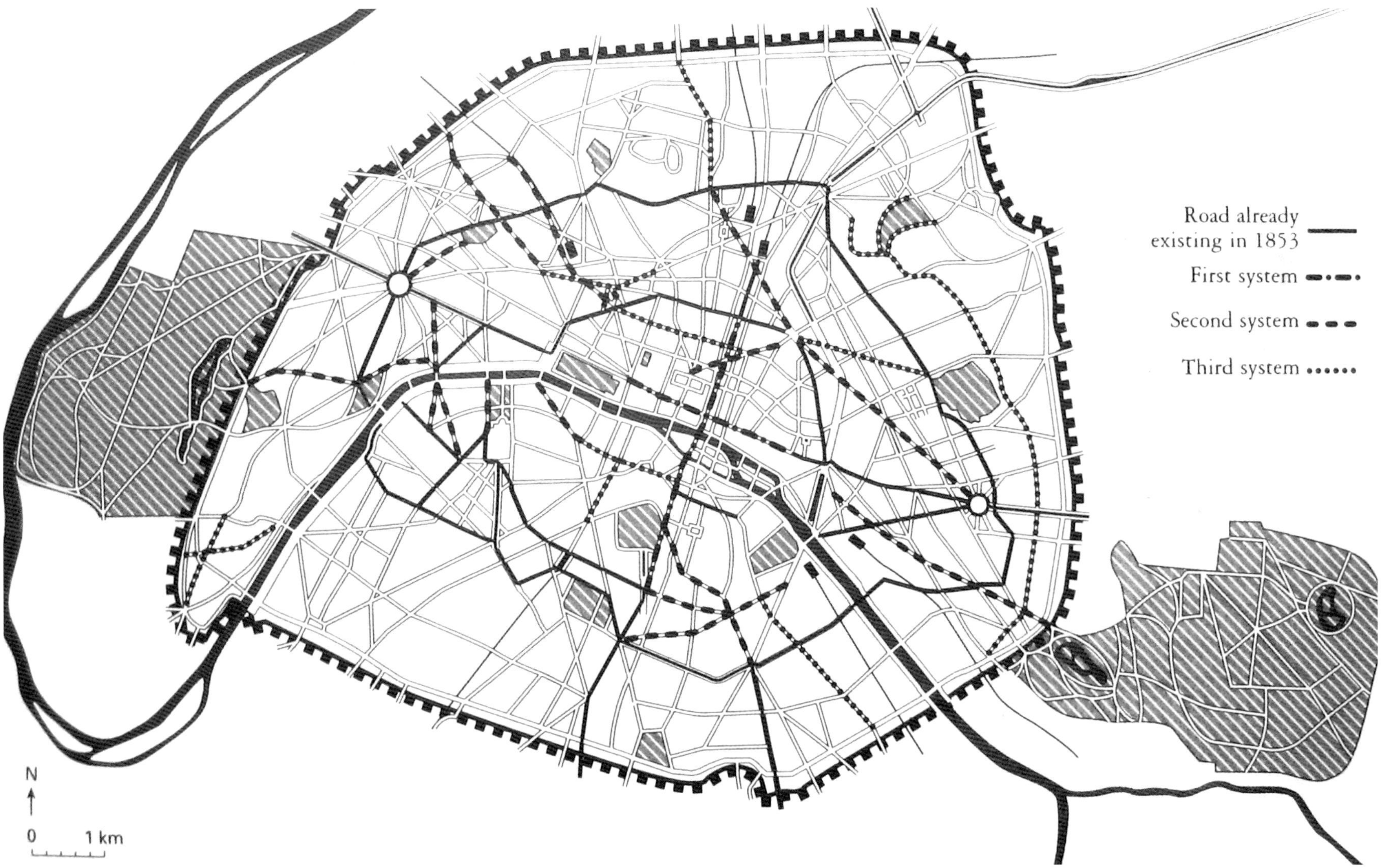

Diagram showing major thoroughfares, parks, urban forests, the River Seine, and the fortification wall from 1840

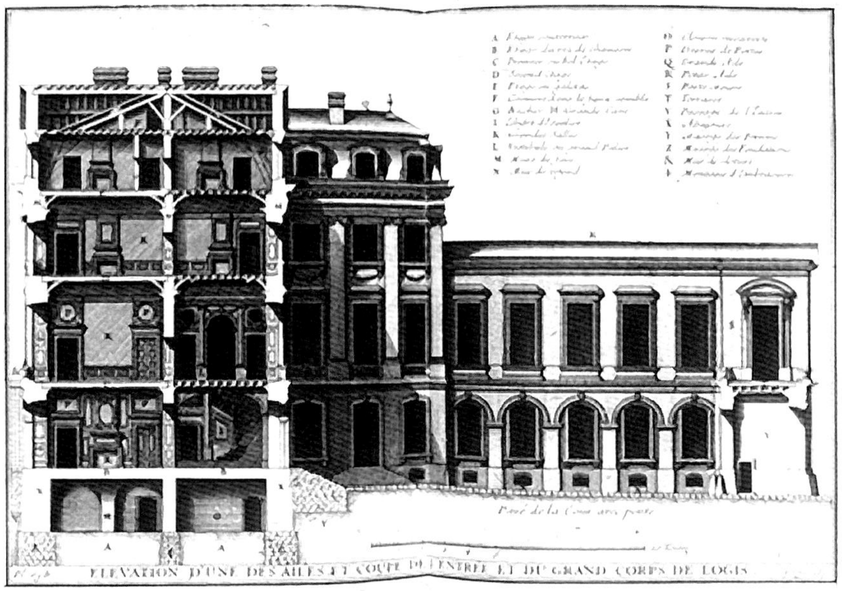

1. Section of a hôtel from D'Aviler, 1691

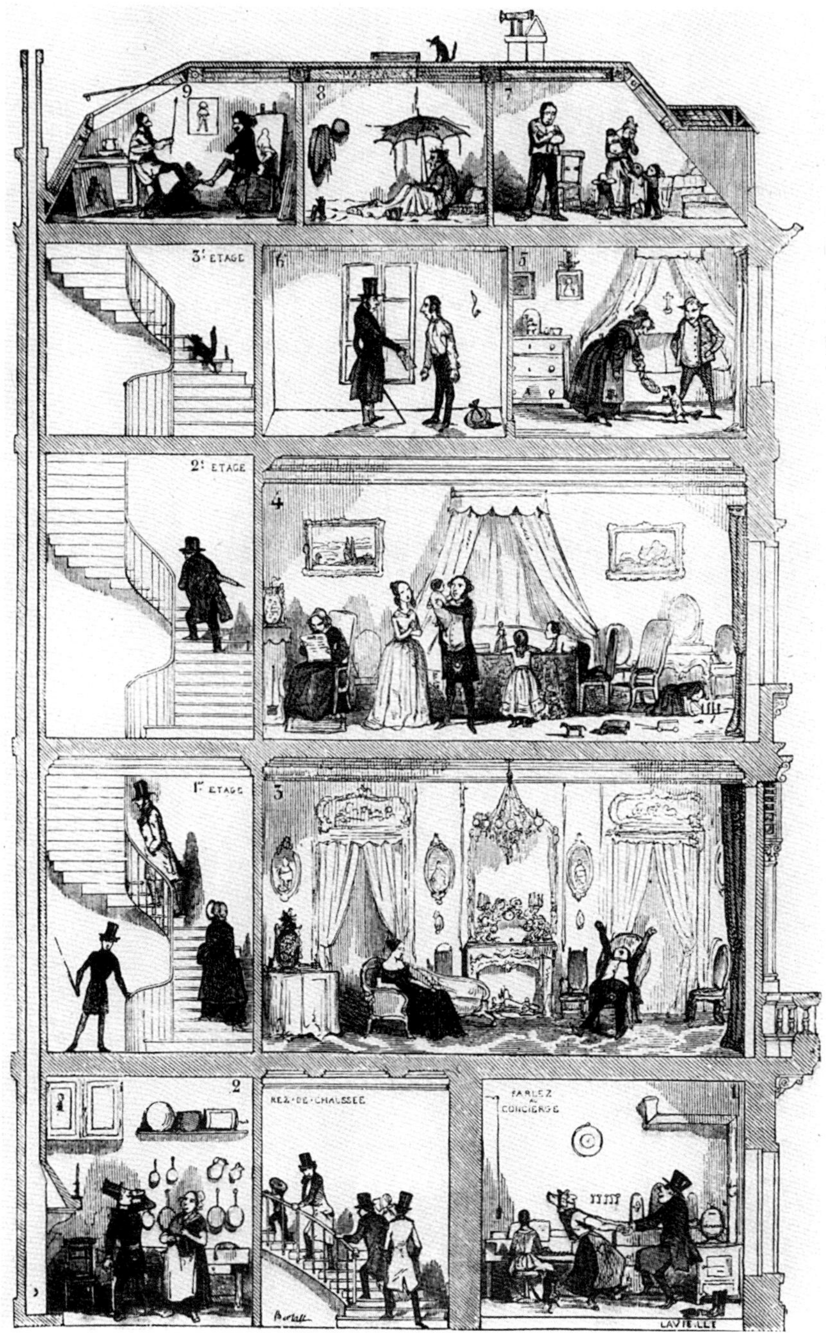

2. "Five levels of Parisian life," from Texier

The Paris Apartment Building

There were apartment buildings in Paris before Haussmann, but the apartment building was not well regarded by preindustrial theoreticians, such as Pierre Patte. The idea of people living above each other was distasteful. The neoclassical family house was regarded as ideal, but the population pressure made this impossible. As a result, the apartment house became a necessity, and the Baroque hôtel provided the model.

Unlike the English row house, the classic Baroque hôtel was organized by section, with extensive apartments arranged horizontally by floor. This was the system of the apartment building. Usually they were five to seven stories high, with the more desirable and expensive units on the lower levels owing to lack of elevators. This resulted in a social and economic mix of private lives within individual buildings, and the street provided public life.

When apartment buildings finally became socially accepted, and the first ones were constructed in New York and Boston around 1870, the Parisian apartment tradition became known as "French flats."

1. *Section of a Parisian apartment building, from* La Magazin pittoresque, *1847*

2. *Elevation of an apartment building, 1858*

1. *Elevation, house on the Boulevard Sebastopol, 1860, a typical building from the Haussmann era*

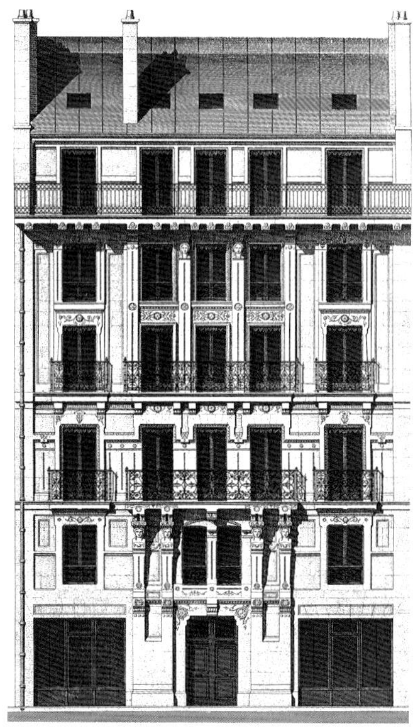

2. *Apartment house of the Second Order, elevation*

Apartment Planning

The public realm took precedence over the private realm in Haussmann's Paris. The virtuoso planning techniques developed in the seventeenth and eighteenth centuries, therefore, proved indispensable for solving the complex geometries that often resulted from cutting straight streets through the tangled medieval pattern of Paris. Indeed, the revival of this distinctly French tradition served well, not only in the nineteenth century, but also well into the twentieth century. Public rooms were disposed along street frontages, and idiosyncracies were absorbed behind.[6]

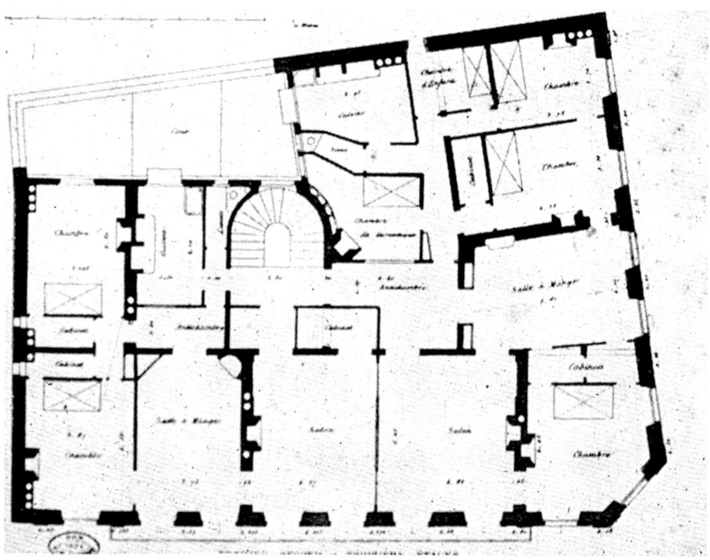

3. *Plan, house on the Boulevard Sebastopol, 1860*

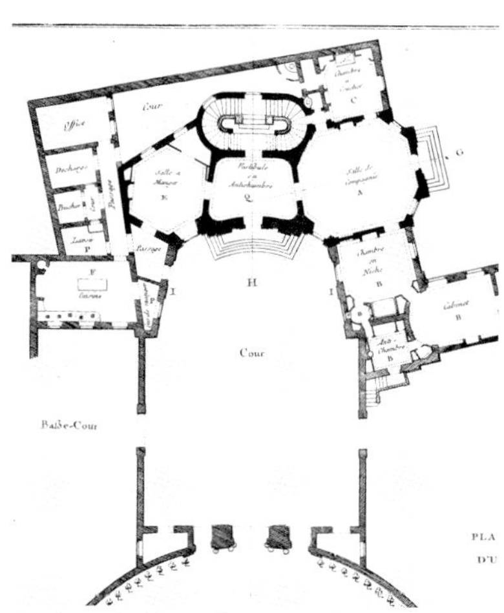

4. *Plan of abbot's house, Villers-Cotteets, 1765*

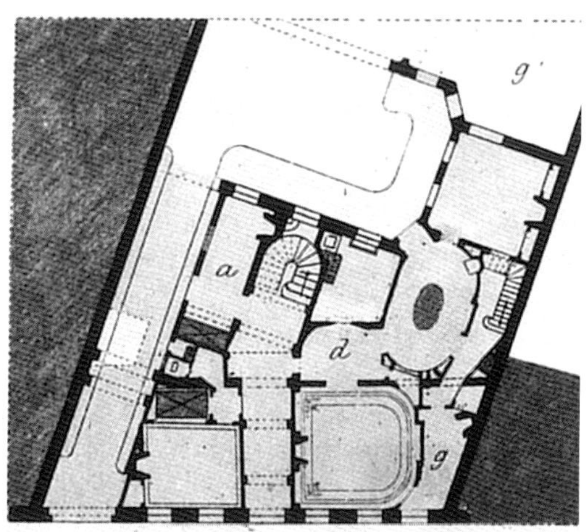

5. *A typical apartment plan from Daly's parallèle*

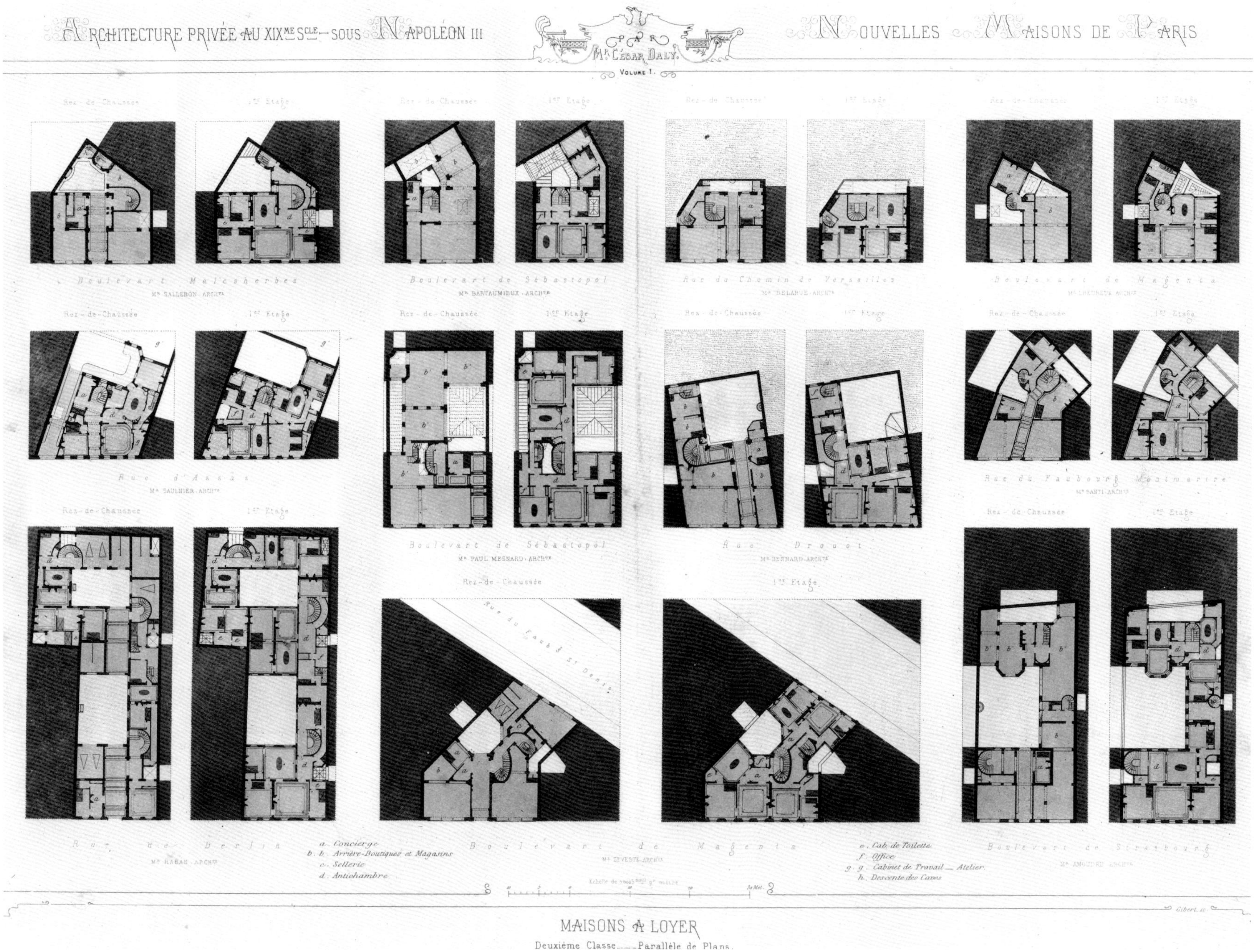

Apartment house plans, César Daly's second parallèle of the Second Order

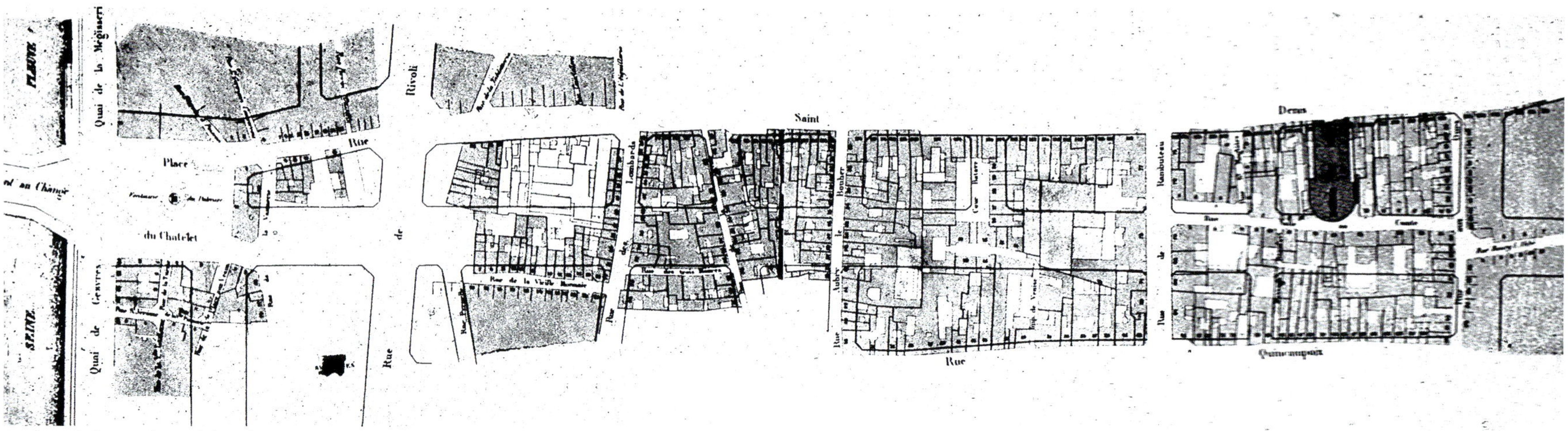

1. Plan of the Boulevard de Sébastopol

2. The cutting of the Boulevard de Sébastopol; demolition of the Rue de la Barillerie in 1859

3. The Boulevard Sébastopol at the end of the 19th century

The Boulevards

Cuts for the new boulevards left wounds in the existing city fabric, which were sealed off by new buildings. Residential typologies were subordinate to the public space. The building blocks provided the background for the open spaces, and Haussmann offered whole streets to developers to achieve homogeneous facades. Additionally, building height regulations were modified in streets wider than 20 meters (66'), to give the streets a more monumental character. Usually, the blocks along the streets were an addition of buildings, rather than one building per block. Typical was an apartment building of six or seven stories. The old buildings that were away from the representative network of boulevards formed a fragmented remnant of old Paris.[7]

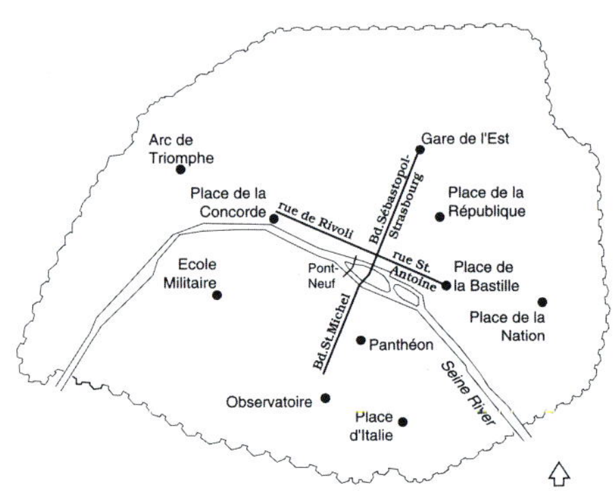

4. Plan diagram of the first boulevards, the Grande Croisée

5. Aerial view looking west along Rue St. Antoine, the eastern extension of Rue de Rivoli

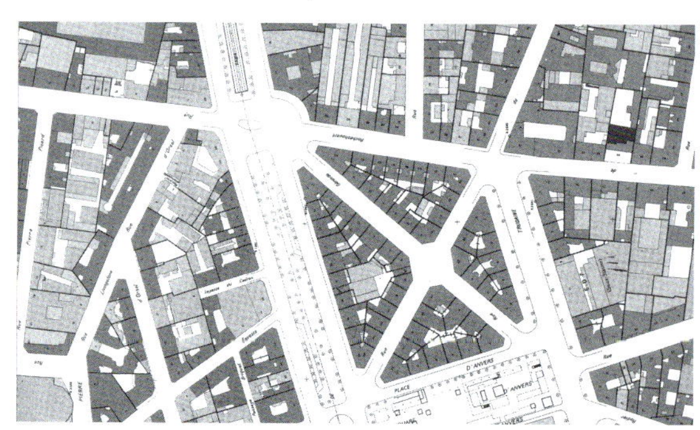

6. Typical pattern of Haussmann blocks

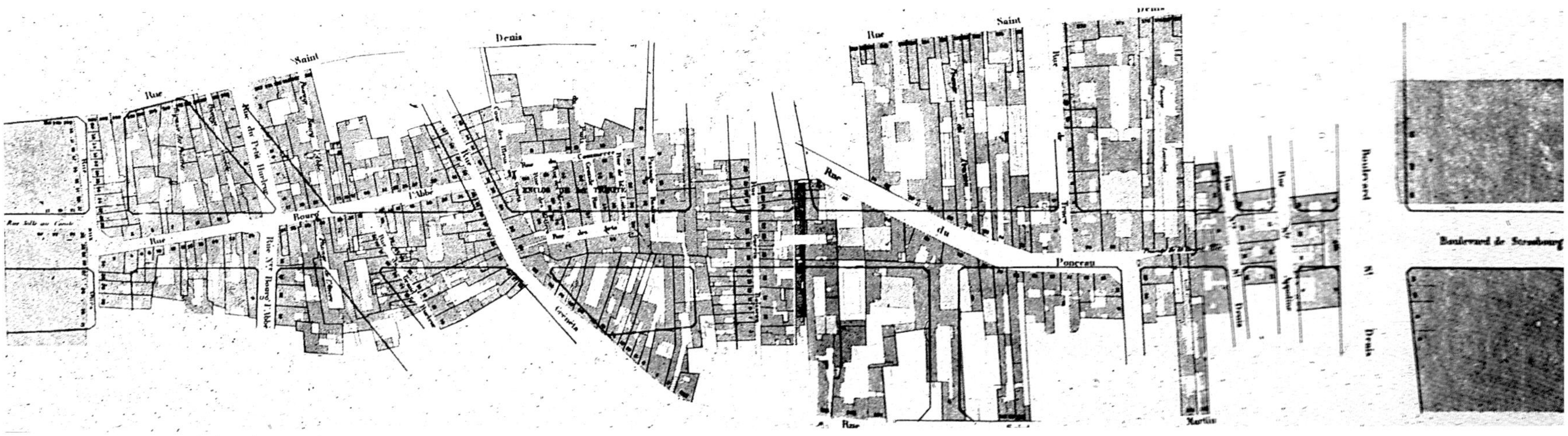

1. Plan of the Boulevard de Sébastopol

2. The Quartier de la Porte Saint-Denis before its transformation

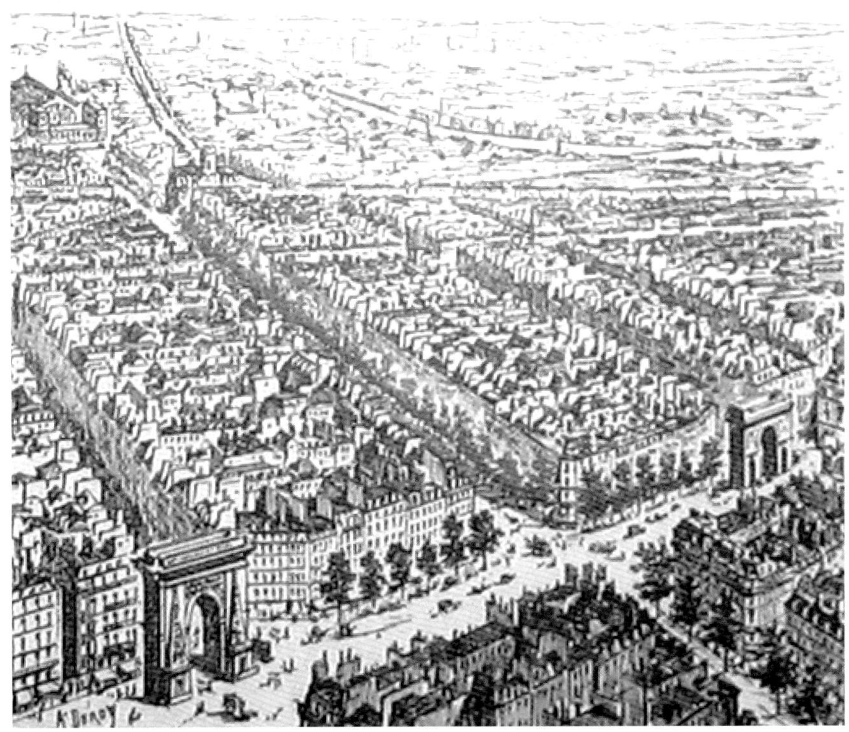

3. The Quartier de la Porte Saint-Denis after the creation of the Boulevard Strasbourg

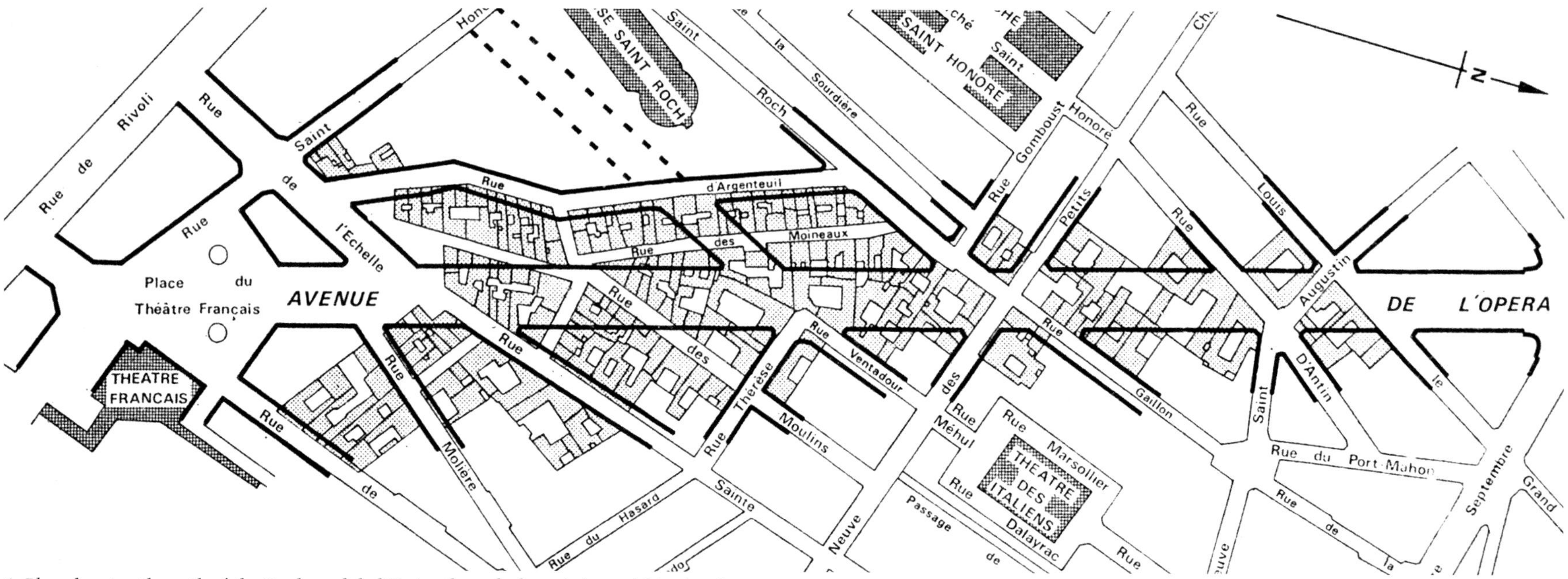

1. Plan showing the path of the Boulevard de l'Opéra through the existing neighborhood

2. Aerial view of the Boulevard de l'Opéra

3. Boulevard de l'Opera, ca. 1880, toward the Louvre

4. Contemporary view of the Boulevard de l'Opéra

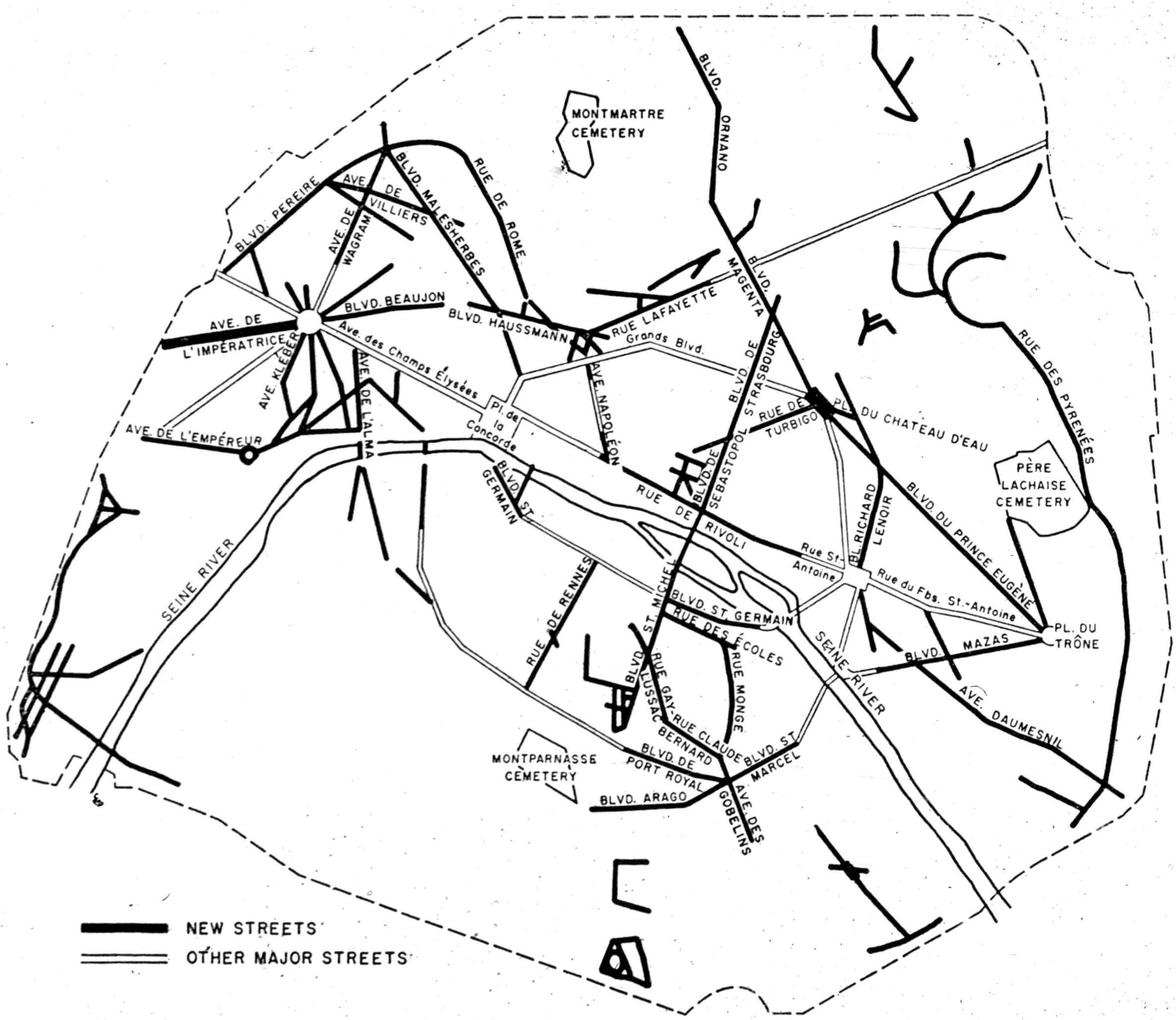

Plan showing the principal new streets in Paris between 1850 and 1870

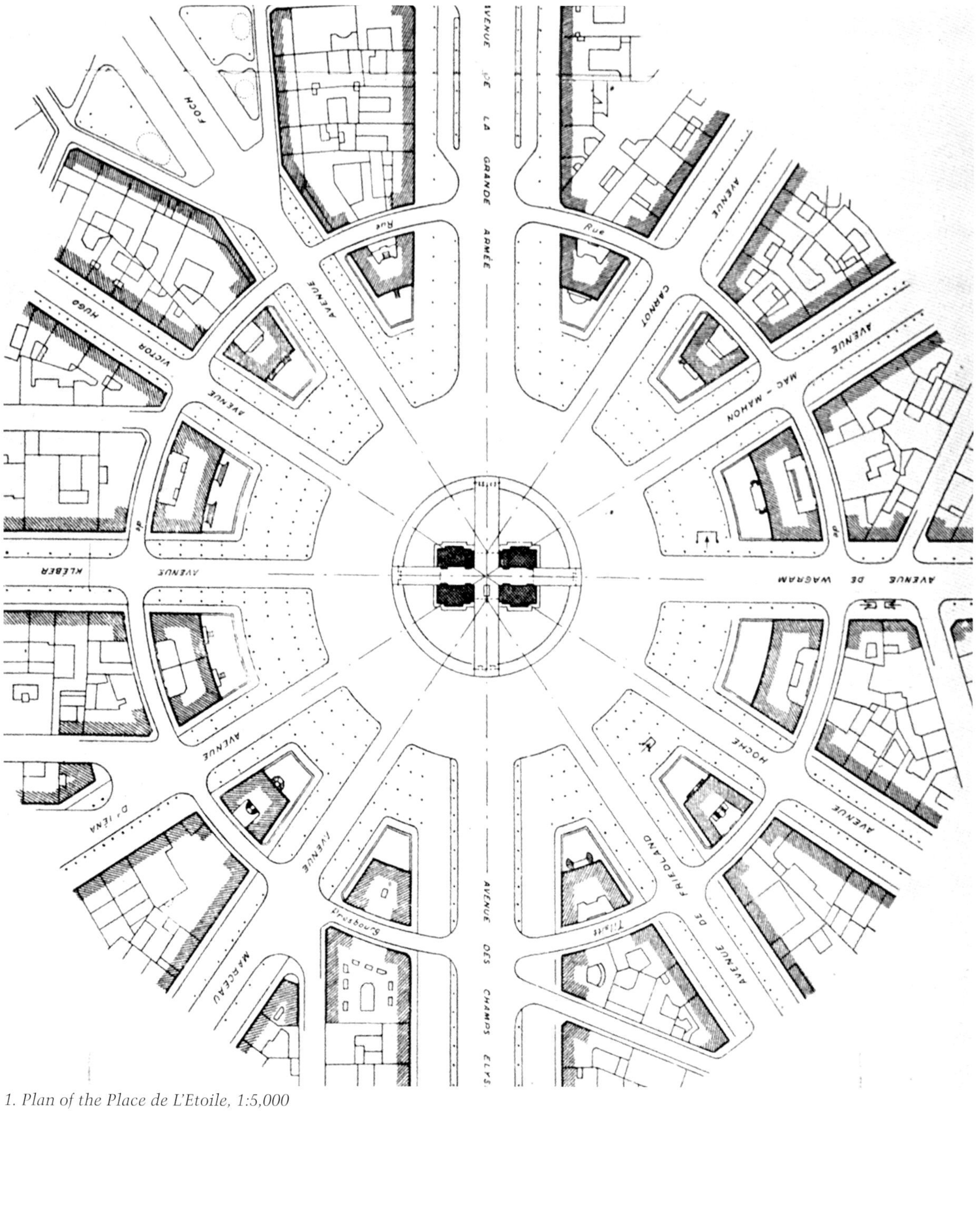

1. Plan of the Place de L'Etoile, 1:5,000

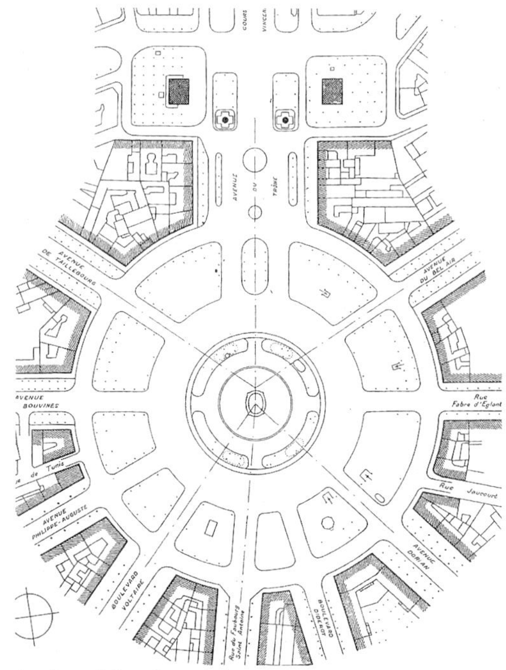

2. Plan of the Place de la Nation, 1:5,000

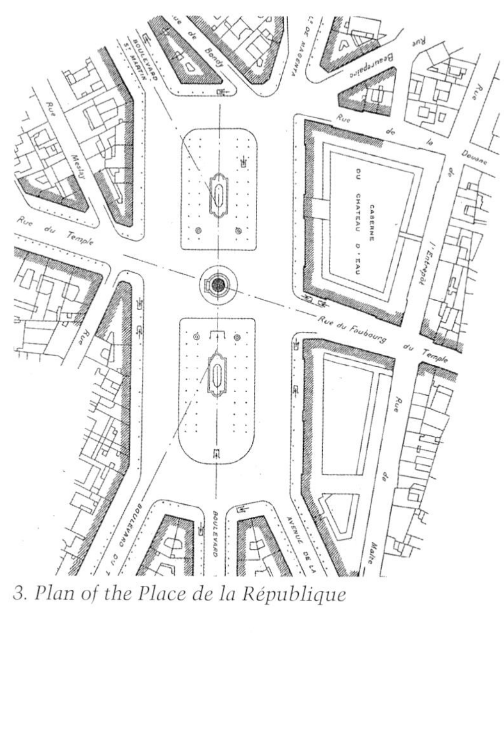

3. Plan of the Place de la République

1. Place de L'Opéra in 1869

Nineteenth-Century Squares

As streets widened to accommodate circulation and nature in the nineteenth century, squares also transformed. Laugier was prescient in the mid-eighteenth century when he said that squares should be penetrated by important streets. Even the eighteenth-century *rond points* had narrow streets and spatial closure. But the *place* became a traffic circle in the late nineteenth century, and the exposed corners of buildings were often rounded—an increasingly common Parisian architectural effect.[8]

4. La Place de Wagram

5. La Rue Scribe

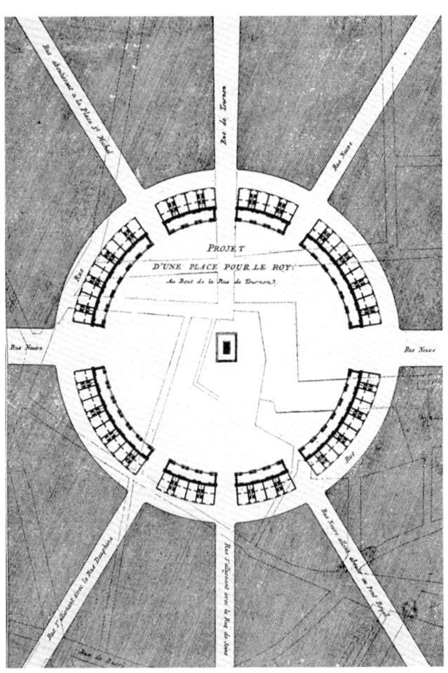

2. Plan for a royal place

3. Aerial view of the Place de L'Etoile

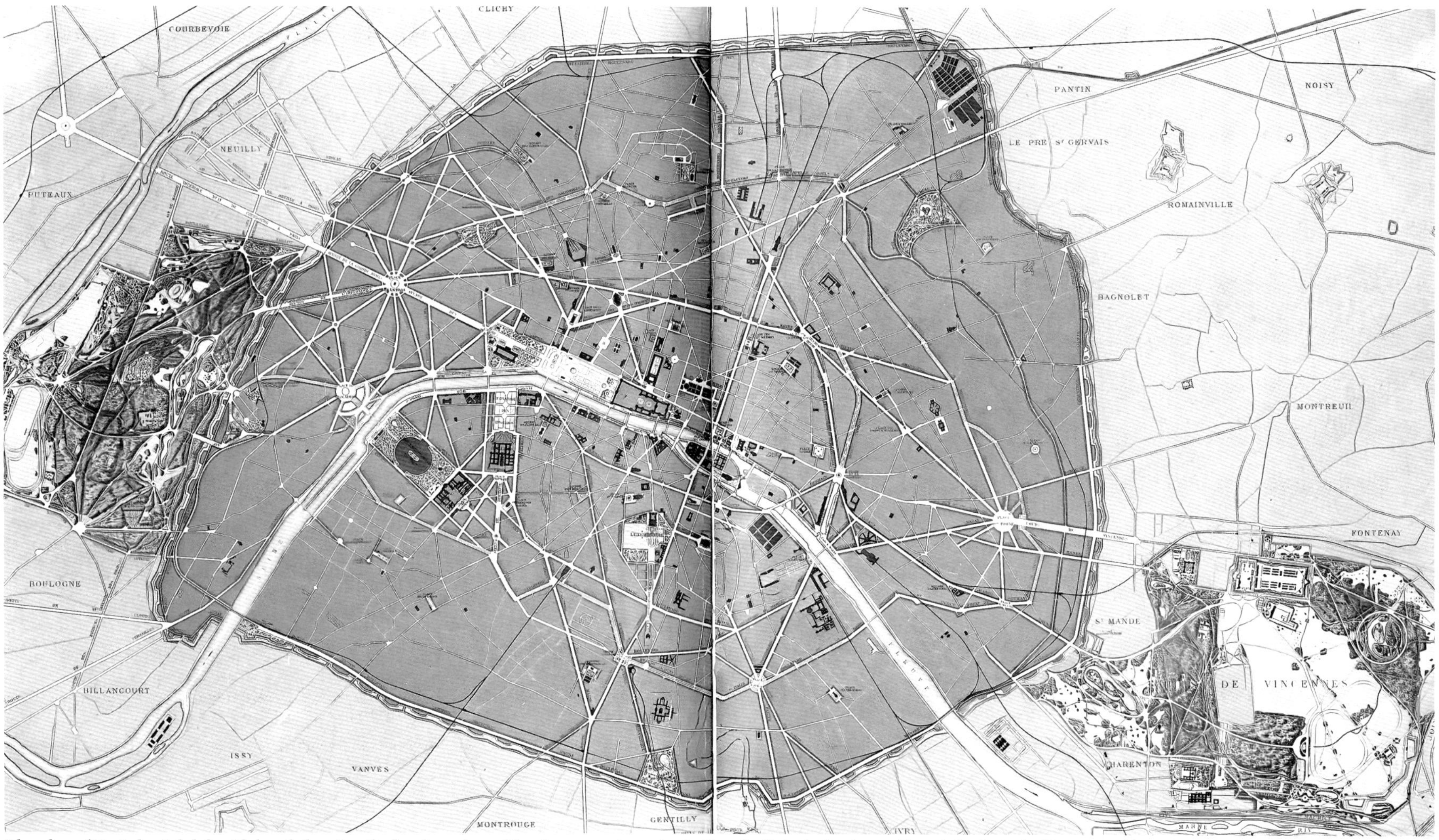

The plan of Paris by Adolphe Alphand showing the boulevards and landscape projects, including the Bois de Boulogne (l) and the Bois de Vincennes (r).

Landscape

For the first time, with the renovation of Paris, landscape entered the city as an aggressive medium of urbanism. A continuous landscape of boulevards, squares, and parks created a new type of city, as published in Alphand's *Promenades de Paris*. The spaces of nineteenth-century Paris provided a robust framework for the city that has endured until today. Within this framework, architecture, landscape, urban design, and infrastructure were interrelated.[9]

Alphand's Paris landscape is a fortuitous blend of two landscape traditions: the formal tradition of the *allée*, the *cours*, and the *promenades*; and the Romantic tradition of the picturesque landscape.

Napoleon III was particularly fond of Hyde Park and the English Romantic landscape, and one of his first initiatives after 1848 was to have Alphand transform the Bois de Boulogne from a geometric hunting wood into a Romantic park for the bourgeoise. Later, the same was done with the Bois de Vincennes. Notably, at the time, both of these were outside the city proper. Within the city, the formal—more urban—tradition prevailed, although some medium-sized Romantic parks, like the Buttes Chaumont and Montsouris, were created.

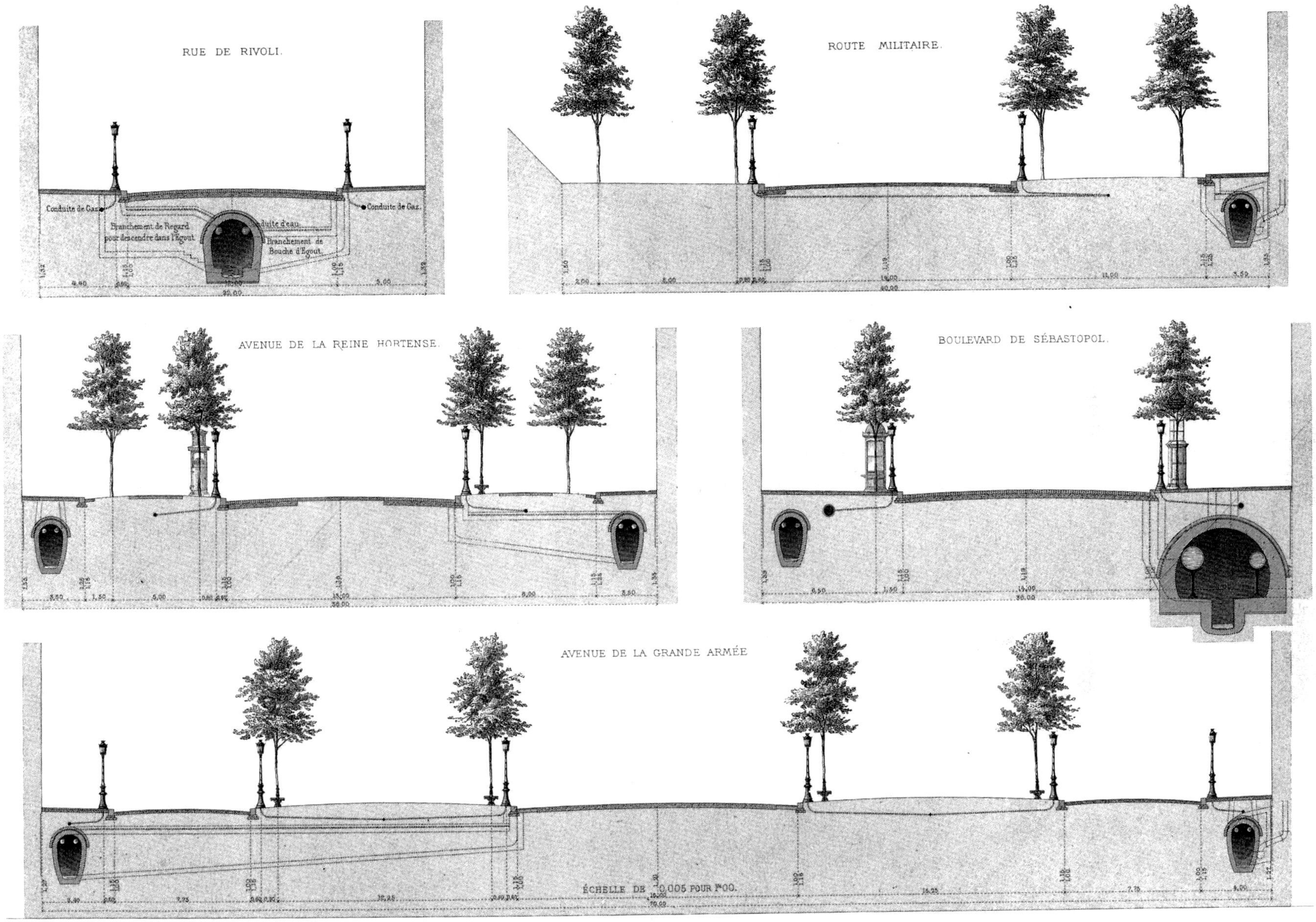

1. Profiles of different streets: Rue de Rivoli, Route Militaire, Avenue de la Reine Hortense, Boulevard de Sébastopol, Avenue de la Grande Armée

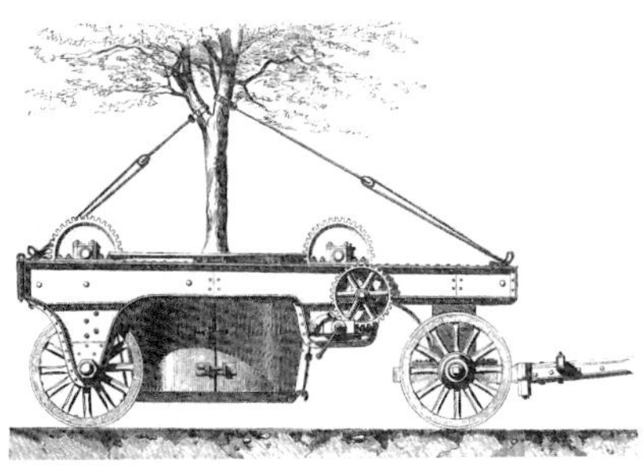

2. Illustration of mechanical tree-planting device

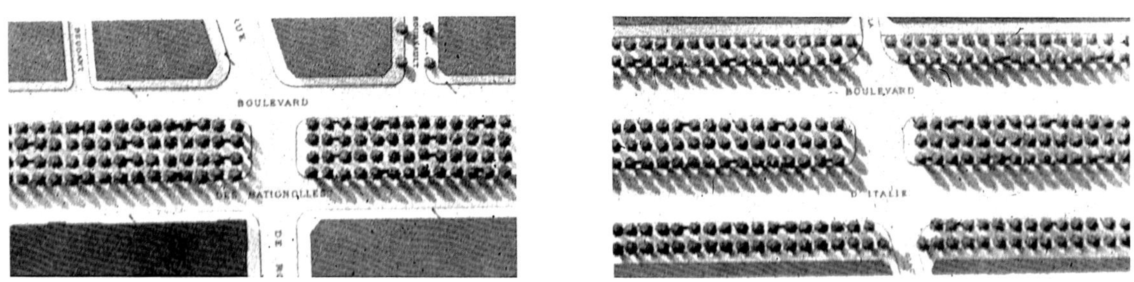

3. Plans of Boulevard tree-planting schemes from Alphand

Tree-Lined Boulevards

Historically, urban streets were relatively narrow and without landscaping. Movement within the city was limited. To accommodate increased population and movement, however, Paris and other cities "loosened." As streets became wider, landscape became an important design component.

The boulevards were wide, monumental, often multilane thoroughfares, with generous numbers of trees and other vegetation, combined with street lighting and underground facilities. Trees were an effective way of articulating various modes of traffic and pedestrians within the same system.

The Rue Rambuteau had cleared the way for the first time in the city's history for a large avenue in the center of Paris, and Parisians were impressed by its width of 13 m (45'). But Haussmann made the Rue Rambuteau a moderate-sized street after creating new boulevards that were 30 m wide (100'), like the Boulevard Sébastopol. Some even resembled linear parks, like the Avenue de la Grande Armée with a width of 70 m (233') or the Rue de l'Impératrice (now Avenue Foch), one of the connectors to the Bois de Boulogne, with 140 m (460').

The boulevards were designed with the engineer and landscape architect Adolphe Alphand. They were not only crucial to facilitate and separate traffic flow, but also to bring in air and light.

1. *L'Avenue de L'Impératrice seen from the entrance of the Bois de Boulogne, around 1870*

2. *L'Avenue de L'Impératrice after its transformation by Alphand*

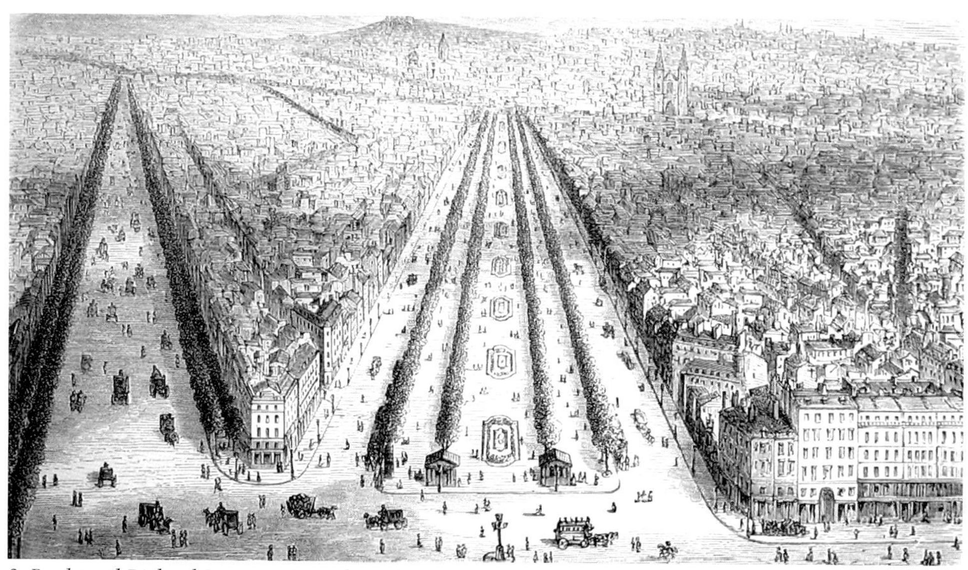

3. *Boulevard Richard-Lenoir cutting through the old city fabric, 1861–1863*

1. Aerial view of the Palais Luxembourg

2. Aerial view of the Rue Scribe

3. Street level view of a boulevard

4. L'Avenue des Champs Elysées from Alphand

5. Bird's-eye view of the Champs Elysées in the 1850s

The Squares

Various landscape designs—from small squares to urban forests—worked as the climaxes of Alphand's *promenades*.

Within their quarters, the squares filled a need for accessible neighborhood parks. Unlike the London squares with limited access, however, the Parisian squares were completely public.

The squares often resulted from a pattern of diagonal streets forming an irregular open space. These leftover spaces were resolved by the landscape design, which might be either formal or picturesque, and the number of spatial conditions required an almost endless variety of solutions.

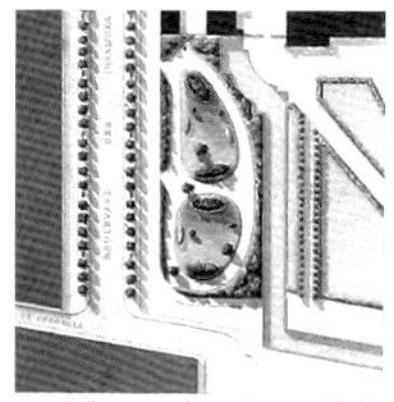

2. Place des Invalides

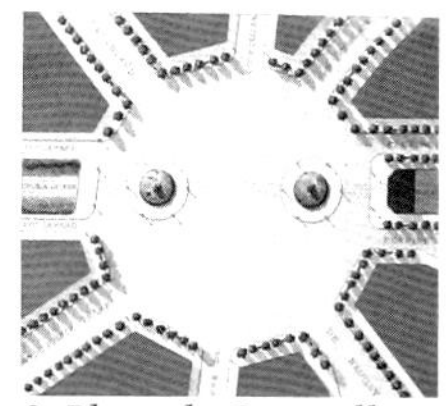

3. Place de Courcelles

4. Place de Prince Eugéne

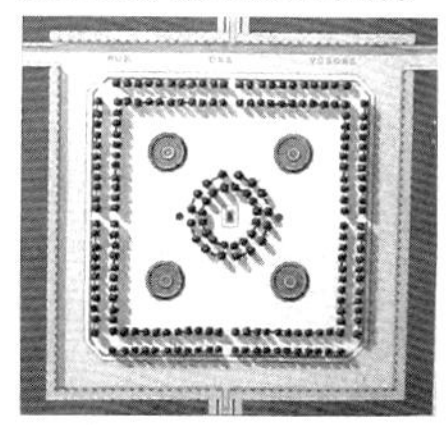

5. Place Royale

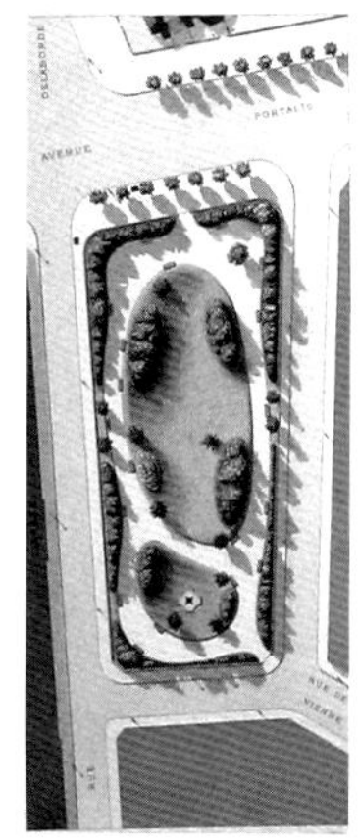

6. Place Delaborde

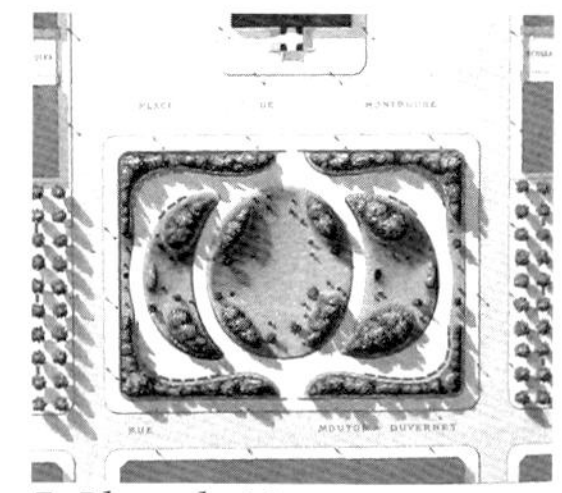

7. Place de Montrogue

8. Place de L'École Polytechnique

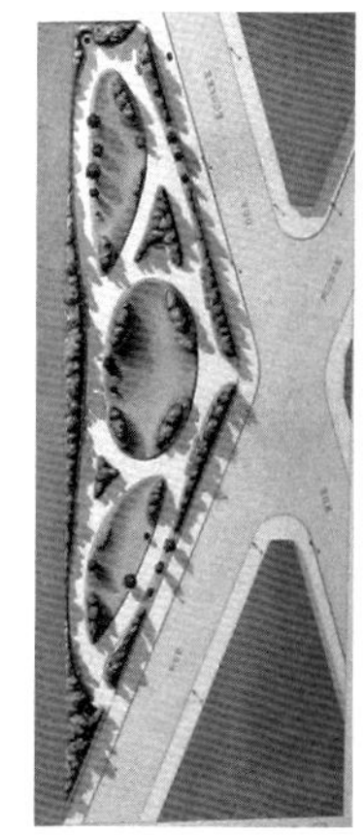

9. Triangular place

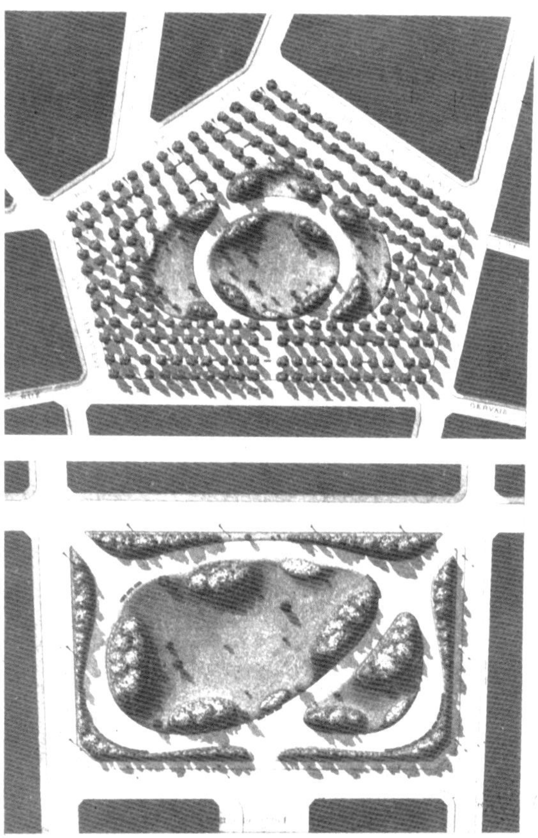

1. Place St. Genevieve and Square Popincourt

10. Bird's-eye view of the Square de Batignolles

1. Plan of the Buttes-Chaumont

4. The Temple of Sibyl

2. Stone bridge to the Temple of Sibyl

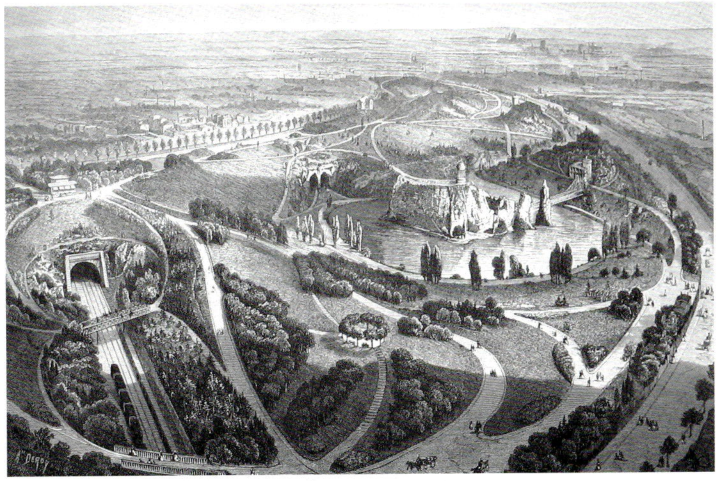

3. Bird's-eye view of the Buttes-Chaumont

The Urban Parks

The city structure of Paris was enriched by several large parks, the most significant being the Buttes-Chaumont. The sixty-two-acre area had been an abandoned quarry that was transformed into a curvilinear landscape, with a mountain crowned by a Temple of Sibyl at its highest point. Another attraction was a large grotto with a thirty-two-meter cascade. Generally the *flâneur* never had to return the way he entered. The park was a reserve of an exaggerated and artificial nature that was more natural than nature itself, dedicated to recreation, pleasure, and entertainment of the citizens. It cost more than all other parks combined.

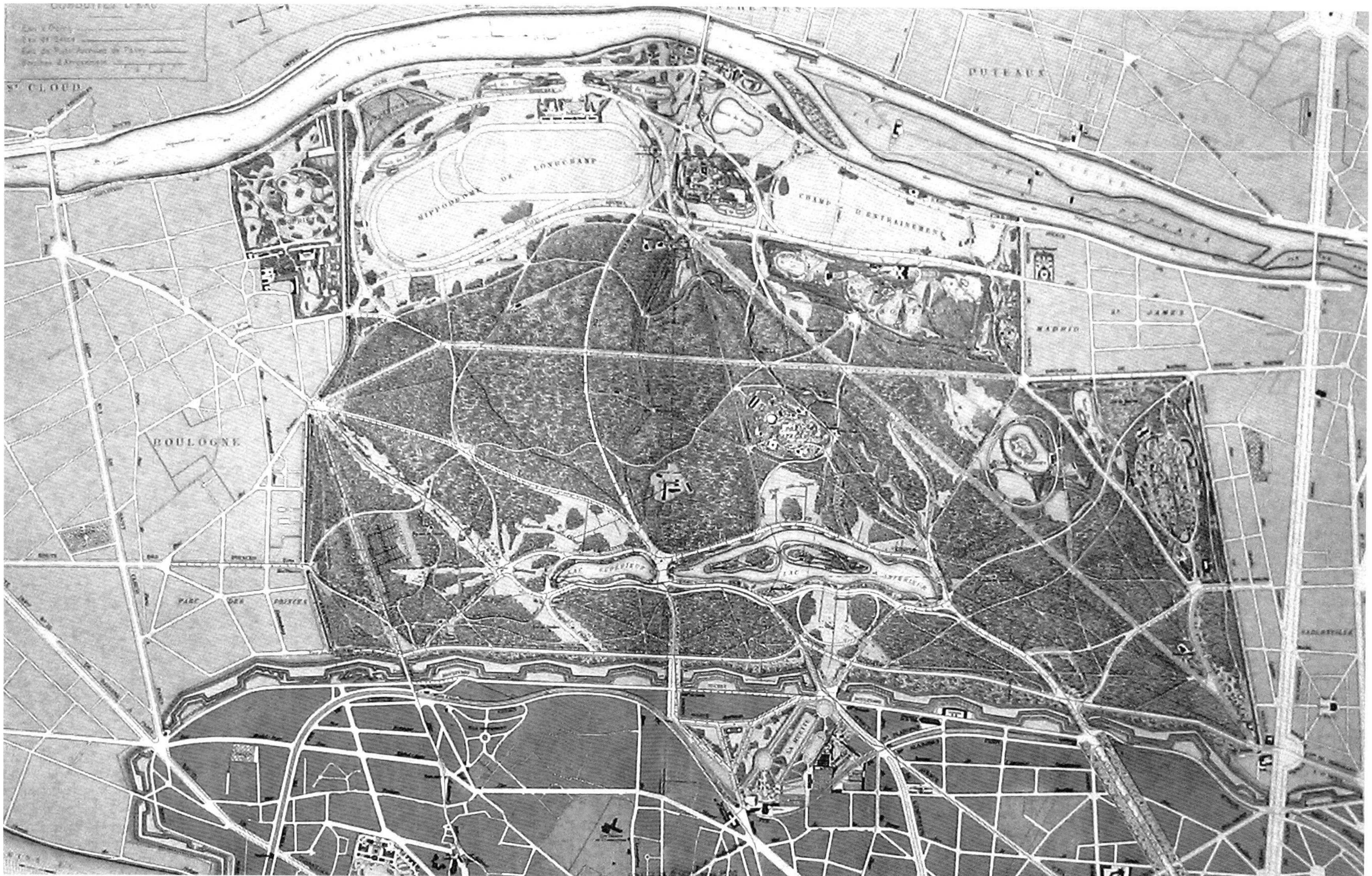

1. The Bois de Boulogne after its transformation by Alphand in the 1850s

The Large Wooded Parks

The Bois de Boulogne had been a hunting reserve for kings until it was transferred from the national government to the city of Paris. In contrast to its geometry of linear axes, Napoleon III was in favor of contemporary English landscape architecture, especially Hyde Park. Alphand therefore transformed the Bois de Boulogne into labyrinthine promenades composed of curves and sinuous lines. Large water features were introduced, which included cascades and grottoes. Pavilions and building ensembles, a hippodrome, and smaller gardens were nested within the park and formed various attractions. The choice and layout of new vegetation gave the area an informal character. These transformations served for the entertainment and recreation of the bourgeoisie. The park had only a few entrances and its boundaries were relatively abrupt. In the west, the river formed a natural boundary; in the east stood the fortification of the city. The northern and southern sides were bordered by large trenches and dense planting.

Later, the design of the Bois de Vincennes followed the example of the Bois de Boulogne, though under different conditions, such as more natural remnants, various military demands, and a location away from the wealthy districts of the city.

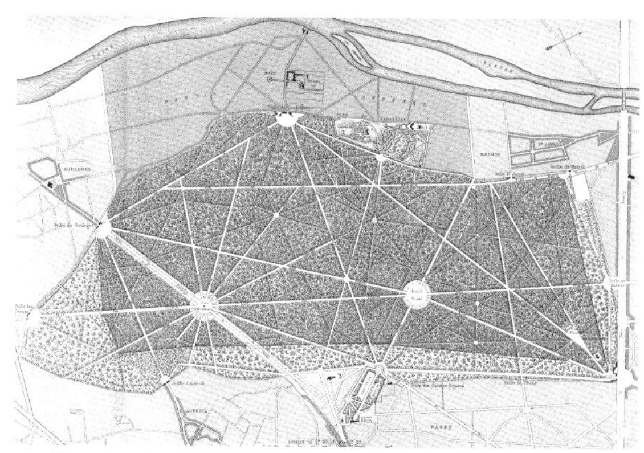

2. The Bois de Boulogne before its transformation

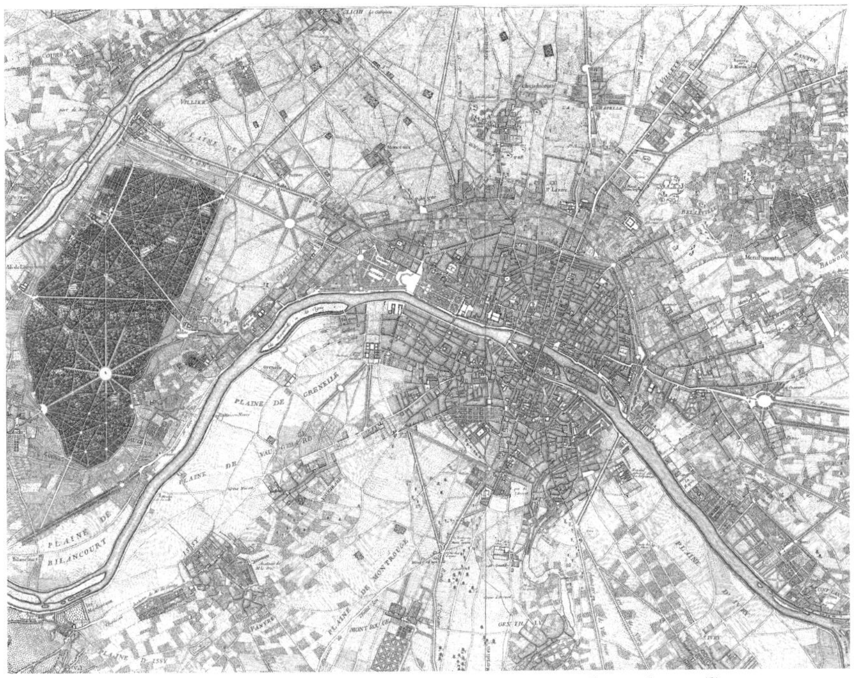

1. The Delagrive plan of the Paris region in 1740: Paris (r), Bois de Boulogne (l)

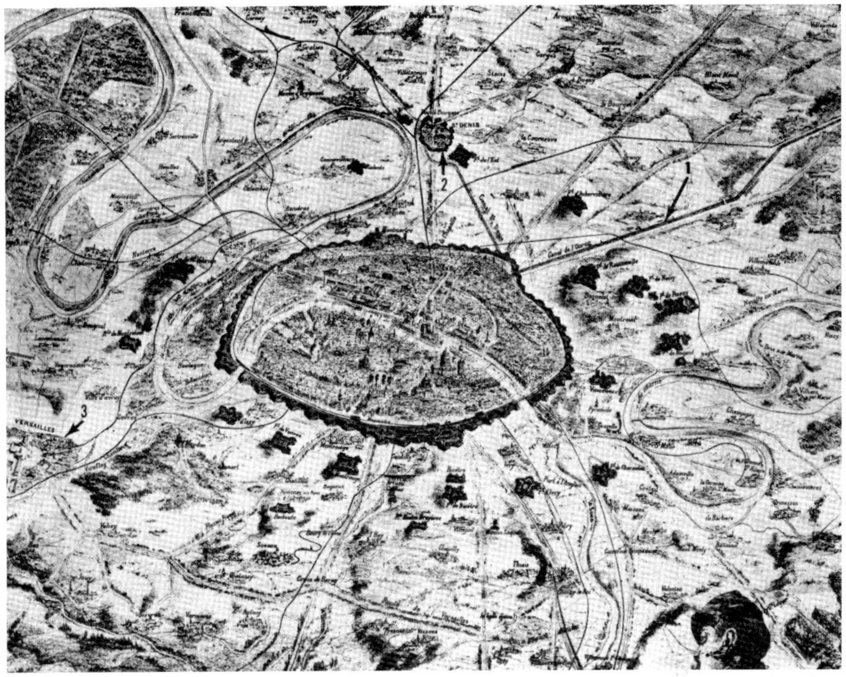

2. Paris and environs, 1870, showing city wall of 1840. The dark lines mark main railroads into the city

Conclusion

Comparing the Delagrive plan of the environs of Paris from 1740 with an illustration of Paris as seen from the air in 1870 shows how the interpretation of the city had changed within a relatively short period of time. The difference is best described by the terms "explosion" and "implosion" by Bacon in *The Design of Cities*. The regime under Louis XIV conceived a city that extended infinitely into the region by axes of avenues. In contrast, the city of Napoleon III was constricted into its fortification walls, although its population had roughly doubled since 1740. Napoleon III saw Paris as a compact city that he wanted to make healthy, monumental, and beautiful.

Indeed, Haussmann, Alphand, and others demonstrated that an industrial city with old roots could be functional, economical, more social, beautiful, even magnificent. They also demonstrated to city planners that civic architecture must be conceived at a large scale, and that the relationship of buildings to the space should be at least as important as the design of individual structures. Moreover, with the work of Haussmann, Alphand, and others, a new attitude toward the architect's duty toward the community was born. It was a conception that was fundamentally different from the École des Beaux Arts, whose teaching was blind to social conditions and site.

Most important was the introduction of landscape as a fundamental component of urban design. Not only could the city be conceived holistically, but this could only be done by including both formal and Romantic landscape types.

Legacy

Haussman and Alphand's Paris served as a model for successive late-nineteenth-century planners and for the City Beautiful movement. It might even be argued that the interest in rationalizing movement led fairly directly to Le Corbusier and the Ville Contemporaine.

It seems to have had a limited effect on Frederick Law Olmsted, however. Olmsted went to visit Alphand, so he was aware of what was happening in Paris. If he was influenced, though, it was only by the Romantic tradition, not the formal one. Thus, if Alphand may be seen as the father of modern urban landscape, Olmsted went on to become the father of suburban landscape.[10]

Castello plan of New Amsterdam in 1660, redrawn by Adams-Stokes in 1916

1. Topography of Manhattan, ca. 1500

2. Dutch row houses, 1620–64

3. View of "New Amsterdam"

Dutch New Amsterdam

Henry Hudson explored the New York Bay area in 1609, and Dutch traders began to arrive in 1614. Dutch settlers arrived in 1624 and founded New Amsterdam on the southernmost tip of what is now Manhattan Island. The plan was irregular, the houses small, and a fortification wall was built along "Wall Street" between the East River and the Hudson River in 1633 (to keep the English out). The population was about 270.[11]

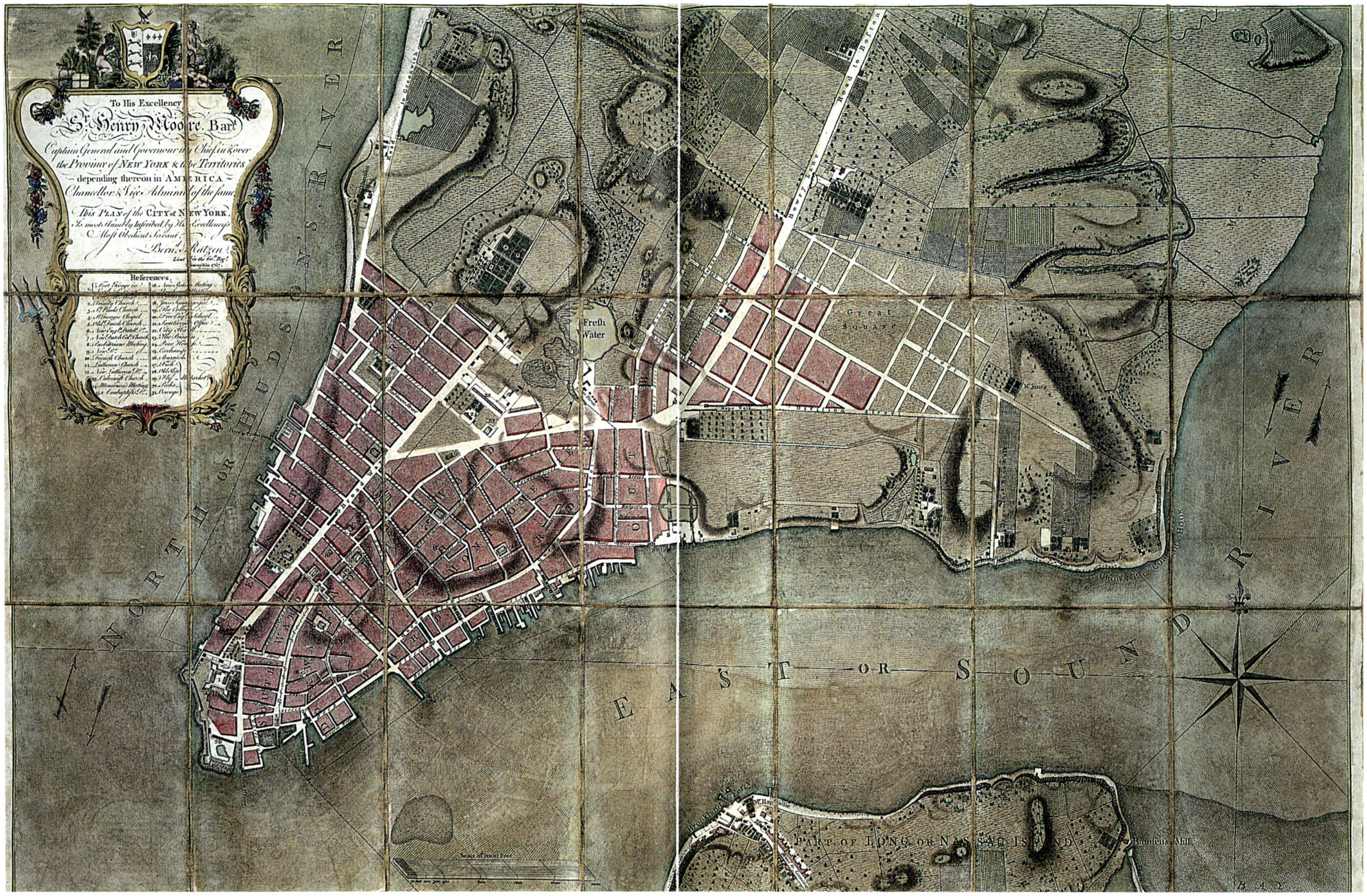

Ratzen plan of British New York, 1776–77

British New York

The British took New Amsterdam from the Dutch in 1664 and renamed it New York. The Dutch retook the city in 1673 and held it for a year, until the British took it again. New York remained British until the close of the American Revolution, when the British left New York City in 1783. By 1790 the population was 33,000.[12]

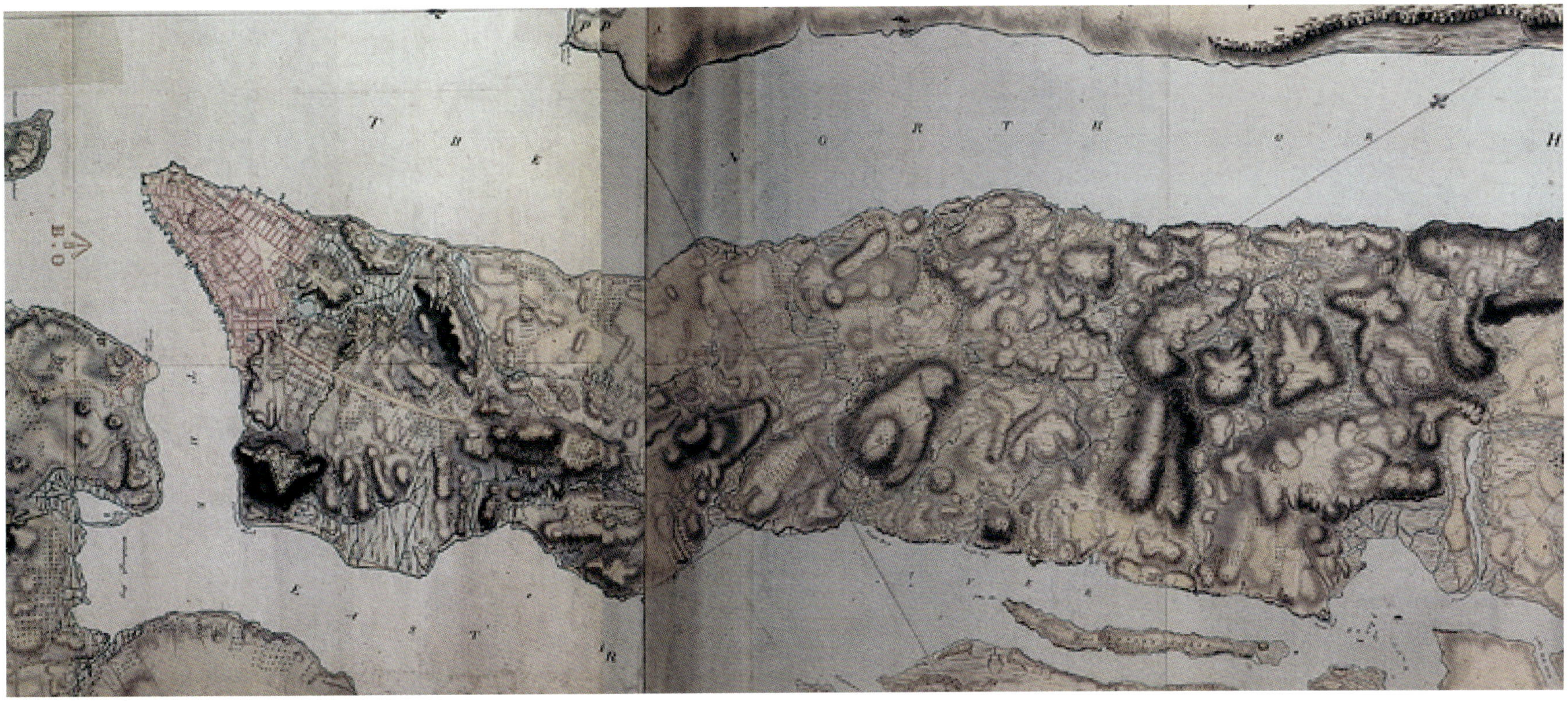

1. British headquarters map, 1782

2. View of the city in 1673, from the Allard Map, 1674

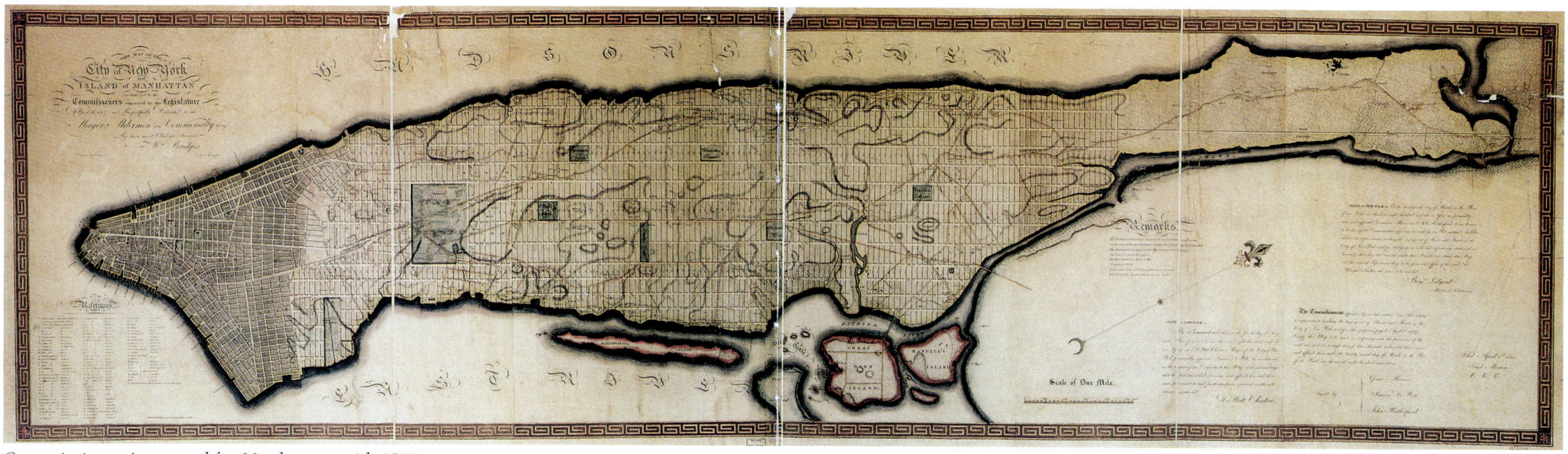

Commissioners' proposal for Manhattan grid, 1811;
"the land it divides, unoccupied; the population it describes, conjectural; the buildings it locates, phantoms; the activities it frames, non-existent."

American New York

The departing British had burned much of New York, but rebuilding began quickly. Between 1790 and 1797 the population grew from 33,000 to 60,000, and the city had grown north almost to present-day 14th Street.

Recognizing the inevitable growth of the city, in 1807 the Common Council requested the New York State legislature to appoint a commission to make recommendations for expansion.

The expansion plan was formulated by an independent three-member commission of influential New Yorkers: Gouverneur Morris, lawyer John Rutherfurd, and surveyor Simeon De Witt. De Witt drafted military maps and was working with Morris on the Erie Canal project.[13]

John Randel, Jr., who mapped the plan, perceived a purposeful Cartesian aesthetic of "symmetry, order and proportion," but the plan was actually based on practical, commercial goals, including: "A free and abundant circulation of air"; "Straight-sided and right-angled houses are the most cheap to build"; disdain for the "circles, ovals and stars, which certainly embellish a plan"; and provision for commercial traffic and maximization of negotiable land through exclusion of service alleys.[14]

The Commissioners' Plan of 1811

The 1811 plan was a regular grid of long, rectangular blocks, extending from 14th Street to 155th Street—a distance of approximately seven miles. The Commissioners' Plan was adopted in 1811 and became the sole basis for the development of Manhattan in the nineteenth century.[15]

The plan did not provide for recreation space and did not acknowledge water or topographic features. As development moved north, up the island, hills were flattened, squatters were displaced, and streams were covered over. Streets and utilities were built ahead of buildings, which followed.

Much has been made of the rigidity and relentless consistency of the plan, but despite the origins in the 25' dimensions of early Dutch houses, the plan has proven to be infinitely flexible. Every known building type can be found in New York, and the skyscraper has transformed the city into one of the modern wonders of the world.

Urban Housing Types

There are three types of New York City housing: the row house, the tenement, and the apartment building. To some degree these evolved chronologically.

1. *View of a typical 25' row house, ca. 1830*

The Row House

The earliest house type in New York was the single-family row house—a party-wall building type. It formed the basis for the 25' x 100' block parcels.

The Tenement

As hundreds of thousands of immigrants poured into New York in the nineteenth century, the row house type evolved into the tenement—a building occupied by more than one unrelated family.

The Apartment Building

The first apartment building in New York, the Stuyvesant, was built on East 18th Street in 1869. Initially, apartment buildings were known as "French Flats."

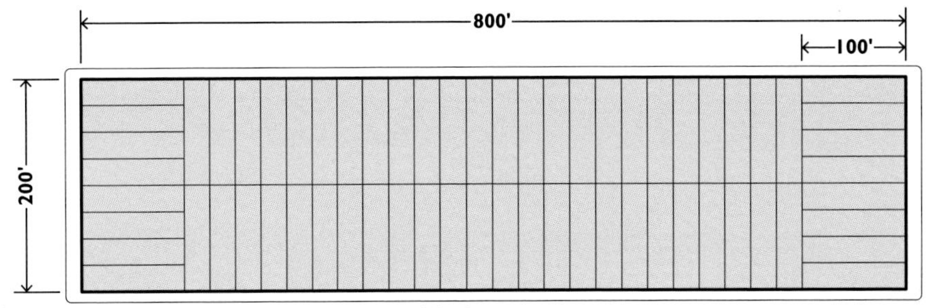

2. *Plan of a typical New York City block*

The Urban Block

The basic unit of the Commissioners' Plan was an urban block 200' x 800', divided into parcels 25' wide x 100' deep. Oddly, this was reminiscent of archaic and classical Greek city blocks, with parcels of about 2,500 square feet. The New York City blocks run east–west and do not have service alleys.

Streets

The east–west streets are typically 60' building face to building face, and the north-south avenues are typically 100' building face to building face. Principal cross-town streets are wider, as are some north-south avenues. Thus, the private area is 68 percent, and the public space for streets is 32 percent.

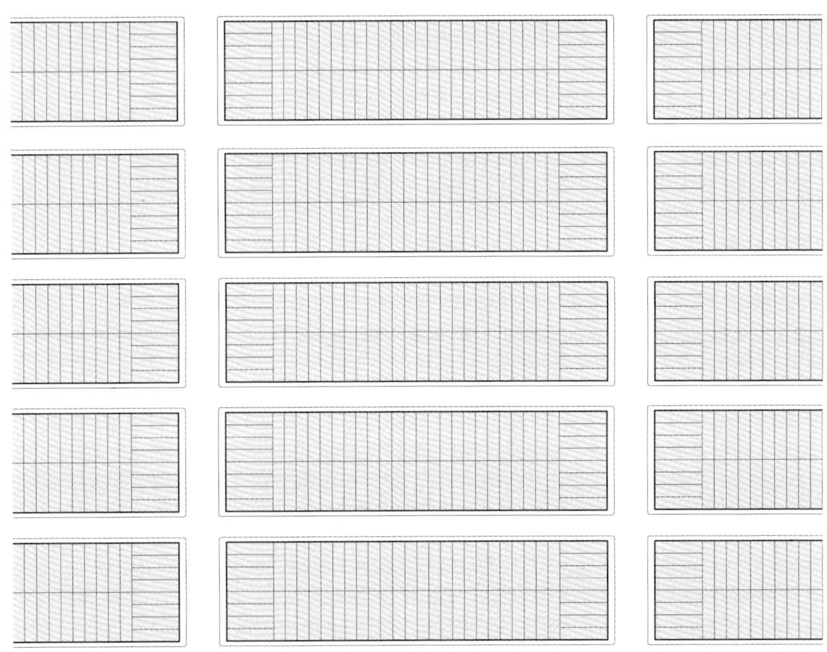

3. *Typical urban fabric of 200' x 800' blocks, 60' streets, and 100' avenues*

1. Dripps Plan I, 1850

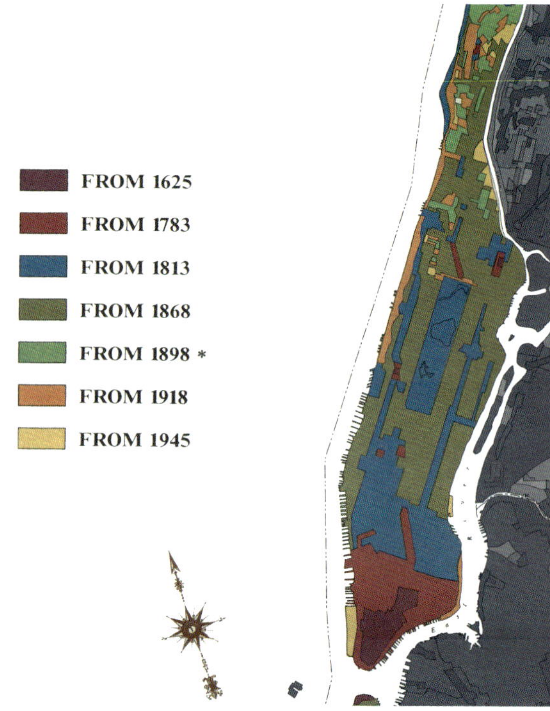

2. Urban development of New York, 1625–1988

Immigration and Expansion

The city had developed to about 12th Street by 1836, and the population was around 300,000. By 1840 the city was to 14th Street, and the population was about 350,000.

The Croton Aqueduct was begun in 1835, just after the disastrous fire, and opened in 1842.[16] This was a major contribution to the health and development of the city. In the decade preceding 1850, rear buildings, slums, and uptown shantytowns absorbed immigrants. In 1850 the population had reached 500,000, and the city reached Madison Square and 23rd Street, as represented on the first Dripps Plan.

In the 1850s, waves of immigration began with 630,000 Germans, Irish, and Scandinavians, and the population would double every twenty years. Between 1880 and 1884 2,000,000 immigrants arrived, and were housed in increasingly dense tenements. The density of the tenement district of the Lower East Side reached 1,000 people per acre in the 1890s, and 1,500,000 lived in tenements.

By 1900 New York was the world's largest city with 3,437,000 people. Tenements housed 2,300,000, with 1,000,000 below 14th Street.

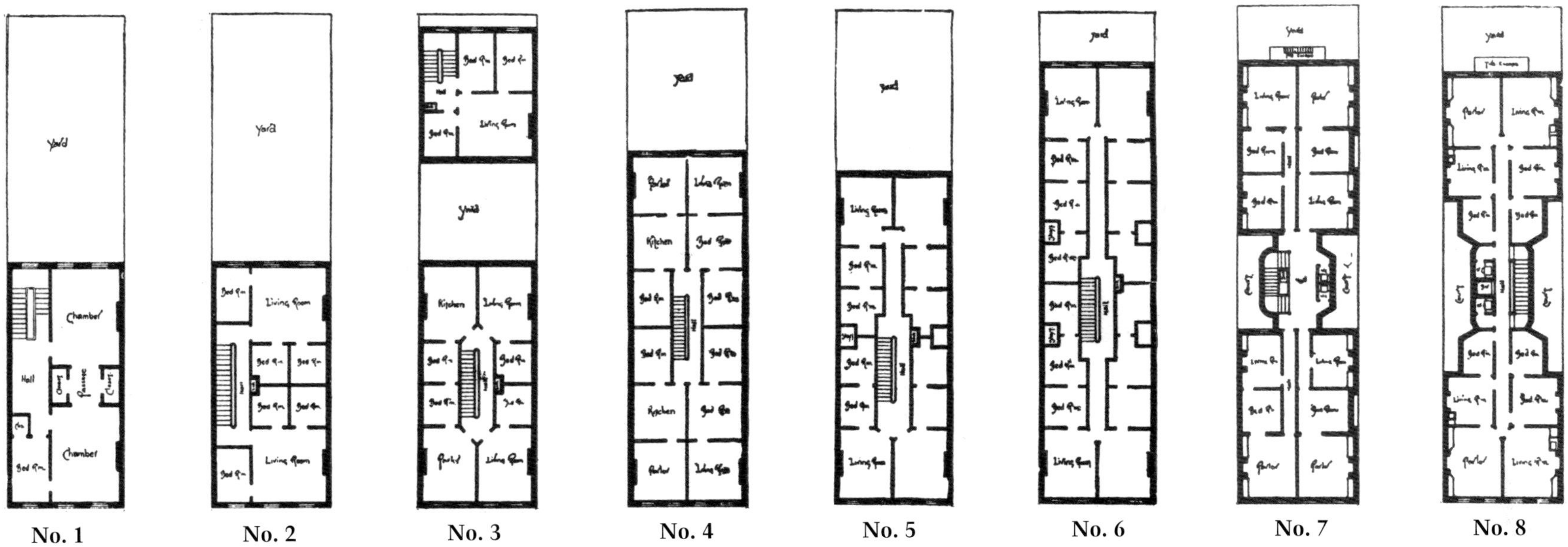

1. The evolution of New York City housing on 25' x 100' lots. Nos. 1-6 before 1879, Nos. 7-8, 1879

1. Plan of an old New York row house on lot, 25' x 100', 2. Plan of an old row house transformed into a tenement house, 3. Two buildings on one lot, 25' x 100', 4. Tenement without light or ventilation except in outer rooms, 5. Type of tenement house showing introduction of light shaft, 6. Typical tenement of the old style, covering 90 percent of lot, 7. Dumbbell tenement plan with small light well and common toilet on each floor, 8. Dumbbell tenement plan with light well configured to get light to all rooms, and with common toilet.

New York Housing Evolution

New York housing evolved from the single-family row house to the multifamily railroad flat (long tenement) before the tenement house legislation of 1879—the revised "Old Law"—that produced the "dumbbell" plan.[17]

There was no public housing authority in nineteenth-century New York. All tenements were built by private developers without restrictions (or scruples).

The plans above illustrate eight steps in the evolution of the New York City tenements, from an original single-family row house to a typical railroad flat that covers 90 percent of a 25' x 100' lot. In many railroad flats, the rear yard was eliminated entirely or might consist of only a few inches. In these tenements, only the rooms on the street received light. A tenement floor often contained eighteen rooms, only two of which received direct sunlight if the facade faced south. The interior rooms did not have any ventilation, unless air shafts were provided. The practice of back building, which was common in Manhattan, could lead to absurd results.

The first (Old Law) Tenement Act of 1867 required fire escapes, and the revised (Old Law) Tenement Act of 1879 required 12' light courts, 65 percent maximum site coverage, and no rear building. The "New Law" Tenement Act of 1901 provided for separate rooms, private baths, larger courts, and 50' x 100' plots.

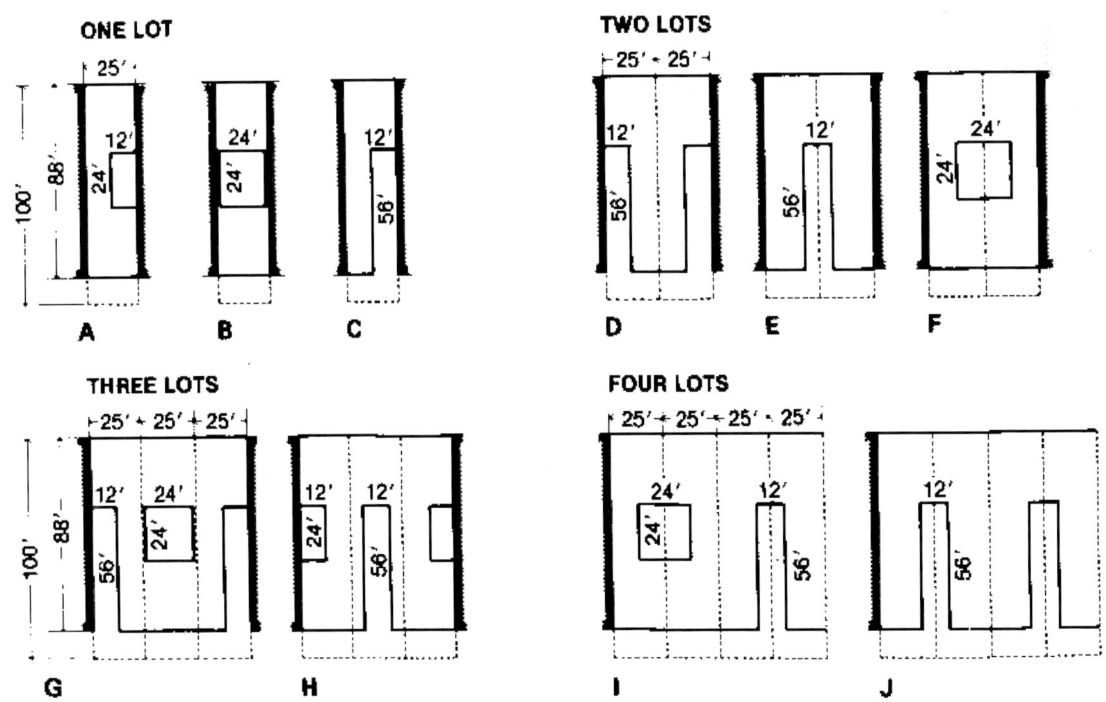

2. Diagrammatic plans based on the "New Law" Tenement Act of 1901

Apartment Buildings

For social and cultural reasons the apartment building came late to New York, as the concept of multiple families living in the same building was unacceptable to upper class New Yorkers. The first apartment building in New York—and the United States—was the Stuyvesant, built on West 18th Street in 1869. The building was designed by Richard Morris Hunt, who had returned from studying at the École des Beaux Arts in 1855, bringing the idea of the Parisian apartment building, or "French Flats," with him. The building type caught on quickly as development pushed north.[18]

Initially, the buildings were party-wall buildings aligned on the street. Gradually, however, they became larger courtyard buildings filling the ends of blocks, or whole blocks. Some, such as the Ansonia, had reentrant courts off the streets, to increase public exposure and perimeter, but they were still urban buildings related to the street.

After the 1916 zoning code, taller buildings like the San Remo and others introduced a distinctly New York skyscraper—one that defined the street on the lower levels, but was towerlike on the upper levels. Anti-urban models began to appear in the 1930s and 1940s and became the norm after the Second World War.

1. The Stuyvesant apartment building, 1869

2. The Bradley, 1877

3. Bryant Park Studios, 1901

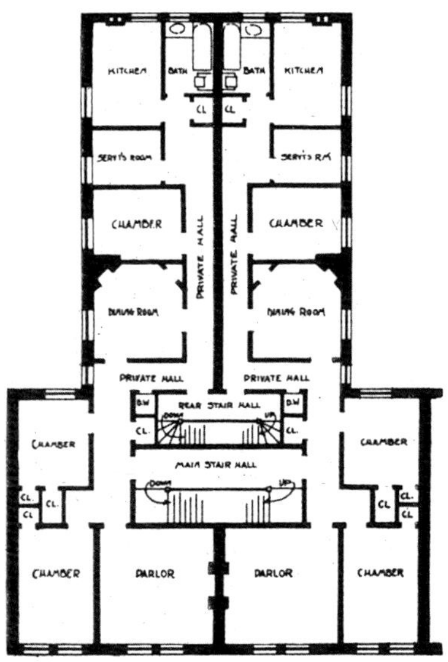

4. Plan of the Stuyvesant

5. View at Madison and 55th Street in 1870, looking northwest toward 5th Avenue and Central Park

1. The Osborne, 1885

2. The Dakota, 1884

3. The Ansonia, 1902

4. The San Remo, 1930

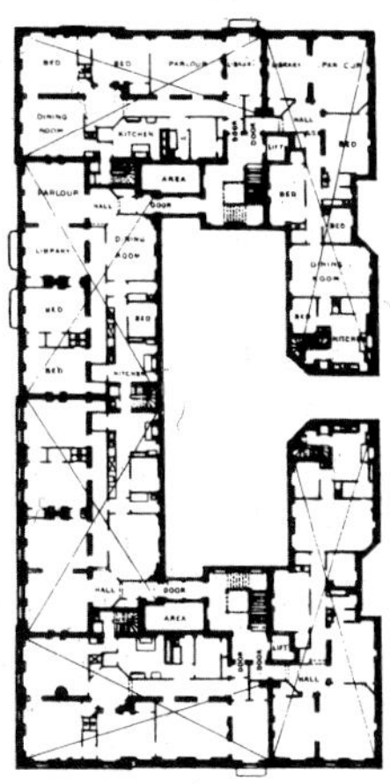

5. Plan of the Van Corlear, 1880

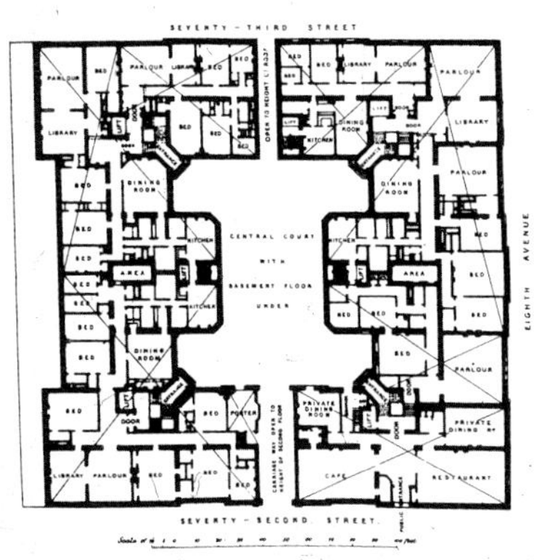

6. Plan of the Dakota, 1884

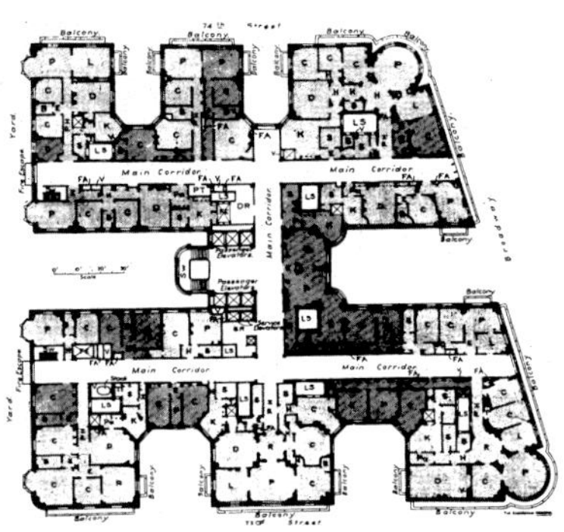

7. Plan of the Ansonia, 1902

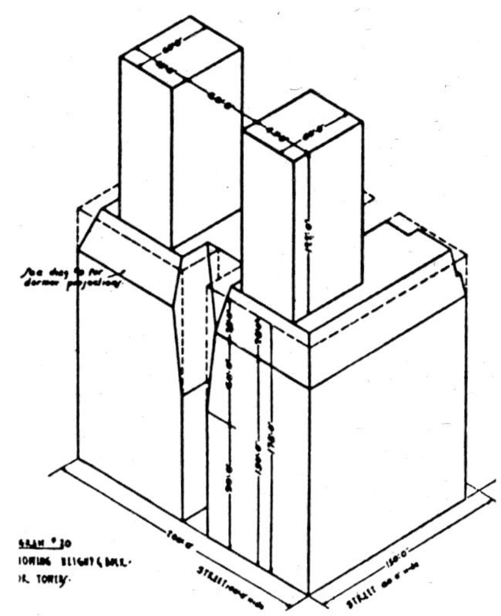

8. Diagram of the step-back zoning code, 1916

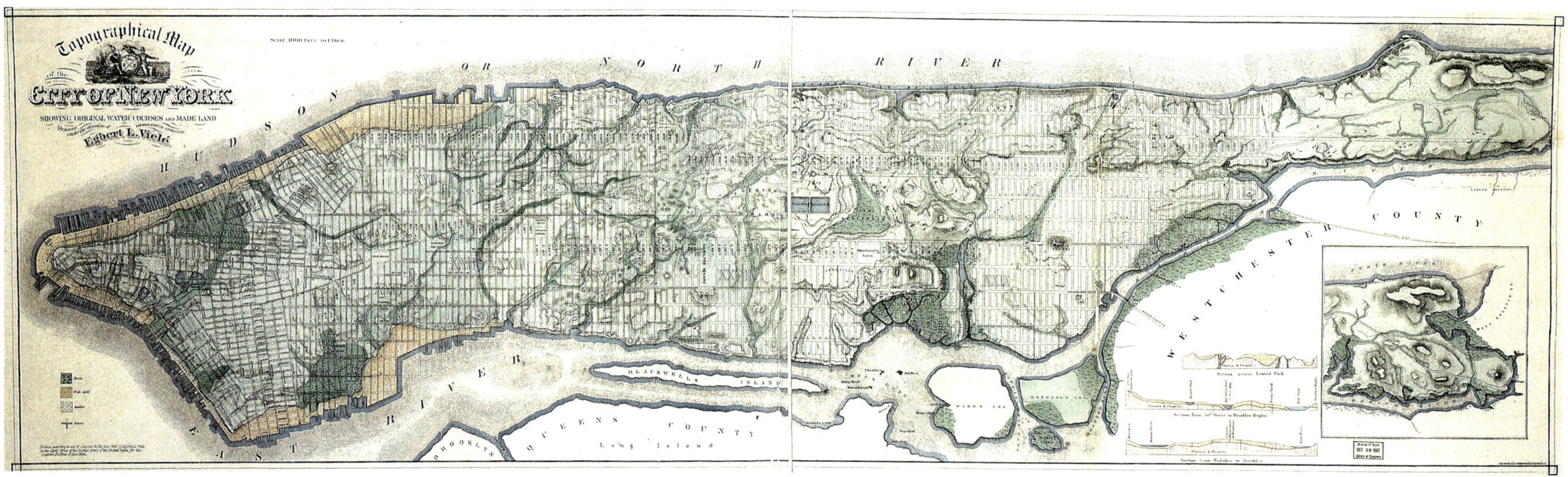

The Viele Water Map, 1856–74

Central Park

In the mid-1800s, there were 500,000 people living in New York City, with most city dwellers housed in crowded, cramped quarters below 38th Street. To escape the din of city life, people sought refuge in such pastoral spaces as Green-Wood Cemetery in Brooklyn.

In 1844, William C. Bryant called for the creation of a large public park. Andrew J. Downing and Bryant pressed officials to set land aside before it was swallowed up by the fast-developing city. Between 1853 and 1856, the commissioners paid more than $5 million for land from 59th Street to 106th Street, between 5th and 8th Avenues.

Egbert Viele was appointed engineer-in-chief of the park, and his first task was to map the terrain with all its water and topographic features. After mapping the park area, Viele continued to map the whole island with the block structure of the Commissioners' Plan superimposed on it. The first part, the plan of lower Manhattan, was published in 1859, the entire island in 1865, and a revised version in 1874.

The plan is remarkably accurate, and since everything was flattened and covered over as development moved north, the plan has been in continual use as a subsurface reference since it was made.[19]

Viele also made a plan for the park in 1856, but in 1857, the independent board of commissioners set aside his plan and sponsored a public competition to design the new Central Park. Viele submitted to the competition, but the commissioners chose the Greensward plan by Frederick Law Olmsted, superintendent of the park work crews, and Calvert Vaux, the British architect who had convinced the commissioners to hold a design competition. The new plan launched the redevelopment of upper Manhattan for the affluent, and the career of Olmsted as a landscape architect. Viele also lost out to Olmsted and Vaux for the design of Prospect Park in Brooklyn, but his Water Map was one of the most important plans of Manhattan.

The varied terrain of the topography set aside for the park invited pastoral, picturesque, and formal landscapes, all of which were included in Olmsted and Vaux's plan. The soil was inadequate to sustain the trees and shrubs Olmsted and Vaux planned, so 500,000 cubic feet of topsoil was carted in from New Jersey. Thirty-six bridges and arches were built and six man-made water bodies, fed from the City's water supply, were created. Most of the landscape of Central Park was completed twenty years after the design competition was announced.

Central Park was the first public park in the United States and Olmsted's first landscape commission. He was thirty-five years old when he won the competition, and it is a masterpiece. In 1872 Olmsted also did the conceptual design for Riverside Park and Drive in Manhattan, and with Vaux, designed Prospect Park in Brooklyn.

The Romantic naturalism of Central Park was an antidote to the city. Even though the park was completely fabricated—completely man-made, in the manner of the Buttes Chaumont—it seemed natural, and was big enough to wall off the city outside. In fact, formally and philosophically the park contained the seeds of the disintegration of the American city. At this point in time, well before the worst of the industrial era—of "filth, congestion, crime, and disease"—the idea of a less dense, less integrated city had emerged in America.

The idea of separating the place of work from the place of living had been around since the early nineteenth century when mechanized transport enabled longer commutes.

Paris also experienced similar increased movement,

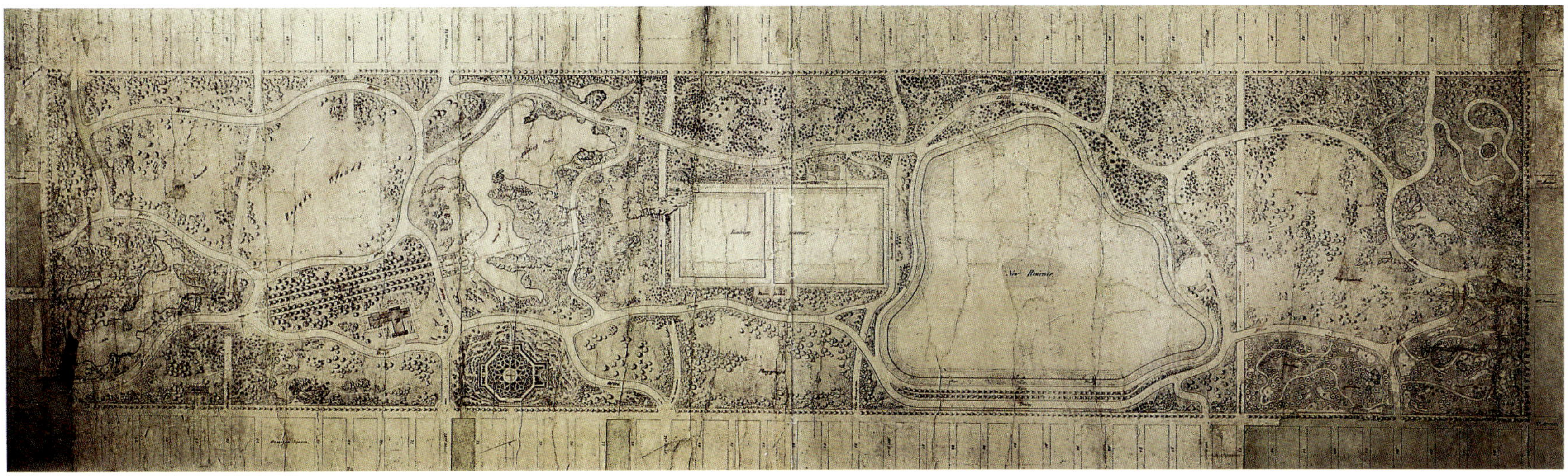

1. The first plan for Central Park, 1856

but in Paris Napoleon III, Haussmann, and Alphand built wider streets to accommodate increased vehicular circulation, whereas in America, with no urban tradition, suburbia and mono-functional zoning were spawned in lieu of the revised, compact city. Schuyler points out that Olmsted felt that "a large part of the ideas of a city, which have been transmitted to us from the period when cities were walled about and necessarily compact and crowded, must be put away."[20] Olmsted believed that the new city should have a compact business district, but that housing should spread out into the natural landscape on a less dense basis.

There is some argument about whether A. J. Downing or F. L. Olmsted is the father of American landscape architecture, but based on his later work such as Riverside, it seems clear that Olmsted is the father of suburbia, and represents the real beginning of the ecological landscape movement. His influence on the Garden City movement and the City Beautiful movement leads more or less directly to Le Corbusier, the "City in the Garden," and ultimately, to Ian McHarg.

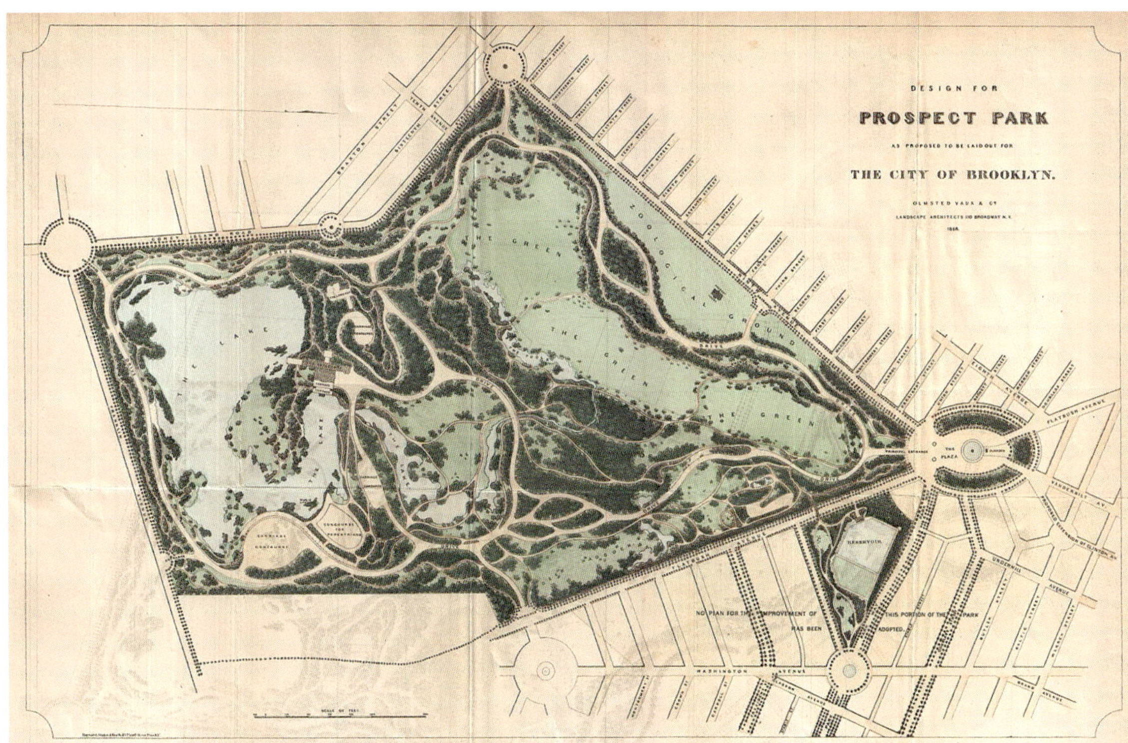

2. Plan for Prospect Park

View of the Long Meadow in Prospect Park, ca. 1890

1. Perspective view of Manhattan in 1850, 39 years after the 1811 plan was adopted

2. Perspective of Manhattan in 1856, with land set aside for Central Park

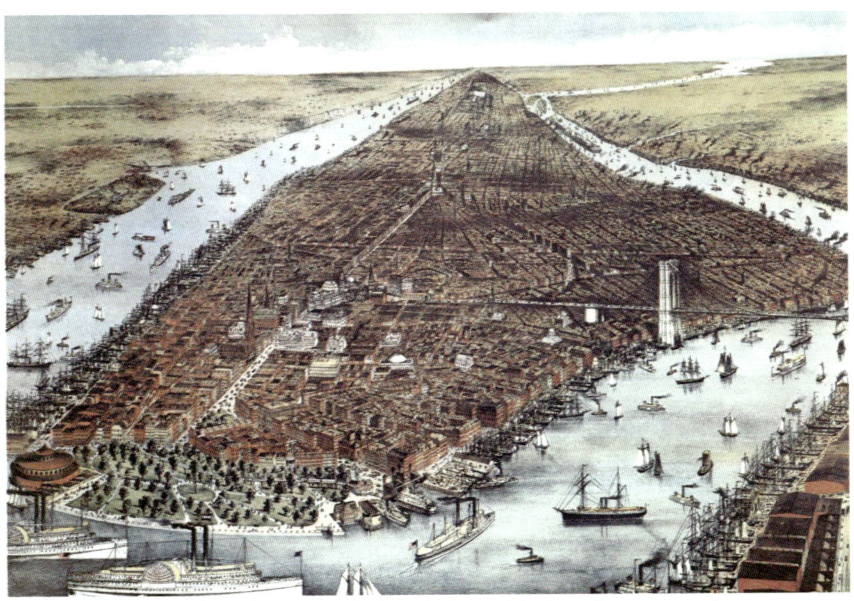

3. Perspective view of Manhattan in 1876, with Central Park under construction

4. Contemporary aerial view of lower Manhattan

2. Plan of Boston in 1833 showing the Back Bay before the Mill Dam and subsequent filling

The Back Bay in Boston

This aptly named neighborhood in Boston derives its name from the body of water that gradually began to disappear in the early nineteenth century. Filling the bay began after construction of the Mill Dam, finished in 1821, had isolated the bay from the Charles River. In 1856 authority was given to proceed according to a plan attributed to the architect Arthur Gilman, and the filling began in earnest.[21]

The plan established five parallel east–west streets: Beacon Street, which was built on the Mill Dam; Marlborough Street; Commonwealth Avenue, which had been widened to 200' plus 20' set-backs, making it 10' wider than the Champs-Elysées in Paris; Newbury Street; and Boylston Street. When completed, the combination of Commonwealth Avenue, the Public Garden, and Boston Common formed an elaborate urban set-piece—an essential component of Boston's civic structure.

The blocks were 240–250' wide, with 20–22' alleys, by 500–550' long. The parcels were not platted, but were sold outright, or by lottery, in increments, beginning at Arlington Street. The parcels varied in width, but the basic module was 25', which was suitable for large row houses—as opposed to the greater width required for the apartment buildings of Paris. Apartment buildings did not begin to appear in Boston and New York until about 1870.

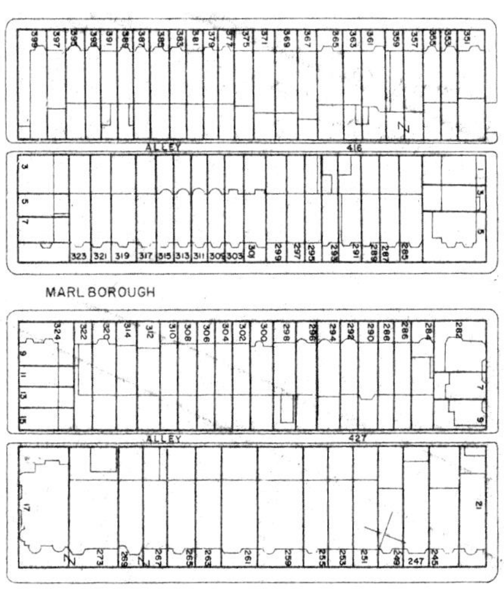

1. Plan of Back Bay blocks showing parcels

3. Plan of Back Bay with 1630 shoreline

1. View of Commonwealth Avenue in 1877

2. View of Commonwealth Avenue completed

3. Aerial plan of Back Bay

4. Aerial view of the Champs-Elysées

5. Aerial view of Back Bay

6. Commonwealth Avenue Park

7. Commonwealth Avenue

8. Aerial view of Back Bay in 1983

"La Catena" view of Florence, 1472, Francesco Rosselli studio

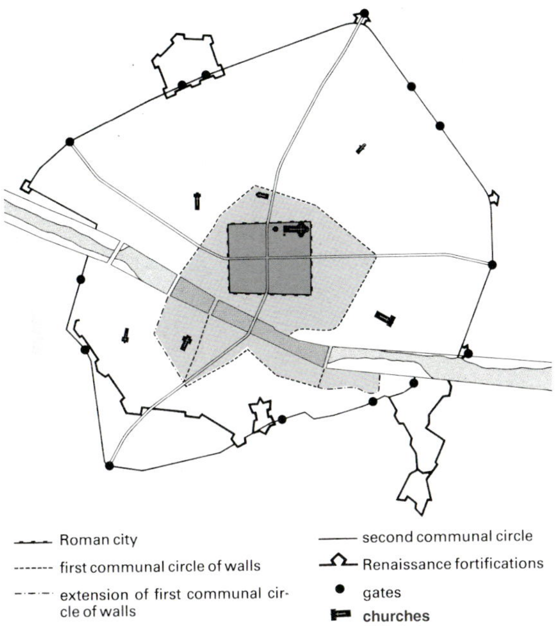

1. *Florentine walls:*
Dark gray = Roman;
Light gray = 1173–75;
Outer = 1284–1333

2. *Piazza della Signoria and Palazzo Vecchio*

Medieval Florence

Between the second and third centuries AD the population of Florence was over 10,000, and the city had a river port, a theater, and an amphitheater.[22] After the collapse of the Roman Empire, the population fell to ca. 1,000, and would not reach 10,000 people again until around 900 AD. But by 1200 the population had increased to 50,000, and by 1300 it was 100,000.[23]

The late 1200s and early 1300s were also of fundamental importance for the long-range urban development of Florence. Three urban iniatives were important: major churches and piazzas were begun outside the twelfth-century perimeter (1173–75), and would later become neighborhood centers; new civic buildings were begun in the Roman core; and new city walls were constructed enclosing a vastly expanded urban area.

The architect, sculptor, and urban planner Arnolfo di Cambio (ca. 1245–1301/10) was central to all three initiatives.[24] He planned the church of Santa Croce in 1295. He began the new Cathedral, Santa Maria dei Fiori, in 1296, and the Palazzo dei Priori (later Palazzo Vecchio) in 1298.[25] These projects established the pattern of the city's neighborhoods, and provided the governmental and religious civic monuments in the city core. Equally important were Arnolfo's new urban walls, constructed between 1284 and 1333.[26] These walls were a major determinant of Florence's urban form. For over 500 years they provided room for internal growth and renovation, as well as defense.

3. *Arnolfo di Cambio's wall, 1284–1333*

1. *Plan of Florence, 1832*

Renaissance Florence

The bubonic plague of 1348 killed roughly half of Florence's population, and the city would not reach previous population levels until the nineteenth century. Thus, expansion did not occur within Arnolfo's walls, and the urban plan appears frozen in time—except for the interventions of the Renaissance.

In addition to the plethora of artistic and architectural additions to the city during the Renaissance, the main urban intervention was the sequence: Palazzo Pitti, Ponte Vecchio, Uffizi, Piazza Signoria, Duomo, Piazza SS. Annunziata. Vasari's elevated connection between the Palazzo Pitti and the Palazzo Vecchio was completed in five months in 1565 for Cosimo I and is a major component of the cross-town sequence.[27]

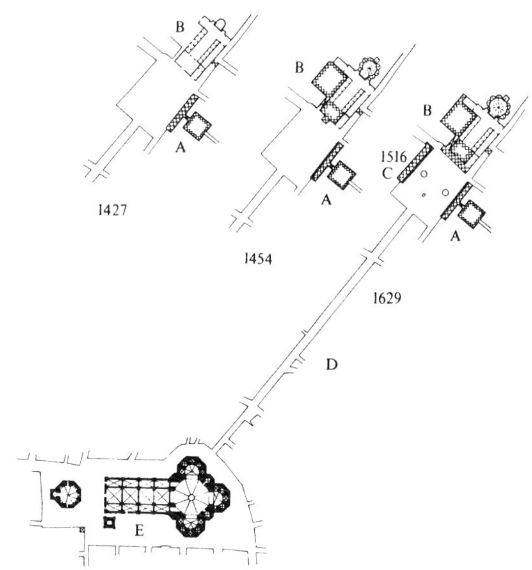

2. *Development plan of the Piazza SS. Annunziata*

1. Plan of Vasari's corridor connecting the Palazzo Pitti and the Palazzo Vecchio, 1565

2. Vasari's corridor and the Ponte Vecchio

3. Palazzo Pitti and Boboli Garden

4. Uffizi

5. Piazza SS. Annunziata

Florence Expansion

Federico Fantozzi's plan depicts Florence in 1843. The extent of the city had changed little since Arnolfo di Cambio's fortification walls greatly enlarged the city between 1284 and 1333. There were still vast amounts of open land within the walls, and open country beyond.[28]

The unification of Italy in 1860, and the subsequent decision to move the capital of the new nation from Turin to Florence, precipitated major plans for expansion and reconstruction. Massive amounts of new housing were required for the expected influx of officials. In 1800, the population of Florence was 100,000. By 1865 it was 150,000, and was expected to grow by another 50,000.[29]

The organization of the Italian government came to Florence in 1865 and began to function within available facilities. At the same time, the architect Giuseppe Poggi was asked to develop an expansion plan.

Plan of Florence, Federico Fantozzi, 1843

Fantozzi Plan of Florence with Poggi's proposed expansion, 1865

Poggi's Florence Expansion Plan

Poggi's expansion plan called for the demolition of the city's fortification wall and its replacement with a tree-lined boulevard punctuated by a series of new squares. Urban blocks of new housing were proposed both "inside" the old wall and "outside." The plan also called for the rebuilding of the ancient market (the Roman Forum) in the medieval core of the city, but curiously, no new state buildings were proposed.

The seat of government was moved to Rome in 1871, and Florence entered a period of economic uncertainty. Nevertheless, the plan was ultimately completed, including the reconstruction of the core.

Poggi's plan is not sophisticated, but it was produced in two months in 1865.[30] Outside the line of the walls, the plan consists of a grid of streets parallel and perpendicular to the viale that replaced the walls. Inside the line of the walls, the plan consists of gridded neighborhoods in undeveloped areas and in the core. Several of these areas have a public space—piazza or park—at the center, as in the Bastide towns, or the Great Estates in London.

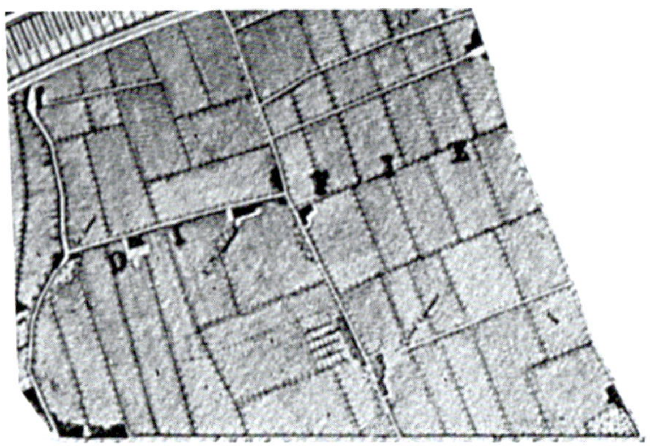

1. Piazza Savonarola area, 1:10,000

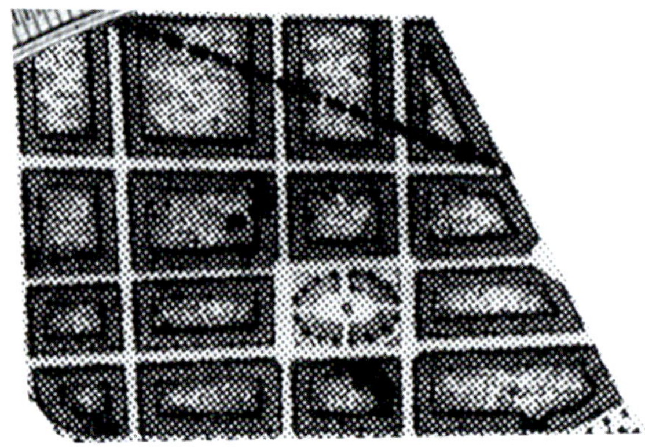

2. Poggi plan, 1:10,000

3. Aerial plan, 1:10,000

4. Piazza D'Azeglio area, 1:10,000

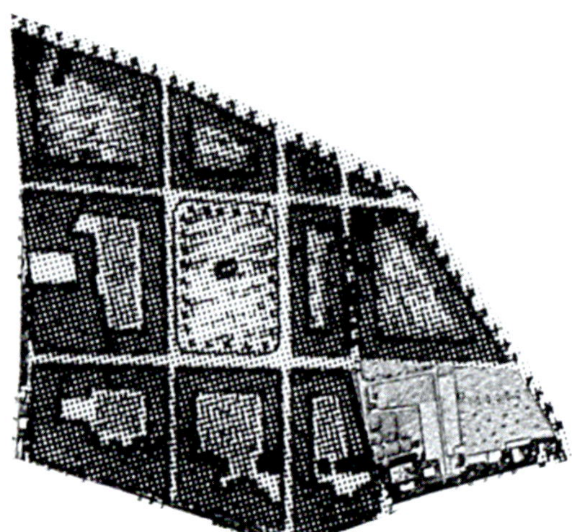

5. Poggi plan, 1:10,000

6. Aerial plan, 1:10,000

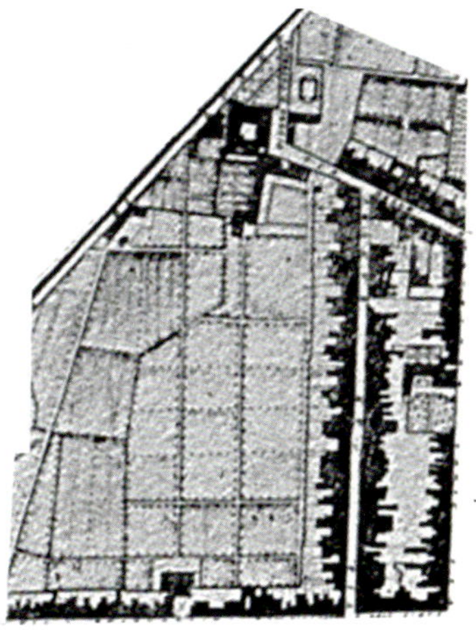

1. Piazza Indipendenza area, 1:10,000

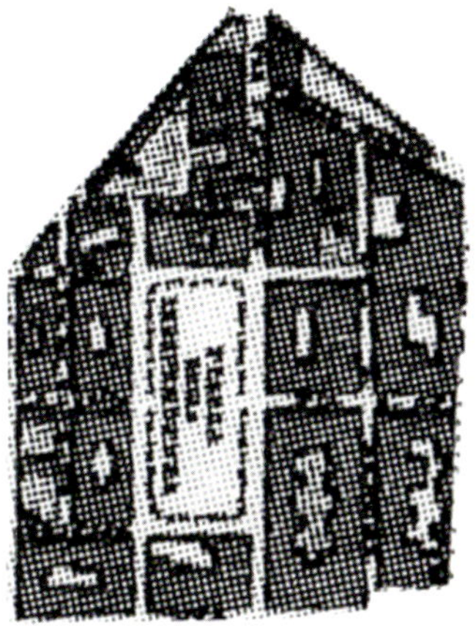

2. Poggi plan, 1:10,000

3. Aerial plan, 1:10,000

Poggi's Urban Fabric

If the various neighborhoods of Poggi's plan are conceptually similar to the Bastides or London's Great Estates, extracting them from their context and comparing them to each other is revealing.

Compared to the historic (Roman) core, Poggi's neighborhoods are almost equal in size, but with very large public spaces, and very large blocks. This is an issue with Florence's earlier urban development as well. Because Florence did not develop incrementally outside the core, and because it developed orthogonally to the Arno River and the Roman system of centuriation, the blocks between the core and Arnolfo's walls tend to be very long, and/or large. There is more open space inside the blocks, but the public space of the streets in this area is the most boring part of the city.

4. West part of core area, 1:10,000

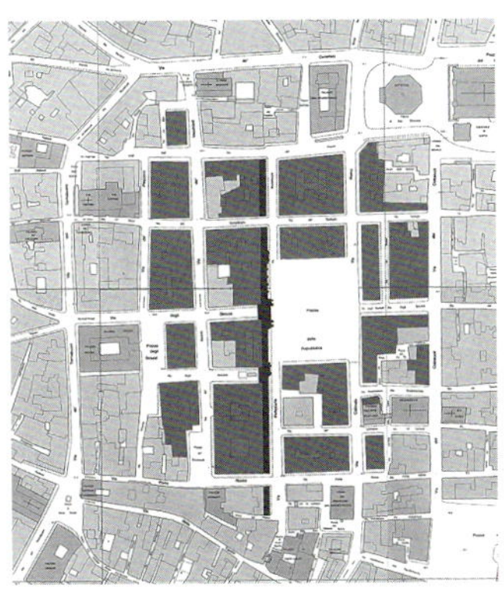

5. Poggi plan, 1:10,000

6. Aerial plan of core, 1:10,000

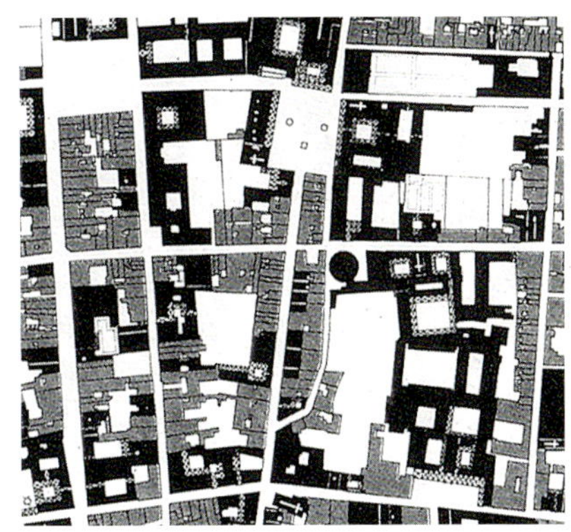

7. Area north of Duomo, 1:10,000

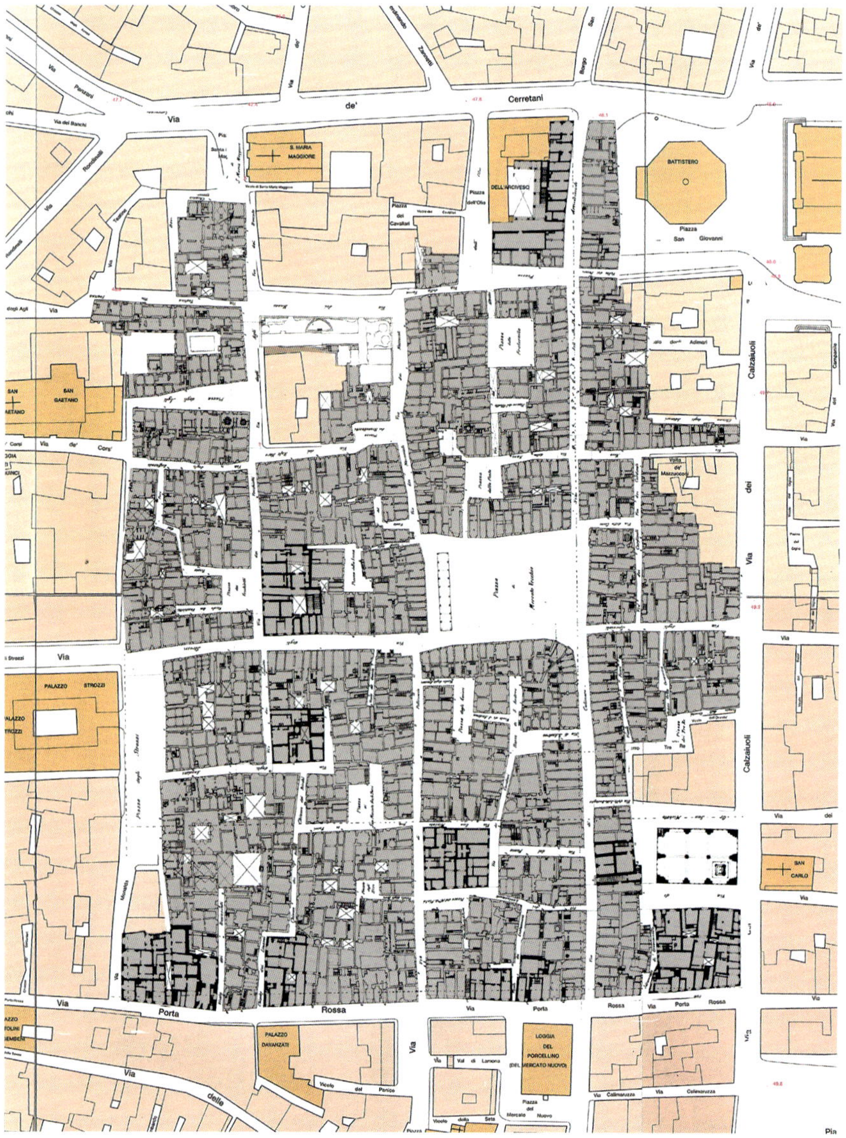

1. Plan of the Mercato Vecchio area scheduled for demolition, 1:3,000

2. Mercato Vecchio

3. Mercato Vecchio

4. Demolition of the Mercato Vecchio

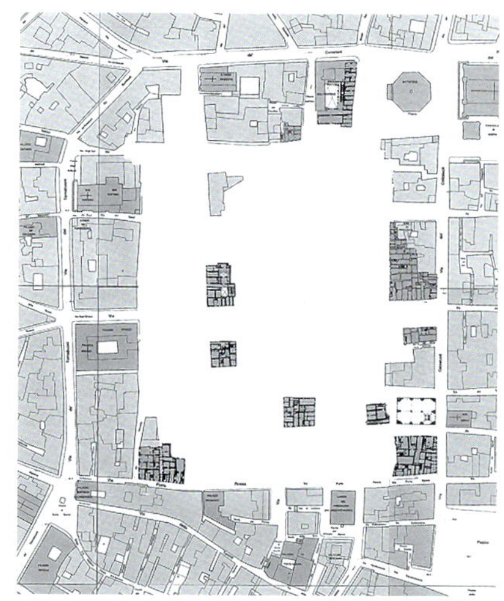

5. Plan after demolition, 1:10,000

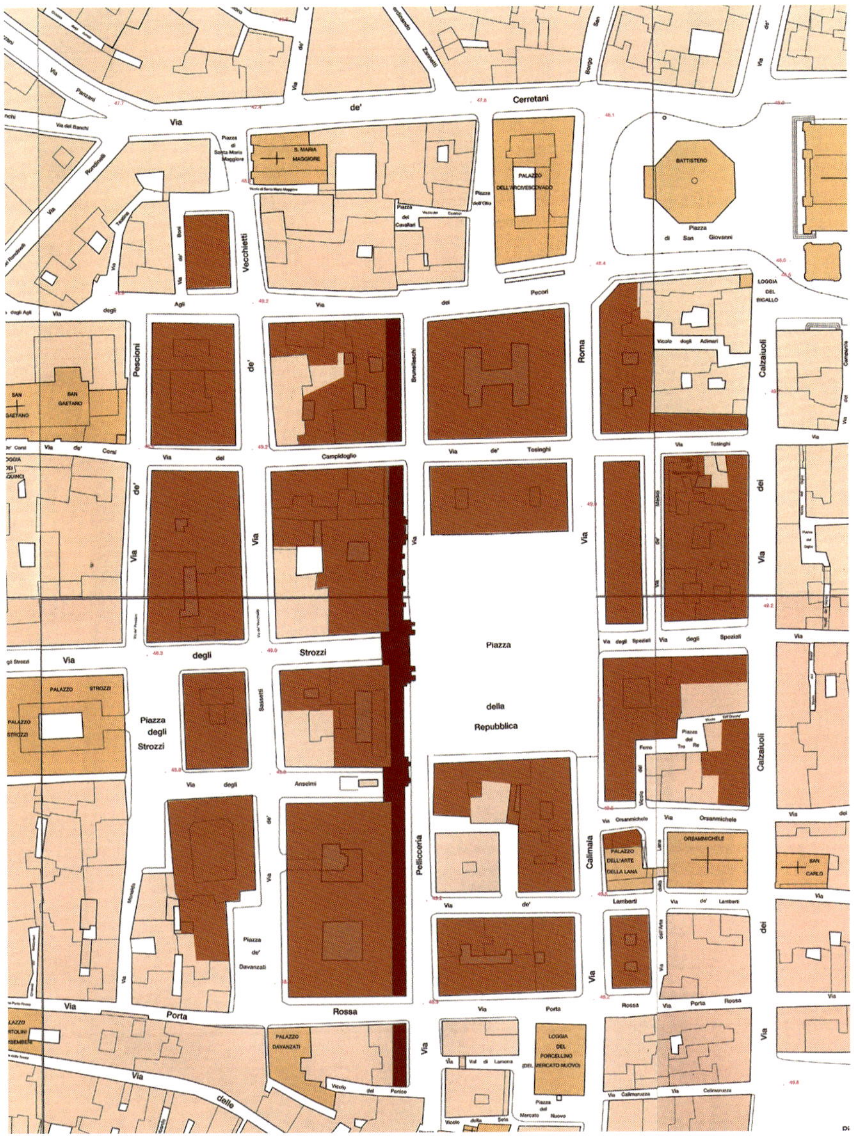

1. *New insertions by Poggi, 1:3,000*

2. *Piazza della Repubblica*

The Renovation of the Core

The medieval fabric in the western half of Florence's core only vaguely followed the original Roman pattern, but it had a porous, small-scale texture of narrow streets and courtyards. The old market, the Mercato Vecchio, occupied the site of the original Roman Forum and was also small: 140' x 220'. The medieval fabric was demolished between 1865 and 1869.[31]

The renovation by Poggi returned the area to a grid pattern closer to the Roman one, but with wider streets and larger buildings. The new Piazza della Repubblica more than doubled the size of the Mercato Vecchio to approximately 260' x 300'. A loggia defines the west side of the space, and runs for 1,000', almost exactly to the limits of the original Roman grid. The central portion of the loggia has a unified facade that relates directly to the piazza.

3. *Loggia*

Dutch engraving of the walled city and plain, 1706

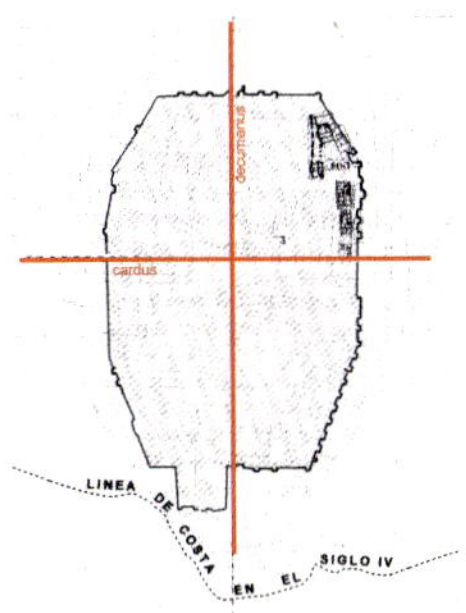

1. Plan of Roman Barcino, ca. 15 BC

2. Plan of the Gothic city with the second wall, 1230

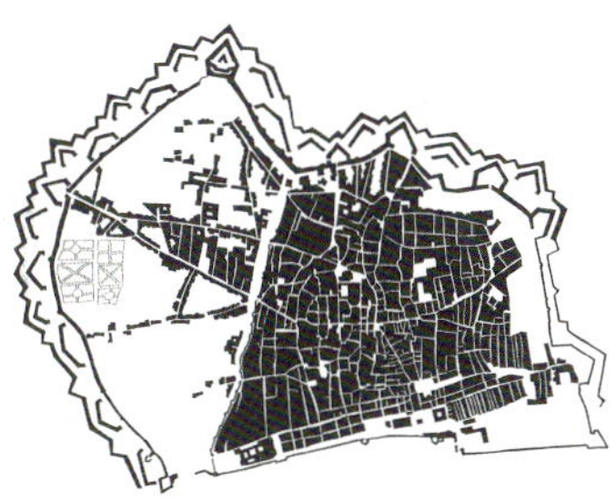

3. Plan showing the third wall, 1359

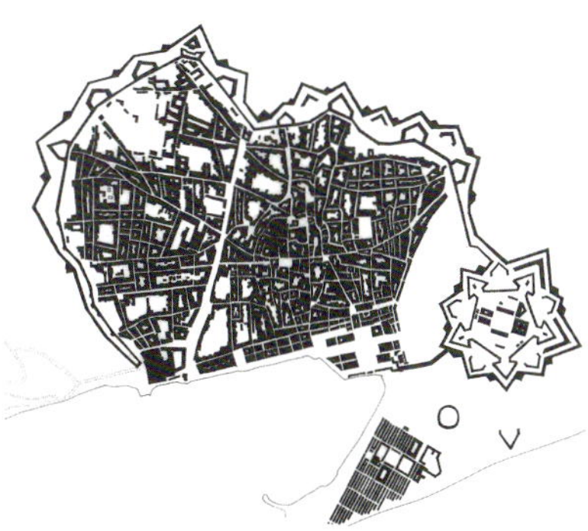

4. Plan with the Fortress and Barceloneta, 1714

Introduction

The city of Barcelona is a remarkable combination of urban unity and beauty, with an almost infinite variety of parts and details. Indeed, it is one of the world's most beautiful cities. It would have been a great city even if it had not been transformed by Ildefons Cerdà (1815–76), planner of the city's nineteenth-century urban expansion, but the identity and form of modern Barcelona is also so closely associated with Cerdà that it is surprising how little attention they have received—at least until fairly recently. Cerdà himself is equally unique. He spent his whole professional life developing a new theory of urbanism and applying it to one city.[32]

Barcelona Before Cerdà

The old city of Barcelona, the Ciutat Vella, developed for over eighteen hundred years before Cerdà's expansion project, which took less than one hundred years. The city's formal Roman origins are still legible in the pattern of urban fabric today, and the Ciutat Vella and Gracia stand in marked contrast to the expansion. The streets and blocks are small and irregular; the buildings are generally smaller; and there are more plazas and public spaces. Arguably, this is still the most beautiful part of the city.

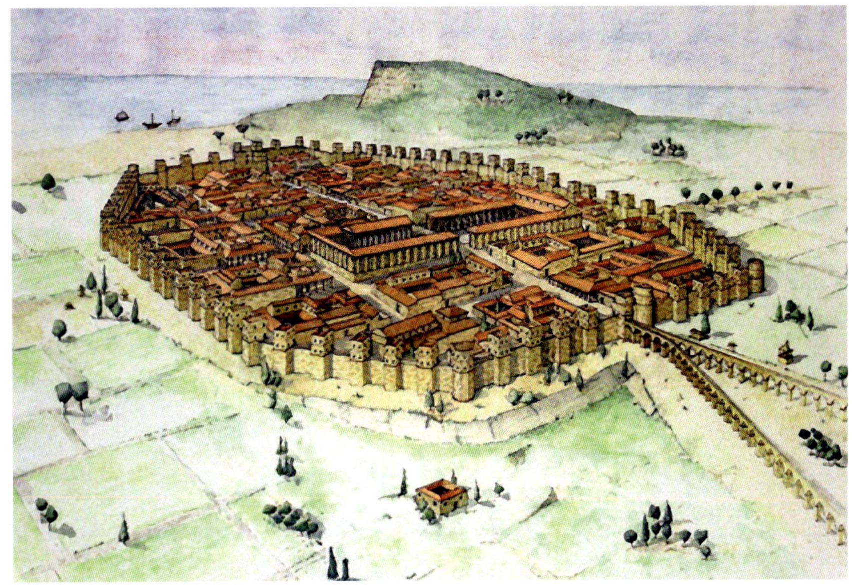

5. Reconstruction of Roman Barcino, ca. 15 BC

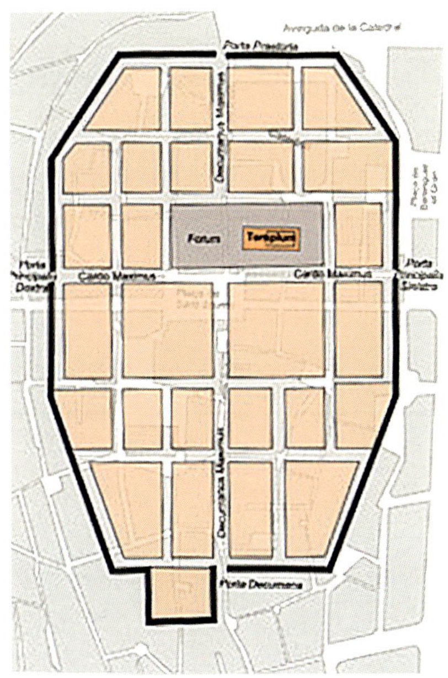

6. Reconstruction plan of Roman Barcino

7. Remains of the Roman wall

Roman Barcelona

The nucleus of contemporary Barcelona was the Roman colony of Barcino, founded around 15 BC on the small hillock, Mount Tabor, near the sea. The Roman Forum was located in approximately the same location as the Plaça Sant Jaume.[33]

Medieval Barcelona

For roughly a thousand years Barcelona remained within the Roman walls, but substantial changes began to happen between 900 and 1200, as European cities began to develop again.

Most of Barcelona's medieval civic buildings were built within the Roman walls, but gradually, development began to occur outside the Roman core, and in 1230 a second wall was built. The western limit was a dry river bed that later became the famous Rambla.

In order to manage the developing city, King Jaume I established the Consell de Cent, in 1249, as the government for "The City of Counts."[34]

The Cathedral was begun in 1298 and finished in 1448. During the fourteenth century the city hall was built along with the council chamber, the Saló de Cent, and the Tinell Room in the Palau Reial dates from the eleventh century.

By 1350 the population was 30,000. Some institutions and less desirable uses grew up outside the western wall, and in 1359 a third wall was built to enclose the area that is still known as El Raval, or suburb.[35] The population was about 34,000. Together, these two areas comprise the Ciutat Vella, or Old City.

4. Extent of the Ciutat Vella within the second wall until 1359

1. The Tinell Room in the Palau Reial, 11th c.

2. Saló de Cent in City Hall, 14th c.

3. Plaça Reial

5. Plan diagram showing the growth of new areas outside the Roman wall

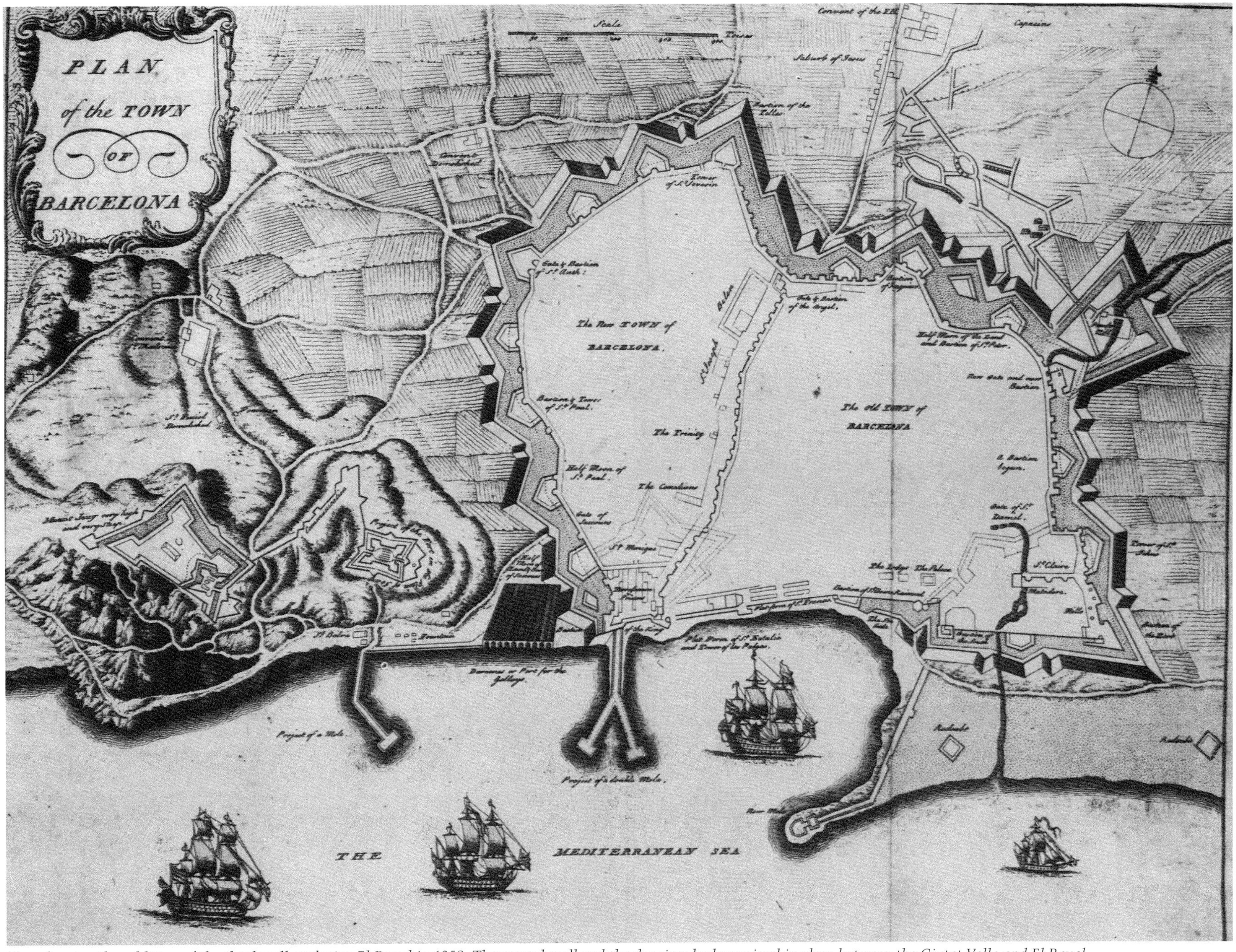

Plan showing the addition of the third wall enclosing El Raval in 1359. The second wall and the dry river bed remained in place between the Ciutat Vella and El Raval

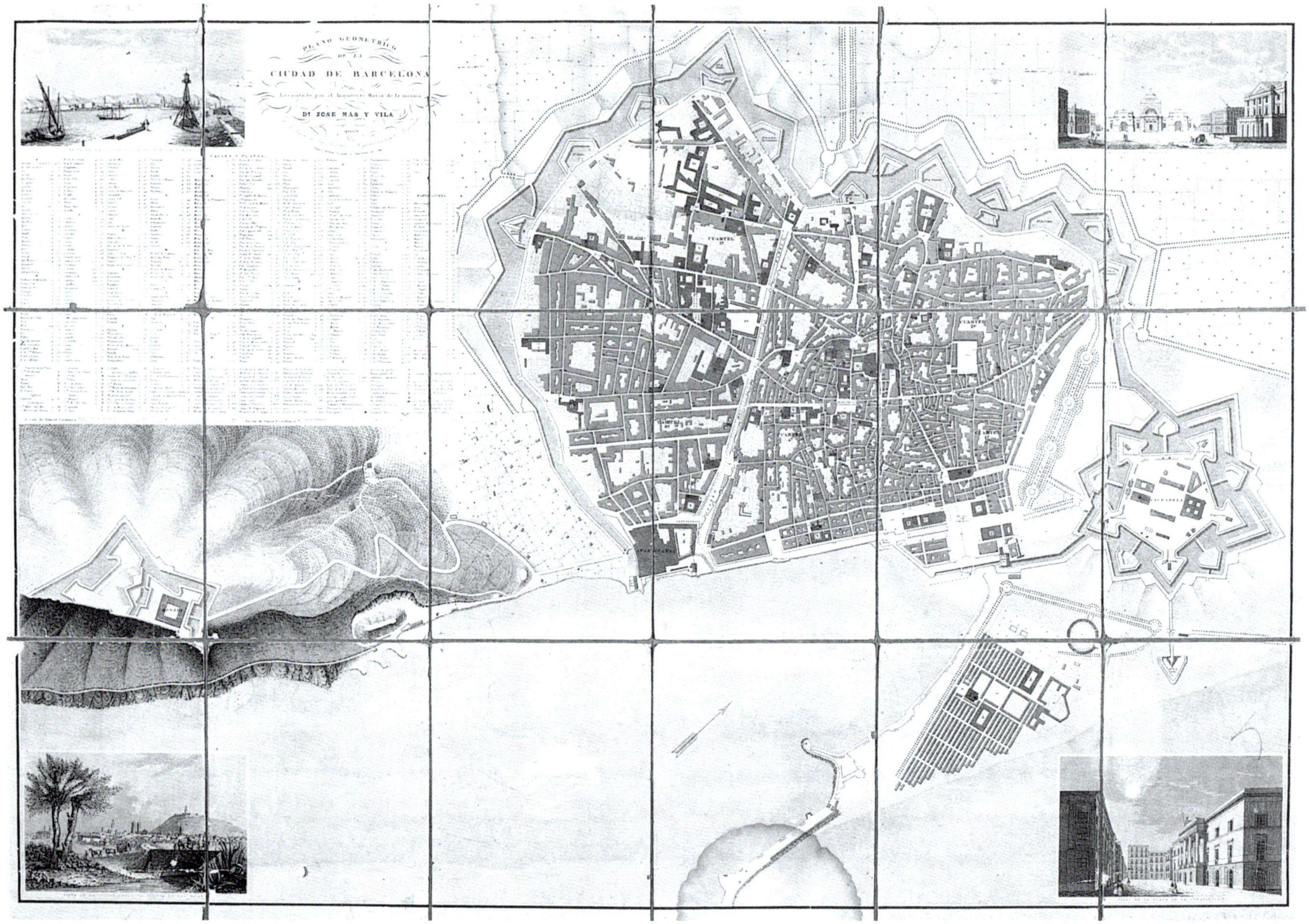

1. Plan of Barcelona in 1842

Eighteenth-Century Barcelona

The War of Spanish Succession (1701–14) did not result well for Barcelona. Philip V captured Barcelona and dissolved the Catalan kingdom in 1716. From then on Barcelona would be subject to Madrid.[36]

Few urban projects occurred in Barcelona in the eighteenth century. The fortifications were reinforced, and in 1715 Philip V had the Ribera neighborhood destroyed in order to build the Ciutadella fortress, the largest in Europe. It was not until 1753 that the displaced population was housed in the newly planned suburb of Barceloneta, between the city and the sea.[37]

Barceloneta

Designed by the military planner Prospéro Verbloom and begun in 1753, Barceloneta is the first planned neighborhood in Barcelona. It is like a mini-Manhattan with very long, narrow blocks. But whereas the typical Manhattan block is 200' x 800' with streets 60' wide, in Barceloneta the typical block is about 30' x 320' with streets 20' wide.

2. Aerial plan of Barceloneta

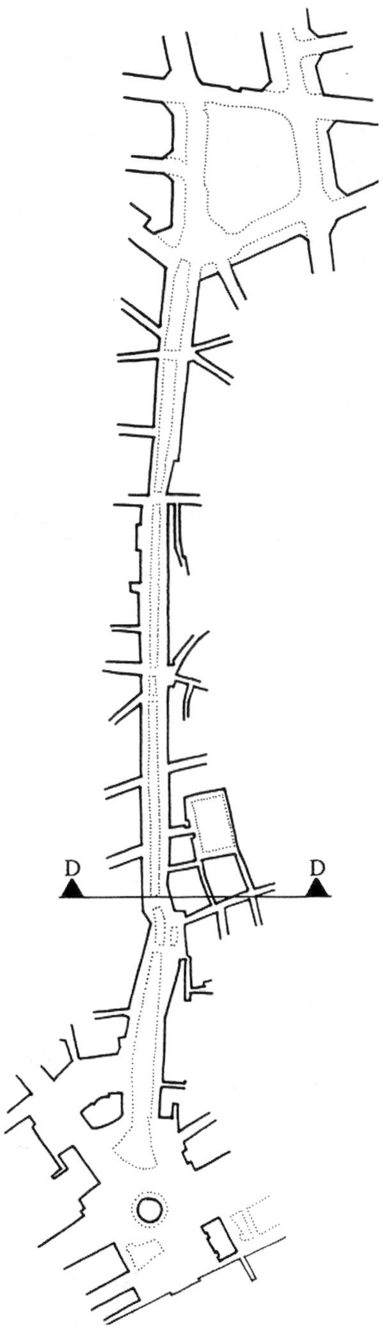

1. *Plan of La Rambla*

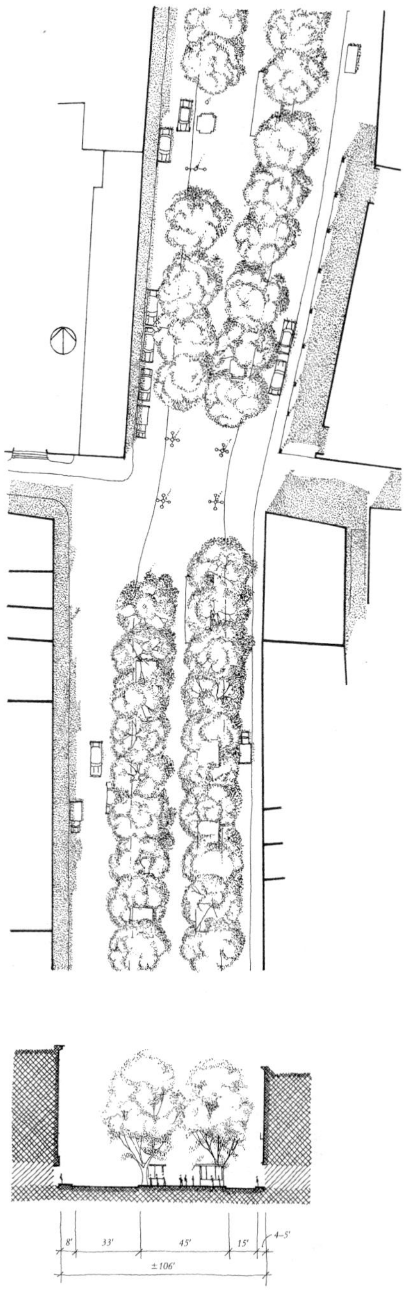

2. *Detail plan and section from A. Jacobs*

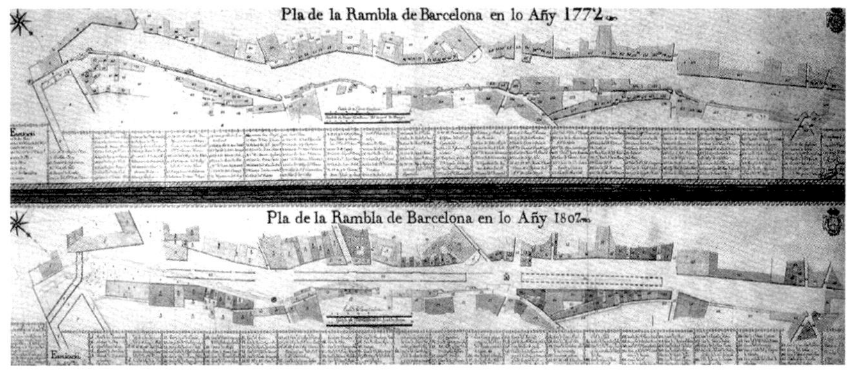

3. *Plan of La Rambla*

4. *View of La Rambla, 1906*

La Rambla

One of the most famous streets in the world began as a river bed skirting the second ring of Barcelona's walls,[38] which remained in place until 1704, when it began to be demolished. In the late eighteenth century, between 1772 and 1807, the realignment was carried out by the engineer Cermeño. Further configuration occurred in the nineteenth century, and the plane trees were transplanted from Girona's Devesa Park in 1850.

The street is approximately 100' wide with an "insert" of a paved pedestrian median about 60' wide, lined on each side with plane trees planted about 20' apart. The Rambla was Barcelona's first great urban space.

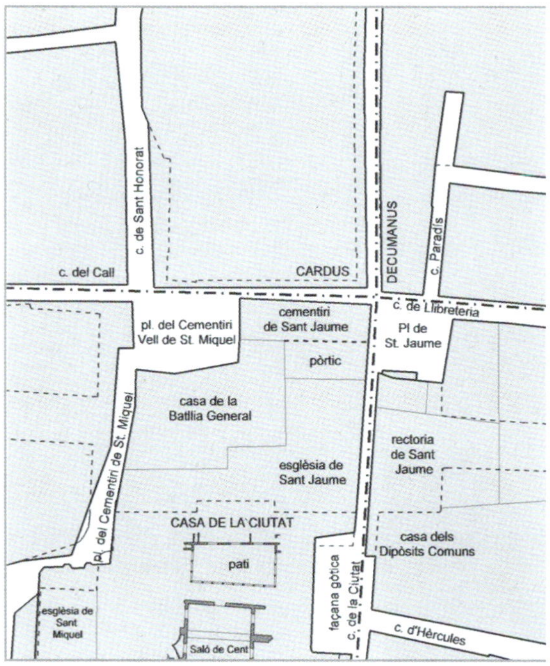

1. Plan of the medieval area before construction of the plaza

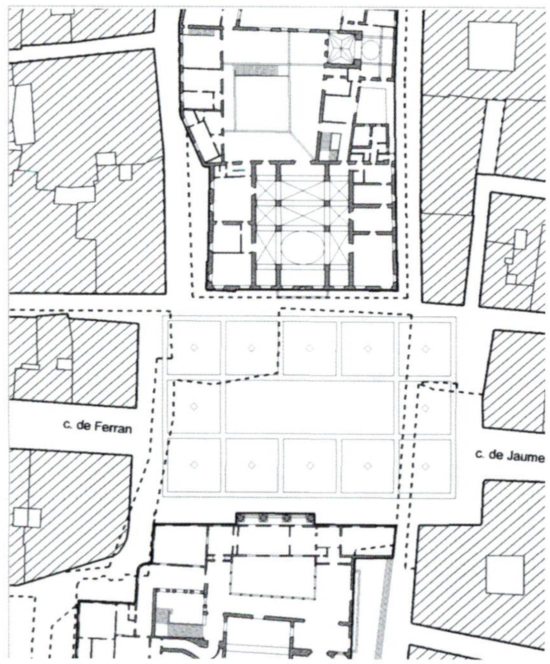

2. Plan of the Plaça Sant Jaume

3. Aerial view of the plaza

Plaça Sant Jaume

The second major space to be developed in the Ciutat Vella was the Plaça Sant Jaume, constructed in 1820–23 approximately on the site of the ancient Roman forum.[39] Carved out of the dense medieval fabric, the plaza is framed on one side by the Generalitat, seat of the Catalan government, and on the facing side by the Barcelona City Hall. Both are medieval buildings with shallow neoclassical facades defining the plaza, which is 145' x 220'. The Carrer de Ferran was opened in 1858.

4. View of the plaza, and the Generalitat

1. Plan of the site in 1842

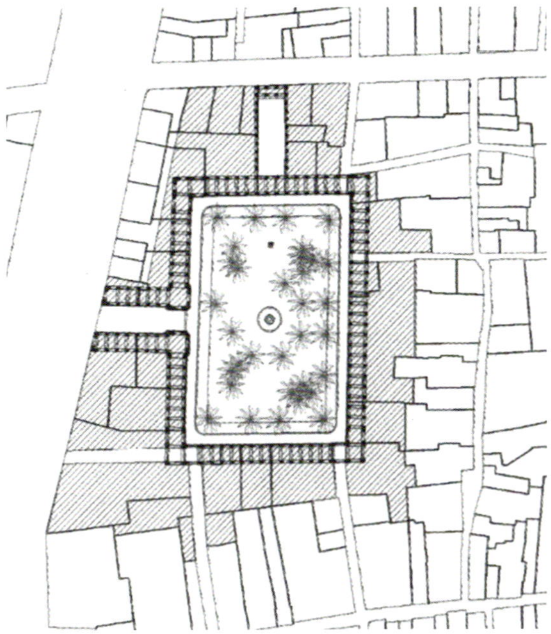

2. Plan of the Plaça Reial, 1:2,500

3. Aerial plan of the Plaça Reial, 1:2,500

Plaça Reial

The third major space to be developed in the Ciutat Vella was the Plaça Reial, designed in 1848 by Daniel Molina on the site of the former Capuchin convent.[40] Today, the plaza is a great outdoor room just off the Rambla, 175' x 270', paved, with a series of palm trees, and surrounded by an arcade and unified facades.

4. View of the arcade

5. View of the plaça

1. *Aerial view of the Rambla and Plaça Reial*

2. *Aerial plan showing the extension of the Carrer de Ferran through the Plaça Sant Jaume*

Nineteenth-Century Barcelona

By 1850 the city of Barcelona, the Ciutat Vella, was nominally complete. El Raval was admittedly deplorable, but had nothing else happened, Barcelona would have been one of the world's great cities. It is still, arguably, the most beautiful part of the city.

With the growing economy in Barcelona after industrialization, trade with the Americas reopened, and a constant growing demand for labor caused an urban migration. By mid-nineteenth century, Barcelona, with a population of 189,000, was one of the most dense cities in Europe, with 856 people per hectare. Hygiene and cholera were major issues, and by 1844 Barcelona City Hall began to call for expansion of the city.

One major problem was the loss of regional independence as a result of the War of Spanish Succession, and the city was controlled by Madrid. Later, this was to be a crucial factor in the selection of Cerdà's expansion plan over the city's choice. Another problem was that the military controlled the land surrounding the city to the north, which had to remain open, as a *glacis*, or cannon-firing no-man's-land. Without Madrid's and the military's permission, the walls could not be torn down, and no expansion could take place.[41]

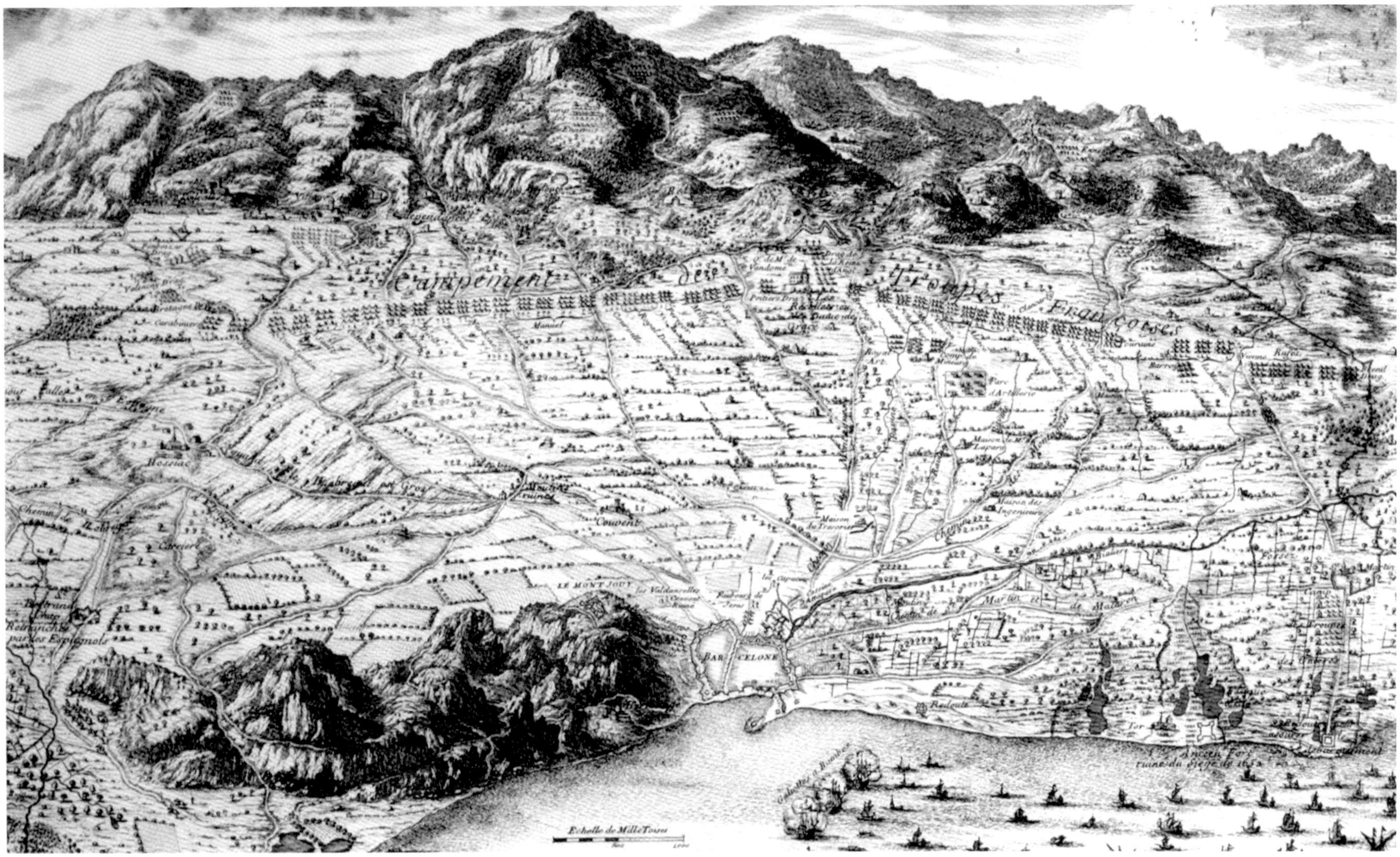

Engraved aerial view of Barcelona and the plain in 1698. The area between the city and the mountains had to remain open for defense.

Cerdà's topographic survey of the area surrounding Barcelona, 1855. The expansion was to absorb several surrounding towns, including Gracia.

Cerdà before the Eixample

Ildefons Cerdà (1815–1876) studied civil engineering in Madrid, and after graduating in 1841 worked as an engineer for the state. In 1844 he was impressed by the new railroads on a visit to Nimes, France, and became interested in cities and the impact of mechanized transportation. He then began to devote himself to the study of city planning, but quickly discovered that nothing had been written and that he would have to do it himself.

In 1849, owing to family deaths, Cerdà inherited the family fortune, which enabled him to resign his position and devote all his time to the study of urbanism. He cited the importance of electricity, circulation, water supply, hygiene, economics, and social justice in the design of the modern city.[42]

Between 1856 and 1858 Cerdà visited Paris four times (once for one year) to study the ongoing urban transformation of Paris by Haussmann. He made copious notes regarding street details, sewers, and financing.

He was also impressed by London's row houses and density, and by New-World urban grids, which were to figure prominently in his planning proposals for the expansion of Barcelona.

Cerdà and L'Eixample

Barcelona City Hall began to call for the expansion of the city in 1844, requesting a "partial expansion." But in 1853, City Hall set up an extension committee, and petitioned Madrid for a major expansion within "natural limits," claiming that "Civilization can develop only within populous cities."

Permission was given, and in 1854 demolition of the walls began. The Civil Governor, Ciril Franquet, asked Cerdà to propose an extension as the "foundation of a new city."

Cerdà knew that a survey of the surrounding area would be required, and since none existed, he prepared one at his own expense. This remarkably detailed topographic survey was completed in one year, 1854–55.[43]

1. Limited expansion plan, Miquel Garriga i Roca, 1858

2. Second-place competition plan, Francesc Soler i Glòria, 1859

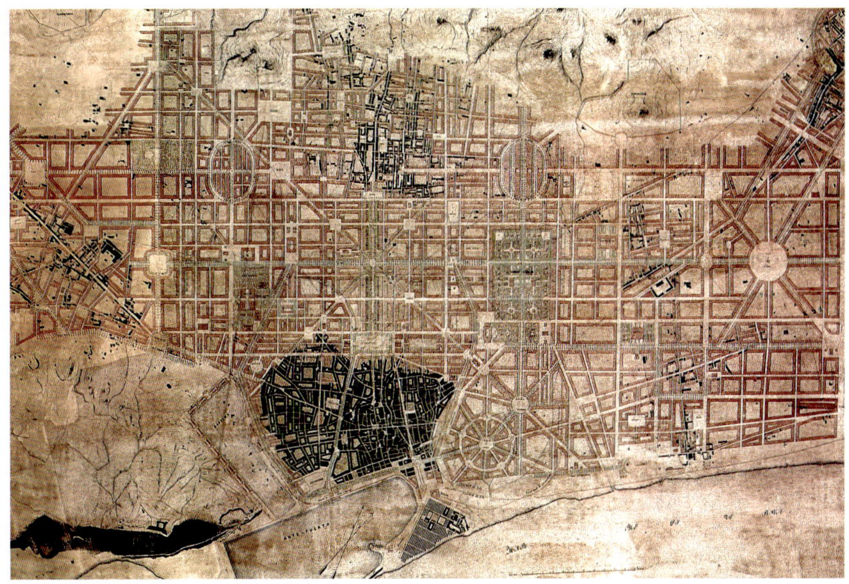

3. Third-place competition plan, Josep Fontserè, 1859

Cerdà's Preliminary Plan, 1855

From November to December 1855 Cerdà prepared a preliminary project—a plan on tracing paper that has been lost—and presented it in Madrid. This set in motion the alignment of Cerdà with the state—the ultimate authority—rather than the city. To make matters worse, in 1856 there was a regime change, and Cerdà was no longer in favor in Barcelona, which exacerbated the division between the state in Madrid and Barcelona City Hall. This had the effect of cementing Cerdà's alignment with the state.[44]

Garriga i Roca's Plan, 1858

After proposals for a public competition in 1855 and 1857 were dismissed, in 1858 City Hall commissioned a plan by a municipal architect, Miquel Garriga i Roca, with the intention of sending it to Madrid for approval. Once again, Cerdà went to Madrid in August, presumably to argue his case and neutralize Garriga i Roca's Plan.

The City's Competition, 1859

In February 1859, the City Council appointed a commission to establish the regulations for the extension, which were to serve as the basis for a public competition. Before the competition could be held, however, Cerdà's plan and theoretical research were well advanced, so he took his project to Madrid to seek approval. Oddly, the city went ahead with the competition even though they did not have the authority over the expansion, and even though they had to put aside the plan they had commissioned by Garriga i Roca. Before the competition deadline for submissions, however, a royal command was issued by the Ministry of Development on June 7, 1859, approving Cerdà's plan, with amendments. City Hall pressed Madrid to withdraw their approval, but Madrid refused.[45]

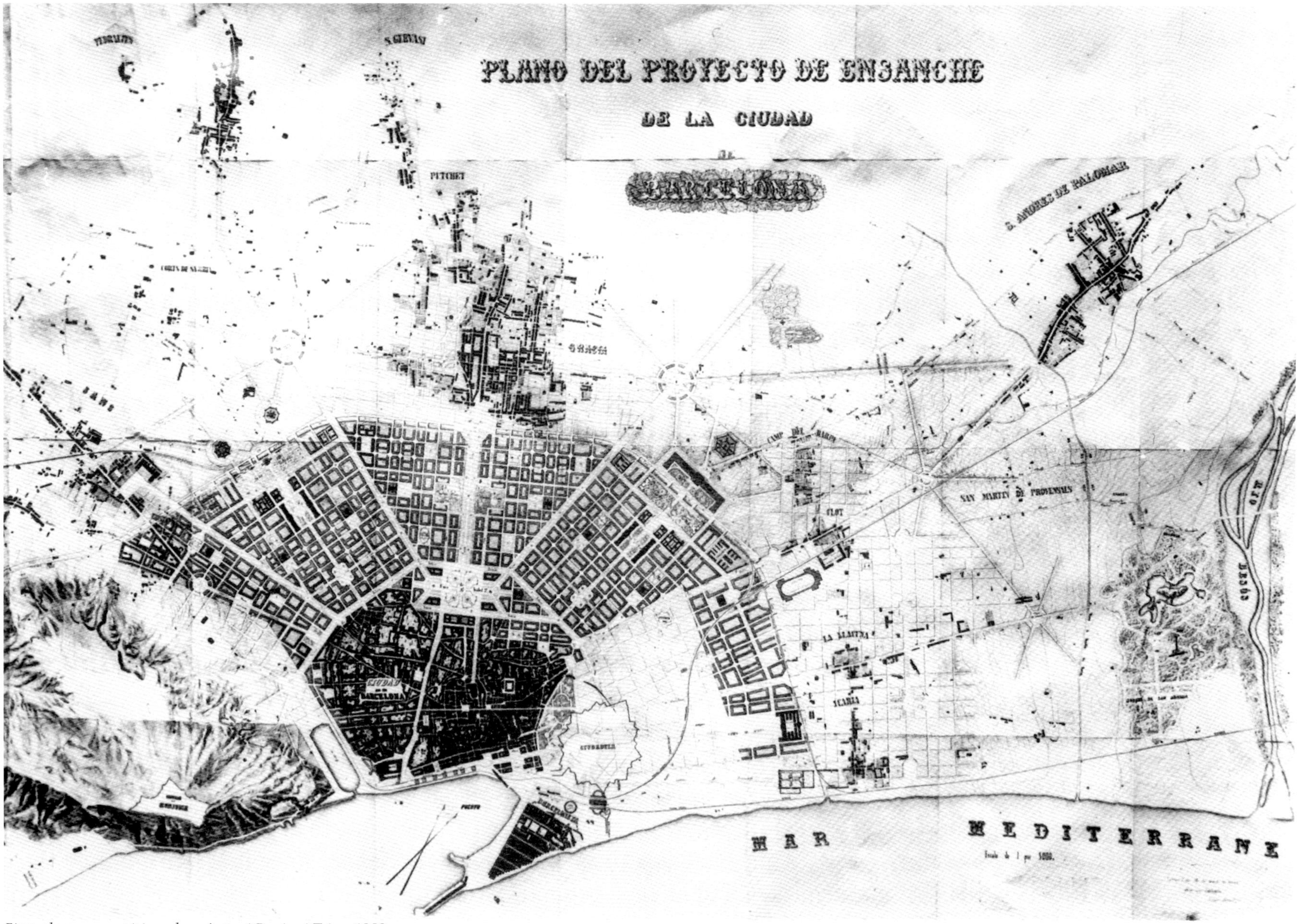

First-place competition plan, Antoni Rovira i Trias, 1859

State approval of Cerdà's Plan

A royal command of July 31, 1859, made it clear that Barcelona had no authority to hold a competition, but could conclude it in order to compare the results with Cerdà's plan.

The winner of the competition was the plan by the architect Antoni Rovira i Trias; the second-place winner was the engineer Francesc Soler i Glòria; and the third-place winner was Josep Fontserè. The three competition plans, as well as Cerdà's plan, were exhibited in City Hall Chambers in October 1859.

Massive controversy ensued, but in January 1860, Cerdà presented his regulations and economic plan to the Ministry of Development in Madrid, and in May 1860, a royal decree confirmed approval of Cerdà's plan for L'Eixample, but not his regulations and economic plan. The decree praised the plan for being not just a plan, but a comprehensive theory of urbanism that could be applied to other urban conditions.

The decree also provided funds to publish the two volumes of Cerdà's treatise on urbanism: *Teoría general de la urbanizatión y aplicación de sus principios y doctrinas a la reforma y ensanche de Barcelona.* This work was published in 1867.

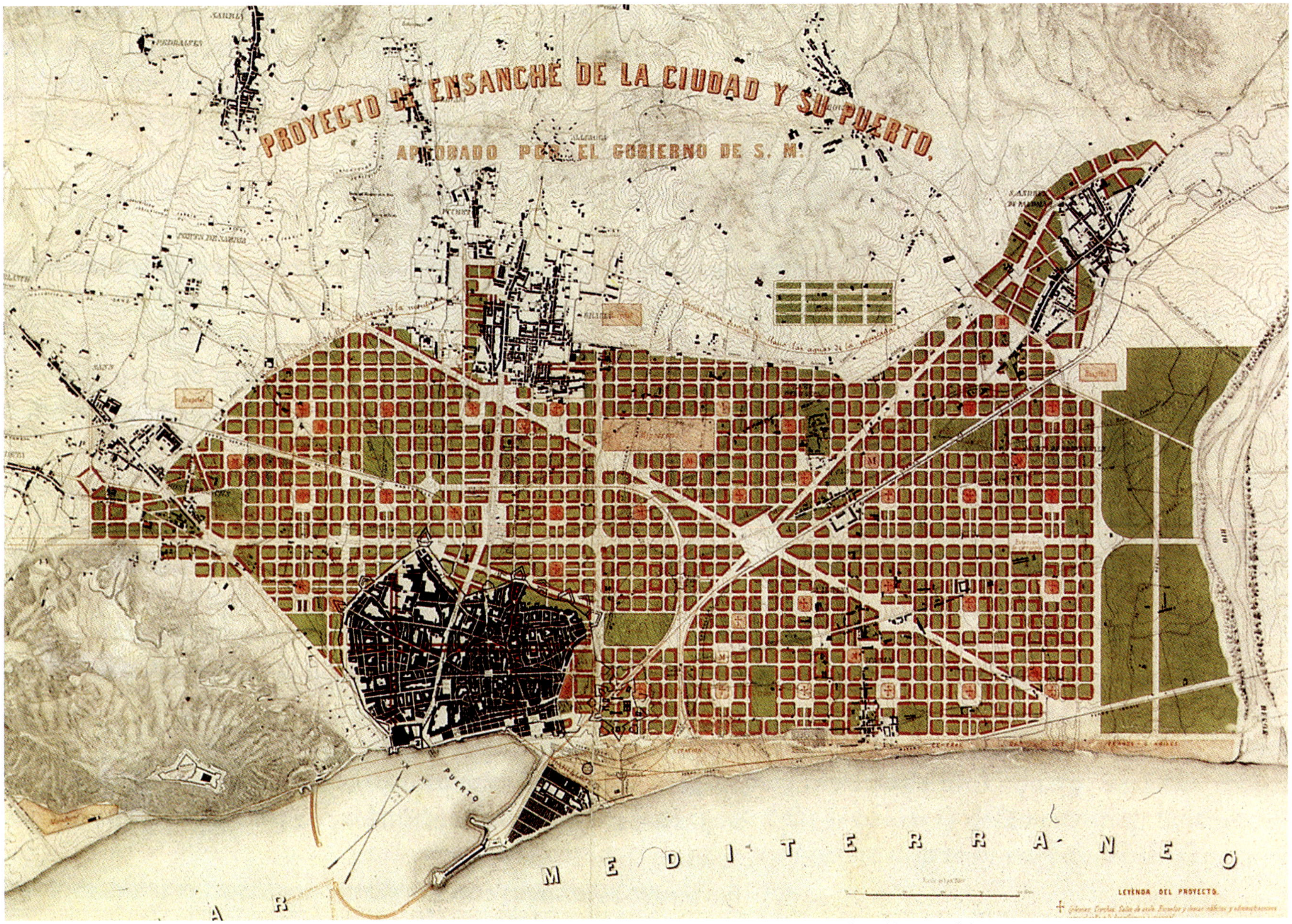

Plan by Ildefons Cerdà, 1859. The plan was approved by the Ministry of Development in Madrid in April 1859. This was confirmed by a royal decree in May 1860.

Cerdà's Plan

Removed from the contemporary circumstances of politics and the competition, the wisdom of Cerdà's plan seems clear. Fontserè's scheme was an orthogonal grid also, but almost frivolous in its Baroque extravagance; Soler i Glòria's plan exhibited a more considered fabric, but the collision of grids is inexplicable; and the competition-winning project by Rovira i Trias was a radial plan, organized in sectors around the old city, leaving out any apparent way of further expansion and incorporation of the surrounding communities.

Cerdà's plan, on the other hand, was an egalitarian grid of square blocks, filling the plain and absorbing the surrounding communities. The grid was parallel to the shore line, and therefore oriented 45 degrees from north. More important, Cerdà's was a comprehensive plan. The product of years of study and development, it incorporated ideas of social justice, housing, hygiene, circulation, relationship to the existing agricultural parcels, and infrastructure. It was also flexible.[46]

Civic Structure

Cerdà's plan called for 66' wide typical streets, with arterials of 164'. Because there are few genuine public plazas in the plan, it is the arterials that provide the civic structure of the city.

The Gran Via de les Corts Catalanes bisects Cerdà's plan from southwest to northeast and connects the Llobregat and Besos Rivers. The Avinguda Diagonal and the Avinguda Meridiana cross in the Plaça de les Glories Catalanes, but the most important umbilical connection is that of the Ramblas and Passeig de Gracia, which connect the Ciutat Vella to Gracia.

Cerdà also proposed cutting new orthogonal streets through the Ciutat Vella, to enmesh it with the Eixample, but most of these were not implemented.

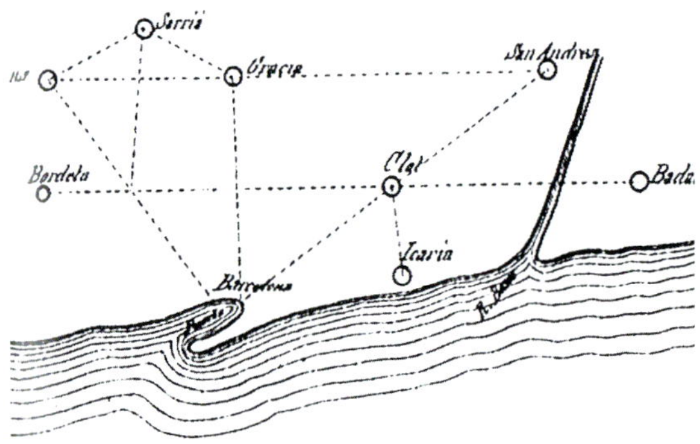

1. Sketch of the layout of Cerdà's Eixample boulevards

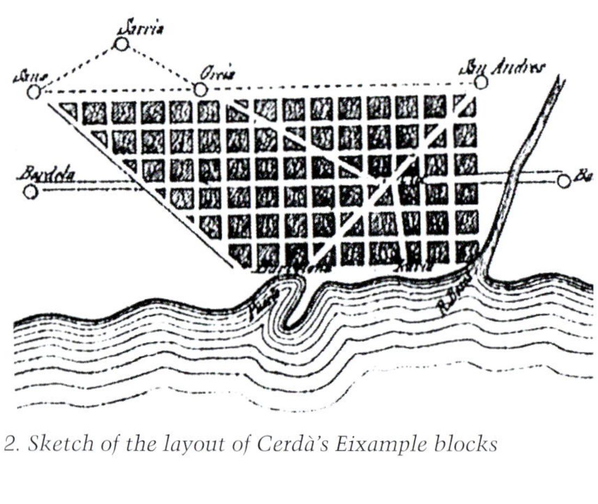

2. Sketch of the layout of Cerdà's Eixample blocks

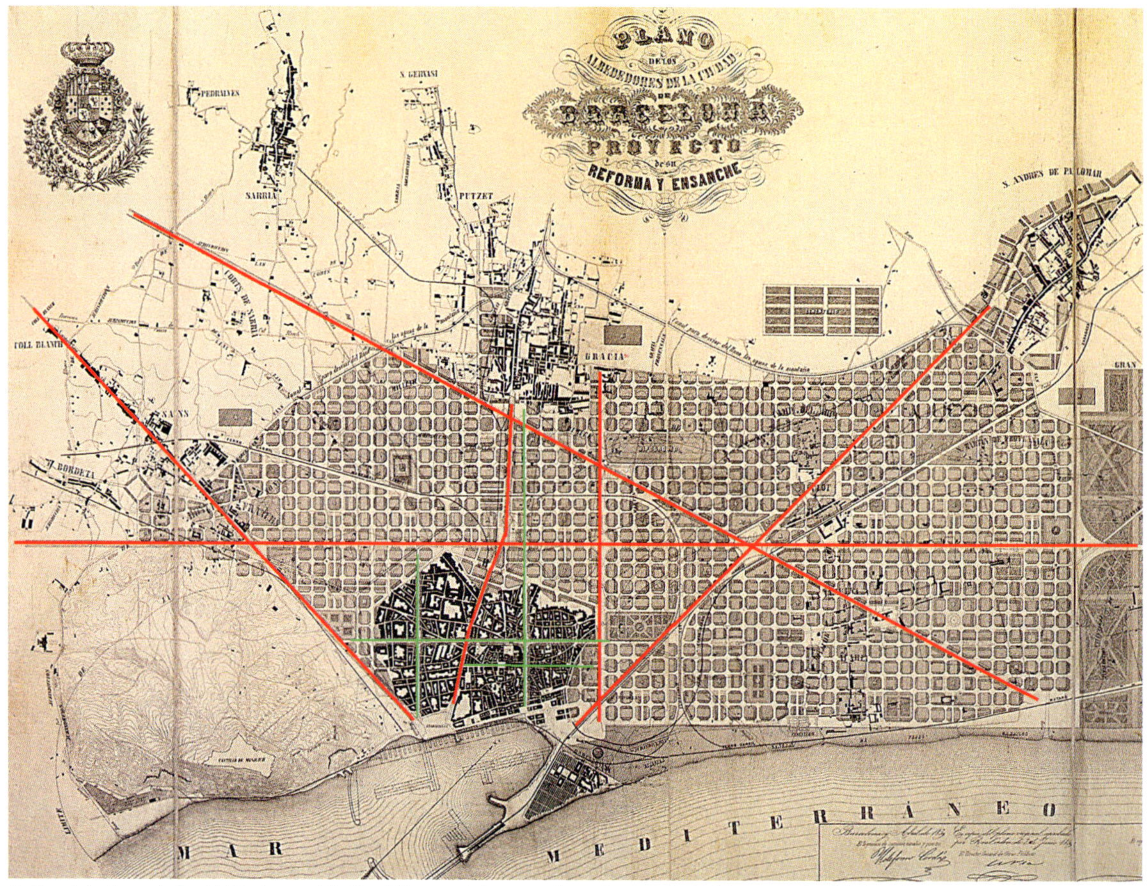

3. Partial view of the 1859 plan, with Cerdà's arterial network and extended old streets highlighted

4. View of a multilane arterial

Aerial plan of the contemporary city

Cerdà's Urban Fabric

The most striking and inventive aspect of Cerdà's plan—indeed, of Barcelona—is his development of the basic urban fabric of the Eixample. Barcelona does not have Paris's elaborate civic structure of heroic spaces. It does not have the discrete neighborhoods of the Great Estates in London. Rather, it has a rich tissue of buildings, blocks, and streets that, together with the topography and the older towns, make it one of the world's most beautiful cities.[47]

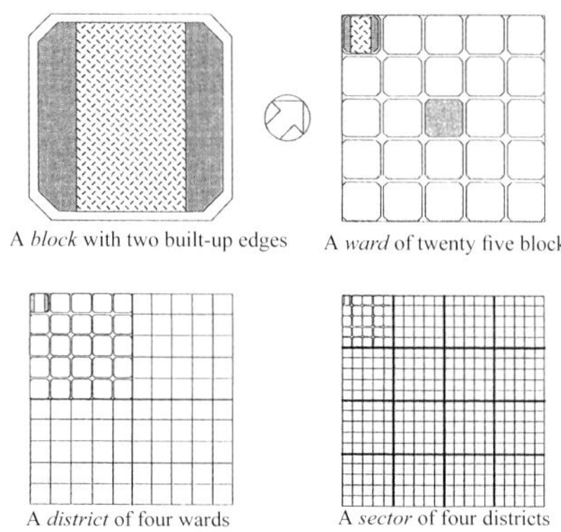

1. The block as a municipal organizational unit

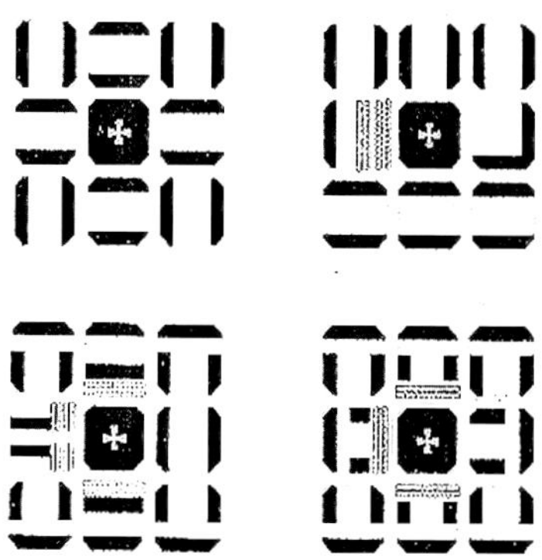

2. Variations of Cerdà's blocks, 1859

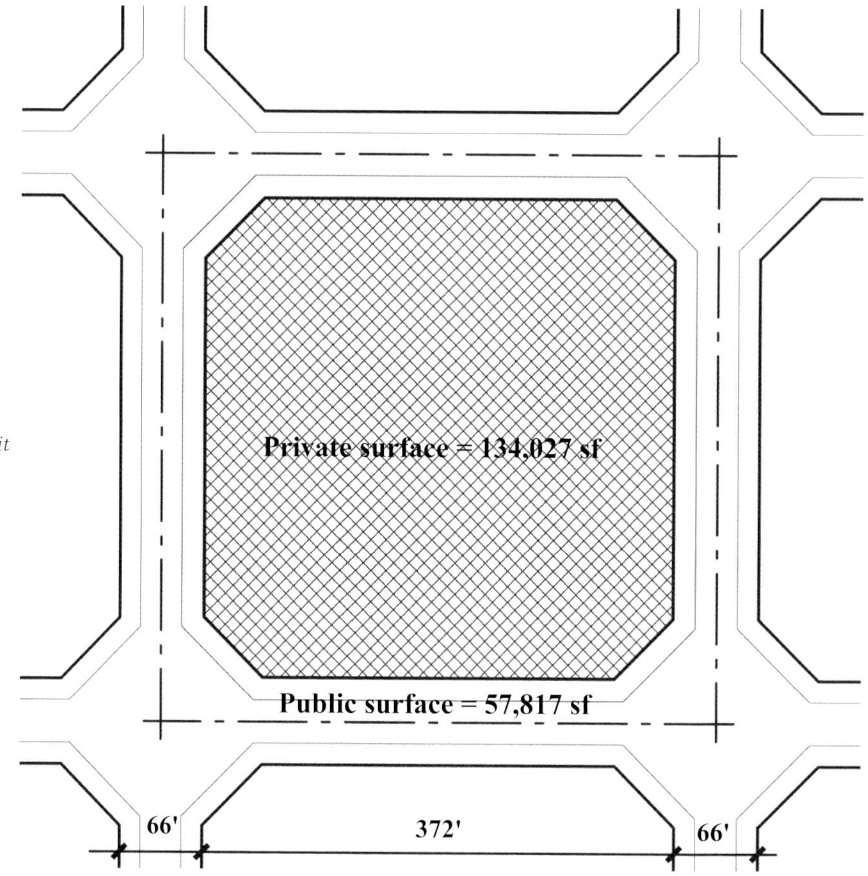

3. Typical block configuration and size, 1859

The Urban Block

The form and dimensions of the basic unit of the plan—*the urban block and its streets*—are the most important aspects of Cerdà's plan.

During Cerdà's twenty years of studying town planning, he researched and illustrated various precedents for block sizes and configurations. In the end he concluded that large, square blocks oriented 45 degrees from the cardinal points were most egalitarian and environmentally beneficial.

His original vision for the urban fabric was to have open blocks with only two sides built equal to 50 percent of the site, and open green space in the center, remarking: "Joining more than two houses to others, and above all, completely closing the space of a block, are monstrosities incompatible with the culture of our century." This was the system illustrated in his 1859 plan, but as soon as the plan began to be implemented, the density increased, and buildings lined all four sides of the block.

The typical Eixample block is 372' square, with chamfered corner faces of 66'. The typical surrounding street is 66' wide with a 33' carriage way, and sidewalks of 16.5' each; i.e., 50 percent for vehicles, and 50 percent for pedestrians. Thus, the public surface area of the streets and sidewalks is 57,817 square feet (30% of the total), and the private surface area of the block is 134,027 square feet (70% of the total).

The buildings that occupy the blocks are different from those that Cerdà originally proposed. In fact, many have changed significantly over the years, and there is a wide range of architectural styles.

The thing that makes Barcelona beautiful, flexible, and resilient, however, is that buildings are generally smaller than blocks; they are limited in height; and they align on the streets. In other words, they are subordinate to the hegemony of the urban realm. Only toward the city's fringes does architecture begin to trump urbanism, and the result is that the quality of the environment declines precipitously.

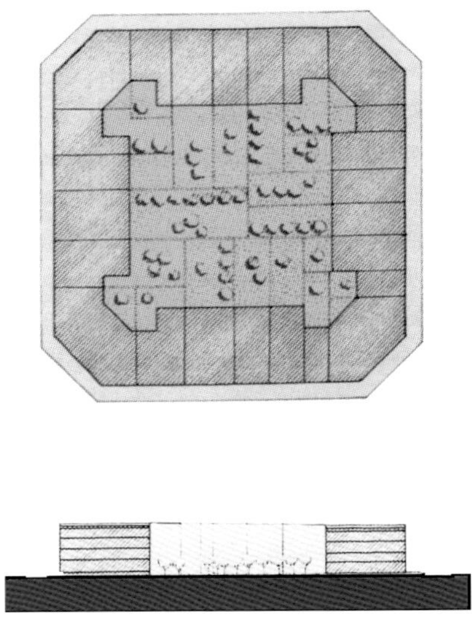

1. Plan and section of proposed regulations

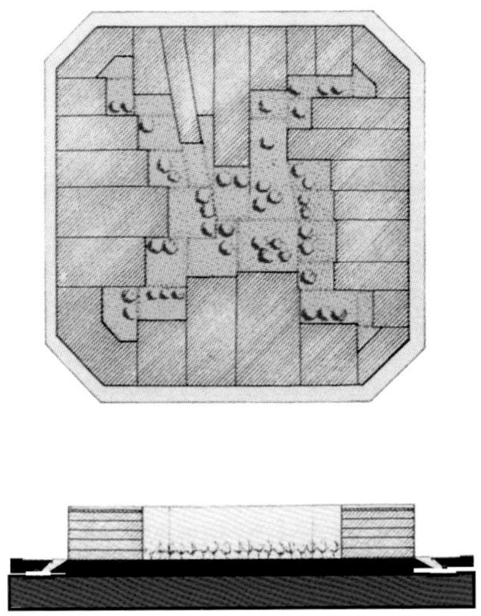

2. Plan and section of 1868–79 regulations

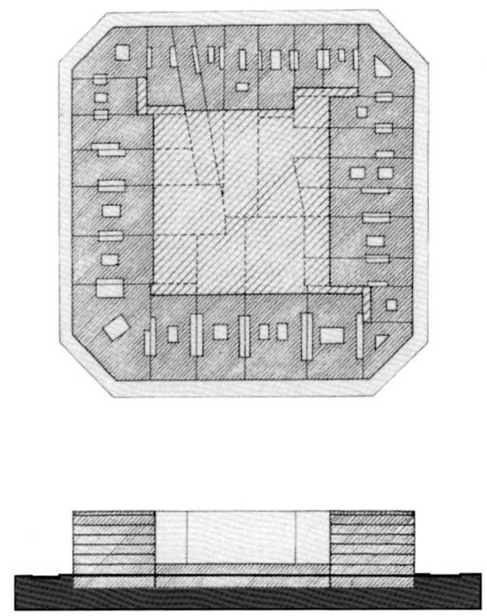

3. Plan and section of 1891–1924 regulations

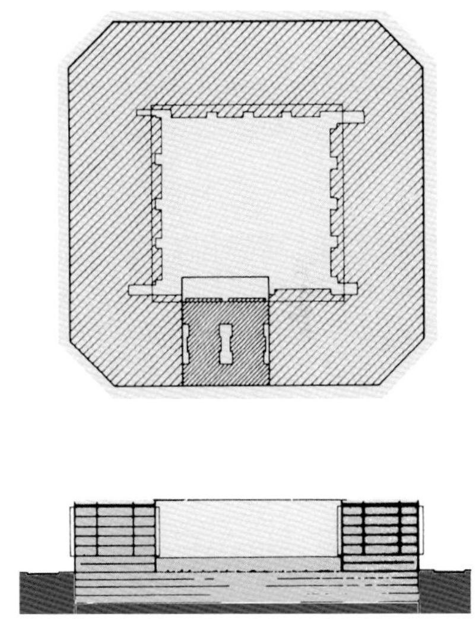

4. Plan and section of 1976–86 regulations

Proposed Regulations, 1860–76

The revised regulations proposed by Cerdà, and later Garriga i Roca, maintained 50 percent coverage of the block by buildings with a height limit of 52.5' (five floors) and an open courtyard. This was subsequently revised to permit a 66' height limit and 70 percent coverage. These proposals would result in a net FAR of ca. 2.1 and 4.2.

Regulations, 1868–79

The 1868–79 regulations allowed four stories with an open courtyard.

Regulations, 1891–1924

The 1891 block regulations allowed 73.6 percent coverage and a building depth of 92'. The height limit was raised from 66' to 75', and the court could be occupied up to 14'. These regulations would result in a net FAR of ca. 5.7.

Regulations, 1924–1976

Between 1924 and 1976 the density increased significantly, as the permitted coverage was 73 percent, the height limit was 80' with two step-back additional floors. The court could be built to 18', with one basement level.

Regulations, 1976–86

In 1976 the permitted coverage was reduced to 70 percent, the height limit was reduced to 68', and construction in the court was reduced to 15'. There was no restriction on the number of basement levels. These regulations would result in a net FAR of 5.5 or more.

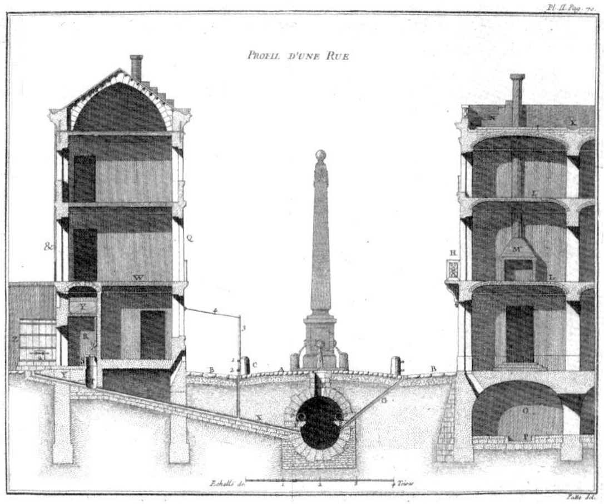

1. Street section, Pierre Patte, 1769

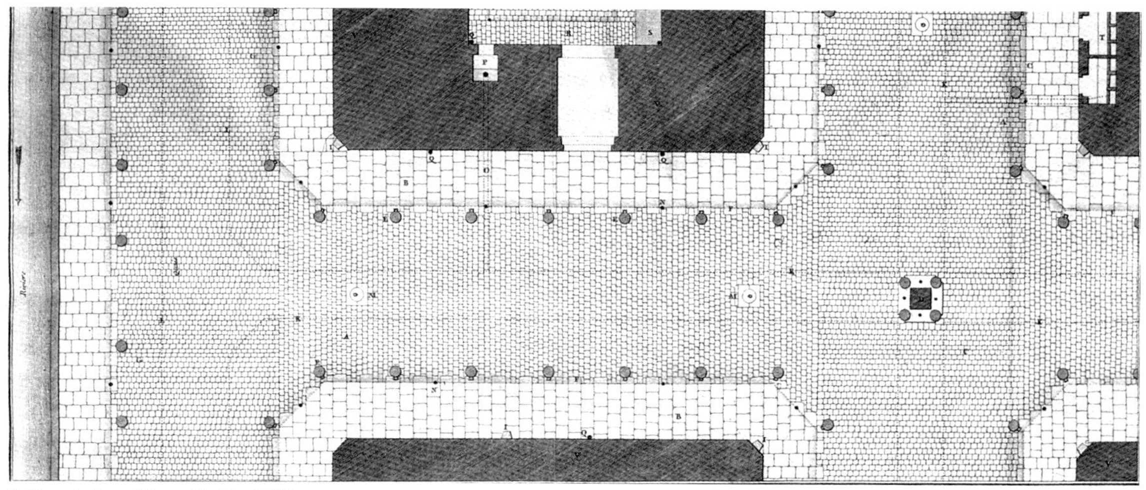

2. Street plan, Pierre Patte, 1769

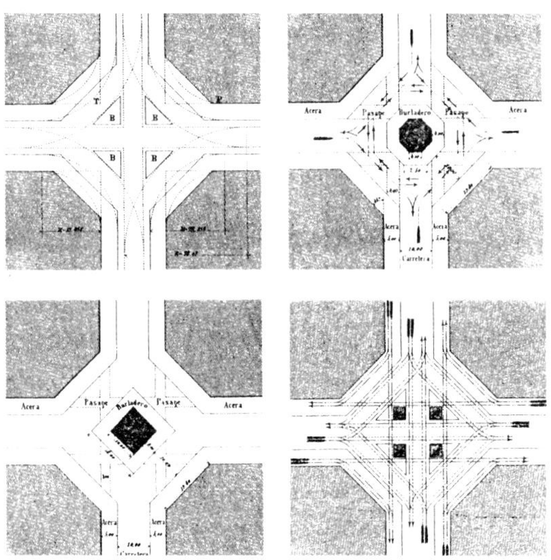

3. Proposals for intersections

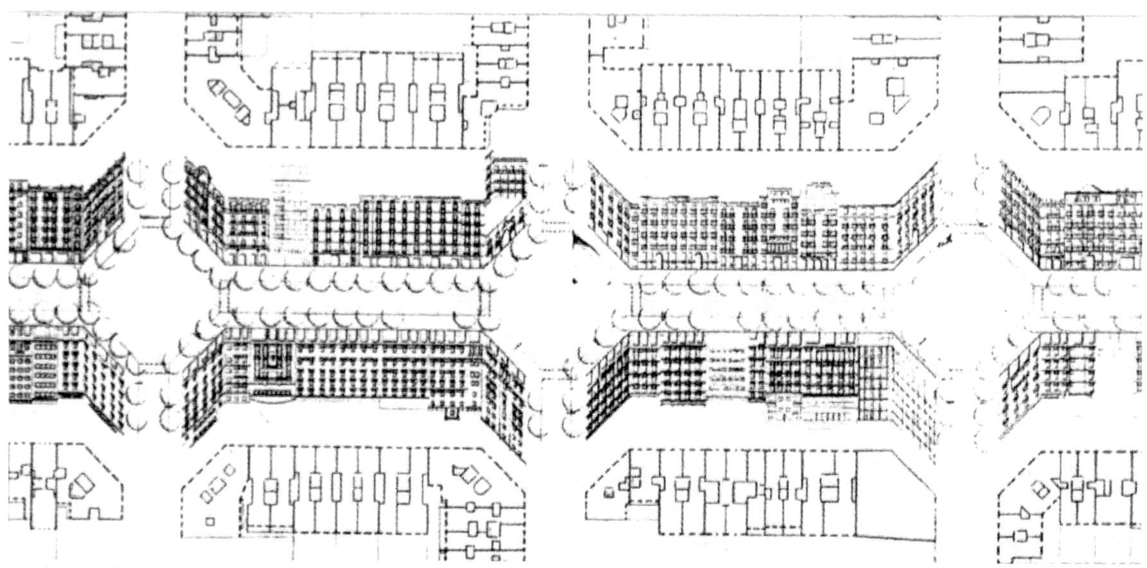

4. Plans and elevations of a typical Barcelona street

The Street

The designed street with integrated infrastructure was fundamentally a mid-nineteenth-century development, but almost a century earlier Pierre Patte had illustrated similar proposals. Cerdà may or may not have known about Patte, but his research in Paris between 1856 and 1858 was detailed and comprehensive. He made detailed drawings of pavements, lighting, tree spacing, sewers, etc.

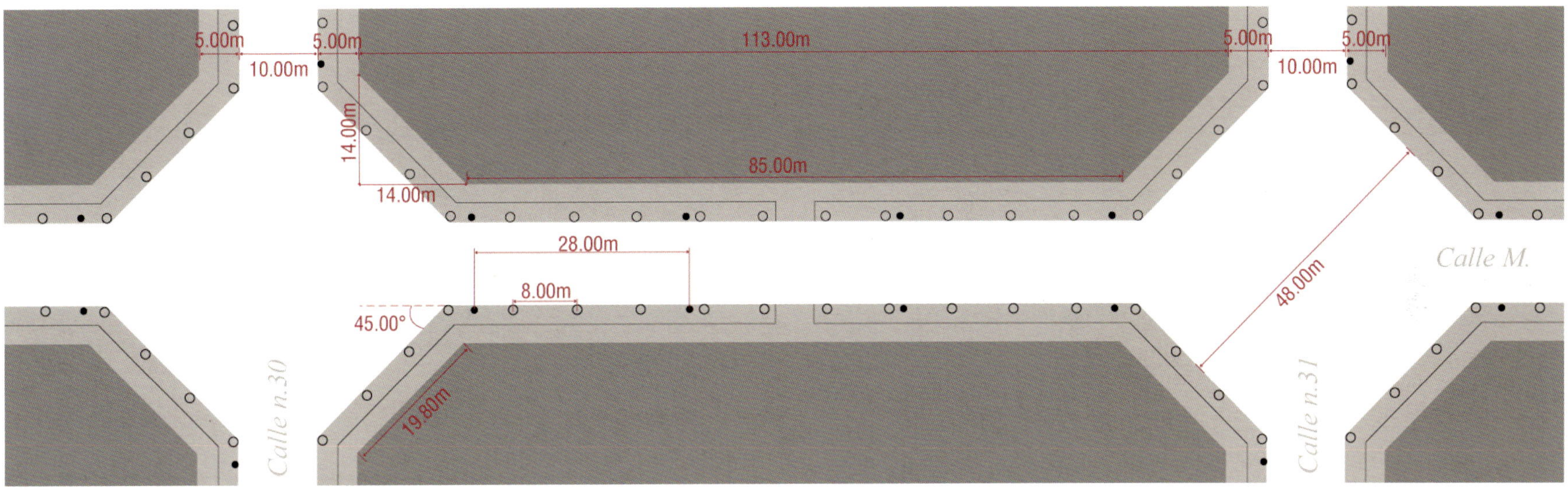

1. Dimensioning of the standard Cerdà Eixample street and block

2. Section of the proposed 35-meter-wide street, 1859

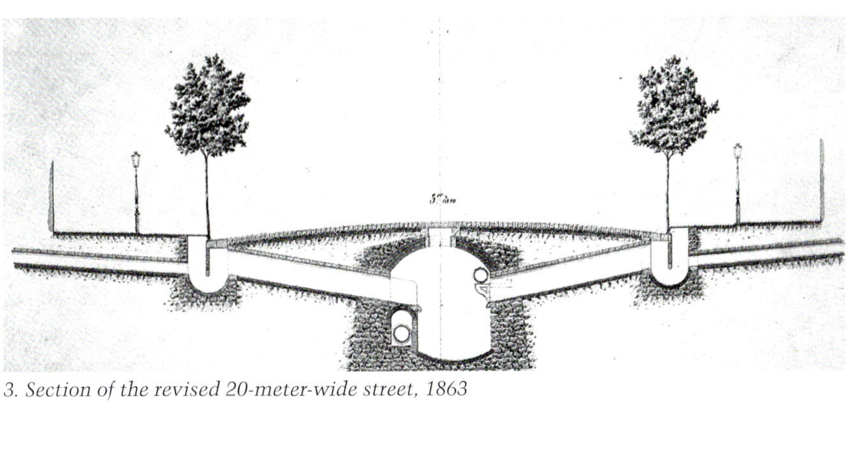

3. Section of the revised 20-meter-wide street, 1863

4. View of a typical Barcelona street

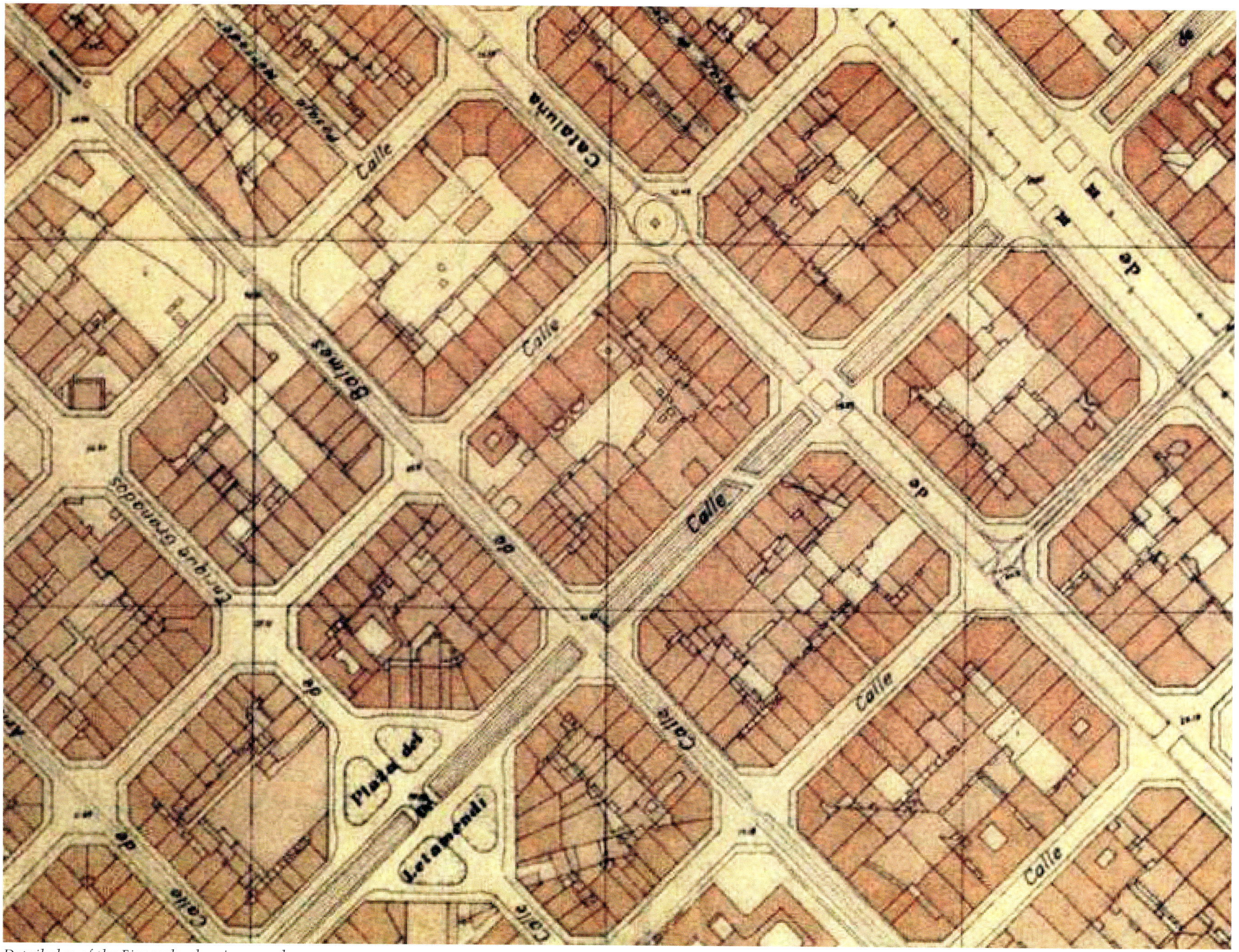

Detail plan of the Eixample, showing parcels

Block Parcels

Generally, the Eixample block is subdivided into 15 to 50 parcels to promote different types of building developments—from less than 2,000 square feet to 6,000 square feet. The standard plot is narrow and very deep, with four fairly truncated square plots on the chamfered corners. The parcel sizing both afforded an efficient means of dividing and selling plots of land for development and provided similar housing and building sizes, as previously seen in the city.

Cerdà's block and street plan was laid over the tangled network of property in the Barcelona plain, resulting in two contrasting patterns of parcels. In the northwest—between the Ciutat Vella and Gracia—a system was developed for compensating property owners, and various sizes of orthogonal plots were auctioned off. To the northwest in the Poble Nou section, the plots were the direct result of the two contrasting grids: that of the blocks and streets and that of the preexisting properties.

The combination of urban plan, parcel system, and building regulations, together with the landscape system, produced an urban fabric that was at once unified and varied—an argument for the hegemony of the public realm.

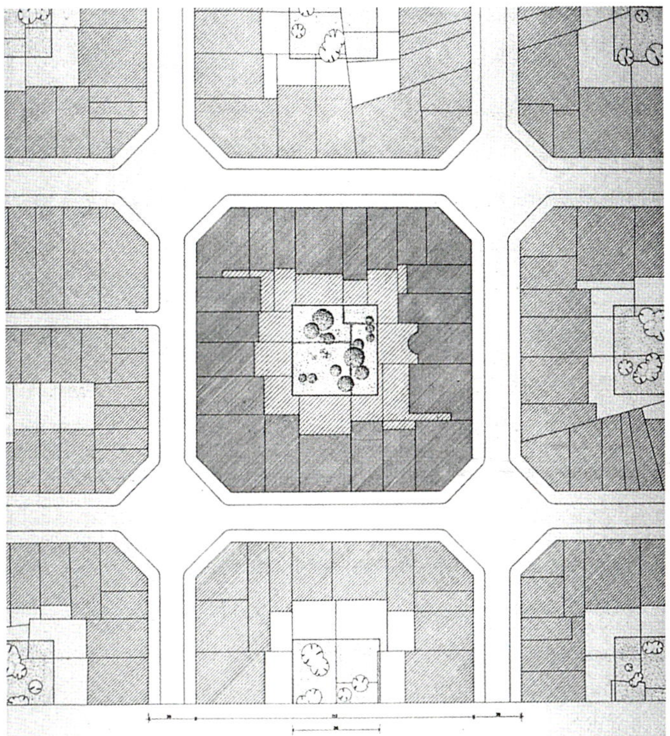

1. Detail plan of the blocks, showing parcels

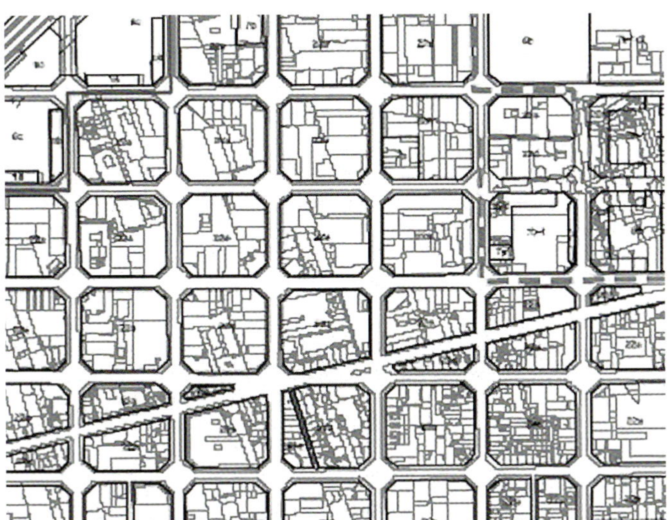

2. Plan of the Poble Nou area showing parcels

3. Aerial view of the urban fabric of the Eixample

1. View of a chamfered block

Building Types

The basic premodern building type was the apartment building, the *casa urbana*, built on a lot between 39' and 52' wide, and extending up to 92' in depth. The Barcelona apartment building is uniquely large and deep. Like Parisian apartment buildings, they are stacked flats, five to six stories high. Typically they range from two to six bays wide and four to five or six bays deep. Because of the depth, the buildings are punctured by small light wells in order to get light and air to the interior rooms. Obviously, these apartments were for large families. Accommodating modern demographics—smaller families and smaller apartments—is a challenge within the typical Barcelona block size, as the units tend to be shallower, thus making it even harder to turn the corners.

Typology and Style

Typology is more important than style when there is hegemony of the public realm, i.e., when buildings are urban types that align on the street and define space rather than suburban free-standing types. Barcelona has a plethora of excellent modern buildings. It also has its share of banal buildings. But the overwhelming impact of the city is its urbanism.

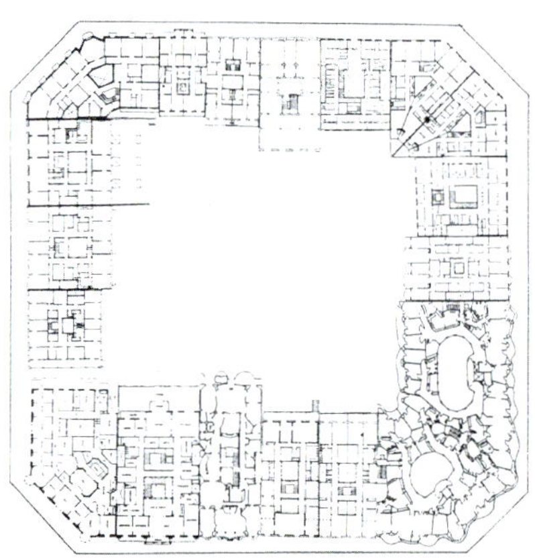

2. Cerdà block with Gaudí's La Pedrera

3. View of a chamfered block

4. Facade of Gaudí's La Pedrera

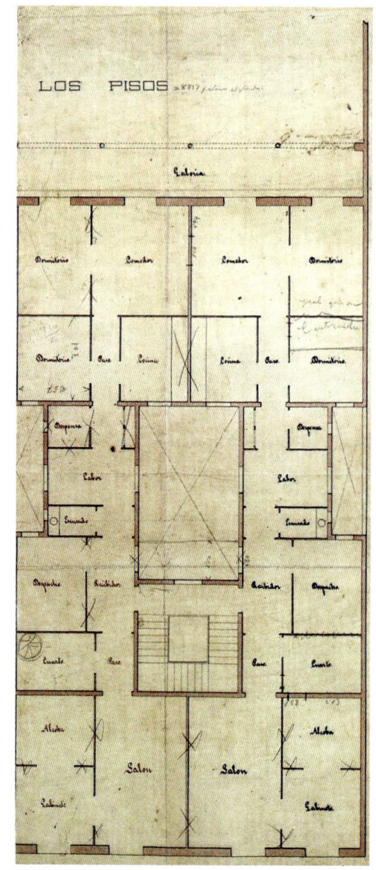

5. Plan of a flat by architect Torres i Grau

6. Facade of the house owned by Josep Cerdà

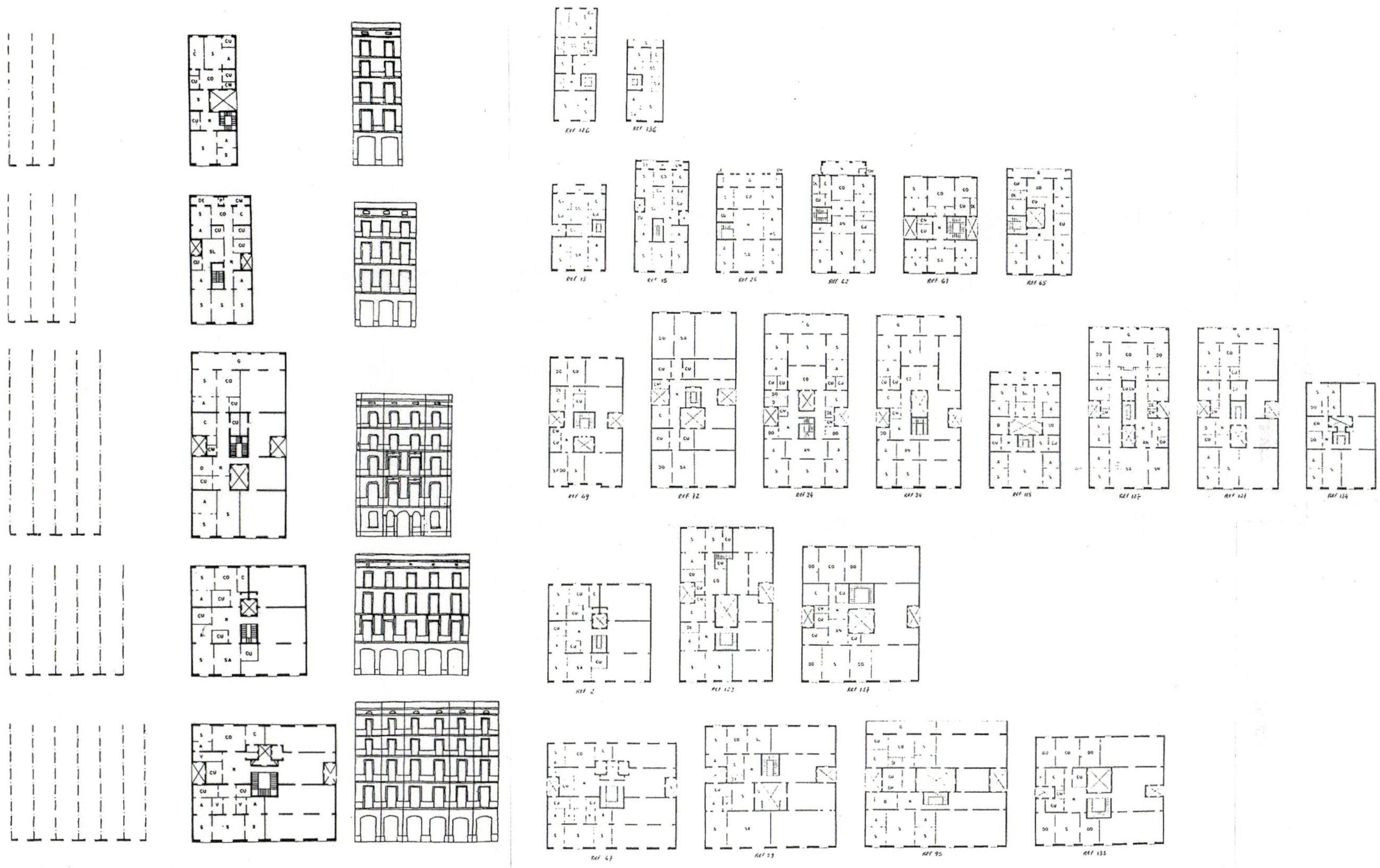

1. Comparison of housing units

2. Building facades

Jaussely plan, begun 1905

Barcelona after Cerdà

In 1903, the Barcelona Council announced an international competition to connect the Eixample to newly annexed towns and surrounding metropolitan areas. A French planner, Leon Jaussely, proposed a plan that both went against Cerdà's influential plan by considering issues of zoning thematics and Taylorization for the first time in European town planning rather than building line planning, and sought to monumentalize the city, including adding green spaces (which were practically non-existent).

The project focused on three specific aspects: the application of zoning of activities, the systematization of green spaces, and the design of the street. The Jaussely plan provided a much more nuanced perspective in limiting building and building forms, as the new "differential bylaws" sought to consider the appropriateness of compatibility of buildings in any one block as well as forms in the city as a whole. So too, the use of fiscal controls on land markets allowed for the replacement of old, crowded, and often unhygienic buildings that Cerdà sought but was unable to achieve through his plan directly.

A lack of funds prohibited the completion of the envisioned parks system. A diluted adaptation would eventually be implemented through the 1917 Romeul Porcel "Connection" plan, while the outer developing territories were able to see the vision partially realized. Through successive plans, Jaussely's concepts for circulation were implemented. The plan "addressed Cerdà's isotropic grid plan by introducing oblique or diagonal elements."

The proposed layout defined several centers throughout the metropolitan area that served as nuclei from which streets radiated in a Beaux Arts style. A hierarchy of streets through boulevards, landscaped avenues, streets, and so forth can be seen today.[48]

Aerial view of Barcelona

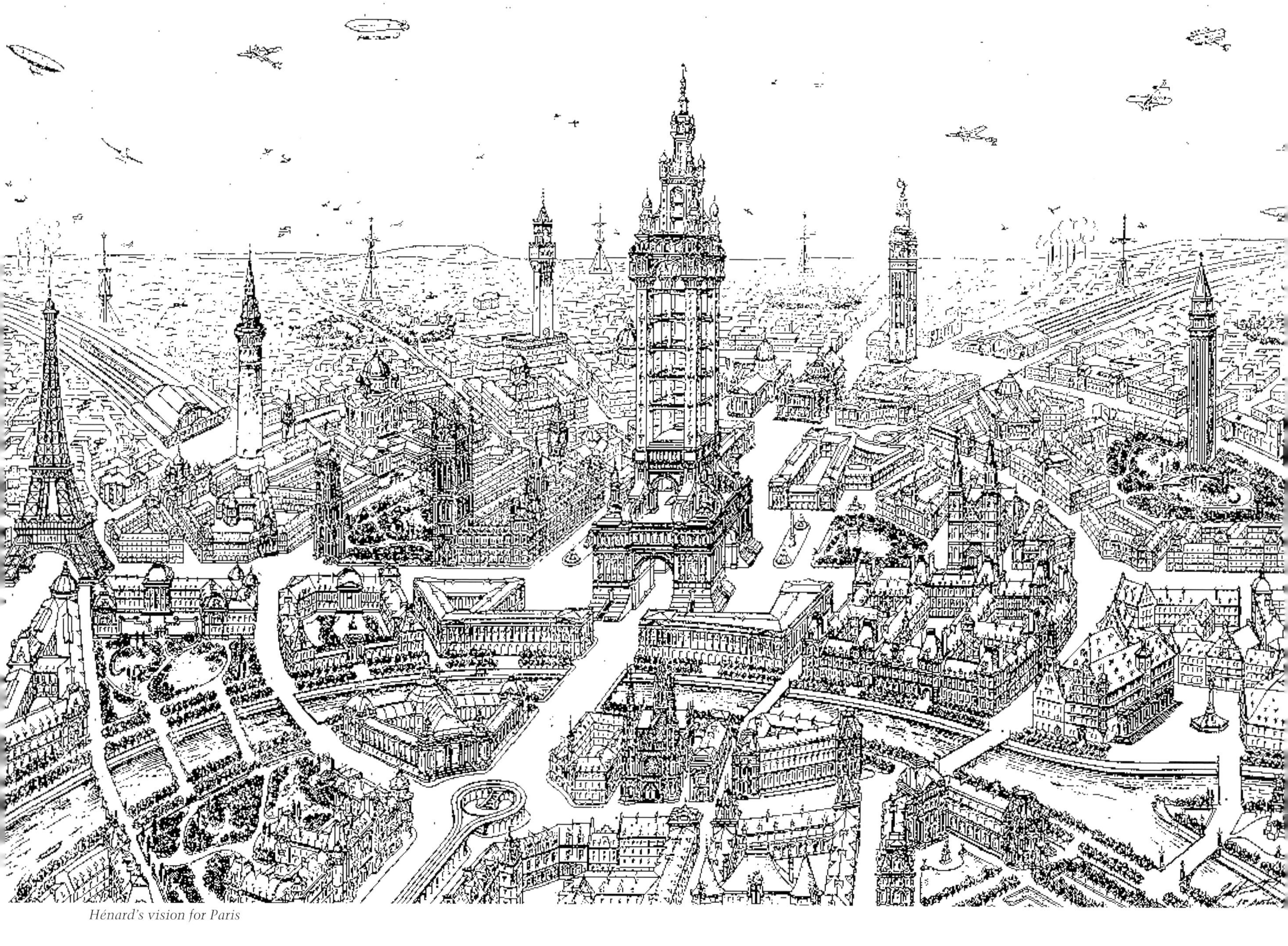

Hénard's vision for Paris

Proto-Modern Urbanists: 1890–1922

By 1890 the effects of rapid urban expansion and increased urban mobility had become central issues for a new generation of planners, and rationalized circulation became a primary determinant of urban form. The roots of this new, rationalistic view of the city, however, are deep. Indeed, Laugier was prescient when in 1753 he wrote comparing the circulation networks of Le Notre's geometric designs for large hunting parks to cities:

> One must look at a town as a forest. The streets of one are the roads of the other; both must be cut through in the same way. Let us carry out this idea and use the design of our parks as plan for our towns. It is only a question of measuring the area and making the same style roads into streets and carrefours into squares.[1]

The connection of straight, rationalized boulevards into an urban network in Paris beginning in 1853 made Haussmann the inspiration for late-nineteenth-century planners. Haussmann's articulation of Paris's network of boulevards from its urban fabric provided a model that allowed planners (primarily German) to focus almost exclusively on circulation as the medium of urban planning. Cerdà produced a comprehensive and integrated urban fabric in his expansion plan for Barcelona, but the streets performed an equal role in the composition.

Another change of enormous consequence was that planners began to produce three-dimensional, architectural illustrations of their plans. Ultimately, in the twentieth century, this would create great confusion about the relationship between architecture and urban planning.

Carriage traffic in Paris

The Proto-Modern Period

This remarkable period of some twenty-five to thirty years may be seen as one of transition between the traditional city and the city of modern architecture. The urban planners of this period still saw the city as comprising rationalized versions of streets and squares and a continuous urban fabric of buildings and blocks—that which had formed the city for centuries. But the seeds were being sown for a complete inversion of urban form.

Notable changes in planning factors included an increased emphasis on the illustration of architectural character, the beginnings of monofunctional zoning, ideas of centralized land management, and a special emphasis on vehicular circulation. In addition, there was an increase in the number of large public buildings required for the expanding bureaucracies of the modern nation-state.

The period was initially centered in Germany, but later spread internationally and encompassed two major planning movements: the Garden City and the City Beautiful.

The Nineteenth-Century Street

If the eighteenth century was the century of the unified square, the nineteenth century was the century of the unified (or designed) street.

In 1753 Laugier's description of what a square should be accurately predicted the transformation from the enclosed eighteenth-century square to the nineteenth-century idea of the square as a traffic intersection:

> For a square to be beautiful ... several streets must lead to it like the roads of a forest to a Carrefour.[2]

This was augmented by a related statement regarding streets:

> The streets of a great town cannot make communication easy and convenient unless they are sufficiently numerous to prevent lengthy detours, sufficiently wide to forestall any obstructions and perfectly straight to shorten the way.[3]

Following Laugier's prescient observations was a continuing series of street developments in the nineteenth century: unified streets such as Rue des Colonnes and Rue de Rivoli, the glazed interior streets of the Galleries, and the boulevards of Haussmann and Napoleon III. The integration of infrastructure and the holistic consideration of Haussmann's Paris boulevards coupled with emerging ideas for mechanized transport led to the idea of the street as a rationalized and mechanized whole in the late nineteenth century.

Paxton's project for the Crystal Way in London in 1855, for example, proposed a covered street above grade, with a transport and service street below grade. This idea would be elaborated in the extreme by Eugène Hénard toward the end of the century, and Edgar Chambliss would invert the idea and propose a street-like linear building snaking through the landscape—unburdened by urban fabric. The modernist city was near.

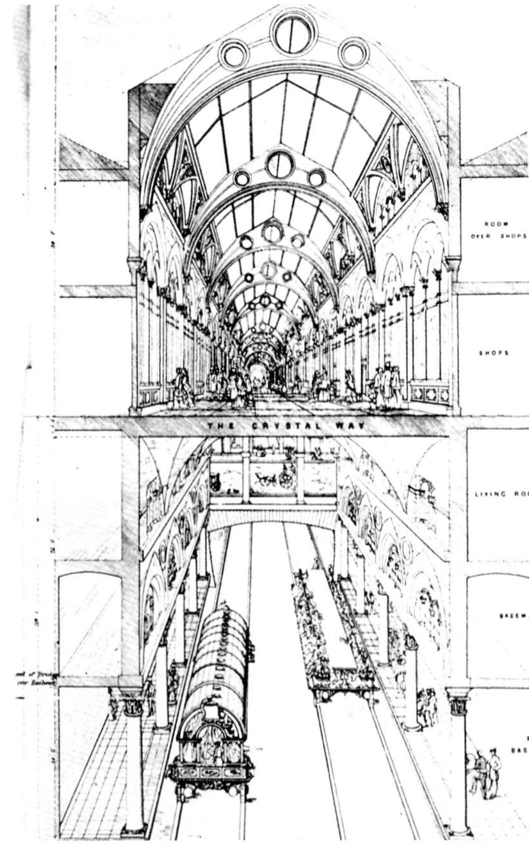

1. Crystal Way section, London, 1855

2. Edgar Chambless, "Roadtown," 1910

1. Stübben, Cologne Extension Plan

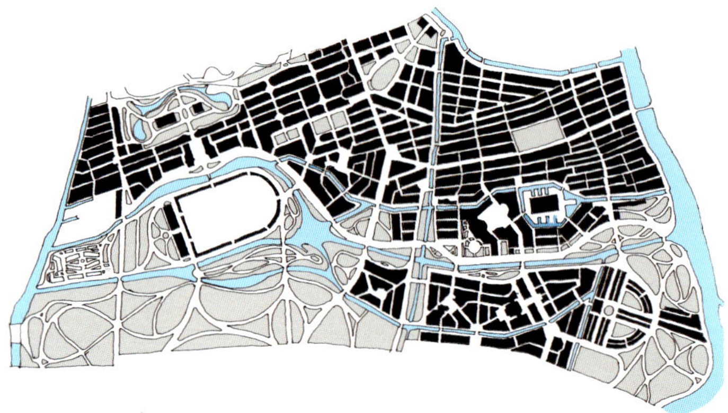

2. Berlage, first Amsterdam South Plan, 1904

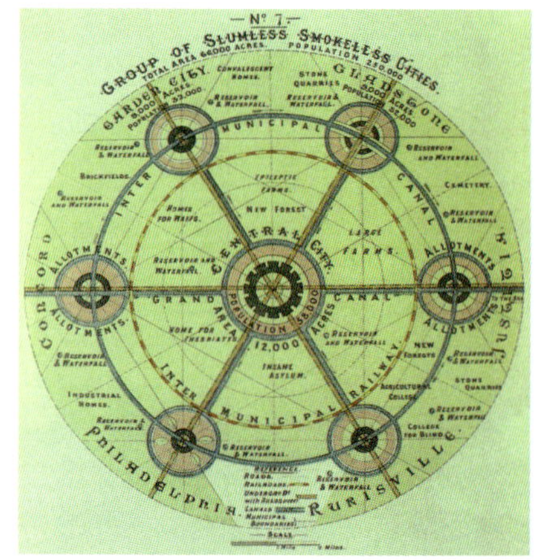

3. Howard, Garden City Diagram

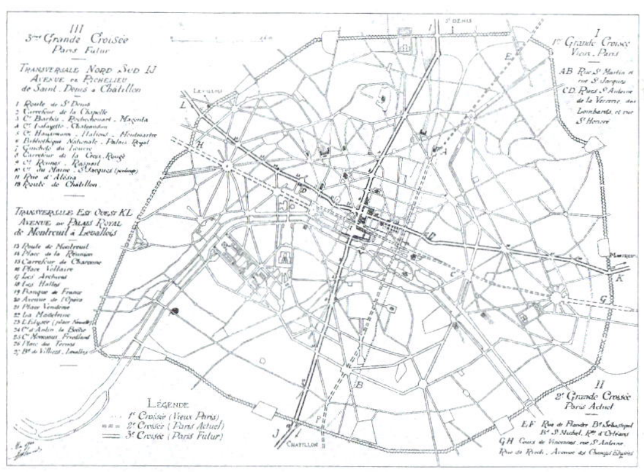

4. Hénard, Paris Plan

5. Berlage, Second Amsterdam South Plan, 1915

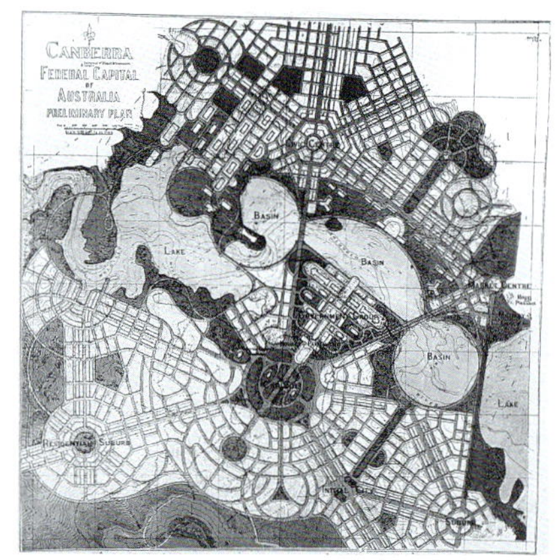

6. Griffin, Canberra Plan

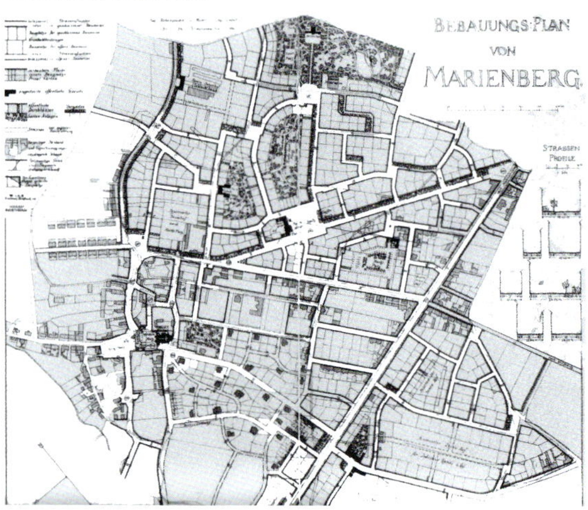

7. Sitte, Marienberg Plan

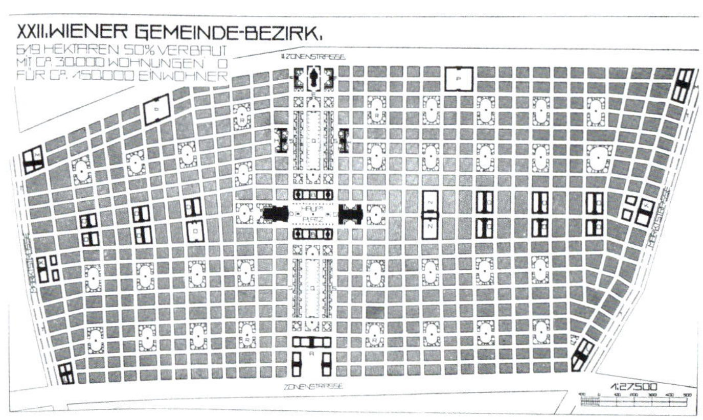

8. Wagner, Vienna Extension Plan

9. Lutyens, New Delhi Plan

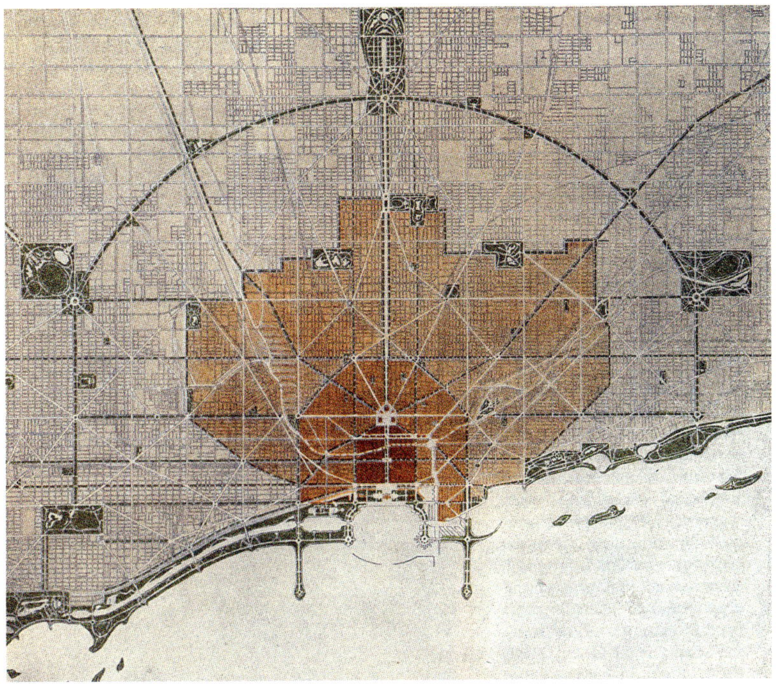

1. Burnham, Chicago Plan

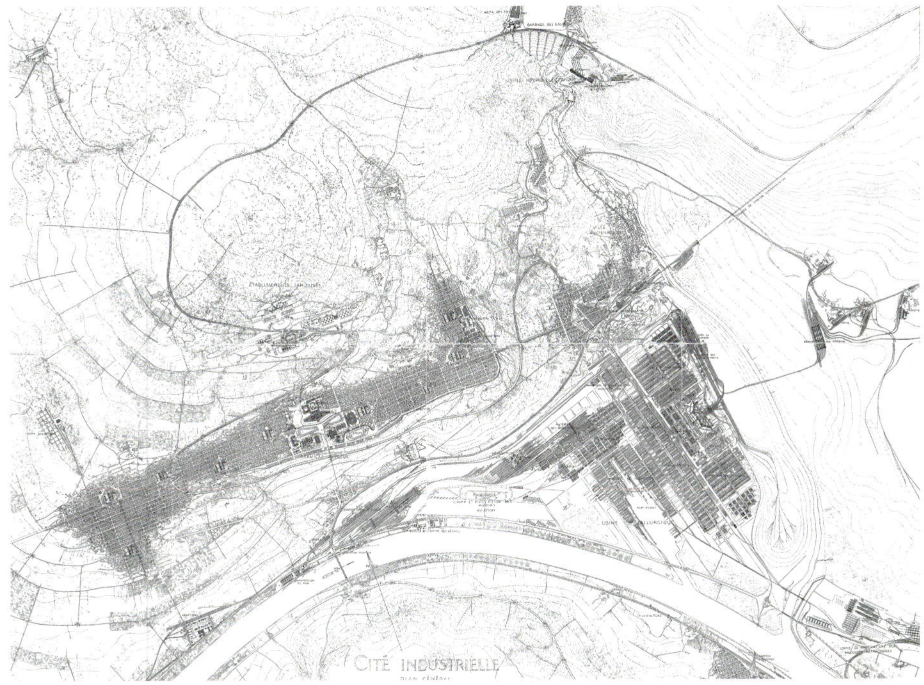

2. Garnier, Industrial City Plan

Proto-Modernist Urban Planners

There are, generally, two generations of urban planners during this period: one, the decade of the 1840s, but extending a bit earlier and later, consisted of Reinhard Baumeister (1833–1917), Otto Wagner (1841–1918), Camillo Sitte (1843–1903), Joseph Stübben (1845–1936), Daniel Burnham (1846–1912), Eugène Hénard (1849–1923), Ebenezer Howard (1850–1928), and H. P. Berlage (1856–1934); the second, the decade centered around 1870, consisted of Edwin Lutyens (1869–1944), Tony Garnier (1869–1948), and Walter Burley Griffin (1876–1944).

Despite their generations, however, a veritable avalanche of plans and publications were produced during the first decade of the twentieth century. Because of this it is easier to summarize their work than to parse it.

All were involved with the traditional city, and ideas about the street, whether mechanized or rationalized, permeated every project. But there were also significant differences.

Wagner, Howard, and Garnier, for example, made theoretical urban plans, whereas the others were practicing urban planners, designing urban interventions, urban extensions, or plans for complete cities.

Perhaps the most important distinction, however, is between Howard's Garden City, Burnham's City Beautiful, and Garnier's so-called Industrial City.

If Howard advocated "the City in the Garden," it was Lutyens and Griffin who advocated "the Garden as the City." It was Garnier, however, who most radically undermined the conventional idea of the city by proposing a garden suburb, and by formally isolating sectors of the city as monofunctional zones.

German planners played a central role in the development of modern city planning in the late nineteenth century. Inspired by the work of Haussmann in Paris, they took a rationalized, pragmatic approach to urban planning—one intended to deal with social, cultural, and health issues and to improve the functioning of expanding cities.

Civic Reform in Germany

The social reform movement, primarily occurring between 1860 and 1914, was a plan to impose order on growing cities that culminated in an ambitious urban attempt to define the social and geographical relationship of different social classes. These efforts represented civic pride and anti-urban sentiment, a notion that increased in varying degrees throughout Germany and worldwide during the next century. Planners in Germany were faced with "promoting the positive aspects of city life," against the backdrop of strong "romanticism and anti-modern cultural pessimism."[4]

The driving forces of civic reform were both control of the authorities over economic development and the desire for social order, in addition to the public health movement beginning in 1860. Public health was the essence of social reform. By the 1890s, the agenda included "nearly all the elements that ultimately composed modern city planning, from water supplies to ambitious attempts to coordinate the layouts of streets, and construction of housing in a healthy and orderly manner."[5] City planning was viewed as the physical means of implementing these ideas.

German Urban Planning

The establishment of urban planning as a scientific field is generally credited to Reinhard Baumeister (1833–1917), who saw planning primarily as a function of vehicular traffic.[6] Joseph Stübben (1845–1936) extended and expanded the field.

Joseph Stübben

Stübben was the preeminent German city planner from 1880 and well into the 1900s, working in more than thirty cities at home and abroad.[7] His approach to planning has been characterized by the term *practical aesthetics*. He sought to create a natural extension of the city fabric that improved upon the existing city and allowed for modern improvements such as traffic, sewage, water, light, and landscape.[8] These ideas were the platform from which he designed and created guidelines for good city planning in his book, *The Handbook for Architecture (Der Stadtebau).*

Stübben first published the *Handbook* in 1890 and subsequent versions in 1907 and 1924 with updated and revised information. The book includes an extensive selection of precedent drawings addressing nearly every aspect of city planning: block sizes, parcels, streets, boulevards, traffic plazas, civic plazas, historic monuments, and numerous practical details for drainage, curbs, and lampposts.

The content and presentation of the *Handbook* distinguishes Stübben as a true city planner, not an architect. He did not draw buildings or invent completely original designs; rather, he collected ideas and examples from sources he deemed acceptable and worthy of proper city design. He was particularly impressed with Haussmann's Paris, which is evident in numerous drawings for radial plazas, diagonal tree-lined boulevards, and triangular intersections.

His success was due not to design brilliance, but rather to his ability to recognize and synthesize many needs and aspirations into a single city plan.[9] He strove to impose a sort of modest order on cities without redefining or compromising rights of property ownership or suggesting radical changes within the city structure.

Stübben's rise to prominence began in 1880, after winning the competition for the design of the Cologne Ringstrasse. From that point he became the most sought-after consultant for city planning in Germany and surrounding countries. He was involved in a large number of projects, and the sheer volume of work helped to propel the German movement to become more international in scope, rendering his own contributions more influential.[10]

While Stübben remained a part of the city planning scene until his death in 1936, his influence began to wane after 1914 and even as early as 1900, when other planning movements focused on smaller-scale humanism, spurred by contemporaries such as Camillo Sitte, began to gain momentum, rendering his radial plazas and sweeping boulevards less appealing. Despite the changing cultural climate, respect for Stübben's contributions continued to be honored, and he was present at numerous International and Town Planning Conferences including that of the RIBA in 1910.[11]

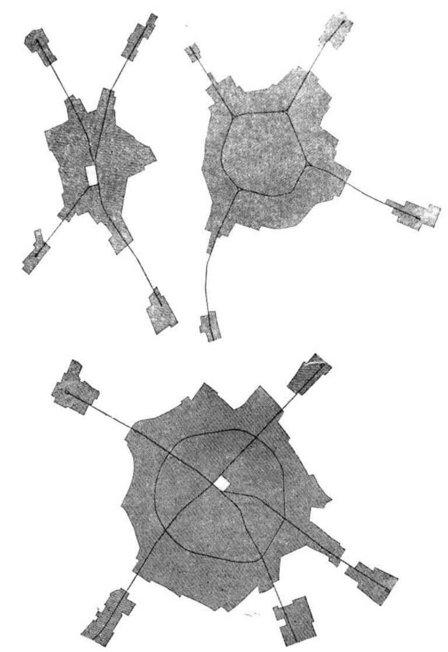

City extension diagrams

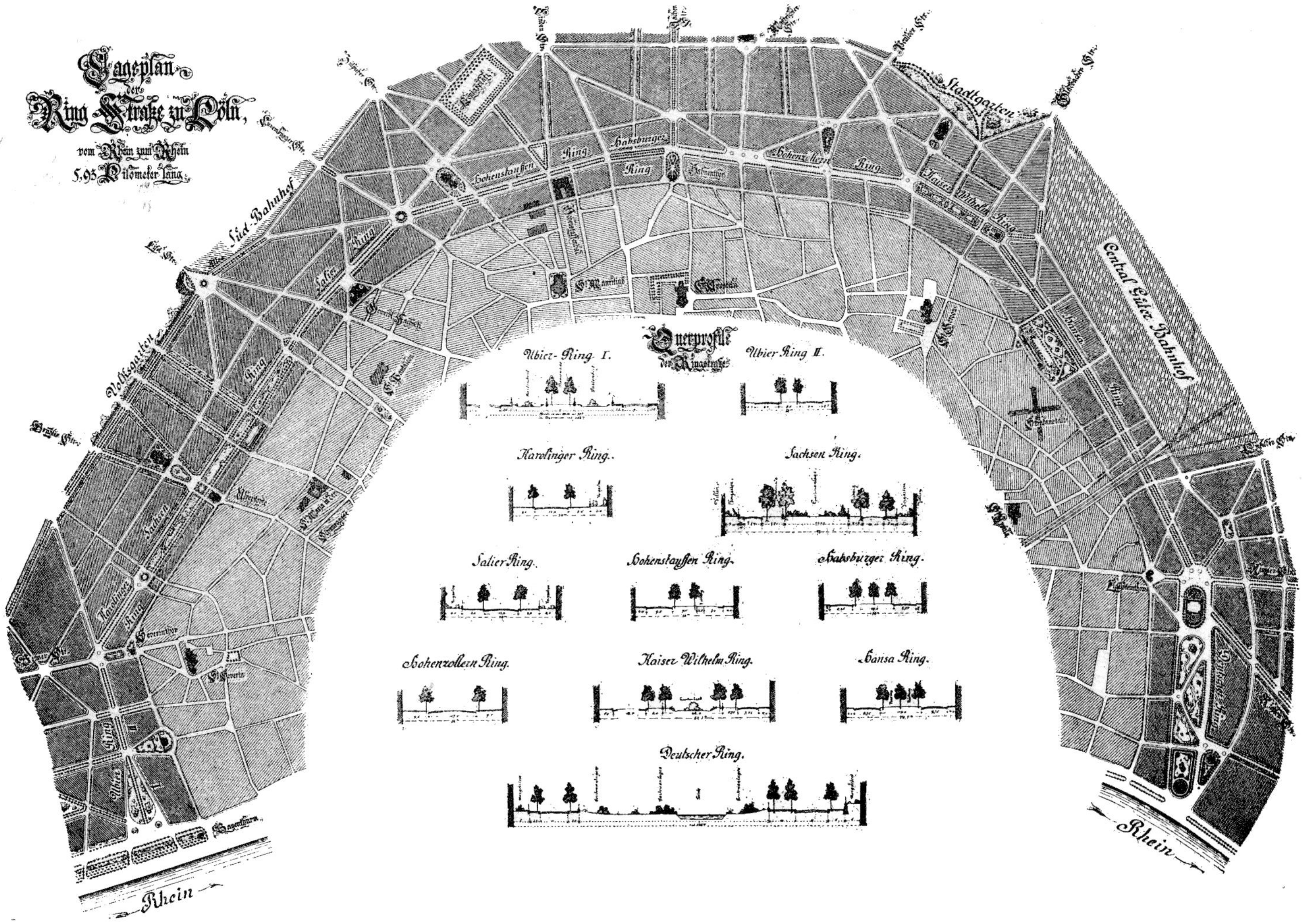

Cologne Ringstrasse: Expansion Plan, Stübben, 1880

Stübben's Early Planning Objectives

Stübben's goals as a planner were aimed at facilitating what he viewed as the natural expansion of the city. He believed that:

> The laying out or spreading out of a city should proceed upon the basis of a well-considered, comprehensive plan. The essential basis of regulated city-building is the establishment of future streets and places. The practical principles of city construction relate to traffic, to building, and to health.[12]

This attitude and the climate of civic and health reform created the framework in which Stübben pursued order in three respects:

1. Orderly circulation of traffic
Construction of wide streets.

2. Sanitary needs
System of drainage and sewers with each street plan. Light and air secured in all parts of the city (This also justified wide streets, parks, and squares.)

3. City Beautification
Aesthetic principles held by city planners and their sponsors: typically, "Haussmanesque or Baroque."[13]

Over time, Stübben's goals changed with the ideals of the planning movement, perhaps most notably in the 1890s when the movement turned toward a smaller, more human scale as a result of the influence of urban designers such as Camillo Sitte.

Streets

According to Stübben the most important duty of streets and squares is to accommodate city traffic in the most perfect manner possible. There are four kinds of streets: radial, ring, diagonal, and by-streets. (Rectangular grids should not be used.)

The width of streets should correspond to traffic requirements. They should be at least 10 m (33') wide, and rarely more than 40 m (131'). Streets with trees should be wider—at least 20 m (66'), but 25–30 m (82–98') is better.

Building heights should not be greater than the width of the street, i.e., maximum 1:1 proportion.

Streets should not be too long—a maximum of 20–30 times their width.[14]

Stübben's Cologne Extension Plan

After winning the competition for the Cologne Ringstrasse in 1880, Stübben assumed the position of city planner of Cologne in 1881 in order to implement the scheme. His extension plan included,

> wide straight, radial, and diagonal streets fanning out from complicated and imposing intersections, a comprehensive sewer system to be hidden underneath them, judicious provisions for greenery along the boulevards and in squares and parks ... all aimed at presenting Cologne with a light, airy, monumental, and prosperous looking Neustadt.[15]

These elements would become the trademark of Stübben's early city extension plans and constitute the major principles illustrated in his *Handbook for City Planning*.

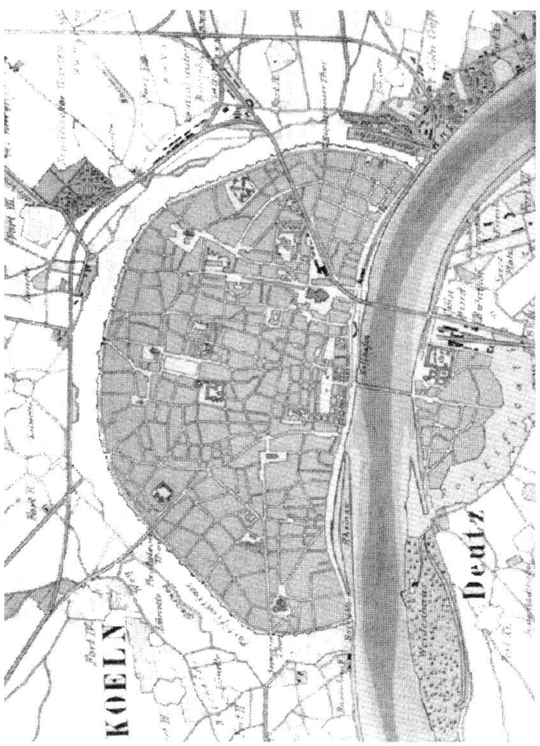

1. *Plan of Cologne before 1881*

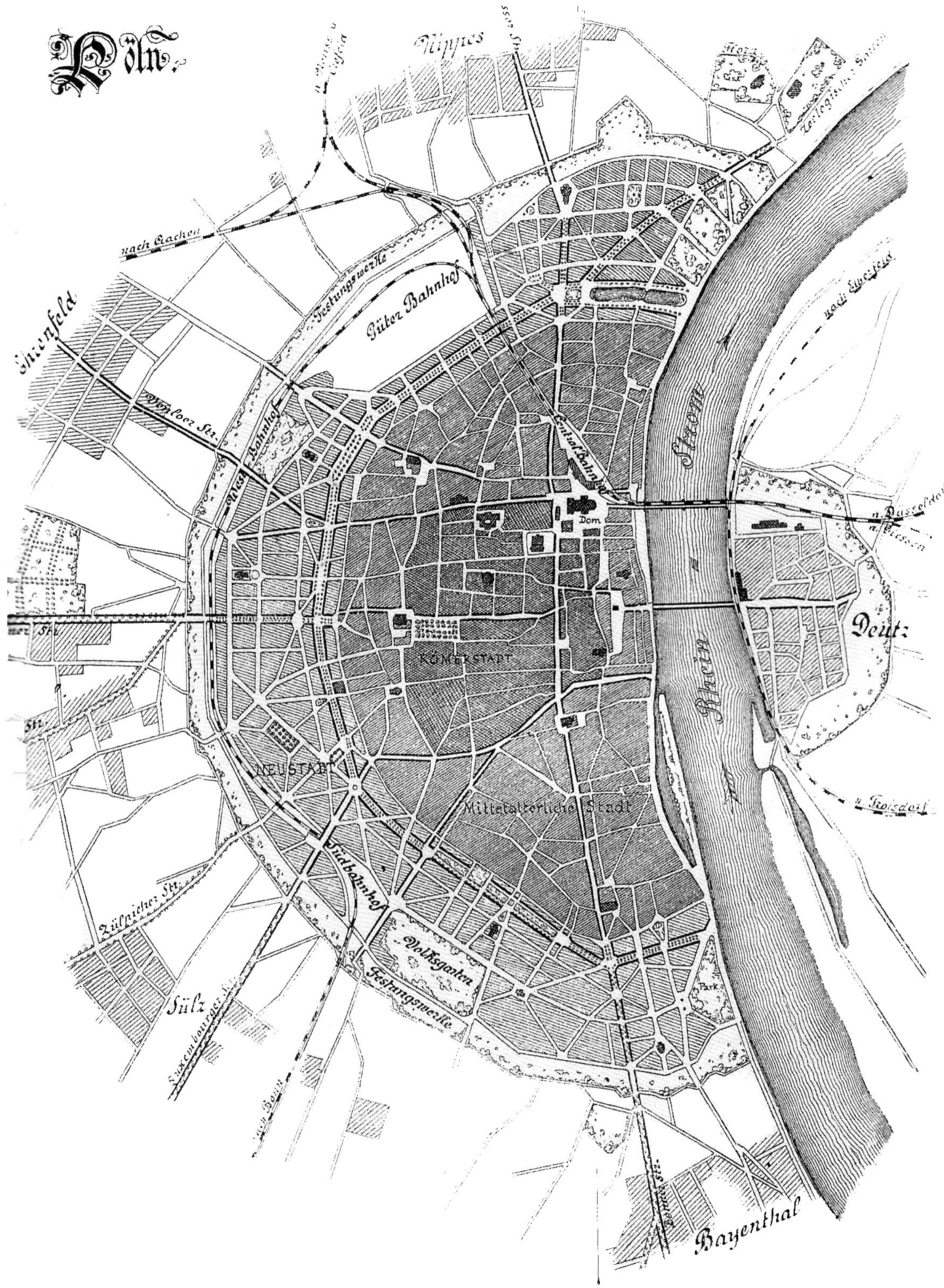

2. *Cologne: Stübben's City Extension Plan (Neustadt), 1880*

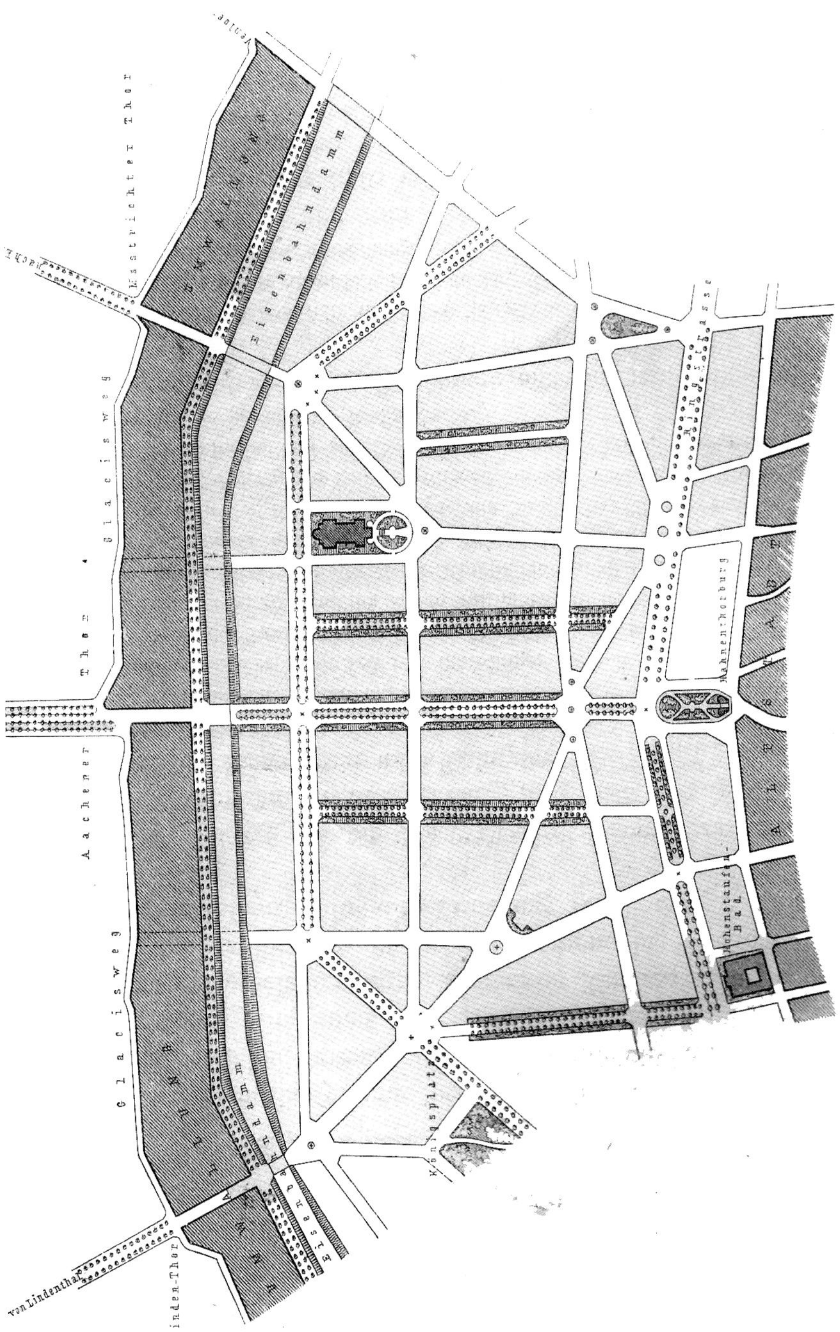

1. *Cologne: Enlarged plan (Neustadt), 1880*

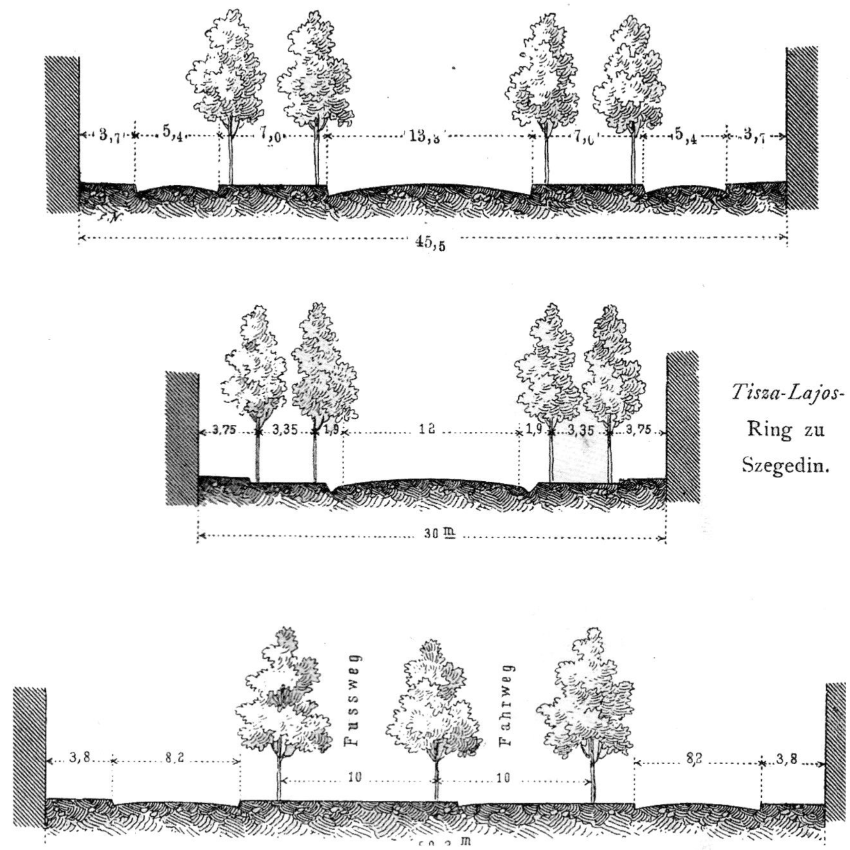

2. *Typical street profiles*

Street Grades and Drainage

According to Stübben the grades of the streets are to be made as convenient as possible: max. 1–10 percent, for the sake of drainage, min. 0.5–0.2 percent. It is desirable that the streets should lie slightly above the general surface (say 1 m). Heights of 3 m are ill advised.[16]

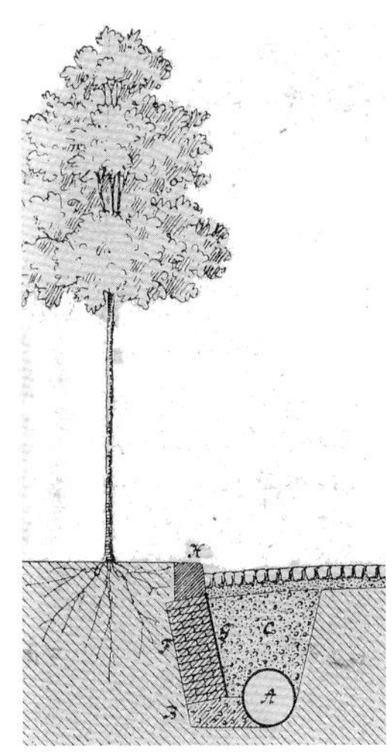

3. *Typical section at street edge*

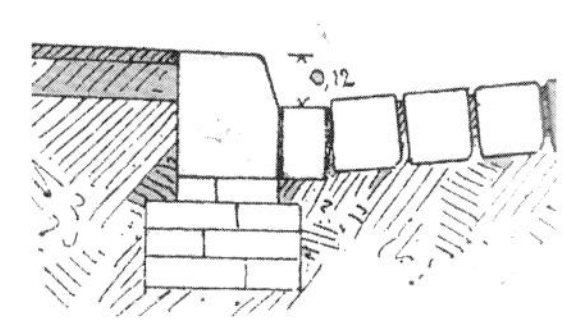

4. *Street Edge Detail*

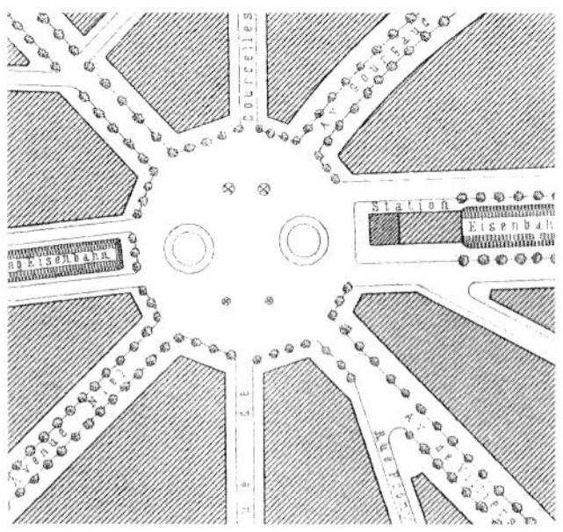

1. Place Pereire, Paris, 1:7500

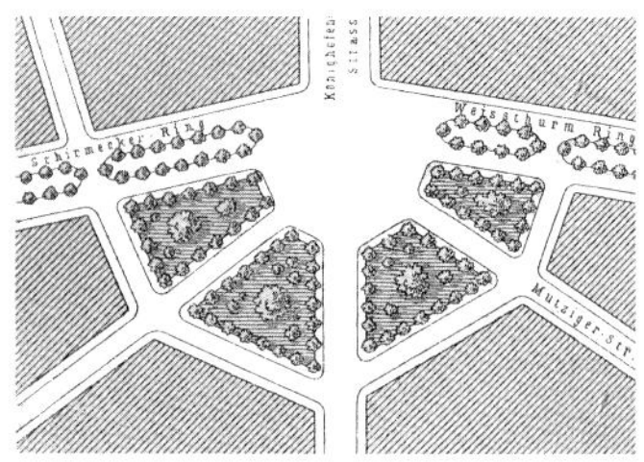

2. Weifsthurmplatz, Strasbourg, 1:7500

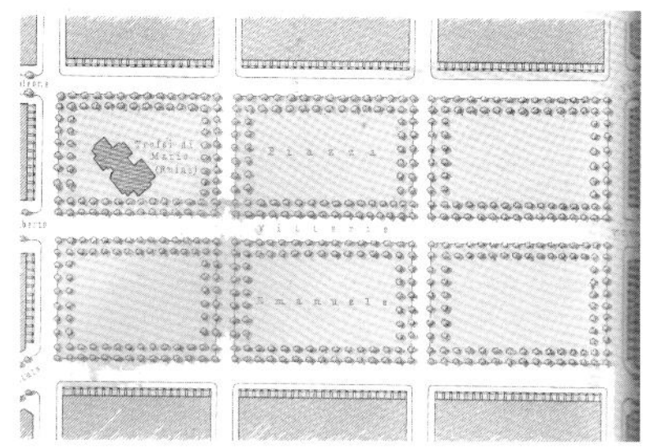

3. Victor-Emanuel-Platz, Rome

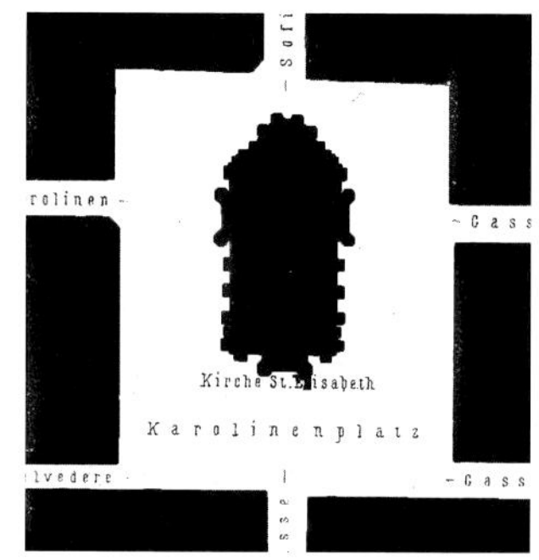

4. Kirchplatz, Vienna, 1:3750

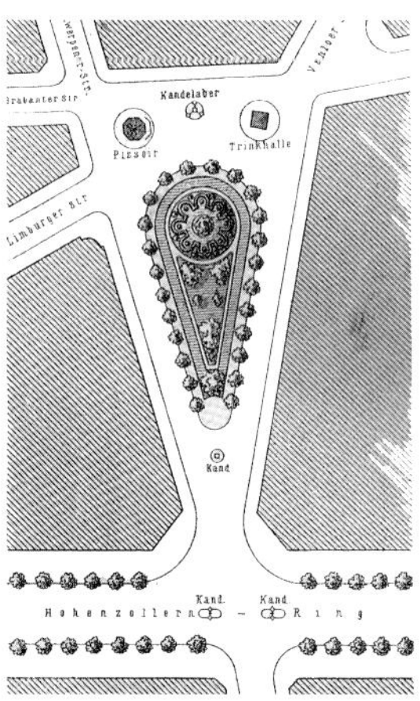

5. Traffic Plaza, Cologne, 1:3750

6. Kaifer-Wilhelm Boulevard, Breslau, 1:2500

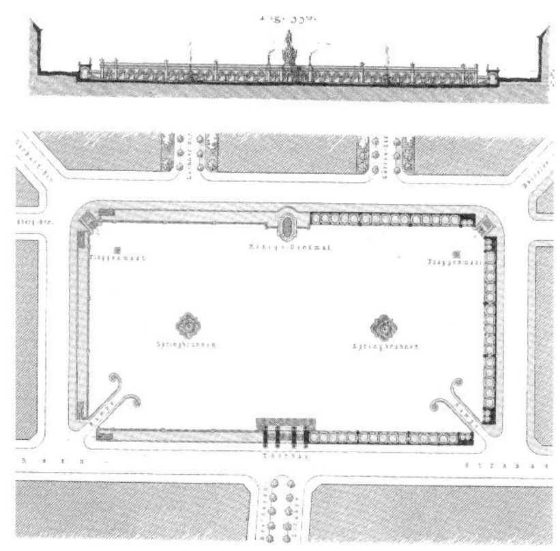

7. Konigsplatz, Cologne, 1:5000

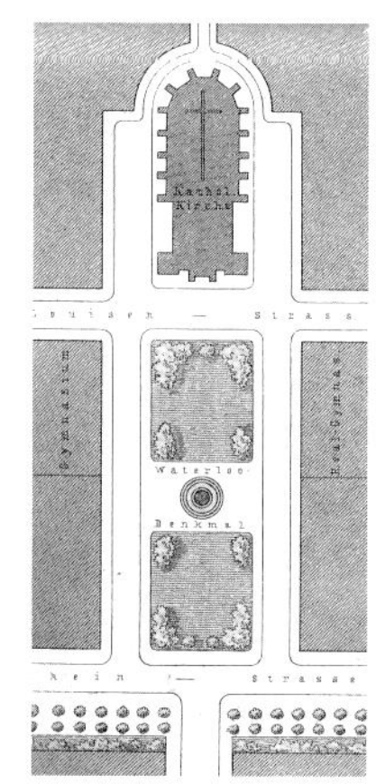

8. Luifen-Platz, Wiesbaden, 1:5000

Squares

According to Stübben squares should not be too large, nor bounded by exactly straight lines, nor have any summits. Squares should be planted with trees and gardens. Business squares require openings on all sides; their surfaces serve walking and driving. All other squares need the closest enclosure possible; travel may be around the square, but not across the space. Public buildings, such as churches, theaters, museums, etc., require an open space, if not all around, at least on three sides.

The determination of squares as traffic areas, as air reservoirs, and as shaded places of recreation will be subordinate to the question of how they may serve as a place of setting up the more important works of architecture and monumental art.

There are four different distances for viewing buildings and statues: a distance equal to the cross-sectional height of the work, for observing the structure itself; a distance equal to double the height, which is essential to comprehend the form of an edifice; a distance equal to three times the height, which includes the work and its surroundings as a composition of buildings; and a fourfold and greatest distance, which produces the effect of picturesque masses and outlines.[17]

1. *Rectangular Block Division, 1:10,000*

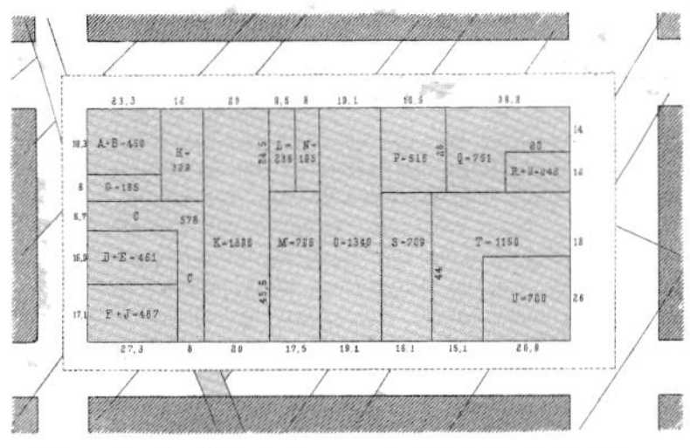

2. *Rectangular parcelization, 1:4,000*

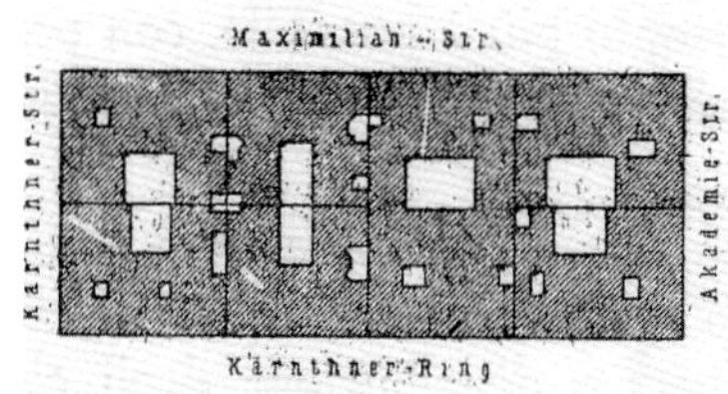

3. *Hauferblock, Cologne1:300*

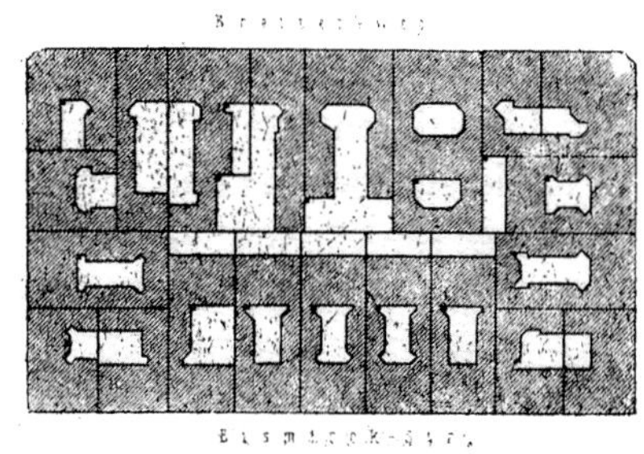

4. *Baublock, Magdeburg, 1:300*

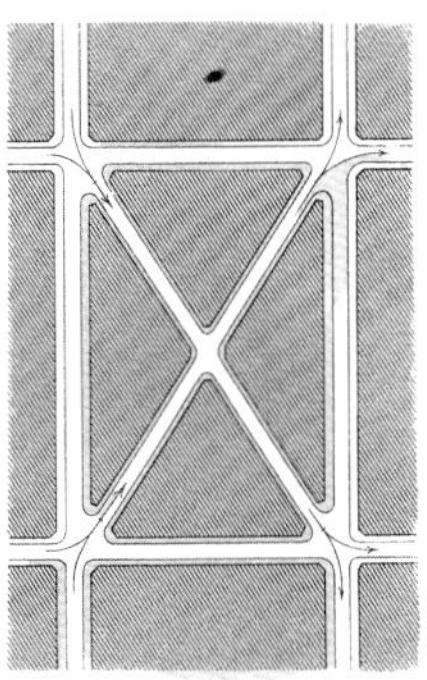

5. *Diaganal Block Division, 1:10,000*

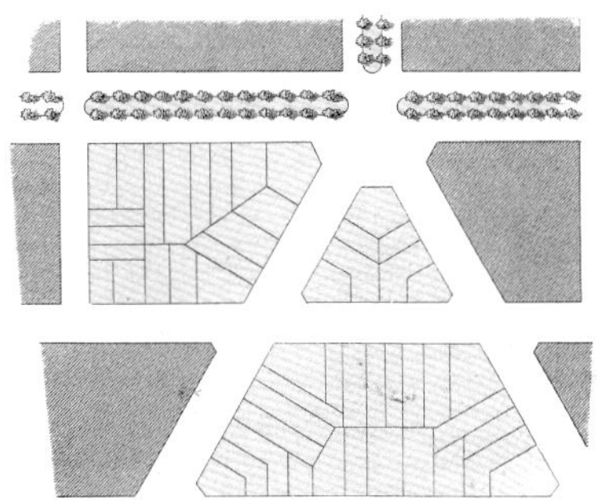

6. *Trapeze Block, 1:5,000*

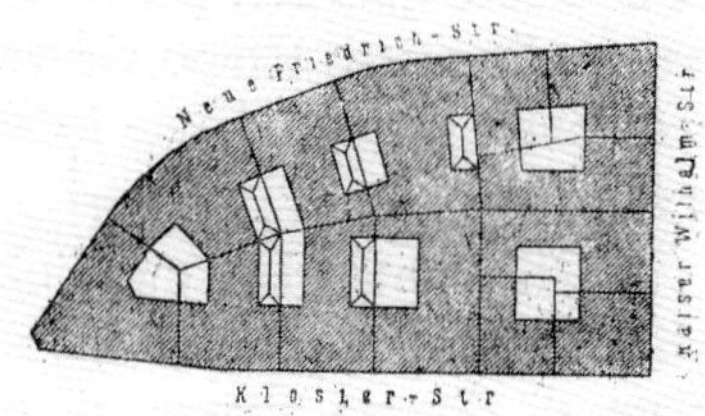

7. *Hauferblock, Cologne, with garden/ courtyard, 1:300*

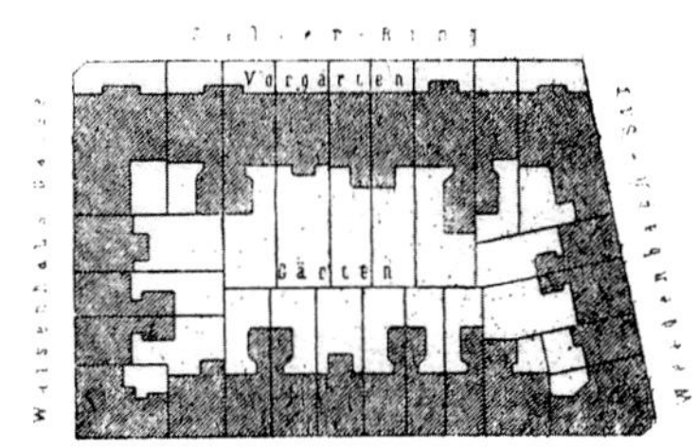

8. *Hauferblock, Cologne, with garden/ courtyard, 1:300*

Blocks

Also, according to Stübben blocks are the result of the street network. There are three shapes of blocks: rectangular, trapezoidal, and triangular. The corners of acute angle blocks should either be rounded or cut off, but leaving enough surface to provide for a facade. The length of blocks should be about 1.5–2.5 times the depth of the block. Medium-size blocks for residences with gardens should be about 80 x 160 m (250' x 500'). Rental and business houses without gardens require about 60 x 120 m (200' x 400'). Blocks for workers' houses require smaller blocks of about 35 x 140 m (115' x 460'). Industrial blocks should be about 100 x 200 m (328' x 656').[18]

Parcels

In right-angled blocks the depth of the block is equal to the depth of two building lots. Parcels should be at right angles to the bounding streets so that the buildings with oblique angles occur only at street corners. The notion that acutely angled blocks are to be generally avoided is incorrect; in the first place, conformity to the plan of traffic lines brings out sharp-angled blocks, and the inconvenience in building is easily overcome, and indeed is availed of to bring about commercial and artistic advantages.[19]

Camillo Sitte

Much has been written about Camillo Sitte: artist, architect, town planner, and urban theorist.[20] Sitte was one of the most uniquely influential figures in the lineage of urban planning—primarily through his urban theory.

Sitte was the first to challenge modernist planning principles, which had been developing since the mid-eighteenth century, and was, in this sense, a revolutionary. He was also (unknowingly) prescient, as variations of his critique would appear periodically throughout the twentieth century.

In 1889, his small book on city planning was published in Vienna, and was an immediate success. *Der Städtebau nach seinen künstlerichen Grundsätzen* (City Planning According to Artistic Principles) has been reprinted many times (in several languages), and continues to be debated and influential more than a century later.[21] Over this time, the book has been used and misused by proponents and opponents alike to such a degree that any real thought or reinterpretation has been almost completely deflected. This has also tended to deflect attention from his actual planning practice, which included projects for Vienna and other northern cities.

Der Städtebau

Sitte's book was a reaction against the prevailing Germanic engineering approach to city planning exemplified by Baumiester and Stübben, in favor of a more spatial version of urbanism that he felt was fundamental to the historic European city.

His critiques of engineers were numerous: opposition toward the architectural impact of sanitation and hygiene measures, obsession with traffic and zoning, and disagreement with the unwavering geometry of straight boulevards, radial plazas, and relentlessly repetitive landscape.

In the introduction to *Der Städtebau,* Sitte states clearly his counterargument that "city planning should not be merely a technical matter, but ... an artistic enterprise." And "It is only in our mathematical century that the process of enlarging and laying out cities has become an almost technical concern." But "this attitude solves only one aspect of the problem ... the other, the artistic aspect, is of at least equal importance."[22]

The original version of *Der Städtebau* did not address the street, urban fabric, neighborhoods, zoning, or landscape. Chapters on the street and landscape were added to some later editions.[23]

Sitte's book is primarily about the public spaces of the city: the principles of historic exemplars, the retrofitting and improvement of existing plazas, the design of new ones, and the grouping of spaces.

Plazas

Two of the precedents for plazas that were cited by Sitte in the introduction to *Der Städtebau* were the Forum at Pompeii and the Forum Romanum in Rome.

He especially calls attention to the "nature of the ancient forum, which was so rigorously closed off from the outside." He also states that "the main requirement for a plaza, as for a room, is the enclosed character of its space."[24] Thus, he firmly establishes the perception of urban space as what is, for him, the essential medium of urbanism.

This was completely counter to the notions of contemporary town planners, so interested in circulation, practicality, and fascination with Beaux Arts emphasis on free-standing, monumental civic buildings. His was an avant-garde position.

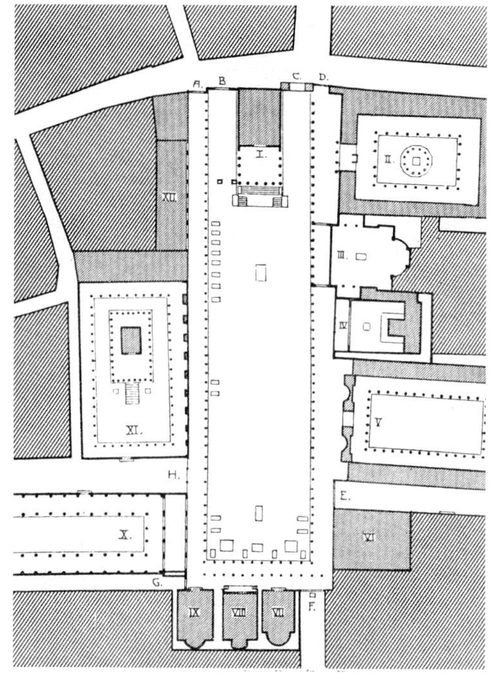

1. Plan of the Forum at Pompeii

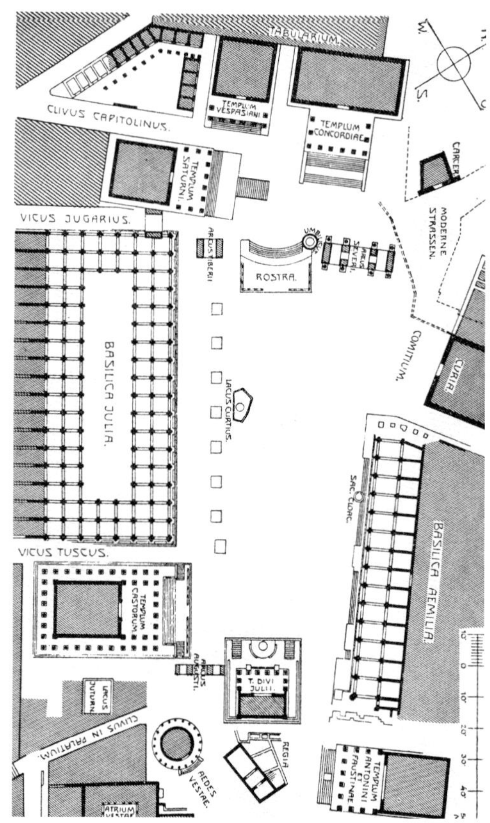

2. Plan of the Forum Romanum

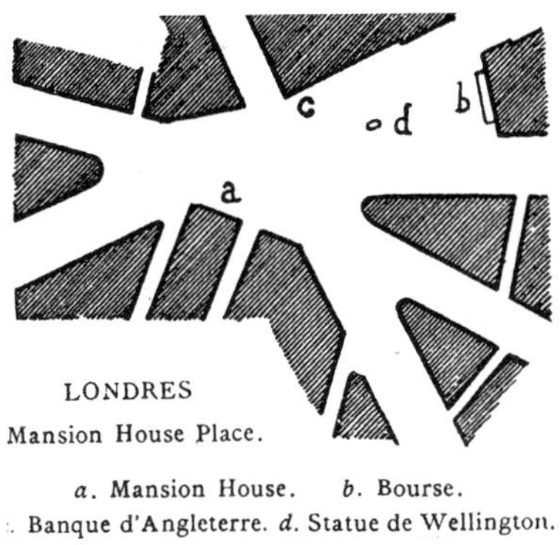

1. Plan of Mansion House Place, London

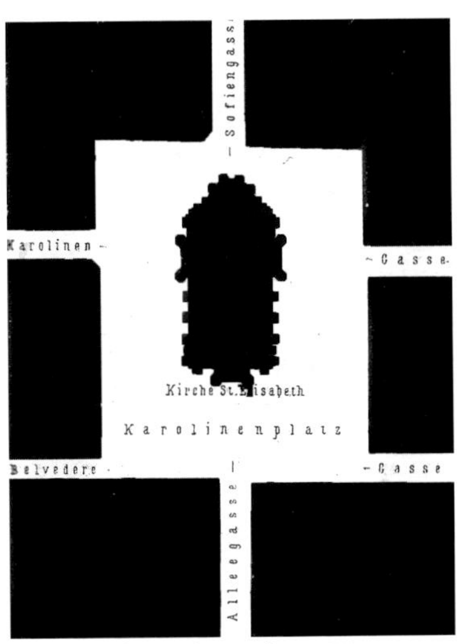

2. Plan of Karolinenplatz, Vienna, from Stübben

Sitte's Critique of Modernist Plazas

Sitte illustrates and severely criticizes various contemporary urban spaces. His harshest criticism is toward open spaces pierced by too many streets, so that they become undefined and consumed by vehicular circulation—traffic intersections rather than plazas. Major criticism is also directed toward symmetrical plazas with monumental free-standing buildings in the center. Finally, he condemns plazas that are too big, such as the open spaces of the Ringstrasse in Vienna.

Sitte's Principles

Sitte cites and illustrates multiple examples of historic squares where the major buildings are embedded in the surrounding fabric, resulting in asymmetrical compositions with adequate spatial closure. His basic principles for the design of plazas were:

Plazas should be enclosed entities

The centers should be kept free

From any viewpoint no more than one street leading out should be seen at one time

Defining buildings should have a proportional relationship to the square

Absolute regularity is unnecessary, and

Plazas should be modest in size

Sitte cites countless examples of plazas based on these principles, including the Piazza della Signoria in Florence and Strasbourg Cathedral and its plazas. Using these principles, he proposed his own revisions to the spaces of the Ringstrasse.

3. Plan of the Piazza della Signoria, Florence

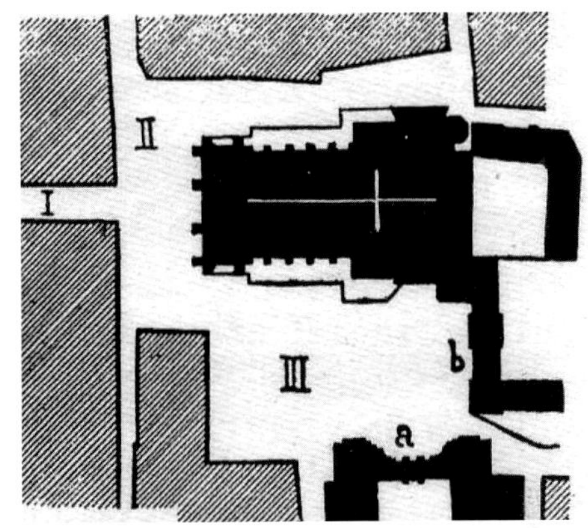

4. Plan of Strasbourg Cathedral plazas

5. Perspective view of Strasbourg Cathedral

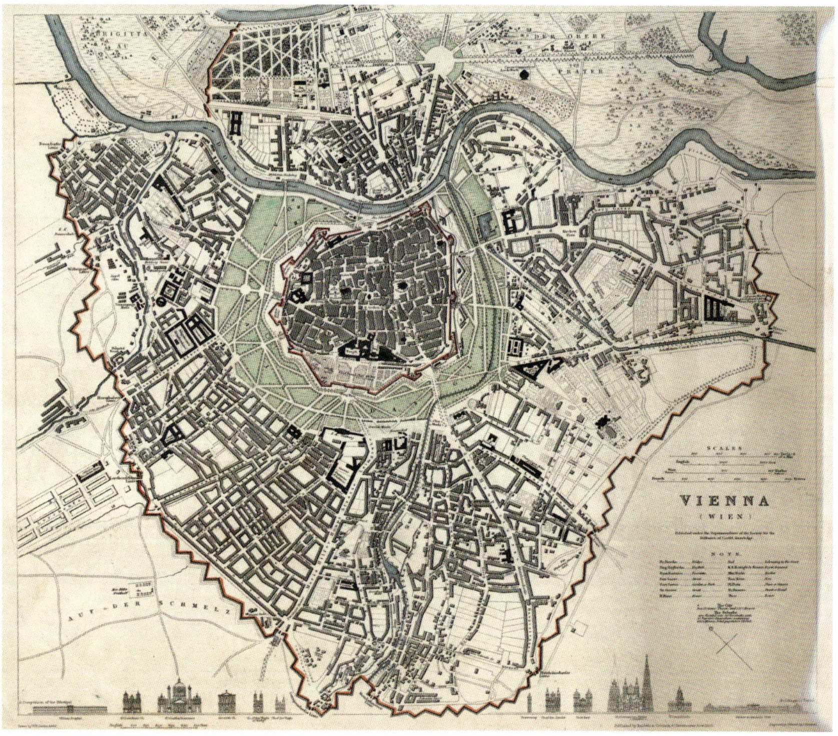

1. Vienna, plan, before demolition of the city walls

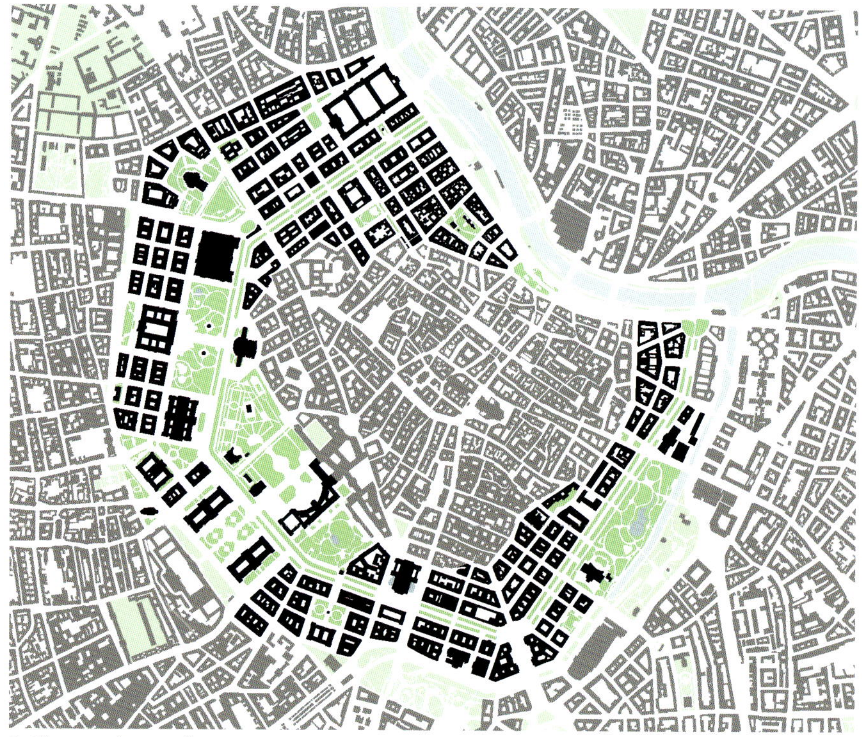

2. Vienna, plan, with Ringstrasse

The Vienna Ringstrasse

By the mid-nineteenth century, central Vienna was still surrounded by defensive walls, and the open space of the Glacis separated the core of the city from the surrounding suburbs. In 1857, Emperor Franz Joseph ordered the demolition of the walls and the construction of the Ringstrasse in the space of the Glacis. Franz Joseph opened the Ringstrasse in 1865, and the project was mostly complete by 1880. A combination of open space, monumental buildings, and urban fabric, the Ring offered Sitte the opportunity for both critique and example.

Sitte's Critique

Sitte begins his critique of the Ring by stating that :

> If all the high expectations ... regarding the future artistic effect of the new layout do not seem to be fulfilled ... at least nothing so far has been completely spoiled. ... Whatever is lacking can still be achieved. The situation at present is that the buildings are successful, but the parceling is not. Luckily, however, there remains enough vacant area so that the shortcomings of the latter can still be rectified.[25]

Sitte then outlines his infill proposals to "correct" the design of the Ringstrasse.

Ringstrasse Buildings and Blocks

Most of the urban blocks of the historic core of Vienna are irregular, and the civic spaces are controlled and modest in size. "The ... forums were of regular shape ... calculated for their visible effect, while all their irregularities were absorbed in the mass of surrounding structures."[26] Most of the urban blocks of the Ringstrasse, however, are rectangular within a regular grid, and except for the Hofburg, the civic buildings are symmetrical free-standing monuments. The resulting open spaces are not only extensive but residual.

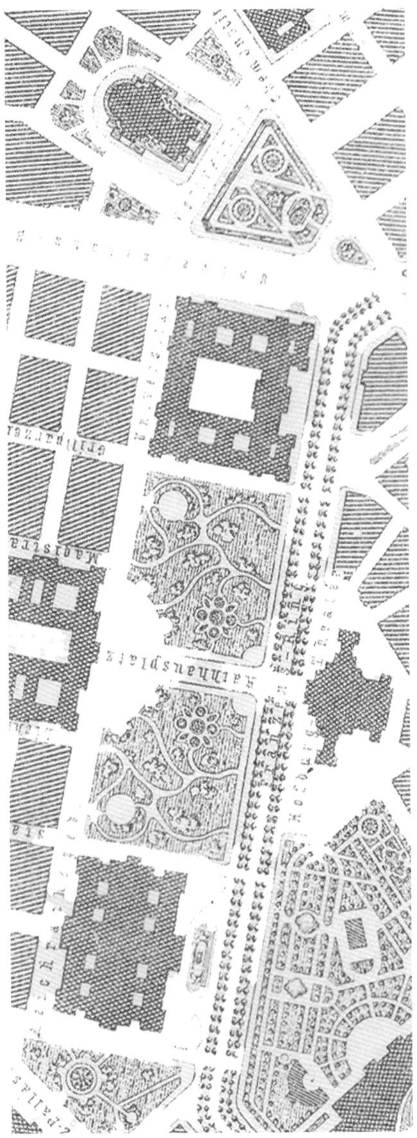

1. *Stübben's proposed Ringstrasse redesign*

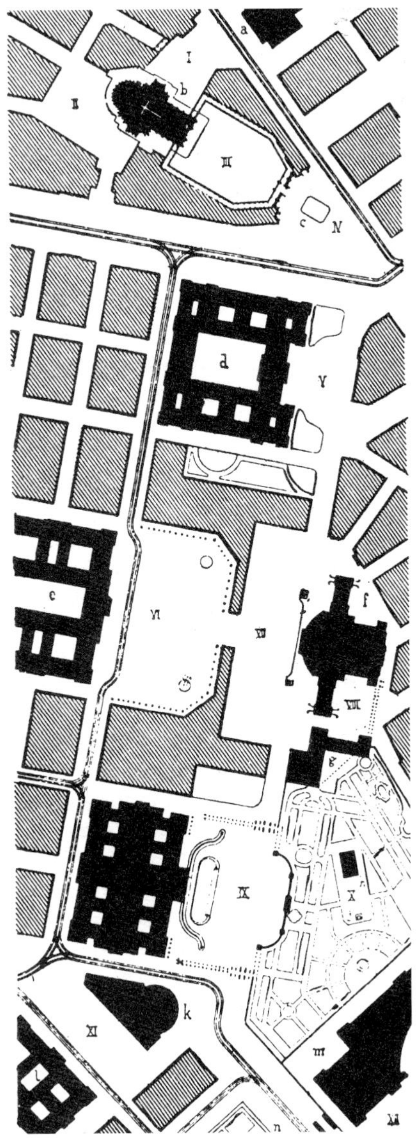

2. *Sitte's proposed Ringstrasse plan*

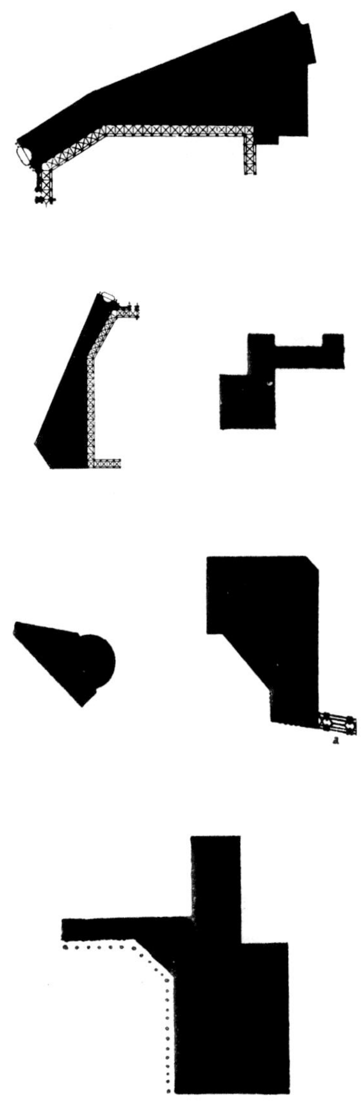

3. *Configurations of Sitte's proposed buildings*

Building Legend

(a) Chemical Laboratory, (b) Votive Church, (c) Site for a large monument, (d) University, (e) Rathaus (City Hall), (f) Burgtheater, (g) Projected new building related to the Burgtheater, (h) Temple of Theseus, (j) Suggested site for the Goethe Monument, (k) Proposed new building, (l) Palace of Justice, (m) New Hofburg construction, (n) Projected triumphal arch

Public Squares Legend

I, II, IV New Plazas around the Votive Church, III Forecourt of the Votive Church, V University Plaza, VI Rathaus Plaza, VII Larger Theater Plaza, VIII Smaller Theater Plaza, IX Plaza in front of Parliament building, X Plaza in the Volksgarten, XI Plaza in front of the Palace of Justice, XII New Hofburg Plaza

Sitte's Buildings

Sitte's proposed plan is what would be called an "urban intervention" today. It is an infill project—like a prosthetic urban suit—that articulates and shapes a series of positively defined, modestly scaled urban spaces. Irregularities are absorbed by oddly shaped buildings whose configurations are determined by the urban context, i.e., from the outside in. The proposed building configurations would never be conceived *a priori*, but only as a result of urban considerations where architecture is subordinate to urban space.

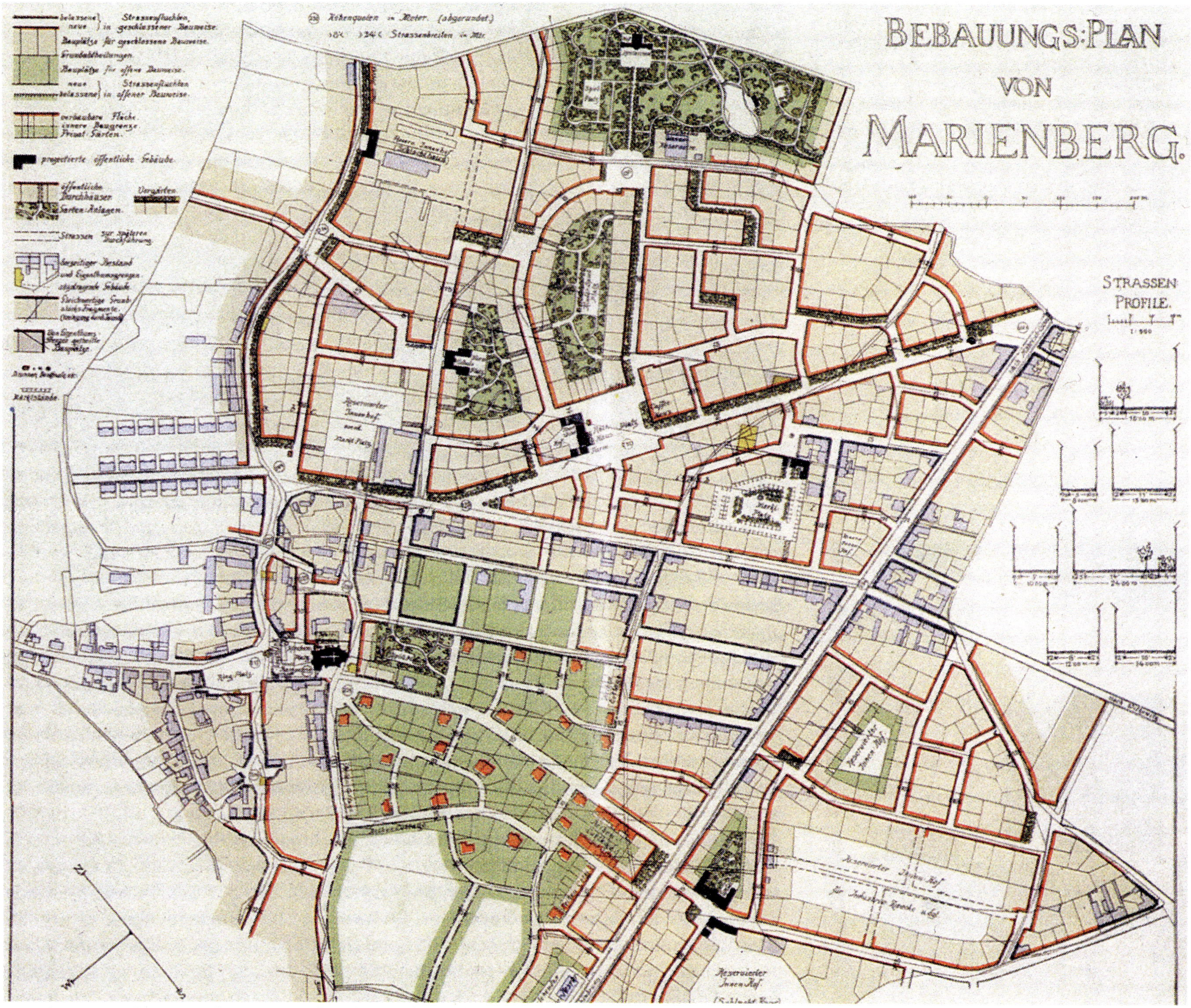

Marienberg, proposed expansion plan, 1904, Camillo and Siegfried Sitte. The natural topography of Marienberg proved so irregular that many adjustments for sloping plazas and forecourts had to be accommodated. The main avenues are straight and the minor streets avoid sharp intersections while adhering as closely as possible to the complicated property lines. Existing streets are outlined in black; new streets are outlined in red; existing buildings are in blue; new public buildings are in black.

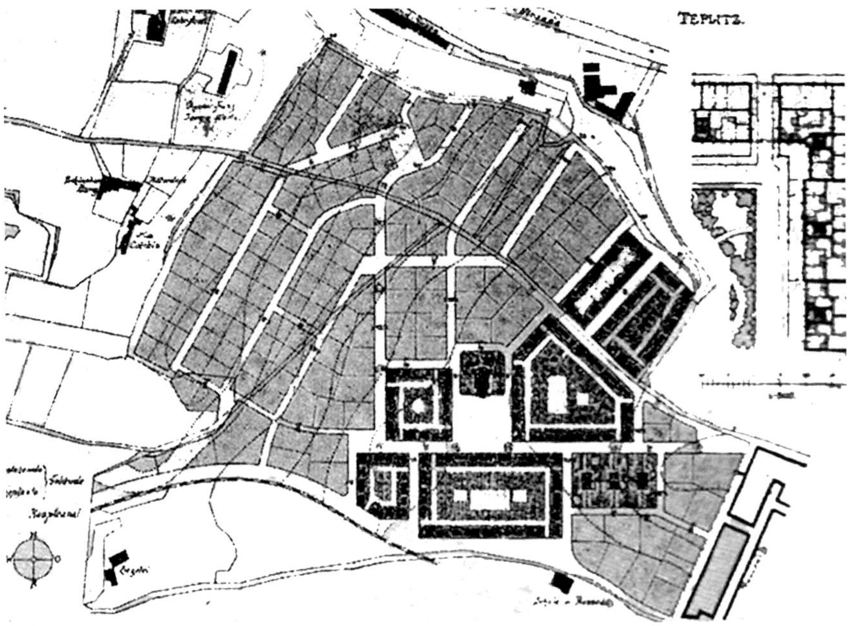

1. Teplitz: Sitte's plan for a subdivision on a large slope adjoining the city

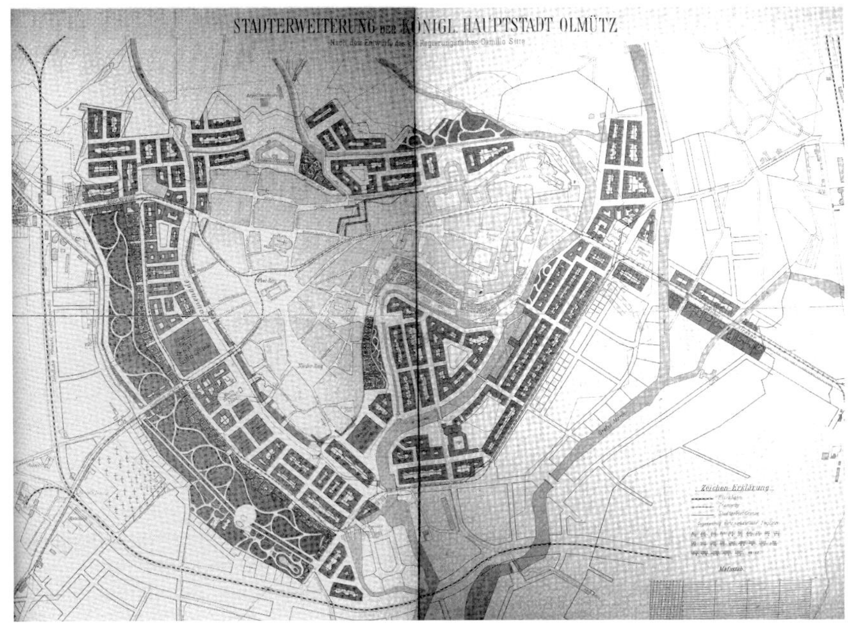

2. Sitte's expansion plan for Olmütz, 1894

Sitte and City Planning Abroad

Sitte's principles made him an intriguing and logical choice for many provincial towns in the Austro-Hungarian Empire. His work had not previously included this region, but this may be because he was not willing to write about places he had not seen himself. In fact, the Austro-Hungarian empire would be the primary place in which he would be afforded the opportunity to propose practical applications of his artistic planning theory.

Sitte approached implementation with careful attention to topography and existing city fabric. He did not recreate Italian piazzas; he created new public spaces, and choreographed movement accentuated by vistas and turns suggested by the natural landscape.

This made Sitte unique among his counterparts. Rather than creating an unrelated geometry and building through brute force, his plans account for nature and humans. Most of Sitte's projects were never realized, but they represent his thoughts at the larger scale. It was not his professional work that cemented his legacy, however, but his little book, *Der Städtebau.*

Sitte's Impact

Sitte's success upon publishing his book was immediate and echoed through the profession of city planning in the Austro-Germanic world. His ideas were used to redraw plans almost instantly, and a few, such as Ludwigshafen and Altona, were even used as examples when Sitte lectured. While not all of his ideas were appropriated correctly, he had a few ardent followers, most notably Karl Henrici, Theodor Goeke, and Theodor Fischer who was a mentor to J. J. P. Oud, Walter Gropius, Paul Bonatz, and Bruno Taut. Fischer was one of the first to consider Sitte the "father of modern city planning" and used his principles in his plan for Munich. By 1905 Sitte's influence had extended to the city plans of Berlin, Munich, Stuttgart, Aachen, Danzig Darmstadt, Dresden, and Vienna.

Even eminent planners of the "old guard" such as Joseph Stübben were influenced by Sitte's ideas. Their relationship was amicable; however, each had their likes and complaints of each other's work. Sitte felt Stübben's *Handbook for Architecture* was a good platform for understanding the numerous issues involved with city planning; however, Sitte did not agree with his positions on traffic strategies, central placement of monuments, and relentless axial geometry. On elements such as the turbine plaza and Sitte's illustration of squares they could agree, and Stübben even began to feature some of Sitte's work in his later editions of the *Handbook.*

Sitte's impact abroad was delayed owing to slow translations of his text. He was first translated into French (with significant alterations)[27] and garnered a small following in Western Europe, and eventually became recognized and praised in the United States.

American Vitruvius: An Architect's Handbook of Civic Art, published by Werner Hegemann and Elbert Peets in 1922, catalogs Sitte's contribution to architecture and has remained an authoritative text illustrating his lineage.

In 1975, Rob Krier's seminal *Stadtraum* (later published in English as *Urban Space*) was dedicated to Camillo Sitte—the first "revival" after half a century of modernist town planning and derision of Sitte.

Amsterdam South

H. P. Berlage believed in the holistic character of architecture and town planning. Like Sitte, he saw urban space as the primary medium of urbanism and the blocks as "filler" between the spaces. But like Stübben, he believed in realistic urban plans.[28]

His first scheme for Amsterdam South was commissioned in 1904 and is in stark contrast to his subsequent two plans. The first plan was more picturesque—more "Sitte-esque"—and was heavily criticized as being like a series of "medieval neighborhoods."[29] Because of the spatial pattern and site features, many of the urban blocks were irregular and gave no indication of architectural form.

In contrast, Berlage's second plan in 1915 owed more to Stübben and to Baroque planning. There was a clear pattern of public spaces, but the streets were straighter, and the blocks were thinner and more regular. Berlage believed in social housing rather than urban villas, and most of the plan is composed of continuous, unified perimeter blocks of apartments.

The final version of Berlage's plan in 1917 was built out during the 1920s. Like the other town plans of this transitional period, Berlage's plan for Amsterdam South was based on centralized land distribution, block-sized parcels, and monofunctional zoning, and the architecture of the plan was unified and illustrated.

Berlage was largely ignored by Le Corbusier and his CIAM colleagues.

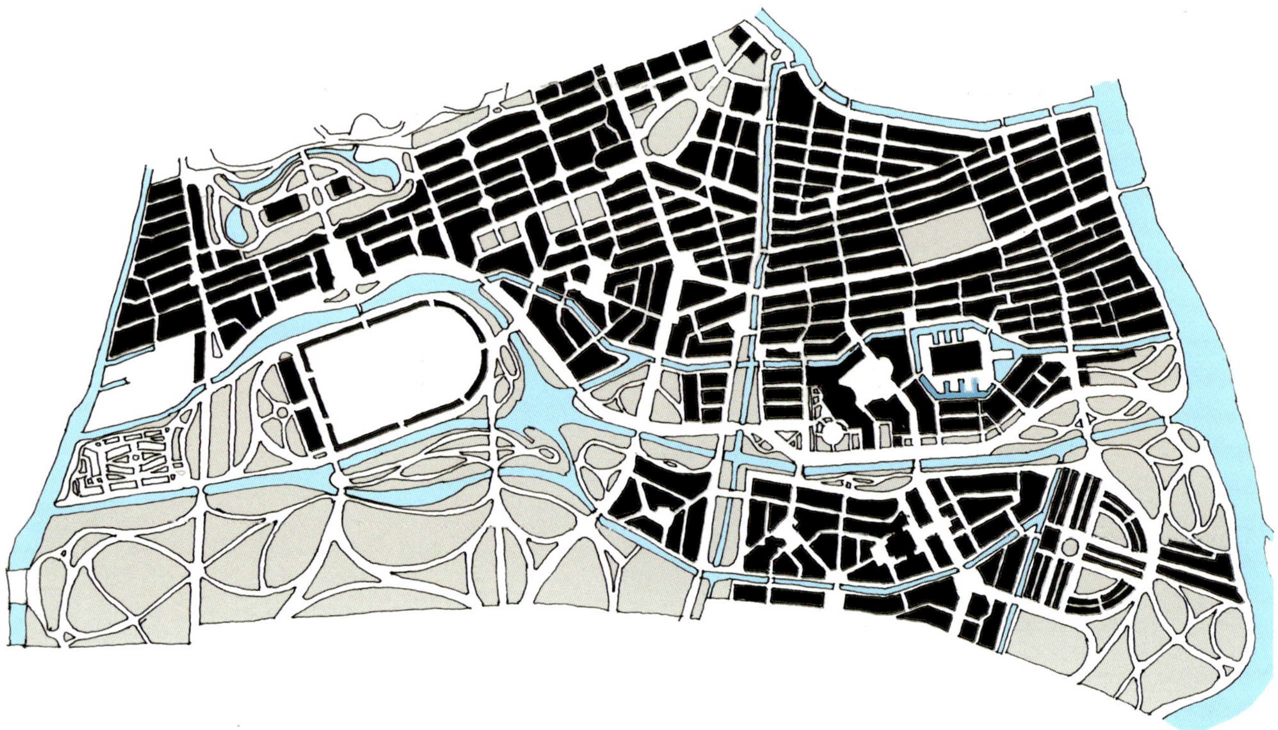

1. Berlage's first plan for Amsterdam South, 1904

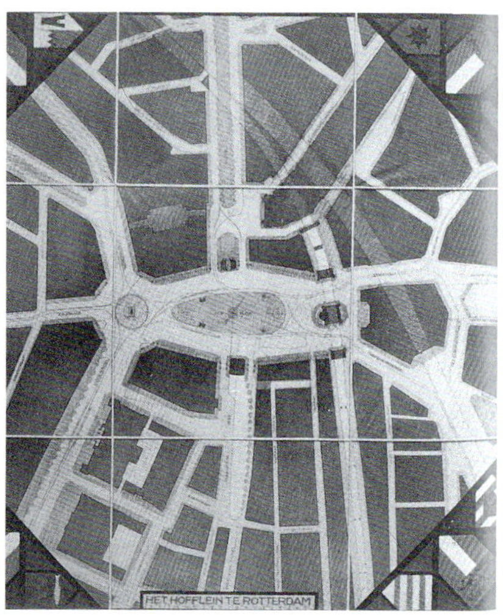

2. First plan for the Hofplein in Rotterdam, 1921

3. Second scheme for the Hofplein in Rotterdam, 1926

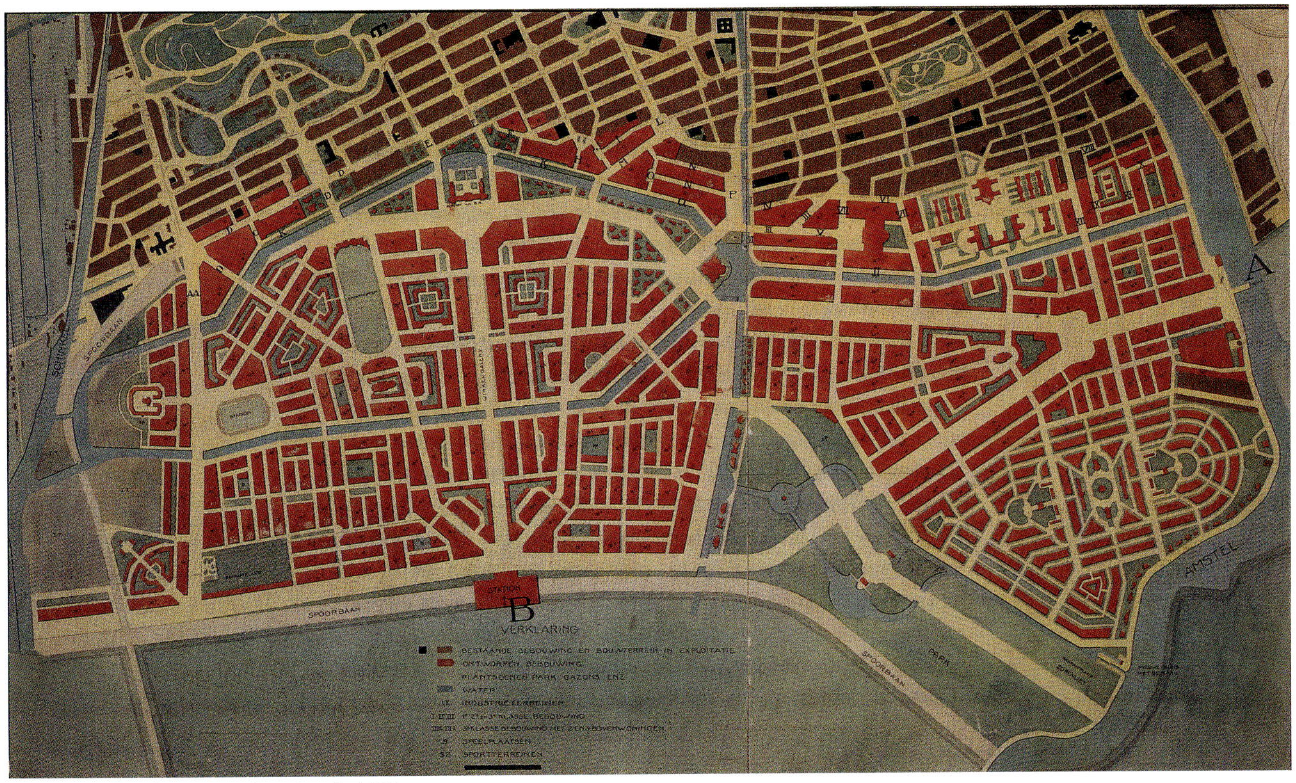

1. Second plan for Amsterdam South, 1915

2. Aerial perspective, 1915

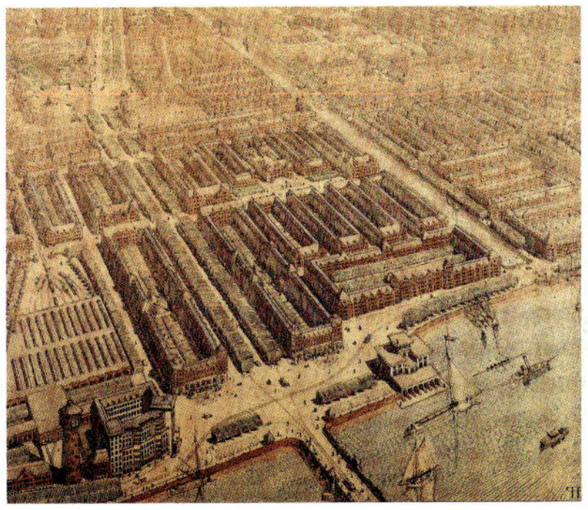

3. Aerial perspective, 1915

4. Final plan for Amsterdam South, 1917

5. Aerial view of Amsterdam South

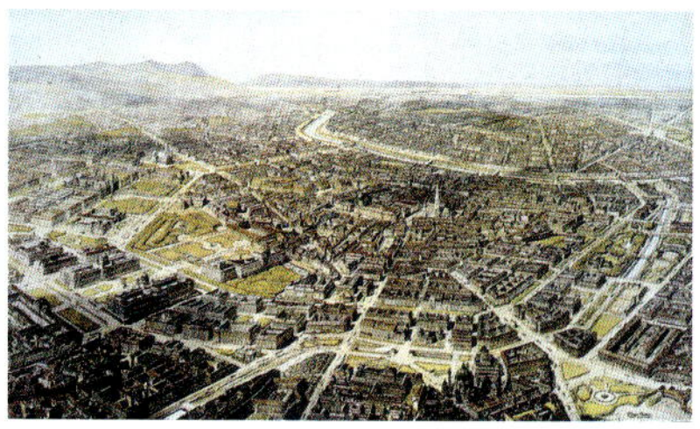

1. Perspective view of central Vienna

Otto Wagner and Vienna

Otto Wagner's study of urban issues began with his submission for the competition for the general regulating plan of Vienna in 1892–1893.[30] His urban ideas were further articulated in his *Modern Architecture* in 1896, and his theoretical plan for the expansion of Vienna was published as *Die Groszstadt* (The Metropolis) in 1911.[31]

Wagner assumed that major cities would double in size by expanding into the surrounding territory, and he cautioned that these suburban areas might be neglected. His general plan for Vienna was therefore a system of streets radiating from the city center superimposed over concentric rings of growth. The resulting network defined dense urban districts of 100,000 to 150,000 people. Radial railways were intended to connect the outlying districts with the center, assuring equal quality between them. Wagner illustrated a detailed plan and aerial perspective for District XXII.[32]

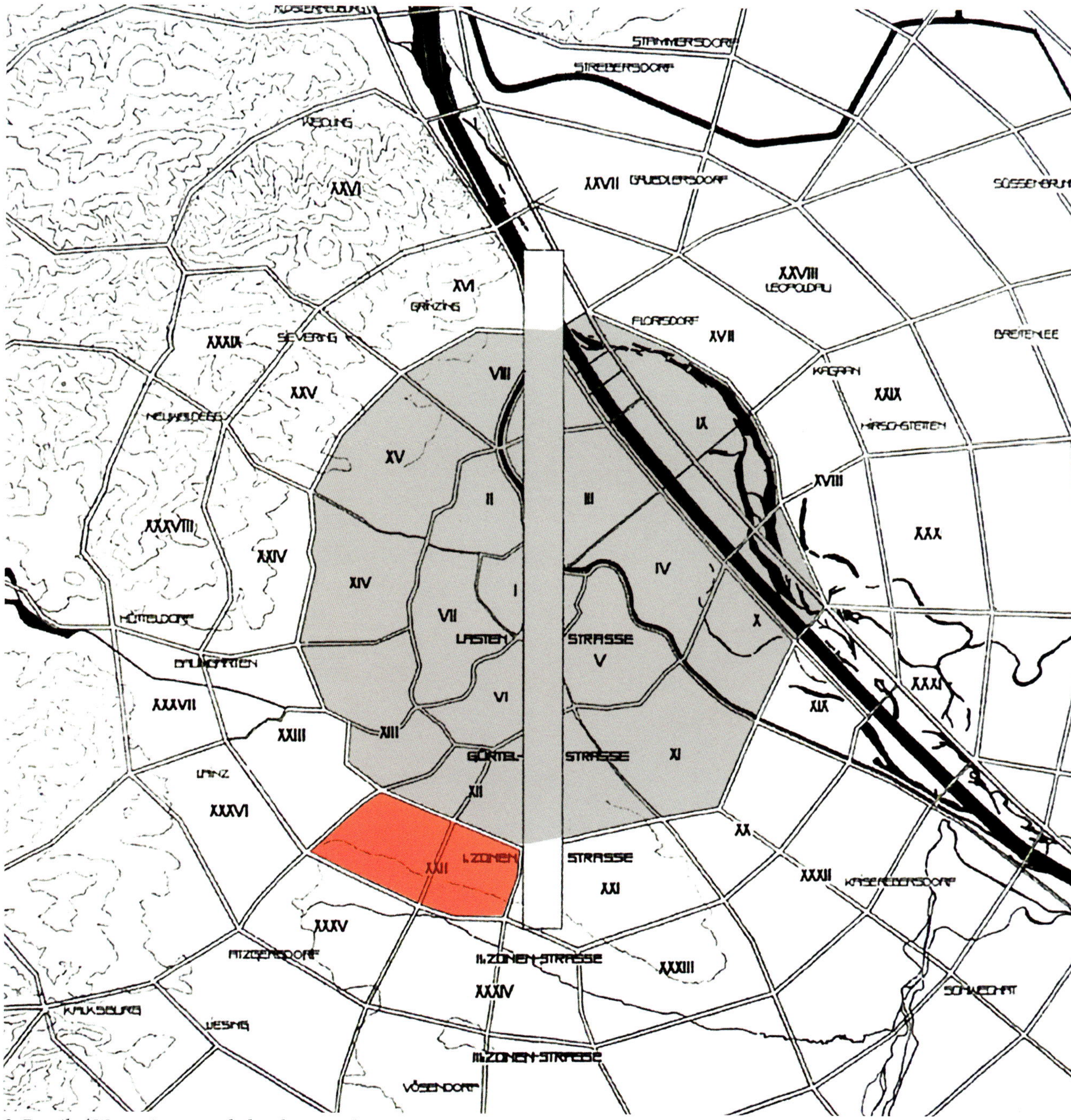

2. Detail of Wagner's proposed plan diagram of greater Vienna, 1:125,000. Gray is central Vienna in 1911, red is district XXII

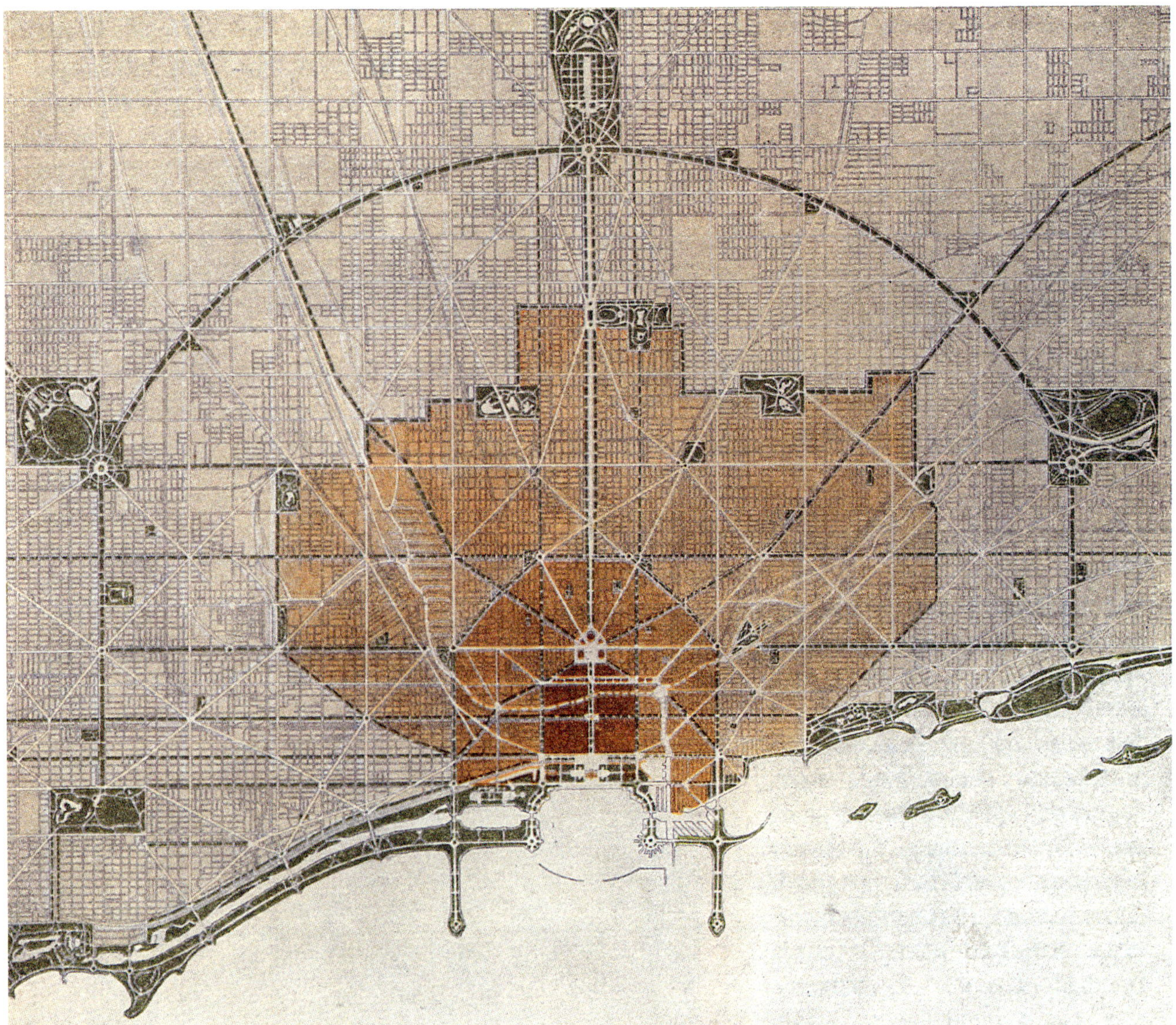

1. Burnham's Plan of Chicago, 1:125,000, 1909

2. World's Columbian Exposition, 1893

Daniel Burnham and Chicago

The 1893 World's Columbian Exposition in Chicago, coordinated by Daniel Burnham, was a rehearsal for Burnham and Edward Bennet's *Plan of Chicago*, published in 1909.[33]

In contrast to the radial Vienna plan, the Chicago plan is more an update of L'Enfant's plan for Washington—a regular grid with superimposed diagonal boulevards, or Paris meets the Midwest. But unlike both Paris and Washington (both cited as exemplars) the Chicago plan was intended as a unified, integrated, comprehensive work.[34] According to Burnham this was unprecedented in city planning. The Chicago plan was developed in much more detail than Wagner's Vienna plan, but its size, scale, symmetry, and total design were among the contributing factors to its failure to be realized.

1. Aerial plan of Vienna inside the Ringstrasse, 1:25,000

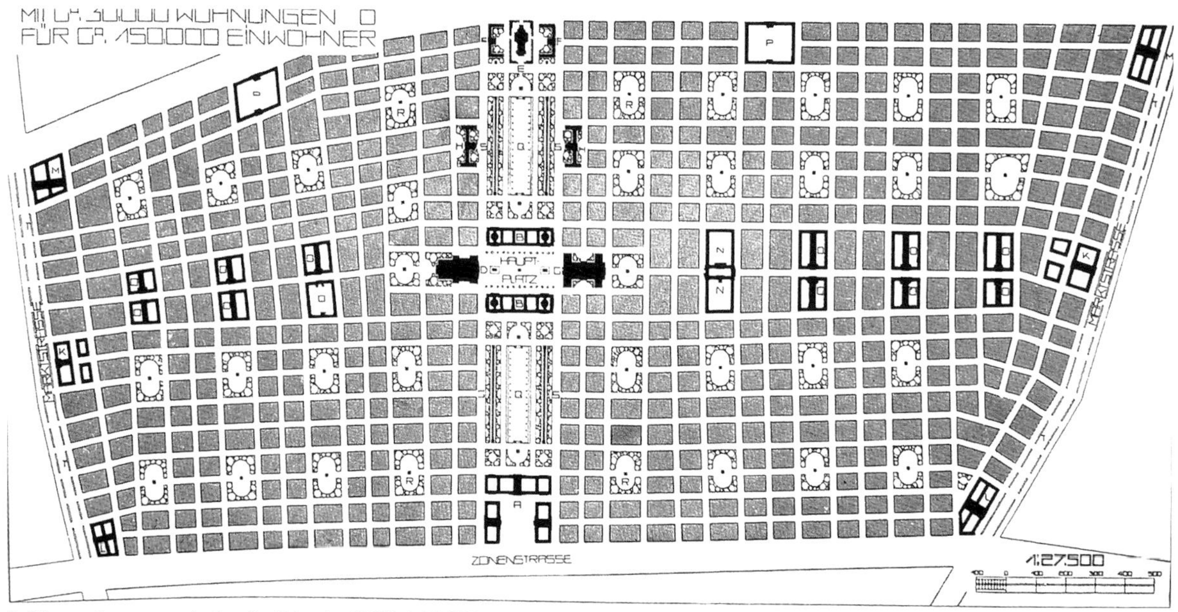

2. Wagner's proposed plan for District XXII, 1:25,000

District XXII Plan

Wagner's plan for District XXII is a more or less regular orthogonal grid of enormous size—about three times the width of Vienna's core inside the Ringstrasse—for ca. 150,000 people.

Urban Fabric

The urban blocks are relatively small and vary in size, but there are two basic types: square, about 60 x 60 m (200' x 200'); and rectangular, about 60 x 104 m (200' x 340'). The blocks are a uniform height of 23 m (75') with internal gardens, and the typical streets are 23 m wide.

Civic Spaces

There are thirty-three neighborhood parks formed by omitting blocks, and a monumental sequence of public spaces and buildings axially organized in the center of the district. (Compare this civic structure to the central Vienna plan.)

Urban Buildings

The basic component of the urban fabric is the six-story apartment building, which Wagner considered the most appropriate modern housing system. Each block contained several buildings, but the effect is uniform.

3. Characteristic six-story apartment building

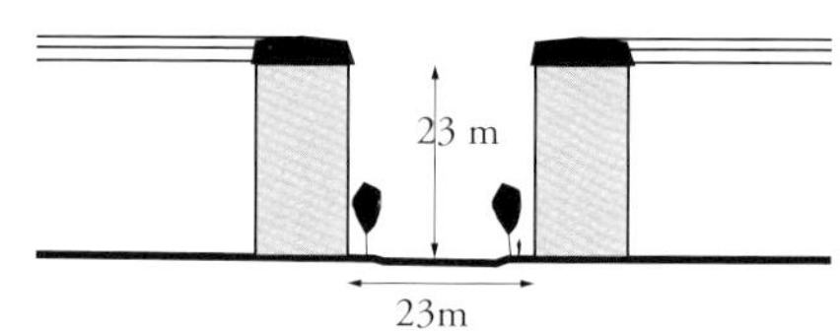

4. District street section

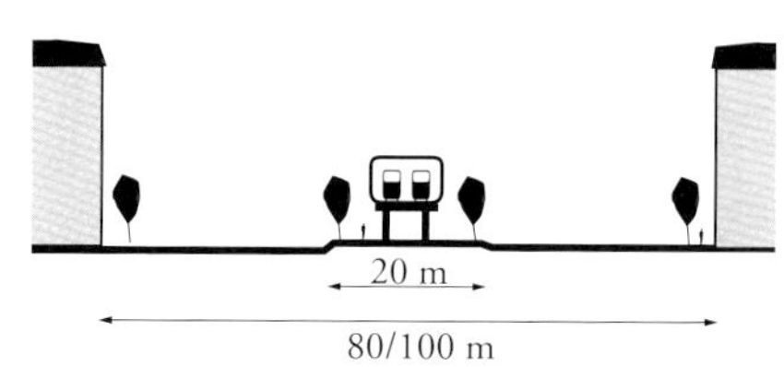

5. Main traffic artery section

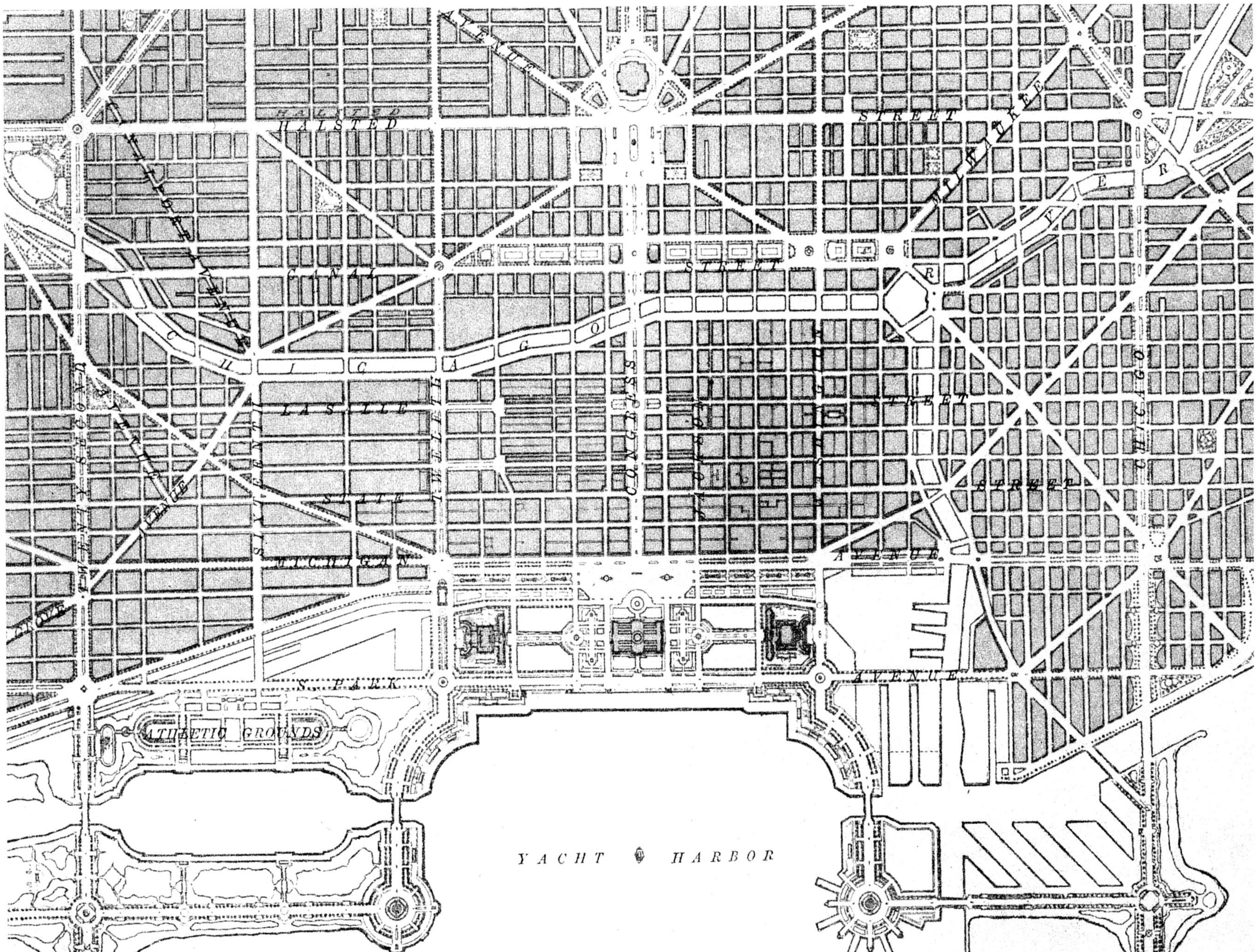

Burnham's proposed plan for central Chicago, 1909, 1:25,000

Vienna and Chicago

Views of Wagner's Groszstadt and Burnham and Bennet's Chicago plans both now seem like quaint but noble snapshots—not of the future they so passionately projected, but rather an innocent last edge of the past. The propensity of planners since 1890 to bind architectural illustrations to their plans finally caught up with them. The previous tradition of drawing urban plans without illustrating architectural development would have served them well, but the dreamy consistency of continuous six-story, load-bearing wall buildings expressed an idealistic order that could not be sustained, as the worlds of architecture, art, and technology had been in revolution for some time.[35]

The elevator, in combination with the steel frame, changed architecture profoundly.[36] William Le Baron Jenney built the first steel frame building in Chicago in 1883–85; Burnham & Root's Reliance Building was built between 1889 and 1895; and Ernest Flagg's Singer Building was built in 1908. All of these preceded Wagner's Vienna plan and Burnham's Chicago plan. Wagner may have been unaware of these developments, but Burnham was central to them. Thus, despite the beginnings of skyscrapers, and despite cubism, Wagner's and Burnham's plans remained rooted in tradition.

1. *Aerial perspective of the District XXII Civic Center in die Großstadt, 1911*

2. *Burnham & Root, Reliance Building, 1889–95*

3. *View of the World's Columbian Exposition, 1893*

1. Aerial perspective of the Chicago Civic Center, painting by Jules Guerin, 1909

2. Aerial perspective of the Chicago Civic Center, painting by Jules Guerin, 1909

3. Burnham, Flatiron Building, 1903

4. Ernest Flagg, Singer Building, 1908

Eugène Hénard

After graduating from the École des Beaux Arts in 1880, Eugène Hénard began his professional career in the office of public works in Paris, where he was primarily concerned with architectural projects.[37] Privately, however, he focused almost entirely on the study of urban problems between 1903 and 1913.[38] For Paris, he proposed a series of radial streets, proposals for traffic intersections, a ring road with housing *a redans*, and a series of new parks. Fascinated with traffic calculations and more highly rationalized services infrastructure, he produced radical ideas for three-dimensional, mechanized street sections. These studies along with his project for the "Cities of the Future" were presented at the London Town Planning Conference in 1910.[39]

Hénard did not share city-planning theory with those of his colleagues interested in the garden city, however. Although a vast, wide ring of parks would eventually be explicit in his proposal for the fortification replacement in Paris, he was committed to the necessity of high-density urban environments. His proposal for the ring road, laced with parks and green space, was sewn together with national routes that radiated out from the center of Paris. His socially inspired idea of improved health and welfare was anchored by the augmentation of small neighborhood parks and nine larger parks. The parks were planned to be spread out into the neighborhoods that especially needed them, and the surrounding housing designed for a range of income groups along boulevards *a redans*.[40]

The park system movement that Hénard proposed was an attempt to bridge the shift in urban scale from walking to riding, while maintaining the effect of being within a park. Hénard was interested in the accommodation of the automobile, which drove him to substitute the experience of the spectator moving through the city at a quick pace for walking, which was clear in his design for the boulevard *a redans*.

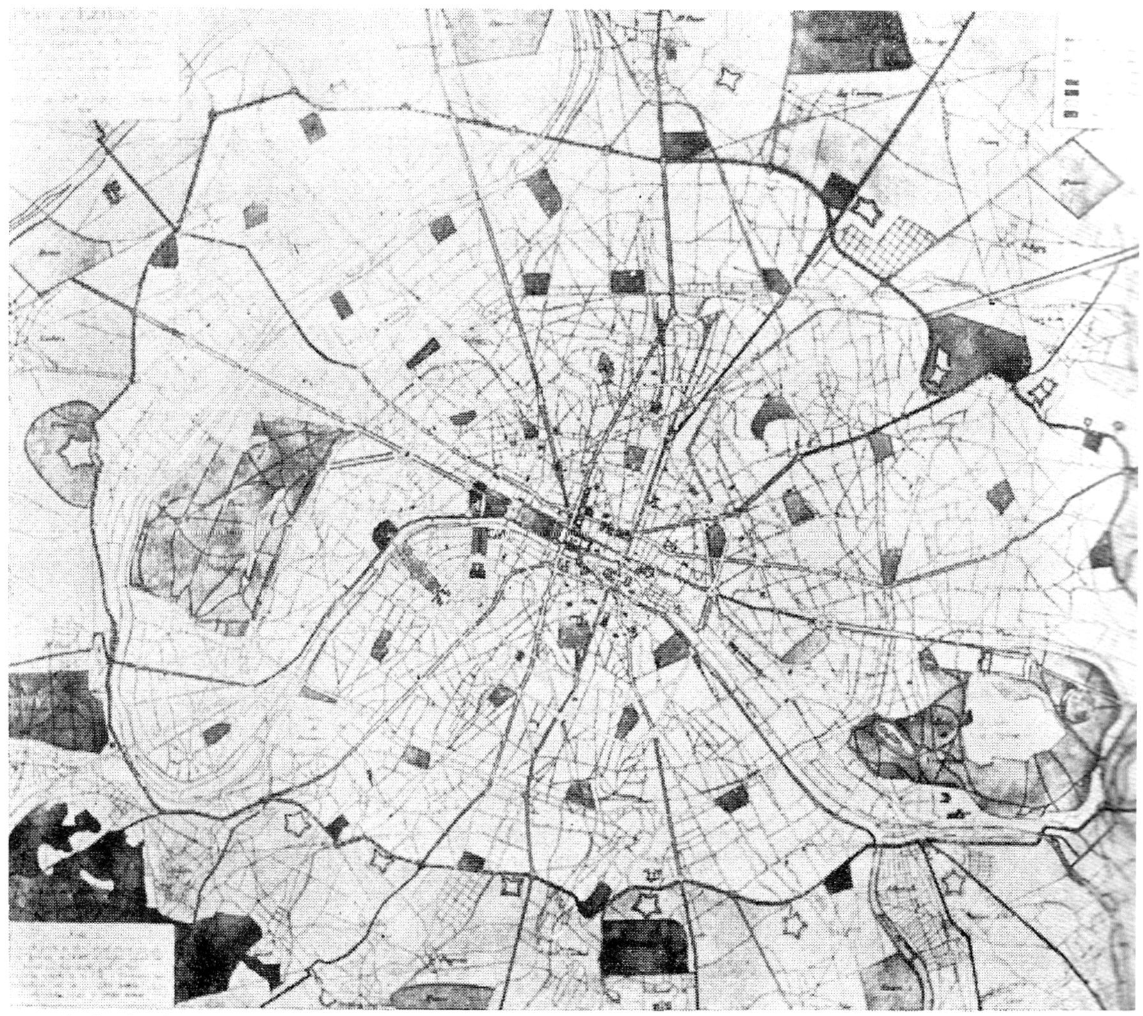

Hénard, plan for the extension and transformation of Paris with a boulevard a redans, *and nine new peripheral parks*

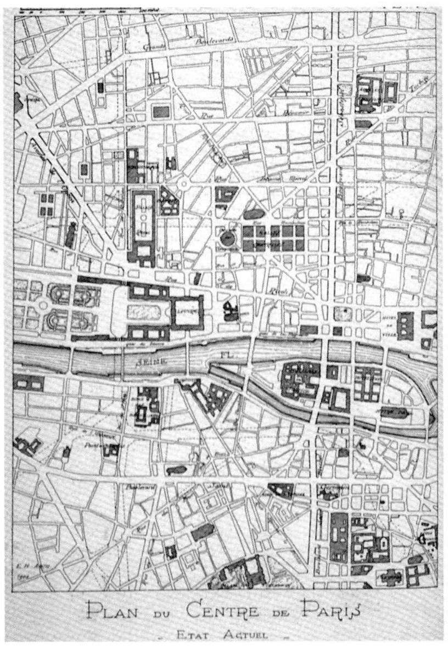

1. Existing plan of central Paris

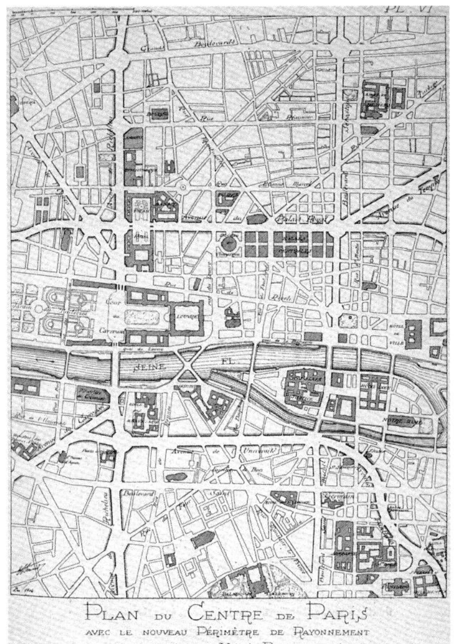

2. Hénard, proposed plan of central Paris

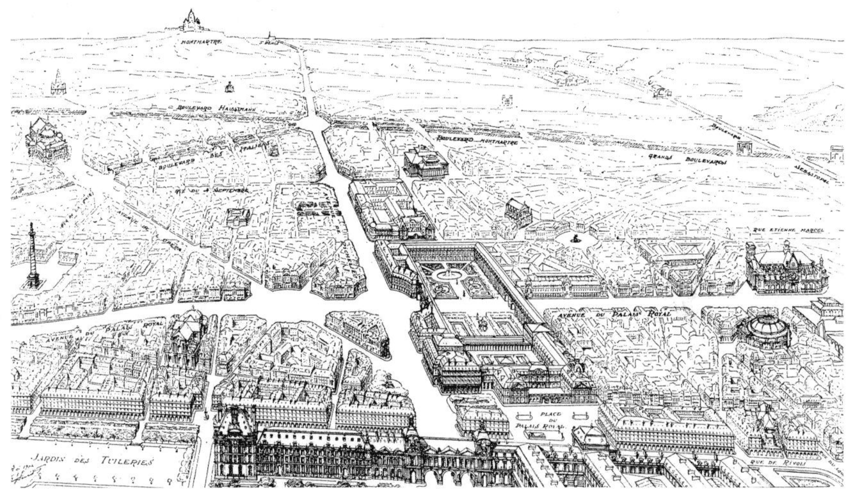

3. Hénard, aerial perspective of proposal for central Paris

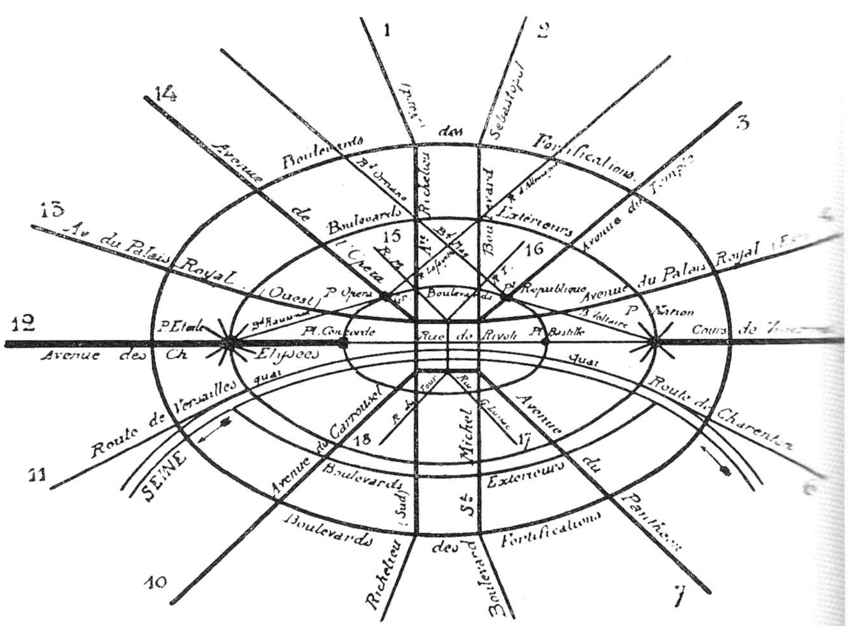

4. Hénard, proposed schematic plan of Paris streets with new radiating diagonals, 1904

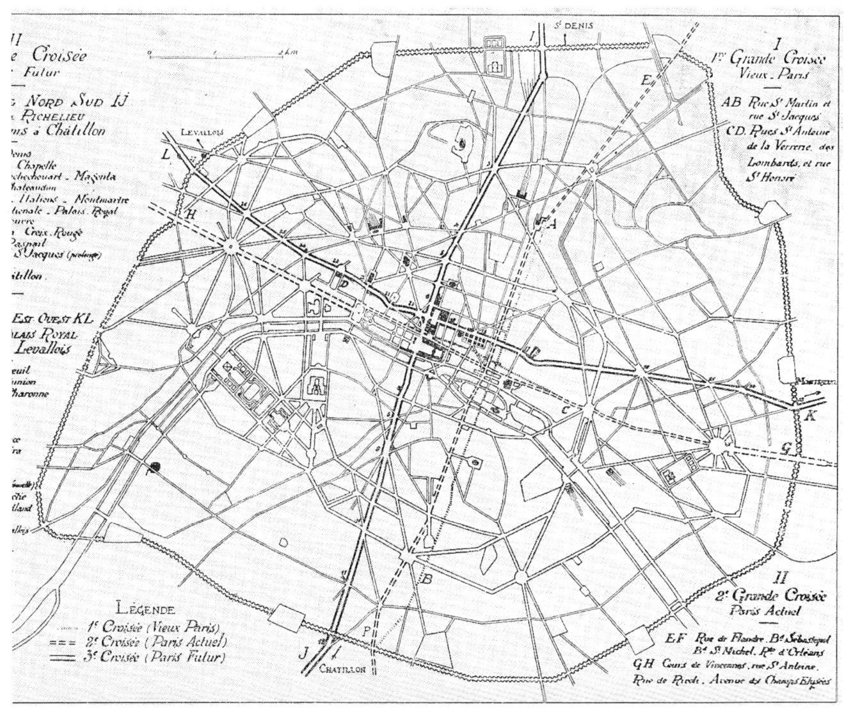

5. Hénard, proposed new grand croisée for Paris (ancient and actual croisée indicated by broken lines; proposed route by solid line), 1904

Traffic Intersections

Hénard published a journal illustrating his studies of traffic and the city.[41] The journal issues are filled with analytical diagrams studying the turning radii of carriages, their functions at intersections, and the types of intersections, as well as algebraic equations for determining the diameters of traffic circles. Typical intersections are illustrated in plan, section, and bird's-eye perspectives showing the architectural character of the buildings. He often proposed grade separation for carriages, and in the large traffic circles, an underpass for pedestrians.

1. Hénard, carriage traffic in Paris

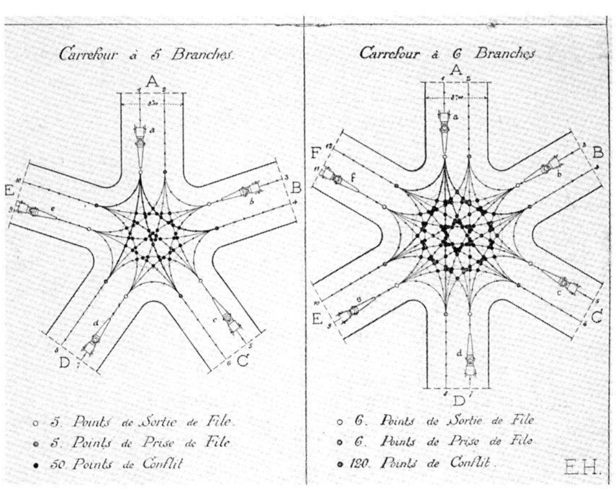

2. Hénard, traffic intersections, 1906

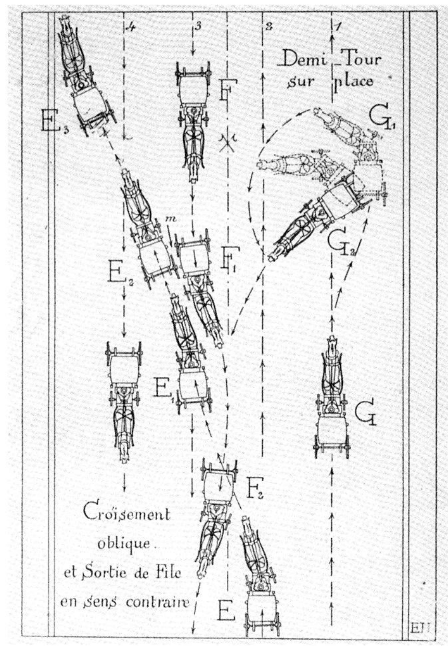

3. Hénard, traffic analysis, 1906

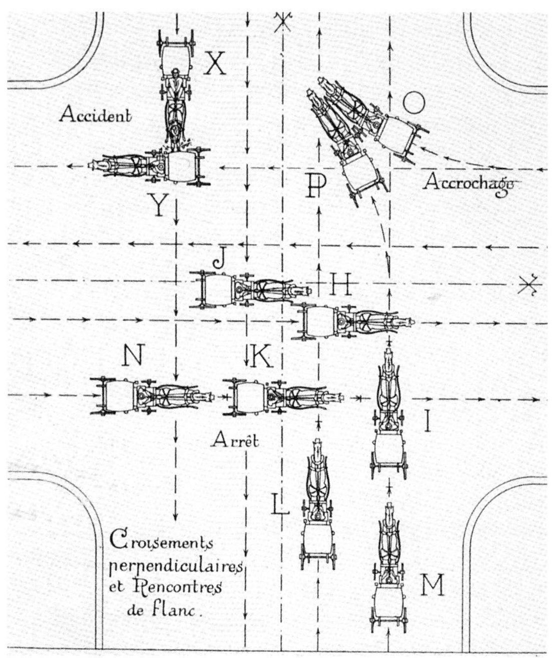

5. Hénard, traffic analysis, 1906

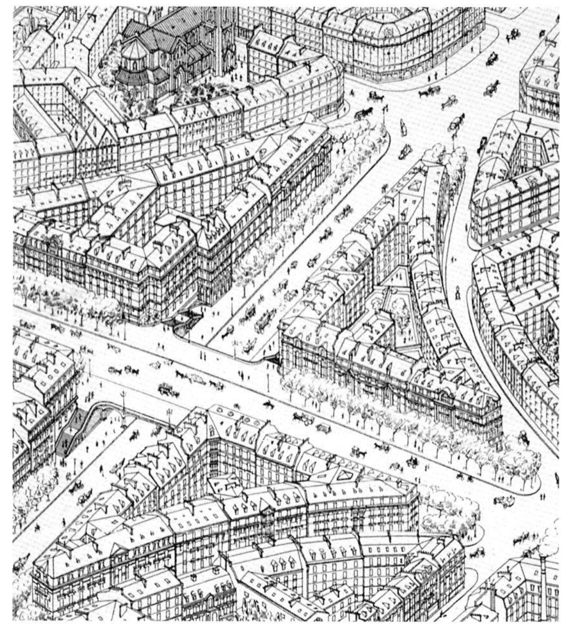

4. Hénard, overpass intersection, 1906

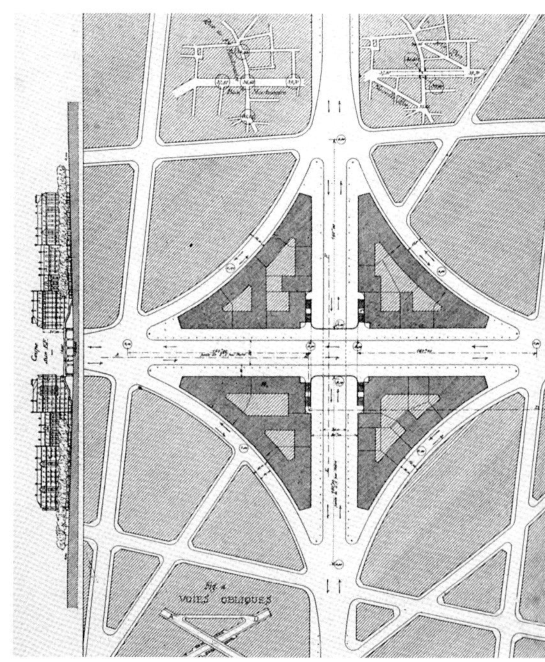

6. Hénard, overpass intersection plan, 1906

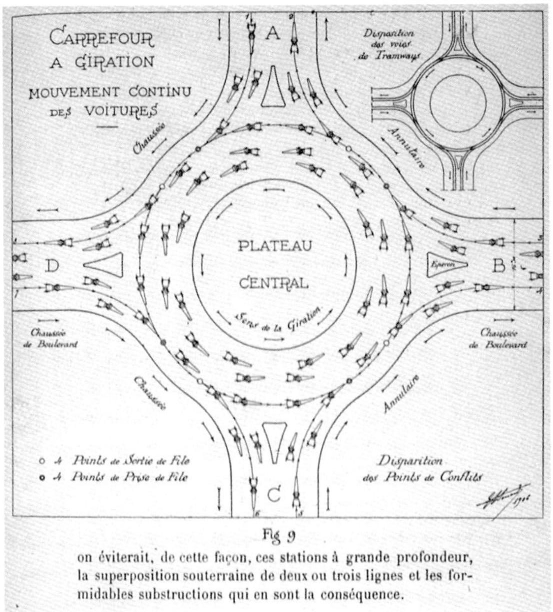

on éviterait, de cette façon, ces stations à grande profondeur, la superposition souterraine de deux ou trois lignes et les formidables substructions qui en sont la conséquence.

1. *Hénard, roundabout analysis plan, 1906*

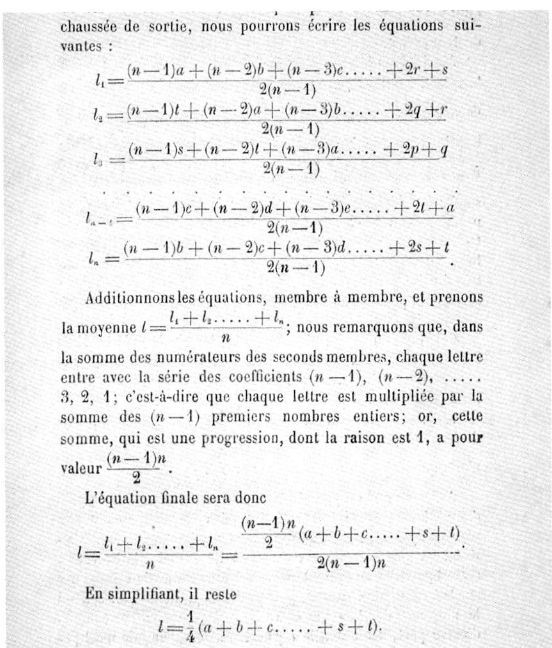

chaussée de sortie, nous pourrons écrire les équations suivantes :

$$l_1 = \frac{(n-1)a + (n-2)b + (n-3)c \dots\dots + 2r + s}{2(n-1)}$$

$$l_2 = \frac{(n-1)t + (n-2)a + (n-3)b \dots\dots + 2q + r}{2(n-1)}$$

$$l_3 = \frac{(n-1)s + (n-2)t + (n-3)a \dots\dots + 2p + q}{2(n-1)}$$

$$\dots\dots$$

$$l_{n-1} = \frac{(n-1)c + (n-2)d + (n-3)e \dots\dots + 2t + a}{2(n-1)}$$

$$l_n = \frac{(n-1)b + (n-2)c + (n-3)d \dots\dots + 2s + t}{2(n-1)}.$$

Additionnons les équations, membre à membre, et prenons la moyenne $l = \frac{l_1 + l_2 \dots\dots + l_n}{n}$; nous remarquons que, dans la somme des numérateurs des seconds membres, chaque lettre entre avec la série des coefficients $(n-1)$, $(n-2)$, ... 3, 2, 1; c'est-à-dire que chaque lettre est multipliée par la somme des $(n-1)$ premiers nombres entiers; or, cette somme, qui est une progression, dont la raison est 1, a pour valeur $\frac{(n-1)n}{2}$.

L'équation finale sera donc

$$l = \frac{l_1 + l_2 \dots\dots + l_n}{n} = \frac{\frac{(n-1)n}{2}(a + b + c \dots\dots + s + t)}{2(n-1)n}.$$

En simplifiant, il reste

$$l = \frac{1}{4}(a + b + c \dots\dots + s + t).$$

2. *Hénard, traffic calculations, 1906*

3. *Hénard, first schematic "roundabout," 1906*

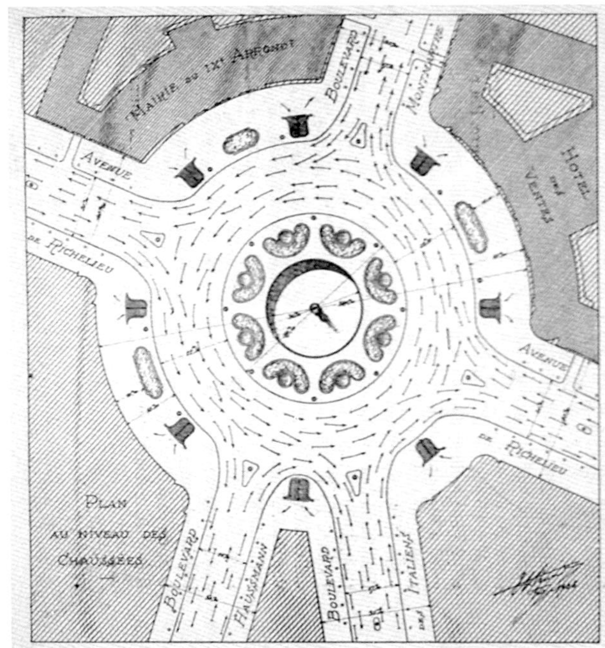

4. *Hénard, roundabout plan, 1906*

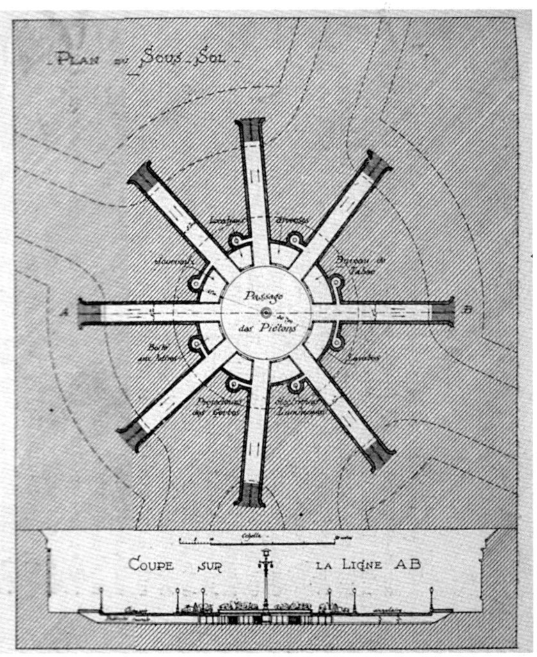

5. *Hénard, roundabout, lower plan, 1906*

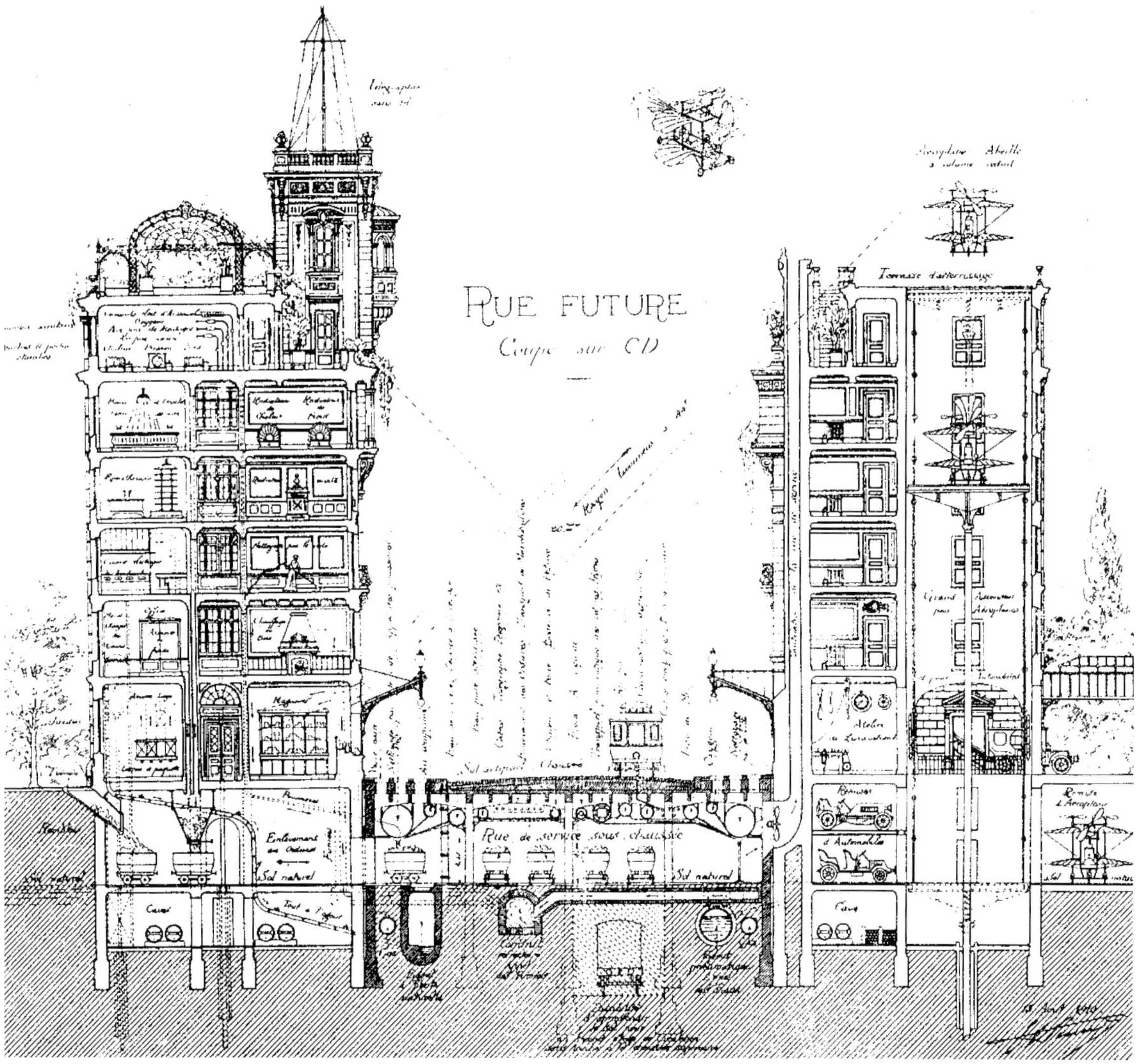

1. Hénard, street of the future section, 1910

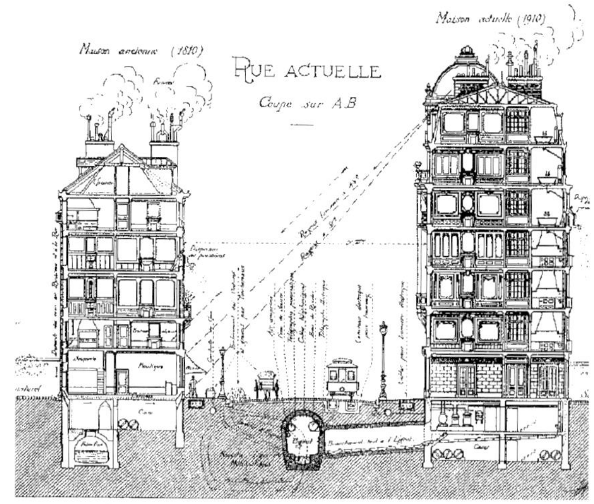

2. Hénard, contemporary street section, 1910

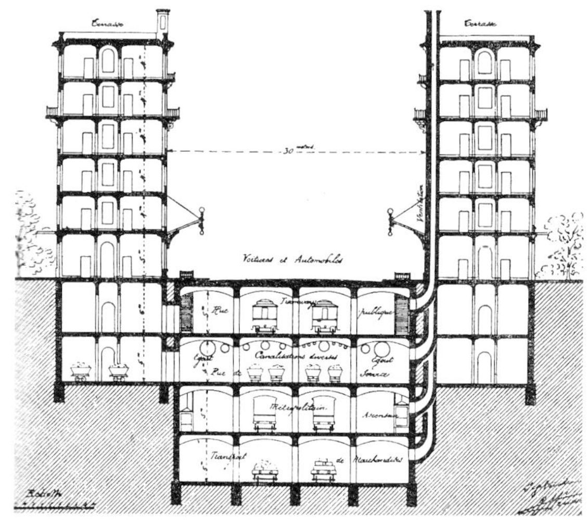

3. Hénard, multilevel street section, 1910

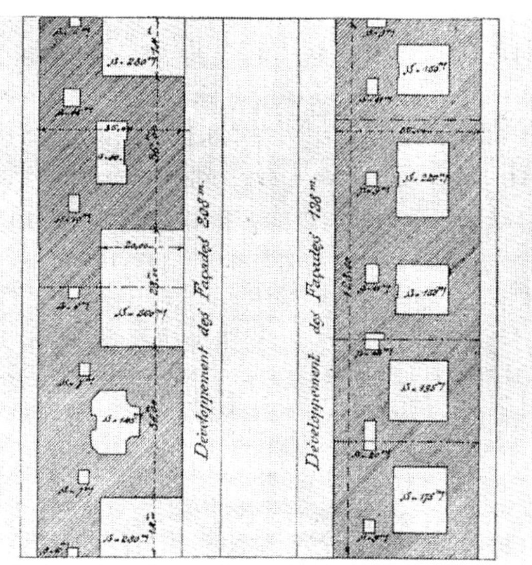

4. Boulevard a redans and a regular boulevard, 1903

Mechanized Streets

Hénard criticized the houses of his time as being improved over the historic houses of Paris, but still problematic because of buried services and polluting chimneys. Instead, he proposed, as the "Rue Future," a raised roadway built like a platform or a bridge, that would carry all of the services in an accessible and expandable way—suspended beneath the roadway. His proposed services included "vacuum cleaning, supply of compressed air, river water, sterilized pure water, petrol and liquid air, conveyance of letters, supply of pure air, together with ... telegraph, telephone, light, power, high-frequency currents, etc."[42] Below this on the lower roadway were two rail lines for long-distance service, and others for local service.

Above grade, a series of courtyard buildings were connected to form re-entrant entry courts off the street *a redans*. The apartment buildings were also to have flat roofs so there could be gardens planted and eventually a landing pad for *aero-machines*.

Another section proposal illustrated four service levels below grade allowing for expansion of other elements conducive to the health and concerns of the inhabitants. Hénard claimed that after constructing the first level, any number of them could be added—simply by building further into the ground. In this scheme he called for the height of the buildings to be equal to the width of the street.

Boulevards and Parks

Around 1910, Hénard called for a critical increase in periphery parks and additional housing. His plan was to gradually build 75,000 apartments, but was stalled until the First World War. He was backed by the Musée Social, a group that was a proponent of the idea

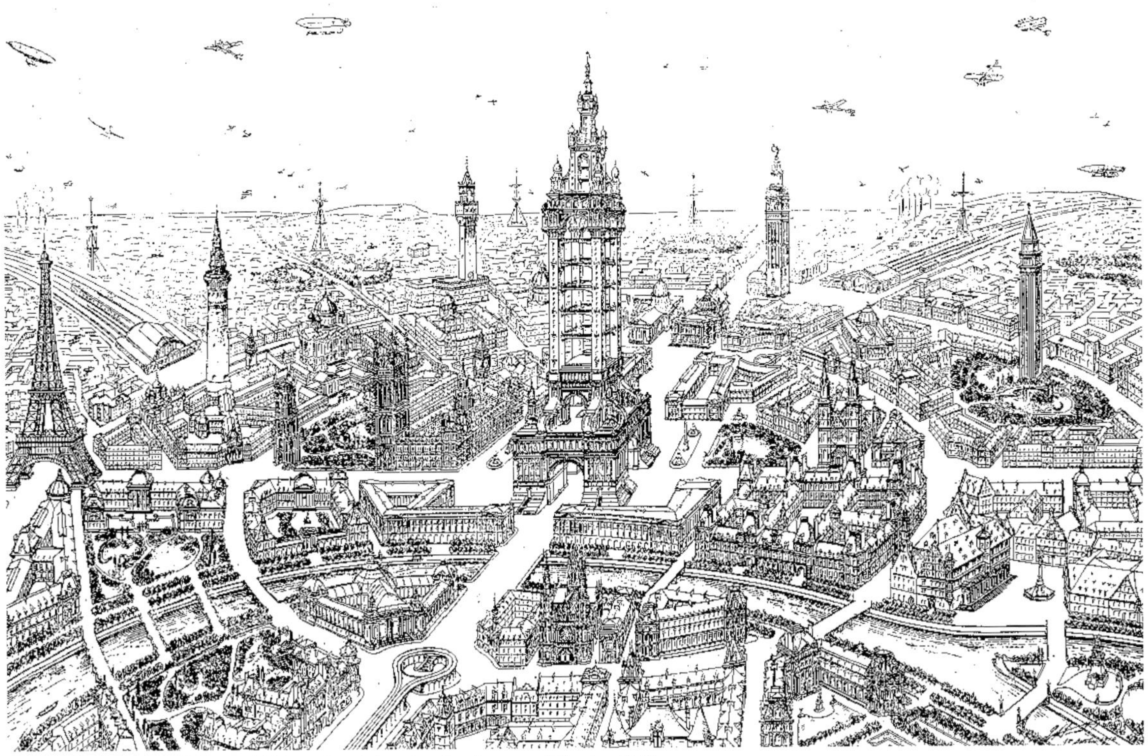

Hénard, aerial rendering of Hénard's vision for the future of Paris, 1910

that Paris and its surrounding region should have a master plan. In 1909, with the help of Jules Siegfried, Hénard advocated for fortification replacement plans with parks and road networks. By 1911, Siegfried authorized a more comprehensive study, right at the time Hénard's health was starting to deteriorate. To assist him, young Frenchmen with experience in urban planning were appointed to help carry out his plans, most notably Albert Agache and Henri Prost. Their study anticipated a massive expansion of Paris and involved neighborhood parks, a boulevard *a redans* along the fortifications, new transversals, and large areas of reserve for future parks throughout the surrounding region. The first usable master plan devised in Paris after World War I was done in 1934 by Henri Prost, one of Hénard's assistants.[43]

The Cities of the Future

In 1904, Hénard conducted an effort to prevent the Counseil Municipal from demolishing the Palais de Machines. Hénard proposed to convert the Champ de Mars into the first in-city airfield; the Palais de Machines as its repair hangar, the Eiffel tower as its signal tower. Additionally, he wanted to include cafes, a concert amphitheater, and sports parks facilities. His efforts failed, and the Galerie de Machines was dismantled. Most important, however, during his investigation, he developed a fascination with airflight. He described his perspective view as follows:

> From out the centre of the city's heart there will arise the colossal orientation tower, soaring to a height of five hundred metres, and crowned by a powerful beacon light. At the base of the tower the historical portion of the city will nestle, with its monuments of bygone days, its old houses, and all its artistic and traditional treasures.
>
> ... the far-reaching revolution brought about in our ideas by aviation opens up such wonderful possibilities that we may indulge the hope that all these things will come to pass. The conquest of the air will herald the reign of universal peace and wealth. The Cities of To-morrow will be more readily susceptible to transformation and adornment than the Cities of Yesterday: they will be built with superb towers which will attract these giant birds from every point of the horizon ... competing with the very clouds themselves.[44]

The remarkable thing about Hénard's vision of the urban future is that it did not propose erasing the traditional city. Rather, it combined the traditional city, modernized circulation and service systems, and modern towers. This was the same urban system prevalent in the United States throughout the 1930s, and until after the Second World War.

Hénard's vision also did not propose mono-functional zoning, but the traditional Parisian neighborhood mix of residential apartment buildings, commercial services, cafes, public facilities, and an urban landscape of boulevards and parks.

The Garden City

Among the many reactions to nineteenth-century urban problems, none has been as far reaching as the concept of dispersal into satellite cities promoted by the Garden City movement, founded in 1898 by Ebenezer Howard. His *To-morrow: A Peaceful Path to Real Reform* was published in 1898 and reissued in 1902 as *Garden Cities of To-morrow*. Howard's concept, with the help of Jules Siegfried, was for independent subcities of 32,000 people separated in open country from a central city of 50,000, but connected by road and rail.[45]

The concept of the garden city devolved rater quickly into the garden suburb, however. Letchworth was built in 1904 by Raymond Unwin and Barry Parker, followed by Unwin's Hampstead in 1909, and Welwyn in 1919. These were the predecessors to low-density suburban developments all over the world.

Despite Howard's admonition that his idea was a diagram, not a plan, its radial, formal characteristics served as the organizing principles for both Lutyen's plan for New Delhi in 1911 and Walter Burley Griffin's plan for Canberra in 1912—both suburban rather than urban.

The fantasy of "the city in the garden" would become a founding principle of the city of modern architecture.

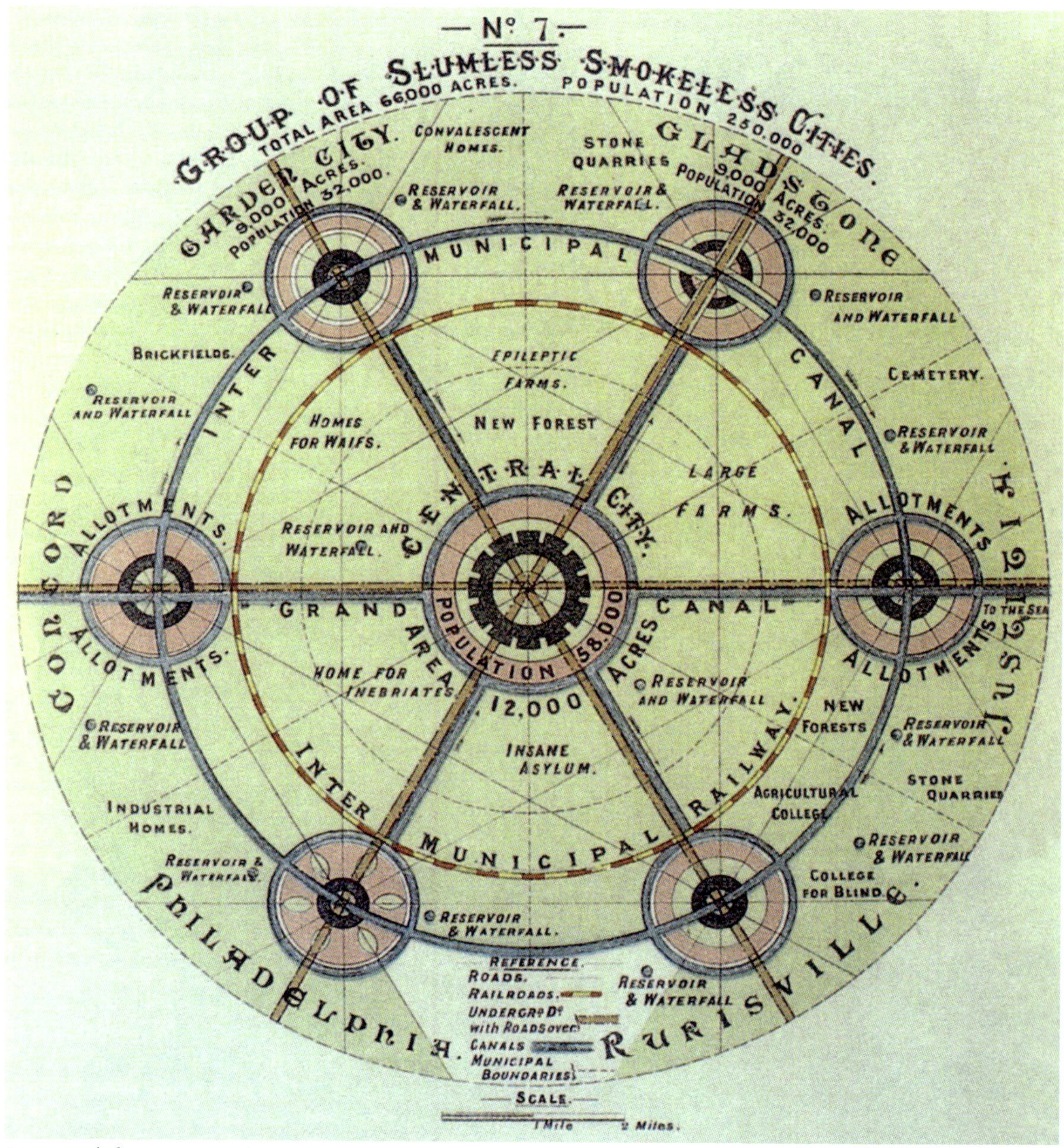

Diagram of Ebenezer Howard's Garden City concept, 1898

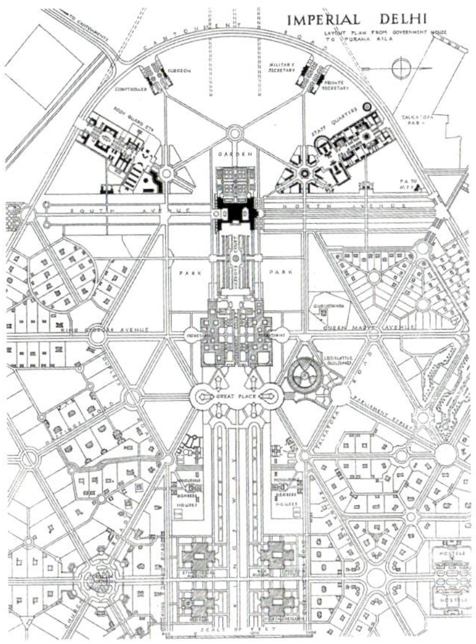

1. Detail plan of Imperial Delhi, 1911

2. Plan of New Delhi, 1911

4. Aerial view of New Delhi

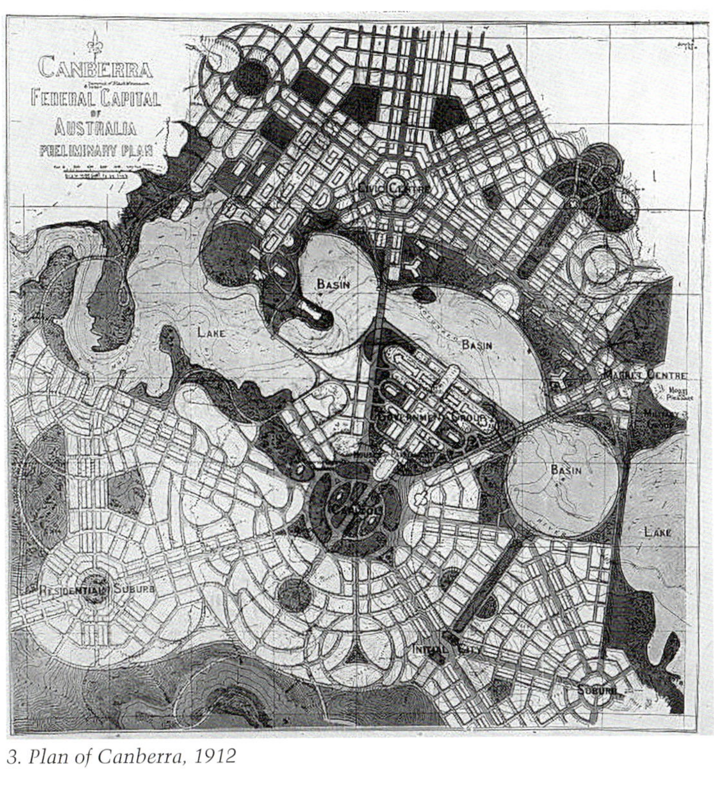

3. Plan of Canberra, 1912

5. Aerial view of Canberra

Tony Garnier's Cité Industrielle

Tony Garnier's reputation is due almost entirely to his design for a theoretical industrial city, *Une Cité Industrielle*, designed for a hypothetical site in southeast France.[46] Garnier's work was admired by Le Corbusier and others for its articulation of urban functions into monofunctional zones dedicated to housing, industry, recreation, and health, and separated by green belts.[47] The Cité Industrielle was thereby a fundamental contribution to the modernist city. Later in the twentieth century, however, the principle of monofunctional zoning would be among the most discredited aspects of modernist town planning.

Background and Theory

Garnier first considered designing an imaginary industrial city in 1898 while studying at the École des Beaux Arts in Paris.[48] In 1899, he won the Prix de Rome, and it was in Rome where he started to develop his vision for the Cité Industrielle. The École called for a more conventional study, however, so when Garnier sent his proposal for the Cité Industrielle in 1901, the academy refused to exhibit it. Finally, after three years, he exhibited it as a supplementary work to his Tusculum reconstruction study in 1904, and he published a two-volume book, *Une Cité Industrielle*, in 1917.

The project was designed for a plateau between high land and a river and comprised four main functions: work, housing, health, and leisure. There were two main development areas, however: the industrial area to the east, and the town above and to the west.

The town contained housing, schools, and a town center with administrative, cultural, and sports facilities. It stretched nearly four miles from one end to the other, consuming an area larger than Manhattan's Central Park.

The factory zone lay approximately one and a half miles away, further down the slope and surrounded by railroad tracks. Arterial roads connected these areas as well as other components, but some workers would have had a commute of close to eight miles.[49]

Three-dimensional illustrations of planning proposals were characteristic of other proto-modernist planners, but Garnier's plan was unequaled in the extent, thoroughness, and beauty of his illustrations.[50]

1. Cité Industrielle perspective view looking east

1. *Ancient City*
2. *Central station*
3. *Residential neighborhoods*
4. *Downtown*
5. *Primary school*
6. *Professional schools*
7. *Health-care institutions*
8. *Station city*
9. *Industrial complex*
10. *Wastewater plant*
11. *Cemetery*
12. *Old Castle & public park*
13. *Slaughterhouses*

2. Cité Industrielle plan diagram

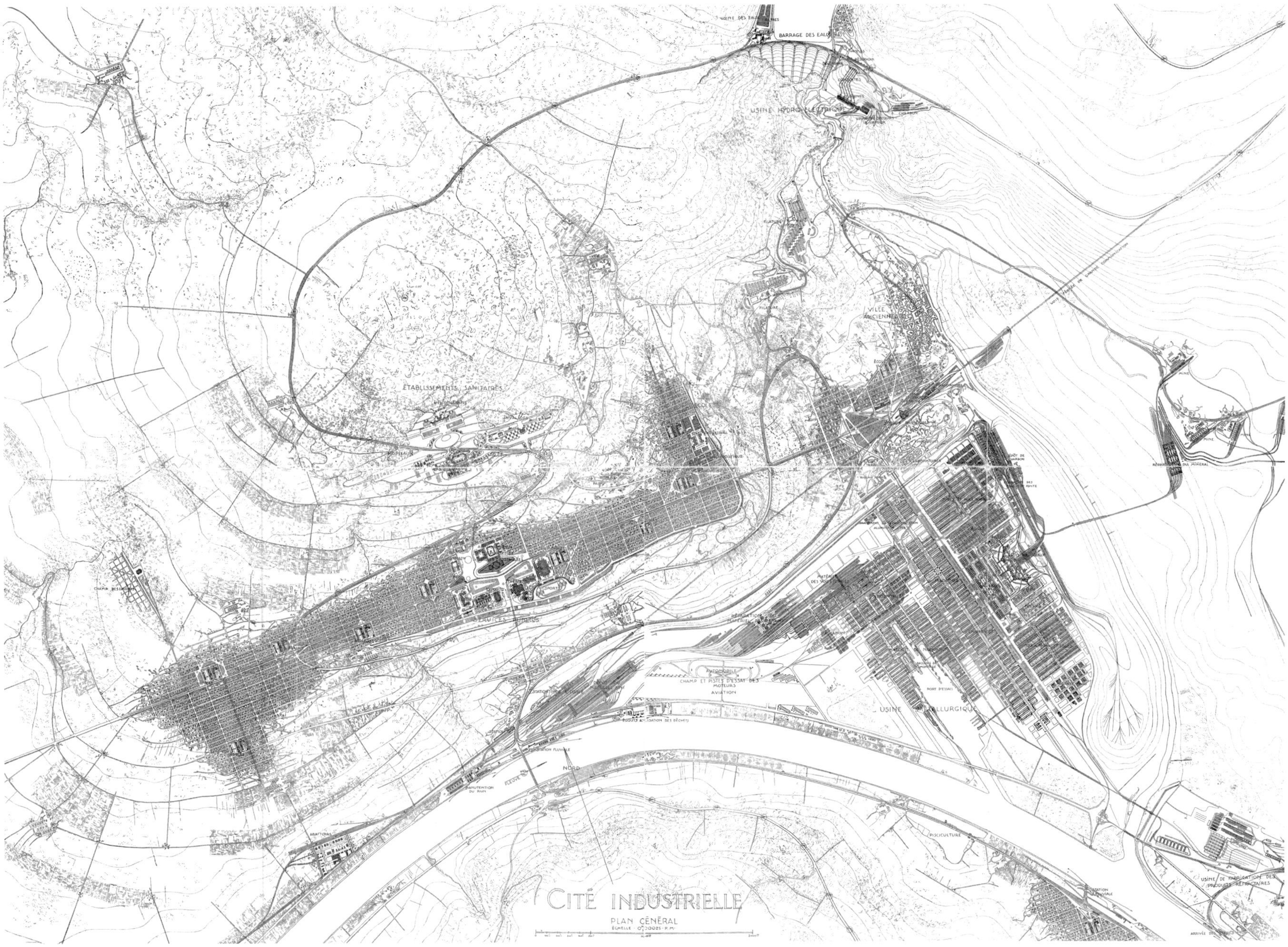

Cité Industrielle plan, 1:50,000

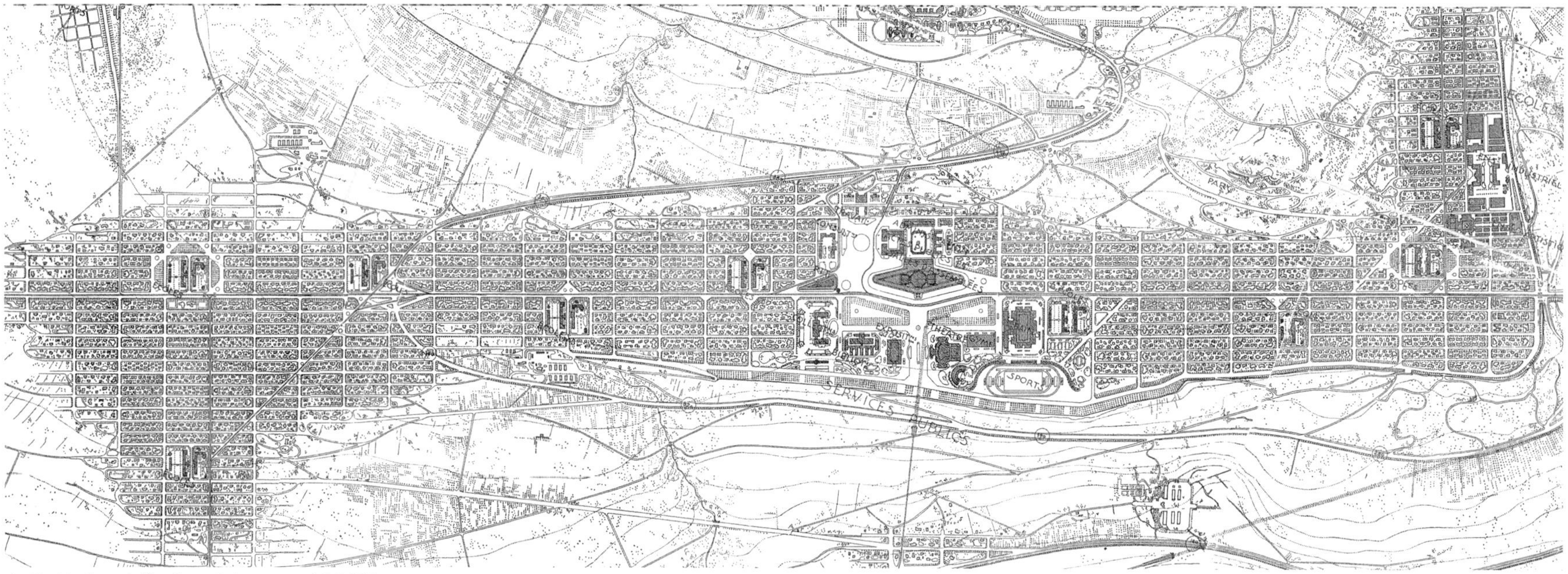

1. Cité Industrielle plan of the town, 1:25,000

2. Plan of Central Park, 1:25,000

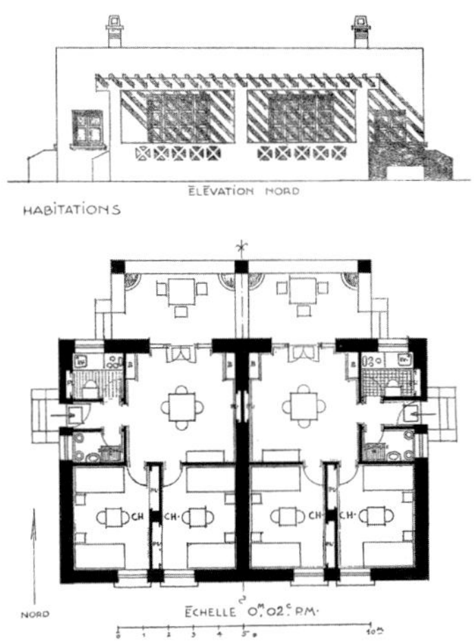

1. *Plan of a small house, 1:400*

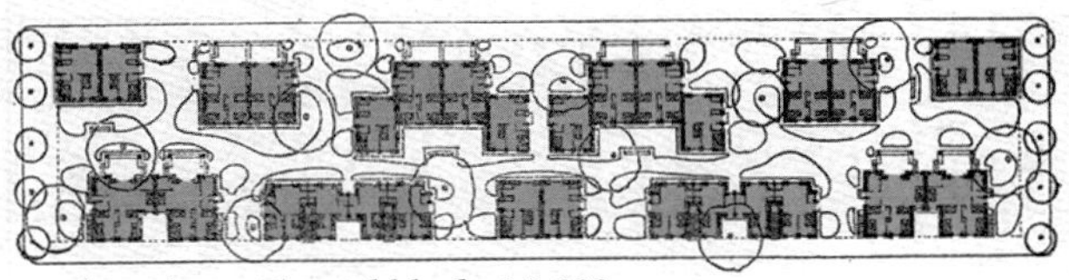

2. *Plan of a residential block, 1:2,000*

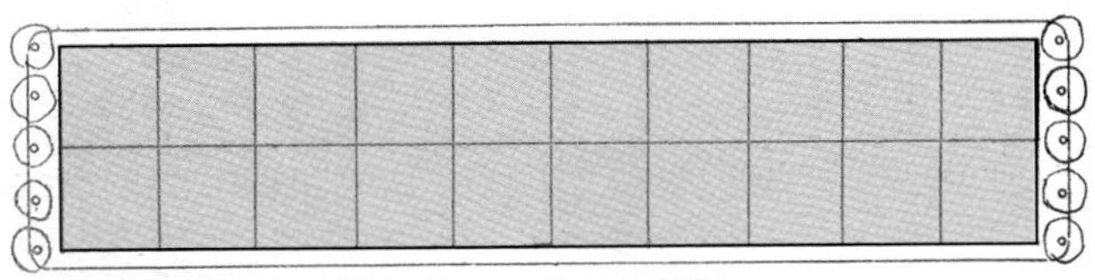

3. *Plan of residential block parcels, 1:2,000*

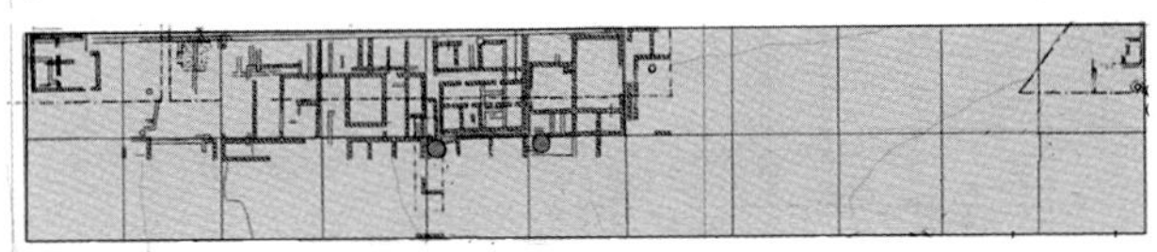

4. *Selinunte, plan of a residential block, 1:2,000*

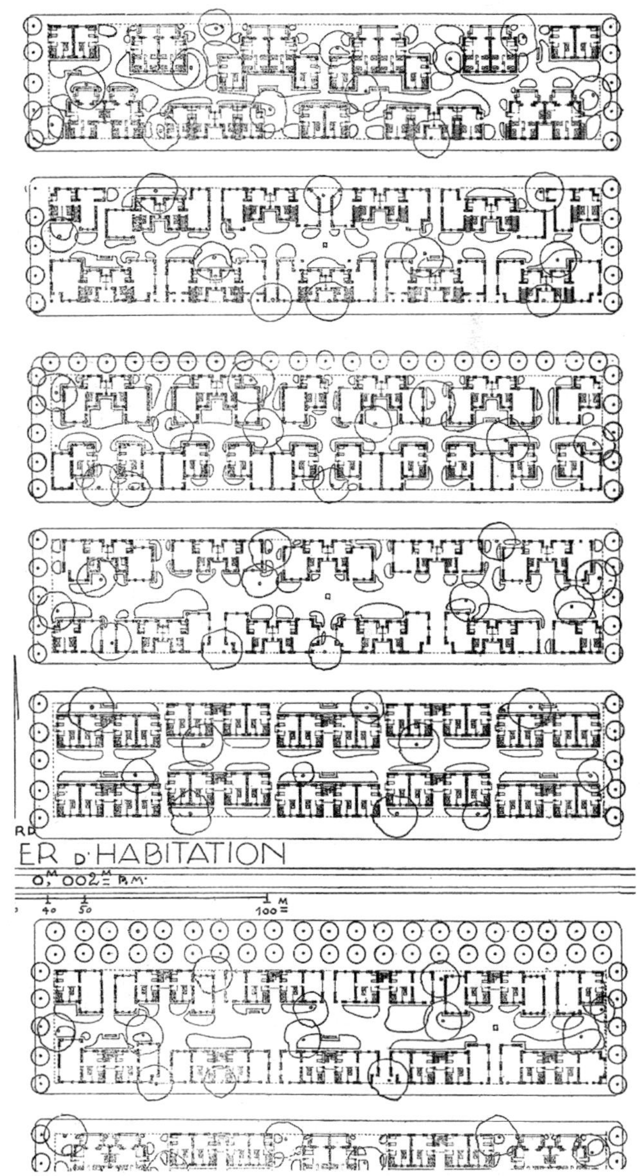

7. *Plan of residential fabric, 1:2,000*

Houses, Blocks, and Fabric

Garnier illustrated a great variety of mostly very tiny, detached houses arranged in a variety of patterns on long, narrow blocks of 30 x 150 m (98' x 192').[51] These blocks were divided into 15 x 15 meter parcels, and were almost identical in size and proportion to classic Greek blocks of courtyard houses such as those of Paestum. Walls, fences, and enclosures around the parcels were not permitted in Garnier's plan, however, so that circulation could occur freely within the picturesque landscape development. This fabric was obviously related to Garden City ideas, and was not urban at all, but suburban. Garnier's plan was thus not an industrial city, but an industrial suburb—*Une Banlieue Industrielle.*

5. *Perspective view of residential area*

6. *Perspective view of residential area*

1. Perspective of the train station

2. Perspective of apartment buildings

3. Perspective of marine area

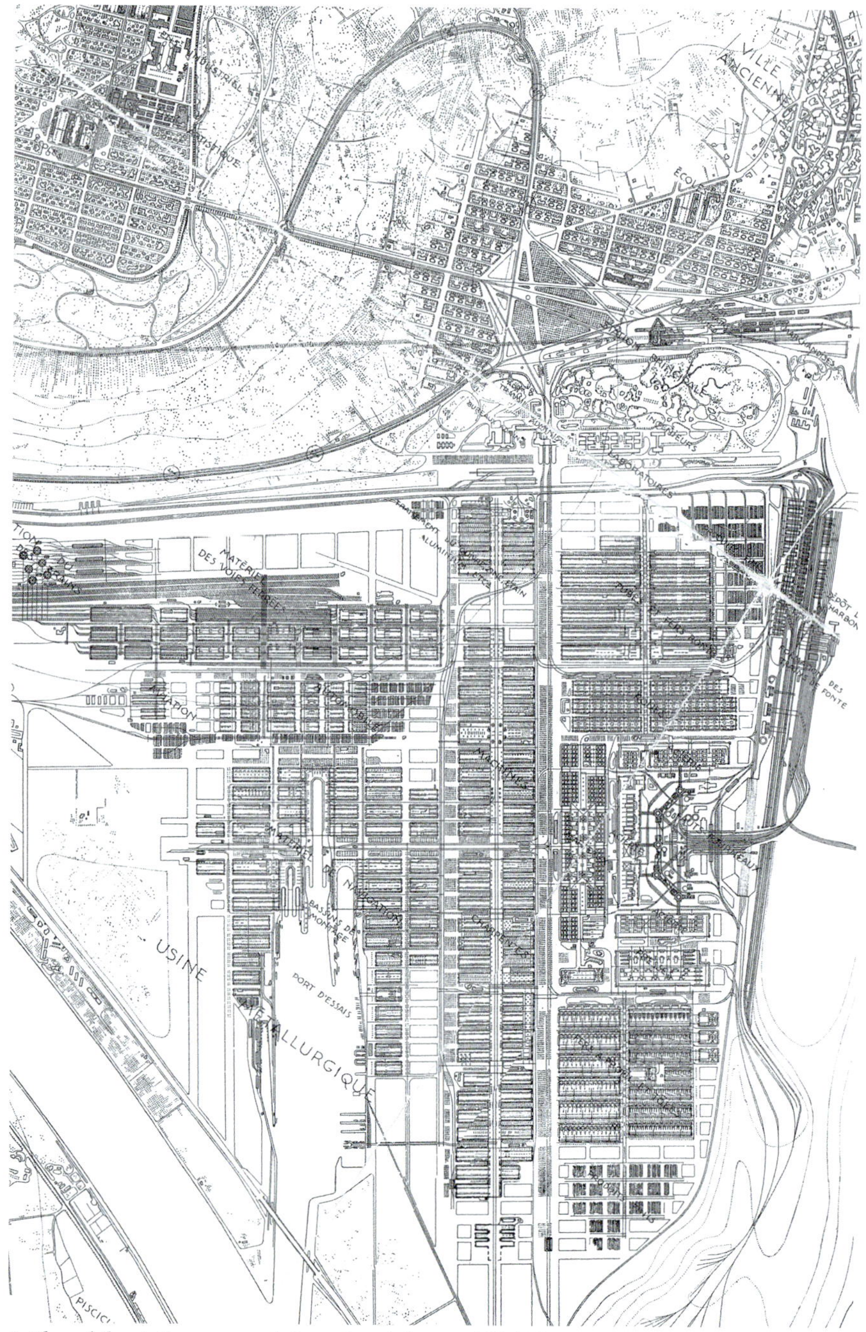

4. Plan of the station area and the industrial zone, 1:25,000

The Station

The rail station is located between the hypothetical existing town and the industrial zone, and all the multistory apartment buildings were concentrated in a grid of long blocks surrounding the station. All connections from the main town pass through this area to connect to the industrial zone.

The Industrial Zone

The industrial zone is also very large—almost two miles square—necessitating extensive vehicular circulation within, as well as vehicular circulation to the river and town through the encircling railway system.

The Town Center

All of the town's civic buildings, except schools, are concentrated in the Town Center, and all are freestanding buildings. The Administrative buildings define a plaza of 110 x 120 m (360' x 394'), but the surrounding spaces are vast—comparable in scale to those of the Forum at Chandigarh.[52]

With the Cité Industrielle, Garnier created a garden suburb of objects, articulated by function, and necessitating vehicular circulation. This was the last link in the urban transformation: from the *Garden in the City* of Paris to the *City in the Garden* of Le Corbusier.

1. *Conference center*
2. *Administration buildings and plaza*
3. *Hotels, restaurants, & workers' organizations*
4. *Sanitary services*
5. *Post office*
6. *Historic archives*
7. *Library*
8. *Exhibitions*
9. *Performing arts*
10. *Outdoor theater*
11. *Gymnasium*
12. *Swimming*
13. *Sports fields*
14. *Tennis*
15. *Primary school*

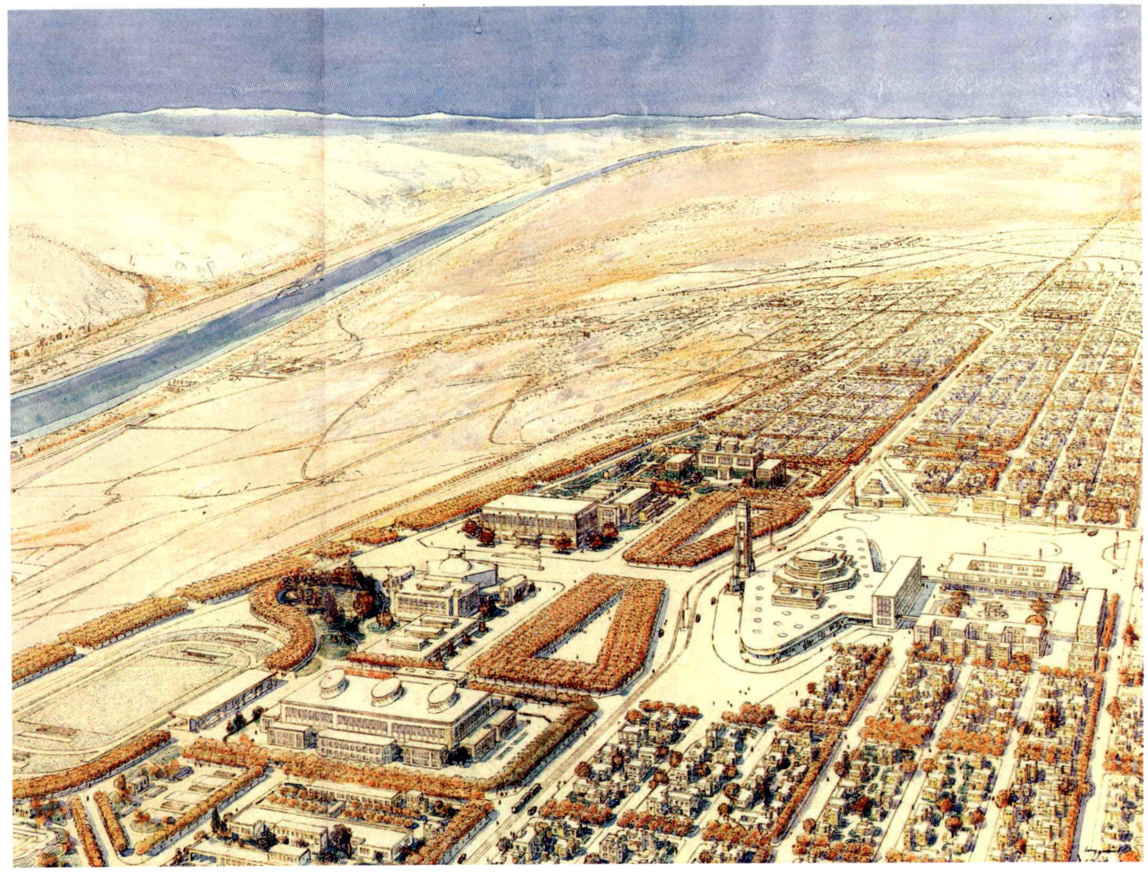

3. Aerial perspective of the town and town center looking west

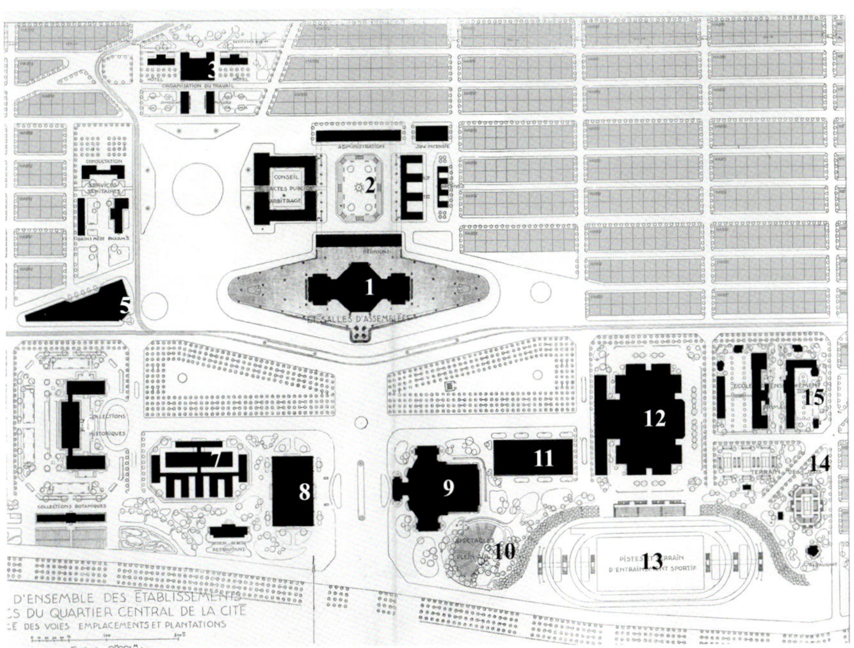

1. Plan of the city center, 1:10,000

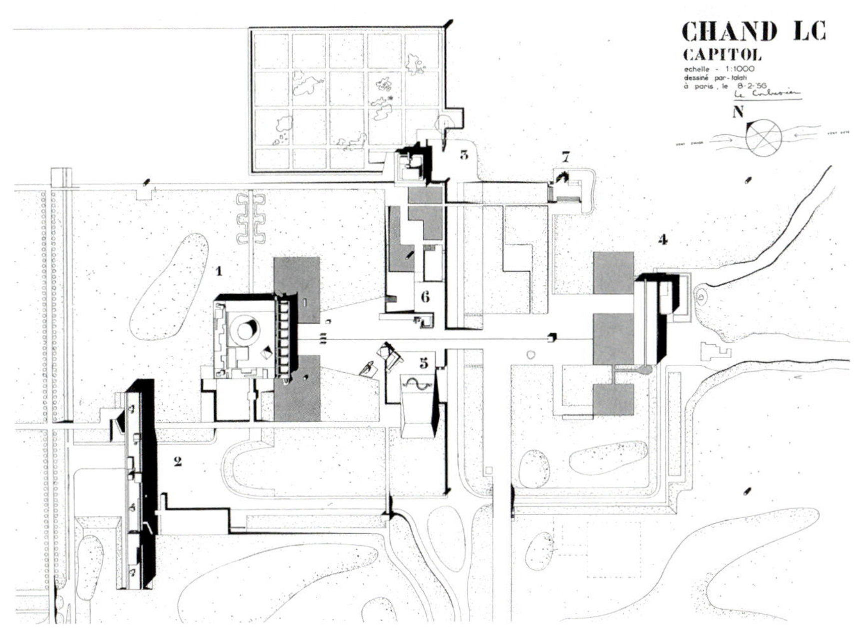

2. Le Corbusier, plan of the Forum at Chandigarh, 1:10,000

Ville Radieuse, Le Corbusier

The Modernist City: 1922–1975

In contrast to the traditional form of cities—that of streets, blocks, and squares—the modernist city of Le Corbusier and his CIAM colleagues was a complete inversion. The street, the square, and the block of varied buildings all disappeared, and consequently, the public realm of legible civic space disappeared.

The modernist city comprised monofunctional zoning, a limited range of free-standing building types, centralized land management, articulate vehicular circulation networks, and continuous Romantic landscape. Indeed, it was the *city in the garden.*

This planning system did not relate well, if at all, to the existing form of cities, and was usually promoted as a necessary replacement.

Le Corbusier and CIAM were the dominant forces in town planning from ca. 1922 through the postwar period of reconstruction, when Team X emerged. Although Team X lasted until 1982, adverse reaction to modernist planning began soon after the end of World War II.

Modernism

The early twentieth century witnessed a revolution in art and culture not seen since the early Renaissance almost 500 years before. New ideas about space[1] and representation infused the arts and again brought architecture and painting into an intimate and fruitful relationship.

Ideas in painting spread rapidly in the years preceding World War I and the Russian Revolution. Invented in Paris, cubism led the way, followed by constructivism in Russia. Both would later have a major influence on architecture and arguably define two strains of modern architecture: one based on discontinuity and frontal, layered space; the other based on continuity and deep diagonal space.

Cubism

Douglas Cooper describes the cubist revolution:

> Between 1425 and 1450 artists throughout Europe ... abandoned the medieval way of representing reality, by means of experiential conceptions, and began to rely instead on visual perception, one-point perspective and natural light. ... And for some four hundred and fifty years European artists followed this same principle until, coming to the end of its pictorial possibilities, Cubism was invented to replace it.[2]

Invented in Paris by Picasso and Braque between 1906 and 1908, cubism shed perspective representation of spatial depth for shallow, layered spatial composition—but composition that was still frontal—and figurative realism for abstraction and fragmentation. Thus, there was both a revolution and a parallel between cubism and art since the Renaissance. Indeed, there was a completely new kind of pictorial space, but one that was related to the past by frontality.[3]

Picasso's *Les Demoiselles d'Avignon* traditionally marks the beginning of cubism in 1906. Picasso never completely abandoned the figure, but in the ensuing years he explored new relationships between figure and field through fragmentation and planarity, as in his *Man with a Guitar*, of 1911–13. Rather quickly, cubism spawned other important movements, including constructivism. It would also provide the basis for purism in the 1920s.

1. Picasso, Les Demoiselles d'Avignon, *1906–7*

2. Kasimir Malevich, Suprematist Painting, *1915*

Constructivism

Kasimir Malevich invented suprematism in 1913 as abstract, non-objective painting. Unlike cubism, where forms and figures are fragmented and melded together with the field of the canvas, suprematism produced pure geometric forms of color that appear to float in indeterminate space—what has often been described by the incomprehensible and unfortunate term "negative space." Suprematism led directly to Russian constructivism, El Lissitzky, and ultimately, to Mondrian, Van Doesburg, and De Stile. These movements favored pure abstraction, and diagonality over frontality. Thus, a certain object-fixation was built into the compositional system, as was continuous, deep space in lieu of shallow, frontal space. Like centralized churches of the renaissance, the isolation of these objects rendered traditional urbanism difficult.

Painting and Modern Architecture

If it can be argued that there were two strains of modernism: one, growing out of Paris and cubism, would include Le Corbusier (the architect), early Mies, Terragni, and Aalto; and the other, more related to Russian constructivism, would include Van Doesburg, Hannes Meyer, and possibly, Frank Lloyd Wright. The first group tended to explore complex and contradictory ideas through compositions exploiting principles of discontinuity; the second group insisted on more unified, consistent, and integrated compositions.[4]

Within this argument Le Corbusier the town planner surely belongs to the second group. In this sense he inculcates a modern version of the Renaissance principles of frontality and centrality, i.e., frontality for urban interventions, centrality for idealized town planning.

1. Le Corbusier, Still Life, 1923

2. Le Corbusier, Villa Savoy, Entry Hall, 1929

3. Le Corbusier, Villa at Garches, 1931

4. Reitveld and Van Doesburg, Study, 1923

5. Reitveld, Schroder House, interior, 1923–24

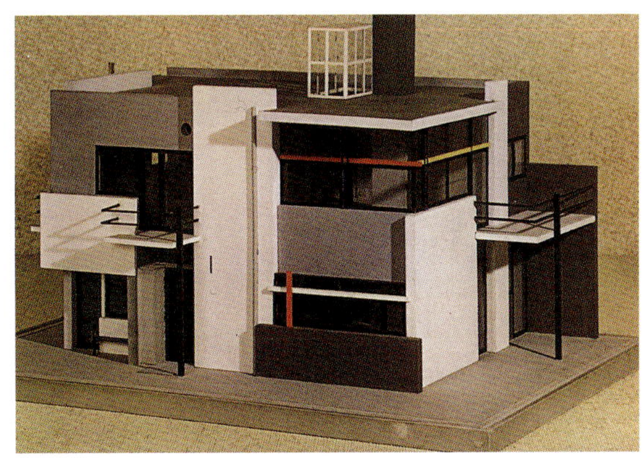

6. Reitveld, Schroder House, Model, 1923–24

7. El Lissitzky, Proun, 1921

8. Melnikov USSR Pavilion, Paris, 1925

9. El Lissitzky, Cloud-iron, 1925

1. Erich Mendelsohn, Einstein Tower, 1920–24

2. Mies van der Rohe, Glass skyscraper, 1921

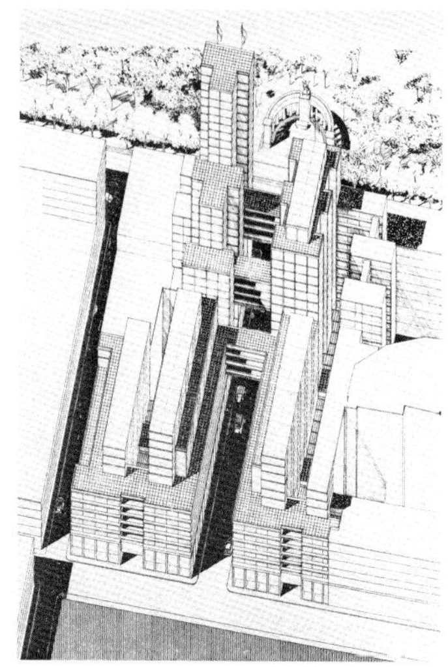

3. H. Meyer, Mexico Bank project.

4. FL Wright, Ward Willits House, 1902

5. Rob Van T'Hof, House, 1916

6. W. Gropius and A. Meyer, Faguswerk, 1911–12

7. Tatlin, Monument to the Third International, 1919–20

8. Bruno Taut, Glass Pavilion, 1914

9. Antonio Sant'Elia, "Cittá Nuova" Project, 1914

Early Modern Architecture

With the hindsight of almost a century, even the most cursory review of early modern architecture reveals the degree to which most architects were absorbed with crafting the architectural object rather than architectural or urban space. Despite differing philosophical persuasions—from functionalism, to constructivism, to expressionism—most buildings and projects were isolated, self-absorbed objects floating in space, with few urban implications. Oddly, the most unlikely exception was by Hannes Meyer, an urban project for a bank in Mexico.

Axonometrics, oblique perspectives, and three-quarter-view photos were the preferred means of representation, Wright being somewhat an exception. External views predominate, as internal space was rarely brought center-stage, Wright again being the exception. The diagonal was preferred over the frontal, and figurative plasticity over planar space. Beyond the fascination with recent industrial process and construction, the roots of object obsession lie deep in the narrative architecture of eighteenth-century neoclassicism.[5]

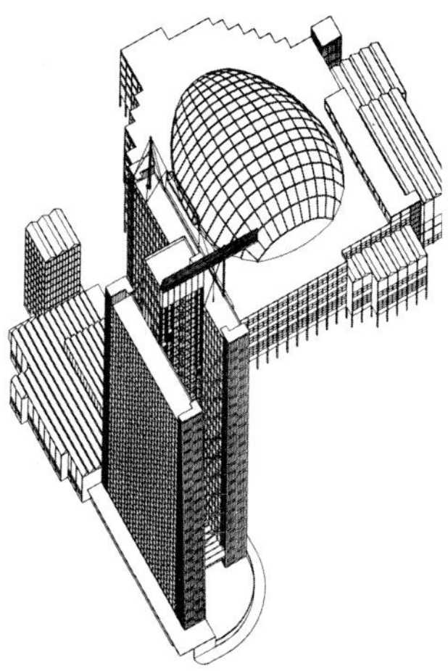

1. H. Meyer, *League of Nations competition, 1927*

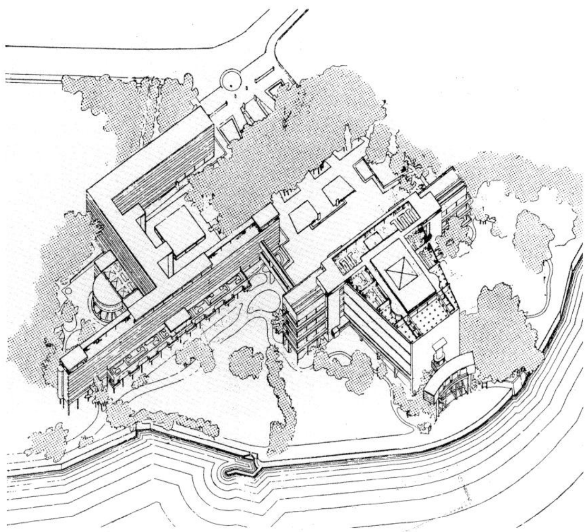

2. Le Corbusier, *League of Nations competition, 1927*

3. Le Corbusier, *Maison Plainex*

4. Maison Plainex, 1927

Two Strains of Modern Architecture

Two entries for the League of Nations competition—those of Hannes Meyer and Le Corbusier—may be used to illustrate the strain of modernism growing out of constructivism versus that growing out of cubism.

Both schemes are drawn in axonometric, but Meyer's scheme is an agitated figure, abstracted from any context. Its emphasis on integration and consistency—on *total design*—belies no hint of external or interior spatial character. Indeed, it is even difficult to determine how to penetrate the composition.

Le Corbusier's project, on the other hand, clearly illustrates its relationship to the land and the lake; it articulates a legible, frontal, sequence of spatial layers on the entry side and an iconic image on the lake side. Other drawings illustrate the discontinuous interrelationship between the structural frame and the spatial idea.[6]

Le Corbusier the Architect

Le Corbusier shared his contemporaries' interest in industrialization, but unlike theirs, his work was embedded in history and the urban fabric of Paris, and it grew out of cubism rather than constructivism. In contrast to the search for consistency, integration, and continuity—again, the *total design*—sought by Wright, Van Doesburg, Gropius, and the Russians, Le Corbusier exploited principles of discontinuity through articulate, independent systems (e.g., structure versus spatial enclosure). His architecture was thus more complex, more spatial, and more urban. He was more interested in frontality and shallow, layered space rather than the oblique, and in urban context rather than the tabula rasa of autonomous buildings. For polemical reasons his publication of the Maison Plainex is cropped to appear autonomous and revolutionary. In reality it has a significant historic pedigree, and an elegant contextual resolution of street-wall misalignment.

5. Palladio, Ca Cogollo, Vicenza, 16th c.

1. Mies, Friedrichstrasse Competition, 1919

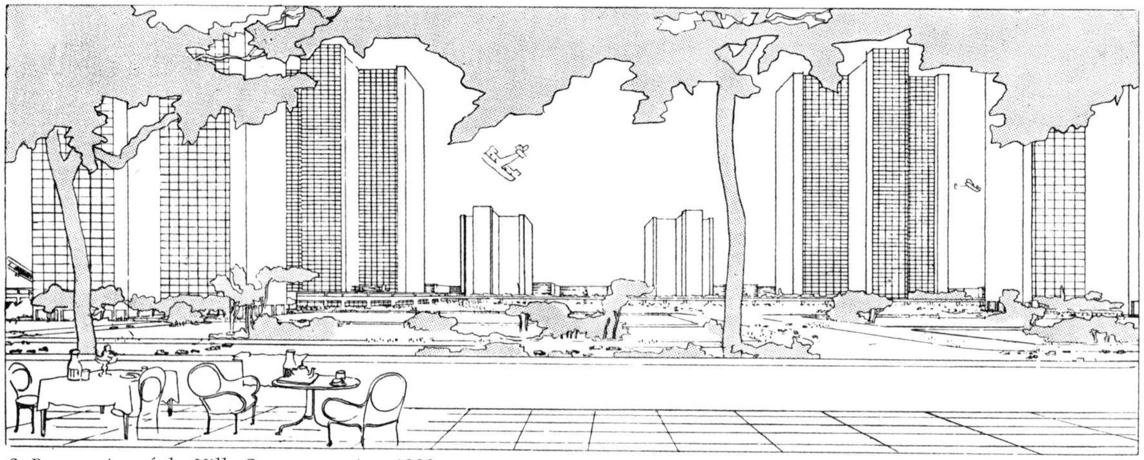

2. Perspective of the Ville Contemporaine, 1922

3. Cass Gilbert, Woolworth Building, New York, 1913

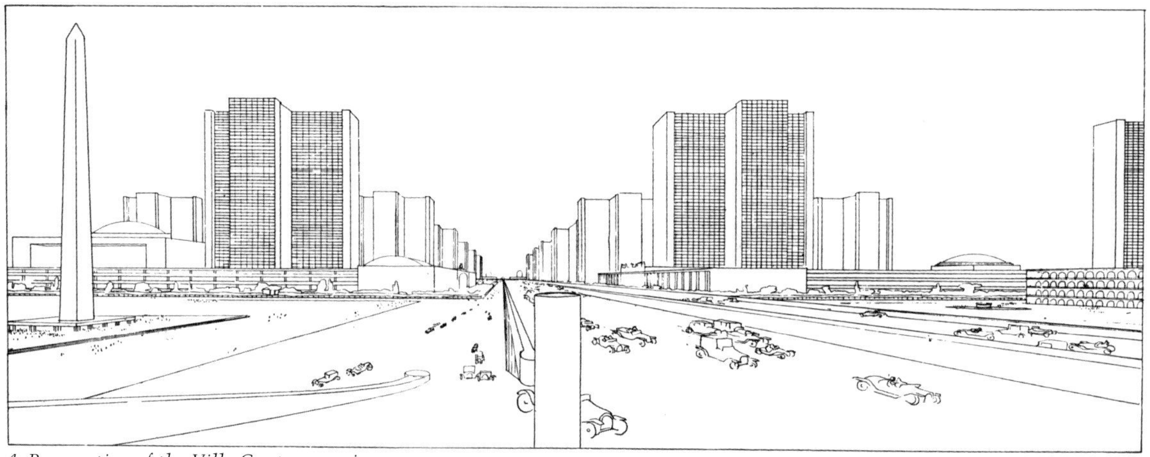

4. Perspective of the Ville Contemporaine

Modern Architecture and the City

The period between 1890 and World War I was a fertile one for the birth of the American skyscraper, including Cass Gilbert's Woolworth Building of 1913. New York City's "step-back" zoning code was adopted in 1916, and the *Chicago Tribune* competition in 1922 opened a new era of skyscrapers in America. But no one had applied these new architectural forms to a new theory of the city. In America, they were simply skyscrapers in the city. Following World War I, modern skyscraper architecture emerged in Europe with Mies' Friedrichstrasse competition entry in 1919, and his Glass Skyscraper project in 1921, neither of which conformed to the city.

Le Corbusier and the Modern City

By the time Charles Eduoard Jeanneret opened his studio in Paris in 1922, he had worked for the European masters of modern architecture, invented the Dom-ino frame in 1914, built the Villa Schwob in 1916, founded *L'Esprit Nouveau* and adopted the name Le Corbusier in 1920. There was no evidence, however, of either radical town-planning ideas or tall buildings in his work.[7] But suddenly, in 1922, he produced the stunning plan for the Ville Contemporaine de 3 Millions d'Habitants.[7] This theoretical plan and its successors—the Plan Voisin for Paris, 1925, and the Ville Radieuse, 1931–33—would revolutionize the world of architecture and town planning. Much of this success came from his influence on the Congrès Internationaux d'Architecture Moderne, or CIAM, founded in 1928.

The Ville Contemporaine

According to Le Corbusier's *Oeuvre Complète de 1910–1929*, in July 1922, the director of the urban section of the *Salon d'Automne*, Marcel Temporal, proposed that Le Corbusier make something for the next salon in November, saying:

> The art of urbanism is the shop, the wrought iron sign, the house door, the street fountain, all that our eyes see in the street. Make us therefore a beautiful fountain or something similar.[8]

Le Corbusier had another idea, and instead, over the next three months made the Ville Contemporaine de 3 Millions d'Habitants.

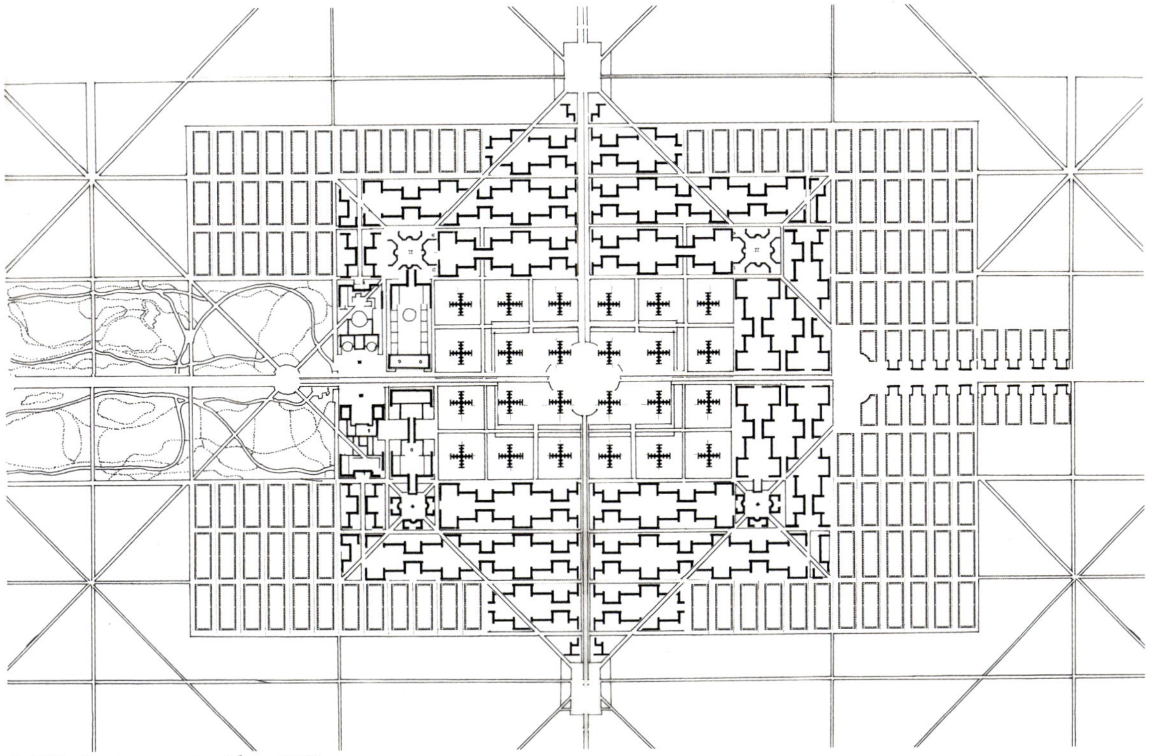

1. Ville Contemporaine Plan, 1922

2. Ville Contemporaine, digital model

3. Ville Contemporaine perspective

4. Ideal City, attributed to Piero della Francesca

Le Corbusier the Town Planner

The Ville Contemporaine was nothing less than the complete urban inversion of all that had come before: form, space, zoning, circulation, coverage, land ownership (parcels), and landscape. Moreover, the Ville Contemporaine was not designed and drawn as a city, but as buildings, i.e., not as space, but as solids.

For centuries the city had been composed of urban buildings that formed blocks, streets, mixed-use neighborhoods, squares, and parks. Le Corbusier's diagram banished the street, the square, and their defining buildings, in favor of a limited range of anti-urban building types, monofunctional zoning, an articulate network of vehicular circulation, and a continuous, picturesque landscape of "towers in the park." Finally, the proposed scale of the Ville Contemporaine was significantly bigger than the city of the past. Traditionally, only the most important civic institutions were articulated free as "narrative" monuments; in Le Corbusier's city of modern architecture, the most prosaic of modern society's institutions were articulated free as icons. What had been space became solids; what had been integrated became articulated; and what had been urban became pastoral.

Le Corbusier the architect was complex, resonant, and contradictory, but Le Corbusier the town planner was simplistic and diagrammatic. His vision, however, was clear and concise, and although it was initially greeted with skepticism, its ideas rather quickly became pervasive. Indeed, it can be argued that he changed the world.

Two Architectural Prototypes

Between 1914 and 1922, Le Corbusier developed the two housing ("unit") types that would be the basis of all his future work: the Maison Dom-ino in 1914, which was based on a columnar frame supporting cantilevered horizontal floor slabs; and the Maison Citrohan in 1920 and 1922, which was based on parallel walls with a double high space in section.

In 1922, these two prototypes were combined in the Immeubles Villas. According to Le Corbusier, the idea came from the monk's cells in the Cistercian monasteries of Pavia and Val d'Ema, in which an outdoor space is defined by the unit.

The first Immeubles Villas apartment block consisted of 120 "villas" (24 per floor), and was illustrated with the Ville Contemporaine. The villa units were organized along both sides of a long, narrow courtyard and were oriented out toward the street.

This was not the scheme shown in the plan for the Ville Contemporaine, however. Rather, the blocks in the plan are bigger, with 68 villa units organized around all sides of the block, and with the villas oriented inward toward a large inner-block courtyard, resulting in much more banal streets.[9]

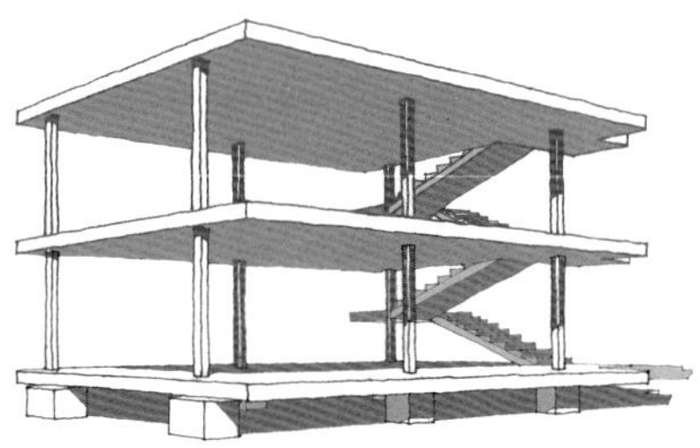

2. Dom-ino frame, 1914

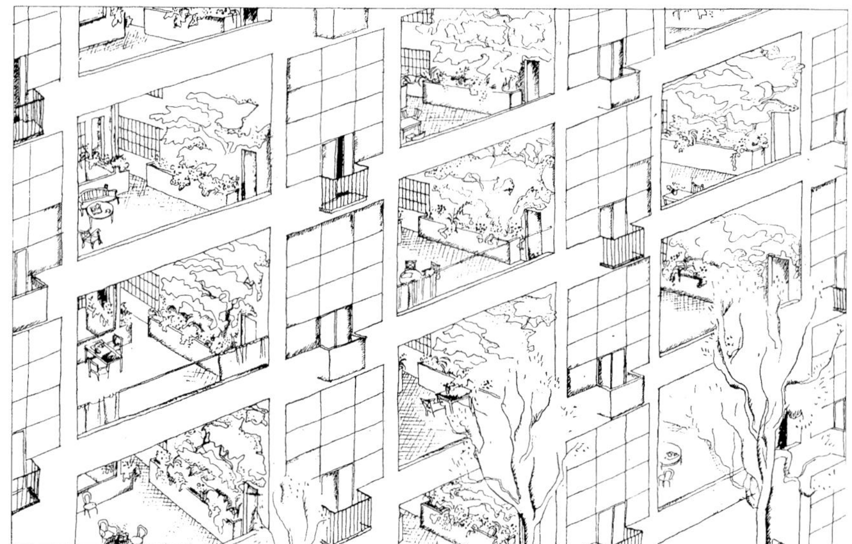

5. Immeubles Villas

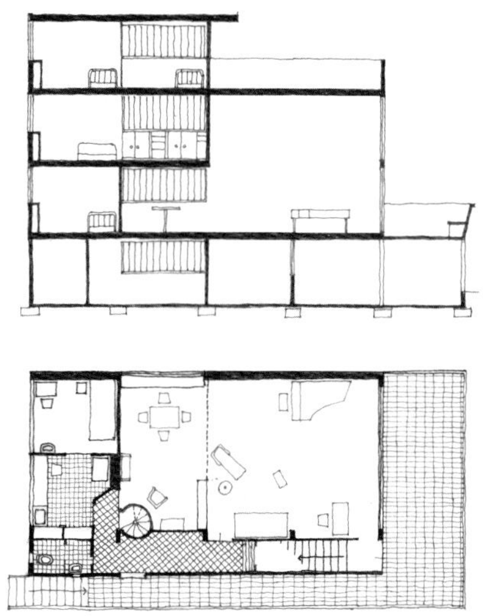

3. Maison Citrohan plan and section, 1920–22

6. Immeubles Villas, 1922

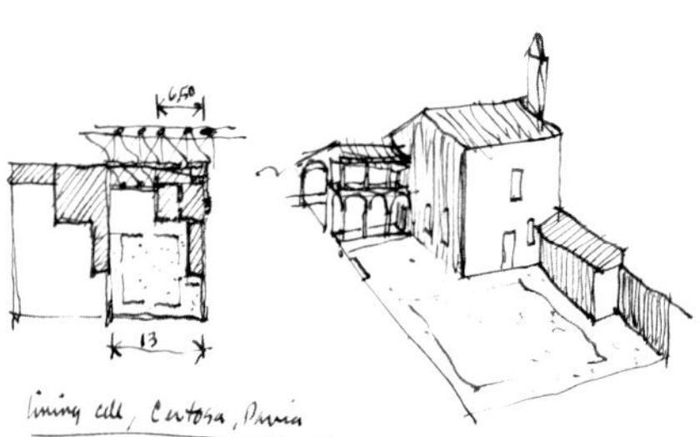

1. Sketch of monk's cell, Certosa

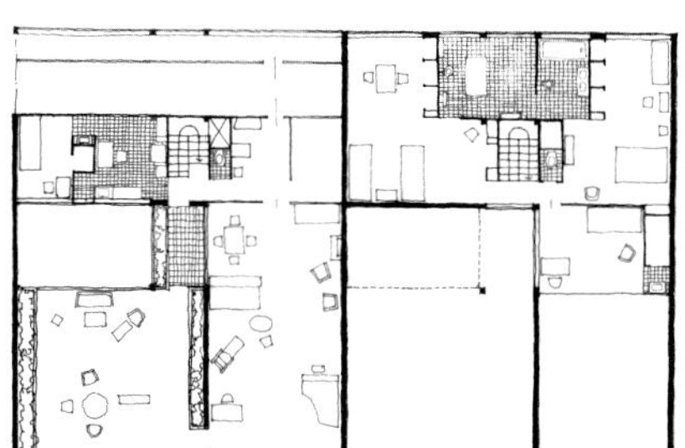

4. Villa Immeubles plan, 1922

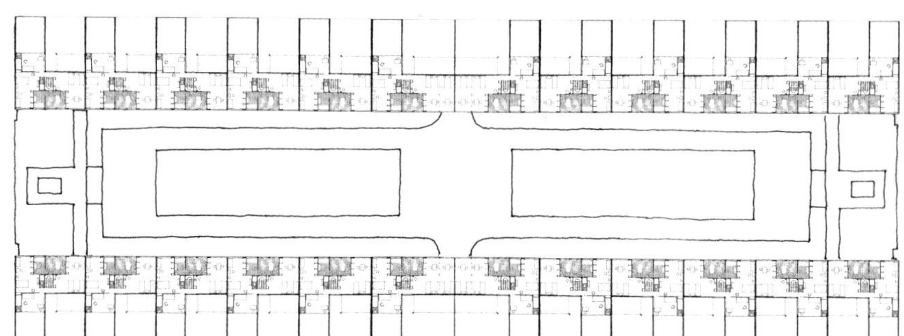

7. Diagramatic plan of first Immeubles Villas scheme, showing second floor level of units

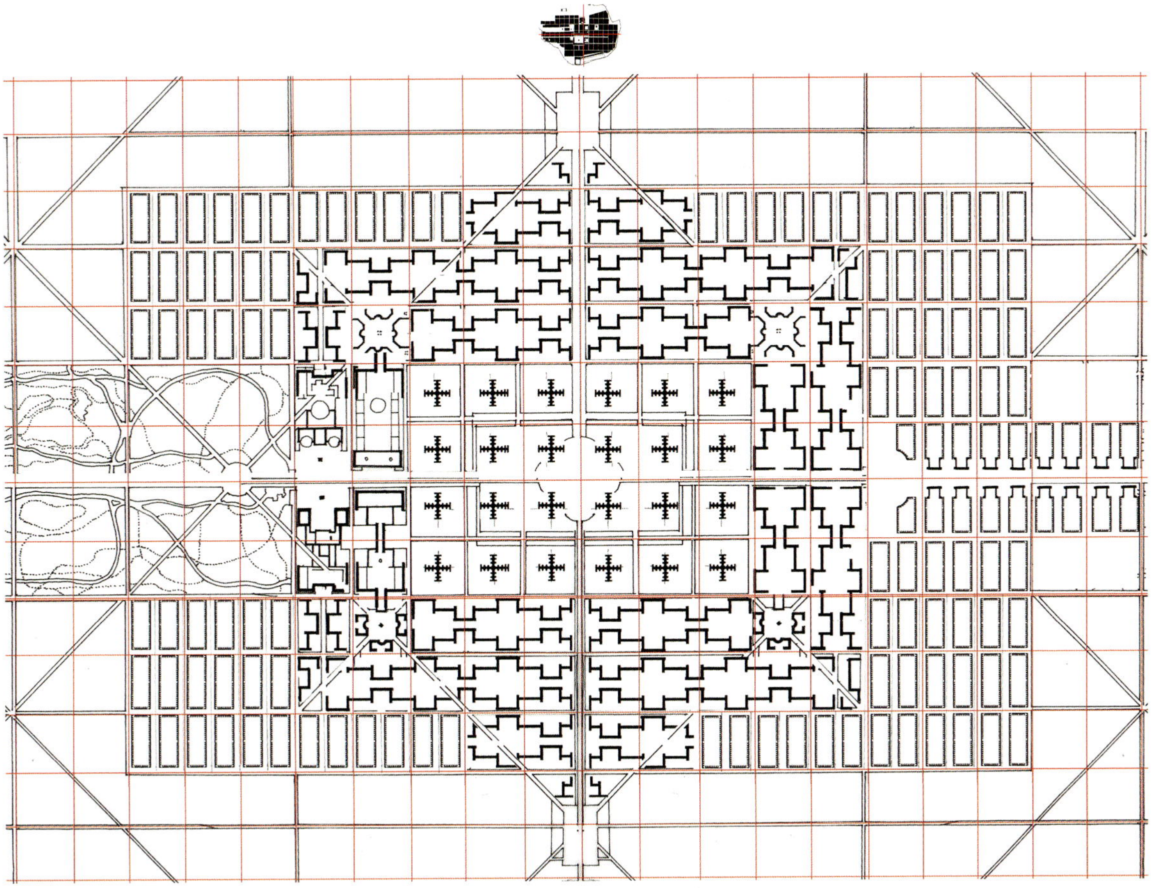

1. Ville Contemporaine plan with 400 m regulating grid with the plan of Priene at the top and at the same scale

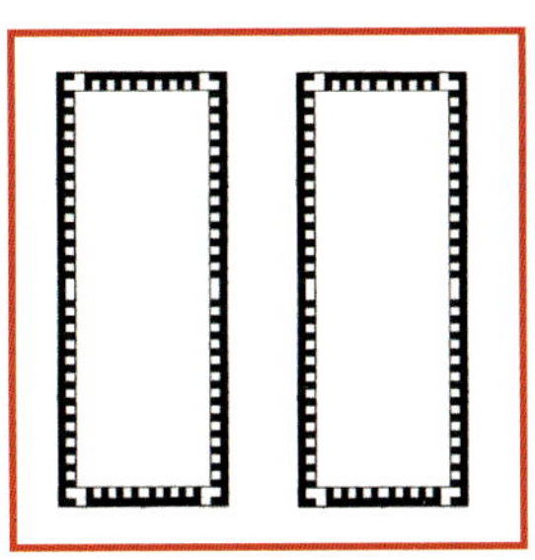

2. Second Immeubles Villas

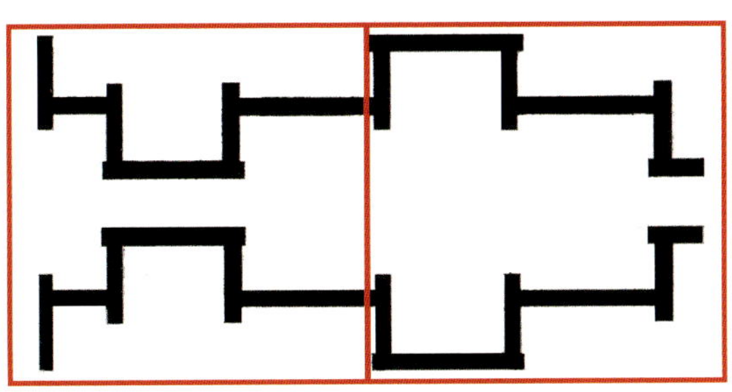

3. Redens, 400 x 800 m grid

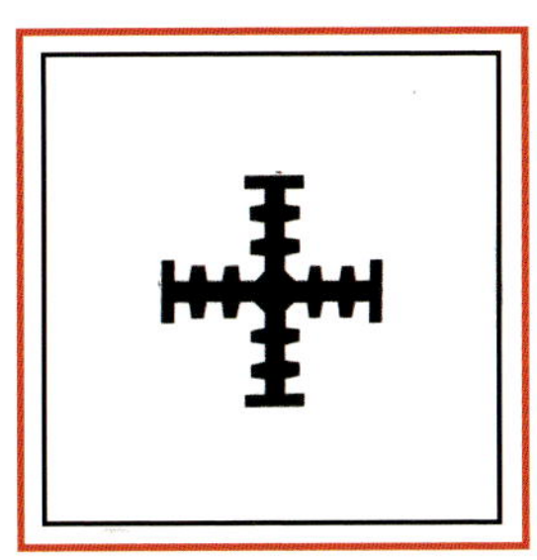

4. Skyscrapers, 400 x 400 m grid

Regulating Lines

The Ville Contemporaine appears to have been organized on a 400-meter grid (1,312'), or approximately a five-minute walk. There is also a 200-meter subgrid. All building types as well as highways are organized by this grid. A multilevel transportation interchange occupies the center of the plan, and a large park connects the center to the surrounding landscape.

Building Types

There are three basic building types in the Ville Contemporaine: (1) cruciform glass towers (24) for business in the center; (2) continuous twelve-story apartment buildings, *a redan*, surrounding the center; and, (3) a zone of Immeubles Villas apartment blocks.[10]

Le Corbusier had built nothing since the Villa Schwob in 1916, but by 1922 all the principles of his future work were in place:

1. The Dom-ino model
2. The Citrohan model
3. The Immeuble Villa model
4. Buildings *a redan*
5. Glass towers
6. The pilotis
7. The free plan
8. The free facade
9. The horizontal window
10. The roof terrace
11. Abstract "industrial" language
12. Centralized property management
13. Monofunctional zoning
14. Articulated vehicular circulation
15. Continuous Romantic landscape

But if Le Corbusier's urbanism continued to be diagrammatic and anti-urban, his architecture became ever more complex, resonant, and contextual. Between 1922 and 1930 he built sixteen houses and other small buildings. Although he would design many subsequent urban plans, he would not realize a single urban plan until Chandigarh, beginning in 1950.

1. Plan Voisin, model

2. Plan Voisin, city center

THE 1925 PLAN VOISIN FOR PARIS

The first urban application of the elements and principles of the Ville Contemporaine was Le Corbusier's Plan Voisin for Paris in 1925. The plan was exhibited in the Exposition des Arts Décoratifs in a diorama attached to a full-scale mock-up of an Immeubles Villa unit called the Pavillon de L'Esprit Nouveau.[11]

Unlike the Ville Contemporaine, the Plan Voisin contained only two building types: the cruciform glass towers, and the buildings *a redan*. (The Immeubles Villas blocks were shown, but were not used in the plan.)

The plan was organized around two major new circulation routes through Paris. These intersected at a right angle—like a great *cardo* and *decumanus*—reminiscent of Hénard's 1904 project for Paris. The major north-south part of the project consisted of a field of eighteen towers occupying approximately 1.4 square miles of the historic center of the city, necessitating its demolition. In place of the multilevel transportation interchange at the center of the Ville Contemporaine is a vast rectangular paved space with two triumphal arches, two obelisks, and a grade-separated intersection—again reminiscent of Hénard.

The western extension of the plan preserves the Palais Royale, the Place Vendome, the Garnier Opera, the Place de la Madeleine, and the Palais Elysèe. Almost everything else is demolished.

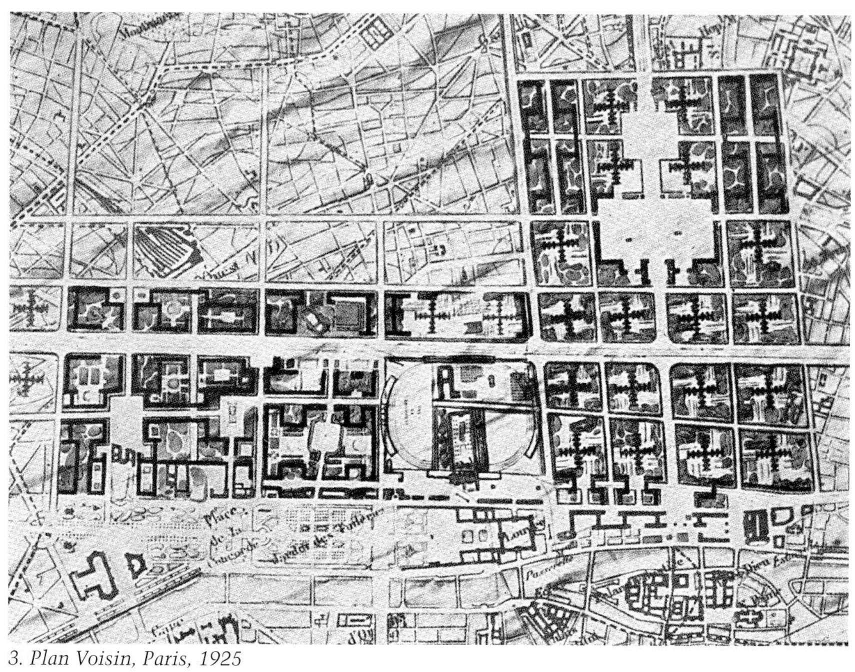

3. Plan Voisin, Paris, 1925

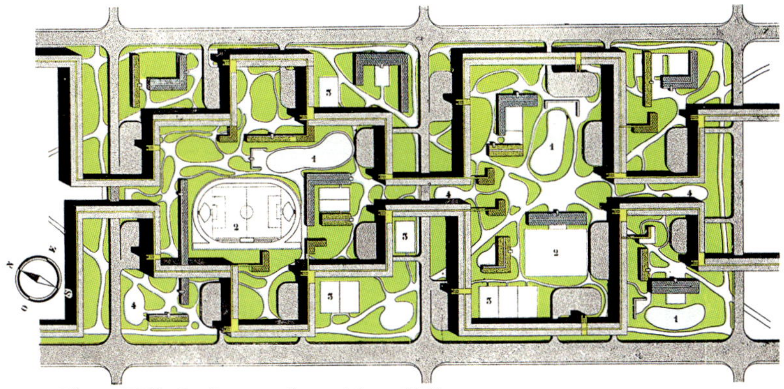

1. Plan of Ville Radieuse redans, 1 in. = 800′

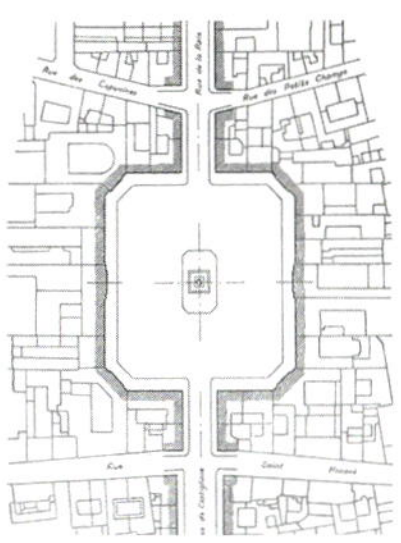

2. Place Vendome, plan, 1 in.=800′

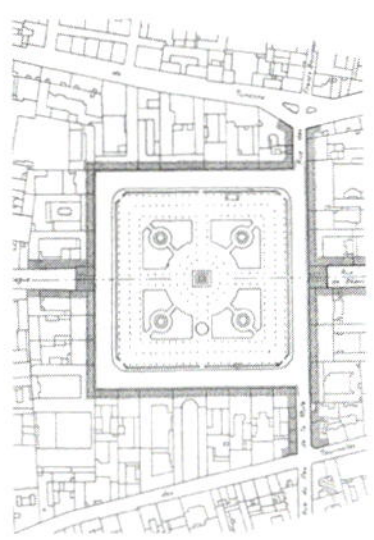

3. Place des Vosges, plan, 1 in.=800′

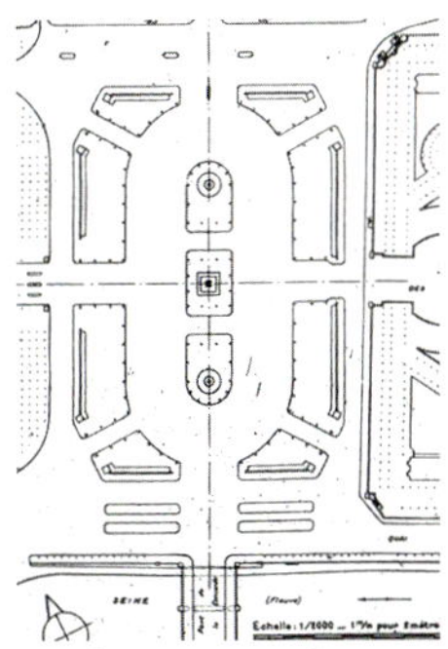

4. Place Concorde, plan, 1 in.=800′

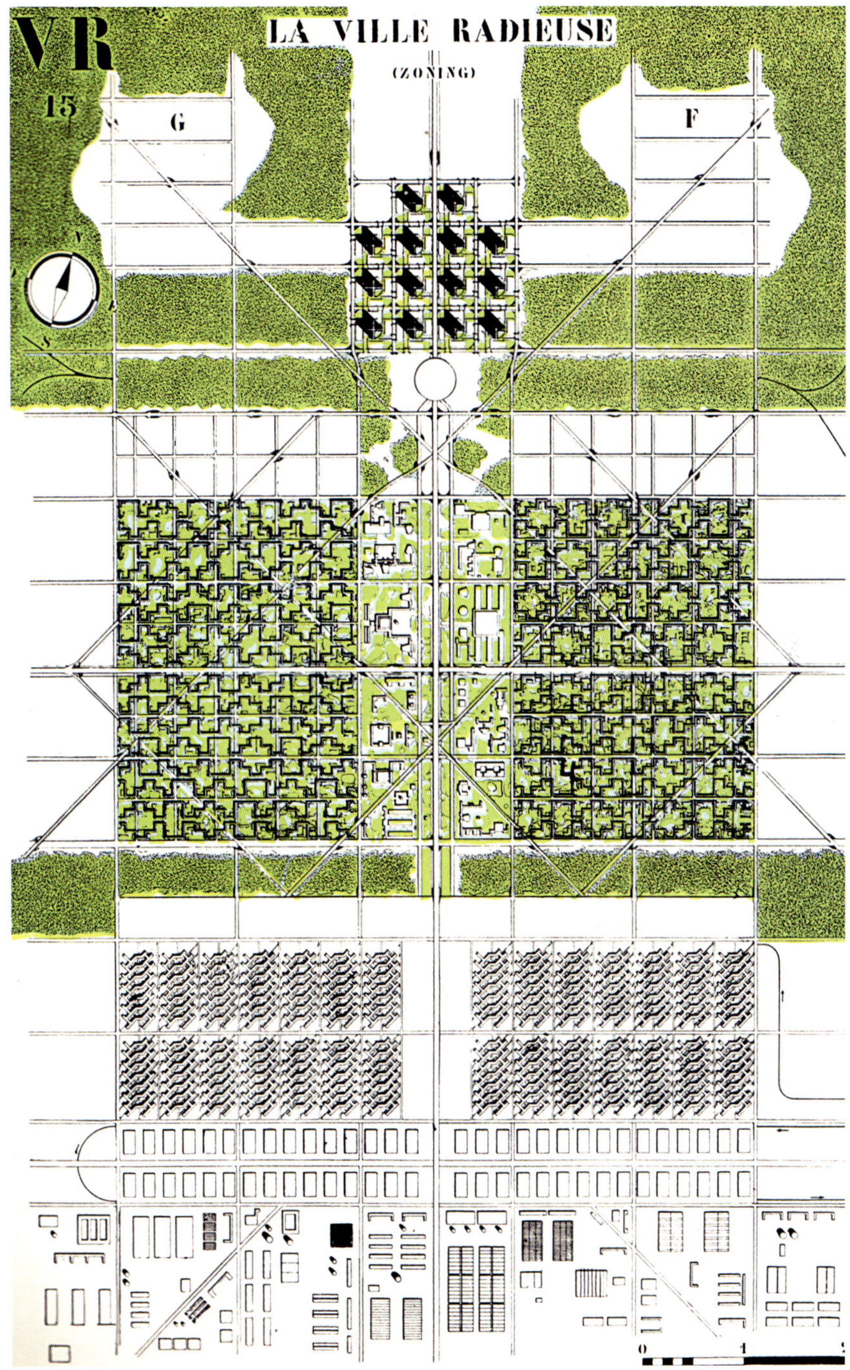

5. Plan of Ville Radieuse, 1931–33

The Ville Radieuse, 1931–33

The Villa Savoye, designed in 1928 and completed in 1931, forms the coda to Le Corbusier's prolific work of the 1920s. For fifteen years—from 1930 to 1945—the combination of the Great Depression and the Second World War would limit his architectural possibilities, and he would focus on town planning.

The sequel to the Ville Contemporaine and the two Voisin plans for Paris was the Ville Radieuse, which was developed between 1930 and 1933, and published in the new journal *Plan* during those years. It was published as a book in 1935.[12] If the Ville Contemporaine was a centralized ideal city diagram, the Ville Radieuse was an axial ideal city diagram (one that would become the formal infrastructure for the plan of Chandigarh in 1950). The cruciform glass towers remained, but were located outside the city as the "head" of the diagram. The dominant themes of the Ville Radieuse were the *redans* apartment buildings and the raised auto circulation network. The Immeubles Villas disappeared.

Parisian squares were the apparent precedents for the original enclosed spaces of the Ville Radieuse redans. The large rectangular space of the original redans is approximately 600′ x 1,000.′ The only Parisian square that is close to those dimensions, however, is the Place Concorde, which is not an enclosed square, but a traffic circle.

1. Porte Molitor, LC, 1933

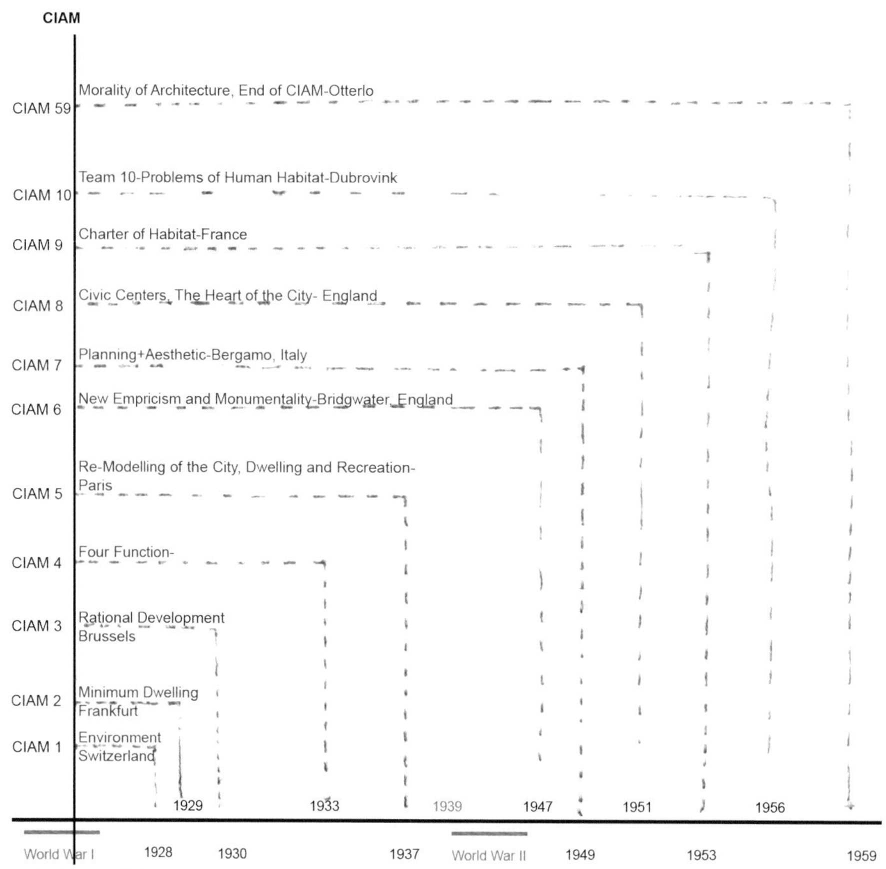

2. Chart of CIAM meetings, 1928–1959

CIAM

Le Corbusier's work can be read as a continuous, unbroken stream despite two world wars and the Great Depression. Much of his success came from this work, but much also came from his influence on the now equally famous Congrès Internationaux d'Architecture Moderne, 1928–1956.[13]

The International Congress of Modern Architecture (CIAM) was founded in La Sarraz, Switzerland, in 1928 to promote modern architecture—ultimately, the international style of modern architecture. The "Urbanism" section of the La Sarraz Declaration identified consolidated land distribution, functional zoning (living, working, recreation), traffic regulation, and building regulations—all underlying principles in the work of Garnier and Le Corbusier.

CIAM 2 was held in Frankfurt in 1929 and focused on the minimum dwelling. Le Corbusier did not attend, but criticized the topic in the third CIAM.

The focus of the CIAM 3 conference in Brussels in 1930 was on rational site planning. Le Corbusier presented his plans for the Ville Radieuse and the beginning of "The Functional City."

The CIAM 4 conference was held in the summer of 1933 aboard the SS *Patris II* in the Mediterranean. It centered on the functional city—the four functions: *dwelling, work, transportation,* and *recreation.* The results of this conference were published by Le Corbusier in 1943 as "The Athens Charter."

The CIAM 5 conference was held in Paris during the 1937 Paris Exhibition with the theme of housing and recreation. Ideas regarding "The Functional City" were presented at the regional, neighborhood, and urban design scales. Le Corbusier exhibited his Athens Charter version of CIAM urbanism and his updated Plan Voisin as the *Plan de Paris 1937* in his Temps Nouveaux pavilion. This was the last CIAM conference until after the Second World War.

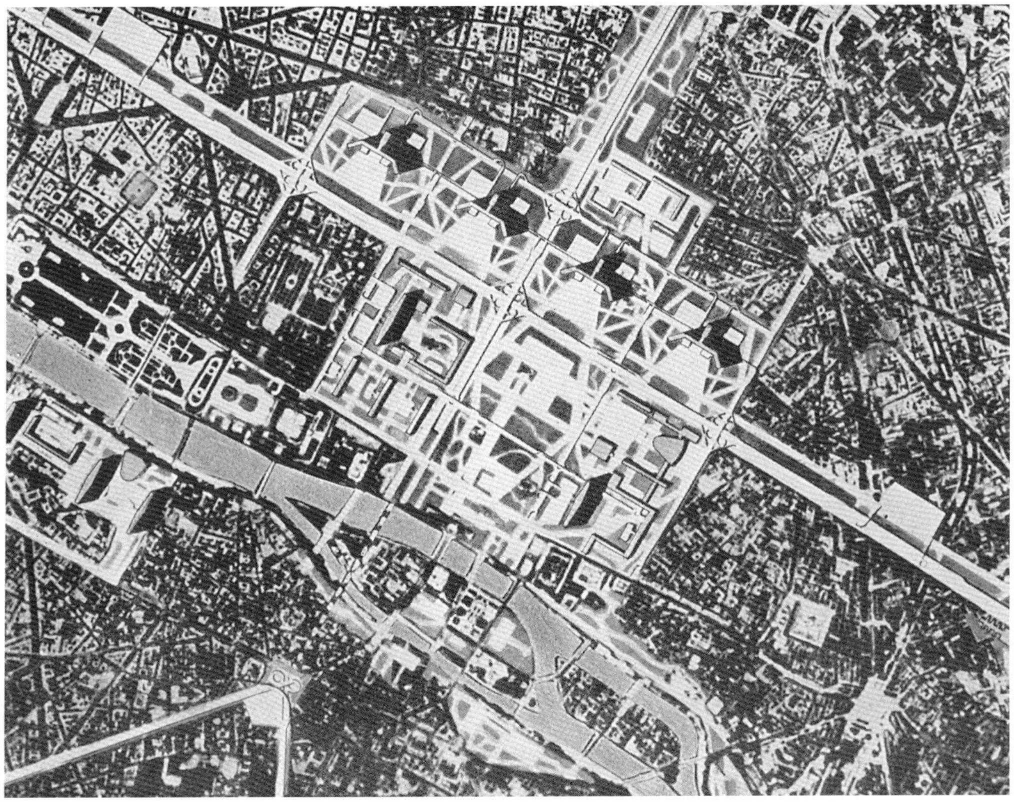

1. Plan for Paris, 1937

The Plan for Paris, 1937

This "revised Plan Voisin" for Paris was exhibited in Le Corbusier's Pavillion du Temps Nouveaux at the 1937 Paris exposition.[14] The area of the plan was reduced from the 1925 version, but the location on the right bank in central Paris was generally the same, and the *cardo* and *decumanus* were retained. The cruciform glass towers were replaced by four "Cartesian skyscrapers," and the *redans* were replaced by freestanding slabs.

Toward the east, however—beyond the Place des Vosges—fragments of the *redans* were collaged into the fabric of Paris with little adjustment. This scheme may be seen as a prelude to the later work of the Smithsons, as well as that of Candilis, Josic, and Woods. It also employed the sectionally interlocking units with skip-stop corridors that would be the system of the Marseilles Block after the war.

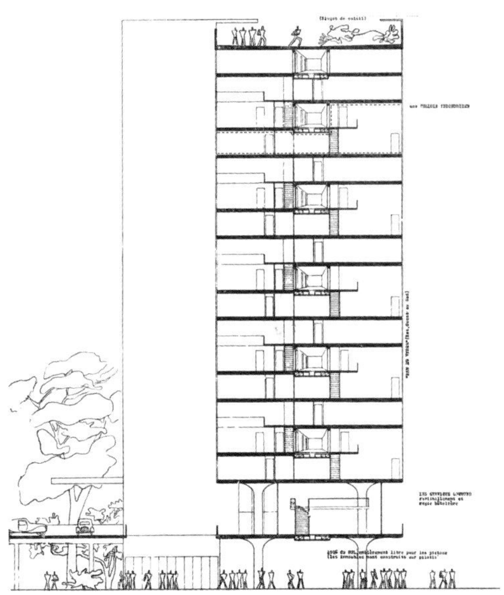

2. Apartment building section

3. Perspective of Ilot Insalubre #6

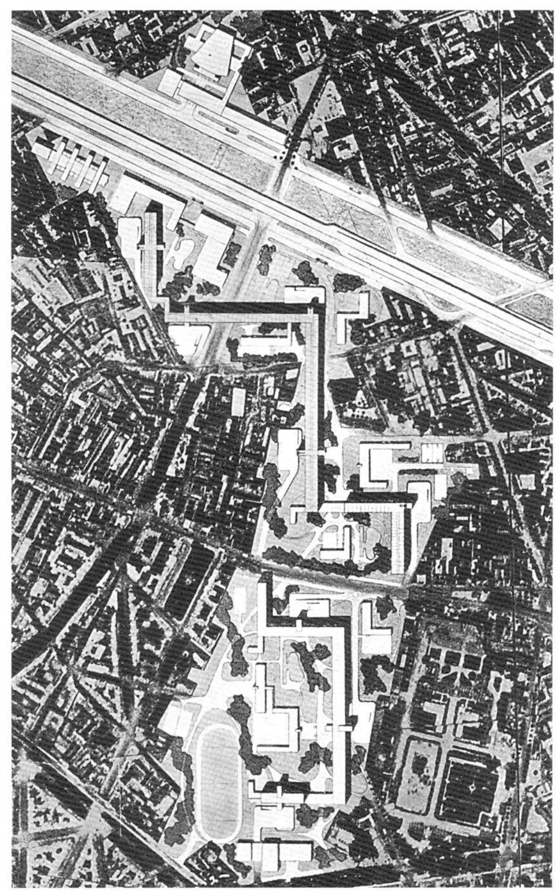

4. Plan for Ilot Insalubre #6, Paris, 1934

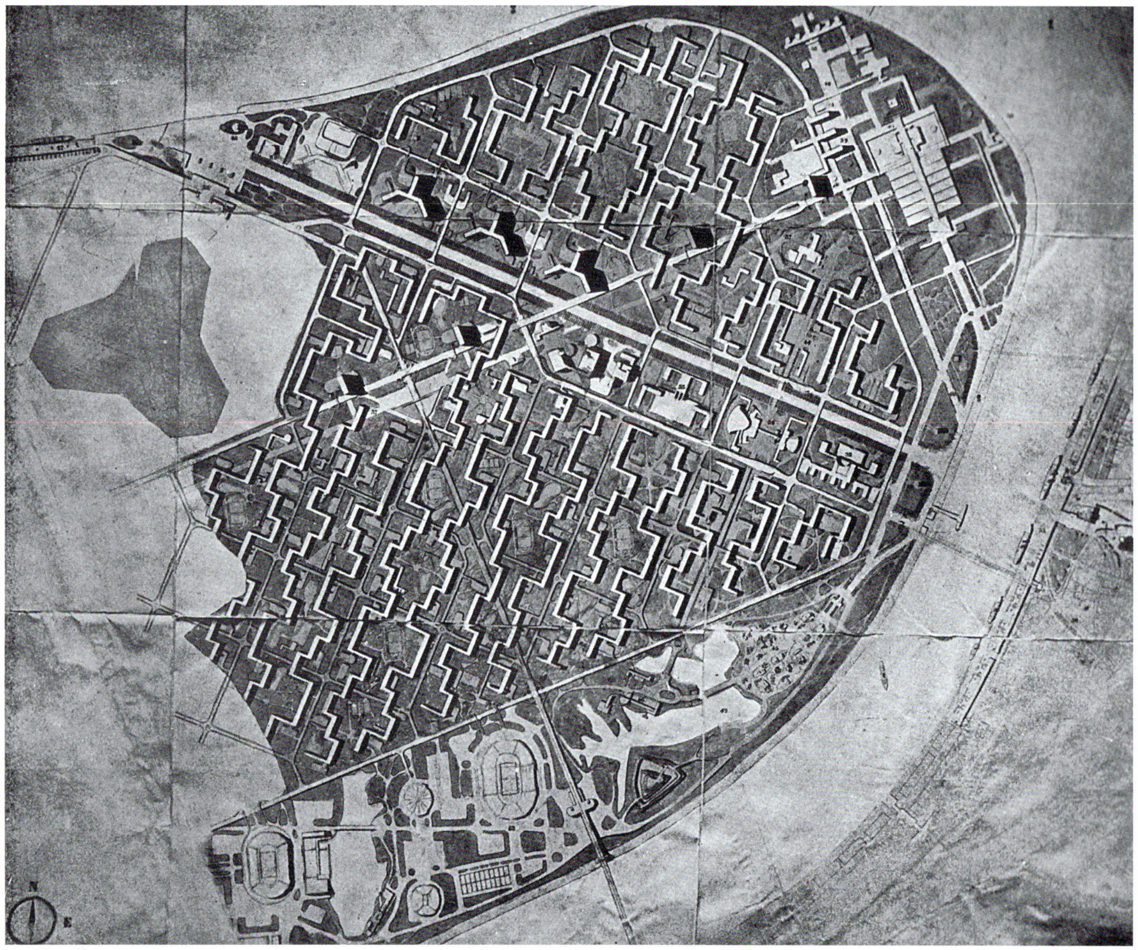

1. Plan for Antwerp, 1934

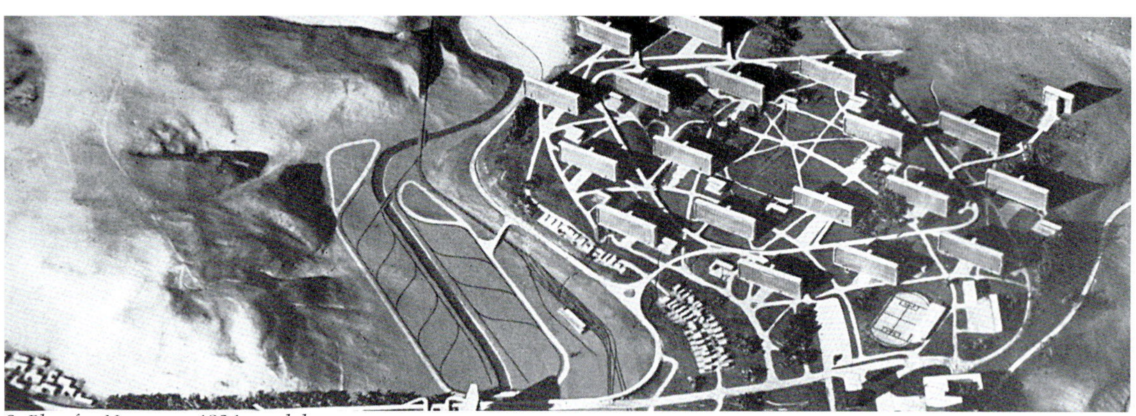

2. Plan for Nemours, 1934, model

3. SDUK Map of Antwerp, 1844

What Were They Thinking?

During the 1930s Le Corbusier produced a series of town-planning projects—all based on CIAM principles. Today, close to a century later, it is still difficult to imagine that the same mind could, and would, produce the architectural and urban sophistication of the Maison Plainex and Porte Molitor projects and, at the same time, the unimaginably grotesque "urban" projects. It is even more incomprehensible that so many followers drank the Kool-Aid and became willingly infected.

The original idea for the *redans* was inspired by the larger spaces of Paris; i.e., clear rectangles of enclosed space with an implicit, private "inside" and a public "outside." In order to produce variety, however, the clear model morphed into a random jig-jag pattern of mega-buildings with illegible spaces and no distinction between the public and private realms. This, in turn, morphed into the more practical high-rise slabs.

Le Corbusier used the rationale that widely spaced buildings were safer than dense areas of urban fabric in an aerial bombardment. He could not have imagined the development of the atomic bomb, however, which completely neutralized this aspect of his rationalization. Nevertheless, the high-rise slab became ubiquitous after the Second World War.

1. Hiroshima USA, painting, 1950

World War II and the Atomic Bomb, 1945

Of the most prominent modern European architects, only Alvar Aalto and Le Corbusier remained in Europe throughout the Second World War, and there were no more CIAM congresses until 1947.

The world's first atomic bomb was developed by the United States and tested in July 1945 at Alamogordo, New Mexico. In August 1945 atomic bombs were dropped on Hiroshima and Nagasaki, Japan—effectively ending World War II and initiating the atomic age. It would be difficult to overestimate the effect of this event—an effect that would last into the present.

The postwar world was partitioned into east–west/communism–capitalism. Russia soon developed its own atomic weapons, and the world settled into the continuing state of tension of the Cold War. In the United States, Manhattan was generally considered to be ground zero—the first target in a nuclear attack by Russia, to be followed by other metropolitan areas. Fear was significant and all pervasive. School children were taught to get under their desks in case of attack; backyard bomb shelters were constructed and stocked; and unpopulated areas were considered to be safer places to live than dense urban environments. Thus, "the bomb" was a major contributor to the psychology of decentralization and disurbanization.

2. Atomic Bomb, Nagasaki, 1945

Prewar Dresden

On the eve of the Second World War Dresden was essentially complete. It had evolved since 1200, with each successive period adding to and enriching the city. Dresden was regarded as one of the most beautiful cities in Europe.

In terms of art, architecture, and urban development, the first half of the eighteenth century was Dresden's golden age. Despite war and political difficulties, under August the Strong and his son August II, the medieval urban fabric of the city was transformed, the city was embellished by a spectacular array of Baroque buildings, and an unsurpassed art collection was assembled. The Zwinger, named after the area between the inner and outer fortification walls in which it was built, was constructed from 1709–32. The old Frauenkirche was rebuilt from 1726–43, and the Hofkirche was built from 1739–51. The crown of the monumental Baroque composition, the Brühlsche Terrasse, was built on the fortification walls along the Elbe in 1738, completing Dresden's orientation to the river.

On February 14, 1945, the "Florence of the North" was annihilated by Allied bombing. Eighty-five percent of the built-up area was destroyed.[15]

1. Central Dresden after Allied bombing, 1945

2. Aerial view of the historic core of Dresden, before World War II looking north

3. Reconstruction plan, Herbert Conert, 1946

4. Plan of Dresden in 1898

5. Reconstruction plan, Mart Stam, 1946

1. Aerial view of the inner city looking south, 1992

2. Aerial view of part of Gorbitz suburb

3. Reconstruction project, Hans Hopp, 1946

4. Plan of Dresden in 1989

Postwar Dresden

During the occupation period between the end of the war in 1945 and the foundation of the GDR in 1949, no reconstruction took place. This was a period of discussion regarding the rebuilding of the city, and both neo-traditional and modernist plans were proposed. Herbert Conert, director of planning in 1945, made the first master plan for reconstruction in 1946. His plan followed the historic spatial and functional pattern of the city. Hans Hopp and Mart Stam also made proposals, but their plans were Corbusian in their utopian aversion to the traditional city.

The period following the foundation of the GDR, 1949–1956, was marked by Soviet influence, the need for the representation of socialism, and an architectural and urban style known as "national traditionalism." The death of Joseph Stalin in 1953, however, freed planners from the slow and expensive burden of national traditionalism.[16]

In the mid-1950s the decision was taken to reconstruct the representational public buildings but leave the ruins of the Frauenkirche as a monument, demolish the ruins of the old city, and build a new socialist city. Modernist fabric in Dresden was composed of three fundamental architectural types: (1) the perimeter block, (2) the slab, and (3) the tower.

Of these three types, only the perimeter block had the capacity to turn the corner, and thereby approximate the traditional urban fabric of blocks, streets, and squares.

Postwar Urbanism

By the end of World War II Europe's cities were devastated, and the partitioning into the communist East and the capitalist West was imminent. Coventry, London, Rotterdam, Hamburg, Berlin, Leipzig, Dresden, Warsaw, and other cities were in ruins.

Demolition had been accomplished. Le Corbusier, his followers, and his CIAM colleagues were ready. No longer could they be accused of destroying historic urban fabric to replace it with the city of modern architecture.

There were two impediments to reconstruction according to modernist principles, however. In the communist East, Joseph Stalin was no supporter of modern architecture, and in the capitalist West, society was generally resistent. Indeed, there was not professional consensus in either the East or West regarding principles of urban reconstruction. It would take the death of Stalin in 1953 to free planners in Dresden to abandon tradition, clear the rubble, and construct a modernist social utopia. In the West, many cities were rebuilt according to previous patterns, but with modern buildings.

1. Cathedrale de St. Dié

St. Dié

From the high-rise slabs of Le Corbusier's plan for Nemours in 1934 to the high-rise slabs of his plan for the small industrial city of Sainte-Dié-des-Vosges in 1945, it would be impossible to imagine that World War Two occurred, and that it destroyed the latter city.

What was new about St. Dié was the heart of the plan—the "Civic Center." This was the urban element that captivaded Gideon, Sert, and others. It was extolled as a new conception of urban space, and references to the Athens Acropolis were inevitable.

An "acropolis" of modern freestanding buildings replaced the agora-inspired city center of the 1925 plan for Paris, while maintaining the *cardo* and *decumanus* of the Ville Contemporaine, the 1925 Paris Plan, as well as the historic plan of Sainte-Dié-des-Vosges.

The residue of pre-war *redans*—the *unités* (half the size of those for Marseilles)—provided the surroundings of the civic center, replacing the urban fabric of the destroyed city.

The plan for the Ville Contemporaine had at least a semblance of urban space defined by the grids of Immeubles Villes and redans. These are both absent from the plan for Sainte-Dié, however. Object buildings cannot make cities, and the forum may be an appropriate precedent for city centers, but the acropolis is not.

Le Corbusier was a master of graphic design. His drawing of the plan for St. Dié, with its spring green figurative shape, conveys the idea of the city in a garden and unifies the sparse built-form of the plan, while the light grey areas successfully evade representing the buildings that remained after the bombing. If the proposed and existing buildings are both shown without color, however, it reveals that the proposal is not really a city at all.

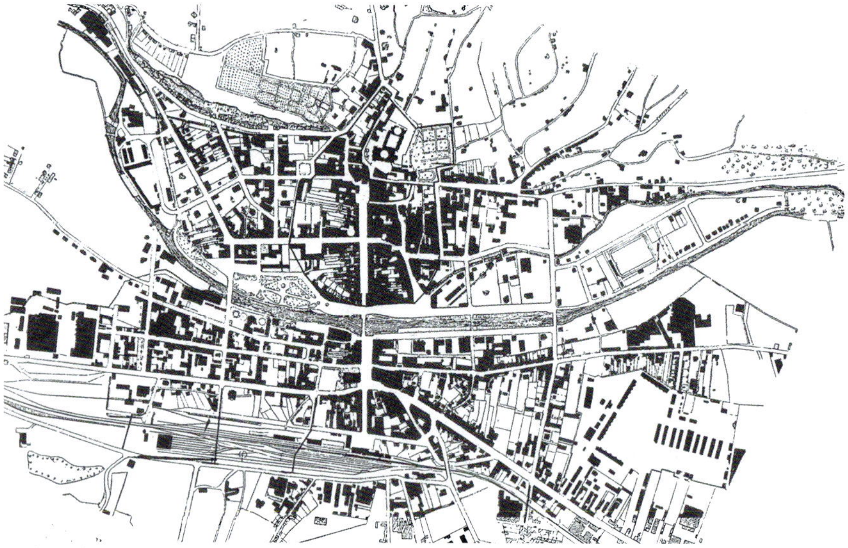

2. Plan of St. Dié before World War Two

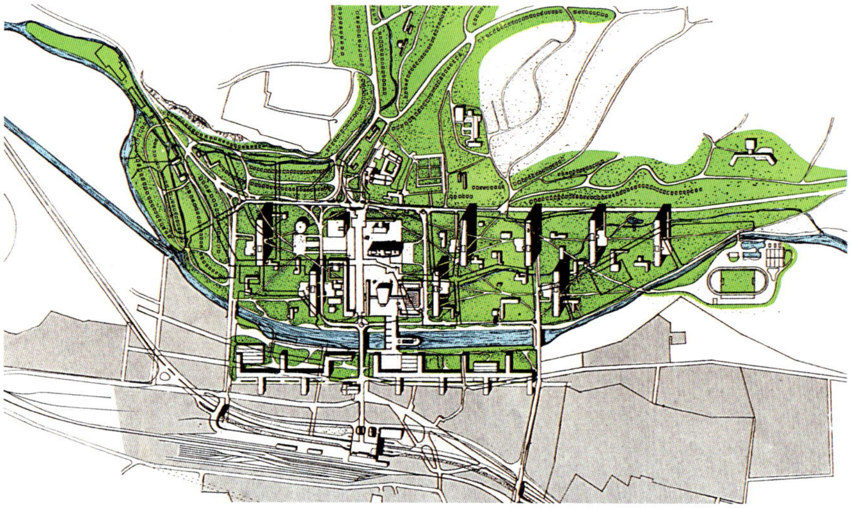

3. Le Corbusier, first proposed plan for St. Dié, 1945

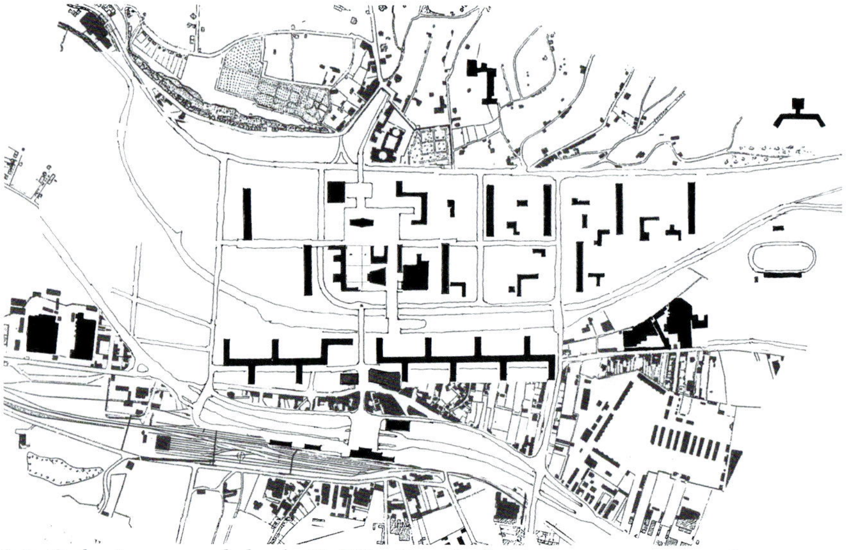

4. Le Corbusier, proposed plan for St. Dié with revised civic center on post-war plan

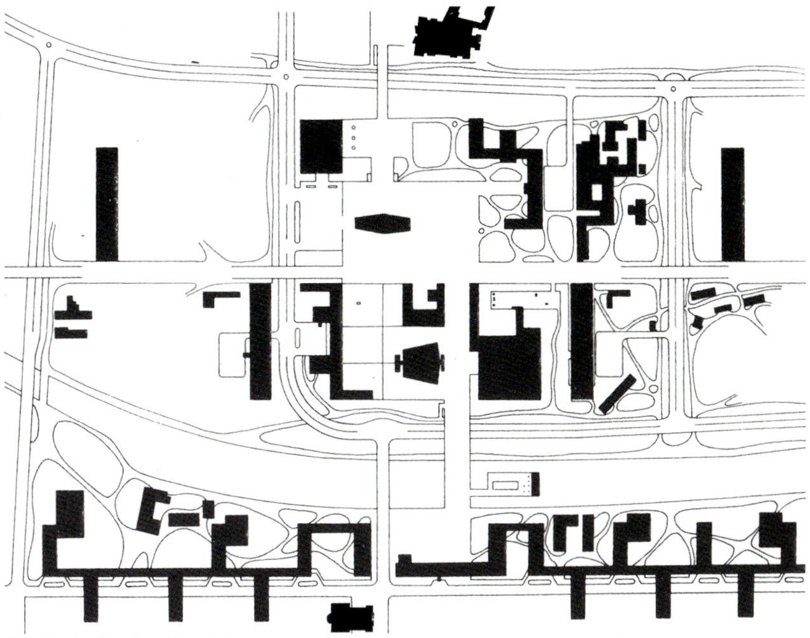
1. Revised plan for the civic center

2. Sketch view of proposed civic center

3. View of St. Dié destruction after the war

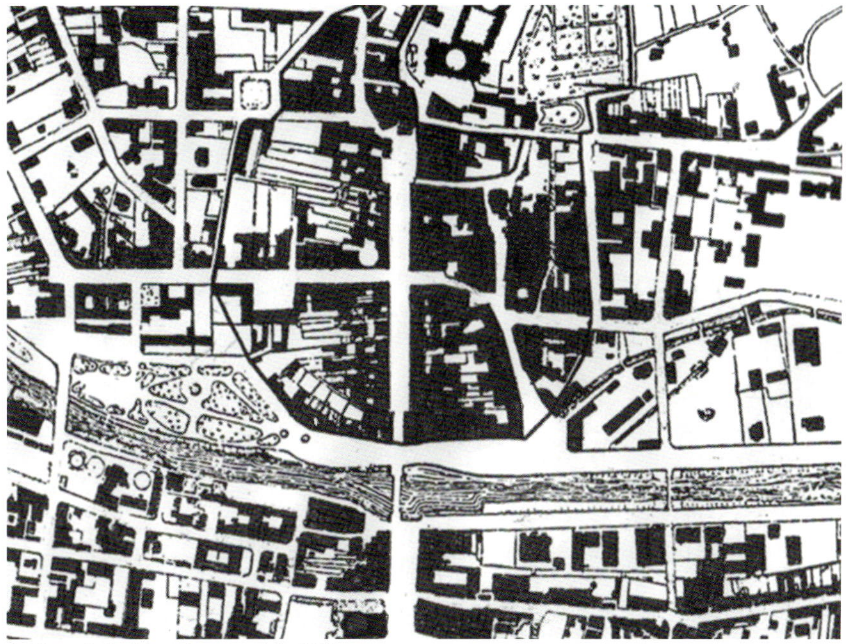
4. Plan of the historic core of St. Dié

5. Pre-war view of Rue de Thiers (the cardo of St. Dié)

6. Post-war view of Rue de Thiers

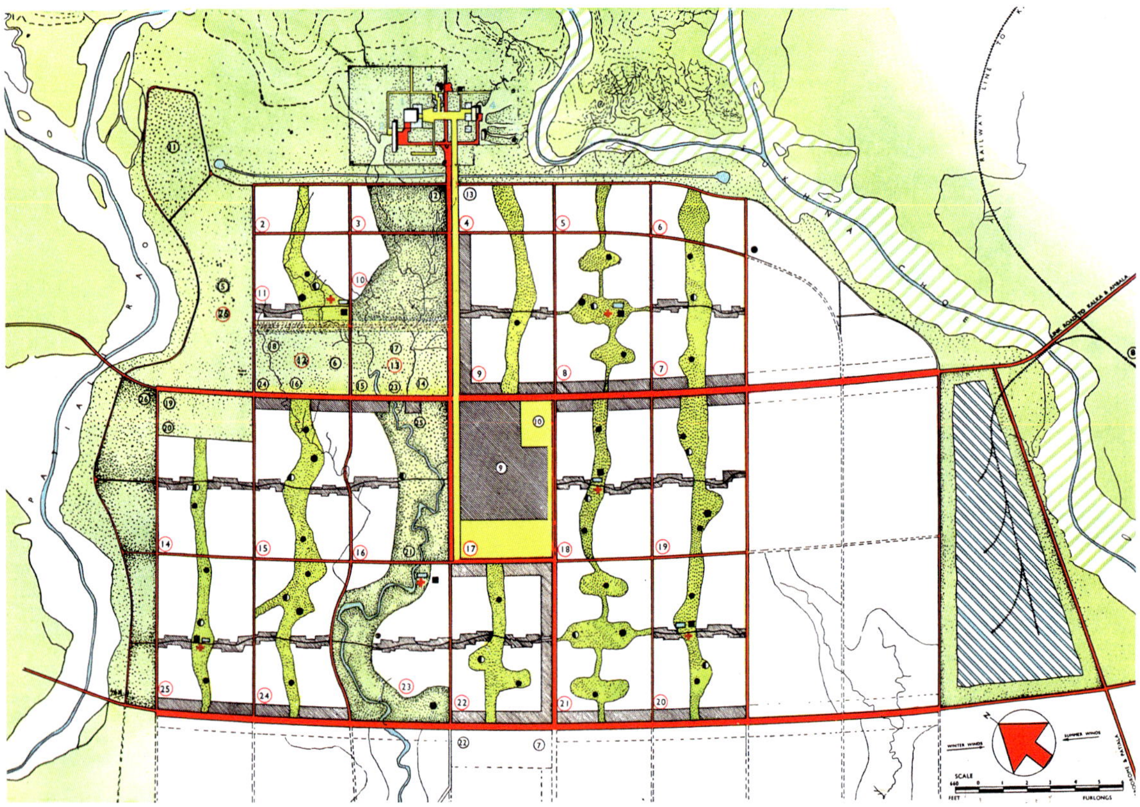

1. Le Corbusier, plan for Chandigarh, 1950

2. Chandigarh, Secrétariat

3. Chandigarh, Assembly Building

4. Chandigarh, High Court

Chandigarh, 1950

In 1945 Le Corbusier's plan for the reconstruction of the town of St. Dié was rejected, which meant that for almost twenty-five years none of his town plans had been implemented.

After Indian independence in 1947, Albert Mayer and Matthew Nowicki were selected to design the new capitol city of the Indian Punjab, and their plans were conceptually developed when Nowicki was killed in a plane crash in 1950. Le Corbusier was selected to replace him, and promptly revised the concept to a more rectangular plan reminiscent of the Ville Radieuse.[18]

The body of the plan is composed of "sectors" that are like self-contained communities measuring approximately 800 x 1200 meters—six times the size of the 400 m grid of the Ville Contemporaine, and about eight times the size of Roman (central) Florence. The dwellings in these sectors are low rise and low density, giving the character of a garden city reminiscent of English New Delhi.

The business buildings are in the center of the plan, but the governmental buildings are organized, like a head, outside the body. Le Corbusier referred to this area as the "Forum," but strictly speaking it is more like an acropolis.

There are no high-rise buildings in Chandigarh, but Le Corbusier's only built town plan is a literal diagram of The Rational City: *living*, *work*, *recreation*, and *circulation*—in addition, centralized planning and land distribution.

1. Skyros, Greece

2. Unité d'Habitation, Marseilles, 1947–52

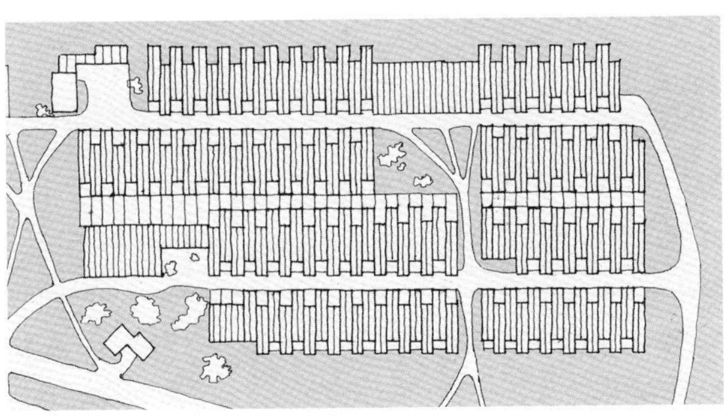

3. St. Baume, Plan, 1948–49

4. Sarabhai house, 1955-56

5. St. Baume, elevation

Postwar Architecture

Le Corbusier's postwar architecture surprised everyone: the Citrohan model replaced the Dom-ino model, and natural materials, including exposed concrete, replaced the industrial materials of his pre-war work. This direct expression of form, structure, and materials had overtones of the vernacular, and of additive composition. An interest in villages and village life emerged. Bernard Rudofsky's 1964 book about vernacular building, *Architecture Without Architects*, was widely circulated.

In 1948–49, Le Corbusier produced two projects for steeply sloping sites on the Côte-d'Azure, Roq et Rob, and St. Baume. Both utilized parallel-wall units organized along streets to form compact "villages" with central squares. In 1947–52, Le Corbusier touted his "Unité d'Habitation" at Marseilles as a "vertical village." These projects had a powerful influence, especially on the members of Team X.[19]

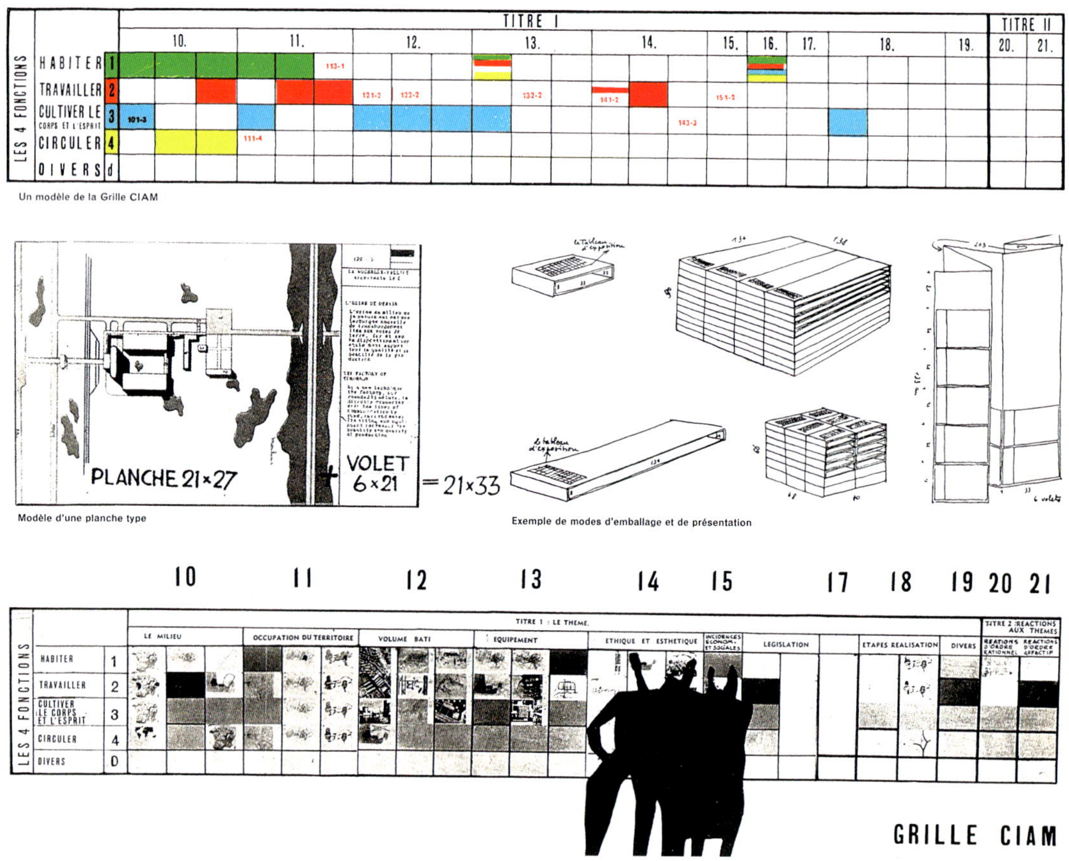

CIAM Grid, 1947

Postwar CIAM

In September 1947, the CIAM 6 congress was held in Bridgewater, England. It was the first CIAM congress in ten years. This congress is generally portrayed as a reorganization meeting with optimism, but little agreement. Le Corbusier had proposed the CIAM "Grid" as a consistent way of organizing and comparing urban projects. The Grid categorized projects based on the four functions of the Rationalist City: living, working, recreation, and circulation. It was approved in 1948, and used in the next congress.

CIAM 7 was held in Bergamo, Italy, in 1949. An important—even prescient—component of this congress was the presentation of José Lluis Sert and Paul Weiner's project for Chimbote, Peru. The project reflected Sert's interest in civic centers and low-rise mat housing.

The theme of CIAM 8, held in 1951 in Hoddeston, England, was "The Heart of the City." Sert presented the plan for Bogota, done with Paul Weiner and Le Corbusier, and Le Corbusier presented the project for Chandigarh.

CIAM had been criticized since Bridgewater, and a younger generation was beginning to press a different agenda. The more elusive aspects of "The Heart of the City" (the city core) contributed to the transformation of CIAM through congresses 9 at Aix in 1953, 10 at Dubrovnik in 1956 (the emergence of Team X), to its demise in Otterlo in 1959.[20]

Team X

Team X (Team Ten) emerged out of dissatisfaction with the goals and structure of CIAM, especially the four functions of the "rationalist city" as outlined in the Athens Charter. The limitations of CIAM principles were painfully evident in the CIAM VIII publication, *The Heart of the City*, in 1952.[21]

The younger generation held an interim meeting in Doorn, Holland, in 1954, intended to outline a new direction for CIAM to be presented at CIAM X in Dubrovnik in 1956. This meeting produced the Doorn Manifesto, which is generally considered the foundational document of the new group, later to be known as Team X. The declaration of the death of CIAM, and the formal announcement of Team X, was made in 1959, at the final CIAM conference in Otterlo. Team X continued to meet informally for discussions of their work. Their last formal meeting was in 1977, and the death of Jaap Bakema in 1981 marked the end of the group. [22]

After the Doorn Manifesto, a more developed document, "Draft Framework 4," was produced by Alison and Peter Smithson for CIAM X. In contrast to the mechanism of the Athens Charter, the Framework 4 proposed: "to study Urbanism as being communities of varying degrees of complexity." These are shown as a "Scale of Association" on a diagram derived from the Scottish town planner Patrick Geddes's "Valley Section.[23] They then proposed that working parties operate in a "field" on the "Scale of Association," i.e., City, Town, Village, Isolated Building.

1. *Team X announces the Death of CIAM at CIAM X at Otterlo in 1959.*

2. *Although over the years associations shifted, intensified, and broke, Team X's core members remained constant. They were Alison and Peter Smithson, Jaap Bakema, Georges Candilis, Giancarlo Di Carlo, Aldo Van Eyck, and Shadrach Woods.*

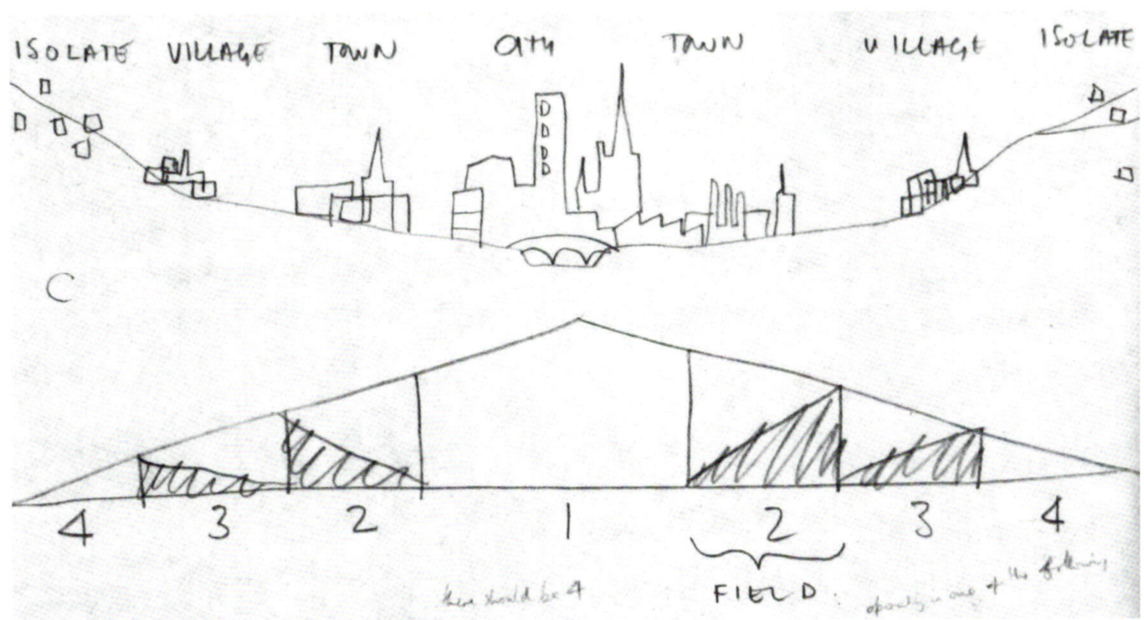

3. *Diagram of "fields" and "scales of association" as illustrated in "Draft Framework 4."*

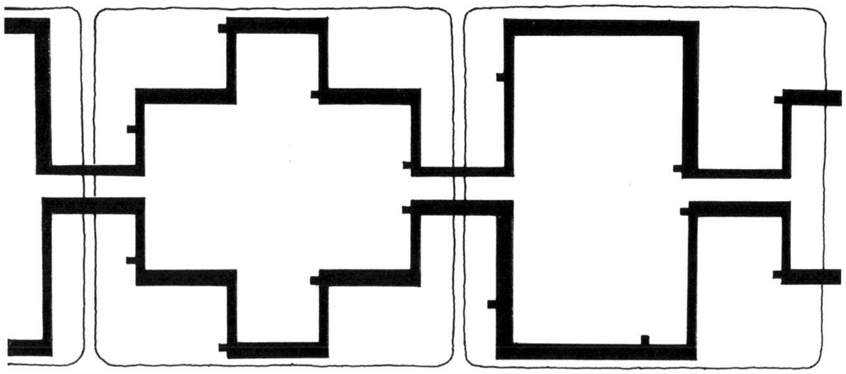

1. Le Corbusier, Ville Verte redans, 1931

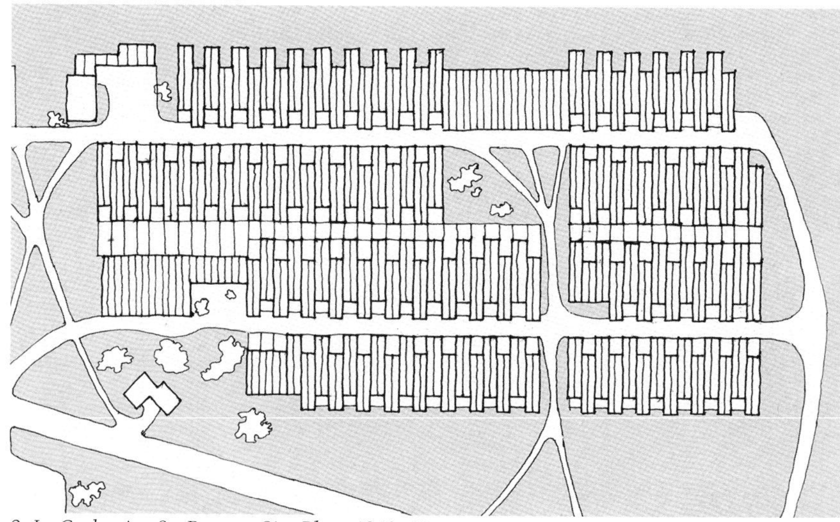

2. Le Corbusier, St. Baume, Site Plan, 1948–49

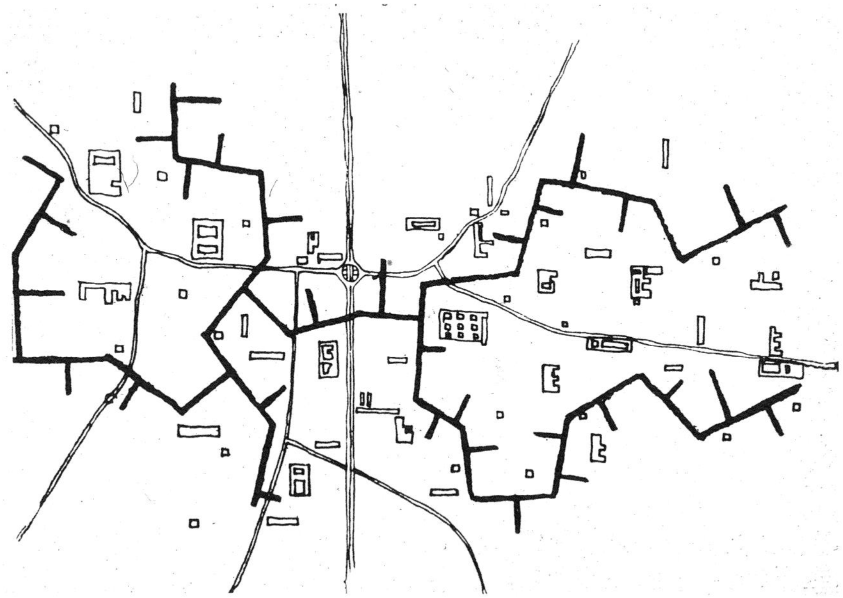

3. Allison and Peter Smithson, "Urban re-identification" diagram, 1952

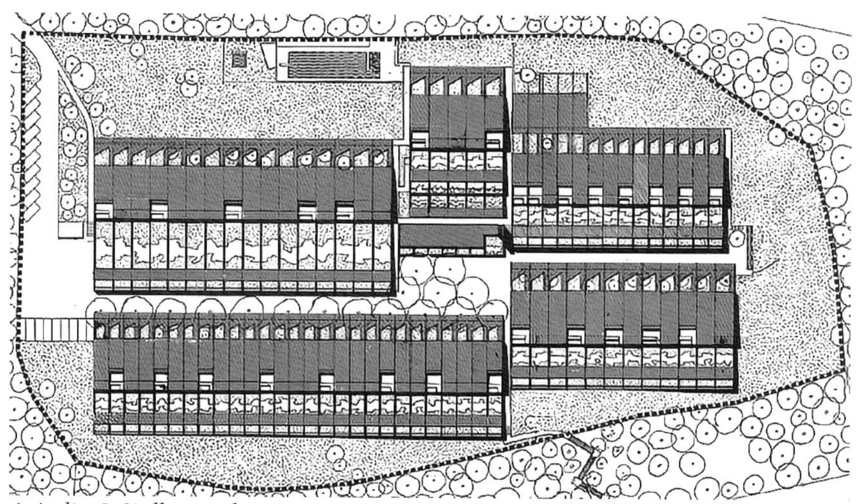

4. Atelier 5, Siedlung Halen, Berne, Switzerland, 1957–61

Team X Principles

The work and theories of Team X may be seen as both a critique and an extension of CIAM principles. In retrospect, however, their critique seems minor, and the continuity greater. The group's objections to CIAM principles centered around CIAM's reduction of urbanism to the four functions—living, working, recreation, and circulation—and the resultant monofunctional zoning. In contrast, Team X argued that cities should support change, and multifunctional activities. Their strategies for achieving this, however, were modifications of CIAM form types derived mostly from the work of Le Corbusier, and if the modernist city promoted by the Athens Charter suffered from the absence of a legible civic realm—of public space—then Team X was at least as inept in the provision of a tangible public realm. Obsessive object fixation—seeing every urban project as an architectural project no matter how large—and their blind rejection of the traditional city prevented them from achieving their own stated goals.

Team X Formal Strategies

Team X deployed three basic form strategies, all derived from Le Corbusier: the linear wall-building, low-rise grids or mats, and spine organizations. These were often combined. All were fundamentally anti-urban, and all mistook architecture for urban design. Consumed by the need for "mass housing," or what they referred to as "habitat," they produced vast architectural compositions on an unprecedented scale—still not solving "The Heart of the City" issue.

1. Candilis, Josic, and Woods, Toulouse University Plan, 1968

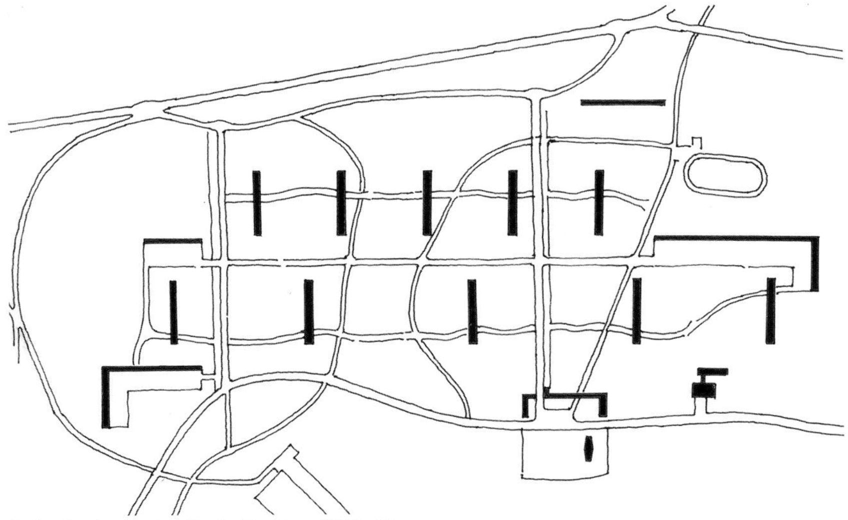

2. Le Corbusier, La Rochelle plan, 1945–46

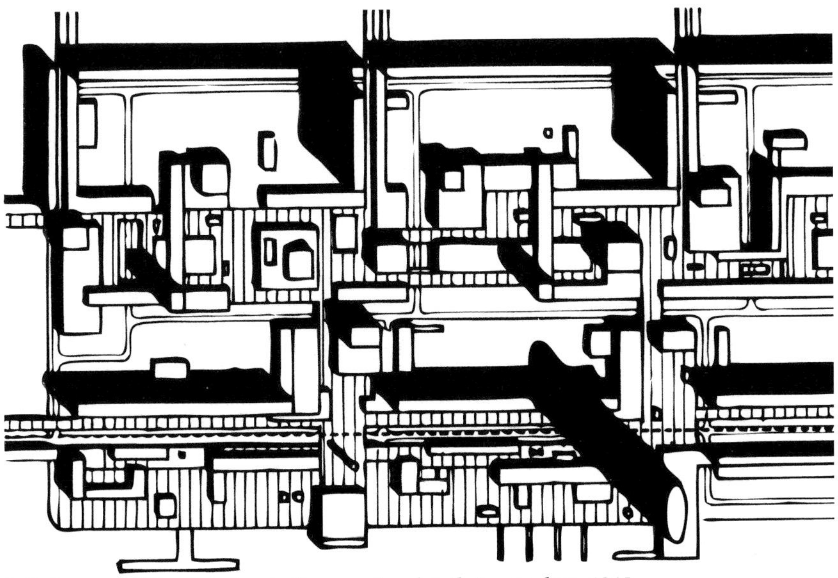

3. Bakema and Van Den Broek, Pampusplan detail, Amsterdam, 1965

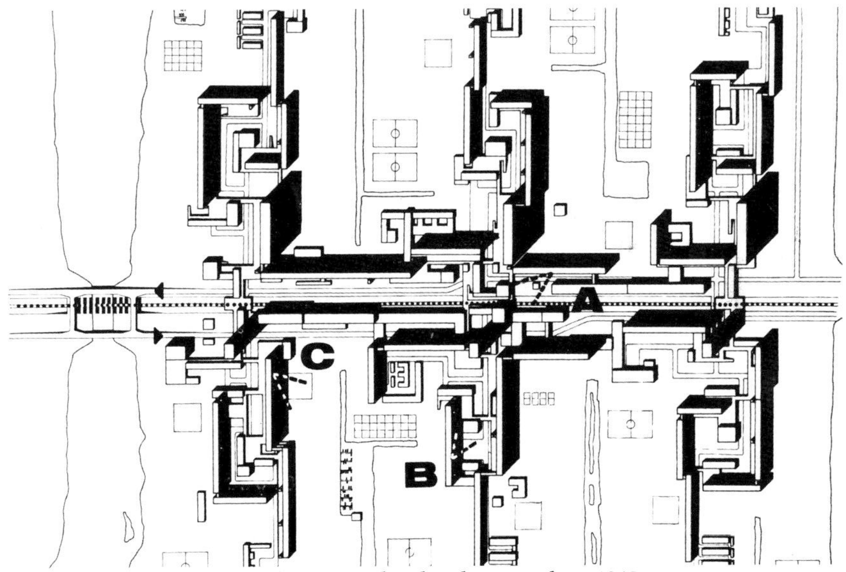

4. Bakema and Van Den Broek, Pampusplan detail, Amsterdam, 1965

Linear Wall-Buildings

The linear building networks developed by the Smithsons[24] and by Candilis, Josic, and Woods were angular networks of continuous slabs with "organic" implications of growth, change, and unpredictability. Like Le Corbusier's redans, they were based on the idea of the "street-in-the-sky," but they contained mixed uses on the lower levels, and often connected to low-rise elements at their extremities. Unlike Le Corbusier's redans, however, they did not have the capacity to define legible space. Consequently, the public areas are a confusing no-man's-land despite the infrastructure of continuous circulation.

Grids and Low-Rise Mats

Le Corbusier's townlike projects sponsored many low-rise, high-density projects such as Atelier 5's Siedlung Halen. In contrast to the angular networks, these projects exhibited rationalized characteristics of urban fabric and community. They also led to the exploration of grids and neighborhoods.

In addition to networks of wall-buildings, Candilis, Josic, and Woods also explored low-rise grids with vague implications of town plans with blocks and covered streets. Bakema on the other hand never made angular networks, but orthogonal mixes of high and low buildings organized into neighborhood units.

Spines

There was frequent discussion of infrastructure within Team X, and Bakema often utilized pedestrian or transit spines as an organizing device. Candilis, Josic, and Woods also used the idea of the spine in their plan for Bochum University, as did Jose Lluis Sert in his New Community plan in 1968.

Haupstadt Berlin Competition

Central Berlin was almost completely destroyed during the Second World War, and although postwar Germany was divided between east and west, the Berlin Wall was not yet constructed by 1957 when an international competition was held for the reconstruction of the central city.

The competition occurred as Team X was emerging from CIAM, and members of both groups submitted entries. The entries by Le Corbusier and the Smithsons offer a snapshot of postwar modernist town planning, and a contrast between CIAM and Team X principles.

Both projects completely abandoned any vestiges of the traditional city fabric, preserving only Schinkel's buildings and the axis of the Unter den Linden.

Le Corbusier's project employed the familiar CIAM principles of monofunctional segregation, elevated motorways, ground-level pedestrian circulation, continuous picturesque landscape, and free-standing object buildings.[25]

The Smithsons' proposed a continuous network of raised, angular, pedestrian decks intersected periodically by small-footprint towers. Vehicular circulation was at ground level.[26]

Given the perspective of over fifty years of hindsight, it is difficult not to regard both projects as naive and destructive.

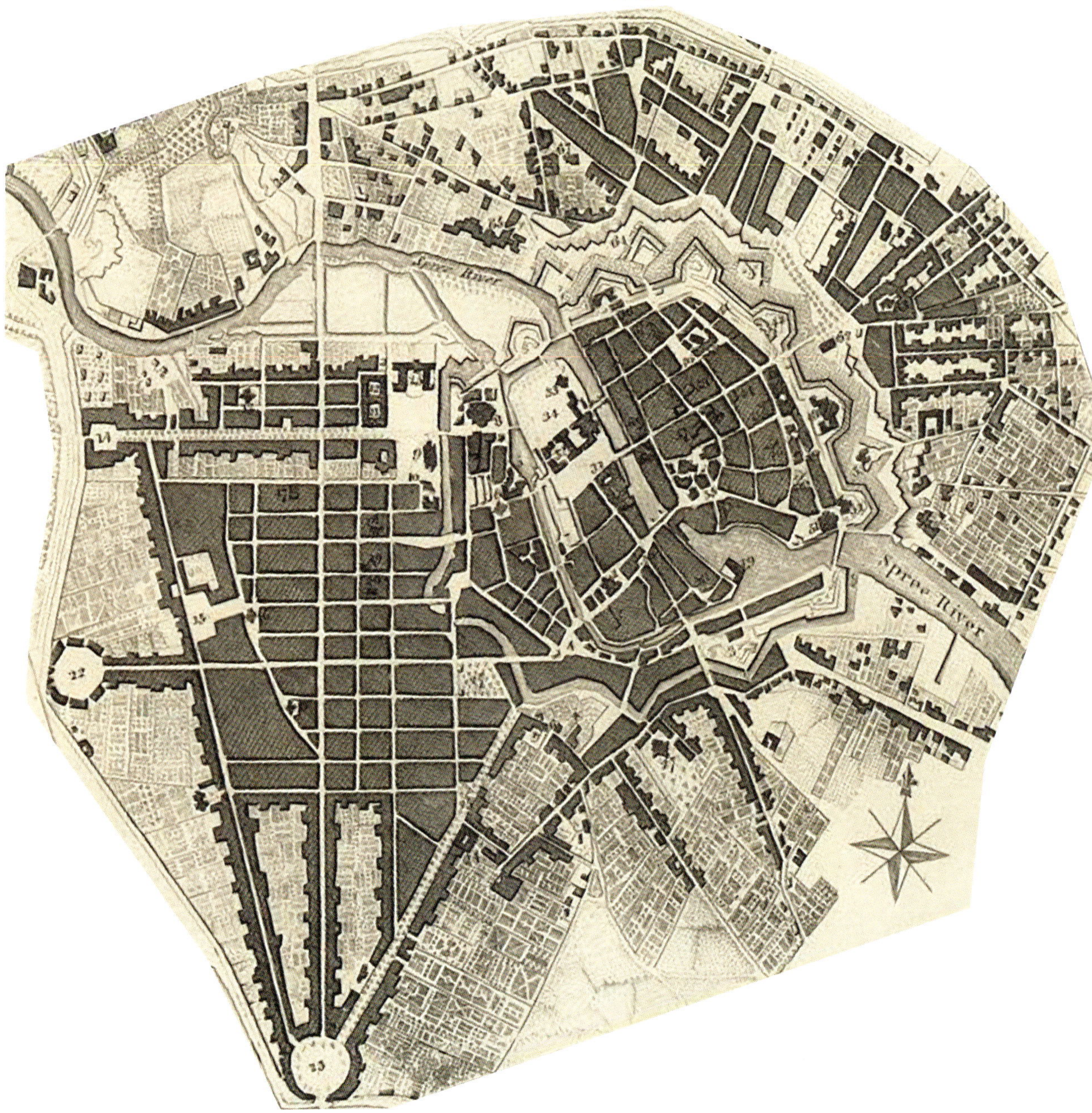

Stockdale Plan of Berlin, 1800

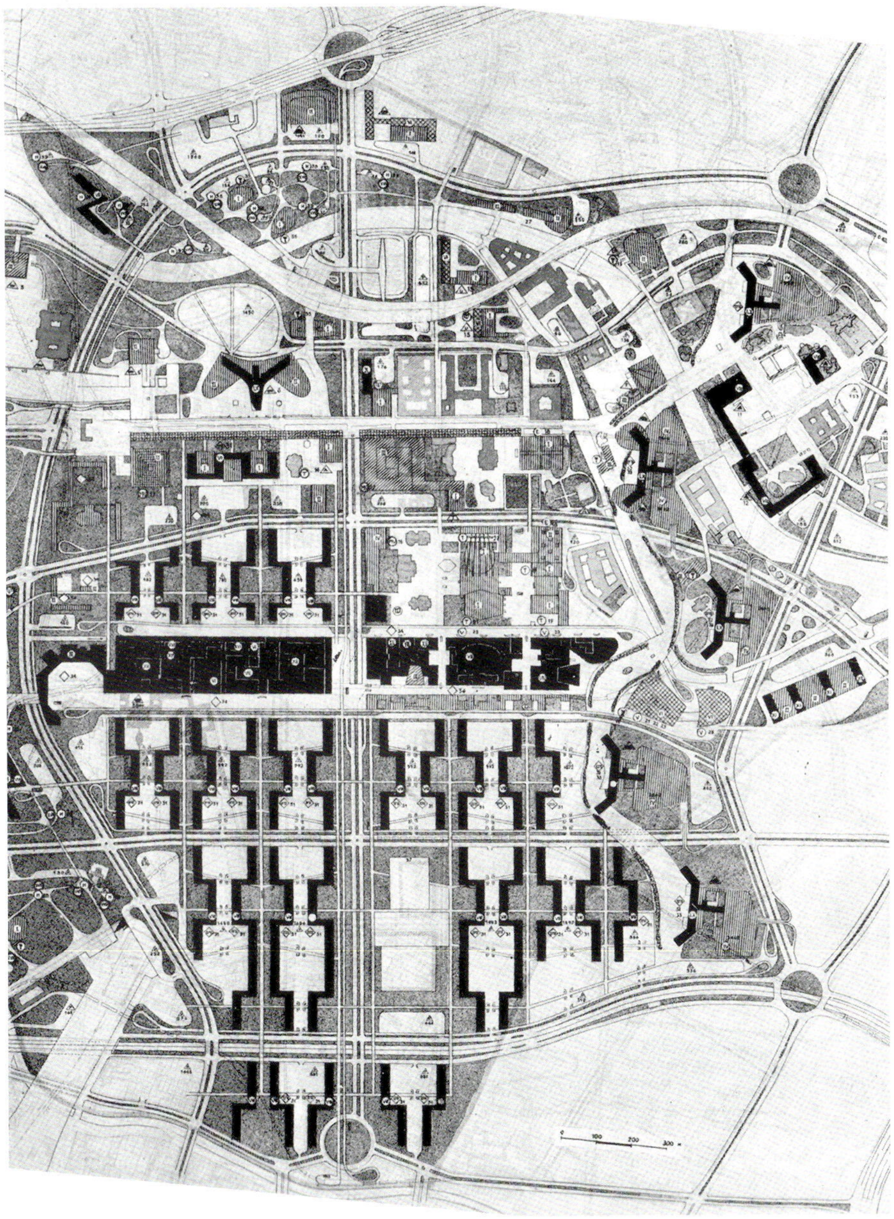

1. *Haupstadt Competition Plan, Le Corbusier, 1957*

2. *Haupstadt Competition Perspective, A. & P. Smithson*

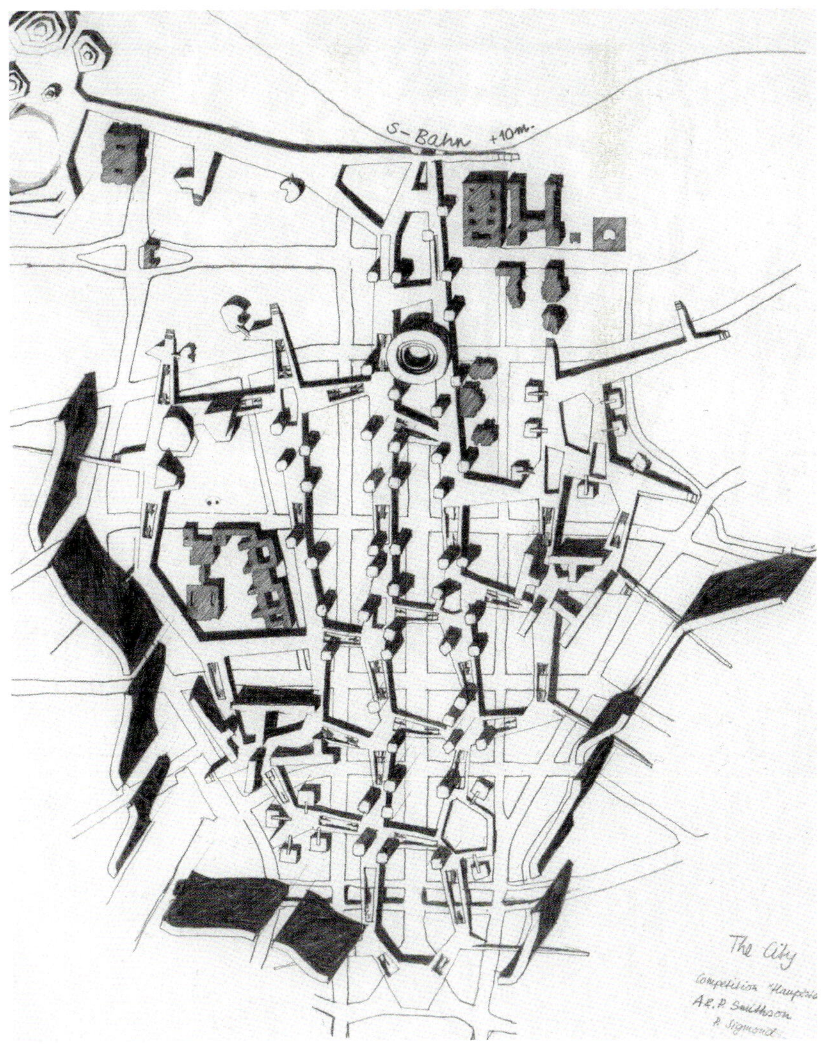

3. *Haupstadt Competition Plan, A. & P. Smithson, 1957*

1. *Edgar Chambless, Roadtown, 1910*

2. *Le Corbusier, Algiers, 1930*

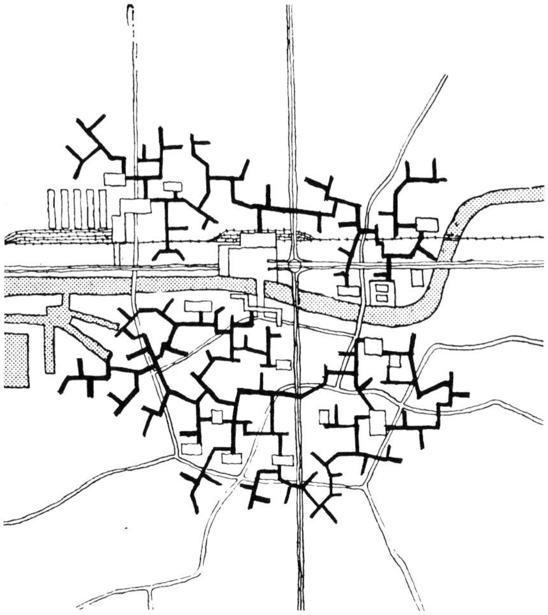

3. *A. & P. Smithson, "Cluster City" diagram, 1952*

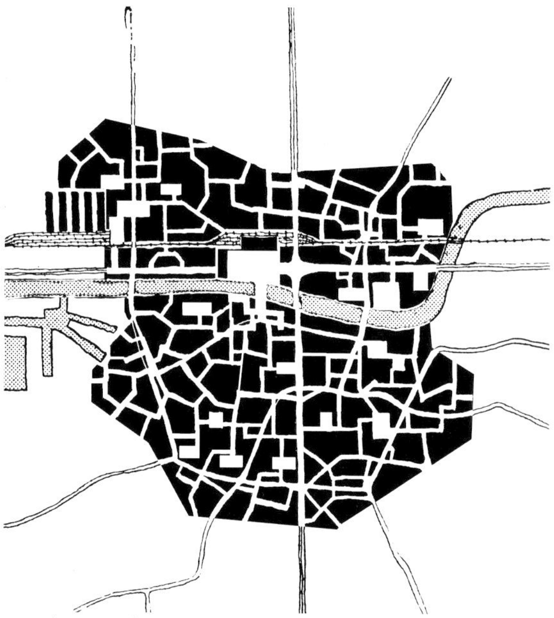

4. *Before, or after, "Cluster City," M. Dennis*

Cities and Streets

From the late nineteenth century, when town planners began to consider urban designs as large-scale architectural problems, the idea of the "building-as-a-street" was pervasive, as the space of the traditional urban street inverted to become a linear building. Michiel Brinkman's Spangen housing project of 1919–21 had an external access gallery, as did Le Corbusier's proposed Villa Immeubles blocks, and in the 1950s, the Smithsons transformed the idea into so-called streets-in-the-air.

5. *Golden Lane Housing montage*

The Golden Lane Housing Competition

At CIAM 9 in 1953, Alison and Peter Smithson proclaimed that "The problem of re-identifying man with his environment ... cannot be achieved by using historical forms of house-groupings, streets, squares, greens, etc., as the social reality they presented no longer exists." Instead, "we propose a multilevel city with residential 'streets-in-the-air.'"[27] Their "Cluster City" diagrams for the Golden Lane competition in 1952 could be seen as an inverted medieval city with its streets and squares turned into buildings.[28]

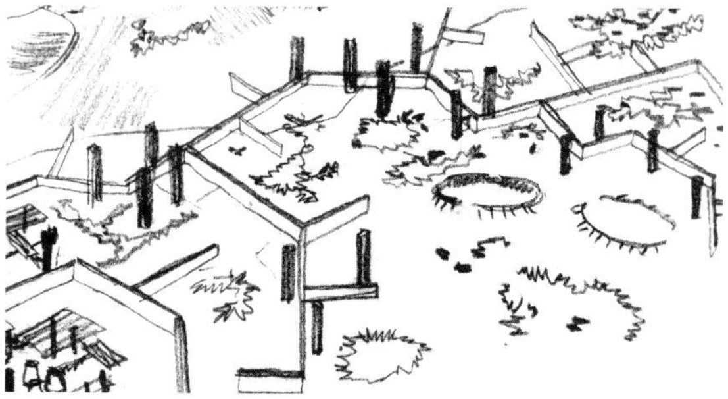

6. *Golden Lane Housing diagram, 1952*

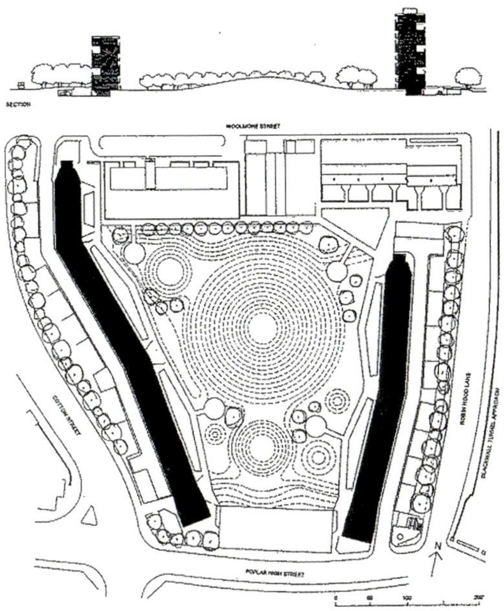

1. Robin Hood Gardens, site plan

2. View from the street

Robin Hood Gardens

The Smithsons used the idea of the "Cluster City" diagram as an angular network of raised decks in their Haupstadt Competition entry in 1957, but nothing was actually realized until their Robin Hood Gardens project, begun in the late 1960s and finished in 1972. Robin Hood Gardens did not form a continuous network, but did utilize exterior galleries as "streets-in-the-air." The project, for low-income immigrants, had problems from the beginning, including lack of maintenance, and is now threatened with demolition.[29]

3. Access gallery

4. Alison and Peter Smithson, Robin Hood Gardens

5. View from the court

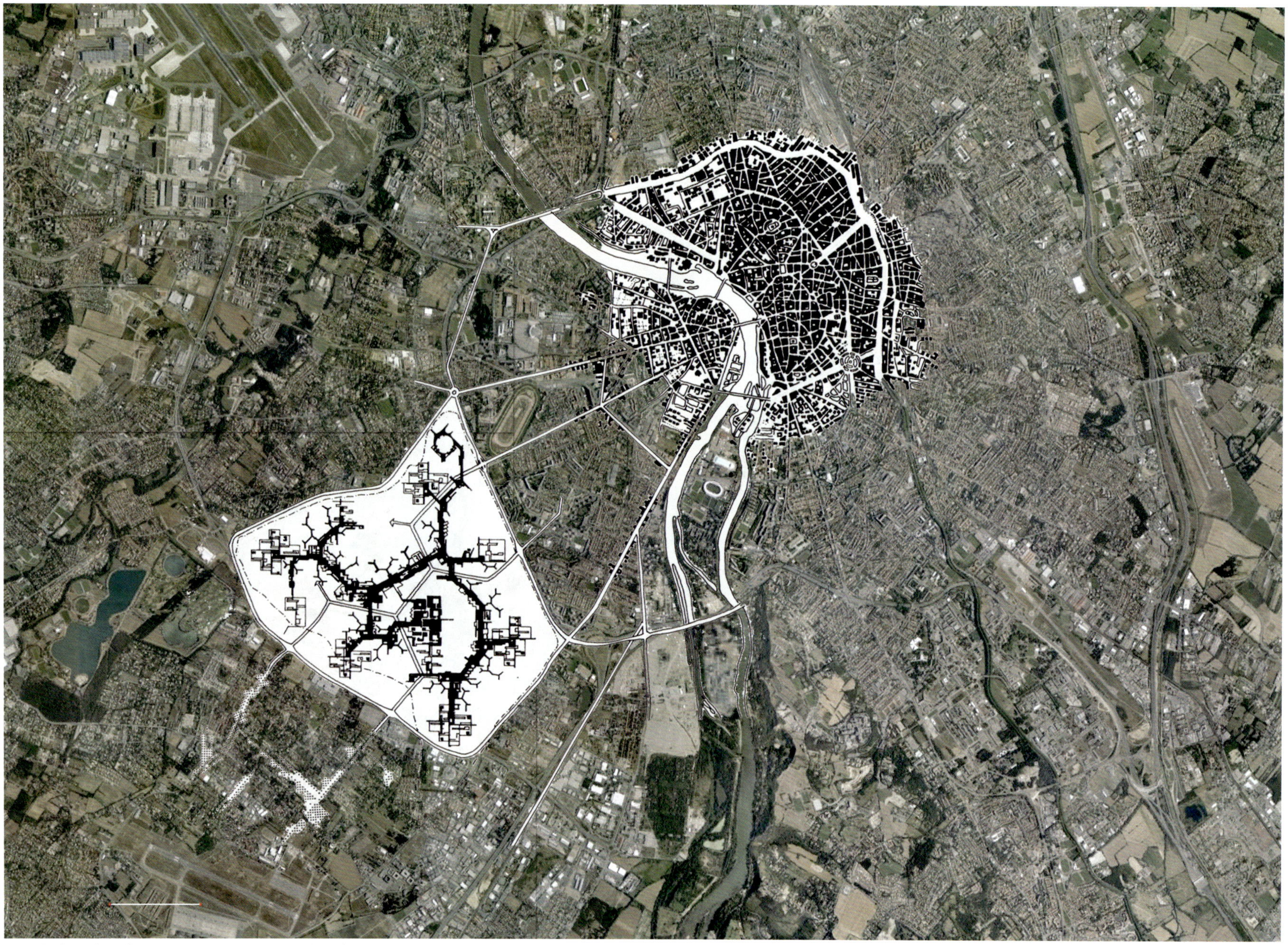

Aerial plan of Toulouse, France, superimposed with the plan of the historic core (upper right), and the plan for Toulouse Le Mirail (lower left), begun in 1961 as a winning competition entry by Georges Candilis, Alexis Josic, and Shadrach Woods

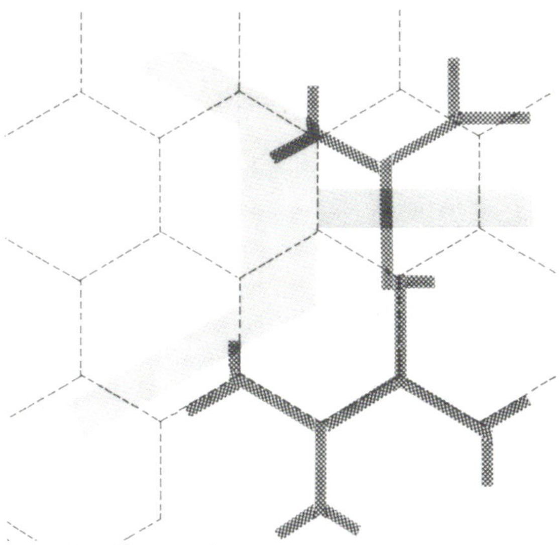

1. Idealized hexagonal network

2. Aerial view of the Bellefontaine neighborhood as constructed. In the foreground are the "patio villas"

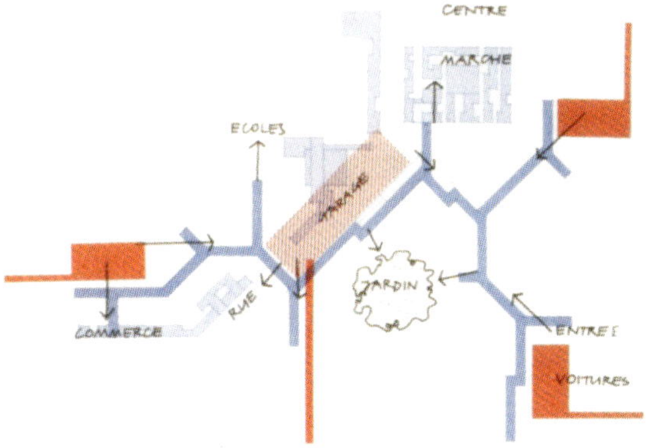

3. Concept sketch

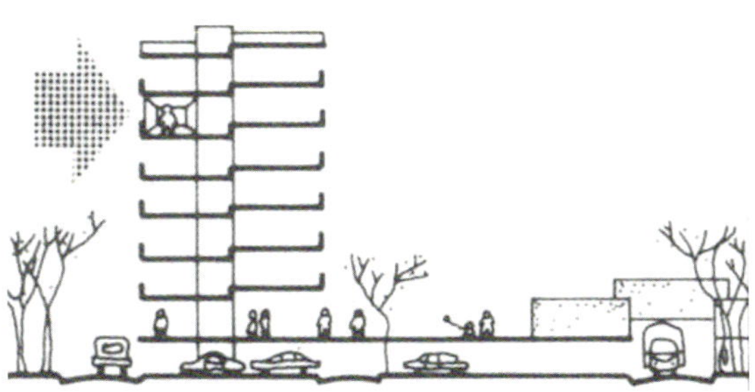

4. Section of "Stem" building

Candilis-Josic-Woods

In the early 1960s, Georges Candilis, Alexis Josic, and Shadrach Woods developed a more regular version of the angular network system outlined by the Smithsons in 1952. Candilis-Josic-Woods's hexagonal system was used for a competition in Bilbao, Spain, in 1962, and for their winning entry in the Toulouse Le Mirail competition for 100,000 inhabitants outside Toulouse, France, in 1961.[30] The competition project for Toulouse Le Mirail was enormous—equal in area to the historic city of Toulouse.

The primary structure of the plan was a hexagonal, treelike network of linear buildings of five, nine, or thirteen floors, with parking on the ground floor, covered by a continuous pedestrian deck containing public functions. The linear buildings—referred to as "Stems" by Shadrach Woods—stepped down in height toward their extremities, with low buildings at the ends, like clusters of leaves on the tree. After the competition, the interstitial areas were filled with mid-rise and courtyard housing, and other public buildings such as schools.

5. Bilbao Competition model

Toulouse Le Mirail Competition, plan, 1961

1. Plan of "Stem" buildings and clusters. Phase I is the right-hand portion of the plan

2. Plan of the pedestrian deck and clusters

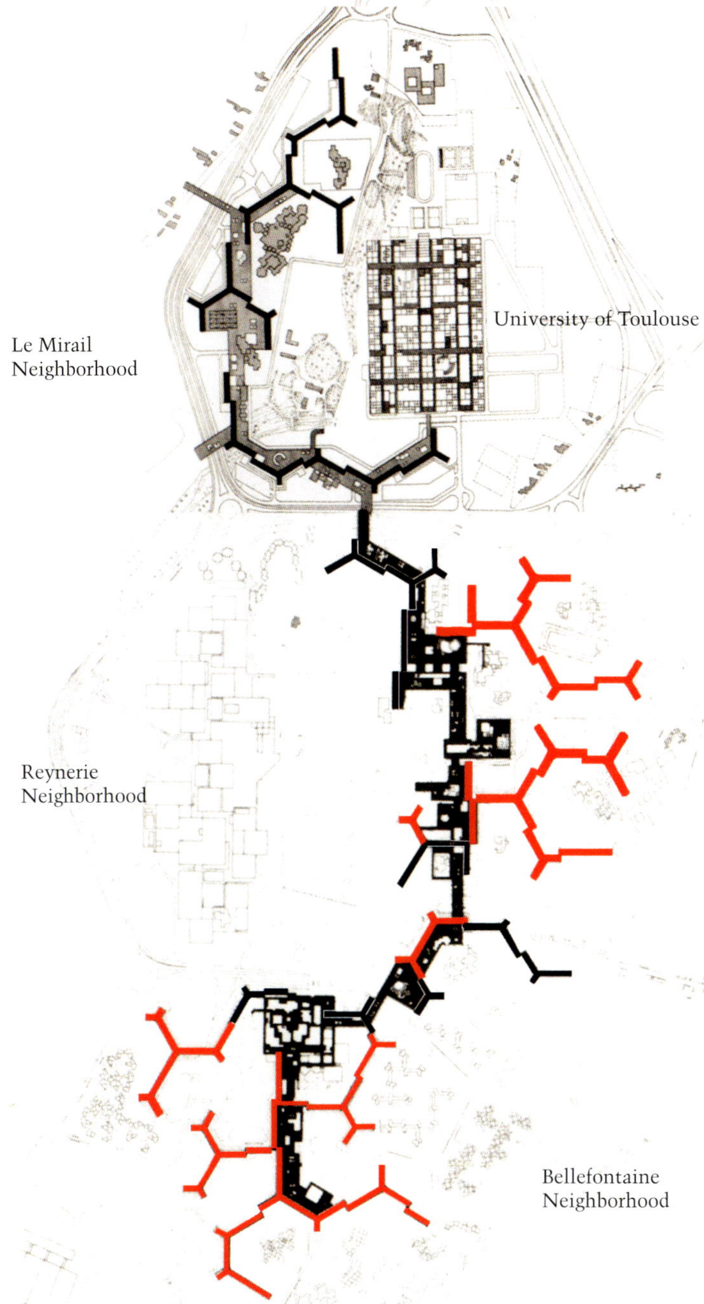

3. Plan of the Phase I design. Only the stem buildings in red were built

1. Aerial view of Toulouse Le-Mirail, Phase I, as constructed

Phase I: Reynerie and Bellefontaine

Phase I consisted of approximately half of the competition project, but only a portion of the Phase I design was actually built. Housing was built in the Reynerie and Bellefontaine neighborhoods, and Toulouse University in the Mirail neighborhood. Although continuous pedestrian decks were designed for Phase I, they were not built as continuous elements, thus isolating the housing blocks. The housing consisted of three types: high-rise apartment buildings, mid-rise apartments, and one-story courtyard houses.

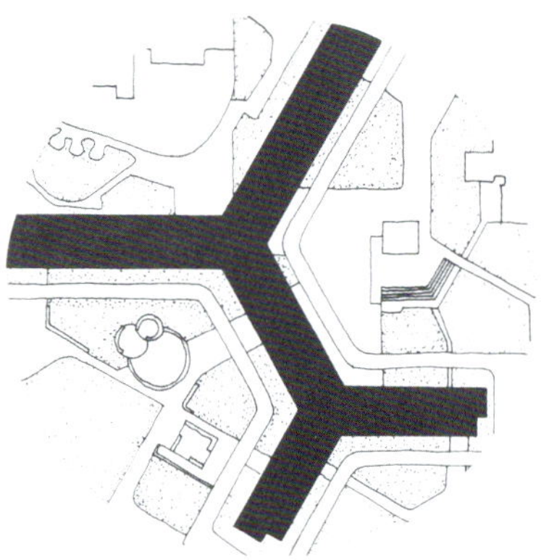

2. Partial plan of the stem building

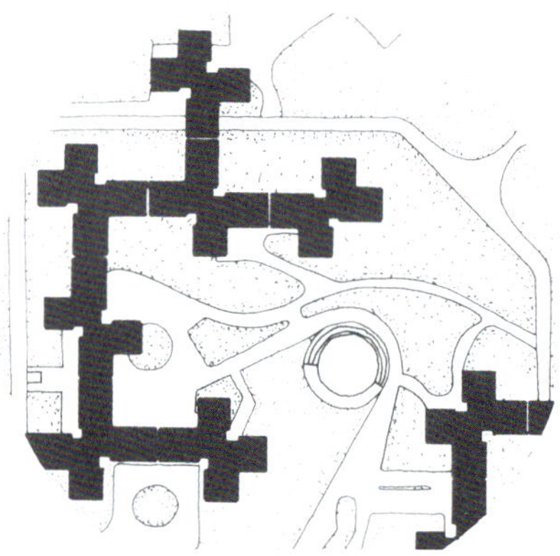

3. Plan of the mid-rise apartments

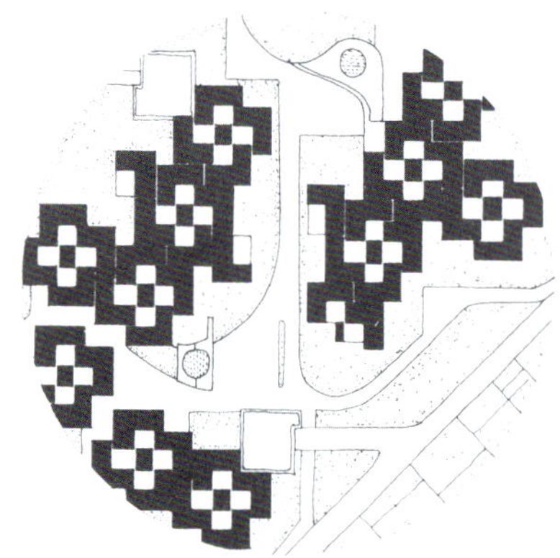

4. Plan of the "patio villas"

5. View of a stem building

6. Mid-rise apartment buildings

7. The "patio villas" are one-story houses for families

Demolition

Toulouse Le Mirail housed low-income immigrants isolated from the city. The project gradually deteriorated, and crime became a major problem, especially in the garages and public areas. As a result, the authorities have demolished large sections of the stem buildings, decks, and garages, thereby reducing the remaining buildings to isolated fragments in a suburban landscape, and eliminating any vestige of the original concept. Contrary to Team X theories, it should be no surprise that urban design as consistent architectural mega-structure could not be accomplished or flexibly sustained.

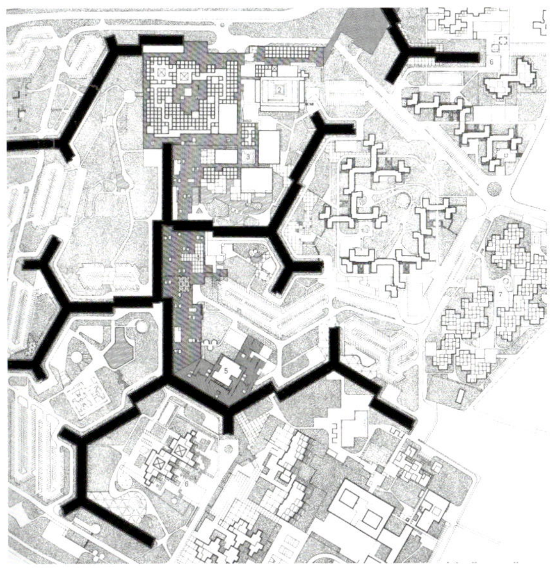

2. Plan of Bellefontaine before demolition

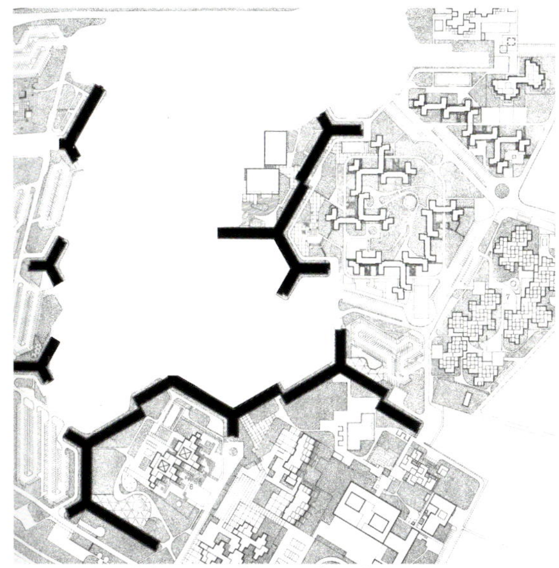

3. Plan of Bellefontaine showing demolition

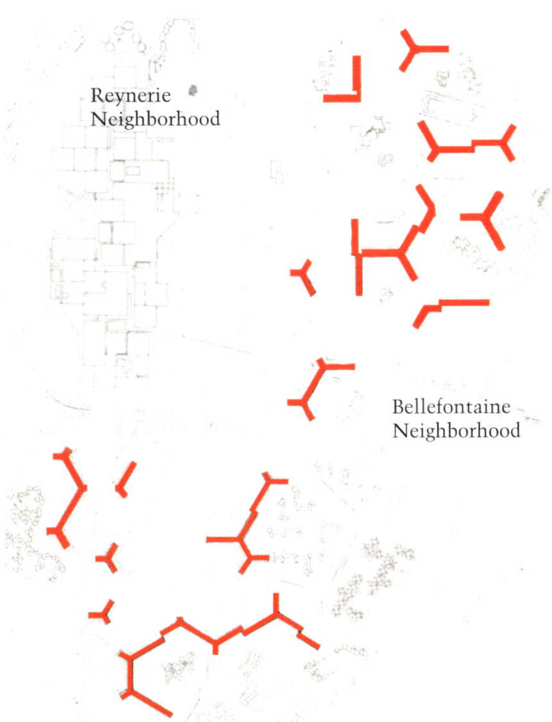

1. Plan of the Reynerie and Bellefontaine stem buildings after demolition

4. Aerial view of the Reynerie and Bellefontaine neighborhoods after demolition

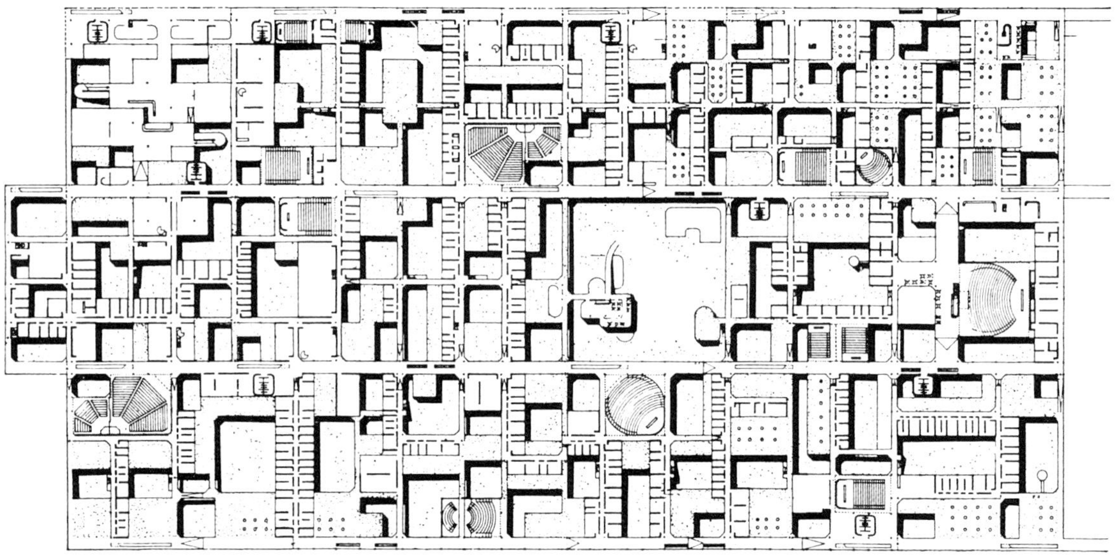

1. Candilis–Josic–Woods, Berlin Free University, plan, 1963–73

2. Berlin Free University, model

Grids

By the early 1960s, the pervasive influence of Le Corbusier's village-like projects and Atelier 5's Siedlung Halen reached Team X—in particular Candilis-Josic-Woods—and they began to experiment with town-like grids and "mat buildings."[31]

Berlin Free University

In 1963, Candilis-Josic-Woods won the competition for the new Free University of Berlin.[32] Their scheme was a low-rise mat-building perforated by open courtyards and organized on a grid. The overall plan was similar to that of a Bastide town, except that the whole plan was designed at one time and was pedestrian only.

Even though the project was completely designed, the circulation and structural systems were intended to allow for flexibility and change. Wall panels could be removed, for example, and rearranged in order to reconfigure the plan.

As executed, and ultimately changed, the project is considerably different from the competition plan.

Frankfurt

The area in front of Frankfurt Cathedral was completely destroyed in World War II. In 1963 Candilis-Josic-Woods entered a competition for the reconstruction of the area. Rather than reconstruct the medieval pattern, they proposed a continuous gridded mat of square blocks approximating the limits of the previous urban fabric.[33]

3. Candilis–Josic–Woods, Frankfurt, model, 1963

4. Frankfurt Cathedral area, prewar plan

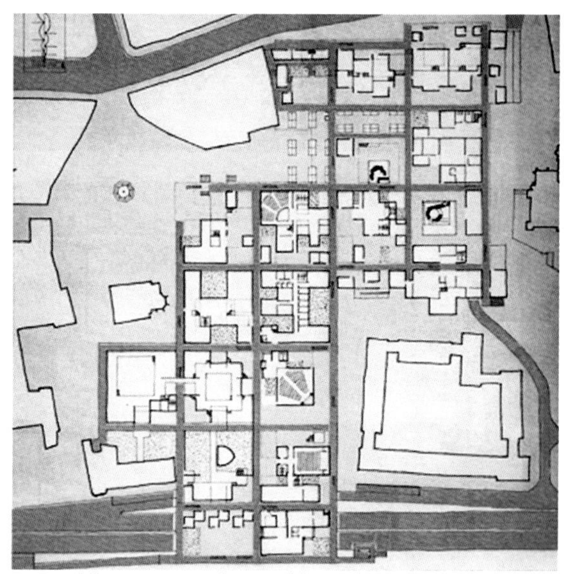

5. Candilis–Josic–Woods, Frankfurt, plan, 1963

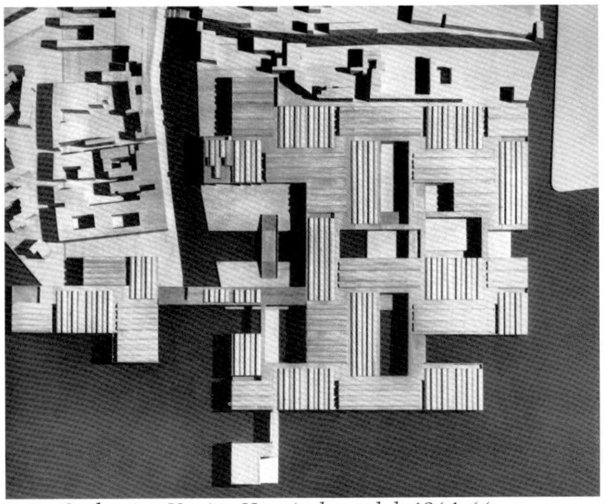

1. Le Corbusier, Venice Hospital, model, 1964–66

Venice Hospital

According to Guillaume Jullian de la Fuente, Le Corbusier sent him to a meeting of Team X to find out what they were doing. When Jullian returned, he said: "Monsieur Le Corbusier, they are making grids." To which Le Corbusier responded: "Well Jullian, we will show them how to make a grid."[34] The Venice Hospital project followed. Jullian completed the drawings after Le Corbusier's death in 1966.

2. Candilis-Josic-Woods, Toulouse University, 1968

3. Toulouse University, model, 1968

4. Candilis-Josic-Woods, Bochum University Competition model, 1962

Toulouse University

The housing projects designed for the Mirail neighborhood of Toulouse Le Mirail were not built, but in 1968, Candilis-Josic-Woods designed a gridded university for this area.[35] The project was similar to the original plan for Berlin Free University in that a network of covered walkways connected blocks of buildings and open courtyards. This project was executed.

Spines

The 1962 Candilis–Josic–Woods competition entry for Bochum University was not a straight spine scheme, but an irregular one.[36] A central sequence moved uphill, forming the backbone for a series of "fingers" and secondary streets spreading into the landscape like a low-rise town. If built, daily circulation and service might have been seriously difficult.

1. *Bijlmermeer, begun in 1966, existing plan detail, 1:20,000*

2. *Bijlmermeer, aerial view before partial demolition*

The Netherlands

After the Second World War, the Netherlands embarked on a massive campaign to rebuild destroyed cities, such as Rotterdam, and provide low-cost housing for immigrants. In Amsterdam this housing development took place well beyond the city core. The most well-known and controversial estate was Bijlmermeer, begun in 1966 southeast of Amsterdam. The primary architectural typology was high-rise slab buildings in a hexagonal pattern similar to Toulouse Le Mirail. The project has been viewed as problematic, and many of the high-rise buildings have been demolished.

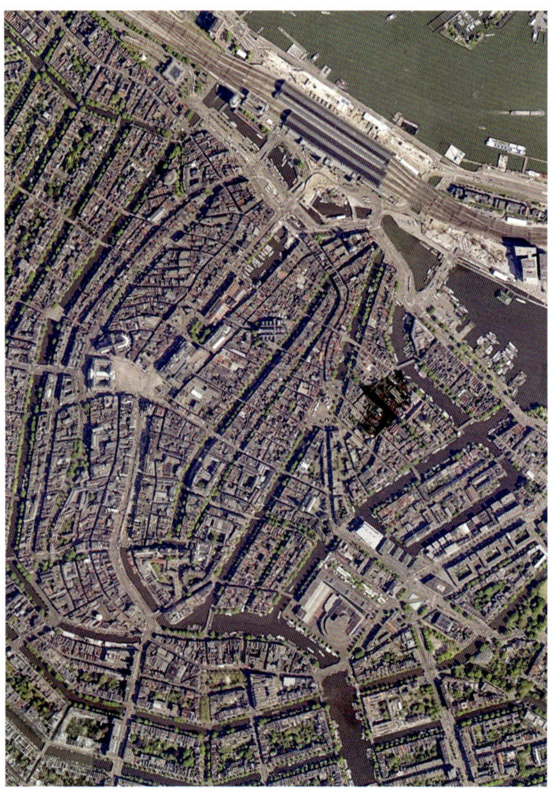

3. *Central Amsterdam, aerial plan, 1:20,000*

4. *Aerial view of central Amsterdam*

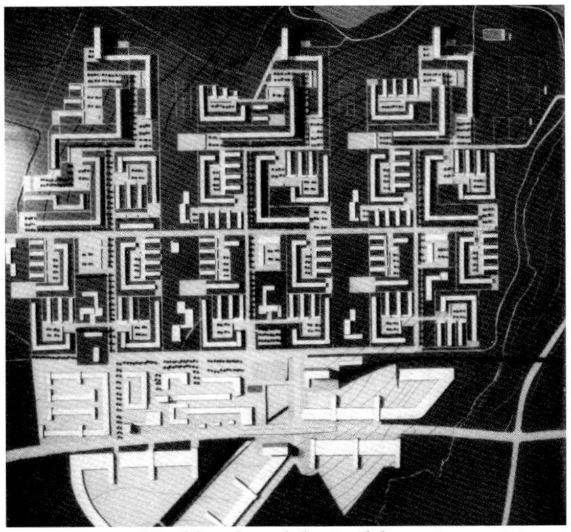

1. Bakema and Stokla, plan of the Steilshoop Competition entry, 1961

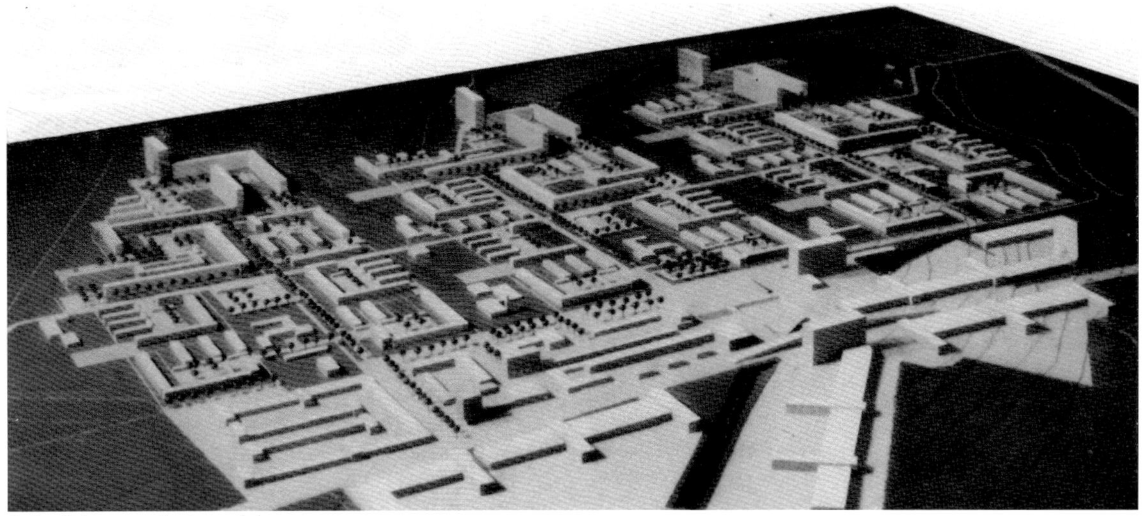

2. Steilshoop project, model

Bakema

Jaap Bakema never used angular networks of buildings like those of Bijlmermeer, the Smithsons, and Candilis–Josic–Woods, but like his Team X colleagues, he did see urban design as large-scale architectural composition. Rather than continuous linear buildings, he favored "neighborhood units" as a blend of architectural typologies: towers, slabs, and low-rise housing. These units were always rectangular and repetitive, often organized along a circulation spine.

The 1961 Steilshoop, Hamburg competition entry by Bakema and Stokla is illustrative.[37] Like a "domesticated" CIAM scheme, three sectors of housing alternate with fingers of open space. Each sector is divided into neighborhoods and connected to public facilities along a major circulation route. Similar characteristics form the 1962–72 't Hool estate in Eindhoven.[38]

3. Van den Broek and Bakema, Aerial view of 't Hool estate

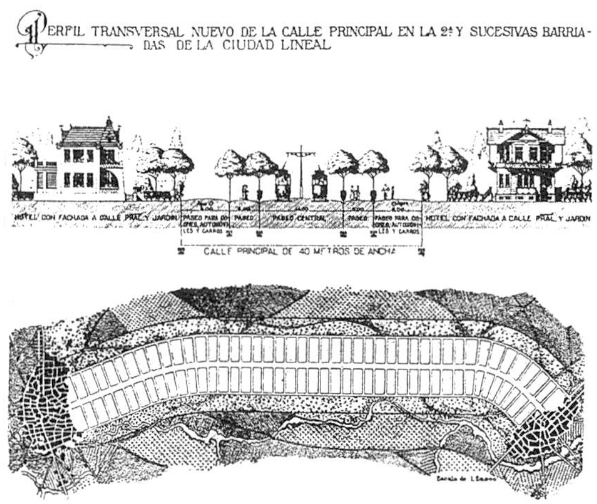

1. Soria y Mata's Linear City diagram

LINEAR "CITIES"

Infrastructure has been an integral part of cities at least since the Etruscans, but in the late nineteenth century infrastructure (and its street) began to be overtly exploited as a form determinant. Arturo Soria y Mata is repeatedly cited for his "Linear City" proposal of 1882, which was intended to replace the city-as-center-and-periphery with an infrastructure framework to connect existing cities. But Soria y Mata's proposal was not a city at all, but a boulevard lined with detached houses.[39]

In 1960, a similar argument was made by Kenzo Tange with his Tokyo Bay housing project.[40] In this case, a ladder of circulation was deployed to support branches of housing and to connect the two sides of Tokyo Bay. The framework was intended to allow flexibility and change, but like other megastructure projects of the 1960s, investment and implementation were prohibitive.

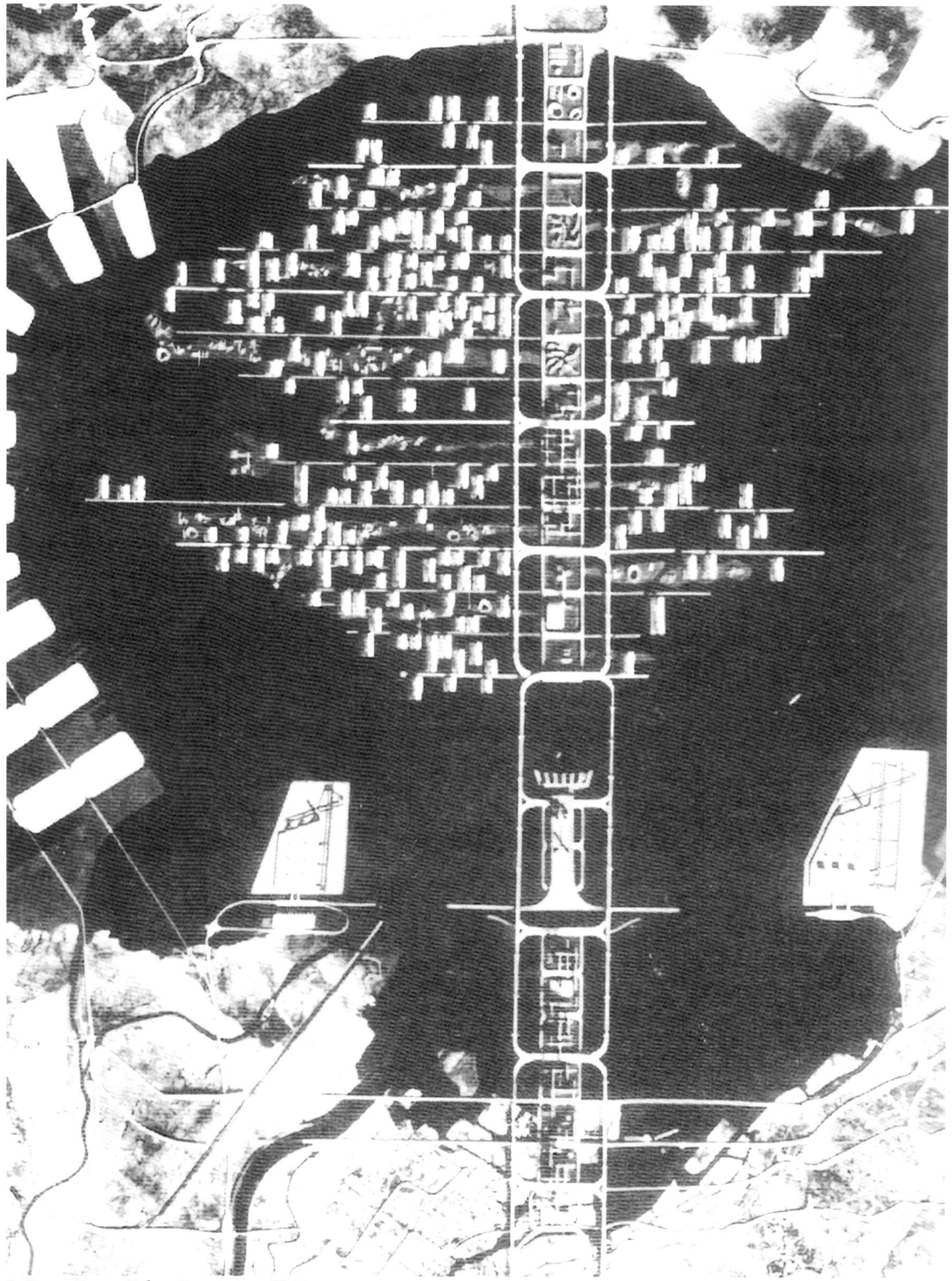

2. Kenzo Tange, Tokyo Bay project, 1960

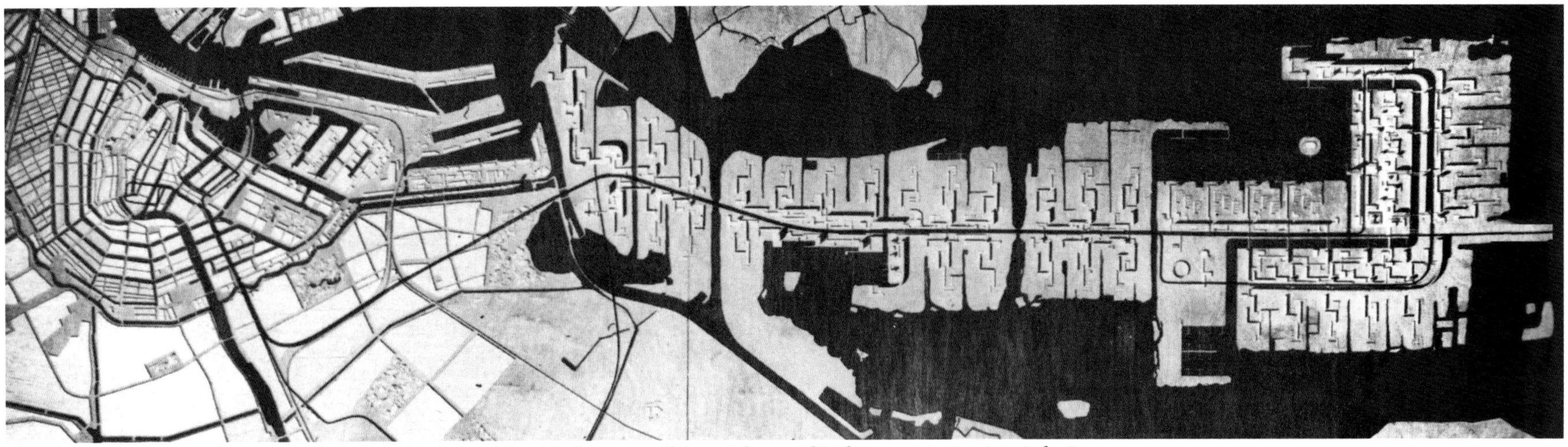

1. Model image showing the Pampusplan project's relationship with the center of Amsterdam, and its linear projection into Lake Ij

Pampusplan, Amsterdam, 1965

Jaap Bakema and Johannes Van den Broek designed the Pampus extension for Amsterdam in 1965 as a reaction to the city's growing population and need for residential areas.[41] The plan extends into the shallow areas of Lake Ij, connecting man-made islands by way of a central transportation artery. The plan's formal basis can be described as linear, although it attempts to create moments of enclosure around public and commercial areas.

The plan includes a variety of building scales, programs, and configurations organized as neighborhood units with interstitial green spaces. A highway and a high-speed monorail form the spine of the composition.

2. Importance was placed on the housing units' access to open space and the lake

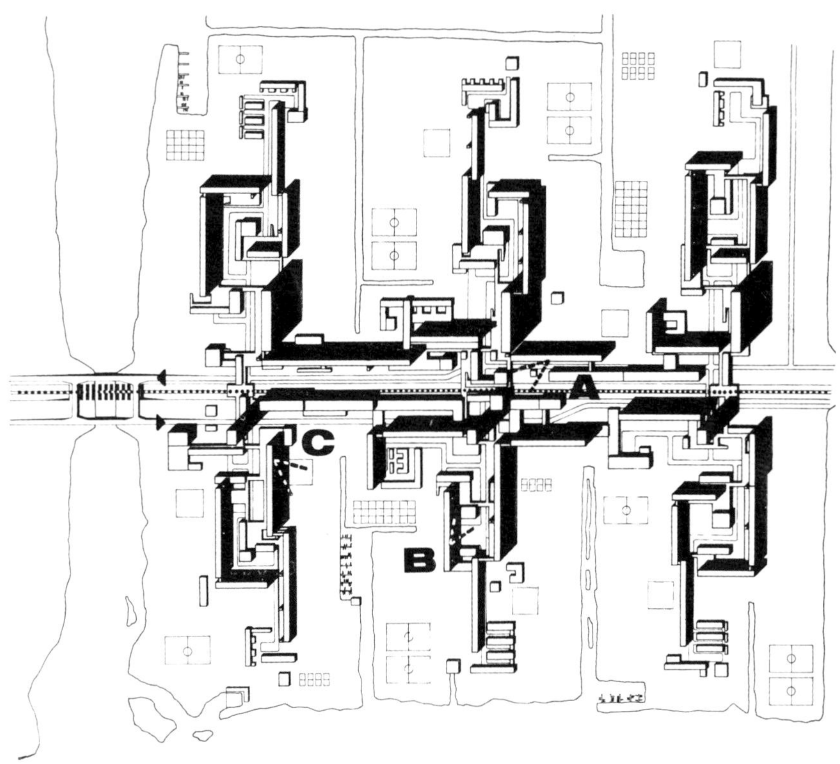

3. Plan of a neighborhood unit, showing the "central artery" (A), "the neighborhood" (B), and open space (C)

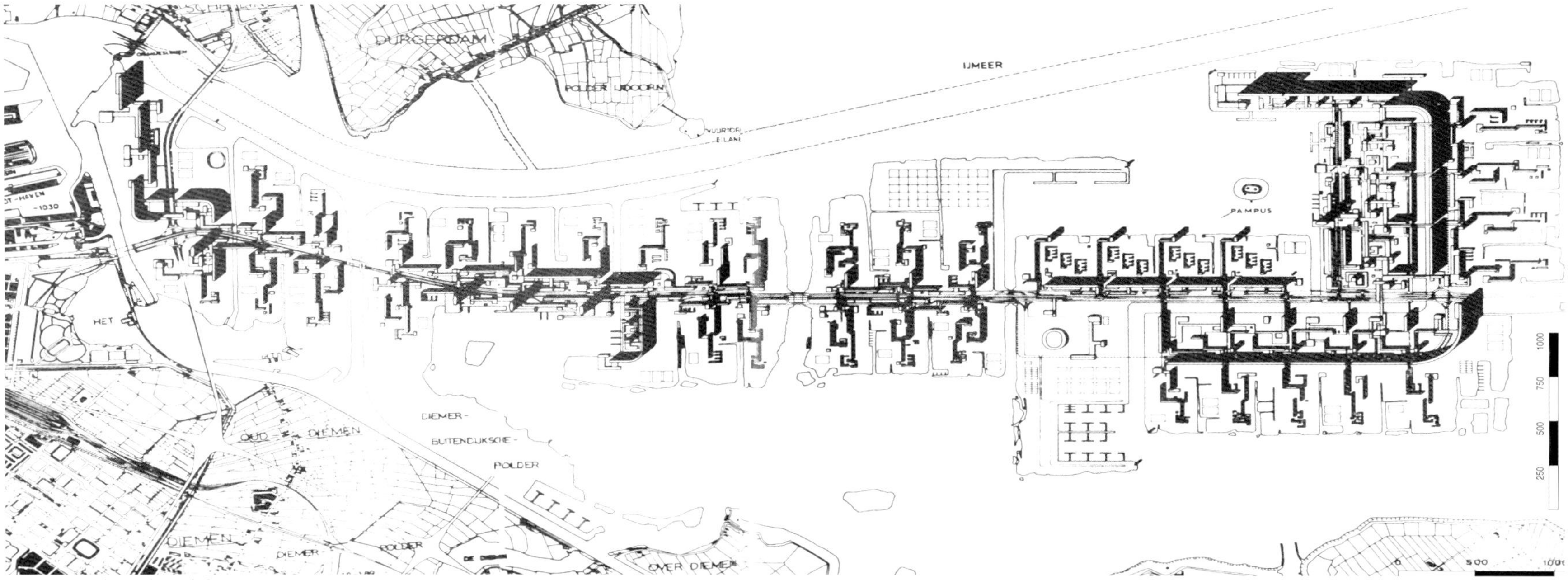

1. Pampusplan, plan of the project

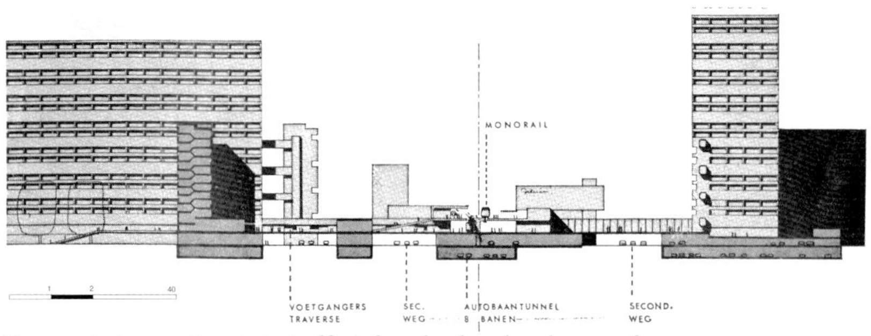

2. Transportation section. Auto traffic is largely placed underground

3. Pampusplan model view showing the transportation artery

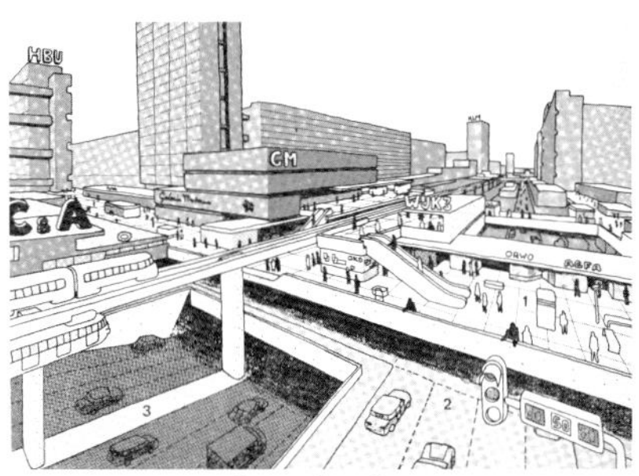

4. Transport node and pedestrian areas

5. Pampusplan, model view looking east

Tel Aviv City Center Competition

Bakema's formal repertoire is illustrated well by both the 1965 Pampusplan for Amsterdam and the 1962 Tel Aviv City Center Competition. Both projects are composed of large, linear wall-buildings, lower linear buildings, slabs, and mat-housing. Multi-level circulation spines provide structure, but the compositions are architectural mega-structures of heroic proportions

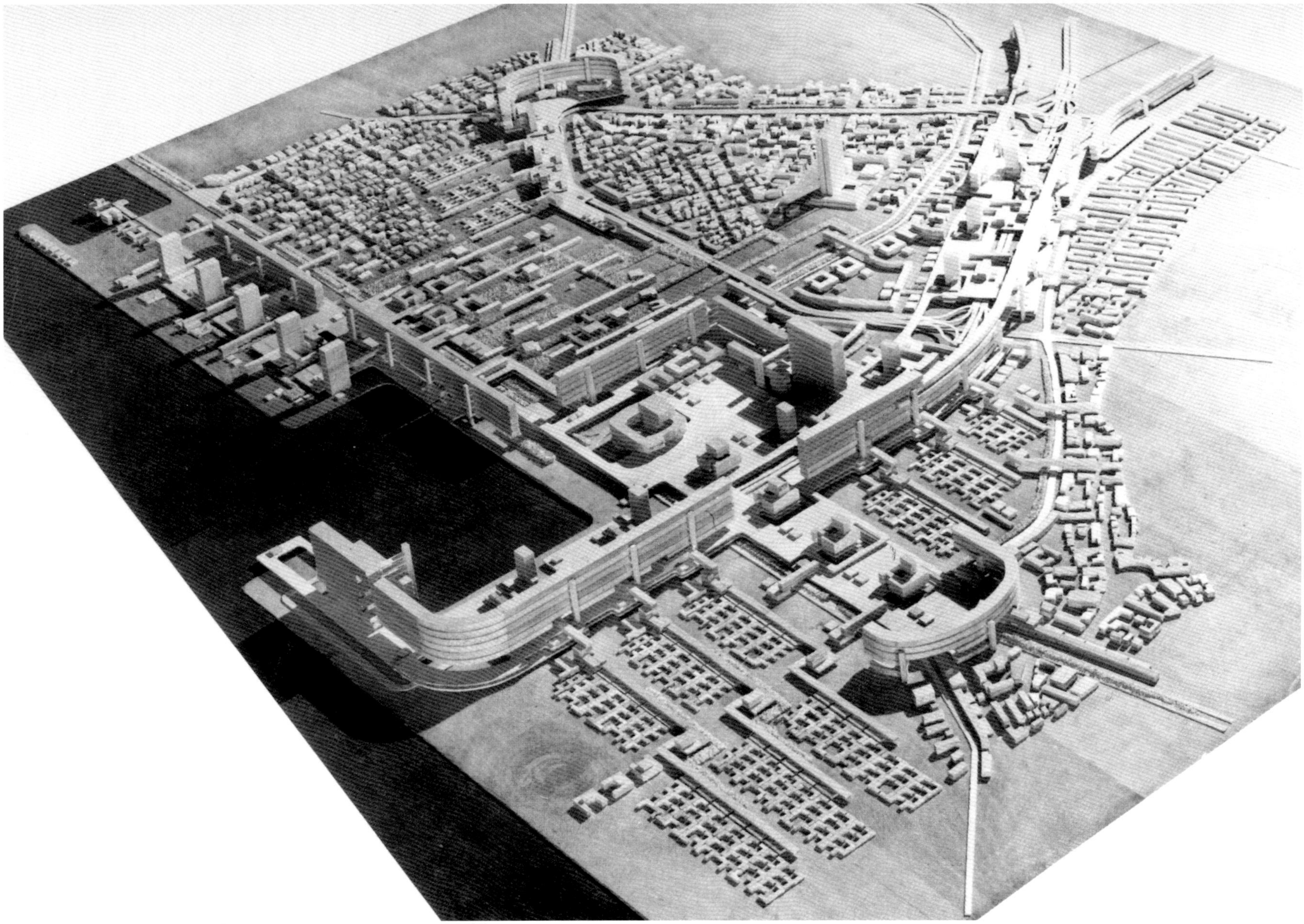

Van den Broek and Bakema, Tel Aviv City Center Competition, model, 1962

Team X in America

With the exception of Shadrach Woods (who lived in Europe), all of the members of Team X were either Europeans or at least non-Americans. Thus, Team X was fundamentally a European movement with little influence in the United States. Gropius and Sert had introduced CIAM precepts at Harvard, but Team X was far less known.

Mathias Ungers had been a popular visiting critic at Cornell University in the 1960s, along with a steady stream of Swiss and English architects, and he became the chair of the Department of Architecture at Cornell University in the fall of 1968.[42] This was a period of social turmoil and confusion. Vietnam, race, institutional authority, and generational conflict conspired to make architectural discussion and production more difficult. Student demonstrations closed Cornell University early in the spring of 1969, and again in the spring of 1970, because of the US invasion of Cambodia. It was into this milieu that Ungers invited twelve members of Team X to Cornell to lecture and teach studios during the academic year 1971–72.[43] Many of their contributions had to do with social issues, and raised pedestrian decks enjoyed a renaissance of sorts, but architecturally and urbanistically their impact was generally small.

A different architectural and urban sensibility had been developing in America since the 1950s. In contrast to the urban theories of CIAM and Team X, a focus on the traditional urbanism of cities was replacing large-scale architecture-as-urban-design.

III. THE POSTINDUSTRIAL CITY: 1975–Present

The reality of modernist city principles became visible in the first decades after World War II. The reconstruction of European cities began, and urban centers in the United States were destroyed under the guise of "urban renewal," and rebuilt according to modernist principles. The Highway Act provided further urban destruction and facilitated suburban sprawl.

Reaction to the social and formal results of modernism came quickly, and by 1975 a new urban sensibility was emerging. Architects and town planners looked to the long-standing centers of their disciplines for guidance in the recovery of the city and urban design. Preservation became a force, as did "advocacy planning." Both were bottom-up resistance to the top-down destruction of urban renewal.

Multifunctional neighborhoods and urban fabric of blocks, streets, and squares again became the elements of urban design, and a public realm was reestablished through a legible structure of civic space. The illustration of architectural character continued, but would rapidly become an issue of "style."

More recently, continued urban growth and ecological issues have expanded the discourse. Indeed, these promise to be major issues in the twenty-first century.

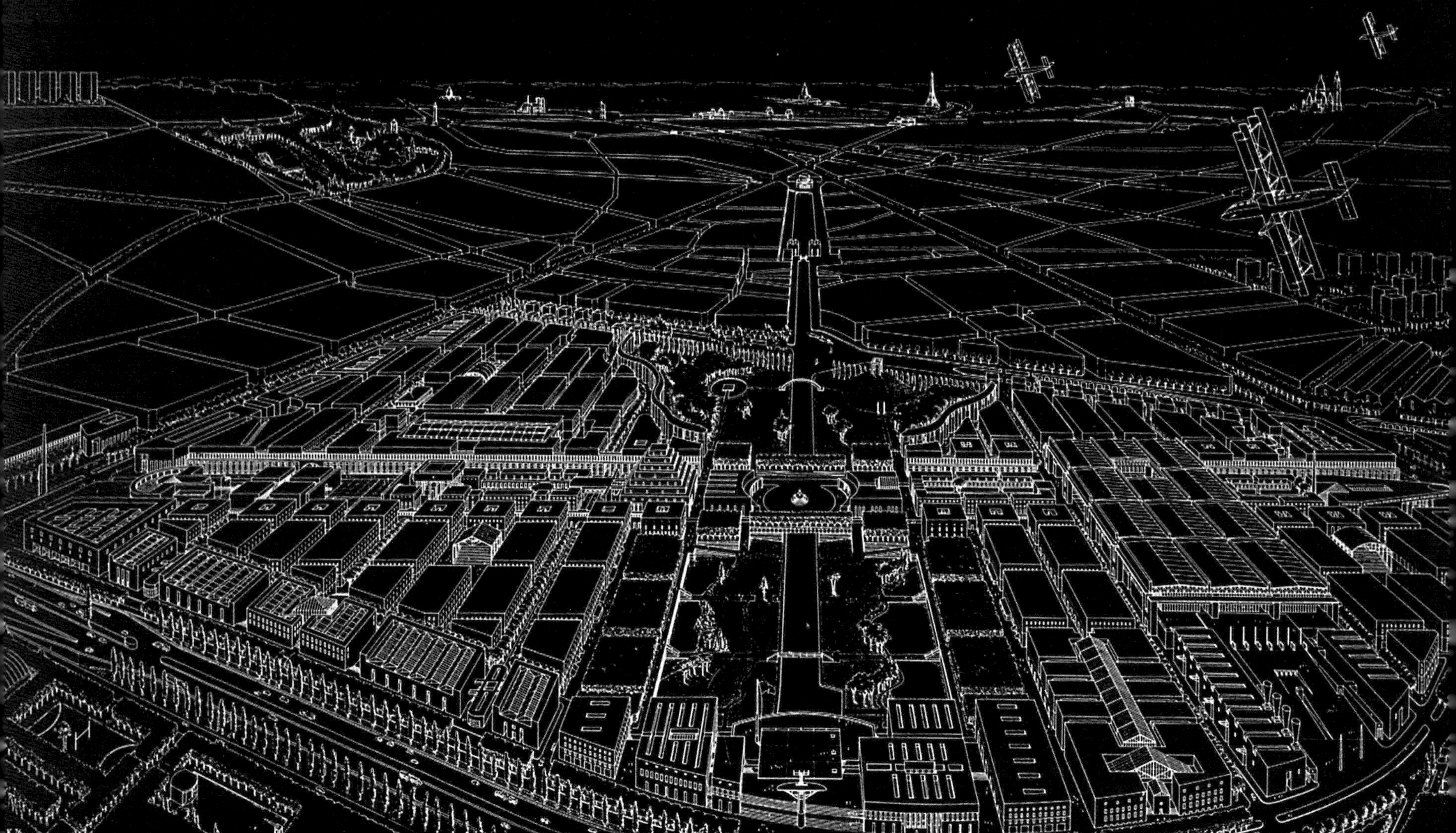

Leon Krier, aerial perspective of La Villette

The Recovery of the City: 1975–2000

By the time Team X ended their discussions in 1981, a completely different urban sensibility had developed—one that stood in stark contrast and resistance to the precepts of CIAM and Team X—the recovery of the city. This new sensibility began to emerge in the 1960s, and in the beginning, theory preceded practice.

Colin Rowe's essays began to be published in the *Architectural Review* in 1947, beginning with "The Mathematics of the Ideal Villa." Jane Jacobs' *The Death and Life of Great American Cities* appeared in 1961; Aldo Rossi's *L'architettura della città*, in 1966; and Robert Venturi's *Complexity and Contradiction in Architecture*, in 1966.

In the 1970s three related urban design positions emerged, all engaged in the study of the traditional city: the rationalists in Europe (Aldo Rossi, the Krier brothers, et al.); the Cornell School (Colin Rowe, et al.); and the populists (Denise Scott Brown, et al. at the University of Pennsylvania). Rob Krier's *Stadtraum* (*Urban Space*) appeared in 1975; Colin Rowe and Fred Koetter's *Collage City*, in 1978; and Denise Scott Brown's essays in the mid-1970s.

Colin Rowe established the Urban Design Studio at Cornell University in 1963, beginning a twenty-year research agenda exploring architecture and the city. In a certain sense the studio sought to develop town planning principles based on those of Le Corbusier the architect rather than those of Le Corbusier the town planner—in other words, based on principles of complexity, discontinuity, and cubism rather than "total design." The classic Buffalo Waterfront Plan was produced as a studio project in 1967.

Rob Krier did similar projects—as urban interventions—in Stuttgart during this period, but it was Leon Krier who drew the whole city, and outlined a comprehensive set of principles for designing the city. These were the complete inverse of Le Corbusier's. Leon's competition entry for La Villette in 1976 was the first in a series of illustrative projects.

Many urban projects were designed, but little was implemented or built until the late-1980s and the 1990s, when built projects proliferated. The New Urbanism movement emerged in the early-1980s focusing primarily on the American town as an antidote to suburban sprawl. New Urbanist principles could be, and were, applied to cities as well as towns, however. Since then, countless international efforts have focused on the urbanism of the city—its form, and culture.

Postwar Urban Design in America

There is no clearer manifestation of the postwar change in urban design theory and practice in America than two projects for the Lower West Side of Manhattan in the decade between 1969 and 1979.

The decade of the 1960s represented the dying gasp of modernism's most extreme version of large-scale architecture as urban design—*mega-structures*. French architectural journals during this time were full of mega-structure projects by Japanese Metabolists and others. The plasticity of beton brut popularized by Le Corbusier's postwar work proved irresistable to architects designing ever larger projects, despite the fact that they could never be achieved financialy, administratively, or politically.

The roots of change lie in the 1960s, but the decade of the 1970s is when the hegemony of architecture over urbanism gave way to the tradition of urban design as a related, but distinct discipline, one in which urbanism regained hegemony over architecture. In order to accomplish a felicitous outcome, architectural and urban guidelines were required, and required to be enforced. This was the case with Battery Park City in Lower Manhattan.

Battery Park City

The first approved plan for the landfill along the Lower West Side of Manhattan was the 1969 plan by Conklin & Rossant: a mega-structure consisting of a seven-story shopping mall running the length of the site with attached slabs and towers. Like other mega-structures of the period it was an all-or-nothing project, and the 1973 recession sealed its fate.

By 1979, architectural and urban sensibilities had changed, and Alexander Cooper and Stanton Eckstut were commissioned to produce a new plan. In contrast to the 1969 architectural mega-structure, the new plan extended the street and small-scale block pattern of lower Manhattan; created a landscaped waterfront esplanade, tree-lined streets, and a series of public parks and open spaces; and developed guidelines to produce incremental buildings on small parcels consistent with the architecture of New York.[1]

The two site plans are also a study in contrast: even though the 1969 plan bridged over the West Side highway and literally connected to the city, it was rendered with heavy shadows as if detached from the (unrendered) city; the 1979 plan rendered Battery Park City and Lower Manhattan equally.

1. Perspective view of the 1969 scheme

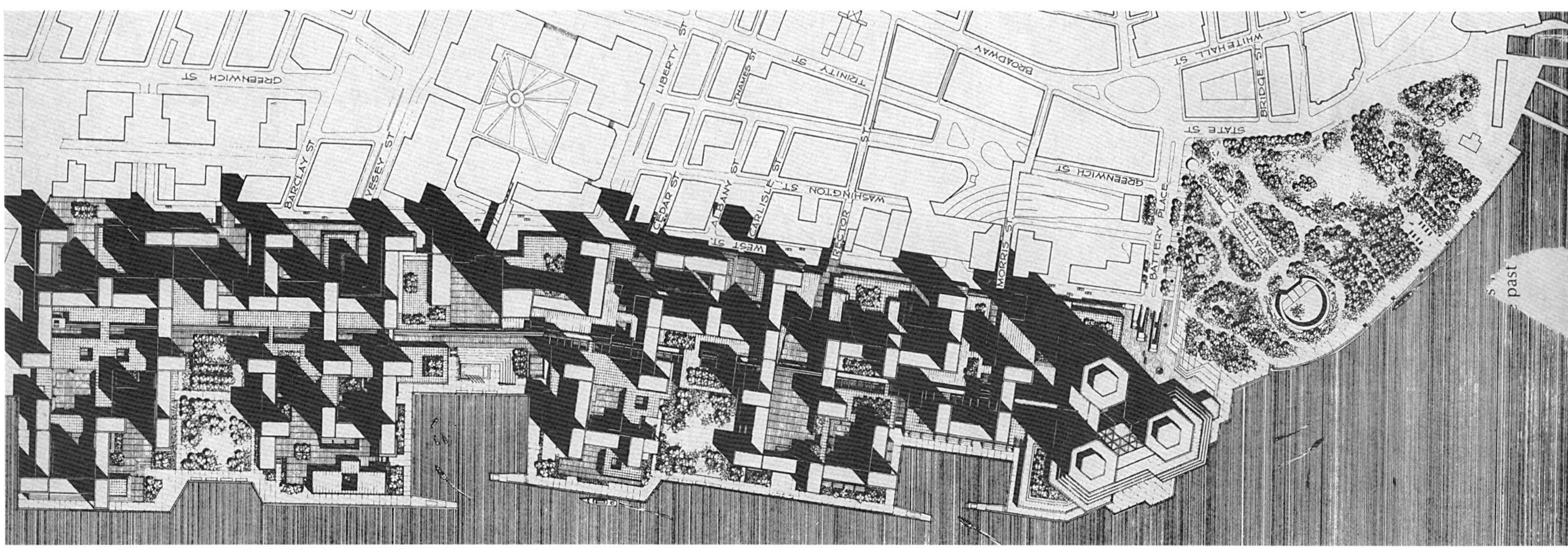

2. Proposed plan for Battery Park City by Conklin & Rossant, 1969

1. View of lower Manhattan

2. Model view of northern development

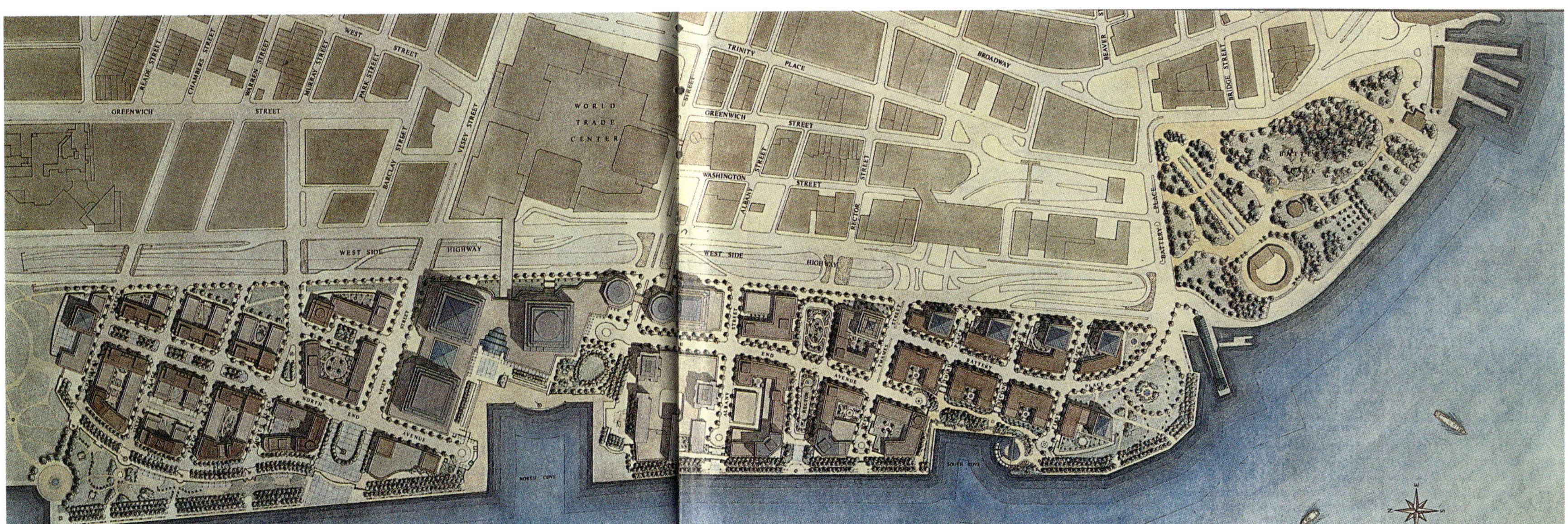

3. Plan for Battery Park City by Alexander Cooper and Stanton Eckstut, 1979

Boston

Battery Park City was a landfill on the edge of Manhattan, which remained intact, but Boston, like many other American cities, suffered major urban destruction during the 1960s and 1970s. Indeed, Boston offers a clear illustration of four factors that had major modernist effects on American postwar urban development:

1. *Urban renewal*
2. *Highway construction*
3. *Suburbanization*
4. *Modern architecture*

Prewar "Old" Boston

Boston was still an intact nineteenth-century city at the end of the Second World War in August 1945. There were no highways, few public housing projects, and no real skyscrapers. The "Old" John Hancock Building opened in 1949; it and the 1915 Customs House Tower remained Boston's two tallest buildings until 1964. The urban fabric was continuous; and although Bulfinch's Tontine Crescent was gone, the city's rather substantial structure of urban spaces still existed. The famous Scollay Square was as lively as ever, and the city possessed a series of impressive civic buildings. In contrast to the destroyed cities of Europe, Boston was ahead of the curve.

The city was physically tired and run down, however. Many buildings were shabby, and many also lacked basic amenities—such as heat and indoor plumbing. Vehicles were continually increasing in number, and circulation in urban areas was difficult. Boston was referred to as "Old Boston."

1. *Customs House Tower, before 1960*

2. *Aerial view of Boston, 1930. This was essentially the state of the city in 1945*

3. *Plan of Boston, 1950*

1. Aerial view of Boston, 1960s

2. Plan of Boston illustrating the amount of destruction caused by urban renewal, 1960

In 1944 William Roger Greeley, a prominent architect, stood up in Faneuil Hall and claimed that Boston had not shared with London the "advantage" of widespread destruction by aerial bombardment, which would clear out the old city and make way for the new.[2]

New Boston and Urban Renewal

The destruction of nineteenth-century urban fabric to build highways was the beginning of urban disintegration in Boston. Greeley's 1944 comment was to prove prescient. By the mid-1960s Boston would, indeed, look as if it had been bombed during the Second World War. Something like 25 percent of the city center was destroyed, much of it under the policy of urban renewal—or, as it later came to be known "urban removal."

Modern Architecture in America

Before World War II American architecture was distinctly different from that of Europe. American architecture, however heroic, was less doctrinaire, more linked to history, and more engaged with the city. In Europe, however, there was a powerful new architecture from at least 1910. This modern architecture was more polemical; it was less linked to the past; it was more abstract; and it was implicitly more anti-urban—rejecting the traditional city. The principles of this new architecture, and its anti-urban implications were well developed by the eve of World War II.

Modernist Architectural Education

In 1937, Laszlo Moholy-Nagy, Mies van der Rohe, Marcel Breuer, and Walter Gropius all immigrated to America and began transforming American architectural education and—after a lag—American architecture and urbanism. Thus, at the time of the redevelopment projects in Boston, architects trained as modernists were selected to design them, and modern architecture—abstract and often anti-urban—appeared.

3. Aerial perspective of proposed Prudential Center

1. *View of Rome from the dome of St. Peters*

2. *Boston, aerial view of throughway construction, 1960s*

Postwar Modernism in America

With the clarity of hindsight it is difficult to comprehend the mentality of the immediate postwar years in America, but the zeal to replace the traditional city with the city of modern architecture was all pervasive. Much of this zeal emanated from the Harvard School of Design under the influence of Walter Gropius. For example, Gropius had invited Martin Wagner to teach at Harvard, and in 1944 Wagner's submission to the Boston Center design competition actually proposed tearing down the whole of central Boston to be replaced with a gigantic "J"-shaped building.

The chilling extent of this arrogance and ignorance is also revealed by Christopher Tunnard when in 1968, he recounted:

> An apocryphal story told by a former head of the American Academy in Rome concerns his showing the well-known view over the city from its terrace to a 'Fellow' fresh from the Harvard architectural school. The young man looked at all this beauty sadly. Shaking his head, he observed: 'What a pity it all has to come down.[3]

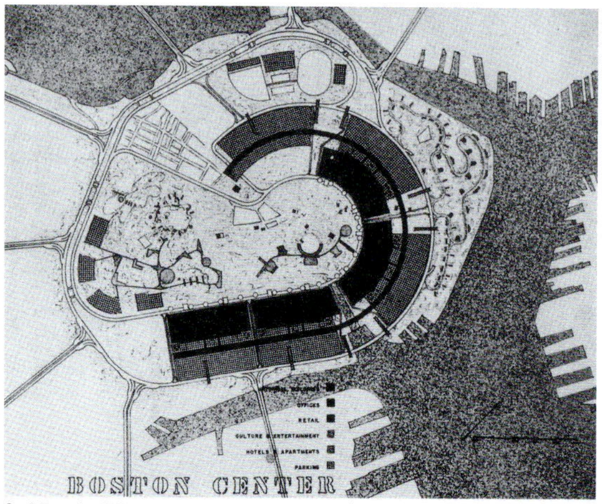

3. *Martin Wagner, Boston Center plan, 1944*

4. *Boston, plan of buildings demolished in 1960s*

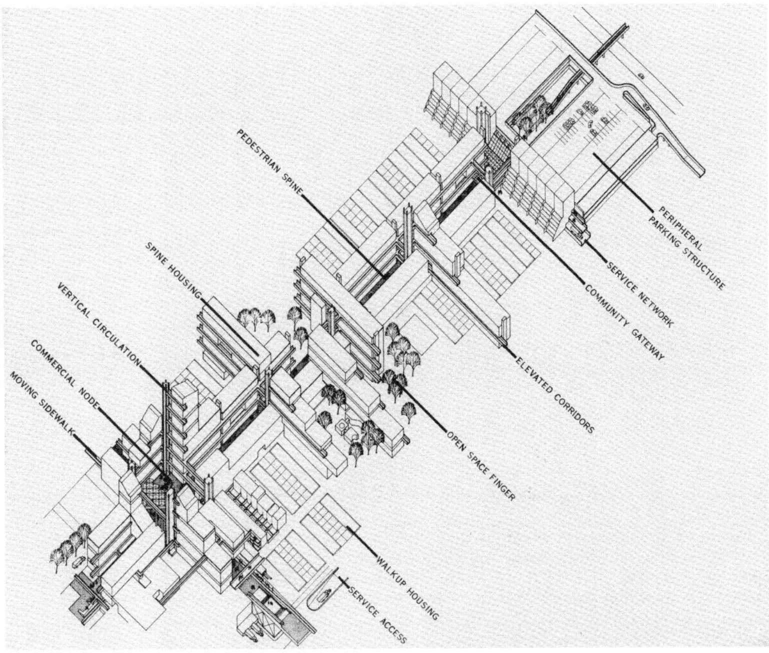

1. Axonometric of the New Community spine, 1968, Sert et. al.

José Sert and Urban Design

Walter Gropius was chair of Architecture at the Harvard Graduate School of Design from 1937 to 1952. José Lluis Sert became dean and chair of Architecture in 1953, and served until 1969.

Sert is credited with introducing the term "urban design" in 1953. He organized the first urban design conference at Harvard in 1956 (coincidentally the end of CIAM) and established the first Urban Design master's degree program in 1960.[4]

Although Sert continued the main values of CIAM, he shifted the focus to walkable neighborhoods and the revitalization of city centers. There was an interest in maintaining existing cities, in courtyard houses, and a mix of building types, but the idea of traditional streets and blocks was absent. The CIAM idea of "towers-in-the-park" was gone, but separation of functions was prevalent. Indeed, the Harvard New Community project of 1968 bears a striking resemblance to the Team X spine projects of Bakema and others.

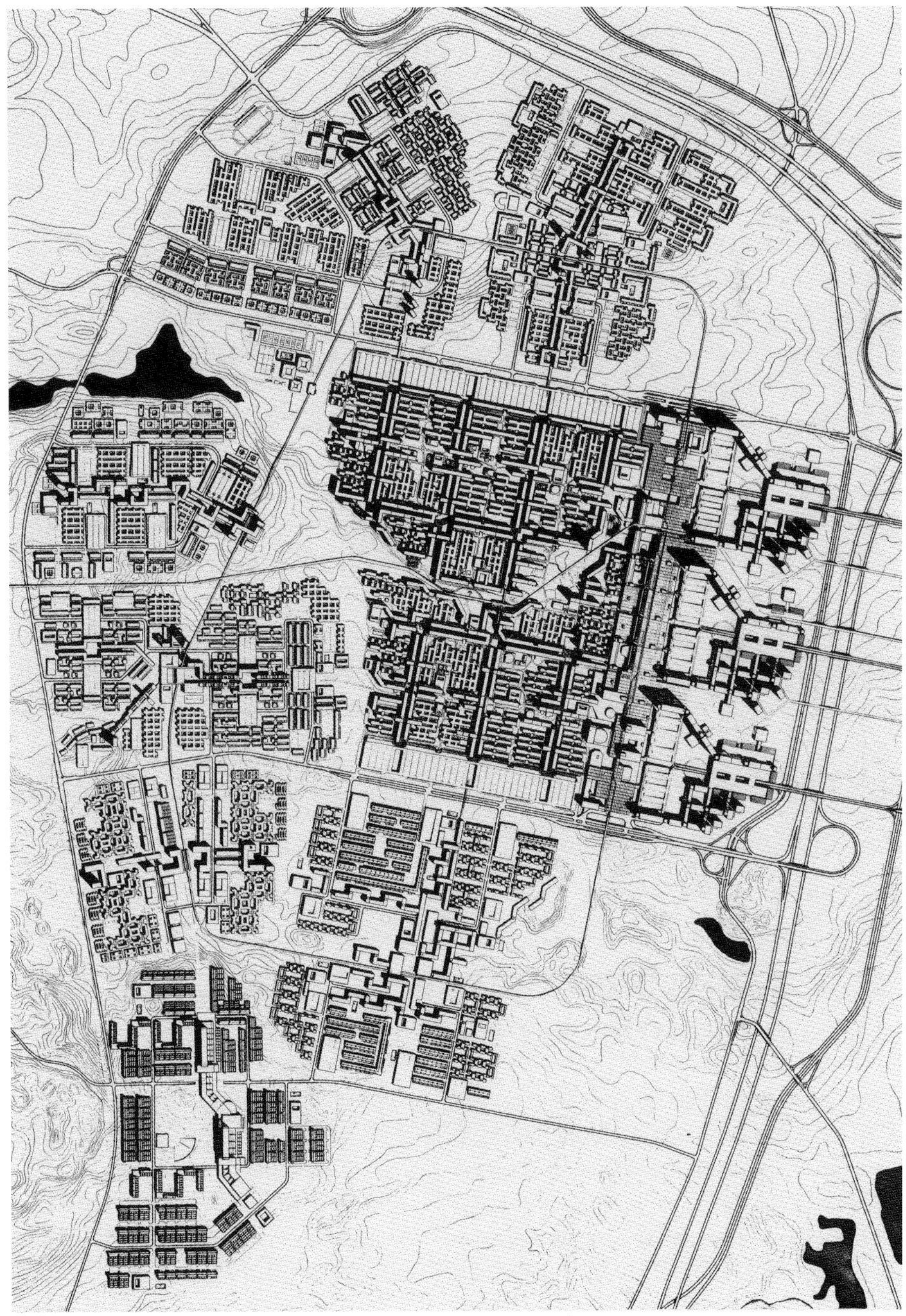

2. The Harvard New Community project, plan, 1968, Sert et. al.

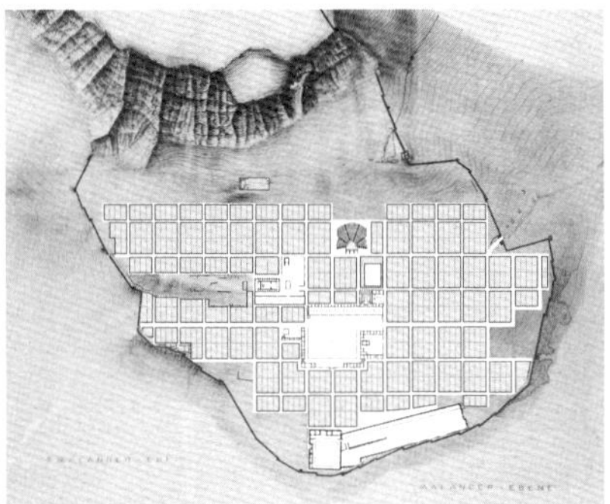

1. Plan of Priene

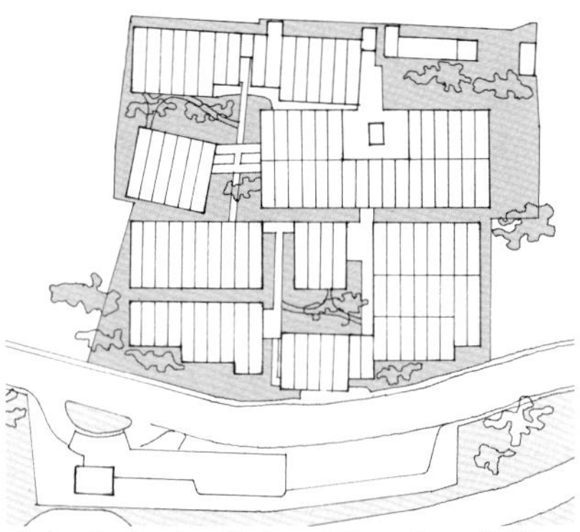

2. Le Corbusier, Rob and Roc plan, 1949

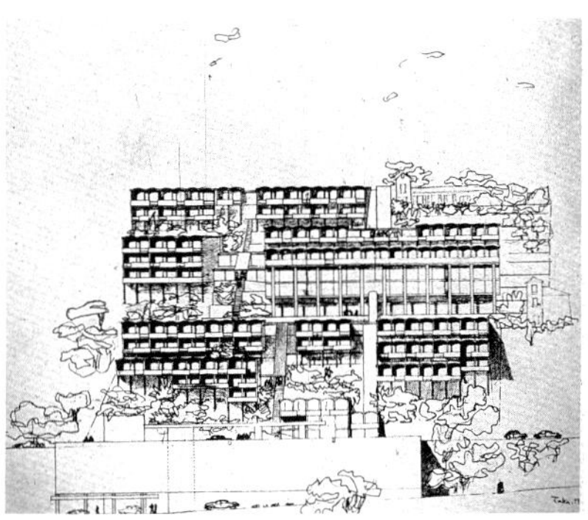

3. Le Corbusier, Rob and Roc elevation, 1949

CIAM 8: The Heart of the City

The eighth meeting of CIAM was held in Hoddesdon, England, in 1951. The topic was the "Core" of the city. The proceedings were published in 1952 as *The Heart of the City: Towards the Humanisation of Urban Life*.[5] Sert began the introductory essay by quoting Ortega y Gasset regarding the *forum* and the *agora*, as the core of the *urbs* or *polis*.[6] Gropius suggested "a retrieval of the right of way for the pedestrian, disenfranchised by the automobile" and spoke of a Mexican village with "a fairly large square with arcades around it," one that "serves as the centre of life for the population."[7] Sert also spoke of the importance of community, neighborhoods, and the right size for neighborhood units. A certain dilemma was apparent, however: the CIAM principles of the four functions of dwelling, working, circulation, and recreation, coupled with the modernist typologies of detached slabs and towers, were incapable of dealing with the "urbanity" of the city—especially the urban core.

Nevertheless, Sert explored more traditional patterns of urbanism with streets, blocks, neighborhoods of low-rise fabric, and urban cores in an effort to transform CIAM principles into a more adaptable urbanism.

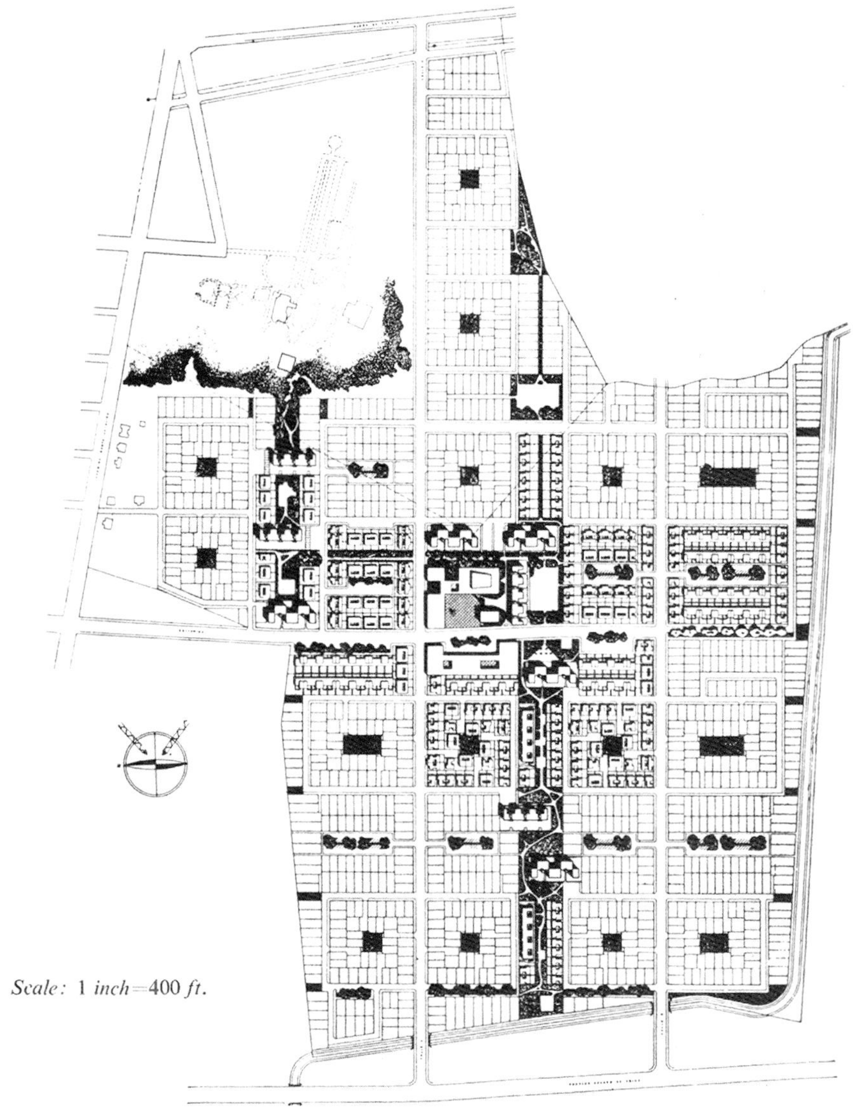

4. Sert and Wiener, Quinta Palatina plan, 1955

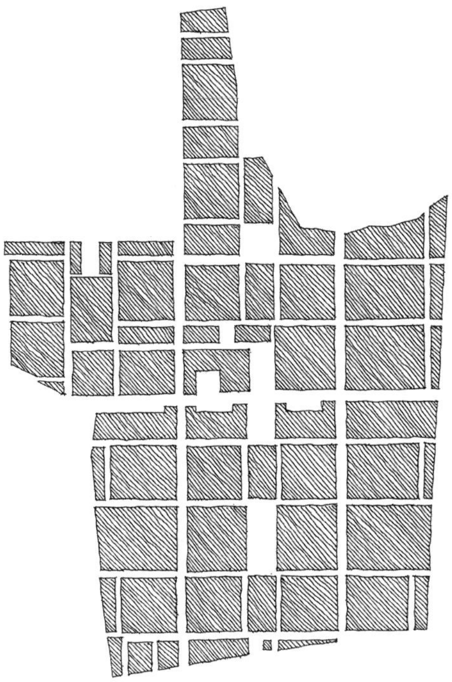

1. *Conceptual urban block and space plan*

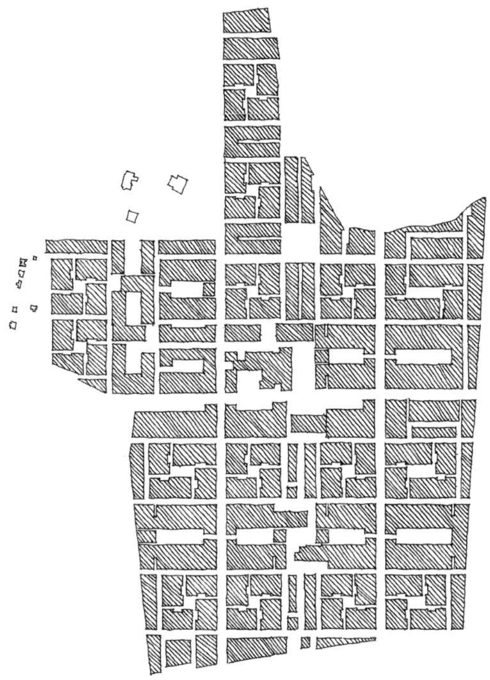

2. *Actual urban block and courtyard plan*

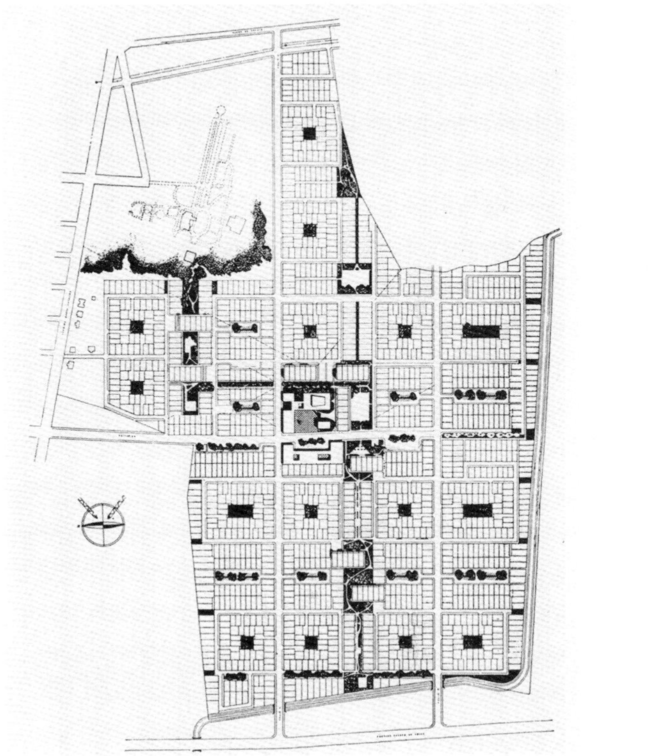

3. *Parcel plan*

Quinta Palatina, Havana Plan

José Sert and Paul Wiener's plan for a neighborhood in Havana illustrates an urban design attempt "towards the humanisation of urban life." This was not without controversy within CIAM, however.[8]

The urban plan is composed of several different fairly large block types—most with a semipublic courtyard in the center. Two dimensions predominate: square blocks about 360' x 360' (110 x 110 m), and rectangular blocks about 360' x 475' (110 x 145 m). These blocks are broken into smaller components pin-wheeling around the central court. Others are unitary with more secluded central courts. The parcels are almost all narrow frontage, row-house type lots about 30–35' wide. If these were filled with party-wall buildings, such as London row houses, or terrace houses, an elegant urbanism with beautiful streets might be expected. But as illustrated, the plan is populated with suburban-type garden houses, and there is no indication that the streets are a developed part of the urban idea.

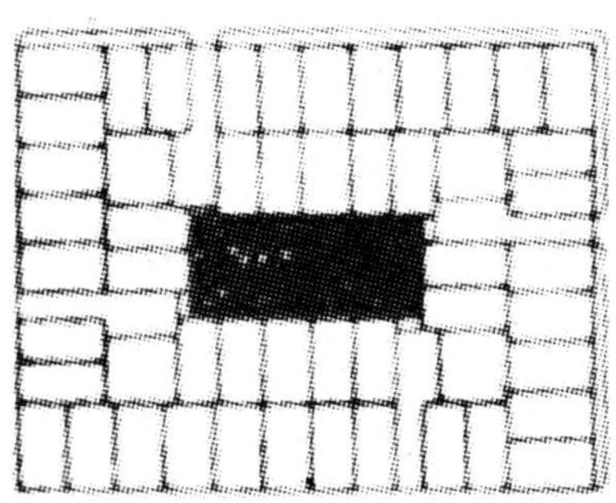

4. *Typical rectangular block and parcels*

5. *Typical square block and buildings*

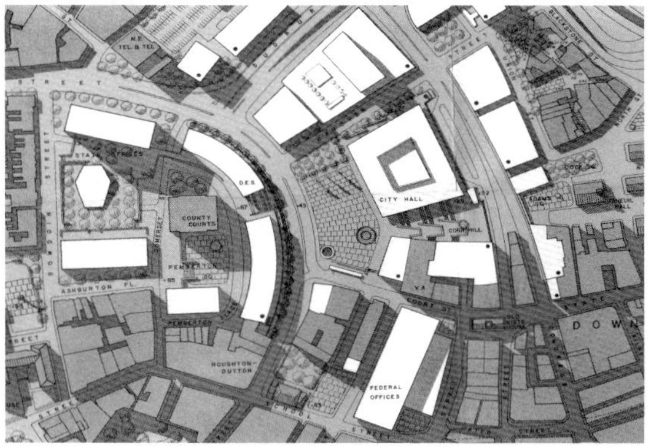

1. *Plan for Government Center*

2. *Model of the Boston Waterfront project*

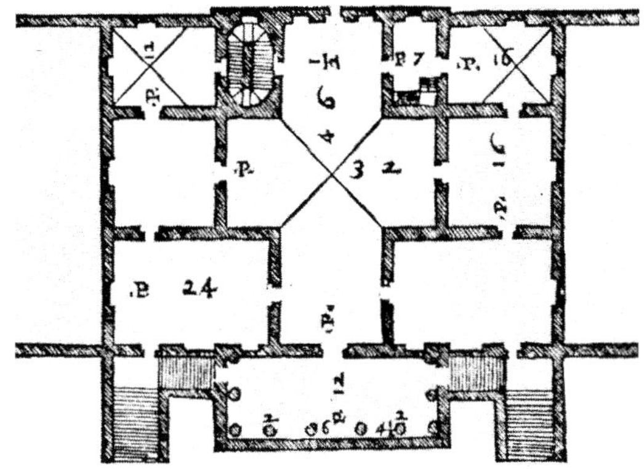

3. *Palladio, plan of Villa Malcontenta*

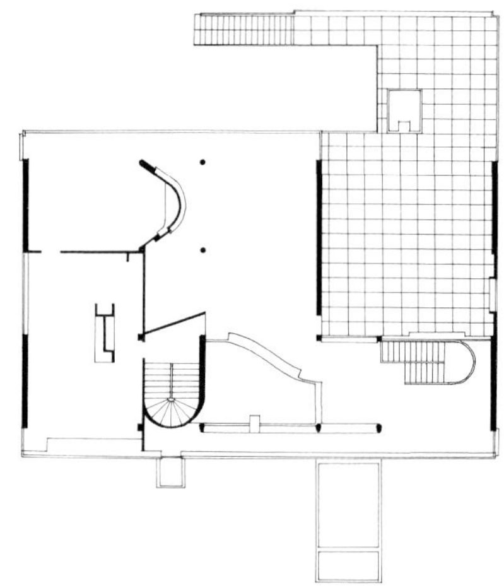

4. *Le Corbusier, plan of Villa at Garches, 1927*

In the years following the end of World War II a modern urban architecture did not yet exist. Rather, this period marked the triumph and proliferation of modern architecture around the globe. Fractured cities, anti-urban buildings, and violent infrastructure became the norm.

Jane Jacobs

Against this background it would be difficult to overestimate the importance of Jane Jacobs's *The Death and Life of Great American Cities* (1961), and her legendary resistance to the plans and policies of New York's Robert Moses.[9]

Preservation and Advocacy Planning

Other alternatives were also emerging. No sooner were the effects of modernist planning principles and practice detected than reaction set in. The 1949 Housing Act provided for "slum clearance."[10] In the same year, however, the National Trust for Historic Preservation was established. The 1954 Housing Act and the 1956 Federal Aid Highway Act provided federal funding for "urban renewal" and highway construction, but in 1964–65 "advocacy planning" arose as a bottom-up antidote to the arrogance and destruction of top-down planning.

Kevin Lynch

Kevin Lynch's landmark book, *The Image of the City*, published in 1960, connected the form of the city with the perceptions of its inhabitants. It identified five elements of perception in the city: *paths* (streets, sidewalks, etc.); *edges* (perceived boundaries); *districts* (sections of the city distinguished by identity or character); *nodes* (focal points, intersections or loci); and *landmarks* (identifiable objects which serve as external reference points).

Little translation is required to connect to the later urban terminology of: *streets, squares, quarters, edges*, and *monuments*. Thus, Lynch's theory stood in stark contrast to the principles of CIAM, Team X, and Sert. Lynch was also a professor at MIT and a practicing planner involved with two contemporary Boston projects: Government Center and the waterfront. Both of these schemes were prescient, but at odds with the prevailing sensibilities.

Government Center: The First Plan

In 1958 the Boston planning department commissioned the architectural firm of Adams, Howard, and Greeley, in collaboration with Jack Myer and Kevin Lynch, to produce a plan for Government Center. Their plan was finished in 1959, and called for the complete redesign of the Scollay Square area.[11] The City Hall was positioned to have a clear front toward Tremont Street, and a clear back on the Congress Street side, and Hanover Street was maintained through to Tremont Street. Although the plan proposed the demolition of many buildings and the removal of streets, the proposed new buildings generally held the street lines—thus relating the new fabric to the old.[12] This project was replaced by a scheme by I. M. Pei (illustrated in the waterfront model).[13]

The Waterfront

The project for the Boston waterfront, designed in 1962 by Sy Minsk, Jack Myer, and Kevin Lynch, was the sister project to the scheme for Government Center. The idea was to connect Beacon Hill and the State House to Boston's waterfront and the sea.[14]

The presence of the vehicular Central Artery made a formidable barrier, but inventive ideas for configuration, and for buildings under the artery would have produced a relatively seamless connection between Beacon Hill and the sea. Not only was significant density proposed for the piers along the waterfront, but the city was brought right up to the Central Artery. This proposal was also not implemented. The density was reduced, and an unsuccessful park was substituted for urban fabric at the water's edge.

Colin Rowe and Architectural Theory

Reactions to modernist architecture also emerged in contemporary architectural theory. After establishing a link between modern architecture and tradition in his seminal articles: "The Mathematics of the Ideal Villa" (1947), and "Mannerism and Modern Architecture" (1950), Colin Rowe taught at the University of Texas (1954–56) where he coauthored "Transparency: Literal and Phenomenal" (1955–56) with Robert Slutzky as well as a more urban article, "Lockhart, Texas," with John Hedjuk.[15]

Robert Venturi's *Complexity and Contradiction* appeared in 1966, as did Aldo Rossi's *The Architecture of the City*. In different ways both of these treatises bound architecture to culture and the city.

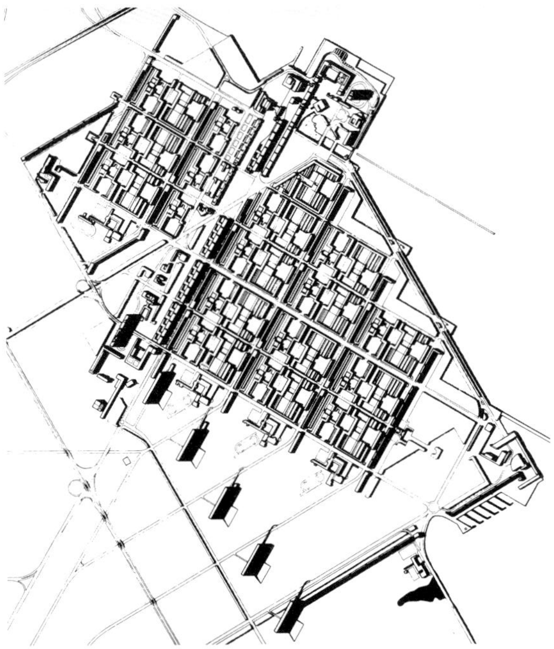

1. Tom Schumacher, thesis, 1966

2. Figure/ground plan of Wiesbaden

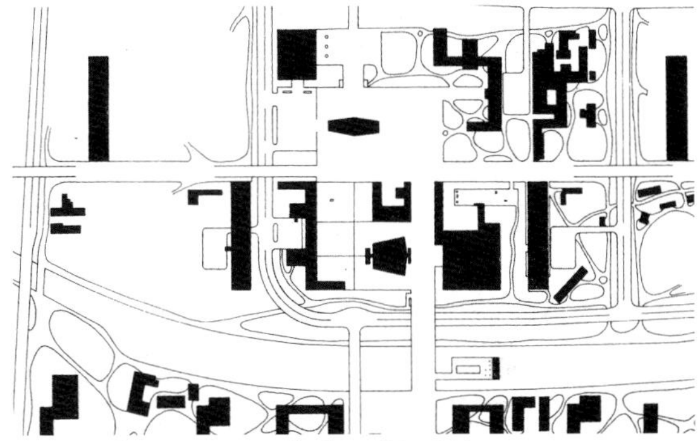

3. Le Corbusier, proposed plan of St. Dié

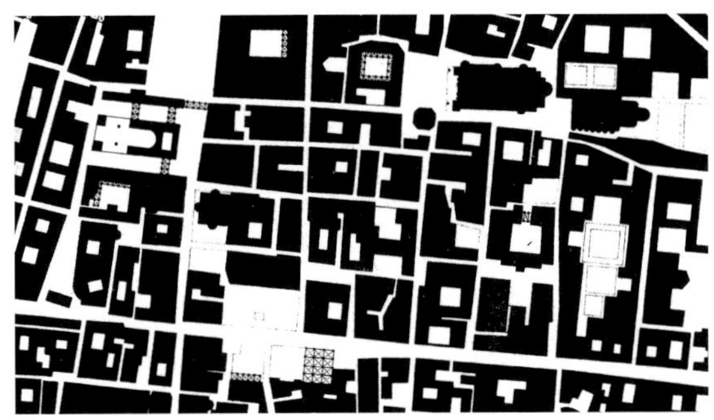

4. Figure/ground plan of Parma

The Cornell Urban Design Studio

Subsequently, Rowe established the Urban Design Studio at Cornell University in 1963. The studio was an opportunity to concretely explore revisionist ideas about the city and architecture's urban role. In contrast to the Urban Design Program established by José Lluis Sert at Harvard in 1956, which was based on CIAM principles, the Cornell studio studied traditional cities and sought to develop an urban architecture that could remake, repair, and extend traditional cities rather than replace them. It sought to apply the cubist complexities of Le Corbusier the architect to city design rather than the simplicities of Le Corbusier the town planner.

In the beginning, Urban Design Studio projects tried to utilize the language of modern architectural types—slabs, wall buildings, and towers—to produce urban fabric. The 1966 thesis project by Tom Schumacher is an early example.[16]

So-called figure/ground plans were used as an efficient technique for exploring formal principles of fields (urban fabric), edges, grids, and urban space.[17] Project cities were sought that provided opportunities for grid collisions, overlapping fields, and a combination of modern and traditional building and space types. Cubist principles that permeated the architecture of Le Corbusier were highly prized, as were city plans with complex spatial characteristics, like that of prewar Dresden.

Representation of the projects was generally limited to plans and three-dimensional volumetric projections such as aerial perspectives or physical models. Architectural language or character was never illustrated.

Rarely were studio ideas simple or straight. Mutually exclusive ideas were almost always simultaneously entertained. Whether they were program vs. paradigm, the ideal vs. the circumstantial, or modern vs. traditional space, a free mannerist juxtaposition of ideas was always the modus operandi. Gradually, as studio plans evolved, these juxtapositions became more and more important as collage replaced overlapping fields.[18]

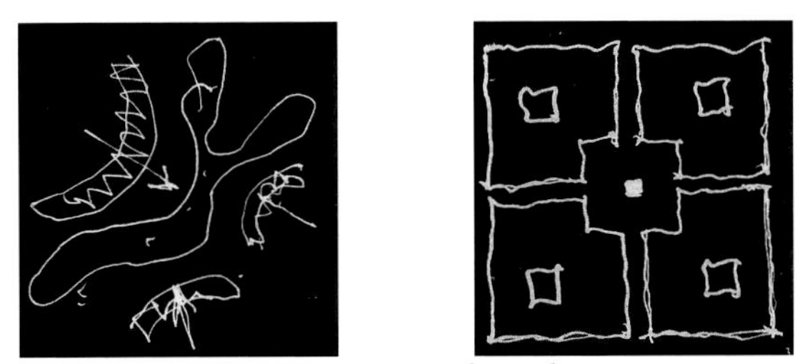

5. Rowe's diagrams of program and paradigm

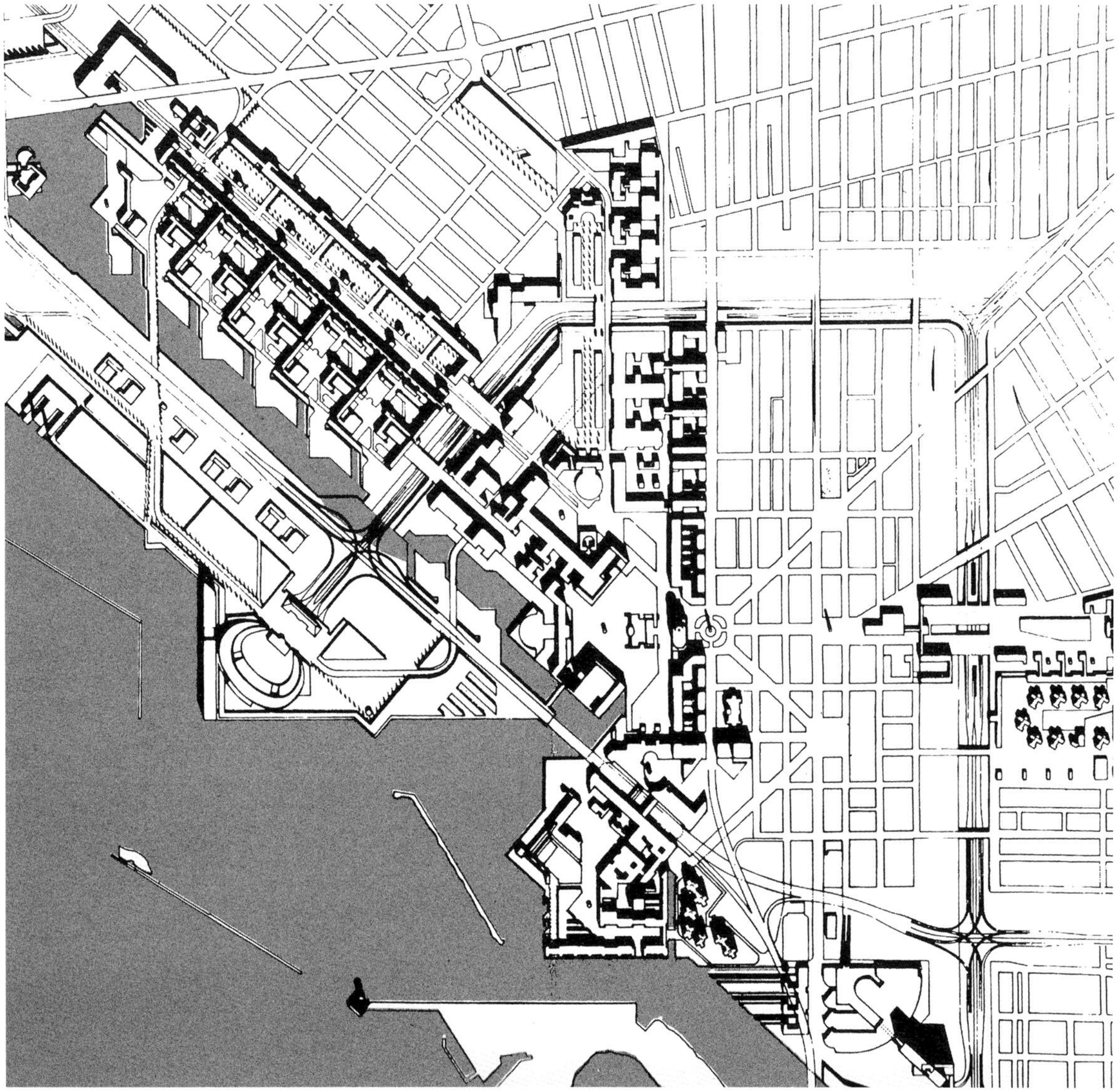

1. Buffalo Waterfront, proposed plan, 1966

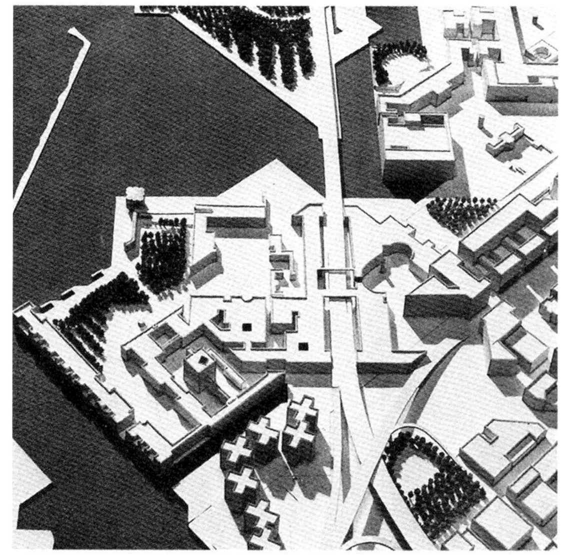

2. Model detail

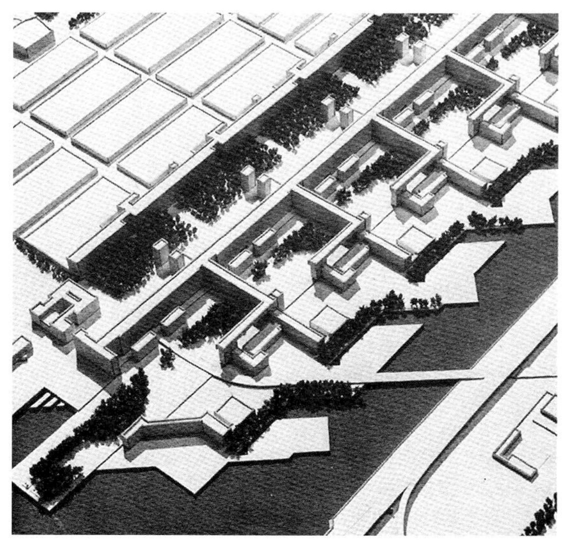

3. Model detail

The Buffalo Waterfront Project

This project, done by the Cornell Urban Design Studio, is located in a problematic area of the waterfront of Buffalo, New York, an area isolated from the city of Buffalo because of the highway. Grids of different alignments collide, creating the sense of an underdesigned, fractured urban environment.[19]

A portion of the project attempted to generate an elaborate fabric of hybrid, thin buildings and courtyards, but traditional urban characteristics were also discernible in the project.

The main design strategy was to extend the existing grid and expand the development to the northwest and southeast. Another goal was to revitalize the waterfront, and for that reason the stadium is sited on the water edge.

Various solutions can be observed for the collision of the different grids, especially in the area closer to the city hall, where the city core is extended by thick, irregular urban blocks, which were capable of resolving odd angles and other unique urban conditions, with the intention of creating hierarchy and focus with continuous open public spaces.

The large linear building with smaller arms to the northwest is a typical example of the research of that time, where linear buildings were used to define the boundaries and provide enclosure as mentioned above. Although the overall design differs from that of the modernist city, the project uses the architectural vocabulary of modern architecture, and the composite buildings of the collision were not yet developed in detail.

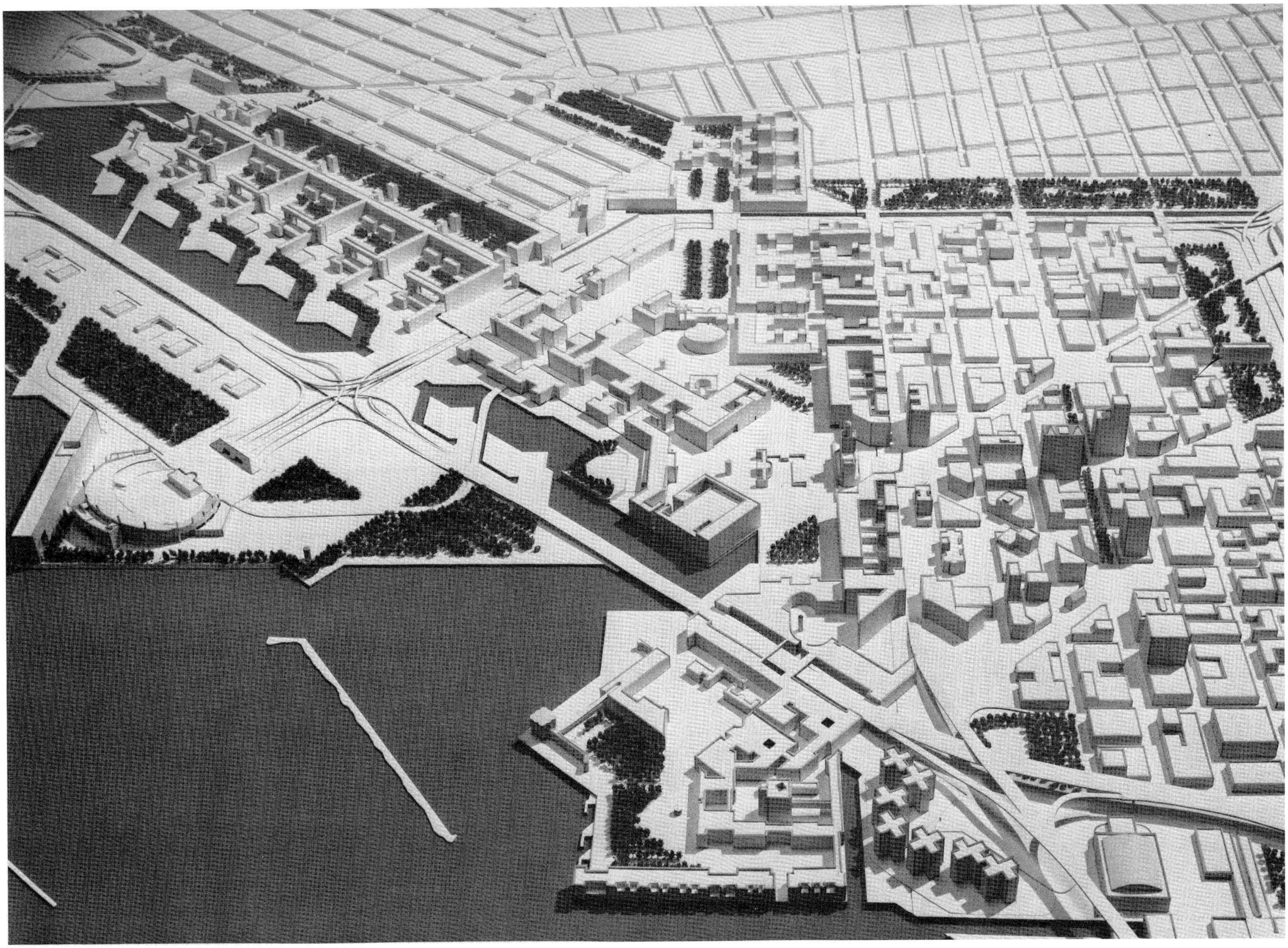

Buffalo Waterfront, model view

1. *Nolli Plan of Rome, detail*

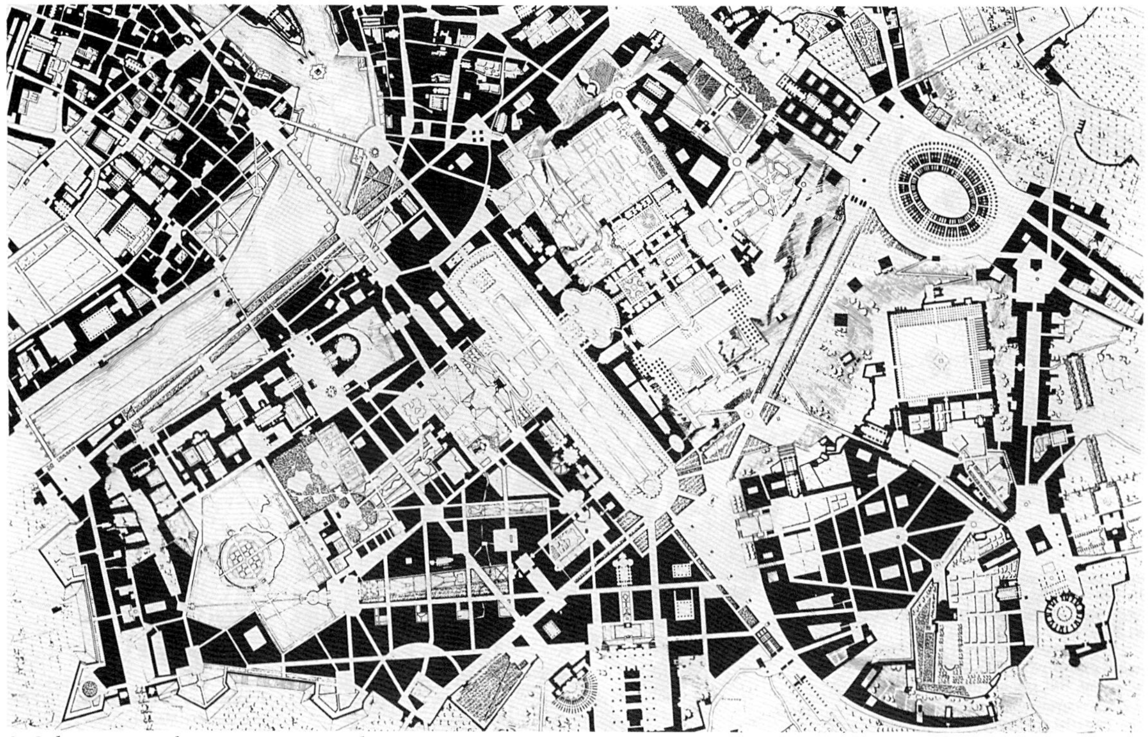

2. *Colin Rowe et al., Roma Interrotta plan*

Roma Interrotta

With the 1978 Roma Interrotta project, a major formal shift can be observed. Formal complexity, discontinuity, and more elaborate block types were evident. There were two related influences: *Collage City* had been published, and research into the French Hôtel had been explored in architectural studios.[20]

In "Urban Design Tactics,"[21] Steven Peterson, one of the authors of the Roma Interrotta project, stated that there are three basic issues of morphology in the discipline of urban design:

1. Space is the essential, prerequisite medium of urbanism;
2. The constituent urban elements are field, texture, street, square, block, and block unit (building); and,
3. The formal strategies of fragments and lines and the tactics of connections provide coherence and relationships among the urban elements.

Peterson also illustrated how irregular urban fabric and blocks can be interpreted by exploiting principles of discontinuity—something regular grids of blocks cannot do. In previous studio projects urban space was often "left-over," as residue between gridded fields. With Roma Interrotta, space could be positively configured and irregularities absorbed by the blocks and buildings.

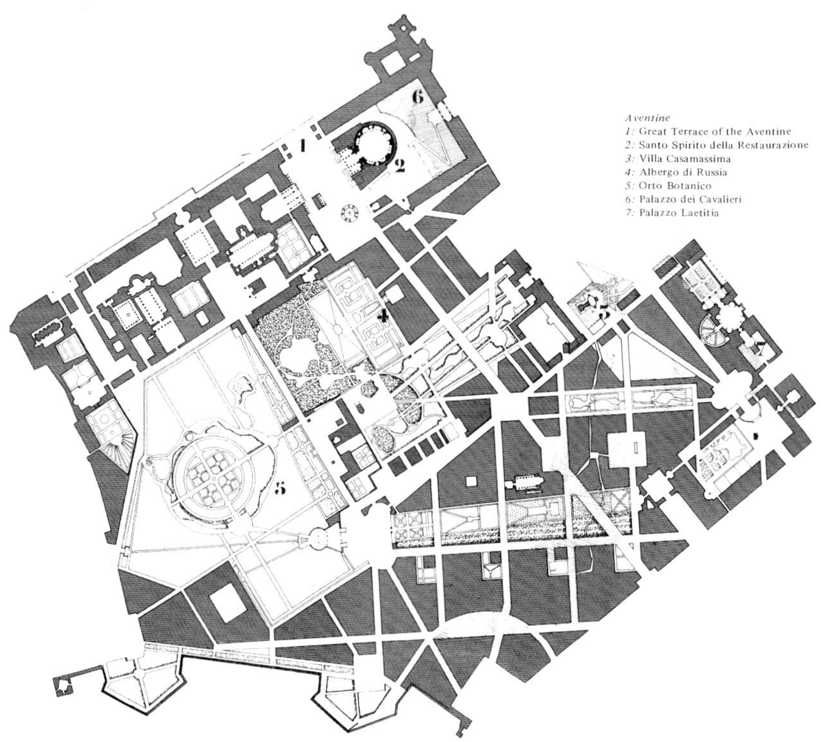

3. *Plan for the Aventine*

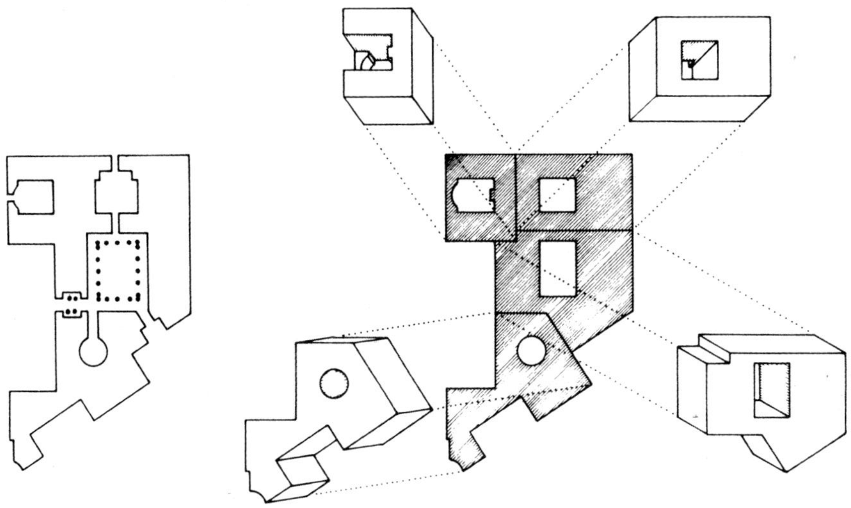

1. Building diagrams

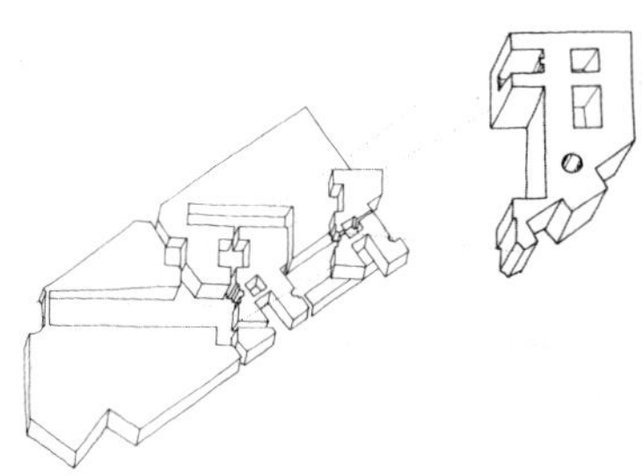

2. Block diagrams

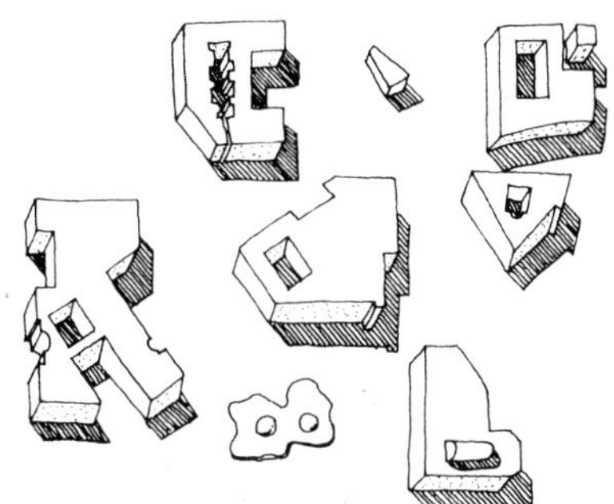

3. Block diagrams

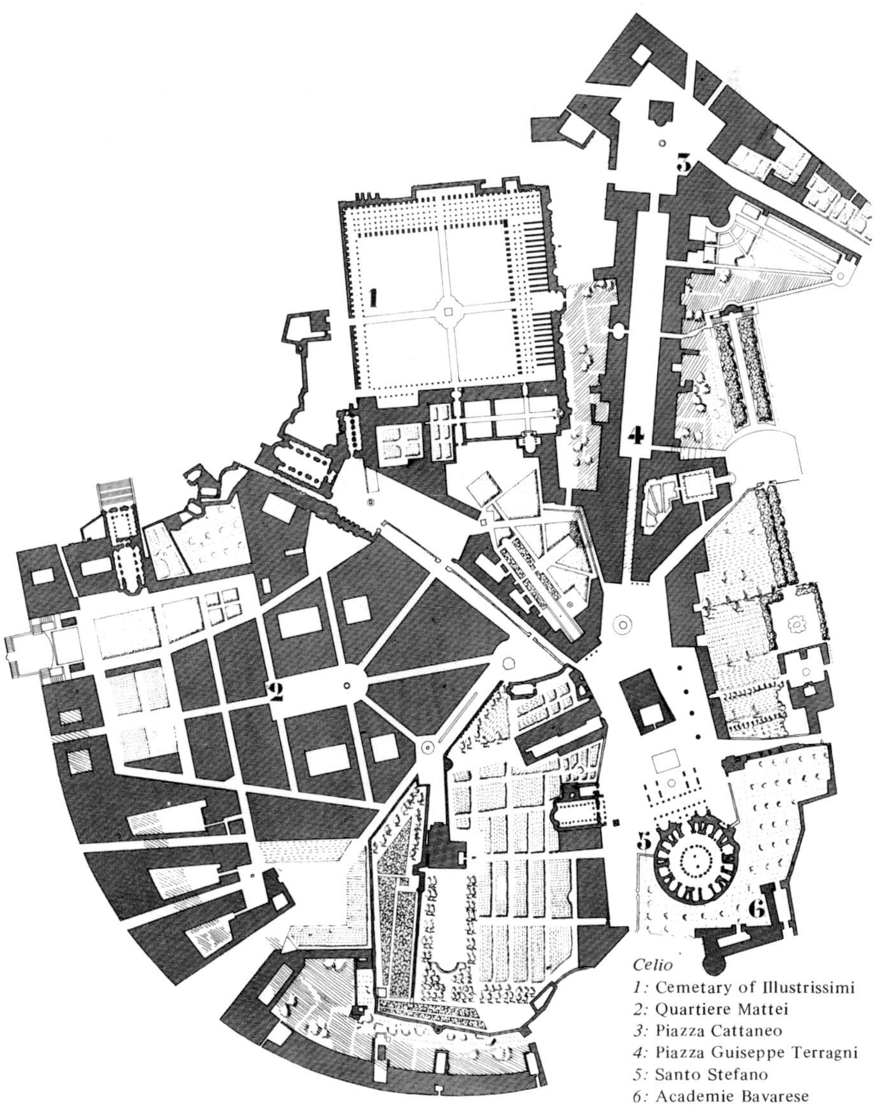

4. Plan for the Celio

Buildings and Blocks

Emphasis on elaborate, figurative urban space tends to produce irregular blocks and fields and, therefore, discontinuity between the space and the urban fabric, resulting in irregular building parcels.

These parcels may, in turn, be resolved by figural courtyards producing discontinuity with their surrounding building fabric. Finally, the principal interior public spaces may be ideally disposed within the building plan, leaving more residual space, or *poché*, to be successively resolved in a similar manner—as in the French hôtel.[22]

This planning system allows great flexibility in the design of urban fabric and an infinite variety of urban architectural types. In contrast to modernist building types that are designed from the inside out, urban building types can be designed from the outside in. Hegemony of the public realm is crucial.

The street is a relic of the centuries, a dislocated organ that can no longer function. The street wears us out. And when all is said and done we have to admit it disgusts us.
Le Corbusier[23]

The first thing to do is to abolish the rue corridor with its rigid lines of buildings and its intermingling of traffic, pedestrians, and residences ... the rue corridor, which life itself condemns, ... belongs to the optical vision of another day.
Siegfried Giedion, 1967[24]

The problem of re-identifying man with his environment (contenu et contenant) cannot be achieved by using historical forms of house-groupings, streets, squares, greens, etc., as the social reality they presented no longer exists.
Alison Smithson, 1968[25]

A city can only be reconstructed in the form of streets and squares and urban quarters.
Leon Krier, 1978[26]

Something went wrong in 1714, or 1750, or 1789, or 1804, with the beginning of the Georgian era or at its end, with the death of Queen Anne or the accession of Queen Victoria, with Andrew Jackson, with Ulysses S. Grant, with the discovery of Pompeii, with the emergence of the Roman Empire, with the collapse of the Roman Empire, with the decline of the middle ages, with the appearance of Brunelleschi, or Michelangelo, or Inigo Jones, or Borromini.

But, now, nous avons changé tout cela. *For we, the protagonists of the new, have scrutinized and discriminated. We know the evil, we have the remedy, ours is the prescription; and, as for you, just you take a good look and a good listen.*

Such, in its time, was one of the primary messages of modern architecture—a primary message of Walter Gropius, Sigfried Gidion, Le Corbusier, and Nikolaus Pevsner.

But, ... the locus of the historical rift valley is now shifted; the bad date is now 1923 ... the bad gestures/propositions are those of CIAM ...

To repeat: the bad date is now 1923, the good date is now 1974, or '75, or '76 ...

Colin Rowe, 1979[27]

European "Rationalists"

Reaction to modernist architecture and planning in Europe began in the early 1970s, and the protagonists announced themselves as "Rationalists." They included, among others: Aldo Rossi, Massimo Scolari, Maurice Culot, Robert Delevoy, O. M. Ungers, and—centrally—the Krier brothers, Rob and Leon.

The unifying factor of the movement was the search for an urban architecture—an architecture of the city—but within the group it was the Krier brothers and Maurice Culot who were most involved with urbanism.

The school of architecture, La Cambre, in Brussels, was an experimental source of urban interventions, many of which were published by Maurice Culot in *AAM, Archives d'Architecture Moderne*, a major publishing outlet for Leon Krier, as was *AD, Architectural Design*.

An exhibition of "Rational Architecture" was organized in London in 1975, and a book, *Rational Architecture*, was published in both French and English in 1978. The anchor of *Rational Architecture* was Leon Krier's article, "The Reconstruction of the City," in which he declared that the "primary concern should now lay with the re-creation of the public realm."[28]

Something had indeed "gone wrong" with the industrial city, and the history and form of the preindustrial city became the source of architectural form and measure.

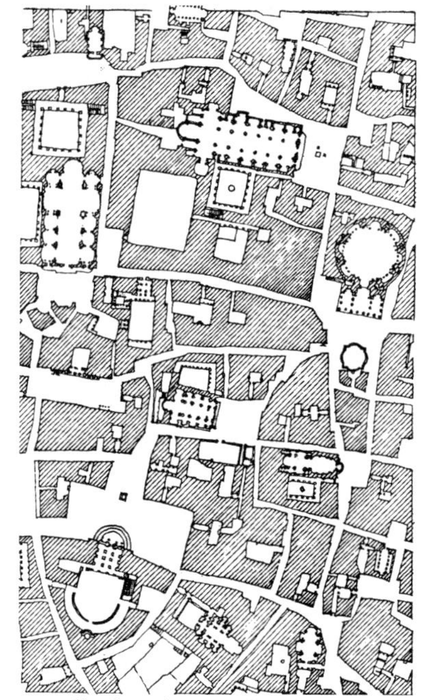

1. *Nolli plan of Rome, detail, 1748*

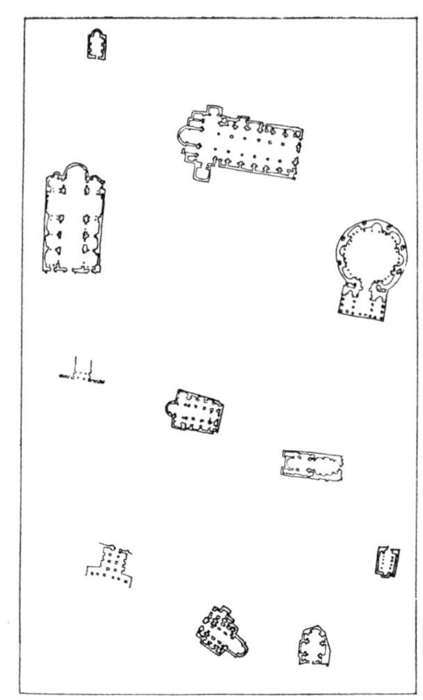

2. *Nolli plan, monuments without fabric*

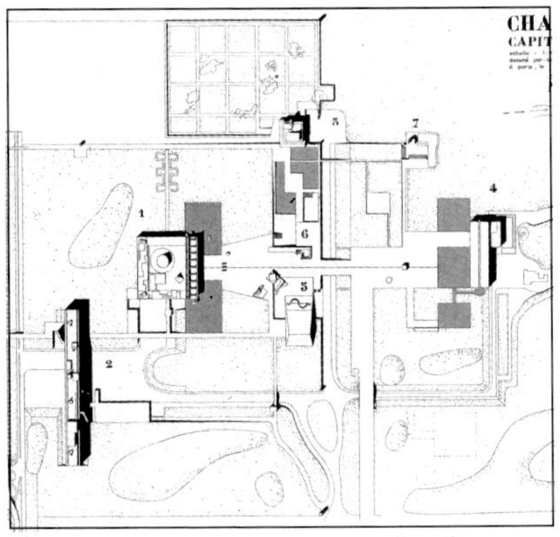

1. *Plan of the Capitol at Chandigarh, 1955*

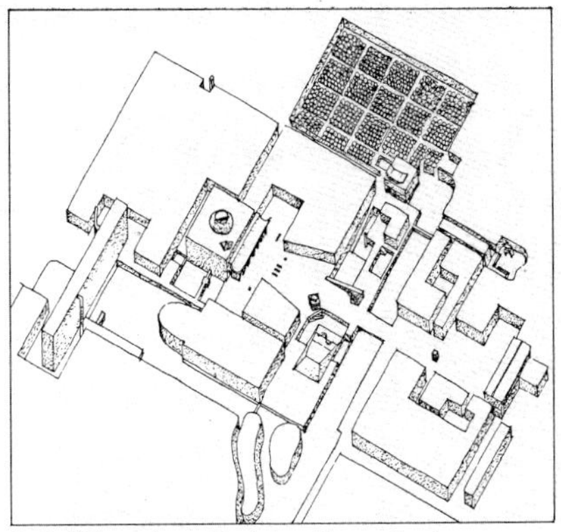

2. *Infill project, Rodrigo Perez de Arce*

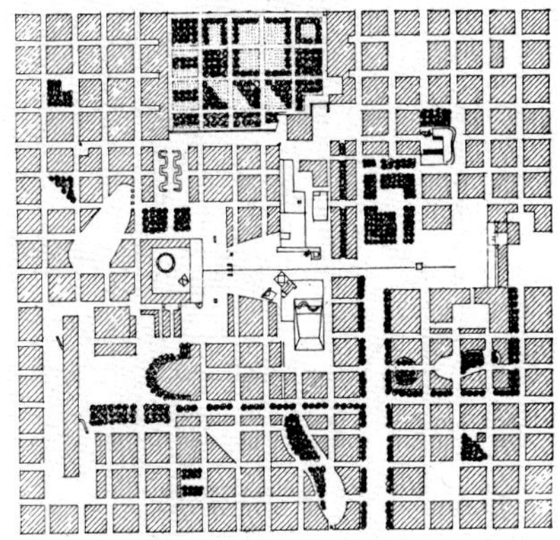

3. *Infill project, Rodrigo Perez de Arce*

4. *View of infill project*

Urban Interventions: Rob Krier

Because of the disintegration of traditional western cities due to war, architects, and planners, many rationalist projects were urban interventions to "correct" the errors of the nineteenth century and of modern architecture, or to reconstruct war-torn areas. The task was to reconstruct rather than replace.

The spaces of Le Corbusier's Forum at Chandigarh are vast, and the government complex lies outside the city proper. Rodrigo Perez de Arce's project to infill the capitol area was therefore a brash but iconic example of the transformation of isolated object-buildings by absorbing them into an urban fabric of streets, blocks, and squares. The resultant new city is a little over one-half mile square.[29]

The Tauentzienstrasse quarter in the 1984 Berlin project illustrates both the repair and completion of the urban fabric in Rob Krier's scheme, as well as the issue of scale and size of blocks in Leon Krier's scheme. Rob's project simply completes the nineteenth-century blocks, while Leon's project reduces the size and scale of the blocks, thereby increasing the frequency of streets and hence the amount of public space.[30]

Leon Krier

The comprehensive prescription for the recovery of the city (the European City) was the agenda of Leon Krier, rather than Rob. The principles would be derived from an analysis of the "innocent" preindustrial European city. In contrast to the Ville Contemporaine, according to Leon, the city should be composed of small blocks, narrow streets, multifunctional neighborhoods (cities-within-the-city), and legible spaces.

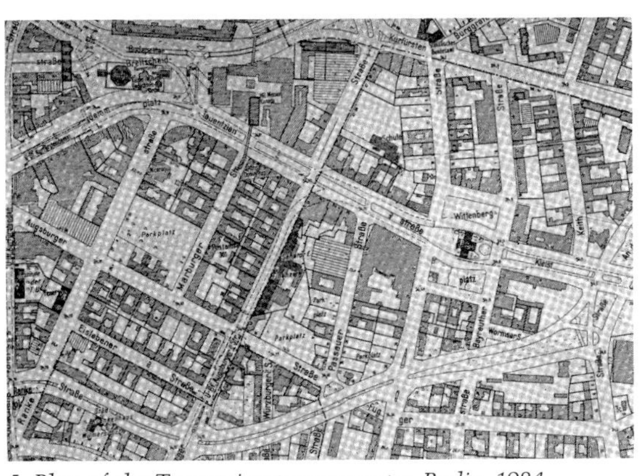

5. *Plan of the Tauentzienstrasse quarter, Berlin, 1984*

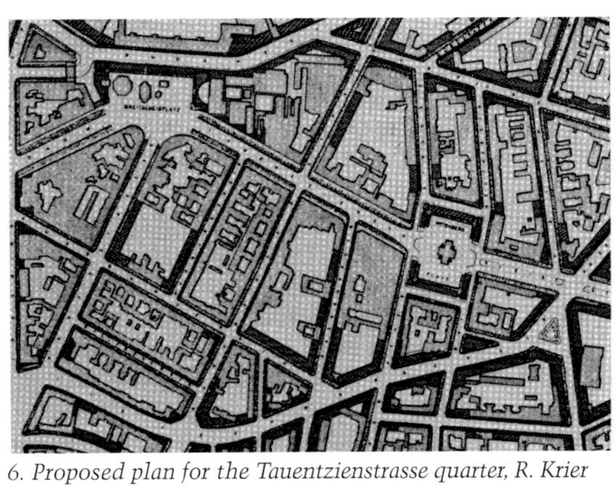

6. *Proposed plan for the Tauentzienstrasse quarter, R. Krier*

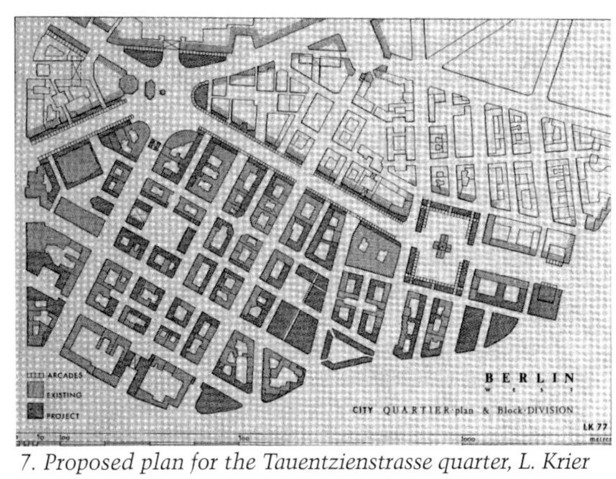

7. *Proposed plan for the Tauentzienstrasse quarter, L. Krier*

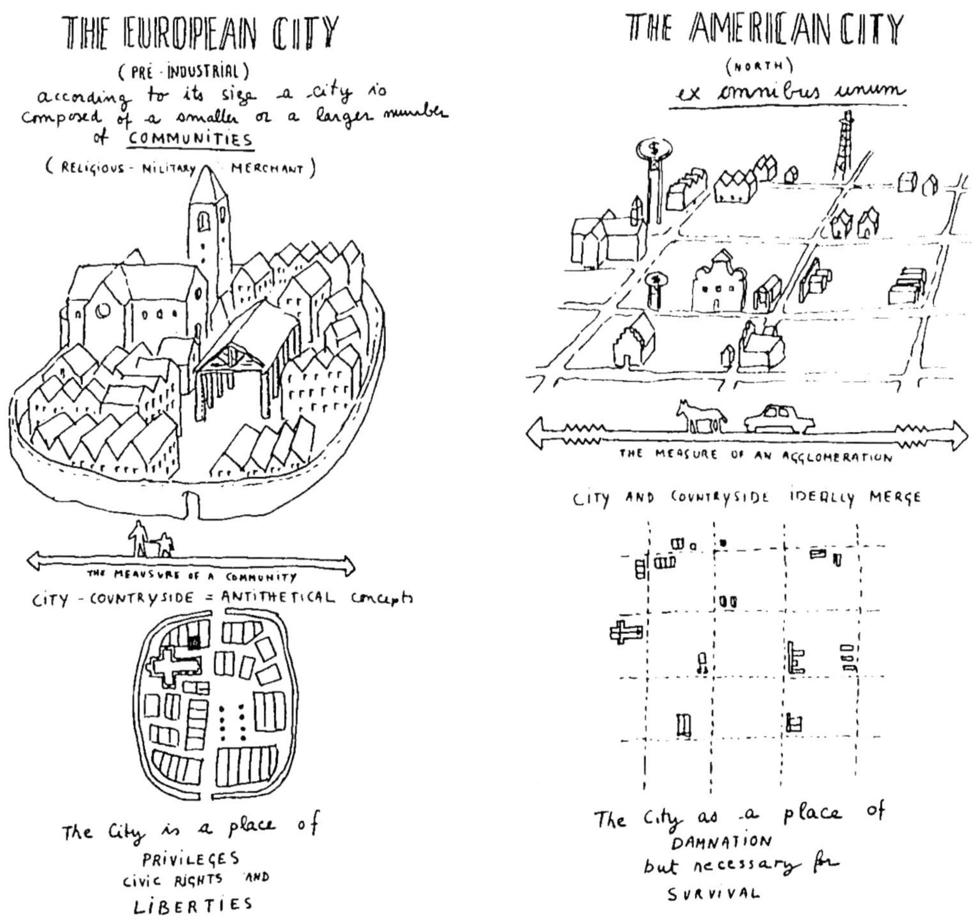

1. European and American cities

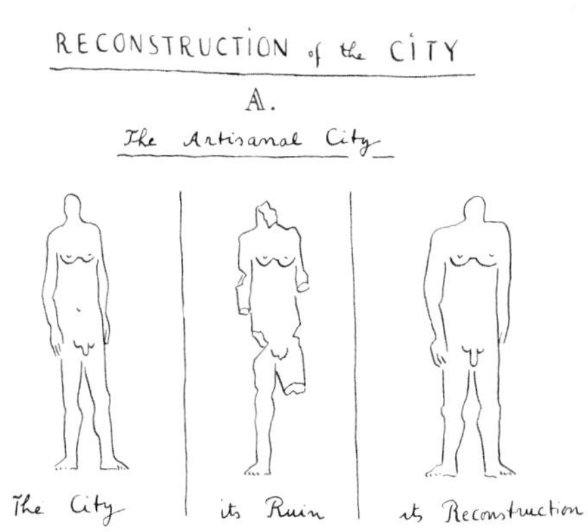

2. The Artisanal city

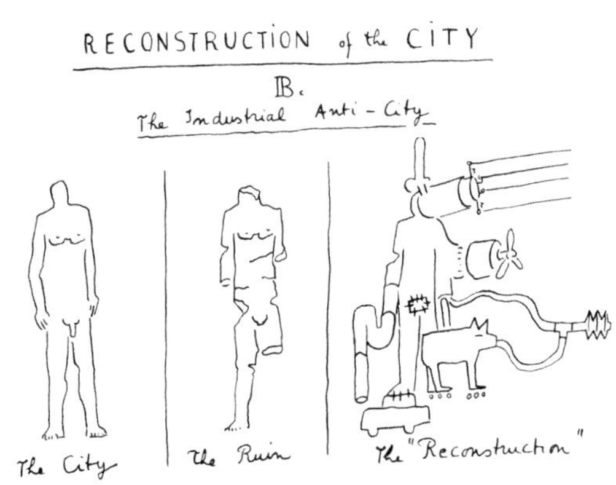

3. The Industrial city

Leon Krier

Leon Krier was not the first to question the tenets of the modernist city, but he was the clearest and most polemically dogmatic. His urban proposals were the exact inverse of a half-century of modernism.

Krier's rationalist colleagues, including his brother Rob, began their onslaught against the disintegration of the traditional European city with local projects—urban "interventions" and "counter-projects." Leon, alone among them, began with the whole city, and was the only one to develop a comprehensive, illustrated theory of the city.[31]

This theory grew out of a reaction against the industrial city—the nineteenth-century city with its dense, overly large blocks, and especially the city of modern architecture, based on the principles of Le Corbusier, CIAM, and Team X, all of which he holds responsible for destroying the city. Krier argues that industrialization disconnected the practice of architecture from the integrity of the urban whole, and turned the contemporary city into a city of objects.

Fundamental is his critique of zoning and the organization of the city through monofunctional zones, which has resulted in the exodus from the city and the propagation of suburban environments and sprawl. He suggests the only real solution is therefore a reversal or inversion of modernist thinking to the preindustrial model to reinstate the city to its former glory.

Krier stresses the importance of designing the urban environment relative to the human scale, informing everything from the organization of civic program through the fabric of the city, the organization and sizes of blocks and streets, to the articulation of the building typologies; he argues that architecture can only be informed by an urban structure that is as considered and rigorously resolved.

He also argues that a mature city's growth should not be a saturated core followed by aimless sprawl, but rather dense multiple centers, which retain a mix of functions and of public and private space. In other words, he stresses growth of the city in a polycentric rather than monocentric manner. These centers, or quarters, are like cities within the city, and their success depends on the retention of the space between buildings, a continuous urban fabric of small blocks, and tight streets. His arguments are all counter to a singular architectural vision.

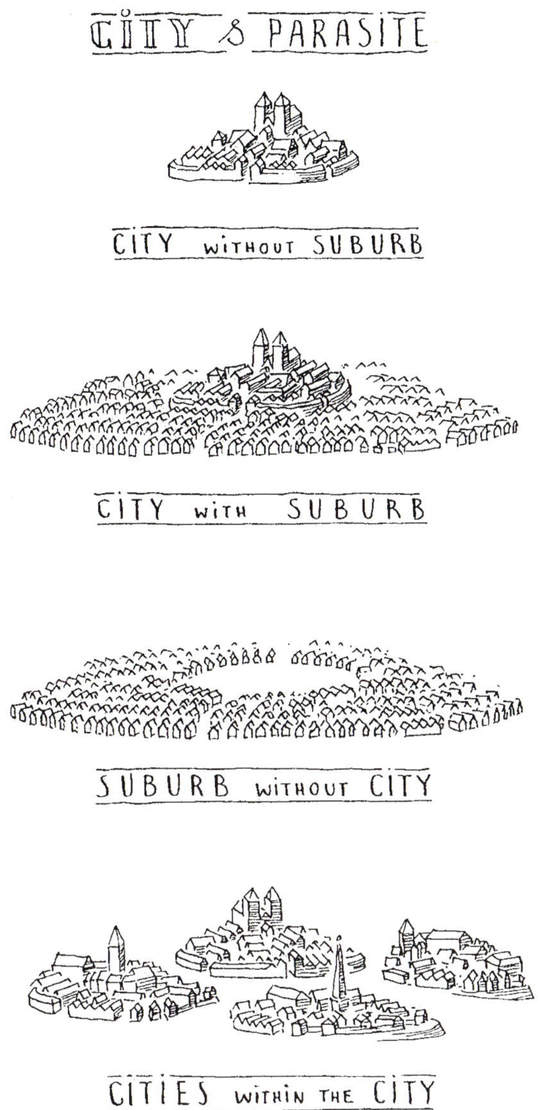

1. Cities and suburbs

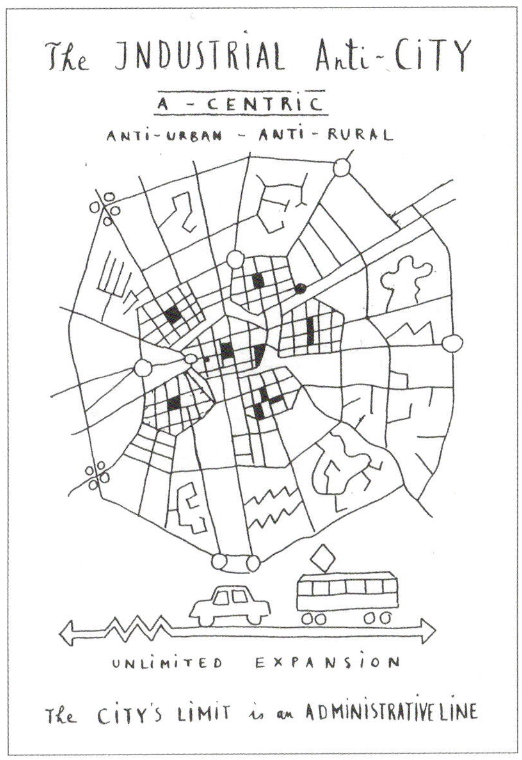

2. The industrial city

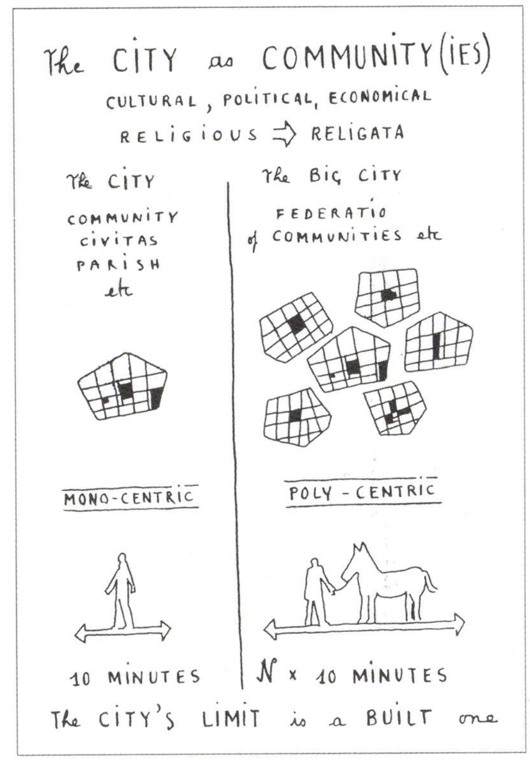

3. The city as community

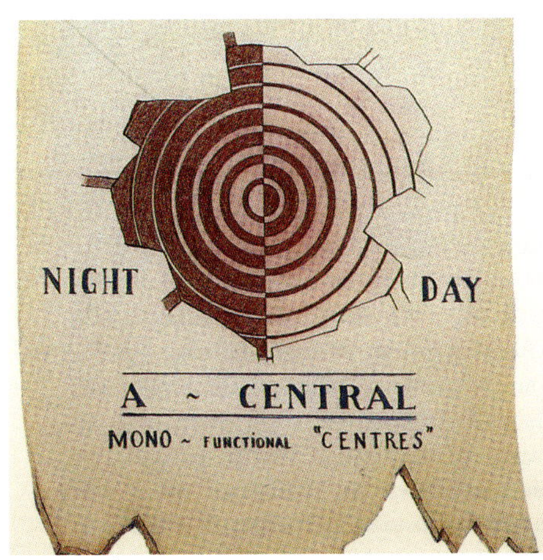

4. Central city

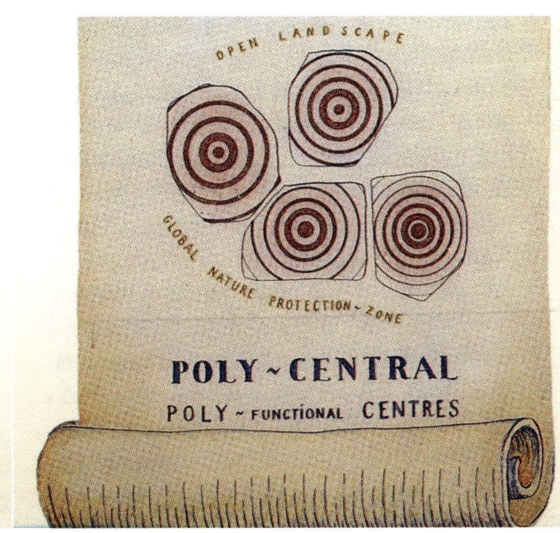

5. Poly-central city

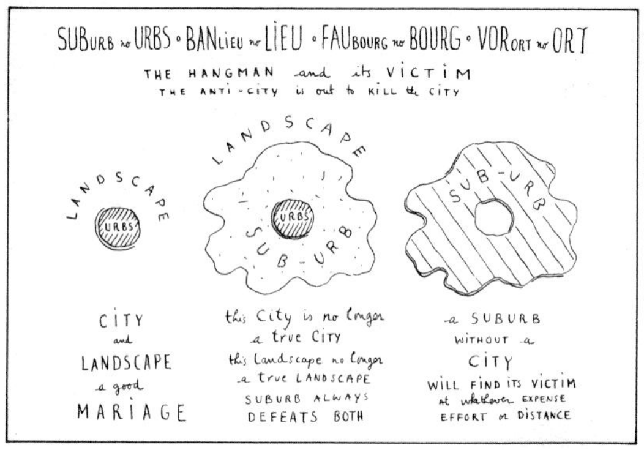

1. City and landscape

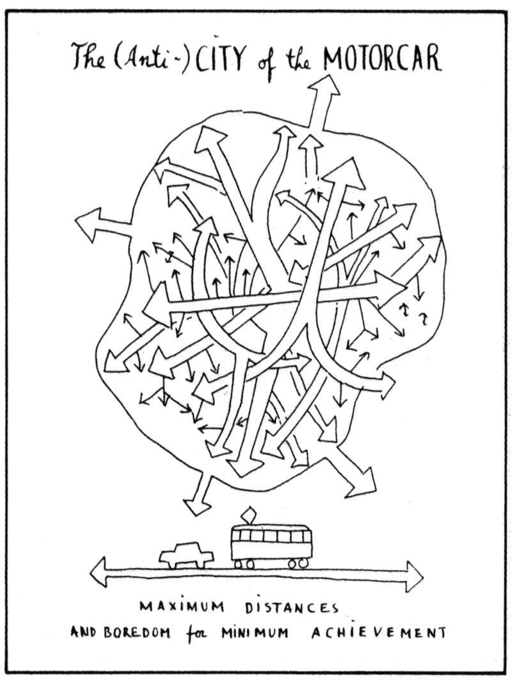

2. City and automobile

The Form of the City

According to Krier, the city, or the city within the city, is composed of monuments and an urban fabric of streets, blocks, and spaces. Together, these form a civic structure—a public realm—of legible spatial sequences and important buildings. The city is compact, with limited vehicular circulation. It should not be blended into the surrounding landscape by suburbia.

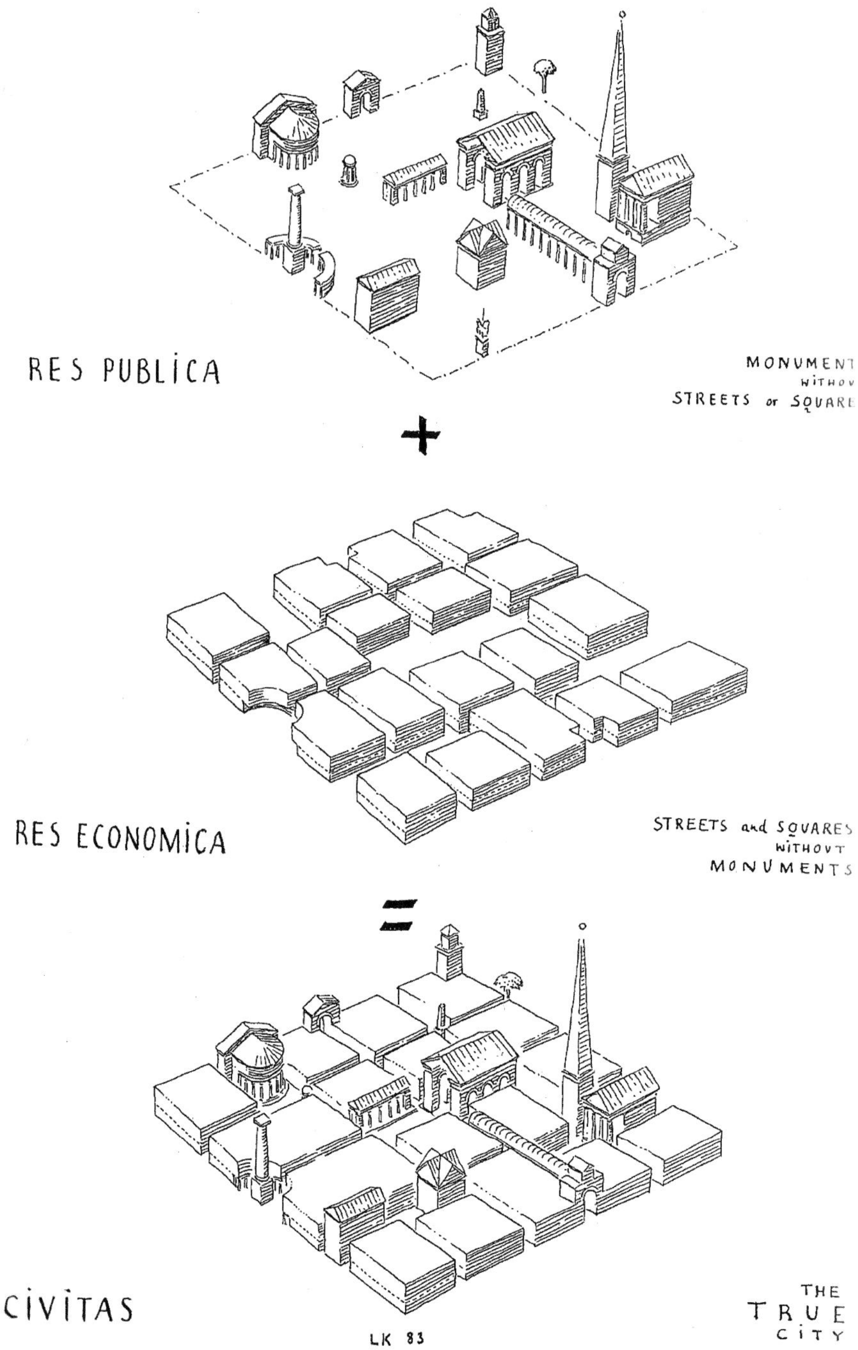

3. Monuments and fabric

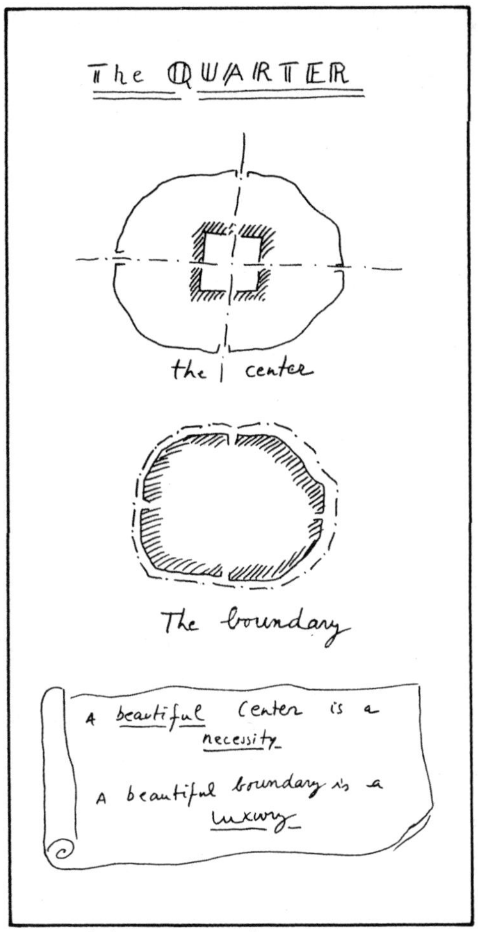

1. Formal characteristics of a quarter

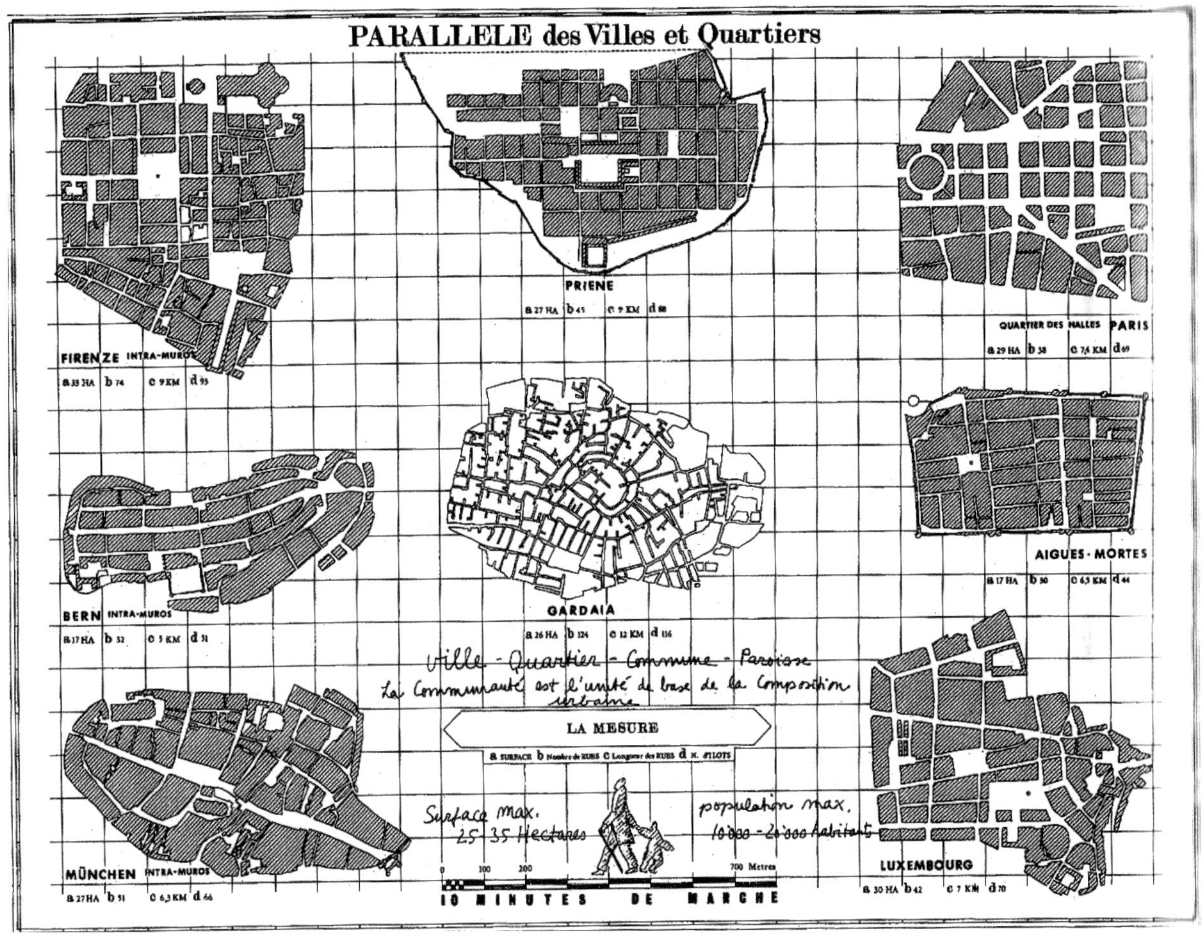

2. Parallel of cities and neighborhoods

QUARTERS: THE CITY WITHIN THE CITY

An urban quarter, or neighborhood, is analogous to a Roman cross-axial town plan in that it has three formal characteristics:

1. *A clear center*
2. *Consistent urban fabric*
3. *A clear edge*

A clear edge is less important.

Krier refers to the city as a federation of autonomous quarters. He argues that the neighborhood, or quarter, can easily accommodate all of the necessary programmatic functions of commerce, industry, residential areas, and culture so that the movement through the city as a whole is limited to an occasional experience, and there is less pressure on the traffic arteries to penetrate the neighborhoods, which function equally well independently. He established the 10-minute walking rule—that anything within a quarter should be accessible within a 10-minute walk. This rule acts as a measure of what the reasonable size of a neighborhood should be, and in turn also emphasizes that the urban environment should be designed with continual consideration of the human scale. Krier goes so far as to specify that the size of a quarter designed to the human scale should not exceed 35 hectares and 15,000 inhabitants to be considered a quarter.[32]

Urban Space

Krier argues that the form of public spaces should not be a matter of personal experiment, but must present a familiar character with dimensions and proportions of the best and most beautiful cities. He identifies four fundamental types of urban space. The first is the indescribable modernist space that is the residue of antiurban architecture. The second is that of the pattern of streets and squares resulting from a grid of typologically classifiable blocks. In the third type, urban blocks are the result of a pattern of streets and squares. The fourth is that of precise, formal space types that are discontinuous from the surrounding fabric.[33]

Urban Blocks

Small blocks are central to Krier's idea of the city. He uses the Spanish quarter of Naples as a good example of how higher densities can be achieved with small block sizes, which improves not only the quality of the buildings (creating more opportunities for windows), but also the quality of the street, through more public space, and thus the general safety of the city.

The other very important advantage of the smaller block is that it plays a significant role in breaking up the continuum of the street. When wider arterial boulevards are drained with multiple smaller streets, smaller block sizes create more animated streets.[34]

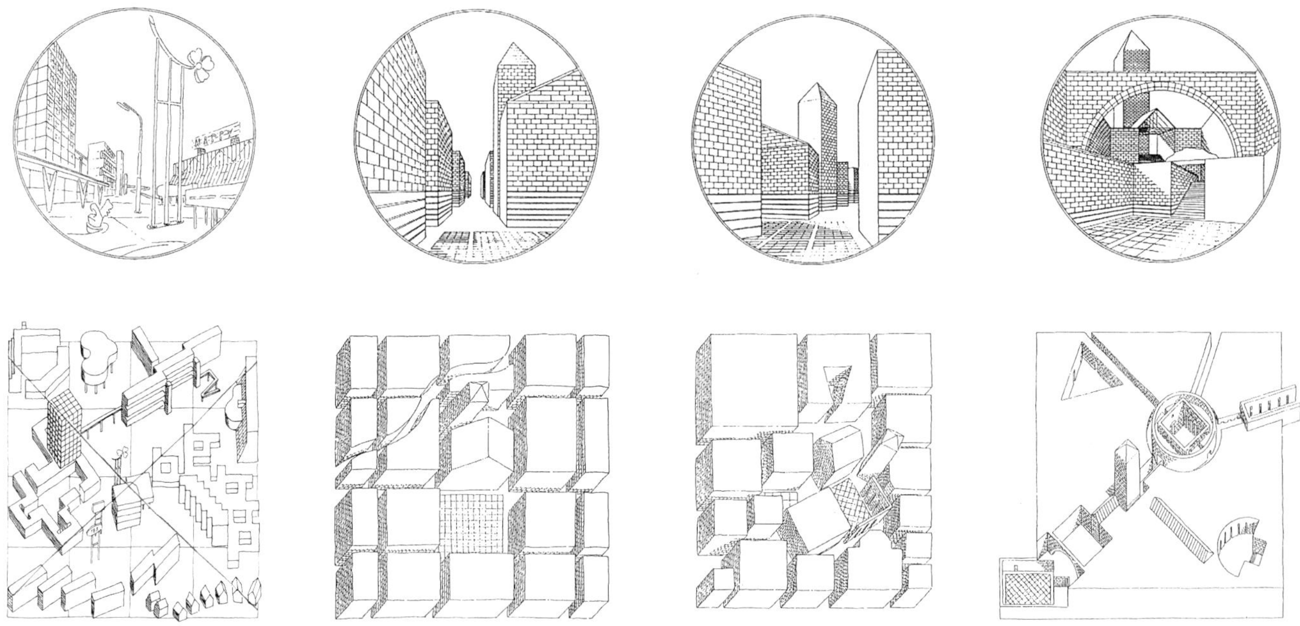

1. Isolated objects, no space *2. Congruent blocks and space* *3. Space results from blocks* *4. Blocks result from space*

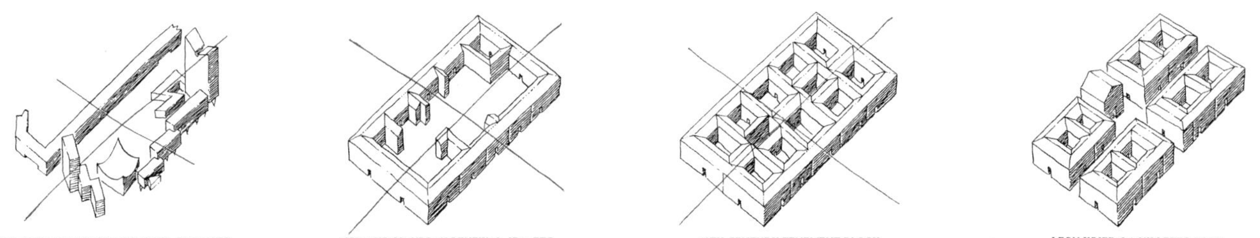

20TH-CENTURY ATHENS CHARTER, CIAM, ETC . . . 1970s AND 80s URBAN RENEWAL, IBA, ETC . . . 19TH-CENTURY TENEMENT BLOCK LEON KRIER, LA VILLETTE (1976); BERLIN CITY (1977), ETC . . .

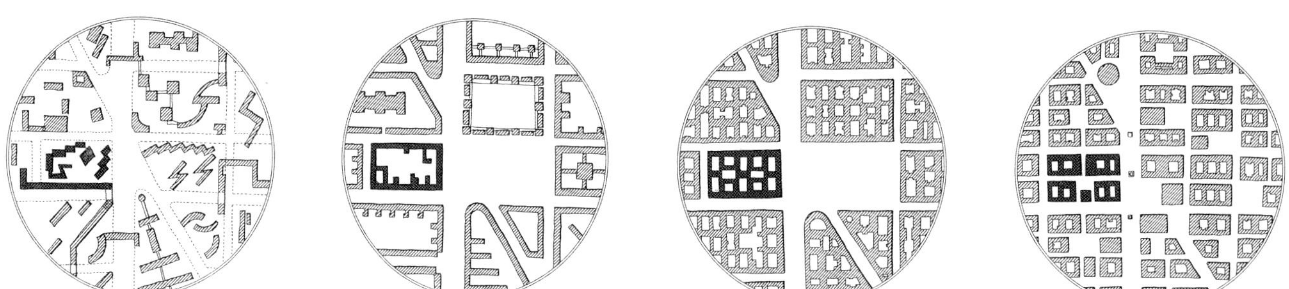

5. Too much public space *6. Too much semipublic space* *7. Too little public space* *8. The correct solution*

1. *The "City"*

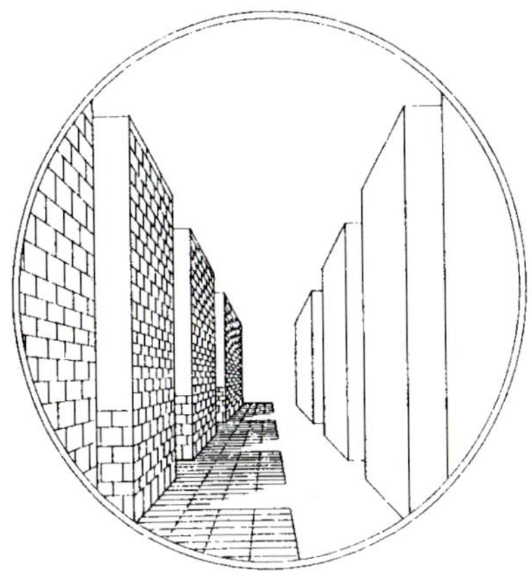

2. *Street with small blocks*

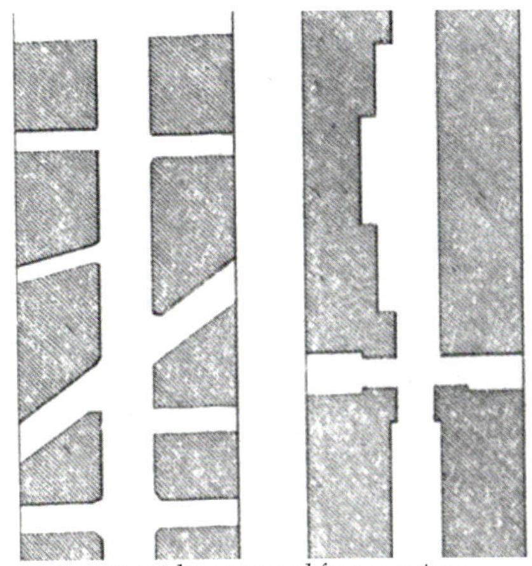

3. *Streets with many and few openings*

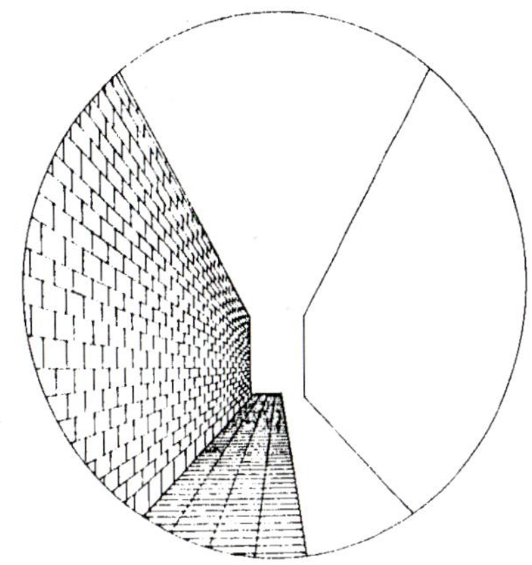

4. *Street with large blocks*

Streets

Along with smaller blocks, Krier advocates smaller streets—pedestrian rather than passage. This theory acknowledged the street as a place and animated it, with varying building typologies and smaller blocks, to avoid the discomforting continuum of endless streets and large blocks, in which the only resemblance to an urban experience is through movement at an automotive speed.

Squares

Krier is surprisingly quiet about urban squares, but he always illustrated their architectural language, which progressed from the stripped-down abstraction of *L'architettura razionale* in the early 1970s, to the emergent neoclassicism of the late 1970s, to the full blown classicism of the 1980s. As his classical language expanded it had a revised impact on his plans.

5. *Royal Mint Square, 1974*

6. *Luxembourg Square, 1978*

7. *Civic space*

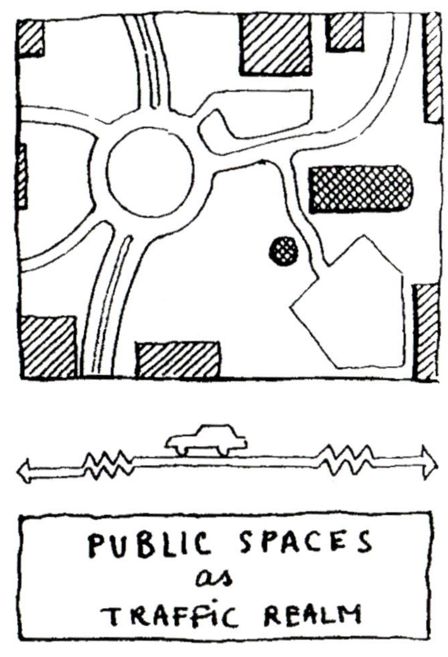

8. *Traffic space*

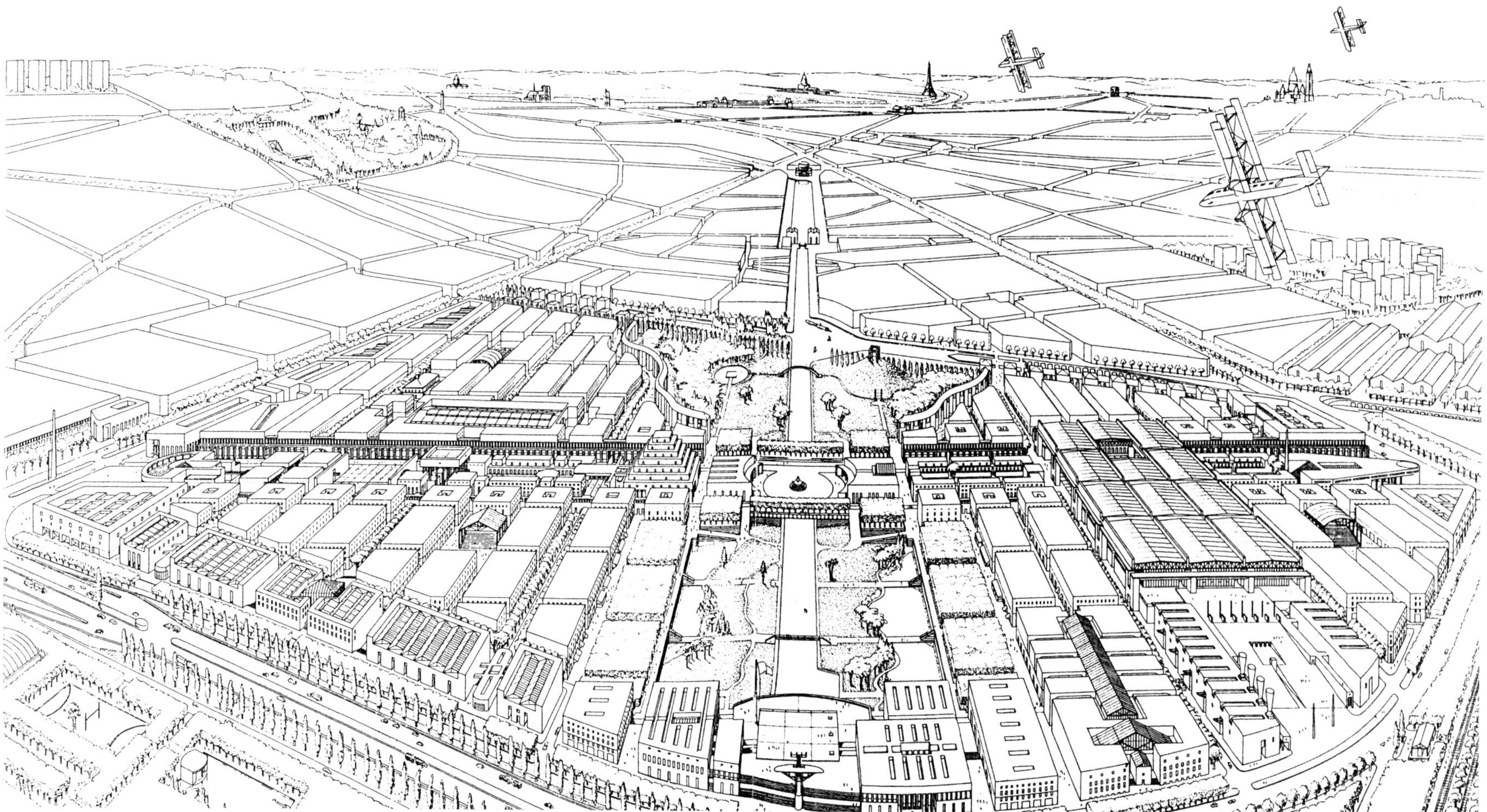

1. Aerial view of La Villette proposal, 1976

2. Le Corbusier, Plan Voisin for Paris, 1925

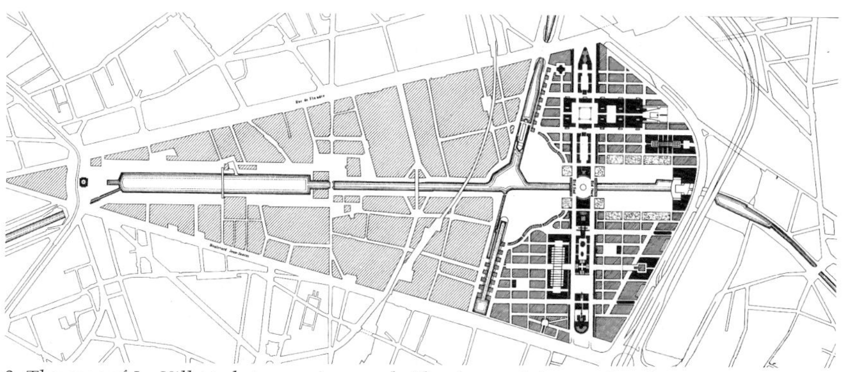

3. The area of La Villette between Avenue de Flandres and Avenue Jean Jaures

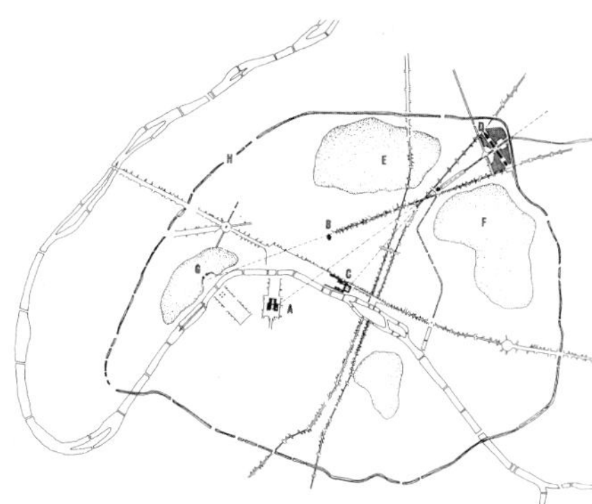

4. Location of La Villette in Paris

La Villette (1976)

The project for the La Villette quarter in Paris was Krier's first comprehensive plan. He not only drew the whole "city within the city," but he related its civic structure to the immediate surroundings and the city of Paris. Urbanistically, it is the antithesis of Le Corbusier's urban plans, such as the Plan Voisin for Paris. The La Villette project is dense, limited in height, and formed of the traditional elements of blocks, streets, squares, parks, etc.—in other words, the exact opposite of the town planning principles of Le Corbusier, CIAM, and Team X.[35]

The most remarkable invention is the figurative sequence of parks that align with the Canal de l'Ourc and the basin de la Villette. This monumental gesture is made of prosaic components rather than cathedrals or other monuments, and is within the Parisian tradition of urban landscapes.

LOCATION OF PUBLIC SPACES KEY

A-GRAND BOULEVARD NORD-SUD
B-PLACE CENTRALE
C-PLACE DE LA MAIRIE(TOWN HALL)
D-SQUARE DES CONGRES
E-PLACE DE QUARTIER
F-MARKET **G**-PERSPECTIVE DES INVALIDES **H**-INDUSTRIAL EXHIBITION LEVELS
I-PUBLIC GARDENS **J**-LAKE
K-METRO EXIT

DISTRIBUTION OF FUNCTIONS KEY

A-CENTRE DE QUARTIER
B-MAIRIE/TOWN HALL
C-CULTURAL CENTRE **D**-MUSUEM
E-CONFERENCE AND EXHIBITION CENTRE
F-HOTELS **G**-BATHS **H**-CASINO
I-MAJOR SHOPS **J**-STREET MARKET
K-OFFICES **L**-ARTISANS
M-INDUSTRY **N**-OFFICES **O**-HIGH SCHOOL
P-CRECHE **R**-HOSPITAL

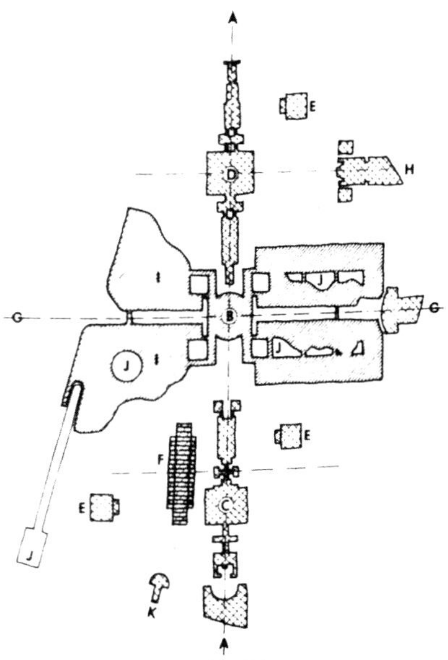

1. Civic structure of public spaces

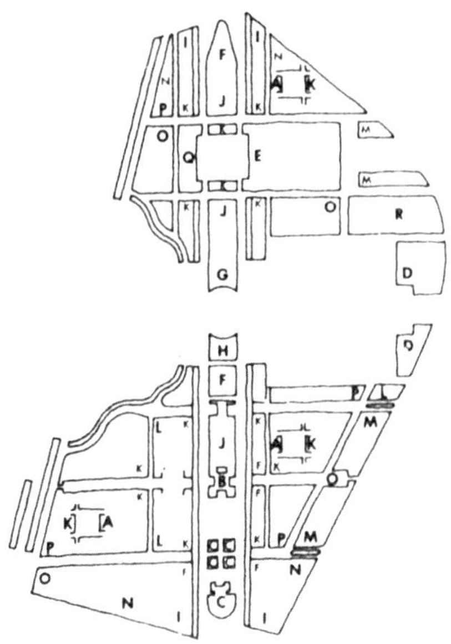

2. Distribution of functions

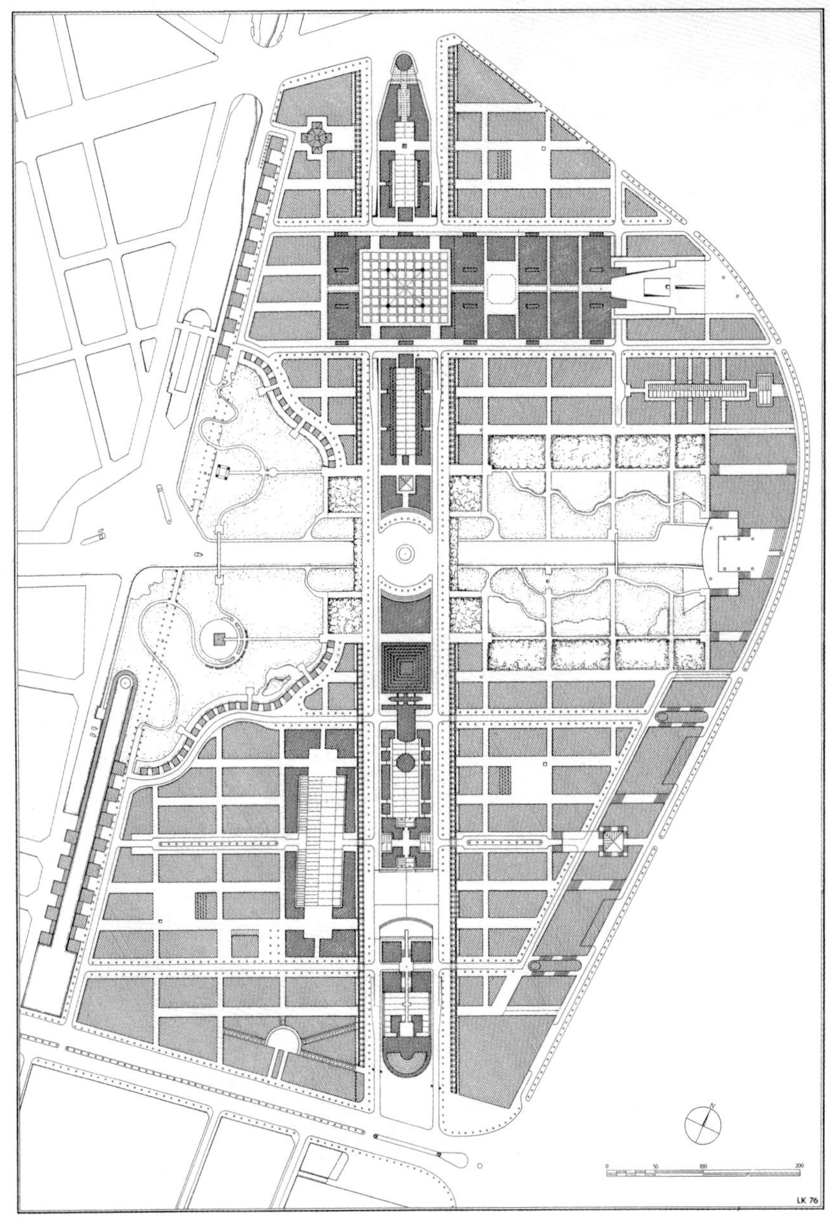

3. Proposed plan of La Villette, 1976, 1:7,500

Civic Spaces: The Park

Public parks and gardens have played a significant role in the Parisian urban environment at least since the time of Haussmann and Adolph Alphand. Their invention of urban landscape—*the Garden in the City*—is a quintessential characteristic of Paris. Since buildings rarely provide individual outdoor space, Parisians make very active use of the public parks and gardens as a relief from the density of the city.

Krier used the geographical characteristics of the great basin of La Villette, and the axis of the Canal de l'Ourc, which is oriented toward Ledoux's monumental cylinder—the Barrière de la Villette—to create the great park. In other words, the park was designed as a natural culmination of the space of the basin as well as the focus of the La Villette neighborhood.

The porous boundaries with the screen of artists studios contain the space without completely gating it off. Rather, the screen transparently links the park to the residential neighborhood behind.

In a time of secular culture, where the idea of the monument has become redundant, Krier was able to create a monumentality in the experience of the park while referencing the monuments dotted across the Parisian landscape in the distance.

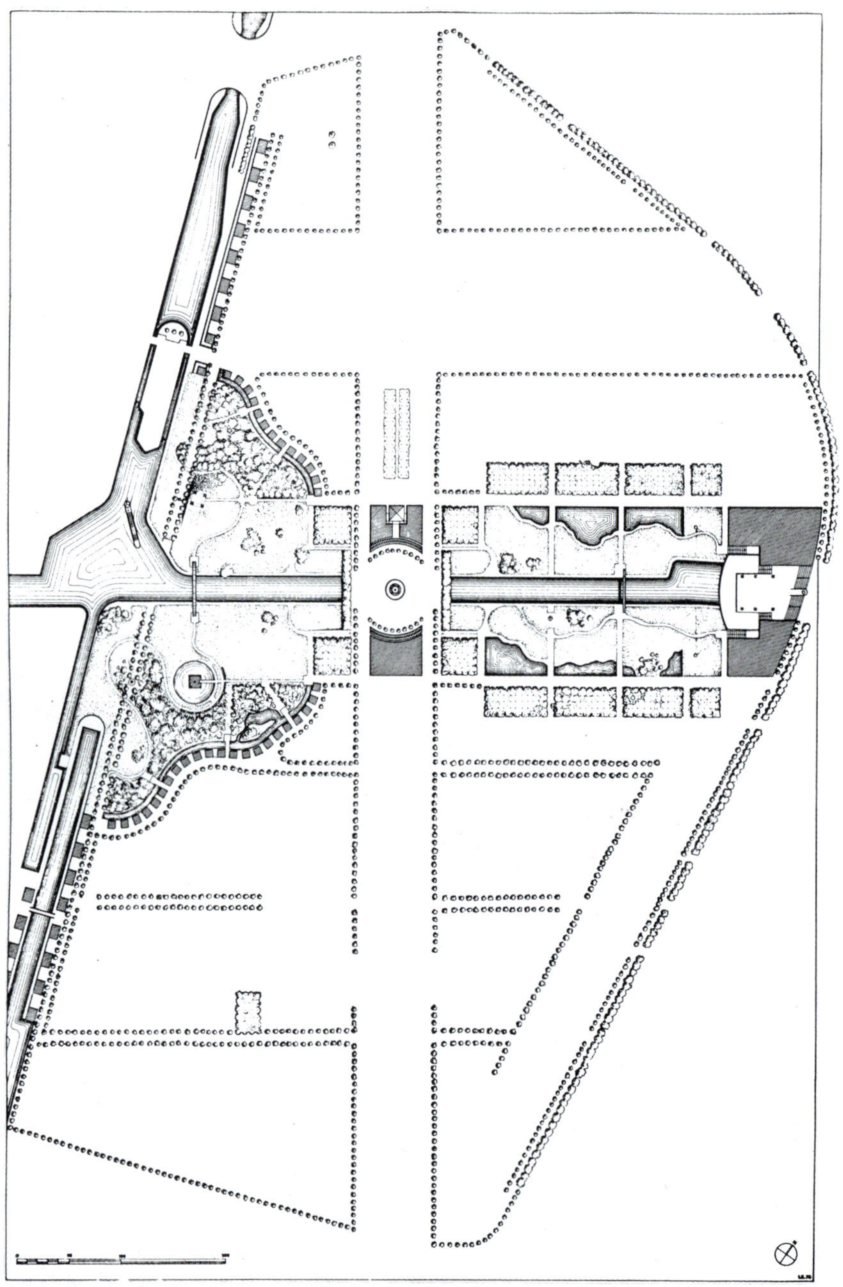

1. *Landscape plan*

2. *View of artists's studios from the park*

3. *View of the park and Paris beyond*

4. *The screen of the park edge*

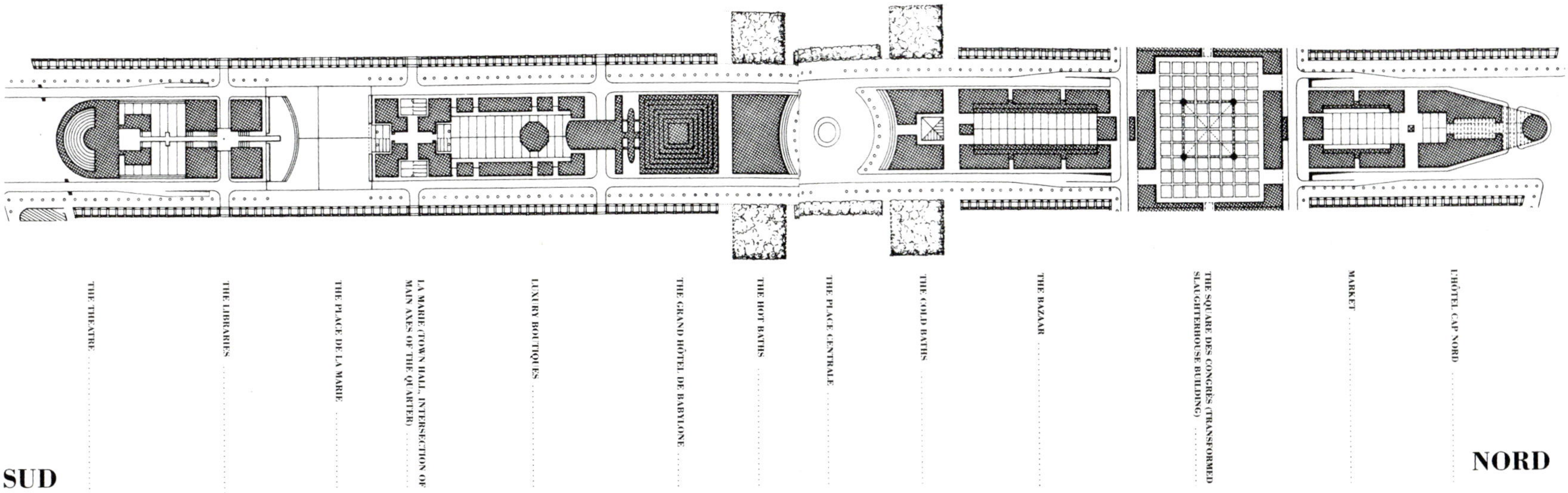

1. The north–south boulevard plan

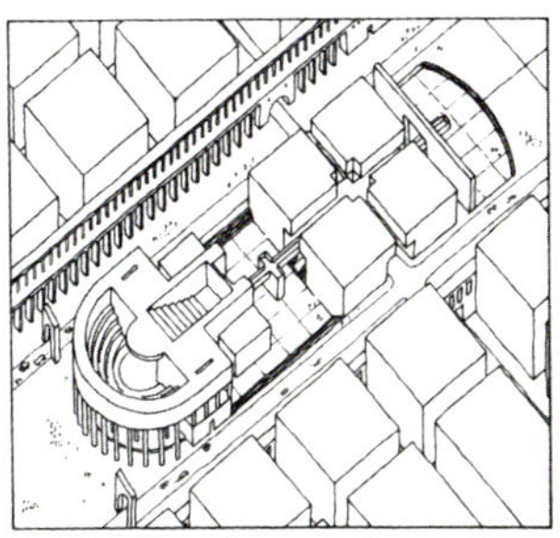

2. The libraries and theater

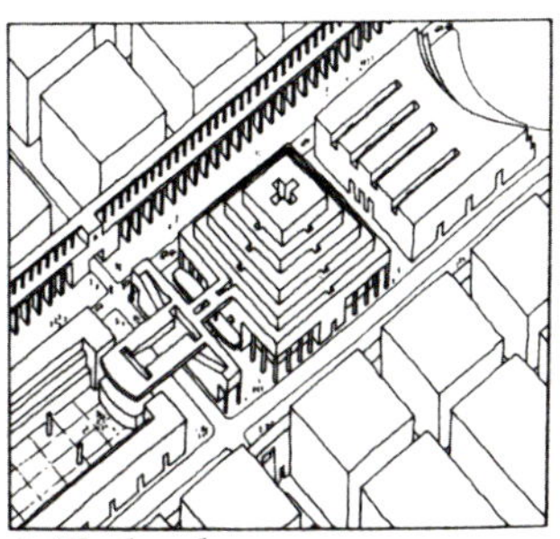

3. The hotel

4. Ledoux's Barrière

5. The stoa of the Grand Boulevard

6. The Square des Congres

Civic Spaces: The Boulevard

The Boulevard Nord–Sud is effectively a one kilometer-long city center. In keeping with the traditions of the median strip in Parisian Boulevards, Krier flanked the Boulevard on either side with parallel avenues for traffic flow, which are 50 meters wide and span the entire length of the Boulevard. The Boulevard is made up of a series of civic and cultural amenities for the quarter. These include the Grand Hotel Cap Nord et de Babylone, the cultural center, the New Town Hall (the Mairie), and the subsequent public spaces of the Place de La Mairie, the Place Centrale, and the Square des Congres. The boulevard sets up the premise for the hierarchy of subsequent streets. The stoa plays a vital role in acting as a buffer zone between the open air public spaces and the beginning of the city fabric. It also creates an interstitial space of activity for commerce and allows for a vertical zoning of program, which Krier feels is the only type of zoning required. The covered space of the stoa emphasizes this transition between the secondary streets which drain traffic into the general city fabric from the Grand Boulevard, while creating an impressively monumental vista along its length, emphasizing the difference between public and private space within the quarter.

7. View of the Place de la Mairie

Luxembourg (1978)

In contrast to the plan for La Villette, which was almost all new or ideal, the plan for Luxembourg is a counterproject that was precipitated by Krier's disgust with the modernist plan for the European Parliament on a plateau across from the historic city. Krier's plan is like a prosthetic urban suit that absorbs and embeds the free-standing modernist buildings into a civic urban environment of humanly scaled blocks, streets, and squares.[36]

Like the blocks of La Villette, the basic Luxembourg block dimension is 30 m (ca. 100'), and the basic street width is 11 m (36'). The Place du Parlement is 70 m x 100 m (ca. 230' x 330').

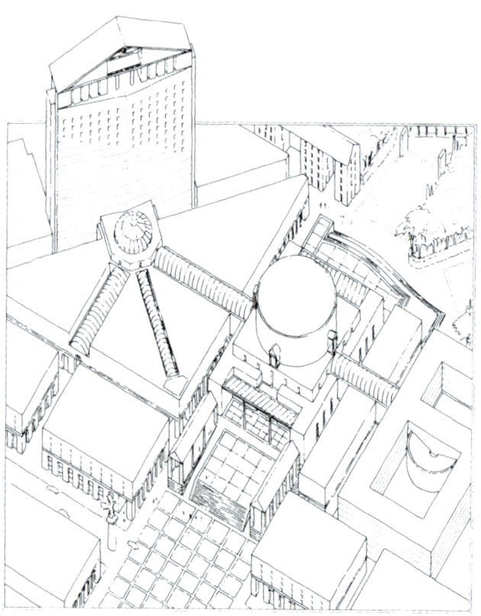

1. Axonometric of the Place du Parlement

2. Aerial view of existing site

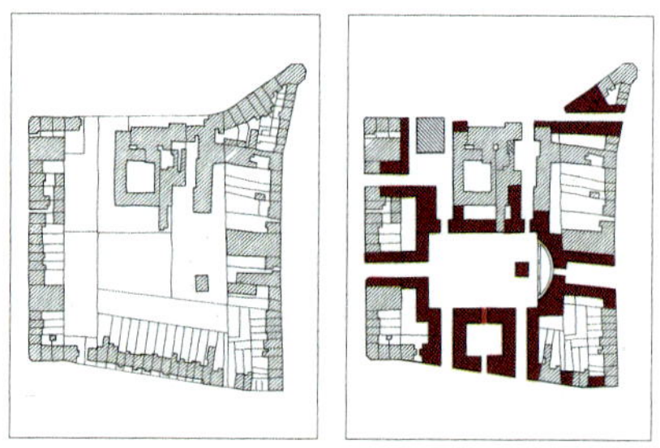

3. Block transformation

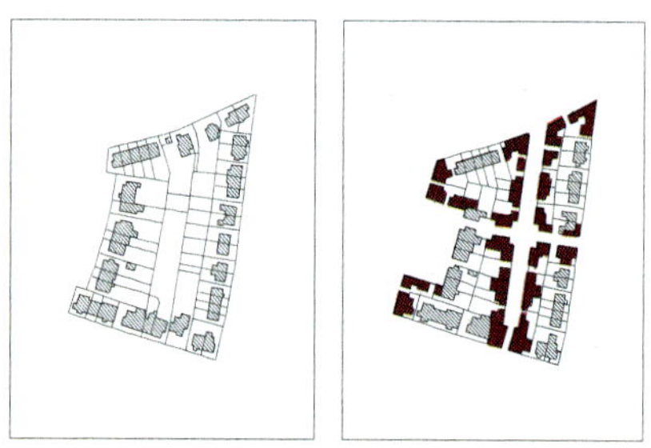

4. Block transformation

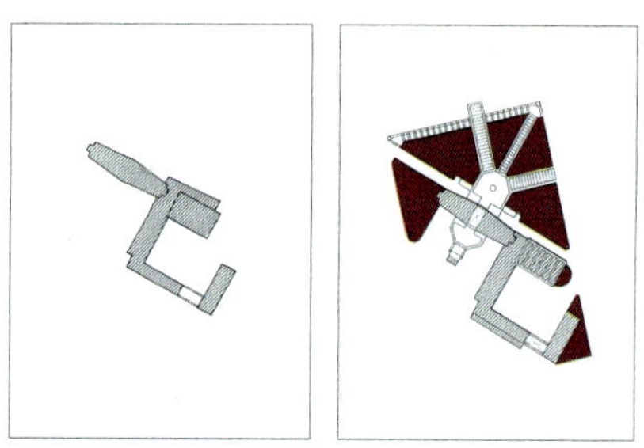

5. Block transformation

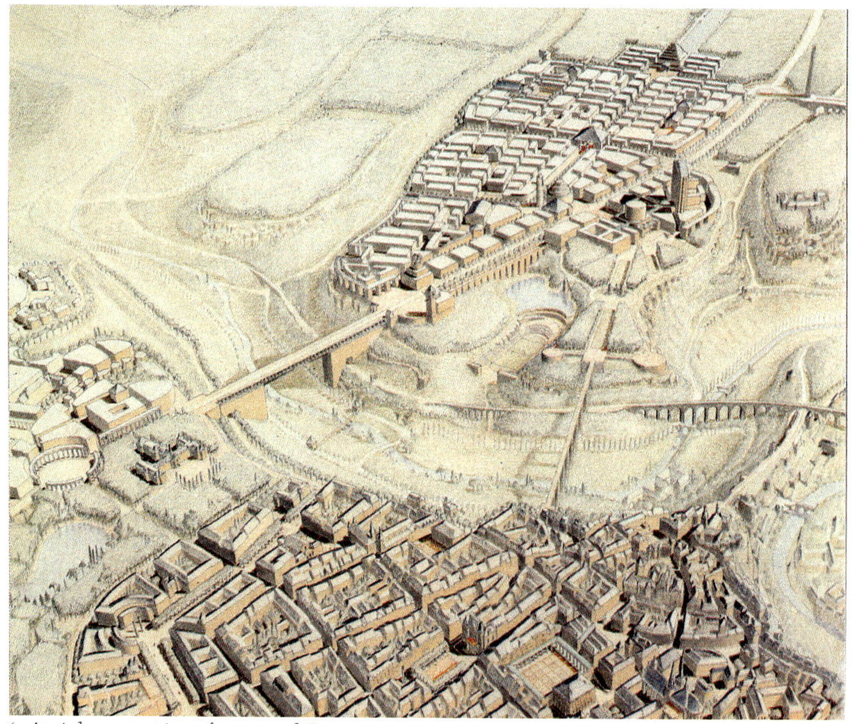

6. Aerial perspective of proposed European quarter

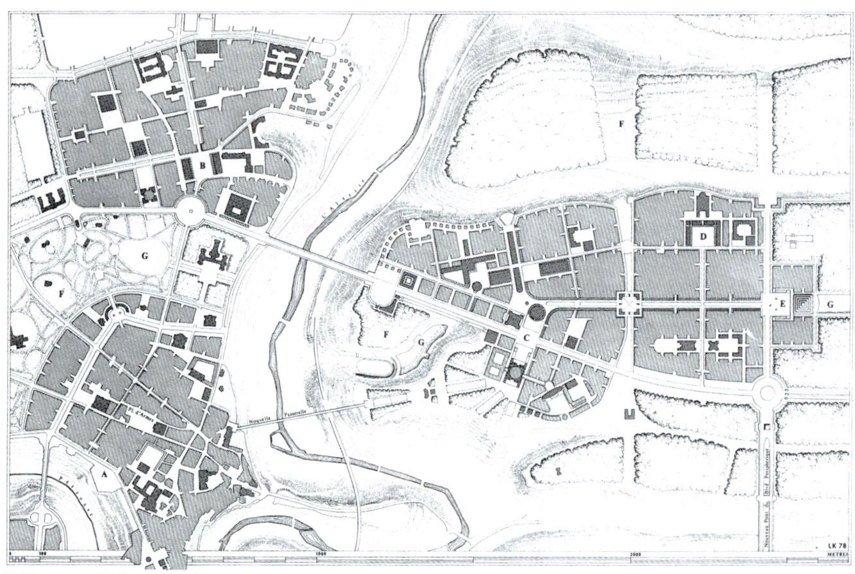

7. Proposed plan of all quarters

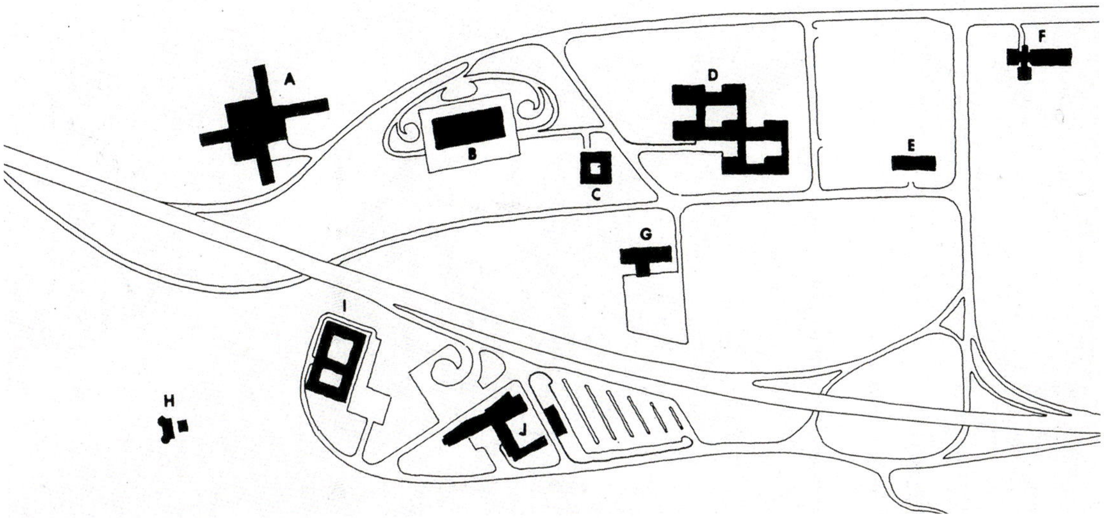

1. Existing plan of European quarter, 1:10,000

3. Aerial view of the proposed European quarter from the old city

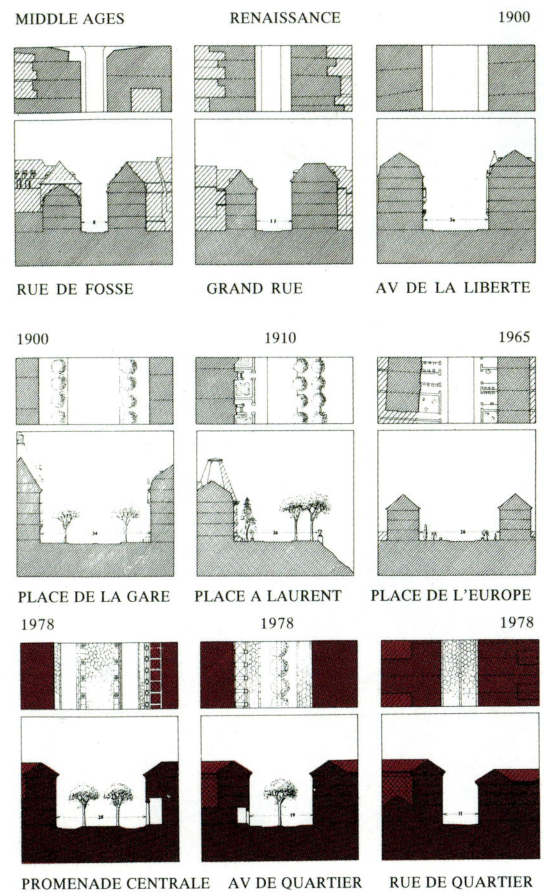

4. Street sections

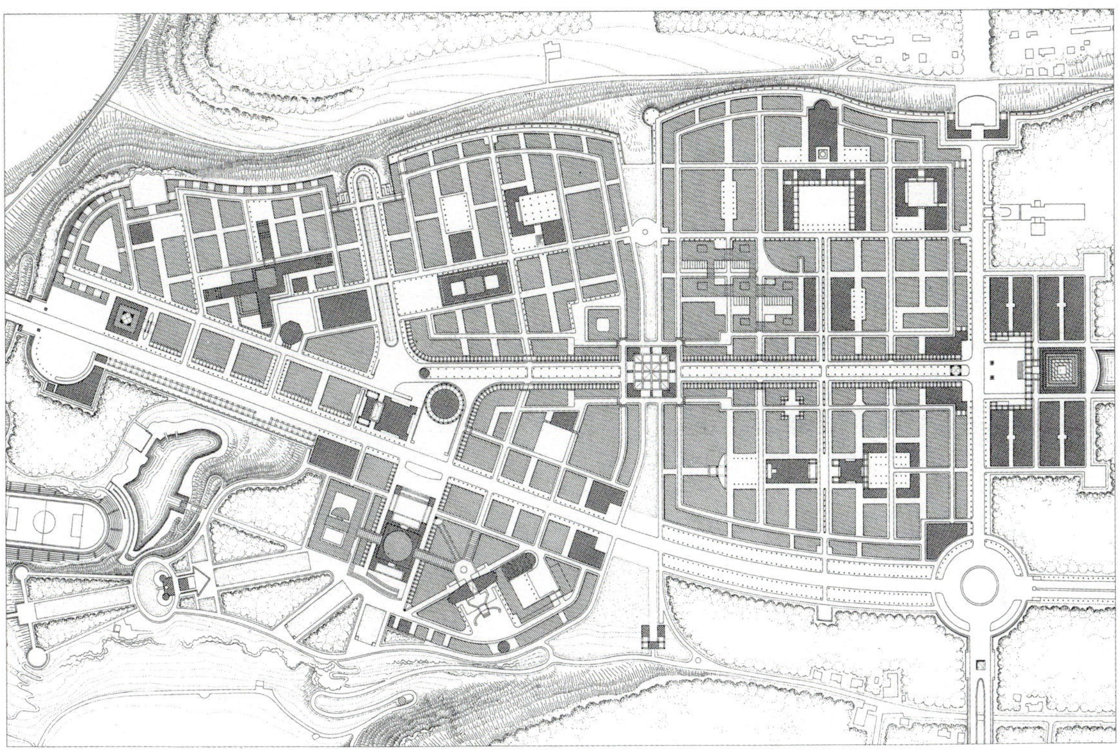

2. Proposed plan of European quarter, 1:10,000

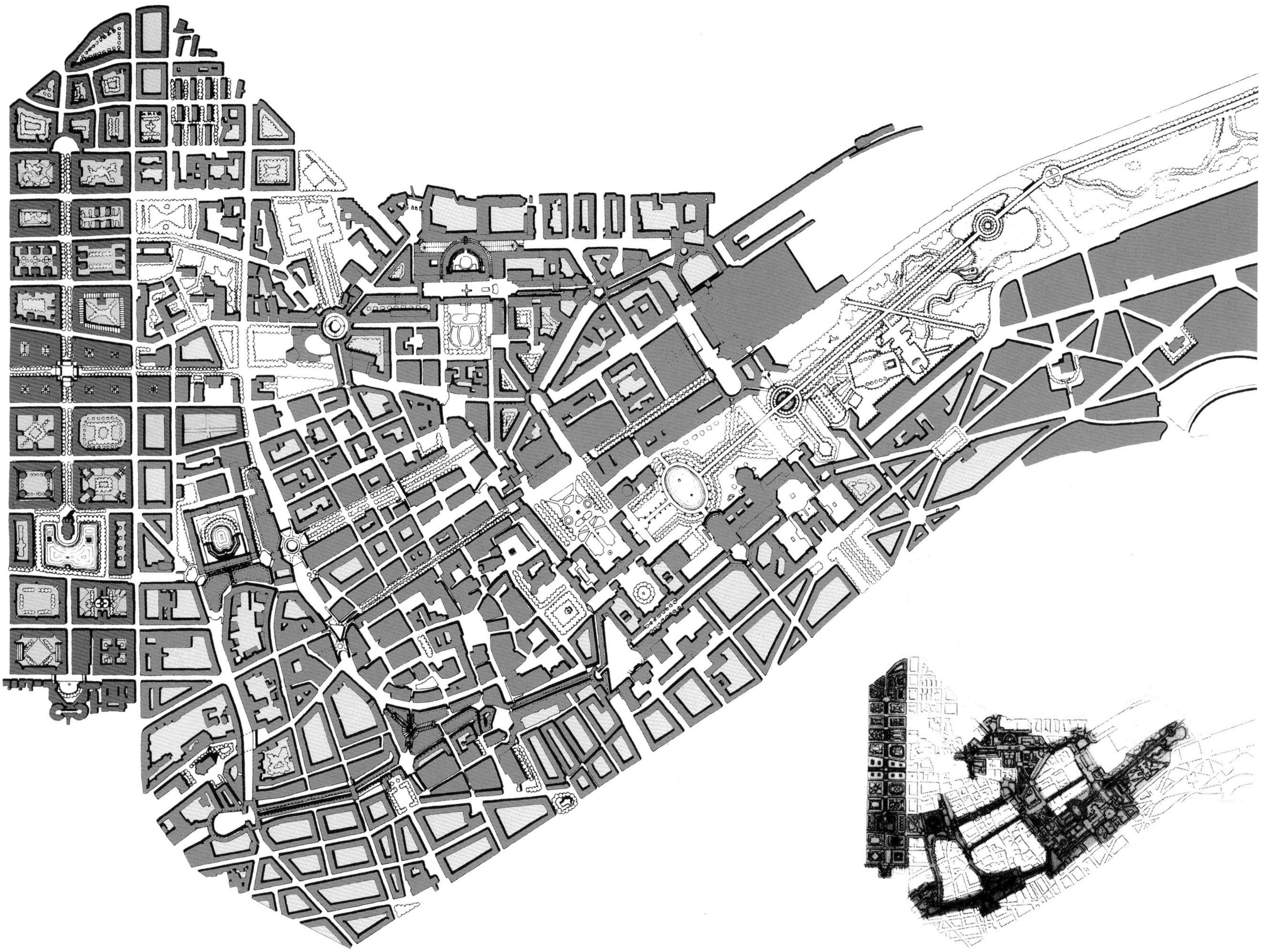

1. Proposed plan of central Stuttgart

2. Replanned areas

Rob Krier and *Stadtraum*

The Stuttgart projects done by Rob Krier's students during the early 1970s, and published in *Stadtraum* (Urban Space) in 1975, focus on the reconstruction of the European city, but they exhibit greater similarity to the principles of Roma Interrotta than to those of Leon Krier. This book, dedicated to Camillo Sitte, had an enormous impact and served as the foundation for Rob's own later work.[37]

In contrast to the destruction at the hands of architects and planners in Boston, Stuttgart had actually been decimated by bombs during the Second World War. In *Stadtraum*, Krier is clear about the demise of urban space—both from bombs and planners—and is equally clear about the need to reconstruct the civic space of the city.

Stadtraum has an overarching argument about the reconstruction of central Stuttgart, but the illustrated design projects are a series of very sophisticated "urban interventions," which are intended to provide important spatial nodes within the city, reestablish the city's civic structure, and reconnect the urban fabric. The formal strategies for accomplishing this are based on principles of discontinuity analogous to those of Roma Interrotta. Figural spaces, such as the Österreichische Platz, for example, stand in sharp contrast with their surrounding urban fields. The tactics, however, are often transformed from modern architecture. Long, thin buildings are used to form streets and spaces rather than blocks, and multiple buildings are often fused into larger agglomerations.

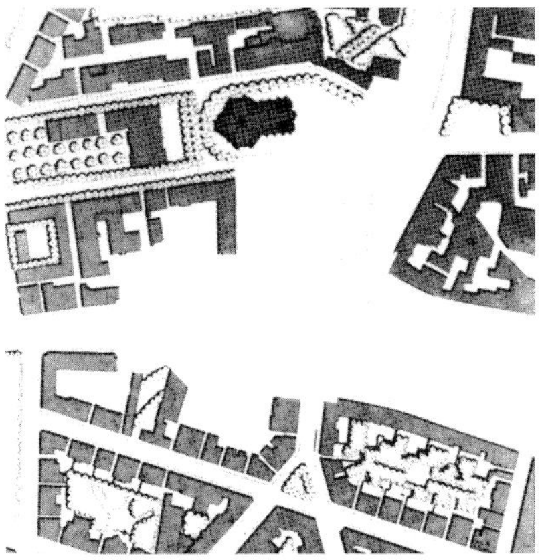

1. *Österreichische Platz, existing plan*

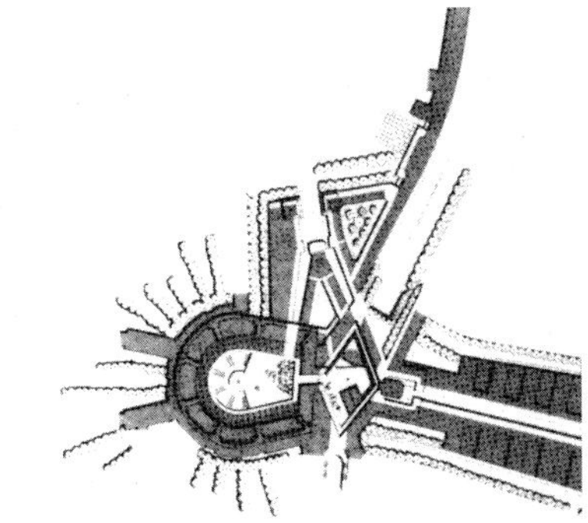

2. *Proposed intervention*

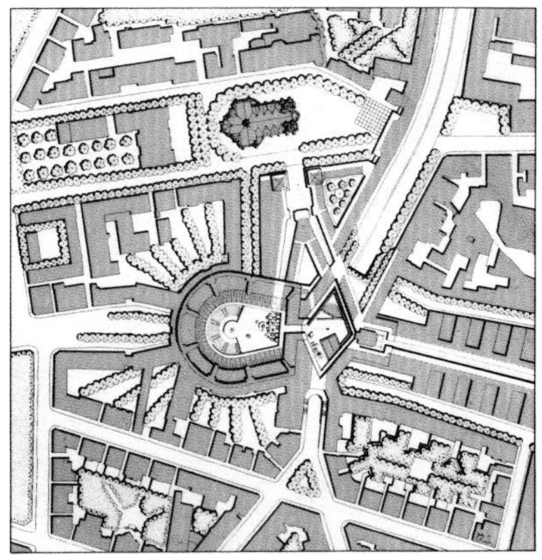

3. *Proposed plan*

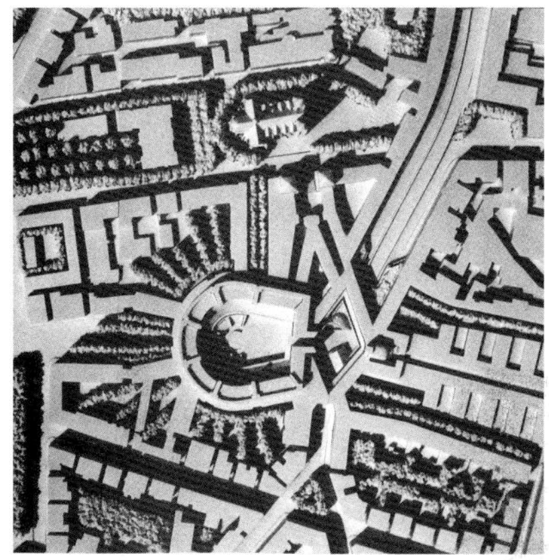

4. *Model of proposed plan*

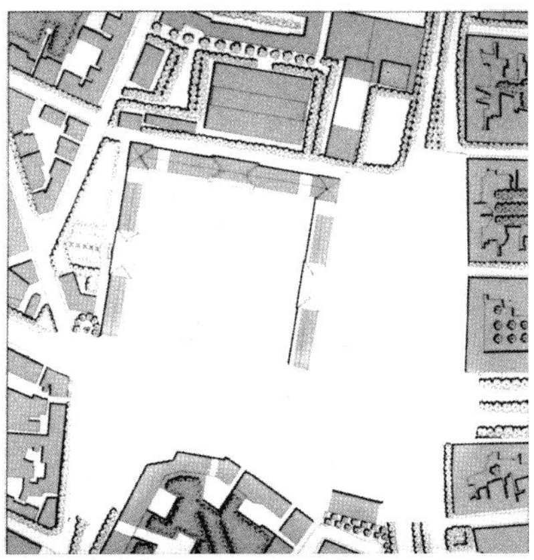

5. *Rotebühl area, existing plan*

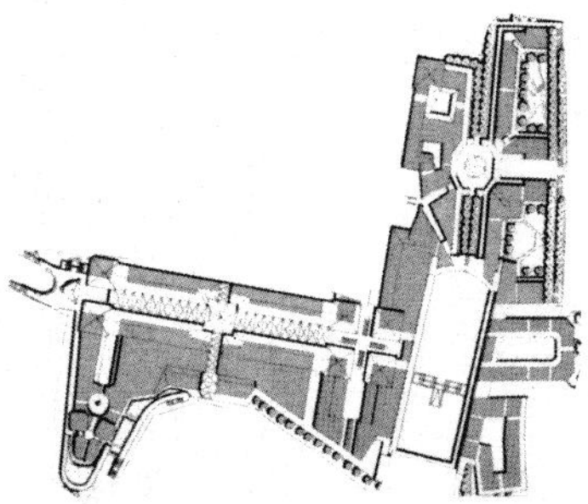

6. *Proposed intervention*

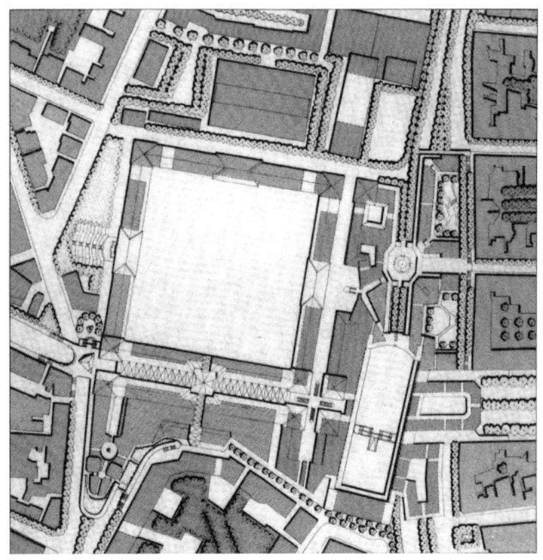

7. *Proposed plan*

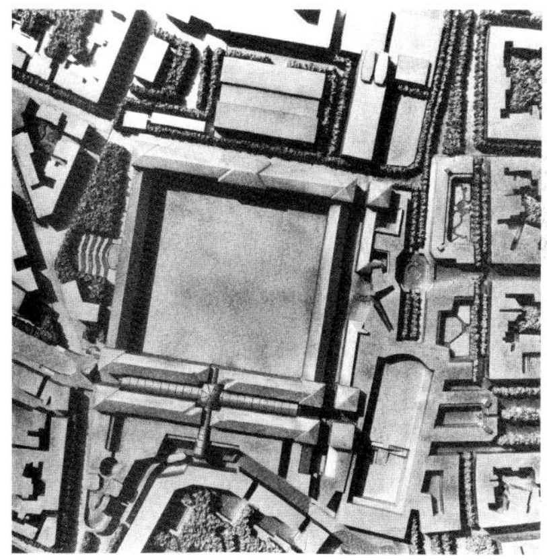

8. *Model of proposed plan*

Urban Interventions

Each major intervention is illustrated by a sequence of four images: existing plan, proposed intervention, proposed plan, and model view of the proposed scheme. Together, these clearly illustrate the principle of discontinuity, or the collision of the ideal (streets and spaces) and the circumstantial (appendages and surrounding fabric).

The primary means of representation are plans and mass models. When architectural language is shown, it is either modest or ephemerally expressionistic.

For all the virtuosity of Rob Krier's Stuttgart interventions and Rowe's Roma Interrotta project, however, neither developed a comprehensive formal agenda for the city—one to stand in complete contrast to Le Corbusier's Ville Radieuse. Rather, they both accepted the traditional city and the idea of the incremental, cumulative city.

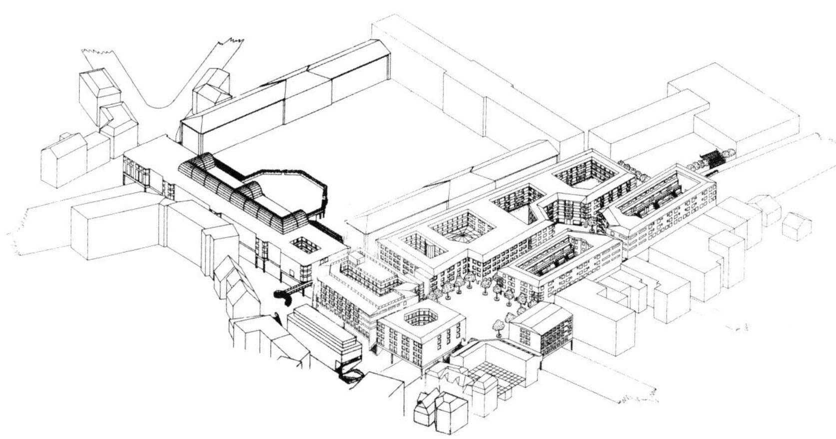

9. *Rotebühl area, isometric view*

The Cornell School

Urban design at Cornell was never involved with the holistic principles and design of towns and cities, such as the work of Leon Krier. Like Rob Krier's work, urban design work at Cornell was involved with fragments—urban interventions—or at most, fields of urban fabric. This situated it at the intersection of urban design and architecture, without succumbing to "urban design as large-scale architecture." It was based on pure urban form, rather than politics, economics, or social issues. It was also not involved with issues of architectural language or style. It always saw the city through an urban lens. It was, however, always steeped in contradiction, discontinuity, fragmentation, and Mannerism. These issues are clearly reflected in the work of Peterson/Littenberg Architects and Koetter/Kim & Associates.

Peterson/Littenberg Architects

Steven Peterson and Barbara Littenberg's extensive urban design work is presented in-depth in their book, *Space & Anti-Space: The Fabric of Place, City, and Architecture*. In addition to commissions, they won several major urban design competitions, including international competitions for Les Halles in Paris in 1979 and the Cité Internationale in Montreal in 1991, and their World Trade Center project in 2002 was the overwhelming favorite of the public in New York City. Les Halles and the World Trade Center projects were conceived as large public spaces with adaptable urban perimeters, while the Montreal project knitted together a series of scattered open sites.

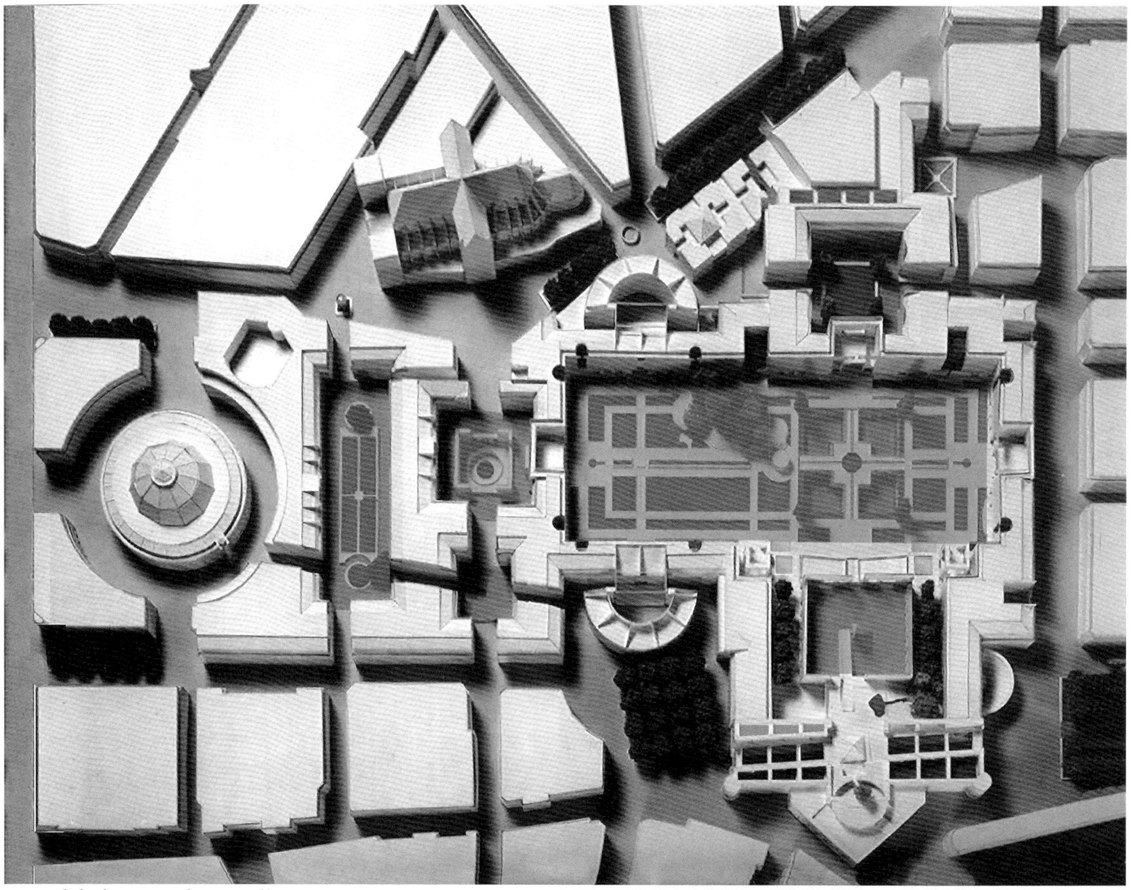

2. Model of proposed Les Halles, Paris

1. Original Les Halles market, Paris

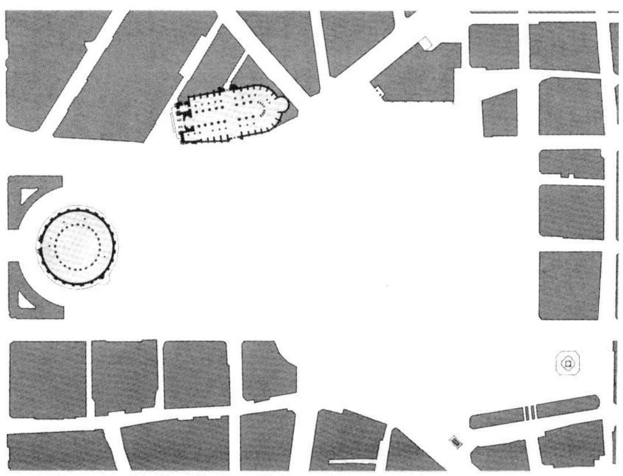

3. Site for Les Halles competition, Paris

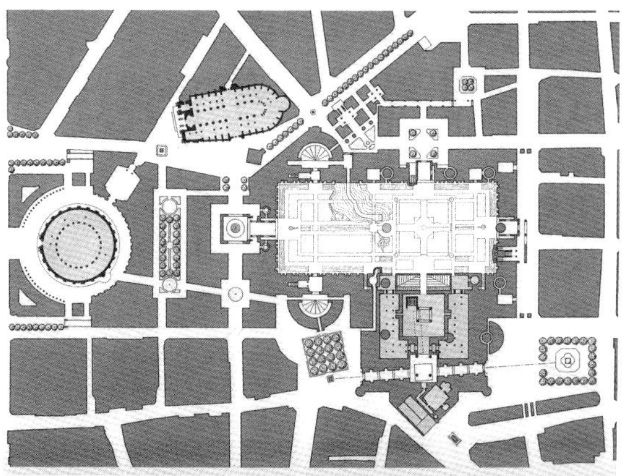

4. Plan of proposed Les Halles

1. Model of proposed World Trade Center

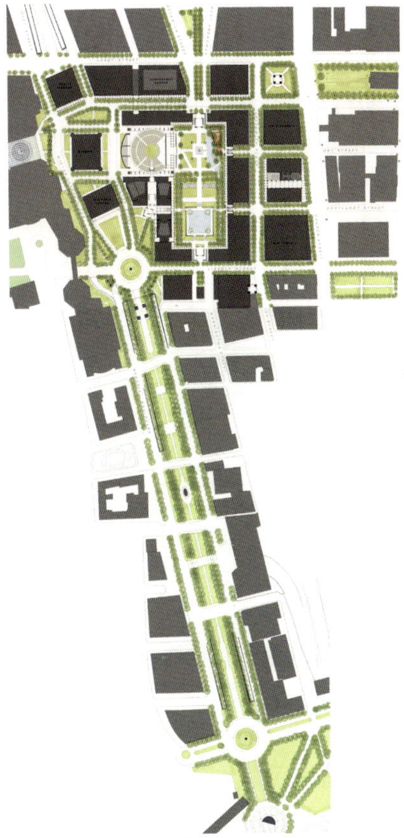

2. Plan of proposed World Trade Center

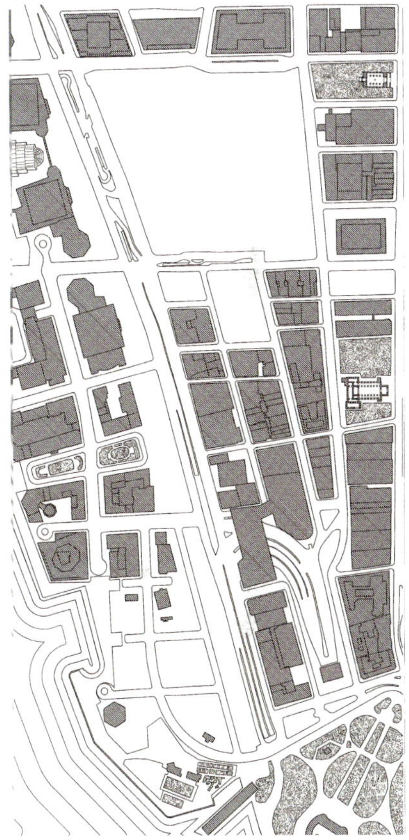

3. Site of proposed World Trade Center

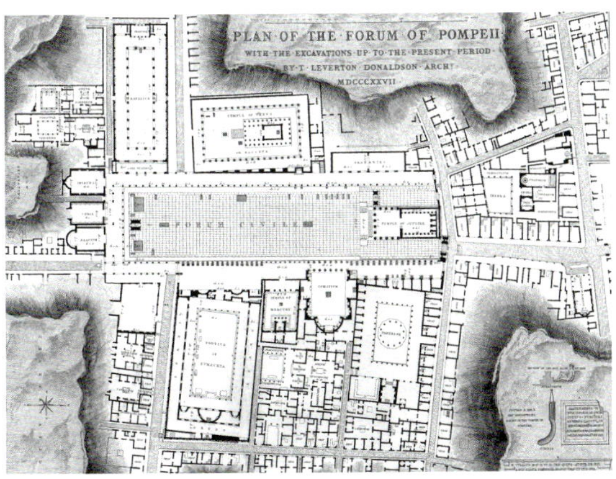

4. Plan of Pompeii Forum

5. Model of proposed Montreal project

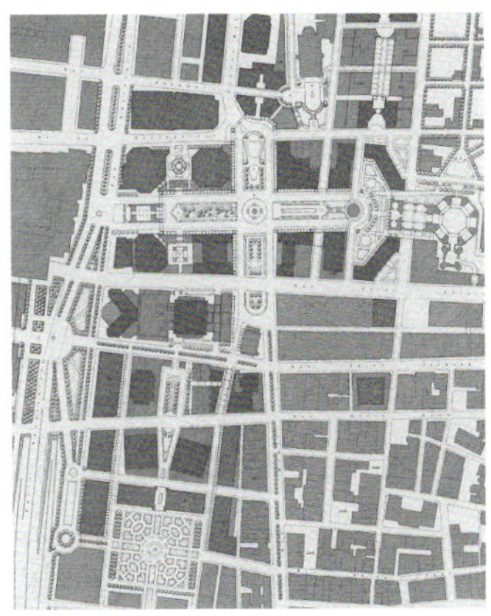

6. Proposed plan of Montreal project

7. Site for Montreal competition

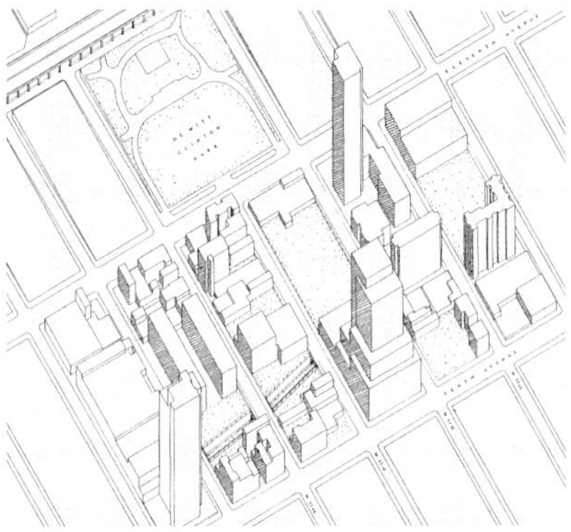

1. *Axonometric view of existing neighborhood*

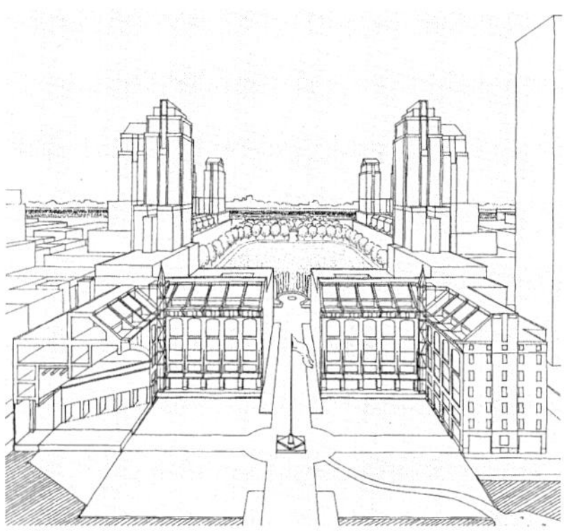

2. *Perspective view of Market Square*

Clinton

The 1984-87 project by Steven Peterson and Barbara Littenberg for Manhattan's Clinton neighborhood is an urban intervention on a concrete architectural scale rather than a comprehensive town expansion plan, but it inculcates all the principles of traditional town planning: definition of streets, continuity of urban fabric, and legible spaces and sequences.[38]

Peterson Littenberg Architects were hired by a neighborhood group to make a counter-proposal to a developer's plan that proposed demolishing the existing buildings for high-rise buildings. The Peterson Littenberg plan preserves all of the existing housing and provides as much new housing as the developer plan. In addition, it articulates the very long blocks by utilizing courtyard buildings and mid-block spaces to create a rich, residential-scaled community.

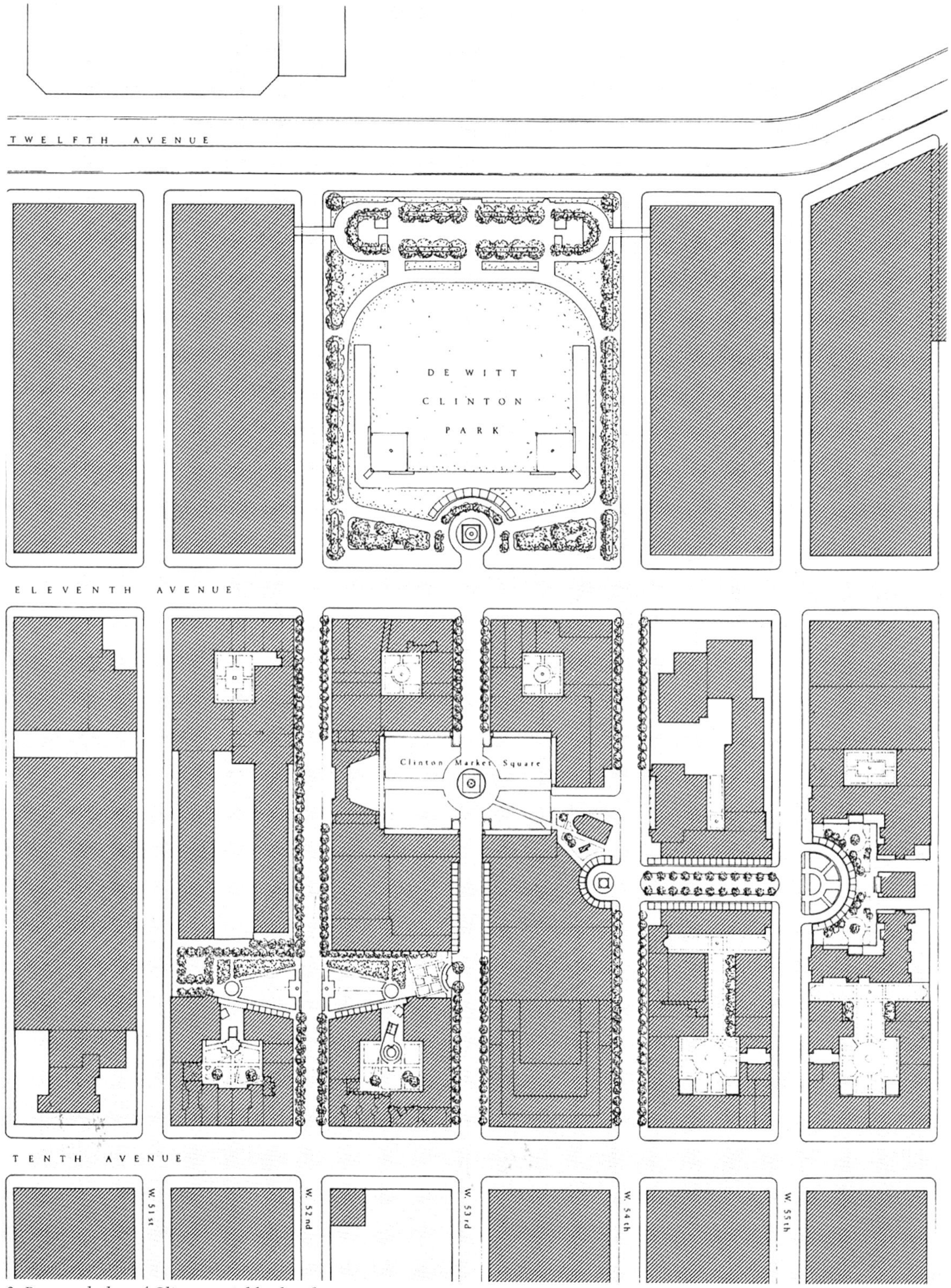

3. *Proposed plan of Clinton neighborhood*

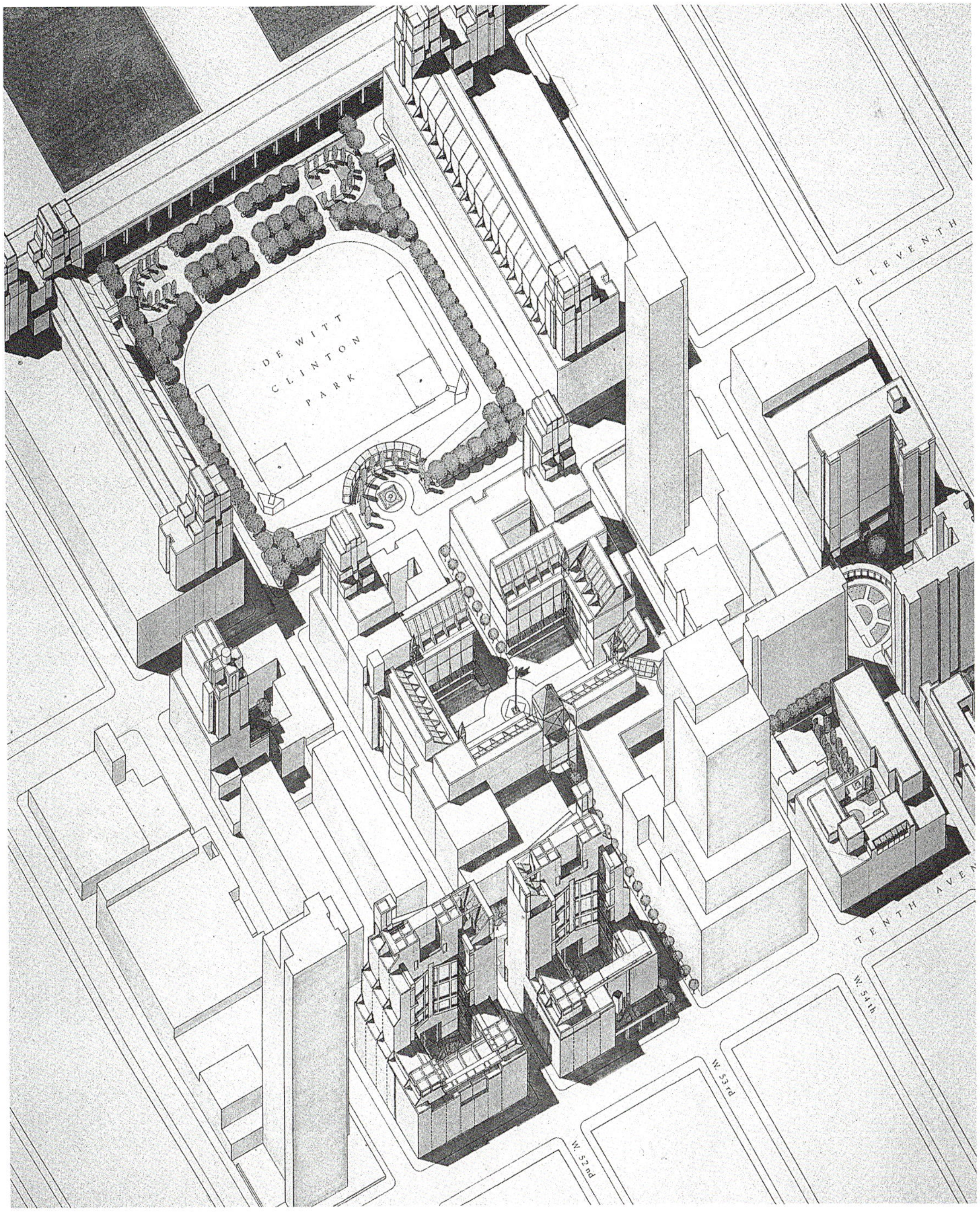

1. Axonometric view of Clinton project

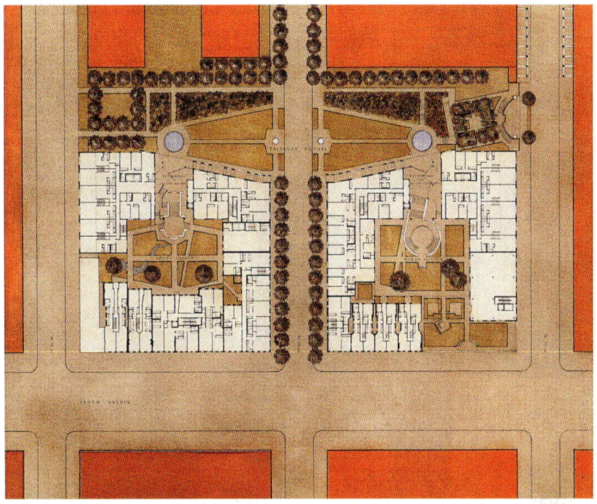
2. Plan of Triangle Square and apartment buildings

3. Model view

4. Model illustrating composite buildings and integration into the urban fabric

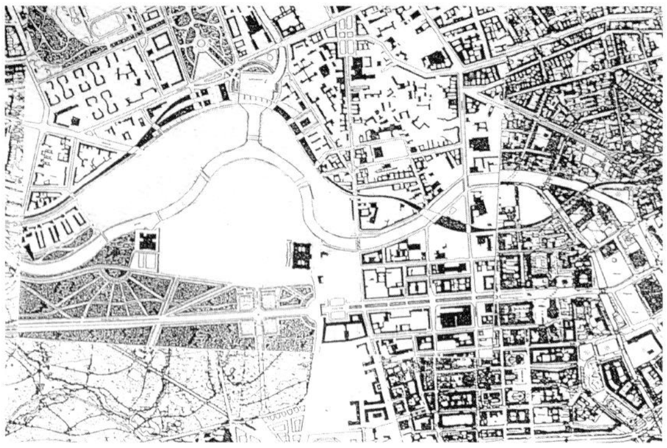

1. *Existing plan*

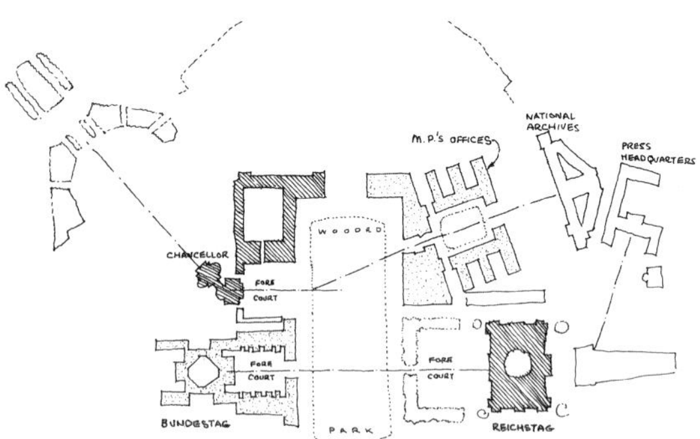

2. *Concept diagram*

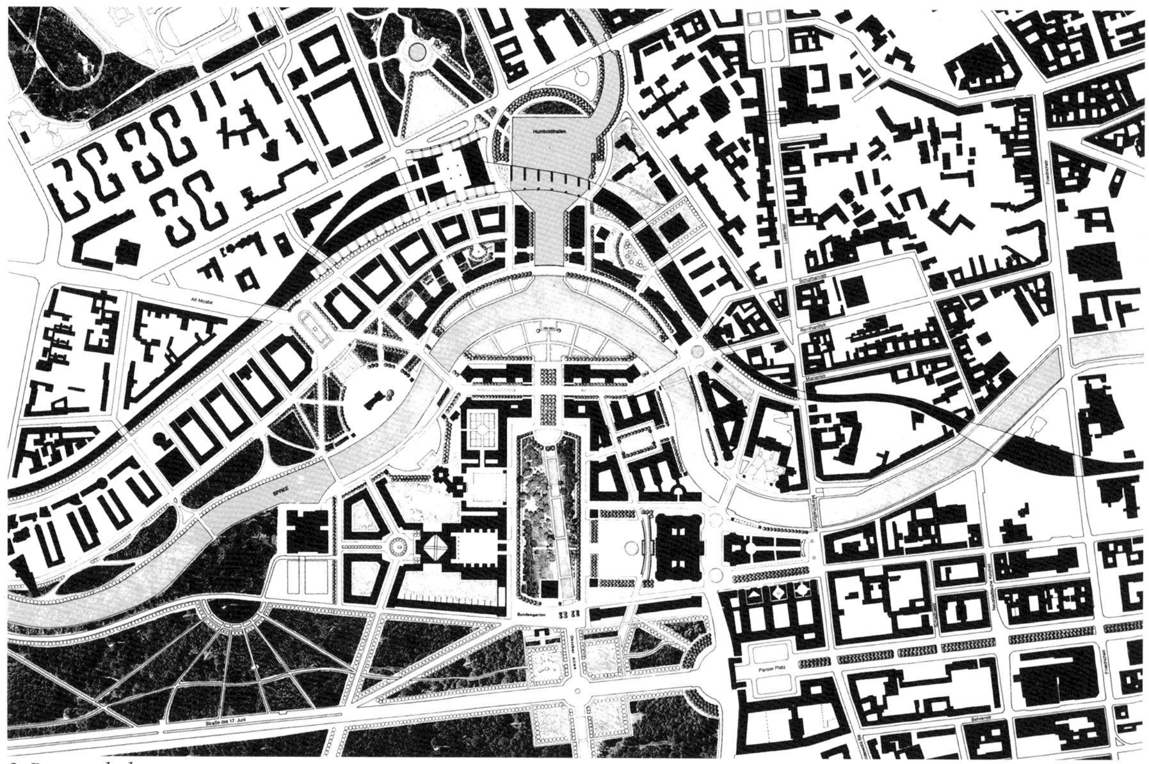

3. *Proposed plan*

Spreebogen Project

In 1997 a competition was held to accommodate the German Federal Government's move from Bonn back to Berlin. The site for the project was a large area outside the Brandenburg Gate between the Tiergarten to the south, the Reichstag (Parliament building) to the east, and the bend in the Spree river to the north.

Rather than the usual monumental buildings and controlling axes, the project by Peterson Littenberg Architects was conceived as an urban extension of the historic core—as a series of urban and garden districts filling the site like a small city.[39]

All government functions are clustered around a large green park linked to the Tiergarten. Each surrounding district is discrete, but links in formal and symbolic ways to the others, and helps define the central Green Park. The idea is similar to that of Hadrian's Villa, where the primary space, the Pecile, is analogous to the new Spreebogen Park.

The diagram of government functions illustrates the variety of visual and formal interaction of the parts. The chancellor's house faces out to the city but is still contained in the federal district. The MP Offices form their own small town square with an internal street leading down to the Reichstag. Another street leads out to the Green Park and relates axially to the National Archives Building across the Spree river. The National Press building relates to the National Archive and overlooks the Reichstag. Each adjacency and minor axis within the whole district is meaningful to the interaction of this complex modern government and its history, thus illustrating how a complex urban fabric can act in subtle and symbolic ways.

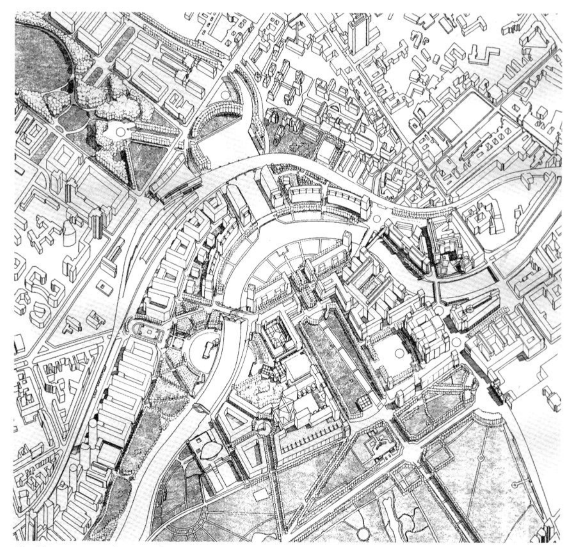

4. *Perspective view*

Model view of proposed scheme

Lake West

The West Dallas Housing Projects occupy a one-square-mile area adjacent to downtown Dallas. It is the largest low-rise project in the country with 3,500 units in almost identical barracks-like two story buildings in a parallel pattern. The units do not face the streets, there is no civic space, and there is little connection to the surrounding street pattern.

The 1981 proposed plan for Lake West by Peterson Littenberg transforms the project into a cohesive community by turning the detached buildings into blocks, providing a new system of streets that the units overlook, a new series of neighborhood squares, and a new civic structure of spaces and public buildings.[40]

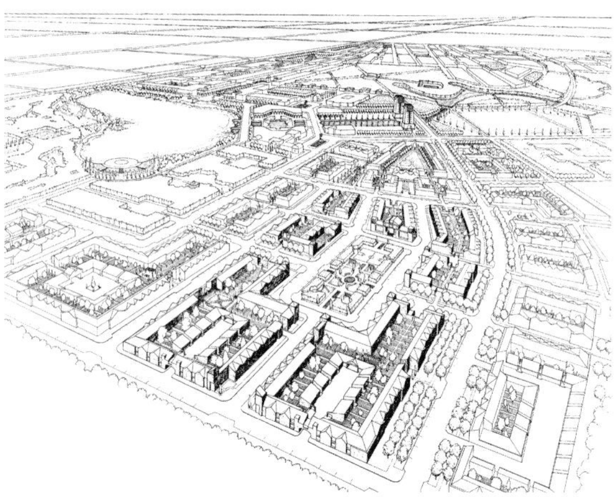

1. Bird's eye perspective of proposed project

2. Aerial view of existing project

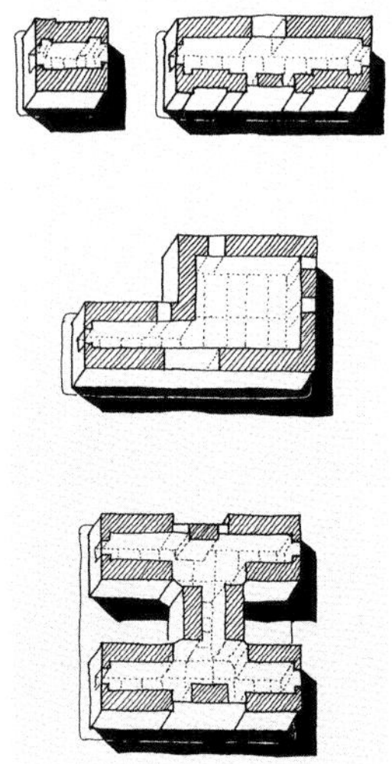

3. Block configurations

4. Existing plan

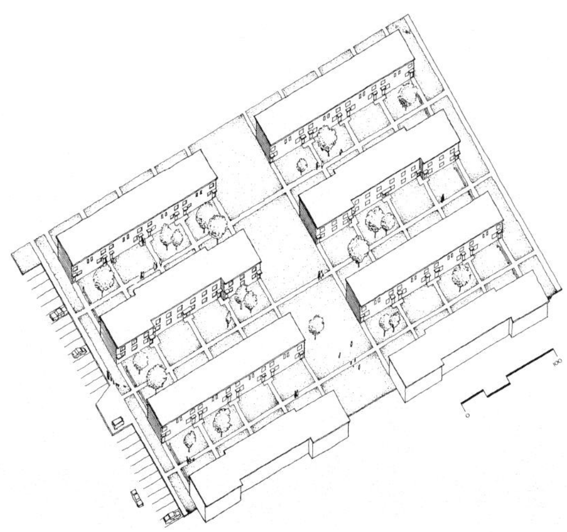

5. Axonometric view of existing buildings

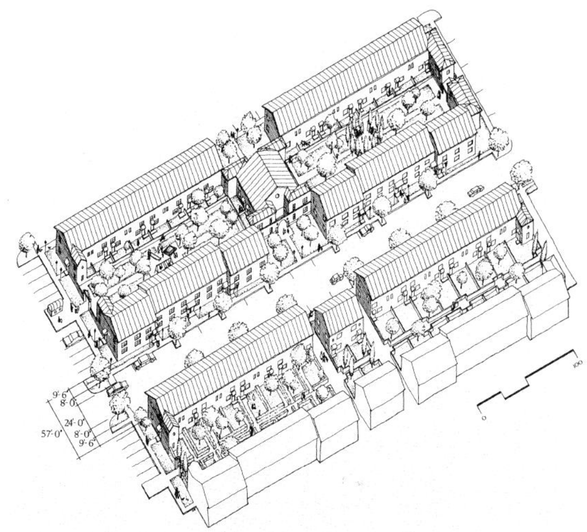

6. Axonometric view of proposed buildings

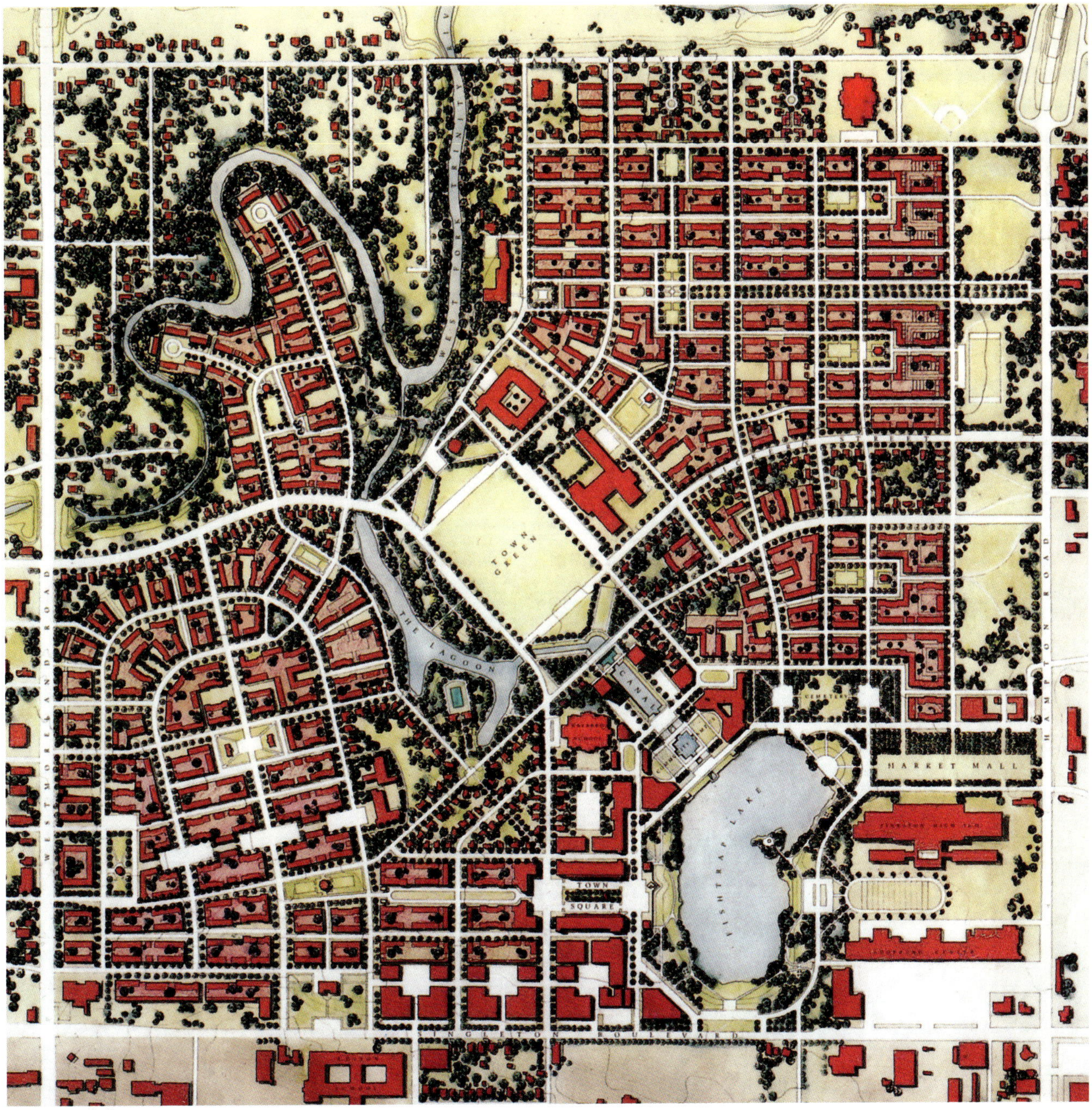

1. *Proposed plan*

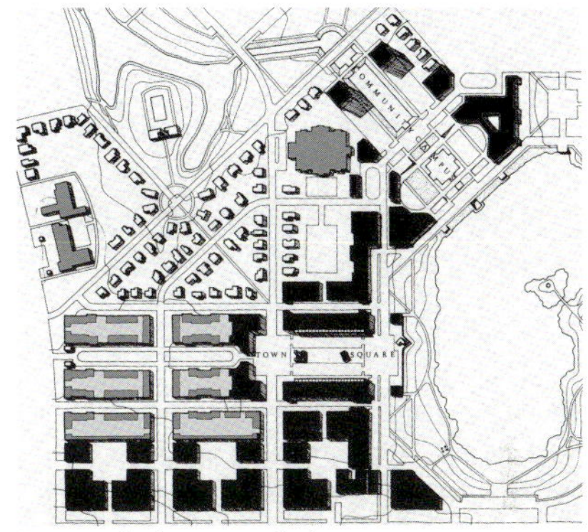

2. *Detail of proposed plan*

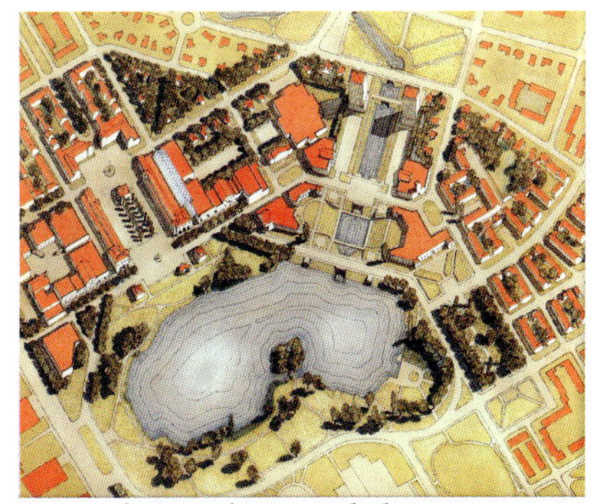

3. *Aerial view of proposed plan*

1. Plan of the Boston projects

Koetter Kim

After moving to Boston in 1978, Fred Koetter established an office with Susie Kim, and they immediately proposed a series of urban interventions to reconstruct tattered parts of the city.[41] The vicissitudes of modern architecture's impact on urbanism had been especially hard on Boston, and no project was more problematic than the Prudential Center. Gropius's original proposal was suave, destructive high modernism, but Luckman's built project was pure suburban shopping center dropped into the dense urban fabric of Back Bay. Luckman's Prudential Center retreated to the center of the site from the street edges, thus producing confused entries and divorcing the project from its urban context.

The Koetter/Kim proposal is like a prosthetic urban suit: it provides new, legible entrances and grand sequences through the site, while reestablishing connections to the surroundings. This was one of the first projects from the "Cornell School" to illustrate a genuine architectural language.

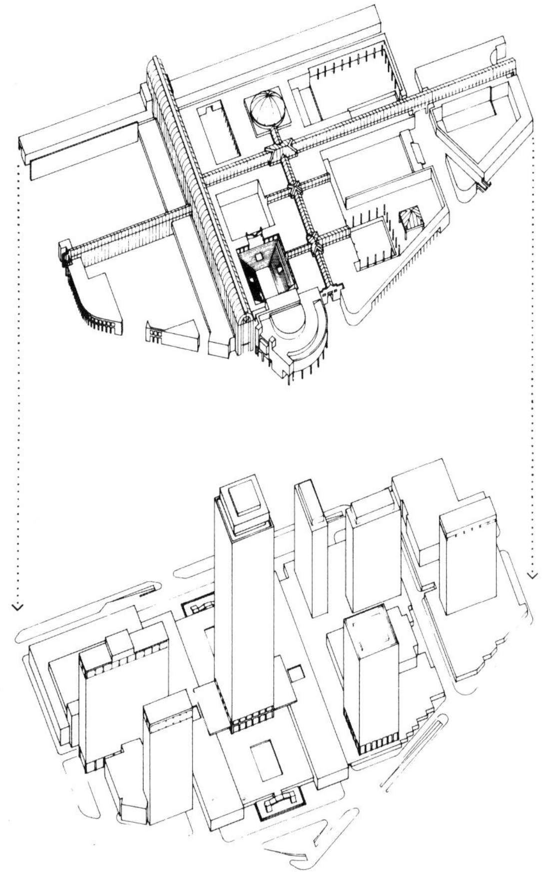

2. Proposed renovation of the Prudential Center

3. Proposed plan for Storrow Terrace

4. Perspective view of Storrow Terrace proposal

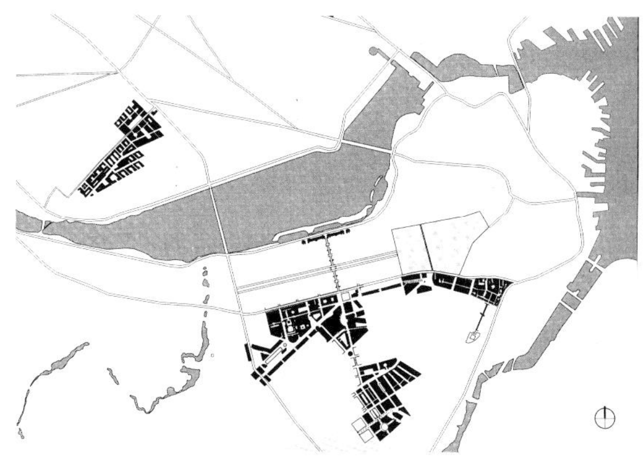

5. Plan of Boston projects, Koetter/Kim

1. Perspective view of the proposed galleria. Drawing by Kelly Wilson

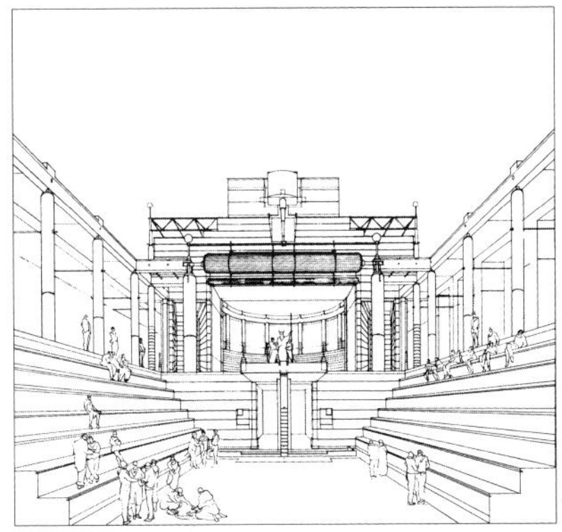

2. View of outdoor theater

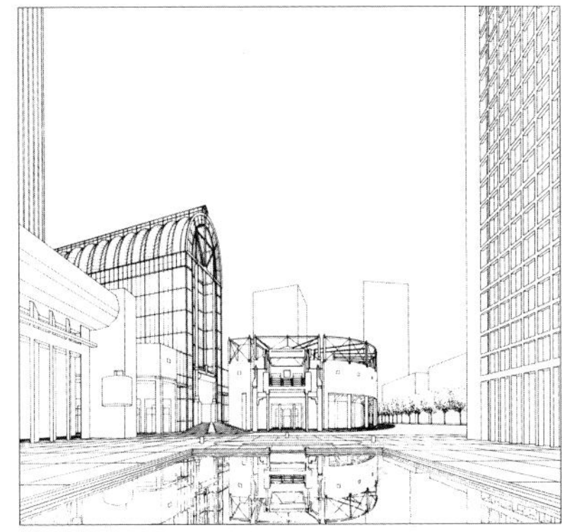

3. View of gallery entrance

4. Proposed Prudential Center by Charles Luckman

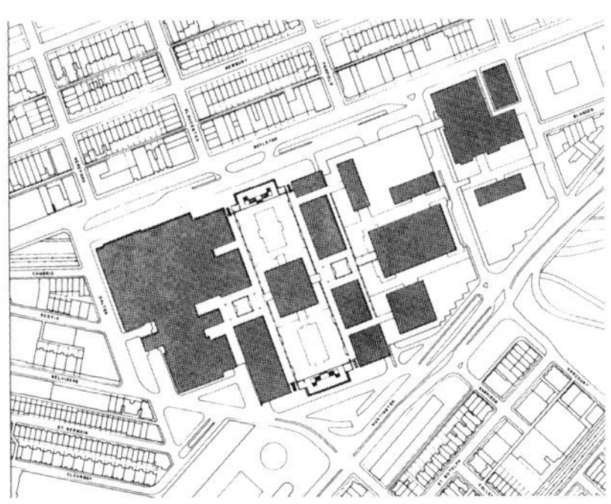

5. Existing plan

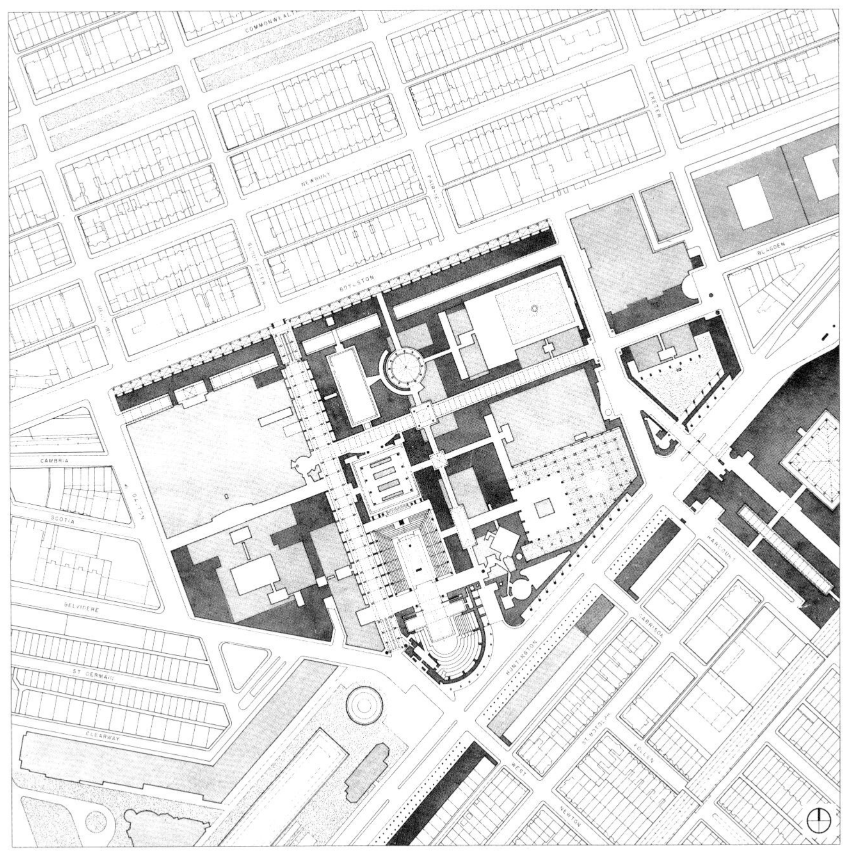

6. Proposed Prudential Center plan

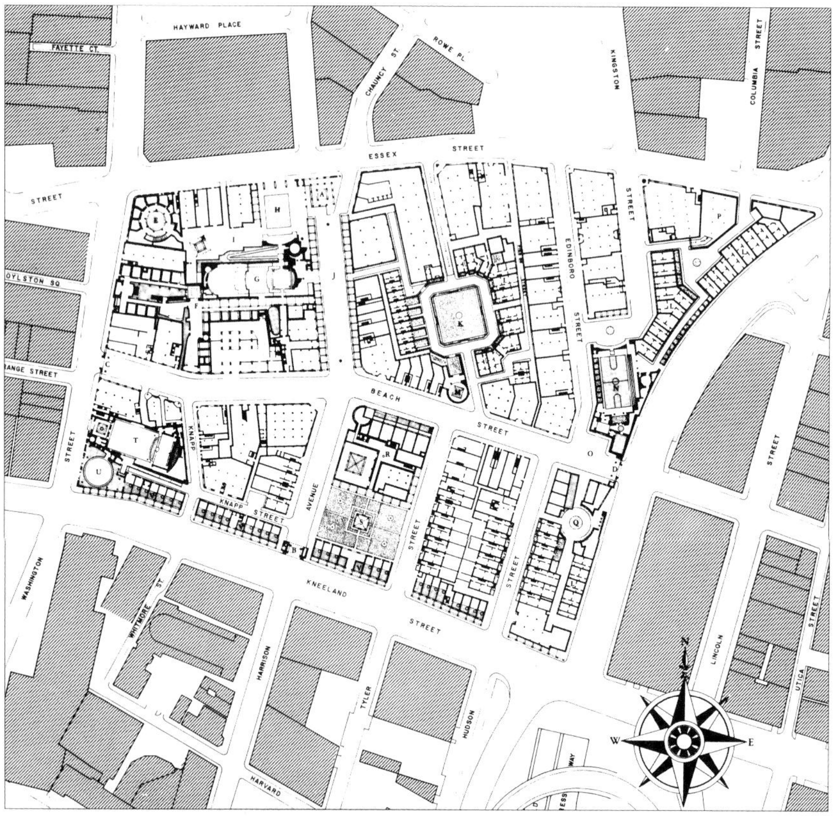

1. *Proposed Chinatown plan*

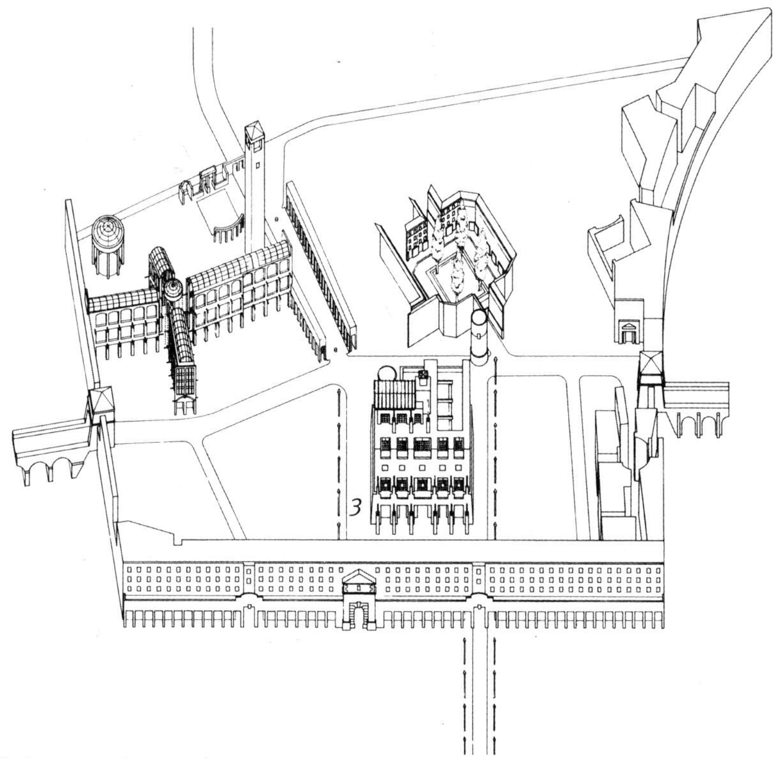

2. *Axonometric view of interventions*

Chinatown

Boston's Chinatown is dense, impacted, and lacks a legible public space structure and clear edges. The Koetter Kim proposal strengthens the edges and provides new gateways, a new town square, and modern housing. Like a small walled town, the proposed project would at once condense and enhance Chinatown's identity through a porous, fine-grained urban fabric and spatial structure.

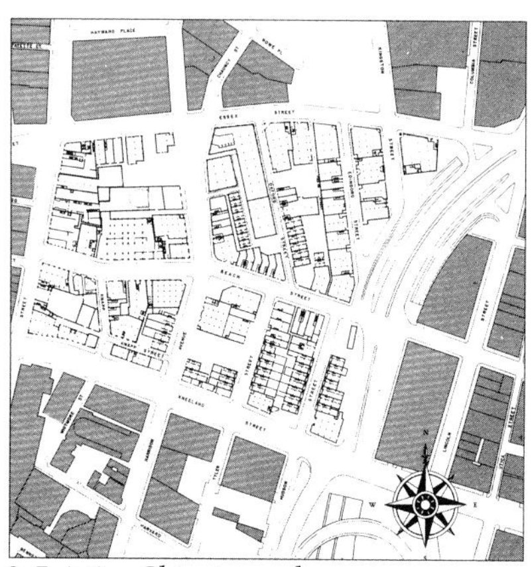

3. *Existing Chinatown plan*

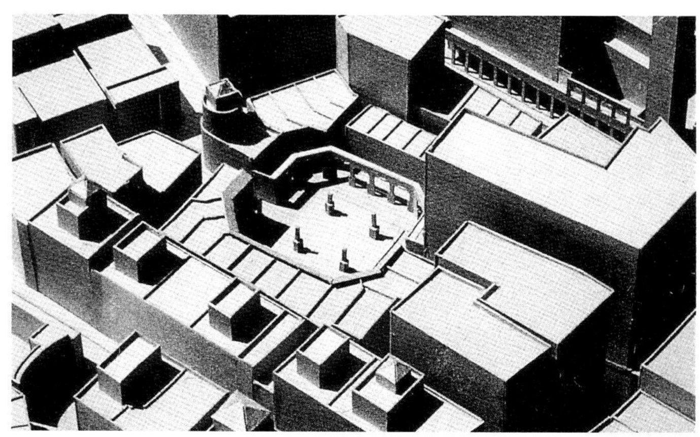

4. *Model view*

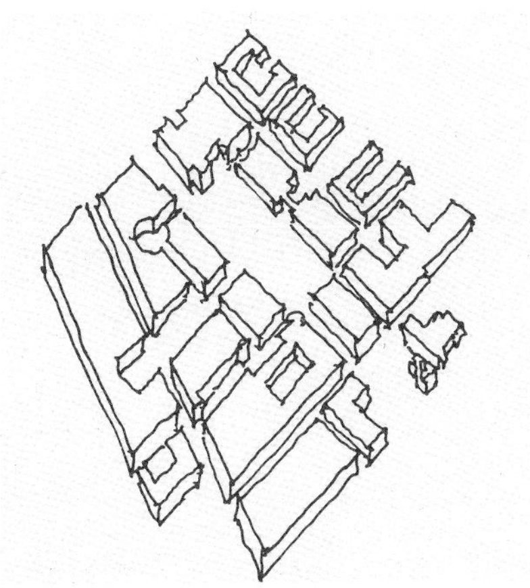

1. *Diagram of fabric buildings*

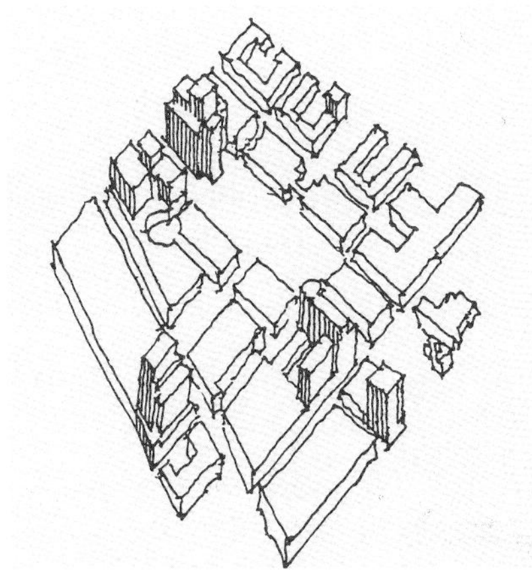

2. *Diagram of tall buildings*

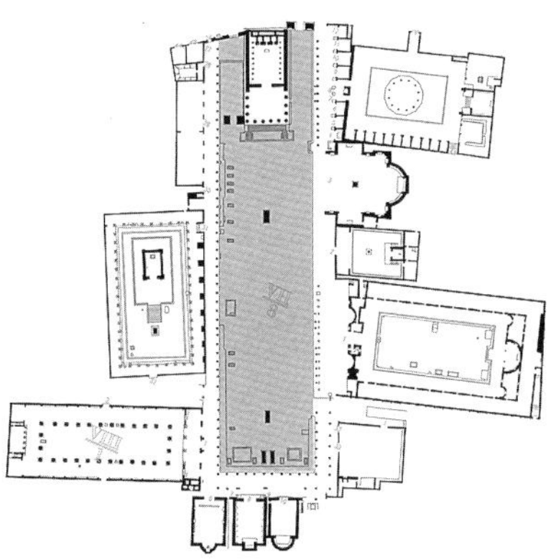

3. *Plan of the Forum at Pompeii*

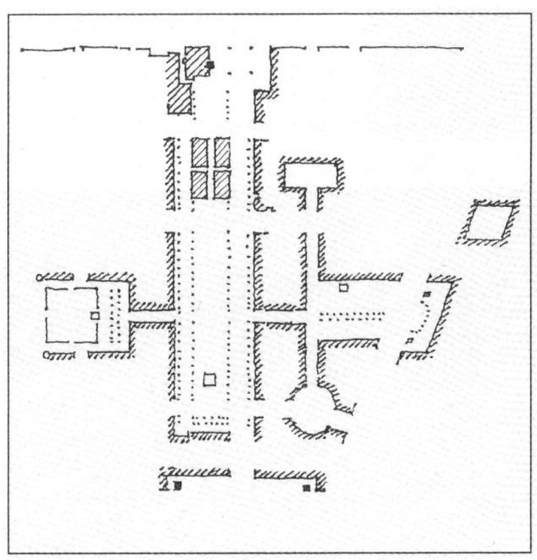

4. *Conceptual diagram*

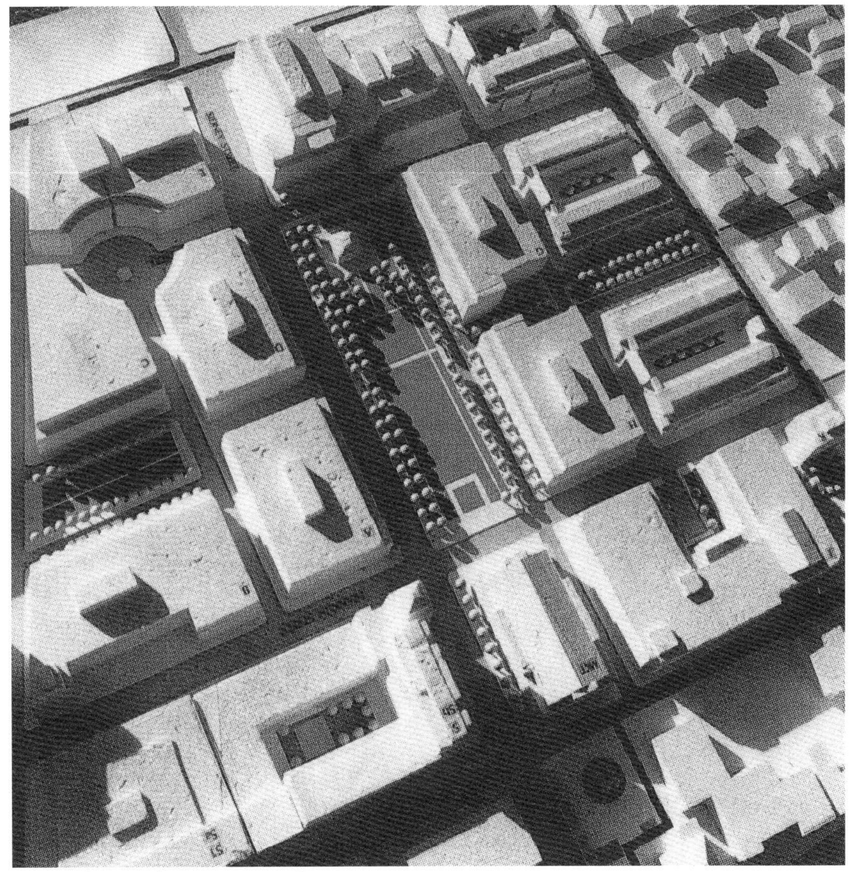

5. *Model view of University Park*

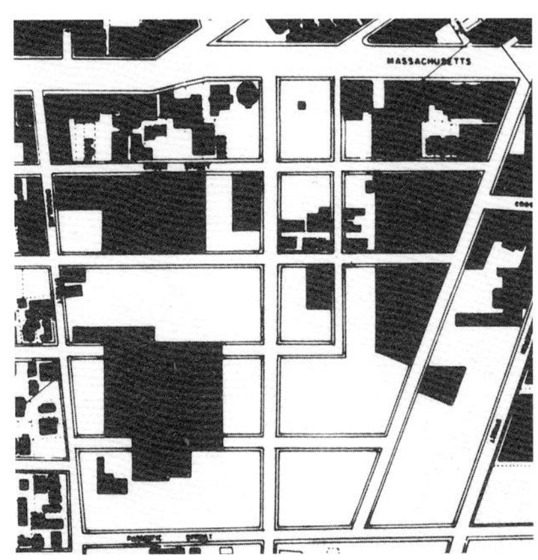

6. *Existing urban plan*

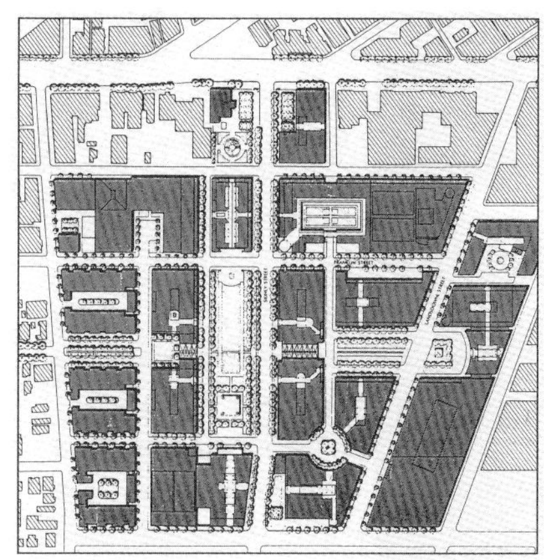

7. *Proposed plan*

University Park

The plan for University Park was intended to revitalize a run-down industrial area of Cambridge between MIT and Central Square.[42] The new neighborhood is organized like a mini-city, in which a large central space is surrounded by normative urban streets and blocks and a series of secondary spaces. The central space connects to Massachusetts Avenue, thus adding another link in the Cambridge civic structure of MIT, Central Square, City Hall, and Harvard Square. Flexible loft buildings establish the urban fabric, which is punctuated by several taller buildings.

Toronto Port Lands

In 2002 Koetter Kim & Associates engaged in a study of Toronto's largely abandoned port area. Toronto was vying for the 2004 Olympics, and this was seen as a stimulus for the redevelopment of this vast area with a prime waterfront location.

Until at least the end of the nineteenth century, a predictable and limited number of building types facilitated town planning and mixed-use neighborhoods. Today the number, complexity, and unpredictability of building types present a challenge to planned towns and major expansions. Indeed, a knowledge of building typologies is essential to urban design today.

In addition to the standard array of office towers, modernist social housing, and one-family houses, Toronto has recently developed a series of hybrid formal typologies—dense, mixed-use, part low-rise, part high-rise. These characteristics are exploited in the Koetter Kim project.

The proposed urban fabric is composed of large blocks with the possibility of multiple subdivision and the capability of accommodating multiple building types, from terrace housing to high-rise housing, laboratory buildings, and big-box retail. Typically, these blocks contain multiple buildings. The edges of the blocks are always defined, and the resultant public realm is integrated with the waterfront environment.

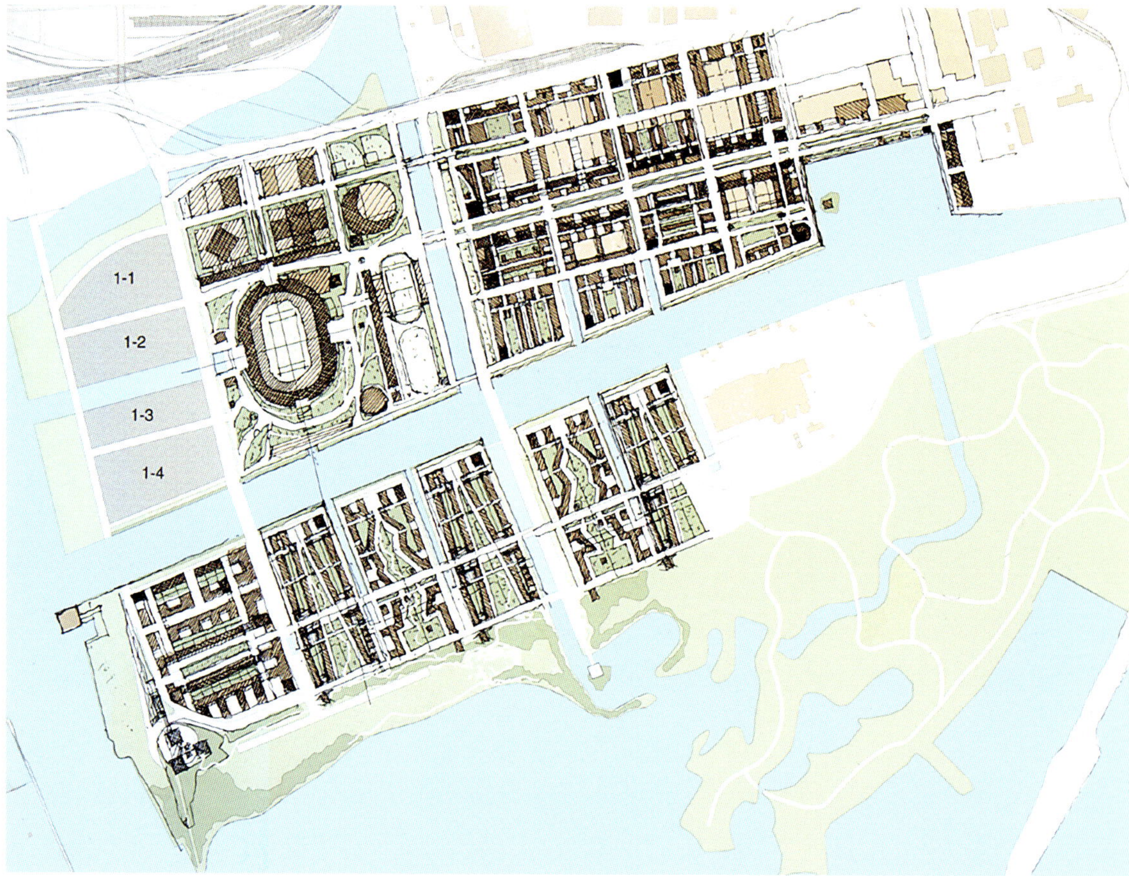

1. Port Lands proposed plan, 2002

2. Aerial view of the Port Lands

3. Perspective view of the canal

4. Perspective view of street

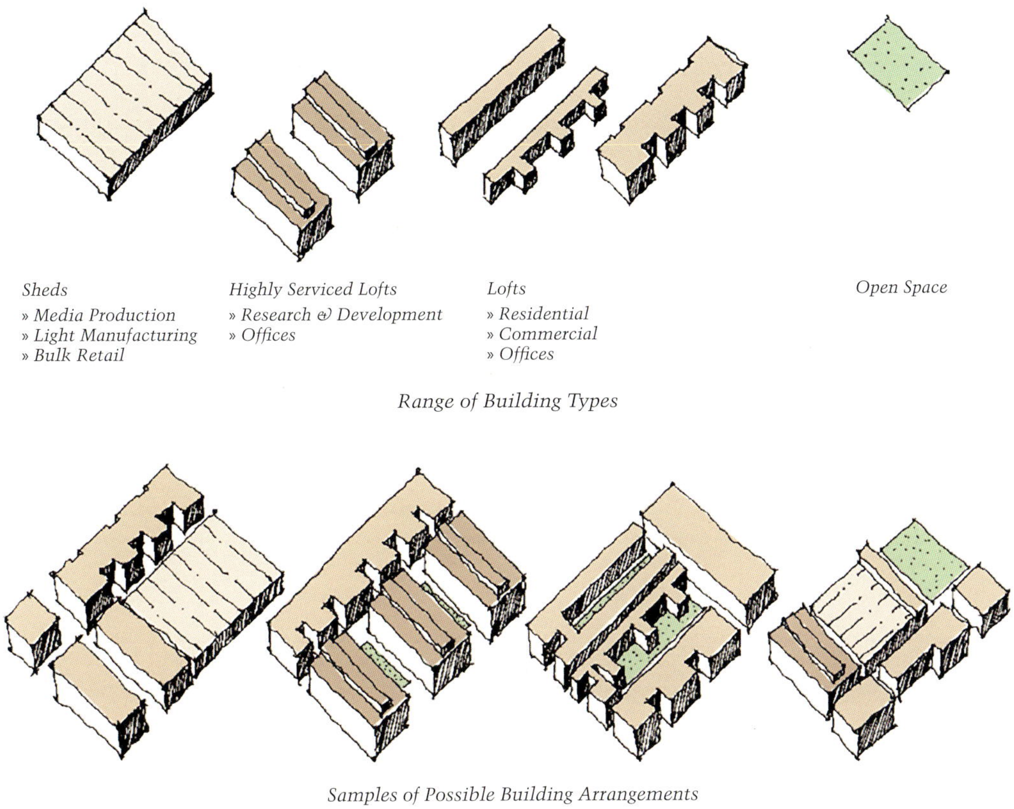

1. Building and block type study

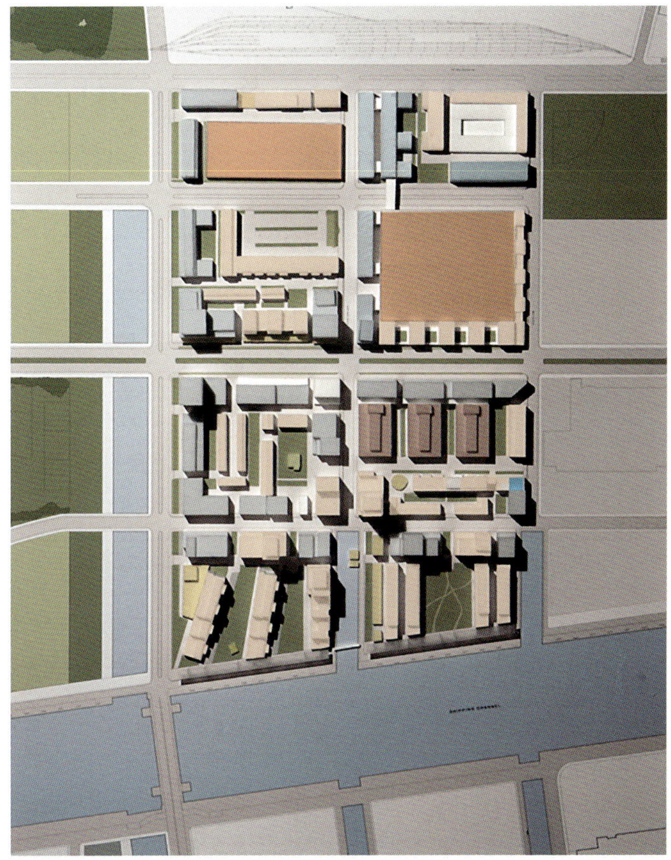

2. Plan of possible block development

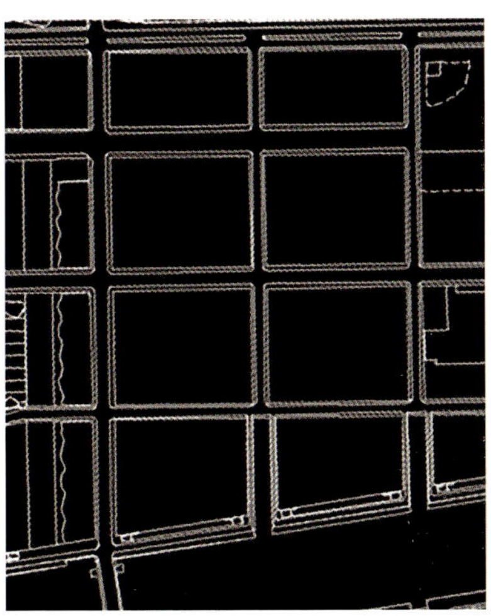

3. Block pattern

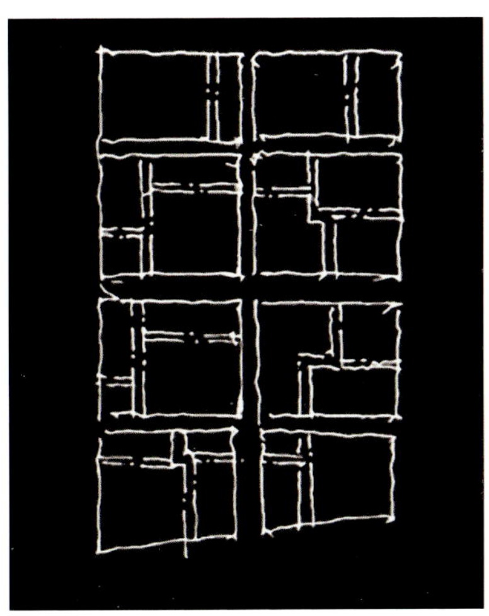

4. Block parcels

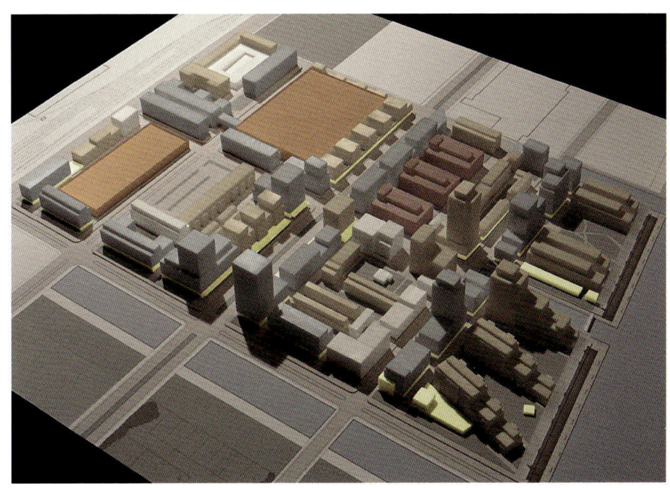

5. Model of possible block development

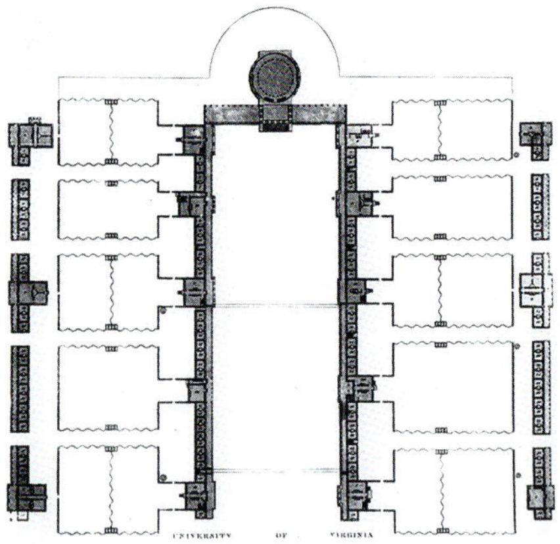

1. Mavrick Plan of Jefferson's design, 1825

2. University of Virginia, the Lawn

3. Carnegie Mellon University, Hornbostle quadrangle

4. Carnegie Mellon University, long-range campus plan, 1992

The Campus as Rehearsal for the City

The prolific postwar building period was no kinder to American campuses than it was to cities, as emphasis on the private realm at the expense of the public realm created a parallel disintegration of campuses and cities. For some two hundred years, Thomas Jefferson's design for the University of Virginia has been a lesson in civics, and in the relationship of architecture and urbanism. Like a physical manifestation of the US Constitution, the "Lawn" represents the balance of civic responsibilities and private prerogative.[43] It is the stable presence of this great public space and its supporting grid that allows the private variations enjoyed by the pavilions and gardens—a rehearsal for the city in a newly formed democracy and a model for future campuses.

It is the landscape–open space structure of American campuses that defines their uniquely memorable qualities. The architectural quality of individual buildings should contribute to enriching the whole, but a collection of anti-urban, individualistic buildings cannot make a campus. Thus, urbanistically contributing buildings and a complementary landscape–open space plan are both required for a beautiful campus—one that promotes urban community and campus life. The American campus is, indeed, a rehearsal for the city. Along with "Elm Street" it is also a genuine American contribution to urbanism.

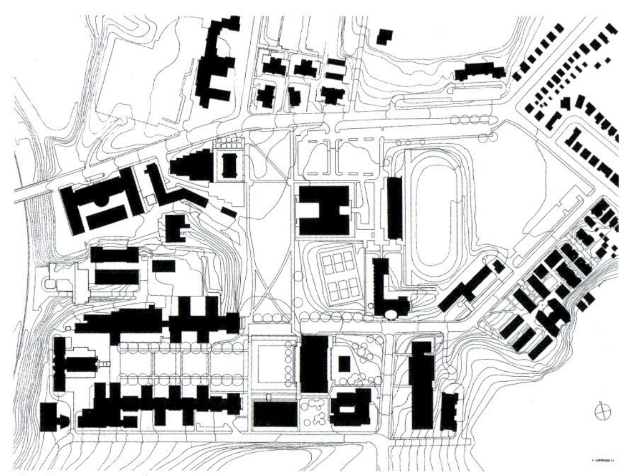

5. Campus plan, 1987

1. Aerial view of the campus in 2000

2. View of the University Center Courtyard

Carnegie Mellon University

Approximately one hundred years after Jefferson's plan, Henry Hornbostle's 1904 plan for Carnegie Tech, later Carnegie Mellon University, followed similar principles. But by 1987 Hornbostle's superb pre-war buildings and campus plan contrasted sharply with the desolation and anti-urban banality of post-war additions to the campus. The 1987 competition-winning project by Michael Dennis and Jeffery Clark proposed a radical restructuring of the campus around a civic structure of new spaces.[44] A new entry quadrangle was defined by a University Center and a Performing Arts Center. A central element of the plan was the proposed reexcavation of a picturesque ravine articulating the old and new parts of the campus. A bridge spanning the ravine connected the new colonnaded entry quadrangle with the Hornbostle quad, and an athletic quad was enclosed by buildings.

3. View of the University Center

4. View of the Athletic Quad

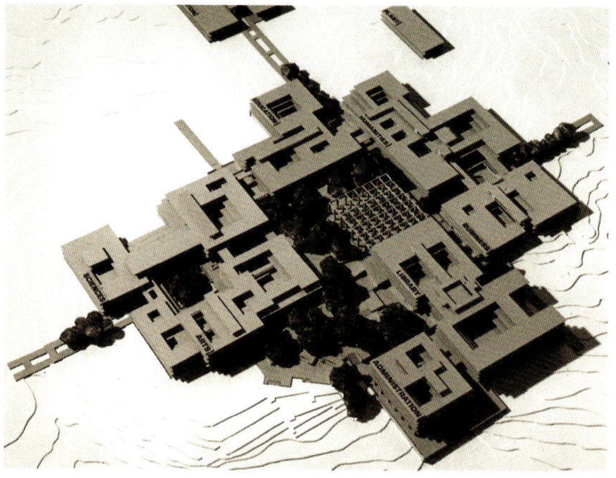

1. Model of the original scheme by O'Neil Ford

2. View of the Sombrilla

University of Texas San Antonio

UTSA was founded in 1970 as a commuter campus on the outskirts of San Antonio, at the edge of the Texas Hill Country. Despite its then-mobile student body, O'Neil Ford planned the initial campus buildings as a tight urban core according to the principles of the Laws of the Indies. An ample central plaza was defined by arcaded buildings and contained a large pavillion-like structure known as the *Sombrilla*. Streets, or *paseos*, pinwheeled out from the plaza in anticipation of future urban growth. Beyond the core, however, the campus form quickly disintegrated as the student body grew and inappropriate suburban buildings were added. By 2007 there were 28,000 students and it was time to transform UTSA into a "real campus."

The new plan by Barnes Gromatzky Kosarek Architects, with Michael Dennis and Associates, returned to the urban principles of the Laws of the Indies to extend the initial O'Neil Ford design into a comprehensive urban plan with an extensive civic structure of quadrangles and streets. The urban framework of blocks, streets, and natural landscape allows for further growth, as well as programmatic and architectural change while maintaining the urban order.

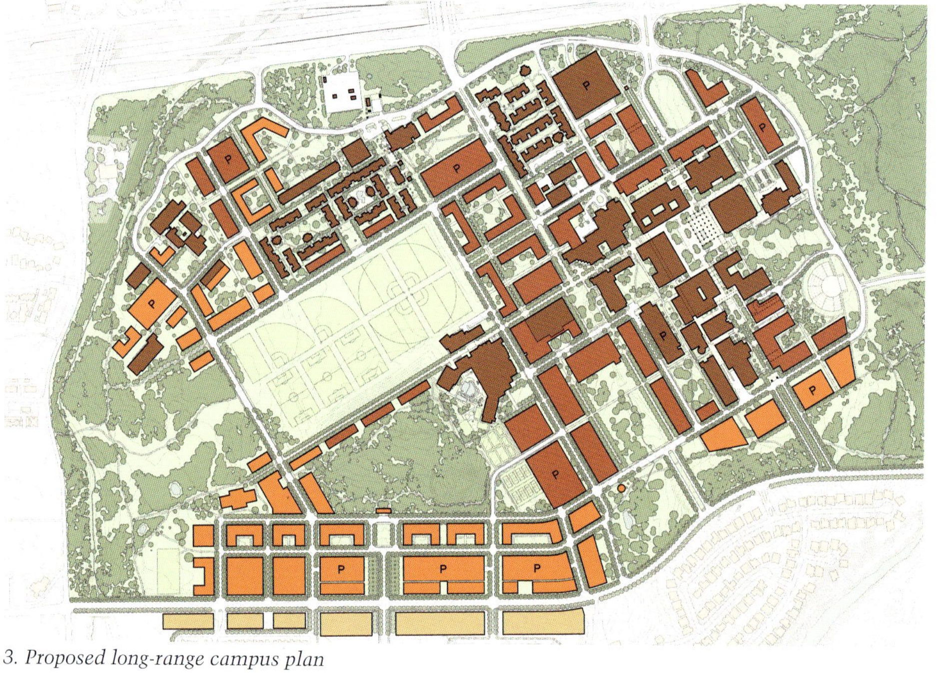

3. Proposed long-range campus plan

4. Proposed long-range landscape plan

1. Campus plan, 2007

2. Aerial view of the campus in 2007

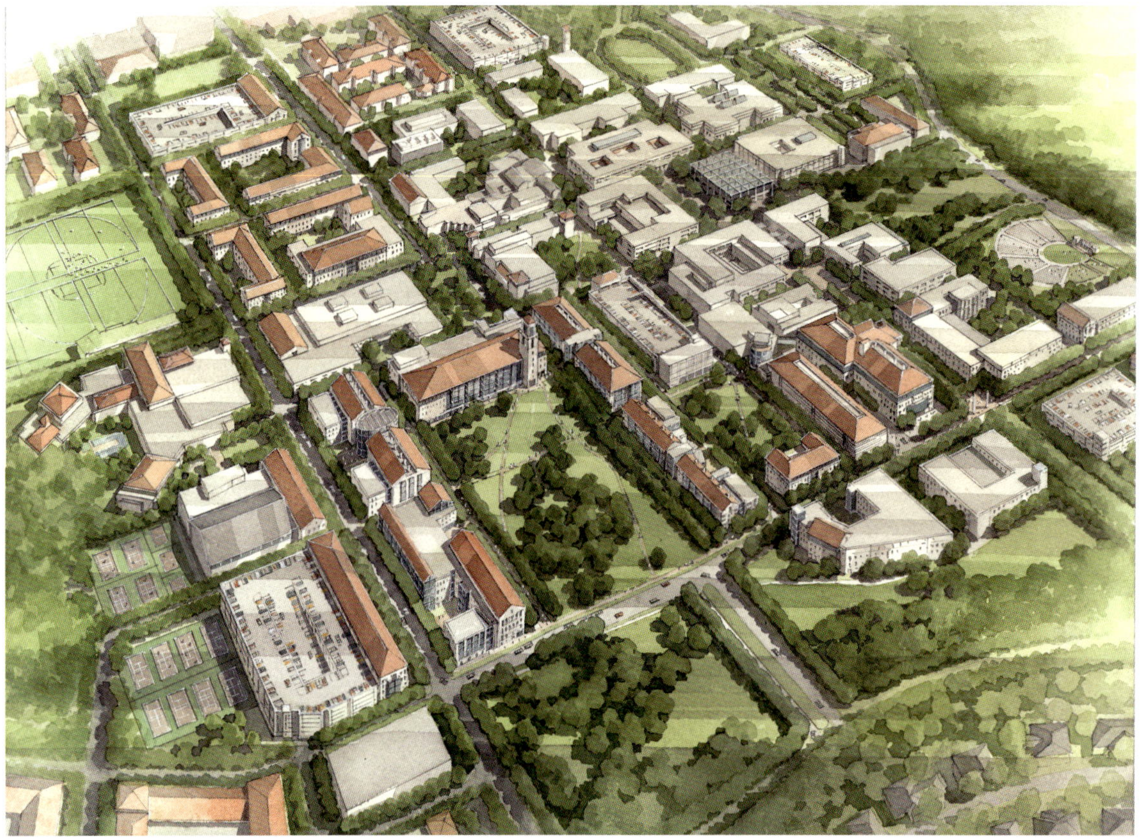

3. Aerial perspective of proposed long-range campus development

4. View of the new campus quadrangle

5. View of an extended paseo

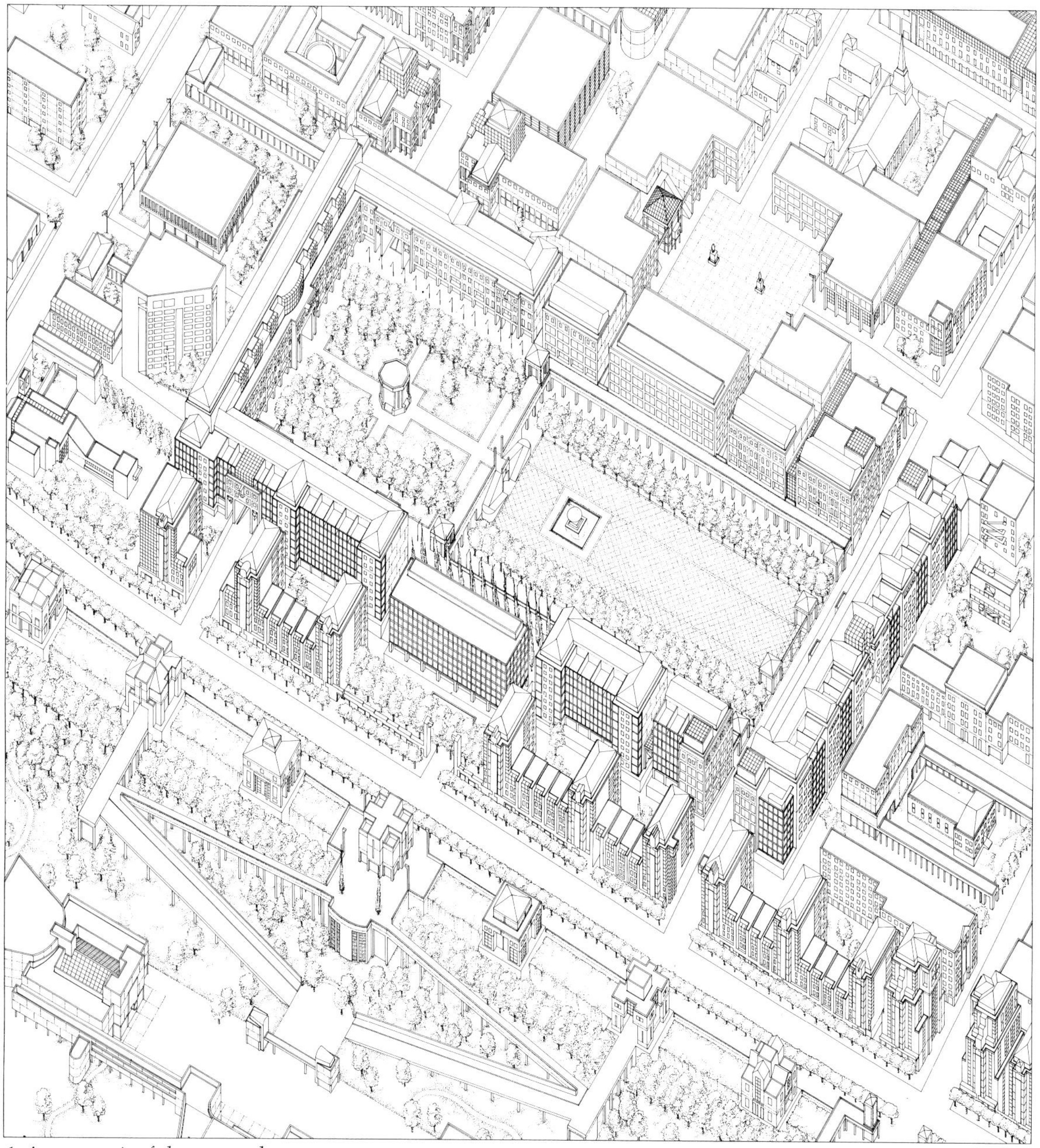

1. *Axonometric of the proposed town center*

Redevelopment of Burlington, Vermont

This project is an early example of the reconstruction of an American town that was semi-destroyed, not by bombs, as in European cities, but by bad planning decisions; i.e., *Urban Renewal.*

Burlington, Vermont is situated on a waterfront lying in ruin since the end of the industrial era. The city has a central business district containing fragments of a grid plan with a wide range of architectural building types, from single-family dwellings to perimeter block structures. The lack of connection between the center and the waterfront was further exacerbated by the demolition of twenty-two acres in the city center and a partially completed zone of object-like buildings constructed in the 1970s—two of them by Mies van der Rohe. These buildings usurp the order of the area without providing a coherent replacement.

The basic strategy of Craig Neely's 1981 project for the inner city is the insertion of a series of new "liner" buildings, connecting the disparate modern office buildings and organizing them into a set of distinct spaces forming a new civic structure. These in turn are linked to the waterfront, where a new park with urban villas overlooks the lake front.[45]

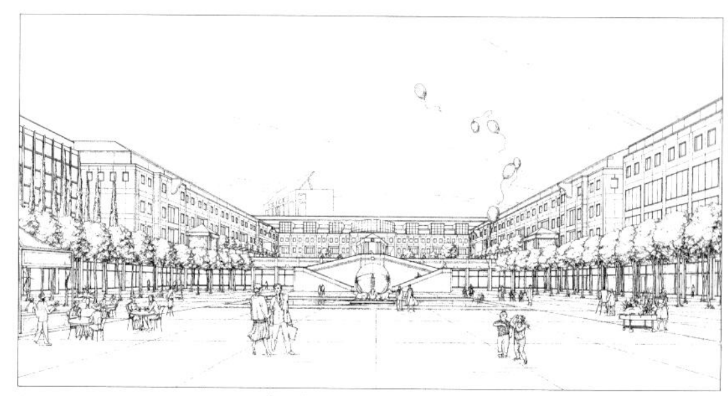

2. *Perspective view of Chittenden Terrace*

3. *Perspective view of the park and lake*

1. Existing town plan

2. Proposed town plan

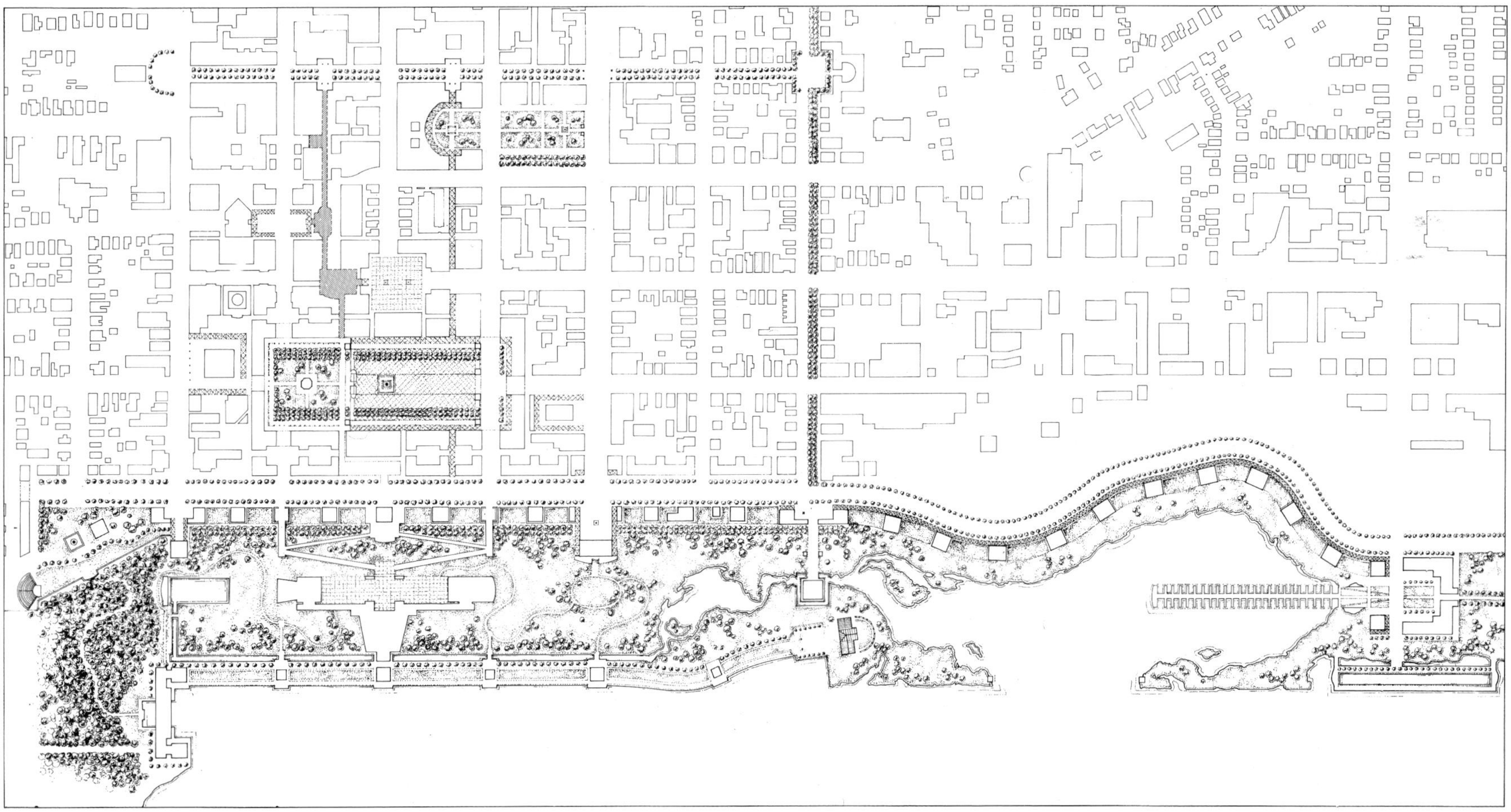

3. Landscape plan

Classical and Vernacular

In the 1980s Leon Krier's town planning became more irregular and village-like, and his architecture became more classical. For example, in his 1982 project for Pliny's Villa and his 1988 project for the town of Atlantis in Tenerife, both are on hilltop sites, which is his argument for irregular plans and picturesque arrangements of buildings; but these characteristics will mark later projects on flat sites as well. Rather, there is a veering away from complex cities with rationalized grids and multiple architectures toward villages as unified, classical, architectural compositions.[46]

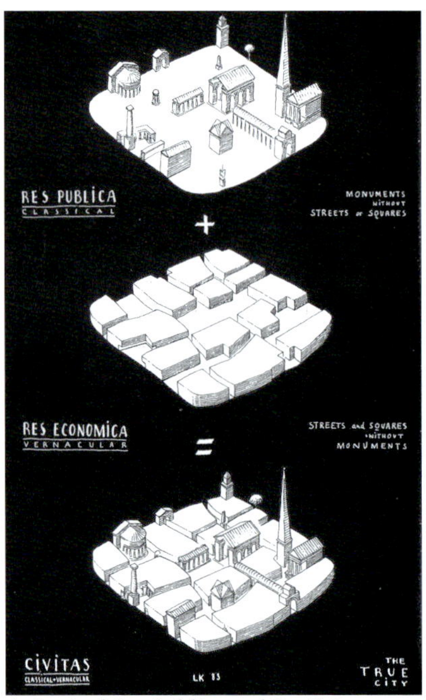

1. Revised Res Publica and Res Privata

2. Model view of Pliny's Villa, 1982

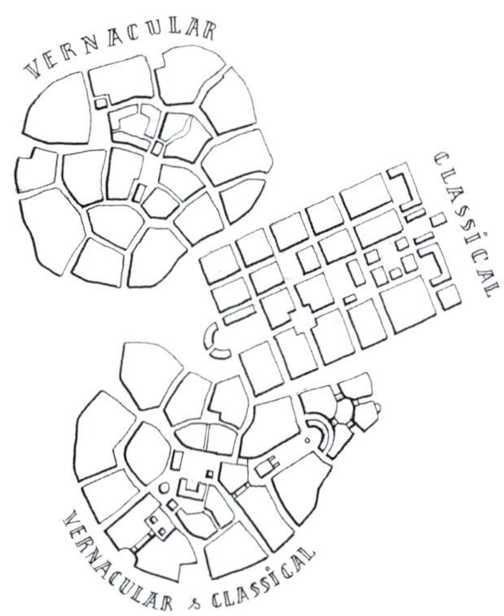

3. Classical and vernacular planning diagram

4. Model view of Atlantis, 1988

5. Model view of the Agora

1. Plan of Atlantis, 1988

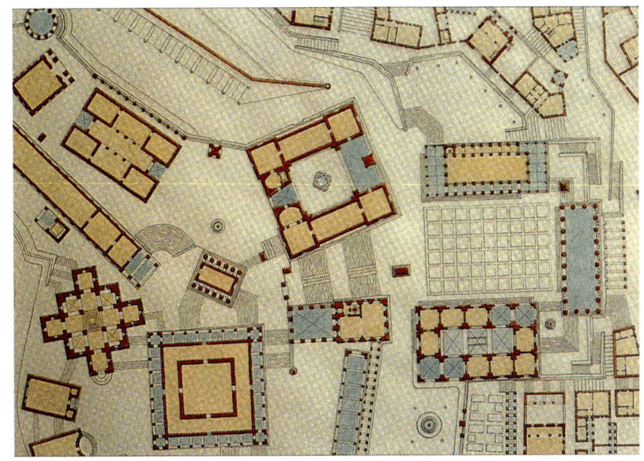

2. Plan of the Agora

3. Aerial perspective of Atlantis

Plan of Poundbury expansion of Dorset, 1988–2025

Poundbury, Dorset

The Poundbury expansion of Dorset by Leon Krier rivals the town of Seaside, Florida, by DPZ, in its power to elicit violent antagonistic reaction from much of the modernist architectural and planning communities.[47]

Poundbury is based on the urban principles developed by Krier in the 1970s: compact, walkable, mixed-use neighborhoods with small blocks, legible civic space, and use of traditional local materials. Unlike Krier's work of the 1970s, however, which illustrated modern rationalist architecture, Poundbury's architecture reflects Krier's intervening turn to classicism and traditional vernacular building. It is this—the stylistic issue, rather more than the planning principles—that precipitates attack by the architectural community, despite the project's success and the general public's preference for traditional architecture.

The Poundbury expansion of Dorset is articulated into four neighborhood phases, each containing a neighborhood center. Two have been completed. All four phases are scheduled to be completed by 2025.

1. Plan of neighborhoods

2. Street view

3. Loggia

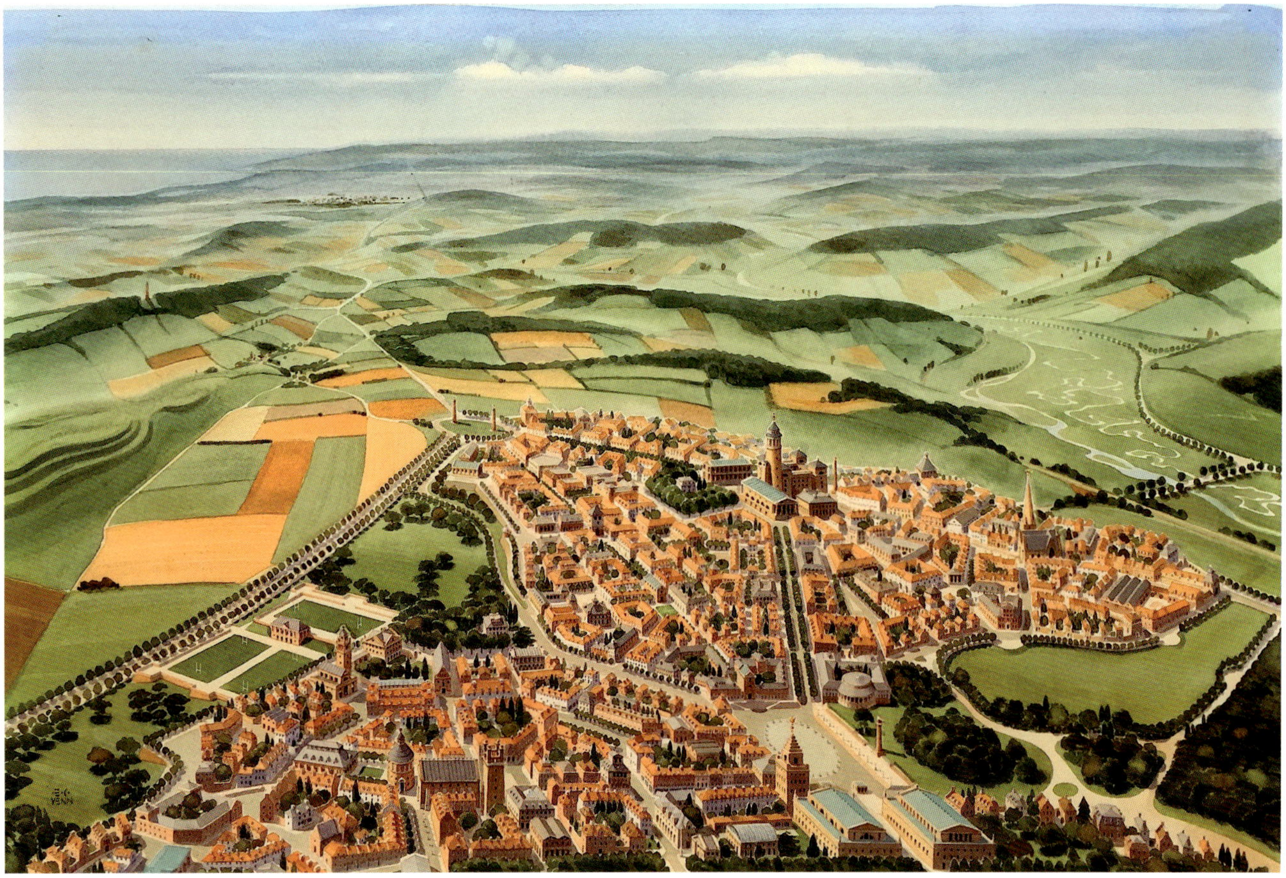

4. Aerial perspective of Poundbury expansion of Dorset

5. View of square from loggia

6. View of square

View of Seaside, Florida

Seaside, Florida

Not since Le Corbusier's Plan Voisin for Paris has such a big fuss been made among professionals as about the tiny beach resort town of Seaside, Florida.

This small-town "Bordeaux-by-the-sea" has become a lightning rod: praised on the one hand by the public and by neo-traditional American town planners, who see it as an optimistic antisprawl model, and on the other hand, vilified by self-proclaimed architectural avant-gardists retching over its "regressive" pitched roofs, picket fences, and upscale socioeconomic community.

Designed in the late 1970s and early 1980s by Andres Duany and Elizabeth Plater-Zyberk (DPZ) for the developer Robert Davis, Seaside has been enormously successful in its own right, as well as serving as the iconic beginning of the movement later known as New Urbanism.[48]

Duany points out two main influences on the design: one was the urban and architectural conventions of Key West and other towns of Florida and the Caribbean; the other was the influence of Leon Krier. Krier first came to south Florida in the late 1970s, and his influence was instant, in terms of both urbanism and classicism. One wonders, however, if there might not have been a reverse influence as well, given Krier's increased drift from rationalism to classicism and focus on vernacular planning in the 1980s: Pliny's Villa, 1981; Atlantis, 1987.

The American Town

In spite of being a seasonal beach community of upscale inhabitants, Seaside represented an urban antidote to suburban sprawl—the American Town. With its form-based code and its potential for liaison with developers, it was a practical, achievable, and marketable alternative to the generic suburb. Unfortunately, however, pitched roofs and picket fences, coupled with the fact that Seaside is a beach town, have so enraged the sensibilities of the architectural avant-garde that attention has been deflected from the town's underlying urbanist principles. To some degree, later towns have been slightly more palatable to the avant-garde, but architects have generally remained immune to urbanism.

1. Aerial view

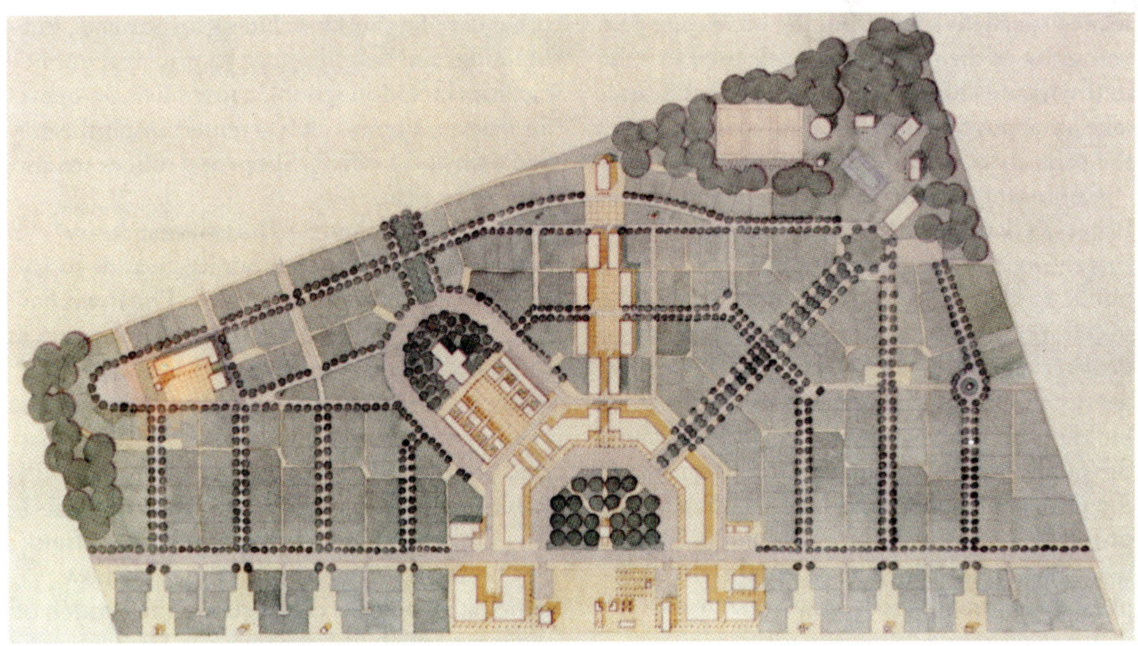

2. Plan of Seaside

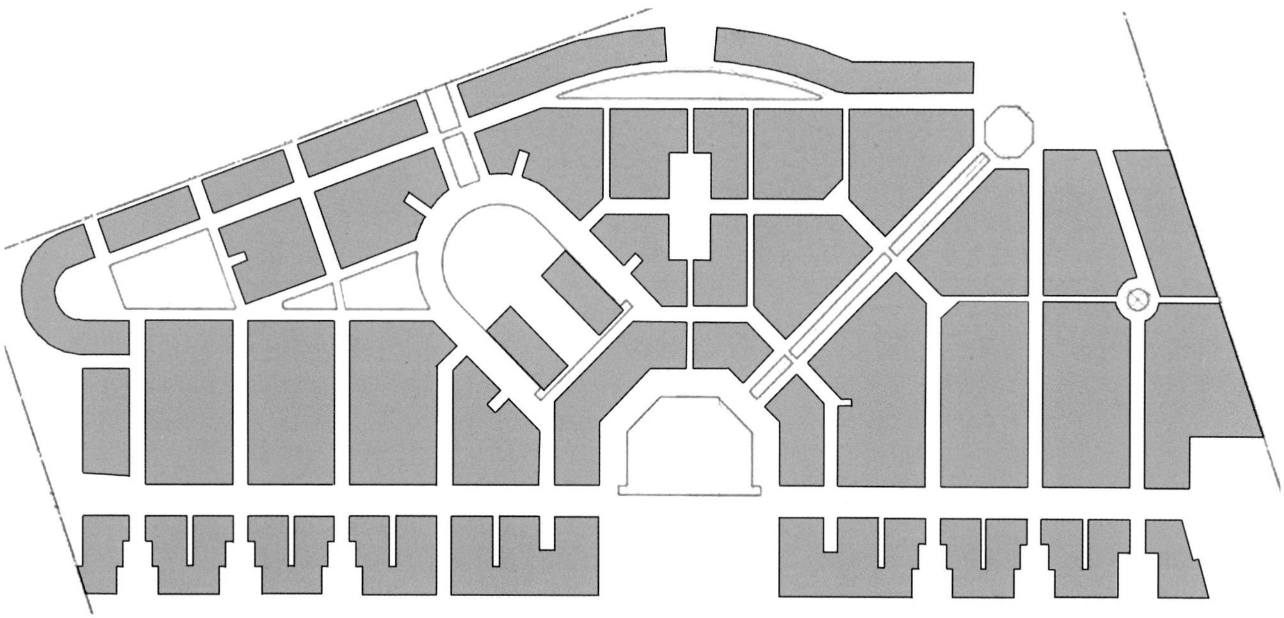

1. Block plan of Seaside, 1:5,000

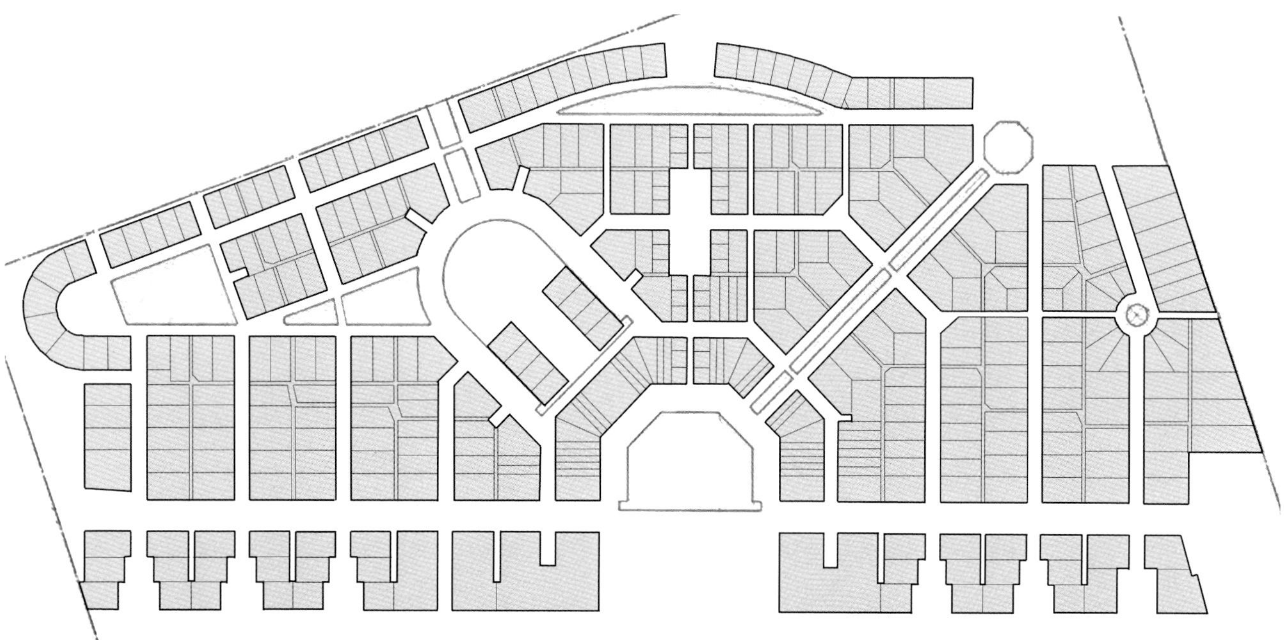

2. Block and parcel plan of Seaside, 1:5,000

Plan and Architecture of Seaside

The block plan and the parcel plan of Seaside might suggest a dense, traditional European city—perhaps a Bastide town, or maybe the neighborhood of a city along the Garonne River in southwest France.

But Seaside is a small American town, made mostly of detached houses, not party-wall buildings, and with picket fences delimiting the boundary between the public realm and the private realm. The transparent acknowledgment of these two realms is the quintessential characteristic of small-town America and reflects the neoclassical origins of the nation.

The three-dimensional architectural and urban development—the third of Conzen's three elements of urban fabric—is controlled by a form-based code that ensures both unity and variety.

Blocks, Streets, and Squares

The typical Seaside block is about 200' wide with lots on each side, facing streets of approximately 40', with on-street parking.

Seaside's Town Square is about 410' wide x 260' deep (with chamfered corners).

The Place de la Bourse in Bordeaux (previously Place Louis XV) is 400' wide x 175' deep as enclosed by buildings, and 230' as paved surface.

1. Aerial plan of Seaside, 1:5,000

2. Seaside street

3. Aerial plan of the Place de la Bourse, Bordeaux, France, 1:5,000

4. Place de la Bourse from reflecting pool

Aerial view of South Jordan, Utah

1. Founders of New Urbanism at CNU I, 1993: front (left to right): Liz Moule, Elizabeth Plater-Zyberk; rear (left to right): Stefanos Polyzoides, Dan Solomon, Andres Duany, Peter Calthorpe

2. Aerial view of suburban Atlanta

3. Aerial view of Tysons Corner

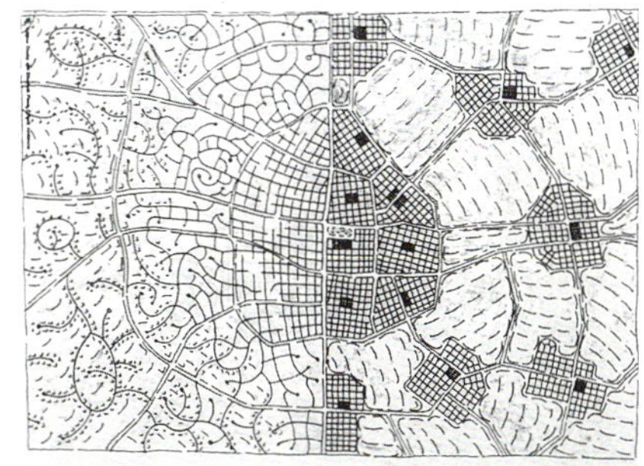

4. Suburbia vs. city and towns, Doug Kelbaugh

The Enemy

Enemies are useful, especially in adolescence, but also in maturity. They help us define who we are by who we are not. They spur us to action, especially in moments of doubt. Having already had some degree of success, a worthy enemy has identity, definition, and noticeable failures. Since ancient times they have often proved invaluable.

The enemy of the modernist planners of CIAM, Team X, and the Harvard Urban Design program was the traditional city, with its streets, squares, civic structure, and vibrant life.

The enemy of the rationalists, contextualists, and populists was the modernist city, with its monofunctional zoning and lack of a public realm and vibrant life.

The enemy of New Urbanism was the idiot cousin of the modernist city: suburban sprawl.

Suburban Sprawl

Suburban sprawl was a genuinely formidable enemy. Following World War II, cheap land and cheap gas fed an almost unlimited American appetite for further and further expansion in an escape from the city to the single-family suburban house. As development moved further out and became less dense, more infrastructure was required, and any sense of community was lost. The American Town ceased to be a model for American life. The private automobile became a necessity rather than a luxury, and as oil usage increased, suburbia became a driving force of American foreign policy.

Congress for The New Urbanism

In the 1980s, a small group of architects and urbanists began to develop an alternative to suburban sprawl through a return to the urban form and principles of the small American town. Compact, walkable communities became the new model, and relationships with developers were the means. The architectural language was traditional and familiar to the average home buyer, but the typology was controlled by form-based codes.

After more than a decade of work and dozens of projects, the Congress for New Urbanism was founded by Peter Calthorpe, Andres Duany, Elizabeth Moule, Elizabeth Plater-Zyberk, Stefanos Polyzoides, and Dan Solomon. The first meeting of the Congress was held in 1993 in Alexandria, Virginia, with approximately 100 attendees—mostly architects and urban designers.[49] Since that meeting, membership has expanded to include developers, politicians, and a wide variety of consultants. Attendance is now around 3,000.

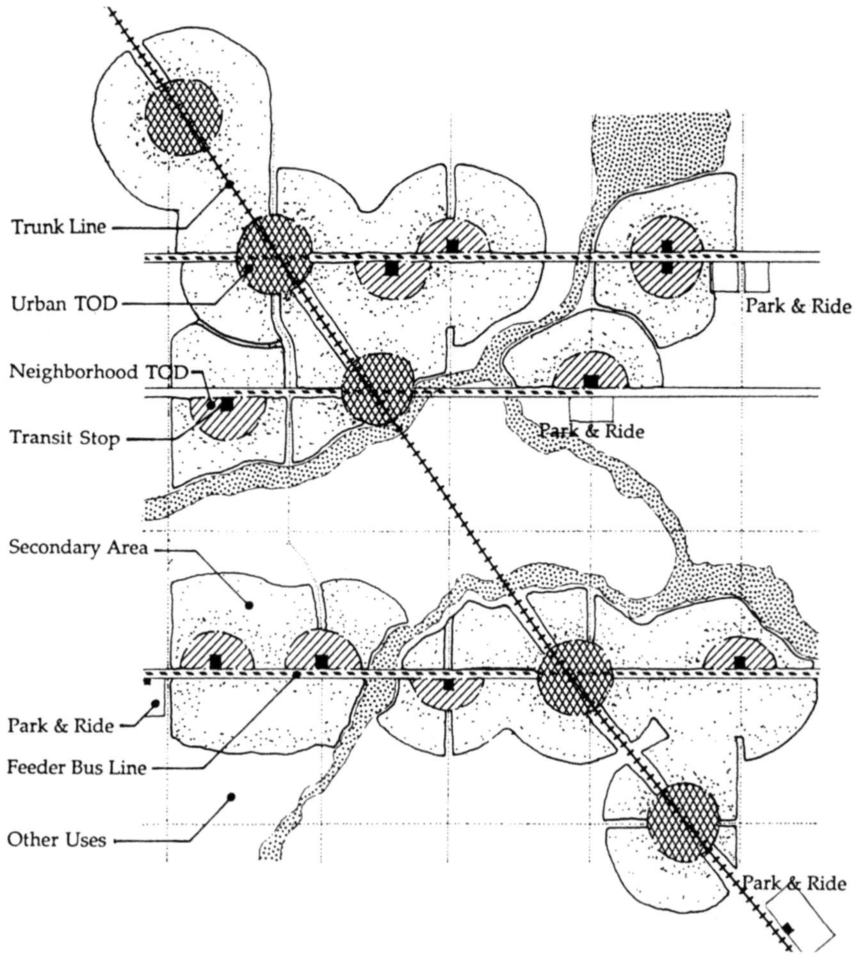

1. *Transit-oriented urban diagram, Peter Calthorpe*

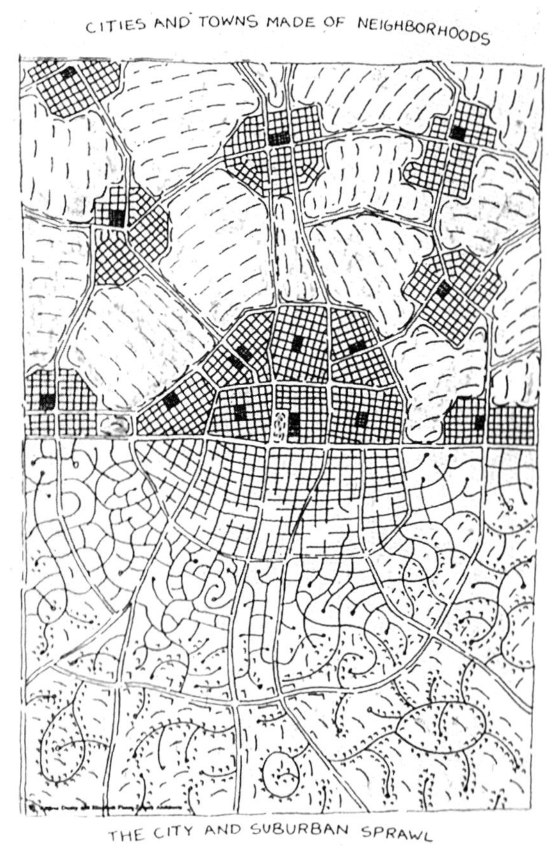

2. *Comparative urban diagram, Doug Kelbaugh*

Urban Principles

The basic principles of New Urbanism are of course not new at all, but are newly articulated from time-tested principles of urban form—most recently from Leon Krier's description of city form and elements. Further, they are not used primarily for city design, but to renovate or produce towns as an alternative to suburban sprawl. The basic principles are clearly elucidated in the introductory essays of Peter Katz's 1994 book: *The New Urbanism: Toward an Architecture of Community*.

Despite the book's subtitle—*Toward an* Architecture *of Community*—there is nothing in it about architecture *per se*, nothing about architectural style, and only glancing references to architectural theory. Notably, the book is not about architecture at all, but about urbanism—the urbanism of cities, towns, and villages. At its core is the reintroduction of the public realm, the civic space of the city, and the emphasis on form and form-based codes, rather than functional zoning. Three essays outline the basic principles of New Urbanism: "The Region," "The Neighborhood, the District, and the Corridor," and "The Street, the Block, and the Building."[50]

The Region

Peter Calthorpe's essay argues that urbanism is now well understood in the city, but that the principles are rarely applied to the suburb; and that the region—the city, the suburbs, and the natural environment—should be designed as a whole. He states:

> In every context ... the quality of new development in a region should follow town-like principles—housing for a diverse population, a full mix of uses, walkable streets, positive public space, integrated civic and commercial centers, transit orientation, and accessible open space.[51]

Two other ideas are crucial to regional planning: urban growth boundaries and transit-oriented development. *Urban growth boundaries* are "the regional equivalent of a defined neighborhood edge. These boundaries create identity for the whole and express the need to preserve nature as a limit to human habitat."[52] *Transit* "can order and formalize the region in much the same way a street network orders a neighborhood. It supports the life of the pedestrian throughout the region."[53]

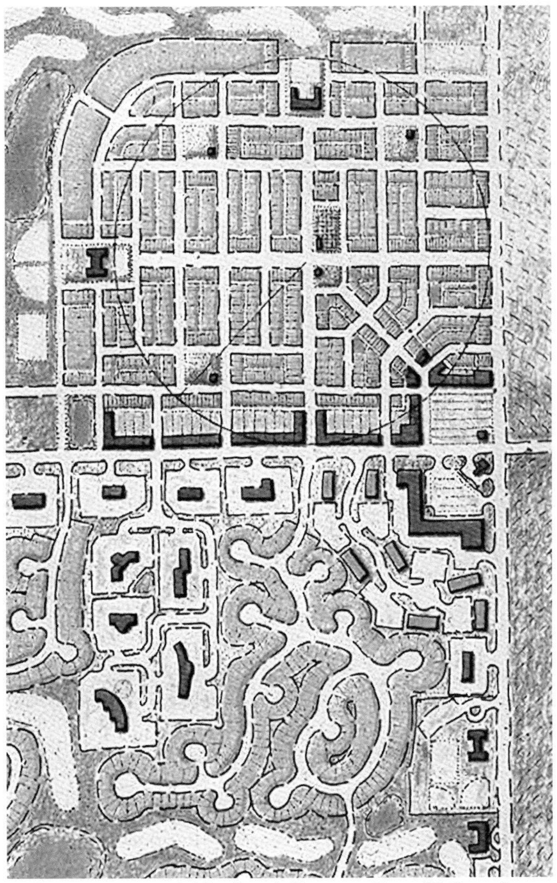

1. Comparative neighborhood diagram, Doug Kelbaugh

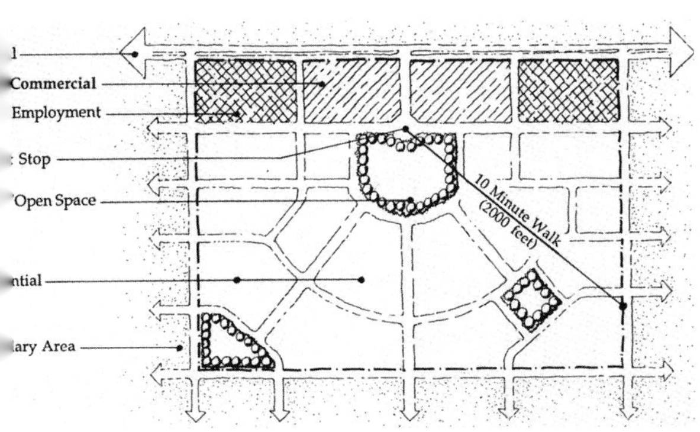

2. Neighborhood diagram, Peter Calthorpe

Neighborhood, District, and Corridor

Andres Duany and Elizabeth Plater-Zyberk point out that, in contrast to suburbia, the neighborhood, the district, and the corridor are fundamental elements of urbanism.

"The following are the principles of an ideal *neighborhood* design:

> 1) The neighborhood has a center and edge;
> 2) The optimal size of a neighborhood is a quarter mile from center to edge;
> 3) The neighborhood has a balanced mix of activities—dwelling, shopping, working, schooling, worshipping, and recreating;
> 4) The neighborhood structures building sites and traffic on a fine network of interconnecting streets;
> 5) The neighborhood gives priority to public space and to the appropriate location of civic buildings."[54]

The *district* may be formally similar to the neighborhood, but is more monofunctional rather than multifunctional. Nevertheless, districts such as theater districts, universities, etc. still allow multiple activities and support public spaces.

Corridors both connect and separate neighborhoods and districts.

Street, Block, and Building

It is telling that Elizabeth Moule and Stefanos Polyzoides discuss the street, the block, and the building in that order, as the *street* is perhaps the most important element of New Urbanism.[55] It was fundamental to the traditional city, and banished by the modernists, but it is again crucial for a complete, functioning public realm. Moule and Polyzoides argue that streets are communal rooms and passages that form a hierarchical spatial network defined by street walls. Building heights need to be proportional to the width of the street, and the landscape and details need to support both pedestrians and vehicles. Street trees help articulate the pedestrian space and scale as well as that of vehicles.

Blocks may be square, rectangular, or irregular, and should be of moderate size. It is important that they allow for a variety of parcels, and permit buildings to align on all edges in order to make a continuous street wall defining the public space of the street.

Buildings are the city's smallest increment of growth. A plan of streets, squares, and parks is made, but "single buildings incrementally introduced into blocks eventually determine the character of open spaces. It is at this most elemental scale ... that architecture and urbanism define each other."[56] Implicitly, this means that, generally, buildings should be smaller than blocks.

Type is usually more important than style. Building types connote function, or use, such as libraries, offices, housing, etc. Architectural types connote form. There are two architectural types: one produces urban fabric, the other monuments.

Urban architecture—that which produces urban fabric—is ensured by "building envelope guidelines that link entitlements with predictable physical and architectural definitions of the public realm."[57] In other words, form-based codes should replace zoning codes. This safeguards the public realm "while allowing significant freedom for the designers of individual buildings. It is in the balancing of such public and private interests and concerns that the future quality of life in the American city lies."[58]

It has been almost twenty years since the publication of *The New Urbanism.* Topics that were lightly touched at the time—landscape, ecology, squares, politics, etc.— have become more developed, but the basic urban design principles remain. They are still applied primarily to suburban conditions, and market preferences for retro-architecture remains an issue for some, but the principles are applicable to urban conditions as well.

A New Village

This 1992 project for Dade County, Florida by Dover, Kohl & Partners is a literal expression of new urbanist principles.[59]

The 100-acre site allows the development of a compact neighborhood within an approximately ten-minute walking shed. (The town is about twice the size of Seaside.) The blocks are small, the streets are tight, and there is a variety of housing types that define the streets. Typical blocks are about 225' x 350' with service alleys and fine-grain parcels.

The town square is about 300' x 350', and is defined by mixed-use party-wall buildings with arcades along the streets and a green park in the center. Smaller parks and squares are distributed throughout the plan—several at residual areas resulting from grid collisions.

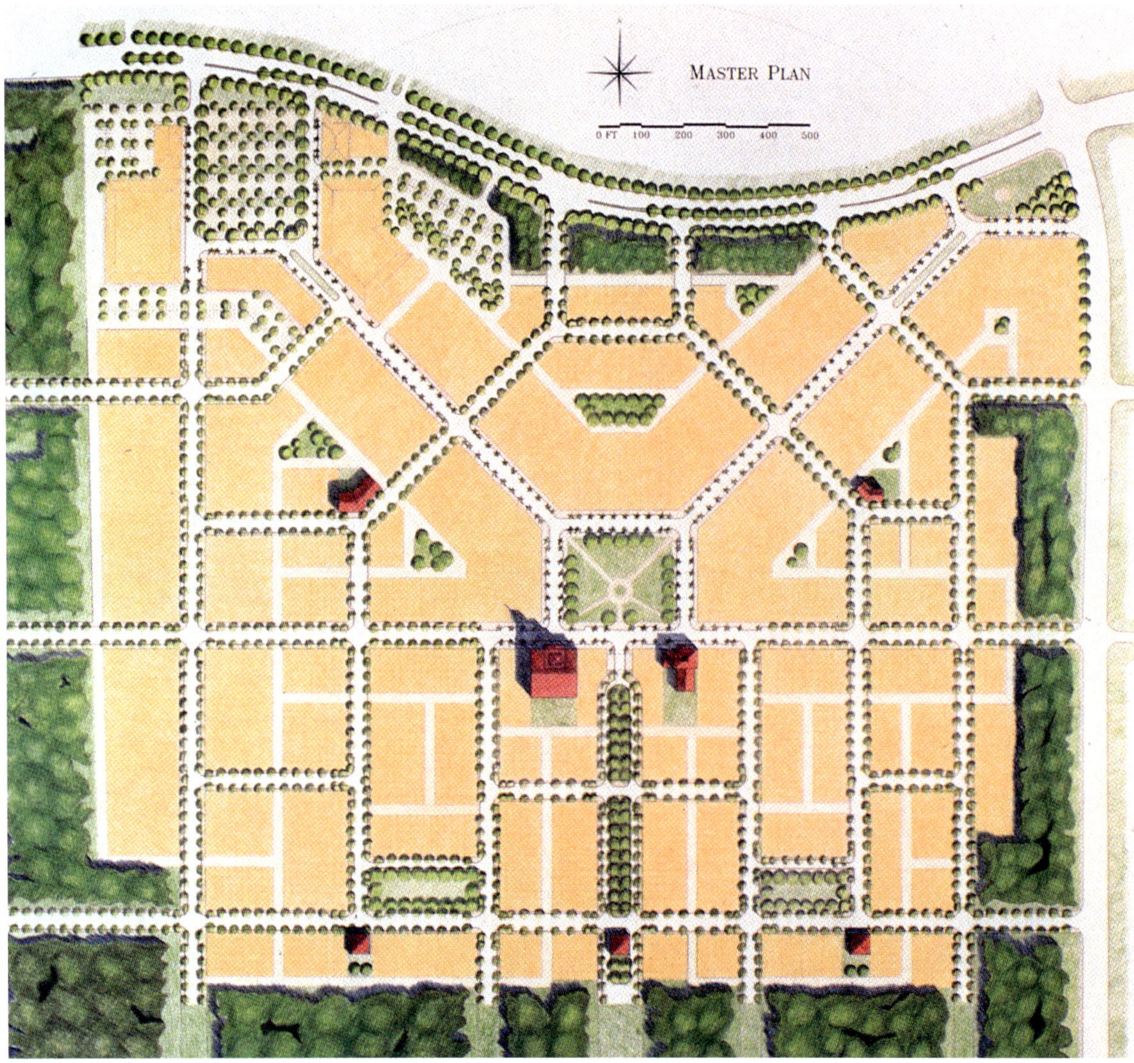

1. Proposed plan, 1:5,000

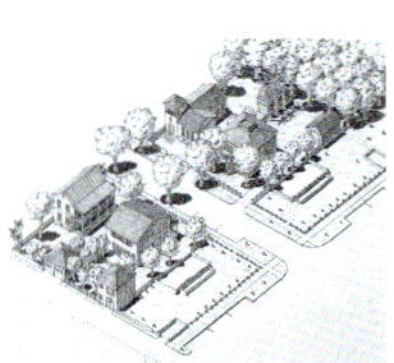

2. Detached houses

3. Row houses

4. Apartments over shops

5. Garden apartments

6. Courtyard apartments

7. Town Square

1. San Diego, proposed regional transit plan

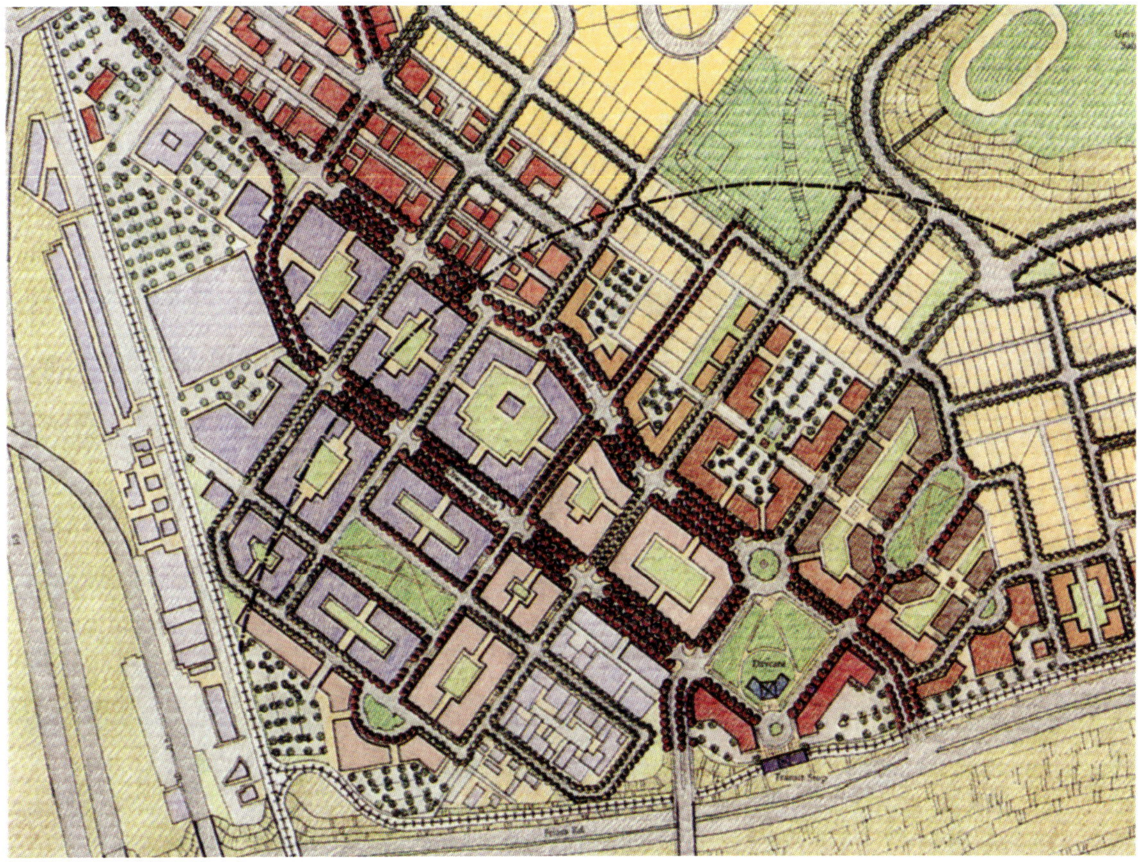

2. Tecolate Road, proposed plan

Transit-Oriented Development

Peter Calthorpe argues for comprehensive regional design as well as the urban design of towns and neighborhoods. In other words, neighborhood developments should be pedestrian-oriented and mixed-use, but should be connected by a regional transit system—as illustrated in his plan for San Diego.[60]

Because adequate density is required to support transit, Calthorpe proposes increased density and public uses concentrated around transit stops. Calthorpe Associates' plan for the redevelopment of the Tecolate Road area illustrates both the town planning principles and the effect of a regional transit connection.

The existing plan is typical of suburban auto-oriented development: huge blocks, segregated functions, little possibility of pedestrian connections, and no public space. The proposed plan accomplishes the opposite.

The existing vehicular street network is at once simplified and extended. The small block pattern of the residential area is extended into the commercial area to form a town plan of fine-grained blocks and tree-lined streets, filled with street-defining urban buildings. There is a hierarchical pattern of public open spaces and a mix of uses. The density is greatest around the town square, which is located adjacent to the transit stop.

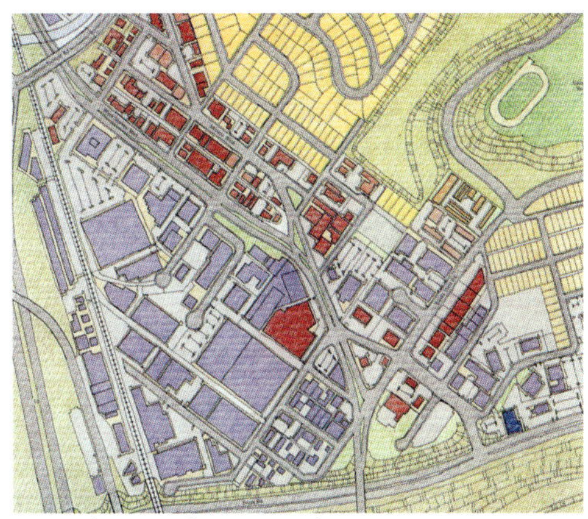

3. Tecolate Road, existing plan

1. *Aerial perspective of Orange Tree Courts*

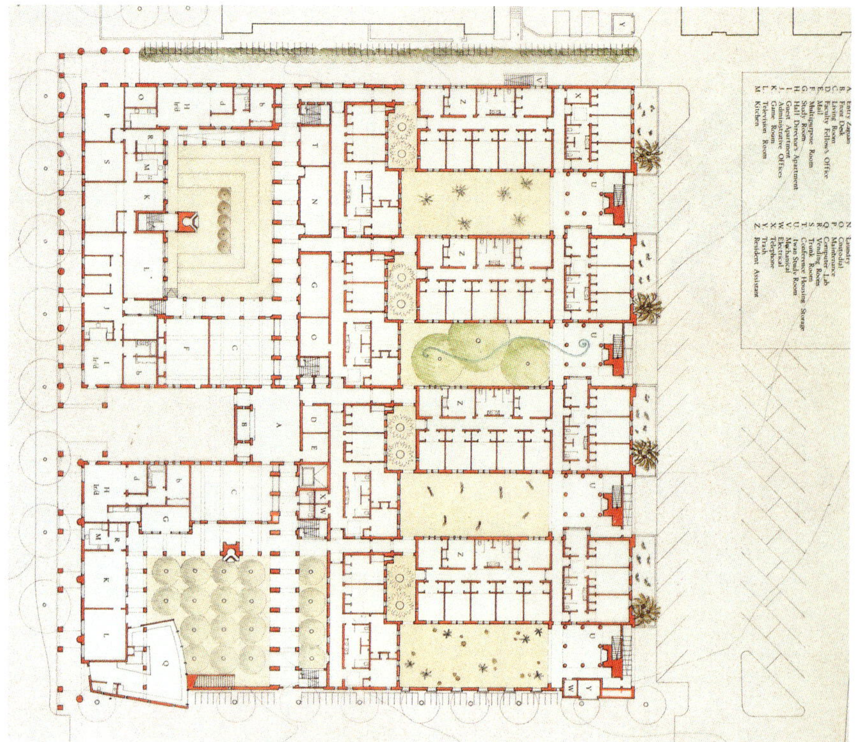

3. *Highland District, proposed plan*

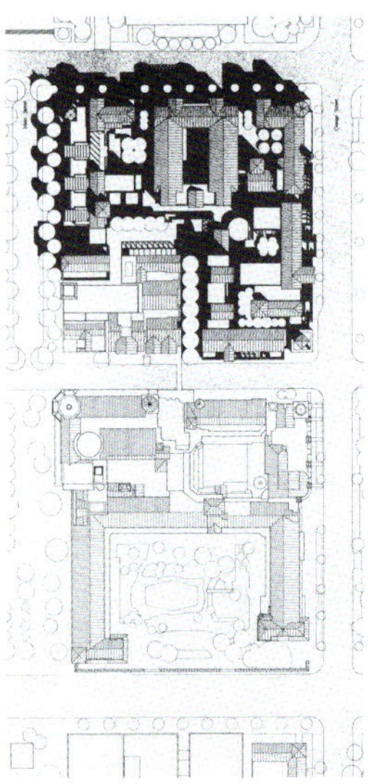

2. *Plan of Orange Tree Courts*

Orange Tree Courts

The 1988 Orange Tree Courts project, by Moule & Polyzoides, is a renovation and reconstruction of a large 335' square urban block across from Riverside, California's historic Mission Inn. The development incorporates the hotel annex and an existing parking garage. It provides 74 living units and office space above retail, offices, and parking entrances at ground level.[61]

The large block size allows for multiple courtyards, and the articulation of five separate buildings.

This project is in many ways a rehearsal for their 1990 Highland District Plan.

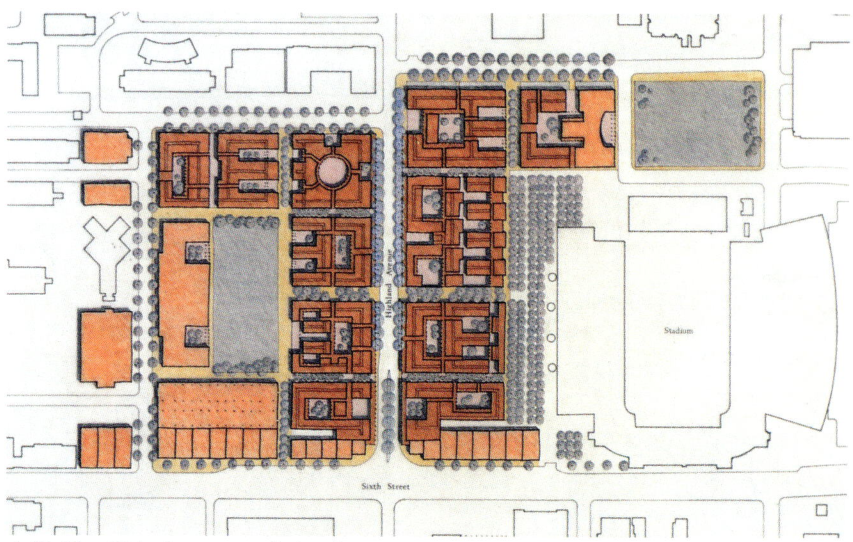

4. *Highland District, proposed site plan*

1. *Aerial perspective of the Highland District*

2. *Aerial plan of courtyard housing at Caltech*

Highland District

The courtyard typology of southern California and the southwest is exemplified by the Avery student housing at the California Institute of Technology in Pasadena, where the office of Moule & Polyzoides is located. It is also the typology for their 1990 Highland District housing for the University of Arizona.[62]

Instead of high-rise dormitories, a rich fabric of low-rise courtyard housing reinforces the urban structure of Highland Avenue as a continuously colonnaded street connecting South Street to the main university mall. In addition to housing for 3,000 students, the project contains street-level retail, classrooms, administrative offices, recreational facilities, and a parking garage.

Like the Caltech example, student rooms are clustered around small courts, shielded from Highland Avenue by larger courts and more public facilities.

Dan Solomon and John Ellis

A native San Franciscan, Dan Solomon is urban. His urban design partner since 1993, John Ellis, is also urban, and the city has provided the framework and principles for their architecture and urbanism.

The Solomon office's work is almost exclusively housing—urban housing—that developed out of San Francisco's narrow party-wall parcels, grew through blocks, into whole blocks, and then into comprehensive town plans, such as that for Coyote Valley near San Jose.

San Francisco

Unlike Manhattan, where the natural topography was erased ahead of the relentlessly advancing practical grid, San Francisco is famous for its grid draped over the topography without regard for slopes; thus producing equally famous precipitous streets and magnificent views—both favorites for car-chase and romantic movies.

1. Aerial view of San Francisco

2. Facade

3. Living Room

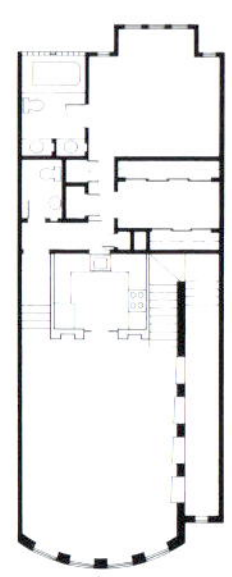

4. Plan

Solomon Townhouse

Dan Solomon's own house is on a typical, narrow San Francisco party-wall site. It consists of a high second living story above a ground-floor garage. The facade is modern, built to the street line, and blends with the other houses to define the street.

5. Through-block street

7. Aerial view of Fulton Grove townhouses

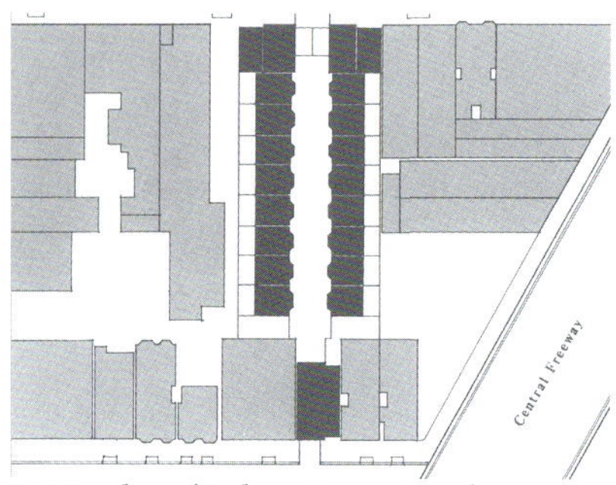

9. Site plan of Fulton Grove townhouses

Fulton Grove, San Francisco

Capitalizing on the precedent of small through-block streets in San Francisco, this project organizes 22 units along a tree-lined street for a density of 44 units per acre. The three-story townhouses have garages and private gardens.

6. Street facade of 101 San Fernando

8. Aerial view of 101 San Fernando

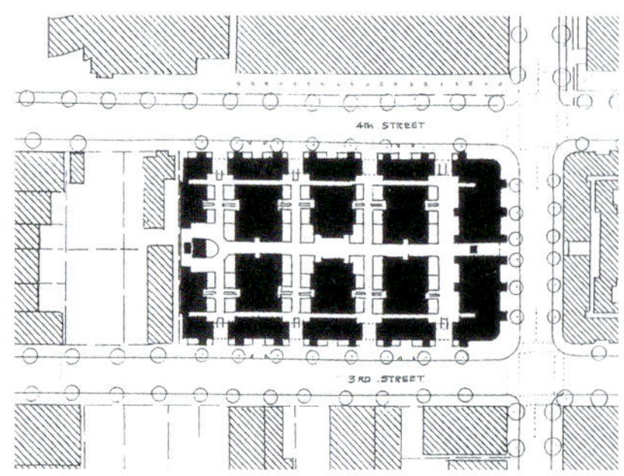

10. Site plan of 101 San Fernando

101 San Fernando, San Jose

This five-story mixed-use project contains 322 units organized as a perimeter block with through-block lanes. It achieves an astonishing 108 units per acre, with 10,000 square feet of retail space and sits over a two-level parking podium.

1. *Downtown blocks, 275' x 413', 1:10,000*

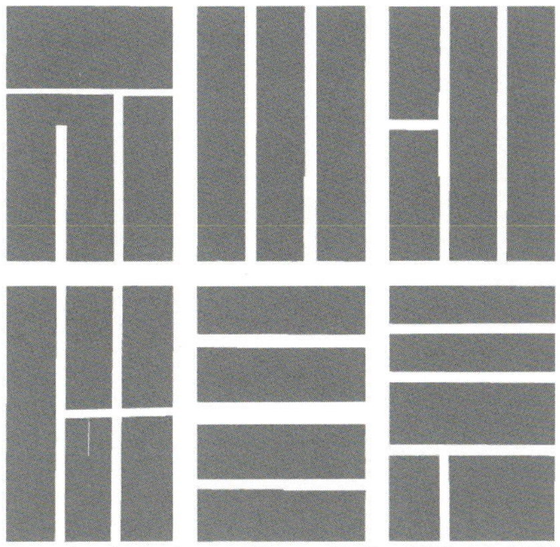

4. *South of Market grid, ca. 630' x 908',1:10,000*

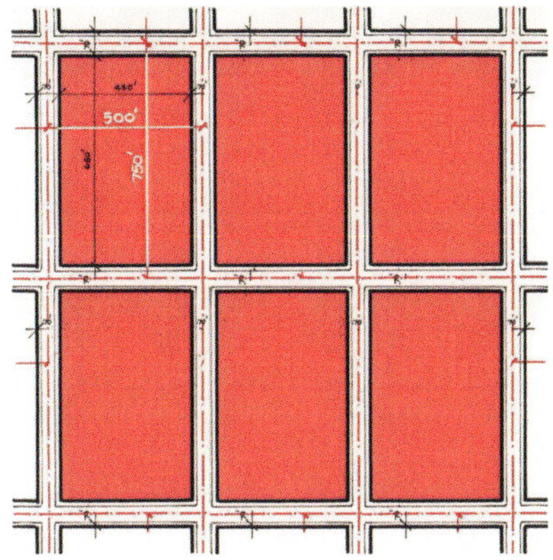

5. *Coyote Valley grid, 500' x 750', 1:10,000*

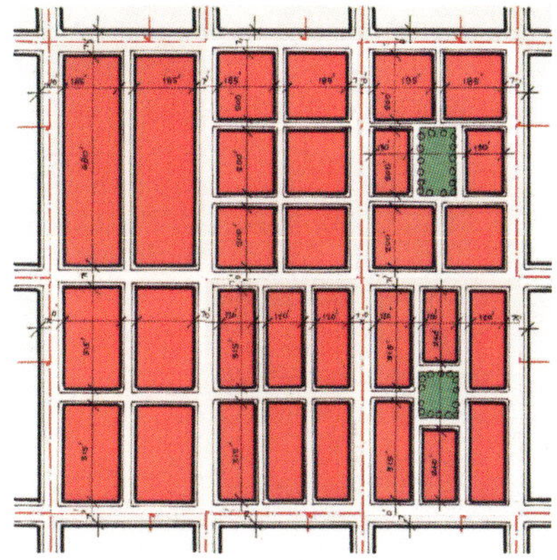

6. *Sample division of Coyote Valley blocks, 1:10,000*

2. *Richmond blocks, 240' x 600', 1:10,000*

3. *Potrero Hills blocks, 200' x 400', 1:10,000*

San Francisco Urban Fabric

The grain of San Francisco is fine, the architecture urban, the squares humanly scaled, the neighborhoods distinct, and large parks provide a civic structure at the scale of the city's stunning landscape.

There are four primary block sizes that form the urban fabric of major parts of the city. The original settlement, now Downtown, was laid out according to the Laws of the Indies and was based on the Spanish land measurement of a vara (2'-9"). The North of Market blocks measured 100 x 150 varas (275' x 412'-6") with 25 vara-wide streets (68'-9"). The South of Market blocks were intended for commercial and industrial use and are four times larger, measuring 200 x 300 varas (550' x 825') with 30 vara-wide streets (82'-6"). These mega-blocks have been divided into a variety of smaller blocks and streets. This is the area where the Solomon office was once located, and may therefore have provided a familiar model as a precedent for the Coyote Valley project.

The later nineteenth-century additions to the city, the Richmond and Sunset District blocks to the west, were laid out to English land measurements, 240' x 600' with 80' wide streets, while the finer-grained Potrero Hills District blocks measure 200' x 400' with 60' and 80' wide streets. The older Spanish districts have mid-block alleys and are among the densest parts of the city.

Parcels and Density

The typical 25'-wide San Francisco parcel has generated the city's characteristic row-houses and stacked walk-up flats. The average net density in the city is approximately 35 units per acre, characterized by two-and three-story-high perimeter block housing, while the denser districts with mid-block alleys can achieve net densities of 75 units per acre in North Beach and Telegraph Hill to as high as 100 units per acre in Chinatown and the Tenderloin district.

Coyote Valley Urban Fabric

The planning module of the Coyote Valley plan is based on a grid of 500' x 750', resulting in an urban fabric of 70' streets and 430' x 680' blocks. These blocks must be divided, however, into at least two smaller blocks and maybe as many as six smaller blocks. This provides the flexibility to accommodate a wide variety of building types, and ensure a small-scale fabric.[63]

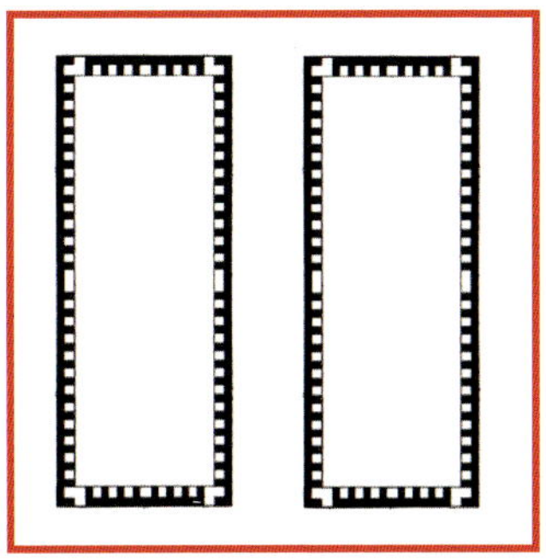

7. *Villa Immeuble grid, 400 m, 1:10,000*

8. *Ville Contemporaine grid, 400 m, 1:10,000*

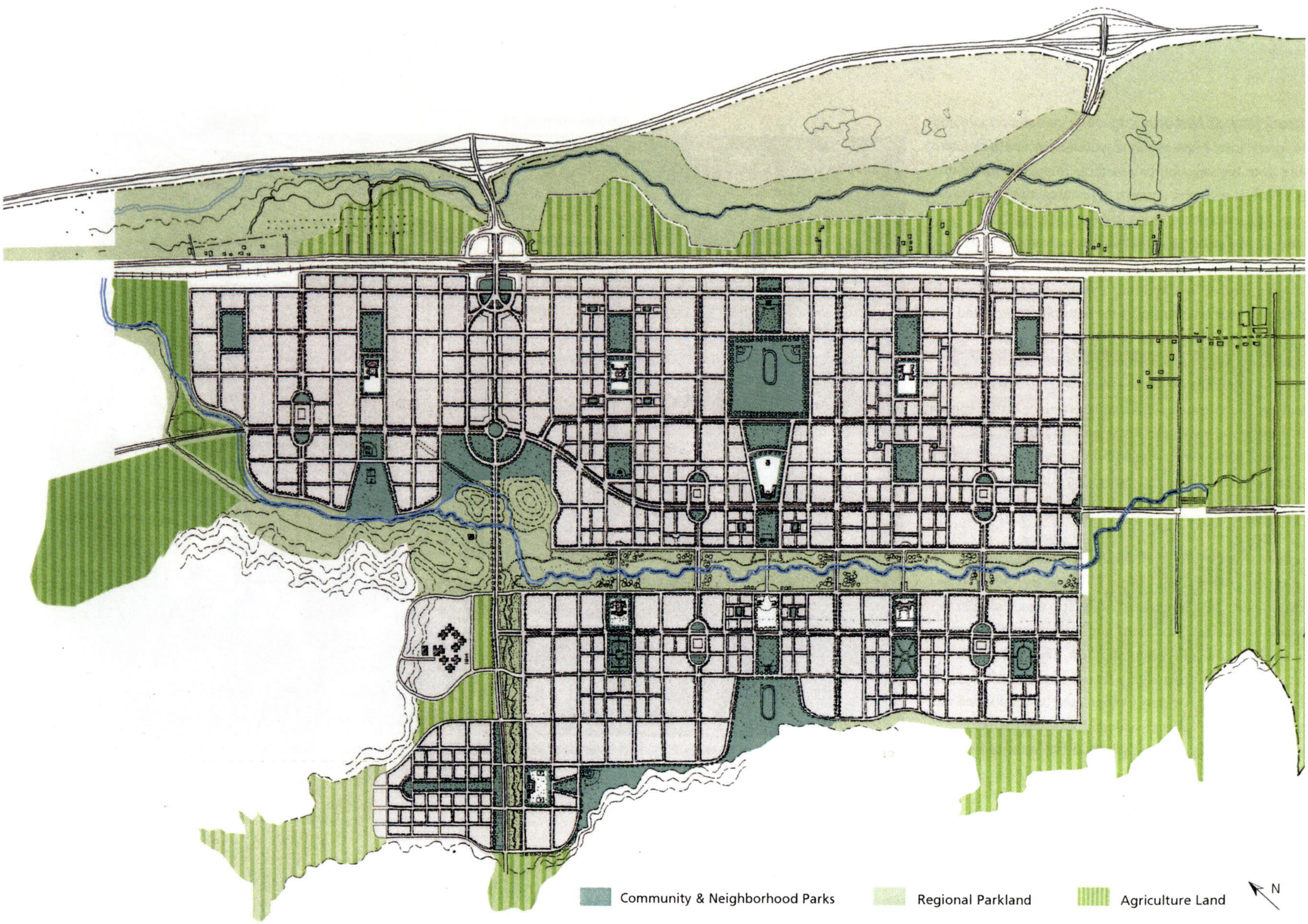

Proposed development plan for Coyote Valley

Coyote Valley Plan

Development of the fertile plain of Coyote Valley can be expected in the near future owing to its proximity to San Jose. Without a plan, however, the valley would likely succumb to sprawl. The proposed plan by WRT Solomon is a more responsible alternative, designed to preserve agricultural land, improve the ecological systems, and establish a compact, walkable community for 80,000 residents. It is also expected that 53,000 jobs will be created.

The town's neighborhoods are organized by the 3:2 planning grid around the reconfigured Fisher Creek, which runs north–south through the town. This green area serves both as an important recreation area and as flood control. Major town parks and greens relate directly to this element.

The town grid also preserves and incorporates the existing roads on the site.

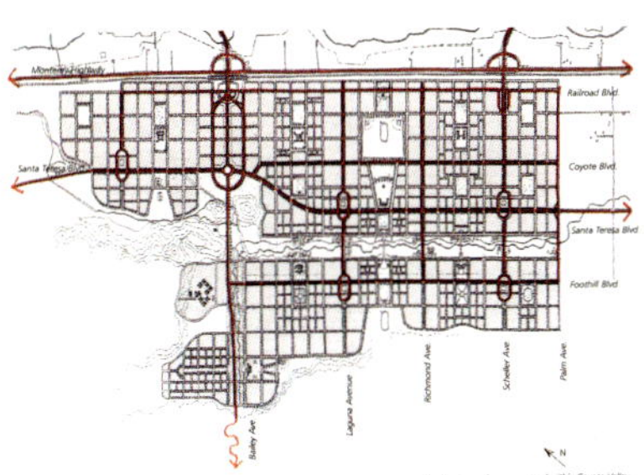

1. Major road network

2. Aerial perspective of proposed plan

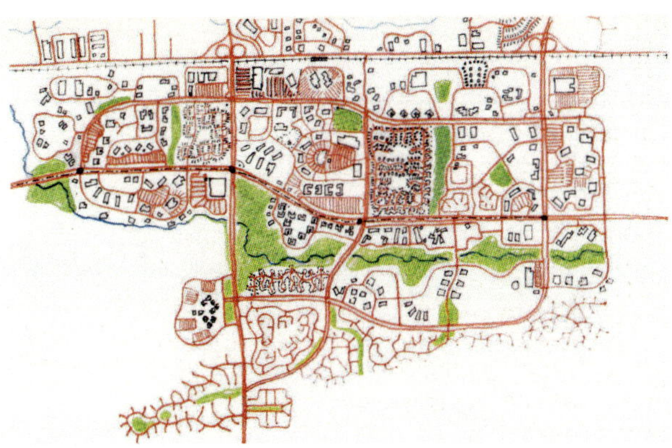

3. Possible sprawl development plan

4. Coyote Valley

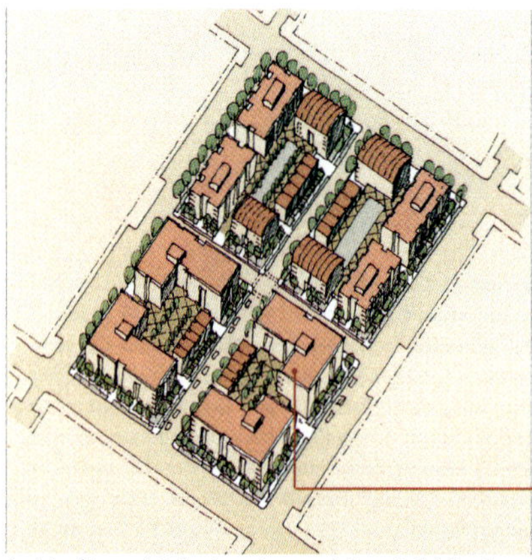

1. *Medium-high-density residential block*

Medium-High-Density Residential
35–45 units/acre

Above a density of 32 units/acre it becomes necessary to provide podium-parking garages—assuming a parking ratio of two spaces per unit. Below this density it is possible to provide either tuck-under wood-frame garages or surface parking, which are substantially less expensive alternatives.

Five-story stacked flats over one-story parking (45 units/acre)

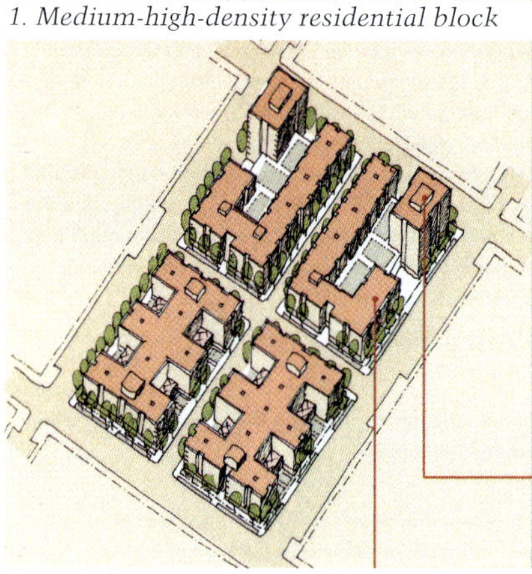

2. *High-density residential block*

High-Density Residential
75–125 units/acre

In order to provide a choice of housing types to accommodate a wide variety of households and create a compact walkable town, certain areas will have higher densities. Higher densities should occur in the town center, neighborhood centers, and along transit routes. Density of 100 units/acre would result in significant population close to shops and services.

Eight-story "below life-safety" mid-rise apartment tower over two-three level parking (100 units/acre)

Six-story stacked flats over two-story parking (75 units/acre)

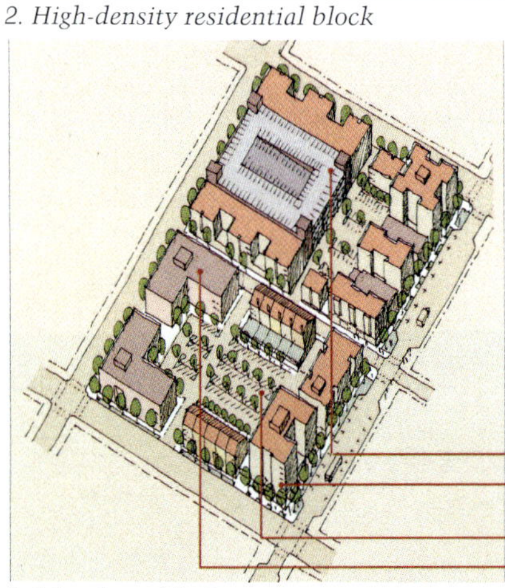

3. *Mixed-use block*

Mixed Use
30–50 units/acre, FAR 2-Commercial

Commercial or residential occurs over ground floor retail. Parking is on-street, on interior surface lots, or in garages. Parking structures are lined with other uses to minimize their impact on the street.

Parking garage with buildings on two sides

Mid-rise residential over ground-floor retail

Mid-block surface parking

Commercial perimeter-block office building

4. *Aerial view of Coyote Valley, East Scheiler neighborhood*

Neighborhoods

Each neighborhood accommodates 10,000 to 12,000 residents in a varied mix of housing types. Parks and open spaces are within easy walking distance, and each neighborhood has a neighborhood center with a dense mix of public and private uses. The neighborhood centers are each located adjacent to a transit line and a major boulevard.

Buildings align on the streets and public open spaces, and the typical 70'-wide street ensures enough closure to make the street a legible public space.

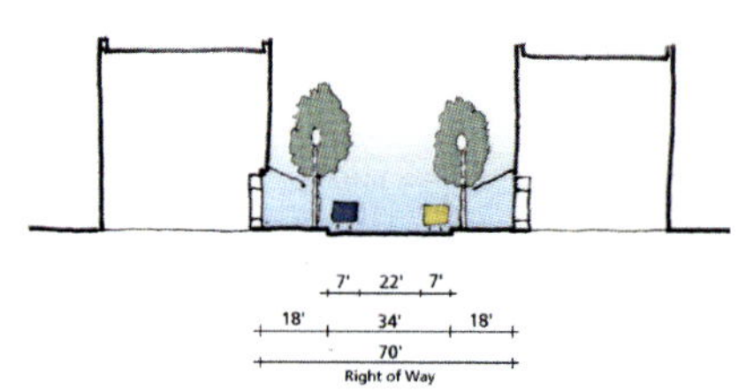

5. *Typical street section*

High-Density Mixed-Use
75–100 units/acre, FAR 3-Commercial

A variety of high-rise office buildings and mid-rise residential are over ground-floor retail. Parking at two cars per 1,000 square feet is on-street, in podiums, or in garages.

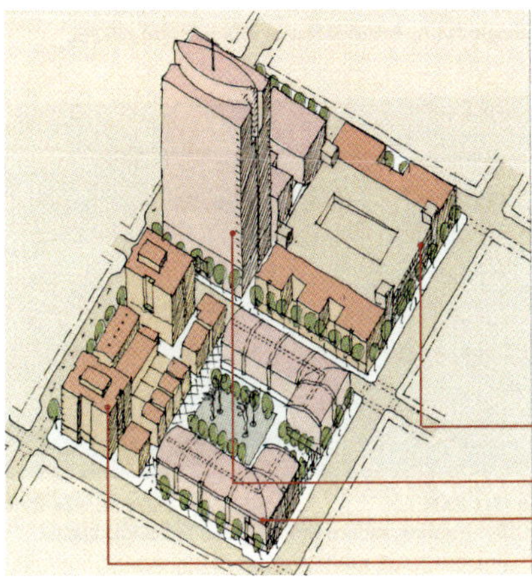

1. High-density mixed-use block development

High-Density Commercial
FAR 3

This density requires high-rise towers in addition to mid-rise buildings. Parking at two cars per 1,000 square feet is on-street and in garages.

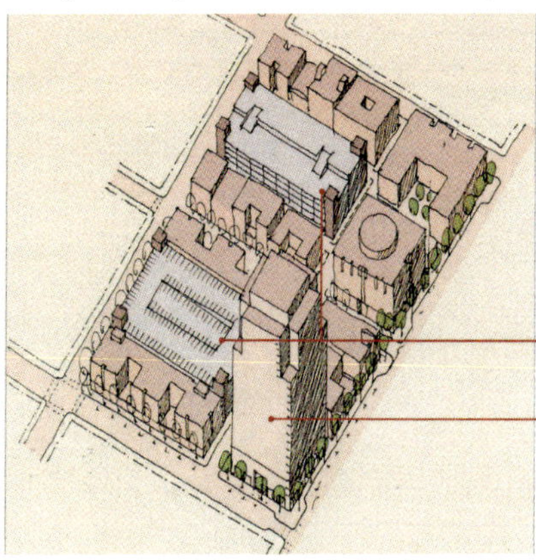

2. FAR 3 Commercial block development

Medium Density Commercial
FAR 2

This development allows mid-rise perimeter-block buildings around courtyards at a code-determined height of 85', i.e., "Below Life-Safety" of six to seven stories. Parking is in parking structures.

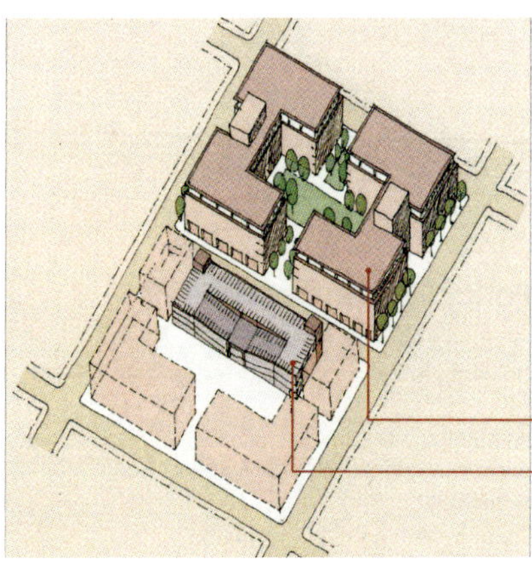

3. FAR 2 Commercial block development

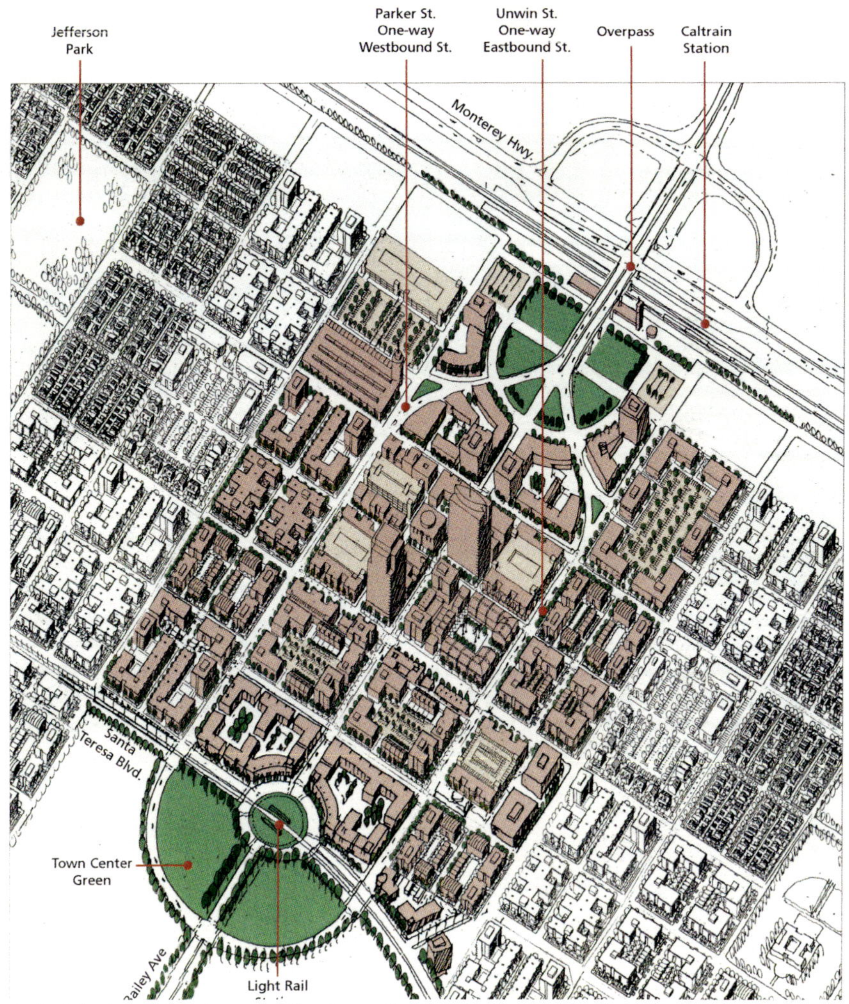

4. Aerial view of the Coyote Valley Town Center

The Town Center

The town center is served by train to the east and by light rail to the west. It is a dense multifunctional area with a mix of mid- to high-rise buildings. All buildings align on the street to define the civic space at the level of the street, with taller buildings rising from the resulting urban matrix.

The large planning module of 500' x 750' allows for a great variety of building and block types.

Bailey Avenue is a two-way central "main street," but the two adjacent streets form a one-way couplet, which carries through-traffic while maintaining a more pedestrian-friendly street width.

Aerial view of the partially completed town

Krier Kohl Architecten

Despite Rob Krier's success with his Berlin IBA projects, realized projects were sparse in the 1980s. Indeed, in the postscript to *Rob Krier: Architecture and Urban Design*, published in 1993, he poignantly describes his disappointment with the lack of realized projects. That, of course, was about to change. Over the course of the next two decades, he and his partner, Christoph Kohl, would design dozens of urban projects in Germany and the Netherlands, and most of these would actually be built.

Kirchsteigfeld

This 1991–1997 project for a major addition to Potsdam, Germany, is the result of a competition won by Rob Krier and Christoph Kohl, and the collaboration of the five other competitors.[64]

The final plan is based on regular streets and squares formed by often irregular perimeter blocks. The block interiors are large open spaces, informally connected. Rather than continuous perimeter buildings, such as those of Amsterdam South, however, the blocks are divided into smaller parcels allocated to different architects in order to achieve variety. All buildings are designed to the code developed by Krier Kohl.

The progression from the initial "urban vision" plan to the final design is striking. The initial plan is like an extract from the 1989 Bussy St. Georges plan—an irregular medieval-like plan with narrow streets and highly irregular blocks, but with an axial, orthogonal overlay superimposed. In the final plan the blocks are bigger and more regular, the streets are much wider, and there are breaks in the block perimeters. Competitors John Ruble and Buzz Yudell described the transformation positively, like "leavening" of bread; that the opening up of the plan allowed it to "breathe, bringing air and sunlight to Krier's earlier solid street walls and closed courtyards."[65] Perhaps, but are the streets not too wide, and is there not too much open space? And, does this (and the colors) not put just a bit too much emphasis on the architecture?

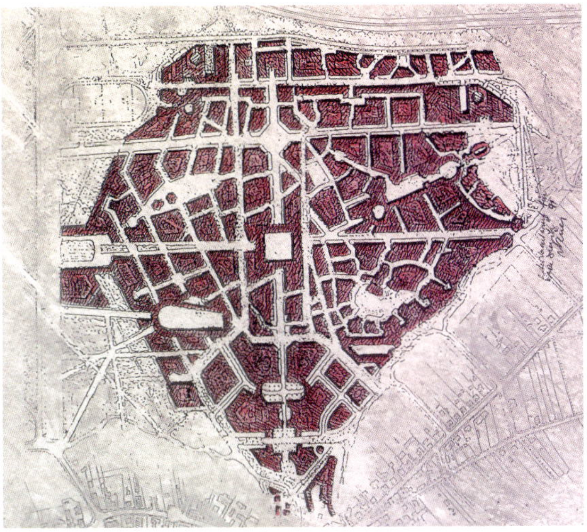
1. Initial "urban vision" plan

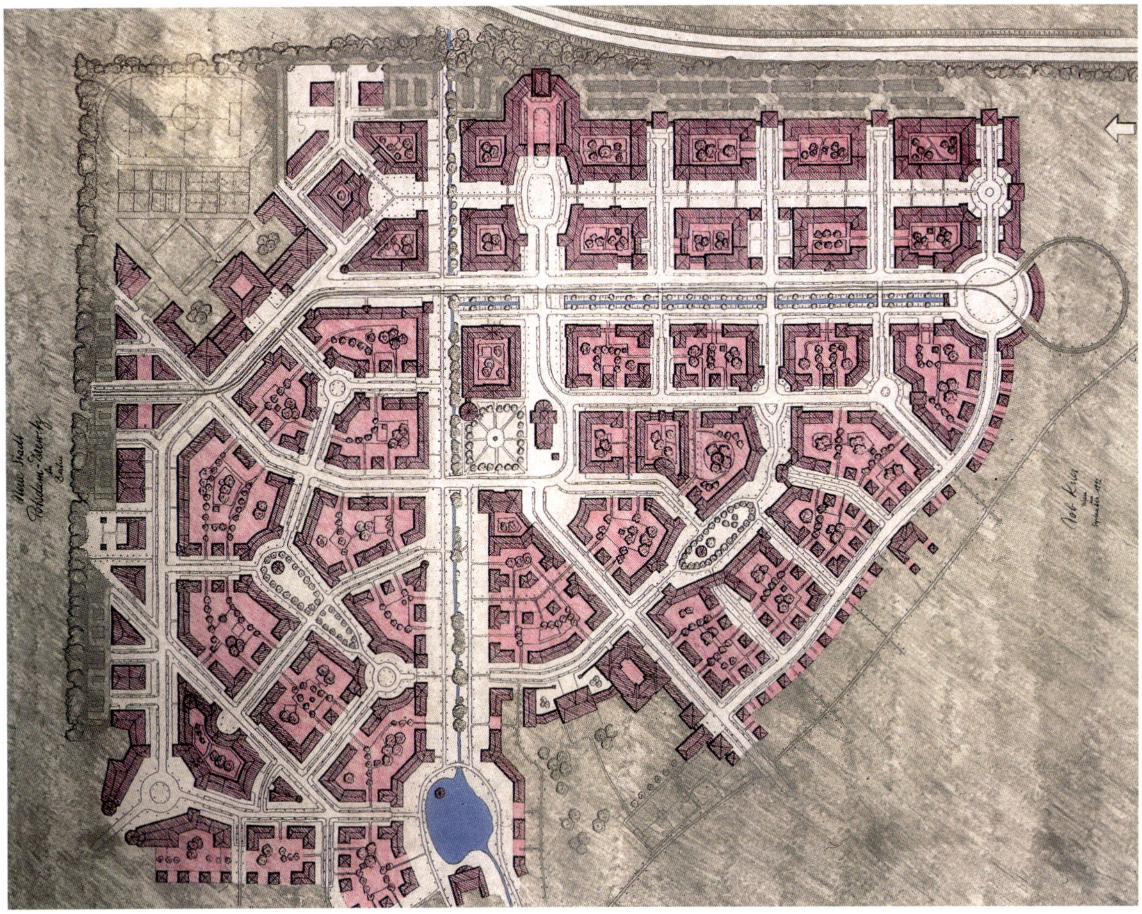
2. Final development plan

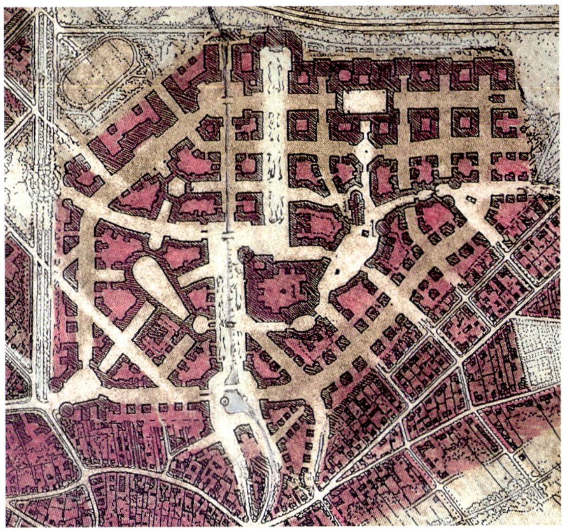
3. Workshop plan

4. Street view

5. View of the pond and "Hirtengraben"

6. The irrigation canal

1. Aerial view of Port Marianne, Montpellier, 1990–93

2. Aerial view of Meander, Amsterdam, 1995–2006

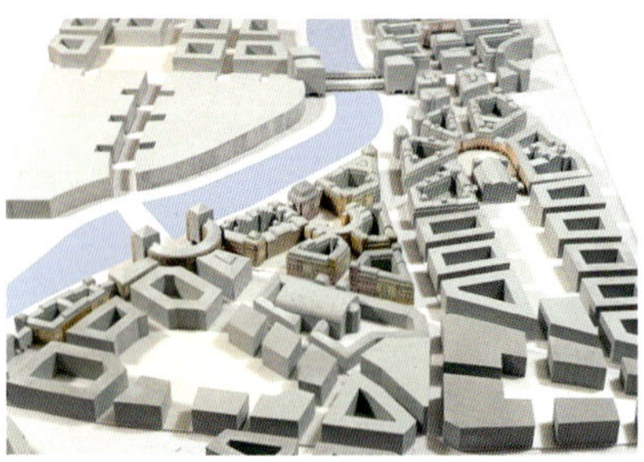

3. Port Marianne, Montpellier, model

4. Pont Marianne, Montpellier, riverfront view

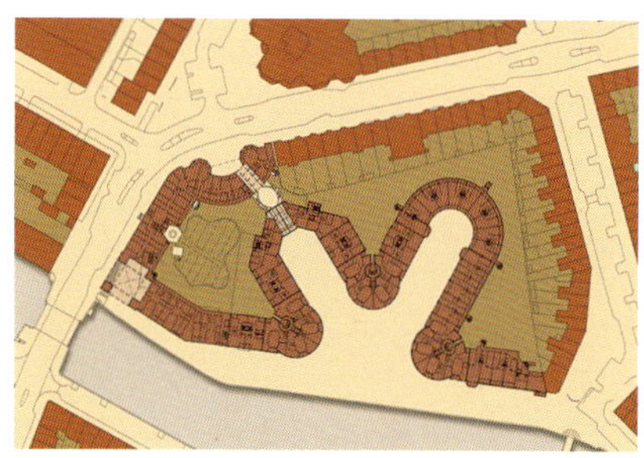

5. Plan of Meander, Amsterdam

6. River front view of Meander, Amsterdam

Port Marianne, Montpellier

Part of a new town master plan by Ricardo Bofill, Krier's project along the river is for 2,800 units of housing, offices, commercial, and public facilities.[66]

Building heights were limited, building parcels were smaller than blocks, and various architects could design no more than four buildings each, and not together. Krier designed the squares and prominent buildings.

Meander, Amsterdam

Built between 1995 and 2006, Meander is an exaggerated version of irregular block/regular spaces. This project orients two "U"-shaped spaces to the canal and city, leaving residual space to the interior of the block.

The units along the two street sides are repetitive and unified, while the "exposed" parts are figurative and unique.[67]

1. Aerial view of Bussum, 2001–2010

2. Model view of Arnhem, 2007–2009

3. Plan of Bussum

4. Canal view of Bussum

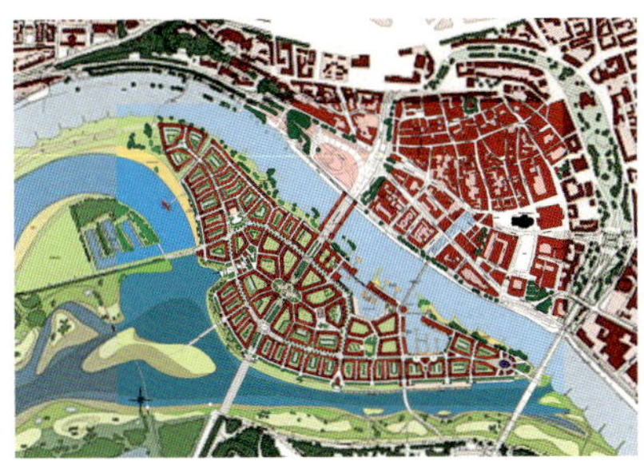

5. Plan of Arnhem

6. Model view

7. Bussum, view of gateway

Bussum, Netherlands

The historic harbor in the center of the Dutch village of Bussum had long been filled, and had a parking lot on top. This project, built 2001–2010, reconstructed the harbor, and public buildings were built across from the existing city hall. A variety of typical Dutch houses line the streets and canal. Each house is slightly different in character and height, but together they support the public space of the town.[68]

Arnhem, Netherlands

In 2007 a competition was held for a nature and recreation area and a new urban quarter across from the historic core of Arnhem, Netherlands. The Krier Kohl project won first prize.[69]

Perimeter blocks with large open interiors form the urban fabric of the island. Two water harbors and a north–south axis articulate the civic structure and connect the three parts of the town.

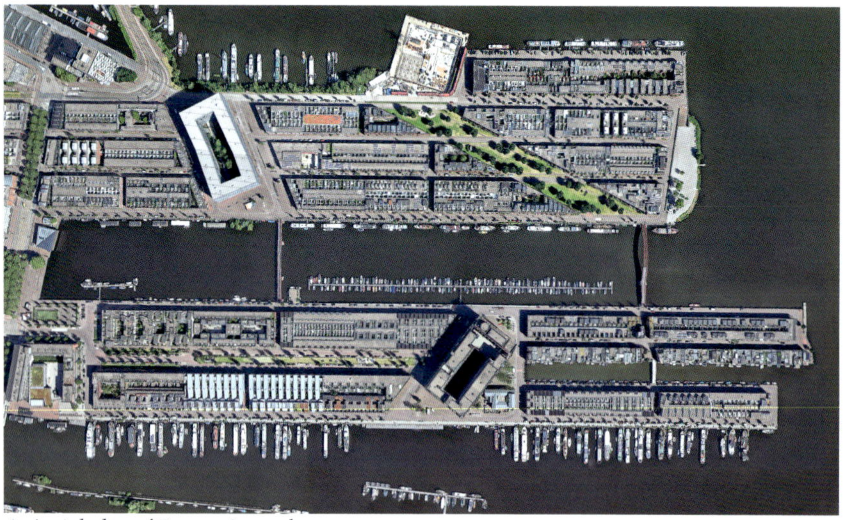
1. Aerial plan of Borneo Sporenburg

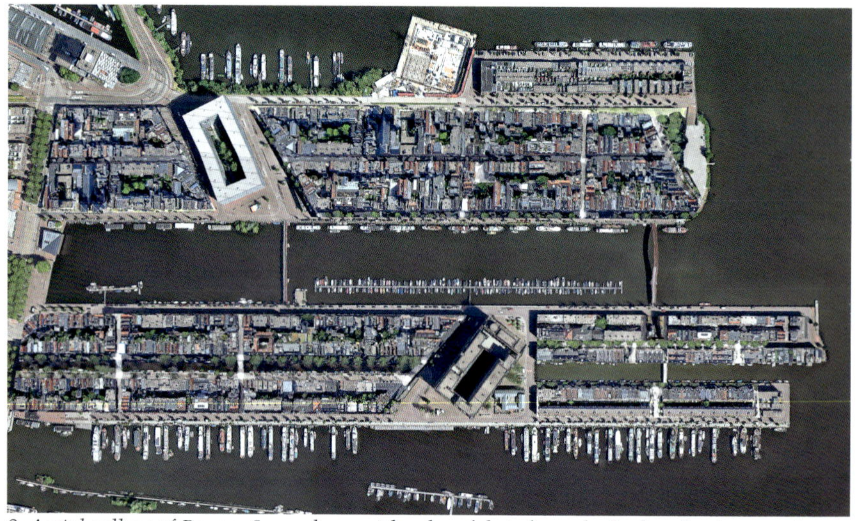
2. Aerial collage of Borneo Sporenburg with urban fabric from the Jordan district superimposed

3. Aerial view of Borneo Sporenburg

4. Borneo Sporenburg row houses facing a major canal

5. London, Bedford Square row houses

Borneo Sporenburg, Amsterdam

Built between 1996 and 2000, West 8's master plan for two peninsulas in Amsterdam returns to the traditional urban system of central Amsterdam, in contrast to the high-rise maga-structures of the modernist Bijlmemeer housing project on the outskirts of the city.

The program required 2,500 housing units. To achieve that density and maintain a predominantly continuous fabric of low-rise buildings, 600 units are accommodated in two large apartment buildings set at odd angles to the strips of low-rise housing.

The peninsulas, or piers, are too narrow to allow for continuous urban fabric of blocks, streets, and squares, but they promote long urban blocks, and streets or canals similar to central Amsterdam and the historic Jordaan district. Except for the two mega-buildings—the "density busters"—the urban plan follows the traditional Amsterdam precedent.

The development guidelines for Borneo Sporenburg's architecture were rigorous. The building heights and frontages along streets and canals were determined, as was the accommodation of autos. Originally, architectural variety was to be achieved by small parcels, and by limiting the number of adjacent buildings by the same architect. Indeed, Borneo Sporenburg is most famous for its smallest component—the wall of narrow row houses overlooking a canal, all by different architects.[70]

After the first phase, however, large development parcels designed by one architect became the norm, and development guidelines for streets and facades appear to have been minimal or non-existent. The result is that much of the site is repetitious with quite grim streets. Repetition in and of itself is not necessarily a problem. For example, London's Georgian terraces are repetitious, and yet they make some of the world's most beautiful urban fabric. On the other hand, large parcels and repetitive, bad facades are street-killers.

Thus, the varied row of canal houses remains the most famous part of the experiment, even though most of the facades are not very good. Following the earlier examples of Rob Krier's work, however, the variety produced by multiple architects is preferable to the continuous banality of much of the rest of the project.

Three major factors conspire in the underdevelopment of the streets, canals, and public spaces: large development parcels, architectural inability to design urban facades, lack of adequate civic space guidelines, and accommodation of private automobiles.

In addition, the project is isolated from the urban core of Amsterdam, with few commercial amenities and offices, thus tending to make it a car-dependent, mono-functional "bedroom suburb," rather than a lively, multi-functional neighborhood like the Jordan. Nevertheless, it is interesting as an experimental modern update of the traditional city.

1. Row houses in the Jordaan district

2. Canal houses in the Jordaan district

3. Canal houses in Borneo Sporenburg

4. Canal houses in Borneo Sporenburg

5. Street view in the Jordaan district

6. Street view in Borneo Sporenburg

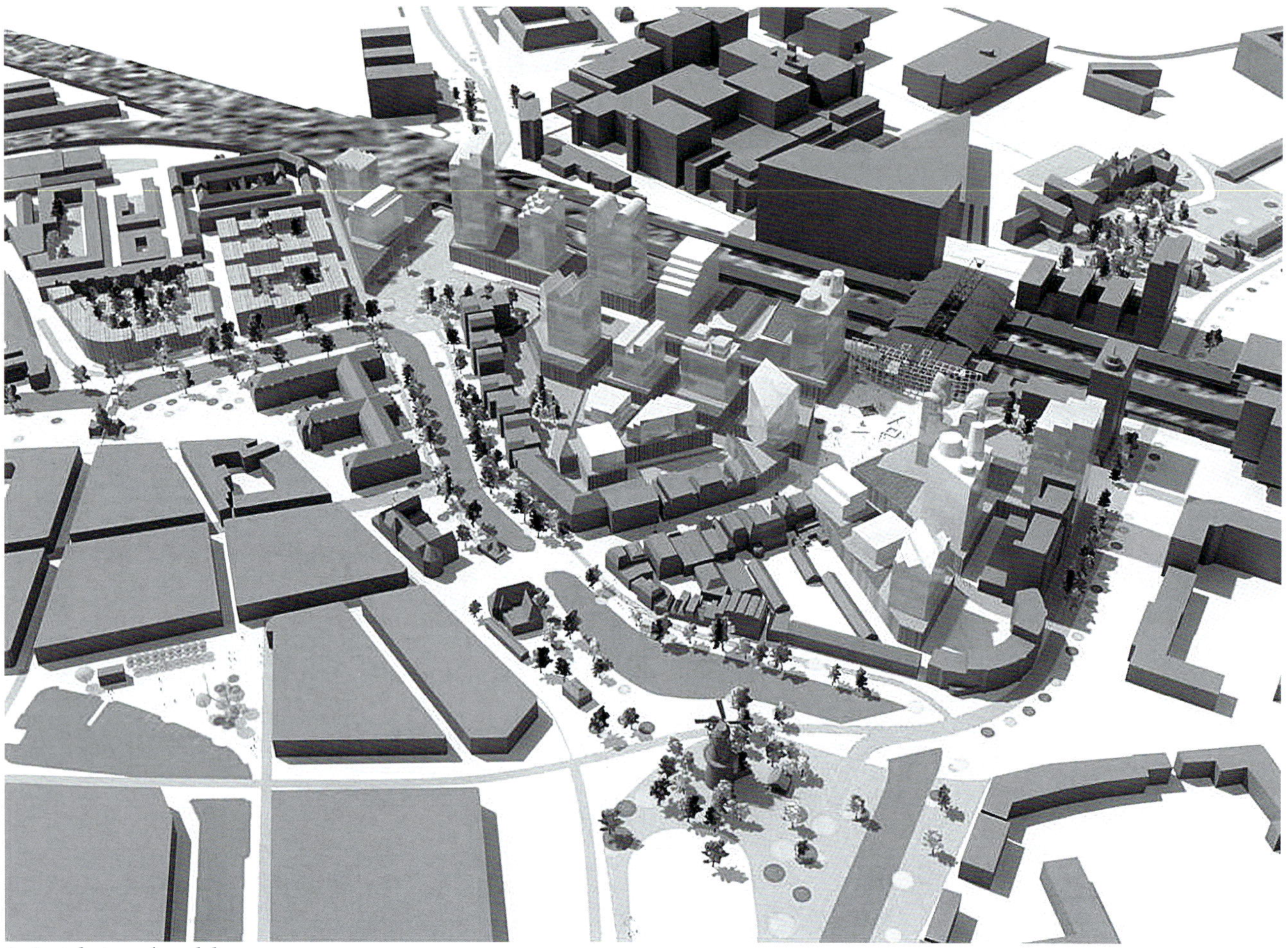

1. *Aerial view of model*

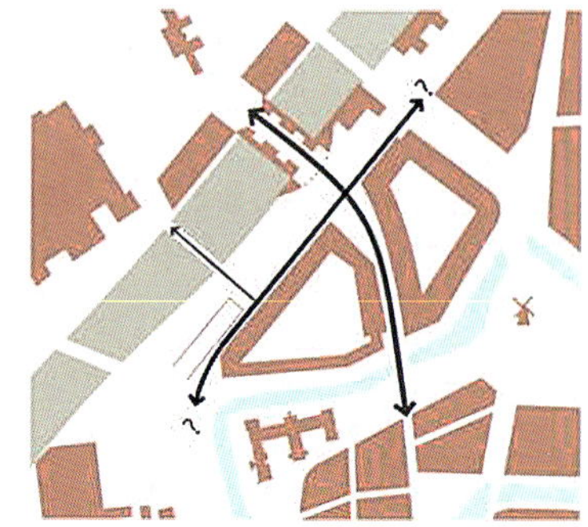

4. *Existing pedestrian circulation*

5. *Proposed pedestrian circulation*

6. *Effect of continuous massing*

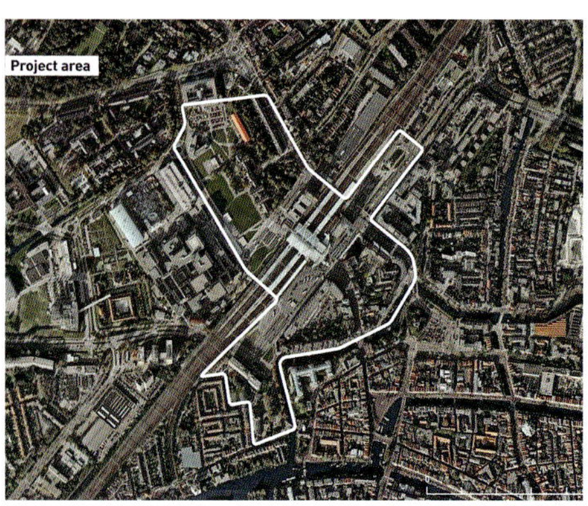

2. *Aerial plan of project area*

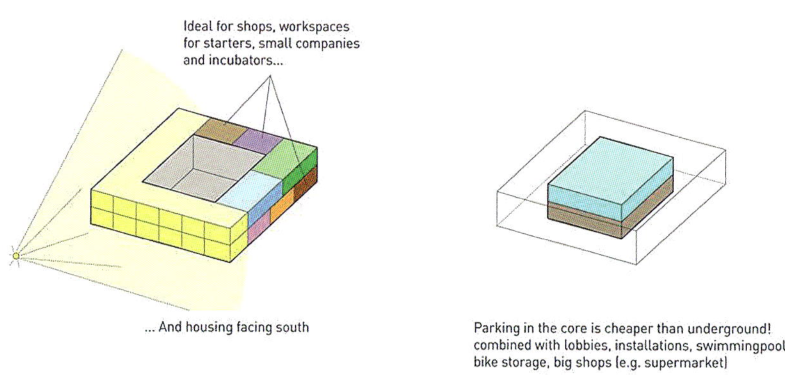

3. *Parking in the center of the block*

7. *Effect of articulate massing*

Leiden

Rients Dijkstra's (PosadMaxwan) 2010 master plan for the station quarter of Leiden is a transformation designed to connect the historic core of the city on the south with a new bio-tech area to the north. The plan consists of 1,000 housing units, offices, commercial, hotel and conference center, and a transportation hub.[71]

The proposed plan is based on smaller blocks and a fine-grained pedestrian network, allowing for more choice and an intimate scale. The building types are also small, with a base that defines the public space of streets and squares and a taller superstructure that steps back from the street—thus adding density while defining the traditional fabric of the town. Parking garages are located in the centers of blocks, surrounded by housing and commercial space facing the streets.

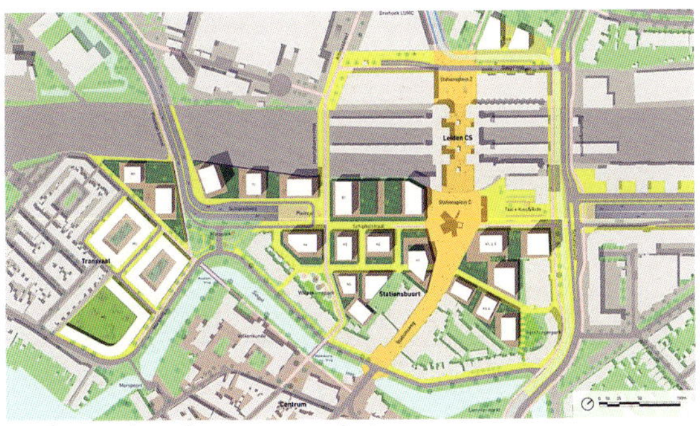

1. Plan with pedestrian circulation

2. Aerial perspective of station plaza

3. Street perspective

4. Plaza perspective

5. Station plaza perspective

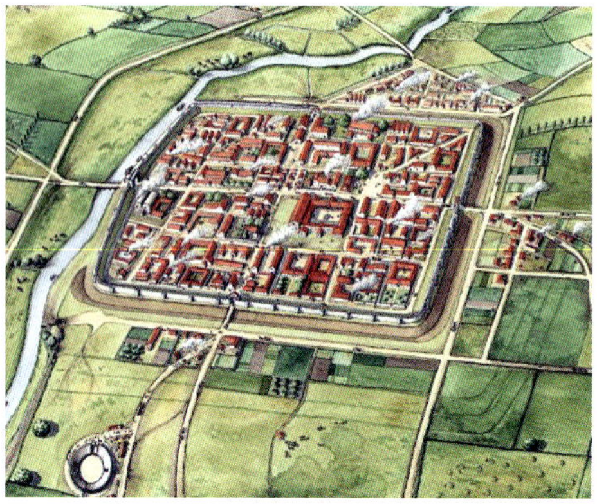

1. Reconstructed view of Roman Venta Icenorum

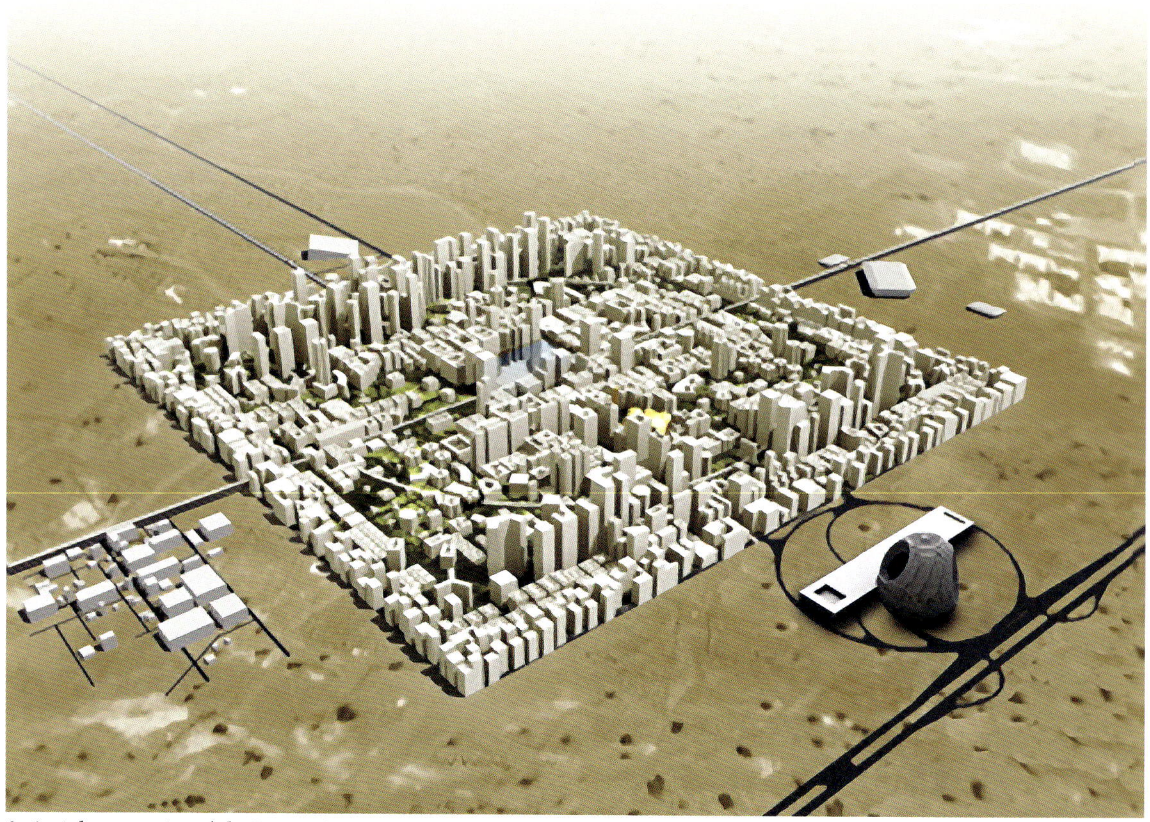

2. Aerial perspective of the Desert City

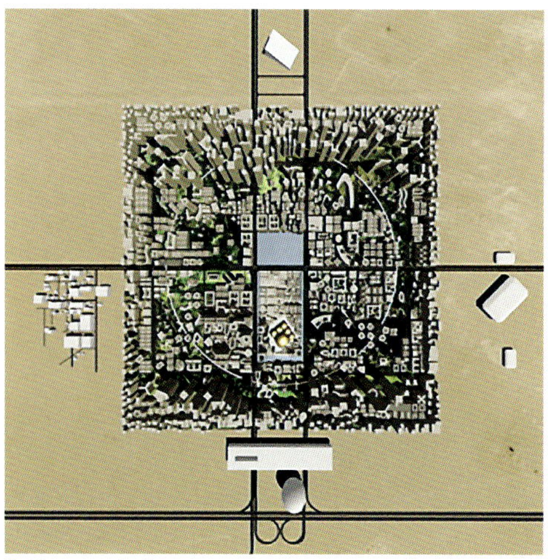

3. Proposed plan

5. Aerial view of Shibam, Yemen

Desert City and Waterfront City

In contrast to the extravagant modernist sprawl of Abu Dhabi and Dubai, Rem Koolhaas and OMA have proposed alternatives in the form of two dense, compact new towns intended to promote the street life typically associated with metropolitan environments.[72]

One of these is a 2006 study for a Desert City outside of Ras al-Khaimah, UAE. In addition to the idea of a finite Roman town, the project has a more direct regional precedent in the famous desert city of Shibam, Yemen. Outside the boundary of the proposed city is the RAK Gateway with the stunning "Death Star."

The second project is the 2008 Waterfront City in Dubai, for the development company Nakheel. An artificial island of tall buildings is surrounded by water and connected to the adjacent very dense neighborhoods by bridges. Another version of the iconic "Death Star" marks the entry from the harbor.

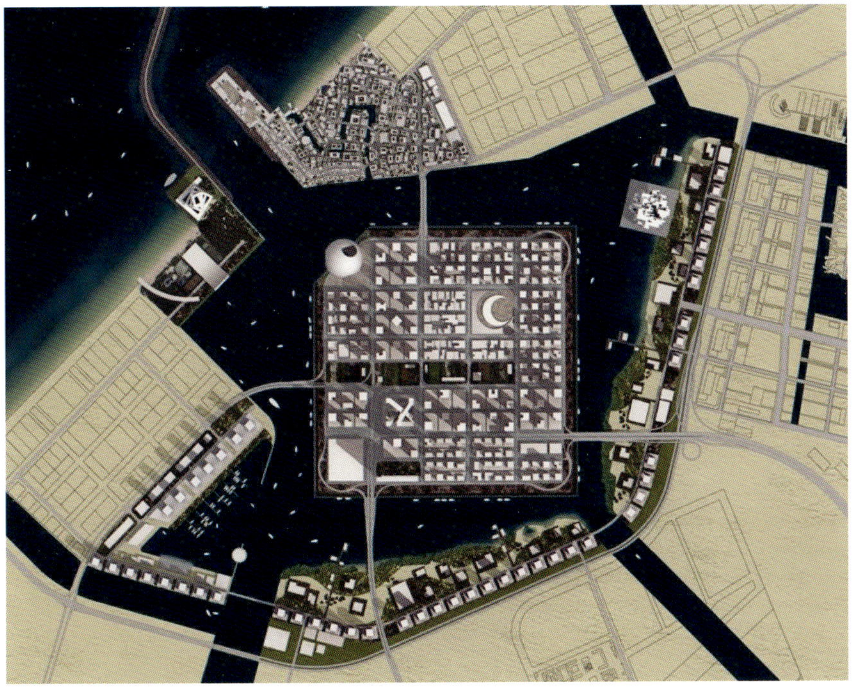

1. Proposed plan detail of Waterfront City, Dubai, 2008

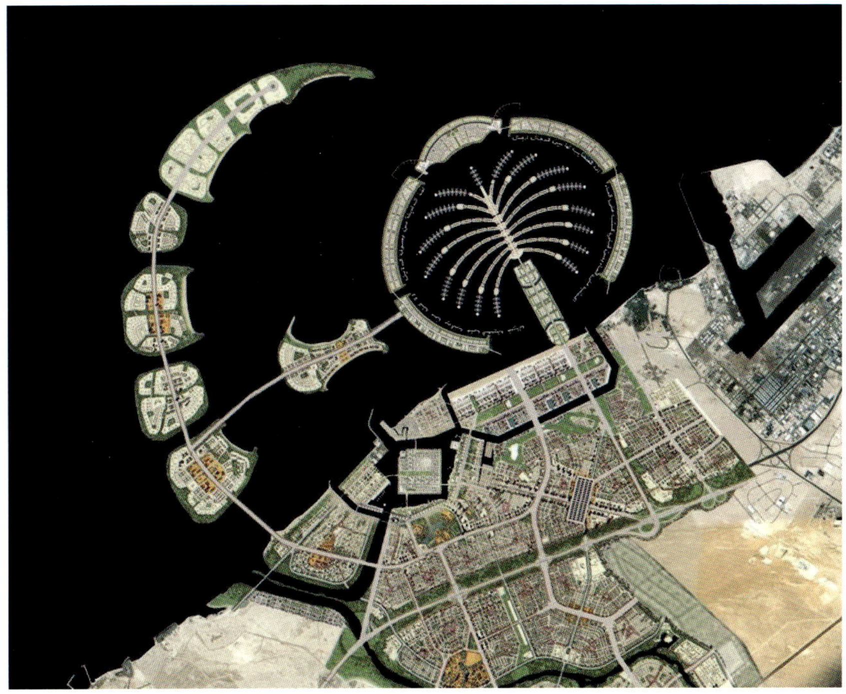

3. Proposed plan of Waterfront City

2. Aerial perspective of proposed Waterfront City

4. Aerial view of the island and harbor

Masdar City, Abu Dhabi

Masdar, 2006, a planned new city in the Abu Dhabi desert by Foster + Partners is modeled after the walled cities of the Arabian peninsula. It is advertised as a sustainable, zero-carbon, zero-waste, car-free environment for 45,000–50,000 inhabitants. It occupies an area of six square kilometers (2.3 square miles).

The city is also planned to host 1,500 businesses and a research university, the Masdar Institute of Science and Technology (MIST). In addition, it is estimated that 60,000 workers will commute in and out every day.

Power will be generated by an initial 40–60-megawatt solar power plant, photovoltaic modules, a 20-megawatt wind farm, geothermal, and a hydrogen power plant. Water consumption is reduced and all water is recycled. A desalinization plant provides fresh water. Transportation within the city will be by battery-powered individual vehicles.

All buildings are limited in height and define high, narrow streets and courtyards. The proposed plan appears to be organized according to monofunctional zones, with housing (white) surrounding the central business area (blue).[73]

The Masdar Headquarters building is by Adrian Smith & Gordon Gill Architecture.

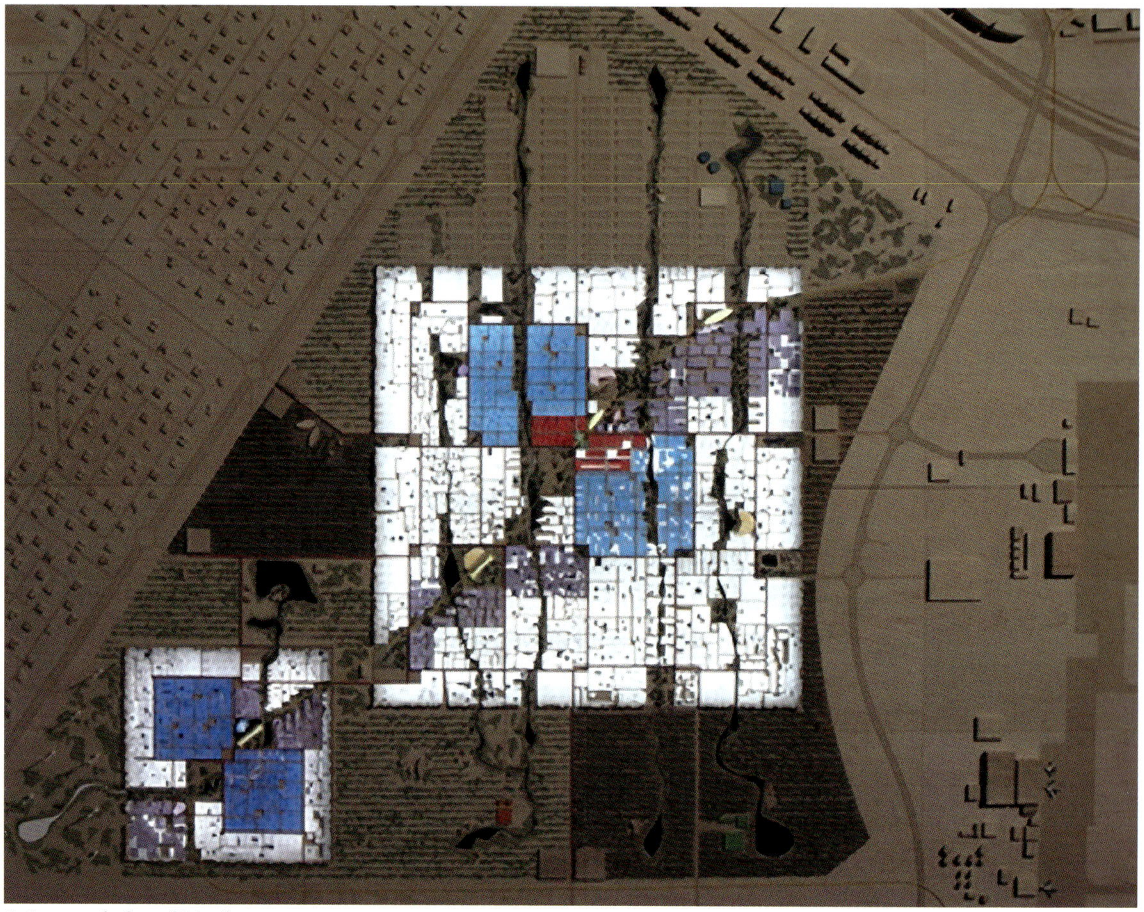

1. Proposed plan of Masdar

2. Interior public space

3. Aerial perspective

4. Perspective of housing

1. Aerial perspective

2. Perspective of headquarters building

3. Perspective under roof canopy of headquarters

4. Aerial perspective of proposed city

Calthorpe Associates

Peter Calthorpe, one of the founders of the New Urbanism group, has become known for his emphasis on transit-oriented development, regional planning, and for his writing, such as: *The Next American Metropolis: Ecology, Community, and the American Dream* (1995); and *The Regional City: Planning for the End of Sprawl* (2001). The early professional work of Calthorpe Associates included dozens of town and regional plans for American communities. In general, they were compact, relatively low-density plans centered around public transit.

In recent years, however, the office's work has become more international, and more genuinely urban—especially in China, where the required densities are far higher than those of the office's earlier work.

This later work has been accompanied by a new book, *Urbanism in the Age of Climate Change* (2011), which organizes now-available data and links it to urban form. Calthorpe states emphatically: "Responding to climate change and our coming energy challenge without a more sustainable form of urbanism will be impossible."[74]

Although he treats of both suburbs and cities, he points out that: "Certainly cities are green. On a per capita basis, they require less land, less auto travel, and less energy, and they emit less carbon.[75] ... Urbanism is the most cost-effective solution to climate change" and "in short, urbanism is the foundation for a low-carbon future and is our least-cost option."[76]

There was an explosion of environmentally detrimental lifestyle in the second half of the twentieth century, and this is reflected in Calthorpe's comparative statistics. Although there are some indications that this trend is reversing, we are stuck with the damage, and rapidly developing parts of the world continue to enlarge the problem. Calthorpe's work abroad is an attempt to reverse this trend.

In contrast to Calthorpe Associates' earlier projects, such as the redevelopment of Stapleton Airport in Denver, Colorado, their Middle-Eastern projects are dense and urban. They utilize traditional building typologies of courtyard houses and tight streets and spaces to create community and relate to the climate. The blocks are urban, with continuous building frontages.[77]

1. *San Ramon, East Bay Area* 2. *Russian Hill, San Francisco*

Suburban Changes:	**1950**	**2005**
Living in Suburbs:	23%	50%
Size of Homes:	980 sf	2,350 sf
Couples with Kids:	44%	23%
Working Women:	1	3

1. Aerial perspective

2. Proposed street

3. Proposed square for Al Wasl

4. Aerial perspective of proposal for Al Wasl, Saudi Arabia, 2007

5. Aerial perspective of neighborhood center, Al Foah, Abu Dhabi, 2009 (with Torti Gallas & Partners)

Urban Principles and Climate Change

The principles of Calthorpe Associates' earlier work have deepened and taken on greater significance with the density and comprehensiveness of their work in China. Their report, *Low Carbon Cities: Principles and Practices for China's Next Generation of Growth*, outlines ideas for transforming urbanism in China, but the principles are applicable in general.[78]

The report identifies eight design principles:

1. *Develop neighborhoods that promote walking;*
2. *Prioritize bicycle networks;*
3. *Create dense networks of streets and paths;*
4. *Support high-quality transit;*
5. *Zone for mixed-use neighborhoods;*
6. *Match density to transit capacity;*
7. *Create compact regions with short commutes;*
8. *Increase mobility by regulating parking and road use.*

These principles work together to reduce auto use, increase transit use, and thereby reduce energy use and carbon output. They also make a more human-friendly urban environment.

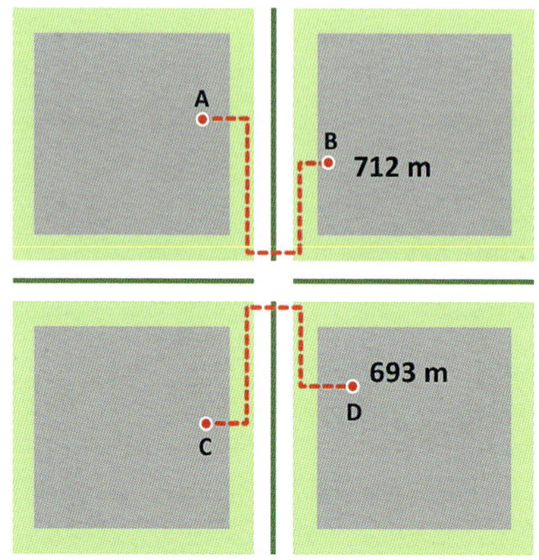

1. Superblock grid (500 m)

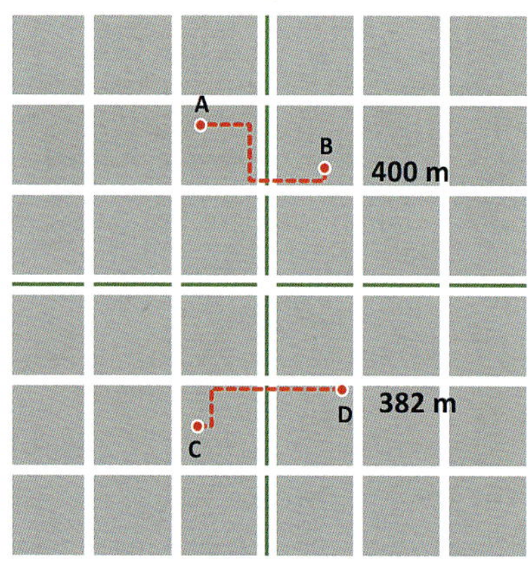

2. Urban network grid

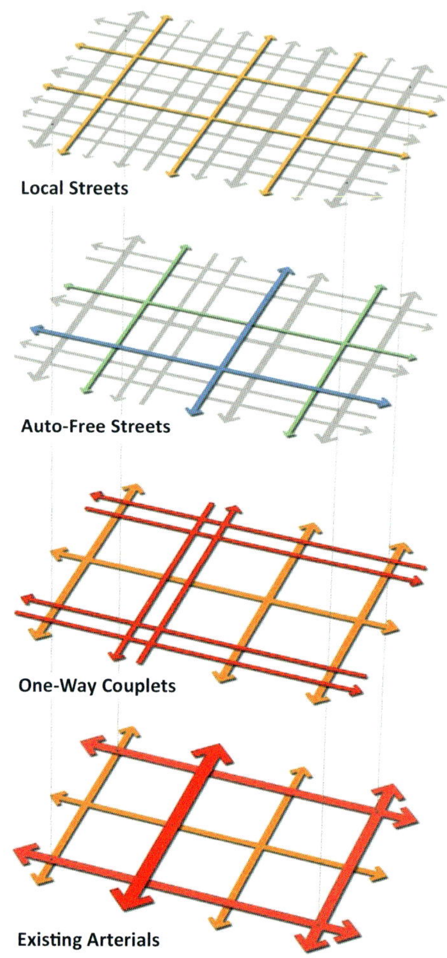

3. Transformation of an arterial grid into an "urban network"

Urban Development in China

In *Low-Carbon Cities* Calthorpe points out several problematic trends, or characteristics, of urban development in China today. These trends have radically increased auto use, and therefore energy consumption and carbon emissions. The same trends have also reduced bicycle use and made pedestrian activity more difficult and dangerous.

Central to current planning strategies in China is the "Superblock," often 500 meters square, surrounded by very wide arterial streets. The order of magnitude of this size block is illustrated by the fact that the entire Roman core of Florence, Italy, will fit inside such a block. A combination of building setbacks and the surrounding arterials turn the blocks into islands rather than urban fabric.

In contrast, Calthorpe proposes smaller blocks, and a finer-grained network of narrower streets. This is enabled by one-way couplets to replace the arterials. It should be noted, however, that even the resulting blocks are still quite large—approximately 147 x 235 m, or ca. 480' x 770', about two New York City blocks. Calthorpe therefore proposes a further subdivision by local, or pedestrian, streets.

These principles were utilized by Calthorpe Associates to redesign the original plan for the new town of Chenggong, Kunming—a city for 1.5 million people.

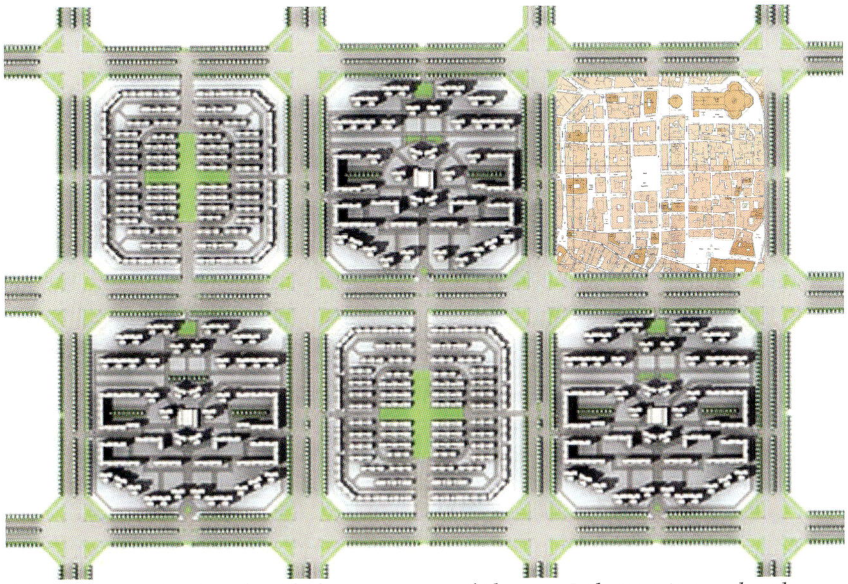

1. Original superblock grid, with the Roman core of Florence, Italy superimposed at the same scale (upper right)

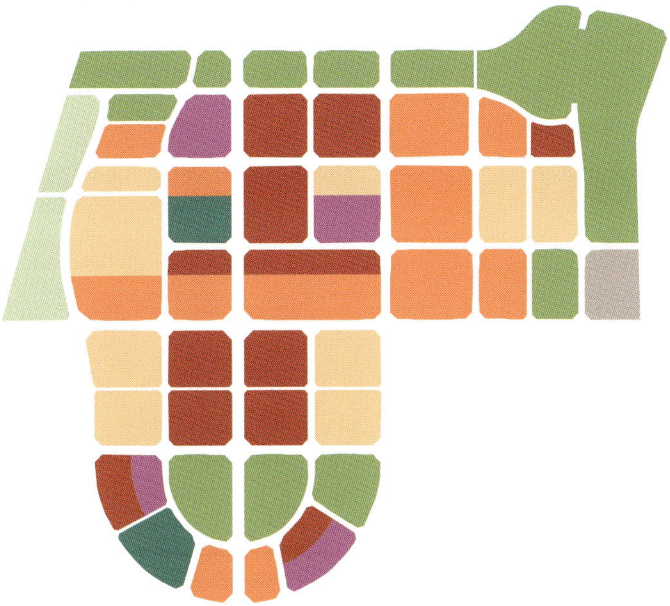

3. Original superblock grid of Chenggong

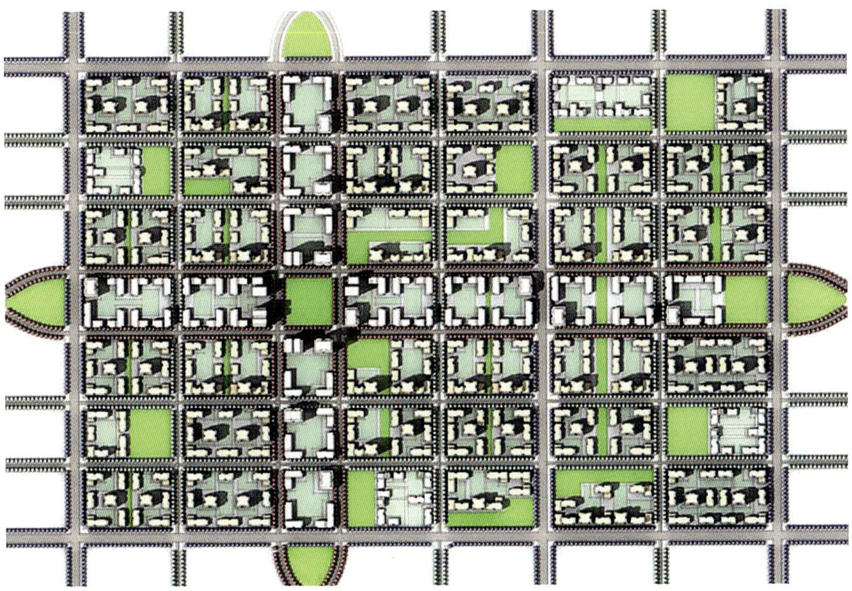

2. Urban network grid

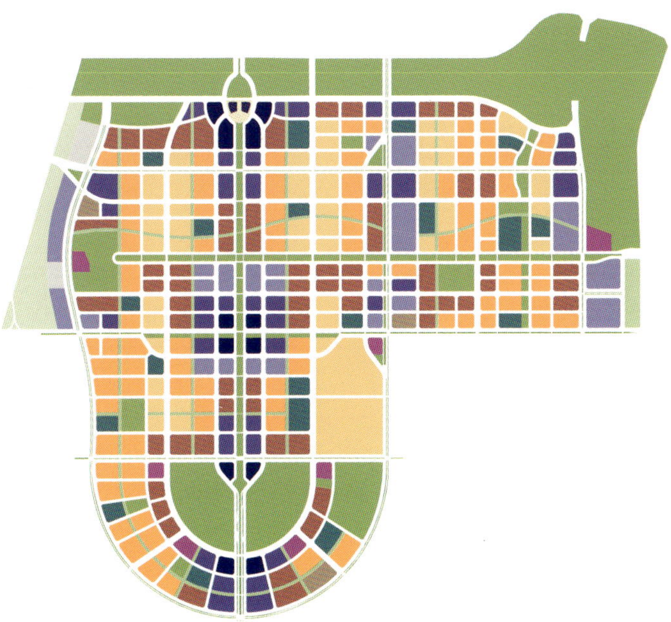

4. New urban network grid proposed for Chenggong

1. Redesigned plan for Chenggong, Calthorpe Associates

2. Aerial perspective of new plan

1. Detail plan of the retail mall

2. Aerial perspective of the retail mall

3. Aerial perspective

4. Aerial perspective at edge of park

Twenty-First-Century Urbanism

Unprecedented environmental and cultural problems confront us in the twenty-first century. Among them: continued population increase, inadequate production of food and water, excessive resource consumption including the end of oil, and waste and pollution resulting in global warming. These problems have all been enabled by technology, coupled with social and environmental irresponsibility. Sprawl, and its progeny, globalization, are at once the cause and result. Refocused technology may help a redirected effort, but alone it is not enough.

Compact, more sustainable communities, a realignment of architecture and urbanism, and the reestablishment of the hegemony of urbanism over architecture will be required. In short, architecture is in desperate need of a larger civic agenda.

Introduction

The turning of a millennium, like the turning of a century, is not of profound consequence in and of itself; other mere stones would serve as well. But it does promote a certain anxiety and speculation, and it allows us to identify and suggest change around it with an assumption of more than normal importance. It also allows us to conveniently, and sometimes more or less correctly, attach labels such as "the industrial age" to the past and "the digital age," or "the age of climate change," or "the urban age" to the future. The year 2000 may be useful in this regard, as there do seem to be profound, if not ominous, changes in process. Of these changes, two interrelated subjects are especially important: *urbanism* and *ecology*.

After the anti-urban antagonism of modernist architecture, the late-twentieth century witnessed the rediscovery of the city, of urban design, and multiple attempts to realign architecture with urbanism. Parallel to these urban initiatives was a slow but significant environmental awakening, the implications of which were not completely clear in the beginning; some fifty years later, however, they have became soberingly clear, and are backed up by solid scientific data.

For the sixth time in 500 million years of "Big History" of Planet Earth, there is an environmental crisis of epic proportions—the possibility of the extinction of life on earth. There have been five previous extinctions, one of which destroyed 96% of all planetary life. The last one, the Fifth Extinction, killed the dinosaurs some 65 million years ago, when there were no humans on earth. We are now within the Sixth Extinction—this one caused by humans. While there are many environmental problems today, the primary driver of extinction is global warming, caused mainly by burning fossil fuels, which is a result of the way we live. This is what will kill life on our planet if we fail to act.

Recent decades have seen an explosion in ecological concerns and information. Books, and books, and books have been written about environmental issues, with many focusing on specific subtopics, from water to food to carbon to economics. But the form of human settlement patterns and its relationship to environmental issues has only recently been brought to the foreground despite its profound effect on the environment. In this regard, two books stand out: Peter Calthorpe's *Urbanism in the Age of Climate Change*, and David Owen's *Green Metropolis: Why Living Smaller, Living Closer, and Driving Less are the Keys to Sustainability*. Both books link statistics and the form of settlement patterns to environmental issues. Both books also point out the environmental advantages of cities.

> "On a per capita basis [cities] require less land, less auto travel, and less energy, and they emit less carbon." And further, "... urbanism is the most cost-effective solution to climate change, more than most renewable technologies." (Calthorpe)

> "Dense cities are scalable, while sprawling suburbs and isolated straw-bale eco-redoubts are not." And, "The environmental problem we face ... is not how to make our teeming cities more like the countryside. The problem we face is how to make other settled places more like Manhattan." (Owen)

Although these two books discuss the general environmental benefits of dense, compact, urban conditions, neither discusses the specifics of urban form—specifics inherent in the traditional city, without any additional technologies.

The recent decades of concern for ecological issues have also been a period of efforts to apply ecological solutions to buildings, and, more recently, to the form of human settlements—to urban design. These efforts have been marked by a veritable "Green Wave" of so-called "Eco-City" designs. Much of this wave is merely overt marketing strategy by design firms seeking to capitalize on ecological trends, with aerial color renderings saturated in so much green landscape that they appear to be inhabited forests. On the other hand, there have also been serious attempts to design sustainable communities based on the best ecological practices.

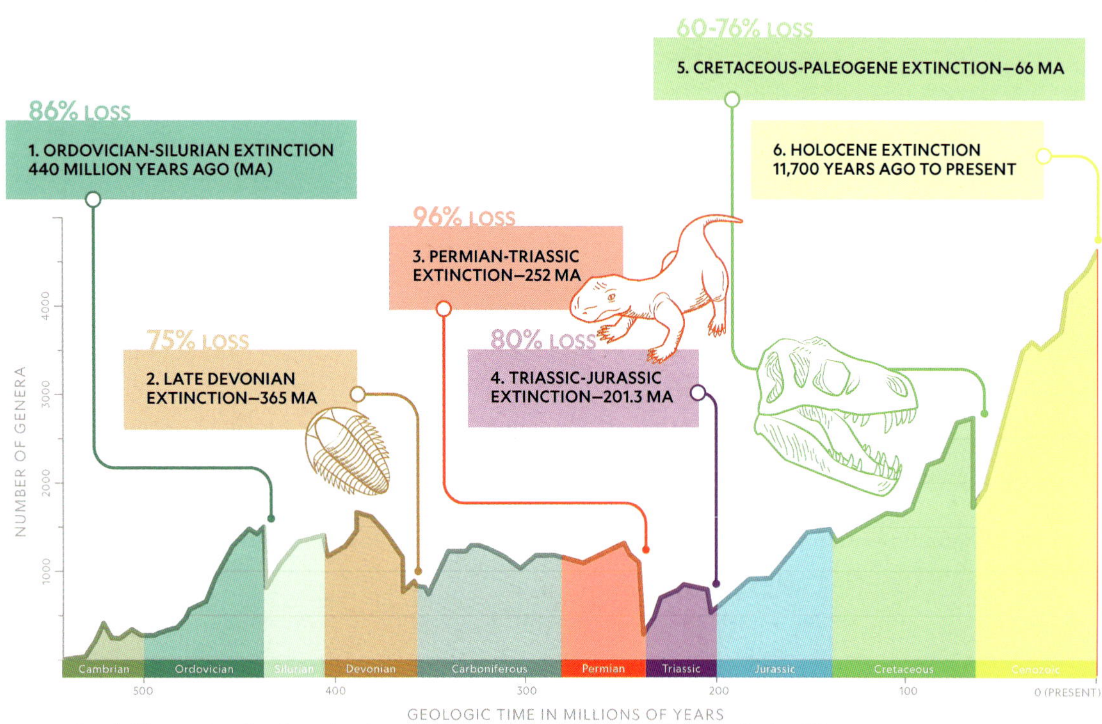

Graph illustrating the six extinctions of life on earth over the last five hundred million years

Harrison Fraker has written about four of these serious, comprehensive, eco-communities in his book, *The Hidden Potential of Sustainable Neighborhoods: Lessons from Low-Carbon Communities.* The book's four case studies are Vauban, in Freiberg im Breisgau, Germany; Bo 01, in Malmö, Sweden; Hammerby Sjöstad, in Stockholm, Sweden; and Kronsberg, in Hannover, Germany. Fraker thoroughly discusses the comprehensive nature of the various "eco-technologies" employed, but there is little discussion of the urban form of these communities or the relationship between their urban form and their ecological principles. The urban form of each of the four communities is different, and very different from that of their respective host cities. This suggests that environmental principles have little, if any, direct influence on the urban form of these communities. Despite all the eco-technology, however, the urban form of these communities is not good; all four exhibit confusion about the relationship of architecture to urbanism, and especially of landscape to both architecture and urbanism.

In contrast, the urban form of the host cities, Freiberg, Malmö, Stockholm, and Hannover is based on traditional urban principles, not the principles of environmental eco-technologies. Yet all four of these cities are not only beautiful, livable, urban environments, but they are also environmentally efficient because they are comprised of neighborhoods that are small, compact, walkable, and multifunctional. Could their environmental performance be further enhanced by eco-technologies? Of course. But it is the basic urban form of these cities that provides the majority of their environmental benefits. Technology can augment these benefits, but, by itself, it cannot make good, urban environments, much less beautiful ones that people love.

This raises the question: what is the relationship of environmental issues to issues of urban form—especially "good" urban form? The argument here is that discussion and design around contemporary environmental issues should begin with good urban form—that of the best traditional cities—with technology as an added benefit.

The Contemporary Ecological Environment

Facts and data regarding the environment are now commonly available, and they indicate that we are in for ominous change during this, the twenty-first century—change that will affect everything about the way we live.[1] If we are to survive, this change will require us to think boldly and in a completely new way to live: smaller, closer, denser, and more simply.

In the course of a little over one hundred years we have become accustomed to the status quo of assumed technical progress, unlimited consumption, and endless growth.

My mother witnessed it all. She was born in 1904. She grew up in a small rural community in north Texas. Her family had no car, no telephone, no indoor plumbing. They raised and grew everything they ate, except for staples such as flour and sugar. When she was twelve her family got the first automobile and the first telephone in their community. She watched the Wright Brothers fly their airplane along the railroad tracks through town, and enthusiastically described the taste of her first Coca Cola. She lived through the Great Depression and two World Wars. She experienced television, jet-travel, and modern medicine. By the time she died in 2001, America had become the lone superpower, cell phones and email were ubiquitous, and "globalization"was an accepted fact.

But the reality of the future will not be the reality of the past century. For example, the continued viability of the large, private automobile, the one-family suburban house, and endless natural resources is an illusion, not a sustainable fact. Blind faith that new technology will save this "reality" is what James Kunstler calls "waiting for Santa Claus." What has changed, and what is the new "reality"? The environment.

There are two major, interrelated environmental crises we face in the twenty-first century: *resource depletion* and *pollution,* primarily the production of carbon, which is a major cause of global warming. Both these crises have been driven by the massive consumption that is the combined result of *population growth* and *lifestyle.*

Population and Lifestyle

The size and lifestyle of the world's human population has been the driver of environmental degradation, and projected population increases will only exacerbate the situation.

Currently, the world population is over six billion. Estimates differ, but the Earth's natural carrying capacity is thought to be between two and three billion people.[2] The "overshoot," currently three billion, occurred between 1950 and 2000 and has been sustained only by technology and by relatively minimal consumption in less-developed parts of the world. As the population increases further, and as a greater proportion of the world adopts a more consumptive lifestyle, the growing overshoot will place an increasingly unsustainable strain on the planet. It is predicted that world population will increase to ten billion by 2050.

Increased efficiencies, such as in the production of food, have supported the overshoot of the past fifty years. But the production of food has reached a plateau, even as less developed parts of the world "catch up" and further increase the global demand. The growing population in China, for instance, has increased grain consumption to the extent that the country now must depend on imports.[3] Further, as China's population demands more protein, increasing amounts of grain and water are required for the production of seafood and animals. China's expected population growth to 2050 produces staggering—unachievable—numbers regarding food requirements.

Population size and growth are important, but the lifestyle of the industrialized world is currently more important in terms of resource consumption and pollution. This will be exacerbated as developing countries become more affluent and demanding of resources. Another familial anecdote illustrates the problem.

One of my early ancestors, Jesse Dennis, died in Jasper County, Georgia in 1818. An inventory of his possessions indicated that he owned one horse, one saddle, one oven and pot, one lot of knives, forks and a coffee mill, one table, three chairs, one churn, a spinning wheel, one lot of cards, twenty barrels of corn, two cows and calves, one stock of hogs, and 350 pounds of bacon. Jesse was a pig farmer. To say he lived a simple life would be an understatement. He had no heating, no air conditioning, no refrigerator, no running water, no hot water, no indoor toilet, no electricity, no gas, no sewer system, no storm water system, no telephone, no television, no movies, no computer, no automobile, no boat, no washer and dryer, no dishwasher, and no sewing machine. It's hard to imagine this today, but Aristotle, Mozart, Michelangelo, and Shakespeare did not have these things either.

Jesse's pigs may have been messy, but Jesse Dennis lived simply out of necessity, and did not contribute to the current crisis caused by global warming. In contrast, Americans live in a state of luxury today, and this contemporary American lifestyle consumes and produces waste to an unprecedented degree. The United States has 4% of the world's population, but we consume 20% of the world's oil, and we have contributed 30% of the world's carbon;[4] we use almost nine times our proportion of the world's resources.

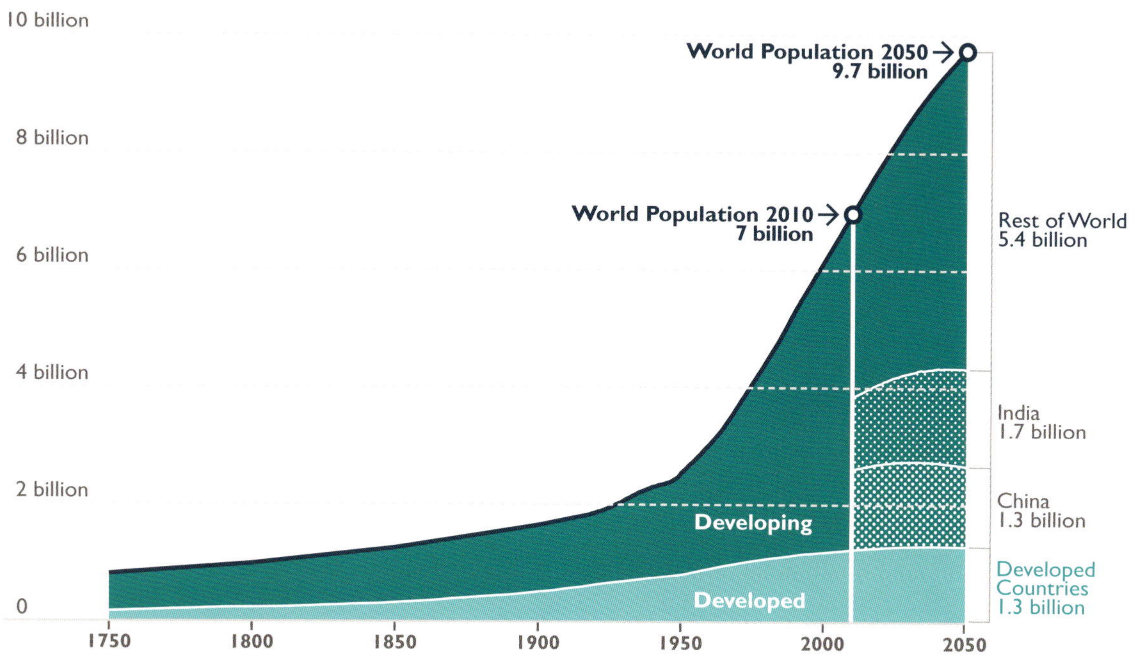

1. Population growth projection

2. Early nineteenth-century farm life

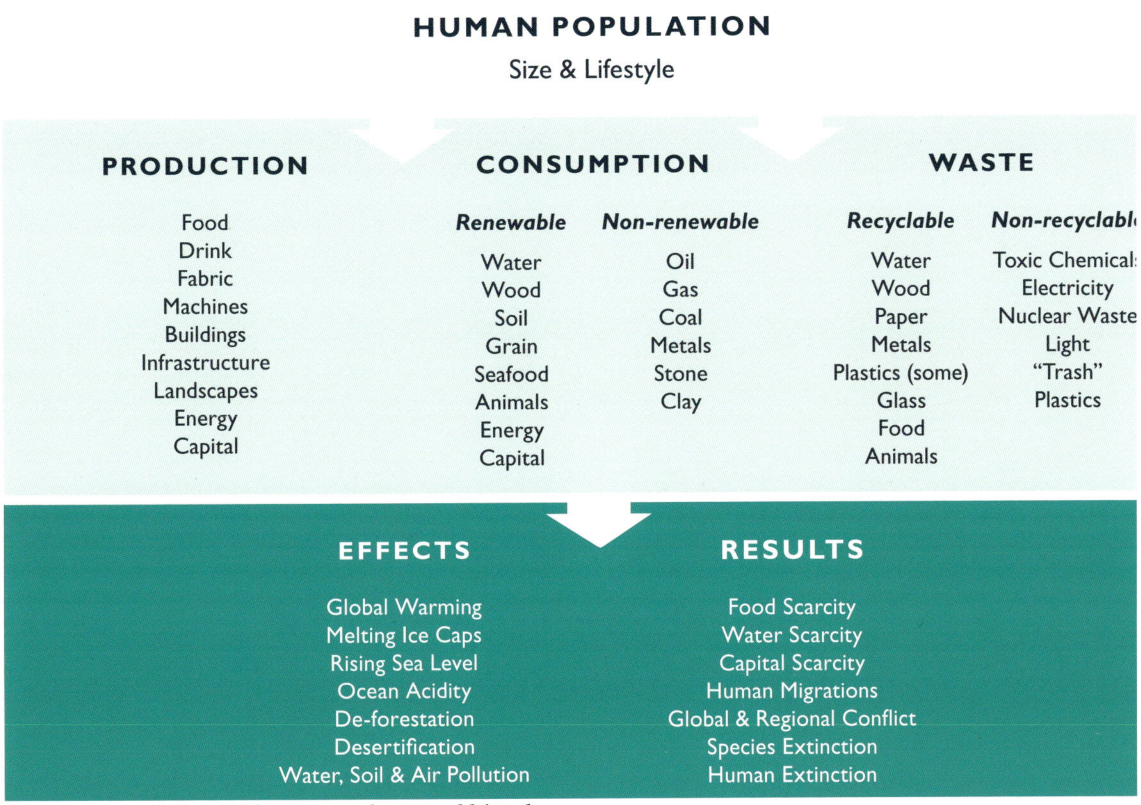

1. Environmental effects of human population and lifestyle

2. Contemporary suburban life

3. Atlanta freeways

Resource Depletion and Pollution

Resource depletion and pollution caused by fossil fuels are the fraternal twin by-products of our consumer society. Over the last one hundred years humans have consumed a staggering proportion of the world's non-renewable resources—especially fossil fuels and metals. In economic terms, it now costs more and more to extract less and less, and this will only increase as we approach depletion. We have also managed to consume renewable resources at a greater rate than their replenishment rate—seafood, soil, forests, and especially water.

The "good news" is that we are rapidly depleting the fossil fuels that have played the biggest role in polluting our planet with atmospheric carbon, which in turn produces global warming and climate change; petroleum and natural gas are projected to be depleted within this century—around the late 2060s. The "bad news" is their depletion will come too late to reverse the damage they have caused.

The most devastating result of population growth, production, and resource depletion is global warming and its consequence, climate change. The very conservative predictions regarding the effects of increasing amounts of carbon emissions—melting ice caps, rising sea levels, increased desertification, ocean acidity, increasingly strong and unpredictable weather conditions, de-forestation, soil erosion, and species extinction—are not only happening, they are happening on an unexpectedly rapid basis. There seems to be a compounding relationship accelerating the process. Forty years ago the problem might have been averted, but there are indications that the process may now be irreversible.[5]

The cause of global warming is not bad storm water management, and it is not cities; it is carbon. Roughly one third of carbon is from buildings and one third from transportation. The Center for Neighborhood Technology in Chicago has pointed out that on a per capita basis, most of the carbon resulting from automobile use is from suburbia, not cities.

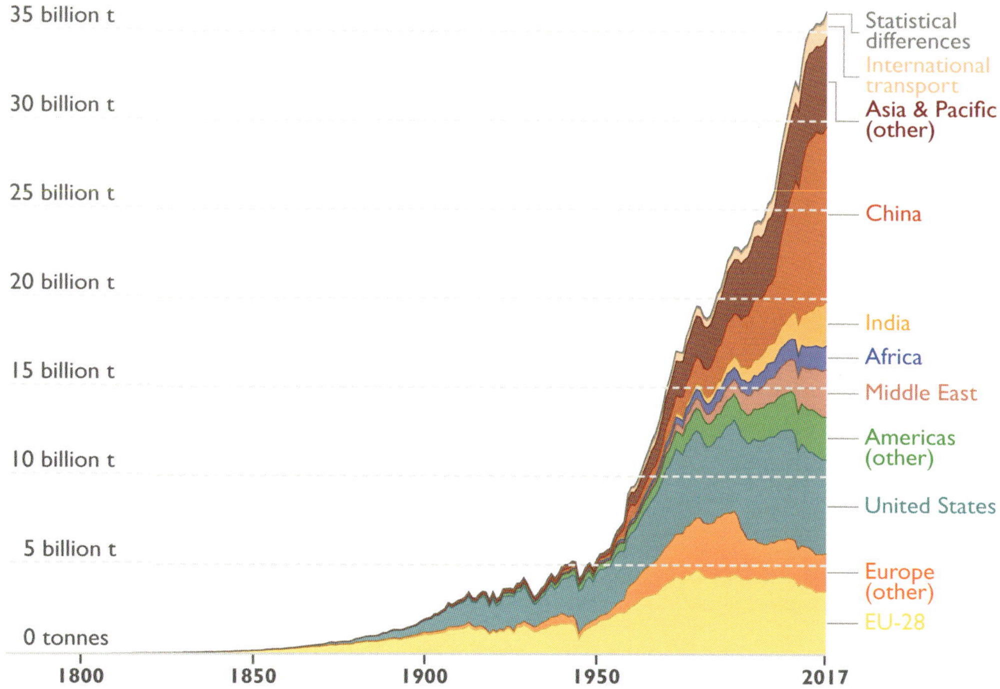

1. Graph of annual CO2 emissions by world region since 1800

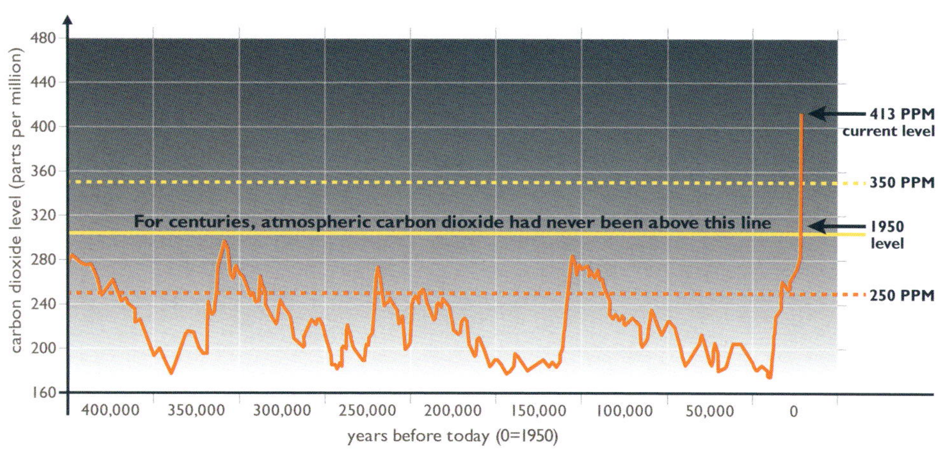

2. Graph of atmospheric carbon levels over 400,000 years

Global Warming

Humans, and our technologies, have precipitated global warming, beginning with the Industrial Revolution near the middle of the nineteenth century. The majority of the problem, however, has occurred since the Second World War. In the century between 1850 and 1950, the world's annual carbon emissions rose from zero to about five billion tons per year, but in the period between 1950 and 2017, carbon emissions increased to 35 billion tons annually. This produced a level of carbon in the atmosphere not seen for 500,000 years. Until 1950, the PPM (particles per million) of CO2 had rarely been above 250 PPM, but since 1950 the level has risen to more than 415 PPM, resulting in an unprecedented rise of global warming—an average of 1°C since the Industrial Revolution. We have already passed a tipping point of warming, thus assuring that the world will not be the same as it was before the Industrial Revolution. Scientists contend that once temperature rise passes 2°C, global warming will be unstoppable, with total disaster looming at 5°C. Further, scientists point out that we only have about a dozen years to take actions to stay below 2°C. Without massive action, humanity is on a path to extinction.

Changing light bulbs and exposing storm water will not solve the problem. Only massive, long-range change in the way we inhabit the planet has any hope of saving us. Is this likely? Maybe not, for many reasons. The problematic aspects of contemporary lifestyle are deeply embedded in most of the world's cultures, and no current government seems capable of dealing with the problem. Nevertheless, we should realistically try. We should begin by thinking long-range, free of the constraints of everyday life—the status quo. We should begin by questioning everything: suburbia, transportation, the economy, systems of government, the role of nature, and more.

So, if we were unconstrained by the practicalities of the status quo of our contemporary lifestyle, what changes could accomplish the goal of staying below two degrees centigrade by 2030–35? The only answer is simple: stop using fossil fuels (source for 86% of

US energy), and, probably, stop consuming meat and dairy. Implementation? Impossible. This would mean stopping all mechanical transportation—fossil fueled vehicles as well as so-called electric vehicles. (Two thirds of electricity is produced by fossil fuels.) It would mean ceasing all mechanical heating, ventilation, and air conditioning. It would mean ceasing to produce cement for concrete, and plastics for computers, medical equipment, sealants, etc. It would mean ceasing to harvest lumber, and ending industrial agriculture. In fact, it would mean ceasing all industrial production, and dismantling all modern military capability. Without the support of gory details, it is clear that should this fantasy actually happen, our contemporary world would disintegrate.

Such an abrupt disruption—and its far-reaching implications—is in fact described in William Forstchen's sobering novel *One Second After*. Although the events in Forstchen's fictional account are the result of an EMP (electromagnetic pulse) rather than the results of industrialization, the implications are remarkably similar. Airplanes crash, cars stop, life support systems go off, and all communication ceases. In an instant, civilization reverts back to the nineteenth century, but not to its now-forgotten knowledge, which must be rediscovered and relearned.

Short of some EMP-level event to force the radical change required, limiting temperature rise to only a two-degree increase in temperature by 2035 appears impossible. If scientists are correct, we are facing a world of unknowable hurt. If the increase reaches a five-degree increase, which is predicted by 2100 if we do nothing, complete disaster becomes unstoppable.

What is the alternative to impending disaster? Everything we know and can conceive is embedded in the Industrial Revolution and the consumption of fossil fuels. If life on our planet is to survive, everything we know will have to change and adapt. Cosmetic actions won't help. This requires a long-range strategy, and a timeline. Everything will have to flow from strategies for energy production, reduced consumption, waste management, and settlement patterns.

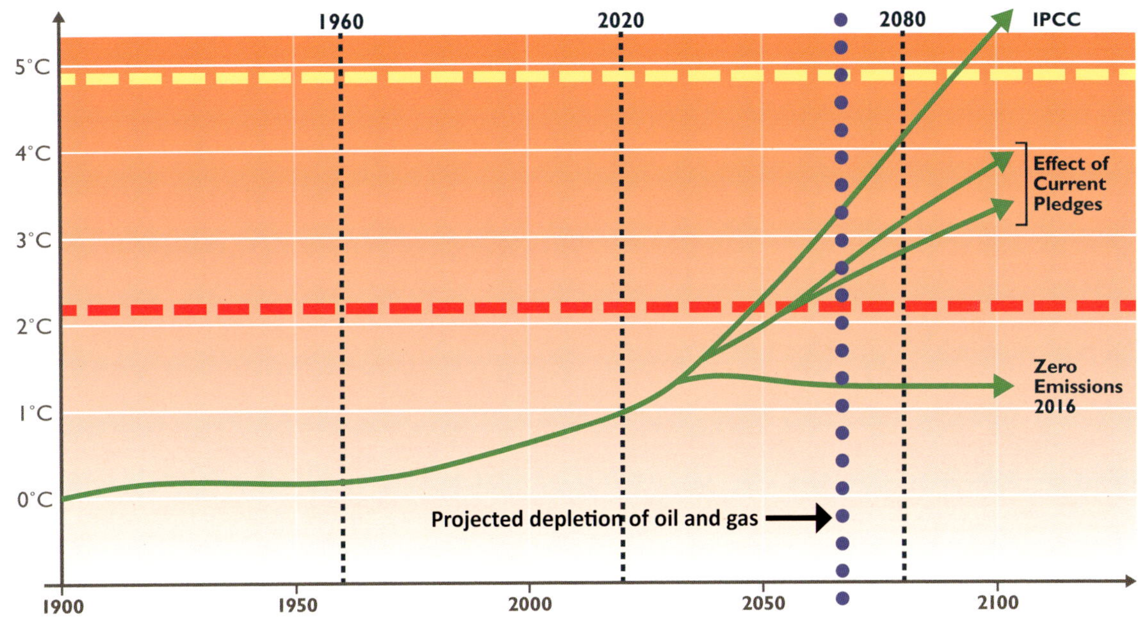

Graph of temperature rise since 1900 and alternate projections to 2100

Energy production:

Natural gas, electricity, and co-generation for both heating and cooling may serve as transitional energy sources to end dependence on fossil fuels, in order to develop various sources of clean, renewable energy. Proposed renewable sources include bio-thermal, wind, solar, hydro, and retrieval of energy from waste. Applications of these sources are discussed in Fraker's book about sustainable neighborhoods. It is unclear whether renewables alone can fulfill our energy needs, but this is based on demand.

Energy consumption:

Despite some initiatives for reduction of energy use, demand continues to rise. Major sources for energy demand are transportation (27%), buildings (38%), and industry (31%). Building demand can be more easily reduced, but transportation and industry are heavily dependent on fossil fuels, which are predicted to be depleted well before the end of the twenty-first century. If demand cannot be sufficiently reduced to be covered by renewables, nuclear is the only other option. Future scarcity and eventual unavailability of fossil fuels will force the issue.

Waste management:

Fraker's book on sustainable neighborhoods outlines several sophisticated strategies for waste management beyond the simple categories of recycle and reuse, including extracting energy in the process.

While these technical solutions to environmental problems are important, far more effective means involve reorganizing our patterns of habitation to reduce consumption. The state of the contemporary built environment does not look promising. The question is whether or not it can be refocused to address contemporary environmental issues, and perhaps produce better urban environments in the process.

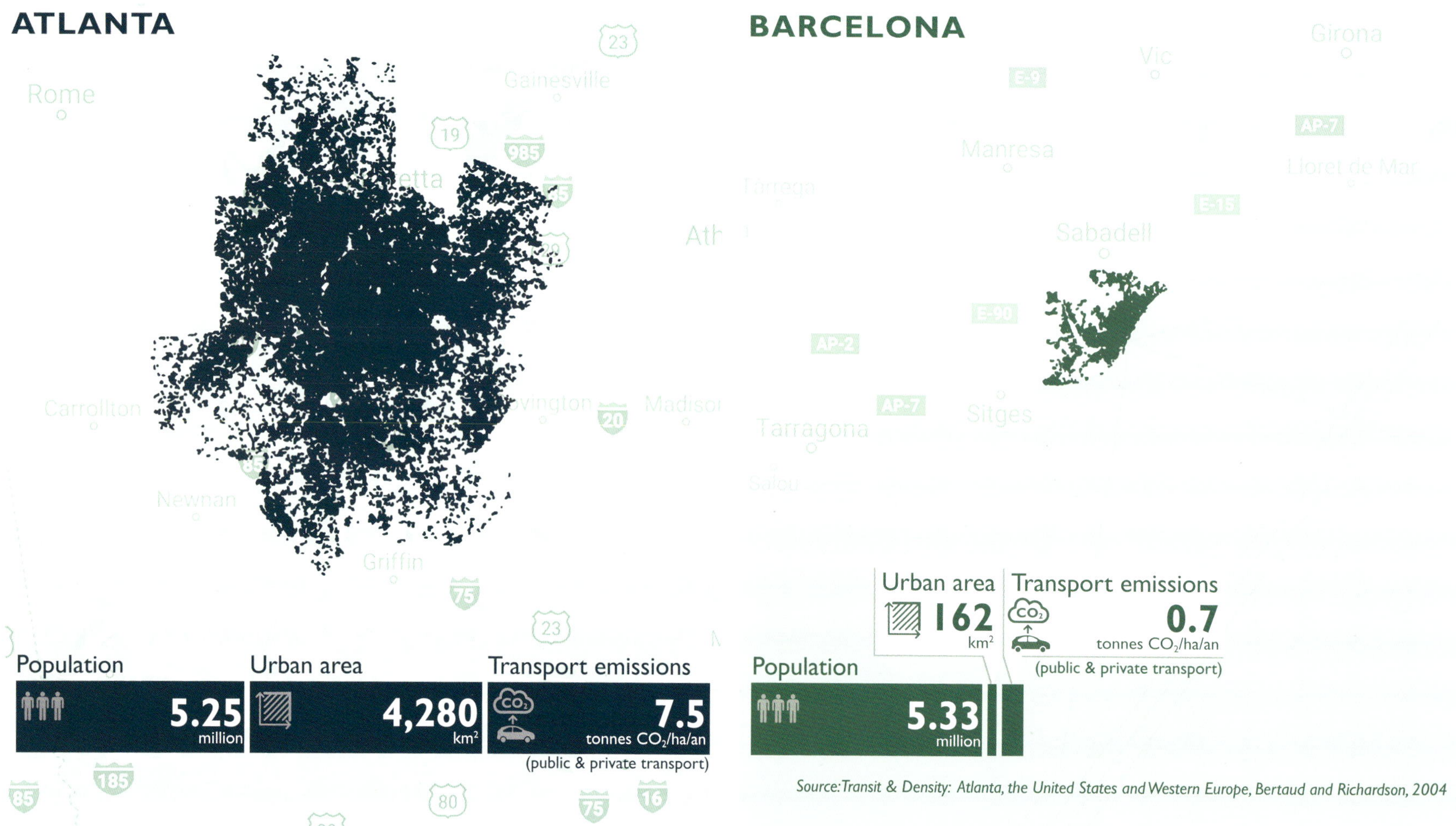

1. Atlanta and Barcelona at the same scale (Atlanta has almost eleven times the per capita emissions of Barcelona)

2. Aerial view of an Atlanta suburb

3. Aerial view of Barcelona

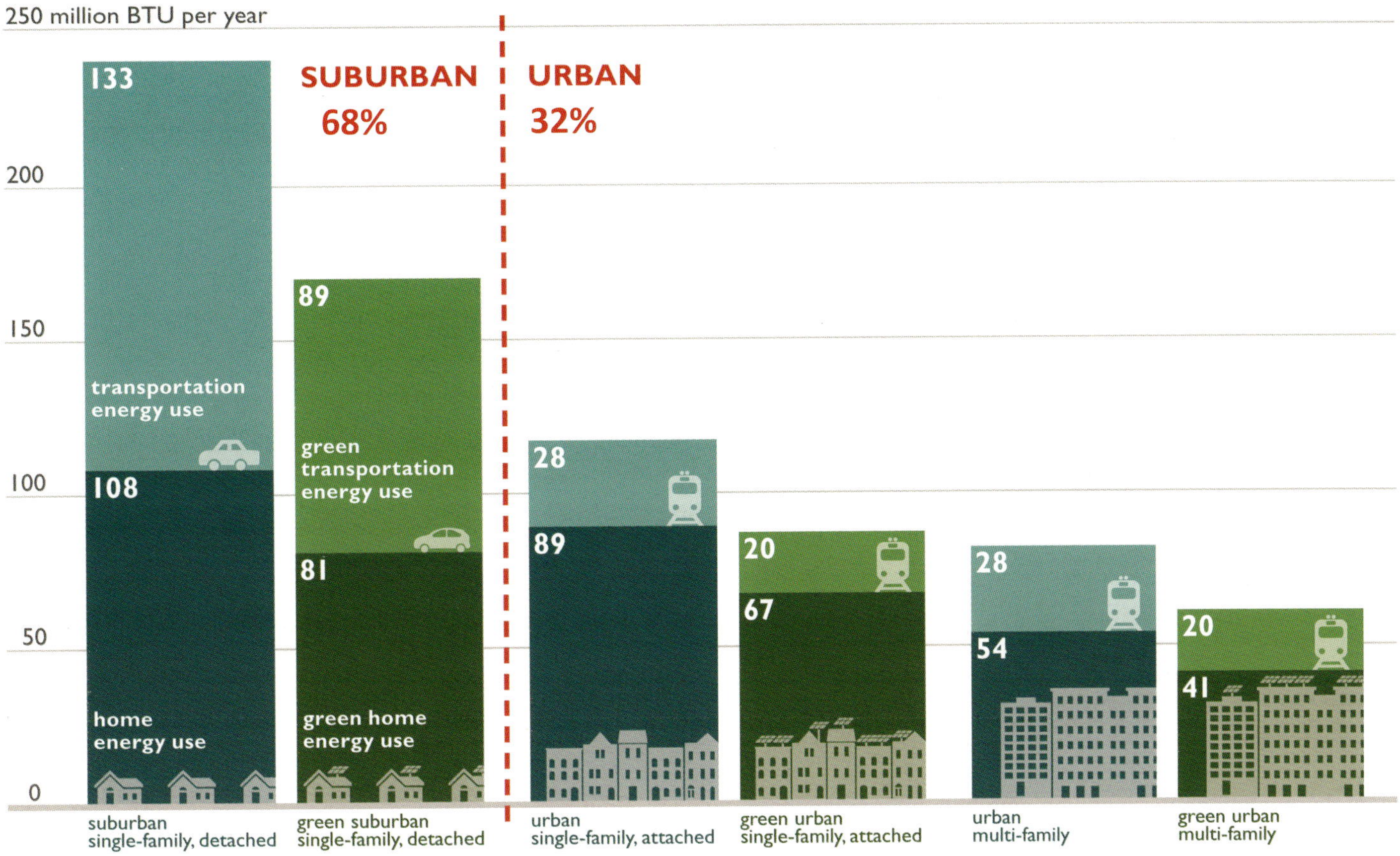

Energy use by household type. (Two-thirds of Americans live in suburban or rural areas.)

Urbanism and the Environment

Given the city's basic efficiency, it is odd that environmental reform efforts inevitably focus on cities rather than the larger context. As David Owen has said, asking cities to improve rather than suburbs is like asking a skinny person to go on a diet. Owen makes an emphatic case that cities are the answer, not the problem, citing New York, Tokyo, and older European cities as being the most ecologically sustainable on a per-capita basis.[8] It is true that cities produce about 80 percent of all emissions, but on a per-capita basis their efficiency is undeniable. Cities have more efficient infrastructure than suburbia, lower carbon footprints on a per-capita basis, and fewer toxins washed into the ground by rainwater. In contrast, suburbs consume more resources, use more energy, and produce more carbon. Suburbs require more infrastructure, more driving, and a military to guarantee access to oil.

Efforts to reform suburbia are understandable—two thirds of Americans live in suburban or rural areas—but they are failure-prone; like a poorly cut suit, suburbia can be improved by a tuck here or there, but the fundamental problem can never be fixed. For example, Barcelona has almost the same population as Atlanta (ca. 5M), but it occupies about 3.8% of the area of Atlanta, and Atlanta's transport emissions are almost 11 times that of Barcelona. City dwellers in Chicago produce only 22 percent of the GHGs generated by automobiles, while suburbanites produce 78 percent.[9]

The environmental performance of cities outpaces not only suburbia, but rural areas as well. Owen points out that sparsely populated Vermont is commonly considered green and efficient, but actually, on a per-capita basis, the opposite is true. Vermonters use more water, three and a half times as much gasoline, and one third more electricity than New Yorkers. They also have a larger carbon footprint and generate more solid waste. Owen says. "The environmental problem we face ... is not how to make our teeming cities more like the countryside. The problem we face is how to make other settled places more like Manhattan."

We should not need an environmental excuse to promote and plan cities; civic responsibility should be enough. But contemporary environmental circumstance suggests that we need to radically transform the way we live. With ample data indicating that cities are the most efficient form of human habitation on a per capita basis, it seems clear that cities are the antidote, enabling us to live more sustainably while supporting and promoting civic life. We don't need "new" ways of forming cities. The form, elements, and principles of cities have been basically the same for centuries, and fortunately the best urban practices and the best environmental practices are not antithetical, but complimentary. After nearly two centuries of traffic-dominated planning, it is imperative to return to an urban form based on humans and resource conservation rather than cars.

The Contemporary Built Environment

The current state of architecture, urbanism, and landscape could not be in a worse position to address the contemporary environmental crisis. In fact, these disciplines are major contributing factors to the problem, as all three are anti-urban. Consequently, when solutions are proposed, they are not only less effective than they should be, but they usually make the problem worse.

There are three primary contributors to the disintegration of the contemporary built environment. The long transformation from embedded urban architecture to the free-standing icons of modern architecture has made urbanism impotent by eliminating the spatial public realm. Parallel to this, the landscape transformation from the city *and* the garden, to the city *in* the garden has further eroded the city. Indeed, in today's context of ecological concerns, landscape may be the most formidable enemy of the city, though disguised as a friend and collaborator. Finally, vehicular circulation has further "loosened" the city. This did not begin with fossil-fueled vehicles, however, but with carriages near the mid-nineteenth century, when work began to be separate from home. The roots of all three of these contemporary issues lie in the eighteenth century, a watershed of modern architecture, urbanism, landscape, politics, and philosophy.

Historically, the city had, for centuries, been a fortified refuge from the dangers of the natural world outside. The city was sacred, nature profane. The formal garden was a man-made artifact, analogous to the city itself, that represented the natural world. In the eighteenth century this began to change. As society began to open up, it became more self-conscious. Laugier's Primitive Hut, combined with the idea of the noble savage inhabiting a romanticized landscape, revolutionized the previous relationship of architecture, landscape, and the city. This was the prelude to landscape's invasion of the city.

Landscape entered the city in the nineteenth century as a complement to urbanism, articulating the urban fabric to define the city of the bourgeoisie. Street trees added definition to wider streets and boulevards, and landscaped squares and urban parks expanded the repertoire of public space in the city. This invasion was not in itself detrimental to urbanism. To the contrary, it produced some of our most beautiful urban environments. But other than this, "nature" does not contribute to urbanity, and solutions to environmental problems are not antithetical to traditional urbanism. Gradually, however, the idea of continuous landscape as a matrix for detached, free-standing buildings has not only become the norm, but is commonly touted as the solution for our environmental ills. But the city is not a pasta dish needing "green pesto sauce" to perform properly.

1. Aerial view of an American suburb

2. The Primitive Hut, Laugier, 1752

Aerial view of Dubai

There are many enemies of the city. Foremost among them are private automobiles, detached single-family houses, suburban sprawl, most architects, professional education, eco-snake oil (greenwash), so-called landscape urbanism, high-rise suburban sprawl, and impotent governments.

Private Automobiles

Humans, not cars, should determine city form. Since about 1850, private vehicles have increasingly had an excessive influence on city form, as have fire trucks and huge buses in recent times. It should be prohibitively expensive to own a private car in the city and very difficult to use one. Sufficient density enables subways and public transit to obviate most of the need for cars.

Single-Family Houses & Suburban Sprawl

The "American Dream" of a single-family suburban house with a lawn, garage, and backyard is the enemy of the city and the environment. Suburbs use a disproportionate amount of land, energy, and infrastructure—not to mention hidden costs, such as the military strength required to secure access to the foreign resources that enable this "freedom of choice."

Since 1950, the suburban population in the United States has more than doubled, but even though the number of suburban couples with children has dropped from 44 percent to just 23 percent, the size of the typical house has more than doubled. The energy consumed by a suburban household (for transportation and buildings) is two and a half to four times that of an urban household, and the emissions for a suburban household are almost four times more than urban households.[10]

Since 1960, the number of miles of highways have increased 235 percent, and it should not be surprising that traffic fatality rates are highest in exurban areas, not cities. Other health issues, such as obesity and diabetes, have been linked to the auto-dependent lifestyle of the suburbs.

Peter Calthorpe sums it up: "Our suburban planning model is a form of growth that no longer fits our demographics, economic needs, or environmental challenges."[11]

1. The American dream, Levittown

2. Postwar advertisement

3. Suburban sprawl, Hot Springs, Arkansas

1. Project, Z.Hadid

2. Popstage, Breda, NL, E. van Egeraat

3. Project in Abu Dhabi

4. Global Urbanism Center, W. Alsop

5. Dancing Towers, D. Libeskind

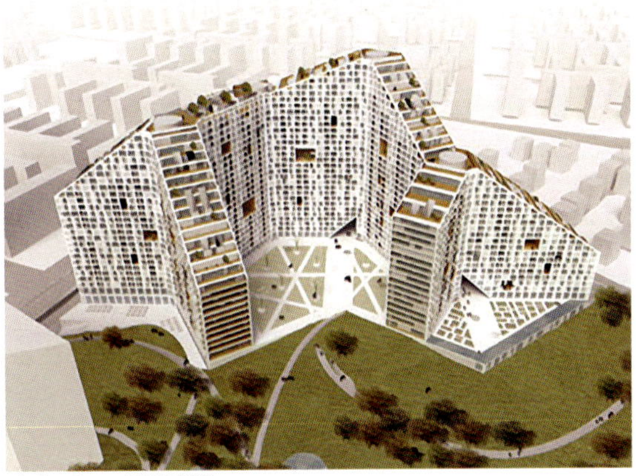
6. Project, MVRDV

7. Project, B.Tschumi

8. Project in China

Contemporary Architecture

It is too soon for a history of early-twenty-first-century architecture, but even a cursory review of contemporary architecture reveals that the most talented architects are still absorbed with crafting the architectural object rather than architectural space, much less urban space. Most buildings and projects are isolated, self-absorbed objects floating in space, with few, if any, urban implications.

Elaborately warped envelopes have replaced the faceted surfaces of machine-age buildings, but the anti-urban characteristics of most contemporary architecture are at least as strong, if not more so, than those of the early-twentieth-century modernists.

Professional Education

There is a reciprocal relationship between contemporary architecture and professional education—as there has always been. Architecture students today are media savvy, however. Thus, they are instantly aware of the latest work of well-known architects, and so are their teachers. It is therefore no surprise that today's architectural education reflects the profession and contains little, if any, education about the city, contemporary environmental issues, or the relationship between city and environment. Unfortunately, the world can no longer afford to have architects that are unable, or unwilling, to address urban and environmental issues.

1. *Yinchuan, Ningxia Hui, China*

2. *Le Corbusier, Ville Contemporaine, 1922*

Urban Sprawl

Outside of the US, the explosive growth of cities in the last two decades has resulted in more new cities and even mega-cities (cities of 10 million people or more) but very few genuinely urban environments. Much of this urban growth has been unplanned, primarily in India, Africa, and South America, but in China it has been planned.

The traditional Chinese city consisted of a hierarchy of streets and a consistent low-rise, low-density urban fabric of courtyard houses. There were a limited number of building types: houses, temples, and palaces, and they were all variations of the same architectural type. With the advent of modern urban development in the late-twentieth century, the traditional model of courtyard housing and narrow streets has been abandoned for very dense high-rise housing of slabs and towers, without a multifunctional connecting tissue of urban fabric.

As extensions of Ville Radieuse, or CIAM, principles, these planned cities qualify as cities in terms of population, but they function as social warehouses instead of urban environments. The basic system consists of very dense mega-blocks of detached buildings surrounded by wide arterials. This system is also auto-dependent, and rising affluence has radically increased the number of vehicles, and consequently, pollution. Like the Ville Radieuse from almost one hundred years ago, the high-rise suburb has most of the ecological deficiencies of the split-ranch suburb but few of the private amenities. And like its shorter relative, it has no civic realm to make it urban.

3. *Typical hutong, China*

Landscape and the City

The fallacy of "Design with Nature," however well-intended, has deep roots. Garden Suburbs, Broadacre City, and the Ville Radieuse all promoted a continuous, horizontal landscape matrix as a setting for detached buildings. The best of the Garden Suburbs had distinct, high-quality landscape development, but the modernist city did not. Nevertheless, the idea of the "horizontal city," against all logic, continued. Ultimately, the so-called Landscape Urbanism movement almost succeeded in erasing even the most obvious urban ideas in favor of a buildingless landscape of process and change. This inexplicable oxymoronic label, *Landscape Urbanism*, professes to replace an urbanistically impotent architecture with landscape that is at once scientific, artistic, and urban. What it actually does, however, is provide anti-urban contemporary architects with a vision of an open, landscape matrix within which to freely sprinkle increasingly narcissistic architectural icons. Now that this movement has passed from serious consideration, we are left with urban damage and the questions: What is contemporary landscape? What is its contribution to urbanism? And, what environmental issues does it address?

In general, contemporary landscape ideas have been major contributors to the dilution of the city, primarily by watering down the public spatial realm. Buildings provide primary spatial definition; properly done, landscape provides secondary spatial definition; improperly done it blurs spatial definition.

In *Space & Anti-Space*, Barbara Littenberg and Steven Peterson point out that with good urban fabric—New York, Paris, Rome, etc.—public space is approximately 30% of the area. An exceptional, but interesting comparison, is that of Barceloneta, (a neighborhood of Barcelona, Spain) and Vauban (a neighborhood of Freiberg im Breisgau, Germany). Both neighborhoods are composed of long, narrow, barracks-like, or Zeilenbau, buildings, but although the proportion of public space in Barceloneta is approximately 50%, Barceloneta is urban, whereas Vauban is not. This is because in Barceloneta the long, thin buildings are close together and define streets. In Vauban, the buildings do not define streets, and the landscape has no spatial character. It is amorphous, like a jungle.

1. Project in Tianjin

Eco-Snake Oil

Otherwise known as "greenwash," eco-snake oil is like the Old-West potion sold by hucksters under the assurance that it would cure "whatever ails you." At its best, it is effective marketing flim-flam. At its worst, it disingenuously deflects attention from more substantive, holistic environmental concerns and solutions. Its ultimate focus is looking green rather than actually being green—or sustainable.

Specimen plants on the roofs of buildings, Italian parsley growing along the facades, and native grasses on the ground planes may look "green," and may even help the heat island effect, but they do little to make a sustainable environment, much less an urban one.

Fortunately, efforts to develop comprehensive, ecologically sustainable communities are emerging.

2. Ken Yeang, project

Urban Form and Ecology

For almost 6,000 years—between ca. 4000 BC and 2000 AD—the language of city form remained essentially the same across countless cultural and architectural variations. In preindustrial cities, contiguous buildings formed urban blocks and defined streets and public spaces. Streets were relatively narrow, neighborhoods were multifunctional and car-free, blocks were modest in size, and landscape occurred in courtyards and the interiors of blocks. There was hegemony of urbanism over architecture. Circumstances have changed, however, and we now refer to these urban forms as "The Traditional City."

In the nineteenth century, traditional cities "loosened" to accommodate increased circulation; blocks became bigger; streets became wider; and landscape appeared in streets, squares, and parks as a supporting compliment to urban form. Cities retained their urban character, however. When cities were planned, it was the pattern of spaces, blocks, and parcels that were designed, not the architecture. The architecture was developed as an integral component of urbanism.

In the twentieth century, the traditional roles of architecture and the city were reversed: architecture achieved hegemony over the city and became articulated from the city. Detached buildings, as updates of neoclassicism, sat freely in the landscape. Rather than the idea of *the garden in the city*, the ideal became *the city in the garden*. Both the Zeilenbau building type and the Garden City (which quickly became the Garden Suburb) were products of the early modern period. Suburban sprawl began in earnest, and sustainability became elusive.

The "rediscovery of the city" in the late-twentieth century was characterized by initiatives to reinterpret the traditional city—but formed by modern urban buildings. These initiatives continue, but in practice, architects' fascination with unique, iconic, autonomous buildings has actually increased. This has been facilitated and enhanced by digital technology, which has made bizarre architectural forms easy. Unfortunately, however, the pursuit of ever more "original" architectural forms has made city design virtually impossible. Urban cities cannot be made by free-standing objects.

"Eco-Cities"

With the rise of ecological awareness in the 1990s, projects all over the world began to be developed and touted as "green cities," or "eco-cities." While many were simply the result of "green-wash" marketing strategies of architects and planners, others were seriously dedicated to real, comprehensive, environmental effectiveness, including, energy efficient buildings, alternative energy production, minimal auto use, transit orientation, and waste management. The four projects described by Harrison Fraker in *The Hidden Potential of Sustainable Neighborhoods* are not cities, however, but experimental districts, or neighborhoods, within established traditional cities. The projects and cities are Vauban in Freiberg im Breisgau, Germany; Bo01 in Malmö, Sweden, Hammarby Sjöstad in Stockholm, Sweden; and Kronsberg in Hannover, Germany. Three of these are discussed below: Vauban, Bo01, and Hammarby.

The focus on the environmental issues of these projects tends to deflect thought about their urban form. In other words, the performative ecological metrics tend to imply a deterministic relationship with urban form where none necessarily exists. For example, all three of these projects have different urban forms, and there is no reason the same ecological solutions could not be applied to traditional city form. This brings center stage the question of the relationship between ecological issues and urban form.

For these reasons the following three studies will compare Vauban, Bo 01, and Hammarby suburbs to the historic cores of their host cities, Freiberg im Breisgau, Malmö, and Stockholm, as well as other urban patterns.

Post-Roman Cities in Northern Europe

Cities, and the intentional planning of cities, in Europe began in Graeco-Roman antiquity—below the Danube and west of the Rhine river. This limit of the Roman Empire was achieved by the time of Julius Caesar in the first century BC, and was practically the same in the time of Diocletian in the fourth century AD. The centers of most of the great cities of Italy, Austria, France, and Spain began as planned grid towns within the Roman world. During this period there were no cities in northern Europe.

With the disintegration of the Roman Empire, cities also disintegrated and did not become important again until around 1000–1200 AD. Most of the famous cities of northern Europe and Scandinavia were founded around 1200 AD. Rather than being established as grid towns like the Bastides of southwest France, these cities grew up on irregular medieval patterns.

These early medieval cities were fortified, dense, and limited in size. Their urban form was characterized by narrow, irregular street networks; long, closed, irregular blocks; small parcels; limited building heights; and irregular squares. They were walkable and multifunctional. Most also had prominent cathedrals and protective fortresses.

The fortifications are long gone, but otherwise the characteristics of urban form—the characteristics of the traditional city—have persisted in these cities to the present day. These original cores within the much-expanded contemporary cities are not only historic, they are often the most beautiful and sustainable parts. Consequently, they may serve as comparative examples in the evaluation of the subsequent additions of so-called "Eco-City" neighborhoods.

1. Map of the Roman Empire with the future locations of northern cities

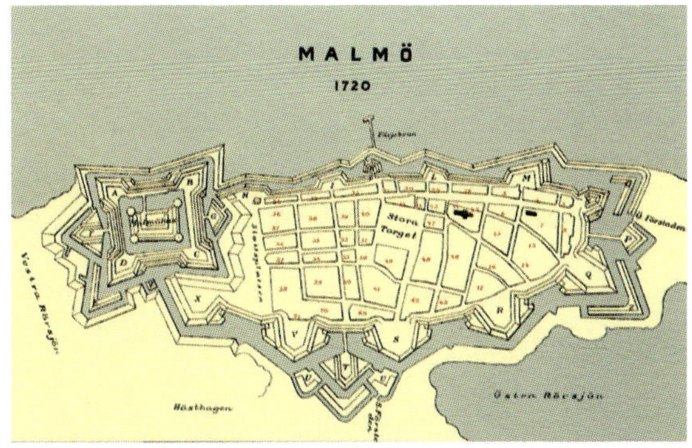

2. Map of Malmö in 1720

3. Map of medieval Freiberg

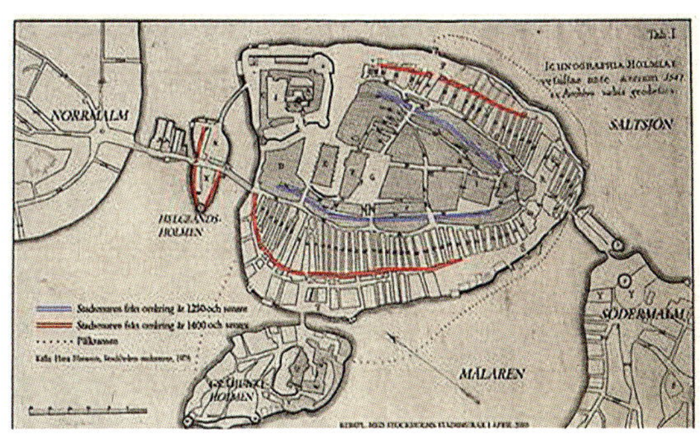

4. Map of medieval Stockholm

Freiberg im Breisgau

Freiberg is nestled into a valley in southwest Germany on the edge of the Black Forest. The city was founded in 1120 as a free market Zähringen town on the Dreisam river. In 1200 the population was about 6,000, when the city's cathedral, the Freiberg Münster, was begun. In the seventeenth century, the city's fortifications were built by the French engineer, Sébastien Le Prestre de Vauban. Today, the historic core of Freiberg, the *Altstadt*, has a population of ca. 7,500. It is a beautiful, livable city that prides itself as being an "Eco-City."

In the Altstadt, buildings define narrow, picturesque, medieval streets lined with ground-floor commercial, and there is a series of lively urban squares. The Altstadt has a series of iconic civic buildings and genuinely multifunctional neighborhoods. In the Altstadt the tram follows the pattern of the city. The architecture of domestic buildings in the Altstadt is generally modest, but the buildings have facades and identity, and collectively they define the public realm. Civic buildings in the Altstadt are more assertive than the domestic buildings, but even when free-standing they define urban space.

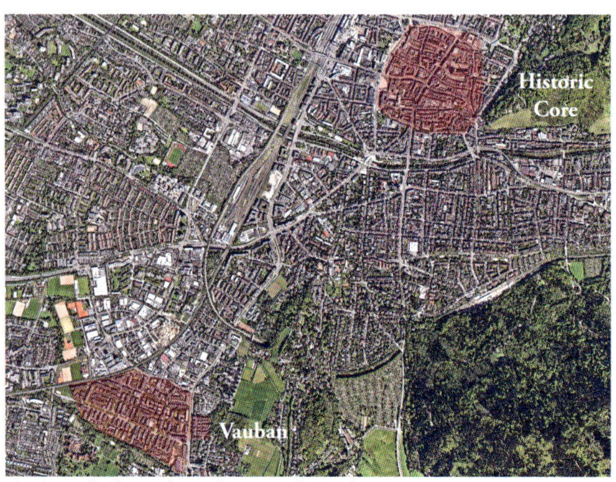

1. Aerial plan of Freiberg and Vauban

2. View of Munster Square in the "Old Town"

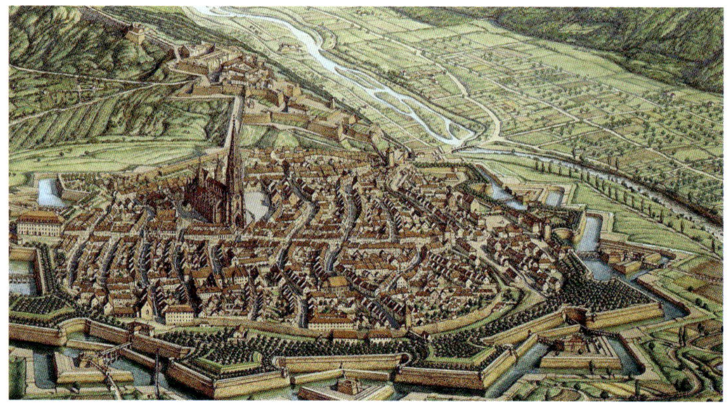

3. Aerial perspective view of Freiberg in 1745

4. Plan of the built fabric of Freiberg Altstadt, 1″ = 1,000′

5. Street view in the Altstadt

6. Traditional row houses in the Altstadt

7. Tram in the Altstadt

8. Row houses and cafes in the Altstadt

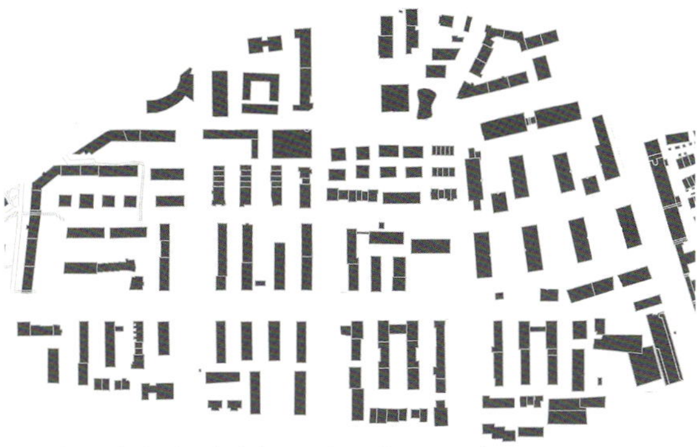

1. *Plan of the built fabric of Freiberg Vauban, 1″ = 1,000′*

2. *Aerial view of Vauban*

Vauban

A former French Army base, the Vauban district is located on the southwest edge of Freiberg. In contrast to the *Altstadt,* Vauban was renovated and developed with modern architecture. It was developed with strong environmental parameters, promotes itself as the first "Eco-City," and is proudly touted as "a sustainable model district." For all its positive environmental achievements, however, Vauban is not urban. It is like a marriage of *zeilenbau planning* and *garden city*, but without the landscape sophistication of the garden city. Vauban, with a population of 5,500, is perhaps sustainable, but it is not a city. It is a bedroom suburb overrun by jungle-like landscape.

Vauban lacks both legible public space and landscape structure. In Vauban no streets or squares are defined; there are only buildings and left-over spaces between the buildings. The buildings are too far apart; they do not make urban blocks or define a legible spatial structure of streets and squares; the architecture is too agressive; and the wild landscape appears to be engulfing a ruin. Even the environmental issues would be improved by more dense, compact urban fabric. Thus, the historic center of Freiberg may be seen as a critique of the Vauban district on both a formal and ecological basis. The architecture of domestic buildings in Vauban is self-referential, and often grotesque. Most public buildings are free-standing objects without sufficient architectural merit and no contribution to legible urban space.

Bad architecture and bad urban design form a lethal combination in Vauban, demonstrating that good ecological intentions and solutions cannot, in and of themselves, create good urban environments.

3. *Modern row houses in Vauban*

4. *"Street" view in Vauban*

5. *Houses and open space in Vauban*

6. *View of street car boulevard in Vauban*

7. *View of Paula Modersohn "Square" in Vauban*

Malmö

Malmö was founded around the middle of the 1200s and became a fortified island over the next centuries with a population of 5,000. By 1875 the original fortified city, *Gamla Staden*, now the Old Town, had expanded to the south, and its civic structure of streets and squares was nominally complete. Malmö had a major ship building industry and an enormous port area. Part of that port, *Västra Hamnen* (Western Harbor) is the site for major new urban development. In Malmö's historic core, the buildings define streets, often with commercial on the ground floor, along with a series of lively urban squares. The old town has a series of iconic civic buildings and genuinely multifunctional neighborhoods. Trees and landscape are confined to squares and courtyards in the old town, as narrow streets do not require street trees to further articulate the space of the street. Malmö's ancient civic structure of streets, squares, and important buildings still forms the anatomy of the city center. The streets maintain a gentle, picturesque, medieval irregularity, and the old town contains six linked major squares:

1. Gustav Adolf Torg: ca. 440' by 525'
2. Lilla Torg ("Small Square"): ca. 175' by 240'
3. Stortorget ("Big Square"): ca. 450' by 475'
4. Church of St. Peter's Square
5. Caroli Church Square
6. The square at the end of Ostergatan (East Street)

The two large squares, Gustav Adolf Torg and Stortorget, are connected by Södergatan, the main shopping street of Malmö, and Stortorget is connected by another street, Hamngatan, across the north canal to the train station. The most beautiful streets in the Old Town are in the western section. They are gently picturesque, with changing, angular views and modest urban facades. But even the streets in the eastern section—those rebuilt in the 1960s and 1970s—define the blocks and provide urban continuity. Architecture in the Old Town ranges from that of modest urban houses, to that of larger urban apartment buildings, to that of more iconic civic buildings, such as the Old City Hall and St. Peter's Church. In every case, architecture supports the public realm by defining urban space.

1. Plan of the built form of Gamla Staden

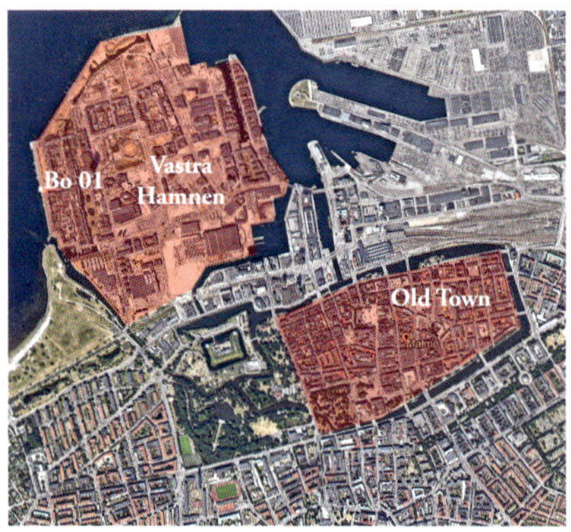

2. Aerial Plan of Malmö and Bo 01

3. Stortorget

4. Street view

5. Street in western part of Old Town

1. *Aerial view of Bo 01*

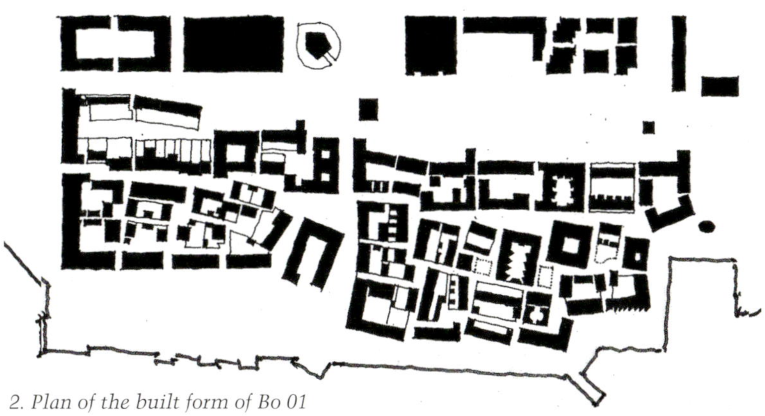

2. *Plan of the built form of Bo 01*

3. *Building in Bo 01*

4. *View of the interior of Bo 01*

5. *Street in Bo 01*

6. *Street in Bo 01*

Bo 01

Bo 01 is a small area of Västra Hamnen, the large port currently undergoing redevelopment. Planning for Bo 01 as an international housing exhibition began 1998, and the first part opened in 2001. Bo 01 continued to develop as a mixed-use residential community based on sustainable principles. It was designed to use 100 percent renewable resources.

Although Bo 01 is often referred to as an "Eco-City," it is actually quite small—about the size of the most western part of the Old Town, *Gamla Väster*, "Old West." Its urban character is very different, however. It is more architectural than urban. In Bo 01 there are many different building heights, and each "block" is either one building or one building style. In addition, each "block" is kicked at an angle. This combination erases any sense of urbanity and continuity—as if architectural toys had been randomly scattered about on a table top.

Like Vauban, no streets or squares are defined in Bo 01; there are only buildings and left-over spaces between the buildings. In Bo 01, architecture trumps urbanism, with most buildings trying to be "special" at the expense of urbanism. This is the result of an architectural plan rather than an urban plan—like an architectural "lego-town" of building blocks, each designed by a different architect and scattered randomly about the site. Rather than an urban order of picturesque, medieval streets, the jagged angles of the housing blocks create too much meaningless, left-over space, and call excessive attention to the narcissistic architecture.

Bo 01 is a perfect example of how a real urban environment cannot be made from excessively differentiated and aggressive architecture. Importantly, most of the ecological solutions developed in Bo 01 have nothing to do with its physical form.

7. *Row houses in Bo 01*

Västra Hamnen

The third-largest city in Sweden, Malmö had a major ship-building industry and an enormous port area. Part of that port, *Västra Hamnen* (Western Harbor) is the site for major new urban development. Bo 01 is just the first phase of the redevelopment. Västra Hamnen is a much bigger area than the Old Town, and is being redeveloped as "The City of the Future."

Three major factors limit the urban development of the area: 1) the number of existing buildings on the site; 2) a mega-grid of arterial roads; and 3) an architectural master plan rather than an urban master plan. Another issue is the isolation of Västra Hamnen. Unlike Gamla Staden with its many connections to neighboring parts of Malmö, Västra Hamnen is like an island, with limited vehicular access. If the development goal of a population of 30,000 is achieved, vehicular circulation in and out will be significant. It is doubtful that Västra Hamnen will achieve either the beauty or the sustainability of the old city of Malmö.

The fantasy collages on the next page are the same scale as the master plan, and illustrate the development potential of Västra Hamnen as a real city.

1. Aerial view of the Main space of Västra Hamnen

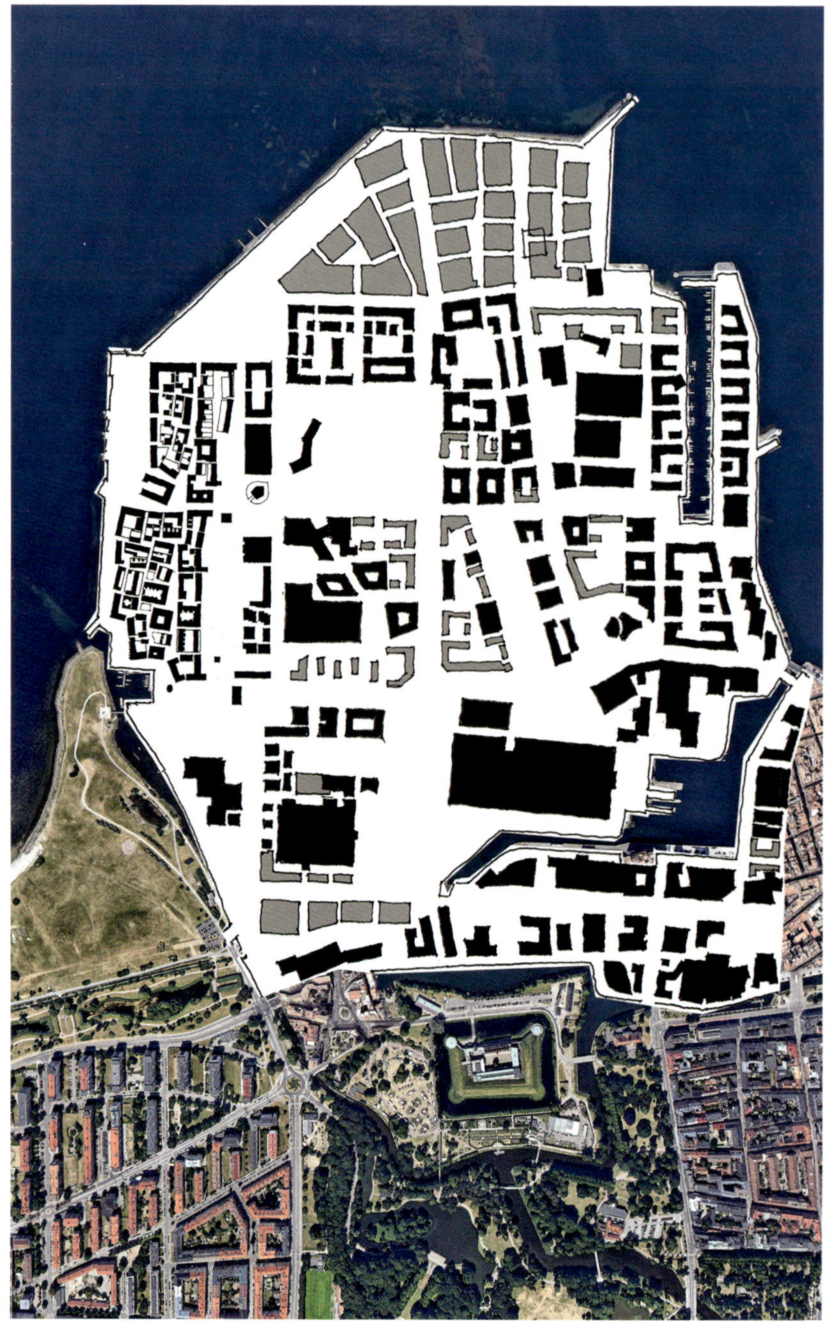

2. Västra Hamnen master plan, 1" = 1,200'

1. Fantasy collage with Malmö "Old Town," 1" = 1,200'

2. Fantasy collage with central Rome, 1" = 1,200'

Stockholm

Stockholm was founded on an island between Lake Mälaren and the Baltic Sea around 1252. The fortified medieval city is indicated in grey in the 1547 plan. As the city prospered, new quarters of long, narrow blocks began to be developed outside the city walls. Much of the medieval urban pattern remains today. The population continually increased, and in the mid-1500s gridded development spread to the mainland.

There are many beautiful streets in Stockholm. They range from narrow widths with modest buildings, to grand tree-lined boulevards defined by equally grand classical buildings. The ground floors may be articulated by commercial activities, but the street walls come straight down to the ground.

In addition to beautiful streets and boulevards, Stockholm has a wide range of beautiful squares and parks. Some of these are landscaped squares, and some are large, irregular urban parks—reminiscent of Paris.

In Stockholm, the urban landscape is a complement to the urban form. In wider streets and boulevards, trees articulate and layer the space of the street. Stockholm also has a wide variety of urban parks.

The architecture of Stockholm ranges from modest, but beautiful, urban buildings to superb examples of the art of architecture—truly history-book buildings.

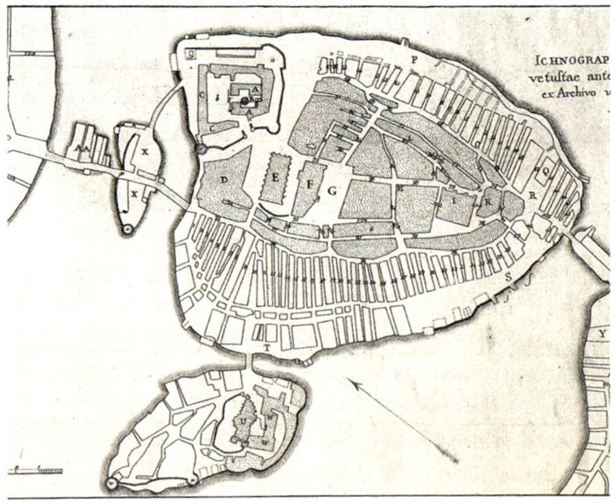

2. Map of Stockholm (Gamla Stan, or Old Town) in 1547

3. Aerial plan of central Stockholm and Hammarby Sjöstad

4. Aerial view of Tegnérlunden Park in Stockholm

1. View of Sagerska Palace in Stockholm

5. Street view in Gamla Stan

6. Boulevard in Östermalm

1. Built-form plan of Hammarby

2. View of proposed building in Hammarby

3. View of buildings in Hammarby

4. Aerial view of Hammarby

5. Aerial view of central space

Hammarby Sjöstad

Hammarby Sjöstad is a contemporary community of about 20,000 people situated on an old industrial site around Lake Hammarby, southeast of Gamla Stan. Planning began in 1990, with serious ecological intentions.

Hammarby occupies a series of linear, waterfront sites without sufficient depth to produce real urban fabric. A comparison with Gamla Stan is revealing, as the whole of Gamla Stan fits within the available real estate on one side of the canal. In fact, the Roman core of Florence also fits.

The biggest problem with this linear organization is the relentless repetition of buildings and blocks. One or two urban "blocks" would not be bad, but nearly twenty of them—close to identical—makes the project into a giant architectural design, as opposed to an urban design with all the variety of traditional cities.

Although the landscape in Hammarby is better than that of Vauban or Bo 01, it lacks clear urban intent. Part of this is due to wide linear zones that are neither parks nor streets. Landscape in these areas tends to be decorative, not complementary.

Hammarby has no squares and no urban parks, only courtyards, linear mall-like areas, and a central area at the bend of the canal. This central area is neither a park nor a square, however, just a mish-mash of random landscape and banal buildings. The result is that the crescent is reduced to a geometric device to resolve the obtuse angle produced by the canal.

The architecture of Hammarby is better than that of Vauban and Bo 01. It ranges from decent developer buildings to really grotesque, anti-urban buildings, but it is also too much architecture and not enough city.

6. Linear landscape in Hammarby

7. Aerial view of blocks

8. View of canal buildings in Hammarby

Eco-Cities and Urban Form

This critique of these eco-communities—Vauban, Bo 01, and Hammarby—is in no way intended to dismiss their laudable environmental initiatives. Such initiatives are indeed imperative for all urban designs if we are to seriously confront the contemporary environmental challenge, and they should be the norm rather than the exception. Perhaps most notable about these eco-projects is that they were actually realized. This represents incredible will and cooperation among multiple entities—not only to initiate these projects, but to bring them to fruition. It reflects enlightened leadership and collaboration, and in a time of widespread climate denial and political obfuscation, it is practically a miracle. Because such solutions run counter to almost every aspect of modern life—particularly modern American life—achieving them will always be a difficult task.

These environmental initiatives, and their interrelationships, are described in easily available material on the internet, and they are covered in detail in several excellent books, including Fraker's, *The Hidden Potential of Sustainable Neighborhoods*; Douglas Farr's, *Sustainable Urbanism* and *Sustainable Nation*; and Doug Kelbaugh's, *The Urban Fix*.

Fraker's book outlines the following topics, describes them specifically for each eco-project, and compares them in Chapter 6, "Observations across Neighborhoods."

Energy: Demand reduction, Renewable sources, Cogeneration (combined district heat and power)
Waste Management and Recycling: Storm water, Sewage, Solid waste, Organic waste
Transportation: Public transit, Limited car use and parking
Materials: Local, Recycled
Landscape: Permeable surfaces, Green Space, Expanded public and private green space, Habitat provision

The question arises how technical solutions to these environmental issues relate to urban form. Are they determinants of urban form? Do they have any impact, or implications, on urban form? Do they suggest a new idea of urban form? Given the intent of Fraker's book, one might surmise that solutions to these topics are in fact significant determinants of urban form. Yet in studying the form and character of the subject neighborhoods, what is notable is their formal diversity—the fact that each of the eco-cities is different from the others, and that none is genuinely urban. This diversity indicates that the urban form of the three case studies is independent from the technical solutions they all employ—that the solutions themselves are not inherently form determinants at all. In fact, the technical solutions all could (and should) be applied to traditional city form, and except for the expansion of green space, most could be deployed retroactively to existing urban conditions as well.

Unfortunately, common interpretations of environmental solutions often degrade cities rather than reinforce them. Too often environmental values are used to replace urban values, which they cannot do. While the eco-communities may be justifiably praised for their environmental achievements, this is not enough. They are not scalable, they are not dense, and they are not urban. The historic centers of Freiberg, Malmo, and Stockholm are undeniably more beautiful than Vauban, Bo01, and Hammarby; moreover, the traditional urban form of these historic cities, coupled with the possible deployment of eco-strategies, offers the potential to rival, perhaps exceed, the environmental performance of their eco-neighborhoods.

The Urban Measure of Things

One of the great, useful, pleasures enabled by contemporary digital technology—specifically Google Earth and Photoshop—is the ability to easily get and adjust the scale of images for comparative purposes. Size matters. Distance matters. *What size is it? What is the texture of the fabric? What is a five- or ten-minute walking shed, especially with an unfamiliar (unvisited) town?* For years, my own measure, my urban yardstick, has been the Roman core of Florence, which represents a five-minute walking shed, roughly a quarter mile, or 1,320'. It has the three characteristics of an ideal town or neighborhood: 1) a clear center, 2) consistent urban fabric, and, in this case, 3) a clear edge.

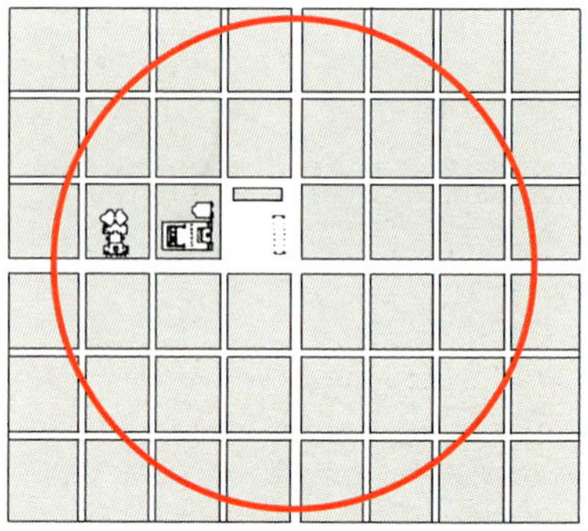

1. *Plan of Roman Florence, 1″ = 800′*

2. *Aerial plan of Roman Florence, 1″ = 800′*

Comparative Plans

Another useful exercise is to collage more extensive aerial plans of existing cities into urban design sites at the same scale. The results are often surprising, and reveal unique ideas and patterns, as well as providing a critique of proposed designs. For example, the following collages—the Marais neighborhood of Paris superimposed on Vauban, and Florence and Bordeaux superimposed on Hammarby—are provocative, even if a bit outrageous. They are urban, however, and they put the actual designs for those areas in sharp relief.

1. Aerial plan of Hammarby with Florence and Bordeaux superimposed, 1″ = 1,000′

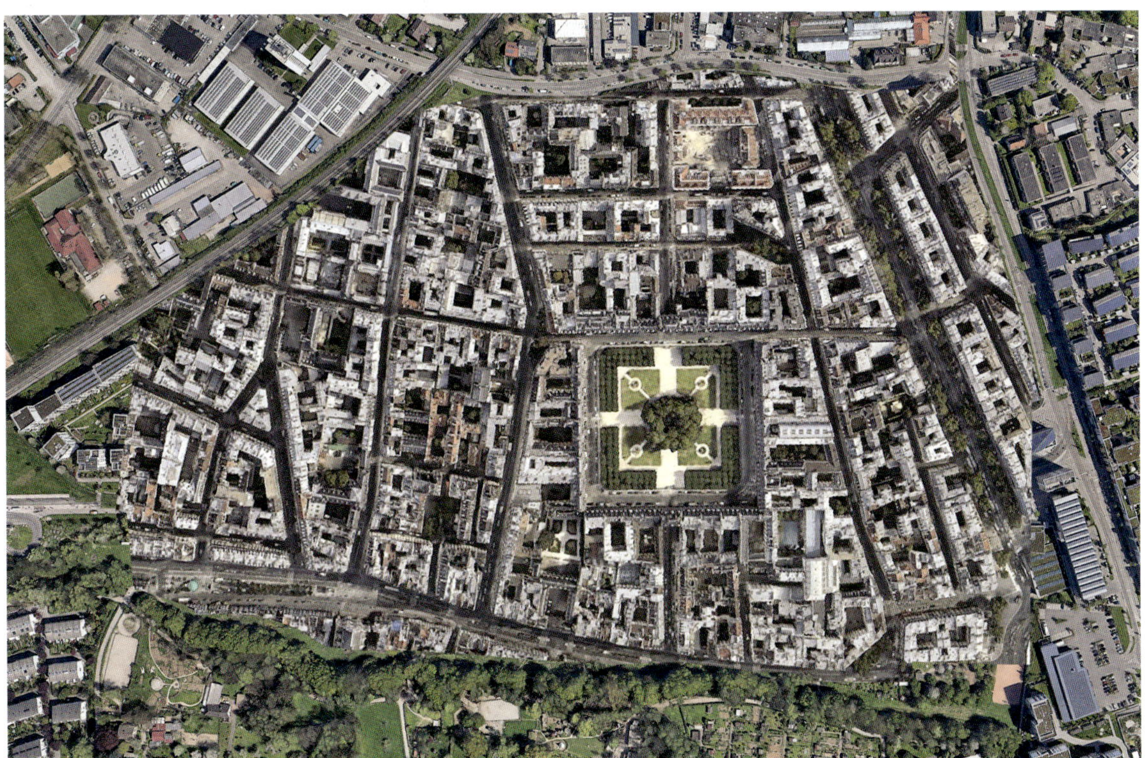

2. Aerial plan of Vauban with Paris Marais superimposed, 1″ = 500′

The Future

Given the contemporary ecological environment, if life on Planet Earth is to survive, our lifestyle and settlement patterns must change—and rapidly. The contemporary state of architecture, urbanism, and professional education is completely inadequate for this challenge, however. The profession is in dire need of reorientation. We need a reintegration of architecture, the city, ecology, and professional education. This will be difficult.

The disciplines of architecture and urbanism have been developing in the opposite direction for well over a century now. The false promise of limitless resources and expansion has produced a heady narcissism that emphasizes private prerogative over civic responsibility. This has destroyed the urbanity of cities, and it is ruining the environment.

A starting point, together with ecological understanding, would be the reexamination of architecture's relationship to the city—to urbanism. This is not an issue of style or language. Great cities—such as Barcelona or Bordeaux—have always absorbed a variety of architectural languages as long as there was hegemony of urbanism over architecture. These, and other great traditional cities, provide a fertile source for future possibilities.

1. Aerial rendering of "downtown" Dubai

2. Aerial view of Sheik Sayed Road

3. "Grass in the desert"

Anti-Ecology and Anti-Urbanism

The most exaggerated discrepancy between ecological responsibility and urban form may be in the Middle-East. Indeed, it is ironic that far-northern cities, with extremely cold climates, have taken initiatives to develop ecologically responsible communities, whereas some Middle Eastern cities, with extremely hot climates, seem to have flagrantly disregarded environmental issues, even though they too have excellent traditional models of adaptation.

The UAE have experienced radical city growth over the last twenty years, and in the process, Abu Dhabi, and to a greater extent Dubai, represent another extreme in the anti-urban problem of contemporary urban sprawl.

It is clear that ecological issues played no part in the design for the new Dubai "downtown." This is a desert environment with mean daily temperatures above 90 degrees F. There is very little water, and no native products other than dates, pearls from the sea, and of course oil and gas (mostly in Abu Dhabi).

The region has a rich architectural and urban tradition that is adapted to the environment with simple means: tight pedestrian streets, shaded courtyards, thick masonry walls, and naturally ventilated buildings—all of which creates a genuine urban fabric. Against this background is the modernist city development of isolated glass skyscrapers (not a great idea for the desert), gigantic anti-urban automobile circulation systems, autonomous air-conditioned shopping centers, monofunctional zones for sports and other uses, and to top it off, an indoor ski resort—*an indoor ski resort!* It is like the Ville Radieuse laundered through Disney Studios. All of this consumption and environmental pollution is enabled by the technology of oil and associated wealth. The financial crisis of 2008 dampened development, and as resource depletion increases, further retreat should be expected.

Ecology and the Traditional City

The historic neighborhood of Bastakiya is less publicized than Dubai City, but it is more interesting. Its traditional urban form is more simply adapted to the environment, with narrow covered streets, enclosed and shaded courtyards, and covered shopping areas contrasting sharply with the indulgence of the modernist city.

1. Covered shopping street in Bastakiya, Dubai

2. View of Bastakiya

3. Shaded courtyard in Bastakiya

4. Shaded street in Bastakiya

Conclusion

It is difficult to end a book like this. The concrete evidence of the past and the present may be described and argued with some degree of clarity, but predictions about the future almost always prove to be quite wrong.

Even if the future cannot be predicted, however, there are facts that can be known and trends that can be identified with some degree of confidence. For example, the environmental and economic trends identified in *The Limits of Growth* in 1972[12] have proven to have tracked more or less as predicted over the last forty years, and we now face unprecedented environmental and cultural challenges that threaten not only the quality of life on our planet but possibly even the continuity of planetary life. Predictions of the future are not required, but an acknowledgment of the facts of the present is. To quote Aldus Huxley, "Facts do not cease to exist because they are ignored."

Excessive consumption of both renewable and nonrenewable resources, population growth, waste, and pollution (including carbon) are crucial facts of our time. They are exacerbated by our nonurban lifestyle, and have ominous implications for our future. At best, radical change will be required, and at worst, if we do not change, the near future could make the centuries of disintegration of the Roman Empire seem like a pleasant interlude.

No excuse—not even pending environmental doom—should be needed in order to produce livable, joyous urban environments. We have several thousand years of excellent precedents to draw upon. But more than a century of destructive urban behavior has produced contemporary architectural and urban conventions that are impotent for twenty-first-century issues, much less for producing quality urban environments. And, when conventions are inadequate, principles become necessary.

Urban life may indeed be the most sustainable form of habitation, but rapid and increasing urbanization, primarily in India, South America, and China, does not suggest livable or sustainable urban futures—nor does continuous horizontal sprawl in the United States. These forms of habitation may technically be cities, or megacities, but they are not urban, because the civic realm is missing. They are simply warehouses for people.

The combination of excessive vehicular circulation and detached buildings have together done more to produce bad urban environments than any other factors—by far. Conversely, the combination of dense, contiguous buildings and streets as narrow as possible would do more to produce good urban environments than any other factor, because urbanism is about the organization of public space, not private buildings.

Oddly, after all the theorizing, everyone knows which are the good cities: Paris, Rome, Bordeaux, Bath, Venice, Barcelona, etc. All are compact, with continuous fabric, tight streets, and fabulous spaces. There is communal life because there is a civic realm.

The basic form guidelines for good, sustainable urbanism are simple:

Dense, contiguous urban buildings forming modestly sized blocks;

Streets as narrow as possible, designed primarily for people, not cars;

A pattern of plazas or squares of moderate size;

Neighborhood and civic parks and gardens;

Mixed-use, walkable neighborhoods;

A legible civic structure of public spaces and buildings; and

Efficient public transportation systems.

These are the time-tested principles characteristic of the cities we love. They are also the principles that make the most sustainable forms of human habitation, and are therefore ideal for the future. They are not the principles of the status quo, however, nor do they account for the role of architecture in urbanism.

Unfortunately, most contemporary urban design today is based on the status quo, not implications of the future. Private automobiles, diesel buses, fire trucks, "iconic" architecture, large development parcels, and mono-functional districts are assumed as factual parameters for contemporary urban design. This all-pervasive condition—the triumph of the private realm over the public realm—has deep roots, but most of the transformation has occurred in a little over a half century. Urban change is slow and incremental, but another fifty or more years will be too late for the environment. Radical change in urban design parameters is needed now.

Perhaps even more problematic, few architects today understand the city and are capable of making urban buildings. Urban buildings require urban typologies and facades, and modern architecture has made this virtually a lost art. Most contemporary architecture reveals a flimsy, confused desperation. It is as if architecture has lost its purpose and dissolved into an ever increasingly overt struggle for media attention. Achieving good, sustainable cities will require not only adherence to good town planning principles but also a parallel transformation of architecture from an autonomous to an urban endeavor. The details and architectural "style" of future cities will necessarily change, but the principles of good urbanism and environmental responsibility will not.

Bordeaux

By definition, not every city in the world can be surrounded by the world's best wines, but even without the wine, the city of Bordeaux would be a superb example of beautiful, sustainable urban life. Architecture, landscape, and urbanism enjoy a mutually reinforcing relationship in Bordeaux, enabling the latest technology, and the latest architecture, to be absorbed with ease into the formal and social fabric of the city. Why shouldn't every city have this quality—if not the wine?

Examples of all the principles of good urbanism can be found in Bordeaux: beautiful streets, a variety of blocks, walkable neighborhoods, a plethora of active squares, wonderful parks, integrated landscape, public transportation, and a superb civic structure. Importantly, many of these are not relics of the past but the result of a recent transformation, beginning in 1995. In just ten years, with the oversight of Mayor Alain Juppé, grimy, moribund Bordeaux was transformed into a sexy, world-class city.

SDUK plan of Bordeaux, 1832

Aerial view of central Bordeaux showing the grand river promenade connecting the Place de la Bourse with the large Place des Quinconces. The Roman/Medieval core is to the left of the view

1. *Night view of the Place de la Bourse and the tram reflected in the water mirror*

Civic Structure

Few cities possess a grand public face such as that of Bordeaux facing the Garonne River. The extended wall of unified river facades is punctuated by the Place de la Bourse, the royal square built for Louis XV, and the huge Place des Quinconces, which are now linked by a spectacular landscape promenade along the river. This urban landscape project by Claire and Michel Corajoud, with a large water mirror by Jean-Max Llorca, replaces a series of abandoned warehouses for the old port along the Quai. The project integrates the circulation infrastructure to extend and connect the city to the river and provide a public promenade between river and city. The water mirror is especially effective. Only about one inch deep, the reflecting pool drains away every fifteen minutes and fog rises to produce an ephemeral cloud of mist. Not since Haussmann's Paris has there been such a felicitous collaboration of architecture, landscape, public space, and infrastructure.

2. *Place de la Bourse, with the reflecting pool, or water mirror*

3. *Tram through the park of the Place des Quinconces*

1. Building facades

2. Pedestrian street

3. Street view

4. Tree-lined street

5. Palais de Justice, Foster + Partners

6. Palais de Justice, Foster + Partners

7. Opéra National de Bordeaux

Buildings

Within Bordeaux only institutional buildings and market buildings are free-standing. Even these usually conform to the spatial matrix of the city. For example, the National Opera fills a block, but the portico defines one side of a square. Even the modernist Palace of Justice aligns on the street and is figurative only on its courtyard side. All other buildings are urban party-wall types of varying widths.

Urban Blocks

The majority of the urban blocks in Bordeaux are modest in size, and are formed of multiple, contiguous buildings. Some building facades are architecturally refined. Others are prosaic. But the style is less important than the continuity of the street wall, for this defines the public spaces of the city. Buildings are sufficiently high and have enough surface area and continuity to define legible streets and squares.

Streets

Most of Bordeaux's streets are defined by four- to six-story building walls, and are only as wide as necessary. Small ones are 12–15' wide, medium ones are 25–30', and large ones are 75–100'. Only larger streets are tree-lined, but all are designed for the traffic they carry. Ground floors are generally articulate, with shops and public facilities that define the "people space" of the city.

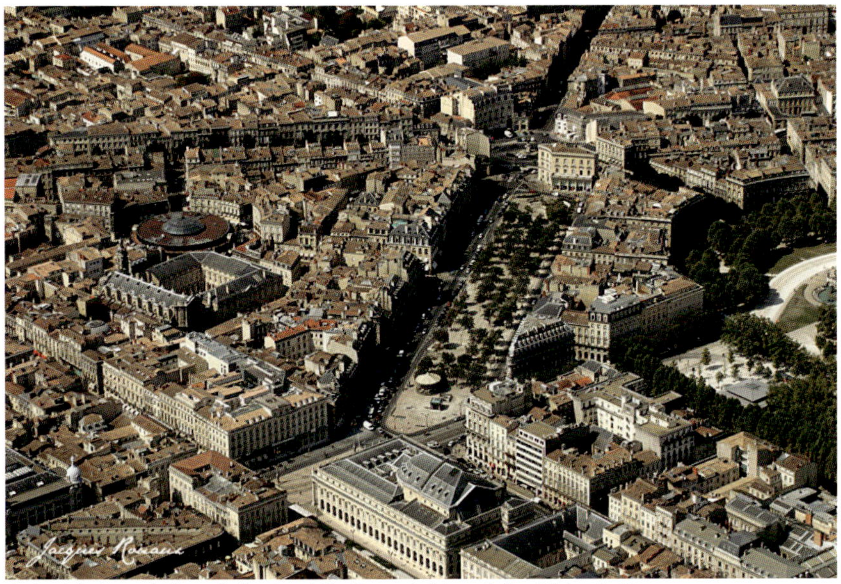

1. Aerial view of Place de la Comédie (lower left), and the Allées de Tourny

2. Place du Parlement at night

3. Neighborhood park

4. Cafe life

5. Aerial view of Place Gambetta

6. Place Camille Jullian

Squares

Bordeaux has a remarkable variety of squares and neighborhood parks of modest size, some offering the possibility of underground parking. The Allées de Tourny, for example, covers a massive underground garage. The size of most squares is modest. Place Camille Jullian is approximately 130' x 175'. Place du Parlement is 135' x 150'. The Allées de Torny is 213' x 1,000'.

Urban Life

It is the presence of a legible, elaborate network of civic space—a public realm—in Bordeaux that facilitates communal life in a way that most American cities cannot. To achieve this, urbanism must have hegemony over architecture, as a city cannot be made with private icons alone. Not since Jane Jacobs has any of this been new news, but now it is an environmental imperative as well as a cultural one.

Model of Imperial Rome

Excursus: Irregular & Composite Plans

With time, both planned and unplanned cities become cumulative cities, in which incremental growth transforms the original pattern. This is true of the planned grid towns of Greece, the Roman Empire, and Manhattan as well as the unplanned irregular towns of Palermo, Venice, Boston, Rome, and the informal settlements of Caracas and Mumbai.

Some Roman-founded cities, such as Florence, Vienna, Barcelona, and Bordeaux, became more picturesque and medieval following the disintegration of the Roman Empire. Their gridded cores softened, and they expanded in irregular ways. Turin, however, is a unique case in that it grew as a series of consistent gridded extensions, with transformations happening within the grids. New York City (Manhattan) and most American cities have also been planned as grids and have expanded as gridded extensions.

The principal subject of this book has been planned towns and expansions. These have always been grid plans, as there have never been irregular planned towns—at least until recently with the work of Rob and Leon Krier. But irregular cities, such as Rome and Venice, are among our most cherished and interesting. Therefore, this section has been included as a stimulant, and to question whether informal, irregular plans might be designed today—or perhaps allowed to develop over time within a larger composite framework.

Plan of ancient Rome

1. Plan of central Boston, 1930

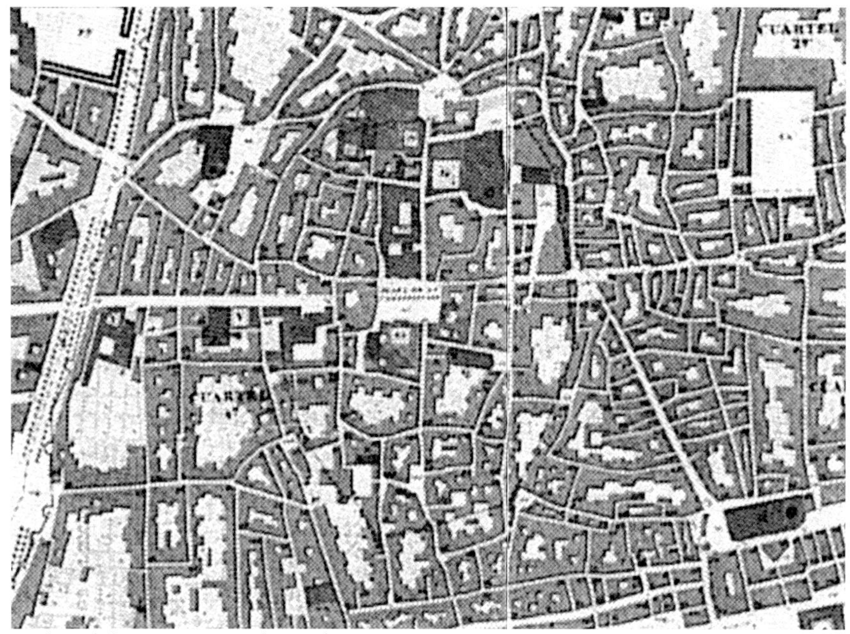

2. Plan of the Roman core of Barcelona

Irregular Plans

Cities with irregular plans are often the most interesting, but historically they were never planned—they were built up incrementally. Thus, they are difficult, if not impossible, to emulate or design.

There are three basic types of irregular plans. Rome of the Empire, for example, was a fantastic collage of designed, ideal set-pieces to which local contingency had to adjust. Another type was originally a planned Roman town such as Barcelona, which was rebuilt over the Roman ruins. Many European cities, such as Paris, Vienna, Florence, Bordeaux, etc., were casually reconstructed over the disintegrated ruins of Roman grid towns. Finally, there were those plans in which modest additions were made incrementally according to culture, law, or terrain. The picturesque irregularity of Islamic cities, for example, was due to culture, law, and the environment. Still others, such as Venice, Palermo, Boston, and many hill towns, were a result of environment and terrain.

Designed Irregular Plans

Until recently there were no designed irregular plans. There were Sitte-inspired picturesque plans, and romantically curvilinear plans, but no irregular urban plans of medieval or Imperial Roman character. In the 1980s, however, both Leon and Rob Krier began to produce irregular urban plans. Leon's were more Roman inspired with detached buildings; Rob's were irregular patterns of perimeter blocks and are very seductive.[1]

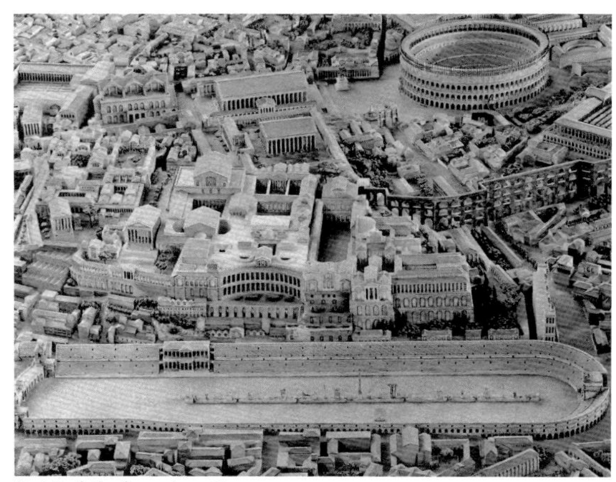

3. Model of ancient Rome

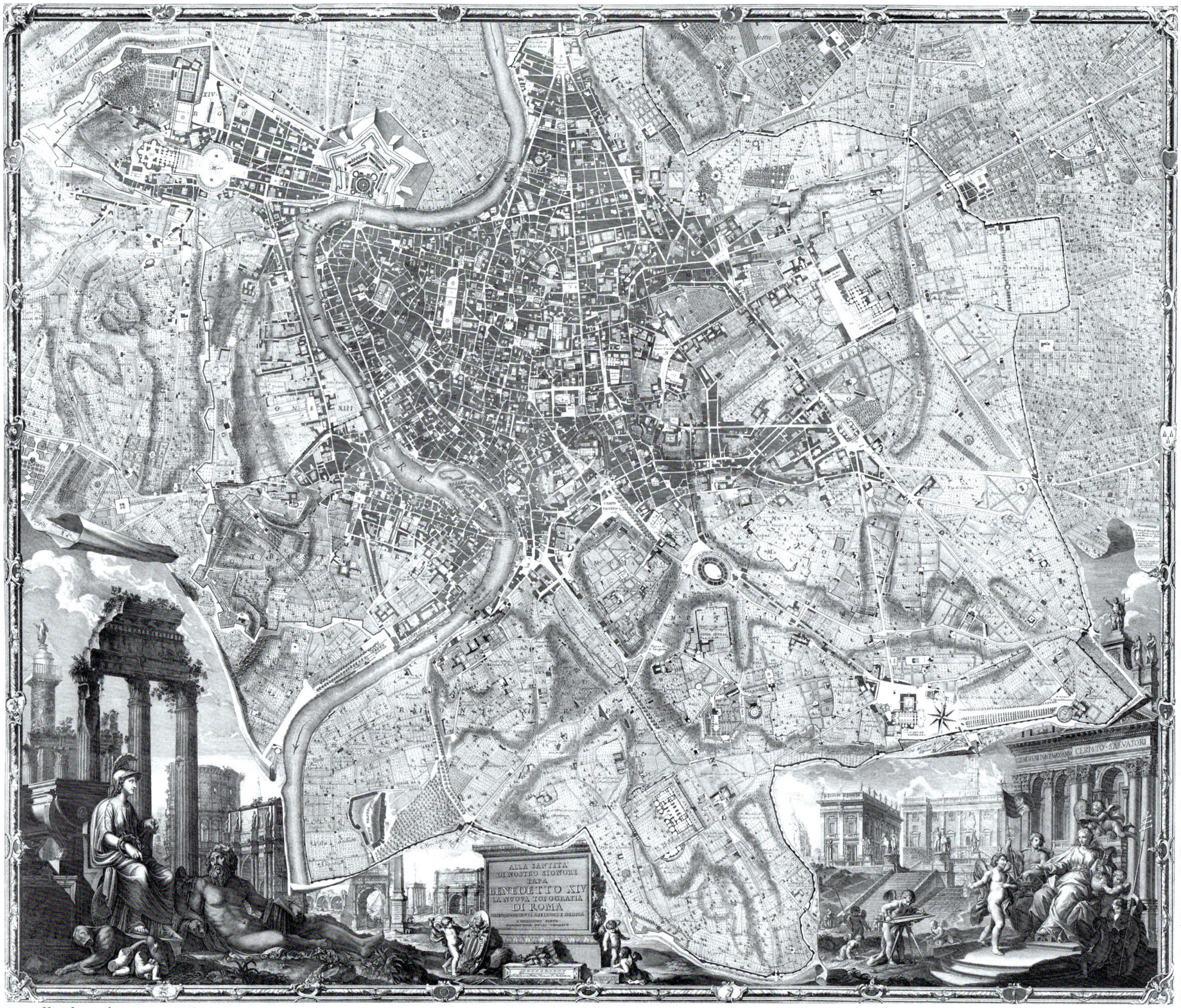

1. Nolli Plan of Rome, 1748

Rome and the 1748 Nolli Plan

Giambattista Nolli's famous plan of Rome was published in 1748. It depicts the city at the pinnacle of its post–Roman Empire, Renaissance, and Baroque development—a state that is still largely intact today.[2]

Nolli's plan is an ichnographic plan—an orthogonal plan—in contrast to the bird's-eye aerial view of its exact contemporary, Bretez's "Turgot" plan of Paris. It is surprisingly accurate and has served as the base for many subsequent plans.

The technique of hatching the urban blocks—the *poché* of the city—emphasizes the civic spatial structure of streets, squares, courtyards, and the interiors of major buildings. In other words, the semipublic spaces of passageways, loggias, courtyards, and theater and church interiors are shown as extensions of the public open spaces of streets and squares. This part of the network would be hidden by an orthographic projection of only the city's solids and voids. It is an excellent system for representing dense, horizontally consistent urban fabric. It is also excellent for representing existing cities, but not for proposed ones.

2. View of Rome

Nolli plan detail

Inhabited part of the Nolli plan superimposed on a contemporary aerial plan of Rome, 1:40,000

Planning versus Incremental Growth

If town planning, or urban design, is the design of the public structure of the city—the streets, squares, blocks, and sometimes the parcels but not the architecture—then the Nolli plan is instructive only on the micro-urban level. Indeed, when the interiors and courtyards are removed to reveal only the open space structure, it becomes apparent that no such urban fabric could be "planned."

Urban Expansion

Little changed in the size of Rome between the mid-eighteenth century and 1870, when the city became the capital of a unified Italy. Until that time the city had developed for over two millennia. Its unplanned, irregular maze of streets and blocks was the residue of countless small negotiations and decisions.

Over the next half-century, however, Rome would expand exponentially via a series of large planned areas, some of which were equal in size to the antique core depicted by Nolli. The first wave of expansion happened within the Aurelian walls in the late nineteenth century, and a second wave occurred in the early twentieth century.[3]

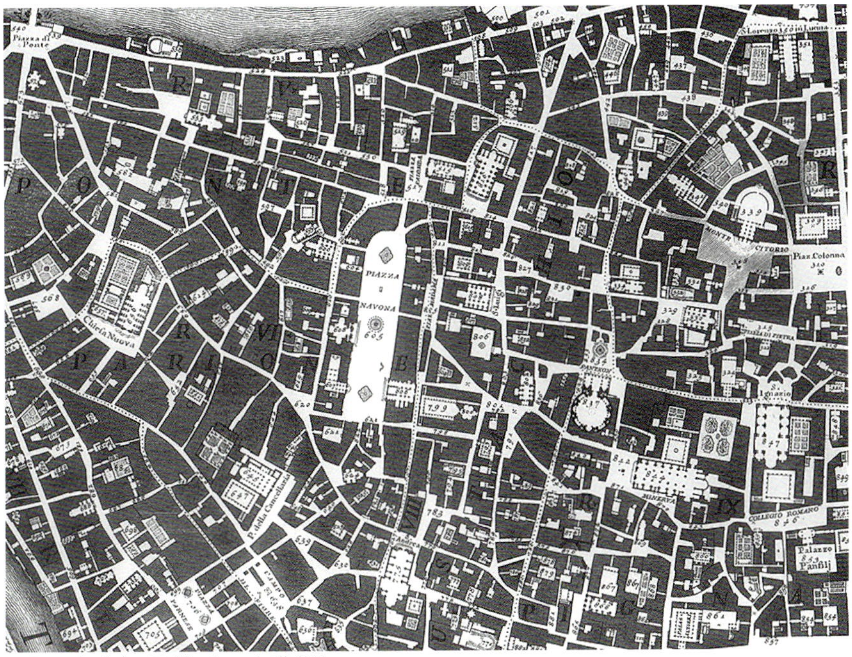

1. Detail of the Nolli plan, 1:10,000

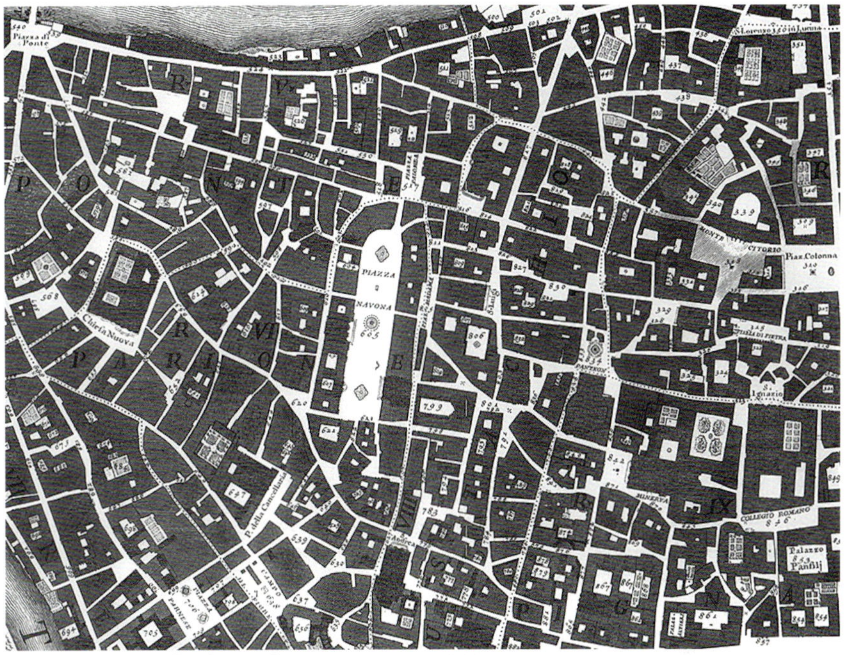

2. Detail of the Nolli plan without interiors, 1:10,000

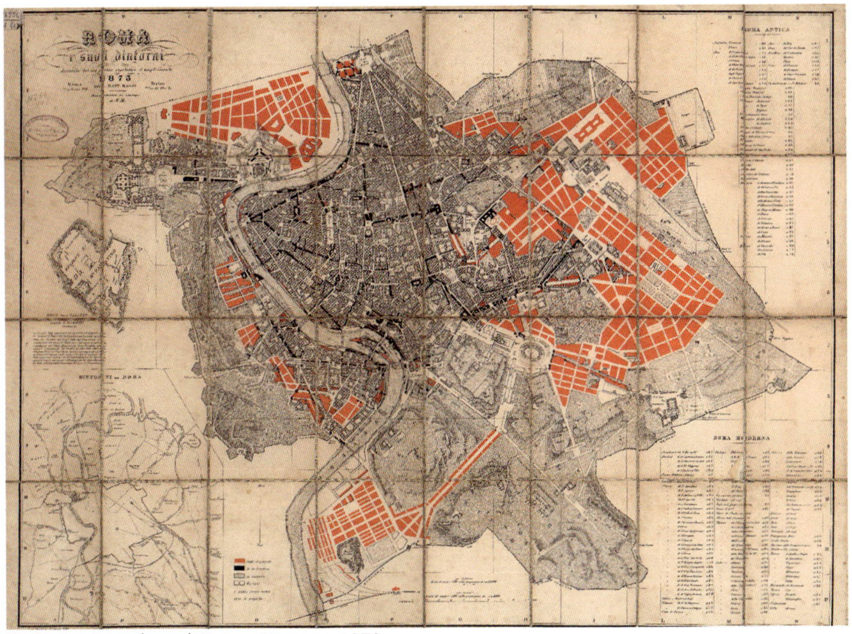

3. Expansion plan of Rome, Viviani, 1873

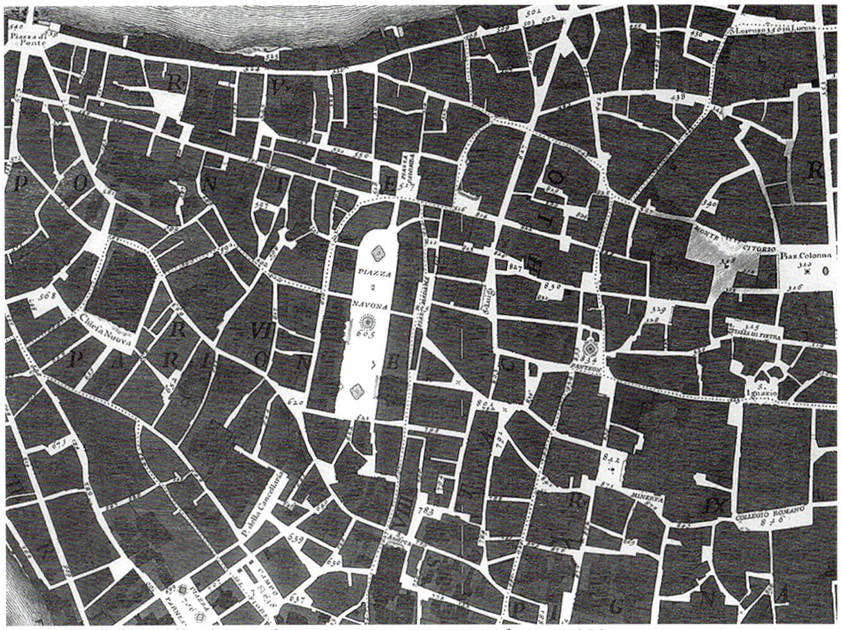

4. Detail of the Nolli plan without interiors or courtyards, 1:10,000

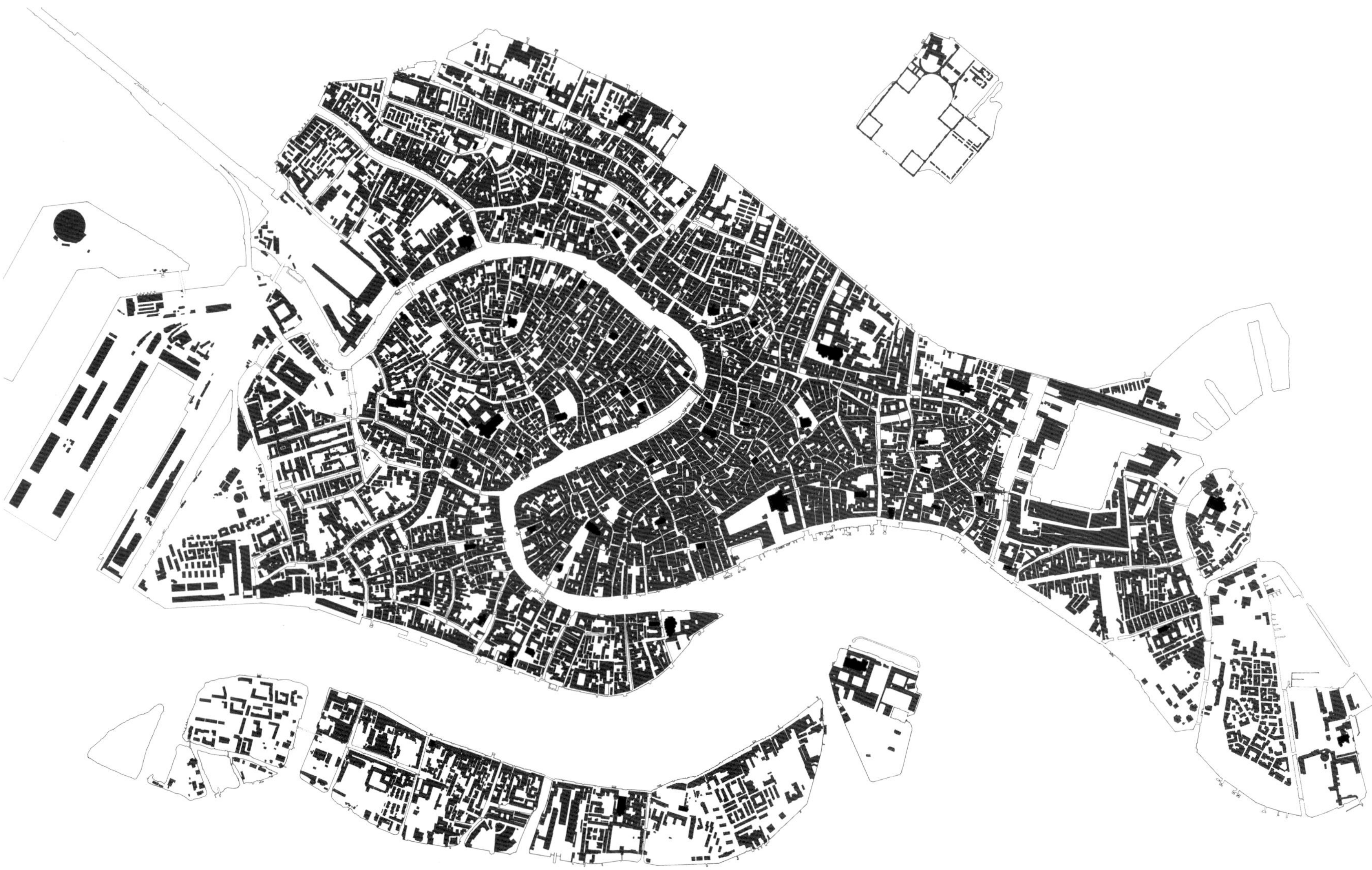

Plan of Venice

Venice and Its Lagoon

Except perhaps for some Islamic cities, Venice is the quintessential irregular plan city, and the water makes it especially unique. The lessons of Florence and New York do not apply; Cartesian it is not. The seemingly impenetrable confusion of its urban pattern is only offset by its dreamy, otherworldly charm. One has to look closely to decipher its form.

If Venice was "planned," it was planned by the pattern of canals lying hidden beneath the surface of the water, the location and configuration of which were known only to the Venetians. Indeed, its form and character grow out of its environment and history rather than a "town plan."

Between the sixth and eighth centuries residents of the Roman coastal centers fled the mainland to escape the Germanic invasions and established themselves on the sandy islands of the lagoon. In 737 the Rialto (now Venice) was established as the administrative center of the region, and in 828 St. Mark was adopted as the patron saint of the city. Until the city surrendered to Napoleon in 1797, the Republic of Venice was never conquered. Its defense was its location in the center of the lagoon. Even Napoleon's cannons could not reach Venice from the mainland, and ships entering the mouth of the lagoon were subject to destruction by a Venetian fortress, or they ran aground in the maze of unseen canals. This effective defense system allowed Venice an internal openness unavailable to cities like Florence and Rome.[4]

1. View of the Venetian Lagoon

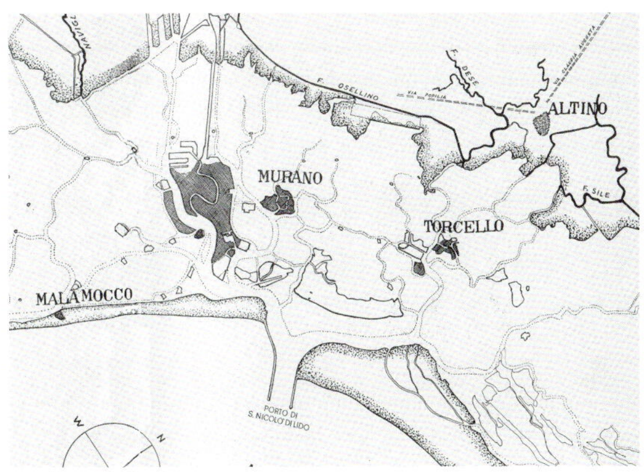

2. Plan of the lagoon

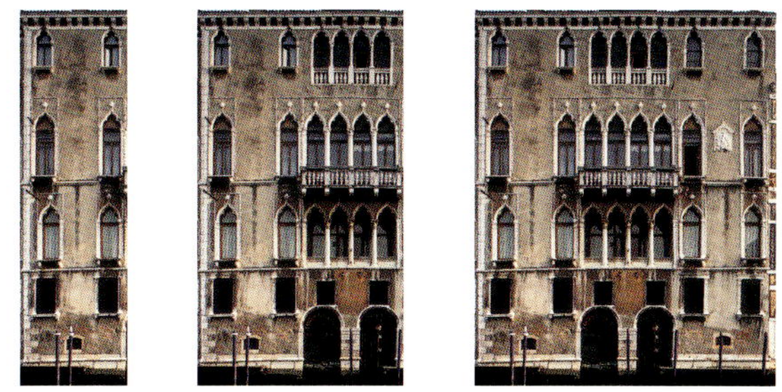

3. Venetian House facade types

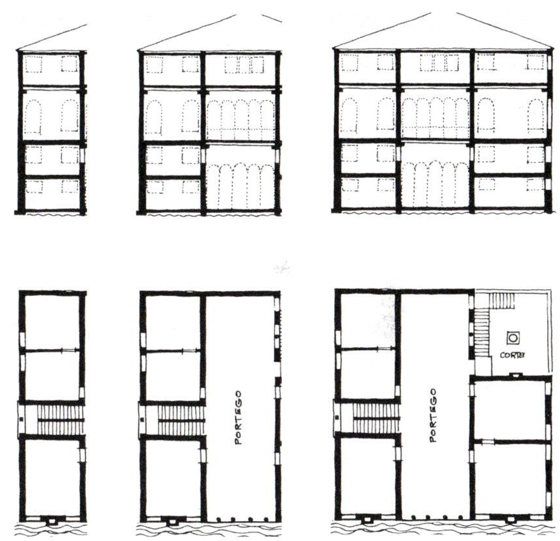

4. Venetian house, plan and section types

The Venetian House

The safety of the lagoon allowed for open facades—more like screens or tapestries than defensive barriers, and the curvilinear canals promoted narrow, deep building plans in irregular patterns. Because of the openness, light could penetrate deep into the house. The ground level and mezzanine were for commercial use, and the upper levels were residential. Many houses had both a water and a land entrance, sometimes through a courtyard.[5]

Plan and Facade Types

Various combinations of basic plan and facade types form the building blocks of Venice. Houses were either one, two, or three bays wide, and were usually quite deep. There were two bay types: one consisting of a series of rooms and a facade with widely spaced vertical windows with a blank panel between them; the other consisting of a long open hall stretching the depth of the building with a facade of mostly glass, with closely spaced vertical windows.

A one-bay house was always the blank panel bay, but never an open bay. A two-bay house could be either two blank panel bays or one blank panel bay and one open bay—such as the Ca D'Oro. A three-bay house would be an open bay between two blank panel bays. The architectural styles changed with the epochs, but the types remained the same for hundreds of years. This is Venice's DNA, providing flexibility, consistency, and endless variety.

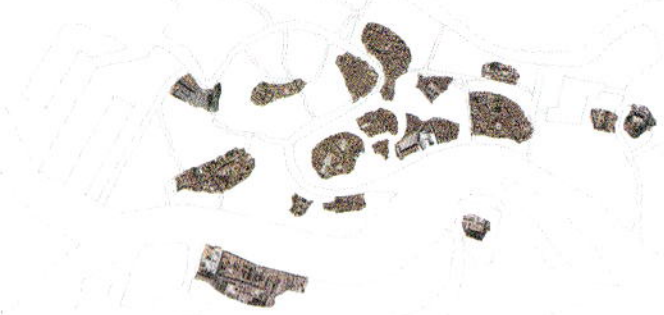

1. Extent of Venice in the 7th c.

2. Extent of Venice to the 9th c.

3. Extent of Venice to the 11th c.

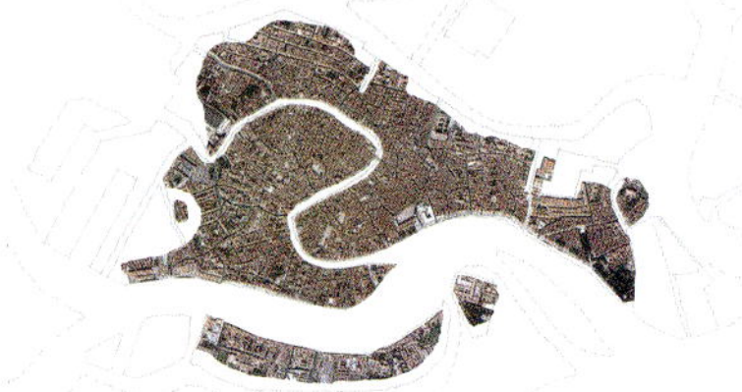

4. Extent of Venice in the 12th c.

5. Extent of contemporary Venice

6. Aerial view of Venice

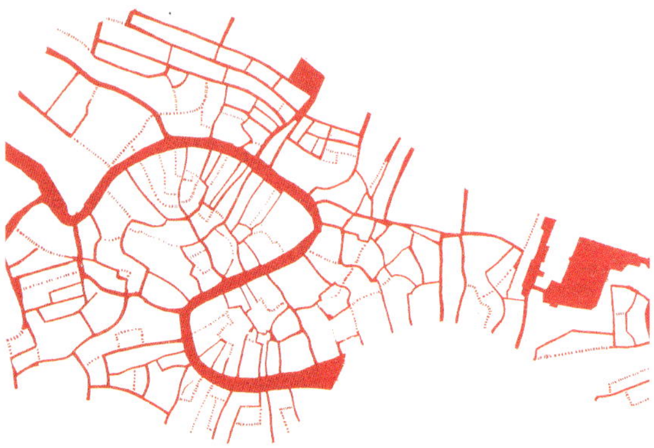

7. Canal and street patterns

8. The Grand Canal

Urban Development

Venice's urban development began with a series of island neighborhoods separated by water. These irregular urban islands were organized around a piazza, or *campo*, with a church and a well. Internally, there were both streets and canals, but as the city gradually expanded, bridges were built to connect the islands. The result is a dual network of streets and canals.[6]

The urban form of Venice is medieval; thus, there are no set-piece boulevards and no regular squares. All of Venice's public spaces, including the Piazza San Marco, are picturesque and irregular.

The plan gives no clue to the urban quality of the city, which is due to its long, incremental, and sophisticated architectural development. But the plan and the architecture are integrally related. No amount of design and planning could produce Venice's high level of art, architecture, and culture. This can only accrue with time and will. But also, no amount of design and planning could produce the plan, as this too required time and circumstance.

Detail plan of Castello area, 1:5,000

1. View of Palermo in 1849, engraving

Palermo

The stunning 1844 plan of Palermo is at first incomprehensible: an apparent melange of irregularity, cut through by a "cardo" and "decumanus." Only the historic development of the plan brings its order into focus.

Palermo was founded between two rivers by Phoenicians from Carthage in the eighth century BC. The original settlement occupied the high ground, but gradually expanded down the slope toward the harbor, and was surrounded by fortification walls. This—the "Phoenician foot"—was the limit of the city through the Roman occupation until Palermo was conquered by the Arabs in 831.

The Arabs first occupied the fortress area, but after troubles with the natives they created a new fortress to the southeast. Gradually the areas north and south of the rivers were built up, and another fortification wall was built.[7]

In the sixteenth century the two rivers were diverted, the river beds were filled in, and these areas began to be built up in an irregular pattern following the terrain.

The main street of the Phoenician city, now the Via Cassaro, was straightened and extended to the sea in the sixteenth century, and in 1600 the cross street, the Via Maqueda, was cut through, completing the city until the mid-nineteenth century when it began to expand to the north.

2. Porta Felice, gateway to the sea from via Cassaro

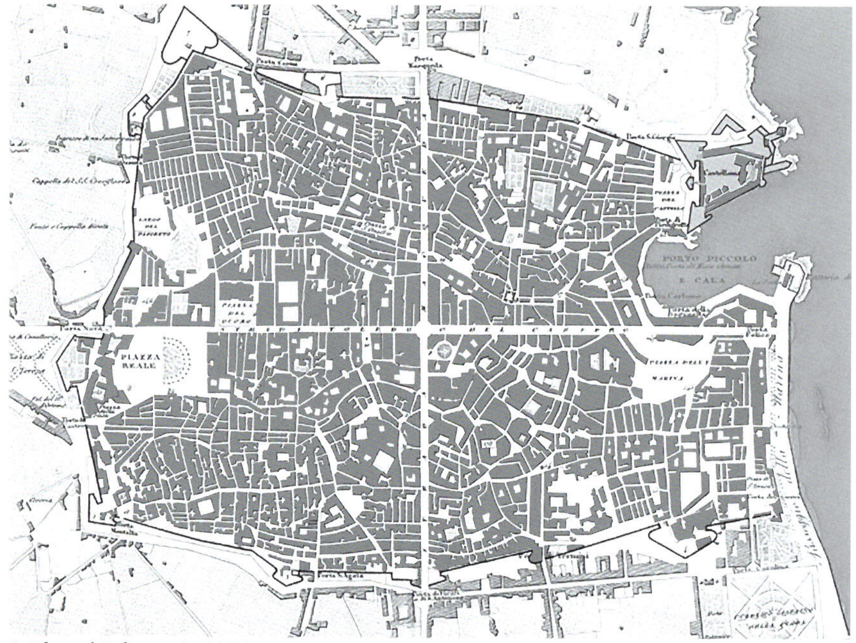

3. Plan of Palermo in 1844

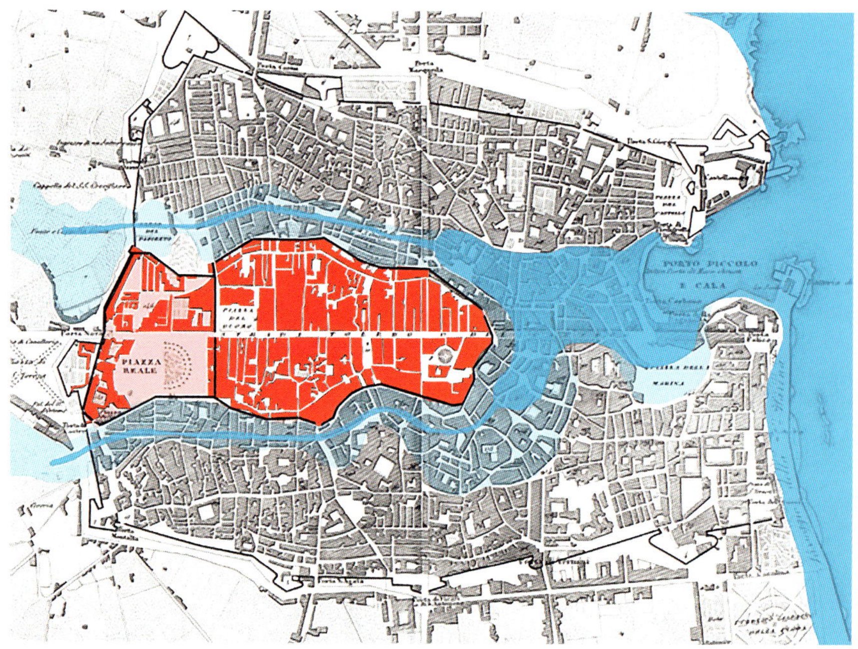

4. Extent of the Phoenician and Roman city

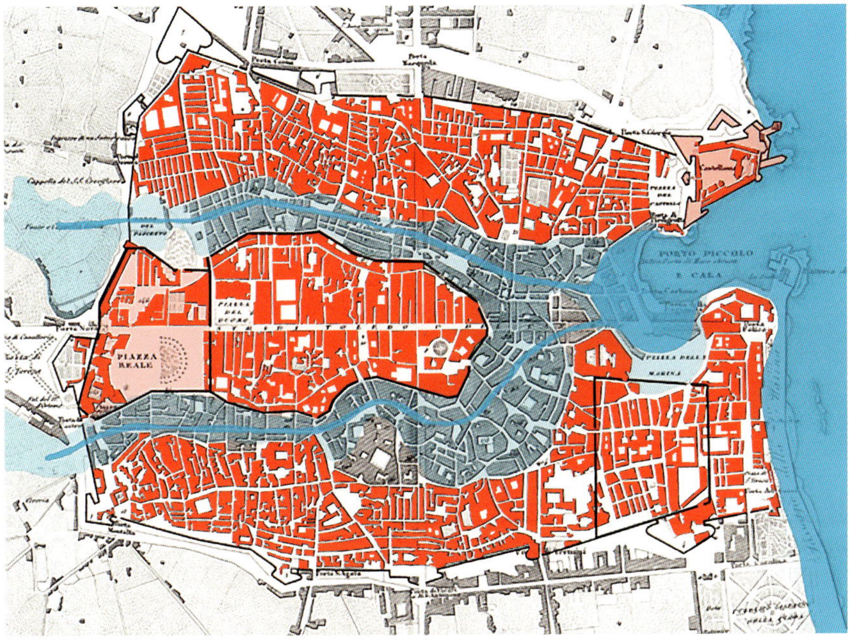

1. Extent of the Arab city

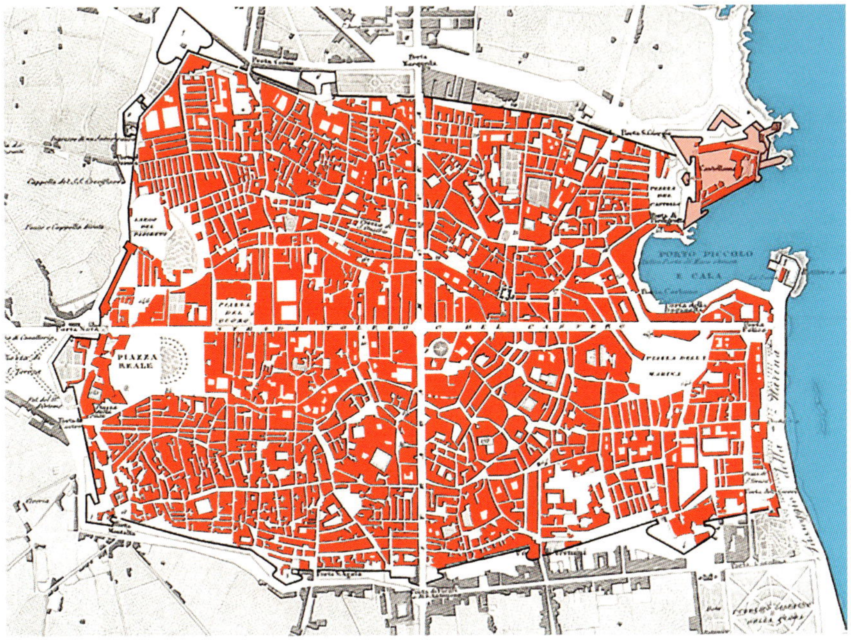

2. Extent of the seventeenth-century city

3. Plan of Palermo, Bambino, 1885

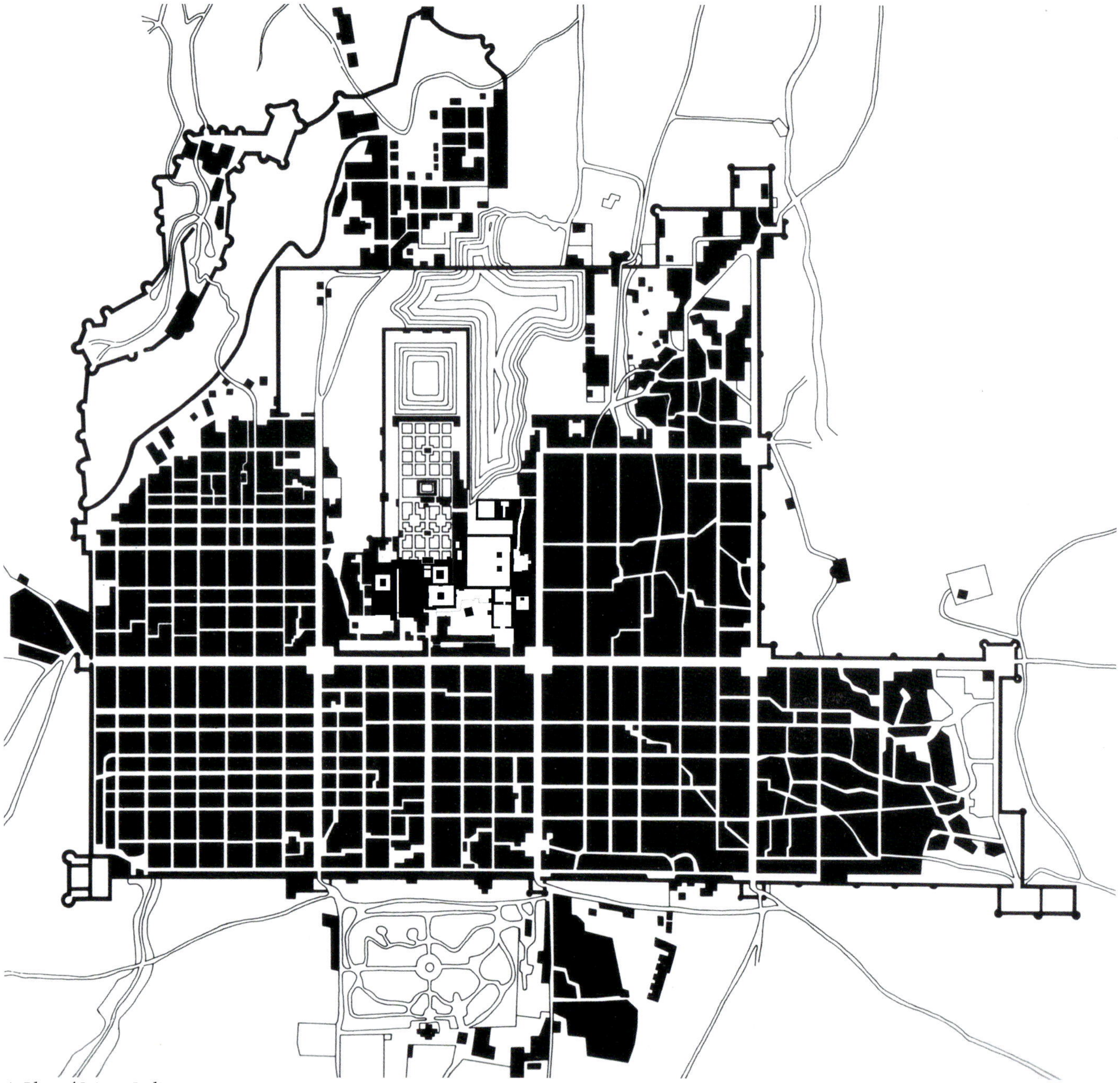

1. Plan of Jaipur, India

2. View of the City Palace and mountain

Jaipur

The desert city of Jaipur in Rajasthan, India, is a planned town founded by Jai Singh II, and designed by Vidyadhar Bhattacharya in 1727. The walled city was originally designed for 60,000 people, but today houses over 600,000.[8]

Conceptually, the plan is a nine-square grid of major streets lined with arcades and shops defining sectors that are about a half mile square. In the actual experience of the city, however, the cerebral clarity of the plan is masked by the vibrant, teeming chaos of contemporary life. Nevertheless, for nearly 300 years the plan has served as a controlling framework for internal change and development.

The royal palace, the City Palace, and its entourage of courtyards and gardens occupy the central two sectors. (The north–south street leading to the palace is a nineteenth-century addition.) The western residential sectors have generally retained their grid patterns, but those to the east have evolved into completely irregular patterns, and the demolition of the eastern parts of the wall allowed them to spread.

1. City Palace garden

2. Core building of the City Palace and courtyard

3. View of major streets and large square

4. Arcade and shops of major street

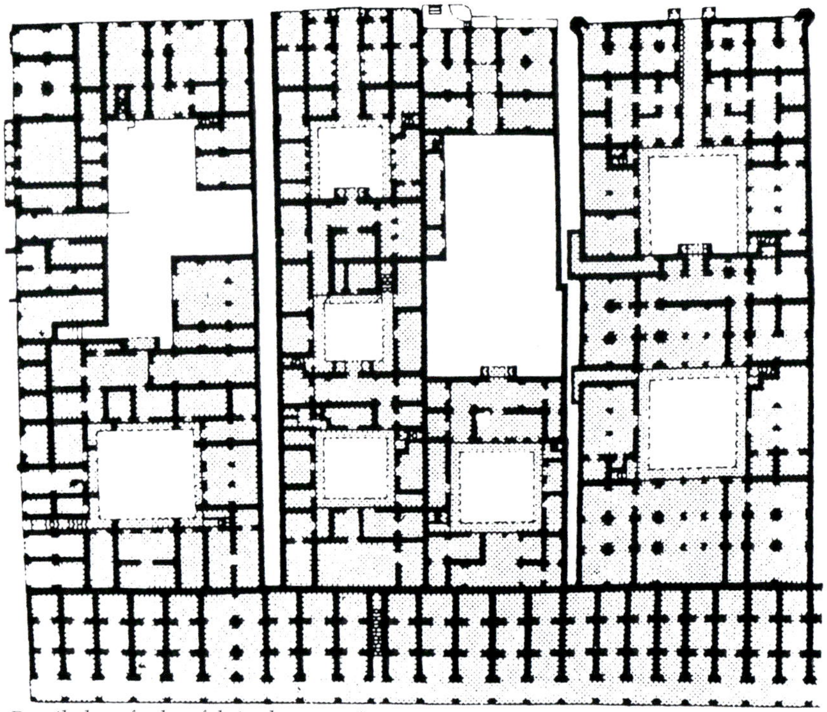

1. Detail plan of urban fabric along a major street

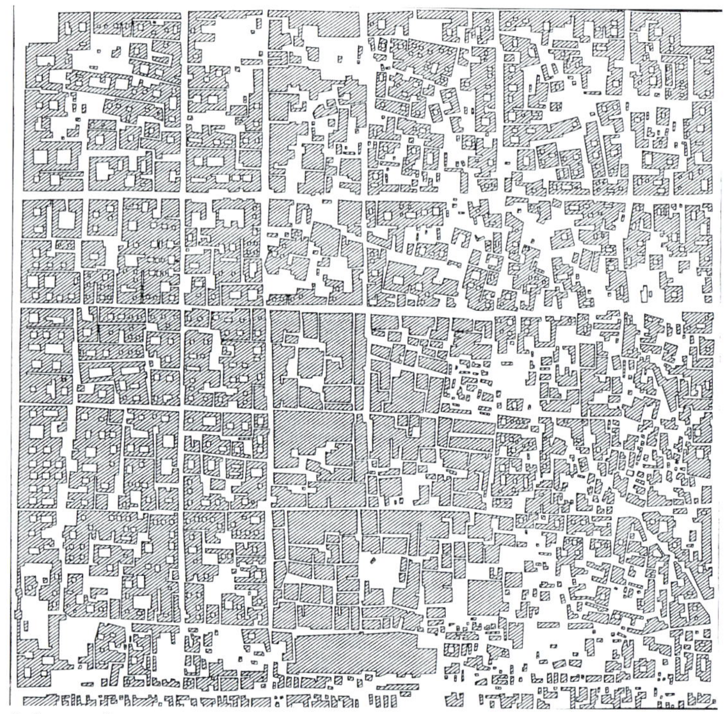

2. Sector plan

3. View of major street

4. View of the Hawa Mahal, Palace of the Winds

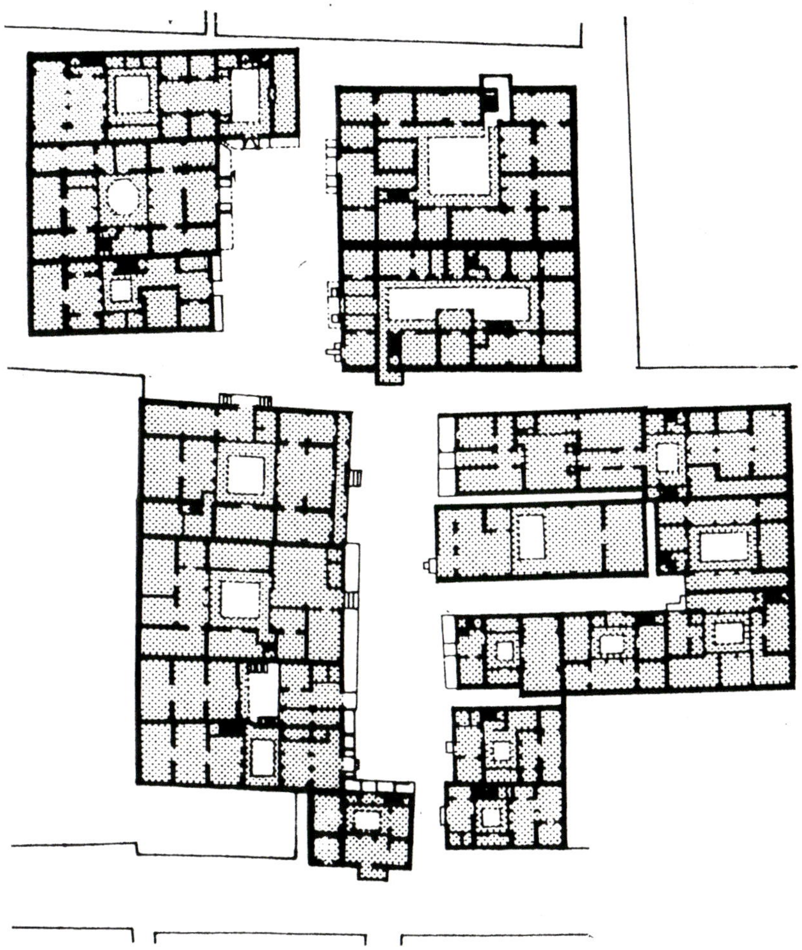

1. Plan detail plan of a sector

2. Aerial view of residential fabric

3. Aerial view of model

Major Streets and Urban Fabric

The city's sectors are bounded by large streets lined with arcades and shops. Houses in the urban fabric behind are not entered from these streets, but from a hierarchical network of secondary streets off the main ones. Thus, there is a progression from private courtyards, to community streets, to sector streets, and finally to large public areas. The sectors are multiuse, with commercial and retail interspersed with residential. A typical configuration is with shops on the ground floor and residences stepping down to rear courtyards. Small temples and shrines are also distributed throughout.

Color

Much of India's Mugal architecture, such as Fatepur Sikri, is made of red sandstone. Jaipur has no red sandstone, however, so the city was painted "pink" in the late nineteenth century for the visit of the English monarch.

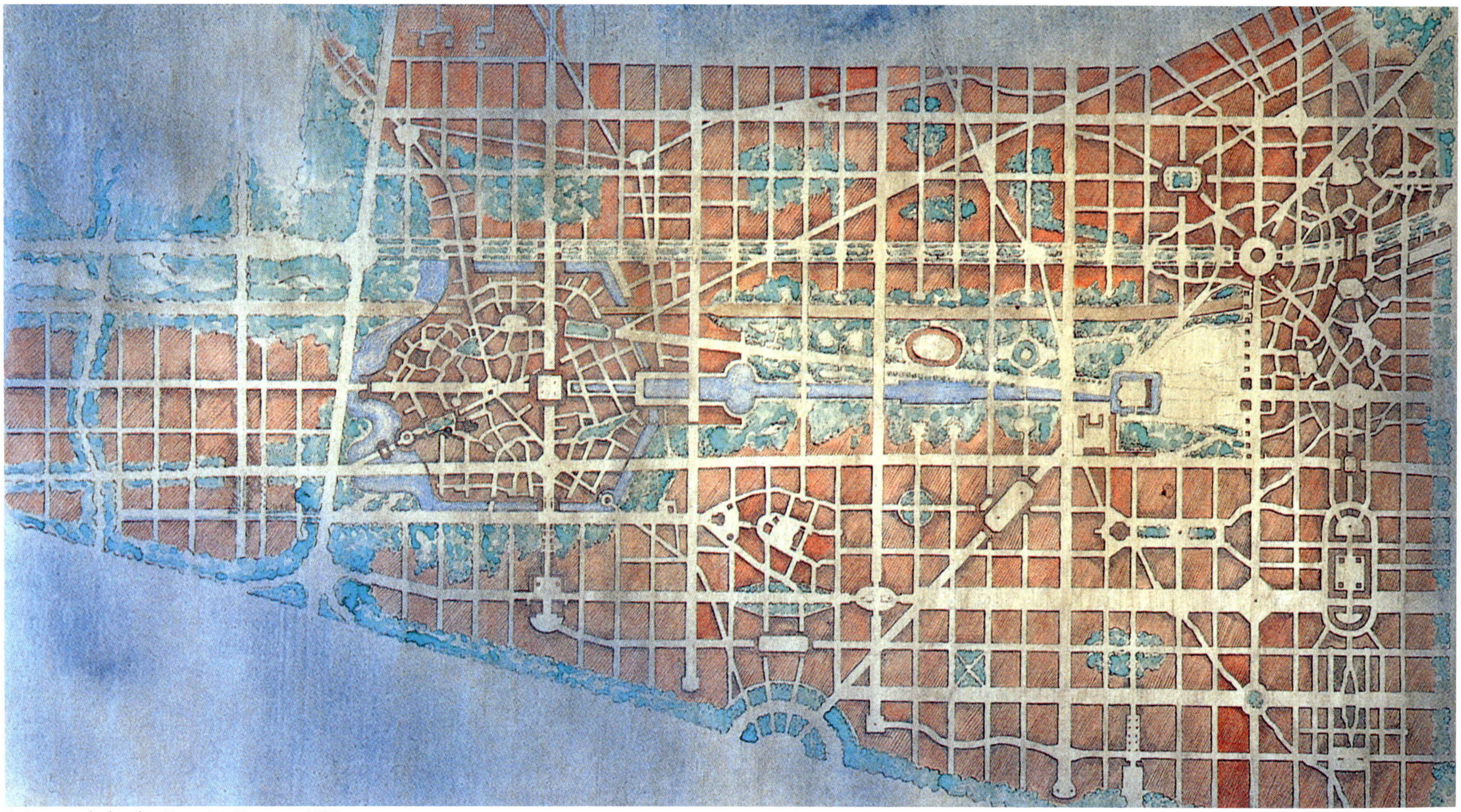

1. *Proposed plan for Bussy St. Georges, 1989*

Irregular Plans

Rob Krier was always more focused on the continuous structure of civic space than his brother, Leon. He naturally favored the perimeter block with its open interior and urban flexibility as the primary element of urban fabric. In other words, Rob made irregular blocks and regular spaces, whereas Leon favored smaller regular blocks and irregular spaces. Both, however, explored irregular plans.

Bussy St. Georges, 1989

Rob's predilection for idiosyncrasy is clear in the 1989 plan for Bussy St. Georges at Marne La Vallée, Paris.

To articulate and enliven the mega-grid developed by the planning authority, Krier Kohl reintroduced preexisting paths and diagonals, and embedded small-scale, irregular neighborhoods into the otherwise banal grid. Despite its obvious elegance, however, the plan was not accepted.[9]

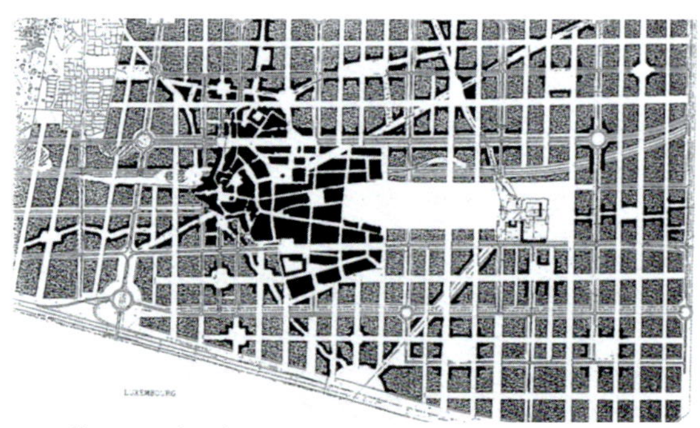

2. *Collage study of Luxembourg into the plan*

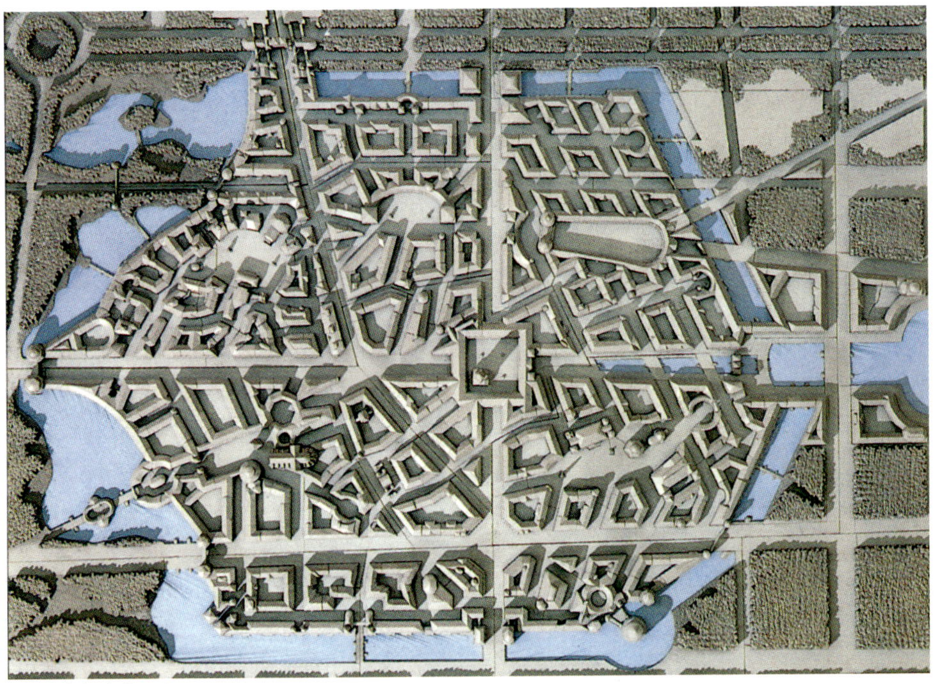

1. *Model of the city center*

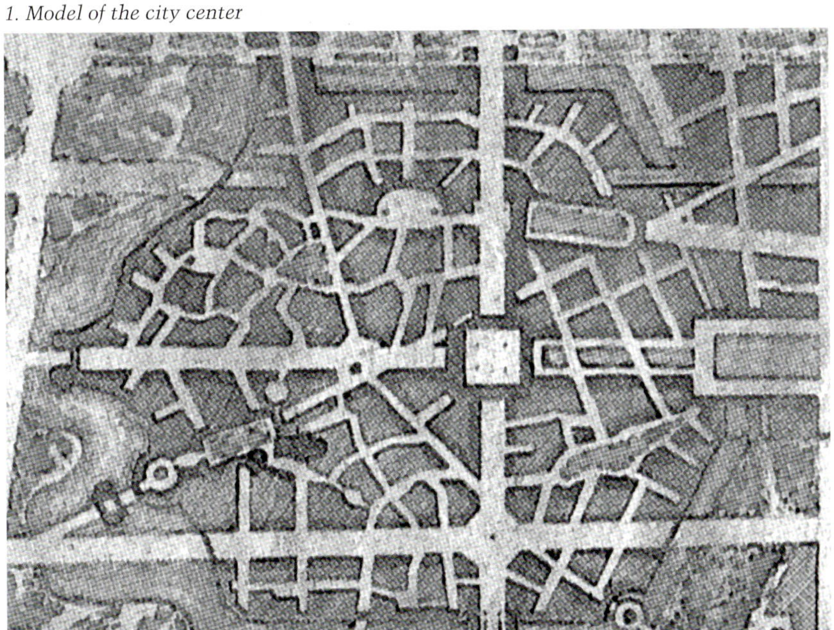

2. *Plan of the city center*

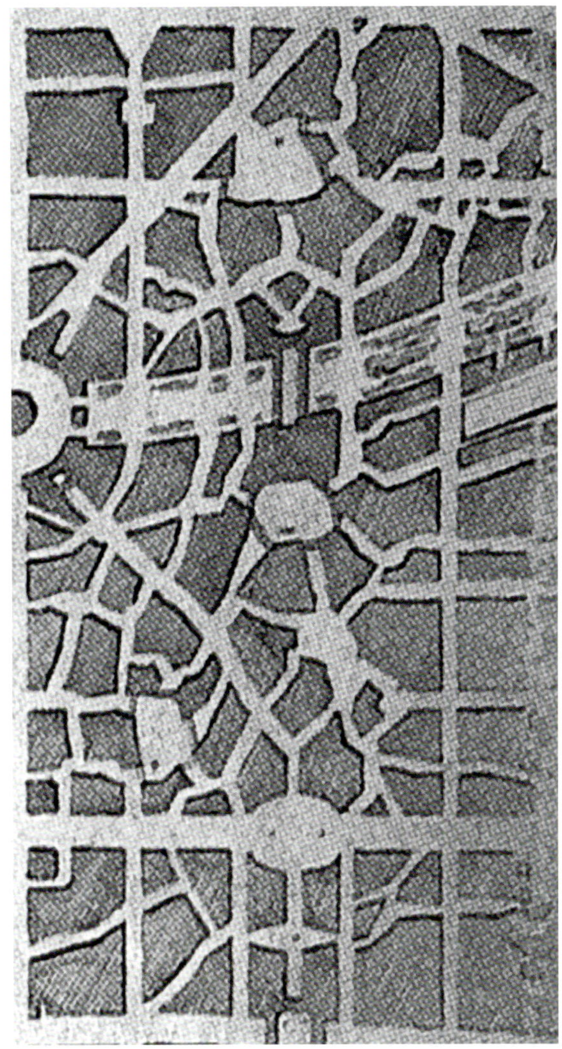

3. *Plan detail of a neighborhood*

Rational versus Artistic Planning

Rob Krier's 1975 book, *Stadtraum* was dedicated to Camillo Sitte, who, in his own 1889 book, *Der Städtebau*, extolled the virtues of irregular medieval plans and asymmetrical urban spaces. Even though Sitte's own plans were fundamentally regular, he promoted planning "according to artistic principles" rather than the street-focused practical planning of Stübben and other German planners. In this sense, Sitte was not reactionary, but revolutionary.

Notes

Foreword

1. Regarding the role of the urban block in city design, Rob Krier states: "the city block is the original cell of every urban design structure. It defines the network of routes around its edges and the building plot structure in the middle" (*Town Spaces*, 11.); and Leon Krier states: "The [urban] building block ... must be identified as the most important typological element in the composition of urban spaces, the key element of any urban pattern" (*Architecture & Urbanism 1967–1992*, 27).
2. See also S. Peterson, "Urban Design Tactics," Roma Interrotta, *Architectural Design* 49, no. 3–4 (1979), 76–81; and "Space and Anti-Space," *Harvard Architecture Review: Beyond the Modern Movement*, 1 (1980), 89–113.
3. W. Worringer, *Abstraction and Empathy: A Contribution to the Psychology of Style* (New York: International Universities Press, 1963). Translated by Michael Bullock from the German: *Abstraktion und Einfühlung* (1908). First published in the United States in 1953.
4. See R. Krier, *Kirchsteigfeld.*

Introduction

1. See H. D. F. Kitto, *The Greeks*, ch. iv.
2. C. W. Westfall. Unfortunately, neither Bill Westfall nor I seem to be able to identify the source of this quote.
3. See Dennis, *Court & Garden.*
4. Kostof, *City Shaped*, 26.
5. For the Uffizi and Vasari's Corridor, see M. Dennis, "Museum as Urban Design," *Perspecta 16*, 1980.
6. Scully.
7. R. Billows, "Cities," *A Companion to the Hellenistic World*, ed. A. Erskine (Malden, MA, and Oxford: Blackwell Publishing, 2003).
8. For Greek blocks and parcels, see Hoepfner; for New York City blocks, see Ballon.
9. Cappelletti.
10. Randolf.
11. See Argan.
12. See Crouch.
13. For Noto, see Tobriner *Genesis of Noto.*
14. Ballon.
15. Summerson, *Georgian London.*
16. See Mumford, *CIAM Discourse.*
17. See Mumford, *Defining Urban Design.*
18. Hurtt.
19. See McKibben, *Eaarth.*
20. See Owen.

I. THE PREINDUSTRIAL CITY

Greek Cities

1. Scully's *Earth* is entirely about this topic.
2. Billows, "Cities."
3. See Mertens, for beautifully illustrated plans.
4. Cherchiai, 62.
5. Mertens.
6. *Priene* is entirely devoted to the city.
7. Hoepfner.
8. *Priene.*
9. Levi, 188.
10. Ward-Perkins, 18.
11. Ibid., 14.
12. Hoepfner.
13. Bacon, 75.

Roman Cities

1. Gutkind, 17. This topic is complicated and controversial. See also Ward-Perkins, 25, and Castagnoli, 14–21.
2. Castagnoli, 100.
3. Brown, 17.
4. Ward-Perkins, 28.
5. Castagnoli, 100.
6. Brown, 1; Ward-Perkins, 27.
7. Ibid., 16.
8. Boëthius, 122.
9. Castagnoli, 100.
10. Fanelli, 193.
11. J.-P. Descoeudres, "History and Historical Sources," *The World of Pompeii*, 9.
12. Ibid., 15–16.
13. Castagnoli, 25–26.
14. H. Geertman, "The Urban Development of the Pre-Roman City," *The World of Pompeii*, 82.
15. Dobbins, 169.
16. Maiuri, 60.
17. Dobbins, conversation.
18. Ibid.

Medieval Bastides

1. Randolph gives a thorough explanation of the legal and procedural issues in the founding of Bastides, with extensive references.
2. Divorne et al. provide an excellent formal and typological analysis of the Bastides.
3. Randolph.
4. Kostof, *City Shaped*, 133.
5. Divorne.
6. Ibid.
7. Bentley, 111.
8. Ibid., 193.
9. Ibid., 56–60.

Renaissance Cities

1. P. J. Gärtner, *Filippo Brunellechi: 1377–1446* (Cologne: Könemann, 1998), 26.
2. M. A. Lavin, *Piero della Francesca: The Flagellation* (New York: Viking Press, 1972).
3. Argan, 11.
4. Ibid., 14.
5. Ibid., 5.
6. Pinto, 50.
7. See, for example, Bacon, 216; Kostov, *City Shaped*, 145; and, M. Bell, Unpublished lecture manuscript: "European Sources for Oglethorpe's Plan of Savannah," given at the Center for Advanced Study in the Visual Arts, National Gallery of Art, March 15, 1999.
8. See, for example, S. Anderson, "Savannah and the Issue of Precedent: City Plan as Resource," in *Settlements in the Americas: Cross-Cultural Perspectives*, ed. R. Bennett (Cranbury: Associated Universities, 1993).
9. The principal town-planning ordinances of "The Laws of the Indies" are reprinted in *The New City*, and in Crouch.
10. For a more extended discussion, see M. Dennis, and A. MacIntosh, "Landscape and the City," in *Landscape Urbanism and Its Discontents: Dissimulating the Sustainable City*, A. Duany, and E. Talen, eds. (Gabriola Island, BC: New Society Publishers, 2013).
11. S. Peterson, lecture at Cornell University, ca. 1972.

Baroque Cities

1. J. W. Reps, *The Making of Urban America: A History of City Planning in the United States* (Princeton: Princeton University Press, 1965), 249. See also S. W. Berg, *Grand Avenues: The Story of Pierre Charles L'Enfant, the French Visionary Who Designed Washington, D.C.* (New York: Random House, Vintage Books, 2008).
2. Tobriner, 11.
3. Ibid., 24.
4. Ibid., 25.
5. Ibid., 27.
6. Ibid., 43.
7. Ibid., 29.
8. Franca, *Citta Dell'Illuminismo.*
9. Youngson.

Great London Estates

1. F. H. W. Sheppard, ed. "The Architecture of the Piazza and St. Paul's Church," *Survey of London, volume 36: Covent Garden* (1970), 64–76. See also J. Summerson, *Inigo Jones* (Harmondsworth: Penguin, 1983), 85.
2. Summerson, *Georgian London*, 39–41.
3. Ibid., 42.

II. THE INDUSTRIAL CITY

Nineteenth-Century Cities

Paris

1. Dennis, *Court & Garden.*
2. M.-A. Laugier, *An Essay on Architecture* (Los Angeles: Hennessey & Ingalls, 1977), 95.
3. For a thorough study of arcades, see J. F. Geist, *Arcades: The History of a Building Type* (Cambridge: MIT Press, 1983).
4. See Alphand, *Les Promenades*; also M. Dennis and A. MacIntosh, "Landscape and the City," ed. A. Duany, and E. Talen; and Jordan.
5. Pinkney.

6. H. Lipstadt, "Housing the Bourgeoisie: César Daly and the Ideal Home," with an introduction by A. Vidler, *Oppositions* 8 (spring 1977), 33–47.
7. P. Panerai et al., "Haussmannien Paris: 1853–82," *Urban Forms: The Death and Life of the Urban Block* (Oxford: Architectural Press, 2005), 1–29.
8. For a compendium of squares, see R. Auzelle, *Encyclopédie de l'urbanisme* (Paris: Vincent, 1947).
9. Alphand, *Promenades*, and Dennis, "Landscape."

New York City

10. W. Rybczynski, *A Clearing in the Distance: Frederick Law Olmsted and America in the 19th Century* (New York: Scribner, 1999).
11. Cohen, 20.
12. Ibid., 84.
13. Schuyler, 18.
14. Cohen, 102.
15. Ibid., 104.1.
16. Ibid., 22.
17. Plunz.
18. Alpern, 12.
19. Cohen, 136.
20. Schuyler, 5.

Boston

21. W. M. Whitehill, *Boston: A Topographical History* (Cambridge: Harvard University Press, 1968).

Florence

22. Fei, 11.
23. Ibid., 33.
24. Arnolfo also planned the Florentine new town, San Giovanni Valdarno.
25. Fei, 41–45
26. Ibid., 41.
27. See M. Dennis, "The Uffizi: Museum as Urban Design," *Perspecta* 16: 63–71.
28. Fanelli, 199.
29. Ibid., 204.
30. Ibid., 202.
31. Ibid., 203.

Barcelona

32. I. Cerdà, *Teoría general.*
33. Busquets, *Barcelona*, 24–28.
34. Ibid., 33–45.
35. Ibid., 63.
36. M. D. Clota, "Considerations on the Cerdà City Layout," *Treballs*, 368.
37. Ibid.
38. Busquets, *Barcelona*, 66.
39. Ibid., 108.
40. Ibid., 110.
41. For a timeline of nineteenth-century developments, see A. Soria i Puig, "The Project and its Circumstances," *Treballs*, 308–324.
42. Ibid., 310.
43. Ibid., 312.
44. Ibid., 313.
45. Ibid., 315–21.
46. Busquets, *Barcelona*, 122–142.
47. See *Treballs*, for a thorough discussion and illustrations of Cerdà's plan and elements.
48. Busquets, *Barcelona*, 191–194.

Proto-Modern Urbanists

1. M. A. Laugier, *An Essay on Archjitecture* (Los Angeles: Hennessey & Ingalls, 1977), 128.
2. Ibid., 95.
3. Ibid., 127.

Joseph Stübben

4. Ladd, 3.
5. Ibid., 40, 43.
6. Ladd, 85, and Collins, 44.
7. Stübben.
8. Ibid.
9. Ladd, 104.
10. Sitte, 45.
11. Stübben.
12. Stübben.
13. Ladd, 104.
14. Stübben.
15. Ladd, 97.
16. Ibid.
17. Ibid.
18. Ibid.
19. Ibid.

Camillo Sitte

20. See especially Collins, *Camillo Sitte*; and Bohl, *Sitte*.
21. There were significant differences in many of the editions. See Collins, *Camillo Sitte*, chapter 7, "The Successive Editions and Translations of the Book," 71.
22. Ibid., 141–2.
23. Ibid., 140.
24. Ibid., 170.
25. Ibid., 279–81.
26. Ibid., 226.
27. Ibid., note 21.

H. P. Berlage

28. Polano.
29. V. van Rossem, "Berlage and the Culture of City Planning," *Hendrik Petrus Berlage*, 46.

Otto Wagner and Daniel Burnham

30. V. M. Lampugnani, "Vienna Fin-de-siècle: Between Artistic City Planning and Unlimited Metropolis," in Bohl.
31. Wagner, "The Development of a Great City."
32. Ibid.
33. Wilson.
34. Burnham, *Plan.*
35. Ibid., Wagner, and Burnham.
36. The Otis safety elevator was invented in 1852 and first used in a building in 1857. Steel developed from 1856, and was used in the first skyscraper, the Home Insurance Building by William Le Baron Jenney, in 1883–85.

Eugène Hénard

37. Wolf, 20.
38. Ibid., 23.
39. Hénard, "Cities of the Future."
40. Ibid.
41. Wolf, 9, 21.
42. Hénard, "Cities of the Future."
43. Ibid.
44. Ibid.

The Garden City

45. Howard, *Garden Cities*.

Tony Garnier

46. Garnier's other works are illustrated in T. Garnier, *Tony Garnier 1869–1948*, (1990).
47. Mariani, 19.
48. See Weibenson for Garnier's background and cultural context.
49. See Mariani for detailed plans.
50. See T. Garnier, *Une Cité Industrielle*, for color illustrations.
51. Mariani.
52. Ibid.

The Modernist City

Le Corbusier & CIAM

1. See Le Corbusier, *New World of Space* (New York: Reynal and Hitchcock, 1948).
2. D. Cooper, *The Cubist Epoch* (London and New York: Phaidon Press Limited, 1971), 11.
3. The concept of frontality was postulated by the nineteenth-century German sculptor Adolf von Hildebrand in *Das Problem der Form in der bildenden Kunst*, 1893, published in English as *The Problem of Form in Painting and Sculpture*, 1907.
4. See Dennis, *Court & Garden*.
5. See C. Rowe and R. Slutzky, "Transparency: Literal and Phenomenal," *The Mathematics of the Ideal Villa and Other Essays* (Cambridge: MIT Press, 1987).
6. See W. J. R. Curtis, *Le Corbusier:*

Ideas and Forms.
7. Le Corbusier, *Oeuvre complète 1910–1929.*
8. Ibid., 34.
9. Ibid.
10. Ibid.
11. Ibid.
12. Le Corbusier, *La Ville Radieuse*, 1935.
13. For CIAM see E. P. Mumford, *The CIAM Discourse on Urbanism.*
14. Le Corbusier, *Oeuvre complète 1934–1938.*
15. For the destruction of Dresden, see F. Taylor, *Dresden: Tuesday, February 13, 1945* (New York: Harper Collins, 2004).
16. For the replanning of Dresden, see *Dresden 1992: Erfahrungen—Perspektiven* (Cologne: R. Müller, 1992).
17. Le Corbusier, *Oeuvre complète 1942–1946*, 132–139.
18. Le Corbusier, *Oeuvre complète 1946–1952*, 116–161.
19. Ibid., 58–65.
20. Mumford

Team X

21. CIAM 8.
22. *Team 10*, 12.
23. Ibid., 42–43.
24. See Cluster City diagram, *Team 10 Primer*, 51.
25. *Le Corbusier 1910–65*, 248–49.
26. *Team 10 Primer*, 56.
27. *Team 10*, 43.
28. *Primer*, op cit, 51.
29. *Team 10*, op cit, 174–77.
30. For extensive documentation of Toulouse Le Mirail, see Gruet; also *Team 10*, 166–69; and 96–97 for Bilbao.
31. See T. Avermaete, "Mat-Building: Team 10's Reinvention of the Critical Capacity of the Urban Tissue," *Team 10*, 307–312.
32. *Team 10*, 135, 186–89.
33. Ibid., 132–34.
34. Conversation with Guillermo Jullian de la Fuente, 1970s.
35. *Team 10*, 164.
36. Ibid., 110–11.
37. Ibid., 93–94.
38. Ibid., 170–73.
39. It is surprising that this oft-reproduced scheme is repeatedly passed off as a "linear city," when it is not urban at all, but suburban.
40. *Team 10*, 292.
41. Bakema, "Stad op Pampus."
42. I also began teaching at Cornell University in the fall of 1968—the same time that Ungers began as Chair of the Department of Architecture.
43. *Team 10*, 180.

III. THE POSTINDUSTRIAL CITY

The Recovery of the City

1. A. P. Latini, *Battery Park City, New York: Principe e tecniche di* Urban Design *attraverso la storia di un modello* (Roma: Officina Edizione, 2001).
2. As quoted in T. H. O'Connor, *Building a New Boston: Politics and Urban Renewal 1950–1970* (Boston: Northeastern University Press, 1993), 67, from R. B. Adams, Jr., *The Boston Money Tree* (New York: Crowell, 1977), 305.
3. Mumford, *Defining Urban Design*, 28.
4. Ibid.
5. *The Heart of the City: Towards the Humanisation of Urban Life*, J. Tyrwhitt, J. l. Sert, and E. N. Rogers, eds. (New York: Pellegrini and Cudahy, 1952).
6. J. L. Sert, "Centres of Community Life," *The Heart of the City*, 3.
7. W. Gropius, "Discussion on Italian Piazzas," *The Heart of the City*, 74.
8. See Mumford, *Defining Urban Design*, 109–113.
9. The introduction to Jacobs's 1961 book begins as follows: "This book is an attack on current city planning and rebuilding. It is also, and mostly, an attempt to introduce new principles of city planning and rebuilding, different and even opposite from those now taught in everything from schools of architecture and planning to the Sunday supplements and women's magazines. It is an attack ... on the principles and aims that have shaped modern, orthodox city planning and rebuilding." In a lecture at the University of Oregon in 1962, the architecture critic for the San Francisco Chronicle and an apologist for modernist planning, Allan Temko, dismissively referred to Jacobs as "a sentimental regressionist." After more than a half-century, however, her prescient book remains surprisingly relevant and vivid.
10. L. W. Kennedy, *Planning the City upon a Hill: Boston since 1630* (Amherst: University of Massachusetts Press, 1992), 159.
11. Adams, Howard, and Greeley Inc., *Government Center—Boston 1959* (Boston: Prepared for the City Planning Board, 1959), 6. See also J. R. Myer, and M. H. Myer, *People & Places: Connections between the Inner and Outer Landscape* (Hanover: Sandwich Publications, 2006), 62–65.
12. Myer
13. Kennedy, 178. See also W. M. Whitehill, *Boston: A Topographical History* (Cambridge: Harvard University Press, 1968), 203–211.
14. Myer, 65–70.
15. Rowe, *Mathematics.*
16. S. Hurtt, "Conjectures on Urban Form: The Cornell Urban Design Studio 1963–1982," *The Cornell Journal of Architecture 2* (Ithaca: Cornell University Department of Architecture, 1982), 63, 86–87.
17. See *The Cornell Journal of Architecture* 2, 1982.
18. Hurtt.
19. Ibid., 88–91.
20. C. Rowe and F. Koetter, *Collage City* (Cambridge: MIT Press, 1979); and Dennis, *Court & Garden.*
21. S. Peterson, "Urban Design Tactics," *Architectural Design 49*, no. 3–4, Roma Interrotta (1979), 76–81.
22. Dennis.
23. *Le Corbusier et Pierre Jeanneret: Oeuvre complète 1910–1929, 118.*
24. Giedion, *Space, Time and Architecture*, 822–823. In the same passage, Giedion continues: "Haussmann's endless streets belonged not only in their architectural features but also in their very conception to the artistic vision born of the Renaissance: optical perspective. Today we must deal with the city from a new aspect, dictated by the advent of the automobile, based on technical considerations, and belonging to the artistic vision born out of our period—space-time."
25. Smithson, *Team 10 Primer*, 76.
26. L. Krier, *Drawings: 1967–1980* (Brussels: Archives D'Architecture Moderne, 1981), xv.
27. C. Rowe, "Introduction," in *Urban Space* (New York: Rizzoli, 1979), 7–8.
28. L. Krier, "The Reconstruction of the City," in *Rational Architecture* (Brussels: Archives D'Architecture Moderne, 1978).
29. *Rational Architecture*, 183.
30. *Archives D'Architecture Moderne*, no. 21, 1981, 79–80.
31. L. Krier, for years a self-described "paper tiger," has been a prolific promoter. This section is derived from the many publications in the bibliography.

32. L. Krier, *Architecture & Urban Design*, 99.
33. The fourth form of public space was used by Rob Krier, but not by Leon.
34. L. Krier, *Houses, Palaces, Cities*, 45–46.
35. L. Krier, *Architecture & Urban Design*, 64–71.
36. Ibid., 88–101.
37. R. Krier, *Stadtraum.*
38. P. Katz, 206–211.
39. Peterson Littenberg Architects.
40. Katz, 146–153.
41. A. H. Koetter, "Monumentalism and the American City," *Harvard Architectural Review* (Cambridge: MIT Press, 1984); *Koetter Kim & Associates: Place Time* (New York: Rizzoli, 1997).
42. Koetter Kim, 34–43.
43. See M. Dennis, "On Campus Design and Planning," *Modulus 23*, 1995.
44. "Urban Design and Planning," *Progressive Architecture*, January, 1989, 113–115; M. Schmertz, "Project Diary: New Architecture for a Classic Campus," *Architectural Record*, August 1997, 54–65.
45. *Cornell Journal of Architecture 2* (Ithaca: Cornell University Department of Architecture, 1982), 130.
46. L. Krier, *Architecture & Urban Design*, 226–245.
47. Ibid., 260–273.
48. Katz, 2–17.
49. Katz.
50. Ibid., xi–xxi.
51. P. Calthorpe, "The Region," *The New Urbanism*, xi.
52. Ibid., xvi.
53. Ibid.
54. A. Duany, and E. Plater-Zyberk, "The Neighborhood, the District and the Corridor," *The New Urbanism*, xvii–xx.
55. E. Moule, and S. Polyzoides, "The Street, the Block and the Building," *The New Urbanism*, xxi–xxiv.
56. Ibid., xxi.
57. Ibid., xxiii.
55. Ibid., xxiv.
59. Ibid., 96–99.
60. Calthorpe, *The Next American Metropolis*, 130–133.
61. Ibid., 160–163.
62. Ibid., 198–205.
63. Solomon, E.T.C., a WRT Company, *Getting It Right: Preventing Sprawl in Coyote Valley*, San Francisco, 2003.
64. R. Krier, *Potsdam Kirchsteigfeld.*
65. Ibid., 9.
66. *Rob Krier: Architecture and Urban Design*, 124–125; also *Town Spaces*, 186–201.
67. R. Krier, *Town Spaces*, 219–233.
68. www.archkk.com/urbanism/.
69. Ibid.
70. www.west8.nl/projects/all/borneo_sporenburg/.
71. www.posdarmaxwan.nl/selected-projects/leiden-cs/#/t_3497.
72. www.oma.eu/projects/.
73. Foster + Partners
74. P. Calthorpe, *Urbanism in the age of Climate Change*, 7.
75. Ibid., 4.
76. Ibid.
77. www.calthorpe.com/international-work.
78. P. Calthorpe, *Low Carbon Cities* (Berkeley: Calthorpe Associates, n.d.

Twenty-first-Century Urbanism

The Contemporary Environment

1. There is greater and greater consensus that the Earth has passed the tipping point into irreversible climate change, leading to serious discussions about a possible sixth extinction. Regarding climate change, see McKibben, 15–27; and Hartmann, 60–83. Regarding extinction, see R. E. Leaky and R. Lewin, *The Sixth Extinction: Patterns of Life and the Future of Humankind* (New York: Anchor Books, 1996); and E Kolbert, *The Sixth Extinction: An Unnatural History* (New York: Henry Holt, 2014).
2. http://8020vision.com/2010/06/21/the-real-population-problem/.
3. See L. R. Brown, *Who Will Feed China: Wake-up Call for a Small Planet* (New York: W. W. Norton & Company,1995); and *Full Planet, Empty Plates: The New Geopolitics of Food Scarcity* (New York: W. W. Norton, 2012).
4. Calthorpe, 5.
5. See note 1 of this chapter.
6. See, M. White, and L. White, *The Intellectual Versus the City: From Thomas Jefferson to Frank Lloyd Wright*, (Cambridge: Harvard University Press and MIT Press, 1962).
7. The United States is the third largest country in the world, with a current population of about 316,000,000 distributed as follows: cities 32%, suburbs 52%, and rural 16%. See, W. H. Frey, Brookings Institution, noted by P. Applebome, in "Suburban Life, Secret or Open, Is Complicated," *New York Times*, Thursday, July 1, 2010. The population is expected to increase by approximately 110,000,000 by 2050. If the current distribution continues the American suburbs would increase by some 57,000,000.
8. Owen; See also D. Kelbaugh, "Landscape Urbanism, New Urbanism and the Environmental Paradox of Cities," in *Landscape Urbanism*, 57–86.
9. Center for Neighborhood Technology, http//:www.cnt.org./media/TOD-Potential-GHG-Emissions-Growth.FINAL_.pdf.
10. Calthorpe, plates 3–5.
11. Ibid.

Excursus: Irregular & Composite Plans

1. See, "The Recovery of the City."
2. Jim Tice and others have made a substantive study of the Nolli plan, sponsored by the University of Oregon, on the web: nolli.uoregon.edu.
3. For expansion plans of Rome, see R. Cassetti, *Roma e Lazio 1870–1945* (Rome: Gangemi Editori).
4. G. Perocco and A. Salvadori, *Civilta di Venezia* (Venice: Stamperia di Venezia Editrice, 1973).
5. Ibid., 361.
6. Ibid.
7. G. Blandi, Palermo: *Storia dello sviluppo urbanistico della citta dalle origini all'eta contemporanea* (Palermo: Edizioni Axon Sicilia, 1998); see also C. De Seta and L. Di Mauro. *Palermo* (Roma-Bari: Laterza, 1980).
8. Conversation with Jaipur city planner.
9. R. Krier, *Rob Krier*, 130–133; also, R. Krier, *Town Spaces*, 34–37.

Bibliography

The following bibliographical references are listed in the sequence of the book's chapters, after the general sources.

General Urban History

Bacon, E. N. *Design of Cities.* London: Penguin, 1967.

Benevolo, L. *The History of the City*. Cambridge: MIT Press, 1988.

Hiorns, F. R. *Town-Building In History: An Outline Review of Conditions, Influences, Ideas, and Methods Affecting "Planned" Towns Through Five Thousand Years.* London: George G. Harrap, 1956.

Kostof, S. *The City Shaped: Urban Patterns and Meaning Through History*. London: Thames and Hudson, 1991.

———. *The City Assembled: The Elements of Urban Form Through History*. London: Thames and Hudson, 1992.

Morris, A. E. J. *History of Urban Form: Prehistory to the Renaissance*. London: George Godwin, 1972.

Triggs, H. I. *Town Planning: Past, Present and Possible.* London: Methuen, 1911.

I. THE PREINDUSTRIAL CITY

Greek Cities

Castagnoli, F. *Orthogonal Town Planning in Antiquity.* English translation by MIT. Cambridge: MIT Press, 1971.

Cerchiai, L., L. Jannelli, and F. Longo. *Greek Cities of Magna Graecia and Sicily*. Verona: Arsenale Editrici, 2004.

Erskine, A., ed. *A Companion to the Hellenistic World*. Malden, MA: Blackwell, 2007.

Foundation of the Hellenic World, Athens & Center for Hellenistic Studies, Harvard University. *Priene,* 2nd edition, Cambridge: 2005.

Hoepfner, W. and E. Schwandner. *Haus und Stadt im klassischen Griechenland.* Munich: 1994.

Kriesis, A. *Greek Town Planning.* Athens: 1965.

Martienssen, R. D. *The Idea of Space in Greek Architecture.* Johannesburg: Witwatersrand University Press, 1956.

Mertens, D. *Città e monumenti dei Greci d'Occidente: Dalla colonizzazione alla crisi di fine V secolo a.C.* Rome: "L'Erma" di Bretschneider, 2006.

Scully, V. *The Earth the Temple and the Gods: Greek Sacred Architecture*, revised edition. New York and London: Frederick A. Praeger, 1969.

Ward-Perkins, J. B. *Cities of Ancient Greece and Italy: Planning in Classical Antiquity.* New York: Braziller, 1974.

Roman Cities

Barnow, Finn. *The City of the Landowner.* Royal Danish Academy of Fine Arts School of Architecture, 2002.

Barton, I. M., et. al. *Roman Public Buildings,* Exeter: University of Exeter Press, 1989.

———. *Roman Domestic Buildings.* Exeter: University of Exeter Press, 1996.

Boëthius, A., and J. B. Ward-Perkins. *Etruscan and Roman Architecture*. Harmondsworth: Penguin, 1970.

Brown, F. E. *Cosa: The Making of a Roman Town.* Ann Arbor: University of Michigan Press, 1980.

Calza, G., and G. Becatti. *Ostia*. Rome: Istituto Poligrafico e Zecca dello Stato S.P.A., 2008. (Revised by M. F. Squarciapino.)

Cappelletti, D. "Between External and Internal Space: *An Urban Transition.*" Thesis, MIT, 2012.

Castagnoli, F. *Orthogonal Town Planning in Antiquity.* English translation by MIT. Cambridge: MIT Press, 1971.

Dobbins, J. J., and P. W. Foss, eds. *The World of Pompeii*. New York and London: Routledge, 2008.

Ellis, S. J. R. ed. *The Making of Pompeii:Studies in the History and Urban Development of an Ancient Town*. Portsmouth, RI: Journal of Roman Archaeology, 2011.

Grimal, P. *Roman Cities.* Wisconsin: University of Wisconsin Press, 1983.

MacDonald, W. L. *The Architecture of the Roman Empire.* New Haven and London: Yale University Press, 1986.

Maiuri, A. *Pompeii*. Rome: Istituto Poligrafico dello Stato, 1954.

Nash, E. *Roman Towns.* New York: J.J. Augustin, 1944.

Sear, F. *Roman Architecture.* London: B. T. Batsford, 1982.

Stambaugh, J. E. *The Ancient Roman City*. Baltimore and London: The Johns Hopkins University Press, 1988.

Vitruvius. *Ten Books on Architecture.* Cambridge: The Press Syndicate of the University of Cambridge, 1999.

Ward-Perkins, J. B. *Cities of Ancient Greece and Italy: Planning in Classical Antiquity.* New York, 1974.

Medieval Bastides

Bentley, J. *Fort Towns of France: The Bastides of the Dordogne & Aquitaine.* London: Tauris Parke Books, in association with KEA Publishing Services, 1993.

Divorne, F., and B. Gendre, B. Lavergne, and P. Panerai. *Les Bastides d'Aquitaine, du Bas-Languedoc et du Béarn: Essai sur la régularité.* Bruxelles: Aux Archives d'architecture moderne, 1985.

Lauret, A. *Bastides: Villes Nouvelles du Moyen Age.* Milan: Etudes & Communication, 1988.

Lilley, K. D. *Urban Life in the Middle Ages, 1000–1450.* New York: Palgrave, Houndmills, Basingstoke, Hampshire, 2002.

Randolph, A. "The Bastides of Southwest France," *Art Bulletin* 77, no. 2 (Jun. 1995): 290–307.

Triggs, H. Inigo. *Town Planning: Past, Present, and Possible.* London: Methuen, 1909.

Renaissance Cities

Argan, G. C. *The Renaissance City.* New York: Braziller, 1970, 1969.

Boscarino, S. *Sicilia Barocca: Architettura e Citta, 1610–1760.* Rome: Officina, 1981.

Cornish, J., and J. Osborne. *Urbino: The Story of a Renaissance City*. Chicago: University of Chicago Press, 2003.

Muntean, L. "Geometries of Power: From Palmanova to the American Grid." *Moreana* 43, no. 166 (2006): 151.

Pinto, J. A. "Origins and Development of the Ichnographic City Plan." *Journal of the Society of Architectural Historians* 35, no. 1 (Mar. 1976) 35–50.

Silvetti, J. *Architectural and urban environments of Sicily = Ambiente architettonici e urbanistici della Sicilia.* Cambridge: Harvard University Graduate School of Design, 1989.

Tobriner, S. *The Genesis of Noto.* Berkeley: University of California Press, 1982.

Whitfield, P. *Cities of the World: A History in Maps.* Berkeley: University of California Press, 2005.

The Laws of the Indies

Crouch, D. P., D. J. Garr, and A. I. Mundigo. *Spanish City Planning in North America*. Cambridge: MIT Press, 1982.

Frontado S, and J. Guillermo. "Las Leyes De Indias: Observations of Its Influence on the Physical Space in the Latin American Colonial Cities." Thesis (M. Arch. A.S.), Massachusetts Institute of Technology, Dept. of Architecture, 1980.

Lejeune, J.-F. *Cruelty and Utopia: Cities and Landscapes of Latin America*. New York: Princeton Architectural Press, 2005.

The University of Miami School of Architecture. *The New City: Foundations*, vol. 1. New York: Princeton Architectural Press, 1991.

Baroque Cities

Noto

Adler, N. L. "Noto, prelude and coda to the rebuilding of a city." *Konsthistorisk Tidskrift* 55, no. 3 (1986): 122–135.

Brambilla, G. *Principi di Insediamento e Logiche di Trasformazione del Disegno Urbano in Sicilia*. Reggio: Iiritie Editore, 2004.

Canale, C. G.. *Noto—La Struttura Continua Della Citta Tardo-Barocca*. Palermo: S. F. Flaccovio, Editore, 1976.

Gutkind, E. A. *Urban Development in Southern Europe: Italy and Greece*. International History of City Development—Volume IV. New York: Free Press, 1969.

Hofer, P. *Noto: Idealstadt und Stadtraum im Sizilianischen 18. Fahrhundert*. Zurich: Instiut fur Geschichte und Theorie der Architektur Eidgenossische Technische Hochschule, 1996.

Ide, J. J. "Noto, the Perfect Baroque City," *Royal Institute of British Architects Journal* 66 (1958): 11–15.

Krämer, A. "Architettura e decorazione: Fonti e modelli del Barocco in Sicilia orientale." *Palladio* 21 (Jan.–June 1998): 47–70.

Mollica, E., and F. Santalucia. "Le chiesa di Santa Maria dell'Arco a Noto: analisi strutturale e criteri d'intervento." *Annali del barocco in Sicilia* 1 (1994): 91–103.

Neil, E. H. "Noto, Idealstadt und Stadtraum im Sizilianischen 18. Jahrhundert" [by] Paul Hofer [book review]. *Journal of the Society of Architectural Historians* 57, no. 4 (Dec. 1998): 471–473.

Silvetti, J. *Architectural and Urban Environments of Sicily, Volume 1*. Cambridge: Harvard University Graduate School of Design, 1989.

———. *Architectural and Urban Environments of Sicily, Volume 2*. Cambridge: Harvard University Graduate School of Design, 1992.

Sitwell, O. "Noto, a Baroque City." *Architectural Review* 76 (Oct. 1934): 129–130, pl. 2–4.

Spinelli, R. "Chiarimenti su un progetto fiorentino poco noto di Andrea Palladio," *Palladio* new ser., v.18, n.35, (Jan.–June 2005):129–137.

Stone, P. "A baroque city in Sicily." *Country Life*, 128, Nov. 1960, 1047, 1049–1050.

Tobriner, S. "Noto's Cassaro an Eighteenth Century Sicilian Street." *American Society of Architectural Historians Journal* 33, no. 2 (May 1974): 169.

———. *The Genisis of Noto: An Eighteenth-Century Sicilian City*. London: A. Zwemmer, 1982.

Lisbon

Abrahamse, C. *Urban Analysis: Lisbon, Portugal*. Cambridge: MIT Unpublished manuscript, 2007.

Bennis, Ed. "Paradise Regained." *Landscape Design* 307 (Feb. 2002):16–19.

Brückelmann, L. "Eine unfreiwillige Lektion—die Baixa Pombalina in Lissabon = An involuntary lesson—the Baixa Pombalina in Lisbon." *Daidalos* 59 (Mar. 1996): 32–45.

Franca, J.-A. *Una Citta Dell' Illuminismo: La Lisbona del Marchese de Pombal*. Rome: Officina Edizioni, 1972.

———. "Le programme éclairé de Pombal: La reconstruction de la Baixa." *Monuments Historiques* 194 (Nov. 1994): 121–123.

Gutkind, E. A. *Urban Development in Southern Europe: Spain and Portugal*. International History of City Development—Volume III. New York: Free Press, 1967.

Edinburgh

Youngson, A. J. *The Making of Classical Edinburgh*. Edinburgh: Edinburgh University Press, 1966.

Edwards, B., and P. Jenkins, eds. *Edinburgh: The Making of a Capital City*. Edinburgh: Edinburgh University Press, 2005.

The Great Estates

London

Archer, J. *The Literature of British Domestic Architecture 1715–1842*. Cambridge: MIT Press, 1985.

Cameron, R., and A. Cooke. *Above London*. San Francisco: Cameron and Company, 1980.

Jackson-Stops, G., and J. Pipkin. *The English Country House: A Grand Tour*. Boston: Little, Brown, 1985.

Jones, E., and E. Woodward. *A Guide to the Architecture of London*. London: Weidenfeld & Nicolson, 1983.

Rasmusssen, S. E. *London, the Unique City*. Harmondsworth, 1961.

Sheppard, F. H. W. *The Survey of London*. London, 1966.

Summerson, J. *Architecture in Britain 1530–1830*. Harmondsworth, 1953.

———. *Georgian London*. Harmondsworth, 1945.

Sykes, C. S. *Private Palaces: Life in the Great London Houses*. London: Chatto & Windus, 1985.

II. THE INDUSTRIAL CITY

Nineteenth-Century Cities

Paris

Alphand, A. *Les Promenades de Paris, histoire—description des embellissements—dépenses de création et d'entretien des Bois de Boulogne et de Vincennes, Champs-Élysées—parcs—squares—boulevards—places plantées, étude sur l'art des jardins et arboretum*. Paris: 1867–73. 1 vol. text and atlas.

Alphand, A., B. Ernouf: *L'art des jardins. Parcs—jardins—promenades—étude historique—principles de la composition des jardins—plantations—décoration pittoresque et artistique des parcs et jardins publics; traité pratique et didactique, par le baron Ernouf*. Paris: J. Rothschild, 1886.

Bacon, E. N. *Design of Cities*, London: Thames and Hudson, 1967.

Carmona, M. *Haussmann. His Life and Times, and the Making of Modern Paris*. Chicago: Ivan R. Dee, 2002.

Choay, F. *The Modern City: Planning in the Nineteenth Century*. New York: Braziller, 1969.

Dennis, M. *Court & Garden: From the French Hôtel*

to the City of Modern Architecture. Cambridge: MIT Press, 1986.
Fredet, J.: *Les maisons de Paris: Types courants de l'architecture mineure parisienne de la fin de l'époque médiévale à nos jours, avec l'anatomie de leur construction, Encyclopédie des nuisances*. Paris, 2003.
Jacobs, A., E. MacDonald, and R. Yodan. *The Boulevard Book*. Cambridge: MIT Press, 2002.
Jordan, D. P. *Transforming Paris: The Life and Labors of Baron Haussmann*. New York: Free Press, 1995.
Loyer, F. *Paris: Nineteenth Century Architecture and Urbanism*, 1st American ed. New York: Abbeville Press, 1988.
Pinkney, D. *Napoleon III and the Rebuilding of Paris*. New York: Princeton University Press, 1958.
Plazy, G. *Le Parc des Buttes-Chaumont*. Paris: Flammarion, 2000.
Saalman, H. *Haussmann: Paris Transformed*. New York: Braziller, 1971.
Waldheim, C., ed. *The Landscape Urbanism Reader*. New York: Princeton Architectural Press, 2006.

New York City

Alpern, A. *New York's Fabulous Luxury Apartments*. New York: Dover, 1975.
Ballon, H. ed. *The Greatest Grid: The Master Plan of Manhattan, 1811–2011*. New York: Columbia University Press and The Museum of the City of New York, 2012.
Cohen, P. E., and R. T. Augustyn. *Manhattan in Maps: 1527–1995*. New York: Rizzoli, 1997.
Cromley, E. *Alone Together: A History of New York's Early Apartments*. Ithaca and London: Cornell University Press, 1990.
Gray, C. "The Commissioners' Plan of 1811: Are Manhattan's Right Angles Wrong?" *New York Times*, October 23, 2005.
Koolhaas, R. *Delirious New York: A Retroactive Manifesto for Manhattan*. New York: Oxford University Press, 1978.
Lockwood, C. *Bricks and Brownstone: The New York Row House, 1783–1929*. New York: Rizzoli, 2003.
Plunz, R. *A History of Housing in New York City: Dwelling Type and Social Change in the American Metropolis*. New York: Columbia University Press, 1990.
Schuyler, D. *The New Urban Landscape: The Redefinition of City Form in Nineteenth-Century America*. Baltimore: Johns Hopkins University Press, 1986.
Scobey, D. *Empire City: The Making and Meaning of the New York City Landscape*. Philadelphia: Temple University Press, 2002.
Wikipedia. Http://en.wikipedia.org/wiki/Commissioners%27_Plan_of_1811#column-one#column-one, 2009.

Boston

Bunting, B. *Houses of Boston's Back Bay: An Architectural History, 1840–1917*. Cambridge: Harvard University Press, 1967.
Kennedy, L. W. *Planning the City upon a Hill: Boston since 1630*. Amherst: University of Massachusetts Press, 1992.
Sammarco, A. M. *Boston's Back Bay*. Dover: Arcadia Publishing, 1997.
Seasholes, N. S. *Gaining Ground: A History of Landmaking in Boston*. Cambridge: MIT Press, 2003.
Shand-Tucci, D. *Built in Boston: City and Suburb, 1800–2000*. Amherst: University of Massachusetts Press, 1999.
Whitehill, W. M. *Boston: A Topographical History*. Cambridge: Harvard University Press, 1968.

Florence

Brucker, G. *Florence: The Golden Age, 1138–1737*. Berkeley and Los Angeles: University of California Press, 1998.
Comune di Firenze. *Atlante di Firenze*. Firenze: Marsilio, 1993.
Fanelli, G. *Firenze*. Roma-Bari: Editori Laterza, 1997.
Fei, S., G. G. Sica, and P. Sica. *Firenze: Profilo di Storia Urbana/Florence: An Outline of Urban History*. Florence: Alinea, 1995.

Barcelona

Busquets, J. *Barcelona: The Urban Evolution of a Compact City*. Barcelona: Actar Distribution, 2006.
———. *Readings on Cerdà and the Extension Plan of Barcelona*. [Barcelona]: Ajuntament de Barcelona, MOPT, 1992.
Cerdà, I. *Teoría general de la urbanización y aplicación de sus principios y doctrinas a la reforma y ensanche de Barcelona*. [Barcelona?]: Instituto de Estudios Fiscales, 1968.
Cerdà, urbs i territori, Planning Beyond the Urban. A catalog of the exhibition Mostra Cerdà, urbs i territori, held September 1994-through January 1995, Barcelona. Madrid: Electa, Fundació Catalana per a la Recerca, 1996.
De Torres i Capell, M. "Barcelona: Planning Problems and Practices in the Jaussely Era, 1900–1930." *Planning Perspective* 7.2 (1992): 211-33.
Fernandez-Alonso. "Cerdà and Barcelona: Research and Plan." Thesis. Massachusetts Institute of Technology, 2008. Sept. 18, 2009. http://hdl.handle.net/1721.1/43909.
Fernández-Armesto, F. *Barcelona: A Thousand Years of the City's Past*. London: Sinclair-Stevenson, 1991.
Fiol Costa, C. "Reticules i diagonals: el pla Jaussely de Barcelona i el pla Burnham de Chicago = Grids and diagonals: Jaussely's 1907 plan of Barcelona and Burnham's 1909 plan of Chicago." Thesis (Ph.D.), Universitat Politècnica de Catalunya, 2007.
Galera, M., F. Roca, and S. Tarragó. *Atlas de Barcelona, Siglos XVI-XX*. Barcelona: A.T.E, 1982.
Hall, T. *Planning Europe's Capital Cities: Aspects of Nineteenth-Century Urban Development*. London: E & FN Spon, 1997.
Hurley, T. "Barcelona." Thesis. Massachusetts Institute of Technology.
Laboratori d'Urbanisme. *Treballs sobre Cerdà i el seu Eixample a Barcelona = Readings on Cerdà and the extension plan of Barcelona*. Barcelona: Ajuntament de Barcelona, MOPT, 1992.
Muntoni, A. *Barcelona 1859: Il piano senza qualità*. Rome: Bulzoni, 1978.

Protomodern Urbanists

Joseph Stübben

Bohl, C. C. *Place Making: Developing Town Centers, Main Streets, and Urban Villages*. Washington, DC: Urban Land Institute, 2002.
Collins, G. R., and C. C. Collins. *Camillo Sitte: The Birth of Modern City Planning*. New York: Rizzoli, 1986.
Hatje-Lexikon der Architektur des 20. Jahrhunderts / herausgegeben von Vittorio Magnago Lampugnani; [Übersetzungen, Gisbert Jänicke (aus dem Finn-

ischen), Thomas Jung (aus dem Italienischen) und Brigitte Weitbrecht (aus dem Englischen und Französischen)]. Stuttgart: G. Hatje, 1983.

Karnau, O. *Herman Josef Stübben, Stadtebau 1876–1930.* Braunscweig/Wiesbaden: Friedr. Vieweg & Sohn Verlagsesellschft mbH, 1996.

Ladd, B. *Urban Planning and Civic Order in Germany 1860–1914.* Cambridge: Harvard University Press, 1990.

Piccinato, G. *La costruzione dell'urbanistica.Germania, 1871–1914.* Rome: Officina, 1974.

Stübben, J. *Der Stadtebau,von J. Stübben.* Darmstadt: A. Bergstrasser, 1890.

———. *City-Building / J. Stubben.* Cambridge: [s.n.], 1911.

———. *Practical and Aesthetic Principles for the Laying Out of Cities/ Excerpts from Der Stadtebau.* Translated/summarized by John W. Reps. Department of City and Regional Planning, Cornell University, Ithaca, New York. http://www.library.cornell.edu/Reps/DOCS/stubb_85.htm.

Camillo Sitte

Bohl, C., and J.-F. Lejeune. *Sitte, Hegemann and the Metropolis: Modern Civic Art and International Exchanges.* London: Routledge, 2009.

Collins, C. C. *Werner Hegemann and the Search for Universal Urbanism.* New York: W. W. Norton, 2005.

Collins, G. R., and C. C. Collins. *Camillo Sitte: The Birth of Modern City Planning.* New York: Rizzoli, 1986. Sitte, C. *City Planning According to Artistic Principles.* Translation of original 1889 Austrian edition. G. R. Collins, and C. C. Collins. *Camillo Sitte: The Birth of Modern City Planning.* New York: Rizzoli, 1986.

Harrison-Moore, A., D. Rowe, et al. *Architecture and Design in Europe and America, 1750–2000.* Malden: Blackwell, 2006.

Hegeman, W., and E. Peets. *The American Vitruvius: An Architect's Handbook of Civic Art.* New York: Princeton Architectural Press, 1988. Originally published: New York: Architectural Book Publishing Co., 1922. Stübben, J. *Der Stadtebau,von J. Stübben.* Darmstadt: A. Bergstrasser, 1890.

Herscher, A. "Stadtebau as Imperial Culture: Camillo Sitte's Urban Plan for Ljubljana." *Journal for the Society of Architectural Historians* 62, no. 2 (Jun. 2003): 212–227.

Jormakka, K., et al. *The Art of the City: From Camillo Sitte to Today.* Tampere: Dept. of Architecture, Tampere University of Technology: Distributor, Juvenes Bookstore, 2006.

Krier, R. *Town Spaces: Contemporary Interpretations in Traditional Urbanism.* Basel: Birkhäuser, 2006.

Peets, E. "Famous Town Planners, II Camillo Sitte." *Town Planning Review* 12, no. 4 (Dec. 1927): 249–259.

Piccinato, G. *La costruzione dell'urbanistica.Germania. 1871–1914.* Rome. Officina, 1974.

Rockcastle, G. "Urban Strategies." *Design Quarterly* 113/114, City Segments (1980): 14–17.

Stephens, H. W. "On Reading Sitte." *Journal of the American Institute of Planners* 12, no. 3 (July, Aug.–Sept. 1946): 30–32.

H. P. Berlage

Gaillard, K., and B. Dokter. *Berlage en Amsterdam Zuid.* Amsterdam/Rotterdam: Gemeentearchief Amsterdam, 1992.

Polano, S. *Hendrik Petrus Berlage.* New York: Rizzoli, 1988.

Otto Wagner

Bernabei, G., & O. Wagner. *Otto Wagner.* Zürich: Verlag für Architektur Artemis, 1986.

Ganz, A., and P. Menconeri. "The Expanding City of Boston Economy." Boston Redevelopment Authority, Research Dept., Community Renewal Program, 1970.

Geretsegger, H., Peintner, M., and Pichler, W. *Otto Wagner, 1841–1918: The Expanding City, the Beginning of Modern Architecture.* New York: Praeger, 1970; Rizzoli, 1979.

Gottmann, J., and J. Patten. *The Expanding City: Essays in Honour of Professor Jean Gottmann.* London: Academic Press, 1983.

Horvat-Pintaric, V., and O. Wagner. *Vienna 1900: The Architecture of Otto Wagner.* London: Studio Editions, 1989.

Mallgrave, H. F. *Otto Wagner: Reflections on the Raiment of Modernity.* Santa Monica, Chicago: Getty Center for the History of Art and the Humanities; distributed by the University of Chicago Press, 1993.

Sarnitz, A., and Gössel, P. *Otto Wagner, 1841–1918: Forerunner of Modern Architecture.* Cologne: Taschen, 2005.

Schorske, C. E. "The Ringstrasse and the Birth of Urban Modernism." *Fin-de-Siècle Vienna.* New York: Vintage Books Edition, 1981.

Wagner, O. "Explanatory Report appended to the plan for the regulation of the Municipality." 1894.

———. "The Development of a Great City (Die großstadt)." *Architectural Record* (1912).

———. *Modern Architecture: A Guidebook for His Students to this Field of Art.* Santa Monica: Getty Center for the History of Art and the Humanities, 1988.

Wagner, O., O. A. Graf, and Otto Wagner-Archive & Drawing Center (New York, NY). "Masterdrawings of Otto Wagner: An Exhibition of the Otto Wagner-Archiv ... the Drawing Center." New York: Otto Wagner-Archiv., 1987.

Wagner, O., W. Zednicek, and K. Sotriffer. *Otto Wagner: Zeichnungen und Pläne.* Vienna: W. Zednicek, 2002.

Daniel Burnham

Burnham, D. H., and E. H. Bennet. *Plan of Chicago.* New York: Princeton Architectural Press, 1993. Originally published in 1908 by the Commercial Club of Chicago.

Roth, L. M. *McKim, Mead & White, Architects.* New York: Harper & Row, 1983.

Wilson, W. H. *The City Beautiful Movement.* Baltimore: The Johns Hopkins University Press, 1989.

Eugène Hénard

Gutkind, E. A. *Urban Development in Western Europe: France and Belgium.* New York: Free Press, 1970.

Hénard, E. *Présentation Jean-Louis Cohen.* Paris: Librairies-imprimeries réunies, 1903–1909.

———. *Etudes sur les trasformations de Paris.* Eight issues between 1903–1909. Nos. 1–3, 1903; nos. 4–5, 1904; no. 6, 1905; nos. 7–8, 1906.

———. "The Cities of the Future," excerpts from *Transactions.* London: The Royal Institute of British Architects (1911), 345–367. Translated/summarized by John W. Reps. Department of City and Regional Planning, Cornell University, Ithaca, New York. http://www.library.cornell.edu/Reps/DOCS/henard.htm.

Wolf, P. M. *Eugène Hénard and the Beginning of Urbanism in Paris 1900–1914.* International Federation of Housing and Planning & Centre de Recherche d'Urbanisme, 1968.

Ebenezer Howard

Howard, E. *Garden Cities of Tomorrow.* London: S. Sonnenschein, 1902.

Tony Garnier

Mariani, R. *Tony Garnier: Une Cité Industrielle.* New York: Rizzoli, 1990.

Pawlowski, C. K. *Tony Garnier: Pionnier de l'urbanisme du XX siecle.* Lyon: Les Creations du Pelican, 1993.

Rovigatti, M. *Tony Garnier architetture per la citta industriale.* Rome: Officina Edizioni, 1985.

Wiebenson, D. *Tony Garnier: The Cité Industrielle.* New York: George Braziller, 1969.

The Modernist City

Le Corbusier and CIAM

Blasi, C., and Padovano, G. *Le Corbusier: La progettazione come mutamento.* Milan: Università statale, 1986.

"CIAM 7 Documents, Bergamo 1949." *Documents of Modern Architecture.* Kraus Reprint, Nendeln, 1949 (CIAM7 1949).

CIAM 8. *The Heart of the City: Towards the Humanisation of Urban Life.* Eds. J. Tyrwhitt, J. L. Sert, and E. N. Rogers. New York: Pellegrini and Cudahy, 1952.

Conrads, U., ed. "Declaration of La Sarraz." *Programs and Manifestoes of Twentieth-Century Architecture.* Cambridge: MIT Press, 1990. (CIAM 1, 1928.)

Curtis, W. J. R. *Le Corbusier: Ideas and Forms.* London: Phaidon, 1986.

Echelle-1. *Le Corbusier Plans 1905-1926.* DVD vol.1, Fondation Le Corbusier, 2005.

______. *Le Corbusier Plans 1945-1949.* DVD vol.10, Fondation Le Corbusier, 2005.

Giedion, S. *Space, Time and Architecture: The Growth of a New Tradition.* Cambridge: Harvard University Press, Fifth Edition, 1967. First published 1941.

______. *A Decade of Contemporary Architecture.* New York: Wittenborn, 1954. (CIAM 6, 1947.)

Gropius, W. "Social Premises for the Minimum Dwelling of Urban Industrial Populations." *Scope of Total Architecture.* New York: Collier Books, 1950. (CIAM 2, 1929.)

Gutkind, E. A. *Urban Development in Western Europe, France and Belgium.* New York: Free Press,1970.

Hoffmann, J. *CIAM Rationelle Bebauungswisen.* Stuttgart: 1931. (CIAM3 1930.)

Le Corbusier. "The City of Tomorrow and Its Planning." Translated from the 8th French edition of *Urbanisme.* New York: Payson, 1928?.

Le Corbusier 1910–65. W. Boesiger and H. Girsbirger Basel: Birkhäuser, 1999.

Le Corbusier et Pierre Jeanneret: Oeuvre complète 1910–1929. Eds. W. Boesiger, and O. Stonorov. Zurich: Girsberger, 1960. First published 1937.

Le Corbusier et Pierre Jeanneret: Oeuvre complète 1929–1934. Ed. W. Boesiger. Zurich: Girsberger, 1957. First published 1937.

Le Corbusier et Pierre Jeanneret: Oeuvre complète 1934–1938. Ed. M. Bill. Zurich: Girsberger, 1958.

Le Corbusier: Oeuvre complète 1938–1946. Ed. W. Boesiger. Zurich: Girsberger, 1961.

Le Corbusier: Oeuvre complète 1946–1952. Ed. W. Boesiger. Zurich: Girsberger, 1955.

Le Corbusier et son atelier rue de Sèvres 35: Oeuvre complète 1952–1957. Ed. W. Boesiger. Zurich: Girsberger, 1958.

Le Corbusier. *The Radiant City: Elements of a Doctrine of Urbanism to Be Used as the Basis of Our Machine-Age Civilization.* New York: Orion Press, 1967.

Mumford, E. P. *Defining Urban Design: CIAM Architects and the Formation of a Discipline, 1937–69.* New Haven: Yale University Press, 2009.

———. *The CIAM Discourse on Urbanism, 1928–1960.* Cambridge: MIT Press, 2009.

Newman, O. *CIAM's 59 in Otterlo.* New York: Universe Books, 1961. (CIAM '59.)

Pedret, A. "CIAM and the Emergence of Team 10 Thinking: 1945–1959." PhD thesis, MIT, Cambridge, 2001.

Scott, F. D. "On Architecture under Capitalism." *Grey Room,* 2002.

Serenyi, P. *Le Corbusier in Perspective.* Englewood Cliffs, NJ: Prentice-Hall, 1974.

Sert, J. L. *Can our Cities Survive?* Cambridge: Harvard University Press; London: H. Milford, Oxford University Press, 1944.

Shane, D. G. "The Street in the Twentieth Century." *Cornell Journal of Architecture* 2 (1983).

Shaw, M. "Promoting an Urban Vision: Le Corbusier and the Plan Voisin." Master of City Planning Thesis, Massachusetts Institute of Technology, Cambridge, 1991.

Tarchópulos, D. "Traces of the Plan of Bogota: Le Corbusier, Sert, and Wiener," *Scripta Nova: Electronic Journal of Geography and Social Sciences* 10, no. 218 (2006).

"World History." *Pearson Education Inc,* http://www.infoplcase.com/ipa.html, viewed Sept. 21, 2009.

http://affordablehousinginstitute.org (viewed October 9, 2009).

http://dome.mit.edu (viewed October 9, 2009).

http://www.iusb.edu (viewed October 9, 2009).

http:// www.arc1.uniroma1 (viewed October 12, 2009).

Team X

Architectengemeenschap Van den Broek en Bakema. *Architektur, Urbanismus = Architecture, urbanism = Architecture, urbanisme.* Stuttgart: K. Krämer, ca. 1976.

Bakema, J., and Van den Broek. "Stad op Pampus: Buiten wonen in de stad." *Country-life in Town.* Amsterdam, Genootschap "Architectura et Amicitia," 1965.

———. *Thoughts About Architecture.* London: Academy Editions; New York: St. Martin's Press, 1982.

Candilis, G. *Toulouse le Mirail: Birth of a New Town/Candilis, Josic, Woods.* Stuttgart: K. Krämer, 1975.

Frampton, K. *Modern Architecture: A Critical History.* London, New York: Thames & Hudson, 2007.

Grinberg, D. I. *Housing in The Netherlands 1900–1940.* Delft: Delft University Press, 1977.

Gruet, S., and R. Papillault. *Le Mirail: Mémoire d'un ville.* Toulouse: Editions Poïésis—AERA, 2008.

Gubitosi, C., and A. Izzo. *Van den Broek/Bakema.* Rome: Officina, 1976.

Lasdun, D., ed. *Architecture in an Age of Scepticism: A Practitioners' Anthology*. New York: Oxford University Press, 1984.

Pedret, A. *CIAM and the Emergence of Team 10 Thinking, 1945–1959*. 2001.

Smithson, A. M. "The Emergence of Team 10 Out of C.I.A.M." *Series AAGS Theory and History Papers*, no.1.82. London: Architectural Assoc. 1982. (CIAM10 1956.)

———. *Changing the Art of Inhabitation: Alison and Peter Smithson*. London: Artemis, 1994.

———. *The Charged Void: Urbanism: Alison and Peter Smithson*. New York: Monacelli Press, 2005.

Team 10 meetings: 1953–1981. Ed. A. M. Smithson. New York: Rizzoli, 1991.

Team 10 Primer. Ed. A. M. Smithson. Cambridge: MIT Press, 1968.

Soria, A. *La Cité Linéaire: Conception nouvelle pour l'aménagement des villes*. Paris: Centre d'études et de recherches architecturales, 1979.

Spellman, C., and K. Unglaub., eds. *Peter Smithson: Conversations with Students: A Space for our Generation*. New York: Princeton Architectural Press, 2005.

Team 10: 1953–81, In Search of a Utopia of the Present. Eds. D. van den Heuvel, and M. Risselada. Rotterdam: NAi, 2005.

———. *Alison and Peter Smithson: From the House of the Future to a House of Today*. Rotterdam: 010 Publishers, 2004.

Woods, S. *Candilis-Josic-Woods: A Decade of Architecture and Urban Design*. Stuttgart: K. Krämer, 1978.

———. *Candilis-Josic-Woods: Building for People*. New York: F. A. Praeger, 1968.

http://www.team10online.org/.

http://en.wikipedia.org/wiki/Team_10.

III. THE POSTINDUSTRIAL CITY

The Recovery Of The City

Postwar American Context

Jacobs, J. *The Death and Life of Great American Cities*. New York: Random House, 1961.

Lynch, K. *The Image of the City*. Cambridge: Technology Press, 1960.

Peterson, S. K., and B. Littenberg. *Space & Anti-Space: The Fabric of Place, City, and Architecture*. ORO Editions, 2020.

Colin Rowe

Caragonne, A. *The Texas Rangers: Notes from the Architectural Underground*. Cambridge: MIT Press, 1995.

Dockery, M. J. "Utopia Reconsidered, Modernism and Urban Form: From the Ville Radiuse to Collage City." http://www.architectureink.com/09-2000/afterthefall.htm.

Frampton, K. *Modern Architecture and the Critical Present*. New York: Thames and Hudson, 1992.

Hays, K. M. *Architecture Theory Since 1968*. New York: Columbia Books of Architecture, 2000.

Harvey, D. *The Condition of Postmodernity*. Cambridge: Blackwell, 1990.

Hurtt, S. "Conjectures on Urban Form: The Cornell Urban Design Studio 1963–1982." *Cornell Journal of Architecture* 2 (1982).

Rowe, C., and F. Koetter. *Collage City*. Cambridge: MIT Press, 1979.

———. *As I Was Saying: Recollections and Miscellaneous Essays*. Cambridge: MIT Press, 1999.

———. "Introduction." *Five Architects: Eisenman, Graves, Gwathmey, Hejduk, Meier.* New York: Oxford University Press, 1975.

———. "Program vs. Paradigm: Otherwise Casual Notes on the Pragmatic, the Typical, and the Possible." *Cornell Journal of Architecture* 2 (1982).

———. "Roma Interrotta." *Architectural Design* 49, no. 3-4 (1979).

———. *The Mathematics of the Ideal Villa and Other Essays*. Cambridge: MIT Press, 1987.

———. "The Present Urban Predicament." *Cornell Journal of Architecture* 1 (1981).

Rowe, C., and R. Slutzky. "Transparency: Literal and Phenomenal Part II." *Perspecta* 13/14 (1971).

Rob Krier

Krier, R. *Stadtraum in Theorie und Praxis*. Stuttgart: Kramer, 1975. Republished in English as *Urban Space*. New York: Rizzoli, 1979.

———. *On Architecture*. London: Academy Editions, 1982, and New York: St. Martin's Press, 1982.

Economakis, R., ed. *Rob Krier: Architecture and Urban Design*. London: Academy Editions (Architectural Monographs No. 30), 1993.

Krier, R. *Town Spaces: Contemporary Interpretations in Traditional Urbanism*. Basel: Birkhäuser, 2003.

Krier, R., and C. Kohl. *Potsdam Kirchsteigfeld: The Making of a Town*. Bensheim: awf-Verl., 1997.

Leon Krier

Economakis, R., ed. *Leon Krier: Architecture & Urban Design, 1967–1992*. London: Academy Editions, 1992.

Isenstadt, S. "Image Renewal: Polemic and Presentation in the Urban Theory of Rem Koolhaas and Leon Krier." *Imaging the City; Continuing Struggles and New Directions.* Eds. Lawrence J. Vale and Sam Bass Warner, Jr. New Jersey: Centre for Urban Policy Research, Edward J. Bloustein School of Planning and Public Policy, 1982.

Krier, L. *Architecture: Choice or Fate.* Windsor: Andreas Papadakis, 1998.

———. *Architecture and Urban Design, 1962–1992.* London: Academy Editions, New York: St. Martin's Press, 1992.

———. *Drawing for Architecture.* Cambridge: MIT Press, 2009.

———. "Houses, Palaces, Cities." *Architectural Design.* Ed. Demetri Porphyrios. London: AD Editions, 1984.

———. *The Architecture of Community*. Washington, DC: Island Press, 2009.

———. "Tradition Today: Traditional Urbanism," *Tradition Today: Continuity in Architecture and Society*. Ed. Robert Adam and Mathew Hardy. Southampton: WIT Press, 2008.

———. "Project for a New Quartier: A City within the City." *Exit Utopia: Architectural Provocations 1956–76*. Munich: Presetel, 2005.

Pawley, M. "Revolutionaries Reconstructing an Old Order: Review of Leon Krier, Architecture & Urban Design 1967–1992." *Blueprint* 101 (Oct. 1993): 46.

Penny, N. "Leon Krier: Architecture & Urban Design" *AA files* 26 (1993).

Rossi, A. *The Architecture of the City*. Cambridge: MIT Press, 1982.

Thompson-Fawcett, M. "Leon Krier & the Organic

Revival within Urban Policy and Practice." *Planning Perspectives* (April 1998).

New Urbanism

Calthorpe, P. *The Next American Metropolis: Ecology, Community, and the American Dream.* New York: Princeton Architectural Press, 1993.
———. *The Regional City: Planning for the End of Sprawl.* Washington, DC: Island Press, 2001.
Duany, A., and E. Plater-Zyberk. *Towns and Town-Making Principles*. Cambridge: Harvard University Graduate School of Design, 1991.
Dutton, J. A. *New American Urbanism: Re-forming the Suburban Metropolis*. Milan: Skira, 2000.
Katz, P. *The New Urbanism: Toward an Architecture of Community*. New York: McGraw Hill, 1994.
Thadani, D. *Visions of Seaside*. New York: Rizzoli, 2013.

Twenty-First-Century Urbanism

The Contemporary Environment

Calthorpe, P. *Urbanism in the Age of Climate Change*. Washington: Island Press, 2011.
———. *Low Carbon Cities: Principles and Practices for China's Next Generation of Growth*. Berkeley: Calthorpe Associates, n.d.
Chakrabarti, V. *A Country of Cities: A Manifesto for an Urban America*. New York: Metropolis Books, 2013.
Gallagher, L. *The End of the Suburbs*. New York: Penguin, 2013.
Hansen, J. E. *Storms of My Grandchildren: The Truth About the Coming Climate Catastrophe and Our Last Chance to Save Humanity*. New York: Bloomsbury, 2009.
Hartmann, T. *The Last Hours of Ancient Sunlight: The Fate of the World and What We Can Do Before It's Too Late*. New York: Three Rivers, 2004.
Heinberg, R. *The End of Growth: Adapting to Our New Economic Reality*. Gabriola Island: New Society, 2011.
Kriken, J. L. *City Building: Nine Planning Principles for the Twenty-First Century*. New York: Princeton Architectural Press, 2010.
Kunstler, J. H. *The Long Emergency: Surviving the End of Oil, Climate Change, and Other Converging Catastrophes of the Twenty-First Century*. New York: Grove, 2005.
Martenson, C. *The Crash Course: The Unsustainable Future of Our Economy, Energy, and Environment*. Hoboken: Wiley, 2011.
McKibben, B. *Eaarth: Making a Life on a Tough New Planet*. New York: Times Books, 2010.
Meadows, D., J. Randers, and D. Meadows. *Limits to Growth: The 30-Year Update*. White River Junction: Chelsea Green, 2004.
Owen, D. *Green Metropolis: Why Living Smaller, Living Closer, and Driving Less Are the Keys to Sustainability*. New York: Riverhead, 2009.
Randers, J. *2052: A Global Forecast for the Next Forty Years*. White River Junction: Chelsea Green, 2012.

Illustrations

Every effort has been made to contact copyright holders, but should there be any errors or omissions, the publisher would be pleased to insert the acknowledgement in any subsequent edition of this book.

R. Adam 141.2 ; A. Alphand, *Les Promenades de Paris*, ... 176, 177.1-3, 178.1-2, 179.4, 180.1-10, 181.1-4, 182.1-2; *Altertumer von Pergamon* 41.2; R. P. de Arce 338.1-2, 339.2-4; Architecture Hub, CC BY-SA 2.0 53.3; Atelier 5 300.4; Author vi.1, xvi.1, xviii.1, 3.1-3 after Tobias, 3.4-5, 6.1, 8.3, 9.3, 10,2-4, 11.1 after Divorne, 11.3, 11.6, 12.3, 13.1, 20.2, 20.5, 21.3-4, 26.1, 27.2, 28.3, 30.3, 32.2-3, 36.1, 38.3, 45.1 after T. Hartmann CC BY-SA 3.0, 54.2, 56.2, 57.3, 59.6-7, 60.2, 64.3, 65 after Dobbins, 67.3-5, 68.1-2, 69.1-2, 69.3-5, 71.1, 71.3, 72.2-4, 72.6, 73.1, 74.2-3, 74.6-7, 75.1-3, 75.5-7, 84.1, 84.3, 84.5-6, 84.8-9, 85.1, 85.3-7, 85.9, 87.4-6, 88.4, 89.1-2, 90.5-6, 91.2, 94, 98.1, 99.5, 100.4-5, 105.1, 109.4, 115.2, 115.4, 115.6, 127.1, 128.1, 129.1-4, 130.2-5, 131.3-8, 134.1-3, 135.1-2, 135.3-4, 136.1, 136.4, 145.1-2, 149.1-3, 150.5-6, 157.1-7, 158, 159.2, 161.3, 162.1-2, 166.1, 168.4, 170.5, 179.3-4, 181.2, 181.4, 189.2-3, 199.6-7, 201.1-5, 204, 205, 206.1-2, 206.4-5, 207.1-2, 207.5, 208.4-5 after *Atlante di Firenze*, 209.1, 209.3, 211.1-4, 215.1, 216.4, 217.4-5, 224.4, 229.4, 233.2, 250.2, 251.3, 281.3, 281.5, 283.1, 284.1-4, 284.7, 288.2, 292.4, 293.4, 294.2, 294.4, 295.1, 295.4-5, 296.2-4, 297.1, 297.3, 300.1-2, 300.4, 301.2, 304.3, 306 after Google, 324.2-3, 325.2, 328.1, 328.4, 330.1-2, 329.1-2, 330.3, 334.3, 351.5, 368.1-5, 369.1-4, 370.1-2, 370.4-6, 371.2-4, 372.1-3, 373.1-3, 383.1 after Katz, 381.4, 400.5, 416, 418.1-2, 419.1, 420.1-2, 421, 422.1, 423, 426.3, 431.1-4, 432.4, 433.1, 434.1, 435.2, 436.2, 437.1-2, 438.2-3, 439.1, 440.1, 441.1-2, 447.2-3, 448.1-6, 448.7, 449.3-4, 449.6, 453.1, 457.1-3, 458, 459.1-4, 460.1-8, 461, 462.2-4, 463.1-2, 464.1-2, 465.1-2, 466.1-4, 467.1-2, 467.3; R. Auzelle and I. Jankovic, *Encylopédie de l'Urbanisme* (Paris, 1947 +) 7.4, 141.3-5, 174.1-3, 287.2-4; Bacon, Clarke, and Koldeway, *Investigations at Assos* (1901) 41.3-4; E. Bacon, *Design of Cities* 202.2; L. Benevolo, *The History of the City* 40.3, 48.2, 48.4, 52.3, 53.1, 59.1-4, 66.2, 118, 119.4; H. P. Berlage 240.2, 240.5, 254.1-3, 255.1-4; Biblioteque Historic de la Ville de Paris 162.3, 163.3; R. Blome 147.1; C. Bonestell 291.1; Boston Atheneum 199.1-2; Boston City Archives 324.1, 325.1, 326.2; Boston Redevelopment Authority 16.4-6, 198.1, 198.3; Braun & Hogenburg 100.3, 144, 156;
F. Brown, *Cosa* 50.1-4, 51.1-4, 74.1; J. E. Bulloz 160.1; D. Burnham, *The Chicago Plan* 241.1, 257.1, 259, 261.1-2; J. Busquets, *Barcelona* 210, 216.1-2, 217.2, 219, 229.2; Calthorpe Associates 384.1, 385.2, 387.1-3, 408.1-2, 409.1-5, 410.1-3, 411.1-4, 412.1-2, 413.1-4, 409.1-2; F. Castagnoli, *Orthogonal Town Planning in Antiquity* 49.3-4, 56, 64.2; P. Cataneo, *Libri* 11.2, 104.1-2; commons.wikimedia.org 61.2, 92, 107.1-2, 100.2-3, 107.3, 195.2; E. Chambliss 239.2, 304.1; F. Chantraine, *Das romische Neuss* 52.2; F. Choay, *The Modern City* 161.1; P. E. Cohen and R. T. Augustyn, *Manhattan in Maps* 184, 185.3, 186, 187.1-2, 190.1, 195.1; Conklin & Rossant 324.1-2; Cooper Ekstut 255.2-3; Corinti 55.2; *Cornell Journal of Architecture* 8.1, 17.4, 333.1-2, 333.4-5, 334.1-3, 335, 336.1; H. Cortez 111.1; Creative Commons, Bernard Gagnon, CCA 41.1, Habib Kaki, CC BY-SA3.0 52.1; 443.4, RillkeBot PD; N. Currier 152; C. Daly, *Revue générale de l'architecture* 168.2, 168.5, 169; E. Dayes 146.1; Delagrive 120.2, 183.1; dezeen.com 442.3; F. Divorne, and B. Gendre, B. Laverne, and P. Panerai, *Les Bastides d'Aquitaine* ... (Bruselles, 1985) 78.2-3, 79.1, 80.1-2, 81, 82.1-3, 83.1-3, 84.2-4, 85.3, 86.1, 87.2-3, 87.7-8, 89.3, 90.1, 91.1; J. Dobbins and P. Foss (eds.) *The World of Pompeii* 67.2, 71.2, 71.4-5;
T. van Doesburg 279.4; *Dresden 1992* 16.1-2, 292.2-3, 293.1; Dover Kohl 386.1-7, Duany Plater-Zyberk 378, 379.1-2, 380.1-2, 381.2; en.wikipedia.org 21.2 (CC BY-SA 3.0),140.1-2, 141.6, 145.7, 154, 70.4; A. Ernouf 164.3; G. Fanelli, *Firenze* 55.5, 202.1; Filarete 99.5; FHW, *Priene* 33, 35.1, 38.4, 39.1-4; © F.L.C. / ADAGP, Paris / Artists Rights Society (ARS), New York 2022 275.2, 279.1-3, 281.2-4, 282.2-4, 283, 284.5-6, 286.1-3, 287.1-2, 289.1-4, 290.1-2, 294.2, 295.4, 296.1, 297.3-5, 298, 303.1, 304.2, 313.1, S. Fong 17.3; Foster + Partners 18.3, 19.1-4, 406.1-4, 427.1-4; Fra Angelo Italia 106.1; P. della Francesca 283.4; Galleria delle Marche 95, 97.1; Gallerie dell'Academia 98.6; J. Gao CC BY-SA 3.0 404.5; T. Garnier, *Une Cité Industrielle* 241.2, 270.1-2, 271, 272.1-2, 273.1-7, 274.1-4, 275.1, 275.3-4; gatag.net 425; A. von Gerken 42.2, 49.1; F. Gilly 159.1; F. di Giorgio Martini 100.1-2; R. Glass 454.2; Google Earth 8.2, 8.4, 9.2, 9.4, 11.4-5, 13.3, 18.1, 54.3, 57.1, 59.5, 67.1, 79.2, 84.7, 85.5, 86.2, 87.1, 88.1-2, 90.2-4, 100.1-2, 105.2-3, 106.3, 111.2, 113.2-3, 114.1-2, 115.5, 123, 132, 133.1-7, 135.4-5, 137, 139.2, 140.3-4, 141.1, 149.5, 150.1-4, 151, 172.2, 175.3, 179.1, 179.5, 199.3, 199.8, 206.3, 206.6, 207.3, 207.6, 214.2, 217.3, 218.1-2, 225, 231.3, 235, 255.5, 258.1, 269.4-5, 293.2, 295.6, 311.4, 314.1-4, 320, 367.1, 372.2, 381.1, 381.3, 382, 384.1, 400.1-4, 401.1-6, 422.2-3, 424.1, 427.2, 432.1-2, 433.2, 434.2, 434.5, 435.1, 435.3-5, 436.1-2, 437.1-2, 438.3-4, 438.6, 439.3-8, 440.2, 441.1-2, 442.2, 446, 449.1, 449.5, 456, 560.6, 465.3; W. B. Griffin 240.6, 269.3; G. Gromort 66.1, 68.4; W. Gropius and A. Meyer 280.6; S. Gruet and Remi Papillault, *Le Mirail: Memoire d'une ville* 307.4, 308, 309.1-3, 310.1-4, 310.7, 311.2-3; J. Gutierrez de Leon 110.1; J. Gwynn, London and Westminster Improved 120.1; Hales Map of Boston 198.2; T. Hamlin 63.2; E. Hawes, *New York, New York* 192.1-2, 192.5, 193.1, 193.4; E. Hénard, *Etudes sur les Transformations de Paris* (1904) 14.2-3, 236, 240.4, 262, 263.1-5, 264.1-6, 265.1-5, 266.1-4, 267; P. Hofer, *Noto: Idealstadt und Stadtraum im Sizilianischen 18 Farhundert*, (Zurich, 1996) 126.1-2, 127.2, 128.2-4, 130.1, 130.6, 131.1; W. Hoepfner and E. Schwandner, *Haus und Stadt* 34.1-2, 35.2-3, 42.1; W. Holar 145.6; E. Howard, *Garden Cities of Tomorrow* 240.3, 268; Institute de France 99.1, 99.2; A. Joli 30.2; J. K. Jordan, *Transforming Paris* 170.4; D. Kelbaugh 383.3, 384.2, 385.1; Koetter Kim & Associates 352.1-5, 363.1-3, 363.5-6, 364.1-4, 365.1-2, 365.4-7, 366.1-4, 367.1-5; G. Kleiner, *Die Ruinen von Milet* 44.2-3; L. Krier 17.1-2, 19.5-8, 322, 339.7, 340.1-3, 341.1-5, 342.1-3, 343.1-2, 344.1-8, 345.1-8, 346.1, 346.3-4, 347.1-3, 348.1-4, 349.1-7, 350.1-7, 357.1-4, 374.1-5, 375.1-3, 376, 377.1-6; R. Krier xiv.1, xv.1, 339.5-6, 352.1-2, 353.1-9, 396, 397.1-6, 398.1-6, 399.1-7, 468.1-2, 469.1-3; Laboratori d'Urbanisme, *Treballs Sobre Cerdá I el seu Eixample* 13.2, 214.1, 221.1-3, 222, 228.4, 231.1, 233.1; A. Lafréry 119.2; *land8. com* 283.2; *Landesamt für Denkmalpflege Sachsen* 293.3; M.-A. Laugier, *Essai sur l'architecture*, (Paris, 1753) 424.2; A. W. Lawrence, *Greek Architecture* 36.3; C. Levy 292.2; Library of Congress 12.1, 122, 188, 194; E. Lissitzky 279.7, 279.9; G. L. Maffei 55.1, 74.5; K. Malevich 278.2; C. McKean 140.5; K. Melnikov 279.8; E. Mendelsohn 280.2; H. Meyer 280.3, 281.1; L. Mies van der Rohe 280.2; moco-choco.com 443.1; Morris 7.1-2; Moule & Polyzoides 388.1-4, 389.1-2; E. Mumford, *Defining Urban Design* 327.1-2, 328.4, 329.3-5; Museo della Civilta Romana 63.3, 334.1, 450, 453.3; Museo Firenze com'era 22.1, 55.3-4, 113.4, 200, 208.1, 208.3; *Museum of the City of New York* 193.2; MVRDV 427.6; J. Myer, *People and Places* 330..1-2; NASA 20.1, 414; *The New City 1* 110.2-3; New York Public Library xi.1; S. Nicholls 12.5, 146.2, 148.2-3; Copyright Office for Metropolitan Architecture, Weena Zuid 158, 3012 NC Rotterdam, The Netherlands 19.9-12, 404.2-3, 405.1-4, A. Palladio 330.4; M. Pallatino, The Etruscans 48.1; P. Patel 116; P. Patte, Monuments 117, 175.2, 228.1-2; P. La Pautre 121; Percier and Fontaine, *Monuments de Paris* 160.2; Peterson Littenberg Architects xii.1, xiii.1, xvii.1, 17.5, 336.2-3, 337.1-4, 354.1-4, 355.1-3, 355.5-7, 356.1-3, 357.1-4, 358.1-4, 359.1-4, 360.1-6, 361.1-3; S. Peterson 112.1; R. Plunz, *A History of Housing in New York City* 185.2, 189.1, 191.1-2, 192.4, 193.3, 193.4-8; PosadMaxwan 402.1-7, 403.1-5; J. Reps, *Urban America* 108.1, *Bird's Eye Views* 197.2-3; G. Rietveld 279.5-6; M. Risselad and D. van den Heuvel (eds.) *Team 10: 1953-81* 299.1-2, 299.3, 301.1, 303.2-3, 307.2, 307.5, 312.2-5, 313.2, 313.4, 315.1-3, 319; J. Rocque, Plan of London 12.2, 12.4, 145.5, 146.3, 148.1; Royal Collection of the United Kingdom 103; H. Saalman, *Haussmann: Paris Transformed* 163.1, 172.3, 178.3, 183.2; Santa Maria Novella 96.2; A. Sant'Elia 280.9; V. Scamozzi 106.2; Scavi di Ostia 49.2; M. Schede, *Die Ruinen von Priene* 36.2, 37.2-3, 38.1; J. C. Shephard and G. A. Jellicoe, *Italian Gardens of the Renaissance* 112.2, 113.3; C. Sitte 240.7, 248.1-2, 249.1, 249.3-5, 251.1-2, 252, 253.1-2; skyscrapercity.com 197.4; J. T. Smith 145.4; A. Smithson, *Team 10 Primer* 300.3, 304.4, 304.6; Society for the Diffusion of Useful Knowledge (SDUK) 4.1, 5.1, 6.2, 108.2, 138, 142, 250.1, 290.3, 445; D. Soloman 384.2-10, 385.1-6, 386.1-5, 387.1-4, 388, 389.1-4; Soria y Mata 316.1; A. Sorrell 52.4; Sting CC BY-SA 3.0 32.1; J. Stübben, *Der Stadtebau* 240.1, 242, 243, 244.1-2, 245.1-4, 246.1-8, 247.1-8, 249.2; Studio Libeskin 427.5; J. Summerson, *Georgian London* 147.4-5; V. Tatlin 280.7; B. Taut 280.8; E. Texier, *Tableau* 163.2, 164.2, 166.2; R. van T'Hof 280.5; Tobriner 125.1-2, 127.2, 131.4; B. Tschumi 427.7; Uratlas 57.4; Vatican Library 119.1; O. Wagner, *Die Grosstadt* 14.1, 14.4, 240.8, 256.2, 258.2, 258.4-5, 260.1; G. B. Ward-Perkins, *Cities of Ancient Greece and Italy* 56.1, 60.1; T. Wiegand, *Milet: Ergebnisse der Ausgrabungen und Untersuchungen seit dem Jahr 1899* (1906) 42.2; F. L. Wright 280.4; A. J. Youngson, *The Making of Classical Edinburgh* 139.4; after Zippelius ii, 3.6, 37.1;

Index